The Richard Godfrey Cup, 1627-28 (see vol. IV, 396)
(© Victoria and Albert Museum, London)

THE HISTORY OF PARLIAMENT

THE HOUSE OF COMMONS 1604–1629

Already published:

The House of Commons 1386–1421, ed. J. S. Roskell,
Linda Clark and Carole Rawcliffe (4 vols., 1992)

The House of Commons, 1509–1558, ed. S. T. Bindoff
(3 vols., 1982)

The House of Commons, 1559–1603, ed. P. W. Hasler
(3 vols., 1981)

The House of Commons, 1660–1690, ed. B. D. Henning
(3 vols., 1983)

The House of Commons, 1715–1754, ed. Romney Sedgwick
(2 vols., 1970)

The House of Commons, 1754–1790, ed. Sir Lewis Namier
and John Brooke (3 vols., 1964)

The House of Commons, 1790–1820, ed. R. G. Thorne
(5 vols., 1986)

The House of Commons, 1690–1715, ed. E. Cruickshanks,
S. Handley and D. W. Hayton
(5 vols., 2002)

The House of Commons, 1820–1832, ed. D. R. Fisher
(7 vols., 2009)

In preparation:

The House of Commons, 1422–1504
The House of Commons, 1640–1660
The House of Commons, 1832–1868
The House of Lords, 1604–1660
The House of Lords, 1660–1832

THE HISTORY OF PARLIAMENT

THE
HOUSE OF COMMONS
1604–1629

Andrew Thrush & *John P. Ferris*

II
CONSTITUENCIES

PUBLISHED FOR THE HISTORY OF PARLIAMENT TRUST
BY CAMBRIDGE UNIVERSITY PRESS
2010

CAMBRIDGE UNIVERSITY PRESS

Cambridge, New York, Melbourne, Madrid, Cape Town, Singapore,
São Paulo, Delhi, Dubai, Tokyo, Mexico City

Cambridge University Press
The Edinburgh Building, Cambridge CB2 8RU, UK

Published in the United States of America by Cambridge University Press, New York

www.cambridge.org
Information on this title: www.cambridge.org/9781107002203

First published 2010

Printed in the United Kingdom at the University Press, Cambridge

A catalogue record for this publication is available from the British Library

ISBN 978-1-107-00219-7 Volume 1 hardback
ISBN 978-1-107-00220-3 Volume 2 hardback
ISBN 978-1-107-00221-0 Volume 3 hardback
ISBN 978-1-107-00222-7 Volume 4 hardback
ISBN 978-1-107-00223-4 Volume 5 hardback
ISBN 978-1-107-00224-1 Volume 6 hardback
ISBN 978-1-107-00225-8 6-volume set hardback

Contents

Maps

Contributors

S.K.A.B.	Sabrina Alcorn Baron
K.E.B.	Karen Bishop
L.B.	Lloyd Bowen
I.C.	Irene Cassidy
B.C.	Ben Coates
A.D.	Alan Davidson
P.A.D.	Anne Duffin
J.P.F.	John P. Ferris
S.H.	Simon Healy
L.M.H.	Lynn Hulse
P.M.H.	Paul Hunneyball
C.R.K.	Chris Kyle
H.J.L.	Henry Lancaster
P.J.L.	Peter Lefevre
V.C.D.M.	Virginia Moseley
G.R.	Glyn Redworth
R.C.L.S.	Rosemary Sgroi
C.T.	Christopher Thompson
A.D.T.	Andrew Thrush
T.M.V.	Tim Venning
P.W.	Paula Watson
G.Y.	George Yerby

Editorial note

The English and Welsh constituency articles are arranged alphabetically by county, with the boroughs similarly grouped under their respective counties. The seven Cinque Port towns (Dover, Hastings, Hythe, New Romney, Rye, Sandwich and Winchelsea) are placed separately at the end of 'England', and are preceded by a general article on all the Ports.

Each article is preceded by a tabular summary of that constituency's electoral history during this period, together with statements concerning the size of the electorate and (in the case of boroughs) the nature of the franchise. The dates of by-elections (which are taken to exclude elections caused by Members choosing a seat having been returned for more than one constituency) appear in italics to distinguish them from all elections. Where seats changed hands during a Parliament, the cause is briefly stated. Explanations of the conventions used in the presentation of franchise details, election results and other matters can be found in the section on 'Method' at the beginning of the Introductory Survey in Volume I.

An asterisk (*) following a name denotes a Member of the House of Commons during the period covered by these volumes, where such inference is not apparent from the surrounding text. A dagger (†) against a name indicates a Member whose parliamentary career lies entirely outside the period 1604-29 and for whom an entry may be found in earlier or later volumes. Members are styled at the head of their biographies according to their status at the time of their first election to Parliament in the period 1604-29. Where two or more Members bear exactly the same name and style they have been differentiated by the addition of roman numerals, for instance John Harris I, John Harris II and John Harris III. This numbering reflects the order in which they first entered Parliament, is specific to this section of the *History* only, and does not reflect a Member's seniority by age or within his family.

Abbreviations

ABBREVIATIONS

Abbreviations in standard usage are excluded from these lists.

I. PRELIMINARY PARAGRAPHS AND TEXT

abp.	archbishop
adm.	admiral
admlty.	admiralty
admon.	administration (probate)
adv.	advocate
aft.	after
amb.	ambassador
appr.	apprentice
art.	artillery
assoc.	association
asst.	assistant
att.	attorney
b.	born
BA	Bachelor of Arts
bap.	baptized
bar.	baron
BCL	Bachelor of Civil Law
Beds.	Bedfordshire
bef.	before
Berks.	Berkshire
bet.	between
bk(s).	book(s)
bp.	bishop
Brec.	Breconshire
bro.	brother
Bt.	Baronet

Bucks.	Buckinghamshire
bur.	*buried*
c.	circa; chief
Caern.	Caernarvonshire
Camb.	Cambridge
Cambs.	Cambridgeshire
capt.	captain
Card.	Cardiganshire
Carm.	Carmarthenshire
ch.	child(ren)
chan.	chancellor
Chas. I	Charles I
circ.	circuit
c.j.	chief justice
cllr.	councillor
co.	county
Co.	Company
coh.	coheir
col.	colonel
Coll.	College
comm(r).	commission(er)
Cornw.	Cornwall
cos.	cousin
c.p.	Common Pleas
cr.	created
ct.	court
cttee.	committee
Cumb.	Cumberland
custos rot.	*custos rotulorum* (chairman of a bench of j.p.s)
d.	died
da.	daughter
DCL	Doctor of Civil Law
DD	Doctor of Divinity
Denb.	Denbighshire
dep.	deputy
Derbys.	Derbyshire
dioc.	diocese
div.	division
Dur.	Durham

d.v.p.	*decessit vita patris* (died in father's lifetime)
E.	East
eccles.	ecclesiastical
educ.	educated
E.I.	East India
Eliz.	Elizabeth
Eng.	England
esp.	especially
Exch.	Exchequer
exec.	executed
f(f).	folio(s)
fa.	father
fell. comm.	fellow commoner
fl.	*floreat* (flourished, used where no life dates known)
Flint.	Flintshire
ft.	foot
gen.	general
gent. pens.	gentleman pensioner
G. Inn	Gray's Inn
Glam.	Glamorgan
Glos.	Gloucestershire
gov.	governor
govt.	government
grandda.	granddaughter
grandfa.	grandfather
grands.	grandson
g.s.	grammar school
gt.	great
h.	heir
Hants	Hampshire
Herefs.	Herefordshire
Herts.	Hertfordshire
hon.	honorary
hosp.	hospital
Hunts.	Huntingdonshire
[I]	Ireland
illegit.	illegitimate
incl.	including

incorp.	incorporated
I.o.M.	Isle of Man
I.o.W.	Isle of Wight
i.p.m.	inquisition *post mortem*
Is.	Island
I. Temple	Inner Temple
Jas. I	James I
j.c.p.	justice, Common Pleas
j.k.b.	justice, King's Bench
j.p.	justice of the Peace
j.q.b.	justice, Queen's Bench
jt.	joint
jun.	junior
j(ust).	justice
k.b.	King's Bench
KB	Knight of the Bath
KC	King's Counsel
KG	Knight of the Garter
kntd.	knighted
kpr.	keeper
Lancs.	Lancashire
ld.	lord
Leics.	Leicestershire
lic.	licence; licensed
Lincs.	Lincolnshire
L. Inn	Lincoln's Inn
LLD	*legum doctor* (Doctor of Laws)
lt.	lieutenant
lt.-col.	lieutenant-colonel
ltcy.	lieutenancy
m .	married
MA	Master of Arts
maj.-gen.	major-general
mar.	marriage
Mass.	Massachusetts
MD	*medicinae doctor* (medical doctor)
Mdx.	Middlesex
Merion.	Merioneth
mo.	mother

Mon.	Monmouthshire
Mont.	Montgomeryshire
mq.	marquess
M. Temple	Middle Temple
N.	North
Neths.	Netherlands
Norf.	Norfolk
Northants.	Northamptonshire
Northumb.	Northumberland
Notts.	Nottinghamshire
nr.	near
o.	only
Oxf.	Oxford
Oxon.	Oxfordshire
p.a.	*per annum* (annually)
parl(s)./parl.	parliament(s), parliamentarian
PC	Privy Councillor
Pemb.	Pembrokeshire
posth.	posthumous
pres.	president
prov.	province
q.b.	Queen's Bench
QC	Queen's Counsel
Rad.	Radnorshire
r.-adm.	rear-admiral
recvr.	receiver
regt.	regiment
R.	River
RN	Royal Navy
roy.	royalist
s.	son
S.	South
[S] or Scot.	Scotland
Salop	Shropshire
sch.	school
sec.	secretary
sen.	senior
settlement	marriage settlement
sgt.	sergeant (Household/military)

sig(s).	signature(s)
sis.	sister
sjt.-at-law	serjeant-at-law
soc.	society
sol.	solicitor
Som.	Somerset
s.p.	*sine prole* (without issue)
sqdn.	squadron
Staffs.	Staffordshire
suc.	succeeded
Suff.	Suffolk
summ.	summoned
Surr.	Surrey
surv.	surviving
Suss.	Sussex
treas.	treasurer
univ.	university
unm.	unmarried
v.-adm.	vice-admiral
vice	*vice* (in the place of)
Virg.	Virginia
visct.	viscount
vol.	volunteer
v.-pres.	vice-president
w.	wife
W.	West
Warws.	Warwickshire
Westmld.	Westmorland
wid.	widow
Wilts.	Wiltshire
Worcs.	Worcestershire
Yorks.	Yorkshire
yr.	younger
yst.	youngest

II. ENDNOTES

The textual abbreviations are also used in the endnotes, where applicable.

acct(s).	account(s)
Add.	Additional mss
admin(s).	*administration(s)*
Admiss.	*Admissions*
AHR	*American Historical Review*
Al. Cant.	*Alumni Cantabrigensis* ed. J.A. Venn (4 volumes)
Al. Ox.	*Alumni Oxoniensis* ed. J. Foster (4 volumes)
antiq(s).	antiquarian; antiquaries; antiquities
AO	Archive Office
APC	*Acts of the Privy Council*
app.	appendix
arch.	archaeological
AS	Archive Service
Ath. Ox.	A. Wood, *Athenae Oxoniensis* ed. J. Bliss (4 volumes)
bdle.	bundle
BIHR	*Bulletin of the Institute of Historical Research*
Bodl.	Bodleian
bor.	borough
Brit.	British
Bull.	*Bulletin*
Burke's LG	*Burke's Landed Gentry*
Cal.	*Calendar*
Cam.	Camden
Cat.	*Catalogue*
Cath.	Catholic
CB	*Complete Baronetage* ed. G.E. C[okayne] (5 volumes)
CBP	*Calendar of Letters and Papers, Borders of England and Scotland*
CCAM	*Calendar of the Committee for Advance of Money* (3 volumes)
CCC	*Calendar of the Committee for Compounding* (5 volumes)
CChR	*Calendar of Charter Rolls*

Cent.	Centre
ch(s)	*charter(s)*
CITR	*Calendar of the Inner Temple Records* ed. F.A. Inderwick (5 volumes)
Col.	*Colonial, America and West Indies*
Col. E.I.	*Colonial, East Indies*
Coll(s).	*Collection(s)*
comp.	compiled by
corp.	corporation
Corresp.	*Correspondence*
CP	*Complete Peerage* ed. G.E. C[okayne] (14 volumes)
CP and CR Ire.	*Calendar of Patent and Close Rolls, Ireland*
CPR	*Calendar of Patent Rolls*
CSP	*Calendar of State Papers*
CTB	*Calendar of Treasury Books*
ded.	dedication
DKR	*Report of the Deputy Keeper of Public Records*
DNB	*Dictionary of National Biography* (1884-1900)
doc(s).	document(s)
Dom.	*Domestic*
DWB	*Dictionary of Welsh Biography*
EcHR	*Economic History Review*
ed.	edited by
EHR	*English Historical Review*
et al.	*et alii* (and others)
et seq .	*et sequitur* (and following)
ex inf.	*ex informatione* (information from)
Fac.	Faculty
fam(s).	family (-ies)
For.	*Foreign*
Gen(eal).	Genealogical
govt.	government
Harl.	Harleian
Her.	*Heraldic*
Hil.	Hilary [law term]
Hist.	History/historical
HJ	*Historical Journal*
HLQ	*Huntington Library Quarterly*

HMC	Royal Commission on Historical Manuscripts
HP Commons	History of Parliament Trust, *House of Commons*
HR	*Historical Research*
IGI	International Genealogical Index
IHR	Institute of Historical Research
illus.	illustrated
inst.	institute
Ire.	Ireland
JBS	*Journal of British Studies*
JMH	*Journal of Modern History*
Jnl.	Journal
Kyle thesis	C.R Kyle, '*Lex loquens*: legislation in the Parliament of 1624' (Auckland PhD, 1993)
L. and I. Soc.	List and Index Society
lib.	library
LP Hen. VIII	*Letters and Papers, Foreign and Domestic, Henry VIII*
m. (mm.)	membrane(s)
Mag.	*Magazine*
Mems.	*Memoirs*
MI	monumental inscription
Mich.	Michaelmas
min(s).	minute(s)
misc.	miscellanea (-aneous; -any)
ms(s)	manuscript(s)
MTR	*Middle Temple Records* ed. C.H. Hopwood (4 volumes)
Mun(s).	Muniment(s)
Mus.	Museum
n	[end/foot]note
N and Q	*Notes and Queries*
Nat.	*Natural*
NH	*Northern History*
n.s.	new series
Oxford DNB	*Oxford Dictionary of National Biography*
p(p).	page(s)
P. and P.	*Past and Present*
par.	parish
paroch.	parochial

PBG Inn	*Pension Book of Gray's Inn* ed. R.J. Fletcher (2 volumes)
ped(s).	pedigree(s)
PER	*Parliaments, Estates and Representation*
PH	*Parliamentary History*
PPE 1604-48 ed. Kyle	*Parliament, Politics and Elections 1604-48* ed. C.R. Kyle (Cam. Soc. ser. 5, xvii)
pprs.	papers
PRO, L. and I.	Public Record Office Lists and Indexes
Procs.	*Proceedings*
Progs.	*Progresses*
pt.	part
Pvte.	*Private*
Q.	Quarter; Queen
r	recto
RCHM	*Royal Commission on Historical Monuments*
rec(s).	record(s)
Reg. PC Scot.	*Register of the Privy Council of Scotland*
Reg. Test.	Registrum Testamentorum, Borthwick Institute, York
rep.	report
repr.	reproduced
rev.	reverend; review; revolution
RO	Record Office
rot./rots.	rotulet/rotuli
Russell, *PEP*	C. Russell, *Parliaments and English Politics, 1621-9*
Sainty, *Judges*	J. Sainty, *The Judges of England, 1272-1990*
Sainty, *Lords Lieutenants*	J. Sainty, *Lieutenants of Counties, 1585-1642*
ser.	series
sess.	sessions
Soton	Southampton
Span.	*Spanish*
spec. ser.	special series
STC	Short Title Catalogue of Printed Books to 1640
stud.	studies
suppl.	supplementary
Top.	*Topographical*
Trans.	*Transactions*

transcr.	transcribed
TRHS	*Transactions of the Royal Historical Society*
UL	University Library
unfol.	unfoliated
unnumb.	unnumbered
unpag.	unpaginated
v	verso
V. and A.	Victoria and Albert Museum, London
Var.	*Various*
VCH	*Victoria County History*
Ven.	*Venetian*
Vis.	*Visitation*
WHR	*Welsh Historical Review*

III. PARLIAMENTARY SOURCES

(a) Published sources

A. and O.	*Acts and Ordinances of the Interregnum* ed. C.H. Firth and R.S. Rait (3 volumes)
Bowyer Diary	*Parliamentary Diary of Robert Bowyer* ed. D.H. Willson
CD 1604-7	'Debates in the House of Commons 1604-7' ed. S.M. Healy in *PPE, 1604-48* ed. Kyle
CD 1621	*Commons Debates 1621* ed. W. Notestein, F.H. Relf and H. Simpson (7 volumes)
CD 1628	*Commons Debates 1628* ed. R.C. Johnson, M.F. Keeler, M. Jansson Cole and W.B. Bidwell (4 volumes)
CD 1629	*Commons Debates for 1629* ed. W. Notestein and F.H. Relf
CJ	*Journals of the House of Commons*
Cobbett, *Parl. Hist.*	*Parliamentary History of England from the Norman Conquest, in 1066, to the Year 1803* ed. W. Cobbett (36 volumes, 1806)
D'Ewes ed. W.H. Coates	*The Journal of Sir Simonds D'Ewes* ed. W.H. Coates
D'Ewes ed. W. Notestein	*The Journal of Sir Simonds D'Ewes* ed. W. Notestein

Ferrar 1624	'The Parliamentary Papers of Nicholas Ferrar, 1624' ed. D. Ransome in *Camden Miscellany XXXIII* (Cam. Soc. ser. 5, vii)
'Hastings 1621'	'Hastings Journal of the Parliament of 1621' ed. E. de Villiers in *Camden Miscellany XX* (Cam. Soc. ser. 3, lxxxiii)
Holles 1624	*The Holles Account of Proceedings in the House of Commons in 1624* transcr. C. Thompson (Orchard Press, 1985)
LD 1621	*Notes of the Debates in the House of Lords 1621* ed. S.R. Gardiner (Cam. Soc. ciii)
LD 1624 and 1626	*Notes of the Debates in the House of Lords 1624 and 1626* ed. S.R. Gardiner (Cam. Soc. ser. 2, xxiv)
LD 1621 and 1628	*Notes of the Debates in the House of Lords* ed. F.H. Relf (Cam. Soc. ser. 3, xlii)
LJ	*Journals of the House of Lords*
Lords Procs. 1628	*Lords Proceedings 1628* ed. R.C. Johnson, M.F. Keeler, M. Jansson Cole and W.B. Bidwell (volume 5, continuation of *CD 1628*)
Nicholas, *Procs. 1621*	[Edward Nicholas] *Proceedings and Debates of the House of Commons in 1620 and 1621* (Oxford, 1766)
Pvte. Jnls.	*Private Journals of the Long Parliament* ed. W.H Coates, A.S. Young and V.F. Snow
OR	*Return of Members of Parliament* (commonly known as *Official Returns*)
Parl. Debates 1610	*Parliamentary Debates in 1610* ed. S.R. Gardiner (Cam. ed. S.R. Gardiner Soc. lxxxi)
Procs. 1610 ed. E.R. Foster	*Proceedings in Parliament 1610* ed. E.R. Foster (2 volumes)
Procs. 1614 (Commons)	*Proceedings in Parliament 1614 (House of Commons)* ed. M. Jansson
Procs. 1625	*Proceedings in Parliament 1625* ed. M. Jansson and W.B. Bidwell
Procs. 1626	*Proceedings in Parliament 1626* ed. W.B. Bidwell and M. Jansson (4 volumes)
Procs. 1628	*Proceedings in Parliament 1628* ed. R.C. Johnson, M.F. Keeler, M. Jansson Cole and

	W.B. Bidwell (volume 6, continuation of *CD 1628*)
Procs. in Opening Session	*Proceedings in the Opening Session of the Long of Long Parl.* ed. *Parliament: House of Commons* ed. M. Jansson M. Jansson
Rich 1624	*Sir Nathaniel Rich's Diary of Proceedings in the House of Commons in 1624* transcr. C. Thompson (Orchard Press, 1985)
SR	*Statutes of the Realm*
Two Diaries of Long Parl.	*Two Diaries of the Long Parliament* ed. M. Jansson

(b) Unpublished parliamentary diaries, 1610 and 1624

'D'Ewes 1624'	Sir Simonds D'Ewes: Harl. 159
'Earle 1624'	Sir Walter Earle: Add. 18597
'Hawarde 1624'	John Hawarde: Wilts. RO, Ailesbury 9/34/2
'Holland 1624', i.	Sir Thomas Holland: Bodl. Tanner 392
'Holland 1624', ii.	Sir Thomas Holland: Bodl. Rawl. D1100
'Jervoise 1624'	Sir Thomas Jervoise: Hants RO, 44M69/F4/20/1
'Lowther 1624'	John Lowther I: Cumbs. RO (Carlisle), D.Lons L2.1
'Nicholas 1624'	Edward Nicholas: SP14/166
'Paulet 1610'	Sir John Paulet: transcribed by Eric Lindquist, Hants RO, 44M69/F2/15/1
'Pym 1624', i.	John Pym: Northants RO, FH50
'Pym 1624', ii.	John Pym: Harl. 6799
'Pym 1624', iii.	John Pym: Add. 26639
'Spring 1624'	Sir William Spring: Harvard Univ. MS Eng. 980

IV. ARCHIVES

AAW	Archives of the Archdiocese of Westminster
Alnwick	Alnwick Castle, Northumberland
Arundel	Arundel Castle, West Sussex
Badminton House	Badminton House, Gloucestershire
Bedford Estate Office	Duke of Bedford's Estate Office, Woburn, Bedfordshire

Beinecke Lib.	Beinecke Library, Yale University, New Haven, Connecticut
BL	British Library, London
BNF	Bibliothèque Nationale de France, Paris
Bodl.	Bodleian Library, Oxford
Borthwick	Borthwick Institute of Historical Research, York
BRL	Birmingham Reference Library
BTRO	Berwick-upon-Tweed Record Office
Castle Ashby	Castle Ashby, Northamptonshire
Cent. Bucks. Stud.	Centre for Buckinghamshire Studies, *formerly* Bucks RO
Cent. Kent. Stud.	Centre for Kentish Studies, Maidstone, *formerly* Kent AO
Chatsworth	Chatsworth House, Derbyshire
CLRO	Corporation of London Record Office
Coll. of Arms	College of Arms, London
CUL	Cambridge University Library
Cumb. RO (Carlisle)	Cumbria Record Office, Carlisle
Cumb. RO (Kendal)	Cumbria Record Office, Kendal
DCO	Duchy of Cornwall Office, London
DWL	Dr. Williams's Library, Gordon Square, London
FSL	Folger Shakespeare Library, Washington DC
GL	Guildhall Library, London
Glamis Castle	Glamis Castle, Angus, Scotland
HALS	Hertfordshire Archives and Local Studies *formerly* Herts. RO
Hatfield House	Hatfield House, Hertfordshire
Hawkins' Hosp.	Sir John Hawkins' Hospital, Rochester Rochester
HEHL	Henry E. Huntington Library, San Marino, California
HLRO	House of Lords Record Office, *now* Parliamentary Archives
HUL	Hull University, Brynmor Jones Library
Hull RO	Kingston-upon-Hull City Archives
JRL	John Rylands Library, Manchester
LMA	London Metropolitan Archives, Northampton Street, London

Longleat	Longleat House, Wiltshire
LPL	Lambeth Palace Library, London
Nat. Marit. Mus.	National Maritime Museum, Greenwich
NE Lincs. Archives	North-East Lincolnshire Archives, Grimsby (*formerly* South Humberside RO)
NLI	National Library of Ireland, Dublin
NLS	National Library of Scotland, Edinburgh
NLW	National Library of Wales, Aberystwyth
NRA	National Register of Archives, Kew
Nott. UL	Nottingham University Library
Oxf. Univ. Arch.	Oxford University Archive (in Bodleian Library)
Roy. Inst. of Cornw.	Royal Institute of Cornwall, Truro
SCL	Sheffield City Library (*now* Sheffield Archives)
Soc. Antiq.	Society of Antiquaries, London
Soc. Gen.	Society of Genealogists, London
St. Bart.'s Hosp.	St. Bartholomew's Hospital, Smithfield, London
T. and W. RO	Tyne and Wear Record Office, Newcastle-upon-Tyne
TCD	Trinity College, Dublin
TNA	The National Archives, Kew
Univ. Chicago Lib.	University of Chicago Library
UCNW	University College North Wales (*now* Bangor University Archives)
Univ. London	University of London, Senate House Library
WAM	Westminster Abbey Muniments
WCA	Westminster City Archives (*now* City of Westminster Archives Centre)
Wm. Salt Lib.	William Salt Library, Stafford
Wilts. Arch. Mag.	Wiltshire Archaeological Magazine Library, Devizes (*now* Lib. Wiltshire Archaeological and Natural History Society Library)
Yorks. Arch. Soc.	Yorkshire Archaeological Society, Claremont, Leeds
Yorks. ERRO	East Riding of Yorkshire Archives and Local Studies, Beverley *formerly* Humberside RO

V. MANUSCRIPT CLASSES CITED AT THE NATIONAL ARCHIVES AND BRITISH LIBRARY

(a) The National Archives

A	Alienations Office
ADM	Admiralty
AO	Audit Office
ASSI	Assize Records
C	Chancery
CHES	Chester
CO	Colonial Office
CP	Common Pleas
CRES	Crown Office Estates
DEL	Court of Delegates
DL	Duchy of Lancaster
DURH	Durham
E	Exchequer
HCA	High Court of Admiralty
IND	Index volumes
KB	King's Bench
LC	Lord Chamberlain
LR	Land Revenue
LS	Lord Steward
PALA	Palace Court
PC	Privy Council
PL	Palatinate of Lancaster
PRO 30	Gifts and Deposits
PRO 31/3	Baschet transcripts
PROB	Probate
PSO	Privy Seal Office
REQ	Court of Requests
SC	Special Collections
SO	Signet Office
SP	State Papers
STAC	Star Chamber
T	Treasury
TS	Treasury Solicitor

WARD   Court of Wards
WO   War Office

(b) British Library

Add.	Additional mss
Add. ch.	Additional charter
Burney	Burney mss
Cott.	Cotton mss
Eg.	Egerton mss
Harg.	Hargrave mss
Harl.	Harleian mss
Lansd.	Lansdowne mss
Loan	Loan mss
Royal	Royal mss
RP	Exported mss (photocopies)
Sloane	Sloane mss
Stowe	Stowe mss

ENGLAND

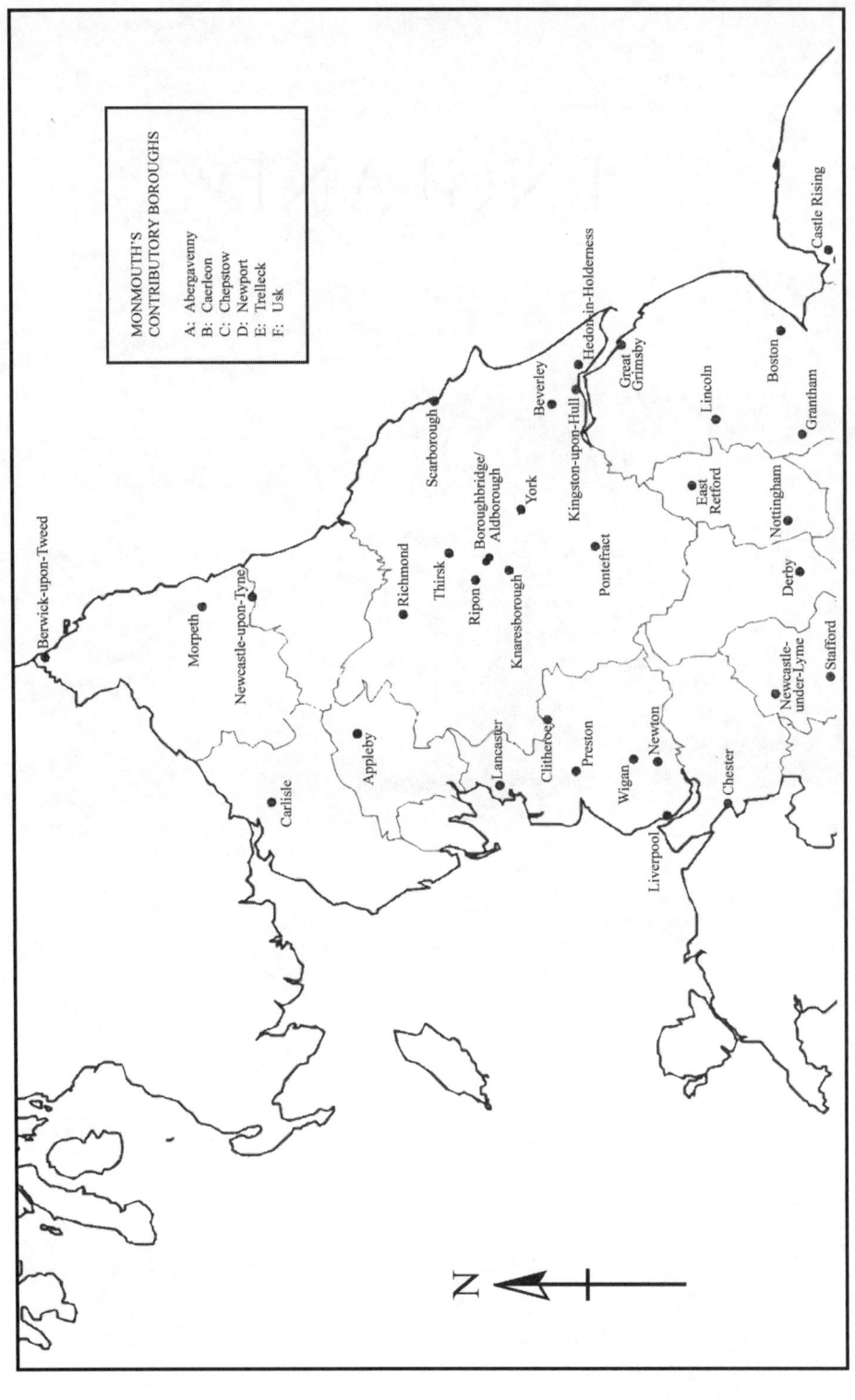

MONMOUTH'S
CONTRIBUTORY BOROUGHS

A: Abergavenny
B: Caerleon
C: Chepstow
D: Newport
E: Trelleck
F: Usk

Berwick-upon-Tweed

Morpeth

Newcastle-upon-Tyne

Carlisle

Appleby

Richmond

Thirsk

Ripon

Knaresborough

Boroughbridge/
Aldborough

Scarborough

York

Beverley

Kingston-upon-Hull

Hedon-in-Holderness

Great
Grimsby

Castle Rising

Lincoln

Boston

Grantham

East
Retford

Nottingham

Derby

Newcastle-
under-Lyme

Stafford

Lancaster

Clitheroe

Preston

Pontefract

Newton

Wigan

Chester

Liverpool

N

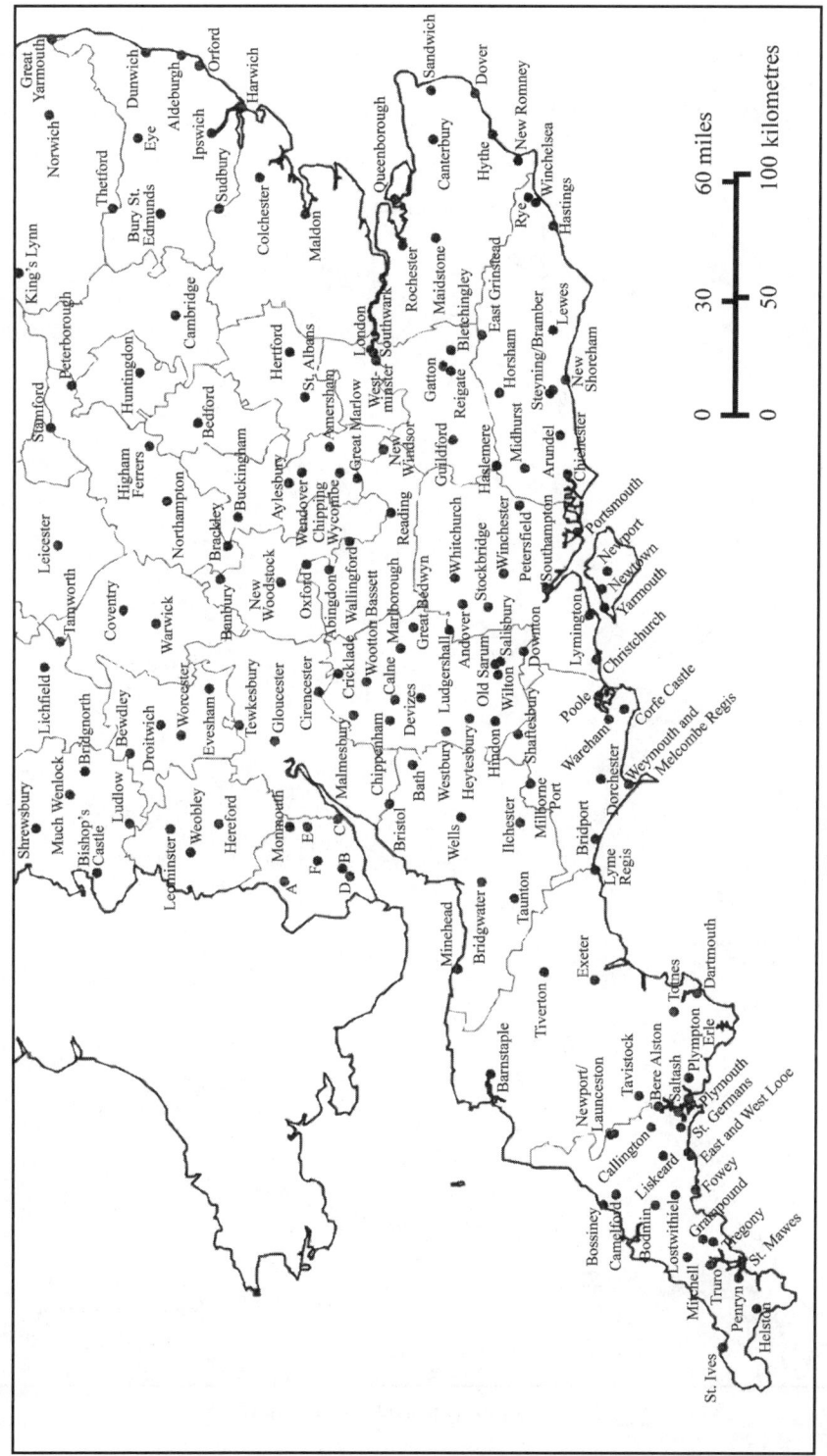

1. English borough constituencies

2. The enfranchised English counties

BEDFORDSHIRE

Number of voters: ?c.1,000

c.Mar. 1604	OLIVER ST. JOHN I
	SIR EDWARD RADCLIFFE
c.Mar. 1614	SIR HENRY GREY
	SIR OLIVER LUKE
11 Dec. 1620	SIR BEAUCHAMP ST. JOHN
	SIR OLIVER LUKE
2 Feb. 1624	OLIVER ST. JOHN II
	SIR OLIVER LUKE
25 Apr. 1625	OLIVER ST. JOHN II
	SIR OLIVER LUKE
c.Jan. 1626	OLIVER ST. JOHN II
	SIR OLIVER LUKE
c.Feb. 1628	OLIVER ST. JOHN II
	SIR OLIVER LUKE

A preponderantly rural county supporting a typical East Midland mixture of sheep and corn farming, with grazing for cattle along the Ouse valley, Bedfordshire's chief products were barley, for malting; woollen yarn for the worsted weavers of Norwich; and butter, sold to London dealers at Woburn.[1] By the later 1620s the county's landowners included six earls (Kent, Bedford, Bristol, Bolingbroke, Cleveland and Peterborough), while another, Sir Edward Radcliffe, 6th earl of Sussex, had only recently sold his estate at Elstow. In an area notably short of borough seats this number of potential patrons might have been expected to provoke stiff competition for the knighthood of the shire, but with the possible exception of 1584 none of the county elections before 1640 seem to have been contested.

Bedfordshire's Elizabethan elections were dominated by the Lords St. John of Bletsoe, who owned nearly 20,000 acres in the north and east of the county, and procured the return of at least one relative at every election during the reign.[2] The Radcliffes of Elstow, just outside Bedford, also stood on at least four occasions. Their estate was relatively modest, but Thomas Radcliffe[†], the unsuccessful candidate at the 1584 election, was backed by his cousin the 4th earl of Sussex (Sir Henry Radcliffe[†]), who probably sponsored the subsequent parliamentary career of Thomas's younger brother Edward*.[3] The Mordaunts and Cheyneys also represented the shire during Elizabeth's reign, but thereafter the Catholicism of the 4th Baron Mordaunt rendered his family unelectable even before his imprisonment for complicity in the Gunpowder Plot; while Henry, Lord Cheyney[†] died without heirs in 1587.[4] Two other major landowners did not field any candidates during Elizabeth's reign: the Grey family, earls of Kent, who owned almost 15,000 acres across the centre of the county, but suffered from a shortage of male heirs; and the Russell earls of Bedford, who acquired 3,000 acres of ex-monastic land at Woburn after the dissolution, but did not settle in Bedfordshire until the later 1620s, and already wielded extensive borough patronage in Devon and Dorset.[5]

At the 1604 general election, as in 1601, Oliver St. John I, heir to the Bletsoe estate, took the senior seat, and Sir Edward Radcliffe the junior. Financial troubles prevented Radcliffe from standing again in 1614,[6] when he was replaced by Sir Henry Grey, heir presumptive to the earldom of Kent. Had St. John, a baron's son, stood again, he would have been expected to settle for the junior seat. Perhaps for this reason he stood aside in favour of his cousin Sir Oliver Luke, who had just succeeded to an estate of 2,500 acres in the east of the county.[7] Luke sat for the junior seat for the remainder of his life, doubtless with the support of his Bletsoe relatives. His cousin, who succeeded as 4th Baron St. John in 1618, paired Luke with his heir, Oliver St. John II, from 1624. The latter, born only in

1603,[8] was presumably considered too young for the county seat in December 1620, when St. John inserted his youngest brother, Sir Beauchamp.

Although the size of the Bletsoe estate gave St. John considerable influence within the shire, his success as an electoral patron during the 1620s was quite remarkable, and owed much to the disinclination of other local landowners to challenge him: Sir John Digby*, 1st earl of Bristol, whose wife held a jointure estate of 1,500 acres near Bedford, confined his electoral patronage to the vicinity of his main estate in Dorset, and the 1st earl of Cleveland, who inherited the Cheyney estate in 1614, is not known to have had any designs on the county seats, although he made an unsuccessful nomination at Bedford in 1628.[9] The only other individual who could have challenged the Bletsoe interest was Sir Henry Grey, who succeeded his father as earl of Kent and lord lieutenant of the county in 1623. However, he had neither heirs to put forward for the county seat, nor interest in challenging the St. Johns, his closest local relatives.

The Bedfordshire electorate was undoubtedly greater than that of the neighbouring county of Huntingdonshire, which may have numbered 2,000 in December 1620.[10] However, in the absence of a contest the number of freeholders attending the county court was probably much lower, perhaps under 1,000. The shire's agricultural interests required little in the way of legislation, and only two bills of local interest were laid before Parliament during the early Stuart period: an Act of 1607 allowed trustees for Robert Thompson, a lunatic with lands near Luton, to make a jointure for his son; and a bill to confirm Luke's purchase of lands in Huntingdonshire, which received a single reading in the Commons on 8 Mar. 1621.[11] In 1626 St. John and Luke were both named to the committee for a bill to restrict the malting of barley in times of dearth (9 Mar.), proclamations for which purpose had caused friction within the county in 1608-9.[12]

[1] BEDFORD; *Agrarian Hist. of Eng. and Wales* ed. J. Thirsk, iv. 491; P.J. Bowden, *Wool Trade in Tudor and Stuart Eng.* 34-6. [2] C142/249/56; 142/376/126. [3] Northants. RO, SS239. [4] *CSP Dom.* 1603-10, p. 258. [5] C142/349/172; 142/435/118. [6] *CSP Dom.* 1611-18, p. 110. [7] *Vis. Beds.* (Harl. Soc. xix), 39; C142/343/177. [8] *Bletsoe* ed. F.G. Emmison (Beds. par. reg. xxiv), 2. [9] C142/309/171; 142/348/135; BEDFORD. [10] HUNTINGDONSHIRE. [11] HLRO, O.A. 4 Jas.I, c.27; Nicholas, *Procs 1621,* i. 133. [12] *CJ,* i. 830b, 833a; STAC 8/18/20.

S.H.

BEDFORD

Right of election: in the burgesses

Number of voters: c.80

c. Mar. 1604	HUMPHREY WINCH, dep. recorder THOMAS HAWES, alderman
30 Nov. 1606	SIR CHRISTOPHER HATTON *vice* Winch, appointed chief bar. [I]
c. Mar. 1614	SIR ALEXANDER ST. JOHN JOHN LEIGH
21 Dec. 1620	SIR ALEXANDER ST. JOHN RICHARD TAYLOR, dep. recorder
21 Jan. 1624	SIR ALEXANDER ST. JOHN RICHARD TAYLOR, dep. recorder
27 Apr. 1625	SIR ALEXANDER ST. JOHN RICHARD TAYLOR, dep. recorder
13 Jan. 1626	SIR BEAUCHAMP ST. JOHN RICHARD TAYLOR, dep. recorder
c. Feb. 1628	SIR BEAUCHAMP ST. JOHN RICHARD TAYLOR, dep. recorder Sir Henry Astry

A Saxon foundation sited at one of the main crossing points on the upper Ouse, Bedford was sufficiently wealthy to build a stone bridge in the twelfth century, paid the surprisingly large sum of £40 for its fee-farm from 1190, and returned two Members to Parliament from 1295. The fee-farm was reduced in 1440 on the ground that a new bridge five miles down river at Great Barford had affected its road traffic, but the town revived under the Tudors, and had a population of about 1,500 by 1603.[1]

Bedford was an assize town and a significant social centre: corporation accounts record regular visits from the bishops of Lincoln and local magnates such as the earls of Kent, Bedford and Sussex, Lords St. John and Mordaunt.[2] The town was also the focal point for local trade in grain, wool and livestock, and its corporation was dominated by maltsters, tanners, glovers and drapers. In the early 1620s the Ouse navigation was extended from St. Ives, Huntingdonshire to Great Barford, which ultimately allowed Bedford's merchants to monopolize the riverborne trade to King's Lynn in coal, grain and hides, although the benefits of this trade did not become fully apparent until the second half of the century.[3]

A borough by prescription, Bedford's corporation included a mayor, an aldermanic bench consisting of all former mayors, two bailiffs and a recorder. Two chamberlains and a host of minor officials were also appointed annually, and in 1610 the corporation established a common council of 13 burgesses to ratify agreements which had formerly been referred to the jury of the court leet.[4] Trading privileges were shared by the burgesses, who were eligible for municipal office, and the ordinary freemen, who were not. The two groups were estimated to number between 100-200 in 1600, but a census taken in 1647 gave a total of 83 burgesses, including a dozen non-resident gentlemen, and 13 freemen.[5] The parliamentary franchise was not questioned during the early Stuart period, and remained ill-defined: surviving indentures are signed by the corporation and Common Council alone, but claim 'the assent and consent of the rest of the burgesses', which presumably excluded the ordinary freemen. It was not until after two bitterly fought elections in 1640 that Parliament awarded the franchise to all male inhabitants.[6]

At the 1628 parliamentary election Richard Taylor, then deputy recorder, insisted that 'I know not of any precedent in the time of the memory of any man when the recorder of this corporation hath been passed by without his own consent'.[7] The custom of returning the recorder apparently become established during the 1580s under Serjeant Thomas Snagge[†], and was continued under his successor, Oliver, Lord St. John[†], who nominated his deputy, Humphrey Winch.[8] St. John possessed sufficient influence as a local landowner to lay claim to the other seat, securing the return of his cousin John Pigot in 1589 and 1593, and his nephew Sir Oliver Luke* in 1597.[9] The only other neighbouring gentleman with any electoral influence was William Boteler[†], who sat in 1586 and doubtless secured the return of his wife's nephew Thomas Fanshawe I* in 1601. Boteler was succeeded by his under-age son Thomas in 1602,[10] which must have temporarily diminished the family's influence at Bedford, and St. John's eldest son was returned for the county in 1604, leaving the second borough seat open to the town's wealthiest inhabitant, alderman Thomas Hawes, whose recently deceased stepmother had been St. John's first cousin once removed.[11]

Winch's appointment as chief baron of Ireland in November 1606 caused him to be deprived of his Commons' seat.[12] His successor as deputy recorder, Edward Rolt, had no known parliamentary ambitions, which left the seat open to Sir Christopher Hatton, a London neighbour of Lord St. John. Hatton was married to one of Fanshawe's sisters and could have been recommended either by William Boteler's widow Ursula, or by Sir Edward Coke*, lord chief justice of Common Pleas and one of the assize judges at Bedford, who was closely involved in his affairs.[13] In 1614 Hatton transferred to Huntingdon, where Lord St. John also had influence, leaving a vacancy at Bedford for one of St. John's younger sons, Sir Alexander. Hawes was by this time an old man, and in the absence of any interest from Rolt, the second seat went to John Leigh, a resident of nearby Caldwell Priory, whose father had represented the borough during the 1550s.

Lord St. John died in 1618, and was succeeded as recorder by his heir Oliver St. John I*, an energetic parliamentary patron who nominated his brothers Sir Alexander and Sir Beauchamp St. John at the next five elections. Rolt was also dead by the time of the next election, and his replacement, Richard Taylor, who was both St. John's deputy recorder and brother-in-law to Sir Thomas Boteler, sat throughout the 1620s.[14] This division of the electoral spoils was challenged in 1628, when Thomas, 1st earl of Cleveland, recently appointed joint lord lieutenant of the shire, recommended his neighbour Sir Henry Astry.[15] Cleveland's service as a Forced Loan commissioner in 1626-7 contrasted sharply with the fate of Lord St. John's brother Sir Beauchamp, who was imprisoned for refusal to pay. The Loan also divided the Bedford corporation, several of whose members, including Stephen Luxford, mayor at the time of the 1628 election, had refused to contribute towards the second half of the Loan in the summer of 1627.[16] Cleveland's support for such a divisive measure is unlikely to have been popular, even among the townsmen who collected the Loan, and in a speech at the hustings in 1628 Taylor implicitly invited the voters to compare Cleveland's stance with that of his patrons, the St. Johns, warning that 'if I be not one that shall be made choice of ... the honour of the honourable lord whose servant I am in this place may ... suffer'.[17]

Bedford MPs were not conspicuously active on their constituents' behalf, although they expressed some interest in issues relating to the town's industries. Hawes, whose eldest son was a tanner, was named to the committee for a bill to regulate the industry (28 June 1604). Sir Alexander and Sir Beauchamp St. John were both named to the committee for the bill to prohibit malting in times of dearth (9 Mar. 1626), while Taylor, who complained about purveyance levied on malt in London (2 June 1626), was appointed to help scrutinize a petition about London's charges for portage of malt (25 June 1628).[18] On 24 Mar. 1621 Taylor spoke at the committee for the bill to prohibit the importation of corn in years of plenty, and he was later named to the committee for a bill regulating coal measures (20 Feb. 1626), which was of significance to the town's merchants, who shipped substantial quantities of coal up the Ouse.[19]

The corporation showed little interest in sponsoring legislation: they were apparently not tempted to seek statutory confirmation of their title to St. John's hospital during a lengthy dispute at the turn of the century, although Taylor may have promoted a proviso to include advowsons in the bill modifying the 1624 Concealments Act (14 Feb. 1626) to prevent any recurrence of this dispute.[20] The town offered to pay for the passage of a bill to make the river Ouse navigable from St. Ives, Huntingdonshire to Bedford in April 1628 as a means of reducing tolls on locks which had been built several years earlier.[21] No such bill was read in the House, but Taylor may have hoped to add a suitable proviso to the Medway navigation bill in committee (added 17 May 1628). The town did not obtain statutory control over the Ouse until 1665.[22]

[1] J. Godber, *Hist. Beds.* 52-6; *VCH Beds.* iii. 1-3; W.M. Wingfield, 'Recusancy and Nonconformity in Beds.', *Beds. Hist. Rec. Soc.* xx. 159. [2] Beds. RO, Bor.B/D6/1. [3] D. Summers, *Gt. Ouse*, 47-50; M. Carter, 'Town or Urban Society? St. Ives, Hunts. 1630-1740', *Societies, Cultures and Kinship, 1580-1850* ed. C. Pythian-Adams, 121-2. [4] *VCH Beds.* iii. 17-19; Beds. RO, Bor.B/B6/7; Bor.B/B7/16. [5] STAC 5/W34/36, answers to Q.6; *Bedford Corp. Min. Bk.* ed. G. Parsloe (Beds. Hist. Rec. Soc. xxvi), 1-2, 149-50. [6] C219/38/19, 219/39/17; D. Hirst, *Representative of the People?*, 99-100. [7] Beds. RO, Bedford bor. uncat. box 60, Richard Taylor file, pp. 53-4, repr. in G.D. Gilmore, 'Pprs. of Richard Taylor of Clapham', *Beds. Hist. Rec. Soc.* xxv. 105. [8] Winch's appointment as deputy can be inferred from Beds. RO, Bor.B/F2/4; Bor.B/F11/4a, p. 70. [9] *Vis. Beds.* (Harl. Soc. xix), 194; *Vis. Hunts.* (Cam. Soc. xliii), 2. [10] *Vis. Beds.* 84-5; C142/268/153. [11] *Vis. Beds.* 53-5; *Sharnbrook* ed. F.G. Emmison (Beds. Par. Reg. xxiv), B38; PROB 11/98, f. 299. [12] *CPR Ire. Jas. I*, 95a; *CJ*, i. 323-4. [13] SIR CHRISTOPHER HATTON. [14] PROB 11/128, ff. 304-5; *Vis. Beds.* 84-5. [15] *Vis. Beds.* 77; *VCH Beds.* iii. 440. [16] *CSP Dom.* 1626-7, p. 44; 1627-8, p. 312; *APC*, 1627, p. 439; 1627-8, p. 217; Beds. RO, Bor.B/A4/4; SP16/75/89. [17] Gilmore, 105. [18] *CJ*, i. 247b, 833b, 919a; *Procs. 1626*, iii. 345; *CD 1628*, iv. 472. [19] *CD 1621*, v. 320; *CJ*, i. 545a, 820a. [20] E112/1/93, 112, 131, 132; 112/68/32, 34; STAC 5/M30/28; 5/W29/28; 5/W34/36; SP16/124/84 (dated 1608-9); *CJ*, i. 819a. [21] *Gt. Ouse Navigation* ed. T.S. Willan (Beds. Hist. Rec. Soc. xxiv), 29-37. [22] *CJ*, i. 893b; Summers, 47-50.

S.H.

BERKSHIRE

Number of voters: unknown

c.Mar. 1604	SIR FRANCIS KNOLLYS I SIR HENRY NEVILLE I
c.Mar. 1614	SIR THOMAS PARRY (expelled the House, 11 May) SIR HENRY NEVILLE I

18 Dec. 1620	SIR RICHARD LOVELACE SIR ROBERT KNOLLYS II
12 Jan. 1624	(SIR) RICHARD HARRISON EDMUND DUNCH
10 May 1625	SIR FRANCIS KNOLLYS I EDMUND DUNCH
c.Jan. 1626	EDMUND DUNCH JOHN FETTIPLACE
c.Mar. 1628	(SIR) RICHARD HARRISON JOHN FETTIPLACE

Described by Thomas Fuller in 1662 as a county 'perfect in profit and pleasure',[1] Berkshire in the early seventeenth century was one of the wealthiest shires in England, as well as being one of the smallest. It owed its prosperity primarily to the fertility of its two principal agricultural districts, the Vale of White Horse, in the north, and the Vale of Kennet, in the south; the cloth industry centred on Reading and Newbury, so vigorous in the sixteenth century, was badly affected by the trade depression of the 1620s. The natural richness of the two vales gave rise to many of the shire's leading gentry families, such as the Dunches of Little Wittenham, the Fettiplaces of Childrey and the Parrys of Hampstead Marshall; while the eastern, or forest, division of the shire, which included the royal Forest of Windsor, boasted families such as the Nevilles of Billingbear, the Harrisons of Hurst and the Lovelaces of Hurley. By comparison, few substantial gentry families were settled in the Berkshire Downs, an area of poor, stony soil which divided the Vale of White Horse from the Vale of Kennet and was fit only for pasturing sheep.[2]

The most prominent figure in Berkshire was the county's lord lieutenant, William Knollys[†], who was successively created Lord Knollys (1603), Viscount Wallingford (1616) and earl of Banbury (1626). His patronage played an important part in the parliamentary elections for those boroughs where he was the high steward, but his influence over the county's parliamentary elections seems to have been less significant. He may have been responsible for the return of his brother Sir Francis Knollys I in 1604 and 1625 and his nephew Sir Robert Knollys II in 1620, but both men were substantial landowners in their own right, and could probably have achieved election without the aid of their illustrious relative.[3] Perhaps the main reason why Knollys was not as influential as one might have expected is that he lived not in Berkshire but in Oxfordshire, at Gray's Court, a few miles across the county border. His tenure of the lord lieutenancy despite his non-residence is explained by a complete absence of indigenous noble families to Berkshire before the 1620s. Even after 1620 the peerage was poorly represented in the county. Francis Norris of Rycote, Oxfordshire and Wytham, Berkshire was created earl of Berkshire in 1621, but he died in January 1624 without male heir. Not until 1627 did Sir Richard Lovelace of Hurley and William Craven of Hampstead Marshall receive baronies, and Craven, an active soldier, was frequently absent abroad. The lack of an indigenous peerage meant that Berkshire's leading gentry families exercised considerable power and influence over the county's parliamentary elections.[4]

Berkshire's elections were always held at Abingdon and were remarkably harmonious affairs. Indeed, of the 17 general elections held between 1558 and 1628, only that of 1571 is known to have been contested. The absence of conflict reflected the fact that the upper echelons of Berkshire society were not riven by serious feuds. It may also have owed something to the availability of parliamentary seats elsewhere for those who wanted them: six of Berkshire's seven borough seats were usually conferred on members of the county gentry rather than on townsmen, for instance.[5] Above all, it suggests that the leaders of county society struck agreements with one another ahead of each election, thereby obviating the need for contests. Certainly, in mid-December 1639 (Sir) Edmund Sawyer*, then a leading figure in east Berkshire, reported that he would be meeting his neighbour Sir Richard Harrison at Twyford before Christmas to consider who in the county should stand for election to the Short Parliament.[6]

Before 1597 Berkshire's seats were usually monopolized by gentry from one area of the county alone. Thus in 1559, 1571 and 1588 all the Members were from the 'Forest', whereas in 1572, 1586 and 1593 they came exclusively from the 'Vale' (meaning either the Vale of White Horse or the Vale of Kennet). Only in 1563 and 1584 did Forest and Vale return one Member each. From 1597, however, the overall picture of representation became more sophisticated. At every general election held between 1597 and 1624 the county returned one Member from the Forest and the other from the Vale. In 1597 the Forest was represented by Sir Henry Norris II, whose father owned Bray, while the Vale was represented by Sir Francis Knollys I of Reading. In 1601 Sir Richard Lovelace of Hurley (Forest), woodward of Windsor Forest and later high steward of Windsor borough, was paired

with his stepson George Hyde of South Denchworth and Kingston Lisle. Sir Francis Knollys I was again returned in 1604, when he was partnered with Sir Henry Neville I of Billingbear (Forest). Neville was re-elected in 1614, and was balanced by Sir Thomas Parry of Hampstead Marshall, chancellor of the duchy of Lancaster (Vale). Neville died in 1615 and his place was taken in 1620/1 by his near neighbour Sir Richard Lovelace, who was returned alongside Sir Robert Knollys II, who dwelt at the aptly named Stanford-in-the-Vale. In the final election of James's reign, Berkshire returned Sir Richard Harrison of Hurst and Edmund Dunch of Little Wittenham, residents of the Forest and Vale respectively. The pattern of elections laid down between 1597 and 1624 seems to form the basis for the observation made in 1695 by James Bertie, 1st earl of Abingdon, that it was 'the ancient custom of the county to have one [Member] in the forest and the other in the vale'.[7]

This neat electoral arrangement was set aside at the beginning of Charles I's reign, as the gentry of the vales, particularly those in the Vale of White Horse, became more assertive. In 1625 and 1626 Berkshire's seats were occupied by Sir Francis Knollys I (Vale of Kennet) Edmund Dunch (Vale of White Horse) and John Fettiplace (primarily Vale of White Horse, but with some lands in the Vale of Kennet). Although the county reverted to its previous practice of creating a balanced ticket in 1628, returning Sir Richard Harrison (Forest) alongside Fettiplace, the Vale of White Horse established a monopoly at the two elections of 1640, when Fettiplace was joined by Henry Marten of Shrivenham. At the Restoration the pattern of electoral politics recognized as normal by James Bertie in 1695 appears to have been re-established.

Change in the pattern of Berkshire's electoral politics was not just restricted to the disappearance of the 'balanced ticket'. Under Elizabeth the senior knight of the shire was invariably drawn from the Forest. The only family able to break the Forest's stranglehold were the Untons, who lived at Wadley, in the Vale of White Horse, and they had done so on only three occasions, in 1572, 1586 and 1593. Forest dominance of the senior knighthood waned dramatically under the early Stuarts, however, for between 1604 and 1640 its representatives were senior knights on just three occasions out of nine: in 1620/1, 1624 and 1628. This further underlines a remarkable shift in the balance of power between Forest and Vale, a shift which is also reflected in the overall number of seats held between 1558 and 1640. During the Elizabethan and Jacobean periods there was an equal division of parliamentary places between Forest and Vale: each held seats on 15 occasions.[8] In the following reign, however, the Forest's influence collapsed completely: between 1625 and 1640 only one seat out of ten was conferred on a Forest resident, Sir Richard Harrison in 1628, whose election may have hinged on his ability to muster the support of his near neighbours in Reading, in the Vale of Kennet.[9]

One possible reason for the rising fortunes of the Vale of White Horse was suggested by Sir Edmund Sawyer in his letter of December 1639. Sawyer observed that because parliamentary elections were always held at Abingdon, on the eastern edge of the Vale of White Horse, 'the men who dwell near there, and who come in the morning and go home at night, are those who usually carry the business'. One might have thought that this would also have been true under Elizabeth, when the Forest had achieved a position of dominance, but Sawyer pointed out that the forest voters were now 'but a handful' compared with those from the Vale, 'and many will make excuses in respect of the long journey and charge'.[10] Sawyer's analysis, if correct, would help to explain why, with one exception, Forest men no longer represented the county after 1624. Reluctance to undertake the long journey to Abingdon may also have extended to the residents of the Vale of Kennet. In January 1624 the members of the corporation of Reading, a borough situated in the heart of Vale of Kennet which had fallen on hard times as a result of the trade depression of the early 1620s, evidently preferred to hold a council meeting rather than attend the hustings at Abingdon. It may be, of course, that the reason that so many of the inhabitants of the Forest region and the Vale of Kennet failed to turn out to vote was that they saw little point in travelling a long distance merely to vote for candidates who were drawn exclusively from the Vale of White Horse. Certainly it is noticeable that the members of Reading's corporation showed no such reluctance to travel in 1628, when their neighbour Sir Richard Harrison decided to stand, for which courtesy they were rewarded with 'a fat buck'.[11]

The motives which led most Berkshire Members to seek election can only be surmised. Sir Francis Knollys I, who was returned in 1604 and 1625, probably wanted a seat because he desired to meet the new monarch, while Sir Henry Neville, who sat in 1604 and 1614, undoubtedly hoped to win royal preferment by cutting a figure on the parliamentary stage. Neville's colleague in 1614, Sir Thomas Parry, was chancellor of the duchy of Lancaster, and as such would have been required to stand. A county seat befitted his rank and

status, although in 1610 he had been forced to settle for St. Albans because Berkshire's seats were already taken. Parry was expelled the House on 11 May for electoral misconduct, but owing to the shortness of the session he was not replaced.

[1] *Fuller's Worthies* ed. R. Barber, 36. [2] C.G. Durston, 'Berks. and its County Gentry, 1625-49', (Univ. Reading Ph.D. thesis, 1977), i. 1; *VCH Berks.* ii. 167, 213. A diagram showing the location of the principal families of the shire from 1625-40 and the four main divisions of the county accompanies C.G. Durston's 'London and the Provinces: The Assoc. bet. the Capital and the Berks. County Gentry of the Early Seventeenth Cent.' *Southern Hist.* iii. 39. [3] This is the conclusion of J.K. Gruenfelder, *Influence in Early Stuart Elections*, 154. [4] Durston, 'Berks.', i. 32-4. [5] The only seat regularly occupied by a townsman was the junior burgess-ship at Reading, which was generally reserved for the borough's recorder. [6] *CSP Dom.* 1639-40, p. 162. [7] BL, Trumbull Misc. ms 29, 4 Sept. 1695, Abingdon to Trumbull. [8] The figure for the Vale includes John Cheyney, MP in 1563, who dwelt in a detached portion of the Downs between Hants and the Vale of Kennet. [9] *Reading Recs.* ed. J.M. Guilding, ii. 415. [10] *CSP Dom.* 1639-40, p. 162. [11] *Reading Recs.* ii. 167, 415.

A.D.T.

ABINGDON

Right of election: uncertain

Number of voters: at least 28

5 Mar. 1604	SIR RICHARD LOVELACE
24 Mar. 1614[1]	SIR ROBERT KNOLLYS II
18/19 Dec. 1620[2]	SIR ROBERT HYDE
10 Jan. 1624	SIR ROBERT KNOLLYS II
3 May 1625	SIR ROBERT KNOLLYS II
9 Jan. 1626	SIR ROBERT KNOLLYS II
23 Feb. 1628	JOHN STONHOUSE

The shire town of Berkshire, Abingdon lay astride a major north-south trade route and was regarded as one of the most beautiful towns in England by some. As well as being a noted centre of the malt trade, it was also an important market for horses, and despite economic decline in the mid-sixteenth century it remained a centre of the cloth trade.[3] In 1556 it received a charter which established a common council consisting of a mayor, two bailiffs, nine other principal burgesses and 16 secondary burgesses. Incorporation did not result in good government, however, for by the early 1590s Abingdon's governors were at loggerheads with each other. In 1599 the corporation ejected three of its members for non-residence and threatened three more with expulsion unless they attended the next meeting. It also repealed all the borough's ordinances as 'many are perished and defaced for lack of good custody of the register wherein they were written' and because 'some [are] holden contrary to the laws and statutes of the realm'. New ordinances were subsequently passed, but by 1605 the municipality was again in turmoil, this time over the annual elections of the mayor and bailiffs, which had degenerated into 'mutinous tumults'. The corporation attempted to limit to 40 the number of ordinary freemen who were entitled to participate, but by January 1614 elections had become so chaotic that the borough's government was 'in danger to be utterly subverted'. Peace was restored in the short term after the corporation ruled that in future the office of mayor should be filled on a rota basis.[4] However, in 1628 a fresh dispute erupted over a secretly held election to the recordership, leading the Privy Council to conclude that the town remained 'troubled with faction, by means whereof things are not carried in so direct and fair a manner as were fit'.[5] Moreover, in 1630 several leading townsmen complained that 'some factious persons' had overturned the ruling of 1614, 'whereby divers inconveniences more mischievous than the first are like to ensue'. Four years later Abingdon was again engulfed in conflict over a mayoral election.[6]

The charter establishing Abingdon's corporation had also granted the town the right to return one Member to Parliament. The franchise was vested in the 'mayor, bailiffs and burgesses', an ambiguous form of wording which was echoed in the borough's election indentures.[7] It left unclear whether freemen who were not members of the corporation were entitled to vote. The election indentures of 1625 and 1628 suggest that they did in practice, as they were made by the 'mayor, bailiffs and burgesses of the borough of Abingdon with the whole assent and consent of all the burgesses there'.[8] On the other hand, the borough minutes reveal that in 1614 at least the franchise was exercised solely by members of the corporation.[9] None of the Members returned between 1604 and 1628 were townsmen. This followed a broad pattern which had been established in Elizabeth's reign but which had been temporarily abandoned in the last three Tudor Parliaments. The exclusion of townsmen suggests that the corporation, and perhaps also the community at large, wished to avoid contests by keeping the town's increasingly bitter politics out of parliamentary elections.

Abingdon was represented in the first Jacobean Parliament by Sir Richard Lovelace. Although from Berkshire, Lovelace was seated some distance from the borough, at Hurley, four miles north-west of Maidenhead. He must therefore have owed his election to a two-fold connection with the borough: his sister had wed the son of Richard Beake, the Member for Abingdon in 1576, while he himself had married the widow of William Hyde, whose uncle Oliver Hyde had represented the seat in 1558 and 1553 and whose son, (Sir) George Hyde[†], dwelt at South Denchworth, nine miles or so from Abingdon. In 1614 Abingdon made its seat available to Sir Robert Knollys II, who had been too young to stand for Parliament at the previous election. Knollys was seated at Stanford-in-the-Vale, nine miles west of Abingdon, but he probably owed his return to his uncle, William, Lord Knollys (William Knollys[†]), who since about 1601 had been the borough's high steward. Sir Robert had almost certainly been raised in the household of his uncle, who later adopted him as his heir. At the following election Knollys was elected junior knight of the shire for Berkshire, thereby clearing the way for the Hydes to reassert their interest at Abingdon. Their representative was Sir Robert Hyde, the stepson of Sir Richard Lovelace and brother of Sir George Hyde. Seated near Wantage, roughly eight miles south west of Abingdon, Hyde was certainly known to the borough, having been one of the commissioners who, in March 1618, had conducted an inquiry into the property belonging to St. Nicholas' church.[10] At the subsequent three general elections Abingdon was again represented by Sir Robert Knollys II, but in 1628 the latter was returned for Wallingford on his uncle's interest. His departure from the scene enabled John Stonhouse, the eldest son of Sir William Stonhouse of nearby Radley, to fill the vacancy.

At Abingdon, any Member not previously chosen was sworn a freemen on the day of his election.[11] Before 1624 the town's election indentures were all written in Latin. None of the surviving indentures for this period bear any signatures, except that of 1604, which was signed by the mayor, the bailiffs and nine other burgesses. Instead they were authenticated by the town's common seal.[12] Between 1597 and 1609 an Abingdon resident, Sir Thomas Smith[†], served as clerk of the parliaments.

[1] A.C. Baker, *Historic Abingdon*, 70. [2] The indenture is dated 18 Dec., but the bor. mins. record that the election was held on the 19th: C219/37/64; Berks. RO, TF41 (microfilm), f. 152. [3] C.G. Durston, 'Berks. and the County Gentry, 1625-49', (Univ. of Reading Ph.D. thesis, 1977), i. pp. 4, 17, 22; *Travels through Stuart Britain: the Adventures of John Taylor, the Water Poet* ed. J. Chandler, 161; *VCH*

Berks. iv. 441; E. Kerridge, *Textile Manufactures in Early Mod. Eng.* 21. ⁴ *Selections from Municipal Chronicles of Abingdon* ed. B. Challenor, 2, 5 and app. pp. x-xii, xvi-xviii; Baker, 50-1, 53, 59. ⁵ *APC*, 1628-9, pp. 226-7, 230-1; *Municipal Chronicles of Abingdon*, 140. ⁶ *APC*, 1629-30, p. 358; *CSP Dom*. 1634-5, p. 217. ⁷ *Municipal Chronicles of Abingdon*, 7. ⁸ C219/39/14; 219/41B/46. ⁹ Baker, 70. ¹⁰ A.E. Preston, *St. Nicholas, Abingdon*, 212. ¹¹ Baker, 70, 72; Berks. RO, TF41 (microfilm), f. 152. ¹² For the 1604 indenture, see C219/35/1/196. For the other indentures, see C219/37/64; 219/38/15; 219/39/14; 219/40/157; 219/41B/46.

A.D.T.

NEW WINDSOR

Right of election: in the corporation

Number of voters: c.30

20 Feb. 1604	SAMUEL BACKHOUSE
	THOMAS DURDENT, under steward
1 Feb. 1610	SIR FRANCIS HOWARD *vice*
	Durdent, deceased
c. Mar. 1614	SIR RICHARD LOVELACE
	THOMAS WOODWARD, under steward
15 Dec. 1620	(SIR) CHARLES HOWARD
	SIR ROBERT BENNETT
10 Jan. 1624	EDMUND SAWYER
	THOMAS WOODWARD, under steward
14 Sept. 1624	SIR WILLIAM HEWETT *vice*
	Woodward, deceased
14 Apr. 1625	SIR WILLIAM HEWETT
	SIR ROBERT BENNETT
9 Jan. 1626	SIR WILLIAM RUSSELL
	HUMPHREY NEWBERY, under steward
23 Feb. 1628	(SIR) WILLIAM BEECHER
	THOMAS HEWETT

New Windsor developed as a royal borough in the shadow of the castle. It received its first charter in 1277 and returned Members intermittently from 1302 and regularly from 1447.¹ A new charter issued in August 1603, on the 'humble petition and request' of Charles Howard, 1st earl of Nottingham, entrusted its government to some 30 brothers of the guildhall, 'of the better and more approved inhabitants', of whom 13 were to be styled 'benchers' and to include the ten aldermen from among whom the mayor was to be chosen.² Both Nottingham and George Villiers, 1st duke of Buckingham, successive constables of the

castle, served as high stewards of the borough, and could expect the nomination to one seat, but on the whole Windsor stood by its resolution of 1572 that the other should go to a townsman, often its under-steward or recorder.³ The indentures were exchanged between the sheriff of Berkshire and the mayor, bailiffs and burgesses. There is no evidence that the borough paid wages to its Members.

In 1604 Nottingham may have exercised his interest in favour of Samuel Backhouse, a London merchant's son who had settled in Berkshire and served as sheriff in 1600. The other Member, Thomas Durdent, was the under-steward. Durdent died in 1607, and was replaced shortly before the fourth session by one of Nottingham's nephews, Sir Francis Howard, a young man of 24 but already an experienced naval officer. By the time of the next election, in 1614, he was at sea, while Backhouse transferred to Aylesbury, leaving his former seat to a more distinguished Berkshire gentleman, Sir Richard Lovelace, who had just replaced Nottingham as high steward.⁴ The junior place went to the new under-steward, Thomas Woodward, whose father had been clerk of the works at the castle and a Member for the borough in 1586. Lovelace took a county seat in the third Jacobean Parliament, making room at Windsor for another of Nottingham's nephews, (Sir) Charles Howard, who held several of 'the offices of Windsor', at the castle and in the forest. Woodward gave way to Sir Robert Bennett, nephew of a former dean of Windsor and later clerk of the works at the castle. Bennett fell 'very desperately ill' during the Parliament, which may explain his failure to sit in 1624. The senior Member then, Edmund Sawyer, was an auditor in the Exchequer whose circuit included Berkshire and who had recently purchased a manor some six miles from Windsor. Woodward regained the junior seat, but died after Parliament was prorogued for the summer. At the ensuing by-election he was replaced by the keeper of Windsor Little Park, Sir William Hewett, who wanted a seat because his conduct as receiver-general for purveyance compositions was under investigation by the Commons. However, the House did not meet again before the death of James I.

When a fresh Parliament was summoned in 1625, Hewett was re-elected, together with the by now recovered Bennett. This was despite a letter of 8 Apr. 1625 from the new high steward, Buckingham, craving Windsor's

> favour in a request which I trust you will not think unreasonable, which is that on my recommendations you will elect Sir William Russell the treasurer of His Majesty's

Navy for one of the burgesses to serve in this approaching Parliament for your town. His known worth and merits speak so well for him that I shall not need to tell you what I believe of him, and being born not far from you, I doubt not you will easily grow confident that he will be very tender of the trust you shall repose in him for the good of your town.[5]

Russell, however, whose father had lived some five miles away and who had himself inherited property in Old Windsor, was chosen in 1626, together with the under-steward, Humphrey Newbery, who was to prove an active Member. Early in the following year Newbery and the mayor were summoned before the Privy Council to account for their arrest of a castle servant. The mayor was immediately discharged, but Newbery, held 'more to be blamed' and accused of 'divers other misdemeanours', was obliged to keep himself ready for further attendance until April 1628.[6] He was accordingly unavailable for election to the third Caroline Parliament. Russell, having resigned his treasurership of the Navy, was replaced in the senior seat by the Buckingham client and clerk of the Privy Council (Sir) William Beecher, for whom the duke had failed to find a seat at Dover; he was the only complete outsider to sit for Windsor in the period. The junior seat went to Thomas Hewett, eldest son of Sir William, who had just completed his education. Neither Beecher nor Hewett is known to have taken notice of the complaint made in Parliament against Richard Montagu, who was said to have kicked out 'the bonfires in Windsor Castle' after the king yielded to the Petition of Right.[7]

[1] VCH Berks. iii. 58. [2] Ibid. 61; Bodl. Ashmole 1126, ff. 83-95v. [3] R.R. Tighe and J.E. Davis, Annals of Windsor, ii. 47; Bodl. Ashmole 1126, f. 46. [4] Tighe and Davis, 47. [5] Add. 37819, f. 11. [6] APC, 1627, pp. 66, 114, 416; 1627-8, p. 372. [7] CD 1628, iv. 291, 298.

A.D.

READING

Right of election: in the corporation

Number of voters: 21 or more

12 Mar. 1604	SIR JEROME BOWES	
	FRANCIS MOORE	
c. Mar. 1614	FRANCIS MOORE	
	ROBERT KNOLLYS	
16 Dec. 1620	SIR ANTHONY BARKER	
	JOHN SAUNDERS	

19 Jan. 1624	SIR FRANCIS KNOLLYS II	21
	JOHN SAUNDERS	16
	(Sir) Robert Knollys	9
	Sir Richard Lydall	0[1]
21 Apr. 1625	SIR FRANCIS KNOLLYS II	
	JOHN SAUNDERS[2]	
16 Jan. 1626	SIR FRANCIS KNOLLYS II	16
	JOHN SAUNDERS	19
	(Sir) Robert Knollys	4
	Sir Edward Clerke	0
	Thomas Turnour	0
	Nicholas Gunter	0[3]
18 Feb. 1628	SIR FRANCIS KNOLLYS II	19
	JOHN SAUNDERS	20
	Sir John Brooke	0
	Edward Ironstead	0
	Thomas Turnour	0
	Nicholas Gunter	0
	Robert Maulthus	0
	William Maulthus	0[4]

Reading, with a population of about 7,000 in the 1630s, was still a prosperous clothing town at the opening of this period, producing high quality woollen fabrics much in demand on the Continent. One of the 23 staple towns created for the wool trade in 1617, it suffered heavily from the trade depression of the 1620s. John Kendrick, a wealthy London cloth exporter who came from a prominent Reading family, bequeathed £7,500 to the borough in 1624, intending to encourage the industry, but the funds were, in the event, misused.[5]

The borough received its first charter in 1253, and returned Members from 1295. It was incorporated in 1542, and reincorporated by Elizabeth, whose charter was confirmed by James in 1604. 'The common council of the borough' consisted of nine capital burgesses, from whom the mayor was chosen, and 12 or more secondary burgesses.[6] William*, Lord Knollys, later Viscount Wallingford (1616) and earl of Banbury (1626), owned a house in Caversham, within two miles of Reading. His brother, Sir Francis Knollys I*, lived in the borough, served as its high steward throughout the period, and was freely accorded the nomination to one seat.[7] The borough persisted in making its own choice for the other nominee despite several attempts by Lord Knollys to control both. The indentures were exchanged between the mayor and burgesses and the sheriff of Berkshire.[8]

Sir Jerome Bowes, who occupied the senior seat in 1604, was the only Member chosen in this period with no apparent connection with either the borough or the county. He evidently owed his nomination to his fellow-courtier, Lord Knollys. Francis Moore, on the other hand, sitting for the third time for Reading, was virtually a native son, having been educated at the local grammar school and risen to the status of a Berkshire country gentleman through his success at the law. There is no evidence that Bowes sought re-election in 1614. This enabled Moore to move up to the senior seat, with one of the high steward's nephews, Robert Knollys, as his junior colleague.

By the time the third Jacobean Parliament was summoned in late 1620, Robert Knollys was serving in the Palatinate. It is likely that it was Wallingford who was responsible for nominating Sir Anthony Barker, whose seat at Sonning lay three miles from Reading, as Barker was subsequently appointed a deputy lieutenant at the viscount's nomination. Moore does not seem to have sought re-election, and was to die the following year. In his stead the corporation chose one of its own members, John Saunders, a Middle Temple barrister like Moore, whose father lived in west Berkshire, but who had himself recently settled at Reading and been elected as a secondary burgess.

In 1623 the borough's steward, Edward Clerke, the equivalent of the recorder in other municipalities, was dismissed for reasons unknown, but set down in '15 articles and matters', and was replaced by Saunders. Wallingford regarded this treatment of his client as a serious affront and secured Clerke's restoration with the assistance of the Privy Council.[9] Saunders was compensated by being appointed 'counsel for this company in matters concerning the corporation', and was re-elected to the next four Parliaments.[10]

On 12 Jan. 1624, after the sheriff's precept had been read, a letter from Wallingford 'was opened and read to the company present, showing my lord's request for nomination of one of the burgesses and both if it may be'. A week later a second letter from Wallingford was read, nominating Sir Francis Knollys II and requesting that his brother Robert, the former Member, now also a knight, 'might have the other place'. Sir Francis headed the ensuing poll, but his brother received only nine votes against Saunders's 16. A fourth candidate, Sir Richard Lydall, received none. He was a local man who had been engaged in a quarrel with Sir Anthony Barker at Sonning, and may have thought himself entitled to replace him. The indenture, returning Sir Francis Knollys and Saunders was made out the following day. After the election one or both of the Members apparently agreed 'to bear mine own charges

in that service, and that the said mayor and burgesses shall stand clear and be acquitted of and from the payment of any wages, fees or duties payable to or for me in that behalf'.[11] On 8 Mar. 1624, on the other hand, the corporation agreed that Thomas Turnour, a former mayor, should 'have his charges borne to go and attend the burgesses of the Parliament, hoping to attain a free trade'. Nothing further is heard of this mission.[12]

In 1625 Wallingford nominated Sir Francis Knollys, but left the other seat to the corporation, 'presuming you will make choice of Mr. Saunders'.[13] Knollys and Saunders were accordingly re-elected without contest on 21 Apr., and both signed the agreement to serve without wages. The indenture was dated three days latter.[14]

On 9 Jan. 1626 Reading received both the sheriff's precept and Wallingford's nomination of Sir Francis Knollys. Three days later, however, when it had been proposed to hold the election, Sir Robert Knollys joined his brother as a candidate, as did the steward Edward Clerke, now also a knight, apparently standing against the Knollys interest. Nothing was done on that day, and any hope that the air would have been cleared by 16 Jan., when the election was held, soon vanished: two further candidates appeared, Thomas Turnour and Nicholas Gunter, both of whom were former mayors. Clerke, Turnour and Gunter received no votes at all, suggesting that they did not even vote for themselves. Sir Francis Knollys and Saunders were re-elected and again agreed to bear 'their own charges'.[15] On this occasion the indenture was backdated to 10 January.[16] On 15 Feb. 1626 the corporation decided 'that counsel shall be forthwith had to have the aid and help of the Parliament to settle the stock' bequeathed by Kendrick, but again nothing seems to have been done.[17] Following the failure of Parliament to vote subsidies, Charles I initiated a Benevolence, but on 31 July, after a meeting 'of the most able men' in the town hall 'concerning the raising of moneys to supply the king's warrants', it was agreed to 'desire there may be a Parliament, for then all men should be bound to pay a part by subsidy and fifteens'.[18]

On 4 Feb. 1628 Reading received a letter from the earl of Banbury, as Wallingford had now become, nominating Sir John Brooke* 'to be one of the burgesses of this corporation for the Parliament', presumably with Sir Francis Knollys. The corporation agreed to answer Banbury and another candidate, Edward Ironside or Ironsted, to the effect that it would stand by Knollys and Saunders. Banbury's letter was read again before the election on 18 Feb., 'and it was the opinion of the whole company that the said earl was therein satisfied by the answer of these letters sent unto him, there being no other letter from the lord since that time'. Further members of the corporation, however, including Turnour and Gunter, chose to put their names forward. Knollys and Saunders, once chosen, again agreed to serve without wages.[19] In April 1628 Clerke 'delivered to Mr. Mayor to be put into book in the hall divers speeches in the Parliament', delivered by the king, the lord keeper and the Speaker, as well as the petition for religion but, it seems, these were returned to him, 'and not put in book'.[20] Early the following year, however, the corporation agreed 'that books of the statutes made in every Parliament' since 1610 'shall be forthwith provided', but again nothing was done and the agreement had to be remade two years later.[21]

[1] *Reading Recs.* ed. J.M. Guilding, ii. 169. [2] Ibid. 231. [3] Ibid. 273. [4] Ibid. 386-7. [5] N.R. Goose, 'Decay and Regeneration in 17th Cent. Reading,' *Southern Hist.* vi. 53-74; SP46/176, ff. 36, 307, 411; Ashmole, *Berks.* ii. 509-47; *Oxford DNB sub* Kendrick, John. [6] *Reading Chs.* ed. C.F. Pritchard, 1, 6-7, 19, 54; *OR.* [7] *HP Commons, 1558-1603,* ii. 417; *Reading Recs.* iii. 58. [8] C219/38/12; 219/39/12; 219/40/159. [9] *Reading Recs.* ii. 115-17, 127; *APC,* 1621-3, pp. 460, 467-8, 508-9, 516-17. [10] *Reading Recs.* ii. 133. [11] Ibid. 168-9; *OR.* [12] *Reading Recs.* ii. 178. [13] *HMC 11th Rep, VII,* 221. [14] *Reading Recs.* ii. 230-1; *OR.* [15] *Reading Recs.* ii. 270-1, 273. [16] *OR.* [17] *Reading Recs.* ii. 278. [18] Ibid. 305-6. [19] Ibid. 384-7. [20] Ibid. 402. [21] Ibid. 446; iii. 47.

A.D.

WALLINGFORD

Right of election: in the freemen[1]

13 Mar. 1604	SIR WILLIAM DUNCH GRIFFITH PAYNE
c. Mar. 1614	SIR CAREW REYNELL SIR GEORGE SIMEON
28 Dec. 1621	SIR GEORGE SIMEON SAMUEL DUNCH
24 Jan. 1624	SIR EDWARD HOWARD II SIR GEORGE SIMEON
7 Mar. 1624	SIR ANTHONY FOREST *vice* Howard, chose to sit for Calne
30 Apr. 1625	SIR ANTHONY FOREST MICHAEL MOLYNS
18 Jan. 1626	SIR ANTHONY FOREST UNTON CROKE
1 Mar. 1628	SIR ROBERT KNOLLYS II EDMUND DUNCH

Wallingford owed its origins and early importance to a ford across the Thames, dominated by a medieval castle. It received its first charter in 1156 and returned Members from 1295. The population was declining in this period and in 1636 was described as only 'a good market town'.[2] The corporation consisted of the mayor, three aldermen, and 16 'burgesses'; but the indentures exchanged with the sheriff customarily included also the commonalty, which appears to have meant the freemen. However, the returns do not name the voters and were unsigned.

The honour of Wallingford formed part of Anne of Denmark's dower, inherited on her death in 1619 by her son Prince Charles, but there is no evidence of royal electoral patronage.[3] In 1614 and 1621 the borough minutes record that one of the Members was 'chosen' by the high steward, suggesting that it was established practice accepted by the corporation for that officeholder to have one seat at each election. At the start of this period the high steward was Sir John Fortescue*, the chancellor of the duchy of Lancaster. He died in 1607 and was succeeded by William Knollys†, the treasurer of the Household, who had been created a baron in 1603 and was raised to the dignity of Viscount Wallingford in 1616, and earl of Banbury in 1626. He had been constable of Wallingford castle since 1584.[4] In 1614 and 1621 the other Member is recorded as having been chosen by the 'company', but in practice the corporation's seat was often awarded to one of two influential local gentry families, the Dunches of Little Wittenham, four miles from the borough, and the Molyns' of Clapcot, a hamlet in the parish of All Hallows, Wallingford. In 1614 the minutes of the corporation make reference to a by-law for the election of the recorder as one of the borough's Members of Parliament. However, Thomas Stampe, recorder from 1584 to 1606, only represented the borough in 1586 and 1588.[5]

It is not clear who the high steward's nominee was in 1604. Sir William Dunch was related to Fortescue by marriage, as well as being the son of Edmund Dunch, who had represented the borough in 1571. Edmund was ineligible to sit himself because he was sheriff of Berkshire, but he was probably sufficiently influential in the borough to secure the corporation's seat. The other Member was Griffith Payne, a purveyor and Household official, who was serving his fourth term as mayor, and had been appointed escheator of Berkshire and Oxfordshire in 1593 thanks to Fortescue's nomination. During the first session of the Parliament Payne distinguished himself by 'a bitter invective' against the bill to control purveyance, and also condemned the House for its proceedings concerning Fortescue's election for Buckinghamshire. After some debate and an apology, he was forgiven the speech, but suspended until his right to sit could be determined, for as mayor he was technically ineligible. In the event he was not restored until the fourth session, and he never stood again. Dunch died shortly before the dissolution, but no by-election occurred.[6]

The election of 1614 was the first in which Knollys was able to exercise his patronage. He nominated Sir Carew Reynell, a courtier and his neighbour in Charing Cross, and added 'if they will bestow the other place upon me if Sir Michael Molyns† or his son have it not, I would name thereto Mr. Emanuel Giffard*'.[7] Neither Molyns appears to have been interested in standing, but it was presumably they who secured the promise of 'the company' to elect their Oxfordshire kinsman, Sir George Simeon, a former recusant. The corporation acknowledged that 'according to order', the recorder, Edward Clerke of Reading, who had replaced Stampe in 1606, should have been chosen for the corporation's seat, but, at the corporation's request, he surrendered his right and consequently Simeon was elected with Reynell.[8]

In 1620 Samuel Dunch, Sir William's younger brother, was 'chosen' by Knollys, and Simeon was again chosen 'by the company', or at least 'the more and greater part of them'.[9] In 1624 Simeon yielded the first place to Knollys's brother-in-law, Sir Edward Howard II, who chose to sit for Calne. At the ensuing election it was presumably Knollys who nominated Sir Anthony Forest, the client of another brother-in-law, the 2nd earl of Salisbury (William Cecil*). Forest was re-elected to the first Caroline Parliament, but Simeon made way for his young cousin, Michael Molyns. In 1626 Forest sat for the third time, the junior seat going to another young man, Unton Croke, a younger son of the great legal family. Croke was presumably the corporation's candidate, but his connection with the borough has not been established. During the Parliament he was granted privilege against the litigious Sir Thomas Whorwood, and reported that he had 'reviled him, saying, he came to be a Member of this House by bribery and corruption'. No further proceedings in the matter are recorded.[10] In 1628 Knollys almost certainly nominated his nephew, Sir Robert Knollys II, and the borough presumably chose Edmund Dunch, Sir William's son, who was

just 25 but had already represented Berkshire in three Parliaments.

[1] D. Hirst, *Representative of the People?*, 215.   [2] *VCH Berks*. iii. 523, 532, 534, 536; J.K. Hedges, *Wallingford*, ii. 217; C219/35/1/199; 219/38/14. [3] *VCH Berks*. iii. 528; Hedges, ii. 113. [4] Berks. RO, W/AC1/1/1, f.88,98v,105;*HPCommons,1558-1603*,ii.417;Hedges,ii.197. [5] Berks. RO, W/AC1/1/1, f. 98v; *HP Commons, 1558-1603*, i. 117; ii. 435. [6] *CJ*, i. 162b, 396b, 406b. [7] *Pprs. of Capt. Henry Stevens* ed. M.R. Toynbee, (Oxon. Rec. Soc. xlii), 37. [8] Berks. RO,W/AC1/1/1,ff. 93,98v. [9] Berks. RO, W/AC1/1/1, f. 105. [10] *Procs. 1626*, iii. 89.

A.D.

BUCKINGHAMSHIRE

Number of voters: up to 360 in 1604[1]

22 Feb. 1604	SIR FRANCIS GOODWIN
	SIR WILLIAM FLEETWOOD II
	  Sir John Fortescue
	    Return of Goodwin rejected by
	    the clerk of the Crown

21 Mar. 1604[2]	SIR JOHN FORTESCUE *vice* Goodwin

16 May 1604	CHRISTOPHER PIGOTT *vice*
	  Fortescue and Goodwin, both
	  elections having been declared
	  void

18 Mar. 1607	SIR ANTHONY TYRINGHAM *vice* Pigott, expelled from the House
c.Mar. 1614	SIR FRANCIS GOODWIN SIR WILLIAM BORLASE
6 Dec. 1620	SIR FRANCIS GOODWIN SIR WILLIAM FLEETWOOD II
28 Jan. 1624	SIR WILLIAM FLEETWOOD II SIR THOMAS DENTON
c.Apr. 1625	SIR FRANCIS GOODWIN HENRY BULSTRODE
c.Jan. 1626	SIR FRANCIS GOODWIN SIR THOMAS DENTON
23 Feb. 1628	SIR EDWARD COKE SIR WILLIAM FLEETWOOD II

Buckinghamshire, a grazing county, was geographically divided into two distinct regions, with the 'mountainous, or rather hilly' Chilterns to the southeast, and the Vale to the north.[3] During the medieval period quarter sessions and most of the county's administrative functions had migrated away from the nominal capital, Buckingham, situated in the north-west, to the more centrally located and prosperous town of Aylesbury, where they remained throughout the early Stuart period.[4] The county as a whole was in several respects slow to define itself as a separate regional entity; the shrievalty was shared with neighbouring Bedfordshire until 1575,[5] and the lord lieutenancy remained vacant after the death of Arthur, 14th Lord Grey of Wilton in 1593, until lord chancellor Ellesmere (Thomas Egerton[†]) was appointed in the aftermath of enclosure rioting in 1607.[6] The attainder of the 15th Lord Grey for complicity in the Bye and Main conspiracies of 1603, and the perpetual absence of the Russell earls of Bedford from their onetime seat at Chenies, left a vacuum of aristocratic leadership in the area. Moreover, at the turn of the seventeenth century many of the county's most distinguished gentry families were relative newcomers. Buckinghamshire estates, located within easy reach of London by either river or road, provided ideal country retreats for statesmen and successful lawyers, including Sir John Croke[†], based at Chilton, Sir William Fleetwood[†] of Great Missenden, Sir John Fortescue of Salden, and Sir Edward Coke, who acquired Stoke Poges by marriage in 1598. These and other recently established names, such as Goodwin of Winchendon, Borlase of Little Marlow, and Denton of Hillesden, would gradually eclipse the longer standing Hampden family of Great Hampden, and crypto-Catholic Dormers of Wing. As a result there was a state of flux in Buckinghamshire's local governance during the early modern period, with frequent shifts in the balance of influence within the county's ruling elite.[7] Religious and familial allegiances created factions whose differences had found expression at the hustings on several occasions during the reign of Elizabeth, although outright contests were generally avoided. Elections had traditionally been held at Aylesbury since at least the early fifteenth century; indentures were usually signed by around 30 electors, although the total number of freeholders in attendance at elections was much greater.[8]

In 1604 the sheriff, Sir Francis Cheyney, summoned the election to Brickhill, in the north-east of the shire, to avoid the plague at Aylesbury. According to Cheyney's subsequent testimony, at the first poll on 22 Feb. Sir Francis Goodwin received 200-300 votes for the senior seat, clearly beating Sir John Fortescue, chancellor of the duchy of Lancaster, whose supporters numbered no more than 60. This upset the general expectation that Fortescue would take the

first seat and Goodwin the second; Goodwin himself 'earnestly persuaded with the freeholders' to reconsider, begging that they 'would not do Sir John that injury'. When they still refused, Fortescue took great offence and stood down rather than accept second place, which would have been beneath the status and dignity of an ancient privy councillor.[9] A further poll was then held, whereupon Sir William Fleetwood II was unanimously elected as the junior Member. Goodwin's efforts on Fortescue's behalf may have been disingenuous, since it was common knowledge that their rivalry dated back to at least the early 1580s. Moreover, each man represented opposing factions among the county elite, with Fortescue, a religious and political conservative, set against a puritan element of which both Goodwin and Fleetwood were prominent adherents.[10]

A considerable delay ensued before the election indenture was delivered to the clerk of the Crown, Sir George Coppyn[†], by which time Fortescue had taken steps to ensure that the result would be overturned. Fortescue first consulted some of his fellow privy councillors, including Ellesmere, Sir Robert Cecil[†], and the lord chief justice Sir John Popham[†], with whose help he concocted a plan to have Goodwin declared ineligible on the grounds of two outlawries against him for small debts in the London Court of Hustings.[11] Official notification that Goodwin was an outlaw was presented to Cheyney on 2 Mar. by the attorney-general (Sir Edward Coke), who penned a certificate to accompany the original return, which was thereby voided. However, Cheyney did not forward these documents to Coppyn until 16 Mar., when Fortescue immediately handed him a fresh writ, already sealed, so that the election process could begin again from scratch.[12] On 21 Mar., two days after the state opening of Parliament, Fortescue was returned unopposed, albeit at short notice and at a time when many of the county elite – presumably including the candidate himself – were absent due to their attendance at events in the capital.[13]

Fleetwood lost no time in raising complaint to the Commons on 22 Mar., demanding that the returns might be examined and Goodwin admitted as a Member.[14] Coppyn and Goodwin were therefore ordered to attend the following day, and after hearing and debating their evidence the Commons resolved on 23 Mar. that Goodwin had been lawfully elected, and should be permitted to take up his seat.[15] In particular, the House refused to accept Goodwin's disqualification as an outlaw, since his alleged offences predated the Act of general pardon passed in 1601.[16] However, the case was far from closed. Four days later the Lords, acting on instruction from above, requested a conference to consider the matter further, which the Commons refused.[17] James I then let it be known that he 'conceived himself engaged and touched in honour', and ordered both Houses to confer, a turn of events that the Commons considered 'so extraordinary and unexpected' that its Members could hardly decide how to react.[18]

From this point onwards Goodwin vs. Fortescue escalated into a serious confrontation over who ultimately had authority to determine the outcome of disputed elections.[19] Although it seems unlikely that either James or the Privy Council would have wished to initiate such a conflict merely in order to increase the number of councillors in the Commons, their high-handed intervention at every stage in the case does imply that there was more at stake than first meets the eye. It has been suggested (although substantial evidence is lacking) that Goodwin and Fleetwood, both of whom had connections at Court themselves, may have been prompted to stand by Fortescue's enemies among the Council, and that the dispute arose not just out of local rivalry in Buckinghamshire, but out of factional in-fighting between the king's conservative, old guard of Elizabethan councillors such as Fortescue, and the mostly Scottish newcomers upon whom favours and rewards had been heaped since James's accession.[20] A more plausible explanation is that the situation may have been deliberately engineered from the outset by Ellesmere, as the latest episode in a long running contention, dating back to at least 1581, between Chancery and the Commons.[21] Certainly Ellesmere seems to have been responsible for placing great emphasis upon a clause in the royal Proclamation of 11 Jan. 1604 which announced that 'persons bankrupts or outlawed' should not be permitted to stand at the forthcoming general election; and it must also have been the lord chancellor who obliged Fortescue by authorizing the writ for the second election.[22] He furthermore seems to have initially convinced the king that upholding the supremacy of Chancery against the Commons' incursions was a matter of royal prerogative. On 29 Mar. James therefore informed a Commons delegation that 'by the law this House ought not to meddle with returns, being all made into Chancery', and ordered them to confer with the judges and report to the Privy Council.[23] James may have hoped, by this decisive stance, to settle the matter quickly so that the Commons could proceed with what he had already told them would be the main business of the Parliament: the Union with Scotland. As Conrad Russell argued, underlying anxiety about the Union was possibly the real reason why both sides considered the Buckinghamshire election to be 'worth a serious dispute'.[24]

The Commons, considering the implications of James's announcement, unrestrainedly expressed alarm. On 30 Mar. Sir Robert Wingfield declared that 'now the case of Sir John Fortescue and Sir Francis Goodwin was become the case of the whole kingdom … the free election of the country is taken away, and none shall be chosen but such as shall please the king and council'. Sir George More warned that it was no longer now 'the case of Sir John and Sir Francis, but a case of great difference between the king and us; wherein we are deeply to consider the consequence, if this pique be bruited in the country abroad, or beyond the seas'.[25] Reports had indeed already been dispatched by the Venetian ambassador, who observed that the Parliament had so far been marred by 'great friction and ill feeling' over the Buckinghamshire election, which had left the king 'greatly disturbed'.[26] Members of the Commons began, one after another, to insist that 'this [House] is a court of record; therefore we ought by all means [to] seek to preserve the honour and dignity of it'; all were adamant that its ancient privileges and autonomy must be maintained. Many were therefore reluctant to meet with the judges, and after heated debate the Commons resolved not to do so, but to put their reasons for supporting Goodwin into a written petition.[27]

James, who had by this time retreated to Royston, expressed his annoyance at the Commons' intransigence, but privately began to doubt whether the course he had embarked upon was really the best way to handle the situation. According to the French ambassador, he confided that he had been given bad counsel, and was persuaded by Henry, earl of Northampton to devise a compromise solution that would restore harmony to the Parliament.[28] Since he had urged the House to debate the Union, and it had so far failed to do so, James now decided not to further jeopardize the Union project by continuing to side with Ellesmere and the Council, in the face of mounting evidence that their case was weaker than he had originally been led to believe. Lawyers in the lower House meanwhile proceeded to interrogate Cheyney on 2 Apr., and to uncover a series of damning revelations about Fortescue and his allies' conduct in the aftermath of the election, including the fabrication of evidence against Goodwin.[29] After the Commons delivered its 'Humble Answer' to the Privy Council, James responded on 5 Apr. by admitting that he had been 'distracted in judgment'; nevertheless he commanded them 'as an absolute king' to confer with the judges, in the presence of his privy councillors 'not as umpires to determine, but to report indifferently on both sides', so that the matter could be settled once and for all. The Commons' amazed silence was broken by Henry Yelverton, who exclaimed that 'the prince's command is like a thunderbolt; his command upon our allegiance, like the roaring of a lion'.[30]

After a brief adjournment of the session for Easter, Sir Francis Bacon reported the king's proposed compromise on 11 Apr.: neither Fortescue nor Goodwin should sit, but a new writ would be issued to elect another senior knight of the shire. On the question of who should adjudicate in cases of disputed elections, he gave assurances that the Commons' privileges 'were not in question ... he granted, it was a court of record and a judge of returns', while also maintaining that Chancery had 'the like power' when Parliaments were not in session, and that whichever court 'that first had passed their judgment, should not be controlled'.[31] The Commons fully assented to this ruling, and immediately passed a formal vote of thanks to the king; the writ for the new election was issued on 13 April.[32]

Despite the fact that Goodwin's election was quashed, the Commons had won a decisive victory, and as James's frustration at the lack of progress with the Union project grew, he privately expressed regret for the concessions he had made.[33] On his express instruction the earl of Northampton wrote on 24 Apr. to a handful of Buckinghamshire justices, requiring them to examine further the 'the ground of that so high and hot an opposition' to Fortescue, and to 'descend into a due consideration of [Goodwin's] carriage at and before his first election'.[34] It is not known whether anything ever came of this investigation, but it was possibly set in motion with the aim of better understanding how to defuse similar situations in future. The selection of men to whom the letter was addressed suggests that Northampton sympathized with Goodwin, and may have been considering ways to compensate him. If so this perhaps explains why Goodwin was nominated by the Privy Council, presumably at Northampton's instigation, for a borough seat at the first opportunity, in February 1606; the timing of this intervention would moreover suggest that it was intended as a gesture of goodwill towards the Commons, since it coincided with a request for a large vote of supply.[35] For their part, some Members of the lower House remained uneasy about the outcome of the Buckinghamshire election controversy and its constitutional implications.[36] The authors of the *Form of Apology and Satisfaction*, which document was drafted towards the end of the first session but never formally submitted to the king, described the Commons' capitulation to the 'middle course' proposed by James as a 'deceiving of ourselves and yielding in our apparent right'. It furthermore reasserted the need to safeguard the Commons' privileges and status as a court of record, particularly in judging elections, against the claims of Chancery.[37] Ellesmere, needless to say, continued many years later to maintain that the Commons had no right to determine election returns; a point he might well have succeeded in establishing in 1604 had it not been for the king's desire to pursue the Union.[38]

The reverberations from the dispute delayed the fresh election in Buckinghamshire for several weeks. When it was eventually held, on 16 May, the seat went to a compromise candidate, Christopher Pigott, who had supported Goodwin in the initial election but was also Fortescue's kinsman by marriage. It is ironic that despite James's efforts to ensure that the earlier election controversy would not displace the Union from the top of the parliamentary agenda, a Member was chosen who, in the third session, went on to deliver an anti-Scots invective so outrageous that he had to be expelled from the House in disgrace.[39] This necessitated a by-election for Buckinghamshire on 18 Mar. 1607, at which Goodwin's first cousin, Sir Anthony Tyringham, was returned. Like Pigott, Tyringham was clearly considered a safe choice, as his ancestors had represented the county as far back as 1295.

The next general election, in 1614, occurred without commotion, perhaps contrary to the expectations of observers. On 17 Mar. John Chamberlain informed his friend (Sir) Dudley Carleton* that 'I have not heard of so much contestation for places in Parliament as falls out this time, yet Sir Francis Goodwin and Sir William Borlase have carried it quietly in Buckinghamshire'.[40] As the result suggests, Goodwin's standing among the county gentry remained undented by the events of 1604. There is no evidence that Ellesmere attempted to use his position as lord lieutenant to exert electoral control in any direction. In any case, there appears to have been a lack of serious challengers: Fortescue was long since deceased, and his successor, Sir Francis†, was a known recusant; Fleetwood showed no inclination to serve on this occasion; Pigott could hardly be chosen again after the disgrace of his expulsion; and Tyringham, believing he was on his deathbed, had made his will only a few weeks earlier.[41]

A bill was introduced in this Parliament to move the assizes and quarter sessions to Buckingham, probably by Sir Thomas Denton, the borough's senior Member. However, two Buckinghamshire magistrates, Sir Jerome Horsey and Sir Edward Hoby, opposed the bill at its first reading on 3 June 1614, and it had no time to progress further before the session was abruptly terminated the following week.[42]

Ellesmere stood down as lord lieutenant in 1616, and was replaced by the royal favourite, George Villiers, future marquess and duke of Buckingham, despite the latter's lack of substantial estates in the county. Although he occasionally took advantage of the borough seats that this position placed at his disposal, there is no record of Buckingham's direct involvement in the selection of knights of the shire at any of the general elections during his lieutenancy. In December 1620 Goodwin and Fleetwood were returned in first and second places respectively; indeed, throughout the period Buckinghamshire voters showed no objection to re-electing previous Members, so that Goodwin was chosen on seven separate occasions over a period of 40 years, while Fleetwood represented the county in four Parliaments. On behalf of the constituency, Goodwin obtained licence on 16 Mar. 1621 to attend the Lords with particulars exhibited from Buckinghamshire against the notorious monopolist (Sir) Giles Mompesson*; and on 21 Apr. Fleetwood presented a petition from the county's grand jury concerning purveyance of carriages, a practice he condemned as 'a greater burthen in many places than an annual subsidy'.[43]

Goodwin served as sheriff in 1623-4 and as such was ineligible to stand at the next election, at which Fleetwood and Denton were returned. It is notable that this, the only occasion on which Fleetwood won the senior seat, took place after Fleetwood had been sacked from the magistrates' bench for obstructing the Palatinate Benevolence, to which he refused to contribute.[44] Fleetwood again pressed for the reform of purveyance of carriages, an issue of high local importance in the counties closest to London, reviving a bill that he had previously steered through the Commons in 1621; however, it was ultimately blocked by the Lords.[45]

Goodwin was twice re-elected as the senior knight of the shire to the first two Parliaments of Charles's reign. He was joined in 1625 by Henry Bulstrode of Horton, whose ancestors had first represented the county in the mid-fifteenth century, and in 1626 Goodwin was paired with Denton. Ahead of the latter election it was rumoured that Fleetwood might be pricked as sheriff of Lancashire, where his family originated, in order to prevent him from re-entering the Commons, but

in the event he avoided this onerous appointment by giving sufficient assurances that he had no intention to stand.[46] Sir Edward Coke was for the same reason assigned to the shrievalty of Buckinghamshire, though he initially refused to take the required oath of office. Coke audaciously defied this attempt to exclude him from the Parliament by having himself returned for Norfolk; however, his eligibility to sit was duly questioned, and the privileges committee, though unable to find any way to let him take up his seat, expressed their sympathy by refusing to sanction a writ to replace him, so that no by-election was ever held.[47] Coke was elected as Buckinghamshire's senior knight of the shire, together with Fleetwood, in 1628.[48]

[1] CJ, i. 161b. [2] CD 1604-7, p. 55. [3] W. Camden, Britannia (1722), i. 308. [4] VCH Bucks. iv. 528-9. [5] List of Sheriffs comp. A. Hughes (PRO, L. and I. ix), 9. [6] E. Viney, 'Bucks. Ltcy.', Bucks. Recs. xix. 118-9; Sainty, Lords Lieutenants, 12. [7] Cent. Bucks. Stud., D138/22/1; A.M. Johnson, 'Bucks. 1640-60' (M.A. thesis, Swansea 1963), app. II; H.A. Hanley, Bucks. Sheriffs, 8-11. [8] C219/35/1/204, 209, 211, 213; 219/37/66; 219/38/2; 219/40/152; 219/41B/71. [9] CJ, i. 161b. [10] L.L. Peck, 'Goodwin v. Fortescue: the Local Context of Parlty. Controversy', PH, iii. 33-56. [11] HMC Hatfield, xvi. 40; HMC Buccleuch, iii. 83; SP84/64, ff. 135v-136; Winwood's Memorials ed. E. Sawyer, ii. 18. [12] CJ, i. 161b. [13] E. Lindquist, 'The Case of Sir Francis Goodwin', EHR, civ. 670-77. [14] CJ, i. 149a. [15] Ibid. 151b-2a. [16] Lansd. 486, ff. 7v-8. [17] CJ, i. 156a. [18] Ibid. 156b. [19] Bodl., Eng. Hist. c. 397, ff. 154-7; State Trials ed. T.B. Howell, ii. 91-114. [20] R.C. Munden, 'The defeat of Sir John Fortescue: Court versus Country at the Hustings?', EHR, xciii. 811-16. [21] A. Thrush, 'Commons v. Chancery: the 1604 Bucks. Election Dispute Revisited', PH, xxvi. 301-9. [22] Ibid. 306; Stuart Royal Procs. ed. J.F. Larkin and P.L. Hughes, i. 66-70. [23] CJ, i. 158b; CD 1604-7, pp. 33-4. [24] C. Russell, 'Eng. Parls. 1593-1606: one Epoch or Two?', in Parls. of Eliz. Eng. ed. D.M. Dean and N.L. Jones, 208, 211-12. [25] CJ, i. 159a-160a; 939a-940b. [26] CSP Ven. 1603-7, p. 142. [27] CJ, i. 160a. [28] HMC Hatfield, xvi. 49, 50; CSP Ven. 1603-7, p. 143; PRO31/3/37, pp. 93, 100; C. Russell, Trevelyan Lectures ed. R. Cust and A. Thrush (forthcoming). [29] CJ, i. 162b-165a, 942a; SP14/7/3; Lindquist, 672, 674-5. [30] CJ, i. 166b, 943a. [31] Ibid. 168a-9a. [32] Ibid. 170b-1b. [33] CSP Ven. 1603-7, p. 150. [34] Bodl., Rawl. D918, f. 35. [35] Peck, 49-50; W. Notestein, House of Commons 1604-10, p. 512; Add. 11402, f. 110. [36] D. Hirst, 'Elections and the Privileges of the House of Commons in the Early 17th Century: Confrontation or Compromise?', HJ, xviii. 851-62. [37] Constitutional Docs. of Reign of Jas. I ed. J.R. Tanner, 221, 224-5. [38] L.A. Knafla, Law and Pols. in Jacobean Eng. 256; Thrush, 308-9. [39] CJ, i. 333b, 336a. [40] Chamberlain Letters ed. N.E. McClure, i. 518. [41] Peck, 52; PROB 11/125, f. 367. [42] Procs. 1614 (Commons), 412, 418; HLRO, Lords main pprs. 3 June 1614; Lipscomb, Bucks. ii. 577. [43] CJ, i. 565a, 585b. [44] SP14/127/44; C231/4, f. 138. [45] CJ, i. 619a, 685a. [46] Procs. 1625, pp. 725-6; Wentworth Pprs. ed. J.P. Cooper (Cam. Soc. ser. 4. xii), 240. [47] Procs. 1626, ii. 12, 33; iv. 134-5, 294, 313, 317. [48] CD 1628, ii. 174.

R.C.L.S.

AMERSHAM

Right of election: inhabitants paying scot and lot

Number of voters: 148 in 1624[1]

aft. 7 May 1624	WILLIAM HAKEWILL
	JOHN CREWE
c. Apr. 1625	JOHN CREWE
	FRANCIS DRAKE
c. Jan. 1626	WILLIAM CLARKE
	FRANCIS DRAKE
c. Feb. 1628	WILLIAM HAKEWILL
	EDMUND WALLER

Amersham, situated 26 miles from London on the road to Aylesbury, was well established by the time of the Domesday survey.[2] Although granted a fair and market by the Crown in 1200, it was never incorporated. The chief municipal officers were two constables, appointed by a borough court; however, no borough records survive that might shed further light on the town's institutions and administration.[3] In the early sixteenth century Amersham was described by John Leland as 'a right pretty market town ... of one street well built with timber'.[4] By 1601 there were around 988 inhabitants.[5] Having previously been a notorious centre of Lollardy, Amersham retained a reputation for puritan nonconformity: in 1624 it was reported that 'the people still lie in their pews, sit with their hats on, and neither kneel at the litany nor bow at the name of Jesus', despite orders to the contrary at the last ecclesiastical visitation.[6]

Amersham first sent Members to Parliament during the reign of Edward I; the earliest surviving returns are dated 1301, but the town's representation lapsed after 1309, most probably as a result of 'decay and poverty'.[7] Efforts to restore the franchise to Amersham, Wendover, Great Marlow, and Hertford were first mooted in the Commons in 1621, Sir George More reporting on 18 May that the privileges committee 'thinketh fit new writs should be granted for these boroughs'.[8] However, the four towns were first required to submit their charters for consideration by the king's counsel.[9] A hearing was assigned for all four boroughs on 24 Nov. 1621, but no further progress was achieved before the abrupt end of the session a few weeks later.[10]

In the next Parliament, in 1624, new petitions were prepared by the lawyer William Hakewill*, who lived near Wendover and was retained as counsel by the three Buckinghamshire boroughs.[11] A precedent had been set by the re-enfranchisement of Pontefract and Ilchester in 1621, and on 4 May 1624 the privileges committee again signalled its support for re-enfranchising Amersham and the other towns which had lobbied in 1621.[12] By this time it was well known that the king was not favourably disposed to increase the size of an already unmanageably large institution, and therefore everything depended on the claim that all four towns had previously sent Members, since 'a borough cannot forfeit this liberty of sending burgesses by non-user'. After searching the archives, John Selden* provided assurances that no other boroughs were eligible for re-enfranchisement on such grounds. Despite its lack of a charter, Amersham was held to deserve full borough status and representation because, in respect of parliamentary money grants, it had always paid tenths rather than fifteenths.[13] Writs were accordingly issued on 7 May.[14] No election indentures survive from this period, but Crown Office lists indicate that the borough was officially described as Agmondesham *alias* Amersham, the former name being that employed in the fourteenth-century returns.[15]

The choice of Members reflects the town's gratitude to Hakewill, who was elected in first place, and the influence of the 3rd earl of Bedford, to whom the manor of Amersham had been granted in 1610.[16] The junior seat was bestowed on John Crewe, the nephew of Sir Ranulphe Crewe* who, from the spring of 1624, assisted Bedford after the latter entered into lengthy negotiations for selling the manor to William Tothill, owner of the adjacent manor of Shardeloes.[17] The precise date of the election is unknown, as the indenture is not extant, but Hakewill had certainly taken his seat by 28 May, when he was appointed to present a petition to the king.

John Crewe was re-elected in 1625, alongside Tothill's son-in-law Francis Drake. In 1626 the senior seat was awarded to William Clarke, a local magistrate and deputy lieutenant based at Hitcham, about eight miles south of the borough, while Drake, who inherited Shardeloes later in 1626, took second place. In 1628 Hakewill was returned again, and the junior seat went to another wealthy Buckinghamshire magnate, Edmund Waller of Beaconsfield, four miles south of Amersham. There is no evidence that Amersham paid the expenses of its Members during the early Stuart period, and probably did not do so since the men returned were all wealthy members of the local gentry.

[1] Anon. 'The Shardeloes Muniments', *Bucks. Recs.* xiv. 282-5.
[2] W.H. Hastings Kelle, 'Amersham', *Bucks. Recs.* ii. 333-53. [3] *VCH*

Bucks. iii. 145. ⁴Lipscomb, *Bucks.* iii. 146-67. ⁵M. Mullins, *Amersham through the Ages*, unfol. ⁶*CSP Dom.* 1623-5, p. 347. ⁷*Bucks. Misc.* ed. R. Gibbs, 239-40; M. McKisack, *Parl. Rep. of Eng. Bors. during Middle Ages*, 10; *CD 1621*, iii. 285-6; v. 380. ⁸*CJ*, i. 624a, b. ⁹*CD 1621*, ii. 380; iv. 360. ¹⁰*CJ*, i. 643b; *CD 1621*, iv. 434. ¹¹J. Glanville, *Reps. of Certain Cases* (1775), p. 88. ¹²*CJ*, i. 697b. ¹³'Earle 1624', f. 169r-v; SP15/43/62, ff. 150-2. ¹⁴B. Willis, *Notitia Parliamentaria Bucks.* 34-5; C231/4, f. 165. ¹⁵*OR.* ¹⁶Hastings Kelle, 336. ¹⁷Anon. 'The Shardeloes Muniments', *Bucks. Recs.* xiv. 281-97.

R.C.L.S.

AYLESBURY

Right of election: in the corporation

Number of voters: 23

9 Mar. 1604	SIR WILLIAM BORLASE
	SIR WILLIAM SMITH
c. Mar. 1614	SIR JOHN DORMER
	SAMUEL BACKHOUSE
21 Dec. 1621	SIR JOHN DORMER
	HENRY BORLASE
6 Feb. 1624	SIR JOHN PAKINGTON, bt.
	(SIR) THOMAS CREWE
27 *Jan.* 1625	SIR ROBERT KERR *vice*
	Sir John Packington, deceased
29 Apr. 1625	SIR ROBERT KERR
	SIR JOHN HARE
c. Jan. 1626	CLEMENT COKE
	ARTHUR GOODWIN
27 Feb. 1628	SIR EDMUND VERNEY
	CLEMENT COKE

Described by Camden as 'a very fair market town, large and pretty populous, surrounded with a great number of pleasant meadows and pastures',[1] Aylesbury, by the later Middle Ages, had usurped Buckingham as the centre of county administration in Buckinghamshire; the assizes, gaol, and county elections were all relocated to the town, which was conveniently situated in the middle of the county.[2] A charter of incorporation in 1554 appointed as the governing body a 'common council', comprising a bailiff, ten aldermen and 12 capital burgesses.[3] In the same year Members were first sent to Parliament. The franchise was limited to the corporation, and the borough's patronage was entirely dominated by the Pakington family as lords of the manor of Aylesbury. Indeed,

during the Elizabethan period the sheriff sent his precept not to the borough but directly to the Pakingtons; the recently widowed Dame Dorothy Pakington therefore completed the return herself in 1572. This somewhat irregular practice had been discontinued by the 1600s, as early Stuart returns were drawn up between the sheriff of Buckinghamshire and the mayor of Aylesbury in the usual way.[4] It is doubtful whether many of the privileges conferred in the borough's charter were ever exercised: the townsmen quarrelled with the Pakingtons over such things as rights of common, and protested that although they were entitled to hold a weekly market they 'durst not make use of their charter'.[5] They finally managed to break the Pakingtons' stranglehold during the Civil War, when the town become a parliamentarian garrison, and the royalist Sir John Pakington, 2nd bt. suffered heavy losses.[6] In the absence of surviving borough records it is impossible to say whether Aylesbury's corporation contributed towards the expenses of its Members during the early Stuart period, but it seems improbable that it did so.[7]

In June 1603 Sir John Pakington, a former favourite of Elizabeth I, entertained the new king and queen at Aylesbury with 'unusual magnificence'.[8] On this occasion Lady Pakington's brother, William Smith, was knighted.[9] Pakington subsequently nominated him for the junior seat at Aylesbury at the general election the following year, and he was returned together with Pakington's distant kinsman, Sir William Borlase of Little Marlow, who took the senior seat. In 1614 a Buckinghamshire gentleman, Sir John Dormer of Dorton, took the first seat, while the second went to Borlase's brother-in-law, Samuel Backhouse; both presumably had Pakington's support. Dormer sat again in 1621, together with Borlase's third son, Henry. Pakington reserved the first seat in 1624 for his son and heir, Sir John, for whom he had purchased a baronetcy in 1620. He was also responsible for ensuring the unopposed return of Thomas Crewe, the prospective Speaker of the Commons, who was obliged to take second place.

A writ was issued for a by-election following the tragic early death in October 1624 of the younger Pakington who, in the parish register, was styled 'the hopes of Aylesbury'.[10] The elder Pakington himself died the following January, leaving his four year-old grandson and heir, John, to the care of trustees including Sir William Borlase and attorney-general Sir Thomas Coventry*. On 27 Jan. 1625 Sir Robert Kerr, a Scottish courtier only recently naturalized, was returned, indicating that Coventry had assumed control of the borough's electoral patronage.[11] Kerr had no opportunity to take up his place before the session was automatically terminated by the death of James I, but he was re-elected at the next general election, at which time the second seat went to Coventry's son-in-law, Sir John Hare, of Stow Bardolph in Norfolk. In 1626, however, Coventry seems not to have intervened in the election, in which both seats were taken by the offspring of leading Buckinghamshire families: Clement Coke, son of Sir Edward*, and Arthur Goodwin, son of Sir Francis*. Coke went on to be re-elected in 1628, but was obliged to concede the first seat to Sir Edmund Verney, whose seat at Middle Claydon lay about ten miles north-west of the town.

[1] *Bucks. Misc.* ed. R. Gibbs, 145-6. [2] Lipscomb, *Bucks.* ii. 27-8; *VCH Bucks.* iii. 1-11; iv. 528-30. [3] M. Weinbaum, *Brit. Bor. Charters*, 7; *Cal. Deeds at Aylesbury* comp. J.G. Jenkins (Bucks. Arch. Soc. v), 5. [4] J.E. Neale, *Eliz. House of Commons*, 174-6; C219/38/5-7. [5] *VCH Bucks.* iii. 9-10; R. Gibbs, *Hist. Aylesbury*, 171. [6] *VCH Bucks.* iii. 7, 10; G. Lamb, 'Aylesbury in the Civil War', in *Bucks. Recs.* xli. 183-9. [7] J. Parker, 'Notes on the Hist. of Aylesbury', in *Bucks. Recs.* v. 432-3. [8] J. Nichols, *Progs. of Jas. I*, i. 192-3. [9] *Vis. Leics.* (Harl. Soc. ii), 66-7. [10] C219/38/6; Gibbs, 142. [11] Gibbs, 139-43.

R.C.L.S.

BUCKINGHAM

Right of election: in the corporation[1]

Number of voters: 13

28 Feb. 1604	SIR EDWARD TYRELL
	SIR THOMAS DENTON
24 Feb. 1606	SIR FRANCIS GOODWIN *vice*
	Tyrell, deceased
c. Mar. 1614	SIR RALPH WINWOOD
	SIR THOMAS DENTON
8 Dec. 1620	SIR THOMAS DENTON
	RICHARD OLIVER
30 Jan. 1624	SIR EDMUND VERNEY
	RICHARD OLIVER
29 Apr. 1625	SIR ALEXANDER DENTON
	RICHARD OLIVER
23 Jan. 1626	SIR ALEXANDER DENTON
	SIR JOHN SMYTHE III
26 Feb. 1628	SIR THOMAS DENTON
	RICHARD OLIVER

The county town of Buckinghamshire from at least the time of the Conquest, Buckingham declined sharply during the medieval period, partly because of its inconvenient location to the north of the shire but also because of the decay of the Norman castle.[2] Administrative functions such as the assizes were removed to Aylesbury, leaving Buckingham, according to Camden, as 'no considerable place', its castle 'seated in the middle of the town upon a great mount, of the very ruins of which scarce anything now remains'.[3] The nadir of Buckingham's fortune was reached in the early sixteenth century, when a fire destroyed many of its buildings, as a result of which the town was highlighted in an Act of 1542 aimed at reversing urban decay.[4] However, the gradual revival of the local economy, based initially on the wool trade, meant that in 1554 the town was granted a charter of incorporation which established a governing body comprising a bailiff and 12 principal burgesses and gave the borough the right to hold regular markets and two annual fairs.[5] Buckingham also acquired its own bench of magistrates. New industries such as lace-making and a bell foundry became established during the later sixteenth century.[6] The earliest surviving borough records include various Elizabethan bye-laws, grants, commissions for gaol delivery, and a memorandum of the queen's visit to the town in 1568.[7] Elizabeth's kinsman Sir John Fortescue*, based at Salden, about ten miles to the east, was the borough's high steward by around 1584, but although he and his son, Sir Francis†, who succeeded as steward in 1606, both represented Buckingham in the Commons during the queen's reign, neither appears to have sought seats there, either for themselves or others, under the early Stuarts.[8]

Buckingham first sent Members to Parliament in 1529, and the franchise was established continuously from 1545 onwards.[9] Voting was restricted to the 13 members of the corporation, whose choice of Members throughout the early Stuart period seems to have been determined entirely by various patrons.[10] It would be easy to suppose that chief among these was (Sir) Thomas Temple†, who bought the lordship of the borough in 1604. This title, which was separate from the manor of Buckingham, brought Temple an annual rent of 40s.; but there is no evidence that he ever exercised direct electoral patronage.[11] Instead Temple seems to have ceded control over elections to his relatives by marriage, the Dentons, whose seat of Hillesden lay about three miles south of Buckingham. Sir Thomas Denton or his eldest son Sir Alexander occupied one of the town's seats in all but one Parliament between 1604 and 1628. The remaining places were made available to members of the local gentry and to outsiders recommended by various Court patrons. In 1604 the senior seat went to Sir Edward Tyrell, whose Thornton estate lay only four miles to the east, while Sir Thomas Denton took second place. Both men were members of the town bench.[12] Following Tyrell's death early in the second session, the Privy Council wrote to the corporation on 21 Feb. 1606 recommending that they elect Sir Francis Goodwin of Upper Winchendon. They were, they declared, 'well persuaded of [his] loyalty and good affection ... towards His Majesty and the state, as also of his sufficiency to discharge whatsoever shall be recommended unto him for the good of that town to which he is by habitation so near a neighbour'.[13] The Council went on to mention that they were aware that 'some mediation' had been used for another candidate, but the latter's identity remains unknown. As the letter itself tacitly acknowledges, this direct intervention by the Council was somewhat unusual. In part it was intended to compensate Goodwin, whose return in 1604 as the senior knight of the shire for Buckinghamshire, though fiercely defended by the House of Commons, had been declared void by the judges and ultimately by the king. However, it may also have been intended as a goodwill gesture towards the Commons, as the Council was hoping to persuade the Lower House to vote a large sum to James, who was by now deeply in debt. Three days after the date of the Council's letter Goodwin was returned at the ensuing by-election.

Denton consolidated his interest by purchasing the manor of Buckingham from Sir Robert Brett* in 1613, and was re-elected at the general election in the following year.[14] The senior seat went to Sir Ralph Winwood, a diplomat who had recently been promoted principal secretary of state. One may strongly suspect that the Privy Council intervened again to solicit the seat on his behalf, although no letter of nomination survives. However, Winwood was the lessee of Goodwin's Westminster town house, and could alternatively have been recommended to the corporation by their former representative.[15] In the Commons, it was presumably Denton rather than Winwood who introduced a bill to fix the county's summer assizes and quarter sessions at Buckingham rather than Aylesbury, but the measure failed to progress beyond a first reading on 3 June as two Buckinghamshire magistrates, Sir Jerome Horsey and Sir Edward Hoby, opposed it; in any case it was lost, along with all other legislation, at the abrupt dissolution four days later.[16] Elected as Buckingham's senior Member to the 1621 Parliament, Denton does not appear to have tried to revive this measure, and

consequently the assizes remained permanently at Aylesbury. The second seat was taken by an outsider, Richard Oliver, servant of the lord admiral, the marquess of Buckingham, who was doubtless able to assert his influence over the borough as Buckinghamshire's lord lieutenant.

In 1623 the lord admiral, now a duke, replaced Sir Francis Fortescue as the town's high steward, and subsequently ensured that Oliver was re-elected to the next two Parliaments. Denton did not represent the borough in 1624, having been elected a knight of the shire, but assigned his interest in the senior seat to his son-in-law, Sir Edmund Verney. In 1625 Denton could have decided to resume his representation of the borough, but he chose instead to make way for his son and heir Sir Alexander, who also took the first seat in 1626. Sir Alexander was joined on the latter occasion by Sir John Smythe III who, despite having enlisted the duke of Buckingham's support, had been unsuccessful at Rochester in his native Kent, and was presumably offered the Buckingham seat instead. In 1628 Sir Thomas Denton reclaimed the first seat, together with Oliver in second place. There is no evidence that Buckingham's corporation paid wages to any of its MPs during this period.

[1] T.A. Hume, 'Bucks. and Parl.', *Bucks. Recs.* xvi. 97. [2] D.J. Elliott, *Buckingham*, 4-14; *VCH Bucks.* iii. 471-80. [3] J.L. Stern, 'Worthies of Bucks.', *Bucks. Recs.* xvii. 3-4; W. Camden, *Britannia* (1722), i. 311. [4] J. Clarke, *Bk. of Buckingham*, 32, 51; *SR*, iii. 875-6; 33 Hen. VIII c.36. [5] Cent. Bucks. Stud. B/Buc/1/1; M. Weinbaum, *Brit. Bor. Charters*, 8, B. Willis, *Hist. Buckingham*, 86-96; *VCH Bucks.* iii. 477. [6] Clarke, 65. [7] Cent. Bucks. Stud., B/Buc/3/1, ff. 354-6, 380; B/Buc/3/2, ff. 28v-32; Elliott, 42-3, 208-9. [8] Elliott, 246; R. Gibbs, *Bucks. Misc.* 86-7. [9] Willis, 41-2. [10] *VCH Bucks.* iii. 477. [11] Elliott, 20; Cent. Bucks. Stud., B/Buc/2/1. [12] C181/1, f. 47. [13] Add. 11402, f. 110. [14] Elliott, 22; Clarke, 69. [15] *Winwood's Memorials* ed. E. Sawyer, ii. 412. [16] *Procs. 1614 (Commons)*, 412, 418; Lipscomb, *Bucks.* ii. 577.

R.C.L.S.

CHIPPING WYCOMBE

Right of election: in the freemen

Number of qualified electors: unknown

12 Mar. 1604	HENRY FLEETWOOD
	SIR JOHN TOWNSHEND
c. Mar. 1614	SIR HENRY NEVILLE III
	WILLIAM BORLASE
18 Dec. 1620	ARTHUR GOODWIN
	RICHARD LOVELACE
2 Feb. 1624	HENRY COKE
	ARTHUR GOODWIN
16 Apr. 1625	HENRY COKE
	THOMAS LANE
28 Jan. 1626	HENRY COKE
	EDMUND WALLER
23 Feb. 1628	(SIR) WILLIAM BORLASE
	THOMAS LANE

Chipping Wycombe was a small town located in a sheltered, well-watered valley on the important route between Oxford and London, and was linked to Great Marlow.[1] Its long-established market, particularly in corn, drew in traders from the capital, Berkshire, Hampshire and Oxfordshire, as well as from Buckinghamshire itself. Cloth-working and lace-making provided employment for a significant section of the population.[2] The architectural record, the presence of a large number of alehouses and inns and the construction of a new 'Gildhall' in 1604, all suggest a period of urban prosperity in the later sixteenth and early years of the seventeenth centuries.[3]

This economic growth may partly explain the granting of successive charters in 1558, 1598 and 1609.[4] Under their provisions, the free burgesses were given a monopoly of trade within the corporation's boundaries, and responsibility for internal government was place in the hands of a mayor, aldermen, bailiffs and the principal burgesses, who were emerging as a common council. When the steward was replaced by a recorder in 1609, this oligarchical structure was complete. By then, however, the cloth trade was about to begin its long-term decline and efforts were already being made by the corporation to exclude 'foreign' blacksmiths and collarmakers, hatmakers and tailors. Butchers were later barred from trading from stalls anywhere other than in the newly erected 'shambles'.[5]

Mortality rates doubled in 1617 and almost did so again in 1624-5 as a result of the plague.[6] From 1623 onwards, meeting the costs of caring for the poor and unemployed became of increasing concern to the corporation and the local magistrates.

The right to return Members lay in the hands of the corporation's resident burgesses. Like many other boroughs, Chipping Wycombe had chosen to send to Westminster members of local landed families well before the end of the Tudor period. The Windsors of Bradenham, the Fleetwoods of Chalfont St. Giles, the Fortescues of Whaddon and the Goodwins of Wooburn had all provided MPs.[7] As steward of the borough, Henry, 5th Lord Windsor, claimed the right to nominate both Members in 1601, and may have done so again in 1604. Certainly Sir John Townshend, a man based in Wales and the Marches, is likely to have been Lord Windsor's nominee. However, Henry Fleetwood, being domiciled in London where he pursued a legal career, may have owed his selection to the first Jacobean Parliament to his connections with the king's chief minister, Lord Cecil (Robert Cecil[†]). Neither man appears to have raised local matters in the Commons.

Lord Windsor died in April 1605, and though his son Thomas, the 6th Lord Windsor, had attained his majority by the time of the 1614 Parliament there is no evidence that he succeeded his father as steward of Chipping Wycombe. It was therefore the case, perhaps, that the borough was left free to choose both its Members. William Borlase of Bockmer and Little Marlow was the son of an active county administrator with recent parliamentary experience. Since he was in his mid-twenties at the time of his election, it may have been intended that his return would form part of his education in public affairs. His partner, Sir Henry Neville III of Billingbear in Berkshire, had no more than the closeness of his father's estate to Chipping Wycombe and, presumably, a willingness to bear his own charges to recommend him. Their relative silence in 1614 was by no means unique.

In 1620 the corporation's choice fell upon Arthur Goodwin of Upper Winchendon, Buckinghamshire and Richard Lovelace of West Drayton and Hillingdon, Middlesex. It is impossible to be certain but Goodwin's position as the son and heir of Sir Francis Goodwin, probably the wealthiest landowner in the county, suggests a desire to win Sir Francis's favour at a time when the latter was serving as a justice for the town. It is doubtful whether anything more was expected of Arthur Goodwin since he remained almost, if not entirely, silent during the Parliament. Similar motives may be suspected in the case of Richard Lovelace, whose daughter had married Henry Coke, the third surviving son of Sir Edward Coke, the great lawyer. Sir Edward lived at Stoke Poges, not far from Wycombe, and may have been the town's honorary high steward.[8] It seems likely that he was responsible for nominating his son's father-in-law to the borough.

Once established, the Coke family's connection with the town endured for the next three parliaments. Henry Coke, who lived in a farmhouse at Stoke Poges in 1622, was again returned for Chipping Wycombe in 1624, 1625 and 1626, even though he had probably moved to his estates in Cambridgeshire and Suffolk during this period and proved a resolutely silent participant in the proceedings of the Commons. If Wycombe's local rulers expected anything more, they left no trace in the surviving records. Arthur Goodwin sat again in 1624.

There was, however, a change when Goodwin failed to sit in 1625. Thomas Lane, who had served as the town's recorder since 1620, replaced Goodwin. Lane had been more active in Wycombe's affairs than any of his predecessors and seems to have been on good terms with Sir William Borlase* rather than Sir Francis Goodwin. This is almost the only clue to local tensions within the town's oligarchy and with local magistrates in this period. Even so, Lane was no more loquacious in 1625 than Henry Coke. Edmund Waller, who sat with Coke for the borough in 1626, could claim better local connections. His father's family resided only a few miles away at Coleshill and his mother was the sister of John Hampden*. Waller, moreover, was educated at High Wycombe grammar school between about 1618 and 1621. Exactly how he came to be chosen is not clear but, like many other Members for Chipping Wycombe, he seems to have observed an almost Trappist vow of silence in the Commons.

In 1628 the corporation again chose men who had previously served. William Borlase, who had sat in 1614 and had since been knighted, reappeared alongside the recorder, Thomas Lane. Borlase was appointed to no committees and was apparently completely silent in the House. By contrast, Lane's legal skills were deployed but not on any matter directly relating to Chipping Wycombe itself.

[1] *VCH Bucks.* iii. 113. [2] L.J. Ashford, *Hist. of Bor. of High Wycombe from its Origins to 1880*, pp. 123-6. [3] *VCH Bucks.* iii. 114-16. [4] J. Parker, *Early Hist. and Antiqs. of Wycombe*, 46-76; *VCH Bucks.* iii. 118; *The First Ledger Bk. of High Wycombe* ed. R.W. Greaves (Bucks. Rec. Soc. xi), 100. [5] *First Ledger Book*, 104, 107, 114, 117, 119-20. [6] J. Skinner, 'Plague Mortality in Bucks. during the Seventeenth Century', in *Bucks. Recs.* xx. 454-9. [7] Ashford, 109. [8] *HMC 9th Rep.* ii. 374.

C.T.

GREAT MARLOW

Right of election: inhabitants paying scot and lot[1]

Number of voters: 245 in Nov. 1640 (franchise extended to all male inhabitants)[2]

aft. 7 May 1624	HENRY BORLASE
	THOMAS COTTON
c. Apr. 1625	THOMAS COTTON
	JOHN BACKHOUSE
c. Jan. 1626	SIR WILLIAM HICKS, bt.
	JOHN BACKHOUSE
c. Feb. 1628	(SIR) JOHN BACKHOUSE
	SIR MILES HOBART

Situated close to the Buckinghamshire-Berkshire border 'where the Thames winds itself round the bottom of the hills', Great Marlow was characterized by Camden as 'a pretty considerable town', which owed its importance chiefly to the confluence of river traffic to London and good road connections to both Reading and Chipping Wycombe.[3] Grants and commissions for the repair of the timber bridge, a structure remarked upon by John Leland when he visited in 1535, can be traced back to at least the thirteenth century, by which time the town had a regular market and two annual fairs.[4] The local economy was sustained mainly by trade in wheat, hides and cloth; the town also had a significant hospitality industry, boasting at least nine registered inns and alehouses in 1577.[5] Elizabeth I honoured Marlow with a visit in 1592; and in 1600 townsman John Rotherham bequeathed £40 towards procuring a charter of incorporation.[6] However, no such charter was ever obtained, and the borough remained under the control of the lords of the manor, the Paget family, based at Beaudesert in Warwickshire. Although William, 4th Baron Paget, was restored to the peerage early in James's reign, he seems to have played no discernable role in regaining the town's franchise, first mooted in the 1621 Parliament and more vigorously pursued in 1624 by William Hakewill*, a local lawyer who had acted on Marlow's behalf since at least 1617 in disputes concerning the repair of the bridge and other charitable causes.[7]

Marlow sent Members to five Parliaments between 1301 and 1307, but thereafter its representation lapsed. On 18 May 1621 Sir George More reported to the Commons that the privileges committee 'thinketh fit new writs should be granted' for the boroughs of Great Marlow, Amersham, Wendover and Hertford, whereupon each town was ordered to submit evidence to the king's counsel. By the time the towns' cases were referred back to the privileges committee on 24 Nov., however, the Parliament was preoccupied with thoughts of war with Spain, and soon thereafter the session was terminated before further progress could be made.[8] In 1624 Hakewill submitted petitions on behalf of the three Buckinghamshire boroughs. Report was made from the privileges committee on 4 May, again in favour of re-enfranchisement, 'of which resolution of the committees His Majesty taking notice did (before the same was reported to the House) send unto the two chief justices', who also certified their assent.[9] Writs were accordingly issued three days later.[10] The exact date of the election is unknown, as is the number of voters at Marlow, since no election indentures or borough records survive for this period. The franchise, left ill-defined in the absence of a charter, was probably limited (as at Amersham) to inhabitants paying scot and lot. This is certainly the implication of a Commons' ruling of 1679, although the vote was thrown open to all male inhabitants in November 1640. The town's only municipal officers, its two constables, acted as returning officers.[11]

It seems likely that Hakewill was assisted in his preparation of the boroughs' petitions by Sir Robert Cotton*, whose library housed most of the early parliamentary rolls and sources of precedents upon which Marlow's case rested.[12] This presumably explains the return of Cotton's son, Thomas, in 1624, together with Henry Borlase of nearby Little Marlow, the younger son of Sir William Borlase*, a leading member of the local gentry who re-endowed the grammar school at Marlow in memory of Henry when the latter died in December 1624.[13] Thomas Cotton was re-elected in 1625, plumping for Marlow rather than Morpeth in Northumberland, where he had also been returned on the recommendation of his father-in-law, Lord William Howard of Naworth. He was joined by a kinsman of Sir William Borlase, John Backhouse, who represented the borough in the first three Caroline Parliaments. In 1626 the other seat went to Sir William Hicks bt., son-in-law of Lord Paget; and in 1628 the borough returned Sir Miles Hobart, owner of the neighbouring manor of Harleyford. It seems unlikely that any of Marlow's Members received wages during the early Stuart period.

[1] T.A. Hume, 'Bucks. and Parl.', *Bucks. Recs.* xvi. 97. [2] D. Hirst, *Representative of the People?*, 99. [3] W. Camden, *Britannia* (1722), i. 309; R. Gibbs, *Bucks. Misc.* 68-9. [4] J. Leland, *Itinerary* ed. L. Toulmin-Smith, i. 111; *VCH Bucks.* iii. 65-70. [5] Cent. Bucks.

Studs. D-X423/1. [6] J.E.L. Wrench, *Hist. Gt. Marlow Church*, 7-13; PROB 11/97, f. 28v. [7] C93/7/3. [8] *CJ*, i. 624a; 643b; *CD 1621*, ii. 380; iv. 360, 434. [9] *CJ*, i. 697b; 'Earle 1624', f. 169r-v; Eg. 2723, f. 104. [10] SP15/43/62, ff. 150-2; B. Willis, *Notitia Parliamentaria Bucks.* 34-5; C231/4, f. 165. [11] Hirst, 86, 99; Hume, 97; *VCH Bucks.* iii. 69-70. [12] Cott., Julius C.III, ff. 316, 317, 334; K. Sharpe, *Sir Robert Cotton*, 189. [13] *VCH Bucks.* ii. 214-15; iii. 66; Wrench, 7-13.

R.C.L.S.

WENDOVER

Right of election: in the burgesses

Number of voters: 33 in 1628[1]

aft. 7 May 1624	JOHN HAMPDEN
	SIR ALEXANDER DENTON
c. May 1625	JOHN HAMPDEN
	RICHARD HAMPDEN
24 Jan. 1626	SIR SAMPSON DARRELL
	JOHN HAMPDEN
29 Feb. 1628	JOHN HAMPDEN
	RALPH HAWTREY

Wendover's development as a market town during the early medieval period was assisted by its location on the high ground at the western edge of the Chilterns and the fact that the main road from Aylesbury to London passed through the parish.[2] Under the Tudors and early Stuarts it increased in prosperity. By 1620 its houses were concentrated around West Street, with further dwellings in North Street and South Street; the church and former manor house lay half a mile to the west.[3] The architectural evidence suggests that the early seventeenth century witnessed building activity both inside and outside the town.[4] The population may have risen from about 500 in the mid-1520s to about 900 by 1660.[5]

The earliest record of Wendover as a borough dates from 1227 or 1228; however the town was never incorporated and remained under the lordship of the owner of the manor. The chief official was the bailiff, who held office for a year; there were in addition two constables.[6] On being sold by the Crown in 1564, Wendover was divided into two manors, namely Wendover Borough and Wendover Forrens. However, by the mid-1570s both were in the possession of the Hawtrey family, whose seat at Chequers was situated some five or so miles to the south west. In 1613 they were owned by Mary, daughter of Sir William Hawtrey and widow of Sir Francis Wolley†, who retained possession of them until her death in the late 1630s.[7]

During the early fourteenth century Wendover returned Members to Parliament three times, but thereafter its representation lapsed.[8] The first attempt to restore the town to the franchise was made in May 1621, when Wendover, along with two other Buckinghamshire boroughs and the town of Hertford, submitted petitions to the committee for privileges and returns. The decision taken by the House in March of that year to restore the franchise to Ilchester and Pontefract may have stimulated their applications. The petitions were reported to the Commons on 18 May by the chairman of the committee, Sir George More, with a recommendation that writs should be issued to all four boroughs. However, on the motion of the solicitor general, (Sir) Robert Heath, the Commons ordered a delay for reflection, after which the boroughs were to submit their charters to the privileges committee, who would also hear the king's counsel. Wendover, of course, did not have a charter, and it is likely that Heath, who was presumably aware that James I believed that the Commons was already too large, was trying to frustrate the borough's petition. On 24 Nov. the Commons ordered that the boroughs should have their hearing at the privileges committee the following Thursday, with the king's counsel present, but the crisis which subsequently engulfed the third Jacobean Parliament the following month, leading to its dissolution, ensured that the case was not reported back to the House.[9]

When the fourth Jacobean Parliament met in 1624 the case of Wendover and the other Buckinghamshire boroughs which had petitioned for re-enfranchisement was raised on 25 Feb. by Sir William Fleetwood II, who sat for the county. The issue was again referred to the privileges committee, at which Heath was to be given a hearing. In the committee Heath, who had apparently been ordered by James to frustrate the cause, tried to delay a ruling. However, thanks to both William Hakewill, who owned a house just outside Wendover from 1616 and acted as counsel for the boroughs, and John Hampden, the most prominent local landowner, who paid the costs, the committee came down in favour of re-enfranchisement. Their recommendation was reported to the Commons on 4 May, which ordered writs to be issued for the return of Members.[10] These were dispatched on 7 May,[11] and although no return now survives the borough subsequently elected John Hampden and Sir Alexander Denton of Hillesden.[12]

Denton probably owed his election to the junior branch of the Hampden family, based at Hartwell in Buckinghamshire. At his death in 1618 Sir Alexander Hampden† of Hartwell owned a Crown lease of Wendover parsonage, two thirds of which he bequeathed to his brother Christopher, who settled in the borough. Sir Alexander Hampden appointed Denton, who had married the daughter of another of Sir Alexander's brothers, overseer of his will.[13]

Hampden was again returned for the borough in 1625, 1626 and 1628, suggesting that he had a prescriptive claim to one of the seats. How far he influenced the choice of Members for the other is unclear. His brother, Richard, was certainly chosen in 1625; however Sir Sampson Darrell, returned for the senior seat in 1626, presumably owed his election to his father-in-law, Christopher Hampden, while Mary Wolley was probably responsible for the return of her kinsman Ralph Hawtrey in 1628.

In 1624 the Commons had 'refused to give any direction for the manner of electing… or who should be the electors' in the newly enfranchised borough. In the only legible return to survive from this period, that for 1628, the parties on the borough side were 33 named individuals, described as burgesses of the borough of Wendover.[14] None of the borough's representatives in the Commons in the 1620s raised matters of local concern.

[1] C219/41B/75. [2] VCH Bucks. iii. 20-31. [3] M. Summerell, B. Samuels, A. Mead and P. Eckett, Bk. of Wendover, 105-6, 108. [4] VCH Bucks. iii. 20-2; Summerell et al. 119-20. [5] Summerell et al. 36. These are rough estimates. [6] VCH Bucks. iii. 22. [7] Ibid. 25. [8] OR. [9] CJ, i. 624a-b, 643b; CD 1621, iii. 286; iv. 360; E. de Villiers, 'Parlty. bors. restored by the House of Commons, 1621-41', EHR, lxvii. 177-8. [10] CJ, i. 673a, 697b; 'Pym 1624', i. f. 51v; Eg. 2723, f. 104r-v; De Villiers, 178-82. [11] C231/4, f. 165. [12] The Names of the Knights, Citizens, Burgesses for the Boroughs and Barons for the Ports (1625), unpag. See also Eg. 2723, f. 104v. This ms was printed, with inaccuracies, in W. Browne, Notitia Parliamentaria (1730), i. 138-41, where Denton's surname is mis-transcribed as Unton. [13] W.H. Smyth, Addenda to the Aedes Hartwellianae, 115-17; HP Commons 1558-1603, ii. 244; Vis. Bucks. (Harl. lviii), 171. The exact nature of the relationship between the two branches of the Hampden family is uncertain, but as it dates from the late 14th cent. was fairly distant by the 17th cent. VCH Bucks. ii. 301. [14] CJ, i. 697b; C219/41B/75.

C.T./B.C.

CAMBRIDGESHIRE

Number of voters: ?2,000 in 1624

16 Feb. 1604	SIR JOHN PEYTON
	SIR JOHN CUTTS
31 Mar. 1614	SIR JOHN CUTTS
	SIR THOMAS CHICHELEY
	Sir John Cotton[†]
	Sir John Cage
28 Dec. 1620	SIR EDWARD PEYTON, bt.
	SIR JOHN CUTTS
22 Jan. 1624	SIR EDWARD PEYTON, bt.
	SIR SIMEON STEWARD
	Sir John Cutts
	Toby Palavicino
	Election declared void,
	5 Mar. 1624
18 Mar. 1624	SIR EDWARD PEYTON, bt.
	SIR JOHN CUTTS
	Sir Simon Steward
	Sir John Cage
12 May 1625	SIR JOHN CUTTS
	SIR EDWARD PEYTON, bt.
1626	SIR EDWARD PEYTON
	SIR JOHN CUTTS
14 Feb. 1628	SIR MILES SANDYS, bt.
	SIR JOHN CARLETON, bt.

Early Stuart Cambridgeshire was, in many respects, two counties in one. The northern hundreds of Wisbech and Witchford comprised the Isle of Ely, a thinly populated area of fenland, large parts of which were wholly inundated during winter, so that, as Camden observed in 1637, it 'resembleth in some sort a very sea'. South of the Ouse, fen gradually gave way to chalk and clay uplands, most of which was flat and laid out into fields for growing corn and saffron. This was the shire proper, densely populated in some areas, especially along the fen-edge, and wooded only on its borders with Hertfordshire, Essex and Suffolk.[1] Before the Reformation the division between Isle and upland was sharply reflected in the county's adminis-tration, as the Isle was under the sway of the bishop of Ely.[2] Even after the Henrician abolition of episco-pal liberties the separateness of the shire's two halves continued to be acknowledged, for from at least 1564 the Isle was accorded its own commission of the peace.[3]

Cambridgeshire was never home to more than a couple of members of the peerage at any one time, principally, it would seem, because 'the degree of manorial fragmentation found there from the Conquest did not encourage strong lordship'.[4] Under Elizabeth, the shire boasted only a single resident noble family, the Norths, whose seat at Kirtling was located on the eastern tip of the county. Roger, 2nd Baron North (Sir Roger North[†]), nonetheless dominated Cambridgeshire, exercising his influence through the office of lord lieutenant, which he occupied from 1569 until his death in 1600. Before 1601 a member of the North family commonly sat as senior knight of the shire, and a county seat was sometimes found for one of Lord North's three deputy lieutenants. Although freeholders from the Isle of Ely were entitled to vote at parliamentary elections, the county's Westminster representation was decided by the more numerous gentry of the shire proper, who invariably returned one of their own number. From at least the beginning of Elizabeth's reign the eastern and western halves of the county south of the Ouse normally shared the seats between them, thereby avoiding the need for a contest. Of the 11 general elections held between 1559 and 1604 inclusive, only three – those of 1571, 1572 and 1593 – failed to strike this balance. The dominance of Lord North meant that the candidate from the eastern half of the shire was normally assigned the senior seat. The exceptions were in 1571 and 1572, when 'west-erners' monopolized both seats, and 1601, when Sir John Cutts the elder held the senior place, which he gained either by taking advantage of the 2nd Lord North's death or by exploiting a newly forged kinship connection with Dudley, 3rd Lord North.[5]

North influence declined generally after the death of the 2nd Lord North in 1600. Barely 18 years old on succeeding to his barony, the 3rd Lord North was considered too young and inexperienced to be appointed lord lieutenant in 1602, when the office was instead conferred on Thomas Howard, 1st earl of Suffolk, whose principal estates lay outside Cambridgeshire. After 1597 no member of the North family represented the county again before 1640, although the 3rd Lord's relatives, the Cutts and the Peytons, regularly secured seats for themselves. John, eldest son of the 2nd Lord North, served as senior knight in 1584 and 1586 but died in 1597, while his brother Henry, who took his place in 1597, subse-quently moved to Suffolk. The family's best prospect for future representation in the Commons lay in Sir Dudley North*, eldest son of the 3rd Lord North. However, Sir Dudley was not born until November 1602 and did not complete his education until 1624.

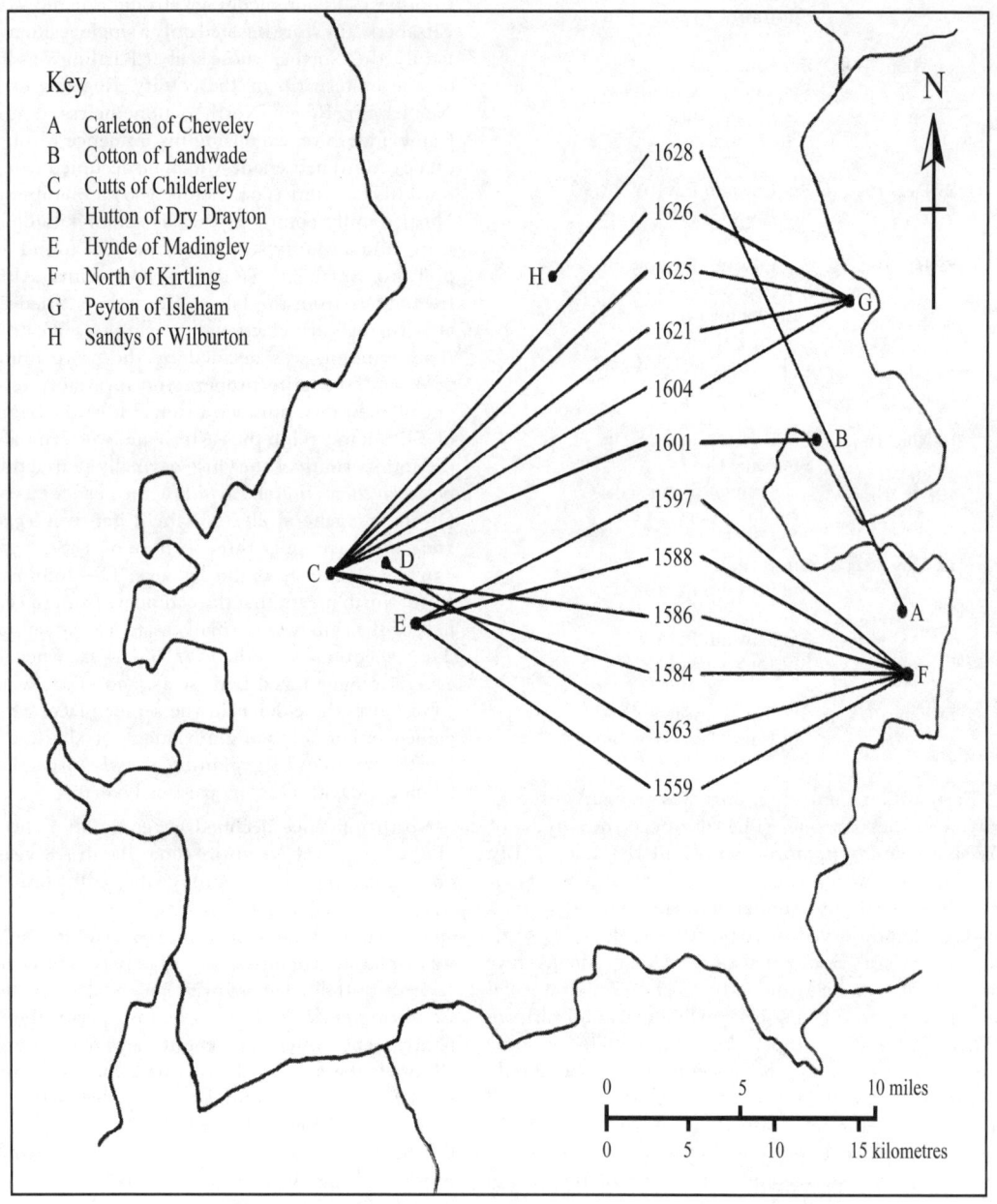

Key

A   Carleton of Cheveley
B   Cotton of Landwade
C   Cutts of Childerley
D   Hutton of Dry Drayton
E   Hynde of Madingley
F   North of Kirtling
G   Peyton of Isleham
H   Sandys of Wilburton

N

1628
1626
1625
1621
1604
1601
1597
1588
1586
1584
1563
1559

H

G

B

A

C

D

E

F

0   5   10 miles

0   5   10   15 kilometres

3. The east-west division of the county seats in Cambridgeshire 1559-1628

Subsequent military service in the Netherlands under the earl of Oxford kept him from seeking a seat until 1628.

The Jacobean period initially saw no departure from the traditional division of the county seats. In 1604 an 'easterner', Sir John Peyton of Isleham, was returned as senior knight, while a westerner, Sir John Cutts the younger, took the junior seat. However, the *status quo* was rudely shattered in 1614, when the county experienced its first recorded contest. Two 'westerners', Sir John Cutts the younger and Cutts's near neighbour and kinsman, Sir Thomas Chicheley of Wimpole, pitted themselves against the easterner Sir John Cotton of Landwade and the westerner Sir John Cage of Long Stowe. Private quarrels undoubtedly helped bring about the contest. Four or five years earlier, the local sewer commissioners had attempted to fine Cage, then sheriff, £1,440 for refusing to levy a rate on the county's towns to pay for a new drain. Although the proposed rate was later deemed illegal and the fine lifted,[6] Cage may have harboured a grudge against the leading sewer commissioners, among them Cutts's father. On the other hand his electoral alliance with Cotton, an active sewer commissioner, perhaps suggests otherwise. Whatever caused the rift between the two camps, the bitterness of the election campaign indicates that the divisions ran deep. Cotton and Cage spread the apparently unfounded rumour that if Cutts were elected the Isle of Ely's inhabitants would forfeit a third of their land to fen drainers, a ploy which allegedly drew support away from their opponents. Cutts and Chicheley, too, employed underhand methods to secure votes: letters allegedly subscribed by them were circulated urging unenfranchised copyholders to vote for them. Cotton and Cage were outraged, and on the eve of the election they persuaded the sheriff, Thomas Baldwin, to order the large number of non-freeholders in Cambridge to stay away from the hustings, which were customarily held in the yard at Cambridge Castle. Cutts and Chicheley, anxious to appear innocent, also publicly disowned the offending circular, sending round to the local inns and taverns urging those not entitled to vote to return home.

The last-minute attempt by Cotton and Cage to weaken their opponents' support failed to prevent Cutts and Chicheley from achieving victory by a margin of at least 500 votes at the view next morning. Two or three hours later, however, the defeated candidates demanded a poll in the full knowledge that many of their opponents' supporters had now gone home. Quite properly, Sheriff Baldwin refused this request as the law required elections to be held before 11 am,

whereupon the two defeated candidates complained to Parliament. When the matter was reported from committee on 19 Apr., sympathy for the petitioners was expressed by Edward Duncombe, who concluded that the circular sent to Cambridgeshire's copyholders could not have been written and distributed without the knowledge and consent of Cutts and Chicheley. However, Sir Maurice Berkeley thought the only substantive issue at stake was the sheriff's failure to scrutinize the voters to determine who was entitled to vote. He nevertheless defended Baldwin, pointing out that the demand for such a survey to be carried out had emanated from just 'one or two', and had been made only after many freeholders had gone home. Sir George More agreed, observing that Cotton had delayed his demand for a scrutiny until the sheriff had gone to dinner. Further unspecified criticism was levelled against Cage by Sir Dudley Digges, a member of the privileges committee and a kinsman by marriage to both Cutts and Chicheley.

As a result of these deliberations the sheriff's return was upheld. This was not the end of the matter, however, for on 14 May, during a meeting of the committee of privileges, Thomas Martin alleged that evidence had emerged of collusion between the sheriff and the victorious candidates in both the recent Cambridgeshire and Huntingdonshire elections. Martin also dismissed the proclamation issued by Baldwin on the eve of the Cambridgeshire election as a mere smokescreen to conceal the purposes contained within the circular addressed to the copyholders. His attack elicited a trenchant defence of Cutts and Chicheley by their counsel, Mr. Richardson, who claimed that the circular was the handiwork of some over-enthusiastic supporters and that his clients had done 'what they could to cross it'. They had subsequently achieved victory by a convincing margin, despite their opponents' attempts to smear them with false rumours about fen drainage. Richardson further argued that it was reasonable to suppose that this majority had been achieved without the aid of unenfranchised copyholders, because both Cutts and Chicheley were residents of western Cambridgeshire, where there were '30 more towns ... than in the east' and consequently 400 or 500 more freeholders. If anyone was guilty of sharp practice it was Cotton, who had waited until the sheriff had gone to dinner before demanding a poll. These arguments seem to have swung the committee behind Cutts and Chicheley, even though Richardson made the astonishing assertion that 'by precedent the west part has usually had both the knights'. Sir Robert Hitcham was satisfied that the two victorious candidates had been 'chosen by the greater number', while Sir Edwin Sandys adjudged the explanations of Cutts and Chicheley more plausible than those of Cotton and Cage.[7]

The failure by Cotton and Cage to dislodge their opponents meant that, for the first time since 1572, both county seats were in the hands of men whose estates lay in the west of the shire. At the 1620 general election, however, the county reverted to its traditional pattern, although it was the 'westerner' Sir John Cutts who obtained the senior seat rather than the 'easterner' Sir Edward Peyton.

Following the death of Sir John Cotton in March 1621 the chairmanship of the county bench was conferred on Cutts, to the fury of Peyton. During the winter of 1617-18 Peyton had temporarily served as *custos rotulorum* himself, and although he had been subsequently forced to relinquish the position to Cotton he had fully expected to succeed Cotton when the latter died.[8] Consequently, when writs for fresh parliamentary elections were issued early in 1624, Peyton determined to deny Cutts the position of knight of shire and to this end he paired with his neighbour, Sir Simeon Steward of Stuntney. In response, Cutts forged his own electoral pact with the impecunious Toby Palavicino of Great Wilbraham, who desired a seat in order to pursue legislation that would allow him to break the entail on his estates.[9]

The election held on 22 Jan. under the auspices of the 22-year-old under-sheriff, Edward Ingrey,[10] was tumultuous. Ingrey twice viewed the assembled voters to gauge the strength of the opposing sides but, considerably shaken after being manhandled by some of Cutts's supporters, he departed the hustings without announcing whom he would return. He was then shepherded by one of Steward's relatives to a tavern occupied by Sir Edward Peyton. There he made out his writ in favour of Peyton and Steward, some of whose supporters stood outside in order to deny entry to their opponents.

The highly irregular manner of the election led Cutts and Palavicino to petition the Commons.[11] Eye-witness statement were subsequently gathered by both sides and submitted to the privileges committee on the afternoon of 4 March. These affidavits, number-ing perhaps as many as 63 documents,[12] have not survived,[13] nor have their contents been reported by parliamentary diarists because the committee refused to admit them as evidence. The lawyers on the commit-tee realized that affidavits were not the unvarnished testimony of witnesses but were the product of careful drafting by counsel acting for each party to a dispute. They were also aware that written evidence was not open to cross-examination, unlike oral testimony,

which afforded the committee the opportunity to watch the witness closely for those 'words, actions, gestures' which 'discover much'.[14] The commit-tee's refusal to accept affidavits also stemmed from a concern to protect Parliament against any renewed attempts to encroach on its authority by the Chancery. Affidavits were sworn before the masters in Chan-cery, and since the practice of returning writs of elec-tion to Chancery had previously been used to suggest that the House was not qualified to determine its own membership, the committee was alert to the possibility that Chancery might use affidavits as a similar weapon against the Commons at some future date.[15]

Having rejected the affidavits, the committee proceeded to take the oral testimony of several key witnesses. Unsurprisingly perhaps, few of those inter-viewed seem to have been genuinely neutral. Indeed, their widely differing accounts served merely to reflect their various loyalties. For instance, Ingrey's servants, Prime and Crofts, claimed that the under-sheriff had arrived at the hustings at around 9 am, whereas Cutts's men, Watson and Oxford, asserted that he turned up at 10, thereby leaving only one hour in which he could legally conduct the election. Watson further claimed that Cutts had 400 more voices than Peyton, whereas Crofts said that Peyton had 200 more votes than Cutts. Despite this unpromising testimony, the committee reached some firm conclusions. Ingrey had arrived in good time and held two views, whereupon a poll was demanded, possibly as many as five or six times. However, he had then left the hustings after Sir Simeon Steward assured him that, since it was past 11 o'clock, he could not legally proceed further. The conclusion of the committee's chairman, John Glan-ville, was thus clear: Ingrey had failed to complete the election by the legally appointed hour. When this finding was laid before the House on 5 Mar., a fresh election was ordered and the serjeant-at-arms was instructed to summon Ingrey.[16]

The hapless under-sheriff was brought to the bar of the House 11 days later, where he was charged by Glanville with failing to make a due election and of being a dependent of Sir Edward Peyton's.[17] So far as is known, the charge of dependency had not previ-ously been mentioned, but Ingrey's failure to conduct a poll, and the fact that he made out his return in Peyton's chamber, strongly suggests that it was justi-fied. Other evidence, of which the committee may not have been aware, appears to point in the same direction. During the second parliamentary election of 1624, and perhaps also during the first, Peyton's headquarters were located in the *Falcon* tavern, whose innkeeper, John Payne, may have been closely related to Ingrey. It is certainly the case that Ingrey later obtained letters of administration in respect of Payne's estate.[18] Perhaps Ingrey was Payne's son-in-law. If so it becomes possible to explain a remark made by Ingrey on the hustings in January 1624. This was that, as he did not know who to return, he 'would be advised by his father-in-law'.[19]

Ingrey naturally denied ever having been Peyton's creature, and rejected the charge that he had failed to declare the result of the election on the hustings. Though he admitted that he had not conducted a poll, he claimed that he had been so manhandled by the agents of Sir John Cutts that he had been prevented from doing so. After hearing this testimony, the House dismissed Ingrey and called in two previously unheard witnesses, Francis Haslock and Henry Peck. Like Ingrey, Haslock claimed 'no dependence upon any man'. He then related that some of Cutts's company had 'pulled the sheriff's cloak off his back, and pulled him very violently when he was going to the poll', so that he had 'lost his papers which he had prepared to take the poll'. Ingrey's account received additional corroboration from Peck, who maintained that the under-sheriff 'did publish in the Castle yard Sir Edward Peyton, Sir Simeon Steward knights of Cambridgeshire before eleven of the clock'.[20]

The neutrality claimed by Haslock, and presumably also by Peck, meant that their testimony was taken seriously. Several Members now entertained considerable doubts concerning the ruling they had previously reached. Sir William Herbert spoke for many when he said, 'either the [under-]sheriff hath offended or we have erred in our judgment to make the election void'. Sir Henry Poole went one stage further, alleging that the new evidence proved that Cutts had 'misused' the election and that Ingrey was blameless. However, some other Members were unimpressed by what they had heard. Francis Brakin, Member for Cambridge, had been present during the county election, and after Ingrey had left the chamber he more or less accused the under-sheriff of lying. Ingrey had refused to carry out a poll, he said, and had left the hustings before publishing the result of the election. Sir John Savile placed a similar lack of faith in the new evidence. Ingrey's misdemeanours were 'proved by worthy gentlemen', whereas the under-sheriff's witnesses were but 'mean men'.[21]

Although a large section of the House now believed that Ingrey was no longer the villain of the piece, there was never any realistic prospect that he would be exonerated. During the two-hour long debate Christopher Brooke put his finger on the reason for this when he said that 'to send away the sheriff is to justify him and condemn ourselves'. Sir Arthur Ingram made the same point with characteristic bluntness: if Ingrey went uncensured, 'how shall we justify sending down a new writ?' The reputation of the House required that Ingrey should be punished. However, instead of fining him, as some suggested, the under-sheriff was ordered to confess his fault, both at the bar of the House and at the next quarter sessions. Furthermore, the serjeant-at-arms was instructed to detain him as a delinquent until after the county election had been re-run to ensure that he could not 'breed a new garboyle', as Sir Edward Giles put it.[22]

Sir John Cutts entered the new election campaign without his former ally, Toby Palavicino. The prospect of incurring the expense of a second election may have unnerved the feckless Palavicino, who withdrew his candidacy, perhaps in return for a promise of support for his bill from Sir Edward Peyton, whose name later headed the list of committee members appointed to consider the measure.[23] In place of Palavicino, Cutts paired with his erstwhile opponent Sir John Cage, who seems to have used his strong bargaining position to demand the right to contest the senior seat. In mid-March more than 1,000 of their supporters descended on Cambridge, where they were distributed among several inns and hostelries hired by the innkeeper of the *Rose and Crown*, Philip Wolf. Over the course of the next three days the supporters of Cutts and Cage ran up a bill of more than £155 for 'meat, drink, wine, diet, lodging for themselves and horsemeat and stable room for their horses'.[24] This sum paled into insignificance by comparison with the bill presented to Peyton and Steward after the election by John Payne and Christopher Hatley, innkeepers of the *Falcon* and *Red Lion* respectively. The cost of housing and feeding them and their supporters for four days amounted to a hefty £248 13s.7d.[25]

The county election of March 1624 was presided over by the sheriff, Robert Audley, and was evidently conducted peaceably. A petition subsequently received by the Commons in late May from several freeholders claiming that the result had been distorted by the votes cast by scholars and fellows of the university, who were not entitled to participate in either county or borough elections, was not acted upon.[26] The outcome of the contest was that Peyton triumphed over Cage, and Cutts defeated Steward. This result was accepted by the Commons, but Cage and Steward refused to pay their share of the election expenses on the grounds that they had been deserted by their allies, whom they belived had secretly reached an accommodation before the election. Peyton naturally denied this accusation, maintaining that Steward had 'gained a great furtherance' at the hustings from his friends, but in fact he had everything to gain striking a deal with Cutts as he could not rely upon repeating his earlier victory, which, in all probability, had only been achieved by suborning the returning officer. Peyton's apparent desertion of his ally represented a double blow to Steward, who was thereby denied a parliamentary seat and lost an important defender of his interests in Parliament. The integrity of his Stuntney estate had been repeatedly threatened by legislation introduced by Lady Jermy, who sought to possess one third of it. In 1621 Peyton had been appointed to the bill's committee, but when a fresh committee was named in April 1624 Peyton's name was conspicuous by its absence.[27]

At the general elections of 1625 and 1626, Peyton and Cutts took it in turns to serve as senior knight. As neither election witnessed a contest, this arrangement was presumably the result of prior agreement. If so, then the secret electoral pact apparently forged between Peyton and Cutts in March 1624 may have formed the basis for the managing of future parliamentary elections in the county. In 1628 neither Peyton nor Cutts seem to have stood for election. Their places were taken by Sir Miles Sandys of Wilburton and Sir John Carleton of Cheveley. The disappearance from the scene of the two men who, between them, had monopolized the county's parliamentary representation since 1621 is difficult to explain. However, it may be linked to the fact that, for the first time since 1597, a member of the North family required a seat at Westminster. Initially at least, North may have expected to represent his native county, but he would soon have realized that to achieve this ambition would require either Cutts or Peyton to stand aside. It is hard to imagine either man accepting the loss of face this would have entailed, whereas it is possible to see how all three men might have reached a collective decision that the simplest solution to their problem was that none of them should stand. If North took some form of self-denying ordinance in respect of his home county it would explain why he subsequently turned to the earl of Arundel for a seat at Horsham.

Sandys and Carleton were obvious compromise candidates. Both men enjoyed the necessary standing in Cambridgeshire, and although Carleton was Cutts' first cousin neither of them represented the shire's older parliamentary families. Carleton had only recently settled in the county, having married the widow of Sir John Cotton. Sandys was longer

established and had made several enemies, but like Carleton he was the first member of his family to dwell in the shire. The decision to hand the county's parliamentary representation to two relative newcomers was probably an important ingredient in avoiding a damaging contest in 1628. The pair's acceptability to the freeholders was undoubtedly underlined by the fact that Sandys represented the western half of the county while Carleton represented the east. However, in one respect Sandys was a peculiar electoral choice. Although his main estate of Willingham was located on the fen edge, he himself resided in the Isle of Ely, where he may have been serving as the bishop of Ely's bailiff.

Cambridgeshire's parliamentary interests were dominated by the issue of fen drainage. Many of the county's most substantial landowners, particularly those on the fen edge and in the Isle of Ely, were keen to drain large tracts of the shire, but proposals to put such schemes into operation were viewed with hostility by both Sir John Peyton and his son Sir Edward. The Peytons took the view that, although they personally stood to benefit from drainage schemes, many of the county's small landowners and copyhold tenants would lose out, as land previously designated as common would inevitably be swallowed up by greedy undertakers. Accordingly, during the first Jacobean Parliament Sir John played a leading role in obstructing fen drainage bills. Following the second reading of a bill to authorize the draining of 300,000 acres in the Isle of Ely (27 Apr. 1607), for example, he and the Cambridge Member, Robert Wallis, presented 'some reasons and petitions ... against the bill'.[28] At around the same time several commoners and landowners entrusted copies of a certificate relating to their petition against fen drainage to Peyton.[29] Sir Edward Peyton followed in his father's footsteps, and in 1621 the authors of a new fen drainage bill, the 3rd earl of Bedford and Sir Francis Fane, allegedly offered him a lump sum of £10,000, or £500 a year if he preferred, to abandon his opposition. Although then in severe financial difficulties, Peyton apparently rejected the bribe outright, and on his return to the chamber he announced his complete disregard for his own financial interests, and branded the bill both 'dangerous' and 'bad for the public'.[30] Peyton again championed the interests of small landholders and commoners in May 1626, when a bill to drain 360,000 acres south of the River Glen was given a first reading.[31] Not until 1628, when Sir Miles Sandys was returned as senior knight, was the county represented in Parliament by an active fen drainer.

[1] *VCH Cambs.* ii. 74-6; M. Spufford, *Contrasting Communities*, 16-17, 22. [2] *HP Commons 1422-1509* (forthcoming), CAMBRIDGESHIRE. [3] C66/998. [4] Spufford, 28. [5] The 3rd Lord North married a sister of Cutts' wife in Nov. 1600: *CP*. [6] *APC*, 1621-3, p. 239; Eg. 2651, ff. 76-7. [7] *Procs. 1614 (Commons)*, 38, 103-8, 239-42; Downing Coll. Camb. Lib., Bowtell ms 11, Metcalfe's Thesaurus, f. 210. [8] C231/4, ff. 54, 56; *Secret Hist. of Jas. I* ed. W. Scott, ii. 441. [9] L. Stone, *Sir Horatio Palavicino*, 310-12. [10] J.K. Gruenfelder, *Influence in Early Stuart Elections*, 15, says it was the sheriff, Robert Audley, who was just 22, but in this dispute the word 'sheriff' commonly referred to the under-sheriff: cf. *CJ*, i. 678a. Stone, 312, calls Ingrey 'Jongrey'. [11] *HMC Rutland*, i. 470. [12] *CJ*, i. 678a. Pym indicates that there were only 30: 'Pym 1624', i. f. 19v. [13] The affidavits entered in the surviving masters' registers (for which see C38) pertain only to law suits. [14] *CJ*, i. 678a; J. Glanville, *Reps. of Certain Cases, Determined and Adjudged by Commons in Parl.* (1775), pp. 84-5. In 1614 the cttee. had expressed similar qualms about the use of affidavits, but there is no evidence that they were actually deemed inadmissible: *Procs. 1614 (Commons)*, 103. [15] *CJ*, i. 678a; Glanville, 85; 'Pym 1624', i. f. 19v. [16] 'Holland 1624', i. ff. 27-9; 'Earle 1624', f. 50r-v. [17] *CJ*, i. 687a; 'Nicholas 1624', p. 129. [18] C2/Chas.I/P56/18; 2/Chas.I/23/36. [19] 'Holland 1624', i. f. 27. Payne's letters of admon. have not been traced. [20] *CJ*, i. 687a-b, 737b; 'Nicholas 1624', pp. 129-30. [21] *CJ*, i. 687b, 737b; 'Nicholas 1624', pp. 130-1; 'Holland 1624', i. f. 56r-v; [22] *CJ*, i. 687b, 737b; 'Nicholas 1624', p. 131; 'Holland 1624', i. ff. 56-7; 'Earle 1624', f. 87v. [23] Stone, 312-13; *CJ*, i. 705a. [24] C2/Chas.I/W88/1. [25] C2/Chas.I/P56/18. [26] 'Earle 1624', f. 197. The Jan. election was blighted in similar fashion: ibid. f. 50v; Glanville, 81. [27] *CJ*, i. 600b, 757a; *CD 1621*, vi. 119. [28] *CJ*, i. 364a. [29] Essex RO, D/Dba O14. [30] *Secret Hist.* ii. 440; *CJ*, i. 611b. [31] *Procs. 1626*, iii. 146.

A.D.T.

CAMBRIDGE

Right of election: in the corporation to 1624; in the freemen from 1625

Number of voters: eight to 1624

15 Mar. 1604	ROBERT WALLIS, alderman JOHN YAXLEY, alderman
23 Mar. 1614[1]	FRANCIS BRAKIN, recorder (SIR) ROBERT HITCHAM
10 Jan. 1621	RICHARD FOXTON, alderman THOMAS MEAUTYS, alderman
30 Mar. 1621[2]	SIR JOHN HOBART II *vice* Foxton, disabled
9 Jan. 1624[3]	FRANCIS BRAKIN, recorder ROBERT LUKYN, alderman
12 Apr. 1625[4]	THOMAS MEAUTYS, alderman TALBOT PEPYS, recorder
27 Jan. 1626[5]	THOMAS MEAUTYS, alderman JOHN THOMPSON
29 Feb. 1628[6]	THOMAS MEAUTYS, alderman THOMAS PURCHAS, alderman

Cambridge became a royal borough under Henry I and returned Members to Parliament from at least 1295, but the town was not formally incorporated until 1605. The composition of the town assembly was not specified in the charter of incorporation, nor was the extent of the franchise.[7] Until 1625, when the corporation resolved that all freemen could vote, Cambridge had one of the most unusual election procedures in the country. The mayor and aldermen on the one hand and common council on the other were required to nominate one selector each. These two selectors were then permitted one hour to choose eight members of the corporation who, in turn, had one hour to select the two Members. If neither the 'two' nor the 'eight' could agree within the hour then the process restarted.[8] The abandonment of this tortuous process in 1625 was probably the result of internal wrangling within the corporation and a desire of the freemen to have a greater say in the town's governance. In 1609 and 1611, and again in the early 1620s, the high steward and Privy Council were forced to intervene to resolve disputes between freemen, councillors and aldermen, most notably over the election as mayor in 1624 of a non-alderman, Thomas Purchas*.[9] In 1632 such differences were finally resolved by a further charter which stated that the corporation was to consist of a mayor, 12 aldermen and 24 common councillors.[10]

In 1601 the corporation declared that, with the exception of the town's recorder, no one would be elected to Parliament unless they had resided in Cambridge for at least a year before the election.[11] In 1604 two aldermen, Robert Wallis and John Yaxley, were accordingly returned. Ahead of the next general election, however, Cambridge came under pressure to elect outsiders and disregard its earlier ruling on residence, as the high steward, lord chancellor Ellesmere (Thomas Egerton I[†]), requested a place for a candidate of his choice. The mayor replied that the corporation had intended to elect the recorder, Francis Brakin, and one of the town's freemen, and he also pointed out that one of the town's counsel, Sir Robert Hitcham*, desired a place. Nevertheless, he assured Ellesmere that the assembly stood 'ready to esteem your honour's desire as a commandment to be observed'.[12] Ellesmere evidently chose not to press the matter, as Brakin and Hitcham were returned.

Ellesmere's successor as high steward, Viscount St. Alban (Sir Francis Bacon*), persuaded the corporation to elect his secretary, Thomas Meautys, in second place in 1621. In order to satisfy the residency requirement, Meautys was made a freeman and an alderman on the day of the election.[13] The first seat went to the mayor, Richard Foxton, whose return was challenged in Parliament on the grounds that it was forbidden for mayors to return themselves. Foxton was therefore unseated.[14] He was replaced by Sir John Hobart at the request of his father, Sir Henry Hobart*, one of Cambridge's legal counsel. Sir John was then made free of the town and elevated to aldermanic status.[15] By the time of the 1624 election, Bacon's influence had waned and Cambridge elected Recorder Brakin again, together with Alderman Robert Lukyn.[16]

For the first Caroline Parliament, Meautys secured the first place, possibly with the support of Sir Thomas Coventry*, who was soon to replace Bacon as Cambridge's high steward. The new recorder, Talbot Pepys, took the junior seat.[17] Meautys served in the following two Caroline Parliaments and was joined in 1626 by one of Coventry's secretaries, John Thompson, and in 1628 by Alderman Thomas Purchas.[18]

Cambridge does not appear to have preferred any legislation to Parliament during this period, although it obviously took an interest in the innumerable bills which concerned the universities and fen drainage. The corporation paid parliamentary wages to its aldermanic MPs at a daily rate of 4s., but the recorder received only half that amount. The records do not reveal any payment of wages to the outsiders who served as MPs.[19]

[1] Cambs. RO, Mun. Rm., Shelf C.7, ff. 43v-4. [2] C.H. Cooper, *Annals of Camb.* iii. 140. [3] Cambs. RO, Mun. Rm., Shelf C.7, f. 125. [4] Ibid. f. 137v. [5] Ibid. f. 146v. [6] Ibid. f. 172. [7] F.W. Maitland and M. Bateson, *Camb. Bor. Charters*, 116-37. [8] Downing Coll. Camb. Lib., Bowtell ms 11, Metcalfe's Thesaurus, f. 77. [9] C.H. Cooper, *Annals of Camb.* iii. 31, 218-19; *APC* 1623-5, pp. 318-19; D. Hirst, *Representative of the People?*, 53. [10] Maitland and Bateson, 136-69. [11] Downing Coll. Camb. Lib., Bowtell ms 11, Metcalfe's Thesaurus, f. 76v. [12] Cooper, iii. 60-1. [13] Ibid. 137 n. 2. [14] Nicholas, *Procs. 1621*, i. 212-13; *CJ*, i. 560a. [15] Cooper, iii. 144. [16] Cambs. RO, Mun. Rm., Shelf C.7, f. 125. [17] Cooper, iii. 176. [18] Ibid. 183-4, 200. [19] Ibid. 137, 169.

C.R.K.

CAMBRIDGE UNIVERSITY

Right of election: in the 'chancellor, masters and scholars'

Number of voters: at least 350

Mar. 1604	NICHOLAS STEWARD	
	HENRY MOUTLOWE	
2 Apr. 1614	SIR MILES SANDYS, bt.	
	SIR FRANCIS BACON	
	Barnaby Gooch	74
	Clement Corbett	64

10 Jan. 1621	(SIR) ROBERT NAUNTON	
	BARNABY GOOCH	
9 Jan. 1624[1]	(SIR) ROBERT NAUNTON	
	BARNABY GOOCH	
30 Apr. 1625	(SIR) ROBERT NAUNTON	
	SIR ALBERTUS MORTON also	
	returned for Kent, 2 May 1625	
by 21 Jan. 1626	(SIR) JOHN COKE	
	THOMAS EDEN II	
11 Mar. 1628	(SIR) JOHN COKE	
	THOMAS EDEN II	

During the early Stuart period Cambridge University consisted of 16 colleges and halls which, between them, housed 2,270 staff, students and servants. The largest college by far, with a population of 340 scholars and servants, was Trinity,[2] which alone was spacious enough to accommodate the Court whenever the king came to visit.[3] During the mastership of Thomas Neville (1593-1615), most of Trinity's medieval buildings were demolished and a new hall erected, the cost of which was met in the first instance by Neville himself, who loaned the college £3,000. Neville's ally in refashioning Trinity was Sir Edward Stanhope[†], one of the college's longstanding fellows. During his lifetime, Stanhope donated £100 for a library, and on his death in 1608 he left a further £700 for the same purpose, plus a small collection of manuscripts and more than 300 books. As a result of the transformation wrought by Neville and Stanhope one observer concluded that Trinity had become 'one of the most goodly and uniform colleges in Europe'.[4]

Attempts to secure parliamentary representation for the universities were made at various times during Elizabeth's reign, but without success.[5] In the absence of such representation the universities were poorly placed to oppose legislation which contravened the ordinances governing individual colleges, or to resist parliamentary assaults on their privileges led by the representatives of the enfranchised boroughs of Oxford and Cambridge. Following the accession of James I in 1603, however, the prospects for enfranchisement markedly improved. James was anxious to please and gratify his subjects, and his learning inclined him to 'favoureth and respecteth the universities'. Sensing that the time was ripe, the attorney-general, Sir Edward Coke*, himself a graduate of Trinity, advised Neville and Stanhope to try a fresh approach. They subsequently contacted the principal secretary of state, Lord Cecil (Robert Cecil[†]) who, as chancellor of Cambridge, was inclined to be sympathetic. The matter was accordingly brought to the attention of James, who signed the appropriate letters patent on 12 Mar. 1604, just seven days before Parliament assembled. These bestowed upon the universities the privilege of returning two Members each, 'who from time to time shall make known to that supreme high court of Parliament the true state of the same university and of each college, hall and hospice there, that no statute or Act may prejudice or injure them generally or any one of them separately, without fair and due notice and information there'. The letters patent further vested the franchise in the 'chancellor, masters and scholars' of the universities. The meaning of this phrase is not entirely clear. It has been argued that 'scholars' should not be taken to include undergraduates, nor even bachelors of arts, but only the holders of higher degrees and bachelors of divinity. The inclusion of the latter is questionable, however, as elections were always held in the senate of the university, a body which consisted exclusively of masters of arts.[6] Whatever the precise composition of the electorate may have been, it seems likely that it included the fellows of each college, of whom there were 350.[7]

The letters patent offered no guidance as to the manner of holding elections, and since Parliament was due to commence within a matter of days neither Canbridge nor Oxford universities had sufficient time in which to formulate their own rules. It was with this consideration in mind that Coke advised Cambridge how to proceed 'for this time'. First, he suggested that the university should avoid choosing a member of Convocation (by which he meant the parliament of the church rather than the governing body of the university), 'for I have known the like to have bred a question'. Secondly, it should refrain from returning the vice-chancellor, because 'he is governor of the university where the choice is to be made'. He proposed instead that it should elect 'some professor of the Civil Law or any other that is not of the Convocation House'.[8] Coke's advice was evidently heeded as two prominent civil lawyers were returned, Henry Moutlowe, professor of Civil Law at Gresham College, London and Nicholas Steward, a judge in the Courts of Admiralty and Delegates. Both men had attained their legal qualifications at Cambridge, while Moutlowe had been a fellow at King's College for over 20 years and had held several university offices. Steward must have seemed an especially good choice, because he was then in favour with Sir Edward Coke. However, neither Moutlowe nor Steward was still technically a member of the university, whereas the king's letters patent required the universities to choose members 'of their own body'.

By 1614 a method of electing the university's parliamentary representatives had been agreed between the college heads, who claimed that there had been disagreements in 1604. Collectively they issued a decree, entitled *De modo eligendi Burgenses*, which proclaimed that the university would follow the rules which governed the annual elections of its vice-chancellor.[9] By this system the senate was offered the choice of one of only two candidates, both of whom had been selected beforehand by the heads. The decree understandably caused consternation among ordinary voters, who desired to exercise the same right to choose from several candidates as they enjoyed when electing the university's chancellor. It was obvious to them that the heads were attempting to gain a large measure of control over the university's parliamentary elections. Equally apparent was the fact that the heads had exceeded their powers by imposing a system without reference to the university's senate. While they were entitled to interpret anything in the university statutes which seemed to them obscure, the heads had no right to act as interpreters of the king's letters patent. Not surprisingly, therefore, the heads' presumption was brought to the attention of the earl of Northampton, who had succeeded Cecil as chancellor of the university in 1612. Northampton entered into a now vanished correspondence with the vice-chancellor on the matter, after which he issued instructions that the university was to elect its burgesses 'after the form of the choice of the chancellor'.[10]

Northampton's ruling was a severe setback to the heads, but they remained determined to control the outcome of the 1614 election. From the detailed account of the election left by the deputy vice-chancellor, Dr. John Duport,[11] it is clear that the heads tried to manipulate proceedings to ensure the election of either the master of Magdalene, Barnaby Gooch, or the vice-chancellor, Clement Corbett, whose selection was in blatant disregard of Coke's earlier prohibition. Their plans were upset, however, by the appearance on the scene of two rival candidates: the attorney-general, Sir Francis Bacon, and Sir Miles Sandys of Wilburton, in the Isle of Ely. Events on the hustings were to show that, although the heads were reluctantly prepared to concede one seat to Bacon, they were determined to thwart Sandys, even though the latter had once been a proctor of the university and had held fellowships at Peterhouse and Queens'.

The election was held at eight o'clock on the morning of 2 Apr. in the university's Senate House.

There the assembled electors were addressed by Duport who, in view of Corbett's candidacy, was obliged to preside. Duport began by reminding his audience that they were required by their letters patent to elect only members of the university, and by statute law to return only residents. These requirements had not prevented the university from electing Mout-lowe and Steward in 1604, however, and by drawing attention to them now Duport was quite obviously trying to exclude Sandys, and perhaps also Bacon, who like Sandys was nonresident. (Bacon, however, had recently been appointed counsel to the university and could therefore claim to be a member of the university). Duport's address was shortly followed by an intervention from one of the masters of arts, a Mr. Browne, who announced that it was rumoured that some among them wished to elect a man 'not eligible by the charter [sic]', and declared his wish that 'there might be none such admitted'. Browne's speech, which seems to have been aimed directly at Sandys rather than Bacon, prompted one of Sandys's supporters to announce that Northampton's secretary had signalled in writing that Northampton wished that Sandys should be returned. Duport endeavoured to brush this damaging revelation aside, declaring that 'he was not to take knowledge of his lordship's pleasure from any private man, having his lordship's own letter to direct him'. As the arguments became more heated, Duport announced that he would void the election of anyone chosen contrary to the king's letters patent, statute law or Northampton's letters addressed to him. Despite this warning, Bacon and Sandys proceeded to top the poll by a large margin, leaving Gooch and Corbett trailing in third and fourth place respectively. An unnerved Duport thereupon ordered the votes to be recounted, so arousing suspicions that he intended to alter the result. He quickly realized his mistake, however, and, faced with large numbers of angry voters whom he feared would turn violent, decided to bring the proceedings to a swift conclusion. Before the recount could be completed, he stepped into his chair, declared Sandys's election invalid on the grounds of nonresidence, pronounced Bacon and Gooch elected, and dissolved convocation. At this there was uproar. Chanting 'you do us wrong' and 'a Sandys, a Sandys!', Sir Miles's supporters made such a din that they could be heard 'a great way off'. Meanwhile, Duport had to be escorted from the rostrum by the bedells. In the ensuing confusion the slips recording the votes cast in favour of Bacon and Sandys were seized by the angry voters, who proceeded to make their way 'in great heaps' towards King's College. There they drew up a certificate in favour of Bacon and Sandys, having,

according to Duport, 'procured aforehand the sheriff or his deputy ... to join with them therein'. The heads, who remained behind, drew up their own return, but were unable to persuade the sheriff or under-sheriff to sign it.[12]

The heads seem never to have protested to the Commons at the return of Sandys, but instead acted to prevent any recurrence of their humiliation. Sometime before January 1621 they again sought to gain control over the nomination process. Their task was undoubtedly made easier by the appointment as chancellor of Thomas Howard, 1st earl of Suffolk, following the death of Northampton in May 1614. As patron of Magdalene College,[13] Suffolk cannot have been insensitive to the electoral humiliation which had been inflicted on that college's master, Barnaby Gooch. Certainly he seems not to have objected when the king, presumably in response to an appeal from the heads, directed that in future elections should be held '*juxta formam electionis procancellarii*'.[14] James's intervention seems to have been accepted with quiet resignation by the rank and file voters. In contrast to the turbulent scenes witnessed in the Senate House in 1614, the election of January 1621 was held 'without tumult or any opposition', according to the registrary, James Tabor. However, soon after Parliament assembled Tabor and the vice-chancellor were made nervous by a rumour, apparently unfounded, that the university's MPs 'are questioned in the Parliament for the manner of their election'.[15]

The heads used their new powers of nomination to bestow the junior seat on Barnaby Gooch. They thereby avenged their earlier humiliation, but given their treatment of Sir Miles Sandys in 1614 their decision to return Gooch was a breathtaking piece of hypocrisy, as the master of Magdalene no longer resided in Cambridge but was now settled at Exeter, where he had been chancellor to the bishop since 1615. The senior seat was conferred upon the king's principal secretary of state, Sir Robert Naunton. The latter was almost certainly nominated by the royal favourite, the marquess of Buckingham, as it was Buckingham's patronage secretary, John Packer*, who notified Naunton of his election.[16]

James's role in establishing a voting system favourable to the heads served to render the university vulnerable to royal interference. Henceforward the university assumed the status of a royal pocket borough, at least so far as the senior seat was concerned. In 1624 Naunton was re-elected, this time at the request of Buckingham's client, lord keeper Coventry (Sir Thomas Coventry*),[17] while the junior seat was again taken by Gooch. At the following election the university bestowed both its seats on government ministers. Naunton, newly promoted master of the Wards, occupied the senior place, while the junior was made available to secretary of state Sir Albertus Morton.

Following the summons of the second Caroline Parliament, Dr. John Collins, the anatomist, evidently offered to bestow a seat upon one of the sons of the university's chancellor, the earl of Suffolk, who was now fast approaching death. On 8 Jan. 1626 Suffolk's wife gently declined the offer as her sons were 'all sure of places in the west country', and instead threw her husband's weight behind the Crown's nominees, Naunton and secretary of state Sir John Coke, 'which are men able to do the university good'.[18] The heads, however, were evidently determined to prevent the Crown from monopolizing both seats as it had in 1625. Since Gooch was now close to death they bestowed the junior seat on the master of Trinity Hall, Thomas Eden II, who had some knowledge of Parliament's workings, having served as a legal assistant to the Lords in August 1625. However, they were willing to accept Morton's successor Sir John Coke for the senior seat in preference to Naunton, perhaps because Coke had enjoyed a distinguished university career at Trinity College, where he had once taught rhetoric. A rumour that Coke was likely to face 'some competition' for the place evidently proved unfounded.[19] Eden and Coke were both re-elected in 1628 without a single vote being cast against them.[20]

Although the university ultimately managed to retain control over one of its seats, the election of a string of government ministers during the 1620s had the effect of weakening its representation in Parliament. Ministers of the Crown were generally far too busy with the king's business to attend to the affairs of the university, which therefore were left to the junior Member. When, in June 1626, the Commons attacked the university for electing Buckingham, now a duke, as its chancellor in succession to Suffolk, it fell to Eden rather than Coke to attempt to lower the temperature of the House.[21] With the notable exception of Coke, those Crown ministers who served for the university were often not even in the House. In 1621 Naunton was under house arrest on the orders of the king, and although he had been released by 1624 he resolved not take his seat unless the king bestowed on him an office of equal or greater importance to the secretaryship, which he had been forced to surrender in 1623. It was not until September 1624 that James conferred the mastership of the Wards on Naunton, but by that time Parliament had been prorogued, never to reassemble. Consequently Naunton did not finally set foot in the Commons as Member for the university until 1625,

in which year his fellow Member, Morton, was kept from Westminster by ambassadorial duties. Morton's absence meant that, for a third Parliament in succession, Cambridge University was deprived of one of its parliamentary representatives. Under these circumstances it is perhaps not surprising that the college heads moved to regain control of the junior seat in 1626.

The successive election of government ministers made a mockery of the idea that membership of the university was a vital qualification for election to the university's seats. Although Naunton, Morton and Coke had all been educated at Cambridge, none were members of their *alma mater* at the time of their election and thus all were technically ineligible. Naunton at least understand this, for in 1621 he considered declining his election on the grounds that he was 'now none of that body'.[22] That said, it should be noted that in 1621 it would have served Naunton's purposes to disclaim his election, as Naunton was then looking for a way to avoid a damaging confrontation between king and Commons over the matter of his confinement. Neither in 1624 nor in 1625 did he express the same sense of disquiet at his eligibility.

A striking feature of Cambridge University's parliamentary elections is that electors were required to record their votes on slips of paper, known as suffrages. These were counted by the procurators, and handed to the official known as the registrary after the election for safekeeping.[23] The registrary, whose presence was required at meetings of the senate, attended parliamentary elections in person, and was the university's archivist.[24] Voting slips were used even when an election was uncontested. Following the 1621 election, at which neither candidate was challenged, the registrary noted that 'all the suffrages are in my custody but seven or eight, that Reding [?the esquire bedell] slyly stole away as they were reading'.[25]

It was unusual for the university to pay its parliamentary representatives wages. The only Member to receive a fee for his services during this period was Henry Moutlowe, a man of such limited means that, as Millicent Rex has remarked, he may actually have needed the money. Until 1606 Moutlowe was paid regularly, at the rate of 5s. a day, but the emptiness of the university's coffers meant that he did not receive the remainder of his wages until 1614. This sum, amounting to £60, was paid in full only because Moutlowe's friend, Dr. John Cowell, had earlier bequeathed £30 to the university to help it pay off the debt.[26]

The interests of the university required it to keep a close eye on the legislative business of the Commons. Evidence that the legislation laid before the Commons was monitored is provided by a single surviving letter written to one of the university's parliamentary representatives by the registrary, James Tabor on 28 Feb. 1621, one month after Parliament had commenced sitting.[27] The identity of the addressee is not stated, but given Naunton's confinement and the undeferential tone of the letter the recipient must have been Barnaby Gooch. Tabor sought to draw Gooch's attention to those bills which concerned the university, to instruct him how to respond to such legislation and to require him to furnish additional information where necessary. The first and most important issue brought to Gooch's attention was that of fen drainage. Tabor had correctly heard that a new fen drainage bill was shortly to be laid before the Commons. This was a matter of keen interest to the university, because it had a direct bearing on the provisioning of the colleges. The waterways in and around Cambridge had begun to dry up as a result of the activities of unscrupulous fen drainers such as Sir Miles Sandys, and consequently it had become increasingly difficult for traders to bring their goods to market. This inevitably led to shortages of foodstuffs and fuel, which in turn led to higher prices, to the anger of the colleges.[28] Tabor was well acquainted with these problems, for as well as being registrary he was clerk to the Cambridgeshire sewer commissioners.[29] Nevertheless, he was ignorant of the contents of the new drainage bill, and was anxious to discover its provisions so that he could acquaint Gooch 'with some material points to be stood upon for us'.

The second item on Tabor's list was a bill for the maintenance of vicars of impropriate parsonages, of which Gooch was advised to take 'some care' because the university owned several parsonages. Gooch was further instructed to oppose a bill to prevent tradesmen from conducting their business without licence from their local corporation, on the grounds that it would be 'against King James's charter, where a scholar or scholar's servant may use any trade without contradiction or composition'. Finally, Gooch was ordered to ensure that the university was granted its traditional exemption from the Subsidy Act.

University interest in the activities of the Commons was mirrored by the Commons' own concern for the business of the university during the later 1620s. In June 1626 several Members expressed distaste at the election of the duke of Buckingham as chancellor of the university. Buckingham's election was interpreted both as a deliberate snub to the Commons, which was then busy drawing up articles of impeachment against the royal favourite, and as evidence of the rising influence of Arminianism within the university.

Speaking for the university, Thomas Eden denied that Cambridge had intended any affront to the House, and claimed that it was free of Arminianism, a defence so unconvincing that it drew from Sir Alexander Temple the caustic response that 'he could as easily believe there was not one whore in the town of Cambridge as that the university was without an Arminian'.[30]

The election of the Arminian Matthew Wren as vice-chancellor of the university in November 1628 can have done little to allay parliamentary suspicions that Cambridge was fast becoming hostile to Calvinism. In February 1629 the Speaker, Sir John Finch II, wrote to both universities requiring them to send up the names of all those university members who had written or published any doctrines contrary to the true or generally received sense of the Thirty-Nine Articles, and to report what punishment, if any, had been inflicted upon them. At Cambridge, Finch's letter resulted in the appointment of an investigative committee. However, it proved unable to compile a detailed return because of the inadequacy of the university's records, and because Wren had circulated a reminder that the recent reissue of the Thirty-Nine Articles forbade members of the universities to explore 'those curious points in which the present differences lie'. The committee's report, such as it was, recorded 14 cases, of which only two were relevant to the issue of Arminianism. It was never presented to the Commons, for by the time it was completed the Parliament had already been dissolved.[31]

[1] CUL, UA, Elect. L.5, no. 3. [2] Harl. 4017, ff. 26v. [3] C.H. Cooper, *Annals of Camb.* iii. 71, 84, 156, 170; LC5/132, p. 91. [4] *Oxford DNB*, xl. 544-5; *HP Commons 1558-1603*, iii. 438; Harl. 4017, f. 18. [5] M.B. Rex, *Univ. Rep. in Eng.* 22, 24-8. [6] Ibid. 60-2; *Cambs. Antiquarian Soc. Procs.* xvii. 208. [7] Calculated from Harl. 4017, *passim*. [8] Rex, 351-2. [9] J. Heywood and T. Wright, *Camb. Univ. Trans.* ii. 258-9. [10] Rex, 58-9; *Cambs. Antiquarian Procs.* xvii. 205. [11] *Cambs. Antiquarian Procs.* xvii. 204-9. [12] CUL, UA Elect L.5 no. 1. The heads' indenture is written on paper rather than parchment, and so may be a copy. The sheriff, Thomas Baldwin, is named as a party to the indenture, but neither his signature nor any other is appended to it. [13] *Misc. Gen. et Her.* (ser. 5), vi. 57. [14] Rex, 355. Rex says that this edict bears the date 28 Feb. 1621, but in fact it is undated: CUL, CUR 50, no.1(a). [15] Rex, 355. [16] *Ct. of Jas. I* ed. G. Goodman, ii. 226. [17] *CSP Dom. 1623-5*, p. 148. [18] King's Coll. Lib. Camb., ms KCAR/1/2/16, vol. iv. no. 59. On Collins see *Oxford DNB*. [19] *HMC Cowper*, i. 252. [20] *Procs. 1626*, iv. 262; Gonville and Caius Coll. Camb., ms T44/249, f. 178. [21] Rex, 112-13; *Procs. 1626*, iii. 370-1. [22] *Ct. of Jas. I*, ii. 226. [23] *Cambs. Antiquarian Soc. Procs.* xvii. 205-7. [24] *Historical Reg. of Univ. of Camb. to 1910* ed. J.R. Tanner, 50. [25] Rex, 355. [26] Ibid. 88; Harl. 7046, ff. 76v-7v; PROB 11/118, f. 87v. [27] CUL, CUR 50, no. 2. Part of this letter only is printed in Rex, 355. [28] CUL, UA, Lett. 11A, no. C18a (fair copy at CUL, T.XII. 1, no. 3); UA, T.XII, no. 17. [29] CUL, UA, T.XII.1, no. 23. [30] *Procs. 1626*, iii. 370-2; iv. 292. [31] N. Tyacke, *Anti-Calvinists*, 51-2; Heywood and Wright, ii. 367-8; Add. 5852, f. 162v.

A.D.T.

CHESHIRE

Number of voters: unknown

27 Feb. 1604	SIR THOMAS HOLCROFT
	SIR ROGER ASTON
c.Mar. 1614	SIR WILLIAM BRERETON
	SIR ROGER WILBRAHAM
11 Dec. 1620	SIR WILLIAM BRERETON
	SIR RICHARD GROSVENOR
1 Feb. 1624	WILLIAM BOOTH
	WILLIAM BRERETON
25 Apr. 1625	SIR ROBERT CHOLMONDELEY, 1st bt.
	SIR ANTHONY ST. JOHN
30 Jan.-2 Feb. 1626[1]	SIR RICHARD GROSVENOR, (1st bt.)
	PETER DANIELL
	John Minshull
c.Feb. 1628	SIR RICHARD GROSVENOR, (1st bt.)
	SIR WILLIAM BRERETON, 1st bt.

Though it was a county palatine, the administration and governance of Cheshire was broadly similar to that of any other shire. Influence and power was largely controlled by the local gentry and administered by the lord lieutenant, deputy lieutenants and magistrates. However, Cheshire remained largely outside the Westminster legal system: it maintained its own courts and justice was administered in the name of the earl of Chester, a title bestowed ever since 1301 on the prince of Wales at his creation. Not surprisingly, the county has been described as an *imperium in imperio*.[2] The senior legal officer was the chamberlain, who presided over Cheshire's Court of Exchequer.[3] In the early seventeenth century this was William Stanley, 6th earl of Derby, who from 1607 also served as lord lieutenant. However, as he was non-resident the office of vice-chamberlain became more prominent.[4] Apart from its separate status, Cheshire was also remarkable for the antiquity of its leading families. 'There is no county in England more famous for a long continued succession of ancient gentry than this of Cheshire,' wrote Daniel King in 1656.[5] Five families could trace their ancestry back to Domesday, while a further 71 had ties to the county stretching back to the thirteenth century or earlier.[6] This, combined with a high proportion of intermarriage, gave Cheshire an insular quality which it was keen to protect.

Elections were held at the Shirehall within Chester Castle. Since its enfranchisement in 1542, Cheshire's representation in Parliament had generally followed a pattern. The senior seat was occupied by a prominent member of the gentry while the junior place went to someone with Court connections. This can be seen both in 1604 and 1614. In the first Jacobean Parliament Sir Thomas Holcroft of Vale Royal served as the senior knight, while Sir Roger Aston, gentleman of the king's bedchamber, took the junior seat. In 1614 the senior Member was Sir William Brereton of Brereton, while his colleague was the master of Requests, Sir Roger Wilbraham. However, from 1620 the pattern changed, perhaps a sign of increasing opposition to the Court. Both Members were drawn from the senior ranks of the Cheshire gentry: Brereton was again returned for the first place and was joined by Sir Richard Grosvenor of Eaton Hall, who lacked Court office. Seats were shared between the leading families on an almost rotational basis, though it was not unusual for someone to be elected more than once: Brereton sat in 1614 and 1620, Holcroft had previously sat in 1593 and 1601, while Grosvenor served in 1621, 1626 and 1628.

The 1624 election again saw Cheshire return two senior members of the local gentry, neither of whom was connected with the Court. This election was remarkable for the fact that the sheriff, Sir Richard Grosvenor, delivered an address to the assembled voters in which he outlined the responsibilities of Members at both local and national levels. His speech provides the first conclusive evidence of the existence of what has been termed 'caucus politics' in the county,[7] as it contains the assertion that the two candidates, William Brereton of Ashley and William Booth of Dunham Massey, represented 'the opinion and resolution' of the leading members of the gentry. Since most of the county's elite were seated behind Grosvenor on the platform, his claim carried great weight, and it is therefore not surprising that Brereton and Booth were unanimously elected, even though Grosvenor was at pains to inform the voters that they had 'free liberty to discover [their] minds'.[8]

This consensual Cheshire politicking, in which senior members of the gentry met before the election and divided the seats between their families, did not survive long into the next reign. The 1625 election appears to have been uncontested with Sir Robert Cholmondeley being returned for the first place and Sir Anthony St. John for the second. However, thereafter Cheshire politics became polarized. One faction was led by those who had (or later acquired) Irish peerages, and included the Breretons of Brereton, the Cholmondeleys and the Needhams. The other group was led by men who had obtained baronetcies, and included the Breretons of Handforth, the Booths, the Wilbrahams and the Grosvenors. This conflict, while part of a wider national controversy, had a substantial impact on Cheshire elections.

In 1626 Grosvenor, who was allied with the 'baronet' group, was unanimously elected to the first place. Two of the baronet group, Peter Daniell of Over Tabley (Grosvenor's son-in-law) and (Sir) William Brereton (1st bt.) of Handforth (Booth's son-in-law) sought the second seat, but were persuaded to draw lots and consequently Brereton was eliminated. Daniell was then opposed by Cholmondeley's brother-in-law, John Minshull. The election itself was described as a 'very great stir such as the like was nev[er] observed in Cheshire before'. Both groups cried out the name of their favourites but the sheriff could not decide who had prevailed. After failing to quiet the proceedings, he adjourned the election from the Shirehall to Flookersbrook Heath, because neither the hall nor the Castle Court were capable of holding the numbers present; he then divided the voters in two and restarted the count, which took two days. Before polling was completed, however, 'it was mediated by gentlemen on both sides and at last it was thus concluded in the Constable's chamber that Mr. Daniell should in loving terms desire Mr. Minshull to yield unto him without any more loss of time and money, which Mr. Minshull was persuaded to do'.[9] Despite the drawn out nature of this contest, it would seem, as Morrill has noted, that 'nothing seems to have been at stake except local prestige and precedence'.[10] In 1628 another contest was envisaged and local traders stocked Chester with supplies, but the 'barons' withdrew at the last minute.[11] Grosvenor was again elected to the senior seat and Sir William Brereton, 1st bt. served with him.

Owing to its palatine status, Cheshire had certain privileges and institutions which it was keen to protect in Parliament. In 1621, for instance, Grosvenor requested the inclusion of the prince of Wales in the concealments bill because he enjoyed *jure regalia* in Cheshire.[12] When the Commons debated whether to enfranchise county Durham, which was also a county palatine, Grosvenor was anxious to ensure that it should not have more Members than Cheshire. During the same Parliament Brereton and Grosvenor both sought to include Cheshire in the bill for fees in courts of justice.[13] Cheshire does not appear to have promoted any legislation on its own behalf during this period, though matters pertaining to Wales or Ireland certainly interested its Members, particularly in 1621, when both MPs fervently supported the Irish cattle

bill which was designed to limit the import of cattle, most of which came through Chester, and the export of specie.[14]

[1] Cheshire Archives, CR63/2/18, unfol. [2] *VCH Cheshire*, ii. 5; W. Stubbs, *Constitutional Hist. of Eng.* i. 294, 392. [3] *VCH Cheshire*, ii. 38; J. Morrill, *Cheshire*, 1-2. [4] *VCH Cheshire*, ii. 38, 54. [5] *Vale Royal of Eng.* (1656) ed. D. King, quoted in Morrill, 3. [6] Morrill, 3-4. [7] *VCH Cheshire*, ii. 107. [8] *Pprs. of Sir Richard Grosvenor* ed. R. Cust (Lancs. and Cheshire Rec. Soc. cxxxiv), 1-7. [9] Cheshire Archives, CR63/2/18, unfol. [10] *VCH Cheshire*, ii. 107. [11] Harl 2125, f. 59. [12] *CJ*, i. 534a; *CD 1621*, v. 18. [13] *CJ*, i. 606a; *CD 1621*, iii. 149; iv. 294. [14] V. Treadwell, *Buckingham and Ire.* 161.

C.R.K.

CHESTER

Right of election: ?in the inhabitants

Number of voters: c.900 in 1628

20 Feb. 1604	THOMAS LAWTON, recorder HUGH GLASIER, alderman
12 May 1606[1]	THOMAS GAMULL, recorder *vice* Lawton, deceased
24 Sept. 1610[2]	SIR JOHN BINGLEY *vice* Glasier, deceased
7 Mar. 1614[3]	EDWARD WHITBY, recorder SIR JOHN BINGLEY
25 Dec. 1620[4]	EDWARD WHITBY, recorder JOHN RATCLIFFE, alderman Sir Thomas Edmondes* John Savage Sir John Bingley
19 Jan. 1624[5]	EDWARD WHITBY, recorder JOHN SAVAGE
9 May 1625[6]	EDWARD WHITBY, recorder (SIR) JOHN SAVAGE
c. Jan. 1626	EDWARD WHITBY, recorder WILLIAM GAMULL, alderman

10 Mar. 1628[7]	EDWARD WHITBY, recorder	631
	JOHN RATCLIFFE, alderman	570
	Sir Randle Mainwaring	C. 300
	Sir Thomas Smith†	C. 300

Chester, situated on the River Dee, was the capital of a palatinate earldom and an important port for the Irish trade, being only 11 miles inland.[8] It received its first charter in 1354, and in 1506 was granted county status. However, Chester Castle and its surrounds (Gloverstone) remained under the authority of the chamberlain of the county palatine. Moreover, in 1541, when the see of Chester was established, the Cathedral precincts also became a separate entity. According to the 1506 charter, the corporation consisted of a mayor, two sheriffs, 24 aldermen and 40 common councilmen, but in fact another group was also involved in the governance of the city, known as the sheriff-peers, who were chosen from among the councilmen. After their election new councilmen were selected, which meant that the sheriff-peers could not return to being councilmen when their term of office ended. However, by custom they continued to attend and vote at corporation meetings, and this meant that the size of corporation tended to vary.[9] Chester also had a recorder and a town clerk, known as the clerk of the pentice.[10]

In the early seventeenth century Chester's population within the city walls numbered around 5,000.[11] The local economy revolved around the leather industry, whose craftsmen comprised approximately 23 per cent of the freemen.[12] Most trade was with Ireland, particularly Dublin. Some links with the Baltic developed during the period, but these were sporadic and did not involve large cargoes.[13] Overseas trade was restricted to members of the city's powerful Merchant Adventurers' Company, founded in 1554.[14] Despite being the dominant port in north-west England, Chester, or rather its corporation, was not wealthy. Rents from city lands, freemen admissions, and fees for grazing cattle on the Roodee accounted for under £100 p.a.[15] Overall income ranged from between £283 in 1607-8 to just £130 in 1616-17.[16] Chester's poverty meant that corporation members were often surcharged to meet extraordinary expenses. King James's visit in 1617 cost around £220, of which £130 was spent on the gift of a standing bowl, £40 on a banquet and £50 in assorted presents to members of the royal entourage.[17] Repairs to the city walls in 1629 also necessitated a levy on Chester's inhabitants.[18]

Although there was substantial contact between Chester and the Crown, especially over the dispatch of royal officials, troops and goods to Ireland, there was surprisingly little interference by the Crown in the city's affairs. The most notable exception was in January 1606, when James attempted to have Hugh Mainwaring elected as Chester's recorder. The corporation reminded the king that only the previous year he had confirmed the city's charter, which gave Chester the right to elect its own recorder. Consequently, James decided 'to forbear to press you any further in the suit'.[19] Relations between the city and successive bishops and the dean and chapter were also generally harmonious, although in 1607 a major disturbance (the 'sword incident') threatened instability.[20] Another substantial disagreement occurred in 1624, when Bishop John Bridgeman tried to make the pews in the corporation church of St. Oswald's 'more uniform and to re-align the pulpit, which was not conveniently situated'. The corporation objected, and the dispute rumbled on until 1638, when Bridgeman caved in.[21] The argument with Bridgeman reflected the emergence of a strong puritan element in the city during the 1620s and 1630s, led by prominent corporation members such as John Ratcliffe, Peter and Robert Ince and the Bruen family, supported by the recorder, Edward Whitby.[22]

Chester first sent representatives to Parliament in 1283.[23] However, Cheshire's status as a palatinate with its own *Parliamentum* meant that Chester did not receive further writs until it was enfranchised by statute in 1543. The two sheriffs of Chester served as returning officers. Before 1620 voting seems to have been restricted to members of the corporation, though the freemen were not excluded either by statute or by the terms of the city's charter.[24] It is not known whether Chester paid parliamentary wages. The city traditionally elected corporation members, one of whom was normally the recorder.[25] Thus in 1604 Recorder Thomas Lawton occupied the senior place and alderman Hugh Glasier the junior. The death of Lawton in 1606 necessitated a by-election, whereupon the new recorder, Thomas Gamull, was elected in his place. However, when Glasier succumbed to the plague during the fourth session of the Parliament he was replaced by Sir John Bingley who, though a native and freeman of Chester, lived in Westminster. Bingley, however, offered to serve without charge,[26] and was elected again in 1614, when he was joined by Edward Whitby, appointed recorder after Gamull's death.

The parliamentary election of 1620 was the borough's first recorded contest and witnessed the first significant attempt to bring outside influence to bear on its seats. In mid-November Thomas, Viscount Savage, one of Cheshire's greatest magnates, nominated his brother John, of Barrow, for the first seat and supported Bingley's request to be re-elected as the junior Member.[27] The Savages enjoyed a long connection with Chester and their father, Sir John, had served as mayor in 1607-8. However, this nomination was swiftly forgotten, for in December 1620 Prince Charles's Council intervened. The prince had been created earl of Chester in 1616 and the Council therefore wrote to William Compton, earl of

Northampton and lord president of Wales, instructing him to propose Sir Henry Carey I*, comptroller of the Household, for the first seat. Northampton complied, though he apologized to the corporation that 'I do well know [this request] to be improper for me to make unto you', he having previously had no connection to the city.[28] The corporation preferred to uphold its tradition of returning the recorder as the senior Member, however, and drafted a response explaining that Carey, as a non-freeman, was ineligible.[29] Before it was dispatched, recorder Whitby and Sir Randle Mainwaring brought news from London that Carey had found a seat at Hertfordshire. They also carried fresh instructions from the Council to substitute Sir Thomas Edmondes*, a privy councillor whose recent attempt to be returned for Middlesex had failed. On 21 Dec. the corporation composed another letter informing Northampton of this turn of events, disingenuously claiming that they would have been willing to accept Carey, though they had 'feared much opposition in the commonalty'.[30]

The election was held on Christmas day, after the corporation met to endorse Whitby and Edmondes as its candidates. This 'selection' was announced to a large crowd outside the Common Hall. However, Whitby then announced that Edmondes, a non-freeman whose candidacy he had, up to this point, appeared to support, was ineligible. Instead he nominated his ally, alderman John Ratcliffe, of whom the mayor, William Gamull, and many others strongly disapproved. Familial and factional rivalries between Whitby and Gamull dated back to 1617, when the corporation, led by the powerful Gamull family, had obtained the dismissal of Whitby's father and brother from the clerkship of the pentice, which they shared. In 1619 there had also been an attempt to oust Whitby himself from the recordership.[31] The corporation's dislike of Ratcliffe was motivated by religion and snobbery, as they described him as a puritan, a 'chief countenancer of factions' and a man whose 'only profession is a beerbrewer'.[32]

Whitby and Ratcliffe achieved a landslide victory at the hustings. The Prince's Council seems not to have been overly concerned at the rejection of their candidate, as Edmondes found a seat elsewhere, but Gamull was furious, alleging that Whitby and Ratcliffe had canvassed among the 'basest sort', many of the crowd being 'labourers, hired workmen and beggars'. He informed the Prince's Council that 'the recorder's tenants and servants out-swayed our good desires and carried the election for Mr. Recorder and Mr. Ratcliffe to be our burgesses, which we could not withstand by

reason of the unappeasable and unruly carriages of this disordered multitude'.[33] Gamull was urged by Sir Randle Mainwaring to petition the Commons for redress, claiming that the corporation could 'easily have procured new writs' had it complained about the lowly status of those who voted for Ratcliffe. However, the corporation ignored requests from both Mainwaring and Viscount Savage to know how many votes each candidate had received.[34] This may suggest that Gamull and the rest of the corporation were actually secretly pleased at the outcome of the election, for though they disliked Ratcliffe outsiders had been excluded and Chester's tradition of returning its recorder had been preserved. Possibly the corporation had even connived with Whitby all along, and the personal animosity between Gamull and Whitby may have been less important than has previously been thought.[35]

The suspicion that the corporation was not displeased at the outcome of the 1620 election is reinforced by events in 1624. On 1 Jan. the Prince's Council instructed Sir Thomas Ireland*, vice-chamberlain of Chester, to nominate Charles's secretary, Sir Francis Cottington*, but on 19 Jan. Whitby was re-elected, along with John Savage, son and heir of Viscount Savage.[36] Following Charles's accession in 1625, Chester was freed from further interference from London. Whitby and Savage sat again in 1625, and in 1626 Whitby was returned with his arch-rival, alderman William Gamull.

In 1627 Whitby caused a further rupture in local politics when he questioned the activities of Robert Brerewood, the new clerk of the pentice. Brerewood was the son-in-law of one of Whitby's staunchest enemies, Sir Randle Mainwaring and a close ally of another of Whitby's antagonists, Sir Thomas Smith.[37] Mainwaring and Smith had been instrumental in removing Whitby's father and brother from clerkship of the pentice, and Whitby sought revenge by petitioning the Privy Council for Brerewood's dismissal. After much wrangling, and with the assistance of Viscount Savage, who was aggrieved that Brerewood had been appointed ahead of his son's servant, Richard Litler, Brerewood was dismissed and the Whitbys reappointed.[38] A bitter contest ensued at the parliamentary election on 10 Mar. 1628, with Mainwaring and Smith standing against Whitby and Ratcliffe:

...[there] was great contention about the burgesses of the Parliament... both parties laboured all the city either freemen or householders to give their voices on one part or other. Yea many were laboured four or five times over. So great was the contention the one seeking to over sway the other many were threatened unless they gave their voices to Sir Randle [Mainwaring] and Sir Thomas [Smith] they should lose their houses. The two knights wrought so with all the country gentlemen that had tenants in Chester to give them their voices. Within the Common Hall had like to have been a mutiny but with much ado it was appeased and each man gave his voice particularly so that Mr. Recorder [Whitby] had 631 voices, Mr. Ratcliffe 570, Sir Randle and Sir Thomas had other 300 and odd apiece and far short which vexed them so to see the recorder so well-beloved that they would not subscribe to the commission which went to London. The like labouring was never seen for a city more divided in faction was never seen.[39]

In 1628 as in 1620, the election contest raised surprisingly few doubts about Chester's franchise.

It is unclear whether Chester pursued many legislative objectives during this period, although under Elizabeth it had frequently promoted bills.[40] During the first Jacobean Parliament the corporation certainly corresponded regularly with its Members at Westminster, and in 1604 it sought an exemption from the provisions of the Tunnage and Poundage bill based upon its charter. However, despite intense lobbying from Glasier and Lawton, the Commons did not approve any dispensation.[41] In 1610 Chester asked its Members to find a way to prevent London merchants from buying and selling goods locally with the same privileges as Chester merchants and to have the impositions removed on yarn imported from Ireland.[42] For the remainder of the period no other correspondence appears to survive.

[1] Cheshire Archives, SIE/7; C219/330/30. [2] Cheshire Archives, SIE/8. [3] Cheshire Archives, SIE/9. [4] Harl. 2125, f. 53. [5] Ibid. ff. 57v-8. [6] Harl. 2150, f. 6. [7] Harl. 2125, f. 59v. [8] A.M. Johnson, 'Political, Constitutional, Social and Econ. Hist. of Chester 1550-1652', (Univ. Oxford D.Phil. thesis, 1970), chap. 1; J. McN. Dodgson, *Place Names of Cheshire*, v. (I:i), 2-7. [9] M.J. Groombridge, *Cal. Chester City Council Mins.* (Lancs. and Cheshire Rec. Soc. cvi), pp. viii-xi. [10] Cheshire Archives, CX/3, f. 108. [11] Johnson, 7. [12] D.M. Woodward, 'Chester Leather Industry', *Trans. Hist. Soc. Lancs. and Cheshire*, cxix. 66, 85-8. [13] W.B. Stephens, 'Overseas Trade of Chester', *Trans. Hist. Soc. Lancs. and Cheshire*, cxx. 23-4; G.M. Haynes-Thomas, 'Port of Chester', *Trans. Lancs. and Cheshire Antiq. Soc.* lxi. 35; T.S. Willan, 'Chester and the Navigation of the Dee', *Jnl. Nth. Wales Architectural, Arch. and Hist. Soc.* xxxii. pt. 1, pp. 64-7. [14] Johnson, 229. [15] Johnson, 91-2. [16] Johnson, 96; Groombridge, 214-9; E.G. James, 'Charity Endowments in Seventeenth and Eighteenth-Cent. Eng.', *JEH*, viii. 153-70. [17] Cheshire Archives, CR60/83, ff. 28v-9; AB/1, ff. 336, 338. [18] Johnson, 7. [19] Cheshire Archives, AB/1, ff. 283, 288-9, 290; AF/7, nos. 4, 7; AF/6, no. 6. [20] Harl. 2173, f. 11; Johnson, 18; R.V.H. Burne, *Chester Cathedral*, 87-8; T. Hughes, 'City against the Abbey', *Jnl. Chester Arch. Soc.* (ser. 1), xii (I), 433-7. [21] Burne, 88-9; Johnson, 18-19; Groombridge, xxii-xxiii; G.T.O. Bridgeman, *Hist. Church and Manor of Wigan*, ii. 295-305, 406-8. [22] J.S. Morrill, *Cheshire*, 19; STAC 8/21/6; CHES 38/48 Ratcliffe to Whitby, 10 May 1620; R.C. Richardson, *Puritanism in NW Eng.* 13, 83. [23] M. McKisack, *Parl. Rep.*

Eng Boroughs during Middle Ages, 7-8. [24] *VCH Cheshire*, ii. 110; *HP Commons, 1509-58*; *HP Commons, 1558-1603*. [25] *VCH Cheshire*, ii. 110. [26] Cheshire Archives, ML/2, nos. 238, 263. [27] Harl. 2105, f. 285. [28] Ibid. f. 275. [29] Ibid. f. 281; J.K. Gruenfelder, 'The Parlty. Election at Chester, 1621', *Trans. Hist. Soc. Lancs and Cheshire* cxx. 37-42; several errors in Gruenfelder's account are corrected by P.M. Hunneyball, 'Prince Charles's Council as Electoral Agent, 1620-24', *PH*, xxiii. 325. [30] Harl. 2105, ff. 271, 279. [31] STAC 8/297/15; Cheshire Archives, CR/374; Harl. 2091, ff. 126v-37; 2105, ff. 152-9, 172, 174-5; Groombridge, xiii. 96, 98-9; D. Hirst, *Representative of the People?*, 197. [32] Harl. 2105, f. 277-v; STAC 8/21/6. [33] Harl. 2105, ff. 277-8. [34] Ibid. f. 283. [35] Gruenfelder, 42; Hirst, 197-8. [36] DCO, Prince Charles in Spain, f. 34v. [37] *Oxford DNB sub* Brerewood; J. Hutchinson, *Cat. Notable Middle Templars*, 30. [38] STAC 8/297/15; APC, 1627-8, pp. 7-8, 164-5, 179-80; SP16/57/12; 58/90; 84/8. [39] Harl. 2125, f. 59v. [40] D.M. Dean, *Law-Making and Soc. in Late Eliz. Eng.* 253. [41] CJ, i. 233b, 237a, 237b, 238a, 239a. [42] Cheshire Archives, ML/6, no. 38; ML/2, no. 233.

C.R.K./R.C.L.S.

CORNWALL

Number of voters: at least 1,500 in 1628

12 Mar. 1604	SIR JONATHAN TRELAWNY SIR ANTHONY ROUS
21 Oct. 1605	SIR WILLIAM GODOLPHIN *vice* Trelawny, deceased
1614	RICHARD CAREW JOHN ST. AUBYN
25 Dec. 1620	BEVILL GRENVILLE JOHN ARUNDELL
1624	WILLIAM CORYTON BEVILL GRENVILLE
29 May 1625	CHARLES TREVANION SIR ROBERT KILLIGREW
1626	WILLIAM CORYTON SIR FRANCIS GODOLPHIN
10 Mar. 1628	(SIR) JOHN ELIOT WILLIAM CORYTON ?John Mohun ?Sir Richard Edgcumbe

A 'demi-island ... besieged ... with the ocean', early seventeenth-century Cornwall largely depended economically on its proximity to the shipping routes between Wales, Ireland, Spain, France and the Netherlands. Despite its poor agricultural land and insubstantial towns, this most westerly of English counties boasted two major trading commodities. The waters around its extensive coastline teemed with pilchards, the bulk of most catches being packed for sale in France and Spain. Equally significant was the mining of tin, England's most important export after cloth at this period. As Richard Carew[†] noted at the turn of the century, through tin Cornwall's 'inhabitants gain wealth, the merchants traffic, and the whole realm a reputation'.[1] However, the county's location also brought with it problems. Mediterranean pirates and 'Dunkirker' privateers posed a constant threat to local shipping and the coastal population, particularly in the later 1620s. From 1625 eastern Cornwall also bore much of the burden of billeting generated by the naval expeditions dispatched from the nearby Devon port of Plymouth.[2]

Cornwall during the early Stuart era lacked a dominant electoral patron. The county had no resident peers until 1625, when a gentleman-moneylender, Sir Richard Robartes, purchased a barony. The greatest landed interest lay with the Crown, consisting principally in the 42 local manors held by the duchy of Cornwall. As the duchy appointed the county sheriff, and also controlled the tin industry through its stannary administration, it might have been expected to wield considerable influence at elections. However, even in 1620 and 1624, when Prince Charles's Council actively exercised its political leverage, nominations were made only to 13 Cornish boroughs where the duchy owned property. The lord warden of the stannaries, the 3rd earl of Pembroke, who was also Cornwall's lord lieutenant, likewise normally limited his attention to borough seats, although his vice-warden and leading client, William Coryton, presumably enjoyed his backing when he became a knight of the shire in 1624 and 1626.[3]

In the absence of significant external pressures, the leading Cornish gentry jockeyed among themselves for the honour of representing their county. Most candidates were both wealthy and active in local government, and were typically drawn from the ranks of the deputy lieutenants, but a lengthy pedigree was also a marked advantage. All but three of the county Members during this period came from families resident in Cornwall since at least the fourteenth century. Of the exceptions, Richard Carew's ancestors had arrived in the 1400s, while Sir Anthony Rous came from ancient Devon stock with estates straddling the county border. Only Sir John Eliot, who owed his fortune to his great-uncle, a Plymouth merchant, could be accounted a genuine newcomer to this elite circle.[4]

Although Cornwall was effectively split into Eastern and Western divisions for administrative purposes, this pattern was not automatically replicated in the choice of Members. Each half of the county was indeed represented in 1614, 1621 and 1626, but both Members in 1604, 1624 and 1628 came from eastern Cornwall, while the west dominated in 1625.[5] However, it is clear that bargains were struck ahead of elections, with prospective candidates lobbying their friends, and testing the strength of potential rivals. For example, in November 1620 John Arundell decided to stand with Bevill Grenville, and sounded out William Coryton, who, it turned out, had been gathering support for his own bid. After an elaborate exchange of courtesies, Coryton agreed to back Arundell and Grenville. Sir Reginald Mohun then informed Arundell that he too was aiming for a county seat, but the latter rebuffed this approach under the pretence that he and Grenville had already engaged themselves to Coryton. These discussions, held discreetly in London, cleared the way for Arundell and Grenville to stand unopposed, and are representative of Cornwall's standard practice.[6]

The surviving election indentures from this period were generally signed only by those gentry who lived close to Lostwithiel, where the county court assembled. The exception to this rule is the indenture for 1628, which was signed by many supporters of Coryton and Sir John Eliot who had come from much further afield for what may have been a contested election. This contrast with normal practice tends to confirm that ordinarily the outcome was a foregone conclusion.[7]

The 1604 election saw the return of two men prominent in local government, the Cecil client Sir Jonathan Trelawny, who had already represented Cornwall in 1597, and the notably pious Sir Anthony Rous. When Trelawny died suddenly during the Parliament's first session, he was replaced by another Cecil protégé, the young Sir William Godolphin, whose electoral success may partly have stemmed from the fact that his father, Sir Francis, was the current sheriff and returning officer.[8] In 1614 the choice fell on John Arundell's nephew and brother-in-law, Richard Carew and John St. Aubyn, neither of whom had yet come into their estates. Arundell presumably backed their return to the Addled Parliament, but at the next general election he presented both of these kinsmen to the borough of Mitchell in order to facilitate his own pursuit of a county seat. As already noted, he faced competition from the newly appointed vice-warden of the stannaries, William Coryton, as well as from Sir Reginald Mohun, who was planning to introduce a private estate bill in the Commons.[9] However, since 1619 Arundell had been leading the county's resistance to the earl of Tullibardine's monopoly of packing, drying and salting fish in Devon and Cornwall. This campaign provided him with a popular platform that his rivals could not match, though he still found it expedient to concede the senior shire seat to the young Bevill Grenville, who could boast recent experience of life at Court. It is possible that Coryton's withdrawal in November 1620 was conditional on Arundell promising to support him at a future election, for in 1624 the vice-warden was returned alongside Grenville, while Coryton's friend Charles Trevanion found Arundell a place at St. Mawes.[10]

The onset of war with Spain changed the dynamic of Cornish politics. In 1625 the county was represented by the courtier Sir Robert Killigrew, who was also captain of a vital coastal fort, Pendennis Castle, and Trevanion, whose home lay close to the English Channel. Arundell, who had recently been removed from the Cornish bench, also attempted to stand, possibly as Trevanion's partner, but was unable to muster enough support.[11] By the time of the next election, parts of the county were grappling with the burden of billeted soldiers. The government was slow to repay the expenses incurred at local level, and Cornwall's best hope of recovering the money lay in the Privy Seal loan which was raised during the winter of 1625-6. It was no coincidence that the county's freeholders returned the two Cornish loan collectors, Coryton and Sir Francis Godolphin, the latter of whom also commanded the Scilly Isles' defences.[12] Once at Westminster Coryton pressed for the reimbursement of Cornwall's billeting costs and campaigned for better naval protection of the Channel coast. However, as a leading client of the earl of Pembroke he was also prominent in the Commons' failed impeachment of the duke of Buckingham.[13]

Following the 1626 Parliament's dissolution, Coryton was replaced as vice-warden by Buckingham's client John Mohun, and also stripped of other local offices. In the following year he and Sir John Eliot were imprisoned in London for opposing the Forced Loan, attracting considerable local sympathy for their resistance to arbitrary taxation.[14] Released in January 1628 ahead of fresh parliamentary elections, Coryton and Eliot promptly announced their intention of standing as knights of the shire. Completely wrong-footed, Mohun launched a rival campaign with Sir Richard Edgcumbe as his partner. With neither side prepared to back down, there ensued an unprecedented period of public lobbying by both camps. Mohun and his allies, who included several deputy lieutenants,

attempted to bully the county sheriff, Jonathan Rashleigh*, and appealed for support from their fellow magistrates, urging the necessity of electing Members who would be acceptable to the government, and thus able to negotiate redress of the county's grievances.[15] By contrast, Coryton and Eliot sought the backing of the ordinary freeholders, playing on their reputation as martyrs for the common good. Experimenting with one novel tactic, Coryton encouraged his supporters to vote by issuing ostensibly neutral 'tickets' to be read in Cornwall's parish churches:

> These are to give you notice that the day for the election of our shire knights is at Lostwithiel on Monday the tenth of March by eight of the clock in the morning, that the freeholders ought to be there to give their voices, those that have forty shillings yearly of inheritance, or for term of their own lives, or for another's life, to which they are requested that there may be a due election.

Perhaps aware that the Mohun faction hoped to cow the voters by summoning the trained bands to Lostwithiel, Coryton and Eliot also arranged for their friends Arundell, Grenville and Trevanion to bring hundreds of their tenants to the election. In the event, Mohun and his associates stayed away from the county court, presumably recognizing that they would not win a poll. Consequently it is not clear whether this election was ultimately contested.[16]

Three days into the new parliamentary session, Coryton produced in the Commons correspondence illustrating the attempt by Mohun and his friends to influence the election's outcome. On 21 Mar. the House agreed that the offenders should be sent for, but it was early May before they finally reached Westminster, by which time several of the group had been spared, and Mohun himself had evaded the Commons' jurisdiction by securing a peerage.[17] Edgcumbe, who had been returned at Bossiney, then made his excuses, leaving just four men to face the Members' wrath. On 13 May John Trelawny and Walter Langdon were sent to the Tower, while Sir William Wrey and Edward Trelawny were placed in the serjeant-at-arms's custody. The Commons' order that all four should make a public submission back in Cornwall was never implemented, and the king released them from detention once the session ended.[18] Of the two victorious Members, Eliot was apparently the more vengeful, maintaining the pressure on Mohun during this session by attacking his record as vice-warden. Coryton, in contrast, largely maintained a dignified silence during the parliamentary investigation, instead addressing local concerns about billeting and martial law. Eliot's bid to revive the inquiry into Mohun's actions in the

1629 session failed in the face of more important business.[19]

[1] R. Carew, *Survey of Cornw.* ed. P. White, 11, 13, 16-17, 19, 34, 45, 51-3; J. Whetter, *Cornw. in Seventeenth Cent.*, 16, 21, 53, 126. [2] A. Duffin, *Faction and Faith*, 128-31, 134. [3] Duffin, 5, 8; *Parl. Survey of Duchy of Cornw.* ed. N.J.G. Pounds (Devon and Cornw. Rec. Soc. n.s. xxv), pp. xv-xvi; J. Doddridge, *Hist. Account of Principality of Wales* (1714), 90; G.R. Lewis, *Stannaries*, 86; P.M. Hunneyball, 'Prince Charles's Council as Electoral Agent', *PH*, xxiii. 319-21, 327; G.K. Gruenfelder, *Influence in Early Stuart Elections*, 129-30. [4] J. Chynoweth, *Tudor Cornw.* 33; F.G. Marsh, *The Godolphins*, 2; D. and S. Lysons, *Cornw.* 222; C. Henderson, *Essays in Cornish Hist.* 187-8; W.H. Tregellas, *Cornish Worthies*, ii. 116-17; J. Polsue, *Complete Paroch. Hist. of Cornw.* i. 263; ii. 370-1; Vivian, *Vis. Cornw.* 11, 68; D. and S. Lysons, *Devon*, p. ccxii; WARD 7/18/162; H. Hulme, *Sir John Eliot*, 17. [5] Carew, 106. [6] SP46/72, f. 147v; SP14/117/55. [7] C219/35/1/150, 181; 219/37/15; 219/39/22; 219/41B/135. [8] *HMC Hatfield*, xi. 405; xv. 303; C219/35/1/150. [9] Vivian, 12, 69; *CJ*, i. 605b. [10] *APC*, 1619-21, pp. 84, 136; M. Coate, *Cornw. in Gt. Civil War*, 85. [11] SP16/521/19. [12] Duffin, 128-9, 145. [13] *Procs. 1626*, ii. 122, 142, 336; iii. 130, 387. [14] SP16/37/91; 16/106/14; *CSP Dom.* 1627-8, pp. 232-3. [15] *APC*, 1627-8, p. 217-18; SP16/106/14; *HMC 1st Rep.* 51, 62; *CD 1628*, ii. 33. [16] SP16/96/36, 48; 16/106/14; *CD 1628*, ii. 375. [17] *CD 1628*, ii. 33-4, 41; iii. 26, 60, 82, 324. [18] Ibid. iii. 376, 386; SP16/108/52. [19] *CD 1628*, ii. 420-1; iii. 32, 623-6, 631-2; iv. 280; *CJ*, i. 925a.

P.A.D./P.M.H.

BODMIN

Right of election: in the mayor and capital burgesses

Number of voters: maximum of 37

26 Feb. 1604	JOHN STONE
	NICHOLAS SPREY
c. Mar. 1614	SIR RICHARD EDGCUMBE
	CHRISTOPHER SPREY[1]
12 Dec. 1620	JAMES BAGG II
26 Dec. 1620	SIR JOHN TREVOR I
c. 10 Feb. 1624	SIR THOMAS STAFFORD
1624	(SIR) CHARLES BERKELEY
30 Apr. 1625	ROBERT CAESAR
	HENRY JERMYN
21 Jan. 1626	HENRY JERMYN
	SIR RICHARD WESTON
4 Mar. 1628	SIR ROBERT KILLIGREW
	HUMPHREY NICOLL

Bodmin traced its roots back to the sixth century, when St. Petroc founded a monastery which served as Cornwall's first Anglo-Saxon cathedral. The town achieved borough status by 1190, and secured its earliest recorded charter of privileges in the mid-thirteenth century. The prestige of its medieval priory, combined with the town's importance as a centre for the tin trade, made Bodmin a focal point for Cornish society, and the western rebellions of 1497 and 1549 both began there.[2] This prominence was scarcely diminished in the early seventeenth century. Richard Carew[†] believed that Bodmin, despite some urban decay, was still Cornwall's largest town, and certainly its weekly market was unrivalled in the county. Quarter sessions and musters were regularly held there, and when large numbers of troops were billeted in the region in the later 1620s, the borough took on a significant share of this burden.[3]

Bodmin's charter of incorporation, granted in 1563 and renewed with minor changes in 1594, provided for a common council comprising a mayor and 36 capital burgesses, of whom 12 possessed the higher dignity of councillor. Appropriately enough, this was Cornwall's largest such body. The borough also possessed a town clerk, who, like the mayor and his immediate predecessor, acted as a municipal j.p. Bodmin's parliamentary franchise, which dated back to 1295, was vested in the corporation. From 1624 the election indentures referred specifically to the mayor and the 'major part of the common council', though it seems unlikely that the abandonment of the looser term of 'burgesses' indicated any tightening of electoral practice. Since the surviving indentures from this period were, with two exceptions, signed only by the mayor, precise voting patterns cannot be determined.[4]

Like several other Cornish boroughs, Bodmin heeded the king's request in 1604 to send local residents to Parliament, and returned two members of the corporation, John Stone and Nicholas Sprey. Ten years later, Sprey was serving as both town clerk and mayor, which doubtless explains how his son Christopher secured election.[5] The other Member in 1614, Sir Richard Edgcumbe, was a Cornish gentleman who perhaps obtained a seat through his kinship with the Prideaux family, which owned land in Bodmin.[6] The pattern of patronage in 1620 is uncertain. James Bagg, a Devon man, may have found backing within the corporation; he was apparently a distant kinsman of the Stone family through his mother, though the actual line can no longer be traced.[7] Sir John Trevor had married into a major Cornish dynasty, the Trevanions, but the key factor may rather have been his Court connections with Sir Robert Killigrew, with whom he had travelled to Spain in 1605.[8] If so, Trevor's election was the first sign of what became a Killigrew stranglehold over the borough's patronage. The basis for Sir Robert's influence has not been established. He seems not to have possessed land in the Bodmin district, nor was he closely related to any of the local landowners except Sir Reginald Mohun*, who held a relatively insignificant manor there.[9] His grip on the borough was such that he might be thought to have held a senior position there, such as the recorder-ship. However, Bodmin's charter at this time did not allow for a recorder or high steward, and Killigrew's known office-holding in Cornwall was limited to the Falmouth and Launceston areas. Whatever the expla-nation, he enjoyed complete control over nominations during the mid-1620s. In 1624 the borough returned his friend Sir Thomas Stafford and his nephew Sir Charles Berkeley. Another of Killigrew's nephews, Henry Jermyn, benefited from his patronage in 1625 and 1626. In the former year he was paired with Killigrew's kinsman by marriage, Robert Caesar.[10] Sir Richard Weston, Jermyn's partner in 1626, was probably nominated as a favour to Killigrew's Court patron, the duke of Buckingham, who had just failed to secure for Weston a seat at Hythe. Killigrew had performed this same service for Buckingham when he returned Sir Edwin Sandys at Penryn in 1625.[11] Of the five indentures which survive from these three elections, four were drawn up with blank spaces left for Killigrew to indicate his choices.[12] Only in 1628 did this stranglehold weaken. Although Killigrew took one seat himself, the other went to Humphrey Nicoll, a local landowner and member of Cornwall's anti-Buckingham faction, which enjoyed widespread electoral success that year.[13]

---

[1] OR. One contemporary list of MPs (Lansd. 1191) states that Richard Connock* was elected at Bodmin in 1614, but this is not supported by other, more reliable lists: *Procs. 1614 (Commons)*, 447, 451. [2] C. Henderson *et al.*, *Cornish Church Guide*, 59-60; J. Maclean, *Trigg Minor Deanery*, i. 122, 208, 219-20; *Bodmin Reg.* comp. J. Walker, 150; G.R. Lewis, *Stannaries*, 44, 61, 106. [3] F.E. Halliday, *Richard Carew of Antony*, 160, 195; *CSP Dom. 1629-31*, p. 21; A. Duffin, *Faction and Faith*, 130. [4] Maclean, i. 211-14; W.P. Courtney, *Parl. Rep. of Cornw.* 227; C219/35/1/179; 219/37/52; 219/38/45. [5] Maclean, i. 236, 239, 294. [6] Vivian, *Vis. Devon*, 621; Maclean, iii. 13. [7] Maclean, i. 312; Vivian, *Vis. Cornw.* 446; Vivian, *Vis. Devon*, 34. [8] Vivian, *Vis. Cornw.* 502; NLW, Carreglwyd mss, I/699. [9] Vivian, *Vis. Cornw.* 268. [10] PROB 11/164, f. 91; Vivian, *Vis. Cornw.* 270; F. Blomefield, *Hist. Norf.* ix. 353; *Vis. Herts.* (Harl. Soc. xxii), 133-4. [11] Add. 37819, f. 17. [12] C219/38/45; 219/39/58; 219/40/256, 281. [13] C142/253/95; C2/Chas.I/N10/19.

P.M.H.

BOSSINEY

Right of election: in the burgesses or commonalty

Number of voters: 18 in 1621

12 Mar. 1604	SIR JEROME HORSEY
	GEORGE UPTON
20 Oct. 1609	GEORGE CALVERT *vice*
	Upton, deceased
c. Mar. 1614	JOHN WOOD
	SIR JEROME HORSEY
2 Jan. 1621	JOHN WOOD
1621	AMBROSE MANATON
17 Jan. 1624	SIR RICHARD WESTON
	THOMAS GEWEN
6 May 1625	SIR FRANCIS COTTINGTON, bt.
	JONATHAN PRIDEAUX
12 Jan. 1626	CHARLES, 2ND LORD LAMBART
	PAUL SPECCOTT
27 Jan. 1628[1]	SIR RICHARD EDGCUMBE
	CHARLES, 2ND LORD LAMBART

A settlement existed at Bossiney by the late eleventh century, when a small Norman castle was constructed there. The village was granted in the mid-thirteenth century to Richard, earl of Cornwall, who provided the borough with its first charter. Like many of the earl's former estates, Bossiney was absorbed into the duchy of Cornwall in 1337. At that time the borough was flourish-ing, but decline set in during the next century, and around 1540 Leland observed a substantial number of ruinous buildings. This situation had presumably not improved 60 years later, since Richard Carew[†] considered the village too small to warrant a description in his *Survey of Cornwall*.[2]

Bossiney was not incorporated until 1685, and consequently local government in the early seven-teenth century was limited to a leet court presided over by a self-styled mayor. The borough had been enfran-chised in 1547, though its geographical insignificance was such that for some years afterwards it was unclear whether its Members were officially representing Bossiney itself or the neighbouring village of Trevena. By 1604 this confusion had been resolved in Bossiney's favour, but as late as 1621 John Wood's election inden-ture displayed an old formula combining the names of both places. The electorate consisted of the burgesses, all of whom were apparently Bossiney property owners, and residents of the borough or the local parish of Tintagel. The alternative term 'commonalty' was used on Jonathan Prideaux's indenture in 1625, a varia-tion which may simply indicate the imprecise nature of the electorate. The number of signatories to the elec-tion indentures varied during this period between six and 18. Many of these voters, including several of the mayors, were unable to write their own names.[3]

Unsurprisingly, external patrons decided the course of Bossiney's parliamentary elections throughout this period. The key figure initially was John Hender[†] of Botreaux Castle, the greatest landowner in the immedi-ate neighbourhood, and the head of a family which was prominent within Bossiney itself. Hender had control-led all nominations since 1586, but he routinely deferred to the wishes of his friend (Sir) William Peryam[†], chief baron of the Exchequer. Accordingly, in 1604 the borough returned two of Peryam's kinsmen, Sir Jerome Horsey, who had already represented Bossiney in 1601, and George Upton.[4] Peryam died in October 1604, and when Upton's own demise in 1609 created a vacancy, Hender found himself under pressure from other quarters. First the borough was approached by Sir John Harington*, either the man returned for Coventry shortly afterwards, or a Somerset kinsman of that name whose family owned a manor near Bossiney. Hender saw off this challenge to his monopoly, but he bowed to the inevitable when lord treasurer Salisbury (Robert Cecil[†]) himself requested the nomination from the mayor and burgesses. Writing to Salisbury on 21 Oct., the day after the by-election, Hender outlined his position:

I have ... had for these 20 years past and more the nomination of the burgesses ... yet is it ... at your good lordship's dispose, whereof [sic] I beseech your good lordship to accept at your servant's hands ... the inden-ture subscribed and sealed together with our seal itself to alter and dispose the same with our allowance and consent at your lordship's pleasure.

Hender's co-operation was not wholly uncondi-tional, however, and he concluded with an ostensi-bly unconnected plea that he should not be chosen as Cornwall's next sheriff. The proffered deal was appar-ently accepted: Hender got his wish, while Salisbury completed the blank indenture with the name of his secretary, George Calvert.[5]

Thereafter, the patronage pattern became signifi-cantly more complex. Hender died in 1611, having divided his lands among his four daughters, and his heirs failed to maintain his stranglehold over the borough. The Botreaux Castle interest was presumably responsible for Horsey's re-election in 1614, but it was not certainly successful again until Hender's son-in-law, Richard, Lord Robartes, secured a place in 1626 and 1628 for his own son-in-law, Charles, Lord Lambart.[6]

Initially, competition came from John Wood, a gentle-man whose house lay just outside Bossiney. Wood was returned in 1614 and 1621, but his family's electoral influence died with him in December 1623, only days before the next Parliament was summoned.[7] By the mid-1620s the lack of a dominant patron was appar-ently common knowledge. In January 1626 Sir Richard Carnsew, who lived around six miles from Bossiney and possessed no obvious status within the borough, was asked to obtain a seat there for his kinsman Richard Hampden*.[8] Nothing came of this, but in fact the borough's vulnerability was already being exploited for the benefit of a rival kinship network, which secured burgess-ships there in all but one election during this decade. Although it is difficult to prove, patron-age in this case was probably exercised by the Pride-aux family of Padstow. (Sir) Nicholas Prideaux[†] was the pre-eminent gentleman in this part of Cornwall, one of the elite group who represented the county on commissions of oyer and terminer, and his administra-tive responsibilities periodically embraced the district around Bossiney.[9] Although he lived some ten miles from the borough, and owned no property there, he and his sons possessed significant estates to the south-west of the town, and this cumulative prestige may well have been sufficient in the prevailing conditions.[10] Certainly a Prideaux connection makes sense of the electoral pattern. Sir Nicholas' brother Edmund, a Devon resi-dent, married a sister of Sir Richard Edgcumbe, who sat for Bossiney in 1628. The borough also returned Edgcumbe's brother-in-law Ambrose Manaton in 1621, and his nephew Paul Speccott in 1626. The fourth member of this group, who sat in 1625, was Jonathan Prideaux, a distant cousin of Sir Nicholas.[11] None of these four men had any other discernible link with Boss-iney or its neighbourhood. Furthermore, Edgcumbe, Speccott and possibly Prideaux were returned by means of blank election indentures, a practice normally associated with external patrons.[12]

Because Bossiney belonged to the duchy of Cornwall, the borough also received electoral nominations from Prince Charles's council in 1620 and 1624. On the first occasion the duchy was firmly rebuffed, and its candi-date, Sir Edward Coke, had to find a seat elsewhere. This resistance was probably inspired by John Wood, who used his Commons platform in 1621 to criticize the duchy's management of its estates. In 1624 the council's nomi-nation of Sir Richard Weston came shortly after Wood's death, and in marked contrast to its earlier behaviour, the borough elected not only Weston but also Thomas Gewen, presumably a secondary duchy nominee since his indenture described him as Prince Charles's auditor. This about-turn probably reflected the influence of yet another minor local landowner, Richard Billing, who, as escheator and feodary to Prince Charles, was jointly responsible for the distribution of the duchy's nomination letters.[13] In 1625 Bossiney again returned a government candidate, Sir Francis Cottington, formerly Prince Charles's secretary. As the duchy made no formal nominations that year, and Billing had died in July 1624, the means by which Cottington obtained his seat are unclear. However, he may well have received the backing of Lord Robartes, who was certainly active as a patron in the following year. In May 1625 Robartes was still in the throes of paying for his recently granted peerage, and his cooperation with the Crown's wishes was therefore to be expected.[14]

[1] OR; Harg. 311, f. 219v. [2] C. Henderson *et al.*, *Cornish Church Guide*, 203-5; J. Hatcher, *Rural Economy and Soc. in the Duchy of Cornw.* 22, 161; *Early Tours in Devon and Cornw.* ed. R. Pearse Chope, 13. [3] J. Maclean, *Hist. of Trigg Minor*, iii. 205-6, 209; *HP Commons, 1509-58*, i. 48; C219/35/1/167; 219/37/40; 219/38/28; 219/39/24. [4] *HP Commons, 1558-1603*, i. 124; E179/88/265; Maclean, iii. 217; C142/519/94; Vivian, *Vis. Devon*, 603. [5] Maclean, iii. 245; J. Collinson, *Hist. and Antiqs. of Som.* i. 128; SP14/48/116; C219/35/1/153; *Ath. Ox.* ii. 522. [6] C142/519/94; Vivian, *Vis. Cornw.* 217, 397. [7] C142/403/65; Maclean, iii. 247. [8] SP46/73, f. 150. Bossiney is referred to in this letter as Tintagel. [9] F.E. Halliday, *Richard Carew of Antony*, 219; C181/3, ff. 136v-7; E179/88/265; SP14/138/116. [10] Maclean, ii. 90; C142/366/188. [11] Vivian, *Vis. Devon*, 618-21, 707; Vivian, *Vis. Cornw.* 142. [12] C219/39/24; 219/40/265; 219/41B/138. Manaton's indenture is lost. [13] DCO, 'Letters and Patents, 1620-1', f. 39v; 'Prince Chas. in Spain', f. 33r-v; *CJ*, i. 531a; C219/38/29; Maclean, iii. 203. [14] Vivian, *Vis. Cornw.* 32; *CSP Dom.* 1625-6, p. 2; *Procs. 1626*, i. 469; SP16/23/118.

P.M.H.

CALLINGTON

Right of election: in the free burgesses or inhabitants

Number of voters: 30 in 1625

10 Mar. 1604	WILLIAM ROLLE
	SIR ROGER WILBRAHAM
c. Mar. 1614	WILLIAM ROLLE
	HUMPHREY WERE
27 Dec. 1620	HENRY ROLLE
	JAMES WRIOTHESLEY,
	LORD WRIOTHESLEY
23 Jan. 1624	HENRY ROLLE
	SIR EDWARD SEYMOUR, (bt.)
22 Apr. 1625	THOMAS WISE
	SIR RICHARD WESTON
18 Jan. 1626	JOHN ROLLE
	SIR CLIPPESBY CREWE
1628	JOHN ROLLE
29 Feb. 1628	SIR WILLIAM CONSTABLE, bt.
bef. 18 May 1628[1]	SIR GEORGE RADCLIFFE *vice* Constable, chose to sit for Scarborough

Callington was the last of the old Cornish boroughs to be enfranchised, and physically was one of the least impressive. Despite being a market town since 1267, and the customary meeting-place for official assemblies within Cornwall's East hundred, the borough was never incorporated, and the chief officer, although known as the mayor, was in reality a manorial reeve. In ecclesiastical terms, Callington was merely a chapelry of the neighbouring parish of South Hill, with which it was also merged for taxation purposes. The town's pleas of poverty during the collection of Ship Money in the 1630s seem to have been genuine.[2] The nature of the parliamentary franchise established in 1584 is unclear, though it is said in the early seventeenth century to have embraced all inhabitants resident for at least a year. Election indentures of this period were usually drawn up in the name of the free burgesses, but one in 1620 referred to the 'inhabitants'. The open nature of the franchise is reflected in the fact that around 50 individual voters can be identified in the election indentures from the 1620s.[3]

The borough's electoral patronage appears to have been shared by three gentry families at this juncture. One seat was controlled by Robert Rolle of Heanton Satchville, Devon, who had purchased the manor of Callington in around 1601. Rolle nominated his brother William in 1604 and 1614, his son Henry in 1620 and 1624, his son-in-law Thomas Wise in 1625, and another son, John, in 1626 and 1628.[4] The second patron was William Coryton*, who lived in the adjacent parish of St. Mellion, and became vice-warden of the Cornish stannaries in 1620, serving under the 3rd earl of Pembroke. In December of that year Callington's second seat went to James, Lord Wriothesley, the son of another prominent courtier, the 3rd earl of Southampton, who may well have requested that Pembroke provide the young man with a burgess-ship.[5] Coryton is likely to have obliged on this occasion, since he certainly presented Sir Clippesby Crewe to the borough in 1626 on the lord warden's instructions.[6] In the purge of the duke of Buckingham's opponents which followed the 1626 Parliament, Coryton lost his position in the stannaries, and subsequently became a prominent Forced Loan refuser. In November 1627 he was identified by Christopher Wandesford* as one of the 'tribunitial orators of the west' who might be approached if Sir Thomas Wentworth* needed seats for his friends, and in February 1628 Callington returned Sir William Constable, one of Yorkshire's leading Loan refusers. On 9 Apr. Constable opted to represent Scarborough instead, and though no official record survives, it is clear that the vacancy was filled by Sir George Radcliffe, another Loan refuser and one of Wentworth's closest associates.[7]

The remaining Members can mostly be identified as nominees of the Trelawny family, who, though not resident in the immediate vicinity, owned the biggest manor in South Hill and the largest share of that parish's advowson.[8] Sir Jonathan Trelawny* is known to have offered burgess-ships to his kinsman Sir Robert Cecil[†] in 1601, and appears to have accepted nominations from him at West Looe in 1604. It is quite feasible, therefore, that he secured a seat at Callington in the latter year for the government lawyer Sir Roger Wilbraham.[9] Trelawny died in June 1604, and the family's interest passed to his son John, who certainly became an active patron at West Looe, and might have played a more prominent role at Callington as well but for Coryton's interventions.[10] A Trelawny connection may also explain the election in 1614 of Humphrey Were, who had strong ties with Tiverton, Devon, where the family were also major landowners. The picture is clearer in 1624, when John's uncle, Sir Edward Seymour, was elected.[11] In 1628 Trelawny himself sought a burgess-ship at Callington while also campaigning with John Mohun* to prevent Coryton from becoming a Cornish knight of the shire, behaviour which doubtless told against him. Whether Trelawny's name was actually put to the borough's voters is not clear, but on 20 Mar., during a Commons' debate on electoral malpractice in Cornwall, Coryton produced a letter of recommendation that Callington had received from the Mohun faction.[12] The remaining Callington Member, Sir Richard Weston, who sat in 1625, was most likely a government nominee, as he had been at Bossiney in 1624, but it is unclear which of the borough's patrons he would have turned to.[13]

[1] T.D. Whitaker, *Life of Sir George Radcliffe*, 159. [2] W.P. Courtney, *Parl. Rep. of Cornw.* 266-7; *Hist. Cornw.* ed. S. Drew, i. 655-6; R. Carew, *Survey of Cornw.* ed. P. White, 104; C219/35/1/158; J. Polsue, *Complete Parochial Hist. of Cornw.* i. 169; E179/88/297; *CSP Dom.* 1639, p. 62. [3] *Hist. Cornw.* i. 656; C219/37/27-8; 219/38/52-3; 219/39/39, 57; 219/40/267, 284; 219/41B/141. [4] C2/Jas.I/R4/25; Vivian, *Vis. Devon*, 654, 791. [5] Polsue, iii. 305; J.K. Gruenfelder, *Influence in Early Stuart Elections*, 129. [6] SP16/523/77. [7] *Wentworth Pprs.* ed. J.P. Cooper (Cam. Soc. ser. 4. xii), 278-9; R. Cust, *Forced Loan*, 38, 61, 197, 201, 219, 227; *CD 1628*, ii. 376. [8] C142/282/82. [9] Vivian, *Vis. Cornw.* 268; *Misc. Gen. et Her.* (ser. 3), iv. 20; *HMC Hatfield*, ix. 405; Gruenfelder, 36. [10] Vivian, *Vis. Cornw.* 476. [11] D. and S. Lysons, *Magna Britannia*, vi: *Devon*, 252; C142/282/82; Vivian, *Vis. Cornw.* 268. [12] *CD 1628*, ii. 33. [13] Gruenfelder, 89, 147.

P.M.H.

CAMELFORD

Right of election: in the burgesses and freeholders or commonalty

Number of voters: 22 in 1626

7 Mar. 1604	ANTHONY TURPYN
10 Mar. 1604	JOHN GOOD
c. Mar. 1614	GEORGE COTTON
	ROBERT NAUNTON
22 Dec. 1620	SIR HENRY CAREY II
	EDWARD CARR
10 Feb. 1624	SIR FRANCIS COTTINGTON
17 Feb. 1624	EDWARD CARR
20 Apr. 1625	THOMAS COTEEL
	SIR HENRY HUNGATE
12 Jan. 1626	EDWARD LYNDSEY
15 Jan. 1626	SIR THOMAS MONCK
by 17 Apr. 1626	?SIR JAMES PERROT *vice* Monck, disabled
26 Feb. 1628[1]	FRANCIS CROSSING
	EVAN EDWARDS

Camelford grew up where the main road traversing north Cornwall crosses the River Camel. Established as a borough by Richard, earl of Cornwall in 1259, in the following century it was absorbed into the duchy of Cornwall, along with the manor of Helston in Trigg to which it had formerly belonged. Despite its strategic location and privileges, Camelford failed to prosper. At the end of the sixteenth century Richard Carew[†] described it as 'a market and fair (but not fair) town', which 'steppeth little before the meanest sort of boroughs for store of inhabitants, or the inhabitants' store'. Not as yet incorporated, the early seventeenth-century borough was apparently run as the personal fiefdom of the leading residents, the Cock family, who had monopolized the mayoralty since at least the 1550s. It is not known whether they were behind a petition presented to the Commons in 1610 concerned with wages in the town.[2]

Camelford returned Members to Parliament from 1547. The nature of the franchise is unclear, but seems to have embraced resident freemen who paid scot and lot.[3] Early Stuart electoral indentures normally refer simply to the 'burgesses' or 'free burgesses', though the terms 'freeholders' and 'commonalty' were also used in 1604. There were at least 43 voters in total during this period. Notwithstanding the Cocks' local dominance, there was considerable competition among the Cornish gentry for control of the borough's seats, and their manipulation of elections is reflected in the indentures. As was customary in Cornwall at this time, separate returns were made for each Member, and in 1604, 1624 and 1626 the two indentures were completed several days apart. Ordinarily a majority of voters signed both documents, but in 1626 only the mayor's name was recorded twice, and appears to have been forged on one indenture. In 1625, 1626 and 1628, Members' names were apparently inserted in pre-prepared 'blank' returns, which had most likely been presented to the relevant patrons by the borough.[4]

Even by Cornish standards, Camelford's patronage pattern during this period is unusually complex, with a large number of evenly matched parties competing for the borough's favours. The Carnsew family, only middle-ranking county gentry but the biggest land-owners in the immediate locality, had made nomina-tions since the 1590s, and probably presented both Members in 1604. Anthony Turpyn, who had also represented Camelford in the previous Parliament, may well have been an associate of their kinsmen the Moncks, while John Good was a family friend.[5] The Carnsews proved unable to maintain their hold over the borough, however, and two new patrons emerged in 1614. One of these was William Cotton, a gentle-man of similar standing, who had acquired lands close to Camelford through his marriage into the Hender family seven years earlier, and doubtless intervened in support of his uncle, George Cotton.[6] The other patron was probably Sir Robert Killigrew*, a leading client of the royal favourite the earl of Somerset and the scion of a major Cornish family, whose father, Sir William I*, held two important duchy of Cornwall estates near Camelford, the parks of Helsbury and Lanteglos.[7] Killigrew's involvement could explain the election of Robert Naunton, a courtier with ties to the earl of Somerset and the Howard clan.

In the elections of 1620 and 1624, a second alliance of Court and gentry figures secured complete control over the borough. On each occasion one seat was claimed by Prince Charles's Council, which exercised the duchy of Cornwall's interest. These nominations were communicated by Richard Billing, the Duchy feodary, who lived at nearby St. Tudy, and held privi-leges of hunting and warren in Helston manor jointly with Nicholas Cock, son of the then mayor of Camel-ford. Billing's local standing, enhanced by his new electoral role, enabled him at both elections to engi-neer the return of one of his kinsmen, Edward Carr.

In 1620 the Prince's Council initially earmarked the other seat for Sir Fulke Greville, and this option was kept open until it became clear that Greville would secure a Warwickshire seat, whereupon a supplemen-tary Duchy nominee, Sir Henry Carey, was elected instead. A similar delay was instituted in 1624, when Sir Francis Cottington was returned at Camelford only after the duchy's original candidate, Sir John Suckling, triumphed at the Middlesex hustings.[8]

The duchy made no further nominations during this decade, and Billing died in July 1624. With these influ-ences removed, the earlier pattern of gentry compe-tition resumed. Sir Robert Killigrew was presumably responsible in 1625 for the election of his nephew, Sir Henry Hungate, and may also have been behind the returns of Edward Lyndsey and Evan Edwards in 1626 and 1628. Both men were servants of the 4th earl of Dorset (Sir Edward Sackville*), who, though he lacked direct ties to Cornwall, could easily have approached Killigrew, who was well known in Court circles as an electoral patron. Killigrew's presumed role in Edwards' election is more problematic, as Sir Robert lost his lease of Helsbury and Lanteglos parks in 1627. However, Killigrew's general prestige in Cornwall throughout this period was probably high enough to enable him to approach the borough without the additional leverage of local property ownership.[9] In 1625 Thomas Coteel almost certainly secured his seat through the mediation of a distant kinsman, Sir Nicholas Prideaux, another leading Cornish gentleman who owned little land near the borough.[10]

In 1626 Sir Richard Carnsew managed to re-assert his family's interest. Though unable to meet Henry Cromwell's* request for him to provide a burgess-ship for Richard Hampden*, he did obtain a place for his cousin Sir Thomas Monck.[11] The Commons' ruling on 24 Mar., that Monck's imprisonment for debt rendered his election invalid, created a vacancy which may have been filled by Sir James Perrot, who was in the Commons by 17 Apr., although no record of an election survives. If Perrot did indeed succeed at Camelford, it probably reflected the influence of his ally the 3rd earl of Pembroke, who as lord warden of the Cornish stannaries found seats for several of his supporters that year.[12] In 1628 the remaining Camel-ford place went to an Exeter resident, Francis Cross-ing, whose links to Cornwall are unclear, although he had sat for Mitchell in 1626. Crossing may have relied on the backing of his kinsman William Hakewill*, who had himself previously represented Mitchell, probably as a nominee of John Arundell* of Trerice. Through his kinsman Crossing was perhaps able to contact Arundell, whose sister had married Sir Richard Carnsew's brother. Alternatively, Hakewill may have recommended Crossing to one of his own distant relatives, Sir Nicholas Prideaux.[13]

[1] OR; Procs. 1626, iii. 10. [2] J. Maclean, Deanery of Trigg Minor, ii. 327-9, 332, 368; Parl. Survey of the Duchy of Cornw. ed. N.J.G. Pounds (Devon and Cornw. Rec. Soc. n.s. xxv), i. 54; R. Carew, Survey of Cornw. ed. P. White, 145; CJ, i. 444b. [3] HP Commons, 1509-58, i. 48; Maclean, 328-9. [4] C219/35/1/178, 183; 219/37/31-2; 219/38/40-1; 219/39/49, 64; 219/40/251, 257; 219/41B/140, 166. [5] HP Commons, 1558-1603, i. 125-6; WARD 7/84/197; SP46/72, ff. 110, 270. [6] Maclean, i. 652-3; C142/519/94. [7] R.E. Schreiber, Political Career of Sir Robert Naunton, 6; E306/4/6. [8] DCO, 'Letters and Patents 1620-1', f. 39v; 'Prince Chas. in Spain', ff. 33v, 34v; Vivian, Vis. Cornw. 32, 93; Maclean, ii. 296, 368. [9] F. Blomefield, Hist. Norf. ix. 353; Vivian, 270; Bedford Estate Office, letter bk. 1, no. 108; C66/2420/3. [10] Vis. London (Harl. Soc. xv), 192; Vivian, 142; Vivian, Vis. Devon, 621; HP Commons, 1558-1603, iii. 252-3; Carew, 172. [11] SP46/73, f. 150; Vivian, Vis. Cornw. 76-7; Vivian, Vis. Devon, 16, 20, 342, 569. [12] Procs. 1626, ii. 356; J.K. Gruenfelder, Influence in Early Stuart Elections, 129-30. [13] HMC Exeter, 124; Vivian, Vis. Devon, 437, 603, 621; Vivian, Vis. Cornw. 12, 77.

P.M.H.

FOWEY

Right of election: in the portreeve and commonalty or burgesses

Number of voters: 37 in 1621

11 Mar. 1604	HENRY PETER	
	FRANCIS VYVYAN	
c. Mar. 1614	SIR EDWARD BOYS	
	JONATHAN RASHLEIGH	
12 Dec. 1620	JONATHAN RASHLEIGH	
	JOHN TREFFRY	
20 Jan. 1624	WILLIAM NOYE	
22 Jan. 1624	SIR ROBERT COKE	
26 Apr. 1625	JONATHAN RASHLEIGH	
	ARTHUR BASSETT	
18 Jan. 1626	WILLIAM MURRAY	
	ARTHUR BASSETT	
7 Mar. 1628	SIR RICHARD GRENVILLE	
	ROBERT RASHLEIGH	

The mouth of the River Fowey forms the best natural harbour on the English coast between Plymouth and Falmouth. This fact, combined with Fowey's close proximity to the duchy of Cornwall's tin coining centre at Lostwithiel, explains the town's rise in the later middle ages as a base for trade, piracy and, on occasion, military expeditions. The latter two activities largely ceased under the early Tudors, but in the early seventeenth century the town quay, 500 feet long, provided a berth for merchant vessels trading with Ireland, Brittany, Gascony and the Netherlands, besides the more distant locations of southern Spain, Naples and Newfoundland. Plymouth was now steadily overtaking Fowey as a port, but the town had improved its economic performance in the later sixteenth century and remained Cornwall's principal merchant community, even though an upsurge in piracy contributed to a sharp decline in its trade between the 1610s and the early 1630s.[1]

Fowey's municipal government was not formally incorporated until 1685, but a recognized structure of Portreeve and burgesses existed as early as the thirteenth century. By then the original manor of Fowey had been divided in two. One half, the so-called 'burgage' manor, was held from the late fourteenth century by the Treffry family, whose house dominated the small town. The other half or 'borough' manor, to which the town's privileges attached, belonged to the nearby Tywardreath Priory until the Reformation, and became part of the duchy of Cornwall in 1540.[2] The parliamentary borough was created in 1571, probably in order to increase Crown or Duchy patronage. The exact nature of the franchise prior to the 1685 charter is uncertain, as the election indentures merely speak of burgesses or the commonalty of Fowey, but it seems to have consisted of freeholders of the borough manor and other tenants paying scot and lot.[3]

The electoral pattern between 1604 and 1628 reflected the local dominance of the borough's leading gentry families, the Rashleighs of Menabilly and the Treffrys. Major players in Fowey's Elizabethan trade revival, the Rashleighs had used their wealth to buy up properties to which burgess votes attached. They are said to have controlled 12 votes in the 1570s and 15 by 1650, the latter figure matching the number of freehold properties in the borough manor which they owned in 1649. Although some of these burgages belonged to a junior branch of the family, based outside Fowey at Coombe, the election results in the early seventeenth century indicate that John Rashleigh[†] and his son Jonathan* could rely on their cousins' co-operation. By comparison, the Treffrys apparently controlled just three or four votes in this way, and the family's influence was further limited by the fact that its head, John Treffry*, inherited as a minor in 1603, coming of age only in 1616.[4] Nevertheless, both families usually exercised greater electoral patronage than the duchy of

Cornwall, which possessed little local leverage beyond the right to appoint the 'borough' manor's officials. Although the Duchy occasionally flexed its administrative muscles, in 1616 accusing John Rashleigh and John Treffry of infringing its rights over the River Fowey, the town was quite capable of ignoring the government's wishes. Twenty years earlier, Rashleigh and William Treffry[+], John's father, had mobilized Fowey against a trade levy introduced to help pay for Plymouth's fortifications.[5]

During this period, Fowey's most successful patrons were undoubtedly the Rashleighs. John Rashleigh, who died in 1624, can be credited with the return of his future son-in-law Francis Vyvyan in 1604, and his son Jonathan in 1614 and 1621. In 1625 Jonathan secured one seat for himself, handing the other to his brother-in-law Arthur Bassett, who sat for Fowey again in the following year. Robert Rashleigh, representing the Coombe branch, took his turn in 1628. The Treffrys probably backed their kinsman Henry Peter in 1604, though their only clear-cut success was John Treffry's return in 1621.[6] The local patrons' double victory in 1621 was especially significant, as the borough thereby rejected the duchy of Cornwall's nominee, William Noye. Three years later, however, the situation was reversed. The Duchy secured one seat for Noye, while Sir Robert Coke was probably nominated by the 3rd earl of Pembroke, lord warden of the stannaries, who enjoyed his own Cornish powerbase within the Duchy.[7] Pressure was evidently applied, as Noye was apparently returned on a blank indenture, while Coke's name seems to have been inserted on the other return only after another name was erased. Neither of the 1624 indentures was signed by John or Jonathan Rashleigh, a complete break with the usual pattern, and the number of signatories, 19, was unusually low.[8]

The Duchy ceased to make nominations after 1624, though this did not mean an end to external interference. When Cornish politics descended into factional struggle during the later 1620s, Jonathan Rashleigh seems to have sided with Pembroke's vice-warden, William Coryton[+], which presumably explains the return of Pembroke's nominee, William Murray, in 1626. Two years later, Rashleigh came under pressure from Coryton's opponents, notably John Mohun[*] and Sir Bernard Grenville[+], which probably accounts for the election of Grenville's son, Sir Richard.[9] It has not proved possible to explain the election in 1614 of Sir Edward Boys, a Kent resident without obvious ties either to Fowey or to the government.

[1] SP16/12/78; J. Keast, *Fowey*, 11, 15, 24-5, 33, 36, 44, 47-8; Carew, *Survey*, 210; E190/1023/14; 190/1033/33; M.M. Oppenheim, *Maritime Hist. of Devon*, 52-3. [2] Keast, 8, 75; (J. Polsue), *Paroch. Hist. of Cornw.* ii. 28; S. Drew, *Hist. Cornw.* i. 665; R. Carew, *Survey of Cornw.* ed. F.E. Halliday, 209. [3] Keast, 44, 78; Polsue, ii. 24; C219/35/1/163; 219/39/27. [4] Vivian, *Vis. Cornw.* 460; Carew, *Survey*, 210; Keast, 44-5; E.W. Rashleigh, *Short Hist. of Fowey*, 29; E317/Corn/15. [5] G. Haslam, 'Duchy and parl. representation', *Jnl. Royal Inst. Cornw.* n.s. viii. pt. 3, pp. 230-1; DCO, 'Letters and Warrants 1615-19', f. 52v; Keast, 49. [6] Vivian, *Vis. Cornw.* 391-2, 460; Vivian, *Vis. Devon*, 47. [7] DCO, 'Letters and Patents 1620-1', f. 39v; Prince Charles in Spain, f. 33v; J.K. Gruenfelder, *Influence in Early Stuart Elections*, 129. [8] C219/38/38-9. [9] SP16/523/77; HEHL, Huntington mss, HM 1554, p. 10.

P.M.H.

GRAMPOUND

Right of election: in the freemen

Number of voters: 14 in 1625

12 Mar. 1604	WILLIAM NOYE
	SIR FRANCIS BARNHAM
1614	SIR FRANCIS BARNHAM
	THOMAS ST. AUBYN
18 Dec. 1620	JOHN HAMPDEN
20 Dec. 1620	SIR ROBERT CAREY
15 Jan. 1624	JOHN MOHUN
1624	SIR RICHARD EDGCUMBE
19 Apr. 1625	JOHN MOHUN
7 May 1625	SIR SAMUEL ROLLE
	Sir Richard Edgcumbe
17 Jan. 1626	EDWARD THOMAS
20 Jan. 1626	THOMAS ST. AUBYN
n.d.	SIR BENJAMIN RUDYARD
	Double return of Thomas and St. Aubyn. THOMAS declared elected, 17 Feb. 1626.[1]
6 Mar. 1626	FRANCIS COURTNEY *vice* Rudyard, chose to sit for Old Sarum
6 Mar. 1628	SIR HENRY CAREY II (Lord Leppington)
7 Mar. 1628[2]	(SIR) ROBERT PYE

Grampound's name derived from the bridge, or *grand pont*, built to carry the main road from St. Austell to Truro across the River Fal. Possibly founded by the earls of Cornwall, who granted it a market and fairs in 1332, Grampound was absorbed into the duchy of

Cornwall in 1337 by Edward III, who provided the borough with its first charter, and made its privileges conditional on payment to the duchy of a yearly fee-farm rent. By the early seventeenth century this rent stood at over £12, a sum which in 1625 constituted almost half the community's annual expenditure.[3] By then Grampound was struggling economically. Towards the end of Elizabeth's reign Carew had found the borough 'but half replenished with inhabitants, who may better vaunt of their town's antiquity, than the town of their ability'. The situation worsened in 1621 when Tregony, a trading rival just three miles distant, acquired a charter of incorporation which threatened to undermine Grampound's privileges. Prince Charles's Council, which then controlled the duchy's central administration, investigated the Grampound burgesses' objections to this grant, but it finally adopted a neutral stance on the issue, and nothing was done to strengthen the borough's own institutions.[4] Although it was regarded locally as a corporation, Grampound's governing structures were in fact still defined by prescription only. Their form is therefore uncertain beyond the existence of a mayor and a body of freemen, perhaps qualified by payment of scot and lot, in whom the parliamentary franchise had been vested since 1547.[5]

In electoral terms, Grampound's comparative weakness made it easy prey to external pressure, though the sheer number of would-be patrons prevented the emergence of one totally dominant figure. Indeed, many of the surviving parliamentary indentures indicate not only competition for seats, but also elements of malpractice. As at most Cornish boroughs, individual returns were routinely prepared for each Member, but even so the gap of nearly three weeks between the two dates for the 1625 election was unusual, as was the outcome, Sir Richard Edgcumbe's name being erased from the second return and replaced by that of Sir Samuel Rolle. In each of the first three Caroline elections, the name of one regular voter, John Hawkins junior, appears as a mark on one indenture, but as a fluent signature on the other. On Sir Robert Pye's return of 1628, even the mayor's signature was forged.[6]

At the start of this period, the duchy apparently expected to secure one seat, the other place being decided by the local gentry. Sir Francis Barnham, a Kent resident, seems to have owed his return in 1604 and 1614 to the lord warden of the Cornish stannaries, the 3rd earl of Pembroke, who controlled the duchy's local administration. In 1620 Sir Robert Carey was nominated at Grampound by Prince Charles's

Council, though he could also expect support from his nephew Charles Trevanion*, one of the biggest local landowners, who lived five miles south of the borough.[7] Barnham's two partners were William Noye, whose patron has not been identified, and Thomas St. Aubyn, who probably relied on a combination of family estates near Grampound and the backing of his kinsman John Arundell*, another Cornish magnate who resided seven miles away at Trerice. Arundell may also have had a hand in John Hampden's election in 1620. The two men were distantly related through Sir Oliver* and Henry Cromwell*, both of whom seem to have used their ties to Arundell and his brother-in-law Sir Richard Carnsew as a means of indirect patronage. Sir Oliver probably arranged Christopher Hodson's burgess-ship at Mitchell in 1614, while Henry requested a Cornish seat for Hampden's brother Richard* in 1626.[8]

In 1624 the Prince's Council nominated Sir Robert Carey's son Thomas, but this time Grampound proved unreceptive, perhaps on account of the duchy's attitude to the Tregony charter. Instead, the borough returned two Cornish gentlemen. One, Sir Richard Edgcumbe, owned a large manor nearby, and had represented Grampound in 1593. The other, John Mohun, belonged to one of central Cornwall's leading families, and was then living around six miles from the borough at Penwarne; in addition, his uncle William Mohun owned a seat close to the town.[9] In the following year the same pairing initially emerged, but although on 7 May Edgcumbe signed an undertaking as a newly-elected Member to pay his own expenses, he was then prevailed upon to withdraw, for reasons unknown, and replaced by Mohun's cousin Sir Samuel Rolle.[10] A more open dispute followed in 1626. Pembroke, anxious to boost his support in the Commons, secured one seat for his ally Sir Benjamin Rudyard, probably through the mediation of his vice-warden, William Coryton*. For the other place, both the former Member St. Aubyn and Edward Thomas, a Mohun nominee, were returned. A petition concerning this election was received by the committee of privileges on 16 February. Even though Rudyard had already created a vacancy by opting to sit for another constituency, the committee decided on 17 Feb. to accept only Thomas' return as sound, and a fresh writ was issued to find his partner. The reason for this verdict was not recorded, but the presence of the suspect Hawkins' signature on St. Aubyn's indenture may have been an issue. Rudyard's replacement, Francis Courtney, should probably be identified as a minor Cornish gentleman with close ties to Coryton.[11] The 1628 election was rather more clear-cut. Henry Carey, brother of Thomas, doubtless owed his seat to his Trevanion ties. Mohun, by now an active supporter of the duke of Buckingham, placed the remaining burgess-ship at his patron's disposal on 17 Mar., ten days after the indenture was drawn up. His recommendation of Sir Robert Pye, a fellow client, for this place was evidently accepted.[12]

[1] *Procs. 1626*, ii. 61. [2] *OR.* [3] *Hist. Cornw.* ed. S. Drew, i. 643; ii. 184; *Parl. Survey of Duchy of Cornw.* ii. ed. N.J.G. Pounds (Devon and Cornw. Rec. Soc., n.s. xxvii), 178-9; Cornw. RO, J/1951. [4] F.E. Halliday, *Richard Carew of Antony*, 216; DCO, 'Letters and Patents 1620-1', f. 143; 'Bk. of Orders 1621-5', f. 14. [5] Halliday, 216; *Hist. Cornw.* i. 643. [6] C219/39/38, 45; 219/40/248, 254; 219/41B/154, 174. [7] *The Ancestor*, ix. 205; DCO, 'Letters and Patents', f. 39v; Vivian, *Vis. Cornw.* 502; *Her. and Gen.* iv. 45. Barnham's 1604 election indenture inaccurately describes him as 'Francis Barnham esq.', which suggests that he was unknown to the borough prior to his nomination: *OR.* [8] C142/423/64; Vivian, 12, 77, 438; SP46/73, f. 150; *Vis. Hunts.* ed. H. Ellis (Cam. Soc. xliii), 79-80; Vivian, *Vis. Devon*, 280; *Vis. Bucks.* (Harl. Soc. lviii), 70-1. [9] DCO, 'Prince Charles in Spain', f. 33v; C142/662/109; C78/344/4; Vivian, *Vis. Cornw.* 325; D. and S. Lysons, *Magna Britannia*, iii: *Cornw.* 70; E179/89/306. [10] Cornw. RO, J/2074; Vivian, *Vis. Devon*, 464, 466. [11] J.K. Gruenfelder, *Influence in Early Stuart Elections*, 129; M.F. Keeler, *Long Parl.* 359; *Procs. 1626*, ii. 7, 55, 61. In 1627 Courtney emulated Coryton in opposing the Forced Loan: *CSP Dom.* 1627-8, p. 231. [12] SP16/96/36; *Liber Famelicus of Sir J. Whitlocke* ed. J. Bruce (Cam. Soc. lxx), 56.

P.M.H.

HELSTON

Right of election: in the freemen

Number of voters: 13 in 1620

29 Feb. 1604	SIR JOHN LEIGH
1604	JOHN BOGANS
3 May 1606	ROBERT NAUNTON *vice* Bogans, deceased
c. Mar. 1614	SIR ROBERT KILLIGREW HENRY BULSTRODE
20 Dec. 1620	WILLIAM NOYE SIR THOMAS STAFFORD
7 Feb. 1624	THOMAS CAREY FRANCIS CAREW I
4 May 1625	THOMAS CAREY FRANCIS CAREW I
18 Jan. 1626	FRANCIS CAREW I FRANCIS GODOLPHIN
6 Mar. 1628	WILLIAM NOYE SIDNEY GODOLPHIN

Helston grew up at a strategic crossroads some eight miles north of the Lizard in western Cornwall, receiving its first borough charter in 1201. Its importance as a trading centre derived largely from the town's proximity to the tin-producing zone, or stannary, of Penwith and Kerrier. Privileged from 1305 as one of the county's five 'coinage' centres, where tin was assayed before sale, Helston had already begun sending representatives to Parliament seven years earlier. In 1337 the local manor became a founding component of the duchy of Cornwall.[1] By the early seventeenth century the bulk of Cornish tin was being produced in the west of the county, and Helston probably overtook Truro as the principal coinage town during the 1610s.[2] Distribution of the metal was controlled mainly by Londoners, who shipped it out from the nearby haven of Helford. Firm evidence concerning Helston's own merchants is scarce, but the Bogans family brought haberdashery and other goods from London, and there was widespread local participation in the Cornish fish-drying industry.[3] Around 1600 Richard Carew[†] described the town as 'well seated and peopled', while in the late 1620s Bulstrode Whitelocke* found it a place 'of much resort, and a great market'.[4]

Although Helston was not yet an independent parish, the borough was incorporated in 1585, the charter providing for a mayor, recorder and an unspecified number of freemen, four of whom served as aldermen. The parliamentary franchise was vested in the freemen, or 'commonalty'. The latter term was employed in the election indentures of 1604 and 1606, but omitted from subsequent returns during this period, which refer only to the mayor and burgesses. However, this variation of form did not apparently signify any change within the electorate. Indentures were signed by the mayor alone, but the commonalty in 1620 included 12 burgesses.[5]

Despite its self-government and comparative prosperity, Helston was almost entirely at the mercy of external electoral patrons during the early seventeenth century, as the surviving parliamentary indentures reveal. Individual returns were made for each Member, and although the same date normally appeared on both indentures, at least one routinely included a blank space where a name was later inserted by whichever patron then held sway. As the Jacobean era dawned the dominant figures were the Killigrew family, influential local gentry with a strong presence at Court. Sir Henry Killigrew[†], bailiff of Helston from the 1570s to his death in 1603, had used his position and personal standing to secure the return of several of his relatives, and probably also to back government candidates proposed by his brother-in-law Lord Burghley (Sir William Cecil[†]).[6] This pattern continued during the first two decades of James I's reign, when the Killigrew interest, now controlled by Sir Henry's brother Sir William*, went virtually unchallenged. His stepson Sir John Leigh was returned in 1604, and his own son Sir Robert was successful ten years later. The other 1614 Member, Henry Bulstrode, obtained his seat on the recommendation of his brother-in-law James Whitelocke*, to whom Sir Robert had first offered the place. Robert Naunton, a client of Burghley's son the earl of Salisbury (Robert Cecil[†]), presumably also relied on the Killigrews when he was returned at a by-election in 1606. The trend was interrupted only by John Bogans, who in 1604 exploited his position as mayor to return himself, a practice condemned by the Commons a few months later.[7]

The early 1620s saw the revival of competition for Helston's seats. The first challenge to Killigrew control came from the duchy of Cornwall, which had a well-established relationship with the town through its ownership of the local manor and its monopoly over the tin trade. Direct involvement in the borough had probably slackened after 1607 when the tin preemption rights began to be farmed out to London-based merchant consortiums, but during the next decade the duchy repaired the town's coinage hall.[8] In 1620, the first elections after Prince Charles's creation as duke, his Council nominated Heneage Finch* for a seat at Helston. The borough felt able to reject him, but did elect the Cornish lawyer William Noye, another duchy nominee, who had failed to secure a place at Fowey. The other seat was secured via a blank indenture by Sir Thomas Stafford, presumably through the mediation of his friend Sir Robert Killigrew.[9]

The remoulding of borough patronage continued in 1624 with the emergence of the Godolphins of Godolphin, cousins of the Killigrews, and major local tin producers, who in previous Jacobean elections had apparently supported Killigrew nominees. The Godolphin estates had been subject to wardship since 1613, and Sir William Killigrew's role as a trustee had doubtless enhanced his local influence. However, following Killigrew's death in 1622, Sir Francis Godolphin*, recorder of Helston, began to assert himself, and no subsequent Killigrew candidates have been identified. In February 1624 Godolphin secured one seat for his nephew Francis Carew, and probably influenced the choice for the remaining place. The Prince's Council requested it for the Speaker-designate, (Sir) Thomas Crewe*, but surprisingly he was turned down in favour of Thomas Carey, who had just been rejected as the duchy's nominee at Grampound. Like Godolphin and Carew, Carey belonged to Prince Charles's Household, so his return on a blank indenture strongly suggests Godolphin intervention. In contrast, a speculative request for a burgess-ship from secretary of state Sir Edward Conway I*, who stood unsuccessfully that year at neighbouring St. Ives, was ignored by the borough.[10]

The duchy made no further nominations during the 1620s, and Godolphin controlled the next two elections. Carey and Carew were both returned again in 1625, and Carew served for a third time in 1626 alongside the young Francis Godolphin, whose wardship was about to expire. In the third Caroline Parliament Francis, now exercising his family's patronage, opted to represent St. Ives and provided one seat at Helston for his brother Sidney. The other place there went to William Noye, who was returned on a blank indenture, presumably with Godolphin backing. Noye's own local standing as the recently appointed steward of Penwith and Kerrier hundreds may also have contributed to his success.[11]

[1] H.S. Toy, *Hist. Helston*, 36, 130, 399-401, 412; G. Haslam, 'Duchy and Parl. Representation', *Jnl. Roy. Institution of Cornw.* n.s. viii. 226. [2] G.R. Lewis, *Stannaries*, 44; E315/354; E306/5/4. [3] G. Haslam, 'Jacobean Phoenix', in *Estates of the Eng. Crown* ed. R.W. Hoyle, 287-8; E190/1022/1; 190/1024/7; 190/1028/5; 190/1030/1. [4] F.E. Halliday, *Richard Carew of Antony*, 227; Add. 53726, f. 37. [5] Toy, 332; C66/1270; C219/35/1/146, 157; 219/37/49; *Vis. Cornw.* (Harl. Soc. ix), 282. [6] SC6/Eliz.I/392; E315/309, f. 147; *HP Commons, 1558-1603*, i. 129. [7] Vivian, *Vis. Cornw.* 268, 270; *Liber Famelicus of Sir J. Whitelocke* ed. J. Bruce (Cam. Soc. lxx), 41; *HMC Hatfield*, xix. 395; C219/35/1/157; *CJ*, i. 245-6. [8] E306/4/6; 306/12, box 1, no. 6; Haslam, 'Jacobean Phoenix', 287. [9] DCO, 'Letters and Patents 1620-1', f. 39v; PROB 11/164, f. 91; C219/37/49-50. [10] *Vis. Cornw.* (Harl. Soc.), 282; Vivian, 68, 184, 268; WARD 9/162, f. 178; DCO, 'Prince Charles in Spain', f. 33v; C219/38/60-1; *CSP Dom.* 1623-5, p. 145. Gruenfelder mistakenly assumes that Conway's letter represented backing for the duchy's nominee: J.K. Gruenfelder, *Influence in Early Stuart Elections*, 89. [11] Vivian, 184; C219/41B/146b; E315/311, f. 9v.

J.P.F./P.M.H.

LAUNCESTON

Right of election: in the commonalty

Number of voters: maximum of 182 in 1604

9 Mar. 1604	SIR THOMAS LAKE I
	AMBROSE ROUS
c. Mar. 1614	WILLIAM CROFT
	SIR CHARLES WILMOT
18 Dec. 1620	THOMAS BOND
	JOHN HARRIS II
22 Jan. 1624	(SIR) FRANCIS CRANE
	SIR MILES FLEETWOOD
22 Apr. 1625	BEVILL GRENVILLE
	RICHARD ESTCOTT
17 Jan. 1626	BEVILL GRENVILLE
	RICHARD ESTCOTT
24 Feb. 1628	BEVILL GRENVILLE
	RICHARD ESTCOTT

Founded by a half-brother of William the Conqueror, Launceston grew up around Dunheved castle, which the Normans built to control the principal northern crossing of the Tamar, Cornwall's eastern border. The town's name referred originally to a neighbouring settlement whose population was encouraged to move to the new citadel, and even in the early seventeenth century the parliamentary borough's official designation remained Dunheved *alias* Launceston.[1] As the focal point of a royal honour, and a strategic base of the earls and subsequently the dukes of Cornwall, Launceston received considerable privileges during the medieval period. A succession of charters provided regular markets and fairs. As the leading town of the tin-producing zone, or stannary, of Foweymore, Launceston was entitled to nominate a quarter of the representatives at Cornwall's stannary parliaments. The county gaol and assize hall were located within the castle, and for many years the quarter sessions were also held there.[2] By the early sixteenth century, decline had set in. The medieval walls were crumbling, significant tin production ceased in the region, and the quarter-sessions were removed to Truro and Bodmin. Nevertheless, Launceston remained the principal market for the wool trade in eastern Cornwall, and by the 1590s Richard Carew† detected 'a new increase of wealth ... in the inhabitants' late repaired and enlarged buildings'. With an adult male population of around 250 people, the town was still one of Cornwall's largest communities, and

during the early seventeenth century it continued to enjoy the dubious honour of receiving tax demands separately from the rest of the county.[3]

Launceston received its first borough charter in the early thirteenth century, and a governing body consisting of a mayor, aldermen and burgesses had emerged by 1319. This arrangement was confirmed when the borough was incorporated in 1555. The Marian charter established a common council comprising a mayor, eight aldermen and an unspecified number of freemen or burgesses, and also provided for a recorder and deputy recorder. In the early seventeenth century the borough enjoyed an annual income of over £200, and was noted by contemporaries for its civic pomp. Uniquely within Cornwall, the aldermen dressed in distinctive red robes, which until 1605 were provided free of charge. The burgesses were certainly capable of defending their privileges. When the neighbouring borough of Newport established a rival wool and yarn market in the early 1620s, Launceston's mayor sued for redress in the Exchequer.[4]

Launceston returned Members to Parliament from 1295. The 1555 charter provided for their election by the mayor and commonalty, the latter term apparently signifying the freemen and burgesses. In 1604 these numbered 182, though it is unclear how many of them participated in early seventeenth century elections, since it was the borough's custom to seal parliamentary indentures rather than append signatures.[5] Except in 1604, individual returns were made for each Member, the standard Cornish practice. However, in contrast to many of the county's boroughs, Launceston's indentures are notable for their uniformity from one election to the next, and for a general absence of tampering with names or dates.[6] This orderliness seems primarily to have reflected the borough's willingness to cooperate with the same external patrons for long periods of time.

During James I's reign, Launceston returned just two Members with local ties, Ambrose Rous (1604) and John Harris (1620). Both men were the heirs to major estates in eastern Cornwall or west Devon, and Rous's father Sir Anthony* later became the borough's recorder.[7] The remaining six Members all possessed Court connections. Thomas Bond (1620) and Sir Francis Crane (1624) were nominated by Prince Charles's council, which on these occasions reminded Launceston of its duty as one of the duchy of Cornwall's own boroughs.[8] Sir Thomas Lake (1604) was a close colleague of secretary of state Lord (Robert) Cecil†, while in 1614 Sir Charles Wilmot was a client of the royal favourite, the earl of

Somerset, as indirectly was William Croft through his father Sir Herbert*. Another decade on, Sir Miles Fleetwood was emerging as a prominent ally of Somerset's successor, the duke of Buckingham.[9] No evidence survives of formal government nominations for these latter four Members, and their places were probably secured through the intervention of the Killigrew family. In 1604 Sir William Killigrew I* possessed unrivalled influence over the borough through his office as constable of Launceston castle, and his leases of Launceston park and the major local manor of Launceston Land. He was also related to the Cecils, and probably found a seat at Penryn for another of their dependents, Sir Richard Warburton, in the same year. By 1614 the constableship and lease of Launceston Land had both been surrendered, but the Killigrews may have kept hold of the park until mid-1624. In the meantime Sir William's son, Sir Robert*, had become manorial steward of Launceston Land, through which role he certainly dominated Newport borough. Given that Sir Robert was himself a client successively of Somerset and Buckingham, it is highly likely that he conveyed their wishes to Launceston corporation in 1614 and 1624.[10]

The new reign saw a dramatic change of pattern, caused by several distinct factors. The first was the rise of the Estcott family, who achieved a dominant position within the corporation during the later 1620s. Richard Estcott, who had already secured a seat at Newport in the 1624 Parliament, became deputy recorder of Launceston early in 1625, and with the backing of his father, a senior alderman, took a seat in the next three elections.[11] His partner on each occasion was Bevill Grenville, whose father owned substantial property in and around the town. In 1621 and 1624 Grenville had served as a Cornish knight of the shire, but in 1625 he required an alternative seat, and Launceston was one of the closest boroughs to his principal residence at Stowe, in north-east Cornwall. The fact that the Grenvilles also had business contacts with the Estcotts probably assisted Bevill's cause.[12] The final, and most puzzling factor, is the collapse of the Killigrew interest. Sir Robert may have lost his position as steward of Launceston Land manor in early 1625, though if so he managed to maintain a hold of sorts over Newport. The advent of a new lessee of Launceston park in 1624 perhaps also helped to tip the scales. Whatever the cause, however, the corporation's subservience to both the Killigrews and the Court emphatically came to an end.[13]

[1] R. and O.B. Peter, *Launceston and Dunheved*, 68, 70; I.D. Spreadbury, *Castles in Cornw.* 17; C. Henderson *et al.*, *Cornish Church Guide*, 137, 198; C129/37/17. [2] *Early Tours in Devon and Cornw.*

ed. R. Pearse Chope, 9; Peter, 74, 105, 109 – 10, 119; F.E. Halliday, *Richard Carew of Antony*, 153; G.R. Lewis, *Stannaries*, 126. [3] Chope, 9; D. and S. Lysons, *Magna Britannia, iii: Cornw.* 189; Halliday, 160, 184; Lewis, 44; A. Duffin, *Faction and Faith*, 7; Cornw. RO, B/LAUS/293/1; *APC*, 1613-14, p. 493; 1621-3, p. 177. [4] Peter, 72, 88, 191-6; Cornw. RO, B/LAUS/112, 179/1; Halliday, 184; E134/20 Jas.I/East.10. [5] Peter, 81, 197-8; Cornw. RO, B/LAUS/293/1. [6] C219/35/1/173; 219/37/16-17; 219/38/32-3; 219/39/25-6; 219/40/259, 271; 219/41B/172-3. [7] WARD 7/58/188; Devon RO, 2527 M/TS 14; Cornw. RO, B/LAUS/296. [8] DCO, 'Letters and Patents 1620-1', f. 39v; 'Prince Charles in Spain', f. 33v. [9] *CSP Dom.* 1611-18, pp. 229, 233; *CSP Ire.* 1611-14, p. 411; V. Treadwell, *Buckingham and Ire.* 59; C. Russell, *PEP*, 168. [10] DCO, 'Duchy Servants', pp. 153, 325; A.F. Robbins, *Launceston P and P*, 106; E134/3 Jas.I/East.11; L.M. Hill, 'Sir Julius Caesar's Jnl.', *BIHR*, xlv. 322; E315/310, ff. 57, 67v; *Parl. Survey of Duchy of Cornw.* ed. N.J.G. Pounds (Devon and Cornw. Rec. Soc., n.s. xxv), i. 73. [11] C2/Chas.I/D51/30; Cornw. RO, B/LAUS/339, 179/1. [12] WARD 7/58/193; Roy. Inst. of Cornw., BRA.B/328/3. [13] E147/3/13; *Parl. Survey of Duchy of Cornw.* i. 73.

P.M.H.

LISKEARD

Right of election: in the corporation

Number of voters: 11 in 1628

10 Mar. 1604	SIR WILLIAM KILLIGREW I
	REGINALD NICHOLAS
c. Mar. 1614	RICHARD CONNOCK
	JOHN GLANVILLE
15 Dec. 1620	SIR EDWARD COKE
	NICHOLAS HELE
20 Jan. 1624	WILLIAM WREY
	NICHOLAS HELE
25 Apr. 1625	WILLIAM CORYTON
	NICHOLAS HELE
23 Jan. 1626	JOSEPH JANE
	SIR FRANCIS STEWART
4 Mar. 1628	JOHN HARRIS III
	SIR FRANCIS STEWART

There was a settlement at Liskeard by around AD 1000. The town received its first charter from Richard, earl of Cornwall in 1240, and like many of the earl's possessions it was absorbed into the duchy of Cornwall in 1337, along with Liskeard manor, castle and park. The borough was important enough to be enfranchised in 1295, and ten years later it was designated as one of Cornwall's five coinage towns, where tin could be assayed. Liskeard's location on a major thoroughfare encouraged its development as a centre for the cloth trade, and in the early sixteenth century Leland considered it to be the county's best market town apart from Bodmin. The privilege of coinage, which had lapsed several centuries earlier, was restored in 1568, though by this time the focus of tin production had shifted to western Cornwall.[1] In 1603 Liskeard processed just 146 pieces of the metal, compared with the 1,251 coined at Truro, and by 1622 the local coinage house was 'much decayed and ruinous'. Indeed Liskeard itself had experienced serious economic contraction. Writing in about 1600, Richard Carew[†] observed: 'coinages, fairs, and markets, (as vital spirits in a decayed body) keep the inner parts of the town alive, while the ruined skirts accuse the injury of time and the neglect of industry'.[2]

Liskeard was incorporated in 1587. The governing body consisted of nine senior or capital burgesses, one of whom served as mayor, and around 15 lesser burgesses. Provision was made for both a chief steward and a recorder, though the latter post was not filled until 1604.[3] The corporation owned a moderate amount of property, and was wealthy enough to retain the services of high-profile lawyers such as Sir John Hele[†], John Glanville* and Henry Rolle*.[4] At least one mayor during this period, John Hunkyn, himself practised in the London courts. However, the corporation was relatively small by Cornish standards, and was weakened at the start of the seventeenth century by factional conflicts. Moreover, most of the burgesses were nonentities; John Harris I* allegedly dismissed them in 1610 as 'base fellows, ... knaves, tinkers and cobblers'. In consequence Liskeard's governors were vulnerable to pressure from the local gentry. As the parliamentary franchise was vested in the corporation, this external interference was reflected in elections.[5]

From the late 1580s the borough's dominant patron was its chief steward, Sir Jonathan Trelawny*, who doubtless controlled the nominations in 1604. The senior Member returned in that year was his wife's uncle, Sir William Killigrew I. Reginald Nicholas' connection with Trelawny has not been absolutely established, but he seems to have been related through his mother-in-law to the Moncks of Devon, one of whom married Killigrew's nephew. Trelawny died in June 1604, leaving a minor as his heir, and his family's influence in Liskeard was abruptly terminated.[6] Subsequent chief stewards were chosen from within the corporation, and Trelawny's ostensible replacement as patron of the borough was the newly appointed recorder, Sir Francis Godolphin[†]. However, the elderly Godolphin lived around 40 miles away, and seems to have taken little interest in Liskeard's affairs. This created a power vacuum, which was exploited by John Harris I, owner of the nearby seat of Lanrest. For much of the next decade Harris sought to manipulate the corporation in his own interests, until he was finally outmanoeuvred in 1612 by John Hunkyn, with the assistance of the duchy of Cornwall's solicitor-general, Richard Connock*.[7] A native of Liskeard, whose family held a local manor and the advowson of Liskeard parish, Connock had just acquired Liskeard Park and so was well placed to act as the borough's unofficial patron. Moreover, Connock had an old score to settle with Harris, since in 1589 his fiancée had jilted him and married Harris instead. During 1612, at Hunkyn's request, Connock launched a duchy inquiry into abuse of Liskeard's charter, and with Harris' allies drawn away to London to defend themselves, Hunkyn secured both the mayoralty and a firm grip over the corporation. His brother-in-law, Edward Chapman, succeeded him as mayor, and presided over the 1614 parliamentary elections, when the burgess-ships went to Connock and the borough's fee'd counsel, John Glanville.[8]

Relations between Harris and the borough were still strained at the start of the next decade, and this probably affected the 1620 election. Connock was now dead, but as the duchy remained a potentially useful counterbalance to Harris' ambitions the corporation willingly accepted a nomination from Prince Charles's Council. At first the council nominated Sir Henry Vane*, but it subsequently replaced him with Sir Edward Coke, one of its high-priority candidates who had failed to secure a seat at Bossiney.[9] The other Commons' seat that year went to Nicholas Hele, whose brother Sir Warwick* had acquired Liskeard Park in 1619. By the time of the next election, in 1624, John Harris was dead, but even his departure from the scene may have had electoral repercussions.[10] The Prince's council again sought to place a nominee, (Sir) William Croft*, but this time the borough had lost its sense of obligation, and declined to accept any duchy candidate. Instead, it opted for William Wrey, the son of Liskeard's then recorder, while the second burgess-ship was again taken by Nicholas Hele.[11] Gentry influence also predominated in the following year, when Hele was returned once more, along with William Coryton, who owned the local manor of Lamellyn. The pattern of patronage shifted once again in 1626. Sir Warwick Hele died shortly before the elections, and although his heirs retained control of Liskeard Park, they exerted no subsequent influence over the borough.[12] One Commons' place was awarded to Joseph Jane, a Liskeard resident whose father was a former mayor of the town. The right of nomination to the second seat was secured by Coryton, this time acting as deputy to the lord warden of the Cornish stannaries, the 3rd earl of Pembroke, who was also the chief steward of Liskeard manor. The borough duly returned Pembroke's client, Sir Francis Stewart. Coryton was presumably also responsible for Stewart's election in 1628, when the remaining place was taken by John Harris III, the son of Liskeard's former *bête noir*. Harris, the under-steward of Liskeard manor and a feoffee of the borough's lands, enjoyed a much more cordial relationship with the corporation. He may also have received Coryton's backing, since Harris' opposition to militia reforms in the following year suggests some association with the Cornish faction which formed around Coryton in the late 1620s.[13]

[1] J. Allen, *Hist. Liskeard*, 13-14, 16-17, 21-2, 55; W.P. Courtney, *Parl. Rep. of Cornw.* 245; G.R. Lewis, *Stannaries*, 44, 106; A. Duffin, *Faction and Faith*, 1, 7; Cornw. RO, B/LIS/13. [2] E315/354; DCO, 'Bk. of Orders 1621-5', f. 75; F.E. Halliday, *Richard Carew of Antony*, 202. [3] C66/1298; Cornw. RO, BK/353; B/LIS/268. [4] Cornw. RO, B/LIS/268, 274, 280, 26/1. [5] STAC 8/164/10; 8/166/10; 8/181/6. [6] *HP Commons, 1558-1603*, i. 130, 589; C66/1298; Vivian, *Vis. Cornw.* 268, 476; *Vis. Glos.* (Harl. Soc. xxi), 117; S. Rudder, *New Hist. of Glos.* 705. [7] C2/Jas.I/L7/35; STAC 8/15/11; 8/164/10; 8/181/6; Cornw. RO, B/LIS/255. [8] STAC 5/C2/15; STAC 8/164/10; C2/Jas.I/ L7/42; E315/76, f. 20; Cornw. RO, CM220; PROB 11/111, f. 323. [9] Cornw. RO, B/LIS/279; DCO, 'Letters and Patents, 1620-1', f. 39v. [10] Vivian, *Vis. Devon*, 464; Vivian, *Vis. Cornw.* 209; *Parl. Survey of Duchy of Cornw.* ed. N.J.G. Pounds (Devon and Cornw. Rec. Soc., n.s. xxv), 78. [11] DCO, 'Prince Charles in Spain', f. 33v; Vivian, *Vis. Cornw.* 564; Cornw. RO, B/LIS/280. [12] C142/662/101; PROB 11/148, f. 2. [13] Vivian, *Vis. Cornw.* 209, 587; SP16/150/74; 16/523/77; SC2/160/47-8; Cornw. RO, B/LIS/282; Duffin, 121.

P.M.H.

EAST LOOE

Right of election: in the mayor and burgesses

Number of voters: nine in 1626

8 Mar. 1604	SIR ROBERT PHELIPS
9 Mar. 1604	SIR JOHN PARKER
1614	SIR REGINALD MOHUN, bt.
	GEORGE CHUDLEIGH
13 Dec. 1621	SIR JOHN WALTER
	SIR JEROME HORSEY
22 Jan. 1624	SIR JOHN WALTER
24 Jan. 1624	PAUL SPECCOTT
23 Apr. 1625	JAMES BAGG II
28 Apr. 1625	SIR JOHN TREVOR I
16 Jan. 1626	(SIR) JAMES BAGG II
24 Jan. 1626	JOHN CHUDLEIGH
4 Mar. 1628	WILLIAM MURRAY
5 Mar. 1628	PAUL SPECCOTT

The larger of the twin settlements at the mouth of the Looe, East Looe existed as a market town and port by the late thirteenth century, and was accounted sufficiently important in 1341 to send a representative, jointly with Fowey, to an assembly at Westminster.[1] In the early seventeenth century the local merchants traded with France, the Low Countries and the Iberian peninsula, but they could no longer compete with their rivals at Fowey in terms of the volume of traffic. Rather, the town's prosperity depended on its weekly markets, and on its fishing fleet, which roamed as far as Newfoundland.[2] Consequently, East Looe was badly affected when the Sallee pirates began raiding the Cornish coast in 1625. In August of that year, 80 of its mariners were captured in just ten days, and the consequent shortage of manpower greatly damaged the local fishing industry. Moreover, the town experienced a series of invasion scares around this time, since the river-mouth was regarded as suitable for a Spanish landing.[3]

In political terms also, East Looe was vulnerable to external pressure. Although the town had been incorporated in 1587, the Common Council consisted of just nine chief burgesses, including the mayor. The reluctance of several burgesses to hold the mayoralty led to a fresh charter in 1623, which addressed this problem and slightly increased the corporation's privileges, permitting the mayors to act as borough j.p.s. In about 1627, however, mayor William Mayowe offended the vice-warden of the Cornish stannaries, John Mohun*, by arresting one of the latter's associates, and was himself summarily imprisoned.[4] By the terms of the 1587 charter, the Common Council also exercised the borough's parliamentary franchise, which had first been established 16 years earlier. Not surprisingly, East Looe's Elizabethan MPs were all outsiders, and the early seventeenth century brought no change to this pattern. None of the Members during this period voiced the borough's economic or security fears in the Commons, and Mayowe's arrest was reported to the House only because a general inquiry was launched into Mohun's conduct as vice-warden.[5]

East Looe's principal electoral patron during these years was Mohun's father, Sir Reginald, who, like his own father before him, held the borough's recordership. At least one nomination in every election can be ascribed to his influence. In 1614 he took one seat himself and secured the other for his brother-in-law George Chudleigh. Sir Robert Phelips in 1604, Sir Jerome Horsey in 1621, and Paul Speccott in 1624 and 1628, were all Mohun's distant kinsmen.[6] In 1626 George Chudleigh turned down the opportunity to sit for East Looe again, handing the vacancy to his son John after first offering it to his Court patron, secretary of state (Sir) John Coke*. As a result of these delays, the seat was not finally filled until around 23 Feb., nearly a month after the official election date.[7] Sir John Trevor, who secured a burgess-ship in 1625, was the uncle and former guardian of Mohun's cousin Charles Trevanion*, and would have known Sir Reginald through the latter's role as a trustee of the Trevanion estates.[8] By 1628 John Mohun had demonstrated his capacity, as vice-warden, to interfere in the borough's affairs, and it was probably he who, through his father or on his own account, obtained a seat for his friend William Murray in that year.[9]

The one clear rival interest to the Mohuns which could operate in East Looe was the duchy of Cornwall, which owned the local manor. However, duchy influence was exerted only in 1621 and 1624, when Prince Charles's Council successfully nominated Sir John Walter.[10] The remaining nominations are somewhat harder to explain. In 1604 Sir John Parker apparently relied on his own local influence as captain of Pendennis Castle, though the fact that his name was entered on his election indenture over an erasure suggests that his candidacy was controversial.[11] James Bagg, who took a place in 1625 and 1626, is said to have been distantly related to the Mohuns through his uncle Thomas Stone, who had represented East Looe in 1572. By September 1626 Bagg was certainly on close terms with John Mohun, but it is not certain that this connection would have served him earlier than this. He might therefore have relied on his burgeoning relationship with the duke of Buckingham, or on his position as vice-admiral of south Cornwall. Whatever means he found to apply pressure, his election in 1625 smacks of malpractice. Although the borough charter allowed for only nine electors, Bagg collected 11 names on his indenture, and comparison with Trevor's return suggests that some of the signatures may have been forged.[12]

¹ T. Bond, *E. and W. Looe*, 1-2, 6. ² J.C.A. Whetter, 'Cornish Trade in the Seventeenth Cent.', *Jnl. Royal Inst. Cornw.* n.s. iv. 391, 395; F.E. Halliday, *Richard Carew of Antony*, 201. ³ T. Gray, 'Turks, Moors and the Cornish Fisherman', *Jnl. Royal Inst. Cornw.* n.s. x. 461, 470; *CSP Dom. 1625-6*, pp. 82-3, 242, 334; *Early Stuart Mariners and Shipping* ed. T. Gray (Devon and Cornw. Rec. Soc. n.s. xxxiii), 67. ⁴ Bond, 3; A.L. Browne, *Corporation Chronicles of E. and W. Looe*, 18-21; *CD 1628*, iv. 4. ⁵ Browne, 18; *HP Commons, 1558-1603*, i. 130-1. ⁶ Vivian, *Vis. Devon*, 190, 707; Vivian, *Vis. Cornw.* 325; *Vis. Dorset, Addenda* ed. F.T. Colby and J.P. Rylands, 2-3; *Vis. Som.* (Harl. Soc. xi), 85; *Russia at the Close of Sixteenth Cent.* ed. E.A. Bond (Hakluyt Soc. xx), p. cxxix. ⁷ *HMC Cowper*, i. 252-3, 257. ⁸ Vivian, *Vis. Cornw.* 324, 502; WARD 9/348; PROB 11/115, f. 113. ⁹ SP16/118/37. In 1628 Mohun appears to have offered the duke of Buckingham a burgess-ship at W. Looe, not E. Looe, as presumed by *Procs. 1628*, vi. 139. ¹⁰ Bond, 57; DCO, 'Letters and Patents 1620-

1', f. 39v; 'Prince Charles in Spain', f. 33v. ¹¹ *CSP Dom. 1603-10*, p. 10; C219/35/1/170. ¹² *HP Commons, 1558-1603*, iii. 450; Vivian, *Vis. Devon*, 34; SP14/147/83; SP16/36/37; C219/39/42, 63.

P.M.H.

WEST LOOE

Right of election: in the burgesses

Number of voters: 8 in 1620

6 Mar. 1604	SIR HENRY GOODYER
	SIR GEORGE HERVEY
21 Oct. 1605	SIR WILLIAM WAAD *vice*
	Hervey, deceased
c. Mar. 1614	JOHN HARRIS I
	SIR EDWARD LEWKNOR II
17 Dec. 1620	CHRISTOPHER HARRIS
27 Dec. 1620	HENEAGE FINCH
4 Feb. 1624	GEORGE MYNNE
9 Feb. 1624	JAMES BAGG II
19 Apr. 1625	EDWARD THOMAS
23 Apr. 1625	JOHN WOLSTENHOLME
13 Jan. 1626	JOHN RUDHALE
1626	JOHN WOLSTENHOLME
4 Mar. 1628¹	JOHN PACKER
	EDWARD THOMAS

West Looe was known originally as Porthbyhan ('little cove' in Cornish), and a corrupted version of this name, Portpighan, still appeared on the borough's election indentures in the early seventeenth century as part of its official title. A settlement existed on the west bank of the Looe by 1243, when it received its first charter. Along with the adjacent manor of Portlooe, the borough was absorbed into the duchy of Cornwall in 1540.[2] Like its larger neighbour, East Looe, the town depended economically on its weekly markets and its fishermen. Around 1600, Richard Carew† observed that West Looe 'hath of late years somewhat relieved his former poverty', but a local gentleman, Sir Bernard Grenville†, reported a heavy burden of poor relief there in 1614. The fishing fleet suffered badly from raids by Sallee pirates in the mid-1620s, and James Bagg II's* survey of Cornish ports in 1626 recorded a solitary 30-ton vessel belonging to the town.[3]

West Looe's poverty was the official reason given for the borough's incorporation in 1574. The charter established a common council of 12 capital burgesses, including the mayor, who were empowered to elect a steward. There was no provision for a recorder, and although the heralds' visitation of 1620 states that John Harris I* held this position it was presumably the office of steward that was intended. The charter also confirmed that the parliamentary representatives of the borough, which had been enfranchised in 1547, were to be elected by the burgesses as a whole. It is possible, however, that a narrower franchise operated in the early seventeenth century. In 1620, the one year for which adequate records survive, the election indentures were signed only by capital burgesses. Of the eight men concerned, the mayor and four others were unable to write their own names.[4]

Not surprisingly, West Looe's governors failed to display any political independence during the early seventeenth century, and the borough's electoral patronage was controlled primarily by the local gentry. Initially the dominant figure was Sir Jonathan Trelawny*, who in 1600 had both acquired the nearby seat of Trelawne and become West Looe's steward. A distant relative of Sir Robert Cecil†, who had assisted with the Trelawne purchase, Trelawny offered burgess-ships to his cousin in 1601, and appears to have repeated this favour in 1604.[5] One seat that year was presented to Sir Henry Goodyer, another of Cecil's kinsmen.[6] The other place went to Sir George Hervey, lieutenant of the Tower, whose nephew Sir George Carew I* was one of Cecil's leading clients.[7] Trelawny died in June 1604, leaving an infant son John. However, the child's wardship was acquired by his mother, presumably with the support of Cecil, the master of the Wards, and the Trelawny electoral interest seemingly continued to function during John's minority. When Hervey also died in 1605, his place was filled by his successor at the Tower, Sir William Waad, whom Cecil had initially nominated for Bere Alston.[8]

In 1614, shortly after John Trelawny came of age, West Looe returned his cousin by marriage, Sir Edward Lewknor II.[9] However, the other seat was claimed by John Harris, who was probably already the borough's steward. Harris maintained his grip on one burgess-ship in 1620, when the corporation elected his son Christopher.[10] This time the competition came not from the Trelawnys but from a third patron, the duchy of Cornwall. Initially Prince Charles's Council nominated Sir Thomas Trevor, but he then secured a place at Saltash, leaving a vacancy at West Looe which was finally filled nearly two weeks later by an alternative duchy candidate, Heneage Finch. The overall pattern

of duchy nominations suggests that the borough deliberately kept one seat available in the interim, and this co-operative behaviour may have owed something to Richard Billing, the long-standing steward of Portlooe manor, who was also one of the duchy's principal electoral agents in Cornwall.[11] In 1624 the Prince's Council nominated Sir John Hobart for a West Looe burgess-ship. When he transferred to Lostwithiel, the borough declined to take another duchy nominee, for reasons which remain unclear. Instead, one place went to George Mynne, a client of the 3rd earl of Pembroke who, as high steward of the duchy of Cornwall, could appeal directly to the corporation despite his exclusion from the prince's electoral machine.[12] James Bagg II, who secured the other seat, appears to have relied on personal ties to Sir Bernard Grenville, who owned the major local estate of Killigarth.[13]

In the later 1620s Bagg emerged as the duke of Buckingham's principal agent in the West Country, working closely with Grenville and John Mohun*. Another prominent figure in this group was Mohun's brother-in-law, John Trelawny, who had succeeded John Harris as steward of West Looe in 1623.[14] Both Grenville and Trelawny seem to have allowed Bagg and Mohun to make nominations at West Looe during the remainder of the decade. Mohun's associate Edward Thomas was returned there in 1625 and 1628, while John Wolstenholme, who sat for the borough in 1625 and 1626, probably relied on Bagg, who would have known the Member's father through the latter's work in naval administration.[15] This patronage framework also created opportunities for other members of Buckingham's circle. John Rudhale, elected in 1626, was brother-in-law to one of the duke's leading clients, Sir Robert Pye*, and Mohun formally witnessed the signing of his indenture.[16] In 1628 John Packer was the beneficiary. On 17 Mar. Bagg presented Buckingham with a burgess-ship at 'Looe' and a shortlist compiled by Mohun, consisting of 'Mr. Packer', Sir Robert Pye and a Captain Heydon. Packer's name was duly inserted in a blank indenture ostensibly drawn up on 4 March.[17]

[1] OR. [2] T. Bond, *E. and W. Looe*, 50, 57; R. Pearse, *Ports and Harbours of Cornw.* 17. [3] R. Carew, *Survey of Cornw.* ed. P. White, 152; *CSP Dom. Addenda, 1580-1625*, p. 541; 1625-6, p. 83; *Early Stuart Mariners and Shipping* ed. T. Gray (Devon and Cornw. Rec. Soc. n.s. xxxiii), 69. [4] A.L. Browne, *Corporation Chronicles of E. and W. Looe*, 97-8; *Vis. Cornw.* (Harl. Soc. ix), 284; *HP Commons, 1509-58*, i. 60; C219/37/53-4. [5] J. Keast, *E. and W. Looe*, 31; DCO, Trelawny ms no. 5 (ref. from James Derriman); Vivian, *Vis. Cornw.* 268, 476; *Misc. Gen. et Her.* (ser. 3), iv. 20; *HMC Hatfield*, ix. 371; xi. 405. [6] *Vis. Warws.* (Harl. Soc. xii), 13, 67; *Vis. Essex* (Harl. Soc. xiii), 39. [7] *Vis. Suff.* ed. Howard, ii. 139; *Winwood's Memorials* ed. E. Sawyer, ii. 59. [8] Vivian, 476; WARD 9/159, f. 161; *HMC Hatfield*,

xvii. 445. [9] Vivian, 268; *Suss. Arch. Colls.* iii. 102. [10] Vivian, *Vis. Devon*, 447-8. [11] DCO, 'Letters and Patents 1620-1', f. 39v; SC2/161/3. [12] DCO, 'Prince Charles in Spain', f. 33v; J.K. Gruenfelder, *Influence in Early Stuart Elections*, 129. [13] Roy. Institution of Cornw. BRA.B/328/3 (ref. supplied by James Derriman). [14] A. Duffin, *Faction and Faith*, 82; Vivian, *Vis. Cornw.* 325; *CD 1628*, iii. 377; DCO, Trelawny ms no. 8. [15] M.F. Keeler, *Long Parl.* 359; SP14/147/3; *CSP Dom.* 1625-6, p. 511. [16] *Vis. Herefs.* ed. Weaver, 92-3; C219/40/247. [17] SP16/96/36; C219/41(B)/157. *CD 1628*, vi. 139 perversely cites Bagg's letter as the explanation for William Murray's election at E. Looe.

P.M.H.

LOSTWITHIEL

Right of election: in the mayor and burgesses

Number of voters: at least 54 in 1625

1604	SIR THOMAS CHALONER
	SIR WILLIAM LOWER
1614	EDWARD LEECH
	SIR HENRY VANE
24 Dec. 1620	(SIR) GEORGE CHUDLEIGH, (bt.)
16 Jan. 1621	SIR HENRY VANE
13 Feb. 1621[1]	EDWARD SALTER *vice* Vane, chose to sit for Carlisle
13 Jan. 1624	JOHN CHICHESTER
	SIR JOHN HOBART II
26 Apr. 1625	NICHOLAS KENDALL
	SIR REGINALD MOHUN, bt.
27 Apr. 1625	(SIR) GEORGE CHUDLEIGH, (bt.)
	SIR HENRY VANE
	Four returns.
21 Jan. 1626	SIR ROBERT MANSELL
	REGINALD MOHUN, bt.
4 Mar. 1628	SIR JOHN CHUDLEIGH
	SIR ROBERT KERR
29 Mar. 1628	SIR THOMAS BAGEHOTT *vice* Kerr, chose to sit for Preston

Lostwithiel was probably founded around the late twelfth century by the Cardinham family, lords of the nearby castle of Restormel, who provided the settlement with its earliest charter. Located on a then navigable stretch of the Fowey river, and near to the tin-producing region, or stannary, of Blackmoor, the town enjoyed early prosperity as a prime distribution-point for the tin trade. The same natural advantages

persuaded Edmund, earl of Cornwall to make Lostwithiel his administrative centre in around 1290, thereby giving the town a pre-eminence within the county which was confirmed by its enfranchisement in the early fourteenth century. When the royal duchy of Cornwall was established in 1337, Lostwithiel immediately became its capital, with the great hall and exchequer constructed by Earl Edmund providing a ready-made base for the duke's officials.[2]

In the early seventeenth century the town still retained many elements of its former prestige. The old duchy 'palace' provided a venue for both the county court and the duchy's stannary court; Cornwall's knights of the shire were elected there, and the stannary convocations or parliaments, to which Lostwithiel sent six representatives, took place there. The town was also entrusted with the county's official weights and measures.[3] However, at the turn of the century Richard Carew observed that all these privileges could still 'hardly raise it to a tolerable condition of wealth and inhabitance'. A few years earlier Camden had found it 'a little town, and not at all populous', compared with nearby Liskeard and Bodmin. The bulk of Cornish tin was now being produced in the west of the county, and Lostwithiel's dominance of this market had emphatically passed to the rival centres of Truro and Helston. Moreover, generations of tin-mining on Blackmoor had caused serious silting of the Fowey river, and even barges could no longer reach the town.[4]

This economic weakness was mirrored by Lostwithiel's government. Although earl Edmund's father had granted the town the status of a free borough, subsequent royal charters did little but confirm existing trading privileges. The chief burgesses began to call themselves mayors during the sixteenth century, but use of this title was ratified only in September 1608, when James I's charter of incorporation finally set up a small common council consisting of a mayor and six capital burgesses. Several considerations prompted the request for this charter. Prior to incorporation, lands bequeathed to the borough had to be vested in trustees. Over time, this role had been virtually monopolized by the Kendall family, minor gentry living both in the neighbouring parish of Lanlivery and in Lostwithiel itself. The Kendalls had come to regard the town lands as an extension of their own property, and it appears that at least some of the income which should have been used for the benefit of the borough was being misappropriated. Indeed, by the early seventeenth century the same family had achieved a financial stranglehold over the town, since they were also receiving the profits from its fairs and markets. The trigger for change may well have been a feud in 1608 between the Kendalls and the then mayor, William Goble, in the course of which 'a very filthy and venomous toad' was dismembered on Goble's pew in the parish church. The mayor apparently applied for the charter without the Kendalls' knowledge, and under its provisions not only was the new corporation confirmed in possession of the disputed lands, but the day for holding the weekly market was changed. Taken by surprise by Goble's tactics, the Kendalls tried to intimidate the corporation and disrupt the new market. However, the borough's officers counter-attacked through the courts, and in 1611 secured a decisive victory in Chancery.[5] Nevertheless, the charter offered only limited independence to Lostwithiel's inhabitants, since it presented them with a new and more powerful gentry patron in the form of Sir Reginald Mohun*, who was named as the borough's recorder. Moreover, the duchy of Cornwall used the grant to confirm its entitlement to a large share of the corporation's profits. Indeed, the duchy made its presence felt at intervals throughout this period. Extensive repairs were carried out to its administrative buildings in 1606, while the prison attached to the Stannary Court was reconstructed in 1620-2. An inquiry into duchy tenancies was conducted there in 1616, and in the following year efforts were made to recover parts of the 'palace' site which had fallen into private hands. Not surprisingly, both Mohun and the duchy played significant roles in early Stuart parliamentary elections.[6]

The precise size and composition of Lostwithiel's electorate at this time is unclear. The 1608 charter makes no mention of the franchise, and the surviving parliamentary indentures normally refer simply to the mayor and burgesses. Although the returns in 1621 and 1624 were apparently signed only by members of the common council, a large number of townsmen participated in the disputed contest of 1625. Signatories other than the capital burgesses also appear on subsequent indentures.[7]

The pattern of electoral patronage at Lostwithiel is more readily discernible. Ordinarily, one seat was taken by a local gentry family or its nominees. In 1604 Sir William Lower relied on his father's substantial property-holdings in the neighbouring parish of St. Winnow, and in the borough itself.[8] During the 1620s Sir Reginald Mohun's recordership allowed him to dispose of places freely among his relatives. His son Reginald and brothers-in-law George and Sir John Chudleigh benefited in 1626, 1621 and 1628 respectively. In 1624 a seat was provided for George Chudleigh's kinsman by marriage, John Chichester.[9]

Lostwithiel's other burgess-ship invariably went to a duchy of Cornwall nominee of some kind. In 1604 the choice fell on Sir Thomas Chaloner, who had recently become governor of the Household of Prince Henry, the newly created duke. In 1614 the lord warden of the stannaries, the 3rd earl of Pembroke, put in his secretary Edward Leech, and presumably also recommended the courtier Sir Henry Vane, who possessed no known ties with local patrons.[10] In both 1621 and 1624 the borough accepted nominees recommended by Prince Charles's Council, though on each occasion the corporation declined to accept the duchy's initial candidate. In 1621 secretary of state (Sir) Robert Naunton* was rejected in favour of Sir Henry Vane, originally the Council's choice for Liskeard. Ironically Vane then opted to sit for Carlisle, leaving his place to be filled by the duchy's unsuccessful nominee for Plymouth, Edward Salter. In 1624 the borough found fault with Miles Hobart, a younger son of the prince's chancellor Sir Henry Hobart*, and instead elected his elder brother Sir John, who had initially been proposed at West Looe.[11] In 1626 Pembroke reasserted himself, and his vice-warden William Coryton* secured the duchy's seat for Sir Robert Mansell. Two years later, the duke of Buckingham probably exerted influence over the duchy machinery to obtain a place for the courtier Sir Robert Kerr. Although documentary evidence for this is lacking, it is significant that at the time of election the vice-warden was John Mohun*, son of Sir Reginald and Buckingham's client. Like Vane before him, Kerr opted to sit elsewhere, and his burgess-ship therefore went to another officer of the king's Household, Sir Thomas Bagehott.[12] The only known contest during this period occurred in 1625. The men elected on 27 Apr., Sir Henry Vane and the now knighted Sir George Chudleigh, represented the usual combination of duchy and Mohun interests, and were most likely the borough's intended choices. However, on 26 Apr. returns had also been made for Nicholas Kendall of Lanlivery, son of one of the former trustees of the town lands, and for Sir Reginald Mohun himself. The probable explanation lies in the fact that Kendall was son-in-law to the then mayor and deputy recorder, Thomas Treffry. The four election indentures show that Vane and Chudleigh received the support of most of the common council except Treffry, who was the only member of the corporation to vote for Kendall and Mohun. This suggests that the mayor had promoted his kinsman, and, failing to win general backing for him, attempted to pre-empt the scheduled election. This conclusion is supported by the fact that Treffry was the sole signatory on Mohun's indenture, as if he were trying to draw the recorder into his scheme by providing him with a seat. A lack of prior consultation on Treffry's part might explain how Mohun and his habitual nominee Chudleigh came to be in competition with each other. An abnormally large number of voters put their names to Vane and Chudleigh's returns, doubtless an indication of the outrage felt in the town at Treffry's behaviour. Vane was able to extricate himself from this dispute by again opting to sit for Carlisle, but Parliament was dissolved before the Commons was able to rule on the three remaining candidates.[13]

[1] C219/37/35. [2] J. Polsue, *Complete Parochial Hist. of Cornw.* iii. 175-6; A. Saunders, *Devon and Cornw.* 40; G.R. Lewis, *Stannaries*, 45, 149; *HP Commons, 1386-1421*, i. 311-12. [3] F.E. Halliday, *Richard Carew of Antony*, 212-13; D. and S. Lysons, *Magna Britannia, iii. Cornw.* 203-4; Saunders, 40; Lewis, 126. [4] Halliday, 212; Polsue, 169; Lewis, 44; E315/354; E306/5/4. [5] Polsue, iii. 169; *HMC Var.* i. 327-7; *HP Commons, 1509-58*, i. 54; C66/1761/1; C2/Jas.I/L18/66; STAC 8/149/21. [6] C66/1761/1; E306/12, box 2, bdle. 24, item 28; DCO, 'Bk. of Orders 1619 – 21', f. 35r-v; 'Bk. of Orders 1621-5', ff. 37v, 75; 'Letters and Warrants 1615-19', ff. 39v-40, 71. [7] C219/37/2,35-6; 219/38/36-7; 219/39/54,56,59-60; 219/40/269,283; 219/41B/118, 148, 169; Cornw. RO, B/LOS 120. [8] WARD 7/58/198. [9] Vivian, *Vis. Cornw.* 325; Vivian, *Vis. Devon*, 177, 190, 719. [10] *HMC Downshire* iv. 193. [11] DCO, 'Letters and Patents 1620-1', f. 39v; 'Prince Charles in Spain', f. 33v; J.K. Gruenfelder, *Influence in Early Stuart Elections*, 89. [12] SP16/523/77. [13] C219/39/54, 56, 59-60; Cornw. RO, B/LOS 120.

P.M.H.

MITCHELL

Right of election: in the portreeve and commonalty or burgesses

Number of voters: 24 in 1626

5 Mar. 1604	WILLIAM CARY
	WILLIAM HAKEWILL
c. Mar. 1614	CHRISTOPHER HODSON
	WALTER HICKMAN
7 Dec. 1620	RICHARD CAREW
	JOHN ST. AUBYN[1]
15 Jan. 1624	JOHN HOLLES
	JOHN SAWLE
3 Mar. 1624	DENZIL HOLLES *vice* Holles, chose to sit for East Retford
20 Apr. 1625	SIR JOHN SMYTHE II
25 Apr. 1625	HENRY SANDYS
16 Jan. 1626	FRANCIS CROSSING
	SIR JOHN SMYTHE II
28 Feb. 1628	JOHN SPARKE
	FRANCIS BULLER
	JOHN COSWORTH

Double return of Buller and Cosworth. COSWORTH declared elected, 21 May 1628.[2]

The town of Mitchell dates from at least the early thirteenth century, when a weekly market was first held. Its location on the main road from Launceston to St. Ives failed to guarantee prosperity, and the town had declined to little more than a village by the time it was enfranchised in 1547, probably at the request of the lord of the manor, Sir John Arundell† of Lanherne.[3] In the early seventeenth century, when it was generally called Michell or Meddishole, the borough remained an economic backwater. There was no corporation, and government lay in the hands of the Portreeve, whose appointment was controlled by the lord of the manor. In accordance with standard Cornish practice, each MP during this period was returned on an individual indenture. The Mitchell franchise varied in scope. Election indentures generally refer to the Portreeve and commonalty, but the term 'burgesses' was used in 1621, 1624 and 1628, apparently indicating a select panel of leading freeholders.[4] Both formulas were employed in 1624 and 1628, but in separate indentures. However, this inconsistency alone is insufficient to explain the fluctuating numbers of signatures and marks on the indentures, with 11 for Richard Carew in 1621, 18 for John Cosworth in 1628, and 24 for Francis Crossing in 1626. Other evidence in the indentures points to conflicting interests in the selection process. It was unusual for both indentures in any one election to be prepared by the same hand, while in 1604 at least, the Portreeve signed one document only. The blank indenture by which Francis Crossing was returned was probably drawn up outside the borough, as a space was left for the Portreeve's name to be filled in.

Electoral patronage at Mitchell was mainly controlled by two local gentry families. The Arundells of Trerice, whose seat lay roughly three miles away, had dominated Mitchell's elections during the last two decades of Elizabeth's reign, taking over from their Lanherne cousins who were disabled by recusancy. John Arundell* of Trerice, who himself sat for the borough in 1597, served as sheriff of Cornwall in 1607-8, and played a leading role in Cornish affairs throughout the early Stuart period.[5] The Cosworth family lived a similar distance from the town, and most of their land was situated in the Mitchell district, which afforded them significant local standing. Edward

Cosworth (*d.* c.1639), a Mitchell burgess in 1588 and a Cornish j.p. and subsidy commissioner,[6] was said by one of his relatives in 1605 to be able to provide the government with a Cornish burgess-ship, by which a seat at Mitchell was probably meant. Arundell and Cosworth were brothers-in-law, and probably co-operated in the selection of candidates, as in other matters. For example, in July 1628 Cosworth was accused of exempting Arundell from subsidy payments.[7] The role of the Cosworth family is readily discernible, as they were frequently the principal signatories of Mitchell's election indentures. Arundell involvement can generally be deduced from kinship ties.[8]

John Arundell was easily the dominant patron at Mitchell throughout this period. In 1604, he can be credited with nominating of his kinsman William Cary, and probably also William Hakewill, whom he seems also to have supplied with a seat at Tregony at the next two elections. Hakewill played a significant role in easing the passage of Arundell's estate bill through the Commons in 1610, the only occasion during this period when a Mitchell burgess was recorded as promoting a local concern. Neither Member received Cosworth backing.[9] In 1614 Arundell was probably pre-occupied with securing Cornwall's shire seats for his relatives Richard Carew and John St. Aubyn, but he most likely provided a place for Christopher Hodson, an associate of his second cousin Sir Oliver Cromwell*.[10] Mitchell's other seat in this Parliament was taken by Edward Cosworth's cousin Walter Hickman.[11] In 1620 Arundell was at the height of his influence in the county, and the selection of Carew and St. Aubyn at Mitchell was probably part of a deal whereby Arundell himself became a knight of the shire.[12]

The picture for the remaining four elections is more confused. In 1624 two families with marginal local standing, the Holleses and Rashleighs, came to the fore. The Holles family owned a minor estate around eight miles from Mitchell. John Holles' real objective was a place at his family borough of East Retford, and once this was achieved he made way at Mitchell for his younger brother Denzil.[13] John Sawle was the grandson of John Rashleigh[†] of Fowey, who also held property close to the borough. However, in this case the key factor was probably the kinship, business and political ties between the Rashleighs and Arundells.[14] From the mid 1620s John Arundell was part of a Cornish gentry network which formed around William Coryton*, and it appears that members of this group used their electoral patronage to do favours for each other. The circle included Sawle's uncle, Jonathan Rashleigh*,

and also Sir Richard Buller*, whose cousin Sir John Smythe was elected at Mitchell in 1625 and 1626. Although Buller was closely related to some minor local landowners, the Vyvyans of St. Columb Major, it is more likely that his connection with John Arundell was the crucial factor.[15] The other 1625 Member, Henry Sandys, was returned five days later than Smythe, and a place at Mitchell was possibly kept open for him at the request of the duke of Buckingham, who had unsuccessfully backed Sandys for a seat at Sandwich a few weeks earlier. However, it is not clear how this nomination was mediated.[16] Francis Crossing may also have owed his return in 1626 to Arundell. An Exeter merchant with no direct links to Mitchell, he was perhaps recommended by his cousin William Hakewill.[17]

In 1628 Mitchell witnessed a disputed election. The Arundell interest was split between Jonathan Rashleigh's brother-in-law, John Sparke, and Sir Richard Buller's son Francis, while Edward Cosworth promoted his son John.[18] Indentures for Sparke and Buller reached Westminster together, and these two were initially seated. However, the subsequent arrival of Cosworth's indenture brought Buller's place under the scrutiny of the committee for privileges, which reported in Cosworth's favour on 21 May. The parliamentary records give conflicting accounts of this report. In one version, Cosworth's election was preferred because his indenture was dated 28 Feb., whereas Buller's dating of 'the last of Feb.' indicated the following day, 1628 being a leap year. However, a fuller description of events states that Buller's name was put forward first, with Cosworth initially attracting less support. On this account, Buller left the election early, believing his place was secured, but Cosworth then won a larger number of votes before polling closed.[19]

[1] Harg. 311, f. 220. [2] *CD 1628*, iii. 511. [3] C.G. Henderson, *Essays in Cornish Hist.* ed. A.L. Rowse and M.I. Henderson, 54–5; *HP Commons, 1509-58*, i. 55. [4] C219/37/1/26; 219/40/263; Henderson, *Essays*, 55; (J. Polsue), *Complete Paroch. Hist. of Cornw.* i. 343. [5] *HP Commons, 1558-1603*, i. 132-3; *List of Sheriffs* comp. A. Hughes (PRO, L. and I. ix), 23. [6] C66/1682; E179/88/299; Cornw. RO, C/969/1; DD.CF/2383. [7] *CSP Dom.* 1603-10, p. 244; 1628-9, p. 333. [8] C219/37/26; 219/38/49; 219/39/43. [9] Vivian, *Vis. Devon*, 157, 159; *CJ*, i. 430b. [10] Add. ch. 39230; *Vis. Hunts.* ed. Ellis (Cam. Soc. xliii), 79-80; Vivian, *Vis. Devon*, 280. [11] *The Gen.* iv. 117; Vivian, *Vis. Cornw.* 104. [12] *APC*, 1619-21, p. 136. [13] *Holles Letters* ed. P.R. Seddon (Thoroton Rec. Soc. xxxvi), 512. [14] Vivian, *Vis. Cornw.* 418; Cornw. RO, DD.R/6; DD.R(S)/1/2, 648. [15] Vivian, *Vis. Cornw.* 57; *Arch. Cant.* xx. 78-9. [16] Add. 37819, f. 11v; J.K. Gruenfelder, *Influence in Early Stuart Elections*, 147. [17] E190/946/6; *HMC Exeter*, 124. [18] Vivian, *Vis. Cornw.* 57, 104, 391. [19] *CD 1628*, ii. 37; iii. 511, 514-6.

P.M.H.

NEWPORT

Right of election: in the freeholders or burgesses

Number of voters: at least 13 in 1628

9 Mar. 1604	SIR ROBERT KILLIGREW
1604	SIR EDWARD SEYMOUR
c. Mar. 1614	SIR THOMAS CHEKE
	THOMAS TREVOR
18 Dec. 1620	SIR EDWARD BARRETT
23 Dec. 1620	SIR ROBERT KILLIGREW
19 Jan. 1624	(SIR) JOHN ELIOT
	RICHARD ESTCOTT
21 Apr. 1625	(SIR) JOHN ELIOT
	PAUL SPECCOTT
12 Jan. 1626	THOMAS GEWEN
	SIR HENRY HUNGATE
18 Jan. 1626	THOMAS WILLIAMS

Double return. GEWEN and HUNGATE declared elected, 17 Mar. 1626.

5 Mar. 1628	JOHN HERNE
	SIR JOHN WOLSTENHOLME
	NICHOLAS TREFUSIS
	PIERS EDGCUMBE
	SIR WILLIAM KILLIGREW II

Double return. TREFUSIS and EDGCUMBE declared elected, 14 Apr. 1628.

Newport sprang up in the shadow of Launceston Priory, and seems to have taken its name from one of the monastery's gateways. In existence by 1274, little more is known about it until 1529, when it was enfranchised. In terms of geography and administration, Newport was the least impressive of the seventeenth-century Cornish parliamentary boroughs. Effectively just a suburb of Launceston, separated from its larger neighbour by only a minor tributary of the Tamar, the village lacked the most basic structures of self-government. Newport allegedly obtained the right to hold a fair and market through a royal charter of 1557, but if this document ever actually existed it provided no other significant privileges. Responsibility for the market lay with a group of 'eight men' drawn from the local parish of St. Stephen by Launceston, and all other issues were settled in the court leet of Launceston Land manor.[1]

One consequence of this primitive institutional framework was an electoral procedure which was apparently unique in early modern England and Wales. With no mayor or portreeve to serve as a returning officer, this function was performed by two 'vianders', who were appointed at the court leet, possibly on the nomination of the manorial steward. Newport's franchise at this time was the subject of dispute. The basic qualification was the ownership of local burgage tenures, possibly combined with payment of scot and lot, and early seventeenth-century parliamentary indentures often refer to 'freeholders' or 'free burgesses'.[2] However, the proper size of the electorate was unclear, and in every election from 1624 to 1628 the vianders sought to return Members solely on their own authority.[3] Such opportunities for the exercise of electoral patronage encouraged non-residents like Thomas Gewen* and Richard Estcott to take on the viander's role, and in 1625 three men laid claim to the two posts. Such confusion undoubtedly contributed to the election disputes which characterized the borough in the later 1620s.[4]

Before 1624 the borough's parliamentary seats were controlled by the Killigrews. At the start of the seventeenth century Launceston Land manor was being leased from the Crown by Sir William Killigrew I*, who in 1601 found his step-son Sir John Leigh* a seat at Newport. In 1604 the borough returned Killigrew's son, Sir Robert, and a nephew by marriage, Sir Edward Seymour.[5] Four years later Killigrew surrendered his lease so that the manor could be used to augment the duchy of Cornwall's estates, but in 1609 Sir Robert became the manorial steward, thereby perpetuating the existing patronage framework. In 1614 one of Newport's burgess-ships went to his distant cousin, Sir Thomas Cheke, while the other Member, Thomas Trevor, probably obtained his seat through the mediation of his brother Sir John Trevor I*, who was one of Sir William Killigrew's colleagues in the king's privy chamber.[6] In 1621 the borough accepted a duchy of Cornwall nominee, Sir Edward Barrett, with Sir Robert Killigrew himself taking the second place five days later.[7]

The 1624 elections brought an abrupt end to this pattern. Barrett was again nominated by the duchy, but on 19 Jan., three days before Launceston meekly handed both its seats to courtiers, the Crown's plans for Newport were swept aside by local interests. One of the vianders, Richard Estcott, exploited his position to secure the return of his own son and namesake. The other place went to Sir John Eliot, whose father-in-law Richard Gedy was doubly equipped to exert influence over the borough, being both a local landowner and the serving sheriff of Cornwall.[8] If Sir Robert Killigrew was taken by surprise on this occasion, as seems likely, he fared no better in 1625. Eliot was again returned, along with Paul Speccott, whose father (Sir) John* had recently acquired the major local seat of Penheale. The election was not straightforward, however, due to a dispute over who the vianders should be. Three indentures were finally sent to London, two for Eliot and one for Speccott. Both of Eliot's named the first viander as William Courtier, but he was associated on one with John White and on the other with Degory Seccombe. In both cases the vianders were the only signatories. Speccott's indenture recorded the vianders as Courtier and White, and included three additional signatures. Since both Seccombe and White wished to elect Eliot, it appears that the underlying issue was one of personal status within the borough, rather than a clash of external patrons. With no actual disagreement about the identity of the Members, Parliament ignored this curious turn of events.[9]

In 1626, however, the Commons was faced with a full-blown election dispute, involving three strands of local patronage. The source of Sir Robert Killigrew's influence at this juncture is unclear, since his stewardship of Launceston Land may well have been terminated in early 1625, when a lease of the manor to the Trefusis family came into effect. Nevertheless he stole a march on his rivals, for on 12 Jan. he secured one place for his nephew, Sir Henry Hungate. At the same time the second seat was awarded to Thomas Gewen, who lived around four miles from Newport. Six days later, Sir John Speccott's supporters swung into action, and a third indenture was drawn up in favour of his son-in-law, Thomas Williams. The Speccott camp then launched a two-pronged attack on the validity of the earlier returns. While Gewen's indenture registered the approval of both the vianders and Newport's freeholders, Hungate had been returned in the name of the vianders only. By contrast, and probably by design, Williams claimed the backing of the 'free burgesses and inhabitants of Newport'. Some residents of the borough duly dispatched a petition against Hungate to Parliament, questioning 'whether election by the generality of the inhabitants or the principal burghers [was] most due'. In the meantime Williams personally pursued Gewen, who, as one of that year's vianders, had returned himself. It is unclear whether this action was directly akin to the recognized abuse of sheriffs and mayors providing themselves with a burgess-ship, but Gewen had clearly experienced some doubts, since he omitted to sign his own

indenture. The anti-Hungate petition came before the committee for privileges on 10 Feb., but was apparently rejected, probably because Sir Henry's indenture followed a locally well-established formula. On 16 Mar. the committee also heard the complaint against Gewen, but reported only that Williams had 'deserted the cause' and that Gewen should therefore be allowed to sit. Whether Williams backed down that same day or sometime earlier is unclear. The fact that neither viander had supported his election may have told against him, while Gewen's behaviour was clearly deemed acceptable in the absence of convincing opposition. Questionable as this verdict appears, the Commons agreed on 17 Mar. to admit both Hungate and Gewen.[10]

During the next two years control over Launceston Land shifted yet again. The Crown sold part of the manor to Paul Speccott in September 1626, and both Killigrew and the Speccotts subsequently acquired further parcels.[11] The 1628 elections brought together many of the strands of patronage and controversy which had surfaced in the previous four years, and resulted in a yet more complex dispute. Five candidates were nominated on 5 Mar., and indentures were drawn up for each of them that day. Local interests were represented by Sir John Speccott's nephew Piers Edgcumbe, Sir Robert Killigrew's son Sir William, and also by Nicholas Trefusis, who certainly owned property close to Newport, and possibly held the lordship of Launceston Land manor itself.[12] There were also two complete outsiders, John Herne and Sir John Wolstenholme. Herne was a colleague at Lincoln's Inn of Richard Estcott, the 1624 Member. Wolstenholme's connection is uncertain, but he may have approached the Estcott family through their cousin (Sir) James Bagg II*, who had recently worked closely with him in preparing naval campaigns. On this occasion one of the vianders was Thomas Estcott, the former MP's brother.[13] His fellow officer was a veteran of 1625, William Courtier. The failure of these two men, the former a Launceston man and the latter a Newport resident, to work together brought about the dispute. Estcott must have received the nominations for Herne and Wolstenholme well in advance, and he presumably hoped to use his position to secure seats for them, thereby emulating his father's behaviour in 1624. He perhaps failed to anticipate the appearance on 5 Mar. of Sir John Eliot, to whom he and Courtier felt obliged to offer one seat. In the event Eliot, who was standing as a knight of the shire, declined this invitation, but he may have indicated at this juncture that he intended to nominate his friend Trefusis. The introduction of a third candidate at this juncture would help to explain why Courtier refused to co-operate when Estcott recommended the election of Herne and Wolstenholme. Undeterred, Estcott inserted his candidates' names on two indentures which had evidently been prepared in advance, and returned them to Westminster on his sole authority. Courtier, unable to frustrate this scheme, instead proceeded to a full-blown election with the freeholders. Eliot now formally proposed Trefusis, who secured a clear majority of votes, and a fresh indenture was drawn up for him, purportedly on behalf of the free burgesses and both vianders though Estcott could not be persuaded to sign it. The second seat was now contested by Edgcumbe and Killigrew, who initially secured four votes each. However, Edgcumbe's kinsman, Ambrose Manaton*, then announced himself as a Newport freeholder and provided Edgcumbe with an extra voice. His credentials were challenged as he was a non-resident but they were ultimately accepted, and so, before the formal election concluded at lunchtime, a further indenture was prepared along the same lines as Trefusis' return. Significantly, Courtier withheld his support from Edgcumbe, whose indenture was not signed by either viander. Later the same day, and apparently after the election was officially over, Killigrew managed to muster two more votes. On the basis of this dubious claim to numerical superiority, Courtier drew up and signed a fifth indenture, in his own name and that of 'the greatest number of the freeholders being inhabitants of the said borough'.[14]

Prior to the opening of Parliament, the indentures for Trefusis and Killigrew were sent up by the sheriff, Jonathan Rashleigh*, who included a certificate affirming the valid return of the former but expressing doubts about the latter. The remaining three indentures arrived by other means. The clerk of the Crown, Sir Thomas Edmondes*, unsure how to handle the situation, declined to record any of the candidates as being duly elected. On 22 Mar. the dispute was referred to the committee for privileges, and later that day Eliot alerted the Commons to the clerk's actions, complaining that Trefusis was being improperly prevented from taking his seat. On 28 Mar. the sheriff's deputy, John Sparke*, confirmed that he had brought up returns only for Trefusis and Killigrew, and the House resolved that they should both be allowed to sit pending the committee's final verdict. Killigrew, however, had also secured an unchallenged burgess-ship at Penryn, and on the same day announced his intention of serving for that borough rather than Newport. Further confirmation of the sheriff's dealings by the deputy clerk of the Crown on 29 Mar. was therefore barely relevant.

The committee's report was finally presented on 14 April. There had clearly been some discussion about the validity of Newport's electoral arrangements, and though the committee arrived at no formal conclusions on this point, it implicitly rejected the vianders' claims to pre-eminence and independent authority. Herne and Wolstenholme were dismissed out of hand, and the report dealt only with the remaining three candidates. The legality of Trefusis' return was re-affirmed, while Edgcumbe became the only man during this period to secure a Newport seat without the backing of a single viander. How far Killigrew's preference for Penryn swayed the committee's decision is impossible to judge. In the meantime, in a splendid gesture of bureaucratic pedantry, the clerk of the Crown issued a writ for an election to fill the 'vacancy' created by Killigrew's withdrawal. The final act of the drama was therefore not the formal declaration that Trefusis and Edgcumbe were duly elected, but rather a procedural motion to stay the unnecessary writ.[15]

[1] W.P. Courtney, *Parl. Rep. of Cornw.* 359; R. and O.B. Peter, *Launceston and Dunheved*, 53-6; *HP Commons, 1509-58*, i. 56; *Cartulary of Launceston Priory* ed. P.L. Hull (Devon and Cornw. Rec. Soc., n.s. xxx), p. xxiv; E134/20 Jas.I/East. 10. [2] *Hist. Cornw.* ed. S. Drew, i. 647; *CD 1628*, ii. 446; J. Polsue, *Complete Parochial Hist. of Cornw.* iv. 169; C219/35/1/161; 219/37/19; 219/40/245. [3] *CD 1628*, ii. 446; C219/38/57; 219/39/53; 219/40/280. [4] E367/240; *Vis. Cornw.* (Harl. Soc. ix), 281; C219/37/18; 219/39/51-2; 219/40/280. [5] E134/3 Jas.I/East. 11; *HP Commons, 1558-1603*, i. 133; Vivian, *Vis. Cornw.* 268, 270. [6] L.M. Hill, 'Sir Julius Caesar's Jnl.', *BIHR*, xlv. 322; E306/12, box 2, bdle. 21, no. 17; E315/310, f. 57; Vivian, *Vis. Cornw.* 268; *Misc. Gen. et Her.* (ser. 3), iv. 20; *Vis. Essex* (Harl. Soc. xiii), 177. [7] DCO, 'Letters and Patents 1620-1', f. 39v. [8] DCO, 'Prince Charles in Spain', f. 33v; C219/38/57-8; Vivian, *Vis. Cornw.* 147, 159; A.F. Robbins, *Launceston P and P*, 127. [9] Vivian, *Vis. Devon*, 707; C54/2428/38; C219/39/51-3. [10] E147/3/13; C219/40/245, 262, 280; *Procs. 1626*, ii. 16, 300, 305. [11] E147/3/13; C66/2424/2; Robbins, 141. [12] Vivian, *Vis. Devon*, 707; Vivian, *Vis. Cornw.* 142, 270; C142/333/13. [13] Vivian, *Vis. Cornw.* 159, 446; Vivian, *Vis. Devon*, 34; *HMC Cowper*, i. 320. [14] C219/41B/116, 142-3, 175, 178; *CD 1628*, ii. 54, 446; Vivian, *Vis. Cornw.* 142, 467; E179/88/301. [15] *CD 1628*, ii. 53-4, 168-70, 188, 444, 446, 453.

P.M.H.

PENRYN

Right of election: in the portreeve and burgesses

Number of voters: 8 in 1610

Mar. 1604	SIR RICHARD WARBURTON
	THOMAS PROVIS
1 Feb. 1610	SIR WILLIAM MAYNARD *vice*
	Warburton, deceased
20 Feb. 1610	SIR EDWARD CONWAY I *vice*
	Provis, deceased
c.Mar. 1614	SIR WILLIAM KILLIGREW I
	FRANCIS CRANE
22 Dec. 1620	(SIR) FRANCIS CRANE
c.Dec. 1620	ROBERT JERMYN[1]
26 Jan. 1624	SIR ROBERT KILLIGREW
	EDWARD ROBERTS
1 May 1625	EDWARD ROBERTS
4 May 1625	SIR EDWIN SANDYS
18 Jan. 1626	EDWARD ROBERTS
20 Jan. 1626	SIR EDWIN SANDYS
3 Mar. 1628	SIR WILLIAM KILLIGREW II
	SIR THOMAS EDMONDES

A settlement existed in the Penryn area before the Conquest, but the town itself allegedly owed its origins to the bishops of Exeter, lords of the local manor, who obtained a borough charter in 1236.[2] Located at the head of a sheltered creek off the great natural harbour of Falmouth Haven, Penryn in the early seventeenth century traded with markets around the globe. Although most of its merchants exported pilchards to France and Spain in return for salt and wine, the port also handled timber and other shipping supplies from as far off as Norway, preserved fruit from Madeira, hides from Brazil, and in 1620 one unspecified cargo from the East Indies. In wartime these goods were supplemented by privateering spoils, some won by Penryn shipowners.[3] However, at the end of the sixteenth century Richard Carew described the place as 'rather passable than notable for wealth, buildings and inhabitants', and argued that it lacked the trade distribution network of its rival Truro, the other port within Falmouth haven. From about 1613 fresh competition emerged in the shape of a new hamlet at Smithick (modern-day Falmouth), just along the bay from Pendennis, which was founded to provide a more convenient source of

shelter and supplies for visiting sailors. Vociferous protests from Penryn's residents failed to persuade the Privy Council to halt Smithick's development, which was advancing apace by the late 1620s.[4]

Just as Falmouth attracted commercial traffic, so the strategically important Haven ensured both the presence of English fleets (in 1625 and 1627) and the attention of hostile shipping, such as a failed Spanish armada in 1596. During the later 1620s there were repeated alarms of impending attack by Spanish or 'Turkish' fleets, while a few years earlier there were clashes inside the Haven between French royal vessels and rebel privateers from La Rochelle. During one incident in November 1625 a Rocheller was even pursued upstream to the Penryn quay.[5] At such moments the inhabitants were largely reliant on the protection afforded by Pendennis Castle, a fortress situated three miles away whose purpose was to guard the Haven mouth and preserve order among visiting ships and mariners. It made sense for the town to cultivate Pendennis' commander, not least because the castle's strategic importance afforded him a voice in London. In 1605, when Thomas Provis sought to be excused from his parliamentary duties, he relied on the then captain, Sir John Parker*, to back his request.[6]

After the Reformation the bishops of Exeter largely ceased to play an active role in Penryn's affairs, though they may have secured the borough's enfranchisement in 1547, and must have agreed to its incorporation in 1621. Little is known about the town's government before this date, except that the principal officer, the portreeve, presided over the local court leet and acted as returning officer at parliamentary elections. The structure established in 1621 – a mayor, 11 other aldermen and 12 assistants – probably reflected earlier arrangements, since a group of leading residents leased Penryn borough manor from Bishop Cotton in 1606 in trust for the town.[7] Early seventeenth century parliamentary indentures refer to the portreeve and burgesses, a terminology which continued unchanged after 1621, when the mayor took over his predecessor's executive functions. A broad scot and lot franchise applied by the late seventeenth century and presumably earlier, but the largest number of voters recorded on an indenture during the early Stuart period was eight in 1610; during the 1620s returns were signed by the portreeve alone, or merely sealed.[8]

Throughout the later sixteenth century, political patronage over the borough lay with the most powerful local gentry family, the Killigrews, whose seat at Arwennack was almost adjacent to Pendennis Castle, which they had captained for over 50 years. As Elizabeth's reign progressed, however, the balance of power shifted within the family from the elder line, which remained in Cornwall but gradually succumbed to debt and criminal charges, to a junior branch headed by Sir William Killigrew I and his brother Sir Henry[†], who made their fortunes at Court, and amassed local political prestige by promoting Cornish issues with the government.[9] At the start of the seventeenth century Sir William, though an infrequent visitor to Penryn, owned a house at Trerose, about four miles south of the borough. By 1638, when they sold up, his heirs had accumulated property in four local parishes and held numerous leases in Penryn itself. While Sir John Killigrew, who inherited Arwennack in 1605, sank ever deeper into debt and antagonized the borough by promoting the development of Smithick, Sir William's son Sir Robert, another courtier, reinforced his father's authority by recovering in 1617 the captaincy of Pendennis which his cousins had forfeited almost 20 years earlier. He was subsequently active in restoring the castle's defences and armaments. Sir Robert's own local dominance was confirmed in 1621 when, despite being essentially a Middlesex resident, he was appointed Penryn's first recorder.[10]

Early Stuart elections saw the borough yield almost entirely to the Killigrews' wishes. The only display of independence came in 1604, when the burgesses elected one of their own number, Thomas Provis, in connection with a forthcoming bill on the West Country fishing trade.[11] Sir William Killigrew placed himself at Penryn in 1614, and provided a burgess-ship for his grandson Robert Jermyn in the following Parliament. In 1624, the first election after Sir William's death, Sir Robert took his turn, and in 1628 he reserved a seat for his own son, Sir William II, who was also contesting Newport. Otherwise, Penryn was placed at the disposal of the family's allies, among whom were their distant kinsmen, the Cecils. The elections of 1604 and 1610 saw the return of three of Robert Cecil's[†] clients, Sir Richard Warburton, Sir William Maynard and Sir Edward Conway I.[12] Sir Robert Killigrew was himself a client of successive royal favourites, Somerset and Buckingham. A connection with the earl of Somerset probably accounts for Francis Crane's election in 1614, if not his re-election seven years later.[13] In 1625 the duke of Buckingham doubtless suggested his client Sir Edwin Sandys, as he was unable to secure him the knighthood of the shire for Kent. Thomas Scott* reported that Sir Edwin 'had never seen Penryn, nor knew the name of it ... nor was a freeman there; nor chosen there, but by Sir Robert Killigrew at London, who for that purpose, or to put in some other if Sir Edwin had sped elsewhere, brought up a blank in his pocket'. Sandys's indenture confirms this statement.[14] Edward Roberts, another Middlesex resident, who was returned with Sir Robert in 1624 and with Sandys at

the next two elections, may also have benefited from his nephew Sir John Franklin's* connections with Buckingham, though presumably direct ties with Killigrew himself were also important. The choice of Sir Thomas Edmondes in 1628 is harder to explain. As treasurer of the Household, Edmondes possessed a wide range of Court connections, and it is therefore difficult to identify who might have recommended him to Killigrew after his failure to win election in Essex.[15]

[1] Harg. 311, f. 219v. [2] J. Polsue, *Complete Paroch. Hist. of Cornw.* ii. 78; R.J. Roddis, *Penryn*, 13-15. [3] E190/1022/12; 190/1026/4; 190/1028/16; 190/1029/14; 190/1030/23; 190/1031/19; *CSP Dom.* 1628-9, pp. 290, 301. [4] F.E. Halliday, *Richard Carew of Antony*, 226; *APC*, 1613-14, pp. 33, 261; 1619-21, p. 130-1; 1629-30, p. 41. [5] *CSP Dom.* 1625-6, pp. 116, 120, 297, 334, 370, 395; 1627-8, p. 359; SP16/12/47iii; Roddis, 55. [6] I.D. Spreadbury, *Castles in Cornw.* 46; *HMC Hatfield*, xvii. 461. [7] *HP Commons, 1509-58*, i. 57; Roddis, 24-5, 32-3, 98; C66/2227/2. [8] C219/35/1/147; 219/39/41, 44; Roddis, 33; Polsue, ii. 91. [9] *HP Commons, 1558-1603*, i. 134; Polsue, i. 150; A.C. Miller, *Sir Henry Killigrew*, 221, 233-6. [10] Polsue, iii. 300; C54/3175/2; Vivian, *Vis. Cornw.* 269; *APC*, 1597-8, p. 281; 1618-19, p. 165; 1619-21, pp. 130-1; 1627, pp. 64-5; 1627-8, pp. 3, 155; *CSP Dom.* 1611-18, p. 516; C66/2227/2. [11] *HMC Hatfield*, xvii. 461. [12] Vivian, *Vis. Cornw.* 268, 270; *Vis. Suff.* ed. Metcalfe, 200; *Vis. Essex* (Harl. Soc. xiii), 39-40; *HMC Hatfield*, xvi. 207; xx. 28; *Winwood's Memorials* ed. E. Sawyer, iii. 130. [13] *Chamberlain Letters* ed. N.E. McClure, i. 358; *Letters and Life of Francis Bacon* ed. J. Spedding, vii. 69; *HMC Downshire*, iv. 266. [14] J.K. Gruenfelder, *Influence in Early Stuart Elections*, 144; Canterbury Cathedral Archives, U66, f. 19; C219/39/44. [15] *The Gen.* v. 302-3; *Mdx. Peds.* (Harl. Soc. lxv), 3; *CP*, iii. 400.

P.M.H.

ST. GERMANS

Right of election: in the inhabitants

Number of voters: at least 35 in 1625

c.6 Mar. 1604	JOHN TROTT
1604	SIR GEORGE CAREW II[1]
c.Mar. 1614	JOHN TROTT
	JOHN ELIOT
25 Dec. 1620	RICHARD TISDALL
	SIR RICHARD BULLER
15 Jan. 1624	SIR JOHN STRADLING, bt.
n.d.	JOHN COKE
22 Apr. 1625	(SIR) JOHN COKE
	SIR HENRY MARTEN
16 Jan. 1626	(SIR) JOHN ELIOT
	SIR HENRY MARTEN
3 Mar. 1628	THOMAS COTTON
	BENJAMIN VALENTINE[2]

Set on the west bank of the Tiddy, a few miles upstream from Plymouth Sound, St. Germans existed by 936, when its church became the cathedral of the Anglo-Saxon diocese of Cornwall. Although the bishops relocated to Devon in 1042, St. Germans Priory remained an important religious site during the Middle Ages, affording the town much of its prestige and prosperity. The decline which set in after the monastery's dissolution in 1539 was noted at the end of the century by Richard Carew[†]: 'the church town mustereth many inhabitants and sundry ruins, but little wealth'. Although privileged with an annual fair, St. Germans lacked any corporate structures, and formal business was conducted by a portreeve appointed each year at the manorial court-leet. At least three of these officers during the 1620s were unable to sign their own name.[3]

How the borough first came to return burgesses to Parliament in 1562 is unclear, and electoral arrangements in the early seventeenth century were relatively ill-defined. The franchise was apparently vested in all householders who had been resident for at least a year, and the portreeve acted as returning officer. The surviving election indentures mostly refer to the 'inhabitants', though the terms 'commonalty' and 'burgesses' were used in 1604 and 1620.[4] The number of voters is difficult to judge. The indentures for 1624 and 1625 include a kind of certificate listing the participants, but much of the text from the former year is now illegible, while in the latter document the roll of 35 names was concluded with the phrase 'etc'. Almost 50 individuals have been identified in the indentures from 1624 to 1628, which accords well with the estimated number of households in the borough at around this time.[5]

Electoral patronage in the early seventeenth century lay exclusively with the local landowners. Half the great manor of St. Germans belonged to the bishops of Exeter, and until 1626 they maintained a firm grip on one seat. In 1604 and 1614 Bishop Cotton placed his son-in-law John Trott, while in 1620 he put forward Trott's close friend Richard Tisdall.[6] Bishop Carey, invited by his tenants in 1624 to make the customary nomination, handed a burgess-ship that year and in 1625 to his brother-in-law (Sir) John Coke.[7] The bishops' principal tenants at St. Germans were the Eliot family, who, although they owned the other half of the manor, were not always able to control the remaining parliamentary seat. At the start of this period they faced competition from another local landowner, George Kekewich of Catchfrench, who had accumulated enormous local prestige in the previous

decade or so through his 'continual large and inquisitive liberality to the poor ... beyond the apprehensive imitation of any other in the shire'. His family had also frequently held the post of portreeve during Elizabeth's reign.[8] In 1604 Kekewich obtained the second seat for his brother-in-law Sir George Carew II, who expected to have to stand down on being appointed ambassador to France in 1605. Indeed, Carew invited his patron, the earl of Salisbury (Robert Cecil[†]), to suggest a new candidate, undertaking to recommend this nominee to Kekewich. However, although Carew formally resigned his seat in September 1605, the Commons seem not to have discussed his case until November 1606, when they decided to let him retain his place pending his return home.[9]

George Kekewich died in 1611, leaving a minor as his heir, and this doubtless helped John Eliot to secure the junior burgess-ship in 1614, in the first election after he succeeded to his own patrimony.[10] However, the Kekewiches recovered their advantage in 1620, when their cousin Sir Richard Buller was returned, leaving Eliot without a seat.[11] This upset seems to have spurred Eliot into action, for in 1622 and 1623 he invested heavily in property in St. Germans borough, effectively ending the Kekewich challenge. Eliot himself sat for Newport in the next two parliaments, through his father-in-law's influence. However, he was most likely responsible for the election in 1624 of the outsider Sir John Stradling, a client of the 3rd earl of Pembroke, while in the following year he provided a seat for his friend Sir Henry Marten, perhaps as a favour to his patron, the duke of Buckingham.[12] It may have been the fierce competition for seats at Newport in 1626 which persuaded Eliot to stand once again in his home borough. However, having presumably already agreed to nominate Marten at St. Germans, he was left with no option but to challenge Bishop Carey's patronage. Sometime in early January the bishop wrote as usual to his tenants, again requesting a place for Sir John Coke, and asking to be supplied with a blank indenture for this purpose. Unexpectedly, the portreeve ruled out any possibility of a blank, and warned that although Coke was likely to be returned, he 'could not make promise, it being a business resting in the wills of others besides himself, and chiefly in Sir John Eliot'. By the time Carey informed Coke on 22 Jan., Eliot and Marten had already been elected. In the event it was a fitting prelude to this stormy Parliament that Eliot entered the Commons by displacing a secretary of state.[13] In the following year he boosted his local standing by having the parish of St. Germans exempted from billeting, and his new-found dominance was confirmed in 1628, when the borough returned his friends Thomas Cotton and Benjamin Valentine.[14]

[1] *HMC Hatfield*, xvii. 339. [2] *OR*. [3] C. Henderson *et al.*, *Cornish Church Guide*, 98-9; R. Carew, *Survey of Cornw.* 61, 127; *Hist. Cornw.* ed. S. Drew, i. 652; C219/37/21; 219/40/261; 219/41B/158. [4] *HP Commons, 1558-1603*, i. 134; *Hist. Cornw.* i. 652; C219/35/1/162; 219/37/21; 219/39/47. [5] C219/38/27; 219/39/47, 55; 219/40/261, 279; 219/41B/146a, 158; *Hist. Cornw.* i. 652. [6] *Hist. Cornw.* 651; *Mdx. Peds.* (Harl. Soc. lxv), 77; PROB 11/152, f. 238. [7] *HMC Cowper*, i. 157; *Vis. Derbys.* (Harl. Soc. n.s viii), 116. [8] *Hist. Cornw.* 651; C142/333/26; Carew, 126-7; *HP Commons, 1558-1603*, i. 134. [9] *HMC Hatfield*, xvii. 339; *CSP Dom.* 1603-10, p. 233; *CJ*, i. 316a, 324a. [10] Vivian, *Vis. Cornw.* 147, 252, 254. [11] Ibid. 56-7, 117, 252. [12] H. Hulme, *Sir John Eliot*, 37-8, 62. [13] *HMC Cowper*, i. 251. [14] *APC*, 1627-8, p. 45; *HMC Cowper*, i. 329; Hulme, 181.

P.M.H.

ST. IVES

Right of election: in the portreeve and burgesses

Number of voters: 13 in 1621

20 Feb. 1604	WILLIAM BROCKE
6 Mar. 1604	JOHN TREGENNA
c. Mar. 1614	SIR ANTHONY MAYNEY
	SIR JOSEPH KILLIGREW
aft. 9 Apr. 1614[1]	THOMAS TYNDALL *vice* Mayney, chose to sit for Cirencester
17 Dec. 1620	LORD JOHN PAULET
16 Jan. 1621	ROBERT BACON
21 Jan. 1624	SIR FRANCIS GODOLPHIN
1624	WILLIAM LAKES
	Sir Edward Conway I*
1 May 1625	SIR WILLIAM PARKHURST
6 May 1625	SIR FRANCIS GODOLPHIN
19 Jan. 1626	WILLIAM NOYE
21 Jan. 1626	BENJAMIN TICHBORNE
aft. 18 Feb. 1626[2]	EDWARD SAVAGE II *vice* Tichborne, chose to sit for Petersfield
4 Mar. 1628	FRANCIS GODOLPHIN
8 Mar. 1628	JOHN PAYNE

St. Ives derives its name from a fifth-century Irish missionary, St. Ia, whose shrine stood in the church there until the Reformation. The peninsula which protects St Ives's harbour from the Bristol Channel attracted settlement from prehistoric times, but the town developed slowly, lacking its own market until the late fifteenth century, and achieving full parochial status only in 1576. Some 20 years later Carew described it as 'of mean plight', and in need of a new pier. Apparently little had changed by 1626, when the town council itself voiced concern about the old pier and the silting-up of the harbour.[3] In the early seventeenth century St. Ives's prosperity depended on the plentiful local fish stocks, the port's principal export commodity, and large quantities of French salt were delivered each year for preserving the catches. Apart from France, seaborne trade was conducted primarily with Ireland and the other Bristol Channel ports; at least some of the cargoes recorded from farther afield, such as Spain, indicate shipping driven in by storms from the English Channel.[4] In 1625 St. Ives played host to English warships returning from Cadiz. Rather less welcome were the Sallee pirates and French privateers which threatened the town and terrorized the all-important fishing fleet during this decade.[5]

By the 1570s, the date of the earliest records, St. Ives was governed by a portreeve and two-tier council of 12 and 24 members respectively. On occasion the council displayed considerable determination in pursuing the town's interests. This was particularly true at the start of the seventeenth century, when a dispute arose between local fishermen, who used a system of land-based 'huers' to alert them to shoals near the coast, and two landowners near St. Ives who began prosecuting the huers for trespass. In January 1603, with the number of cases mounting, the council decided to support the defendants financially. It then successfully promoted a bill 'for the better preservation of fishing', designed specifically to protect customary West Country practices, in the first session of the 1604 Parliament.[6] However, an attempt in late 1604 to strengthen the council's legal status by obtaining a charter of incorporation came to nothing, this privilege not being granted until 1639, and for the remainder of this period the councillors apparently restricted their ambitions to lesser objectives such as repairing the town quay and opposing increased tithes.[7]

St. Ives was enfranchised in 1558, probably at the request of the 2nd earl of Bedford (Francis Russell[†]). The borough was coterminous with the parish, and is usually described as having enjoyed a scot-and-lot franchise, though it appears that in the early seventeenth century only the portreeve and the 12 senior councilmembers normally signed the parliamentary indentures.[8] In 1604, in response to the 'huers' dispute, St. Ives returned one of its own leading residents, John

Tregenna, who helped to steer the town's fishing bill through the Commons, but these circumstances were exceptional. Ordinarily the voters accepted external nominations, a pattern established by Bedford in the early days of the borough's existence. The principal patron was the 'lord' of St. Ives, an honorary position deriving from ownership of the largest local manor, Ludgvan Lese. For much of the sixteenth century the lordship had been shared, but by 1600 it was vested solely in William Paulet, the 4th marquess of Winchester, who backed the 1604 bid for incorporation and was recognized as having a special position of influence within the borough.[9] Winchester probably secured at least one seat in each of this period's elections. His nominees included his own son, Lord John Paulet (1621), and a leading figure in his household, Sir Anthony Mayney (1614), but the connections between Winchester and his other candidates were frequently more tenuous than this.[10] Edward Savage, returned in 1626, was a cousin of Lord John Paulet's wife, while John Payne, the 1628 nominee, was Savage's brother-in-law.[11] Mayney's close friend Sir William Parkhurst was provided with a place in 1625, while in 1604 and 1626 nominations went to gentlemen from the marquess's home county of Hampshire, William Brocke and his nephew by marriage Benjamin Tichborne. Like the Paulets, the Tichbornes were mostly Catholic.[12] The borough made no attempt to disguise its subservience to Winchester's wishes. Individual returns were made for each Member, invariably bearing different dates, which in 1604 and 1621 diverged by several weeks. Moreover, for Brocke, Paulet and Parkhurst, blank indentures appear to have been submitted to the marquess.[13] The consistent presence of a Paulet candidate in each election, and Winchester's success in submitting a second nominee in 1626 after Tichborne opted to sit elsewhere, make it probable that William Lakes in 1624 and Mayney's replacement, Thomas Tyndall, were also placed by the marquess, though this remains a matter of speculation as their identity has not been firmly established.

The strength of the Paulet interest effectively left only one St. Ives seat available to other would-be patrons. The Killigrew family, who dominated the western Cornish boroughs in the first three Jacobean Parliaments, secured a place in 1614 for a junior member, Sir Joseph Killigrew, who as the duchy of Cornwall havener, or customs officer, also enjoyed direct ties with the port. Robert Bacon in 1621 most likely drew on the same source for his nomination, since his kinsman and patron lord chancellor St. Alban (Sir Francis Bacon*) was closely related to the Killigrews.[14] Following the death of Sir William Killigrew I* in 1622, his family's influence declined somewhat,

the void being filled by the Godolphins of Godolphin House, Breage, located some eight miles south west of St. Ives. Ruigh's assertion that the Godolphins exercised influence at St. Ives through a junior family member based at Treveneage, St. Hilary, slightly closer to the borough, appears to be unsubstantiated. Sir Francis Godolphin and his nephew Francis were returned three times between 1624 and 1628. They probably also backed the candidature in 1626 of William Noye, whose somewhat humbler family lived ten miles from the borough at St. Buryan, though the lawyer conceivably also drew on his close ties with the Paulets. Since Noye was returned on a blank indenture, the possibility that Winchester achieved a double success that year cannot be ruled out.[15] The strength of the Killigrew and Godolphin influence over St. Ives proved unassailable by rival interests. The duchy of Cornwall, which kept a toe-hold on the borough through its ownership of the small manor of Porthia Prior, nominated high-profile candidates, Sir Lionel Cranfield* and Sir Julius Caesar*, in 1620 and 1624, but its wishes were apparently ignored on both occasions.[16] The Godolphins faced a rather more serious challenge in the latter year from Arthur Harris, a gentleman living around five miles from the town, who attempted to obtain a place for his relative, secretary of state Sir Edward Conway I*. However, as Harris reported to their mutual kinsman John Verney on 25 Jan., he failed in his endeavour by a single vote.[17]

[1] Procs. 1614 (Commons), 36. [2] Procs. 1626, ii. 69. [3] J.H. Matthews, Hist. St. Ives, i, 16, 27, 31, 47, 183; C. Henderson et al., Cornish Church Guide, 112; F.E. Halliday, Richard Carew of Antony, 231. [4] E190/1021/4; 190/1022/18; 190/1024/16, 20; 190/1025/5, 7, 17; 190/1030/28; E306/8/19. [5] CSP Dom. 1625-6, pp. 20, 185; 1628-9, pp. 106, 175, 501; Addenda 1625-49, p. 132. [6] Matthews, 146, 468; CJ, i. 976a, 985b, 986b, 989b; SR, iv. 1048-9. [7] Matthews, 183, 187-8, 193; HMC Hatfield, xvi. 351. [8] HP Commons, 1558-1603, i. 135; W.P. Courtney, Parl. Rep. of Cornw. 61; C219/37/22; 219/39/31; 219/40/264; 219/41B/153, 164. [9] Matthews, 468; HP Commons, 1509-58, i. 58; C2/Jas.I/W23/16; SC6/Chas.I/382; HMC Hatfield, xvi. 351. [10] C219/37/22; PROB 11/124, f. 360. [11] Vis. Cheshire (Harl. Soc. xviii), 204; Harl. 2075, f. 31; CP, xi. 204; xii. 768. [12] PROB 11/151, f. 132v; Vis. Hants (Harl. Soc. lxiv), 126; W. Berry, Hants Genealogies, 31-2. [13] C219/35/1/166; 219/37/22; 219/39/31. [14] Matthews, 176; Vivian, Vis. Cornw. 268; Vis. Essex (Harl. Soc. xiii), 39-40; Letters and Life of Francis Bacon ed. J. Spedding, i. 299. [15] R.E. Ruigh, Parl. of 1624, p. 108; Add. 4223, f. 85; CSP Dom. 1631-3, p. 180; C33/144, f. 554v; Bp. of London Mar. Lics. 1611-1828 ed. G.J. Armytage (Harl. Soc. xxvi), 118; C219/40/246. [16] G. Haslam, 'The Duchy and Parl. Representation', Jnl. Royal Institution of Cornw. n.s. viii. pt 3, pp. 226, 229; DCO, 'Letters and Patents 1620-1', f. 39v; 'Prince Charles in Spain', f. 33v. [17] CSP Dom. 1623-5, p. 145; SP14/158/47. Gruenfelder mistakenly links Harris's efforts to Caesar, the Duchy nominee: J.K. Gruenfelder, Influence in Early Stuart Elections, 89.

P.M.H.

ST. MAWES

Right of election: in the mayor and burgesses

Number of voters: 20 in 1624

c. 10 Mar. 1604	DUDLEY CARLETON
1604	JOHN SPECCOTT
c. Mar. 1614	SIR NICHOLAS SMITH
	FRANCIS VYVYAN
13 Dec. 1620	WILLIAM HOCKMORE
20 Dec. 1620	EDWARD WRIGHTINGTON
15 Jan. 1624	JOHN ARUNDELL
1624	WILLIAM HOCKMORE
6 May 1625	SIR JAMES FULLERTON
	NATHANIEL TOMKINS chose to sit for Christchurch, 11 July 1625
17 Jan. 1626	SIR HENRY CAREY II
	WILLIAM CARR
2 Mar. 1628	HANNIBAL VYVYAN
5 Mar. 1628[1]	THOMAS CAREY

Situated on a creek to the east of Falmouth Harbour, St. Mawes was a small fishing village notable only for its ancient chapel dedicated to St. Maudutus, and the royal castle built in the 1540s to protect the bay from French raiders. Although one indenture in 1625 referred to 'St. Maudes', the chapel was derelict by 1621, when Parliament was petitioned unsuccessfully for its restoration. Local government was limited to a manorial court leet, held before a portreeve chosen annually by the manor's tenants. The borough, which returned two Members from 1563, covered approximately two-thirds of the village, with the franchise exercised by the portreeve or 'mayor' and a handful of freeholders. St. Mawes followed the Cornish custom of returning individual indentures for each Member. Three of the mayors recorded in election indentures of the 1620s were unable to sign their own name.[2]

Although the borough returned some local candidates to Parliament under Elizabeth, the majority of its representatives then appear to have been government nominees. In the early seventeenth century, however, two Cornish families emerged as the borough's principal patrons. The Vyvyans, whose seat at Trelowarren lay about nine miles south-west of St. Mawes, had provided one MP there in 1597, and were effectively hereditary commanders of St. Mawes Castle.[3] The Trevanions were major landowners who lived nine

miles to the east at Caerhayes. Their kinsmen included the Careys and Trevors, who were prominent at Court and within the Duchy of Cornwall's administration. Both the Vyvyans and the Trevanions were numbered among Cornwall's wealthiest gentry, and the rivalry between them was highlighted in 1632 when Hugh Trevanion secured (Sir) Francis Vyvyan's* dismissal from the captaincy of St. Mawes Castle.[4]

At the outset of this period Charles Trevanion* of Caerhayes was a minor, and his family's patronage devolved in the first two Jacobean elections on the trustees of his estates. Sir Reginald Mohun*, the senior trustee, was particularly well-placed to impose his own preferences, for his half-brother William owned the manor of Bogullas *alias* St. Mawes. In 1604 the borough elected Sir Reginald's brother-in-law John Speccott, and ten years later returned his niece's husband Sir Nicholas Smith. Dudley Carleton, the other 1604 Member, seems to have relied on his government contacts, perhaps securing his nomination through another of Trevanion's trustees, Sir John Trevor I*.[5] In 1614 Francis Vyvyan obtained the second seat for himself, and four years later strengthened his leverage over the borough by purchasing Bogullas manor. He almost certainly arranged the election in 1620 and 1624 of his distant relative William Hockmore, the Duchy of Cornwall's auditor.[6] Gruenfelder has suggested that Hockmore was nominated by Prince Charles's Council, but in fact the Duchy possessed no direct influence over St. Mawes. By contrast, Edward Wrightington, a client of lord chancellor (Sir Francis) Bacon*, probably did rely on government patronage for his nomination in 1620, though it is unclear how this was mediated at local level. His indenture is dated seven days later than Hockmore's, and was prepared separately, probably outside St. Mawes, by someone ignorant of the customary formula for describing the borough's electorate; the burgesses are called the 'commonalty', and 'mayor' was later inserted in place of some other title.[7]

Charles Trevanion came of age in about 1615. By the mid-1620s he belonged to the Cornish gentry faction which looked for leadership to the lord warden of the stannaries, the 3rd earl of Pembroke, and his vice-warden, William Coryton*. From 1624 until 1628 Trevanion seems to have placed at least one St. Mawes burgess-ship at their disposal. The first beneficiary was another of Coryton's allies, John Arundell, whose election in 1624 probably helped to clear the way for Coryton himself to take a Cornish county seat. In 1625, with Trevanion and Arundell standing together for the county, St. Mawes returned Coryton's kinsman Sir James Fullerton, for whom Pembroke found a seat at Portsmouth in the following year.[8] The name of Fullerton's intended partner was erased from the election indenture to make room for Nathaniel Tomkins, a royal servant who, ironically, chose to sit elsewhere and was not replaced. Tomkins was a future opponent of the Forced Loan, and a close associate of Sir Robert Phelips*, then emerging as a critic of the government.[9] In 1626 St. Mawes returned Trevanion's cousin Sir Henry Carey, who supplied the Parliament with information discrediting Buckingham. William Carr has not been certainly identified, but he was probably a groom of the bedchamber who owed his nomination to Pembroke, the lord chamberlain, rather than to Buckingham, as Gruenfelder has speculated. Trevanion doubtless provided a place in 1628 for Carey's brother Thomas, and presumably also supported the election of Sir Francis Vyvyan's brother Hannibal, who helped lead the parliamentary attack that year on John Mohun*, the leader of Cornwall's pro-Buckingham faction.[10]

---

[1] *OR*. No indenture has been found for John Speccott or for William Hockmore in 1624. [2] J. Polsue, *Complete Paroch. Hist. of Cornw.* ii. 303-4, 308; C. Henderson *et al.*, *Cornish Church Guide*, 115; C219/37/25; 219/38/62; 219/39/50; 219/40/252; W.P. Courtney, *Parl. Rep. of Cornw.* 81. [3] *HP Commons, 1558-1603*, i. 136; I.D. Spreadbury, *Castles in Cornw.* 42-3. [4] Vivian, *Vis. Cornw.* 502; A. Duffin, *Faction and Faith*, 24; *CSP Dom.* 1631-3, p. 439. [5] PROB 11/115, ff. 113, 114v; C142/218/43; Vivian, *Vis. Cornw.* 325; *Dorset Vis. Addenda* ed. Colby and Rylands, 3. Gruenfelder misidentifies Smith as a customs official: J.K. Gruenfelder, *Influence in Early Stuart Elections*, 86. [6] C54/2372/48; Vivian, *Vis. Devon*, 472, 789; Vivian, *Vis. Cornw.* 93. [7] Gruenfelder, 88; C219/37/24-5. [8] Duffin, 73-4, 77; Vivian, *Vis. Devon*, 174; Gruenfelder, 128. [9] C219/39/66; Som. RO, DD/PH 219/64, 67. [10] *Procs. 1626*, iii. 123; LC2/6, f. 37v; Gruenfelder, 147; *CD 1628*, ii. 404.

P.M.H.

SALTASH

Right of election: in the free burgesses

Number of voters: at least 11

11 Mar. 1604	THOMAS WYVELL
	SIR PETER MANWOOD
c. Mar. 1614	RANULPHE CREWE
	SIR ROBERT PHELIPS
14 Dec. 1620	(SIR) THOMAS TREVOR
	SIR THOMAS SMYTHE
26 Jan. 1624	(SIR) THOMAS TREVOR
	FRANCIS BULLER
2 May 1625	SIR RICHARD BULLER
	FRANCIS BULLER
20 Jan. 1626	SIR RICHARD BULLER
25 Jan. 1626	SIR JOHN HAYWARD
3 Mar. 1628[1]	SIR RICHARD BULLER
	SIR FRANCIS COTTINGTON, bt.

The borough of Saltash was created in the thirteenth century out of the great feudal honour of Trematon, and formed part of the ancient demesnes of the duchy of Cornwall. The town grew up on the western bank of the Tamar, below Trematon castle, and this favourable location on the edge of Plymouth Sound ensured its status as one of Cornwall's principal ports.[2] In about 1610 Saltash possessed at least 15 ships, which traded with France, Spain, Portugal and Newfoundland.[3] The antiquary Richard Carew[†], who lived barely two miles away at Antony, reckoned that the borough contained between 80 and 100 households at the end of the sixteenth century, and noted a recent increase in building-work, a reflection of the 'competent wealth' of the residents.[4] Two of Saltash's captains turned to privateering in the later 1620s, but the wars with Spain and France also brought economic disruption and the burden of billeting sick soldiers. In 1628 the mayor was summoned before the Privy Council for obstructing impressment in the town.[5]

Under its charter of incorporation, granted in 1585, Saltash was governed by a mayor, recorder and 10 aldermen. The charter also confirmed an anomalous situation whereby the borough, though much quieter than the bustling port of Plymouth, enjoyed extensive rights and jurisdictions over the whole of Plymouth Sound and its tidal tributaries.[6] Additional Duchy of Cornwall profits arising from the Tamar and its ferry crossing were granted to the mayor and burgesses by Elizabeth I, Prince Henry, and, in 1618, by Prince Charles.[7] In 1625, Plymouth attempted to secure some of these privileges for itself, citing Saltash's failure to conduct an expensive salvage operation in Catwater Harbour, but the latter's corporation successfully argued that such a transfer was not in the Duchy's interests.[8]

Saltash first returned Members to Parliament in 1547. The franchise was vested in the free burgesses, but the actual number of voters in the early seventeenth century is difficult to gauge, as election indentures were signed only by the mayor.[9] The pattern of patronage at the start of this period is also hard to establish. The Carews of Antony had exercised a steady influence over the borough throughout Elizabeth's reign, and thus it was probably Richard Carew who provided a place in 1604 for Sir Peter Manwood, a fellow member of the Society of Antiquaries. The other seat in this election went to a local gentleman, Thomas Wyvell.[10] In 1614 Saltash awarded one of its burgess-ships to the Speaker-designate, Ranulphe Crewe, who probably relied on the backing of the 3rd earl of Pembroke, steward of the duchy of Cornwall. Sir Robert Phelips, who secured the other place, may have been able to call on the support of his distant kinsmen, the Bullers, who lived a few miles outside Saltash at Shillingham. It is unclear whether Phelips' seat was kept open for him while he unsuccessfully contested the Somerset county election.[11]

In contrast, the electoral developments of the 1620s are clear-cut. By the start of this decade Sir Richard Buller had become recorder of Saltash, the first holder of this office who can be identified, and he dictated most of the nominations for the next five elections.[12] Buller himself took one seat between 1625 and 1628, while his son Francis was returned in 1624 and 1625. Sir Thomas Smythe, who sat in 1621, was Buller's uncle by marriage, while Sir John Hayward (1626) was the recorder's brother-in-law. Smythe's own brother, Sir Richard, was receiver-general of the duchy of Cornwall, and a combination of this link to the Bullers and Saltash's own deep obligations to the Duchy ensured that the borough accepted nominations from Prince Charles's Council in 1620 and 1624.[13] Although objections were raised to the Duchy's initial choice of candidate in 1620, Sir Oliver Cromwell*, the borough agreed to a compromise figure, Sir Thomas Trevor, who was also returned at the subsequent election.[14] Only in 1628 was there a direct challenge to the Buller monopoly. Despite the recorder's opposition, the mayor was persuaded by his friend (Sir) James Bagg II* to secure the return of another Court figure, Sir Francis Cottington.[15]

[1] OR. [2] *Parl. Survey of Duchy of Cornw.* i. ed. N.J.G. Pounds (Devon and Cornw. Rec. Soc. n.s. xxv), 126; R. Pearse, *Ports and Harbours of Cornw.* 13; I.D. Spreadbury, *Castles in Cornw.* 22. [3] E190/1023/16; 190/1024/3, 15. [4] R. Carew, *Survey of Cornw.* ed. P. White, 132. [5] *CSP Dom.* 1628-9, pp.65, 299, 304, 441; E190/1031/5, 10; A. Duffin, *Faction and Faith*, 132. [6] C66/1265; Pearse, 14; Carew, 132. [7] J. Polsue, *Complete Parochial Hist. of Cornw.* iv. 136; *Parl. Survey of Duchy of Cornw.* 129. [8] *CSP Dom.* 1623-5, pp. 437, 462-3, 465. [9] *HP Commons, 1509-58*, i. 58; C66/1265; C219/37/29. [10] *HP Commons, 1558-1603*, i. 137; *Archaeologia*, i. p. xiv; C2/Chas.I/W63/13. [11] *Vis. Som.* (Harl. Soc. xi), 85; *Dorset Vis. Addenda* ed. Colby and Rylands, 2; Vivian, *Vis. Cornw.* 56-7; C142/356/108. [12] *Vis. Cornw.* (Harl. Soc. ix), 284. [13] Vivian, *Vis. Cornw.* 57; *Arch. Cant.* xx. 77-9; *Misc. Gen. et Her.* (ser. 5), iv. 80. [14] DCO, 'Letters and Patents 1620-1', f. 39v; 'Prince Charles in Spain', f. 33v. [15] SP16/100/47.

P.M.H.

TREGONY

Right of election: in the portreeve and commonalty in 1604; in the mayor and capital burgesses thereafter

Number of voters: at least 17 in 1604; 9 in 1626

5 Mar. 1604	HENRY POMEROY
	RICHARD CARVETH
c.Mar. 1614	WILLIAM HAKEWILL
	THOMAS MALET
18 Dec. 1620	WILLIAM HAKEWILL
24 Dec. 1620	THOMAS MALET
15 Jan. 1624	PETER SPECCOTT
7 Feb. 1624	AMBROSE MANATON
7 May 1625	SEBASTIAN GOOD
	SIR HENRY CAREY II
19 Jan. 1626	SIR ROBERT KILLIGREW
	THOMAS CAREY
27 Feb. 1628[1]	JOHN ARUNDELL
	FRANCIS ROUS

Tregony sprang up at the highest point of the River Fal navigable by medieval shipping. A manorial court leet was recorded there in the Domesday survey, and the town had achieved borough status by 1201, its government lying in the hands of a portreeve or mayor. The manor was granted by William I to the Pomeroy family, who obtained for the town the privileges of holding fairs and a weekly market, and who also constructed a castle and parish church. In the later Middle Ages, however, the river silted up, drowning the church and part of the town, and rendering Tregony an economic backwater. During the sixteenth century the castle also fell into disuse, mirroring the Pomeroys' own decline in local status.[2] Although the borough claimed to have sent representatives to Westminster in 1294 and 1306, its parliamentary history effectively dates from 1559, when it was enfranchised, probably at the behest of Francis Russell[†], 2nd earl of Bedford, who largely controlled the nomination of burgesses until his death in 1585. Thereafter, the borough's patronage increasingly lay with two gentry families, the Pomeroys and, more especially, the powerful Trevanions, who lived some four miles distant at Caerhayes.[3]

The early seventeenth century saw little change to this basic pattern. Except in 1604, the franchise remained vested in Tregony's mayor and eight capital burgesses, whose position as the town's governors was confirmed by the 1621 charter of incorporation. The borough's acquisition of a recorder, town clerk and other dignitaries apparently made it no less vulnerable to outside pressure, which continued to be exerted particularly by the Trevanions.[4] The Pomeroy family's electoral influence effectively ceased in 1609, when it sold Tregony manor, although Henry Pomeroy*, who lived in the town, served as mayor in 1620, and his brother Hugh became town clerk two years later. A legal dispute prevented the new lords of the manor from establishing their title until at least 1622, and they played no discernible part in the borough's elections. Their role as patrons descended to John Arundell* of Trerice, another leading Cornish gentleman, who lived around nine miles from the town, and in 1622 became the borough's first recorder.[5]

At the time of the 1604 election the lord of Caerhayes, Charles Trevanion*, was a minor aged nine or ten, and this may help to explain Tregony's choice of Henry Pomeroy and another local resident, Richard Carveth. In marked contrast to earlier elections, a single indenture was used to return both men. The franchise was also broader than usual, as the indenture, which used the unfamiliar terminology of 'portreeve and commonalty' to define the electorate, was signed by at least 17 voters. In all subsequent elections during this period, the customary narrow franchise was employed, and individual indentures were returned for each Member. In 1621, and again in 1624, there were substantial gaps in time between the two returns, which suggests a tame electorate awaiting instructions.[6] On the former occasion this delay is surprising, since Tregony returned the same men as it had in 1614, William Hakewill and Thomas Malet. Hakewill probably enjoyed Arundell's backing, having previously sat for Mitchell, where Arundell was the principal patron, while Malet belonged through his mother to the junior branch of the Trevanion family.[7] The Members who sat in 1624, Peter Speccott and his uncle Ambrose Manaton, were both from gentry families in east Cornwall, but neither possessed personal ties to the borough. Instead, they may have owed their election to William Coryton*, the powerful vice-warden of the Cornish stannaries. By the mid-1620s both Arundell and Charles Trevanion seem to have joined Coryton's gentry faction, thereafter making seats available to the vice-warden's allies at boroughs where they possessed influence, such as Tregony and St. Mawes. Speccott's political views at this juncture are not known, but Manaton was a strong supporter of Coryton by 1627 at the latest, and therefore probably benefited from his electoral patronage.[8]

In the 1625 elections, Trevanion can be credited with providing a seat for his cousin Sir Henry Carey,

who subsequently became a vocal critic of Pembroke's rival the duke of Buckingham, while Sebastian Good, a London lawyer, probably benefited from a family connection with John Arundell.[9] The Trevanion-Arundell axis suffered a partial set-back in the following year, as Tregony returned Sir Robert Killigrew, a Buckingham client who had stood against them in the 1625 Cornish county poll. However, Trevanion was able to bring in Thomas Carey, Sir Henry's brother, as his partner. In the 1628 elections Arundell was himself chosen as the borough's senior Member. Francis Rous, another gentleman from east Cornwall and an outspoken government critic in this Parliament, probably owed his place at Tregony to the same political considerations which operated in 1624, though he cannot be linked directly to Coryton and his allies.[10]

[1]OR. [2]J. Polsue, *Complete Paroch. Hist. of Cornw.* i. 278, 282, 284; M.W. Beresford, *Eng. Medieval Boroughs*, 82; C. Henderson *et al. Cornish Church Guide*, 207; I.D. Spreadbury, *Castles in Cornw.* 40. [3]Polsue, i. 284; *HP Commons, 1558-1603*, i. 137-8. [4]*Vis. Cornw.* (Harl. Soc. ix), 285; C219/37/47; 219/38/51; 219/40/249; C66/2246/16. [5]C2/Jas.I/L10/14; Cornw. RO, J/2080. [6]C219/35/1/168; 219/37/47-8; 219/38/50-1. [7]Vivian, *Vis. Cornw.* 504. [8]A. Duffin, *Faction and Faith*, 77; SP16/68/16. [9]Vivian, 502; *Procs. 1626*, iii. 123; SP46/72, f. 110. [10]Duffin, 77; *CD 1629*, pp. 12-14.

P.M.H.

TRURO

Right of election: in the mayor and burgesses

Number of voters: maximum 25

6 Mar. 1604	THOMAS BURGES I
	HENRY COSSEN
c.Mar. 1614	THOMAS RUSSELL
	THOMAS BURGES II
18 Dec. 1620	BARNABY GOOCH
21 Dec. 1620	JOHN TREFUSIS
26 Feb. 1621	SIR JOHN CATCHER *vice*
	Gooch, chose to sit for
	Cambridge University
15 Jan. 1624	RICHARD DANIEL
	THOMAS BURGES II
8 May 1625	HENRY ROLLE
	WILLIAM ROUS
16 Jan. 1626	HENRY ROLLE
	FRANCIS ROUS
8 Mar. 1628[1]	RICHARD DANIEL
	HENRY ROLLE

Truro sprang up in the early twelfth century at the juncture of two major roads and a navigable tributary of Falmouth Haven, and began sending burgesses to Parliament in 1295. A key factor in the borough's development was its close proximity to the tin-producing region, or stannary, of Tywarnhaile. From around 1300 Truro was west Cornwall's principal location for 'coinage', the obligatory pre-sale testing of the metal's purity, and when tin production in this part of the county dramatically increased in the sixteenth century the town's prosperity rose commensurately. As a venue for the Cornish stannary 'parliament' and quarter sessions, Truro had also become a significant administrative centre, and the borough's incorporation in 1589 confirmed its local standing. In the following decade Richard Carew[†] rated it as the county's wealthiest community.[2] During the early seventeenth century Truro's merchants supplemented the profits from tin by trading in the standard commodities of the region, such as fish and wine, as well as luxury goods shipped in from London. In 1619 Richard Daniel's[*] brother Jenkin was selling a full range of cloths from canvas and fustian to 'cobweb' lawn and black silk lace.[3] Few Truro merchants owned ships, a fact cited by the corporation as evidence of poverty when confronted by demands for Ship Money in 1620. Indeed, a 1626 survey of Cornish shipping recorded only one vessel belonging to the town. However, although Truro remained comparatively small, with a population of around 900, there are no clear indications of economic decline before the wars of the later 1620s, which disrupted the tin trade.[4]

Under the terms of the 1589 charter, Truro's corporation consisted of a mayor and 24 burgesses, of whom four were aldermen, along with a recorder and numerous minor officers. The corporation owned several properties in and around the borough, thus enjoying a measure of financial clout, and it was not slow to defend the town's interests, protesting to the Privy Council in 1620 about Ship Money demands, going to law to protect its lands in 1623, and defying the local deputy lieutenants over control of the Truro militia in 1626.[5] The parliamentary franchise was vested in the corporation, and the mayor, the sole signatory to election indentures, acted as returning officer. Compared with most Cornish boroughs during this period, Truro experienced relatively little pressure from rival interests seeking control of electoral patronage. By the seventeenth century the local manors were fragmented, and most of their gentry owners, such as the Edgcumbes, Arundells, St. Aubyns and Trevanions, lived too far away to exert real influence. Only two gentry families counted for much in the town – the Robarteses, immensely wealthy former merchants who owned Truro's largest dwelling and entered the peerage in 1625, and the Boscawens, who held the recordership by 1620 and resided some four miles from the borough at Tregothnan. However, neither family apparently made nominations to the borough until the mid-1620s.[6]

Of the men elected to Parliament in 1604 and 1614 at least three, Henry Cossen and the two Burgeses, belonged to Truro's corporation, while the fourth, Thomas Russell, was probably a town resident. Events in 1621 were more confused, as, probably for the only time during this period, the election indentures were dated several days apart, suggesting that there had been a contest or that external pressure had been exerted. The second man returned, John Trefusis, was a gentleman living six miles from the town who enjoyed ties with the Boscawens. Barnaby Gooch, the other Member, was chancellor of the diocese of Exeter, but his connection with Truro has not been established. When Gooch opted to sit elsewhere he was replaced by Sir John Catcher, whose brother was an alderman. In 1624 Thomas Burges II was again chosen, along with a former mayor, Richard Daniel, but thereafter the corporation was represented directly only once more, when Daniel resumed his Commons seat in 1628.[7] Between 1625 and 1628 inclusive, the recorder, Hugh Boscawen, apparently nominated Henry Rolle, a kinsman by marriage. William and Francis Rous, a nephew and uncle returned in 1625 and 1626, doubtless relied on the influence of Sir Richard Robartes, as William was his son-in-law. This emerging gentry dominance of the borough's parliamentary seats probably indicated not so much a decline in the corporation's strength as an increase in pressure from external candidates, prompting action by patrons who would otherwise have been content to allow the town freedom of choice.[8]

[1] OR. [2] V. Acton, Hist. Truro, i. 15-16, 20, 26, 28, 58, 62, 65; G.R. Lewis, Stannaries, 126-7, 149; A. Duffin, Faction and Faith, 109; F.E. Halliday, Richard Carew of Antony, 217. [3] Acton, 62; E190/1021/6; 190/1022/21; 190/1025/13; 190/1028/2, 10; 190/1030/30; Cornw. RO, D183/1a. [4] APC, 1619-21, p. 241; Early-Stuart Mariners and Shipping ed. T. Gray (Devon and Cornw. Rec. Soc. n.s. xxxiii), 74; J. Palmer, Truro in Seventeenth Cent. 3; CSP Dom. 1627-8, p. 46; Harg. 321, f. 321v. [5] C66/1334; Palmer, 14; APC, 1619-21, p. 241; 1626, p. 332; C2/Jas.I/T7/64. [6] C66/1334; C219/38/44; Palmer, 12-14; Vis. Cornw. (Harl. Soc. ix), 285. [7] C2/Jas.I/C8/63; 2/Chas.I/C72/19; Vivian, Vis. Cornw. 464-5; Vis. Cornw. (Harl. Soc.), 285. [8] Vivian, 47, 397, 413; Vivian, Vis. Devon, 654.

P.M.H.

CUMBERLAND

Number of voters: unknown

6 Mar. 1604	WILFRID LAWSON
	EDWARD MUSGRAVE
c. Mar. 1614	(SIR) WILFRID LAWSON
	SIR THOMAS PENRUDDOCK
19 Dec. 1620	SIR GEORGE DALSTON
	SIR HENRY CURWEN
10 Feb. 1624	SIR GEORGE DALSTON
	FERDINAND HUDDLESTON
3 May 1625	SIR GEORGE DALSTON
	PATRICIUS CURWEN
c. Jan. 1626	SIR GEORGE DALSTON
	PATRICIUS CURWEN
4 Mar. 1628	SIR GEORGE DALSTON
	(SIR) PATRICIUS CURWEN, (bt.)

The remote and sparsely populated county of Cumberland was transformed by the Union of the crowns in 1603 from a border province into a backwater. News of the accession of King James precipitated a final outburst of pillage and looting by numerous border clans, among whom the Graham family was the most notorious; it was reported that in one 'busy week' there had been '40 towns burnt, 500 felonies and murders'.[1] George Clifford, 3rd earl of Cumberland, as warden of the west and middle marches, was entrusted with the task of restoring order; he received a grant of the Grahams' main estates and around 150 of their adherents were transported to Ireland.[2] The confiscated lands were eventually bought back in 1628 by Sir Richard Graham*, who had made a career at Court, and was anxious 'to reform vice' in the region.[3]

The Cliffords had traditionally shared the patronage of county elections with the Dacres of Naworth, whose estates had recently passed, by marriage, to Lord William Howard, a notorious Catholic. Elections were held at Carlisle Castle, a seat of the Cliffords; however, after the death of the 3rd earl in 1605 his successors resided outside the county, on their Yorkshire estates; and the influence of Lord Henry Clifford* was further diminished by a bitter feud over Cumberland's legacy.[4] Both Howard and Clifford became renowned for their determination to overthrow the custom of tenant right, whereby rents were artificially held down out of consideration of the need to provide armed retainers to defend the now obsolete border. As in West-

morland, this was a source of tension among the local gentry. Several old families including the Curwens and Musgraves felt persecuted by Howard; however, the resulting emnities found little expression in county elections, and outright contests were avoided.[5]

At the 1604 county election two leading members of the local gentry were returned; there is no evidence that either Cumberland or Howard were directly involved. The senior seat went to Wilfrid Lawson, a long serving magistrate and client of the 9th earl of Northumberland, while the second place was filled by Edward Musgrave of Hayton Castle. Presumably because Lawson was given 'great countenance' by Northumberland, 12 electors, headed by Sir Nicholas Curwen[†], wrote to the earl on 6 Mar. 1604 asking him to intercede with the king and Lords on the county's behalf for an exemption from any subsidy that might be voted, 'in regard of the great spoils and losses which we of late in the county have sustained'.[6] To this they added two wishes, which were to be 'rid of the bad men of the borders' and to have 'liberty to use our lands to our most profit and commodity as others in other parts of England being in the like case'.[7] The poverty of the border shires was acknowledged in the reduced sums demanded on Privy Seal loans in Cumberland and Westmorland after the end of the first session of the Parliament.[8] Peace was gradually restored by a series of border commissions, in which Lawson played a prominent role; Sir Edward Phelips*, reporting from the northern circuit in 1609, was able to point to marked decreases in capital offences and in recusancy.[9]

Lawson was re-elected in 1614, while Howard asserted his influence by nominating an outsider, the courtier Sir Thomas Penruddock, as the junior knight of the shire. Penruddock, a suspected Catholic, was an adherent of Howard's kinsman, Lord Arundel; he was also Musgrave's brother-in-law, and although his main estates lay in far distant Hampshire, he inherited his mother's jointure lands in Cumberland on the eve of the elections, which was presumably enough to make him acceptable to the electorate, despite being unknown in the region.[10] The king passed through Cumberland on his Scottish progress in 1617, although the disdainful attitude of many of his English subjects is reflected in John Chamberlain's observation that the county was 'said to be impassable for coaches, besides [having] incommodious lodgings and other inconveniences'.[11]

Sir George Dalston, a local magistrate and governor of Carlisle, was elected as the senior knight of the shire in every Parliament of the 1620s. He was on good terms with Howard, whose support he presumably enjoyed.[12] He was joined in the 1621 Parliament by Sir Henry Curwen of Workington, a local campaigner against tenant-right, who needed no patron to press his claims to a county seat, at least among the gentry. Howard may have tried to extend his influence in the 1624 elections, by backing Ferdinand Huddleston of Millom Castle, a notorious playboy with 20 outlawries against his name, for the junior seat.[13] Although not yet convicted of recusancy, Huddleston's religion was suspected; and his election must be regarded as a last and singularly ill-judged assertion of Howard's patronage.[14] Although Huddleston probably never took his seat, a petition was presented against him but thrown out by the privileges' committee according to the precedent set in the case of Sir Francis Goodwin*.[15] In the first three Parliaments of Charles's reign Cumberland was represented by Dalston and Curwen's son Patricius; the latter and Lawson were the only two of the seven knights of the shire who sat in this period whose religion was clearly Protestant.[16] Dalston informed the Commons in 1624 that there were 'no papists but the lady of Sir Thomas Lamplugh' in the county and may have helped Huddleston to evade the fate of Musgrave, who was later presented for recusancy.[17] The county's muted opposition to extra-parliamentary taxation during Charles's reign is apparent in the report by Lawson and Patricius Curwen to the Cliffords as early as October 1625 that Privy Seal loans would yield no more than £320 from a total of 20 donors, most of whom sought to be excused because 'the county is poor and the subsidy is [still] collecting'.[18]

[1] CJ, i. 1015a; VCH Cumb. ii. 282-4; P. Williams, 'The Northern Borderland under the Early Stuarts', in Hist. Essays Presented to David Ogg ed. H.E. Bell and R.L. Ollard, 4-6, 11-12. [2] HMC Hatfield, xvii. 289; CSP Dom. 1603-10, p. 78. [3] CSP Dom. 1619-23, p. 339; 1628-9, p. 198. [4] HMC Le Fleming, 12-15. [5] STAC 8/161/16; M. Campbell, Eng. Yeomen, 148-50; Naworth Household Bks. ed. G. Ornsby (Surtees Soc. lxviii), 424-5. [6] CSP Dom. 1603-10, p. 268. [7] Cumb. RO, D/Lec. 169, (Curwen and others to Northumberland, 6 Mar. 1604). [8] CSP Dom. 1611-18, p. 92. [9] CJ, i. 1014b; CSP Dom. 1603-10, p. 543. [10] D. Howarth, Lord Arundel and his Circle, 12, 43, 52-3, 88. [11] Chamberlain Letters ed. N.E. McClure, ii. 79; VCH Cumb. ii. 285. [12] Naworth Household Bks. 8; Hutchinson, Cumb. ii. 454-5. [13] APC, 1625-6, p. 89; Glanville, Reps. 124. [14] CJ, i. 706a. [15] Ibid. 714a; 'Nicholas 1624', f. 239v. [16] J.F. Curwen, House of Curwen, 151; C.B. Phillips, 'Gentry in Cumb. and Westmld. 1600-65', (Lancaster Univ. Ph.D. thesis, 1973), p. 38. [17] CJ, i. 706a; 'Nicholas 1624', f. 179; Procs. 1626, ii. 138. [18] HMC 3rd Rep. 39.

J.P.F./R.C.L.S.

CARLISLE

Right of election: in the freemen

Number of voters: over 200 in 1619[1]

6 Mar. 1604	THOMAS BLENNERHASSETT
	WILLIAM BARWICKE
c. Mar. 1614	GEORGE BOTELER
	NATHANIEL TOMKINS
20 Dec. 1620	SIR HENRY VANE
	GEORGE BOTELER
10 Feb. 1624	SIR HENRY VANE
	EDWARD AGLIONBY
3 May 1625	SIR HENRY VANE
	EDWARD AGLIONBY
c. Jan. 1626	SIR HENRY VANE
	RICHARD GRAHAM
25 Feb. 1628	RICHARD BARWIS
	RICHARD GRAHAM
	?Sir Henry Vane

Carlisle, situated on the river Eden about six miles from the north-west coast, had long served as a strategic point on the border with Scotland, as the administrative centre of the West March, and as a port of trade with Ireland. The city's governing body, established by an ordinance of 1445 and confirmed on 1 May 1604, consisted of a mayor, 11 other 'worshipful persons' or aldermen, and 24 councillors.[2] Admission to the freedom, which gave the right to vote in parliamentary elections, was controlled by eight guilds, but was apparently easily obtained; a list dated 1619 contains over 200 names, including some local gentry, of whom the most prominent was Sir John Dalston†.[3] Carlisle seems to have been reasonably prosperous in the early seventeenth century, since the omission of the port of Carlisle from the great farm of the customs cost the Crown over £700 a year, according to the estimate of (Sir) Lionel Cranfield* in 1612; great quantities of hides, it was later alleged, passed through on their way to Scotland.[4] Furthermore, relations between the cathedral and corporation were harmonious; when the lecturer's annual stipend was doubled in 1627 to £40, two-thirds of the increase was provided by the dean and chapter and the remainder by the municipality, with two aldermen, Edward Aglionby and William Barwicke, acting as trustees.[5]

Although Carlisle's military importance ceased with the Union of the crowns in 1603, gunners continued to be appointed to the castle, which was leased by George Clifford, 3rd earl of Cumberland, the warden of the West and Middle marches. The Crown held considerable property in the borough, which for much of the period was in jointure to successive queens.[6] For this reason parliamentary patronage was shared between the Cliffords and the Court and so, with the exceptions of 1604 and 1628, at least one outsider was returned to each Parliament of the period.

In 1604 the borough returned two townsmen, Thomas Blennerhassett and William Barwicke, to the first Stuart Parliament. The names of the mayor and both bailiffs, with about 40 other citizens, appear on the indenture. It can only be assumed that Cumberland, who died in the following year, had declined to nominate any candidate. His brother Francis Clifford*, who succeeded as 4th earl, never resided at Carlisle, nor did the earl of Dunbar, the next warden of the marches; local victualling trades were therefore hard hit by the absence of great households, as they complained in 1606.[7] The corporation attempted to buy out the Crown rights in the demesne and socage lands attached to the castle in 1610, but were thwarted by Henry, Lord Clifford*, with the help of his father-in-law, lord treasurer Salisbury (Robert Cecil[†]).[8]

No doubt the expense of sending and maintaining two citizens in distant Westminster for five sessions took its toll on the city's finances, and at the next election two outsiders were returned. Henry, Lord Clifford presumably nominated his friend George Boteler for the first seat, and the second went to a courtier, Nathaniel Tomkins. Before the king visited the city on his way back from Scotland in 1617, the merchant guild met, and agreed upon a list of four demands, for 'a licence for transporting of wool and woolfells ... to have a nobleman to live in Carlisle Castle ... to have one of the three sittings of [the Council in the North at] York once a year to be kept in Carlisle ... and to create one university in this poor city'.[9] However, only one of their wishes was granted; Clifford did inhabit the castle for a time in 1618, but his real interests were distant, and there is no indication that his visit was repeated.[10]

Boteler was re-elected in 1620, while the second seat went to another courtier, Sir Henry Vane, who was also chosen to serve in the next three Parliaments. In 1624 and 1625 he was accompanied by a prominent townsman, Edward Aglionby. The latter served his fourth term as mayor in 1625-6, and as returning officer at the next general election no doubt assisted

the return of his kinsman Richard Graham, who had risen in the service of the duke of Buckingham. Graham was re-elected in 1628, but Vane lost the senior seat, perhaps after a contest, to Richard Barwis, a local gentleman of puritan leanings who had recently been admitted to the freedom of the city.

[1] Cumb. RO (Carlisle), Ca2/319. [2] *Royal Charters of Carlisle* ed. R.S. Ferguson, 3, 112-13. [3] Oldfield, *Rep. Hist.* iii. 260, 263, 266. [4] *HMC Sackville*, i. 288; E134/21 Jas. I/Mich.24; *APC*, 1626, pp. 401-2. [5] Cumb. RO (Carlisle), Ca 2/120. [6] SP14/50/93; C.B. Phillips, 'Gentry in Cumb. and Westmld. 1600-65', (Lancaster Univ. Ph.D. thesis, 1973), p. 240. [7] SP14/22/3. [8] Ferguson, 128; E134/22 Jas. I/Mich.25. [9] *Carlisle Mun. Recs.* ed. R.S. Ferguson and W. Nanson (Cumb. and Westmld. Antiq. and Arch. Soc. extra ser. iv), 95. [10] *CSP Dom.* 1611-18, pp. 480, 537; *APC*, 1618-19, p. 445.

J.P.F./R.C.L.S.

DERBYSHIRE

Number of voters: unknown

16 Feb. 1604	SIR JOHN HARPUR
	WILLIAM KNYVETON
c. Mar. 1614	HENRY HOWARD
	SIR WILLIAM CAVENDISH I
28 Dec. 1620	SIR WILLIAM CAVENDISH I
	(LORD CAVENDISH)
	SIR PETER FRESCHEVILLE
22 Jan. 1624	SIR WILLIAM CAVENDISH I
	(LORD CAVENDISH)
	SIR JOHN STANHOPE II
14 Apr. 1625	SIR WILLIAM CAVENDISH I
	(LORD CAVENDISH)
	SIR JOHN STANHOPE II
c. Jan. 1626	SIR WILLIAM CAVENDISH I
	(LORD CAVENDISH)
	JOHN MANNERS
16 Mar. 1626	SIR JOHN STANHOPE II *vice* Cavendish, called to the Upper House
13 Mar. 1628	(SIR) EDWARD LEECH
	JOHN FRESCHEVILLE

Remote from London and dominated by the barren Pennines, Derbyshire boasted great natural beauty but little tillage, deriving most of its wealth from coarse wool and minerals. The Cavendish and Manners families had extensive interests in the lead mines, which by 1600 supplied nearly half Europe's needs, while the Freschevilles profited on a lesser scale as ironmasters. Although the duchy of Lancaster covered more than half the shire, the Crown exerted little political influence.[1] So small a county was always in danger of falling under the control of a great territorial magnate, and until 1618 it was dominated by the Talbot earls of Shrewsbury, whose vast empire, based at Sheffield in the West Riding, also extended into Nottinghamshire and Staffordshire. However, Gilbert Talbot[†], the 7th earl, was frequently opposed by William Cavendish[†], the son of his formidable step-mother, 'Bess of Hardwick', the dowager countess of Shrewsbury. The earl of Shrewsbury remained lord lieutenant until his death in 1616, but his position was weakened by the imprisonment of his wife in 1611 for conniving at the flight of Lady Arbella Stuart, a possible pretender to the throne.[2]

Elections were held in the county town. Signatures on the surviving indentures varied between six in 1625 and 26 in the following year.[3] In 1604 Shrewsbury's agent for his Derbyshire lands, Sir John Harpur, was returned as senior knight of the shire, but the influence of the dowager countess can be discerned in the election for the remaining seat of William Knyveton, the son of her half-sister and principal confidante, Jane Knyveton née Leche. Cavendish, who did not stand, was probably more interested in a seat in the House of Lords, which he purchased in the following year when he was created 1st Lord Cavendish of Hardwick.[4] By the time of the 1614 election Harpur was unable to stand again, as his reputation had been blasted by a long Chancery suit, in which the 5th earl of Huntingdon, assisted by the 1st earl of Chesterfield and Sir Thomas Gerrard*, compelled him to disgorge the surplus of the charity established by their ancestor, Sir John Port. His place was taken by Henry Howard, who had recently acquired property in the county by marriage and was son of the lord chamberlain and brother-in-law to the royal favourite, the earl of Somerset. The second seat was bestowed upon Sir William Cavendish, the eldest son of William, Lord Cavendish. Sir William Cavendish had recently come of age, and was impelled to seek election because of his debts.[5] Knyveton was unable to stand again for the county, as Bess of Hardwick had died in 1608, and without her support his family could aim no higher than a borough seat. Shrewsbury was succeeded in his title by his 'bad brother' Edward[†] in 1616, and two years later by a fourth cousin, a Catholic priest. The lieutenancy went to lord Cavendish, and the Derbyshire estates to the three daughters of the 7th earl and their husbands, William, 3rd earl of Pembroke, Sir Henry Grey*, and Thomas, earl of Arundel. In 1618

Lord Cavendish became the 1st earl of Devonshire, and in the following year Sir William Cavendish, now usually known by the courtesy title Lord Cavendish, was joined with his father in the lieutenancy.[6]

At the next election, in December 1620, Cavendish took the senior seat, which he monopolized for the rest of his Commons career. As Howard was now dead, his colleague in the third Stuart Parliament was Sir Peter Frescheville, 'the person of most principal account and … the greatest power of any of the gentry in that county',[7] who had been closely associated with the 7th earl of Shrewsbury.[8] However, following his service in 1621, Frescheville seems to have had no further parliamentary ambitions, and in 1624 Cavendish was re-elected with Sir John Stanhope II. Cavendish introduced a bill on 9 Apr. to abolish the lead tithe in the High Peak Hundred of Derbyshire. Payment of this duty was the source of a long-running dispute between the lead miners and the lessees of the tithes, which had already been the subject of extensive litigation and appeals to the Privy Council. After receiving a second reading on 17 Apr., the bill was committed. Although Cavendish was named to this body, neither he, nor any other of its named members, attended the only recorded meeting of the committee. The lead miners petitioned the Commons in support of the bill while their opponents published a broadside detailing the case against. On 12 May John Wylde* reported that the committee 'thought fit to have it no further proceeded in', whereupon the House rejected the bill.[9]

The 1624 members were re-elected to the first Caroline Parliament. On 23 June the knights and burgesses of Derbyshire were appointed to help consider the bill to confirm an agreement between the king and the tenants of Macclesfield, across the border in Cheshire, and consequently Cavendish and Stanhope attended at least one meeting of the committee.[10] In 1626 Cavendish was returned with John Manners, who owned a large Derbyshire estate in his own right and had a good chance of succeeding to the earldom of Rutland. A few weeks later Cavendish's succession to the earldom of Devonshire allowed Stanhope to take the senior seat.

Following attempts to collect a benevolence in August 1626, the Privy Council were informed of widespread refusal to contribute in Derbyshire other than 'by way of Parliament'.[11] However, collection of the Forced Loan proved more successful, for on 27 July 1627 Francis Coke, one of the Derbyshire commissioners, reported to his brother (Sir) John Coke* that £2,750 had been paid into the Exchequer and that refusers were few and poor. Nevertheless, as late as September Stanhope and Sir George Gresley* had still not paid their assessments.[12] Among the active commissioners were Sir Peter Frescheville, John Manners and Devonshire, whose co-operation with the Forced Loan does not seem to have diminished his standing in Derbyshire politics. In 1628 he obliged his political mentor Pembroke by securing the election of Sir Edward Leech, a newcomer to the county who had started life in the service of the Herberts. Leech was returned along with Sir Peter Frescheville's son John, Devonshire's kinsman by marriage. A bill was introduced to settle Devonshire's lands, but Leech seems to have raised objections and complained that 'it was well known Devonshire used him not well at the committee', suggesting that the earl or his representatives had been critical of him while presenting evidence before the committee.[13]

[1] J.R. Dias, 'Lead, Soc. and Pols. in Derbys. before the Civil War', *Midland Hist.* vi. 39. [2] Sainty, *Lords Lieutenants*, 17; J.R. Dias, 'Pols. and Administration in Notts. and Derbys. 1590-1640' (Oxford Univ. D.Phil. thesis, 1973), pp. 203, 209. [3] C219/39/68; C219/40/72. [4] Dias thesis, 87, 244. [5] C2/Jas.I/C9/64. [6] Sainty, *Lords Lieutenants*, 17. [7] G. Holles, *Mems. of Holles Fam.* ed. A.C Wood (Cam. Soc. ser. 3. lv), 160. [8] Dias thesis, 86. [9] 'Hawarde 1624', p. 241; *CJ*, i. 758b, 769a, 787b; Kyle thesis, 466-8; C.R. Kyle, 'Attendance Lists', *PPE 1604-48* ed. Kyle., 214; A. Wood, *Pols. of Soc. Conflict*, 175, 231-7. [10] *Procs. 1625*, 226; Kyle, 'Attendance Lists', 227. [11] SP16/35/90; SP16/72/21. [12] E179/93/355; SP16/72/21; SP16/79/67. [13] *CD 1628*, iv. 19.

V.C.D.M.

DERBY

Right of election: in the freemen

Number of voters: unknown

16 Feb. 1604	JOHN BAXTER, town clerk
	EDMUND SLEIGH
c. Mar. 1614	SIR GILBERT KNYVETON
	ARTHUR TURNOR
28 Dec. 1620	TIMOTHY LEVINGE, recorder
	EDWARD LEECH
c. Jan. 1624	(SIR) EDWARD LEECH
	TIMOTHY LEVINGE, recorder
17 Apr. 1625	(SIR) EDWARD LEECH
	TIMOTHY LEVINGE, recorder
c. Jan. 1626	SIR HENRY CROFTS
	JOHN THOROWGOOD
11 Mar. 1628	PHILIP MAINWARING
	TIMOTHY LEVINGE, recorder

At the end of the sixteenth century Derby had a population of between 2,000-2,500 with clothworking as its staple industry.[1] It was a royal borough before the Conquest, though its first surviving charter dates only from 1204.[2] Since 1337 the town had been governed by two bailiffs, chosen annually by the freemen. Power to elect a recorder was added in 1446 and by the 1590s there was also a town clerk, sometimes referred to as the steward or under steward of the borough.[3] In 1612 the borough's high steward, Gilbert Talbot[†], the 7th earl of Shrewsbury, procured a new charter which placed town government in the hands of a self-selecting corporation of 24 chief burgesses, two of whom were to be chosen annually as bailiffs, and 24 assistant burgesses, together with a recorder and town clerk.[4] As the county town, Derby customarily hosted the assizes, although in 1610 they were transferred to Ashbourne following a 'great affray' between Sir Philip Stanhope, later earl of Chesterfield, and (Sir) George Gresley (1st Bt.)*, in which the inhabitants became involved. This was probably a revival of the 1590s feud between the 7th earl of Shrewsbury, with whom Gresley was closely connected, and the Stanhope family.[5]

Derby's electoral history stretched back unbroken to 1295. Elections were held in the guildhall and returns were made in the name of the bailiffs and burgesses until 1628, when the formula was changed to bailiffs and chief burgesses.[6] Parliamentary wages were certainly paid in 1597 to Henry Duport[†], the future recorder, but it is not known whether the practice continued.[7] Except in 1626, the corporation seems to have been free to choose at least one Member itself. However, it seems also to have been amenable to nominations from the magnates who successively occupied the office of high steward, the 7th and 8th earls of Shrewsbury, and (from 1617) the 3rd earl of Pembroke.[8] None of the county gentry sat for the borough, except Sir Gilbert Knyveton in 1614.

In August and September 1603 several prominent townsmen were involved in enclosure riots on commons belonging to the borough. These arose after the corporation rented out the commons, previously utilized by the town's freemen, to private individuals. Attempts by the earl of Shrewsbury to mediate failed and the dispute continued into the following year, when some of the rioters were indicted at the assizes.[9] However there is no evidence that this dispute spilled over into the 1604 election, when two townsmen were returned, John Baxter, the town clerk, and Edmund Sleigh, a merchant of possibly puritan inclinations.[10] Neither Member appears to have promoted legislation on behalf of the town, but in February 1610 Derby's drapers resolved to seek their support for a bill against interlopers promoted by the Coventry Drapers' Company, which was subsequently rejected at its first reading (24 February).[11] Baxter was dead by the following election, by which time Sleigh's health may also have been failing. Under these circumstances, the corporation might have been expected to offer a seat to Duport, who was still recorder, but he was now at odds with its members. In 1614, therefore, the corporation returned the 7th earl of Shrewsbury's henchman Sir Gilbert Knyveton for the senior seat. It was also induced by Henry Howard*, a younger son of the 1st earl of Suffolk and owner of extensive estates in Derbyshire, to elect as its other Member Suffolk's counsel, Arthur Turnor. Both men took out their freedom only after they had been returned.[12]

Howard's death in 1616 deprived Turnor of his patron, and before the next election Duport was replaced as recorder by Timothy Levinge, who proved his worth by launching a protracted Chancery suit for the recovery of a legacy left to the poor of the borough. He also acted for the corporation in a pre-emptive action against Duport to foreclose any demand for parliamentary wages and fees.[13] Levinge consequently took the senior seat in the third Jacobean Parliament, accompanied by the earl of Pembroke's secretary Edward Leech, another outsider, who was probably sworn as a freeman after the election. Although the return was dated 28 Dec., both men may have been elected a few days beforehand, as on 31 Dec. Henry Hastings, 5th earl of Huntingdon stated that Leech 'was chosen upon Monday last was sennight'.[14] Levinge and Leech were re-elected in 1624 and 1625, though in reverse order, as Leech had been knighted and acquired an estate in the county.

In 1626 Derby elected Pembroke's new secretary, John Thorowgood, and Sir Henry Crofts, a kinsman of Pembroke's ally, Sir William Cavendish I*. Following the dissolution, the townsmen were initially unanimous in refusing to subscribe to the royal benevolence demanded over the summer. However, there was little or no resistance to the Forced Loan, for by 1 Sept. 1627 the bailiffs reported that the full sum of £96 6s. 8d. demanded had been paid into the Exchequer.[15] In 1628 the borough returned Philip Mainwaring, a follower of Pembroke's brother-in-law, the earl of Arundel. Levinge resumed the second seat.

[1] E. Lord, 'Trespassers and Debtors: Derby at the end of the Sixteenth Century', *Derbys. Arch. Jnl.* cxvii. 97. [2] R. Simpson, *Coll. of Fragments Illustrative of Hist. and Antiqs. of Derby*, 28. [3] *British Bor. Chs.* ed. M. Weinbaum, 21; R. Clark, 'Derby "Town Chronicle" 1513-1698', *Derbys. Arch. Jnl.* cxviii. 175, 183; *HMC Rutland*,

i. 363. [4] C66/1909/4. [5] Clark, 176; W.T. MacCaffrey, 'Talbot and Stanhope: An Episode in Elizabethan Pols.', *BIHR*, xxxiii. 76-85. [6] C219/35/1/67; 219/37/82; 219/39/70; 219/41B/101. [7] C3/306/115. [8] Clark, 177. [9] Ibid. 176, 183. [10] PROB 11/127, f. 163. [11] Salop RO, 1831/14; *CJ*, i. 399a. [12] HEHL, HA5458. [13] C78/351/1; C3/306/115. [14] HEHL, HA5458. [15] SP16/33/131I; *CSP Dom.* 1627-8, p. 327.

V.C.D.M.

DEVON

Number of voters: unknown

28 Feb. 1604	SIR THOMAS RIDGEWAY EDWARD SEYMOUR[1]
27 *Jan. 1607*	SIR JOHN ACLAND *vice* Ridgeway, vacated his seat
c. Mar. 1614	SIR EDWARD GILES JOHN DRAKE
12 Dec. 1620	SIR EDWARD SEYMOUR, (bt.) JOHN DRAKE
3 Feb. 1624	SIR WILLIAM STRODE JOHN DRAKE
26 Apr. 1625	SIR FRANCIS FULFORD FRANCIS COURTENAY
21 Jan. 1626	JOHN DRAKE JOHN POLE
c. Feb. 1628[2]	JOHN BAMPFIELD SIR FRANCIS DRAKE, bt.

Devon, England's third largest county, was noted in the early seventeenth century both for the wildness of its upland moors and the enterprise of its inhabitants. The population at this time has been estimated at around 234,000. At least 5,000 of the adult males engaged in fishing, the fleets bringing in rich catches of pilchards and herrings from coastal waters, and regularly venturing as far as Newfoundland. Arable farming was concentrated on the southern lowland region, with great efforts made to maximize yield through enclosure and the intensive use of fertilizers. Northern and eastern parts were largely given over to cattle and sheep, the latter producing the wool which fed Devon's flourishing cloth industry.[3] The county was particularly noted for its fine baize and kerseys, mostly produced in the north and around Exeter, though coarser cloths were also manufactured at such centres as Tavistock, Totnes and Okehampton. Much of this material was shipped to France and Spain, via the major south coast ports of Plymouth, Dartmouth and Exeter. Indeed, Thomas Westcote claimed that Devon's local dominance in this trade had encouraged a great population increase, which left the county barely able to feed its own inhabitants.[4]

In administrative terms, Devon was remarkably unified considering its size. Except in times of plague, quarter sessions and assizes were always held at Exeter Castle, which was also the setting for the county's parliamentary elections. This cohesiveness also extended to religion. Recusancy was an insignificant problem, largely confined to a handful of gentry families such as the Courtenays. Puritans were much more numerous, and while still a small minority of the total population, they were similarly prevalent at gentry level, and probably dominated the county bench. Neither of Devon's lords lieutenant during this period, the 3rd earl of Bath and the 4th earl of Bedford (Sir Francis Russell*), showed much interest in local politics, so the choice of shire knights lay with the gentry. There were apparently no contests during this period, and nominations were probably agreed ahead of the elections, a common practice in neighbouring counties.[5]

Considered as a group, the shire knights were highly representative of Devon's gentry leadership. They were all resident in the south of the county, where the bulk of the major seats were located, and many of them were closely related. Sir Francis Drake (1628) was both the son-in-law of Sir William Strode (1624), and the brother-in-law of John Bampfield (1628), who was in turn the first cousin of Sir Francis Fulford (1625). Again, Francis Courtenay (1625) was the brother-in-law of John Pole (1626), and son-in-law of Sir Edward Seymour (1621), himself the son of the 1604 shire knight Edward Seymour. Many of them belonged to Devon's oldest families. Fulford and Sir John Acland could trace their forebears back to the twelfth century, the Poles and Bampfields had been locally prominent since the fourteenth century, while the Courtenays were descended from the medieval earls of Devon.[6] Those who could not boast such a long pedigree were generally distinguished by wealth or active service in county government. Edward Seymour, who had already twice served as a shire knight under Elizabeth, was the grandson of Protector Somerset, and owned more than 16,000 acres. John Drake and Sir Edward Giles were considerably less affluent, but both men were mainstays of local administration, and were also noted for their puritan leanings, another factor common to many of these Members.[7]

In 1604 the senior seat was taken by Sir Thomas Ridgeway, who had recently been appointed to Anne of Denmark's Council, and whose brother-in-law, Sir John Stanhope I*, was vice-chamberlain of the Household. His partner was the more experienced and equally well-connected Edward Seymour. The latter undoubtedly hoped to use this platform to help push through a private estate bill, but the two Members also had urgent county business to attend to in London. Around the time of the Commons' Easter recess, Ridgeway and Seymour appeared before the Board of Greencloth to explain why Devon had fallen behind with its purveyance composition payments, thereby pre-empting government intervention.[8] However, Ridgeway's Court ties worked both ways, and during the same session he was recruited by Stanhope to help rally support for a measure favoured by Lord (Robert) Cecil[†], probably the bill to confirm the Crown's grant of Berwick-upon-Tweed castle to the chancellor of the Exchequer, Sir George Home. Stanhope duly reported to Cecil that Ridgeway and another kinsman, Sir John Holles*, would 'use their best endeavours' during a vital debate, noting that 'Ridgeway, who is strong with his Devonshire crew, assures me of a good party'.[9]

In June 1606 Ridgeway became Irish treasurer-at-wars, and in the following November the Commons resolved that his seat was now vacant. He was replaced by Sir John Acland who, like Seymour, had private business to promote. His 1607 bill to appropriate the revenues of a Devon prebend to other charitable purposes failed to complete its passage, but in 1610 he won approval for an alternative measure to encourage Devon husbandry by establishing 200 apprenticeships in the county.[10]

Acland was the last Member during this period to make private legislation his priority, and for the next three Parliaments the shire knights more conspicuously pursued issues of general interest to the county. John Drake sat in all of these sessions, presumably a sign that he was viewed locally as an effective spokesman, though his local standing must also have benefited from the 1616 marriage of his son, Sir John*, to a kinswoman of the royal favourite, Buckingham. Drake was accompanied in 1614 by Giles, who had recently completed a successful shrieval term, in 1621 by Sir Edward Seymour, who was now head of his family, and in 1624 by Sir William Strode, who had first sat for the county in 1597, and had since established a formidable Commons' reputation as a borough Member.[11] In the Addled Parliament, Giles proved the more vocal spokesman on local matters. He apparently combined forces with Sir William Strode (then sitting as a Plymouth burgess) to attack the French

Company, whose patent posed a threat to Devon's cross-Channel trade. He also highlighted the impact of the disastrous Cockayne Project on the county's cloth industry, and firmly opposed impositions. Drake was presumably reflecting his fellow magistrates' concerns when he emphasized the need for local supervision of alehouses, and criticized the procurement from superior courts of bonds to keep the peace.[12] In the next two Parliaments Drake twice commented at length on the impact of low corn prices on his poorer constituents, and attacked Devon recusants, singling out Sir William Courtenay†. Still a keen advocate of local autonomy, in 1621 he provided damaging evidence of (Sir) Giles Mompesson's efforts to undermine magistrates' jurisdiction over alehouses, while three years later he delivered a letter of complaint from Devon about the number charitable briefs being directed to the high constables.[13] Seymour in 1621 denounced the local grievance of tithes imposed on fishermen, which had allegedly caused 'a great decay of mariners'. Strode, whose participation in the final Jacobean Parliament was apparently cut short by illness, spoke strongly in favour of an anti-Catholic war, but seems not to have raised any specific West Country grievances.[14]

Drake may have alienated local opinion by his sustained criticism of Sir William Courtenay, whose Protestant son Francis replaced him as Devon's junior knight in 1625. The senior seat on that occasion went to Sir Francis Fulford, an active figure in local government. Neither man had previously entered the Commons, and perhaps for this reason they made little impact on the first Caroline Parliament. In the following year Devon was gripped by the plague, and the shire election was poorly attended by the county elite, judging from the signatures on the return. Drake, whose ties to Buckingham were by now a mixed blessing, represented his county for the last time in 1626, but he barely touched on local matters, merely confirming that another Devon gentleman, Sir Thomas Monck, had been improperly elected. Drake's junior partner was a near neighbour, John Pole, who had not yet had much impact on local affairs, and was similarly inactive in the Commons.[15]

In the later 1620s Devon was seriously burdened by the billeting associated with the military expeditions to Cadiz and the Ile de Ré, and in 1628 the county returned as its junior Member Sir Francis Drake, who was at the forefront of efforts to tackle this crisis. He was accompanied by his brother-in-law, John Bampfield, a deputy lieutenant who had recently succeeded to one of Devon's largest estates. Surprisingly, it was Bampfield who was appointed in the Commons to help draft a petition to the king about the payment of outstanding billeting debts, whereas Drake is not known to have commented directly on his county's problems.[16]

[1] SP14/7/82.II. [2] OR. [3] T. Risdon, *Survey of Devon*, 3, 8, 11; M. Wolffe, *Gentry Leaders in Peace and War*, 3-4; M. Stoyle, *Loyalty and Locality*, 14; *Agrarian Hist. of Eng. and Wales* ed. J. Thirsk, iv. 72, 75-6. [4] E. Kerridge, *Textile Manufactures in Early Modern Eng.* 18, 25, 27, 103; *Agrarian Hist.* iv. 73; T. Westcote, *View of Devonshire in 1630*, p. 60. [5] Wolffe, 4; C219/37/79; Stoyle, 18, 21-2. [6] Vivian, *Vis. Devon*, 39-40, 247, 380, 603, 703, 719. [7] Ibid. 702-3; H. St. Maur, *Annals of the Seymours*, 435; C142/296/110; 142/444/76; D.S. Katz, *Philo-Semitism and Readmission of Jews to Eng.* 19; J. Prince, *Worthies of Devon*, 422. [8] *CJ*, i. 185a; A.H.A. Hamilton, *Q.Sess. from Queen Eliz. to Queen Anne*, 36-9. [9] *HMC Hatfield*, xvi. 264. [10] *CJ*, i. 339b, 415a; *SR*, iv. 1157-9. [11] Vivian, 297, 703. [12] *Procs. 1614 (Commons)*, 128-9, 157, 281, 304, 392, 420. [13] Nicholas, *Procs. 1621*, i. 56, 71-2; ii. 89; 'Nicholas 1624', ff. 137, 177; *CJ*, i. 776a. [14] *CJ*, i. 527a; 'Spring 1624', p. 56. [15] D. Hirst, *Representative of the People?*, 203; C219/40/143; *Procs. 1626*, ii. 356; Vivian, 603. [16] *CSP Dom. 1625-6*, pp. 95, 184, 291, 375; 1627-8, pp. 358, 406; Wolffe, 112; Vivian, 39-40; *CD 1628*, iv. 280.

T.M.V./P.M.H.

BARNSTAPLE

Right of election: in the freemen

Number of voters: unknown

27 Feb. 1604	THOMAS HINSON
	GEORGE PEARD
c. Mar. 1614	JOHN GOSTLIN
	JOHN DELBRIDGE
12 Dec. 1620	JOHN DELBRIDGE
	PENTECOST DODDRIDGE
20 Jan. 1624	JOHN DELBRIDGE
	PENTECOST DODDRIDGE
25 Apr. 1625	JOHN DELBRIDGE
	PENTECOST DODDRIDGE
23 Jan. 1626	SIR ALEXANDER ST. JOHN
	JOHN DELBRIDGE
21 Feb. 1628	SIR ALEXANDER ST. JOHN
	JOHN DELBRIDGE

Founded in Saxon times at the head of the Taw estuary, Barnstaple developed into north Devon's principal town, and indeed the county's third richest urban community after Exeter and Plymouth. Although its medieval walls had crumbled by the early seventeenth century, the contemporary historian

Thomas Risdon described it as 'fair built, and populous withal, ... pleasantly and sweetly situate[d] ...; whose streets, in whatsoever weather, are clean and fairly paved'. In 1634, the population was estimated to be almost 8,000.[1] Barnstaple's prosperity derived from trade. Its fairs and markets were regarded as the best in the surrounding area, and it was then the only place in Devon where goldsmiths operated apart from Exeter. However, the mainstay of the local economy was cloth. For several centuries the town had been one of the county's leading centres of textile production. Although the traditional English fabrics were falling out of fashion by the late Tudor period, Barnstaple had responded to the demand for the 'new draperies' by developing a coarse, Flemish-style baize.[2] This commodity, along with other local cloths, was exported in large quantities to western France, Spain, Portugal and the Atlantic Islands. From around 1608 Barnstaple baize was exempted from the payment of impositions in order to encourage the nascent industry. The port's shipping also played a significant role in exploiting the new fishing grounds off the North American coast, and in supplying the early colonies in Virginia and Bermuda, which paid in kind with tobacco.[3]

Despite these many successes, the prevailing wisdom in early Stuart Barnstaple was that the town was on the brink of decline. Despite a major dredging exercise in 1603-5, the harbour was gradually silting up, and by the late 1620s it was so shallow 'that it hardly beareth small vessels'. Consequently, there was mounting concern at the emergence of two commercial rivals, the nearby ports of Bideford and Minehead. Freak flooding in the Bristol Channel in January 1607 caused around £2,000-worth of damage to the town. In the following decade piracy became a serious problem, and the local merchants claimed in 1619 that they could not find the full £500 requested by the government to help fund a naval campaign against the Barbary corsairs.[4] Barnstaple was badly affected by the general slump in the cloth trade at the start of the 1620s, and it was claimed in 1621 that the number of active looms had fallen from 1,000 to just 200. To complicate matters further, sporadic civil war in France disrupted trade with Barnstaple's biggest single market, La Rochelle, leading the corporation to complain in 1622 that many merchants currently had goods trapped there by a blockade. The situation deteriorated further when England went to war against Spain and then France from 1625. With normal commerce effectively suspended, the overall volume of Barnstaple's trade dropped dramatically, despite attempts to boost exports to Ireland and America. The billeting of troops there after the Cadiz expedition

imposed another significant burden on the town, which had spent out £781 on these unwelcome visitors by February 1627. Two months later, the corporation declined to supply two ships demanded by the government for the new fleet assembling at Portsmouth, Hants.[5]

Barnstaple's earliest surviving charter was granted by Henry II. The borough was incorporated in 1557, with the same privileges confirmed in 1596. The corporation was governed by a common council of 25 capital burgesses, from whose number a mayor and two aldermen were elected annually by secret ballot. William Bourchier, 3rd earl of Bath, the most important local landowner, was elected as recorder in 1596 even though this office was not provided for in the borough's charters. This omission was rectified in 1611 by a further charter, whereupon Bath was re-elected on James I's instructions.[6] The borough dealt confidently both with powerful neighbours and with central government. Well aware of the town's importance as a significant source of customs revenues, and as a vital communications link between England and Ireland, the corporation regularly lobbied the Privy Council, seeking both privileges and redress of grievances. In addition to obtaining tax concessions for the baize industry, it secured an investigation at the 1607 assizes into a dispute between the town and a troublesome Devon magistrate, as well as special powers in 1626 to organize its own local militia, in the face of an invasion threat. However, the government evidently tired of the town's assertiveness by 1628, when *quo warranto* proceedings were begun against the corporation, apparently resulting in a £100 fine.[7]

Barnstaple first sent representatives to Parliament in 1295. Elections were held at the guildhall, with the mayor acting as returning officer. The early Stuart indentures were invariably drawn up in the name of the mayor, aldermen and burgesses, and were normally validated simply with the borough seal, though the mayor also signed the return in 1628. Parliamentary wages were paid intermittently, but only ever to the corporation's own nominees, who seem not to have recovered their full expenses.[8] Under the terms of an agreement reached in 1566, the Chichesters of Raleigh, one of the most important local gentry families, were entitled to nominate one of the burgesses at each election. However, while Robert Chichester exercised this privilege as late as 1601, he is not known to have done so subsequently.[9]

In 1604 Barnstaple elected men who had both represented the borough previously. Thomas Hinson was the earl of Bath's receiver-general, and put his master's interests before those of his constituents, to the extent that between 1605 and 1608 he repeatedly attacked the town's recent harbour improvements in the courts. George Peard, in marked contrast, was the borough's fee'd counsel, and he acted as the borough's voice in the Commons, notably in March 1610, when he complained at length about local problems with piracy.[10] In 1614 Bath successfully nominated another of his local clients, John Gostlin, who left no mark on the Parliament's records. Gostlin's partner was a merchant and former mayor of Barnstaple, John Delbridge, who was returned for the borough in every remaining election during this period. He became one of the most prominent and outspoken West Country spokesmen in the Lower House, particularly on any matters affecting his constituency's trade. His stinging attacks in 1621 on the local impact of impositions forced Sir Lionel Cranfield to produce statistics in the Commons on Barnstaple's recent customs revenues. Delbridge also frequently criticized the town's commercial rivals, particularly the Merchant Adventurers and the New England Company, highlighted restrictions on key commodities such as tobacco and wine, and pursued other general grievances like piracy and billeting.[11] Bath is not known to have made a nomination in 1621, but the borough in any case preferred to given its second seat that year to another local merchant and sometime mayor, Pentecost Doddridge, perhaps spurred on by the prevailing crisis in the cloth industry. Doddridge was also returned with Delbridge in 1624 and 1625, though he contributed very little to the proceedings of these three parliaments. The pattern of patronage reverted in 1626 and 1628 to its earlier form, with the borough electing Sir Alexander St. John, brother-in-law to the 4th earl of Bath. It is unclear whether this development simply marked a resurgence in the Bath interest, or whether the town opted to secure the services of a prominent local militia officer in response to the current billeting emergency. However, St. John was apparently content on both occasions to let Delbridge air Barnstaple's grievances as usual.[12]

[1] W.G. Hoskins, *Devon*, 327-8; T. Risdon, *Survey of Devon*, 327; *CSP Dom*. 1634-5, p. 172. [2] Risdon, 328; J.F. Chanter, 'Barnstaple Goldsmiths' Guild', *Reps. and Trans. Devon Assoc*. xlix. 174; Hoskins, 328; E. Kerridge, *Textile Manufactures in Early Modern Eng*. 96, 103-4, 107. [3] E190/939/4; 190/940/2, 4; 190/942/13; 190/944/8; 190/947/5; *HMC Downshire*, ii. 336; *CSP Dom*. 1623-5, p. 496. [4] Risdon, 328; *CJ*, i. 416a; *CSP Dom*. 1634-5, p. 173; *Barnstaple Recs*. ed. J.R. Chanter and T. Wainwright, ii. 134; *APC*, 1618-19, p. 410. [5] *CJ*, i. 633b; *CSP Dom*. 1619-23, p. 398; 1627-8, pp. 43, 141; E190/947/5. [6] J.B. Gribble, *Memorials of Barnstaple*, 255-7, 281, 384; M. Weinbaum, *British Borough Charters 1307-1660*, p. 22; *Barnstaple Recs*. i. 89; ii. 13. [7] *CSP Dom*. 1625-6, p. 363; 1634-5, p. 173; Gribble, 288-9, 294, 629; *HMC Hatfield*, xvi. 6; *Barnstaple Recs*. i.

228; ii. 65. [8] Hoskins, 329; C219/37/7; 219/41B/106; *Barnstaple Recs*. ii. 103. [9] *HP Commons 1558-1603*, i. 143-4. [10] *Vis. Suff*. ed. Howard, i. 192; Gribble, 287, 289-91; *Barnstaple Recs*. ii. 113; *CJ*, i. 404b. [11] J. Roberts, 'Armada Ld. Lt.', *Reps. and Trans. Devon Assoc*. ciii. 114; Gribble, 202; *CJ*, i. 527a, 586b; Nicholas, *Procs. 1621*, ii. 139-40; *CD 1621*, iii. 246; 'Nicholas 1624', ff. 25v, 194; *Procs. 1625*, p. 268; *Procs. 1626*, ii. 150, 154; *CD 1628*, ii. 304, 310. [12] Gribble, 202; *Vis. Beds*. (Harl. Soc. xix), 194; *Barnstaple Recs*. ii. 201.

T.M.V./J.P.F./P.M.H.

BERE ALSTON

Right of election: in the mayor or portreeve and burgesses

Number of voters: 15 in 1626

27 Feb. 1604	Sir Arthur Atye Sir Richard Strode
22 Oct. 1605	Humphrey May *vice* Atye, deceased
1614	Thomas Crewe Sir Richard White
5 Jan. 1621	Thomas Keightley Sir Thomas Wise
21 Jan. 1624	Sir Thomas Cheke William Strode
28 Feb. 1624	Thomas Jermyn *vice* Cheke, chose to sit for Essex
21 Apr. 1625	Sir Thomas Cheke William Strode
18 Jan. 1626	William Strode Thomas Wise
25 Feb. 1628[1]	William Strode Thomas Wise

Bere Alston originated in the late thirteenth century as a small mining settlement within the manor of Bere Ferrers. Granted a market in 1295, and established as a borough shortly afterwards, it passed with the manor into the possession of the lords Willoughby de Broke, and, in 1522, descended to the 2nd lord's coheirs. Still barely more than a large village, Bere Alston was enfranchised in 1584 'at the request of William, marquess of Winchester and William, Lord Mountjoy, chief lords of the town and borough', who initially divided the electoral patronage between them. From 1588, however, in a move that foreshadowed the formal partition of the Willoughby lands in the following decade, Mountjoy became the borough's sole patron. This role was duly inherited in 1594 by his brother, Charles Blount[†], 8th Lord Mountjoy, the distinguished lord deputy of Ireland whose services were rewarded in 1603 with the earldom of Devonshire.[2]

Bere Alston's vulnerability to external pressure manifested itself clearly in the borough's early seventeenth-century election indentures. Returns were normally made in the name of the mayor and burgesses, but the use in 1605 of the alternative term 'portreeve' for the chief officer reflected the absence of the formal structures enjoyed by incorporated boroughs. The character of the indentures was also markedly inconsistent from one election to the next, in both the layout of the text and the choice of language. In 1624 the original indenture was made out in Latin, but at the ensuing election English was employed. Comparatively few of the electors, including the mayors, were able to sign their own names.[3]

For reasons which are unclear, the Blount family generally proved unable to enforce its monopoly over Bere Alston's seats during this period. In 1604 Devonshire successfully nominated his client, Sir Arthur Atye, but the other place went to Sir Richard Strode, eldest son of a prominent local landowner, Sir William Strode*. Atye died at the end of the year. On 3 Oct. 1605 the earl of Salisbury (Robert Cecil[†]) wrote to the borough, requesting that the vacancy be filled by the newly appointed lieutenant of the Tower, Sir William Waad, whom he described as 'a gentleman of very good experience and sufficiency in His Majesty's service, and capable to further anything that may tend to the particular good of your town'. Salisbury added: 'if otherwise you have disposed of your election, my desire is that you will send me word by this bearer, that I may in time provide for some other place for him'. The burgesses evidently replied that they had already made their choice, for Waad was returned at West Looe on 21 Oct., while the next day Bere Alston's seat went to Humphrey May, Devonshire's former gentleman usher.[4]

In the following year, Devonshire died, having placed his estates in trust for the benefit of his eldest illegitimate son, Mountjoy Blount. May himself was one of the trustees, while the overseers of Devonshire's will included the 3rd earl of Southampton. Both men exploited these connections to put forward candidates at Bere Alston.[5] In 1614 Blount secured the election of Sir Richard White, a longstanding member of Southampton's circle. The other burgess-ship went to Thomas Crewe, a notable government critic who conceivably also enjoyed the earl's backing.[6] However,

from this point on, the borough's patronage was once again divided. Although Blount provided a seat in 1621 for Thomas Keightley, one of Southampton's colleagues on the Virginia Company's board, the other place went to Sir Thomas Wise, a Devon gentleman who had probably quite recently acquired property in Bere Alston. Although both elections were held on the same day, Keightley and Wise were returned on separate, albeit matching indentures. As this was the only time that the borough adopted this practice, which was uncommon in Devon, it may indicate uncertainty on the part of the electors over how to respond to Wise's arrival on the scene.[7]

The 1624 general election saw the revival of the Strode interest, with Sir William's younger son William returned at Bere Alston for the first time. Thereafter William represented the borough in every succeeding Parliament until his death in 1645. The senior seat in 1624 initially went to Blount's brother-in-law, Sir Thomas Cheke, but when he opted to sit for Essex he was replaced by Humphrey May's kinsman, Thomas Jermyn.[8] In the first Caroline Parliament Cheke was again returned, and this time he served alongside Strode, but thereafter the Blount interest failed. The 1626 indenture indicates that a show of strength was mounted at the election by the local gentry, as, contrary to the usual pattern, it was signed by Sir Thomas Wise, Sir William Strode and the latter's son-in-law, Sir Francis Drake*. The outcome was the return of William Strode and Wise's son William. The same Members were elected in 1628. Curiously, Strode's name was inserted on the indenture over an erasure. While it is possible that this points to the existence of a third, unidentified candidate and a contested election, the more likely explanation is a tussle over which man took the senior seat, Wise being socially superior but the Strode family enjoying greater local prestige. If the order of the names on the indenture was simply reversed, then it was certainly to Strode's advantage that his sister's father-in-law, Walter Yonge[†], was the presiding sheriff.[9]

[1] OR [2] W.G. Hoskins, Devon, 332; J.J. Alexander, 'Bere Alston as a Parl. Borough', Reps. and Trans. Devon Assoc. xli. 153; HP Commons, 1558-1603, i. 144-5. [3] C219/35/1/128, 137; 219/38/65, 72; 219/41B/112. [4] E214/243; Vivian, Vis. Devon, 719; The Gen. n.s. ix. 177; Hatfield House, ms 112.101; OR; CSP Ire. 1603-6, p. 49. [5] PROB 11/108, f. 2v. [6] Oglander Mems. ed. W.H. Long, 187; Letters and Life of Francis Bacon, ed. J. Spedding, iv. 365. [7] Recs. Virg. Co. ed. S.M. Kingsbury, i. 213; C219/37/13-14; 219/40/150. [8] Vivian, 719; CP, ix. 549; xii. 405-6; Vis. Essex (Harl. Soc. xiii), 177; Vis. Suffolk ed. Howard, i. 295-6. [9] C219/40/150; 219/41B/112; Vivian, 299, 719, 791, 840.

J.P.F./P.M.H.

DARTMOUTH

Right of election: in the freemen

Number of voters: at least seven in 1628

23 Feb. 1604	THOMAS HOLLAND THOMAS GOURNEY
c. Mar. 1614	THOMAS HOLLAND THOMAS GOURNEY
11 Dec. 1620	WILLIAM NYELL ROGER MATHEW
20 Jan. 1624	WILLIAM PLUMLEIGH WILLIAM NYELL
c. Dec. 1624	ROGER MATHEW vice Nyell, deceased
30 Apr. 1625	JOHN UPTON ROGER MATHEW
19 Jan. 1626	JOHN UPTON ROGER MATHEW
23 Feb. 1628	JOHN UPTON ROGER MATHEW Robert Dixon

From its foundation in the twelfth century, Dartmouth was important for its deep natural harbour, in a sheltered location close to the Dart estuary. A base for major mercantile and military voyages during the Middle Ages, the town first returned Members to Parliament in 1298, and secured the right to elect its own mayor in 1341.[1] As the Dart silted up during the sixteenth century, Dartmouth prospered at the expense of Totnes, further upstream. By 1600 it was Devon's second busiest coastal port after Plymouth, with a rapidly expanding population of around 2,000. Local trade revolved around two principal commodities, cloth and fish. Devon dozens were exported mainly to France, but vast quantities of Newfoundland fish were sent as far afield as the Mediterranean and the Canary Islands. Even though many of the merchants engaging in this trade were actually from rival centres such as Totnes and Exeter, the early seventeenth century was one of Dartmouth's most lucrative eras. Only in the late 1620s, when war with France and Spain disrupted trade and the town was burdened with billeted troops, did the local economy experience decline. In 1627 the corporation twice rejected Crown attempts to requisition ships, alleging poverty.[2]

Dartmouth was governed by a mayor, two bailiffs and 12 common councillors, an arrangement confirmed when the borough was enfranchised in mid-1604. This charter also provided for a recorder, town clerk and numerous minor officers.[3] Parliamentary election indentures, which still employed the borough's old composite title of Clifton Dartmouth Hardness, were made out in the name of the mayor, bailiffs and burgesses, and were normally sealed but not signed, thereby obscuring the true size of the electorate.[4] The records for parliamentary wages are incomplete, but the majority of Members were paid, the standard rate apparently being 5s. a day.[5]

Dartmouth's corporation maintained the firmest possible grip over electoral patronage, and normally returned prominent figures from its own ranks to Westminster. Other would-be patrons were invariably rebuffed. In 1614 the borough was approached by several notables, including its high steward, Henry Howard, earl of Northampton, and the Devon magnate Sir George Carey[†], but it refused them all. As the corporation explained to the earl:

> sundry knights and gentlemen of worth by their letters and friends had solicited us that they might serve for this place in this Parliament, and upon making known their desires unto the burgesses and commons of this town for that purpose called together, it was by them all with one voice agreed and resolved that in hope their grievances might be better made known and themselves thereof relieved, they would be at the charge to send burgesses of their place having equal feeling with themselves of the same.[6]

In 1628 a subsequent high steward, the 1st earl of Manchester (Sir Henry Montagu*), nominated his servant Robert Dixon, but met with the same response:

> both privately before and publicly at the election we acquainted the commons who have their voices in the election as well as we. ... But they intreated us to signify to your honour ... that you desire not to prejudice their freedom of election which they have anciently enjoyed, and according to which they have usually made choice of men free of the corporation, and well known unto them.[7]

In point of fact, the corporation was being ingenuous when it blamed the ordinary burgesses for rejecting these overtures. The common council was just as resistant to the commonalty having any say in the nomination process. This oligarchic prejudice was expressed firmly in Parliament in 1624 by William Nyell, the town clerk, during a debate on voting rights at Dover, Kent: 'if it be lawful for every freeman to have a voice, then the more debased and poorer men will choose the burgesses'.[8] Nyell's comment may well have reflected mounting tensions in Dartmouth between the corporation and commonalty, for in 1625 the borough unexpectedly returned an outsider, the local landowner John Upton.[9] His election was forced through by the ordinary burgesses, and this prompted the corporation on the day before the 1626 election to pass a resolution designed to prevent the same thing happening again. This 'constitution' asserted that Dartmouth had customarily chosen men 'free of the borough', and not 'strangers who rather seek the place to the end to pry into their liberties and to sway and rule over the town'. Nevertheless,

> of late some of the freemen of this borough ... out of a contentious and malicious and turbulent humour ... forgetting their oath and duty to this town and opposing themselves to the government thereof ... have practised among themselves and with others ... to make choice of foreigners ... such as in no way acquainted with the town ... its customs, nor experienced in its trades ... nor what may tend to the benefit whereof.[10]

In fact, this move failed to stop Upton's re-election, and he was also returned in 1628, though he never received parliamentary wages, and was evidently not trusted to promote the borough's business in the Commons.

One of the clearest signs that Dartmouth took parliamentary representation seriously is the small number of men dispatched to Westminster during this period. Thomas Holland and Thomas Gourney, both of whom held the mayoralty, served in the 1604-10 and 1614 Parliaments. William Nyell proved himself an effective spokesman in 1621 and 1624, before dying between the prorogation and dissolution of the latter session.[11] Roger Mathew, Nyell's colleague in 1621, was ineligible at the next election, which he presided over as mayor, but he was elected in late 1624 to replace Nyell. In the event, that Parliament did not reconvene, but Mathew went on to partner Upton in every session from 1625 to 1629. In 1624, when Mathew was temporarily unavailable, he was replaced by William Plumleigh, another sometime mayor.

Neither Holland nor Gourney contributed much to debate during their time in the Commons, but they were clearly trusted to handle important business behind the scenes. For example, Gourney stayed on in London after the 1604 session to conclude negotiations for the borough's new charter, while in 1610 the two Members collected an impressive selection of documents detailing the protests in the House against impositions.[12] In subsequent Parliaments, one Member seems to have been nominated as Dartmouth's principal spokesman. Nyell fulfilled this role

in 1621 and 1624, while Mathew took the lead in 1626 and 1628, almost by default, given the circumstances of Upton's elections. In 1621 Nyell possibly introduced the bill against extortionate customs officials, which Mathew also supported. With Dartmouth's cloth trade in mind, Nyell condemned the pretermitted custom, and vigorously attacked the monopolistic ambitions of the London Merchant Adventurers.[13] He had also clearly been briefed to defend Plymouth's bill to preserve free access to the Newfoundland fisheries, in the face of privileges recently granted to Sir Ferdinando Gorges'[†] New England Company. Accordingly, Nyell collaborated with John Glanville on this issue, providing the House with detailed information about the fishing trade, and repeatedly calling for the offending patent to be examined.[14] In 1624 Nyell himself introduced a bill with the same objectives, though the measure failed to become law despite his best efforts to promote it. He also resumed his campaign against the Merchant Adventurers, whom he accused of damaging English trade.[15] The onset of war in the middle of this decade changed Dartmouth's priorities. Accordingly, in the 1626 and 1628 Parliaments Mathew spoke mainly about the threat posed to local shipping by pirates and privateers, the disruption of trade with France, and the problem of soldiers billeted in south Devon. In 1628 he also brought in yet another bill about Newfoundland fishing, which passed the Commons but was lost in the Lords.[16]

[1] W.G. Hoskins, *Devon*, 179, 382-3; P. Russell, *Dartmouth*, 10. [2] T. Gray, 'Fishing and the Commercial World of Early Stuart Dartmouth' in *Tudor and Stuart Devon* ed. T. Gray, M. Rowe and A. Erskine, 174-5, 177-8, 181-2, 189-90; E190/938/11; 190/942/12; 190/947/1; Hoskins, 384; *CSP Dom.* 1627-8, pp. 46, 148. [3] *British Bor. Charters 1307-1660* ed. M. Weinbaum, 24. [4] C219/35/1/123; 219/39/79; 219/41B/110. [5] Devon RO, DD62050, 62109, 62126, 67913. [6] Devon RO, DD61850; SM1989, f. 20; C.F. Patterson, *Urban Patronage in Early Modern Eng.* 246. [7] Devon RO, SM1989, f. 34. [8] 'Nicholas 1624', f. 108. [9] C142/650/140. [10] Devon RO, SM2004, f. 7. [11] PROB 6/11, f. 128. [12] Devon RO, DD61708, 67721, 67723-5. [13] *CD 1621*, ii. 78; iii. 185-6; Nicholas, *Procs. 1621*, i. 330, 333; *CJ*, i. 620b. [14] *CJ*, i. 591b-2a, 644a, 651a; *CD 1621*, iii. 82; Nicholas, ii. 96-7, 178. [15] *CJ*, i. 673a-b; 'Earle 1624', ff. 14v-15, 54v-5; 'Pym 1624', i. f. 59; iii. f. 37. [16] *Procs. 1626*, ii. 91, 132, 298, 379, 385; *CD 1628*, ii. 87; iii. 310; iv. 201.

G.Y./P.M.H.

EXETER

Right of election: in the freemen

Number of voters: unknown

6 Mar. 1604	GEORGE SMITH JOHN PROWSE
1614	JOHN PROWSE THOMAS MARTIN
c. Dec. 1620	JOHN PROWSE IGNATIUS JOURDAIN
1624	NICHOLAS DUCK JOHN PROWSE
1625	NICHOLAS DUCK IGNATIUS JOURDAIN
1626	IGNATIUS JOURDAIN JOHN HAYNE
4 Mar. 1628[1]	IGNATIUS JOURDAIN JOHN LYNNE NICHOLAS MARTIN Nicholas Spicer Adam Bennett

Double return of Jourdain and Martin. JOURDAIN declared elected, 26 Mar. 1628

Founded by the Romans, Exeter flourished through its strategic location on the River Exe, which provided ready access to both the English Channel and most of Devon. Probably England's fourth largest provincial town at the start of the seventeenth century, with a population of around 9,000, it played host to the Devon assizes and Admiralty court, while its cathedral served a diocese covering both Devon and Cornwall.[2] 'The emporium of the western parts', according to the contemporary writer Thomas Westcote, Exeter was the main outlet for cloth produced in north and east Devon and west Somerset. Rising demand for 'new draperies' such as kerseys and perpetuanas made it the country's third wealthiest port until the prolonged economic depressions of the 1620s. The city's merchants ventured as far as Spain, Italy, the Canary Islands, Guinea, Newfoundland and the Baltic, but the mainstay of the local economy was the cloth trade with France, which typically accounted during this period for around half of Exeter's exports. A considerable quantity of Devon cloth was finished in the city's fulling mills, which were powered by water diverted

from the Exe, and textile workers as a whole formed the second largest group among Exeter's freemen. However, the dominant force in the city was its merchant body, incorporated since 1560 as the Exeter French Company. Not only did this organization enjoy a monopoly over the city's wholesale trade with France, but its members invariably formed a majority within Exeter's corporation, which accordingly pursued policies designed to further the Company's interests.[3]

A borough since the twelfth century, early Stuart Exeter possessed the full panoply of civic offices and privileges. Power rested with the 24-member common council, a self-perpetuating oligarchy comprising the city's wealthiest inhabitants. The mayor, recorder and aldermen were all local magistrates. As a county in its own right from 1537, Exeter also possessed its own sheriff and deputy lieutenants, while the corporation enjoyed jurisdiction over the cathedral enclave, much to the annoyance of the ecclesiastical authorities. This administrative independence was jealously guarded. In 1622 Bishop Carey of Exeter sought appointment as a city magistrate, but the corporation's energetic lobbying in London eventually thwarted his proposal, and a new charter in 1627 specifically ruled out this option.[4] Conspicuous during this period for its internal unity, the common council ordinarily also had considerable financial resources at its disposal, derived from its property portfolio and its exclusive management of the city's markets. With a typical annual budget of between £800 and £1,100, the corporation not only undertook large capital projects such as the construction of a new guildhall in the 1590s, but could also fund legislative initiatives at Westminster.[5]

Exeter was represented in Parliament from the late thirteenth century. As with most aspects of civic life, the choice of Members normally rested with the common council. Although the earls of Bedford owned a house in the city, and the corporation invariably chose as its high steward leading peers such as the 1st earl of Salisbury (Robert Cecil[†]) and the 3rd earl of Pembroke, there is no evidence of external patronage. Exeter's early Stuart Members were all corporation figures, usually prominent merchants serving on the common council, though in 1624 and 1625 the borough returned its recorder, Nicholas Duck. In the selection process, personal ability counted for as much as seniority of office. John Prowse, Exeter's most active Member during this period, was merely a middle-ranking common councilman when first elected in 1604, while John Hayne in 1626 had only just joined the corporation.[6] Parliamentary wages were paid at a standard rate of 4s. a day, with allowance made for travelling time and costs. In exceptional circumstances, the common council also voted additional rewards, as in 1608, when Prowse received £20 as compensation for 'his great labour and hindrance' while attending the Commons.[7]

The normal procedure during elections was for the common council to nominate two candidates, who were then approved by voters at the county court. Ostensibly the franchise was vested in Exeter's freemen. The city's freeholders were also allowed to vote in 1588, but there is no clear evidence of this wider electoral body thereafter, and only freemen were allowed a voice under the 1627 charter. The 1604 election return, the sole surviving indenture for this period, merely refers to the mayor and bailiffs, the borough's traditional officers.[8] Ordinarily the common council's nominees were endorsed without argument, but at times of economic hardship rifts tended to emerge between the corporation and the commonalty. In 1604 the latter proposed their own candidates, forcing the common council to concede a poll, though on this occasion the corporation's nominees emerged victorious. A similar situation developed in the later 1620s. According to one report, the freemen forced the election in 1625 of a controversial alderman, Ignatius Jourdain, against the corporation's wishes. On balance, this claim seems doubtful, but the events of the next two elections are unambiguous. When Exeter succumbed to a catastrophic plague epidemic in the autumn of 1625, Jourdain was virtually the only magistrate to remain in the city, his colleagues having fled for their own safety. His heroic efforts to preserve order and tend the sick earned him the lasting gratitude of the masses, and when the corporation failed to propose him for a seat in the 1626 Parliament, the commonalty both nominated and elected him. In retaliation, the common council ruled in the following September that the ordinary freemen would be liable for the parliamentary wages of any further Members that they themselves put forward.[9]

In a further bid to restore its monopoly over nominations, the corporation in February 1628 devised an official shortlist of four names, to allow the commonalty a limited degree of choice, and enjoined the sheriff, John Hakewill (the brother of William Hakewill*), to reject additional nominees. In the event, Jourdain was again proposed as a rival candidate, after Hakewill conceded that such a move was permissible, and in the ensuing poll he emerged victorious alongside the corporation's first-choice nominee, John Lynne. The common council declined to accept

this verdict, and a double return was made to Westminster, with Lynne paired on one indenture with Jourdain, and on the other with the next most popular corporation candidate, Nicholas Martin. Both sides in this dispute apparently also petitioned the Commons, the corporation asserting that its tactic of making four nominations was in fact a long-established custom. On 26 Mar. the House ruled in Jourdain's favour, but in January 1629 his case again came before the committee for privileges, since the common council was refusing to finance him, in line with its ruling of 1626. Under pressure from the Commons, the corporation backed down, but as late as June 1629 it still aimed to recover Jourdain's wages from the commonalty, and finally abandoned this policy only in the following October.[10]

Lynne's election as mayor of Exeter in September 1628 further antagonized the Commons, which refused to allow him to resign his seat so that he could attend to his civic duties.[11] However, such negative behaviour was uncharacteristic of the corporation, which normally sought during this period to engage constructively with Parliament. Enough evidence survives to demonstrate that Exeter's Members corresponded regularly with the common council about developments at Westminster. For example, during the second sitting of 1621, John Prowse and Ignatius Jourdain sent at least five letters, reporting on progress with legislation, particularly supply, the Commons' advice to the king to break off the Spanish treaties, and the disastrous dispute with James over Members' freedom of speech.[12] In 1624 Prowse warned the corporation of the impending disgrace of the lord treasurer (Sir Lionel Cranfield*), Exeter's assistant high steward, and sent down a copy of the king's reply to the Commons' petition against recusants. Four years later, the corporation received copies of the Petition of Right, the Remonstrance against Buckingham, and Charles I's prorogation speech of 26 June.[13]

Such reports were vital, for, as often as not, Exeter's Members arrived at Westminster with specific business to pursue. On several occasions, this involved legislation. The 1606 Act for free trade with Spain, Portugal and France threatened the interests of the city's merchants. Prowse failed to obtain a proviso to protect the privileges of the Exeter French Company, so an explanatory bill was introduced during the 1606-7 session specifically to reaffirm the terms of the Company's charter. Despite considerable opposition in the Commons, the bill received the royal assent.[14] Presumably buoyed up by this success, Exeter's corporation promoted further legislation during the first session of 1610, to protect a recently renewed weir which played a vital role in channelling water to the city's fulling and grist mills. This bill was designed to silence troublesome local opponents of the weir, and the corporation left nothing to chance. Prowse was instructed on 23 Apr. to 'attempt by all the means he can to obtain an Act of Parliament for the settling of the same weir where it is', and he clearly kept the common council abreast of developments. On 22 May, with the bill in committee in the Commons, the corporation began planning for its passage through the Lords, and four days later wrote to the earl of Salisbury asking him 'to give strength to it if it happens to come to the Upper House'. Curiously, they also decided to lobby the 3rd earl of Essex who, as a minor, was not yet attending the Lords, and had no obvious connection with the city. In the event, Salisbury was not named to the Lords' committee, but the bill successfully passed into law at the end of the session. Prowse's expenses for this episode, approved on 14 Aug., shed further light on the lobbying process. He spent in total £64 10s. 6d. Of this amount the lord chancellor (Thomas Egerton†) and the Commons' Speaker, Sir Edward Phelips, each received £10, the clerk of the Parliaments (Robert Bowyer*) £7, and the clerk of the Commons £4. Sums of £10 10s. were also bestowed on the Commons' serjeant-at-arms, and an unnamed civil lawyer. A 'supper for divers gentlemen of the House to make use of their help' came to £1 12s., while 'breviates to deliver abroad' cost £1. Prowse gave 5s. to the keeper of the Exchequer chamber 'where the committees sat', and spent 7s. 6d. on copies of the committee lists for both Houses. Clearly, the process of smoothing a bill's path was well understood. Indeed, the corporation already recognized the value of good relations with key officials, having agreed on 23 Jan. 1610 that the Exeter Members should present the Commons' Speaker with a hogshead of Malaga wine or claret and a baked salmon pie, 'in token of their goodwill'.[15]

The city is not known to have initiated any further legislation during this period, though it perhaps contemplated such a course in 1624, when the bishop of Exeter rejected the corporation's request for a new school. Nicholas Duck, who had been negotiating with the bishop, certainly pondered this option, but concluded in late April that 'to move yet in the Parliament ... would be but a hazard to expend money upon a doubtful event', since the Commons was already fully occupied with bills and petitions. Nevertheless, the corporation undoubtedly recognized Parliament's value as a forum for complaints. When Prowse on 24 Feb. 1621 raised the issue of abuses committed by the patentees for licensing alehouses, persuading the Commons to summon the offenders, he was

reiterating arguments already fruitlessly presented by the corporation to the Crown's law officers during the previous few months.[16] Duck was surely speaking on the city's behalf on 1 Aug. 1625, when he criticized a pardon granted to some Exeter Catholics. Similarly, John Hayne's eloquent pleas in 1626 for a speedy end to the current embargo on trade with France (1 Mar., 17 Apr.) conveyed the desperation of a merchant community economically crippled by this dispute.[17]

It seems likely that Exeter's Members occasionally collaborated with colleagues in the Commons over issues of shared interest. Prowse's nomination on 27 Mar. 1610 to the committee for Sir John Acland's* apprenticeships bill may well have reflected the corporation's backing for the proposed scheme, under which Exeter stood to benefit. In 1626, several Devon boroughs apparently worked together in the Commons to raise grievances about the alnage of clothing and the prisage of wines. No parliamentary evidence for this lobbying now survives, but in the following October the Privy Council, having noted this activity, invited Exeter corporation and other interested parties to make representations to it. Similarly, in 1621 Prowse sponsored a bill to promote the manufacture of new draperies, which seems to have been submitted to Parliament by a Devon gentleman, Walter Morrell, but which was obviously to Exeter's advantage.[18]

The corporation during this period displayed an impressive ability to respond to events as they emerged in Parliament. While it is possible that Hayne used his own initiative on 25 Mar. 1626 in tendering a proviso for Exeter to the bill on exports of dyed and dressed cloth, it is more likely that he first consulted the corporation. In March 1607 Prowse sent down for comment a copy of the bill to regulate weights and measures in market towns, while in April 1614 the common council ordered the urgent dispatch of 'instructions to the burgesses of this city touching their late letters'.[19] A bid in 1604 by the dean and chapter of Exeter to remove the cathedral enclave from the city's jurisdiction prompted a particularly vigorous reaction. Tipped off by Prowse and George Smith that legislation on this issue was expected, the corporation ordered on 21 Apr. that the Members should block 'any bill ... preferred in this Parliament against the city's liberties'. The next day, it wrote to Lord (Robert) Cecil complaining that the dean and chapter 'do now pretend ... to exhibit a bill first into the higher House of this present Parliament, that they may be exempted from us, and be annexed both in possessions and persons to the county of Devon'. The anticipated legislation on the 'boundaries of the county of the city of Exeter' indeed received its first reading in the Lords on 21 Apr., but was lost in committee. Nevertheless, this was doubtless the unnamed bill that the corporation ordered to be entered in its Act Book in the following September. Clearly anxious that the measure might be revived in the next parliamentary session, the common council in December 1604 also appointed a committee, including the two Members, to prepare arguments against the 'suit of the dean and chapter depending in the Parliament House'.[20]

The level of briefing that Exeter's Members could expect was most fully demonstrated in 1624. For once the corporation was still preparing its agenda when the session opened, but on 13 Mar. it authorized a letter to Prowse and Duck, instructing them 'to prefer such grievances as are now sent up by John Chappell from the merchants, ... together with some other grievances touching the state of the city'. One item was doubtless the Exeter merchants' petition against the composition for grocery in the new Book of Rates, referred to in Sir Edwin Sandys' report from the committee for trade on 2 April. However, the Commons' records reveal only part of the city's programme. On 24 Apr. Prowse reported that he had 'possessed the House of Parliament with such things as do most touch the merchants in the burthen of their trade, as they have advised'. He had also secured two readings for a new bill on perpetuanas, while correctly anticipating that it would be lost in committee for lack of time. Stalemate had been reached over the unpopular pretermitted custom, because it touched on the king's prerogative, but he remained hopeful of some concessions. According to Chappell, who had remained in London to assist the two Members, and himself wrote back three days later, other target issues were the prisage of wines, imposts on sugar exports, and the customs allowance on certain types of Devon, Dorset and Somerset cloth. It is worth noting that both of these letters dwell at length on discussions with the bishop of Exeter about the proposed new school, a timely reminder that the corporation's business in London routinely extended beyond the confines of Westminster.[21]

[1] *Procs. 1628*, vi. 150. [2] W.T. MacCaffrey, *Exeter 1540-1640*, pp. 6, 8; P. Clark and P. Slack, *English Towns in Transition 1500-1700*, p. 83. [3] T. Westcote, *View of Devonshire in 1630*, p. 135; W.B. Stephens, *Seventeenth-Cent. Exeter*, 3, 6-9; E190/937/6; 190/947/3; MacCaffrey, 61, 146, 162; W.B. Stephens, 'Merchant Companies and Commercial Policy in Exeter', *Reps. and Trans. Devon Assoc.* lxxxvi. 138-40. [4] MacCaffrey, 16-17, 19, 21, 28-9; C.F. Patterson, *Urban Patronage in Early Modern Eng.* 135-7, 289. [5] MacCaffrey, 22-3, 33, 56-7, 69. [6] Ibid. 222; Westcote, 147; Patterson, 247; Devon RO, ECA Act Bk. 6, p. 118; Act Bk. 7, p. 693. [7] Devon RO, ECA Act Bk. 7, pp. 129, 647; *HMC Exeter*, 321. [8] MacCaffrey, 222-4; C219/35/1/135. [9] D. Hirst, *Representative of the People?*, 203-4; *CD 1628*, ii. 121, 136;

Procs. 1628, vi. 150. [10] Hirst, 204; *CD 1628*, ii. 119, 121, 136; *Procs. 1628*, vi. 150; F. Nicolls, *Life and Death of Mr. Ignatius Jurdain* (1654), p.19; Devon RO, ECA Act Bk. 7, pp. 711, 729, 740-1; *CJ*, i. 924b, 926b; *HMC Exeter*, 189; Vivian, *Vis. Devon*, 437. [11] *CJ*, i. 920a, 924b; [12] *HMC Exeter*, 76-7, 109-13. [13] Ibid. 114, 138, 184-8; Patterson, 39. [14] *CJ*, i. 275a, 324b, 326b; *SR*, iv. 1148. [15] Devon RO, ECA Act Bk. 6, pp. 403, 414; *CJ*, i. 429b; *HMC Exeter*, 321; SP14/54/77; *LJ*, ii. 623b; *SR*, iv. 1173-4. [16] *HMC Exeter*, 137-8; *CD 1621*, ii. 133; Devon RO, ECA Act Bk. 7, pp. 384, 400. [17] *Procs. 1625*, p. 375; *Procs. 1626*, ii. 170; iii. 3, 5, 11. [18] *CJ*, i. 415a; Devon RO, ECA Act Bk. 6, p. 387; *APC, 1626*, p. 337; *CD 1621*, ii. 294; Kyle thesis, 108. [19] *Procs. 1626*, ii. 367; *HMC Exeter*, 78; Devon RO, ECA Act Bk. 7, p. 120. [20] Devon RO, ECA Act Bk. 6, pp. 126, 147, 156; SP14/7/51; *LJ*, ii. 283b. [21] Devon RO, ECA Act Bk. 7, p. 539; *CJ*, i. 752b; *HMC Exeter*, 113, 137-8, 166.

G.Y./P.M.H.

PLYMOUTH

Right of election: in the mayor and commonalty

Number of voters: 37

24 Feb. 1604	SIR RICHARD HAWKINS
	JAMES BAGG I
c. Mar. 1614	SIR WILLIAM STRODE
	THOMAS SHERWILL
11 Dec. 1620	JOHN GLANVILLE
	THOMAS SHERWILL
28 Jan. 1624	JOHN GLANVILLE
	THOMAS SHERWILL
23 Apr. 1625	JOHN GLANVILLE
	THOMAS SHERWILL
20 Jan. 1626	JOHN GLANVILLE
	THOMAS SHERWILL
c. Feb. 1628	JOHN GLANVILLE
	THOMAS SHERWILL

A settlement from Saxon times, Plymouth derived its prosperity from its strategic location at the head of one of the best natural harbours in south-west England. Its prominence as both a port and a royal naval base dated from the thirteenth century. During Elizabeth's reign the town came into its own as the launch pad for English exploration of North America, and the regular departure point for military expeditions against Spain, not least the fleet that harried the 1588 Armada. Between the 1530s and the accession of James I, Plymouth almost doubled in size, and the early seventeenth-century population numbered around 7,000.[1] By the late 1610s, the port was accounted the sixth wealthiest in the country, its merchants trading with the Low Countries, northern and western France, Portugal and Spain, the Canary Islands, Italy, North Africa, Newfoundland and Virginia.[2] One reason for its prosperity was that it served as the main outlet for the Devon cloth manufactured at Tavistock. An even more important commodity was the fish caught in North American waters. During the early seventeenth century the port continued to serve as the customary starting point for transatlantic colonial ventures, such as the short-lived Plymouth Company's New England plantation of 1606-8. However, in general the local merchants viewed American colonists as potential rivals in the lucrative fishing trade, and the New England Company, which from 1620 claimed a monopoly over the vital waters, aroused fierce opposition within the town.[3]

One legacy of the decades of conflict with Spain was Plymouth's firm support for godly Protestantism. This fervour did not yet extend to outright separatism, and the Pilgrim Fathers failed to attract new recruits when they passed through in 1620. Nevertheless, the town was markedly sympathetic towards non-conforming ministers, and many of the leading merchants and corporation members inclined to puritanism.[4] The government disapproved of such tendencies, but continued to value Plymouth as a base for military operations. However, compared with the Elizabethan era, when war against Spain had been accompanied by lucrative privateering activity, the campaigns at the start of Charles I's reign brought few tangible local benefits. Between the spring of 1625 and early 1628, life in the town was repeatedly disrupted by the soldiers billeted there in connection with the expeditions to Cadiz and the Ile de Ré. The troops' presence coincided with a major plague outbreak in 1625-6, which claimed up to 2,000 lives. Trade inevitably suffered during the war, compounding the already serious problem of piracy, and in February 1627 the corporation alleged that these twin difficulties had recently cost the town £44,000. Understandably, relations between Plymouth and the government at the end of this decade were at a low ebb.[5]

Plymouth was incorporated by Henry VI, with subsequent charters augmenting the borough's privileges. At the start of James I's reign, the town was governed by a corporation consisting of a mayor, 12 aldermen and 24 common councilmen. The mayor, recorder and one other alderman acted as magistrates within the borough, which was exempt from the jurisdiction of the main Devon bench. These rights were confirmed by the king in November 1614, while a further charter of March 1628 allowed for two

more aldermen to serve as j.p.s.[6] While not entirely free from internal squabbles, the corporation was generally united in the face of external threats. In 1616-17 Prince Charles attempted to exercise authority over the waters of Sutton Pool, Plymouth's inner harbour, which formed part of the duchy of Cornwall's medieval estates, but after a protracted legal battle the prince leased the harbour to John Sparke* and another townsman. Relations were periodically strained between the corporation and the governor of Plymouth fort, Sir Ferdinando Gorges[†], especially once he became the leading figure in the unpopular New England Company. Efforts by Devon's vice admirals to interfere in the port's operations were also firmly resisted.[7]

Plymouth first sent representatives to Parliament in 1298. In principle the franchise was vested in the whole of the borough's commonalty, but in practice by the early seventeenth century it was exercised exclusively by the corporation. Two of the surviving indentures from this period were signed by the mayor, but the rest simply carried the borough's seal. Plymouth's Members normally received wages at the generous rate of 6s. 8d. a day, though after the 1621 session John Glanville was presented instead with a silver ewer and basin worth £33 17s. 6d.[8]

During Elizabeth's reign, the borough quite frequently accepted nominations from a variety of external patrons, but this practice ceased entirely in the early Stuart period. Only five men sat for Plymouth during these years, of whom three were drawn from the town's merchant community; the other two were recorders of the borough. Sir Richard Hawkins, who took the senior seat in 1604, was then head of the town's leading merchant dynasty, and something of a local hero, as he had only recently returned home after nearly a decade imprisoned in Spain. Contrary to parliamentary convention, he was returned to the Commons while serving as the borough's mayor. His partner was James Bagg I, a former mayor, who had also represented Plymouth in 1601. During the next few years, both men contrived to fall out with the town, Hawkins through his role as Devon's vice admiral, Bagg on account of his corrupt practices as a customs official and his insolent behaviour towards his fellow corporation members.[9] Accordingly, in 1614 the borough opted for a fresh choice, electing its current recorder, Sir William Strode, and another former mayor, Thomas Sherwill, who possessed a fearsome reputation, both for his puritan zeal and for the vigour with which he defended Plymouth's privileges. Sherwill retained his seat through six consecutive parliaments, accompanied from 1621 by Strode's successor as recorder, John Glanville, who proved to be an equally indefatigable champion of the borough's interests. So well did the latter entrench himself in this role that he was even elected in 1626 while absent in Ireland, too ill to travel.[10] Prince Charles's Council twice sent down nominations, on the strength of the prince's claim to Sutton Pool, but there is no evidence that the candidacies of either Edward Salter* in 1621 or Sir Richard Smythe in 1624 were taken seriously by the corporation. According to one apocryphal account, the duke of Buckingham also attempted to secure a seat for one of his clients, perhaps in the late 1620s, but, if the episode ever occurred, nothing came of this either.[11]

The corporation's surviving records shed no significant light on Plymouth's parliamentary agenda, but it is possible to isolate some issues in which the borough took a conspicuous lead in the Commons. In 1614 Strode was the prime mover behind the attempt to overturn the patent of the French Company of London, which interfered with Plymouth's cross-Channel trade. Ironically, it may well have been Strode's reluctance to attack his friend Gorges' New England Company six years later that led to his resignation as recorder.[12] His successor, Glanville, promoted a bill in 1621 for free fishing in American waters, which was designed specifically to cancel out the New England Company's monopoly. He continued this battle in the next two parliaments, in 1624 also persuading the House to rule that Gorges' patent was a grievance.[13] During the 1625 Oxford sitting both Members combined forces to denounce the navy's failure to protect merchant shipping, while in the 1626 session Sherwill was particularly vocal on the twin threats posed by Turkish pirates and Dunkirker privateers. In 1628 Glanville raised local concerns about the abuse of martial law in respect to billeted soldiers, while Sherwill once again presented evidence from Plymouth on the inadequacies of the Navy's coastal patrols.[14]

[1] C. Gill, *Plymouth: a New Hist.* i. 32-3, 57, 66, 136, 154, 157-63, 176, 196; ii. 7. [2] W.B. Stephens, *Seventeenth-Cent. Exeter*, 8; E190/1023/16, 18; 190/1029/19. [3] Stephens, 3; Gill, ii. 7, 10-12; K.R. Andrews, *Trade, Plunder and Settlement*, 326-8; APC, 1618-19, pp. 289-90; 1619-20, pp. 158-9; 1621-3, p. 51; *CSP Dom.* 1619-23, p. 344. [4] Gill, ii. 5-6; R.N. Worth, *Cal. Plymouth Municipal Recs.* 145. [5] *CSP Dom.* 1625-6, pp. 23, 77, 83, 95, 184, 291, 319; 1627-8, pp. 29, 50, 466, 564; APC, 1625-6, pp. 99-100; 1627-8, p. 5; SP16/43/35; L.F. Jewitt, *Hist. Plymouth*, i. 166. [6] Gill, i. 95-7, 213; Worth, 2, 22; Jewitt, i. 136, 169-70. [7] E. Coke, *Reps.* xi. ff. 94-6; Gill, i. 33, 189-90, 199; Worth, 121, 139, 150-1, 218; *CSP Dom.* 1619-23, p. 344. [8] Gill, i. 67; C219/35/1/125; 219/37/12; 219/38/68; 219/39/76; 219/40/145; *Trans. Plymouth Institution*, v. 563-4; W. Devon RO, W132, f. 149; Worth, 153. [9] *HP Commons, 1558-1603*, i. 147; Gill, i. 124-5, 136;

Worth, 22-3, 145-6, 216; APC, 1613-14, pp. 411-12; Coke, xi. ff. 93v-7v. [10] Worth, 23, 85, 205; DWL, J. Quick, 'Icones Sacrae Anglicanae', ff. 403-4, 414; SP16/20/23; *Lismore Pprs.* ed. A.B. Grosart (ser. 1), ii. 173, 177. [11] DCO, 'Letters and Patents, 1620-1', f. 39v; 'Prince Chas. in Spain', f. 33v; DWL, Quick, f. 403. [12] *Procs. 1614 (Commons)*, 58-9, 79, 117, 128; *CSP Dom.* 1598-1601, p. 275. [13] *CD 1621*, ii. 294; iii. 81; *CJ*, i. 630a; 'Spring 1624', p. 39; 'Nicholas 1624', f. 82v; 'Pym 1624', i. f. 59; *Procs. 1625*, p. 274. [14] *Procs. 1625*, p. 460; *Procs. 1626*, ii. 122, 361; *CD 1628*, iii. 308; iv. 208.

J.P.F./P.M.H.

PLYMPTON ERLE

Right of election: in the freemen

Number of voters: unknown

27 Feb. 1604	SIR WILLIAM STRODE SIR HENRY BEAUMONT II
4 Apr. 1604	JOHN HELE *vice* Beaumont, chose to sit for Leicester
22 Oct. 1605	SIR WARWICK HELE *vice* Hele, deceased
1614	SIR WARWICK HELE SAMPSON HELE
11 Dec. 1620	SIR WILLIAM STRODE SIR WARWICK HELE
24 Jan. 1624	SIR FRANCIS DRAKE, bt. JOHN JACOB
22 Apr. 1625	SIR WILLIAM STRODE SIR WARWICK HELE
24 Jan. 1626	THOMAS HELE WILLIAM STRODE
c. Mar. 1626	SIR WILLIAM STRODE *vice* Strode, chose to sit for Bere Alston
25 Feb. 1628	(SIR) THOMAS HELE, (bt.) (SIR) JAMES BAGG II

Plympton Erle grew up around a castle belonging to the earls of Devon, who granted the settlement's first borough charter in 1194. It became a coinage town, a centre for processing Dartmoor tin, in 1328, but local production of this metal declined in the late medieval period, when Plympton was also outstripped economically by the nearby port of Plymouth. By the early seventeenth century the castle had fallen into decay, though the townsfolk still enjoyed a measure of prosperity. Besides the 'much frequented market every Saturday', there were two or three fairs each year, and the local tradesmen had diversified into such activities as wool-combing, tanning and brewing. The adult male population stood at 159 in 1641.[1]

Plympton was incorporated in 1602, with authority vested in a Common Council consisting of the mayor and eight principal burgesses. Other officers included a bailiff and recorder. The Elizabethan charter also confirmed a broad parliamentary franchise which embraced all the freemen.[2] In the early seventeenth century election returns were normally drawn up in the name of the mayor, bailiff and burgesses, although the 1620 indenture was made between the sheriff of Devon and the mayor alone, and simply confirmed that the election had been held with the burgesses' consent. As only the mayor signed these returns, the actual number of voters is unclear.[3] Plympton first sent representatives to Parliament in 1295. For the next two centuries at least the borough's dominant patrons were the Courtenay family, the earls of Devon, who owned not just the castle and its attendant honour, but also the local manor. However, in 1556 the Courtenay estates descended to four coheirs, none of whom was able to exercise the same degree of influence.[4] This vacuum was exploited by the Strode family of Newnham, in the neighbouring parish of Plympton St. Mary, who seem to have nominated all but one of the borough's Members in the last four Elizabethan Parliaments.[5] Their only rival was Sir John Hele[†], whose main seat lay five miles south of Plympton, at Wembury. Having acquired a quarter-share of the castle, manor and borough from one of the Courtenay heirs in 1589, Hele brought in his son in 1601. He further strengthened his position in 1602, when he became the borough's recorder.[6]

The elections for the Jacobean and early Caroline parliaments confirmed that the Strodes had lost ground as patrons of Plympton, though they normally still controlled one seat. Sir William Strode, who had already represented the borough in 1601, was again returned in 1604, 1621 and 1625, while his son-in-law, Sir Francis Drake, served as the senior Member in 1624. When the election was held for the 1626 Parliament, Strode was fully occupied as a commissioner for billeting and martial law at Plymouth, and apparently left his options open by securing seats for his son William at both Plympton and Bere Alston. However, on 18 Feb. William opted to sit for the latter borough, and his father was promptly returned for Plympton in the resultant election.[7] (Sir) James Bagg II, who took the second seat in 1628, probably owed his nomination to Sir William, as the two men had recently collaborated closely in local government. However, Bagg's ownership of Saltram House, another of the gentry houses near Plympton, may have afforded him some independent leverage.[8]

In 1604 Plympton's second seat was initially awarded to Sir Henry Beaumont II, a Leicestershire landowner who presumably owed his nomination to Sir John Hele. No definite connection between the two men has been established, but Hele and Beaumont's father, Francis[†], were contemporaries at the Inner Temple, and also served simultaneously as serjeants-at-law. Moreover, as Beaumont himself attended the Inner Temple, it is not improbable that the two men knew each other.[9] Beaumont, however, subsequently opted to sit for Leicester, whereupon Plympton returned Hele's son John. A further election was called in October 1605 following John's death, and this time the borough chose their recorder's eldest son, Sir Warwick Hele. Having inherited his father's property in 1608, Sir Warwick went on to represent Plympton in 1614, 1621 and 1625. In the first of these Parliaments he was partnered by his cousin, Sampson Hele, a show of electoral strength made easier by Sir William Strode's decision to sit for Plymouth that year.[10] In 1624 the second seat went to John Jacob, a secretary to lord treasurer Middlesex (Sir Lionel Cranfield*). The circumstances are unclear, but Jacob may have been nominated by Sir Warwick, who appears to have been on familiar terms with the lord treasurer.[11] In January 1626 the Hele estates descended to a minor, Sir Warwick's nephew, and the family's interest at Plympton passed to a cousin, Thomas Hele, who owned substantial property near the borough, and had himself returned there in 1626 and 1628.[12]

[1] W.G. Hoskins, *Devon*, 461; G.R. Lewis, *Stannaries*, 90, 149n; J.B. Rowe, *Plympton Erle*, 383, 386, 388; T. Westcote, *View of Devonshire in 1630*, pp. 65, 384-5; *Devon Protestation Returns, 1641* ed. A.J. Howard, 235-6. [2] Rowe, 111-16. [3] C219/37/8; 219/38/75; 219/40/147. [4] Hoskins, 461; Rowe, 16-17, 22-4. [5] *HP Commons, 1558-1603*, i. 147-8; ii. 211, 247; iii. 340, 420. [6] Rowe, 24, 114. [7] Vivian, *Vis. Devon*, 719; *Procs. 1626*, ii. 69. [8] H. Hulme, 'Sir John Eliot and the Vice-Admiralty of Devon', *Cam. Misc.* xvii. pt. 3, p. 29; Hoskins, 463. [9] Nichols, *County of Leicester*, iii. 656; *CITR*, i. 302, 356, 421, *Order of Sjts.-at-Law* ed. J.H. Baker (Selden Soc. suppl. ser. v), 499, 517. [10] Vivian, 461-2, 464. [11] *CJ*, i. 641a. [12] Vivian, 464, 466; C142/423/79.

J.P.F./P.M.H.

TAVISTOCK

Right of election: in the freeholders

Number of voters: at least 16 in 1624

4 Mar. 1604	SIR GEORGE FLEETWOOD
	EDWARD DUNCOMBE
c. Mar. 1614	FRANCIS GLANVILLE
	EDWARD DUNCOMBE
14 Dec. 1620	FRANCIS GLANVILLE
	SIR BAPTIST HICKS, bt.
27 Jan. 1624	JOHN PYM
	SAMPSON HELE
25 Apr. 1625	(SIR) FRANCIS GLANVILLE
	JOHN PYM
17 Jan. 1626	JOHN PYM
1626	SIR JOHN RADCLIFFE
27 Feb. 1628	(SIR) FRANCIS GLANVILLE
	JOHN PYM

A village existed at Tavistock by the tenth century. An important Benedictine abbey was founded there in late Saxon times, and the monks encouraged the settlement's development, obtaining grants of markets and fairs. Borough status was probably achieved during Henry II's reign. Located on the western edge of Devon's tin-mining zone, Tavistock was a stannary town from 1305. In the early Stuart period it was still the county's busiest centre for coinage, the official processing of tin for sale, even though production in Devon had now significantly declined. At this juncture, the town also boasted thriving markets for corn and cloth, production of the latter commodity having replaced tin as the mainstay of the local economy.[1] However, in marked contrast to this relative prosperity, administrative structures remained primitive. Tavistock was not incorporated until 1682, and the borough was still governed in the early seventeenth century on essentially manorial lines, though a rudimentary council, the 'Eight', had begun to exert some influence in the town's affairs.[2]

Tavistock first sent representatives to Westminster in 1295, and had a regular voice in the Commons from the mid-fourteenth century. The parliamentary franchise was vested in the freeholders. The election indentures of 1604 and 1620 were made out in the name of the borough's burgesses only, but subsequent returns invariably also mentioned the bailiff. In both 1620 and 1624 the indentures were signed by at least some of the voters, but ordinarily they simply carried the borough's seal. The normal practice was for both Members to be returned on a single indenture, but in 1626 separate returns were made, of which only one survives. The borough consistently accepted nominations from external patrons, and, unsurprisingly, its particular concerns were never voiced in the Commons by its representatives.[3]

Tavistock's principal patrons in the early Stuart period were the Russell family, who had become lords of the manor after the dissolution of the monasteries. They controlled at least one seat in every election. Their only competitor was Francis Glanville*, a local gentleman resident at Kilworthy, a mile from the town, who also owned a significant amount of property in the borough.[4] In 1604 Edward Russell, 3rd earl of Bedford, took both places, instructing his local agent on 8 Feb. to 'deal earnestly with the Eight of Tavistock for Sir George Fleetwood and Ned [Edward] Duncombe, whom I have specially recommended for burgesses of that place'. Fleetwood was Bedford's kinsman and neighbour, while Duncombe was one of his servants. Ten years later, the first seat was taken by Glanville himself, while Duncombe again served as the junior Member.[5]

In 1617 the earl made over the bulk of his estates to his heir-presumptive, Sir Francis Russell*, who henceforth exercised his family's patronage at Tavistock. Glanville again took the senior seat in 1621, when he was partnered by Sir Baptist Hicks, who probably owed his place to the mediation of Lady Russell's cousin, the 5th Lord Chandos (Grey Brydges†).[6] The principal beneficiary of Russell patronage for the remainder of the decade was Sir Francis' up-and-coming client, John Pym. In 1624 Pym was also returned at Chippenham, but having finally opted on 10 Mar. to sit for Tavistock, he represented the borough in the next three parliaments as well. His junior partner in 1624 was Glanville's brother-in-law, Sampson Hele. At the next election Glanville himself took the senior burgess-ship for the third time, obliging Pym to settle for the second seat. However, Russell achieved a clean sweep in 1626, securing the return of both Pym and Lord Chandos' longstanding friend, Sir John Radcliffe. It is unclear whether the absence of a Glanville candidate and the use of separate indentures points to a genuine electoral battle, or simply a failure by Glanville to make his accustomed nomination this year. In 1628 the normal pattern was restored. Russell, now 4th earl of Bedford, successfully recommended Pym yet again, but Glanville himself took the senior seat.[7]

[1] W.G. Hoskins, *Devon*, 485-6; T. Greeves, 'Four Devon Stannaries', *Tudor and Stuart Devon* ed. T. Gray, M. Rowe and A. Erskine, 41, 52-3, 58, 64; T. Westcote, *View of Devonshire*, 371; S.K. Roberts, *Recovery and Restoration in an Eng. County*, pp. xvi-xvii. [2] Hoskins, 486; H.P.R. Finberg, 'Borough of Tavistock', *Reps. and Trans. Devon Assoc.* lxxix. 136-7; Beds. RO, R3/9. [3] *OR*; *HP Commons, 1509-58*, i. 74; C219/35/1/129; 219/37/11; 219/38/76; 219/39/81; 219/40/144; 219/41B/111. [4] D. and S. Lysons, *Devon*, 475; J. Prince, *Worthies of Devon* (1810), pp. 424-5; C142/271/158. [5] Beds. RO, R3/9; Lipscomb, *Hist. and Antiqs. of Bucks.*, iii. 227; R. Clutterbuck, *Hist. and Antiqs. of Herts.* ii. 107; *CP*, ii. 75-6; vi. 185-6; *CD 1621*, vii. 414-15, 430-1. [6] C. Russell, 'Parl. Career of John Pym', in *Eng. Commonwealth 1547-1640* ed. P. Clark, A.G.T. Smith and N. Tyacke, 150; *CP*, iii. 126-7. [7] Russell, 150; *CJ*, i. 732b; Vivian, *Vis. Devon*, 411; *HMC Downshire*, ii. 400; *HMC De L'Isle and Dudley*, iv. 219.

J.P.F./P.M.H.

TIVERTON

Right of election: in the corporation

Number of voters: 25

20 Dec. 1620	JOHN BAMPFIELD
	JOHN DAVIE
22 Jan. 1624	(SIR) GEORGE CHUDLEIGH, (bt.)
	HUMPHREY WERE
25 Apr. 1625	(SIR) ROWLAND ST. JOHN
	JOHN FRAUNCEIS
c. Jan. 1626	JOHN DRAKE
	PETER BALL
6 Mar. 1626	RICHARD OLIVER *vice* Drake, chose to sit for Devon
20 Feb. 1628	PETER BALL
	JOHN BLUETT

Throughout the medieval period Tiverton was an insignificant settlement, which lay in the shadow of a castle held by the earls of Devon, and possessed only minimal privileges. It was not until the Courtenay family lost most of their power and lands in the mid-sixteenth century that the town escaped this seigneurial stranglehold, and began to achieve economic growth and political independence.[1] During the Elizabethan period Tiverton became Devon's major centre for the manufacture of cloth, particularly kersies. It has been estimated that the population rose by more than one-third in response to this boom, reaching about 4,000 by the first decade of the seventeenth century, at which point the local cloth industry which was believed to be providing work for at least 8,000 people.[2] The cloth was mainly exported to Spain and

France, and such was the self-confidence within the trade that Tiverton was one of five towns to refuse outright the government's suggestion of a London-based French Company in 1609.[3] This era of prosperity lasted into the mid-1620s, by which time the population had apparently risen sharply again to about 6,000, making Tiverton probably Devon's next most important municipality in size and importance after Exeter. Indeed, the assizes were held there in 1626, when a plague outbreak forced their removal from the county town.[4] Nevertheless, by that stage, kersies were losing their market dominance to new cloths such as serges, and trade also suffered in the final years of the decade through the wars with Spain and France, and the accompanying burdens of billeted troops and higher taxation.[5]

This continuing economic success was all the more remarkable for the fact that Tiverton experienced devastating fires in 1598 and 1612, which virtually destroyed its residential infrastructure.[6] The desire to guard against such catastrophes in the future, by providing the town with the protection of municipal authority and law, was the prime motivation behind Tiverton's incorporation in 1615. The charter created an oligarchy consisting of a mayor, 12 capital burgesses, and 12 assistant burgesses, and also provided for the borough's enfranchisement. Although it has been claimed that Tiverton elected two representatives in 1604 on a 'potwalloper' franchise, there is no surviving proof of this episode, and no return was made to Westminster that year. Under the terms of the 1615 charter, the power to elect the borough's two Members was vested exclusively in the corporation.[7] The surviving election returns from this period were all written in Latin, and bore the borough's seal but no signatures. In 1626 the indenture relating to Richard Oliver's election was endorsed: 'deliver this to Mr. Phillips, clerk of the Crown, over the New Exchange in the Strand, with 2s. for the fee'.[8]

Tiverton during this period had no dominant electoral patron. The corporation itself never returned men from its own ranks, but none of the local gentry managed to exert more than a temporary influence either. The principal landowners in the district were probably the Mohun family of Cornwall, who held 'the most entire or largest part' of the much divided manor of Tiverton. However, their only discernible successes came in 1620 and 1624, when they secured the return of their kinsmen John Davie and Sir George Chudleigh.[9] Davie was partnered by John Bampfield, who lived 12 miles from the borough, and most likely relied on the backing of his cousins, the Giffords of

Tiverton Castle, the town's most imposing residence. They may also have assisted the elections in 1626 and 1628 of their distant relative Peter Ball.[10] Sir George Southcote of Calverleigh, three miles from Tiverton, exercised patronage in 1626, possibly nominating his acquaintance John Drake, who subsequently opted to represent Devon instead, and certainly arranging the election of his replacement, Richard Oliver, the duke of Buckingham's receiver-general. Southcote perhaps also lent his support in 1624 to his friend Humphrey Were, the borough's former recorder, who owned a minor property four miles from Tiverton.[11] John Fraunceis and John Bluett, who sat in 1625 and 1628 respectively, were both minor local landowners with strong ties to the borough.[12] Sir Rowland St. John, the other 1625 Member, has not been linked to any local patron, but was possibly nominated by his associate Sir Francis Russell*, lord lieutenant of Devon.[13]

Scarcely any of Tiverton's Members demonstrably attempted to represent the borough's interests in Parliament. Davie and Chudleigh both undoubtedly entered the Commons with a legislative agenda, but the measures concerned were the two bills in 1621 and 1624 to settle the estates of the Mohun family, which they supported in debate.[14] Only Peter Ball is known to have spoken up for his constituents. In 1626 he reminded the House of the money still owed to the inhabitants of Devon and other counties in connection with the soldiers billeted there. Two years later, he again addressed the abuses arising from billeting, supporting moves to petition the king for relief.[15]

[1] J. Youings, 'King James's Charter to Tiverton' (*Reps. and Trans. Devon Assoc.* xcix), 147-56; W.H. Hoskins, *Devon*, 495; M. Dunsford, *Hist. Mems. of Tiverton*, 99-100. [2] Hoskins, 495; Dunsford, 34, 408, 464; Youings, 156. [3] *CSP Dom.* 1603-10, p. 516; A. Friis, *Alderman Cockayne and Cloth Trade*, 165. [4] Dunsford, 46, 462-4. [5] W. Harding, *Tiverton*, 50-52. [6] Youings, 156. [7] Dunsford, 415; Harding, 49. [8] C219/37/10; 219/38/73; 219/39/80; 219/40/62; 219/41B/109, 113. [9] Dunsford, 100; Vivian, *Vis. Devon*, 190, 719. [10] Vivian, 39-40, 227, 399-400. [11] *CSP Dom.* 1625-6, p. 312; PROB 11/145, f. 389v; *HMC Hatfield*, xxiii. 199. [12] Dunsford, 183; D. and S. Lysons, *Devonshire*, 252, 276. [13] PROB 11/212, ff. 225v-6v. [14] *CJ*, i. 623b, 687a; Nicholas, *Procs. 1621*, ii. 86. [15] *Procs. 1626*, ii. 128; *CD 1628*, ii. 369.

G.Y./P.M.H.

TOTNES

Right of election: in the mayor and burgesses

Number of voters: at least 34

23 Feb. 1604	WALTER DOTTYN
	CHRISTOPHER BROOKING
1614	NATHANIEL RICH
	LAWRENCE ADAMS
8 Dec. 1620	SIR EDWARD GILES
	RICHARD RODD
26 Jan. 1624	SIR EDWARD GILES
	ARTHUR CHAMPERNOWNE
19 Apr. 1625	SIR EDWARD SEYMOUR, (bt.)
	SIR EDWARD GILES
23 Jan. 1626	ARTHUR CHAMPERNOWNE
	PHILIP HOLDITCH
21 Feb. 1628	SIR EDWARD GILES
	THOMAS PRESTWOOD

Founded as a Saxon burh, Totnes benefited from its strategic location at the western end of Foss Street, eight miles from the sea on a navigable stretch of the River Dart. The main outlet for tin coined at the nearby stannary town of Ashburton, Totnes also became a centre of cloth production, particularly of Devon 'straits'. For much of the sixteenth century it was accounted the second wealthiest community in the county, its merchants trading with western France and the Iberian peninsula in particular.[1] These patterns of activity continued into the early Stuart period, but economically Totnes was starting to lose ground to its local rivals. Tin production in Ashburton Stannary had now declined sharply, but the debris from the remaining mines silted up the Dart, making it harder for large ships to reach Totnes quay. Accordingly, the commercial focus began to shift downstream to the rapidly expanding port of Dartmouth. However, while many Totnes merchants operated there, new commercial opportunities seemed to pass them by. Few acquired a stake in the lucrative Newfoundland fisheries, and Totnes also failed to respond to the latest trends in cloth manufacture, the so-called new draperies. In 1636 the town was still rated as Devon's fifth richest, but by now many of the wealthier merchants were scaling down their trading ventures and instead investing in land.[2]

Totnes received its first borough charter from King John, and was incorporated in 1505. Initially the governing structure consisted of a mayor, recorder and a single council of burgesses. However, in 1596 power was concentrated in the hands of the town's leading merchants when a further charter redefined the corporation as a governing body of 14 'masters', including the mayor, with an inferior council of 20 burgesses. These masters formed a closed oligarchy, filling vacancies in their ranks by co-option, and nominating the mayoral candidates. The lesser burgesses petitioned the Privy Council against this new system in the following year, but their complaint was rejected.[3]

Ever since the Model Parliament of 1295 Totnes had enjoyed regular representation in the Commons. Early seventeenth-century election returns were made in the name of the mayor and burgesses. In 1626 the indenture was signed by the mayor, Nicholas Wise, but ordinarily the borough seal was the only authenticating mark employed. This customary absence of voters' signatures may well indicate that the 'masters' dominated the electoral process. However, the franchise was formally vested in the burgesses as a whole, and in 1616 the corporation asserted that, upon reports of a Parliament, a meeting of townsmen was summoned to discuss the choice of Members. There is no evidence that successful candidates during this period received wages.[4] In terms of electoral patronage, the corporation was relatively independent. Since 1559 the lords of the manor, the Edgcumbes of Mount Edgcumbe, Cornwall, had leased their manorial rights to the mayor and burgesses, and although the family ostensibly retained the privilege of nominating one Member unless both seats were taken by townsmen, this claim was in practice unenforceable. Sir Richard Edgcumbe*, who had himself represented Totnes in 1589, wrote to the borough in February 1616 noting that a Parliament was expected, and requesting one seat should there be an election (which, in the event, there was not). Even though his father-in-law, Sir George Carey[†], was then recorder, Edgcumbe was still rebuffed by the corporation, which replied simply that it had already decided to return two of its own members.[5]

Ordinarily during this period, at least one seat was taken by a townsman. In 1601, indeed, two corporation members were returned, and this pattern was repeated in 1604, when the choice fell on Walter Dottyn and Christopher Brooking, both former mayors, who had recently played key roles in defending the borough's management of the local almshouses. At Westminster they were probably responsible for the introduction in March 1606 of a bill to confirm lands granted to corporations for charitable purposes, but the measure failed to complete its passage through the Commons.[6]

Their successor in 1614 was Lawrence Adams, who was probably one of the 'masters', since he became mayor in the following year. Like Dottyn and Brooking, he had already represented the borough's interests in the capital, delivering a letter in 1613 to the earl of Northampton, the borough's high steward, which complained that local merchants were being penalized by the new, London-dominated, French Company. There is no evidence that Northampton made any effort to redress this grievance, even though Totnes could quite correctly state that Parliament had in 1605-6 guaranteed free trade with France.[7] Despite this impasse, the earl wrote to the borough in February 1614, requesting the nomination of one Commons' seat. The corporation, with a superficial show of great regret, responded that it was unable to comply, as one place was reserved for a townsman, and the other was in the gift of the recorder, Carey, who declined to relinquish this privilege. The latter's choice fell on his kinsman by marriage, Nathaniel Rich. Carey died two years later, and there is no evidence that his successor as recorder, William Bastard, attempted to make nominations.[8]

For the 1621 Parliament Totnes returned another former mayor, Richard Rodd, but awarded the senior seat to Sir Edward Giles, a prominent Devon gentleman resident just outside the town, who had already sat for the borough in 1597. Giles had doubtless won local favour by attacking the French Company in the Commons in 1614. He proved himself an effective advocate of Totnes's interests in 1621 as well, addressing a range of economic concerns, including the impact of impositions on the Devon kersey industry, an issue that had already prompted the town's merchants to petition the Privy Council.[9] Giles's usefulness in this regard doubtless assisted his re-election by the borough in 1624, and may also have influenced the corporation's decision to offer the second seat not to a townsman but to another local gentleman, Arthur Champernowne of Dartington Hall, who himself possessed commercial interests. Giles retained his hold over the borough's electorate in the following year, but was this time partnered by another major Devon figure, Sir Edward Seymour, who owned the barony of Totnes, and lived just three miles from the town at Berry Pomeroy.[10] In 1626 Giles is not known to have stood, and the corporation once again returned one of its own members, Philip Holditch. The senior place went to Champernowne, whose value to the town was enhanced by his current role as a Devon billeting commissioner, in which capacity Totnes also sought his assistance later in the year. Holditch and Champernowne left no mark on the Commons' records that year, but clearly conducted business of some sort on their constituents' behalf, for they wrote to the corporation from London. Conceivably they joined in the complaints made by several Devon towns during the Parliament against abuses committed in the alnage of cloth, but no firm details of these protests have been found. In 1628 Giles resumed his accustomed seat, and protested vigorously in the Commons against billeting. He was partnered by another corporation member, Thomas Prestwood, who was apparently content to let Giles represent the borough's interests.[11]

[1] W.G. Hoskins, *Devon*, 504; T. Westcote, *View of Devonshire in 1630*, p. 412; T. Greeves, 'Four Devon Stannaries', in *Tudor and Stuart Devon* ed. T. Gray, M. Rowe and A. Erskine, 43; E. Kerridge, *Textile Manufactures in Early Modern Eng.* 27; P. Russell, *Good Town of Totnes*, 45-6. [2] E190/938/11, 14; 190/942/12; 190/943/10; Greeves, 45; T. Gray, 'Early Stuart Dartmouth', in *Tudor and Stuart Devon* ed. Gray, Rowe and Erskine, 175; Russell, 57, 61; Hoskins, 506; E179/102/463. [3] D. and S. Lysons, *Devonshire*, 532; M. Weinbaum, *British Bor. Charters 1307-1660*, pp. 27-8; *HP Commons, 1558-1603*, i. 149; E. Windeatt, 'Totnes Mayors', in *Reps. and Trans. Devon Assoc.* xxxii. 111; *APC*, 1597-8, pp. 168, 507. [4] Lysons, 532; *OR*; W. Cotton, *Antiqs. of Totnes*, 10; C219/35/1/126; 219/40/146; Devon RO, 1579A-O/12/9. [5] Russell, 54; Devon RO, 1579A-O/12/8-9; Vivian, *Vis. Cornw.* 142. [6] *HP Commons, 1558-1603*, i. 149; Devon RO, 1579A-O/10/17, 20-1, 23a; *CJ*, i. 277a, 312a. [7] Devon RO, 1579A-O/16/32, 35; *SR*, iv. 1083; *APC*, 1613-14, p. 206; C.F. Patterson, *Urban Patronage in Early Modern Eng.* 253. [8] E. Windeatt, 'Totnes Mayors', *Western Antiquary*, x. 147-8; Devon RO, 1579A-O/12/5-6; *Vis. Essex* (Harl. Soc. xiii), 277-8; Harl. 3959, f. 16; *Vis. Devon* (Harl. Soc. vi), 334. [9] T. Risdon, *Survey of Devon*, 166; *Procs. 1614 (Commons)*, 129, 405; *CD 1621*, ii. 75-6; *CSP Dom.* 1611-18, pp. 548, 554. [10] C142/232/69; P. Russell and G. Yorke, 'Kingswear and Neighbourhood', *Reps. and Trans. Devon Assoc.* lxxxv. 68; Windeatt, *Western Antiquary*, x. 148. [11] Devon RO, 1579A-O/7/1/20; *APC*, 1626, pp. 337-8; *CD 1628*, ii. 80, 253; iv. 283.

G.Y./P.M.H.

DORSET

Number of voters: over 1,000 in 1626

c. Feb. 1604	SIR THOMAS FREKE
	JOHN WILLIAMS[1]
c. Mar. 1614	SIR MERVYN AUDLEY
	SIR JOHN STRANGWAYS
11 Dec. 1620	SIR JOHN STRANGWAYS
	SIR THOMAS TRENCHARD
2 Feb. 1624	SIR JOHN STRANGWAYS
	(SIR) GEORGE HORSEY
	Sir Nathaniel Napper
25 Apr. 1625	(SIR) WALTER EARLE
	SIR NATHANIEL NAPPER

30 Jan. 1626	SIR GEORGE MORTON, bt.	
	SIR THOMAS FREKE	
	John Browne II	
	Morton's election declared void, 17 Feb. 1626	
27 Feb. 1626	SIR GEORGE MORTON, bt.	511
	John Browne II	498
25 Feb. 1628	SIR JOHN STRANGWAYS	
	(SIR) WALTER EARLE	

One of the smaller English counties, Dorset in this period largely depended for its prosperity on its 'great flocks of sheep', the basis of the local cloth trade, though it was also the country's leading producer of hemp and flax, the raw materials for rope and fishing nets. The extensive coastline boasted several good harbours, notably at Poole and Weymouth. Although its ports were less important than those of neighbouring Devon and Hampshire, there were strong trading links with France, while Poole was a major base for the burgeoning Newfoundland fisheries. Shire elections were held at Dorchester, the county town, which was notable principally for its ancient earthworks and the puritan leanings of its residents.[2]

Predictably, the men who represented Dorset in this period were drawn from the county's wealthiest families. All nine had already received the honour of knighthood by the time of their election, except for John Williams, who was dubbed before the 1604 Parliament met, and Sir George Morton, the county's first baronet. A lengthy pedigree was doubtless also an advantage, but it was not essential. Though Sir John Strangways' ancestors had owned land in Dorset since the fifteenth century, Sir Thomas Freke was a second-generation resident, whose father had purchased his estates with the proceeds of a successful Exchequer career.[3] For administrative purposes the county was split into Eastern and Western divisions, but this bifurcation had no effect on the selection of the knights of the shire, which was normally agreed in advance by the leading gentry in order to avoid contests.[4] In contrast to the Elizabethan era, when local peers apparently influenced some elections, there is no firm evidence of aristocratic pressure during the early seventeenth century. The earls of Suffolk, who held the lieutenancy for most of this period, were non-resident, while the 1st earl of Bristol (Sir John Digby*), who lived at Sherborne, was a newcomer who spent much of his time abroad on embassies, or at home in disgrace.[5] Indeed, the disputed 1626 election, in which Dorchester residents almost imposed their own candidate, suggests that the gentry's grip on the selection process was threatened more from below than from above.[6]

Dorset's first three Jacobean elections passed off without incident, the county's choice falling each time on men linked in some way to Sir George Trenchard[†], arguably the leading local gentleman of the late Elizabethan period. His son Sir Thomas was returned to the 1621 Parliament, while his son-in-law Sir John Strangways sat both in that assembly and that of 1614. Sir Thomas Freke and John Williams, who served in the 1604-10 Parliament, were evidently also on close terms with Trenchard, for they each subsequently married one of their children to Sir George's offspring. Only Sir Mervyn Audley, the senior knight in 1614, did not belong to this kinship group. However, he was a close friend of Strangways, and may also have been encouraged to stand by his relative Sir Francis Bacon*, then attorney-general.[7]

The electoral dominance of this gentry alliance was finally challenged in 1624. By now Sir George Trenchard was in his mid-seventies, his mantle of leadership having apparently passed to Strangways, who was elected for a third consecutive time. Although the latter's grandfather had achieved the same feat in the 1550s, no one since had sought to monopolize a Dorset seat to this extent, and Sir John's latest success effectively triggered a contest for the second place. According to Edward Pitt*, most observers expected Strangways' partner to be Freke's son-in-law, Sir George Horsey, who himself came from a long line of Dorset shire knights. However, a challenge was mounted by Sir Nathaniel Napper, an increasingly active figure in county government, who did not belong to the Trenchard-Strangways clique.[8] Although from the outset Napper's chances looked slim, his opponent took no chances. As William Whiteway II* recorded:

> Sir Nathaniel Napper stood for the place, being promised that Sir George Horsey should not stand, and thereupon leaving most of his freeholders behind. The cry was very confused, so that the sheriff swore the freeholders that came to give their voices, and Sir Nathaniel lost it by 70 voices. But the contrary faction had such a blot cast upon them for their double-dealing that they will not easily wipe it off.[9]

Not surprisingly, the 1625 election marked a sea-change in local politics. Strangways opted for a borough seat, his reputation now further diminished by his close association with the earl of Bristol, who was then effectively under house arrest for his part in the abortive Spanish Match negotiations. Horsey, presumably still in bad odour from his earlier

trickery, seems not to have sought membership of the Commons at all. In their place, the county returned Napper and Sir Walter Earle, another independent figure within Dorset's elite. This verdict was shortly afterwards endorsed by the 1st earl of Suffolk, who promoted both men to the rank of deputy lieutenant at the expense of Strangways and Sir George Trenchard.[10]

Notwithstanding this double snub, in 1626 an unrepentant Strangways achieved a remarkable comeback. Although he again chose to represent a borough, he also made a determined effort to manipulate the shire election. His preferred candidate was his relative Sir George Morton, who at the time was not actually living in Dorset, and was therefore unlikely to be a popular choice. Accordingly, when the gentry gathered at Blandford Forum to settle on two nominees, Strangways left the meeting before any decision had been reached, and instead primed his supporters simply to vote at Dorchester as directed on the day. However, this strategy almost backfired. When the voters gathered on 30 Jan., there was general agreement that the senior place should go to Sir Thomas Freke, 'in respect of his age and gravity', but Strangways was slow to announce Morton's candidacy. With the second seat apparently still wide open, the Dorchester freeholders seized the initiative, and nominated one of their own neighbours, John Browne II*. From the surviving accounts of this election, it is unclear whether Browne himself was expecting this development. As the clamour increased for him to be chosen, he 'disclaimed the place and got out of the company', encouraged by his father, Sir John Browne, who was reportedly reluctant to offend Strangways and his allies. Browne's position was indeed difficult, for he was both Strangways' brother-in-law and Morton's kinsman. Nevertheless, the Morton camp proved unable to shout down Browne's supporters, and a poll became necessary to settle the result. Strangways was clearly rattled by the turn of events, and pressured the aged sheriff, Francis Chaldecot, into agreeing that voters must swear that they had actually been present at the reading of the election writ. This oath was then rigidly applied to Browne's supporters, but not to Morton's. Even so, despite further frantic efforts to recruit additional voters for Sir George, and with the final count conducted in a local tavern to restrict the number of witnesses, Morton was eventually deemed to have beaten Browne by a single vote.[11]

When the Parliament met, Browne's friends petitioned the Commons, which ruled on 17 Feb. that

Morton had not been properly elected, not least because of the imposition of an illegal oath on the voters. The resulting election was again fought between Morton and Browne, but Strangways' manoeuvring had alienated some members of his own circle, including Sir George Trenchard, who now threw his support behind Browne, his son-in-law. However, Strangways remained resolutely behind Morton, who was also supported by Sir Thomas Freke. Once again the election went to a poll, and as before the sheriff demonstrated bias towards Morton. Browne allegedly mustered more votes than his rival, only to have many of them suppressed, but at the end of the day 'Mr. Browne was found to have but 498 voices and the baronet 511'. This time the result went unchallenged.[12]

Strangways' actions in dividing his own supporters might have been expected to end his own hopes of representing the county again. However, the political climate was transformed in the next 18 months by the introduction of unpopular government measures. In July 1626 the Dorset bench confounded the Privy Council by presenting a constitutional argument against a new levy of shipping, securing a reduction of one-third in the assessment on the county. Soon afterwards, the Forced Loan pushed both Strangways and Sir Walter Earle into the role of martyrs, as they were imprisoned for publicly opposing this arbitrary taxation. Earle achieved particular fame as one of the Five Knights who contested their detention in the courts. Billeting of soldiers in the county proved to be another oppressive burden, and by the time of the 1628 election the clamour for reform had become deafening. As the two Dorset men most closely identified with resistance to the Crown's policies, Strangways and Earle were returned unopposed, living up to expectations in the Commons by delivering vigorous attacks on billeting and the Forced Loan.[13]

[1] SP14/7/82 II. [2] Camden, *Britannia* (1772), i. 169, 171; J.H. Bettey, *Dorset*, 48-9, 75, 77, 80, 102; *William Whiteway of Dorchester* (Dorset Rec. Soc. xii), 71. [3] Hutchins, *Dorset*, ii. 660-1; iv. 89, 99. [4] *Dorset Q. Sess. Order Bk.* ed. T. Hearing and S. Bridges (Dorset Rec. Soc. xiv), p. ix; J.K. Gruenfelder, 'Dorsetshire Elections, 1604-40', *Albion*, x. 2. [5] *HP Commons, 1558-1603*, i. 149; *CP*, ii. 320; xiiA. 464, 467. [6] Gruenfelder, 8. [7] *HP Commons, 1558-1603*, iii. 526-7; *Vis. Dorset* (Harl. Soc. xx), 94; *The Ancestor*, x. 198; Hutchins, ii. 524, 714; C.B. Herrup, *A House in Gross Disorder*, 12. [8] *OR*; Add. 29974, f. 76. [9] *William Whiteway of Dorchester*, 58. [10] Ibid. 72. [11] *Vis. Dorset*, 79, 94; Hutchins, ii. 595; *Som. and Dorset N and Q*, iv. 23. [12] *Procs. 1626*, ii. 55, 61-2; *Som. and Dorset N and Q*, iv. 24. [13] *APC, 1626*, pp. 130-1; R. Cust, *Forced Loan*, 167, 233; Gruenfelder, 10-11; *CD 1628*, ii. 286, 361.

J.P.F./P.M.H.

BRIDPORT

Right of election: in the burgesses and commonalty

Number of voters: 15 between 1614 and 1626

27 Feb. 1604	SIR ROBERT MELLER
	JOHN PITT
c. Mar. 1614	SIR WILLIAM BAMPFIELD
	JOHN JEFFERY
21 Dec. 1620	JOHN STRODE
	JOHN BROWNE II
23 Jan. 1624	ROBERT BROWNE
	WILLIAM MUSCHAMP
3 May 1625	(SIR) JOHN STRODE
	SIR LEWIS DYVE
12 Jan. 1626	SIR LEWIS DYVE
	SIR RICHARD STRODE
5 Mar. 1628	FRANCIS DRAKE
	JOHN BROWNE II
	Thomas Powlett
	Bampfield Chafin

Election declared void, 12 Apr. 1628

22 Apr. 1628	THOMAS POWLETT
	BAMPFIELD CHAFIN

Bridport received its first charter in 1253, and was represented in the Model Parliament. Cordage and linen thread formed the town's staple products, and the Act of 1529 requiring local farmers to sell all their hemp there was among the statutes renewed in 1624 and 1628. Though Bridport hosted the Dorset quarter sessions until its incorporation in 1619, and was home to nearly 1,500 communicants, its houses were 'more old than fair', and its harbour 'altogether choked with the sands' by the early seventeenth century.[1] The franchise was vested in the burgesses and commonalty. Judging from a leet book of 1638, the potential voters may have numbered over 400. However, between 1614 and 1626 elections were monopolized by the chief burgesses or corporation, a body of just 15 men. Parliamentary returns were made by the two bailiffs 'with the whole assent and consent of the burgesses'.[2]

The borough's principal electoral patron was Sir George Trenchard[†] of Wolveton, one of Dorset's leading gentlemen, who secured at least one seat in every election during this period. His nominee in 1604 was his step-sister's husband, Sir Robert Meller. The second place went to John Pitt, the only townsman returned in the early seventeenth century. Over 40 of the commonalty participated in this election, apparently because Pitt required parliamentary wages from the borough. At the opening of the second session of 1610 it was claimed that one of the Bridport Members was incurably sick. However, the motion for a new writ was defeated on 24 Oct., and it is not known whether Meller or Pitt was the anonymous invalid. Both men lived on for a number of years.[3] In 1614 the borough elected Trenchard's brother-in-law, Sir William Bampfield, who was partnered by John Jeffery, the younger brother of a local gentleman.[4]

Over the next few years religion began to play a significant role in Bridport politics. By 1613 a flourishing conventicle, attracting over 100 worshippers, had been established there under the spiritual guidance of John Traske, 'a young, hot-headed and excommunicated minister', and John Sacheverell, 'a young schoolmaster and preacher of the same sect or opinion'. Lay leadership was provided by a feltmaker called Robert Millar, who by sheer force of character achieved a dominant position in the borough.[5] It was later alleged that 'Millar, whiles he lived, bore the greatest sway of any in the said town of Bridport', and that 'he and his friends most prevailed in electing [as] the bailiffs of the said town [such] as best pleased him'. It was Millar who obtained the incorporation of the borough in 1619 at a cost of £150, more than twice the sum he was authorized to spend. In the new charter the town clerk and four ex-bailiffs were dropped from the council, and of the 15 'capital burgesses', who formed a self-perpetuating body, ten were members of Traske's congregation. Controversially, the charter also permitted the bailiffs to act as justices of the peace within the borough, on the grounds that there were no county magistrates resident in the neighbourhood. John Strode, Sacheverell's ecclesiastical patron, had already been appointed recorder in 1618, and now retained this position.[6]

At the election of December 1620, Strode himself took the first seat, while the second went to Trenchard's son-in-law, John Browne. In 1624 Sir George secured the nomination of both burgess-ships, his choice falling on Browne's cousin, Robert Browne, and William Muschamp, the brother-in-law of Trenchard's step-son, Bampfield Chafin. With Millar acting as senior bailiff in the following year, Strode regained his seat, but he was accompanied by Sir Lewis Dyve, stepson of the 1st earl of Bristol (Sir John Digby*), and the husband of Trenchard's granddaughter. In 1625 Bridport's commonalty requested the right to participate in the election, but were denied.[7]

The 1626 election saw competition for Bridport's seats. Dyve was again returned, smoothing his path by bestowing on the borough 'one silver salt-cellar ... to be delivered from elder bailiff to elder bailiff at the end of their year for ever, to serve to stand upon their tables at their court dinners and feasts'. However, shortly after the corporation had promised Dyve a place, it received a letter from Bristol's enemy, the duke of Buckingham, asking them to elect the latter's servant Edward Clarke* and Sir Richard Strode, a Dorset gentleman. Although Strode had long been at odds with his kinsman John Strode over a disputed inheritance, he was also one of John Traske's patrons, which rendered him acceptable to the rest of the corporation. Accordingly, Sir Richard secured the junior seat 'by the consent of all that have here voices in our election, he being a man whom we well know, and did incline to make choice of him before'. Curiously, on this occasion the election return was dated 12 Jan., four days before Buckingham's nominations arrived, and two days before the corporation claimed to have chosen Dyve. Perhaps this was an attempt to avoid subsequent complaints. The duke was not notified of Clarke's rejection until 28 Jan., and the news was evidently not well received. When the Parliament met, Sir Richard Strode accused Dyve of obtaining his seat by corruption, but on 21 Feb. Dyve was cleared, having satisfied the House that his gift to the borough had not influenced the result.[8]

Millar died in the plague which struck Bridport in the following autumn, and his removal from the scene emboldened his enemies there, for in Michaelmas term 1627 the new charter was challenged in the Exchequer, though not overturned.[9] Consequently, at the next election in 1628 the corporation was again opposed. Its preferred candidates were John Browne, representing the Trenchard interest, and Francis Drake, who had possibly been nominated by his cousin, John Drake*, another of Traske's admirers. As usual the commonalty were not summoned to the election, but they attended anyway, and threw their support behind rival candidates, Thomas Powlett, a minor local gentleman, and another Trenchard kinsman, Bampfield Chafin.[10] The corporation returned Browne and Drake regardless, but were forced to defend the narrow franchise after a petition was lodged with the Commons. They presented to the privileges committee 'a certificate of disclaimer under the hands of 80 commoners, ... and affirmed they could have proved it by 40 commoners more'. In response, the rival camp produced four earlier returns which demonstrated that the commonalty had participated in former elections, and one of the bailiffs was alleged to have conceded this point privately. Accordingly, the election was declared void on 12 Apr., and Powlett and Chafin were returned at the ensuing election.[11]

[1] Hutchins, *Dorset*, ii. 7; T. Gerard, *Survey of Dorset*, 19, 22-3; *SR*, iv. 1235; v. 28; E134/3Chas.I/Mich. 48. [2] *CD 1628*, ii. 428-30; Dorset RO, B3/E6; Hutchins, ii. 7; C219/37/92. [3] Hutchins, ii. 10; iii. 326; *Vis. Hants* (Harl. Soc. lxiv), 10; *CD 1628*, ii. 428; *Procs. 1610* ed. E.R. Foster, ii. 387. [4] Hutchins, iii. 565; *Som. Wills* ed. F. Brown, v. 61. [5] STAC 8/214/2; PROB 11/150, f. 281. [6] E134/3Chas.I/Mich. 48; Hutchins, ii. 7; Dorset RO, MW/M4. [7] Hutchins, ii. 556; iii. 565; iv. 43; *Oglander Mems.* ed. W.H. Long, 80; C219/39/90; *Vis. Dorset* (Harl. Soc. xx), 94; *CD 1628*, ii. 429. [8] Hutchins, ii. 12; SP16/19/69; C78/534/2; C3/415/119; D.S. Katz, *Philo-Semitism and Readmission of Jews to Eng.* 31; C219/40/216; *Procs. 1626*, ii. 60, 62, 82. [9] PROB 11/150, f. 281; *CSP Dom.* 1625-6, p. 483; E134/3Chas.I/Mich. 48. [10] Vivian, *Vis. Devon*, 297; Katz, 19; Hutchins, ii. 281. [11] *CD 1628*, ii. 37, 397, 404, 428-30.

J.P.F.

CORFE CASTLE

Right of election: in the burgesses and commonalty

Number of voters: at least 8 in 1620

26 Feb. 1604	SIR JOHN HOBART I EDWARD DACKOMBE
c.Mar. 1614	SIR JOHN DACKOMBE JAMES WHITELOCKE
aft.9 Apr. 1614[1]	SIR THOMAS TRACY *vice* Whitelocke, chose to sit for New Woodstock
31 Dec. 1620	SIR THOMAS HATTON SIR THOMAS HAMMON
31 Jan. 1624	SIR FRANCIS NETHERSOLE SIR PETER OSBORNE
10 May 1625	SIR PETER OSBORNE SIR FRANCIS NETHERSOLE
27 Jan. 1626	SIR ROBERT NAPIER EDWARD DACKOMBE
13 Mar. 1628	SIR FRANCIS NETHERSOLE GILES GREENE

The little town of Corfe was dominated by its castle, which Elizabeth I granted to her favourite Sir Christopher Hatton[†]. At his request the town was enfranchised in 1572 and incorporated four years later. The corporation consisted of a mayor and a bailiff, elected annually, and an uncertain number of 'barons', the title given to all those who had served as mayor. The Isle of Purbeck, in which Corfe is situated, still provided excellent sport, including red deer, and there were a number of resident gentry families, notably the Dackombes. The franchise was broad; although election indentures during this period typically listed around six corporation members, returns were made 'with the consent, assent, express agreement and nomination of all and singular the other barons and burgesses with the commonalty'.[2]

The dominant electoral patron during this period was Lady Hatton, the widow of Sir Christopher's nephew and heir. In 1604 she still seems to have been on reasonable terms with her second husband, Sir Edward Coke*, and they agreed on Sir John Hobart, a Norfolk man like Coke, who frequently acted as Lady Hatton's London agent. On 10 Mar. the corporation, describing themselves as 'your worship's unknown yet kind poor friends', wrote to Hobart to say that they had elected him at Coke's request. They hoped that by Sir Edward's 'good counsel and direction a grant from his excellent Majesty may (if possible) be had for the corroboration and confirmation of the ancient liberties of our borough'. However, nothing came of this implied request.[3] In 1614 Lady Hatton nominated James Whitelocke without his privity, as he recorded: 'I was absent in the circuit when she sent my name, and when I came to her to take notice of it she told me she did it lest an honest man should be left out'. Whitelocke 'gave her thanks for it, and yielded up the place to her again', preferring to sit on his own interest for Woodstock, where he had defeated a candidate of the 1st earl of Montgomery (Sir Philip Herbert*), probably Sir Thomas Tracy. Perhaps by arrangement with Montgomery, Tracy replaced Whitelocke at Corfe.[4]

In 1617 Coke agreed to abandon all his claims to Corfe Castle in his wife's favour.[5] Left entirely to her own devices, at the 1620 election Lady Hatton presented a seat to her first husband's cousin, Sir Thomas Hatton. In 1624 and 1625 she won control of both seats, which she handed to Sir Peter Osborne, one of Sir Thomas's friends, and the diplomat Sir Francis Nethersole. The latter was nominated by the duke of Buckingham, who was then trying to induce Lady Hatton to hand over her Purbeck property to her son-in-law, Sir John Villiers. In 1626 Lady Hatton's hold over the borough was temporarily broken, but she again apparently swept the board in 1628, when Nethersole was once more returned, this time with

Giles Greene, one of Lady Hatton's tenants and local agents.[6]

Corfe's other principal patron was a townsman, Edward Dackombe, described by the corporation as 'a man of sufficient ability and livelihood' when he was himself elected in 1604. Ten years later he arranged the return of his distant cousin, John Dackombe, while in 1620 he nominated Sir Thomas Hammon, who had married his mother-in-law. Thereafter, his local influence declined, but he again took the second seat in 1626. The other Member in that year was Sir Robert Napier, who may have relied on the backing of another Dorset gentleman, his kinsman Sir Nathaniel Napper*.[7]

[1] *Procs. 1614 (Commons)*, 37. [2] Hutchins, *Dorset*, i. 471-2; T. Gerard, *Survey of Dorset*, 54; C219/40/210. [3] *Not. Parl.* ii. 98-99. [4] *Liber Famelicus of Sir J. Whitelocke* ed. J. Bruce (Cam. Soc. lxx), 40-1. [5] *APC*, 1616-17, p. 274. [6] *CB*, ii. 97; PROB 11/236, f. 264; R.E. Ruigh, *Parl. of 1624*, pp. 82-3; SP16/20/23; *CSP Dom.* 1633-4, p. 564. [7] *Not. Parl.* ii. 498-9; *Vis. Dorset* (Harl. Soc. xx), 35; *The Ancestor*, ii. 212; *Burke Commoners*, ii. 639-41.

J.P.F.

DORCHESTER

Right of election: in the burgesses

Number of voters: at least 11 in 1625

27 Feb. 1604	MATTHEW CHUBBE JOHN SPICER
c. Mar. 1614	FRANCIS ASHLEY GEORGE HORSEY
13 Dec. 1620	SIR THOMAS EDMONDES JOHN PARKINS
3 Mar. 1621	(SIR) FRANCIS ASHLEY *vice* Edmondes, chose to sit for Bewdley
26 Jan. 1624	WILLIAM WHITEWAY I RICHARD BUSHROD
9 May 1625	(SIR) FRANCIS ASHLEY WILLIAM WHITEWAY I
26 Jan. 1626	RICHARD BUSHROD MICHAEL HUMFREY
19 Apr. 1626	WILLIAM WHITEWAY II *vice* Humfrey, deceased
25 Feb. 1628	DENZIL HOLLES JOHN HILL

Originally a Roman settlement, Dorchester returned two Members to the Model Parliament, and received its first charter in 1337. It was described in 1610 as 'an ancient and populous borough where the assizes for the county are usually holden, and whither the knights and gentlemen of the shire do often repair upon sundry occasions of service of the king's majesty and the county', including the Dorset elections. As the shire town, it housed the county gaol, rebuilt in 1624. It also boasted a free school, a bookseller, and, from around 1631, a municipal library.[1] The richest town in early Stuart Dorset, with a population of around 2,000, Dorchester operated weekly markets and four annual fairs. Operating through the nearby port of Weymouth, its merchants were particularly active in the cloth trade, exporting local fabrics to much of the Continent, especially France. In 1621 a company of freemen was established specifically to prevent the interference of London mercers.[2]

Dorchester was governed by two bailiffs and 15 capital burgesses, an arrangement preserved by the borough's 1610 charter of incorporation, which also provided for a recorder. The bailiffs, elected annually, also presided over parliamentary elections, in which the franchise lay with the wider body of burgesses, later defined as contributors to scot and lot. Surviving election returns for the period give no real clue as to the number of voters, but it must have been considerably higher than the 11 or 12 men who signed the 1625 indenture. Ordinarily the returns were devoid of signatures, and except in 1604 did not even supply the bailiffs' names.[3]

With one exception, George Horsey, all of Dorchester's Members during this period were men with strong local ties. However, in 1604 the borough experienced some difficulty in finding enough candidates, eventually settling on two experienced former bailiffs, John Spicer and Matthew Chubbe. The latter, who had already represented the borough in 1601, was most reluctant to do so again, 'alleging ... the disability of his body to endure that service', and 'offering to some other to be chosen five pounds towards his charge to serve therein'. His objections overruled, he applied for leave shortly after the Parliament opened, and when this strategy also failed, he persuaded the borough in June 1604 to write to the Speaker, requesting a writ for them to elect a replacement. If this letter was actually delivered Chubbe's proposal must have been rejected, as he thereafter seems to have fulfilled his obligations. However, his recalcitrance might explain why parliamentary wages were apparently paid only to Spicer, who received £60 at some point during this Parliament.[4]

In 1605 Dorchester's Holy Trinity parish acquired a new rector, the fervently Calvinist John White, with whom Chubbe was soon at odds.[5] This antagonism was manifested in the Commons during the first session of 1610, when Dorchester promoted a bill to re-allocate the revenues of the depopulated parish of Frome Whitfield, Dorset to charitable purposes in Dorchester. Chubbe, who was then a trustee of these funds, must have consented to the bill, which proposed that the money should be used for 'the maintenance of a preacher, a free school, and nine poor people of the almshouse'. The measure was committed on 16 Feb. and reported ten days later by William Hakewill. However, it then met with objections in the Lords, where it was described as 'so full of imperfections, as the same could not well be proceeded in'. Accordingly, a new bill was drafted, which specified that the money would be used to augment the living of Holy Trinity parish, with a proportion reserved for the benefit of the school and almshouses. When the bill was brought down to the Commons, Chubbe vigorously opposed it 'with a long speech' during the second reading debate on 7 June. He was added to the committee, but despite his obstruction the measure passed with only minor amendments, receiving the Royal Assent at the end of the session.[6]

John White was by now proving to be an inspirational preacher, who attracted a devoted following both in and around Dorchester. His objective was a thoroughgoing reformation of the town, and his opportunity came when a devastating fire in 1613 consumed nearly half the houses there. This disaster was widely seen as an act of divine punishment for ungodly behaviour, and local puritans began to promote White's programme more energetically. This included some impressive acts of philanthropy, but also involved a crackdown on the idle poor, symbolized by the establishment of a workhouse in 1616. A number of the key figures behind this new institution, such as John Parkins*, William Whiteway I*, and Richard Bushrod*, soon achieved prominence within the corporation, which by the early 1620s was dominated by puritan reformers.[7] Many of this close-knit group were also heavily involved in another of White's projects, the Dorchester New England Company, which aimed to establish a puritan colony in America. Bushrod obtained the initial licence in 1623, while the governing committee included William Whiteway II* and John Hill*.[8]

The impact of these changes was not felt immediately at Westminster. In 1614 the borough elected Francis Ashley, who had become Dorchester's recorder three years earlier, and George Horsey, a prominent Dorset gentleman whose ties to the borough have not been established. Although Ashley strongly admired White, later leaving him £100 in his will, there is no firm proof that their friendship helped his cause on this occasion.[9] Again, the election for the 1621 Parliament was probably not entirely to the reformist corporation's liking. Although John Parkins was returned on 13 Dec. 1620, he was paired with Sir Thomas Edmondes, treasurer of the king's Household. The latter had been nominated by Prince Charles's Council, on the basis that the lordship of Dorchester had been granted to the prince three years earlier. According to William Whiteway II, Ashley had been intended to take that seat, but stood aside in favour of Edmondes. However, when the treasurer subsequently opted to sit for Bewdley, Ashley was returned in the resultant election.[10]

For the remainder of the decade, Dorchester's godly leaders were free to advance their own favoured candidates. William Whiteway I sat in both 1624 and 1625, partnered by Bushrod and Ashley in turn. In 1626 the corporation again opted for Bushrod, who was returned with Michael Humfrey, father of the Dorchester Company's treasurer. When Humfrey died during that Parliament, he was replaced by William Whiteway II. John Hill took the junior seat in 1628, the senior place going to Ashley's son-in-law, Denzil Holles. By now Dorchester's population was growing increasingly angry at abuses committed by soldiers billeted in the local district, and the damage to the town's trade caused by war and piracy. Accordingly, when Holles was imprisoned for protesting against the government on the riotous final day of the 1629 session, he retained the borough's support. John White attempted to visit him in the Tower, and after his release the corporation presented him with a standing-cup worth 20 marks, in recognition of 'his service done [during] the last Parliament'.[11]

[1] D. Underdown, *Fire From Heaven*, 7, 99, 188; *OR*; *Brit. Bor. Charters 1307-1660* ed. M. Weinbaum, 29; HLRO, Lords Parchments, f. 32; *Municipal Recs. of Dorchester* ed. C.H. Mayo, 413, 564, 581-2. [2] Underdown, 8, 11; T. Gerard, *Survey of Dorset*, 69; *Municipal Recs. of Dorchester*, 385-91. [3] Underdown, 7, 23; Hutchins, *Dorset*, ii. 356; C219/35/1/131; 219/39/88; 219/41A/41. [4] *Not. Parl.* ii. 415-16; *CJ*, i. 152a; Hutchins, ii. 356. [5] Underdown, 25-7; STAC 8/44/17. [6] J. Savage, *Dorchester*, 186-7, 191; *CJ*, i. 394a, 400a, 435b, 436b; *LJ*, ii. 563b, 567b, 605a, 614b. [7] F.R. Troup, *John White*, 40, 257-8; Harl. 6715, ff. 18, 20; T. Fuller, *Worthies*, iii. 25; Hutchins, ii. 330, 341; Savage, 219-20. [8] Troup, 59; *William Whiteway of Dorchester* (Dorset Rec. Soc. xii), 61. [9] *Municipal Recs. of Dorchester*, 452; PROB 11/171, f. 11. [10] C219/37/85, 89; P.M. Hunneyball, 'Prince Charles's Council as Electoral Agent, 1620-24', *PH*, xxiii. 325; E371/724/126; *William Whiteway of Dorchester*, 33-4. Whiteway mistakenly states that Ashley was elected in Dec. 1620, and then

resigned his seat on 13 Jan. 1621. [11] *William Whiteway of Dorchester*, 61, 108; *Municipal Recs. of Dorchester*, 675-6; *Strafforde Letters* (1739) ed. W. Knowler, i. 40, 42; *CSP Dom.* 1628-9, p. 543.

J.P.F./P.M.H.

LYME REGIS

Right of election: in the freemen and freeholders

Number of voters: at least 12 in 1628

25 Feb. 1604	SIR GEORGE SOMERS
	JOHN HASSARD
24 Feb. 1610	SIR FRANCIS RUSSELL *vice*
	Somers, employed abroad
	GEORGE JEFFERY *vice*
	Hassard, vacated his seat
c. Mar. 1614	SIR EDWARD SEYMOUR, (bt.)
	GEORGE BROWNE
16 Dec. 1620	JOHN POULETT
	ROBERT HASSARD
5 Feb. 1624	SIR JOHN DRAKE
	ROBERT HASSARD
c. Oct. 1624	WILLIAM WYNN *vice*
	Hassard, deceased
19 Apr. 1625	JOHN DRAKE
	THOMAS PARAMOUR
23 Jan. 1626	(SIR) WALTER EARLE
	THOMAS PARAMOUR
25 Feb. 1628	CHRISTOPHER EARLE
	THOMAS PARAMOUR

Located in the extreme west of Dorset, Lyme Regis received its first charter in 1284, and sent Members to the Model Parliament. In the early seventeenth century, notwithstanding the town's frequent pleas of poverty, it was a flourishing community of nearly 2,000 people, 'well-built, and enriched by the conveniency of the Cobb, which is an harbour that the inhabitants with much industry and charge have built in the sea'. The charges levied for maintenance of the Cobb were confirmed by statute in 1585. Although its merchant ships rarely ventured much beyond the English Channel, Lyme's economic hinterland included the Somerset town of Taunton, and it boasted the highest average customs revenues of all the Dorset ports.[1]

Lyme was incorporated in 1559, the charter providing for a mayor, recorder, and up to 16 capital burgesses. By the early Stuart period the mayoralty had become a major financial burden, and on two occasions the post had to be filled by a customs official. In municipal elections the vote was exercised by the corporation, freemen, and freeholders, a total of 56 people in 1606. The precise nature of the parliamentary franchise is less certain, as the surviving parliamentary returns mention only the 'burgesses'. However, the freeholders are said to have participated in 1614, while the mayor, 11 other capital burgesses, and 12 freemen took part in the preliminary election of George Jeffery in December 1609.[2] In the early years of James I's reign there is evidence of factionalism within the corporation, much of it apparently stirred up by John Geare, who arrived in Lyme as a schoolmaster and 'unbeneficed preacher', and from 1609 held the local living. However, it is unclear to what extent this impacted on the town's politics.[3]

In 1604 the borough had important business in Parliament, namely the provision of funds for the repair of the Cobb, and accordingly opted for two Members with strong local ties. Sir George Somers was the son of a Lyme Regis merchant, as well as being a distinguished mariner with useful contacts. John Hassard was the most senior member of the corporation. Although neither Member was recorded as speaking during the 1604 session, and extension of the Cobb Act was opposed on 5 June by Richard Martin*, the statute was duly renewed by Parliament for another ten years.[4] Meanwhile, Hassard also used his time in London to arrange the renewal of the borough charter, which was re-granted in June 1604. However, the new provisions failed to win the approval of the corporation, which accused Hassard of departing from his instructions, and of introducing a clause which made him, *de facto*, a magistrate for life.[5]

At the opening of the next session Somers announced that his colleague was disabled by gout, but on 9 Nov. the House resolved that Hassard should continue to serve.[6] Although Hassard seems to have attended thereafter, he apparently absented himself from the 1606-7 session, and was again ill in early 1610. By now Somers was overseas on Virginia Company business, leaving Lyme, in effect, unrepresented. The borough took matters into its own hands, and on 30 Dec. 1609, without waiting for a writ of by-election, selected as Hassard's replacement George Jeffery, the son of a local landowner, and himself a 'very good friend' of Lyme's searcher of customs, Arthur Gregory.[7] When the Commons reassembled Jeffery's father, Sir

John*, presented a petition on the borough's behalf, whereupon Hassard's disability was finally accepted. Moreover, after much debate about Somers' absence, both seats were declared vacant on 14 February. This outcome may not have been intended by the corporation, which on 15 Feb. resolved to acknowledge Jeffery as 'the sole and only man for burgess of the Parliament for our town'. Nevertheless, he was duly elected nine days later, along with Sir Francis Russell, an outsider whose ties with the borough have not been established. At the same time the corporation took steps to renew the charter in a form more to its liking, the principal change being the vexed question of who could exercise magistrate's powers.[8]

In 1614 Lyme awarded one of its seats to the borough's recorder, George Browne. The other Member, Sir Edward Seymour, may have been nominated by John Drake*, lord of the manor of Lyme Abbots, who was possibly clearing the way for his own election as a Devon shire knight by providing an alternative seat for Seymour, one of his principal rivals. Predictably, it was Browne who spoke for the borough in the Commons, on 21 May successfully opposing the bill introduced by (Sir) Walter Earle* to develop a rival harbour at Axmouth, Devon.[9]

The election of 1620 may have been contested, but if so no firm details have emerged. On 18 Dec. the corporation resolved that:

> if Mr. Anthony Ellesdon, mayor, shall be in any sort questioned or put to any expenses at any time hereafter concerning the election of the burgesses or any one of them which were chosen upon Saturday last to serve at the next Parliament, ... the said Anthony Ellesdon's charges shall be borne and defrayed at the general charge of the whole corporation.[10]

On this occasion, the senior seat went to John Poulett, owner of the nearby manor of Marshwood, who had become a freeman of the borough in the previous year. The other place went to Robert Hassard, great-nephew of the 1604 Member, but now a London resident. Hassard was re-elected in 1624, by which time he was recognized in Dorset as a 'courtier', but Drake's son, Sir John, replaced Poulett. The Cobb Act was again renewed during this Parliament.[11] Hassard died in the following September, while the Commons was still technically in recess, and a new writ was issued by Chancery. At the consequent by-election, for which the return does not survive, the borough bestowed the vacancy on William Wynn, a servant of lord keeper Williams, but he never took his seat, for the Parliament was dissolved by the death of James I.[12]

In 1625 John Drake himself was returned for the senior seat, alongside Thomas Paramour, a servant of his kinsman, lord treasurer Marlborough (Sir James Ley*). Thereafter, Lyme's patronage was divided between Drake and Sir Walter Earle, who owned an estate five miles away at Bindon, Devon. Paramour retained his seat in the next two Parliaments. In 1626 Earle himself took the other place 'with unanimous assent and consent', having clearly been forgiven for his Axmouth project. Sir Walter stepped up to represent Dorset in 1628, but instead nominated his brother Christopher, who would succeed Browne as recorder of Lyme Regis three years later.[13]

[1] Hutchins, *Dorset*, ii. 41, 65; *OR*; *CSP Dom.* 1619-23, pp. 19, 35, 156; 1627-8, p. 46; C2/Jas.I/G10/38; T. Gerard, *Survey of Dorset*, 10-11; SP16/138/11; Dorset RO, DC/PL/B/7/1, f. 107. [2] G. Roberts, *Municipal Gov. of Lyme Regis*, 22, 24, 27-8, 369; C219/41A/38; Dorset RO, B7/D1/1, p. 33. [3] *Procs. Dorset Nat. Hist. and Arch. Soc.* lxxii. 125; Dorset RO, B7/D1/1, pp. 26, 29, 36, 42. [4] *CJ*, i. 986a; *SR*, iv. 1051. [5] Roberts, 71-2; Dorset RO, B7/D1/1, p. 33; Lansd. 91, f. 129. [8] *CJ*, i. 392a-3a; Dorset RO, B7/D1/1, 34; Roberts, 72-4. [9] C142/444/76; *Procs. 1614 (Commons)*, 313-14. [10] Dorset RO, B7/D1/1, p. 61. [11] Hutchins, ii. 262-3; Dorset RO, B7/B6/11, p. 13; *William Whiteway of Dorchester* (Dorset Rec. Soc. xii), 58; *SR*, iv. 1235. [12] C231/4, f. 170. [13] R. Lockyer, *Buckingham*, 74-5; C142/251/169; C219/40/215; Hutchins, iii. 502.

J.P.F.

POOLE

Right of election: in the burgesses and commonalty

Number of voters: at least 11 in 1620

Mar. 1604[1]	EDWARD MAN
	THOMAS ROBARTS
c.Mar. 1614	WALTER EARLE
	SIR THOMAS WALSINGHAM II
18 Dec. 1620	(SIR) WALTER EARLE
	(SIR) GEORGE HORSEY
Jan. 1624	(SIR) WALTER EARLE
	EDWARD PITT
	?Christopher Anketill
9 May 1625	SIR JOHN COOPER, bt.
	JOHN PYNE
c.Jan. 1626	CHRISTOPHER EARLE
	JOHN PYNE
3 Mar. 1628	SIR JOHN COOPER, bt.
	JOHN PYNE

Poole received its first charter in 1248, and was represented in Parliament from 1362, though the borough did not return Members regularly until the mid-fifteenth century. Under its 1568 charter of incorporation, Poole also achieved administrative independence from the county of Dorset, the lord lieutenant alone retaining authority over the town.[2] The largest and wealthiest port in early Stuart Dorset, it was described by one contemporary as 'handsomely built and well provided with shipping'. Poole's prosperity derived primarily from its involvement in the Newfoundland fisheries; by comparison, the town struggled to compete in the wine trade with Southampton, Hampshire, which was exempt from prisage.[3] However, this heavy reliance on one industry carried risks. Much of the processed fish was sold to France and Spain, and the town was badly affected when war and piracy disrupted this trade at the start of Charles I's reign. In just two or three years, around 20 ships and over 200 mariners were lost, with the port's customs receipts in 1626 reportedly reduced to a mere 8s. Although some merchants like Thomas Robarts* profited from privateering, that can have done little to stem the general economic decline. The Dorset antiquarian Thomas Gerard, writing around 1630, considered Poole to be 'much fallen from the pristine glory, yea, and so much that now the houses begin to decay for want of dwellers'.[4]

Under the Elizabethan charter, the corporation consisted of a mayor and 11 assistants, a recorder, and – because of Poole's county status – a sheriff. This body also leased the impropriate rectory and advowson from the Crown for an annual rent of £12, giving it additional influence over the town's religious life. Parliamentary elections were held at the guildhall, presided over by the sheriff, who made his returns direct to the clerk of the Crown in Chancery. The size of the electorate during this period is uncertain, but there were reportedly around 80 voters as early as 1568, and the number is unlikely to have fallen at least until the crisis of the late 1620s. Nevertheless, the participants listed in the returns were generally corporation members, who evidently mediated electoral patronage in the borough.[5]

In the 1604-10 Parliament Poole was represented by two resident merchants. Edward Man was actually referred to as 'gentleman' on the election indenture, but it is he, rather than his colleague Thomas Robarts, who is known to have received wages 'for attendance at Parliament'. The small recorded sum of £14 10s. was presumably only a part payment, but its precise timing is unclear.[6] Thereafter, the borough invariably returned outsiders. In 1614 Man was apparently prevailed upon by his brother Bartholomew, a resident of Rochester, Kent, to arrange the election of Sir Thomas Walsingham, the heir to a great Kentish estate.[7] The junior seat that year went to Walter Earle, one of Dorset's wealthiest gentlemen, who lived just five miles from the borough, and had recently come of age. Earle, who was knighted in 1616, sat again in 1621 and 1624, and successfully nominated his brother Christopher in 1626.[8]

The second place in 1621 was taken by (Sir) George Horsey, whose wife was the great-niece of Poole's recorder, Richard Swayne†.[9] The recorder also exerted influence over the following election. On 11 Jan. 1624 Edward Pitt informed his father, (Sir) William Pitt*, that he was seeking a seat at Poole:

> thither hath my uncle Swayne written on my behalf, but as yet received no answer. But I perceive by a letter from my uncle [John] Bramble ... that there is a good inclination in five or six of the chief [men] of the town (whereof the mayor is one) to join me with Sir Walter Earle, who is undoubtedly to be one [Member]; but there are two or three strong competitors that hope and labour to be joined with him, Sir Nathaniel Napper*, and young Mr. Christopher Anketill who liveth in the town.

Four days later, Pitt reported that the corporation had responded positively to Swayne's approach, 'and put by their other suitors, with answer that they are already resolved for the disposing of their places'.[10] Napper duly opted to contest a county seat instead, though Anketill conceivably possessed enough local standing to persist with his candidacy. A cousin of John Anketill*, and the heir to a debt-racked Dorset gentry family, he held municipal office at Poole, and a little later arranged for his brother Henry to obtain the perpetual curacy. Nevertheless, it was Earle and Pitt who finally prevailed that year.[11]

With the new reign began John Pyne's long connection with the borough, which was broken only by the expulsion of the Rump in 1653. Although a Somerset resident, he had strong local associations through his mother's family, the Hanhams of Wimborne Minster, Dorset, and had also shared chambers at the Middle Temple with Christopher Earle.[12] Pyne took the junior seat in the first three Caroline Parliaments, his colleague in 1625 and 1628 being Sir John Cooper, a Hampshire gentleman who was most likely recommended by his wife's uncle, Sir Francis Ashley*. Cooper's successes ostensibly interrupted the Earle interest at Poole, but Sir Walter and Ashley were both prominent figures in the Dorset puritan community, and possibly reached an understanding on these two occasions.[13]

[1] C219/35/174 (mislabelled as Pembroke). [2] *British Bor. Charters 1307-1660* ed. M. Weinbaum, 31-2; *OR*; J. Sydenham, *Poole*, 179. [3] J.H. Bettey, *Dorset*, 67, 80; 'Description of a Journey Made into the Western Counties' ed. L.G. Wickham Legg, *Cam. Misc. XVI* (Cam. Soc. ser. 3. lii), 68; E134/7 Jas.I/Mich. 27. [4] *CSP Dom.* 1619-23, p. 25; SP16/51/55-6; 16/61/13; 16/103/43; T. Gerard, *Survey of Dorset*, 85. [5] Sydenham, 177, 189, 294-5; C219/37/96; 219/41A/108. [6] C219/35/2/174; Dorset RO, Poole corp. audit bk. 1587-1637. [7] *MTR*, 611; *Arch. Cant.* xx. 10. [8] C142/251/169; Hutchins, *Dorset*, iii. 502. [9] *Vis. Dorset* (Harl. Soc. xx), 1, 41; Hutchins, ii. 453. [10] Add. 29974, ff. 74, 76. [11] Gerard, 92; Sydenham, 236, 303; Hutchins. iii. 61; *Som. and Dorset N and Q*, iii. 1, 48; A.G. Matthews, *Walker Revised*, 308-9. [12] *Som. and Dorset N and Q*, xxxi. 29; *MTR*, 634. [13] *Vis. Wilts.* (Harl. Soc. cv-cvi), 233.

J.P.F./P.M.H.

SHAFTESBURY

Right of election: in the burgesses and inhabitants

Number of voters: at least 13 in 1625

26 Feb. 1604	ROBERT HOPTON
	JOHN BODEN
c. Mar. 1614	SIR MILES SANDYS, 1st bt.
	HENRY CROKE
17 Apr. 1614	SIR SIMEON STEWARD *vice* Sandys, chose to sit for Cambridge University
22 Dec. 1620	THOMAS SHEPPARD
	WILLIAM BEECHER
6 Mar. 1621	PERCY HERBERT *vice* Beecher, chose to sit for Leominster
	RALPH HOPTON *vice* Sheppard, expelled the House
18 Jan. 1624	JOHN THOROWGOOD
	WILLIAM WHITAKER
25 Apr. 1625	JOHN THOROWGOOD
	WILLIAM WHITAKER
23 Jan. 1626	JOHN THOROWGOOD
	WILLIAM WHITAKER
16 Feb. 1626	SAMUEL TURNER *vice* Thorowgood, chose to sit for Derby
20 Feb. 1628	SIR JOHN CROKE
	JOHN THOROWGOOD

Shaftesbury received its first charter in 1252, and sent two Members to the Model Parliament. A survey of 1615 described the borough as lying between 'a deep country full of pasture, yielding plenty of well-fed beeves, muttons, and milch-kine, and ... a high champion country, yielding store of corn, sheep, and wool; so the town is made a great vent for the commodities on either part'. Another contemporary observer, Thomas Gerard, noted it as 'a fair thoroughfare, much frequented by travellers to and from London; governed by a mayor, well inhabited, and accommodated with a plentiful market on the Saturday'. Gerard lamented the total disappearance of the abbey, once the richest nunnery in England, which left 'a fair turreted house' of the 1st Lord Arundell of Wardour as the town's 'greatest ornament'.[1]

Shaftesbury was the normal venue for Dorset's summer quarter sessions, and three resident lawyers, John Boden, Thomas Sheppard and William Whitaker, represented the borough during this period.[2] Religious divisions within the town must have been quite pronounced. The local vicar, Thomas Cooper, who was described as 'a favourer of popish-affected persons', was presumably acceptable to the Catholic Lord Arundell. Conversely, Shaftesbury was also home to a separatist church, whose members regarded Anglican worship as being insufficiently Protestant. At least three of them served on the borough's corporation, and endorsed parliamentary election returns during the 1620s. These indentures were normally made out in the name of the mayor and burgesses, though the 'inhabitants' were also mentioned in 1604 and 1625. In the former year, Members were returned 'with the assent and consent of and for the whole borough'.[3]

Shaftesbury's principal electoral patron was the 3rd earl of Pembroke, the lord of the manor, at whose court leet the mayor had to be sworn in.[4] However, Lord Arundell was almost certainly able to exert influence occasionally, and the borough was independent enough to accept nominations from other quarters as well. In 1604 the first seat was taken by Robert Hopton, heir to a great Somerset estate and presumably Pembroke's nominee.[5] He was partnered by John Boden, who had already represented Shaftesbury in 1601, and who enjoyed longstanding ties to Arundell's family. Boden probably also enhanced his own local standing by offering to return to the borough its guildhall and other municipal property, which he had held since 1585. A month after the election, most of these buildings and lands were conveyed to trustees, who subsequently transferred them to the borough. Meanwhile, Shaftesbury was granted a new charter in July 1604, which established a corporation of the mayor and 12 capital burgesses, and named Boden as recorder.[6]

In 1614 the borough returned three outsiders. The junior seat was awarded to Henry Croke, whose brother, Sir John*, had married the heiress of Payne's Place, Motcombe, around two miles north of Shaftesbury. The first choice as senior Member, Sir Miles Sandys, 1st bt., was a Cambridgeshire man, and when he opted to sit for Cambridge University, he was replaced by Sir Simeon Steward, another landowner from the same county. They were probably both recommended by the 1st earl of Suffolk, who was lord lieutenant of Cambridgeshire as well as Dorset.[7]

At the 1620 election patronage was probably shared between Pembroke and Arundell. The latter presumably helped secure the first seat for the local lawyer Thomas Sheppard, who was later described by Simonds D'Ewes[†] as a 'base, jesuited papist'. The junior place was taken by the diplomat William Beecher, whose extensive connections at Court may well have included Pembroke. However, Beecher then opted to sit for Leominster, while Sheppard was expelled from the Commons for ridiculing a bill on Sabbath observance. At the ensuing election, Pembroke doubtless nominated his cousin Percy Herbert, and probably also Robert Hopton's son, Ralph.[8]

At this juncture a long-standing dispute between Pembroke and the borough over market dues came to a head. Although a new charter, drafted by the earl in 1620 to strengthen his influence, failed to pass the great seal, the corporation was technically dissolved at Michaelmas 1621, when his steward refused to swear in the newly elected mayor. The corporation, now £200 in debt, appealed to Arundell for assistance, but eventually had to come to terms with Pembroke, who enjoyed unquestioned patronage over one parliamentary seat for the rest of the decade.[9] At the next four elections the borough returned the earl's secretary, John Thorowgood, and when in 1626 the latter chose to sit for Derby instead his place was filled by an alternative Pembroke client, Samuel Turner.[10] From 1624 to 1626 the other seat went to another Shaftesbury lawyer, William Whitaker, who seems also to have enjoyed ties to Pembroke.[11] In 1627 Whitaker became the borough's recorder, but he probably squandered his local popularity by promoting the enclosure of the nearby Gillingham forest, a project which allegedly much impaired the town's market 'by reason of the straitening, diverting, and stopping of ways'. At the 1628 election, he was replaced by Sir John Croke, who had recently headed a commission to hear complaints against the enclosure.[12]

[1] Brit. Bor. Charters 1307-1660 ed. M. Weinbaum, 32; OR; Hutchins, Dorset, iii. 7; T. Gerard, Survey of Dorset, 91-2. [2] Dorset Q. Sess. 1625-38 ed. T. Hearing and S. Bridges (Dorset Rec. Soc. xiv), 25, 47, 98. [3] Som. and Dorset N and Q, xiii. 160-2; C219/35/1/116; 219/39/94; 219/40/214; 219/41A/37. [4] SP14/130/128. [5] Vis. Som. (Harl. Soc. xi), 57. [6] HMC Hatfield, vi. 161; C.H. Mayo, Shastonian Recs. 6-8, 53; Hutchins, iii. 14. [7] Lipscomb, Bucks. ii. 189; Wilts. Vis. Peds. (Harl. Soc. cv-cvi), 209; E112/71/158; Vis. Cambs. (Harl. Soc. xli), 11; CP, xii. pt. 1, p. 464. [8] D'Ewes Diary, 1622-4 ed. E. Bourcier, 142; J.K. Gruenfelder, Influence in Early Stuart Elections, 126, 146; CJ, i. 525a; Vis. Som. 57. [9] Mayo, 9, 44-8, 52; SP14/130/128. [10] CSP Dom. Addenda, 1625-49, p. 113. [11] Procs. 1626, ii. 12. [12] CSP Dom. Addenda, 1625-49, p. 205; E178/5256; Hutchins, iii. 649.

J.P.F.

WAREHAM

Right of election: in the burgesses and freeholders

Number of voters: at least 14 in 1620

27 Feb. 1604	SIR ROBERT NAPPER
	FRANCIS JAMES
c. Mar. 1614	JOHN FREKE
	WILLIAM PITT
24 Dec. 1620	(SIR) WILLIAM PITT
	JOHN TRENCHARD
2 Feb. 1624	(SIR) WILLIAM PITT
	JOHN TRENCHARD
23 Apr. 1625	(SIR) WILLIAM PITT
	JOHN TRENCHARD
20 Jan. 1626	SIR NATHANIEL NAPPER
	EDWARD LAWRENCE
22 Feb. 1628	SIR JOHN MELLER
	GERARD NAPPER

A substantial medieval town, Wareham was important enough to begin sending representatives to Parliament in 1302. However, by the early seventeenth century it had long been superseded as a port by Poole, and was noted chiefly for 'fair houses inhabited as much by gentlemen almost as by tradesmen'. The continuing existence of five parishes attested to its former prosperity, but these benefices now provided only a meagre living for most of the incumbents.[1] Still merely a borough by prescription, Wareham was governed by a mayor, six 'burgesses', two constables, and a steward. The relatively informal nature of these arrangements evidently confused Francis James*, who, after nearly three decades of dealings with the town, mistakenly referred to the burgesses as aldermen or assistants.[2] Wareham's election returns were generally made out in the name of the mayor and burgesses, occasionally also referring to other freeholders or free tenants, but the precise scope of the franchise is unclear.[3]

During the Elizabethan era, Wareham's electoral patronage had lain primarily with the Rogers family of Bryanston, a major Dorset gentry line. However, their influence was declining by the turn of the century, and was not felt at all in the early Stuart period. In 1604 the borough returned two of the county's best-known lawyers, Sir Robert Napper and Francis James, apparently without any local gentry intervention. Six years later, a group of townsmen purchased Wareham manor from the Crown, thereby removing any prospect of political pressure from the government. Nevertheless, new gentry patrons then emerged to dominate the borough's elections for the remainder of this period.[4]

William Pitt, who had acquired four of Wareham's advowsons, sat for the borough in every Parliament from 1614 to 1625. On the first of these occasions he was partnered by his kinsman John Freke. He also unsuccessfully requested a seat in 1624 for his son Edward*. However, he squandered his influence in the town through a prolonged dispute with the inhabitants over his ecclesiastical patronage. Shortly after the 1625 election he appointed one of his own relatives to two of the livings, despite local pleas for some of these benefices to be amalgamated, and his family's political interest was lost until after the Restoration.[5]

Pitt's colleague in 1621 was John Trenchard, who owned the manor of Bestwall, just outside the town. He retained his seat in the next two Parliaments, in 1624 benefiting from the canvassing of Sir Francis Ashley*.[6] In 1626 Trenchard in turn lost out to two rival gentlemen with strong property interests in the Isle of Purbeck, Napper's son Sir Nathaniel, and the latter's kinsman, Edward Lawrence. Napper also secured one seat in 1628 for his son Gerard, but the senior Member on that occasion was Trenchard's cousin, Sir John Meller.[7]

[1] OR.; T. Gerard, *Survey of Dorset*, 57; *Procs. Dorset Nat. Hist. and Arch. Soc.* lxxv. 115-17. [2] Hutchins, *Dorset*, i. 82; PROB 11/127, f. 343. [3] C219/35/1/118; 219/37/94; 219/39/92. [4] *HP Commons, 1558-1603*, i. 154-5; Hutchins, i. 82. [5] *Procs. Dorset Nat. Hist. and Arch. Soc.* lxxv. 115-17; *The Ancestor*, x. 194-5; Add. 29974, ff. 74, 76, 154; 29976, f. 93. [6] Hutchins, i. 415-16; Add. 29974, f. 76. [7] Hutchins, iii. 125, 236; *Vis. Dorset* (Harl. Soc. xx), 64; *Vis. Hants* (Harl. Soc. lxiv), 10.

J.P.F.

WEYMOUTH & MELCOMBE REGIS

Right of election: in the freeholders

Number of voters: at least 22 in 1604

1 Mar. 1604	THOMAS BARFOOT, mayor SIR JOHN HANHAM ROBERT WHITE, alderman ROBERT MYDDELTON Edward Reynolds
12 June 1610	WILLIAM CECIL Visct. Cranborne *vice* Barfoot, deceased
16 June 1610	BARNARD MICHELL *vice* White, vacated his seat
c. Mar. 1614	SIR CHARLES CAESAR ROBERT BATEMAN BARNARD MICHELL JOHN ROY
21 Dec. 1620	MATTHEW PITT, alderman GILES GREENE JOHN FREKE CHRISTOPHER EARLE
19 Jan. 1624	JOHN FREKE ARTHUR PYNE MATTHEW PITT, alderman THOMAS GIEAR, alderman
10 May 1624[1]	SIR THOMAS MYDDELTON II *vice* Pitt, deceased
22 Apr. 1625	SIR JOHN STRANGWAYS SIR THOMAS MYDDELTON II ARTHUR PYNE BARNARD MICHELL
Aug. 1625[2]	GILES GREENE *vice* Myddelton, chose to sit for Denbighshire
20 Jan. 1626	SIR JOHN STRANGWAYS ARTHUR PYNE BARNARD MICHELL, alderman GILES GREENE
27 Feb. 1628[3]	HUGH PYNE SIR LEWIS DYVE SIR ROBERT NAPIER HENRY WALTHAM, alderman

Melcombe Regis received its earliest known charter in 1280, and returned Members to Parliament from 1319. Weymouth, which lay just across the estuary of the River Wey, was a somewhat older settlement. However, it developed municipal structures more slowly, and did not regularly achieve a voice at Westminster until Richard II's reign. The two boroughs were united by Act of Parliament in 1571, and incorporated under a mayor and two bailiffs, six aldermen, and 24 common councilmen. This arrangement was elaborated by a new charter in 1616, which somewhat restricted the role of the wider freeman body in the corporation's affairs. The parliamentary franchise lay with the borough's freeholders, and in consequence of the Elizabethan merger, the combined borough of Weymouth and Melcombe Regis was the only constituency other than London to boast four Members.[4]

In the early seventeenth century, the two towns prospered from trade with Newfoundland, 'where they have had 80 sail of ships and barks', and France, from whence their merchants returned 'laden with wine, cloth, and divers other useful commodities'. By the end of this period customs revenues were thought to have reached the impressive annual figure of £3,000. The corporation kept in touch with Exeter and Dartmouth over matters of common interest, and periodically displayed considerable self-confidence, for example rejecting the government's proposal in 1609 for a new, unified French Company. Nevertheless, the wars of the later 1620s inevitably disrupted trade, and in 1627 the borough claimed that it was unable to supply the king with two ships.[5]

Ordinarily, the corporation reserved two places in each election for its own Members during this period. Thomas Barfoot in 1604 was actually the serving mayor, and therefore returned himself in breach of parliamentary convention, though this irregularity went unremarked in the Commons. He was partnered by a future mayor, Robert White. Similarly, John Roy (1614), Matthew Pitt (1621 and 1624), Thomas Giear (1624), and Henry Waltham (1628), all held this office at some point in their municipal careers. Barnard Michell (1610, 1614, 1625, 1626) and Giles Greene (1621, 1625, 1626) both held the lesser post of bailiff, and accordingly also returned themselves in 1610 and 1621 respectively, again without sanction.[6] In 1625, for reasons which remain unclear, the corporation resolved to elect just one local resident, though in the event the normal quota was restored a few months later when Greene was returned. Otherwise, the 1628-9 Parliament was the only occasion when the corporation had just one representative in the Commons. It appears that only Weymouth residents could expect parliamentary wages. No evidence survives prior to

1624, when Pitt and Giear both received 3s. 4d. a day. In the following year Michell was awarded the same daily rate, though Greene was obliged to agree prior to his election to cover his own expenses. The corporation's financial reserves were presumably reduced by 1626, for Michell was paid only 2s. 6d. a day for that session. The arrangements made in 1628-9 are not known.[7]

Weymouth's remaining seats went to outsiders, though many of these men possessed close ties with the town. Robert Myddelton in 1604 and Robert Bateman in 1614 were former residents who had married into the same local family, the Mounsells; Thomas Barfoot was their wives' stepfather. This connection still held good a decade later, presumably helped by Myddelton's generous bequest of £100 to the town in 1616. His nephew, Sir Thomas Myddelton, was returned in 1624, while the latter's brother-in-law, Sir Robert Napier, secured a seat in 1628.[8] Links to the corporation were also an advantage. Hugh Pyne owed his election in 1628 to his status as the borough's recorder, and had already on that basis secured a seat for his son Arthur in the previous two Parliaments. Similarly, Christopher Earle in 1621 may have approached the corporation through his colleague in King's Bench, Giles Greene.[9] Nevertheless, such ties were no guarantee of success. Edward Reynolds, who had already represented the borough in 1601, was originally a local man, but found himself rebuffed in 1604, Mayor Barfoot apparently regarding him as too 'factious' to qualify for a seat. Admittedly, Reynolds did not help his own cause by endlessly vacillating over whether or not to stand.[10]

Comparatively few of the local gentry became Weymouth burgesses in the early Stuart era. Sir John Hanham, the son of a former recorder, probably secured his return in 1604 through the influence of near kinsmen resident just outside the borough. John Freke, who sat in 1621 and 1624, lived just four miles from Weymouth, while Sir John Strangways, senior Member in 1625 and 1626, had a seat seven miles distant. One of Dorset's most prominent gentry figures, Strangways also arranged the election in 1628 of his son-in-law, Sir Lewis Dyve.[11] Thus the corporation was relatively unaccustomed to approaches from outside the borough, which helps to explain the confusion that ensued when the government made a nomination in 1610. Two places at Weymouth had just fallen vacant, through Thomas Barfoot's death and Robert White's incapacity, and when the writ was sent down for a by-election to replace the latter Member, it was accompanied by a letter from Sir Julius

Caesar*, requesting the borough to elect William Cecil, Viscount Cranborne. At first the corporation demurred, responding on 13 June that Caesar's message had arrived too late, and that the borough had already settled on an alternative candidate. However, within three days the inadvisability of rejecting the son of lord treasurer Salisbury (Robert Cecil†) had been recognized. Accordingly, the corporation wrote again to Caesar, explaining that Cranborne's anonymous rival had now withdrawn, and that the voters had agreed to elect the young viscount instead. Realizing that Cranborne might already have made alternative arrangements, they left their options open by sending up Barnard Michell with two blank indentures, dated 12 and 16 June, so that the matter could be resolved in London. The final outcome was that Cranborne took one seat, and Michell the other. Confusingly, though, the viscount was officially returned in place of Barfoot, rather than White, and his name was therefore entered on the indenture of 12 June, creating the impression that he was actually returned the day before the corporation confirmed that he had been rejected. Having achieved his objective on this occasion, Caesar presumably intervened again in 1614 when his son, Sir Charles, was returned.[12]

Weymouth pursued a specific agenda in Parliament only intermittently during this period. In 1604 the borough promoted a bill to convert the chapel-of-ease at Melcombe Regis into a full parish church. This would save the congregation from having to resort for major services to the less convenient church at Radipole, which would simultaneously lose its parochial status. Two of the borough's Members had a direct interest in the measure. Thomas Barfoot undertook to provide a house to serve as the new parsonage, while Sir John Hanham was presumably concerned to guard the interests of his young cousin, James Hanham, who owned the advowson of Radipole. In the event, no Weymouth Members were included when the measure's committee was appointed on 27 Apr., though the bill and committee list were delivered to Barfoot four days later. Amid concerns that this legislation did not provide adequate financial security for the rector of Radipole, the bill was rejected on 17 May. However, a revised version was brought in on 25 May, and this passed smoothly onto the statute books. The rector, who had sought to block the bill, remained unhappy with the outcome, and in the 1605-6 session a new measure 'for the relief of the parson of Radipole' was brought into the Commons, but lost in committee, apparently without the direct intervention of the borough's representatives.[13] In 1626 a further bill to establish a further church or chapel in Weymouth was

introduced. Sir John Strangways was named personally to the committee on 25 Feb., though the borough's other Members were also entitled to attend. The bill was ordered to be engrossed on 23 Mar., but it then proceeded no further.[14]

In 1624 Matthew Pitt and Thomas Giear provided the Commons' grand committee on trade with a letter from Weymouth complaining about the new imposition on groceries. Pitt further informed the committee on 6 Apr. that his constituents were being overcharged by the collectors of the pretermitted custom on cloth. Moreover, Giear supplied evidence that was used against lord treasurer Middlesex (Sir Lionel Cranfield*), testifying on oath that Weymouth merchants were prevented from landing cargoes unless they paid the composition for purveyance of groceries.[15] Giles Greene was doubtless also relaying complaints from his constituents during the 1626 Parliament, when he repeatedly protested against the government's failure to protect merchant shipping in the English Channel.[16] During this same session, the mayor of Weymouth, Henry Russell, was summoned before the Commons on 20 Feb. for breaching parliamentary privilege by arresting a servant of Richard Bushrod*.[17] In general, however, the borough's affairs attracted little attention at Westminster, to the extent that when Hugh Pyne died during the recess of the 1628-9 Parliament, no known steps were taken in the House to fill the vacancy.[18]

[1] Eg. 784, f. 41. [2] *Weymouth and Melcombe Regis Min. Bk.* ed. M. Weinstock (Dorset Rec. Soc. i), 9. [3] *OR*. [4] Hutchins, *Dorset*, ii. 430, 449; *HP Commons, 1386-1421*, i. 375-6, 386; M. Weinbaum, *British Bor. Chs.* 33; *Not. Parl.*, ii. 436 [5] T. Gerard, *Survey of Dorset*, 35; E134/5 and 6 Chas.I/Hil. 29 (deposition of John Bond); Dorset RO, Weymouth corp. order bk. ff. 45, 73, 88; SP14/45/95; SP16/50/58. [6] C219/35/1/115, 121; 219/37/91. [7] *Weymouth and Melcombe Regis Min. Bk.* 7, 9-10; Dorset RO, corp. order bk., f. 93. [8] Dorset RO, P243/RE1; J.E. Griffith, *Peds. Anglesey and Caern. Fams.* 285; *Vis. Beds.* (Harl. Soc. xix), 184-5; PROB 11/127, f. 514. [9] *Vis. Som.* ed. Weaver, 67; Hutchins, iii. 502; STAC 8/295/30. [10] *HP Commons, 1558-1603*, iii. 286; SP14/1/48; 14/6/74, 82, 85, 96. [11] Hutchins, ii. 440, 478, 662-3; *The Ancestor*, x. 198-9. [12] SP14/55/20, 23; C219/35/1/119, 121. [13] Hutchins, ii. 478; iii. 231; H.J. Moule, *Docs. of Bor. of Weymouth and Melcombe Regis*, 192-5; *CJ*, i. 187b, 212b, 259a, 962a, 980a; *SR*, iv. 1059; Dorset RO, Weymouth bor. mss S58, S189. [14] *Procs. 1626*, ii. 86, 125, 349. [15] Cobbett, *Parl. Hist.* vi. 265; 'Spring 1624', p. 194; 'Nicholas 1624', ff. 115v-16. [16] *Procs. 1626*, ii. 97, 105, 108, 137, 142-3, 260. [17] Ibid. ii. 72-3 (the mayor is misidentified here as being Henry Michell). [18] WARD 7/78/139.

J.P.F./P.M.H.

ESSEX

Number of voters: at least 1,200[1]

6 Mar. 1604	SIR EDWARD DENNY SIR FRANCIS BARRINGTON
8 Jan. 1605	SIR GAMALIEL CAPELL *vice* Denny, called to the Lords
by 17 Mar. 1614	SIR ROBERT RICH SIR RICHARD WESTON
19 Dec. 1620	SIR FRANCIS BARRINGTON, bt. SIR JOHN DEANE
10 Feb. 1624	SIR FRANCIS BARRINGTON, bt. SIR THOMAS CHEKE
3 May 1625	SIR FRANCIS BARRINGTON, bt. SIR ARTHUR HERRYS
10 Jan. 1626	SIR FRANCIS BARRINGTON, bt. SIR HARBOTTLE GRIMSTON, bt.
4 Mar. 1628	SIR FRANCIS BARRINGTON, bt. SIR HARBOTTLE GRIMSTON, bt.
6 Jan. 1629	ROBERT RICH, LORD RICH *vice* Barrington, deceased

Described by Norden as 'fat, fruitful and full of profitable things', Essex was one of the richest counties in England. The south-eastern corner was famed for its dairy farming, particularly its huge cheeses, 'wondered at for their massiveness and thickness'; corn production thrived in the north-west; and the area close to the Suffolk border abounded in hops. The cloth industry, concentrated at Colchester, Witham, Coggeshall, Braintree, Bocking, Halstead and Dedham, was also well represented, forming a sizeable part of the county's economy. In 1629 Essex's clothiers claimed that as many as 50,000 of the county's residents were dependent upon the cloth industry. Modern research puts the true figure at around 29,000, but even so this represented around 30 per cent of the shire's estimated population.[2] Coggeshall reputedly made the best white cloths in England, while the new draperies manufactured at Colchester were renowned for their quality throughout the seventeenth century.

The greatest and wealthiest landowners in Essex were the Rich family, earls of Warwick from 1619, whose principal seat of Leez Priory was situated in the centre of the county. In 1619 the 2nd earl (Sir Robert Rich*) inherited a total of 64 Essex manors.

The only other family to hold as many as 30 manors in the county were the Petres of Ingatestone Hall.[3] Despite their landed dominance, the Rich family rarely achieved electoral success at county level under Elizabeth, their path being frequently barred by the Petres and, between 1584 and 1593, by Sir Thomas Heneage[†] of Copt Hall. However, in 1595 Heneage died without direct male heir, and after 1597 the Petres rendered themselves ineligible for election by their recusancy. The only remaining obstacle to the Rich family's electoral ambitions was Sir Henry Maynard of Little Easton, former secretary to the Cecils, who, in 1601, took the senior county seat. However, in 1604 Maynard was prevented from standing, having been pricked to serve as sheriff.

At the beginning of James's reign the longstanding ambition of the 3rd Lord Rich (Robert Rich[†]) to achieve control of the county's elections received added impetus. A well known puritan, Rich probably helped to organize the survey of the Essex clergy compiled shortly after James's accession, which detailed the unfitness of a majority of the county's ministers.[4] This survey was intended for presentation to the king, but as its conclusions were also to be made available to the Commons it was important that Rich should exercise his electoral influence.[5] Rich backed his estate steward, William Wiseman, at Maldon, and perhaps also Wiseman's colleague, Sir Edward Lewknor I. So far as the county election was concerned, his choice for the senior seat settled upon his puritan neighbour, Sir Francis Barrington. The junior place was to be left to Sir Gamaliel Capell, a middle-ranking member of the county's gentry, unconnected with either Rich or Barrington.

Shortly after Parliament was summoned on 31 Jan., Rich apparently consulted several of the county's leading figures, and secured their agreement to return Barrington as senior knight.[6] However, sometime before 11 Feb., Barrington learned that Sir Edward Denny of Waltham Abbey also wanted this place, presumably to further the financial interests of his neighbour, Sir Christopher Hatton* of Ilford, the heir of his wife's late brother-in-law, Sir William Hatton *alias* Newport[†]. Denny was the son-in-law of Sir Thomas Cecil[†], later 1st earl of Exeter, and so was related by marriage to the master of the Wards, Sir Robert Cecil[†]. Barrington was in London when he learned that Denny intended to stand, and consequently in early February he held a meeting with the chairman of the Essex bench, Sir Thomas Mildmay[†] of Moulsham, at the Inner Temple. Mildmay, however, refused to reaffirm his support, but asserted instead that he would neither 'be led nor driven for any man's pleasure, but where I had liking to give my voice, there I would give it'.[7] Mildmay was presumably piqued that Lord Rich's steward wanted the seat at Maldon that the borough's corporation had previously promised to his son Thomas†.[8] Fearful that Mildmay was now considering switching his support to Denny, Barrington subsequently expended considerable energy attempting to persuade Mildmay to honour his original promise, but without success.[9]

Barrington probably left for Essex on 11 Feb., when he left a letter at Mildmay's London residence. He was followed from the capital shortly thereafter by Lord Rich. *En route*, Rich visited Sir Anthony Cooke† at Gidea Hall, who pledged Barrington his whole-hearted support. On reaching Chelmsford, where the election was to be held, Rich reserved two hostelries in Barrington's name in case of a contest. From there he also contacted many of the county's leading gentry and the corporations of Maldon and Colchester. This was partly to advertise them of the correct date of the forthcoming election (6 Mar.), which had been misreported, and partly to gauge the extent of the support for Barrington. By 15 Feb. Rich had returned to Leez Priory, where he compiled an optimistic report for Barrington. So far as he could learn, all the freeholders of Hinckford Hundred apart from Sir Thomas Gardiner 'stand firm with us', while the voters of Rochford and Dengie hundreds, where Rich held extensive lands, 'will not cross us much'. Thanks also to the efforts of Lord Darcy, 'all the divisions between Braintree, Witham and Harwich' had also assured Barrington of their support. Rich, moreover, had suborned the officer of the 5th earl of Sussex, the county's non-resident lord lieutenant. This official had sent out a letter in Sussex's name regarding the election which had not met with Rich's approval, but Rich now caused him 'to write a new letter to my liking', which he had drafted. Matters were apparently proceeding so smoothly that Rich, anxious to avoid unnecessary expenditure on provisions for their supporters, advised Barrington to 'send somebody to listen' in case their opponents decided to throw in the towel.[10]

Lord Rich's satisfaction was, however, a trifle premature. On 20 Feb. Barrington protested that Mildmay, the dominant landowner in the Chelmsford area, had taken up most of the town's inns on behalf of Denny, thereby preventing Barrington from accommodating his own supporters. Mildmay retorted that the inns he had reserved were intended to be used by himself and his friends rather than by Denny and his

followers, and he indignantly demanded to know 'who hath any [au]thority to except against me in so doing in mine own town'. He also chided Rich and Barrington for threatening to cause a contest in a county not noted for them. His reminder that it was their duty 'as good patriots' to avoid factional behaviour came close to a demand that Barrington withdraw.[11]

Barrington's electoral prospects received a further setback a few days later. On 23 Feb. the Privy Council informed the sheriff and the county's magistrates that the king was dismayed to learn that, despite a recent Proclamation which prohibited canvassing, his wishes had not 'in any part of the realm been less regarded and obeyed than in ... Essex', where the voters had 'divided themselves into parties'. The Council deplored the fact that 'some persons do seek to be elected by soliciting their friends and writing letters to most of the towns and principal freeholders of the county to favour and prefer them to be elected knights of the shire', seeing in this behaviour the likely cause of 'great disorder at the time of the election'. They also disapproved of the candidates' practice of compiling 'calendars' of voters' names to identify the strength of their support. Maynard and his colleagues were therefore ordered to report offenders, and to notify the county's freeholders of the king's displeasure 'as soon as possible', so that they might then proceed to 'a free election'.[12] Although neither Barrington nor Rich were mentioned by name, it was clear that the letter was primarily directed at them. Indeed, when Rich learned of its contents he concluded that Denny's supporters had been 'forced to seek for letters to the lords'.[13] He was undoubtedly aware that Denny, through the Cecils, was well connected at Court and enjoyed the open backing of at least one signatory to the Council's letter, the lord chamberlain, Thomas Howard, 1st earl of Suffolk, whose seat of Audley End lay in the north-west of the county, close to Saffron Walden. The day after the Council penned its missive, Suffolk wrote menacingly to Saffron Walden's leading citizens, most of whom were his tenants, rebuking them for promising their support to Barrington 'without my privity'. Suffolk demanded that they transfer their 'free consents and voices to my good friend Sir Edward Denny' or else 'I will make the proudest of you all repent it, be you well assured'.[14]

The Council's intervention may have prompted several voters who had previously promised Barrington their support to transfer their allegiance; on 29 Feb. Rich referred to several former supporters who had 'retracted' as a result of the activity of their opponents.[15] These desertions undermined the confidence of the members of Barrington's inner circle, among them Barrington's steward, whom Rich found to be 'somewhat more dismayed than there was cause of doubt'.[16] Consequently, Rich kept a tight grip on the election campaign, even when he was forced to travel to Newmarket to consult his physician at the end of February. However, it was easy to exaggerate the threat posed by Denny, who was, after all, not a major Essex landowner. In the first place, Rich and Barrington retained the loyalty of the majority of their supporters, including Sir Anthony Cooke, who wrote to Rich signifying his 'firm resolution in this business'.[17] Secondly, the Council's intervention on behalf of Denny was a sign of desperation, as Rich himself clearly understood: 'they knew themselves the weaker side, that have used this means'.[18] Indeed, by 28 Feb. it would seem that, for all their 'great boasts and brags',[19] Denny and his supporters were staring defeat in the face. Led by Mildmay, and probably also by Sheriff Maynard, a former client of the Cecils, Denny's followers now bent their efforts towards finding a way to prevent their candidate from being humiliated. Fortunately for them, Rich and Barrington were prepared to help Denny save face rather than force a contest which Barrington would easily win.

On 28 Feb. Rich and Maynard wrote separately to Sir Gamaliel Capell, the sole candidate for the junior seat, asking him to withdraw. At around the same time Maynard, prompted by Mildmay, summoned an emergency meeting of the county's magistrates for 10 o'clock the next day (the 29th).[20] This created the illusion that the solution which subsequently emerged sprang from the magistracy as a whole rather than from the initiative of one individual.[21] Maynard also wrote to Rich suggesting that Capell should be pressed to support Barrington, as Maynard feared that a fourth candidate might emerge if Capell complained that he had been badly treated.[22] The next morning, perhaps while the justices were still sitting, Capell signified by letter to Barrington that he would stand aside as Rich and Maynard had requested, declaring himself pleased to be spared his share of the election costs, which is 'likely to be extraordinary'.[23] Meanwhile, Maynard and 11 of his fellow justices met at Chelmsford. Apparently ignorant that Capell, who was absent through illness, had already agreed to withdraw, they penned their own letter asking him to stand down. Having done this, Maynard suggested that Barrington and Denny should draw lots at Brentwood on the day before the election (i.e. the 5th) to decide which of them should occupy pride of place. Barrington, who had now arrived, agreed to this proposal, but as Denny was not present he continued to gather supplies for his

supporters at Broomfield Hall, the seat of Lord Rich's receiver of provision rents, John Pake, which lay just outside Chelmsford.[24] Surprisingly, Barrington failed to relay news of the magistrates' proposal to Lord Rich, who was in Cambridgeshire, so that as late as 1 Mar. Rich fully expected that there would be a contest for the first place.[25]

The threat of a contest was not finally lifted until 2 Mar., when Barrington learned that Denny had accepted the magistrates' proposal.[26] The reason for the delay probably lies in a letter written by Maynard to Barrington after the magistrates met on 29 February. By then both Barrington and Denny were now assured of a seat, but Maynard evidently still hoped to achieve the prime place for Denny, even though the idea of drawing lots had been his. He therefore wrote to Barrington offering to meet both candidates for dinner sometime over the weekend to resolve the matter of precedence amicably and spare the county's freeholders from journeying to Chelmsford.[27] However, Barrington, who must have been aware that Maynard was partisan, had no intention of allowing himself to be talked into conceding first place. On 1 Mar. he therefore declined the offer, claiming that he had some private business that required urgent attention.[28] Barrington's refusal to meet Denny earlier than 5 Mar. forced Denny's hand. He now had to agree to draw lots or face losing the battle for first place at the hustings. He chose wisely, as it was Barrington who ultimately drew the short straw. Ironically, Denny served in the Commons only briefly, being elevated to the peerage in October 1604. His replacement was the previously disappointed candidate, Sir Gamaliel Capell, who apparently stood unopposed.

It was not until 1614 that Lord Rich finally achieved his ambition of securing control over the premier seat. Following a quiet election, the senior knighthood of the shire was conferred on his eldest son Sir Robert, now old enough to take over from Barrington, who was left without a seat. The junior place went to Sir Richard Weston, the wealthy owner of a large Essex estate.[29] Lord Rich died in 1619, but his eldest son, now the 2nd earl of Warwick, tightened his family's grip on the county election. This was traditionally held at Chelmsford,[30] but in December 1620 it was moved to Braintree, where Warwick owned the principal manor.[31] There the senior county seat was conferred on Barrington, while the junior place was awarded to a prosperous member of the north Essex gentry, Sir John Deane, whose way was cleared by the absence abroad of Sir Richard Weston. Although not directly connected to Warwick, Deane was a puritan, whose circle of friends included the puritan Winthrops, who were loosely connected with Warwick through an earlier marriage between the elder John Winthrop and the daughter of one of the 3rd Lord Rich's bailiffs.[32]

Warwick's control over county elections continued unchallenged until 1628. Barrington was returned for the senior seat at every election during the 1620s, and was replaced after his death by Warwick's eldest son, Robert, Lord Rich. As for the junior seat, this was made available by Warwick to his son-in-law Sir Thomas Cheke in 1624, and to his tenant Sir Arthur Herrys in 1625. In 1626 and 1628 Warwick allowed it to be occupied by Sir Harbottle Grimston, whose energy as a deputy lieutenant during the invasion scare of 1625-6 may have impressed him. Grimston was so closely identified with Warwick that he was among the principal victims of the purge of the commission of the peace and the lieutenancy after Warwick fell out with the royal favourite, the duke of Buckingham, in 1626.

Buckingham's earlier friendship towards Warwick had helped to ensure the uncontested election of the earl's clients in 1625,[33] but his enmity placed in jeopardy Warwick's control of the county election in 1628. As in 1626, Warwick intended to bestow his favour upon Barrington and Grimston, both of whom enjoyed great popularity for having refused to subscribe to the Forced Loan. However, Buckingham's allies in the county moved swiftly to thwart his plan. Soon after Parliament was summoned, the king's surveyor-general (Sir) Thomas Fanshawe I*, and the privy councillor Sir Thomas Edmondes*, 'privately procured the writ for Essex and the sheriff to come to Stratford [Langthorne]', a small town situated in south-western Essex close to the country estates of both Fanshawe and Edmondes and away from Rich influence. There they evidently intended to hold the election in secret, and either to return themselves jointly or to ensure that one of them was returned alongside Sir Richard Weston, who certainly contemplated standing. Warwick's supporters got wind of this plan, however, and descended in such large numbers on Stratford Langthorne that the sheriff claimed that he had yet received the writ and could therefore not hold the election.[34] This outcome represented a humiliating reverse for Warwick's enemies, but Warwick was also damaged, as the episode highlighted his own earlier behaviour in transferring the county election to Braintree. By the end of February he had conceded that, for the first time since 1620, the election would be held at Chelmsford.[35]

After the failure of the pre-emptive strike launched by Fanshawe and Edmondes, the leaders of the anti-Warwick faction in Essex canvassed energetically on behalf of their candidates, 'both by their letters and otherwise'. However, Fanshawe and Edmondes themselves were careful to secure seats elsewhere. On 1 Mar., a few days before the election was scheduled to take place, three members of this group, exercising their authority as magistrates, issued a circular to the county's high constables implying that they were acting on the orders of the Privy Council. The constables were to bring as many freeholders as possible to Chelmsford, where the latter were to be instructed to vote for such candidates 'as shall be agreed upon by the more part of the justices of the peace of this country there assembled'. This letter so alarmed the high constable of Tendering Hundred that he showed it to his neighbour, Sir Harbottle Grimston, but like the conciliar letter procured by Denny's supporters 24 years earlier, this circular was a symptom of its authors' desperation. Moreover, Warwick had already taken steps to ensure that support for his candidates was artificially swollen, having arranged for various poor men to become voters by purchasing sufficient amount of freehold land on a temporary basis.[36] Barrington and Grimston were consequently returned without even a token contest. In the aftermath of the election, the Council punished two of the three magistrates responsible for the letter to the constables, the crypto-papist Sir Thomas Wiseman and his friend Sir William Maxey, for their presumption.[37]

---

[1] *Procs. 1628*, vi. 146-7. [2] J. Norden, *Speculi Britanniae Pars: An Historical Description of Essex* ed. H. Ellis (Cam. Soc. ix), 7-9; *VCH Essex*, ix. 81; *Maynard Ltcy. Bk. 1608-39* ed. B.W. Quintrell, 252-5; W. Hunt, *Puritan Moment*, 3, 11. [3] Hunt, 15, 161. [4] Rich had helped draft the 1586 Dunmow petition to Parliament protesting against Abp. Whitgift's replacement of godly ministers for non-subscription: M.E. Bohannon, 'Essex Election of 1604', *EHR*, xlviii. 396. Extracts from the Jacobean petition are in *HMC 8th Rep.* ii. 27-8; the original is in LPL, 2442. We are grateful to Christopher Thompson for drawing the petition, and its significance, to our attention. [5] Add. 38492, f. 62, appears to be the strategy document under which the Essex survey was conducted: *ex inf.* C. Thompson. [6] Eg. 2644, f. 130. [7] Ibid. f. 131. [8] Essex RO, D/B 3/3/205/1. [9] Eg. 2644, ff. 130-1. [10] Ibid. f. 128. [11] Ibid. f. 131. [12] Ibid. f. 135. [13] Ibid. f. 149. [14] Ibid. f. 138. [15] Ibid. f. 149v. [16] Ibid. f. 151. [17] Ibid. f. 151v. [18] Ibid. f. 149v. [19] Ibid. f. 149. [20] Ibid. ff. 134, 149v, 153; C. Thompson, *Parlty. Selection and Election of 1604*, pp. 7-8. [21] For the view that the magistracy prevented a contested election through collective action, see M.A. Kishlansky, *Parlty. Selection*, 67. For a detailed demolition of this case, see Thompson, 7-8. [22] Eg. 2644, f. 149. [23] Ibid. f. 143. Capell sent the letter to Barrington rather than Rich because he was temporarily unaware of the latter's whereabouts. Barrington then forwarded the letter to Rich, who, on the 29th, acknowledged its receipt 'this morning': ibid. f. 149. [24] Ibid. f. 153. For the identification of Pake, see Thompson, 9. [25] Eg. 2644, f. 151. Kishlansky believes that Rich was present at the justices' meeting of 29 Feb., but the Robert Rich who attended was a namesake of Stondon Massey: Kishlansky, 69, n. 65; Thompson, 9. [26] Eg. 2644, f. 153. [27] Ibid. f. 145. [28] Ibid. ff. 147v-8. [29] *Chamberlain Letters* ed. N.E. McClure, i. 518. [30] *APC*, 1588, p. 298. [31] C219/37/98 (*ex inf.*

C. Thompson); C. Thompson, 'New Evidence on John Winthrop of Groton's Essex Connections and the colonization of Massachusetts', *Suff. Review*, n.s. xxvi. 25. Warwick had also bought up a considerable amount of commercial property at Braintree a few years earlier: Harl. 3959, f. 12 (*ex inf.* C. Thompson). [32] Thompson, 'New Evidence', 25. [33] *Procs. 1625*, pp. 682-3. [34] *Procs. 1628*, vi. 146-7. Quintrell asserts that Fanshawe and Edmondes twice attempted to hold the election at Stratford Langthorne, a perception arising from the fact that the two accounts of their stratagem are dated 13 days apart. The author of the second of these accounts made it clear that he was conveying old news ('I make no doubt but you have already heard ...'): B.W. Quintrell, 'Gentry Factions and the Witham Affray, 1628', *Trans. Essex Arch. Soc.* (ser. 3), x. 122. [35] *Procs. 1628*, vi. 147. [36] Ibid. 147-8; Quintrell, 123, [37] *APC*, 1627-8, pp. 350, 352, 354, 358-9, 361. Wiseman had previously been assured by Warwick that the matter would not be reported: Add. 34679, f. 61.

A.D.T.

COLCHESTER

Right of election: in the corporation until 1625; in the freemen aft. 1625

Number of voters: 42 bef. 1625

5 Mar. 1604	ROBERT BARKER, town clerk
	EDWARD ALFORD
7 Mar. 1614	ROBERT BARKER, town clerk
	EDWARD ALFORD
14 Dec. 1620	WILLIAM TOWSE, town clerk
	EDWARD ALFORD
22 Jan. 1624	WILLIAM TOWSE, town clerk
	EDWARD ALFORD
19 Apr. 1625	WILLIAM TOWSE, town clerk
	EDWARD ALFORD
	Sir John Hobart II*
	(Sir) Alexander Radcliffe*
6 Jan. 1626	SIR HARBOTTLE GRIMSTON, bt.
	WILLIAM TOWSE, town clerk
16 Feb. 1626	SIR ROBERT QUARLES *vice*
	Grimston, chose to sit for Essex
6 Mar. 1628[1]	SIR THOMAS CHEKE
	EDWARD ALFORD
	SIR WILLIAM MASHAM, bt.
	Double return of Alford and Masham. MASHAM declared elected 28 Mar. 1628

An ancient walled town situated atop a hill overlooking the river Colne, Colchester in the early seventeenth century was the manufacturing centre of the new worsted draperies in Essex and had the largest population of any town in the county.[2] The borough obtained its first known charter in 1189, which allowed it to choose its own bailiffs, who had previously been royal appointees. Edward IV awarded the town a fresh charter in 1462, which authorized the burgesses to elect their own magistrates and created the recordership, an office which, from 1579, equated to that of high steward elsewhere. It also established a ten-strong aldermanic bench, from which two bailiffs were chosen, and set up a 32-strong common council divided into two tiers of equal size. Elected annually by the wealthier freemen, these 42 principal officers formed the corporation. From 1283 the borough enjoyed parliamentary representation by prescription.[3]

During the early seventeenth century Colchester was wracked by a series of fierce quarrels between its native inhabitants and its Dutch-speaking community, which numbered more than an eighth of the total population of around 11,000.[4] Established in the mid-1560s by refugees escaping Spanish persecution in the Low Countries, the Dutch Congregation had been warmly welcomed by a government desperate to arrest the crisis in the cloth industry. Whereas the English produced heavy broadcloths suitable only for export to northern Europe, the Dutch were skilled in manufacturing the lighter and cheaper worsteds, notably baize and says, popular in southern as well as northern Europe. As a result of the privileges granted to the Dutch by the Crown in the early 1570s, Colchester grew prosperous, as did the smaller, neighbouring clothing towns. By 1620 baize-making provided the single greatest source of employment in Colchester, and the town's baize was highly regarded for its quality.[5] However, by 1604 Dutch success had aroused native jealousy.[6] A principal cause of friction stemmed from Dutch insistence on the right to inspect and seal all newly manufactured baize and says, including those of native workmen. English workers were also angered by the failure of their Dutch counterparts to serve apprenticeships in accordance with the requirements of the 1563 Statute of Artificers; by their insistence on levying taxes on English cloth production; by their use of foreign vessels to export their goods; and by their practise of trades other than clothmaking, such as weaving and stool-making, for which they were not legally qualified. In 1616 the Privy Council upheld several of these complaints, demanding, for instance, that goods be transported in English bottoms as the law required. However, it maintained the Dutch right to inspect and seal all new cloths, thereby helping to preserve Colchester's reputation for high quality manufacturing.[7]

Hostility towards the Dutch community united the borough's English majority, but the corporation and ordinary freemen were otherwise frequently at loggerheads. By 1603 a dispute over the municipal franchise had developed. In 1612 an attempt to increase the number of free burgesses eligible to vote was blocked by the corporation, which in turn was prevented from reducing the number of voters by the freemen.[8] Not surprisingly, the Dutch community exploited these disturbances to obtain royal confirmation of their privileges in October 1612.[9] Matters came to a head three years later, when the freemen, allegedly egged on by Sir John Sammes* of Wickham Bishops, displaced two aldermen and seven common councillors, prompting the corporation to appeal to King's Bench. The matter was referred to the attorney-general, Sir Francis Bacon*, who ordered the restoration of the ousted corporation members.[10] For several years thereafter the quarrel remained dormant, but in 1624 the corporation rashly tried to limit the electorate to its own members.[11] In response, perhaps, the freemen raised the stakes by seeking to widen the parliamentary franchise. Parliamentary voting rights was a subject on which the town's charters remained silent, but customarily the franchise had been restricted to the aldermen and common council.

The freemen scored an early success in their battle for the franchise. Writing in April 1625, the town's bailiffs explained to the lord chief justice, Sir Henry Hobart*, that they had been unable to effect the election of his eldest son because 'the company, consisting of a multitude', had instead acclaimed the town clerk, William Towse.[12] However, by the time of the 1628 election the corporation had decided to fight back. While the freemen gathered in a downstairs room to elect Sir Thomas Cheke and Sir William Masham, members of the corporation assembled separately upstairs, where they chose Cheke and Edward Alford. Their decision was supported by the sheriff, who returned only the names of Cheke and Alford, whereupon the ordinary burgesses complained to the Commons' committee for privileges. At the ensuing hearing, the corporation argued that its power to pass ordinances, enshrined in the town's charters, allowed it to determine the extent of the parliamentary franchise. However, the corporation failed to mention that, ever since 1588, its parliamentary indentures had declared that its representatives were elected by 'the bailiffs, aldermen, Common Council with one unanimous consent of the commons'. Counsel for the corporation attempted to shrug off this inconvenient fact by alleging 'that the commons is here mentioned but as involved in the Common Council, to whom they

had given their right'. This was entirely unconvincing, because, as was pointed out, the bailiffs alone chose the Common Council, so how could it be argued that the commons had empowered the Common Council to act on their behalf? There was no answer to this, and consequently, on the recommendation of the committee for privileges, Sir William Masham was seated by the House.[13] A humiliated corporation six weeks later resolved to petition Parliament and to seek 'the most learned counsel they can get upon the charter'.[14] However, Colchester's franchise was not reconsidered by the Commons before the dissolution of March 1629.

Colchester was not accustomed to returning townsmen to Parliament. Indeed, under Elizabeth townsmen had been elected on just three occasions: in 1593 (Martin Bessell), 1597 and 1601 (Richard Symnell). Instead, from 1584 it usually returned its town clerk, an experienced lawyer. Consequently James Morice (1584-97), Robert Barker (c.1598-1618) and William Towse (1618-?34) all regularly sat, although only Barker lived nearby, at Monckwick. Twice only did the borough fail to return its town clerk. The first occasion was in 1597, when the town clerk's deputy, Richard Symnell, was elected following Morice's death. The second was in 1628, when it was apparently decided that Towse, being 77 years of age, was too old to serve in Parliament again. This represented something of a *volte face*, as three years earlier Towse had been rebuked for asking to be allowed to stand aside. When he did sit, the town clerk was invariably awarded the senior place. The single exception was in 1626, when the first seat was conferred on Sir Harbottle Grimston, a prominent local landowner. Grimston, however, stepped down after he was elected the junior knight of the shire and was replaced by Sir Robert Quarles, a landowner from the other side of the county, whose connection with the borough has not been established.

Colchester's recorder played an important part in the borough's parliamentary elections, since he enjoyed the right to appoint the town clerk.[15] Robert Barker and William Towse owed their positions respectively to Robert Cecil†, 1st earl of Salisbury, and Thomas Howard, 1st earl of Suffolk. Cecil, moreover, should probably also be credited with the responsibility for the election in 1604 of the junior Member, Edward Alford, a Sussex resident who owned no property in Essex. This is because Alford's father Roger† had served as secretary to Lord Treasurer Burghley (Sir William Cecil†).[16] Alford's association with Colchester proved so successful that it continued long after Cecil's death. Indeed, it was not until 1626, when he was pricked to serve as sheriff of Sussex, that he ceased to be returned for the borough.

Between 1604 and 1625, then, Colchester conferred its senior seat on the town clerk and its second place on Edward Alford. Consequently there was little scope for outsiders other than the recorder to influence the outcome of elections. This was evidently well understood by the 1st earl Rivers, who was based at nearby St. Osyth's, for, so far as is known, Rivers sought to influence Colchester's voters only at county elections.[17] As late as 1625, when Towse asked to be allowed to stand aside, the borough refused to countenance candidates nominated by the lord lieutenant, Robert Radcliffe, 5th earl of Sussex, and lord chief justice Hobart. Instead the freemen were reportedly 'much discontented' at Towse for being 'so earnest in his request'.[18] Not until 1626, when Alford was disabled from standing, were outside nominations considered.

In 1628 Towse's inability to serve created an opening for the 2nd earl of Warwick (Sir Robert Rich*), the most extensive landowner in the county, whose parliamentary patronage already extended to Essex's other constituencies. In place of Towse, Colchester's voters chose Warwick's son-in-law Sir Thomas Cheke. Warwick's role in Cheke's election is necessarily speculative, but like Quarles, Cheke came from the other side of the county, and the earl was certainly responsible for procuring a seat for Cheke at Harwich in December 1620.[19] Warwick's influence may have been exercised through his younger brother, the 1st earl of Holland (Sir Henry Rich*), who had been appointed to the recordership in 1627.[20] The corporation intended that the second seat should revert to Edward Alford, whose term as sheriff had now ended. However, Warwick evidently wanted it for Sir William Masham. Although not directly linked to Warwick, Masham was the son-in-law of one of the earl's most important allies in the county, Sir Francis Barrington*. To many of Colchester's ordinary freemen, Masham may have seemed a more attractive candidate than Alford, as he had been imprisoned for refusing to pay the widely unpopular Forced Loan.

Colchester's parliamentary elections were held at the town's moot hall, and were presided over by the county sheriff. Election writs did not always reach the town promptly. In 1625 Colchester's bailiffs complained that the writ took seven days to arrive,[21] which meant that the borough's election was not held until 19 Apr., one week later than at Maldon (though this was still much earlier than at Harwich, where the corporation delayed proceedings until 26/27th April). Successful candidates were not necessarily expected to attend the hustings. In 1628 Alford was informed by post of his controversial election, as was Sir Thomas Cheke. However, once notified, newly elected parliamentary burgesses were expected to travel to Colchester to swear the oath of a freeman if they had not previously done so. This requirement dismayed Cheke at least, who had hoped to take the oath at Chelmsford while attending the county assizes rather than make the long journey to Colchester from south-western Essex.[22] The loss of most of the borough's financial records makes it difficult to say whether parliamentary wages were usually paid, but the surviving accounts for 1620-1 suggest that they were not.[23]

Unusually, the corporation's minute books indicate, by means of prick marks, which of its members voted at parliamentary elections. In some cases, the record of election in the minute book is followed by the voters' signatures. In 1614 no signatures were required. Instead, each name recorded is accompanied by up to six unexplained prick marks and crosses. The minute books reveal that turnout at parliamentary elections was initially high: in 1604 all but two of the borough's 42 voters attended the hustings, while in 1614 the entire electorate seem to have appeared.[24] During the 1620s, however, absenteeism increased. In 1620 eight corporation members failed to cast their votes, while in 1624 the figure rose to 11. The worst attended elections of the period, however, were those of 1626. Fourteen members of the corporation failed to vote at the general election in January, while at the election in the following month there were 16 absentees.[25] It seems unlikely that the cause lay in the severe plague outbreak which affected Colchester in 1626, as the first victims were not buried until June.[26] Even in 1628, when the corporation might have been expected to mount a show of strength against the freemen, nine members refrained from voting. Uniquely, the record of the 1625 election indicates not merely the number of absentees – there were eight – but also the reason for their non-appearance, which included sickness and the duties of serving as a churchwarden.[27]

In May 1607 Colchester's bailiffs wrote to Salisbury, the borough's recorder, urging him to support a bill concerning the manufacture of woollen cloth, which had received a first reading in the Lords five days earlier.[28] The fact that Salisbury was approached only after the bill was read makes it unlikely that this particular piece of legislation, which failed to progress, originated in Colchester itself. The 1607 clothing bill was by no means the only legislation in which the inhabitants of Colchester expressed an interest during this period. In March 1610 Edward Alford was petitioned by 16 of the borough's ketchmen in favour of a bill introduced by Lowestoft aimed at curbing the jurisdiction claimed by Great Yarmouth over the East Anglian herring industry. The ketchmen asserted that, unless the bill was enacted, 'we shall be enforced to leave our ancient trading with the fishermen'. Alford responded by proposing in the Commons that the bill be committed, and by helping to organize the campaign in its favour. Multiple copies of manuscripts supporting the bill's proposals and opposing the privileges conferred by royal charter on Yarmouth in 1608 are certainly located among his surviving papers, which also include a copy of the bill itself and other related documents.[29] However, despite his efforts, Alford proved unable to secure a third reading.

The enthusiasm with which Alford promoted the Lowestoft fishing bill may help to explain his remarkable electoral success at Colchester, which returned him to Parliament on five successive occasions. Alford continued to demonstrate a willingness to serve his constituents after 1610, for in 1621 he attempted to steer through the Commons a bill to allow the town to re-pave its streets[30] and raise taxes to pay for the maintenance of its haven, which was so silted up that the landing place was becoming inaccessible. Based perhaps on a measure laid before the Commons by the borough in 1593, the bill was drawn up by William Towse on the corporation's instructions.[31] It received its first reading on 21 Feb., when Alford pointed out the adverse effects on the local economy and the king's customs which would follow if the harbour was not repaired. However, the bill immediately encountered stiff resistance because of its proposal to raise funds by imposing duties for a 15-year period on goods landed in the port. Sir William Strode thought 'it was pity it should trouble the House' as 'it lays more tax than ever I knew bill' and merchants complained 'that there are too many impositions already'. Someone else grumbled that 'divers places were to bear the charge which should have no part of the benefit'. However, Alford received invaluable support from Sir Dudley Digges, who drew attention to the lack of harbours on the Essex coast. Despite calls to reject the measure, Digges persuaded the House 'with much ado' to allow the bill a second reading on the grounds that the criticisms which had been voiced 'extended to parts of the bill, not to the whole'.[32]

It was not until 5 May that the bill received a further hearing, when it again came under fire for cutting across the House's aim to free trade from unnecessary burdens. Furthermore, it was claimed that the town itself would not benefit, as merchants would choose to go elsewhere rather than pay Colchester's landing charges. Finally, Sir Henry Poole complained that 'it was unworthy the greatness of the House to take care of the paving of streets'. Once again the responsibility for rebutting these charges fell to Alford. There were, he said, plenty of merchants who were prepared to testify both to the necessity of the proposed taxation and their willingness to pay, and if the bill, once enacted, was found to produce harmful effects to Colchester's economy the town would abandon its levy of increased duties on imports. As for the claim made by Poole, Alford pointed out that the House had previously authorized the paving of the Strand, St. Giles and Drury Lane. Thanks to this robust defence, the bill was committed, although the committee included critics of the measure, such as Strode and William Noye, as well as its leading advocates, Alford and Digges. The committee's meetings were adjourned at least twice, which perhaps left insufficient time before the sitting ended on 4 June to allow the bill a third reading. No attempt to revive the measure appears to have been made after Parliament reassembled in November.[33]

When the Colchester paving and harbour bill was reintroduced in 1624, Alford played a critical part in ensuring its success, as did William Towse. In stark contrast to the slow progress made in 1621, the bill proceeded from first to second reading in just four days.[34] There was now considerable more sympathy for the bill than in 1621, perhaps because of the continued crisis in the cloth industry. This was reflected in the committee's composition, as it seems to have contained fewer opponents of the bill than its predecessor. In addition to Alford and Towse, who were specifically named, the committee appointed on 14 Apr. consisted of all other burgesses of port towns, many of whom were likely to be sympathetic towards Colchester's problems, and the knights and burgesses of Essex, Suffolk and Norfolk. These categories excluded some of the bill's most vigorous opponents, such as Strode, Member for Devon, and Sir Henry Poole, Member for Oxfordshire. When the measure was reported by Towse on 26 Apr. the only alteration made by the committee seems to have been a proviso added for the benefit of Thomas Lucas of Colchester. This was not included in the final version of the bill and its content remains unknown.[35] It was not until the bill received its third reading on 4 May that it came under attack, and even then the only opposition was voiced by Sir James Perrot, Member for Pembrokeshire, who cautioned against setting a precedent of laying impositions upon imports. In reply, Alford argued that the legislation posed no danger as the proposed impositions were to be levied by consent, but he failed to respond to the retort, 'that this consent was of the inhabitants only and the burden extended to all as well as [sic] strangers as inhabitants'.[36] Nevertheless, the House passed the bill and ordered it to be sent to the Lords that afternoon.[37]

Once in the Upper House the bill apparently received more critical scrutiny than it had in the Commons. Three provisos were added, two of which went some way towards remedying the defect identified by Perrot, as they excluded foreigners and members of the Cinque Ports from payment of the proposed duties. The third proviso ordered the town's bailiffs, who were to receive the money raised by the legislation, to draw up annual accounts for submission to four magistrates.[38] Despite these alterations, the committee was sympathetic to the bill, partly, perhaps, because its members included Lord Howard de Walden (Theophilus Howard*) the son of the borough's recorder, and Samuel Harsnett, bishop of Norwich,[39] who had been born in Colchester, served as the town's school teacher before studying divinity and was appointed rector of Shenfield, Essex by the Lucas family. Harsnett spent some time at Colchester during the mid-1620s, and on his death in 1631 he bequeathed his entire library to the corporation in trust for the use of the local clergy.[40] Reported on 22 May 1624, the bill received a third reading two days later and shortly thereafter was returned to the Commons, where the amendments were approved on the 26th. The measure received the Royal Assent on the 29th.[41]

[1] Essex RO, D/B5 Gb2, ff. 42, 131v; Gb3, ff. 1, 33, 44, 52, 68v. [2] W. Hunt, *Puritan Moment*, 3. [3] *VCH Essex*, ix. 48-9, 52, 54, 56, 111. [4] Ibid. 67. [5] Ibid. 81-2; R. Cust, *Forced Loan*, 264-5; E. Kerridge, *Textile Manufactures in Early Modern Eng*. 95. [6] *APC*, 1601-4, p. 506. [7] Ibid. 1613-14, pp. 238-9; 1615-16, pp. 381-2, 404, 420-3, 590, 633; 1616-17, pp. 59-60, 89-90, 96-8, 121, 303-4; *CSP Dom*. 1619-23, pp. 247, 381; 1629-31, p. 200; *Reg. of Baptisms in Dutch Church at Colchester* ed. W.J.C. Moens (Huguenot Soc. xii), iii-iv, xi-xiii; Essex RO, D/B5 Gb2, ff. 150, 158, 160r-v. [8] Essex RO, D/B5 Gb2, ff. 109v-12v, 115v-18v; *VCH Essex*, ix. 114. [9] *Dutch Church at Colchester*, xi-xii. The English considered these to have been obtained 'surreptitiously': *APC*, 1615-16, p. 590. [10] Essex RO, D/Y 2/4, pp. 23, 241. [11] *VCH Essex*, ix. 115. [12] *Procs. 1625*, p. 680. [13] Essex RO, D/B5 Gb3, f. 70; *CD 1628*, ii. 162-3, 169. [14] Essex RO, D/B5 Gb3, f. 73. [15] Essex RO, D/Y 2/8/69. [16] R. Zaller, 'Edward Alford and the making of Country Radicalism', *JBS*, xxii. 61. [17] *Procs. 1625*, pp. 682-3; *Procs. 1628*, vi. 146. It has been claimed, incorrectly, that Rivers 'regularly claimed a right to intervene in the disposal of freeholders' votes in nearby Colchester': Cust, 262. [18] *Procs. 1625*, pp. 680-1. [19] Harwich bor. ms 109/1. [20] D. Hirst, *Representative of the People?*, 200; C181/3, f. 216v. [21] *Procs. 1625*, p. 680. [22] Essex RO, D/Y 2/4 (mis-transcribed by *Procs. 1628*, vi. 138). [23] Essex RO, microfilm T/A 465/109, ff. 1-5v. [24] Essex RO, D/B Gb2, ff. 42r-v, 131r-2. [25] Ibid. D/B Gb3, ff. 1r-v, 33r-v, 51v-2, 53v-4v. [26] I.G. Doolittle, 'Plague in Colchester, 1579-1666', *Trans. Essex Arch. Soc*.(ser. 3), iv. 136. [27] Essex RO, D/B5 Gb3, ff. 44v, 69. [28] *HMC Hatfield*, xix. 138; *LJ*, ii. 511a. [29] Harl. 6838, ff. 226v-7, 228v-31, 232-41, 243-5,

247-8, 249v-52; *CJ*, i. 410a. [30] The town had been paved, at least in part, by 1473: *VCH Essex*, ii. 335. [31] Essex RO, D/B5 Gb3, f. 1v. For the 1593 bill, see *Procs. in Parls. of Eliz. I* ed. T.E. Hartley, iii. 134, 149. [32] Nicholas, *Procs. 1621*, i. 72-3; *CD 1621*, ii. 111-12; iv. 83. [33] *CD 1621*, iii. 171, 250, n.39; iv. 306-7; *CJ*, i. 609b, 621a. [34] *CJ*, i. 761a, 766b. [35] Ibid. 690b, 775a. [36] Ibid. 697b; 'Pym 1624', f. 87. [37] *CJ*, i. 698a, 782b. [38] HLRO, O.A. 21 Jas. I c. 68. [39] *LJ*, iii. 386a. [40] *Oxford DNB sub* Samuel Harsnett; Essex RO, D/Y 2/4/159, 163, 167; *CSP Dom*. 1625-6, pp. 111, 117. [41] *LJ*, iii. 400b, 403b; *CJ*, i. 711b, 712a.

A.D.T.

HARWICH

Right of election: in the corporation

Number of voters: 32

c.25 Apr. 1604[1]	SIR RICHARD BROWNE THOMAS TREVOR
29 Oct. 1605[2]	JOHN PANTON *vice* Browne, deceased
14 Mar. 1614[3]	SIR HARBOTTLE GRIMSTON, bt. SIR ROBERT MANSELL
aft. 11 Apr. 1614[4]	SIR CHARLES MONTAGU *vice* Mansell, opted to sit for Carmarthenshire
29 Dec. 1620[5]	SIR THOMAS CHEKE EDWARD GRIMSTON
27 Jan. 1624[6]	(SIR) NATHANIEL RICH CHRISTOPHER HERRYS
26 Apr. 1625[7]	CHRISTOPHER HERRYS
27 Apr. 1625[8]	(SIR) EDMUND SAWYER
10 Jan. 1626	(SIR) NATHANIEL RICH CHRISTOPHER HERRYS
26 Feb. 1628	(SIR) NATHANIEL RICH CHRISTOPHER HERRYS
20 Oct. 1628[9]	HARBOTTLE GRIMSTON *vice* Herrys, deceased

In 1614 the author of *England's Way to Win Wealth* described Harwich as 'a royal harbour' and 'a proper town', whose dry beach made it an ideal location from which to put to sea fleets of fishing busses to compete with the Dutch, 'there being no place in all Holland comparable'. However, this potential remained unexploited, local fishing activity being limited to three or four vessels which caught cod and ling off Iceland every year. The town's principal trade was the shipping of coal from Newcastle to London, but an attempt to erect a staple for seacoals in the port was scotched by the Privy Council on the advice of Newcastle's aldermen in 1616.[10] In 1618 the newly appointed navy commissioners briefly considered developing Harwich as a naval base, only to be advised that it was 'not a fit port except for ships on special service',[11] and in 1629 the captain of a large naval warship denounced Harwich as 'that dangerous harbour' after his vessel almost ran aground there. Nevertheless, two smaller royal ships were successfully repaired at Harwich in 1627, and three ships of 250 tons or more were built there between 1625 and 1638.[12] Moreover, for a century after 1665 the port served as a naval building yard.[13]

Its limited economic activity meant that Harwich during the early seventeenth century was far from prosperous. In 1610 the town, together with the neighbouring village of Dovercourt, boasted only 40 subsidymen, whose total contribution to a single subsidy amounted to just £8 2s.[14] Faced with the demand for a Forced Loan in January 1627, the corporation not surprisingly pleaded penury, 'having neither any common lands to maintain the ordinary charge thereof, and very small in comparison of [sic] other places, [there being] no personal estates of lands or goods, whereof our subsidy books, though over-rated, may give assurance'.[15] The Crown was eventually forced to admit the force of these arguments, and in 1637 Harwich was required to provide only £20 in Ship Money, compared with the £300 and £70 demanded from Colchester and Maldon respectively.[16] Yet, despite its poverty, Harwich was of considerable strategic significance. Following the outbreak of war with Spain in 1625, (Sir) John Coke* drew attention both to its suitability as an enemy landing site and the inadequacy of its defences. His concern, coupled perhaps with a visit to Harwich by the duke of Buckingham in November 1625, prompted the partial repair of the town's fortifications and a lengthy mobilization of the Essex militia.[17]

At the beginning of the seventeenth century Harwich remained an unincorporated, unfranchised borough, although its earliest charter was dated 1318.[18] In 1601, however, the town was granted its own commission of the peace, and that same year it attempted, unsuccessfully, to return Members to Parliament.[19] By the beginning of James's reign Harwich had acquired powerful allies: lord chancellor Ellesmere (Thomas Egerton I[†]), was *custos rotulorum*

of its newly created bench, and the attorney-general, Sir Edward Coke*, brother-in-law of the local lawyer Serjeant Robert Barker*, was the town's recorder.[20] It was doubtless with the help of Ellesmere and Coke that, on 18 Apr. 1604, Harwich was granted a fresh charter. Previously it had been governed by a portreeve, but now it was empowered to form a corporate body consisting of a mayor and common council, comprising eight aldermen (from whom the mayor was to be chosen annually) and 24 capital burgesses. In addition, the town was permitted to return two burgesses to Parliament.[21]

The cost of the new charter was considerable, for although the king waived all charges his servants were less generous and lawyers' fees had to be met. At least £72 was raised, though the only surviving account of expenditure records payments of just £13 4s., including 8s. 'bestowed at times on Sir Richard Browne's men and Mr. Serjeant Hay'.[22] Browne was a former clerk of the peace for Essex with family ties in the county, and his help in procuring the charter undoubtedly explains his subsequent election to Parliament by a grateful corporation. He had taken his seat by 26 Apr. 1604,[23] although the writ authorizing the holding of an election was only issued the day before. His fellow burgess was Thomas Trevor, a recently qualified barrister from Denbighshire. Trevor may have been loosely connected with Ellesmere, whose many offices included that of steward of the lordship of Denbigh. If so, then his election was perhaps the corporation's way of rewarding Ellesmere for allowing their charter to pass the great seal. The lord chancellor's assistance was certainly acknowledged following Browne's death in May 1604, for Harwich chose as Browne's replacement Ellesmere's secretary, John Panton. The record of this by-election in Harwich's minute book is revealing, because it demonstrates that the corporation, unused to parliamentary electoral practice, thought that it was also re-electing Thomas Trevor, who had not been unseated by Browne's death.

Gratitude for services rendered may well explain the corporation's decision to elect Sir Robert Mansell in 1614. Mansell was treasurer of the Navy, and enjoyed considerable influence over the lord high admiral, the 1st earl of Nottingham (Charles Howard I[†]). Shortly before a new Parliament was summoned, in January 1614, the corporation instructed two of its members 'to travel to Sir Robert Mansell, knight, about the business of the town'.[24] The nature of this business was unspecified, but at around the same time Alderman Gooding was paid £7 'at his going to London about the vice admiral', and an additional 36s. was laid out 'about the Admiralty' on his return.[25] From this it would seem as though Mansell was enlisted by the town to help it acquire the right to Admiralty jurisdiction, which it did not enjoy under the 1604 charter.[26] These rights had originally been conferred by Edward IV on the duke of Norfolk (d.1476), but by the beginning of the seventeenth century they had passed to the town's recorder, Sir Edward Coke who, perhaps as a result of Mansell's mediation, authorized the town to exercise them on his behalf in December 1614.[27] Mansell preferred to represent Carmarthenshire at Westminster rather than Harwich, a mere borough. His place was taken by Sir Charles Montagu, whose wife was the sister of Sir George Whitmore, a London alderman who had purchased the manor of Harwich from the Crown in 1604.[28]

Montagu's fellow burgess was Sir Harbottle Grimston, bt. Elected at the same time as Mansell, Grimston was settled at Bradfield Hall, situated just over three miles from Harwich. During the 1620s his local standing gave him control of one of the borough's seats, although he himself did not represent the town again until the Long Parliament. His eldest son Edward was returned there in December 1620, while his son-in-law Christopher Herrys took a seat at each of the four subsequent parliamentary elections. When Herrys died in 1628, he was replaced by Grimston's second son, Harbottle.

From 1620 the remaining seat was usually in the gift of the 2nd earl of Warwick (Sir Robert Rich*), the principal landowner in Essex and also the county's vice-admiral. In December 1620 Warwick thanked the corporation for electing his brother-in-law Sir Thomas Cheke.[29] Evidence from the corporation minute book, in the form of a crossing out, suggests that the town set aside an earlier decision to return their former Member, Sir Charles Montagu, who had already been elected for Higham Ferrers. Warwick's interests were represented in 1624, 1626 and 1628 by his cousin and man of business, Sir Nathaniel Rich. Only in 1625, when the corporation chose the Exchequer auditor Sir Edmund Sawyer, did Warwick's interest waver. Sawyer probably owed his seat to a former business association with (Sir) William Whitmore*, brother of Sir George and relative by marriage of Sir Charles Montagu. His election occurred on the day after the town chose Christopher Herrys to be their other burgess, which suggests either that his was a late application or that the members of the corporation initially disagreed among themselves regarding his suitability.

Most of the town's financial records are now lost, but the surviving chamberlain's account for 1613-14 does not record the payment of parliamentary wages. The expenditure of 5s. on crayfish sent to Sir Harbottle Grimston that year may have been a courtesy bestowed annually on a local gentleman of standing rather than a gratuity in lieu of wages.[30] None of the Members returned to Parliament by Harwich appear to have voiced concerns of special interest to the town apart from Herrys. In February 1626 he declared, during a debate on the neglected state of the country's coastal defences, that Harwich 'had neither bullets, guns nor powder', and that the newly erected fort on Landguard Point lacked both gunners and munitions.[31] Herrys was almost certainly speaking to a brief prepared by his father-in-law, who had recently been put in charge of repairing Harwich's defences.

---

[1] No indenture survives; this is the date of the writ: OR. [2] OR. Harwich bor. ms 98/3 f. 6 conveys the impression that the election was held on the Feast of St. Andrew (30 November). [3] Harwich bor. ms 98/3, f. 26v. [4] Ibid. f. 27. This is the date of the warrant. The date of the election is wrongly given in the corp. minute bk. as 24 Mar. 1614, a clerical error compounded by the fact that the year date has been crossed out and replaced with '1615'. [5] OR, but see below n. 27. [6] Ibid. [7] Harwich bor. ms 98/3, f. 42. [8] OR. This is the date on the indenture, which records the election of both Herrys and Sawyer. [9] OR. [10] Printed in Harl. Misc. iii. 401; Trin. House of Deptford Trans. ed. G.G. Harris (London Rec. Soc. xix), 55, 100; APC, 1615-16, p. 537. [11] BL, uncatalogued ms (formerly Derbys. RO, Coke ms C95/42); Jacobean Commissions of Enquiry ed. A.P. McGowan (Navy Recs. Soc. cxvi), p. xxii. [12] SP16/147/18; BL, uncatalogued ms (formerly Derbys. RO, Coke ms C160/12); VCH Essex, ii. 282. [13] P. Morant, Hist. and Antiqs. of Essex (1768), i. pt. 2, p. 500. [14] E179/111/572. [15] SP16/52/13. [16] SP16/358, f. 1v. [17] CSP Dom. 1625-6, pp. 89-90, 93, 96, 101-4, 106-8, 112, 115, 125, 138, 226, 229, 371, 452; VCH Essex, ii. 282. [18] Morant, i. pt. 2, p. 500. [19] L.T. Weaver, The Harwich Story, 33; Procs. in Parls. of Eliz. ed. T.E. Hartley, iii. 324; C193/32/13. [20] C181/1, f. 50. [21] Anon, Charters Granted to Bor. of Harwich (1798), pp. 7-8, 29-30. [22] Ibid. 40-1; Harwich bor. ms 109/3. [23] CJ, i. 185b. [24] Harwich bor. ms 98/3, f. 24. [25] Harwich bor. ms 99/1. [26] Weaver, 26. [27] B. Carlyon Hughes, Hist. Harwich Harbour, 26; Harwich bor. ms 144/2. [28] Vis. Salop (Harl. Soc. xxix), 499; Weaver, 27; M. Gray, 'Exchequer officials and the Market in Crown Property' in Estates of the Eng. Crown ed. R.W. Hoyle, 125. [29] Harwich bor. ms 109/1. It is puzzling that the letter was written eight days before the corp. minute bk. and the returned indenture suggest that Cheke was actually elected. [30] Harwich bor. ms 99/1. [31] Procs. 1626, ii. 136, 140.

A.D.T.

MALDON

Right of election: in the freemen

Number of voters: 89 in 1625

aft. 20 Feb. 1604[1]	SIR EDWARD LEWKNOR I	
	WILLIAM WISEMAN, recorder	
	?Thomas Mildmay[†]	
4 Nov. 1605	THEOPHILUS HOWARD,	
	LORD HOWARD DE WALDEN vice	
	Lewknor, deceased	
25 Jan. 1610	SIR JOHN SAMMES vice	
	Wiseman, deceased	
19 Feb. 1610[2]	SIR ROBERT RICH vice	
	Lord Howard de Walden, called	
	the Upper House	
9 Mar. 1614[3]	SIR JOHN SAMMES	
	CHARLES CHIBORNE, recorder	
20 Dec. 1620[4]	SIR JULIUS CAESAR, high steward	
	SIR HENRY MILDMAY	
		2nd seat
22 Jan. 1624	SIR ARTHUR HERRYS	-
	SIR WILLIAM MASHAM, bt.	47
	Sir Henry Mildmay	42[5]
12 Apr. 1625	SIR ARTHUR HERRYS	
	SIR HENRY MILDMAY	
4 July 1625	SIR WILLIAM MASHAM, bt. vice	
	Herrys, chose to sit for Essex	
11 Jan. 1626	SIR WILLIAM MASHAM, bt.	
	SIR THOMAS CHEKE	
28 Feb. 1628[6]	SIR HENRY MILDMAY	
	SIR ARTHUR HERRYS	

Situated on a hill overlooking the confluence of the rivers Blackwater and Chelmer, Maldon was an ancient port town of approximately 1,000 inhabitants.[7] Unlike Colchester or nearby Witham, it failed to develop a significant textile industry,[8] and its trade with the Continent was on a decidedly small scale.[9] Though well placed to exploit the North Sea fisheries, Maldon possesed very few vessels. Indeed, as late as 1624 its entire fleet consisted of five small hoys manned by 18 mariners, two of whom were aged 14.[10] However, its economy flourished during the second half of the sixteenth century. One reason for this was that in 1554 and 1555 the town was rewarded for its loyalty to Mary Tudor with charters of incorporation,[11] which gave it

the right to hold a weekly court of record. Empowered to hear cases without limit or value between private individuals, this court generated badly needed revenue for the corporation and attracted valuable commercial activity, enabling merchants to raise loans on security, transfer credits or debts, contract for supplies and engage in litigation.[12] Another reason for Maldon's economic transformation was a substantial growth in the volume of coal landed at the town's hythe.[13] Rising population levels in south-east England, coupled with dwindling supplies of fuel timber, combined to create a ready market for the town's coal distributors, whose interests were vigorously championed by the borough against those of neighbouring Heybridge.[14]

The tolls generated by the hythe provided a valuable source of income for the corporation, but the hythe itself was expensive to maintain. In 1596 the tower of St. Mary's church, which housed the harbour beacon, collapsed and the money for its repair was not raised before 1628.[15] In 1611 a Maldon linen draper testified that despite the corporation spending more than £100 in repairing the hythe and the town's two bridges, 'there have [been] greater ships of late years come up thither than now can, in respect that the said haven is decayed and landed up'. The corporation's principal source of income for maintaining the hythe, aside from £120 bequeathed by Alderman Breeder in 1609, was a property sales tax peculiar to Maldon known as landcheap. In 1610-11 this duty was resisted in the Exchequer by Thomas Sprignell, lord of the manor of Little Maldon, who argued that it was applicable only in the adjacent manor of Much Maldon. Ironically, being the owner of Maldon hythe and a major coal importer, Sprignell himself stood most to gain from the payment of landcheap.[16]

By the terms of its Marian charters, Maldon's government was vested in the hands of a Common Council consisting of eight aldermen, of whom two were elected annually to serve as bailiffs, and 18 head-burgesses. The right to return Members to Parliament had been exercised since 1332, and the Marian charters did no more than confirm this. However, in January 1559, exploiting its new authority to make by-laws, the Common Council ordered the franchise to be restricted to its own members and an additional 12 burgesses of its choice, thereby excluding the vast body of freemen who had traditionally been entitled to vote.[17] This attempt to disfranchise the bulk of the commonalty ultimately failed. When the earl of Leicester tried to nominate both Members in 1584 he was informed by the bailiffs and aldermen that 'our election standeth upon the consent of a great multitude', whose support could not be assured.[18]

It has been claimed that Maldon customarily gave one of its parliamentary seats to its high steward or his nominee.[19] Between 1559 and his death in 1583, the town's first high steward, Sir Thomas Radcliffe[†], 3rd earl of Sussex, certainly influenced the borough's parliamentary elections. However, none of the Members elected after Sussex's death appear to have owed their seats to his successor, Robert Devereux, 2nd earl of Essex. Moreover, while the next high steward, Sir Thomas Mildmay[†], obtained the backing of the common council for his son Thomas in 1604, the commonalty preferred instead to return the borough's recorder, William Wiseman. The next high steward, Sir Julius Caesar, chancellor of the Exchequer 1606-14 and master of the Rolls 1614-36, fared no better in the short term, as neither of the candidates returned in 1614 owed him their places.

At the general election of December 1620, however, Caesar proved more successful. He not only obtained the senior seat for himself but was almost certainly responsible for securing the junior place for the master of the Jewel House, Sir Henry Mildmay, whose estate at Wanstead lay too far from Maldon to have given him independent electoral influence. However, Caesar's electoral success is unlikely to have stemmed simply from the fact that he was high steward. Gratitude for services rendered was surely the decisive factor, as Caesar had not only taken a close interest in the Exchequer proceedings against Thomas Sprignell, but on his advice Maldon had resolved in 1618 to erect a bar across the Blackwater to prevent vessels going to Heybridge until they had paid the toll for passing the hythe.[20] Naturally, however, this sense of gratitude quickly evaporated. Shortly before the 1624 election Caesar was warned by Maldon's bailiffs that they could not guarantee a place for his nominee, Sir Henry Mildmay, as many of the town's freemen were 'now affected to men of quality near to our township'.[21] This prediction proved accurate, for in the ensuing contest Mildmay was defeated by Sir William Masham by 47 votes to 42. Caesar remained undeterred, however, and in 1625 he again nominated Mildmay, who this time proved the popular choice.[22] Neither of the successful candidates owed their places to Caesar in 1626. Mildmay was again returned in 1628, when, for the first time, he was awarded the senior seat. However, it seems likely that it was Mildmay's position at Court rather than Caesar's influence which proved important on this occasion. Following his election Maldon sent Milday various messages at Wanstead before

Parliament began. Their contents are unknown, but in all likelihood the corporation had elected Mildmay with the aim of persuading him to use his Court connections to lobby on their behalf regarding a company of Irish soldiers which had been billeted on them. In a petition addressed to the Privy Council written about three weeks before Mildmay's election, the townsmen complained that the troops 'command in our houses as if they were our lords and we their slaves', committing assaults and forcing householders to stay indoors.[23] An initial attempt to persuade the government to order the removal of these soldiers had ended in failure. Within a week of Mildmay's election, however, orders were issued for them to be transferred to Witham.[24] Mildmay's role in bringing about the Privy Council's change of heart is suggested by the borough's payment of 30s. to his servant for 'bringing letters from the Council and the lord lieutenant for the removal of the Irish soldiers'.[25]

Before 1619 Maldon's recorder had a strong claim to one of the borough's parliamentary seats. In 1604 the recorder, William Wiseman, was returned even though the bailiffs and aldermen supported Sir Thomas Mildmay's son. After Wiseman's death in January 1610, Maldon overlooked its new recorder, Charles Chiborne, in favour of a local landowner, Sir John Sammes. This was probably because it had been forced to disappoint Sammes at an earlier by-election after the Privy Council had urged the borough to return the son of lord treasurer Suffolk, Theophilus Howard, Lord Howard de Walden. Chiborne was passed over again at a second by-election in the following month, when the borough returned Sir Robert Rich after Lord Howard de Walden was summoned to the Lords. Chiborne's turn nevertheless came in 1614. During the 1620s the town's recorder, John Wright, was never elected to Parliament because, as clerk of the Commons, he was ineligible to sit.

As in the Elizabethan period, no townsman was returned to Parliament between 1604 and 1629, and the only members of the local gentry to receive seats were Sir John Sammes, who lived three miles away at Langford Hall, and Sir Arthur Herrys of Creeksea, who owned property at nearby Woodham Mortimer. Religious considerations undoubtedly swayed many of Maldon's puritan-minded voters more than the proximity of candidates to their borough. Despite the fact that Sir Edward Lewknor I was seated at Denham in West Suffolk, his godly credentials assured him of the senior seat in 1604. Likewise, the principal attraction to the borough of Sir William Masham, who lived in western Essex, was undoubtedly his religious

leanings, evidenced in part through his family connections. Returned on three occasions during the 1620s,
Masham was nominated each time by his father-in-
law Sir Francis Barrington*, a well-known puritan.[26]
Masham's rival in 1624, Sir Henry Mildmay, proved
acceptable to Maldon on three occasions. In part, as
we have seen, this was because he was the nominee of
the borough's high steward, but his religious views
must also have played some role in his adoption, as he
was one of just eight speakers in 1628 who are known
to have condemned Arminianism explicitly in the
Commons.[27] Given the shared religious outlook of
Mildmay and Masham, it is scarcely surprising that
the contest between them proved so close. Soundness in religion, just as much as the fact that he was the
borough's recorder, undoubtedly improved William
Wiseman's electoral chances in 1604. On the other
hand, religion played little part in the election of
Theophilus Howard in 1605, who was foisted on the
borough by the Privy Council. Whether the religious
views of Sir John Sammes were important in securing
him a seat in January 1610 is unknown. Described by
Maldon's bailiffs as 'a man well esteemed of', Sammes
was so popular that, in 1605, he would almost certainly
have taken the seat vacated by Lewknor's death had he
not agreed to stand down in favour of Lord Howard de
Walden at the bailiffs' request.[28]

Maldon's puritan inclinations enabled the Rich
family of Leez Priory, the largest landowners in Essex,
to exercise electoral influence in the borough. Employment by the Rich family undoubtedly strengthened
the hand of William Wiseman, who in addition to
being the borough's recorder and a godly magistrate,
was also Lord Rich's estate steward. Wiseman subtly
reminded the corporation of this connection after
its members warned him in February 1604 that they
intended to favour Thomas Mildmay. 'I have some
particular business in Parliament for a matter of great
importance', he wrote, 'as some of honour and great
worships in this shire do well know'.[29] The matter he
referred to was probably a bill regarding the debts of
the Elizabethan lord chancellor, Christopher Hatton
(Christopher Hatton I[†]), a measure of particular interest to Sir Robert Rich, who had married the daughter of Hatton's nephew and heir, Sir William Hatton.
Wiseman died in January 1610, and although his
replacement was not a member of the Rich family or
one of its clients, the summoning to the Lords of Lord
Howard de Walden in February allowed the entry
into the Commons of the eldest son of Lord Rich,
Sir Robert Rich, later 2nd earl of Warwick. During
the 1620s the Rich family's candidate at Maldon was
usually Sir Arthur Herrys, who leased several Essex

properties from Warwick. However, when Herrys was
returned for Essex with Warwick's support in 1625, his
place was taken at Maldon by Sir William Masham,
who was connected to Warwick through the latter's ally,
Sir Francis Barrington. In 1626 Cheke was prevented
from sitting in the Commons by virtue of being sheriff
of Essex. This meant that his place was taken by
Warwick's brother-in-law, Sir Thomas Cheke of Pirgo.
However, he resumed his place as a Maldon burgess in
1628, although he was forced to accept the junior seat
after the senior position was bestowed upon Mildmay.

Prospective Members of Parliament for Maldon
were expected to take the oath of a freeman before they
were elected, and to attend the hustings in person.
The oath was usually administered at the time of the
election, but in the case of Lord Howard de Walden,
whose affairs at Court kept him from attending, an
officer was sent to his London lodgings and he was
elected in his absence.[30] In 1624 Masham also failed
to appear on election day as he was not formally sworn
a freeman until four days later.[31] Parliamentary elections were held at the town's moothall, where the
Common Council met, to which those entitled to vote
were summoned by bell. In 1624 the bellman, John
Cowell, was paid 6d. 'for proclaiming the meeting of
all free-burgesses at the moothall ... about the choice
of burgesses for the Parliament'.[32] Letters of nomination addressed to the bailiffs were brought to the attention of Common Council before the election, and then
to the assembled voters at the hustings.[33] The county
sheriff or his deputy served as the returning officer.
He was not normally rewarded for his pains, though
in 1604 and 1628 the under-sheriff was paid 8s. and
4s. respectively, and in 1604 an additional 3s. was given
to the messenger who bore the Proclamation summoning Parliament.[34] During the mid-1620s completed
indentures were sent to Westminster in a box, which
cost 4d. in 1624 and 8d. in 1626.[35] In 1625 the amount
spent in boxing up and sealing the indentures for that
year's parliamentary elections came to an astonishing
4s. 10d.[36] Despite this extravagance, Maldon's parliamentary representatives were unpaid. New Year gifts
of sugar loafs were nevertheless presented to Sammes
and Chiborne in 1615, and to Mildmay and Herrys
in 1629. In 1625 a servant belonging to Masham was
given 20s. after Masham sent a buck to the town. The
same sum was given to one of Mildmay's servants in
1628 for a book which 'much concerned the good of
this borough'.[37] During the 1620s the borough kept
in close contact with its Members at Westminster. In
1624 Masham received a packet of letters sent by the
bailiffs, and received a visit from the town's serjeant of
the mace, as did Mildmay in 1625.[38]

[1] Essex RO, D/B 3/3/205/1. [2] OR. [3] Essex RO, D/B 3/1/19, f. 70v. [4] OR. [5] Essex RO, D/B 3/3/392/18. [6] OR. [7] W.J. Petchey, *A Prospect of Maldon*, 23. [8] Ibid. 12-13, 109. [9] E190/598/14. [10] Essex RO, D/B 3/3/405. By 1629, as the Caroline war with Spain neared its end, the number of mariners had been reduced to 15: SP16/155/31. [11] *CPR*, 1553-4, pp. 137-9; 1554-5, pp. 95-7. [12] Petchey, 130; R. Tittler, 'Incorporation of Boroughs', *Hist.* lii. 38. [13] Petchey, 148. [14] Ibid. 143-5. [15] Ibid. 13-14. [16] Ibid. 77-8; E112/80/180; E134/9Jas./Mich.38; E124/13, ff. 129v, 137, 149. [17] Petchey, 248-9. [18] Essex RO, D/B 3/3/205/6. [19] B.W. Quintrell, 'Govt. of Essex, 1603-42' (London Ph.D. thesis, 1965), p. 32. [20] Lansd. 167, f. 282; Essex RO, D/B 3/3/205/10. [21] Essex RO, D/B 3/3/392/67. [22] Add. 12496, ff. 106, 108v. [23] *CSP Dom.* 1627-8, p. 549. [24] *APC*, 1627-8, pp. 264, 282, 335-6. [25] Essex RO, D/B 3/3/297, rot. 11. [26] Essex RO, D/B 3/3/658. [27] N. Tyacke, *Anti-Calvinists*, 133. [28] *HMC Hatfield*, xvii. 455. [29] Essex RO, D/B 3/3/205/1. [30] *HMC Hatfield*, xvii. 455, 469. [31] Essex RO, D/B 3/3/392/53. [32] Essex RO, D/B 3/3/108, rot. 11. [33] Add. 12496, f. 106. [34] Essex RO, D/B 3/3/275, rots. 6, 8; D/B 3/3/297, rot. 12. [35] Essex RO, D/B 3/3/108, rot. 12; D/B 3/3/295. [36] Essex RO, D/B 3/3/294. [37] Ibid; D/B 3/3/283, rot. 8; D/B 3/3/298, rot. 8; D/B 3/3/297, rot. 10. [38] Essex RO, D/B 3/3/108 rots. 11, 12; 3/3/294.

A.D.T.

GLOUCESTERSHIRE

Number of voters: unknown

7 Mar. 1604	SIR THOMAS BERKELEY
	SIR RICHARD BERKELEY
30 May 1604	JOHN THROCKMORTON *vice*
	Sir Richard Berkeley, deceased
c. Mar. 1614	SIR WILLIAM COOKE
	RICHARD BERKELEY
20 Dec. 1620	SIR ROBERT TRACY
	MAURICE BERKELEY
14 Jan. 1624	SIR THOMAS ESTCOURT
	JOHN DUTTON
	Robert Poyntz
20 Oct. 1624	(SIR) MAURICE BERKELEY *vice*
	Estcourt, deceased
	Robert Poyntz
4 May 1625	(SIR) MAURICE BERKELEY
	JOHN DUTTON
c. Jan. 1626	SIR ROBERT TRACY
	SIR ROBERT POYNTZ
5 Mar. 1628	SIR ROBERT POYNTZ
	NATHANIEL STEPHENS

Few counties could vie with Gloucestershire in the antiquity of its families. The Berkeleys, the Tracys and the Poyntzes were all well established before the Plantagenets. Throughout the Jacobean period, though not under Elizabeth, the county's dominant electoral interest was that of the Berkeleys. Henry, 7th Lord Berkeley was a popular local figure, and on James's accession, doubtless with the aid of his former brother-in-law, Lord Henry Howard, he became Gloucestershire's lord lieutenant. This disappointed the expectations of the 5th Lord Chandos (Grey Brydges[†]),[1] who enjoyed the sobriquet 'king of Cotswold' from the splendour of his hospitality but was compromised (however unjustly) in the Bye Plot.

In 1604 Lord Berkeley's son, Sir Thomas, and his cousin, Sir Richard of Stoke Gifford, were elected at Gloucester Castle.[2] Sir Richard had been prominent in county administration throughout the last reign, but neither he nor Sir Thomas had ever sat in Parliament before. However, Sir Richard was now a septuagenarian, and he died in the sixth week of the Parliament, leaving a son of unsound mind. The by-election was held at Tetbury, on the eastern edge of the county, probably under the auspices of (Sir) Thomas Estcourt, who signed the indenture in first place.[3] Estcourt was to be one of Lord Berkeley's executors, and doubtless promoted the election of John Throckmorton of Lypiatt, one of whose uncles had married into the Berkeley family. Throckmorton thus regained the seat that he had held in the last Elizabethan Parliament. By the time of the 1614 general election, the situation had altered dramatically. Throckmorton had sold his Gloucestershire estate (in 1610) and both Sir Thomas Berkeley and the 7th Lord Berkeley were dead and the 8th Lord Berkeley was a minor. The senior seat was taken by Sir William Cooke, a hereditary official of the Court of Wards who had married a Gloucestershire heiress; but he probably owed his election to his position as Lord Berkeley's chief executor. The junior seat went to Sir Richard Berkeley's grandson Richard. Lord Chandos, who had succeeded to the lieutenancy,[4] played no known part in this or the subsequent election. Cooke died in 1619, and his seat was taken in the third Jacobean Parliament by Sir Robert Tracy, the heir to the Toddington estate. Richard Berkeley, who seems to have involved himself in pecuniary difficulties by an ambitious plantation venture, yielded the second seat to his son Maurice, 'then not 22 years of age'. During this Parliament the Gloucestershire clothiers made 'great complaint' against the Merchant Adventurers for their unwillingness to buy cloth.[5]

In 1624 John Dutton, a man of great wealth and the third of his line in Gloucestershire, was 'agreed and admitted, without contradiction, to be chosen in the first place'.[6] For the other seat Estcourt, now in control of the Berkeley interest while the 8th Lord (George the Traveller) was engaged in linguistic studies abroad, was challenged by Robert Poyntz, who seems to have taken over his family's estate while his father languished in a debtors' prison. The sheriff summoned the county court to Painswick, but delegated his responsibilities to the under-sheriff, an inexperienced youth. On the day of the election 'Estcourt yielded the choice, acknowledged it publicly that the other two were chosen, and commended the county for it'; two hours later Tracy's father, who had been out of politics since the Essex rising, demanded a poll. 'The place a little church; a great throng. Those that named Poyntz, ... though far off, delivered in papers by ten at a time'. Their candidate was defeated by 152 votes, and Estcourt, in accordance with social precedence, was awarded the senior seat.[7] Poyntz subsequently petitioned the Commons against this outcome on several grounds. Besides the venue and the waiver he alleged that

> some few freeholders, who had pronounced for Mr. Poyntz, went away after the poll demanded, and before their names or voices were taken or recorded; and some other freeholders, which came to the place after 11 of the clock, while the election was then in hand, were admitted to give voice, and numbered for Sir Thomas Estcourt.[8]

Estcourt's counsel replied that 'the place was appointed three weeks before, and where the country court had usually been kept for three or four years', that Estcourt's disclaimer was 'but in modesty', and that those who failed to register their votes 'were no freeholders, but such as knew that when they came to their oath they should not be allowed'.[9] John Glanville, reporting from the committee for privileges in Estcourt's favour, observed that no man 'being lawfully chosen' could 'by any unwillingness or refusal of his own make himself incapable'. Those freeholders who had left early had only themselves to blame, and those who arrived after the poll had begun must be allowed to vote, 'for all favour is to be afforded in allowing voices to as many freeholders as reasonably may be had for the choice of those by whose voices in Parliament they and their heirs are to be bound for ever'.[10] Estcourt, despite his 'modesty', proved to be the most active Gloucestershire Member of the period, but he sat only once as he died on 4 July 1624 on his way home from Westminster. Poyntz, anxious to expunge the memory of his earlier defeat, contested the ensuing by-election, but he was again thwarted, this time by (Sir) Maurice Berkeley. Since the House did not meet again before the king's death, it was not called upon to sit in judgment on Poyntz's ingenious

scheme to keep some of Berkeley's voters away from Painswick by summoning the subsidy commission to meet 18 miles away.[11]

Berkeley and Dutton were re-elected to the first Caroline Parliament. Sir Robert Tracy regained the senior seat in 1626, and Poyntz was at last allowed to take his turn. Although the 8th Lord Berkeley was by now of age he played little part in Gloucestershire affairs in this period, he travelled abroad extensively and accumulated large debts, consequently the Berkeley electoral interest was in eclipse in the later 1620s.[12]

The Forced Loan aroused particular hostility among the Gloucestershire gentry. In early 1627 the earl of Northampton and Sir John Bridgeman were sent by the Privy Council to Gloucestershire to stir the commissioners into action. At a meeting on 17 Feb. Northampton and Bridgeman found that of the 25 commissioners who attended 12 refused to have anything to do with the loan, although the remaining 13 were more co-operative.[13] Six of the refusers, (Sir) Maurice Berkeley, John Dutton, Sir Robert Poyntz, Henry Poole* Thomas Nicholas* and Nathaniel Coxwell, were summoned to appear before the Privy Council and were subsequently purged from the bench and imprisoned.[14] Following his release in January 1628, Poyntz stood for election once again, and was rewarded with the senior seat. The junior place went to Nathaniel Stephens, who had also refused to co-operate with the collection of the Loan, though unlike Poyntz he had not been imprisoned.

[1] *HMC Hatfield*, xv. 230-1. [2] C219/35/1/84. [3] C219/35/1/9. [4] Sainty, *Lords Lieutenants*, viii. 21. [5] Nicholas, *Procs. 1621*, ii. 41. [6] J. Glanville, *Reps. of Certain Cases Determined and Adjudged by Commons in Parl.* (1775), p. 100. [7] 'Earle 1624', ff. 124v-5. [8] Glanville, 100-1. [9] 'Earle 1624', f. 125. [10] *CJ*, i. 759a; Glanville, 101-3. [11] W.B. Willcox, *Glos.* 29. [12] *Oxford DNB sub* Berkeley, George, 8th Baron Berkeley. [13] SP16/54/28, 28.I. [14] *APC*, 1627, pp. 125, 374; BRL, 603503/72.

A.D./B.C.

BRISTOL

Right of election: in the corporation and resident freeholders[1]

5 Mar. 1604	GEORGE SNYGGE, recorder
	THOMAS JAMES
11 Nov. 1605	JOHN WHITSON, alderman, *vice* Snygge, appointed to office
c. Mar. 1614	THOMAS JAMES, alderman
	JOHN WHITSON, alderman

c. Dec. 1620	JOHN WHITSON, alderman
	JOHN GUY, alderman
c. Jan. 1624	JOHN BARKER
	JOHN GUY, alderman
c. Apr. 1625	NICHOLAS HYDE, recorder
	JOHN WHITSON, alderman
c. Jan. 1626	JOHN WHITSON, alderman
	JOHN DOUGHTY, alderman
17 Mar. 1628	JOHN DOUGHTY, alderman
	JOHN BARKER

Bristol, as the Privy Council reminded it in 1620, when demanding a contribution of £2,500 towards the cost of a naval expedition, was 'a port that ever hath been reputed to be the second of the kingdom'.[2] With a population about one-twentieth of that of the capital, it came, indeed, a poor second; but it was foremost among the outports in its resentment of London's trading monopolies, 'as if God had no sons to whom he gave the benefit of the earth but in London'. A great part of its trade lay with the Iberian Peninsula, and in the later sixteenth century the leading Bristol merchants had been forced to join the Spanish Company, leaving their own Society of Merchant Venturers, incorporated in 1552, moribund or defunct.[3] Bristol also looked westward to America, and the Newfoundland Company was inspired by one of its Members, John Guy, although it too was largely funded and controlled by Londoners. The port received its first charter in 1155, becoming a separate county with its own sheriff in 1373. The charter of 1499 added a second sheriff and established a council of 43, of which six members were aldermen, and also provided for a recorder who was to be one of the aldermen. Bristol became a cathedral city in 1542, and in 1581 the number of aldermen were doubled at the expense of the common councillors. Confirmatory charters were secured in 1604 and 1626 which did not change the local constitution.[4] Bristol was exempted from the jurisdiction of the lord admiral,[5] but subject to the lord lieutenant of Somerset for militia purposes. However it maintained its independence in its choice of Members, even when the earl of Pembroke combined the lieutenancy with the high stewardship of the city.[6] The franchise lay in the corporation and 'such others as are freeholders resident'. Three of the city's seven Members in the period had passed the chair, and all save the two recorders, George Snygge and Nicholas Hyde, were also prominent members of the Society of Merchant Venturers, which was refounded or revived in 1605.[7] Like the corporation, the society expected the

Members to act for it in and out of Parliament, although it was careful to phrase its instructions as requests. Bristol paid them at the generous rate of 4s. a day, and was always ready to refund extraordinary expenses, including the occasional butt of sack for Mr. Speaker.[8]

Bristol had been accustomed to reserve one seat for its recorder, and in 1604 it accordingly returned Snygge for the third time. It fell to his colleague, Thomas James, a leading Spanish merchant, to open Bristol's campaign against purveyance during the first session, and he also took charge of the general free trade bill. Snygge, appointed a baron of the Exchequer in October 1604, resigned the recordership. His replacement as recorder was Lawrence Hyde I, who was nominated by the earl of Salisbury (Robert Cecil†).[9] Hyde was already sitting in the Commons for Marlborough, and Snygge's seat was taken by John Whitson, another Spanish merchant, James's deputy mayor, William Ellys†, seven other aldermen and 33 'citizens and burgesses' signing the indenture.[10] On 31 Dec. 1605, before Whitson could take his seat, the corporation gave its blessing to the revival of the Merchant Venturers,[11] and in February 1606 the Members vainly sought to include a proviso to preserve the Company's monopoly in the bill for free trade into Spain, Portugal and France.[12] A year later they were instructed to seek royal or conciliar approval for a wharfage tax imposed by the corporation.[13] After the dissolution of Parliament, the corporation sent Whitson back to London to offer the Crown 1,000 marks to purchase Bristol castle, which had become a refuge for outcasts and criminals; but he was unsuccessful.[14] Bristol lavishly entertained the queen when she visited Bath in 1613, and was greatly dismayed at the exaction of wines and other goods for her Household.[15] Hyde, however, may have used the occasion to angle for the senior post on her legal staff, and it is unlikely that he stood for Bristol at the next election. When James and Whitson were re-elected they were instructed to demand repayment from the Exchequer,[16] and shortly after the dissolution of the Addled Parliament Hyde resigned his recordership in favour of his brother Nicholas, who is not known to have sought a seat, here or elsewhere, in the next two elections.

Thomas James died in 1619, but Whitson was re-elected to the third Jacobean Parliament, with Guy, who had recently returned from his Newfoundland venture, as junior Member. They were instructed by the corporation to seek a renewal of the city's commission for Admiralty,[17] and by the Society of Merchant Venturers, with the corporation's approval, to use their 'best endeavour' to secure parliamentary confirmation of its charters. It presumed 'that the several burgesses of Gloucester, Tewkesbury, Worcester, Bewdley, Shrewsbury and all other towns bordering upon Severn will readily assist you in this affairs'.[18] No such bill was introduced, but both Members were active in Bristol's interests. Guy wanted its Admiralty rights protected in the seamarks bill, and tenaciously defended the interests of the Newfoundland settlers in connection with the bill for free fishing off the American coast. Both Members were concerned to protect Bristol's exports, of which lead and calf-skins were said to be the chief.[19] Whitson strove to except the latter from the monopolies bill, while Guy blamed excessive taxation for the decline of the Mendip lead mines. In 1624 the senior seat was taken by John Barker, one of Whitson's trustees, but Guy was re-elected to the junior seat. Between the Parliaments he had been employed in negotiations about the castle, and in a further protest against purveyance claims as revived by lord treasurer Middlesex (Sir Lionel Cranfield*). The Bristol Members gave sworn testimony accordingly in the impeachment proceedings against Middlesex, but again they failed to meet the request of the Merchant Venturers for parliamentary sanction or protection.

Nicholas Hyde at length claimed the senior seat in the first Caroline Parliament, and was joined by Whitson, now a septuagenarian. On the day Parliament met the corporation decided to instruct them to make suit to the Council to prevent Londoners attending Bristol's fair 'during the time that the sickness shall continue'.[20] Shortly before the dissolution Whitson was 'desired at his coming to confer both with my lord of Arundel and with the lord treasurer' about a lease of the castle.[21] Nothing has come to light concerning the context of the careful minute in November of the 'laudable and ancient custom' whereby the parliamentary franchise was limited to the corporation and the resident freeholders.[22] Hyde was not re-elected in 1626, and Whitson again moved up to the senior place, the junior seat going to John Doughty, another of his trustees. During the Parliament they were instructed to 'deal for the castle';[23] increasing preoccupation with this problem may account in part for the noticeable decline in parliamentary activity. In 1628 Doughty was re-elected with Barker, his kinsman and partner. After the first session they 'brought in six paper books containing the several arguments made in Parliament house of the liberty of the subjects', which the corporation ordered should be entered into 'some of the register books of this city there to remain of record'.[24] When they returned to Westminster for the second session, they were ordered to seek a fresh commission of Admiralty and to continue the negotiations for the castle,[25] which was at last transferred to the corporation in 1630.[26]

[1] Bristol RO, common council procs. 1608-27, f. 133v. [2] APC, 1619-21, p. 121. [3] P. McGrath, Merchant Venturers of Bristol, 10, 19-20, 26, 52-53. [4] Cal. of Chs. etc. of the City and Council of Bristol, comp. J. Latimer, 3, 77; Bristol Chs. ed. R.C. Latham (Bristol Rec. Soc. xii), 2, 4-5, 140, 144; W. Barrett, Hist. and Antiqs. of City of Bristol, 119. [5] Bristol Chs. 70. [6] Sainty, Lords Lieutenants, 31; Bristol Lists comp. A.B. Beaven, 231. [7] McGrath, 22. [8] Bristol RO, mayor's audit bk. 1610-13, p. 33; common council procs. 1608-27, f. 95. [9] Bristol RO, common council procs. 1598-1608, pp. 100, 102. [10] C219/35/1/93. [11] Recs. Relating to Soc. of Merchant Venturers ed. P.W. McGrath (Bristol Rec. Soc. xvii), 3-6. [12] CJ, i. 275a. [13] Bristol RO, common council procs. 1598-1608, pp. 132, 135. [14] Bristol RO, common council procs. 1608-27, ff. 21v-2; J. Latimer, Annals of Bristol in Seventeenth Cent. 43. [15] Latimer, 48-50. [16] Bristol RO, common council procs. 1608-27, f. 45v [17] Ibid. f. 92. [18] Recs. Relating to Soc. of Merchant Venturers, 9-14. [19] HMC Hatfield, xxi. 123. [20] Bristol RO, common council procs. 1608-27, f. 126v. [21] Ibid. f. 128. [22] Ibid. f. 133v. [23] Ibid. f. 137. [24] Bristol RO, common council procs. 1627-42, f. 6v. [25] Ibid. f. 11. [26] Bristol Chs. 150; Latimer, 113.

A.D.

CIRENCESTER

Right of election: in the burgage holders 1604-21; in the inhabitant householders 1624-8

Number of voters: c.65 in 1604-21

c. Mar. 1604	RICHARD MARTIN ARNOLD OLDISWORTH	
7 Apr. 1604	EDWARD JONES vice Martin, chose to sit for Christchurch	
16 Jan. 1610	SIR ANTHONY MAYNEY vice Jones, deceased	
c. Mar. 1614	SIR ANTHONY MAYNEY ROBERT STRAUNGE	
29 Dec. 1620	SIR THOMAS ROE THOMAS NICHOLAS	
20 Jan. 1624	SIR WILLIAM MASTER HENRY POOLE (Sir) Maurice Berkeley* John George	35 30
23 Apr. 1625	SIR MILES SANDYS HENRY POOLE	
21 Jan. 1626	SIR NEVILLE POOLE JOHN GEORGE	
c. Mar. 1628	SIR GILES ESTCOURT, bt. JOHN GEORGE	

Cirencester had flourished as a centre of the woollen industry under the firm control of the local Augustinian Abbey.[1] Wool continued to play a vital part in the local economy, and therefore the town suffered badly from the trade depression of the 1620s: in 1628 it was reported to have 1,200 poor in need of relief.[2] The parish of Cirencester, which included a significant part of the surrounding countryside, had a population of about 2,760 in 1603.[3] The borough, which had never been incorporated, was governed by a bailiff, two constables and 14 wardsmen nominated annually in the court leet.[4] Parliamentary representation was only intermittent before 1571.[5] The returning officer was the bailiff, who was appointed by the lord of the manor. Until 1615, when he sold it to Sir Henry Poole[†] of Sapperton, the lordship of the manor belonged to the 1st Lord Danvers.[6] As both Danvers and Poole had strong Wiltshire connections, Cirencester provided fewer parliamentary opportunities for the Gloucestershire gentry than might have been expected. After the manor was sold candidates were drawn from a more restricted geographical area, within a six mile radius of the town, but a more elevated social class. Many of them owned property in the borough, and the Straunges and Georges had roots in the town stretching back before the Dissolution, though the Master family of Cirencester Abbey were more recent arrivals. The attempt of the younger branch of the Berkeley family to establish an interest met with limited success.[7]

In 1604 Richard Martin, a rising young lawyer of Devon origin, was returned for the first seat, presumably on the interest of Lord Danvers. The second seat went to Arnold Oldisworth, who came from one of the local families and was then about to take up his reversionary interest in the clerkship of the Hanaper. When Martin chose to sit for a Hampshire borough, he was replaced by Edward Jones, a former colleague of Oldisworth in the service of the Dudley family and an experienced carpet-bagger, who was to spend much of his time working to secure a Crown grant for Danvers. Jones died in 1609, and his replacement, the Kentishman Sir Anthony Mayney, was closely connected to Danvers' cousin the marchioness of Winchester and related to Oldisworth through the Arnold family.[8] Mayney was re-elected in 1614, but Oldisworth, perhaps preoccupied with his increasingly embarrassed financial position, gave way to another kinsman, Robert Straunge, whose grandfather had been the last abbatial bailiff. Straunge owned 'a great house' in Cirencester as well as an estate four miles away.

Straunge did not seek re-election in 1620, although he continued to play a role in electoral politics as his name

heads the signatories on the indenture.[9] As Sir Henry Poole had died soon after his purchase, and his son Henry was probably on his travels, the senior seat went to Sir Thomas Roe, a kinsman by marriage of the Berkeleys, whose mother lived at Rendcomb, five miles north of Cirencester. The remaining seat went to Thomas Nicholas whose wife, a wealthy widow, had brought him an estate within two miles of the town. Nicholas also acted as trustee for Lord Danvers's brother Sir John*, with whom Roe, coincidentally, had been closely associated in the Virginia Company. Both Nicholas and Roe may therefore have been able to appeal to any residual Danvers interest. Notwithstanding his departure on an ambassadorial posting during the summer recess, Roe proved Cirencester's most active Member during the period; he spoke forcefully against the dishonest practices of the cloth trade's middlemen in debate on the bill for free trade in wool, and some years later he founded an apprenticeship charity in the borough.[10]

In 1624 Henry Poole was accorded the first place as of right, 'by most voices, without contradiction',[11] but there were three candidates for the other seat, all in their twenties: Sir William Master, whose sister had married Oldisworth's heir; Roe's nephew (Sir) Maurice Berkeley*; and Oldisworth's nephew John George, a townsman by birth and a barrister of the Middle Temple.[12] The borough was not accustomed to contests, and therefore 'the opinion of a neighbouring serjeant at law' – possibly John Bridgeman of Nympsfield – was sought on the franchise, 'who set it under his hand, that he thought only the freeholders of the lands within the borough ought to have voice'.[13] The election was attended, 'albeit, in truth, he had nothing to do in the matter', by the same youthful under-sheriff who had presided six days previously over the contested county election,[14] and by Master's friend Sir Thomas Estcourt.[15] The bailiff initially declared that Master had 'the greatest number of voices of the inhabitants present', but the various competitors and their friends were agreed that only the freeholders were entitled to vote and persuaded the under-sheriff to announce this publicly.[16] Berkeley, who seems to have been the most insistent on the limited franchise,[17] now demanded a poll of the freeholders.[18] Those inhabitants who were not freeholders now left, while the rest of the assembly adjourned from the town hall to the spacious perpendicular church where the freeholders were sworn.[19] Estcourt later testified that during the poll 'the bailiff sat in the chief place, the [under-] sheriff at his feet'.[20] George withdrew at this point, and Master emerged with 35 votes to Berkeley's 30.[21] The assembly now returned to the town hall, where 'it was solemnly propounded by the bailiff to the whole assembly to know whom they would have in the first place, who answered all, "Mr. Poole", without a negative voice; and for Sir William Master, in like sort, in the second place'.[22] Master's knighthood in fact gave him precedence on the indenture, which was signed in first place by one Edward Master, presumably a kinsman.[23]

Following this outcome Berkeley's supporters in the town petitioned the Commons against 'the sinister practice and procurement' of the under-sheriff, who was thought to have favoured Master because he had previously returned Master's friend, Estcourt, for the county.[24] However, John Glanville, Lady Master's uncle, reported from the committee for privileges that the under-sheriff had acted merely as 'a clerk of minister' to the bailiff, who had overseen the management of the election himself. The committee also found that franchise lay in the inhabitants rather than the freeholders, and that consequently the election had properly ended after the bailiff had declared that Master was the choice of the inhabitants. The subsequent agreement by the candidates to poll the freeholders, the early departure of some of the inhabitants, the unlawful administering of an oath to the freeholders and their subsequent polling 'did not impeach the election', as these events were merely 'surplusage and idle'. Had anyone demanded and been refused a poll of the inhabitants at any time before Master 'was the second time, and finally, declared burgess', the election would have been invalid, but this, the committee noted, had not happened.[25] The order of the House, that where a borough had no charter or custom the franchise should lie with the householders rather than the freeholders, was subsequently copied into the Cirencester parish records.[26]

In 1625 Poole again yielded precedence on the indenture to his social superior, Sir Miles Sandys, a young man who lived at Brimpsfield, eight miles away, but whose father had recently acquired an estate within Cirencester's six-mile limit. According to one diarist, a petition was presented to the committee for privileges after the 1626 election,[27] but nothing is known of the contest that prompted it. Poole had given his interest to his distant cousin and brother-in-law, Sir Neville Poole, who himself lived four miles across the Wiltshire border. He and George, whose address was given as Cirencester, were returned 'with the whole assent and consent of the rest of the burgesses'.[28] George maintained his hold in 1628, when he brought in a bill 'for the better uttering and venting of white cloth'. His senior colleague, Sir Giles Estcourt, came from the Wiltshire branch of the family, and owed his seat to his brother-in-law Master, who was then serving as sheriff of the county.

[1] VCH Glos. ii. 80-83. [2] W. St. Clair Baddeley, Cirencester, 242; CSP Dom. 1627-8, p. 568. [3] P. Clark and J. Hosking, Population Estimates of English Small Towns (Cent. for Urban Hist. Working Pprs. v), 55. [4] S. Rudder, New Hist. of Glos. 352; E178/959. [5] HP Commons, 1558-1603, i. 163-4. [6] J.D. Thorp, 'Hist. of the Manor of Coates', Trans. Bristol and Glos. Arch. Soc. l. 213. [7] E.A. Fuller, 'Cirencester', Trans. Bristol and Glos. Arch. Soc. ix. 334-43; W. St. Clair Baddeley, Cirencester, 250. [8] Vis. Glos. (Harl. Soc. xxi), 4. [9] C219/37/112. [10] VCH Glos. vii. 227. [11] J. Glanville, Reps. of Certain Cases Determined and Adjudged by the Commons in Parl. (1775), pp. 105-6. [12] 'Earle 1624', f. 152v. [13] Glanville, 105. [14] Ibid. 108. [15] 'Earle 1624', f. 153. [16] Glanville, 106. [17] 'Earle 1624', f. 152v. [18] Glanville, 106. [19] Glanville, 106-7. [20] 'Earle 1624', f. 153. [21] Ibid. f. 152v. [22] Glanville, 107. [23] C219/38/93. [24] Glanville, 104. [25] CJ, i. 708a; Glanville, 107-11. [26] Gloucester RO, P86/1/IN6/3, f. 79v. [27] Procs. 1626, ii. 55. [28] C219/40/49.

A.D./B.C.

GLOUCESTER

Right of election: in the freemen

Number of voters: about 500[1]

Feb. 1604	NICHOLAS OVERBURY, recorder JOHN JONES, alderman Thomas Machen, alderman
c. Mar. 1614	THOMAS MACHEN, alderman JOHN BROWNE I, alderman Nicholas Overbury, recorder Christopher Capell, alderman
28 Nov. 1620	JOHN BROWNE I, alderman ANTHONY ROBINSON
c. Jan. 1624	JOHN BROWNE I, alderman ANTHONY ROBINSON
11 May 1625	CHRISTOPHER CAPELL, alderman JOHN BROWNE I, alderman
17 Jan. 1626	CHRISTOPHER CAPELL, alderman JOHN BROWNE I, alderman
12 Feb. 1628	JOHN BROWNE I, alderman JOHN HANBURY

Founded by the Romans at the first easy crossing place above the mouth of the Severn, Gloucester remained 'at the centre of a communication network stretching north-south along the Severn valley and east-west towards London and Wales'. It suffered from the general decline in the textile industries, but was still the prosperous marketing centre for grain from the vales of Berkeley, Gloucester and Tewkesbury, shipping wheat and malt to Bristol, the West Country, Wales and Ireland. Indeed, it managed to support a dozen great inns and a score of lawyers.[2] Gloucester had become a separate county in 1483 and a city in 1541 on the creation of the bishopric.[3] During the sixteenth century it had also acquired its own deputy lieutenants, although the office of lord lieutenant was held conjointly with that of Gloucestershire.[4] Municipal government was vested in a council of 40, of whom the 12 most senior were the aldermen. All the aldermen were ex officio magistrates, and every year they elected one of their number as mayor.[5]

Under the early Stuarts Gloucester maintained its independence in its choice of its Members. Neither the high steward nor lord lieutenant played any discernible role in elections and not even the recorder was guaranteed a seat. Members of the corporation virtually monopolized the city's parliamentary representation: four of the city's seven Members in this period had passed the chair by the time of their election, and only one Member, John Hanbury, held no municipal office at all. The franchise lay in the freemen, 'near 500 persons' in 1624, who assembled at a county court held at the Guildhall, also called the Booth Hall. Before the 1620s the corporation alone nominated the candidates, a practice which was described by the mayor in 1604 as 'according to the ancient usage'.[6] However, one of the nominees was rejected in 1604 and both were laid aside in 1614. Thereafter the corporation may have relinquished control of nominations as elections during the 1620s seem to have been uncontested. However there was increasing friction between Gloucester and the hundreds of Dudstone and King's Barton, known as the 'in-shire', which were governed and taxed from the city.[7] Gloucester paid its Members at the standard rate, raising the money by a special levy. By 1610, many freemen had become reluctant to pay, and were threatened with disfranchisement.[8]

The contested election to the first Stuart Parliament took place against a background of strife within the governing body, conflict which was carried into Star Chamber. The mayor, Thomas Rich, was accused of seeking office so that he could be revenged on alderman Payne, landlord of the already ancient *New Inn*, 'with whom he was then in law, and [on] some others that he liked not'.[9] Whether or not this was true, Payne was dismissed from the corporation on 16 Dec. 1603, and subsequently appealed to the Privy Council. Rich was in London defending the corporation's actions when Gloucester's sheriffs, of whom there were two, received the writ for the election.[10] The sheriffs informed the aldermen of the receipt of the writ and a meeting was held to consider suitable candidates.[11] Alderman John Jones, a friend of Payne's and registrar of the diocese,

arrived at the meeting armed with a copy of the king's proclamation of 11 Jan. 1604, which required each constituency to elect only residents, and proceeded to cast doubt on the eligibility of the newly appointed recorder, Nicholas Overbury, who lived outside the city. 'Carried away with an ambitious humour', he then proposed himself to his colleagues instead. However, his colleagues concluded that Overbury was certainly eligible and decided to nominate both him and Thomas Machen, the father-in-law of Thomas Rich, who was acting as deputy mayor during the latter's absence. On 13 Feb., the day before the election was due to be held, the Common Council met, chaired by Machen, and upheld the aldermen's decision to exclude Jones, whose own candidacy was described as contrary to the king's proclamation for 'the well choosing of knights and burgesses ... void of any factious humour or dependency'. Instead, Overbury and Machen were endorsed as the persons 'most fittest to be nominated'. It was further agreed 'that every one of the same council should signify the same agreement to their neighbours and persuade them to assent thereunto to the end there might be a quiet and peaceable election'.[12] Jones acquiesced at the meeting, but supported by Payne he subsequently appealed directly to the electorate, sending his sons, servants and officials of the Consistory Court around the taverns and alehouses of the city promising 'to deal very liberally and bountifully' with those who voted for him. He also promised to procure legislation to resolve a number of minor economic grievances, in particular 'that no person should make malt within the said city which had any other trade' and that peas should only be grown in the gardens of the city rather than in the surrounding corn fields. He also pledged to procure more fairs for the city.[13]

Rich arrived back in Gloucestershire on the night of 13 Feb. to find the city in uproar. Indeed, he subsequently alleged that Jones and Payne 'had raised a great tumult and stirred up a great many of the rude and simplest burgesses'. Perhaps at Jones's urging, or perhaps because he feared that the corporation's candidates were about to be defeated, he immediately summoned another meeting of the Common Council, which assembled the following day. Overbury's eligibility was again questioned; the mayor was said to be doubtful 'whether the summons given by his deputy is lawful'; and information was taken, evidently from Machen or his supporters, 'that there hath been labouring to the contrary of that which was yesterday agreed and consented unto'. Rich is also said to have claimed that the writ had been lost. Following these discussions it was agreed that a new writ should be sought from the lord chancellor, that the county court should be adjourned for a fortnight, and that 'the burgesses attending at the Booth Hall' should be dismissed 'till new warning be given, and the sheriffs to be defended from any danger'.[14] Dismissing the voters promised to be difficult, however, as Jones (according to Machen) had marshalled his supporters, including not only 'the meaner sort of burgesses', but 'great numbers of strangers and others such as had no voices in the same election to the number of 200 persons at the least'. This rabble had assembled in 'several inns, taverns and alehouses' and was to be found 'drinking and carousing in very disorderly manner' at Jones's expense. After the mayor and sheriffs entered the hall, Jones's supporters followed in a 'very disorderly and riotous manner ... shouting and crying out ... Jones, Jones for a burgess'.[15] Rich told the burgesses to depart and the sheriffs adjourned the county court. Nevertheless Jones treated the meeting as a victory providing two barrels of strong beer for his supporters, ringing the bells of St. Mary de Crypt, and organizing a demonstration against the mayor and aldermen. Two days later the Common Council approved a letter to the lord chancellor for a new writ. Whether this request was ever granted is unknown, but a further meeting of the freemen was held on 28 Feb., at which Rich allegedly threatened to imprison those who would not support Machen. However, one of the sheriffs was the bishop's stepson, John Browne I, and thus belonged to Payne's faction, and not surprisingly therefore Jones not Machen was returned alongside Overbury.[16]

It has been suggested that the 1604 election dispute resulted from a clash between Gloucester's puritan oligarchy and a popular anti-puritan party. Certainly religion played some part: Jones, whom Rich described as being 'dependent upon the bishop', voiced fears that episcopal jurisdiction 'would be called in question' in Parliament and sought election in order 'that he might join with others that were in like case to make their party as strong as they might'. (His opponents, though, argued that he was motivated by self-interest, and that his true motive for standing was to safeguard his own position and secure his lease of church property).[17] However, there is also evidence that factionalism cut across religious divisions, for according to Rich, Payne's supporters on the Gloucester bench included the puritan Christopher Capell as well as Jones.[18]

There is no evidence that Jones tried to fulfil his campaign promises. A bill for relieving preachers and ministers in Gloucester and Norwich was brought in during the first session, but ordered to sleep, and when it was revived during the second session it seems only to have concerned Norwich.[19] The city may also have been specifically concerned with the bill to reduce

obstructions to navigable rivers, for which Overbury took the chair. Besides his parliamentary wages, he was paid £23 6s. for expenses incurred in obtaining a new charter for the city in 1605, which contained a few minor modifications to the old one.[20]

Jones was not considered for re-election in 1614, but the Common Council, presumably on the recommendation of the aldermanic bench, resolved that Overbury and alderman Christopher Capell were 'persons most fittest to be nominated burgesses'.[21] They were rejected by the freemen in favour of Machen and Browne, now also an alderman. Machen's failure to receive official endorsement for his candidacy in 1614 is in striking contrast to the events of 1604, and suggests that Gloucester's politics were remarkably fluid, and not polarized into clearly definable 'popular' and 'corporation' factions.

By the time of the 1620 parliamentary election Machen was dead, and though Overbury remained recorder his employment as a Welsh judge must have lessened his interest in Gloucester's affairs. Moreover, he was by now over 70. Browne was re-elected to the first seat, while the junior seat went to his brother-in-law Anthony Robinson, who was still only a common councilman. About 100 citizens are named on the return.[22] At a council meeting on 10 Dec. 1620, about a fortnight after the sealing of the indenture, Robinson agreed 'for the good of the city and at the entreaty of this house', to resign his seat to Henry Gibb, a naturalized Scottish courtier who had been entertained in Gloucester at the corporation's expense in the previous year.[23] The sheriffs, who were present, promised 'to make the return accordingly', and the corporation bound itself 'to save master sheriffs and Mr. Robinson harmless from any penalty or danger for the same.[24] However, the freemen may have refused to consent to this arrangement, or the corporation may have had second thoughts over the penalties that might be incurred for such a manifest irregularity. In any event Gibb did not take the seat. Instead he was voted a piece of plate to the value of £20, bearing the arms of the city. On the same day Browne and Robinson were ordered to take counsel's opinion about the renewal of the charter, possibly to strengthen the city's grip on the in-shire.[25] The city also petitioned the Commons against Sir John Townshend*, who had a patent for concealed lands, for suing one of the city hospitals. Townshend claimed that the hospital had been 'superstitiously founded' and that it was therefore forfeited to the crown by virtue of legislation passed at the Reformation.[26]

In 1623 the local gentry of the in-shire, the Guises of Elmore and Sir Robert Cooke† of Highnam Court, procured from the Crown a commission of association, entitling them to sit as justices at the quarter sessions for the city.[27] They also demanded the right to vote at the next election, and threatened to promote a bill in Parliament to establish a knight of the shire for the in-shire to give them separate representation. Consequently, following the 1624 election, when the 1621 Members were re-elected, the corporation instructed its parliamentary representatives to protect its interests.[28] The best lawyers were consulted at great expense, and Gibb's help at Court was enlisted. His loyalty to the king forbade him to press for the revocation of the commission of assistance, and his search for a compromise was thwarted by the refusal of the corporation 'to accept of any conditions whereby the gentlemen of the county may be admitted in the society of government'.[29] The town clerk, himself a member of the Guise family, appealed to his elder brother Sir William Guise to be reasonable, warning him that Gloucester would not surrender its rights, and that if he persisted he would create 'an hereditary quarrel between the city and your house'. He also advised against the scheme 'for a knight' as burdensome, 'and to overthrow the charters of a city in Parliament will be very difficult, in regard in that body three for one are burgesses and not knights and must favour corporations because it may be their own cases'.[30]

In 1625, and again in 1626, Capell took the senior seat and Browne was relegated to second place. Before going up to Westminster in 1626, the two Members, both of whom were deputy lieutenants, signed a letter to the 1st earl of Northampton, the city's lord lieutenant, excusing their failure to implement the 1625 Privy Seal loan. They explained that the city was impoverished by the trade depression, and by 'the late great and yet continuing plague, [and] the excessive number of poor, chiefly occasioned by the decay of clothing'. They also cited the burden of the subsidies voted in 1625 and the prospect that further taxes would soon be voted, 'wherein we nothing doubt but His Majesty's demands shall receive all possible satisfaction'.[31] Capell died during this Parliament, but no writ was issued for a by-election. In 1627 Gloucester acquired a new charter, settling its claims over the in-shire, and declaring that 'to remove doubt, the burgesses shall elect two burgesses of Parliament who shall also be knights of the shire for the county of the same city'.[32] In the following year Browne was re-elected to the senior seat. His colleague, John Hanbury, a Worcestershire iron-founder, owed his election solely to the fact that he was Capell's son-in-law, although he had been given the freedom of the city in the previous year. A copy of the Remonstrance drawn up by the Commons in 1628 against the continued levy of Tunnage and Poundage without parliamentary consent was copied into the municipal records.[33]

[1] Glos. RO, GBR B8/12/1. [2] P. Clark, '"The Ramoth-Gilead of the Good": Urban Change and Political Radicalism at Gloucester 1540-1640', *Eng. Commonwealth 1547-1640* ed. P. Clark, A.G.R. Smith and N. Tyacke, 168, 170, 172, 180. [3] T. Rymer, *Foedera*, vi. pt. 3, pp. 69-71. [4] Sainty, *Lords Lieutenants*, 32. [5] *VCH Glos.* iv. 54, 84. [6] STAC 8/228/30. [7] STAC 5/A20/11. [8] Glos. RO, GBR B3/1, f. 232. [9] STAC 8/4/9. [10] Glos. RO, GBR, B3/1, f. 200; STAC 8/228/30. [11] STAC 8/207/25. [12] Glos. RO, GBR B3/1, f. 201v; STAC 8/207/25; STAC 8/228/30. [13] STAC 8/207/25; STAC 8/228/30. [14] Glos. RO, GBR, B3/1, f. 201; STAC 8/207/25. [15] STAC 8/207/25. [16] Glos. RO, GBR, B3/1, f. 201; STAC 8/207/25; 8/228/30. [17] Clark, 184; STAC 8/207/25, 8/228/30. [18] STAC 8/228/30. [19] *CJ*, i. 245a, 249a, 261b. [20] Glos. RO, GBR B3/1, f. 218; *Cal. of Recs. of Corp. of Gloucester* comp. W. H. Stevenson, 36. [21] Glos. RO, GBR B3/1, f. 253v. [22] C219/37/111. [23] Glos. RO, GBR B3/1, f. 462. [24] Ibid. f. 476v. [25] Ibid. f. 478v. [26] Nicholas, *Procs. 1621*, i. 218. [27] Glos. RO, GBR B8/12/5. [28] Glos. RO, GBR B3/1, ff. 497-8v. [29] Glos. RO, GBR B8/12/7. [30] Glos. RO, D326/Z1. [31] Glos. RO, GBR H2/2, p. 67. [32] *Cal. of Recs. of Corp. of Gloucester*, 40-5. [33] Clark, 181.

A.D./B.C.

TEWKESBURY

Right of election: in the freemen

Number of voters: about 360 in 1640

Apr. 1610[1]	SIR DUDLEY DIGGES
	EDWARD FERRERS
c. Mar. 1614	SIR DUDLEY DIGGES
	SIR JOHN RADCLIFFE
21 Dec. 1620	SIR DUDLEY DIGGES
	GILES BRIDGES
c. Jan. 1624	SIR DUDLEY DIGGES
	SIR BAPTIST HICKS, bt.
28 Apr. 1625	SIR DUDLEY DIGGES
	SIR BAPTIST HICKS, bt.
	Sir Robert Tracy*
20 Jan. 1626	SIR DUDLEY DIGGES
	SIR BAPTIST HICKS, bt.
11 Mar. 1628	SIR BAPTIST HICKS, bt.
	SIR THOMAS CULPEPER
4 June 1628	SIR WILLIAM HICKS, bt. *vice*
	Hicks, called to the Upper House

Tewkesbury lay in a peninsula of Gloucestershire, between Herefordshire and Worcestershire, at the confluence of the Severn and the Avon, and was described by Camden as 'a large and fair town ... famous for the making of woollen cloth and smart-biting mustard'.[2] The mustard brought little more than fame and the woollen industry had greatly declined by the seventeenth century, when the primary occupation was the carrying trade with Bristol and Gloucester and the most important local industries were leather-working and maltmaking.[3] The town, which was obliged to maintain bridges over the Avon and Swilgate, received its first charter in the twelfth century, and was incorporated in 1575 as the 'bailiffs, burgesses and commonalty of the borough'.[4] Following the incorporation the borough was repeatedly in conflict with the steward of the manor, which was then owned by the Crown. This was partly resolved by a re-incorporation in 1605, under which the borough was granted a separate commission of the peace. Five years later, apparently under pressure from the Crown, it bought the manor for £2,450, and paid a further £438 for a new charter. This enfranchised Tewkesbury, extended its authority over the whole hundred and liberty, enlarged the corporation to two bailiffs, 24 principal burgesses and 24 assistants, and increased the number of justices from four to six.[5] The bailiffs acted as returning officers, and the returns were made 'with the whole assent and consent of the rest of the burgesses', nine signed the indenture in 1626 and 15 in 1628.[6] The corporation itself clearly managed the elections with a view to the protection of its investment, as the new constituency was closed to the Gloucestershire gentry, who would scarcely have sympathized with the town's ambition to transfer responsibility for maintaining its bridges to the county. Worcestershire and Herefordshire gentry were not handicapped in this way, and the influence of the Sandys family of Ombersley in Worcestershire may be suspected in some elections.

The charter was issued on 23 Mar. 1610, and the first writ seven days later.[7] The corporation provided one Member, Edward Ferrers, a London Mercer born near Tewkesbury, whose elder brother William, also a Mercer, had advanced most of the money for the purchase of the manor. The charter named both brothers principal burgesses, and Edward high steward. Lord treasurer Salisbury (Robert Cecil[†]), who had arranged the sale and himself held property in the neighbourhood,[8] recommended Sir Dudley Digges, a young Kentish gentleman recently returned from his travels and a kinsman of Sir Samuel Sandys*. He was to become one of the leading Parliament-men of the period and, perhaps under Salisbury's guidance, he showed a ready grasp of the realities behind his return, sending Tewkesbury £160 'by way of thankfulness', to purchase lands for the endowment of the free grammar school which had been founded in 1576 by William Ferrers.[9] Digges remained a 'benefactor and a worthy good friend',[10] and was accordingly assured of re-election throughout the period. Ferrers seems to have been satisfied with a couple of sessions in Parliament, for in 1614 he was replaced by Sir John Radcliffe, standing

on the interest of the lord lieutenant, Grey Brydges[†], 5th Baron Chandos, known as 'the King of Cotswold'. Radcliffe moved up to Lancashire for the 1620 election and consequently Chandos nominated his cousin Giles Bridges as 'a worthy gentleman and neighbour, known to many of you'.[11] He probably secured an unopposed election by recommending to Sir Francis Russell* for a seat at Tavistock the great financier Sir Baptist Hicks, who had acquired an independent interest in the borough by buying the domestic buildings of the abbey. When the 1621 Parliament met, Digges undertook to procure an Act to charge the county with the cost of repairing Tewkesbury's bridges, which had been seriously damaged by flooding three years earlier. He managed to steer the bill through committee, despite the claim of other Gloucestershire Members that it was 'against law and equity' to spread the cost, but it never reached the Lords, still less the statute book.[12] According to a later petition addressed o the justices of assize, one of the knights of the shire, possibly Sir Robert Tracy, privately offered the borough £200 'by way of compensation'.[13] Early in the Parliament, Digges's fellow Tewkesbury Member, Giles Bridges, was suspended for being a partner of the infamous patentee (Sir) Giles Mompesson*, and was not restored to his seat until 21 November. Lord Chandos died in August 1621, leaving a minor as his heir, whereupon the family interest at Tewkesbury lapsed. Bridges subsequently sat for his native Herefordshire.

In 1624 Hicks took over the seat previously held by Bridges, and held it until he was raised to the peerage four years later. On his death in 1629 it was recorded by the town clerk that 'the only cause' of Hicks's 'great bounty towards us' had been his repeated election.[14] In 1625 Tracy, the one Gloucestershire gentleman known to have aspired to a Tewkesbury seat, was rejected by the corporation in Hicks's favour, prompting his indignant protest that 'tis not he who brings most in his truest love, but brings most in his purse, shall be accepted'. He still hoped to challenge the 'stranger' Hicks at the election, pointing out to his friend Roger Dowdeswell of Pull Court that, as knight of the shire in 1621, he had not opposed the bridge bill for fear of harming the borough's interests.[15] The subsequent return of Digges and Hicks ran in the name of the 'burgesses and commonalty'.[16] Both men were re-elected in 1626, but when Digges achieved a Kent county seat in 1628 Hicks moved up to the first place. The junior seat thereupon went to a Kentish knight, Sir Thomas Culpeper, evidently on Digges's recommendation, though Culpeper was closely connected with the Sandys family. Ennobled as Viscount Campden on 5 May 1628, Hicks was replaced in the Commons by his nephew, Sir William Hicks.

[1] *CJ*, i. 418a. [2] W. Camden, *Britannia* (1772) ed. E. Gibson, i. 281.
[3] F. Redmond, 'Bor. of Tewkesbury 1575-1714' (Birmingham MA 1950), pp. 79-85; *VCH Glos.* viii. 137, 142, 144. [4] *VCH Glos.* viii. 147; *CPR*, 1572-5, pp. 526-8. [5] Redmond, 4-6; J. Bennett, *Hist. Tewkesbury*, 208; C66/1811/1, 2; *VCH Glos.* viii. 147-9. [6] D. Hirst, *Representative of the People?*, 209-10; C219/40/127; 219/41A/119. [7] *OR*. [8] J. Smith, *Men and Armour for Glos. in 1608*, p. 115. [9] Glos. RO, TBR A1/1, f. 42; Bennett, 222. [10] Glos. RO, TBR A1/1, f. 42. [11] Glos. RO, TBR B26. [12] *VCH Glos.* viii. 114; *CJ*, i. 542b, 609b, 631a. [13] Glos. RO, TBR A1/1, f. 35. [14] Glos. RO, TBR A1/1, f. 48. [15] Glos. RO, D760/36. [16] Glos. RO, TBR A1/1, f. 18.

A.D.

HAMPSHIRE

Number of voters: about 2,700 in 1614[1]

5 Mar. 1604	SIR ROBERT OXENBRIDGE I	
	SIR WILLIAM JEPHSON	
21 Mar. 1614[2]	SIR RICHARD TICHBORNE	1673
	SIR WILLIAM UVEDALE	1657
	Sir Henry Wallop	1028[3]
18 Dec. 1620	SIR HENRY WALLOP	
	SIR JOHN JEPHSON	
12 Jan. 1624	SIR DANIEL NORTON	
	SIR ROBERT OXENBRIDGE II	
2 May 1625	ROBERT WALLOP	
	SIR HENRY WHITHED	
9 Jan. 1626	SIR HENRY WALLOP	
	ROBERT WALLOP	
3 Mar. 1628	SIR HENRY WALLOP	
	SIR DANIEL NORTON	

Often referred to as the county of Southampton, Hampshire was of great strategic importance, both for its port and naval base at Portsmouth, and for its extensive forests which supplied timber for the dockyard. Its chalky soil and heath land provided for a local economy based on pasture and arable farming. The cloth industry of Winchester, erstwhile capital of England following the Conquest, declined after the Black Death, but the cathedral city remained the regional centre for local government and administration.[4] County elections were held at Winchester Castle, leased in this period by Sir Richard Tichborne*, who, despite his family's reputed Catholicism, afforded hospitality to James I several times. Traditionally the bishop and the Paulet marquess of Winchester had each nominated candidates for the knights of the shire. However, neither did

so under the early Stuarts. In the case of the Paulets this was a result of the imbecility of the fourth marquess of Winchester and the recusancy of the fifth. The indifference of the bishop is harder to explain. Thomas Bilson, bishop between 1597 and 1616, may have exercised an indirect influence through his son-in-law and steward, Sir Richard Norton*, but there is no evidence that his successor, Lancelot Andrewes, showed any interest in the elections of the 1620s. During James's reign the mantle of electoral patron passed instead to Hampshire's lord lieutenant, Henry Wriothesley, 3rd earl of Southampton, who held office from 1604 until his death in November 1624. The next lord lieutenant, the 1st Viscount Conway (Sir Edward Conway I*) was less successful, however, and even found it difficult to obtain borough seats for his sons.[5]

Since early Elizabethan times the county gentry had been divided on religious lines. Those of a puritan persuasion were pitted against a mixture of less godly Protestants and those who still inclined to Catholicism. These differences came to a head in 1614, when, in the only contested election of the period, the church papist Sir Richard Tichborne* bested the wealthy puritan Sir Henry Wallop*, an upset that closely mirrored the defeat of Wallop's father in a by-election in 1566. Thereafter the puritans gained the upper hand, and Wallop, the richest commoner in the county, who had refused a peerage in 1610, ultimately established a firm hold on the senior seat.[6]

In 1604 both Members came from relatively new and minor families. Sir Robert Oxenbridge, a courtier's son-in-law, had recently been honoured with a royal visit; although an Anglican himself his family connections probably made him acceptable to the old Catholic gentry.[7] Sir William Jephson, who took the second seat, was presumably nominated by Southampton, with whom he had longstanding connections.[8] Ahead of the 1614 election Sir Richard Tichborne announced his intention to stand, and according to his later testimony, he approached various local gentlemen of 'worth and quality', all of whom declined to compete except Wallop, who gave 'an uncertain and doubtful answer'.[9] Tichborne then secured the support of Southampton, as did Sir William Uvedale, a well-connected courtier whose cousin, Sir Richard Norton, was sheriff. Wallop himself approached Southampton only to find that he had left it too late to obtain the latter's nomination. He therefore decided to canvass his own support, and on 10 Feb. wrote to one of his kinsmen: 'there is a resolution for a Parliament speedily, and never more need of sending honest men thither, and persons well affected in religion. I pray reserve your freeholders' and friends' voices undisposed of till I may advise you of these things'.[10] Wallop's reference to religion was clearly aimed at Tichborne, who later complained of 'slanderous rumours'. Wallop in return alleged that the sheriff, Norton, as the bishop of Winchester's steward, had so far abandoned impartiality during the campaign as to extract pledges of support for Tichborne from suitors at the bishop's manorial courts, and was prepared to risk a £100 fine for a rigged election. Even copyholders were approached, according to Wallop's account, and when some objected that this was illegal, the canvassers threatened 'that they would be even with them, and would sit on their skirts, with many other words of terror'.[11] The increasing bitterness of the contest alarmed the gentry, and a meeting was held to persuade one of the candidates to stand down, 'for the maintenance of love and amity'. The drawing of lots was suggested, to which Tichborne agreed, but Wallop refused to co-operate. On 2 Mar. some of the gentry drafted a letter to Southampton, informing him that

> the most part of us now assembled at the assizes for this county have conferred of our election for the Parliament, and moved Sir Henry Wallop, whom the freeholders generally affect for that employment, to be one. We doubt not but your lordship will approve our choice in respect of his own worth and the common opinion conceived of his love to the country, yet gladly if time would have given us leave [would we] have been advised by your lordship.

The letter was never sent because of Tichborne's understandable objection to the postscript, which suggested that 'your lordship may dispose of him'.[12] The canvas therefore continued with undiminished vigour, attracting the attention of London gossipmongers, including John Chamberlain.[13] Southampton wrote to the deputy lieutenants regretting that he could not endorse Wallop without breaking his word to Tichborne and Uvedale, and urging them to support his candidates.[14] Wallop nevertheless seemed to have amassed a large following, as he informed his ally Sir Henry Whithed* on 11 Mar. that he had already mustered 1,000 voters. Six days later his friend Sir Daniel Norton* had pledged 130 freeholders, and Sir William Dodington I* a further 40, 'notwithstanding many threats used by the other'.[15]

On the day of the election Tichborne allegedly used his control of the castle to admit his supporters at an early hour, so that 500 of Wallop's voters were physically unable to enter. Tichborne countered that, on the contrary, his electors could gain access only through a side door because Wallop's supporters were blocking the main entrance. His story was corroborated by Norton, who testified that when he tried to read

the writ at 8 a.m. Wallop's supporters raised 'a little banner or flag wherein was made the letter W', and began an incessant chant of 'Wallop, Wallop, Wallop', so that it was an hour before he could make himself heard. On the view, Norton was prepared to declare Tichborne and Uvedale elected, but he acceded to Wallop's demand for a poll. During this protracted process 500 of Wallop's supporters, hungry and exhausted, left the hustings unpolled and were denied readmission, or so it was claimed. The sheriff was further charged with admitting unqualified and plural votes for Tichborne, to which he replied that all had been obliged to file through a wicket gate under the scrutiny of Oxenbridge and Whithed. Wallop was absent when the result was declared on the following morning. Although he was first said to have polled 1,283 votes, this was subsequently reduced to 1,028, over 600 behind Tichborne and Uvedale.[16]

Although defeated, Wallop was assured of a seat in the Commons, having obtained a place at Stockbridge under controversial circumstances. He nevertheless immediately commenced proceedings against Norton in Star Chamber, thereby echoing the aftermath of the 1566 by-election, in which his father had been defeated in similar circumstances and had likewise sued the sheriff. However, this lawsuit contravened the Commons' right to determine the validity of all returns, and consequently, when the Stockbridge election result was challenged in the Commons, William Beecher* magnified the case against Wallop by bringing it to the attention of the House. He also tried to obtain an order requiring Wallop to petition the Commons instead.[17] The case outlasted the Parliament, with no known result. In the long term it probably had the effect of deterring future opposition to Wallop, who was returned for Hampshire unchallenged in 1620, together with Southampton's nominee, Sir John Jephson.

In 1624 the puritan Sir Daniel Norton took the first seat while the second went to Oxenbridge's son.[18] Wallop reasserted his electoral influence in 1625 by securing the return of his son, Robert Wallop, at the unusually young age of 24, together with Whithed, his friend and kinsman. This triumph was consolidated in 1626 when the two Wallops, father and son, achieved the unusual feat of monopolizing both seats. No doubt they were responsible for presenting Tichborne and his father as unfit for county office because of their recusant wives. In 1628 Wallop was re-elected with Sir Daniel Norton, whose house, conveniently close to Portsmouth, was Charles I's residence during the preparation of the Ile de Ré expedition in the summer of 1627, and again in 1628 when Buckingham was assassinated while assembling his forces to relieve La Rochelle. No county was worse affected than Hampshire by the problems of billeting and military disorder in 1627-8, and both knights of the shire protested in the Commons about this, and about the recent appointment of the Arminian Richard Neile as bishop of Winchester.[19]

[1] STAC 8/293/11. [2] Ibid. [3] Ibid. [4] D.A Hinton and A.N. Insole, *Hants and I.o.W.* 1-16; J.S. Furley, *Hants Q. Sess. in Seventeenth Cent.* 16. [5] *CSP Dom. Addenda, 1625-49*, p. 51. [6] E179/175/486. [7] J. Nichols, *Progs. of Jas. I*, i. 250. [8] *HMC Hatfield*, xi. 20. [9] STAC 8/293/11. [10] Hants RO, 19M61/1317. [11] STAC 8/293/11. [12] *Whithed Letter Bk.* (Hants Recs. Ser. i), 113. [13] *Chamberlain Letters* ed. N.E. McClure, i. 518, 521; T.L. Moir, *Addled Parl.* 35-6; Hants RO, 44M69/E4/28, f. 39v. [14] *Whithed Letter Bk.* (Hants Recs. Ser. i), 114. [15] Ibid. 115. [16] STAC 8/293/11. [17] *Procs. 1614 (Commons)*, 397. [18] R.E. Ruigh, *Parl. of 1624*, p. 126. [19] L. Boynton, 'Billeting in I.o.W.', *EHR*, lxxiv. 23-40; R. Cust, *Forced Loan*, 122-5.

V.C.D.M./R.C.L.S.

ANDOVER

Right of election: in the corporation

Number of voters: 24

6 Mar. 1604	SIR THOMAS JERMYN
	THOMAS ANTROBUS
c. Mar. 1614	RICHARD VENABLES
	PETER NOYES
7 Dec. 1620[1]	JOHN SHUTER, steward
	RICHARD VENABLES
22 Nov. 1621	ROBERT WALLOP *vice*
	Venables, deceased
7 Jan. 1624	ROBERT WALLOP
	JOHN SHUTER, steward
29 Apr. 1625	SIR HENRY WALLOP
	JOHN SHUTER, steward
24 Jan. 1626[2]	LORD HENRY PAULET
	JOHN SHUTER, steward
29 Feb. 1628	ROBERT WALLOP
	RALPH CONWAY

Andover, in north-west Hampshire close to the border with Wiltshire, received a charter as early as 1175 and sent Members to Parliament intermittently between 1295 and 1307. Although benefiting from its proximity to Weyhill fair, one of the largest in the region, the borough had no significant industries, and fell into decline in the late medieval period; its parlia-

mentary representation lapsed and was not restored until 1586.[3] In 1599 Andover obtained a new charter, vesting town government in a corporation consisting of a bailiff, a 'steward' or recorder, ten 'approved men' and 12 capital burgesses.[4] The charter did not specify the franchise, but it was effectively monopolized by the corporation.[5] The 4th marquess of Winchester, who held extensive property in the town, including the watermill, exerted no influence on elections except on one occasion, in 1626.[6] The 3rd earl of Southampton, as lord lieutenant of Hampshire, may have nominated both candidates in 1604. He became the borough's high steward two years later, but made no further attempt to use his interest there.[7] Instead, electoral patronage during the rest of the period was dominated by the rich gentry Wallop family of Farley Wallop, 15 miles east of Andover.

The Members returned in 1604 were both strangers to the borough: Sir Thomas Jermyn, a courtier who had fought alongside Southampton in Ireland,[8] and Thomas Antrobus, a London lawyer who settled in the county soon after the election. In 1610, Richard Venables, one of the 'approved men', sued the corporation in Chancery for misappropriating funds to the detriment of the poor, with whom the town was 'much oppressed'. They dismissed his claims as merely 'a show to the world that his charity and devotion should exceed others', and may have bought him off by promising a seat in the next Parliament.[9] Another of their number, Peter Noyes, was returned with Venables in 1614. Venables was re-elected in 1620, yielding the senior seat to his cousin John Shuter, steward of the borough. Venables died in August, and at the ensuing by-election Robert Wallop, the under-age son of Sir Henry Wallop, was chosen with 'the whole assent and consent of the approved men and burgesses'. Wallop and Shuter were re-elected in 1624.

In the first Caroline Parliament Sir Henry Wallop was returned with Shuter. Although there is no evidence that the town paid wages to any of its representatives during the early Stuart period, the corporation disbursed 5s. to celebrate Sir Henry Wallop's birthday with music on 13 Oct. 1625.[10] In 1626 the borough chose as its senior Member Lord Henry Paulet, a younger son of the 4th marquess of Winchester, with Shuter re-elected to his fourth Parliament. Robert Wallop was re-elected in 1628, and the junior seat was solicited by Hampshire's lord lieutenant, the 1st Viscount Conway (Sir Edward Conway I*), for one of his sons. Conway wrote on 2 Feb. 1628 to Wallop's cousin, Sir Thomas Jervoise*, that 'I am in some distress where to provide a burgess place for my son Ralph', and asked for his assistance at Andover. Jervoise controlled extensive Hampshire estates including the advowson of Upper Clatford, adjoining the town. On 15 Feb. Conway was able to write to the Andover corporation that he had been informed by Jervoise 'how much I am beholding to you for your good affection towards me and your readiness to make choice of a son of mine to serve you as one of the burgesses in the next Parliament'.[11] Ralph Conway was duly returned.

[1] C219/37/217. [2] C219/40/239. [3] VCH Hants, iv. 345-51; Woodward, Hants, iii. 173; D.K. Coldicott, Elizabethan Andover, 9-10. [4] Andover Charters ed. E. Parsons, 1, 18-19, 20, 24; R.A. Jones, Andover Members, 6, 8. [5] V. Hodges, 'The Electoral Influence of the Aristocracy 1604-41' (Columbia Univ. Ph.D. thesis, 1977), pp. 401, 425. [6] Hants RO, 37M85/8/CD/1. [7] Hants RO, 37M85/4/AC/2, unfol. [8] CSP Carew, 1589-1600, p. 311. [9] C2/Jas.I/V1/3. [10] Hants RO, 37M85/4/AC/5, f. 25. [11] Procs. 1628, vi. 124.

J.P.F./R.C.L.S.

CHRISTCHURCH

Right of election: in the corporation

Number of voters: c.10

11 Mar. 1604	RICHARD MARTIN
	NICHOLAS HYDE
c. Apr. 1614	SIR THOMAS NORTON
	HENRY BRITTON
8 Jan. 1621	SIR GEORGE HASTINGS
	NATHANIEL TOMKINS
29 Jan. 1624[1]	NATHANIEL TOMKINS
	SIR GEORGE HASTINGS
	?John Eltonhed
28 Apr. 1625	NATHANIEL TOMKINS
	SIR THOMAS WILSFORD
c. July 1625	SIR EDWARD BOYS vice
	Wilsford, chose to sit for
	Canterbury
20 Jan. 1626	NATHANIEL TOMKINS
	ROBERT MASON I
18 Feb. 1628	NATHANIEL TOMKINS
	(SIR) HENRY CROKE

Christchurch, a small coastal town of no economic significance, had never received a royal charter. Its municipal officers were not far removed from manorial officials, and such self-government as it possessed

rested on the tacit agreement of the lord of the manor.[2] It first sent representatives to Parliament in 1571. The franchise was restricted to the mayor, formerly the lord's portreeve, and the 'burgesses'.[3] About eight of them usually signed the indenture.[4] The main electoral patron of the borough in this period was the Catholic Thomas Arundell, later 1st Lord Arundell of Wardour, who bought the castle and hundred in 1601 from Henry Hastings, a kinsman of the earl of Huntingdon. Hastings continued to lease the priory and fishing rights from the duchy of Cornwall.[5] After Prince Charles's creation as Prince of Wales there was an attempt by the Prince's Council to investigate the extent of the duchy's rights at Christchurch, but the survey confirmed that Arundell had preeminence and the Prince's Council does not seem to have contemplated making nominations for the borough in either of the parliaments in which it did so elsewhere.[6]

For the last Elizabethan Parliament Hastings unsuccessfully nominated John Foyle† and Henry Hyde†.[7] In 1604 the townsmen proved anxious to elect Foyle, a thriving attorney from the neighbouring Dorset town of Shaftesbury,[8] but he asked to be spared, 'the time falling out so inconvenient for me I cannot by any means attend without great prejudice unto myself and many my good friends'. To take his place he recommended Hyde's brother Nicholas, another lawyer and 'a very sufficient gentleman'. Although he admitted that Nicholas lived in Wiltshire, and was thus non-resident, he declared that he 'is every way a fit man agreeable to the Proclamation' that had recently been issued by James I requiring that the laws governing elections be strictly applied.[9] Foyle may have consulted Arundell about his chosen replacement, as Arundell later claimed to have supported Hyde's candidature. For the first seat Arundell certainly nominated Richard Martin, his legal counsel, who wrote to the mayor on 14 Feb. requesting the place 'in respect of that love which you owe to so honourable a landlord (whose furtherance and consent herein I am assured of) as also for that information you may have by him and others of me, being one of the Temple'. He went on to ask the borough 'to put in my name according to the custom of your election as well as though I were present in person; and that you with the rest of your brethren will be pleased to give me notice of this your so favourable courtesies'. He ended by undertaking to do the borough any service in his power.[10] Arundell wrote briefly on Martin's behalf six days later, but received the evasive reply that the writ had not yet arrived. On 2 Mar., with elections proceeding apace and no word from Christchurch, he reiterated his recommendation of Martin, who had meanwhile taken the precaution of securing his return at Cirencester. Arundell's anxiety proved groundless in the event, and Martin and Hyde seem to have been returned unopposed.[11]

In 1614 Arundell wrote to the mayor that 'whereas at the last Parliament you did grant unto me the nomination of both your burgesses, ... now I do again desire that I may have the nomination of both your burgesses ... being so near a neighbour unto you and meaning, God willing, to live amongst you'. Promising to bear the Members' charges himself for the 1614 Parliament, he recommended Sir Thomas Norton of Northwood Chasteners and Henry Breton (Britton) of Slyfield. Norton's connection with Arundell is unknown, but Britton, who only the previous year had been in trouble for his religion, was related to him through the Wriothesleys.[12] Arundell proved successful in his request for both seats, but in the next Parliament it is not clear whether he nominated just one or both candidates, as no letter of nomination survives in respect of the senior seat. This was bestowed on Arundell's kinsman, Hastings's son Sir George, then resident in the borough. Arundell's first choice for the second seat was Sir Robert Phelips*, who may have requested the nomination in case his candidature at Bath was unsuccessful. However, by 6 Jan. Phelips was sure of the other seat. Consequently he asked Christchurch, on Arundell's authority, to defer the election. If this had already taken place the borough should send to the sheriff to have the indenture cancelled, otherwise it would be short of a Member when Parliament opened.[13] In Phelips' stead Arundell recommended his London neighbour Nathaniel Tomkins, Phelips's confidant and a servant of the prince of Wales.[14] The election took place the following day, the Members being returned by the 'common assent' of the 'burgesses'.[15]

Tomkins moved up to the senior seat at the next election, though still a mere 'gentleman', and held it for the rest of the period. Arundell wrote to the mayor of Christchurch on 21 Jan. 1624, undertaking that Tomkins would serve *gratis*; he added that Hastings had asked for his nomination to the second seat, but pleaded ill-health as an excuse for deferring his decision.[16] Arundell may have been unwilling to allow Hastings to establish a lien on the seat, for three days later he nominated John Eltonhed, yet another Middle Temple lawyer, adding that 'for my cousin, Sir George Hastings, I have writ unto him, which I hope will give him satisfaction'.[17] Although the sheriff's copy of the indenture, which is now illegible, was endorsed

26 Jan., the election seems to have been deferred for three days following the arrival of Arundell's letter, and the mayor's copy is therefore correctly dated 29 January.[18] Hastings's local connections proved decisive, and in what was presumably a contested election he and Tomkins were returned by 'common assent'. Hastings, in his letter of thanks, waived payment.[19]

In 1625 Arundell nominated Tomkins and Sir Thomas Wilsford.[20] However, Wilsford chose to sit for Canterbury. Ahead of the ensuing election Arundell recommended another Kentishman, Sir Edward Boys, as his replacement.[21] At the 1626 election Arundell confined his interest to one seat, though he was later assured that he might have had both. Tomkins was returned with Robert Mason, a London lawyer of Hampshire origin, who was the son-in-law of John Foyle.[22]

Arundell's nominees for the 1628 election were Tomkins, by this time clerk extraordinary of the Privy Council, and (Sir) Henry Croke, whose brother Sir John sat for Arundell's borough of Shaftesbury. Croke may have recommended himself to Arundell by his slackness, as clerk of the pipe, in pursuing recusants. On 6 Feb. Arundell's agent wrote to the mayor: 'his lordship hopes by this time you have received the writs, and therefore hath sent this messenger of purpose to attend the ending [sic] thereof, and that you would send him away withal as soon as with conveniency you may'. Arundell as usual promised that both Members would serve without charge.[23]

[1] Dorset RO, DC/CC F 1/5. [2] *VCH Hants*, v. 86-89. [3] Dorset RO, DC/CC B 2/1/1; DC/CC A 2/1; DC/CC A 2/2. [4] Dorset RO, DC/CC F 1/3–F/1/7. [5] E112/121/337; *VCH Hants*, v. 92. [6] *VCH Hants*, v. 87-88; P.M. Hunneyball, 'Prince Charles's Council as Electoral Agent', *PH*, xxiii. 316-35. [7] Dorset RO, DC/CC, acc. 7998, unfol. (Hastings to Mayor 13 Sept. 1601; Bindon to Mayor, 6 Oct. 1601). [8] Dorset RO, DC/CC C 1/23. [9] Dorset RO, DC/CC, acc. 7998, unfol. (Foyle to Mayor, 28 Feb. 1604). [10] Ibid. (Martin to Mayor, 14 Feb. 1604). [11] Ibid. (Arundell to Mayor, 20 Feb. 1604, 2 Mar. 1604). [12] Ibid. (Arundell to Mayor, 14 Feb. 1614). [13] Ibid. (Phelips to Mayor, 6 Jan. 1621, to William Goldwire, 7 Jan. 1621). [14] H. Lawson, *Geneal. Colls. Illus. Catholic Fams.* 234; Dorset RO, DC/CC, acc. 7998, unfol. (John Talbot [Arundell's agent] to Goldwire, 7 Jan. 1621). [15] Dorset RO, DC/CC F 1/4. [16] Dorset RO, DC/CC, acc. 7998, unfol. (Arundell to Mayor, 21 Jan. 1624). [17] Ibid. (Arundell to Mayor, 24 Jan. 1624); *M. Temple Admiss.* i. 90. [18] C219/38/200; Dorset RO, DC/CC F 1/5. [19] Dorset RO, DC/CC, acc. 7998, unfol. (Hastings to Mayor, 31 Jan. 1624). [20] *Procs. 1625*, pp. 679-80. [21] C231/4, f. 189v; Dorset RO, DC/CC, acc. 7998, unfol. (Arundell to Colgill, 16 June 1625). [22] Dorset RO, DC/CC, acc. 7998, unfol. (Arundell to Mayor, 3 Feb. 1628). [23] Ibid. (Arundell to Mayor, 3 Feb. 1628, William Woodesson [Arundell's agent] to Mayor, 6 Feb. 1628).

V.C.D.M./R.C.L.S.

LYMINGTON

Right of election: in the freemen

Number of voters: 21 in 1625

		1st seat	2nd seat
3 Mar. 1604	THOMAS MARSHALL		
	THOMAS SOUTH		
12 Mar. 1614[1]	PHILIP FLEMING		
	CHARLES THYNNE		
5 Jan. 1621	SIR WILLIAM DODINGTON I	3	
	HENRY CAMPION		10
	Sir John Mill, bt.*	1	
	John More II		5
19 Jan. 1624	NICHOLAS FERRAR	11	
	JOHN MORE II		10
	Henry Campion	7	7
12 Apr. 1625	JOHN BUTTON	18	
	JOHN MILL		10
	JOHN MORE II		10
	Sir William Uvedale*		0
	Herbert Dodington		0
	Henry Campion		0
	Nicholas Ferrar		0

Double return of Mill and More

18 Jan. 1626	HERBERT DODINGTON
	JOHN MORE II
3 Mar. 1628	HERBERT DODINGTON
	RICHARD WHITHED

Lying on the Hampshire coast opposite the Isle of Wight and almost surrounded by the New Forest, Lymington was known chiefly for its salterns, which in this period supplied nearly all the west of England.[2] Although granted a seigneurial charter before 1216, the borough was never incorporated, and first sent Members to Parliament in 1584. It was governed by a mayor, who was assisted by a town clerk, serjeant, and recorder.[3] The high steward, Sir Henry Wallop*, traditionally had some influence in borough elections, and this continued to be sporadically exercised during the early Stuart period, although competition for seats between various members of the local gentry became increasingly heated from 1621 onwards.[4] The 3rd earl of Southampton, as lord lieutenant of Hampshire, could have made nominations, but the only occasion on which he apparently did so was in 1624. There is no evidence that wages were paid to any of the Members returned during this period.

The two Members returned to the first Stuart Parliament in 1604 were drawn from the local gentry, and were already freemen before the election. Thomas Marshall, who took the first seat, may have enlisted Wallop's support, while Thomas South, in second place, was a lawyer who later served as recorder of Lymington. In 1614 Philip Fleming of Newport, Isle of Wight, was returned in first place, with Charles Thynne, a resident freeman and salt patentee. Both seats were contested at the next general election. Sir William Dodington of Breamore, regarded as 'one of the worthiest knights of these parts', probably had the support of his fellow puritan and friend, Wallop, and defeated Sir John Mill, 1st bt.*, of Newton Bury, by three votes to one for the senior seat; most voters, reluctant to offend either magnate, must have abstained. The second seat was won by Henry Campion, whose father had acquired the two manors of Old and New Lymington in 1609, beating John More II, one of Thynne's partners in the salt monopoly and also a tenant of the earl of Southampton, by ten votes to five.[5] In 1624 Southampton, anxious to defend the Virginia Company charter in the Commons, nominated Nicholas Ferrar, the Company's deputy, for the first seat, and perhaps supported More, who was also a shareholder, for the second. Campion, who was in financial difficulties, stood for both seats, polling seven votes for each, which was insufficient. An entry in the town records allowing 6s.1d. for taking the indenture to the earl's residence at Tichfield suggests that both Members were returned in their absence.[6]

Seven names were put forward at the next general election, in 1625. John Button, the brother-in-law of the town's recorder, South, was unanimously elected in first place with 18 votes. More and Campion both stood again, while Ferrar seems to have been nominated as a compromise, perhaps without his knowledge. The other contenders were Sir William Uvedale*, a courtier and Hampshire magnate with as yet no firm electoral base; Mill's 18-year old son and heir, John; and Dodington's second but oldest surviving son, Herbert. More polled ten votes, including his own, for the second seat, tying with Mill; no votes were cast for either seat for Campion, Dodington, Ferrar or Uvedale. A second poll was held, but the result was unchanged. This produced a double return, but as he explained on the indenture, the mayor refrained from giving Mill his casting vote because he was under age, and left it to the Commons to decide. The case was one of the many still outstanding when Parliament was dissolved.[7]

In 1626 Dodington and More were returned 'with one consent'.[8] Dodington, probably fearing another contest, also stood successfully for Downton, opting for Lymington on 9 Feb. 1626.[9] Dodington stood again in 1628, and was joined by Richard Whithed, a friend of John Button who had protested with him against the Forced Loan.[10] It may have been as a sign of royal displeasure that on 27 May orders were given for billeting a regiment upon Lymington.[11]

[1] Hants RO, 27M74A/DBC1, p. 108. [2] R. Warner, Colls. for Hist. of Hants, iv. 16. [3] VCH Hants, iv. 640-4. [4] E316/3/191. [5] Hants RO, 27M74A/DBC1, p. 123; VCH Hants, iv. 646. [6] Hants RO, 27M74A/ DBC1, p. 135; R.E. Ruigh, Parl. of 1624, pp. 124-5. [7] Hants RO, 27M74A/DBC1, p. 137; C219/39/176. [8] C219/40/233. [9] CJ, i. 816b. [10] P. Haskell, 'Ship Money in Hants', in Hants Studies ed. J. Webb et al. 91, 104. [11] Add. 21922, f. 137v.

V.C.D.M./R.C.L.S.

NEWPORT I.o.W

Right of election: in the freemen 1604; in the corporation 1608[1]

Number of voters: 24 in 1608

13 Mar. 1604	RICHARD JAMES JOHN ASTELL
30 Mar. 1614	SIR RICHARD WORSLEY, bt. JOHN SEARLE
3 Jan. 1621	SIR RICHARD WORSLEY, bt. SIR WILLIAM UVEDALE
6 Dec. 1621	PHILIP FLEMING vice Worsley, deceased
27 Jan. 1624	CHRISTOPHER BROOKE PHILIP FLEMING
9 Mar. 1624	SIR JOHN DANVERS vice Brooke, chose to sit for York
5 May 1625	(SIR) NATHANIEL RICH PHILIP FLEMING
16 Jan. 1626	SIR CHRISTOPHER YELVERTON PHILIP FLEMING
18 Feb. 1628	SIR CHRISTOPHER YELVERTON PHILIP FLEMING Sir Edward Conway II* Sir Edward Dennys*

Lying at the head of the Medina estuary, adjacent to Carisbrooke Castle, where the captain of the Isle of Wight resided, Newport was the most populous

and prosperous of the three island boroughs.[2] Its seigneurial charter, confirmed by Queen Elizabeth in 1559, vested authority in two bailiffs and an indeterminate number of 'burgesses' or freemen.[3] Newport had returned one Member to the Model Parliament, but the franchise thereafter lapsed until 1584, when it was restored at the suit of the captain.[4] In gratitude the borough gave him the right to nominate one Member, and extended the privilege to his successors until 1626, when they ignored the recommendation of the 1st Viscount Conway (Sir Edward Conway I*). Elections were held in the guildhall.[5]

In 1604 an obscure lawyer, John Astell, was returned for the junior seat, perhaps at the behest of the then captain, the 3rd earl of Southampton. The senior seat was taken by a townsman, Richard James, who had represented the borough in the previous two parliaments. In 1608 the borough was incorporated at the insistence of Southampton and Sir Thomas Fleming I*, a native of the town and now lord chief justice, but against the wishes of the principal gentlemen of the Isle, such as Sir John Oglander*, who resented the growing independence of the townsmen.[6] Henceforth the common council, consisting of the mayor and 23 'chief burgesses', engrossed the franchise. Under the new charter Astell was appointed recorder for life and John Searle, a local barrister, continued as town clerk, although he was later suspended from office for attempting to prove that the Crown owned certain of the town's lands.[7] On 30 June 1610 a petition about wages was received by the Commons, probably from James, who had been arrested for debt during the previous recess. As the House did nothing James began an action for £74 in the courts; but after the dissolution he accepted the corporation's offer of £32.[8] By 1611 Astell, whose finances were scarcely less desperate, had ceased to function as recorder, though he could not be removed from office without his own consent.[9]

In 1614 Sir Richard Worsley stood for election, perhaps with the backing of the earl of Southampton. On 19 Mar. 1614 the corporation unanimously resolved to grant him the freedom. There may initially have been disagreement over the choice of the faithless Searle as his colleague; but 11 days later it was decided that he should 'absolutely stand burgess', and he was returned with Worsley 'with a general consent'.[10] On his return from Westminster, Worsley presented the corporation with a buck, and he subscribed generously in October 1614 to the building fund for a free grammar school on a site given by Sir Thomas Fleming II*.[11] He was re-elected to the third Stuart

Parliament 'with a general consent'. The mayor had to cross the Solent to Titchfield (charging the town 20s. for his expenses) to receive Southampton's nomination for the other seat, which, it transpired, was for Sir William Uvedale, a rising courtier from a great Hampshire family.[12] Perhaps in recompense for according the junior seat to Uvedale, the corporation afterwards spent £3 on gifts for Southampton.[13]

Shortly after the end of the first sitting, on 26 June 1621, Worsley died of smallpox, and on 13 Nov., ahead of Parliament's recall, Newport held an assembly to decide whether to replace him with Fleming's brother Philip, a town resident, or with an outsider. 'A general answer was made by the whole company above-named that they thought no man so fit as Mr. Fleming', and he was duly returned.[14] Subsequently appointed deputy-steward of the Isle, he was re-elected to every Parliament of the 1620s. In December 1623 Newport voted to give Southampton a hogshead of wine for Christmas, and at the following election his nominee Christopher Brooke, a director of the Virginia Company, was 'freely elected and chosen' with Fleming.[15] When Brooke opted for York, he was replaced 'by a general consent' with Sir John Danvers, also prominent in the Company. Both Members were returned in their absence with the proviso that they should take out the freedom as soon as possible, but neither seems to have done so.[16]

Southampton died later in the year, and was immediately succeeded as captain by Conway, although the appointment was not ratified until 8 Dec. 1625. Conway had no previous ties with the island, and his management of electoral patronage there proved inept. On 14 Apr. 1625 Newport voted him 'the courtesy of a choice of a burgess for the Parliament for this present'.[17] Too busy as secretary of state to visit the island himself, Conway relied on his deputy lieutenants, Oglander and Sir Edward Dennys*, to promote his candidates. By 2 May they were able to assure him of the boroughs' compliance, and Newport duly returned his nominee (Sir) Nathaniel Rich.[18]

On hearing ahead of the 1625 Parliament that the corporation intended to renew its charter, probably to enable it to replace Astell, Oglander drafted a furious letter berating the townsmen for neglecting to consult him, and adding 'I have been persuaded to write unto my Lord [Conway] to cause a stop therein till his Lordship or some of us his officers may know and be made acquainted with your intentions'.[19] The charter was not renewed, though Oglander's hostility probably reduced the influence which as a freeman and part-time resident he might have expected to

exercise in elections. He incurred further unpopularity by rating the island for the Forced Loan.[20] On 12 Jan. 1626 Fleming complained to Conway that 'the poor town of Newport ... is more charged with privy seals than Southampton or Salisbury'.[21] Conway promised an impartial hearing, and informed him that he had nominated (Sir) John Suckling* for the next Parliament at Newport, threatening reprisals if he were refused. He added that he had already asked Oglander and Dennys to inform the borough of his recommendation.[22] According to Oglander, however, Francis Beale*, a new resident who was 'wont to drink sack' with the corporation, persuaded them to return his nephew Sir Christopher Yelverton.[23] The townspeople may have hoped that Beale's brother-in-law (Sir) Henry Yelverton* would as a judge be able to assist them with their charter. It was recorded in the ledger-book on 16 Jan. that Yelverton and Fleming had been returned 'by a general consent' as required by the writ of summons, which was transcribed in full.[24] Fleming protested to Conway that the election had taken place during his absence, and proposed that 'rather than it shall frustrate my lord's desires, that interest which I have shall be rendered back, and I will gladly stand down if a new election may be made'.[25] This unorthodox offer proved unnecessary, however, since Suckling was successful at both Sandwich and Norwich.

The Isle of Wight was heavily burdened with the billeting of soldiers during the summer of 1627, leaving the inhabitants less inclined than ever to defer to the captain's wishes at the next election.[26] By nominating his own son, a colonel whose regiment was stationed just across the Solent, as candidate for Newport, Conway demonstrated his complete insensitivity to the strength of local feelings.[27] He informed the corporation on 1 Feb. 1628 that his patronage was 'rather for your good and benefit than any other respects', and assured them that his son had 'a good affection to serve you, and he shall have my best assistance to put that forward for your good'.[28] He also informed Oglander and Dennys the following day that 'I rely on Newport for my son, and make no other provision for him', expecting them to prevail upon the townsmen.[29] However, Dennys had redeemed his popularity by his tireless efforts to free the island from troops, and on 6 Feb. 1628 the corporation recorded that 'upon motion made by Sir Edward Dennys to be a burgess of the Parliament House no man contradicteth'.[30] Eleven days later Oglander lamented Conway's decision to transfer his son's nomination from Yarmouth to Newport, 'where (do what I can) he will, I fear, miss it'. He relayed that the mayor 'after a churlish manner' claimed to have received Conway's nomination too late; 'and to myself on the 16th of this month, being importunate with him, his answer was, they were resolved not to choose your son – other reason I could have none of him'.[31] Instead Newport resolved on Yelverton and Dennys, despite the absence of the former in Italy. Oglander mistakenly reported that Fleming had been chosen by Yarmouth, but at the election the following day Yelverton and Fleming were 'freely and indifferently' returned for Newport, and Dennys, probably smarting at his rejection, for Yarmouth. The corporation again recorded that the election was in conformity with the writ of summons, which it appended in translation from the original Latin.[32] An angry response from Conway warning that 'I cannot be of so gentle disposition as to do courtesies where I receive disrespect and discourtesies' arrived too late to make any difference.[33] According to Oglander he made good the implied threat by authorizing the billeting of the Scottish regiment in the island, 'which was the greatest revenge (and slavery to the inhabitants) that ever was'.[34]

Conway may have hoped that Yelverton's enforced absence abroad would necessitate a fresh election. He bore Yelverton no grudge, and soon afterwards helped him to secure a post in Queen Henrietta Maria's Household.[35] The prospect of a further election receded, however, after Conway's son was summoned to the Lords, an unprecedented honour for a viscount's heir, and on 19 May the Commons refused a motion for a fresh writ, despite being informed that Yelverton was in France.[36]

[1] C66/1735; I.o.W. RO, NBC 45/2, f. 20. [2] VCH Hants, v. 253, 256, 257, 259. [3] I.o.W. RO, NBC 45/2, f. 11. [4] Ibid. f. 39. [5] Ibid. f. 16. [6] I.o.W. RO, NBC/1/31; C66/1735; Oglander Mems. ed. W.H. Long, 107, 108. [7] I.o.W. RO, 16a/30, ff. 5, 21v. [8] CJ, i. 444b; I.o.W. RO, 16a/30, f. 9. [9] I.o.W. RO, 16a/30, f. 22; STAC 8/71/11. [10] I.o.W. RO, 16a/30, ff. 35, 37. [11] Ibid. f. 38; VCH Hants, ii. 391; v. 264. [12] I.o.W. RO, 16a/30, f. 153. [13] Ibid. f. 151. [14] Ibid. ff. 164v, 165. [15] Ibid. f. 190v; I.o.W. RO, NBC 45/2, f. 52v. [16] I.o.W. RO, NBC 45/2, ff. 55, 55v. [17] I.o.W. RO, 16a/30, f. 205. [18] I.o.W. RO, OG/BB/74. [19] I.o.W. RO, OG/BB/73. [20] Royalist's Notebk. ed. F. Bamford, 12-13. [21] SP16/523/13. [22] SP16/523/14. [23] L. Boynton, 'Billeting in the I.o.W.', EHR, lxxiv. 29. [24] I.o.W. RO, NBC 45/2, f. 59; 16a/30, f. 215. [25] SP16/523/27. [26] Boynton, 29. [27] CSP Dom. 1627-8, p. 181. [28] SP16/92/4. [29] Procs. 1628, vi. 156-7. [30] I.o.W. RO, 16a/30, f. 225. [31] Procs. 1628, vi. 172-3. [32] Ibid, 173; I.o.W. RO, NBC 45/2, f. 60. [33] Procs. 1628, vi. 157. [34] I.o.W. RO, OG/BB/155. [35] SP16/100/93. [36] CJ, i. 900a.

V.C.D.M./R.C.L.S.

NEWTOWN I.o.W

Right of election: in the burgage-holders

Number of voters: 19 in 1640[1]

10 Mar. 1604	SIR JOHN STANHOPE I WILLIAM MEUX
c.Dec. 1605	THOMAS WILSON vice Stanhope, called to the Upper House
c.Mar. 1614	SIR HENRY BERKELEY GEORGE STOUGHTON
c.Apr. 1614	WILLIAM HIGFORD vice Stoughton, chose to sit for Guildford[2]
8 Jan. 1621	JOHN FERRAR SIR THOMAS BARRINGTON
19 Feb. 1621	SIR WILLIAM HARINGTON vice Ferrar, chose to sit for Tamworth
c.Jan. 1624	(SIR) GILBERT GERARD, (bt.) GEORGE GARRARD
22 Mar. 1624	SIR THOMAS BARRINGTON vice Gerard, chose to sit for Middlesex
27 Apr. 1625	SIR THOMAS BARRINGTON THOMAS MALET
21 Jan. 1626	SIR THOMAS BARRINGTON THOMAS MALET
4 Mar. 1628	SIR THOMAS BARRINGTON ROBERT BARRINGTON Thomas Malet

Newtown, lying east of Yarmouth on the north coast of the Isle of Wight, was sustained mainly by its oyster fishery and saltern.[3] Under the town's seigneurial charter of 1393, which was confirmed in 1598, the governing body consisted of the mayor, town clerk, sergeant, constable, and an indeterminate number of 'chief burgesses', from whose number the mayor was chosen annually.[4] The chief burgesses were themselves recruited from the burgage-holders who, since 1584, when the three Isle of Wight boroughs were enfranchised, formed the electorate.[5] At first the captain of the Isle controlled both seats: in 1601, for example, Lord Hunsdon (Sir George Carey[†]) requested blank indentures so that he could return two nominees on the town's behalf.[6] However, under James I, Hunsdon's successor as captain, the 3rd earl of Southampton, shared his patronage at Newtown with members of the local gentry, notably Sir John Meux of Kingston.[7] By the end of the period Meux's relations by marriage, the Barringtons, an Essex-based family that owned substantial properties on the Isle of Wight, had acquired a dominant interest in the borough's elections. There is no evidence that Newtown paid wages to any of its MPs during this period.

On 4 Feb. 1604 Southampton wrote to Meux recommending 'my two good friends whose names [I] shall send you very shortly'.[8] The courtier Sir John Stanhope I was presumably one of these nominees, but the junior seat was taken by Meux's son William, the only islander to sit during this period. When Stanhope was raised to the peerage in 1605 he was succeeded by Thomas Wilson, secretary to the earl of Salisbury (Sir Robert Cecil[†]) and the translator of Gorge de Montemayor's *Diana*, which he had dedicated to Southampton. At the general election in 1614 Southampton presumably supported the nomination of George Stoughton, nephew to the chief steward of the Isle of Wight, Adrian Stoughton*.[9] The senior seat was taken by Sir Henry Berkeley, whose wife was sister-in-law to a prominent member of the island gentry, Sir Richard Worsley*. When Stoughton opted to sit for his native borough of Guildford, Southampton does not appear to have made any further nominations, and the place was filled by Meux's brother-in-law, William Higford.[10]

In 1621 Southampton nominated John Ferrar, a London merchant, who shared his concern to defend the Virginia Company against anticipated attacks in the Parliament. Ferrar was returned as the senior Member, pushing Sir Thomas Barrington, Meux's brother-in-law, into second place despite his status as the heir to several burgages in the town and to 'the best manor in our Island'.[11] When Ferrar chose to sit for another constituency, he was replaced by a servant of Prince Charles, Sir William Harington, who had failed to obtain a seat at Leicester. Southampton nominated another Virginia Company member, George Garrard, at the next general election in 1624, but was only able to secure him the second seat at Newtown. The first went to Barrington's brother-in-law Sir Gilbert Gerard, in case he was defeated in his own Middlesex constituency. This turned out to be unnecessary, and Barrington was elected to replace Gerard on 22 Mar. 1624.

Southampton died later in the year, and in the remaining elections of the period his successor Viscount Conway (Sir Edward Conway I*) nominated

Thomas Malet, his legal adviser, who was returned in second place alongside Barrington in both 1625 and 1626.[12] Malet, however, emerged from the second Caroline Parliament branded as a supporter of the duke of Buckingham, and his future electoral prospects were further weakened by the unpopularity of billeting in the Isle. Nevertheless, it was with undiminished confidence that Conway wrote on 2 Feb. 1628 to the island's deputy lieutenants nominating 'my cousin Malet for Newtown ... with some such other as I shall hereafter think of, or you find cause to name for the good of the island'. That same day Conway also wrote to the mayor and townsmen asking them to 'make choice of such burgesses as I have thought of to be both able, willing, and ready to advance anything that shall be for the good of the island or that particular corporation'. He did not think it necessary to name the candidates whose identities would be disclosed by his deputies:

> And as you shall perceive that I do principally respect your advantage and good in furnishing you with so good ministers to serve you usefully and profitably, so I shall take your application to me in this as a testimony of your good wills to me and confidence in me, and an obligation upon me to endeavour the welfare of your town.[13]

Sir John Oglander*, who had the thankless task of managing Conway's patronage, informed Conway on 17 Feb. that 'the mayor of Newtown is not yet come home, but divers of the burgesses were very willing to grant your lordship's desire'.[14] In the event Newtown, in common with the other boroughs on the Isle of Wight, defied Conway's recommendations and instead returned Barrington and his brother Robert. Both men undoubtedly benefited from the fact that their father, Sir Francis Barrington*, had stoutly resisted the Forced Loan.

[1] I.o.W. RO, JER/BAR/3/9/8. [2] *Procs. 1614*, pp. 459, 467; *OR Index*, app. pp. xxxix, xl. [3] *VCH Hants*, v. 265, 266, 267. [4] I.o.W. RO, JER/BAR/3/9/1-5. [5] M. Weinbaum, *Borough Charters*, 47. [6] *Oglander Mems*. ed. W.H. Long, p. xiii. [7] Add. 46501, ff. 142-5v. [8] Add. 46501, f. 202. [9] I.o.W. RO, OG/BB/26. [10] *Vis. Berks*. (Harl. Soc. lvi), 249. [11] *Royalist's Notebk*. ed. F. Bamford, 137. [12] SP16/523/14. [13] *Procs. 1628*, vi. 157, 158. [14] Ibid. 173.

V.C.D.M./R.C.L.S.

PETERSFIELD

Right of election: in the burgage-holders

Number of voters: unknown

10 Mar. 1604	SIR WILLIAM HERVEY I
	SIR WILLIAM KINGSWELL
c. Mar. 1614	SIR WALTER TICHBORNE
	EDWARD SAVAGE I
30 Dec. 1620[1]	SIR RICHARD NORTON
	SIR JOHN HIPPISLEY
16 Jan. 1624	SIR JOHN JEPHSON
	SIR JOHN HIPPISLEY
25 Apr. 1625	SIR WILLIAM UVEDALE
	SIR JOHN JEPHSON
20 Jan. 1626	SIR WILLIAM UVEDALE
	BENJAMIN TICHBORNE
29 Feb. 1628	SIR WILLIAM UVEDALE
	BENJAMIN TICHBORNE

Situated on the edge of the South Downs, Petersfield was a prosperous market town and centre for the local clothing and leather tanning industries.[2] A borough by prescription, its government was vested in a mayor, constable, bailiff and two aldermen and tithingmen, and it regularly sent Members to Parliament from 1547. The franchise was confined to the burgage-holders, with the mayor acting as returning officer.[3] A handsome town mace survives, dated 1596.[4] Although never incorporated by royal charter, the inhabitants asserted in 1610 that Petersfield had been 'time out of mind an ancient borough'; their claims to independence were nevertheless insufficient to defeat the lord of the manor, Sir Thomas Hanbury, an Exchequer auditor, who successfully prosecuted them in the Exchequer for the rights to certain waste lands.[5] Hanbury was probably responsible for thwarting the borough's subsequent attempt to obtain a charter, which was drawn up in 1612 but never passed the seals.[6] He exercised no influence over the borough's elections during the early Stuart period, which were dominated by the Nortons of Rotherfield, although Sir Richard Norton only once used his patronage on his own behalf.[7]

In 1604 the electors 'by one assent and consent' returned Sir William Hervey I, keeper of St. Andrew's Castle, situated on the coast, and Norton's kinsman, Sir William Kingswell, the highest rated subsidy payer in the town.[8] Norton was probably responsible for nominating Sir Walter Tichborne in 1614, and the junior seat went to Edward Savage I, a Hampshire magistrate who was in desperate need of parliamentary privilege. In 1620 Norton reserved both seats for himself and his brother-in-law Sir John Hippisley, the marquess of Buckingham's 'principal favourite'.[9] Hippisley sat again in 1624, this time with Sir John Jephson; both men had recently accompanied Charles and Buckingham to Spain. Jephson in turn sat again in 1625, though he conceded the senior seat to Norton's cousin Sir William Uvedale. In the last two parliaments of the reign Uvedale was joined by Benjamin Tichborne, son of Sir Walter. There is no evidence that Petersfield pursued any legislation during the early Stuart period, and its Members, most of whom were drawn from the Hampshire gentry, presumably served without wages.

[1] C219/37/218. [2] *VCH Hants*, iii. 111-16. [3] R.S. Atcheson, *Rep. of Case of Petersfield*, 10-11. [4] E.M. Yates, *Petersfield in Tudor Times* (Petersfield Pprs. v), 24. [5] E134/6Jas.I/Mich.1; Atcheson, 13-16. [6] *VCH Hants*, iii. 114-15. [7] E.A. Minty, *Hist. Petersfield*, 30. [8] C219/35/2/14; Yates, 22. [9] *Chamberlain Letters* ed. N.E. McClure, ii. 152.

V.C.D.M./R.C.L.S.

PORTSMOUTH

Right of election: in the corporation

Number of voters: 48 in 1575; 38 in 1627[1]

8 Mar. 1604	SIR OLIVER ST. JOHN
	RICHARD JENVEY
27 Jan. 1607	JOHN CORBET *vice*
	St. John, appointed to office
c. Mar. 1614	JOHN GRIFFITH II
	GEORGE THORPE
19 Dec. 1620	SIR DANIEL NORTON
	SIR BENJAMIN RUDYARD
29 Jan. 1624	SIR WILLIAM UVEDALE
	SIR BENJAMIN RUDYARD
29 Apr. 1625	SIR BENJAMIN RUDYARD
	SIR DANIEL NORTON
17 Jan. 1626	SIR WILLIAM HARINGTON
	THOMAS WHATMAN
c. Feb. 1626	SIR JAMES FULLERTON *vice*
	Harington, chose to sit
	for Hertford
3 Mar. 1628	OWEN JENNENS
	WILLIAM TOWERSON II

Portsmouth's strategic position and fine natural harbour made it an ideal naval base, although the presence of the garrison and its governor were occasionally a source of friction with the townsmen. Camden noted that 'in war-time it is much frequented, at other times scarce at all, the inhabitants being more attentive to war and navigation than to trade'.[2] The borough received its first charter in 1194, and was incorporated with a governing body specified only as the 'mayor and burgesses' in 1600.[3] Two Members were first sent to Parliament in 1295; the franchise was confined to the corporation, and elections were held in the guildhall.[4] Electoral patronage was dominated by the governor, who usually nominated one, and sometimes both, Members. During the 1620s Sir Daniel Norton*, who lived seven miles away at Southwick and held the lease of the town's two rectories, also exerted a claim to one of Portsmouth's seats.[5]

In 1604 the 1st earl of Devonshire (Sir Charles Blount†), who was both governor and high steward of the town, nominated his kinsman Sir Oliver St. John for the senior seat. The second Member, Richard Jenvey, was an obscure townsman whose wages of 4s. a day for five sessions, plus 20s. for horse hire as required, must have proved an exceptional drain on the borough's resources.[6] On Devonshire's death in 1606 the corporation invited the 1st earl of Salisbury (Robert Cecil†) to accept the high stewardship, while the king appointed Sir Francis Vere† as the next governor.[7] At the start of the third session of the Parliament in November 1606 a writ was issued for a by-election to replace St. John, who had been appointed master of the ordnance in Ireland. The corporation offered the nomination to Salisbury, and as a result the latter's client John Corbet was elected the following January.[8] William Herbert, 3rd earl of Pembroke, became governor following Vere's death in 1609, and held the post for the rest of the period.[9] Soon after his appointment the corporation presented him with a list of grievances, and requested that soldiers should be forbidden to exercise trades or keep alehouses, that their dependants should not become a charge on the borough, and that the constables should have the right of pursuit throughout the garrison.[10] Pembroke's answer was conciliatory but the corporation, alarmed by a report that he intended to have his powers increased by patent, appealed to Salisbury.[11] They also asked Salisbury's furtherance for a bill to establish a customs house at Portsmouth. No such bill was ever introduced in Parliament, presumably because it was not needed, as Salisbury, the lord treasurer, seems to have acted on his own authority to establish a customs house before his death. At any event, the first port book registering customs entries at Portsmouth dates from Christmas 1612.[12]

Following Salisbury's death in May 1612 the office of high steward appears to have fallen into abeyance. Relations between the garrison and the town remained somewhat strained, and in the absence of a high steward, the mayor and brethren petitioned the Privy Council to arbitrate in the summer of 1613.[13] The Council's involvement in its affairs may help to explain the corporation's decision to return, at the general election in 1614, John Griffith II, secretary to one of the most important members of the Council, Henry Howard, earl of Northampton. Certainly neither Northampton nor Griffith had any other discernable link with the town.[14] The second seat went to George Thorpe, a board member of the Virginia Company, in which Pembroke was a leading partner. In December 1620 Norton claimed the first seat, together with Pembroke's most valuable henchman, Sir Benjamin Rudyard in second. Both were elected with the 'whole assent and consent' of the corporation.[15]

Royalty twice graced Portsmouth with visits in 1623, once when James came to inspect the fleet in August, and once when Prince Charles returned from his doomed trip to Spain in October.[16] In the 1624 elections Pembroke, now lord chamberlain, nominated both Members; possibly Norton, who was chosen as a Hampshire knight of the shire, may have surrendered his patronage at Portsmouth in return for the earl's support in the county elections. The first seat went to Sir William Uvedale, a courtier who lived at Wickham, eight miles north of Portsmouth, and Rudyard was re-elected in second place. Rudyard moved up to the first seat in 1625, while Norton took the second.

In September 1625 the corporation petitioned the Privy Council for a renewal of its privileges, and asked for a monopoly of tobacco imports and of exports to New England. Nothing came of the request, and in the following month the town's administration was paralysed by a severe outbreak of plague.[17] Ahead of the 1626 election Rudyard recommended his brother-in-law Sir William Harington, Pembroke's lieutenant, who was returned with the recorder, Thomas Whatman.[18] In the event Harington was also elected at Hertford, leaving a vacancy at Portsmouth. A new writ was issued on 11 Feb., and Harington's place was taken by the Scottish courtier Sir James Fullerton, also a member of the Pembroke circle.[19]

Despite two further plague outbreaks, Portsmouth was chosen as the embarkation point for the military expeditions to the Ile de Ré and La Rochelle, and the duke of Buckingham, in his role as lord admiral, made his headquarters at the house of William Towerson II.[20] The corporation capitalized on the royal favourite's presence by suing for a new charter, granted on 17 Nov. 1627. This established a council consisting of the mayor and 12 senior aldermen, and also formally recognized the recorder and the other municipal officers.[21] By the time of the next election Pembroke, whose nephew had recently been betrothed to Buckingham's infant daughter, may have agreed to let Buckingham choose Portsmouth's candidate. The mayor wrote to the lord admiral's secretary Edward Nicholas* on 6 Feb. 1628 that 'I dare promise nothing until the summons and warrants be out and come to us' but gave an assurance that 'upon my lord his grace's letter to us we shall think ourselves happy to grant his grace's request'.[22] In the event the corporation with 'the whole assent and consent of the rest of the burgesses', returned two of their own number, Towerson II and Owen Jennens, both of whom were local admiralty officials. They were probably selected at the behest of Buckingham's client, Lord Conway

(Sir Edward Conway I*), secretary of state and vice admiral of Hampshire and the Isle of Wight.[23]

[1] VCH Hants, iii. 177-8. [2] Portsmouth Pprs. xv. 6; W. Camden, Britannia (1772), i. 217. [3] VCH Hants, iii. 176-7, 181. [4] C219/38/201. [5] Winchester Coll. muniments, 15256B, 15257-8. [6] Portsmouth RO, CEI/3, f. 47; CSP Dom. 1603-10, p. 64; Portsmouth Recs. ed. R. East, 627. [7] HMC Hatfield, xiii. 103; HMC Buccleuch, i. 106. [8] HMC Hatfield, xix. 7. [9] Portsmouth Recs. 637. [10] Add. 33283, ff. 85-6. [11] HMC Hatfield, xxi. 190-1. [12] HMC Hatfield, xxiv. 209. [13] APC, 1613-14, pp. 105-6; Portsmouth Recs. 155. [14] L. Levy Peck, Northampton, 36-7. [15] C219/37/216. [16] Oglander Mems. ed. W.H. Long, 17; CSP Dom. 1623-5, p. 93. [17] APC, 1625-6, pp. 165, 184, 244. [18] V.A. Rowe, 'Influence of the Earls of Pembroke on Parlty. Elections, 1625-41', EHR, l. 243. [19] C231/4, f. 195. [20] APC, 1626, p. 33; 1627, p. 390; CSP Dom. 1627-8, p. 205; R. Lockyer, Buckingham, 375. [21] Portsmouth Recs. 585. [22] Procs. 1628, vi. 159. [23] C219/41A/85.

V.C.D.M./R.C.L.S.

SOUTHAMPTON

Right of election: in the freemen

Number of voters: about 40

2 Mar. 1604	SIR THOMAS FLEMING I SIR JOHN JEFFERY, alderman
c. Dec. 1605	SIR THOMAS FLEMING II *vice* Fleming, appointed to office
c. Mar. 1614	SIR THOMAS FLEMING II THOMAS CHEKE I
4 Dec. 1620	SIR THOMAS FLEMING II HENRY SHERFIELD
26 Jan. 1624	SIR JOHN MILL, bt. HENRY SHERFIELD
9 Mar. 1624	THOMAS BOND *vice* Sherfield, chose to sit for Salisbury
c. Apr. 1625	SIR JOHN MILL, bt. GEORGE GOLLOP, alderman
16 Jan. 1626	SIR JOHN MILL, bt. GEORGE GOLLOP, alderman
10 Mar. 1628	JOHN MAJOR, alderman GEORGE GOLLOP, alderman

Southampton, once a major trading port, received its first charter in the reign of Henry II, and sent Members to the Model Parliament in 1295.[1] Incorporated in 1445, the town's government was vested in a mayor, sheriff, recorder, two bailiffs, a steward, two constables, and a fluctuating number of aldermen, or ex-mayors.[2] The franchise was extended to all freemen, but admission to the freedom, which conferred the right to trade, was tightly controlled, and the electorate never rose above 40 in this period.[3] Although described in 1635 as a 'rich merchant and sweet maritime town', whose 'fabrics and inhabitants are fair, neat, beautiful, straight and handsome', Southampton's prosperous appearance masked a prolonged period of economic decline, exacerbated in the later years of the sixteenth century by the war with Spain.[4] The monopoly of sweet wine imports, vigorously defended throughout the period, brought a steady income but no real wealth, most merchants preferring to pay the forfeiture and trade elsewhere. Although dissatisfied with their charter, the corporation seems to have been unable to afford the cost (estimated at up to £350) of a new grant, preferring instead to confirm their privileges by Act of Parliament and *inspeximus*.[5] The corporation controlled nominations to both seats and only once, under protest, returned a Member with no official or residential connection with the town.[6]

A royal visit on 20 Oct. 1603 brought no enlargement of the town's privileges, and the corporation's attempt two months later to negotiate a monopoly of trade with Venice proved fruitless.[7] At the general election of 1604 the former recorder, solicitor general Sir Thomas Fleming I, a nearby resident who had represented the borough in 1601, was returned while the second seat was taken by Sir John Jeffery, the most enterprising Southampton merchant of the age. The Commons declared Fleming's seat vacant on 9 Nov. 1605, following his appointment as lord chief baron, and at the ensuing by-election his son was returned as his replacement.[8] On 9 Apr. 1606 the imposition on serges at Southampton was included in a list of grievances considered by the Commons; and the town's sergemakers also petitioned lord treasurer Salisbury (Robert Cecil[†]).[9]

In the next session the corporation decided to procure statutory confirmation of the freemen's exclusive right to trade. They were motivated to do so by a protracted and costly lawsuit brought against them by a London citizen, John Davies, whom the corporation had fined for attempting to trade goods they described as 'foreign bought and sold' in Southampton some six or seven years previously. Although Fleming was doubtless useful in obtaining his father's support, he seems to have taken no part in securing the passage of the bill, which was entrusted to the recorder, William

Brocke*, who sat for St. Ives, and Jeffery. It received its first reading on 29 Apr. 1607 and, after substantial amendments in committee, it was reported by Brocke on 5 June.[10] The measure proved so contentious that Southampton retained Thomas Richardson* to answer the objections of London's merchants, who claimed that under their charter they had the right to buy and sell in all cities of England. The corporation also spent £22 14s. on 'a piece of plate given to an honourable person' to further the bill.[11] Despite the Londoners' attempts to delay the bill until it 'may fall asleep and die', the borough ultimately proved successful, probably because of the strength of the free trade lobby in the Commons at this time.[12] The bill was sent up to the Lords on 11 June, where the 3rd earl of Southampton assisted its progress by ensuring it was read immediately and by ensuring that he was named to the committee.[13] It finally received the Royal Assent on 25 July.[14] In total the corporation had spent over £100, which was raised by a levy on local merchants.[15] However, the Act afforded no protection to Southampton merchants when, in 1608, the new royal butler, Sir Thomas Waller*, sued for arrears of prisage, a long-neglected duty, on wine imports. At first no exception was made, but Brocke managed to negotiate a composition of 500 marks, to be financed by loans from the leading merchants.[16] After petitioning the king, the town was granted, on 6 Feb. 1609, an exemption for the future.[17]

Brocke died in 1611 and was succeeded as recorder by Thomas Cheke I, who took the second seat in the Addled Parliament, while the younger Fleming was re-elected in first place. In 1615 Cheke secured confirmation of Southampton's monopoly of sweet wine imports, which was threatened by the Levant Company's charter.[18] Nevertheless the town's concerted defence of its commercial privileges did little to improve its fortunes in the long term. This is evidenced by Southampton's failure to raise £300 demanded by the Privy Council in February 1619 to help pay for an expedition to suppress the pirates of Algiers; the borough at first yielded only £92 3s. 4d., and eventually struggled to raise their contribution to £150.[19]

By the end of 1615 many observers expected the king to summon another Parliament to meet in the New Year, and consequently the corporation wrote in December 1615, and again in February 1616, offering the senior seat to Sir Thomas Lake I*, a native of the town and a privy councillor, who had assisted them in the prisage negotiations.[20] However, by the time the election actually took place, in December 1620,

Lake was out of office and did not stand for the Parliament. Fleming II was therefore re-elected, accompanied by the town's new recorder, Henry Sherfield. Southampton's sweet wine monopoly was mentioned during the monopolies debates, when on 15 Mar. it was reported that Southampton's previously more extensive privileges had been found void by the judges early in Elizabeth's reign, and since then allowed only for sweet wines imported by strangers.[21] On 21 Apr. 1621 a delegation of Southampton traders presented a petition against the alnage patentees to the committee for trade, which was already considering various measures concerning the manufacture and export of cloth, and may have incorporated the Southampton merchants' points into a general bill 'for the true making of woollen cloths'.[22]

At the next election, in 1624, the senior seat went to Fleming's brother-in-law Sir John Mill, who lived two miles away on the other side of the Test estuary. Sherfield, returned for the junior seat, opted to sit for Salisbury in Wiltshire, and recommended William Peaseley, the son-in-law of the secretary of state, (Sir) George Calvert*, in his stead. The corporation's response was initially favourable, but after second thoughts they informed Sherfield on 15 Feb. 1624 that 'if we should elect a stranger we must nevertheless send up a solicitor for the town, which would be chargeable, we think it therefore more convenient to make choice of one of our own company'.[23] It is ironic therefore that the seat eventually went to Thomas Bond, a minor government official with no local connections who, as an investor in the Virginia Company, may have been recommended by the Company's governor, the earl of Southampton, or by Sir Edward Conway I*, secretary of state, whom he had recently helped after a traffic accident.[24] The corporation seems to have soon regretted this decision, for they resolved on 9 Apr. that in future any freeman who voted for an outsider would be expelled. They reiterated their resolution on 15 Apr. 1625, and returned Alderman George Gollop to the first two Caroline parliaments, together with Mill, who may have been reckoned a part-time resident.[25]

The billeting of troops in 1627-8 was deeply unpopular in Southampton as throughout the county, and the borough therefore reacted with predictable hostility when Conway, now a viscount, who had succeeded the earl of Southampton as lord lieutenant of Hampshire, wrote recommending an outsider, Sir Francis Annesley*, ahead of the elections in 1628.[26] Sir Henry Whithed*, a Hampshire magistrate and former knight of the shire, also requested a seat; but

as a commissioner for both the Forced Loan and billeting he had won no friends in Southampton. The corporation immediately rebuffed both, and when Conway restated his request they responded on 26 Feb. that 'we cannot herein satisfy your lordship's expectation without apparent breach of our oaths and exposing ourselves to public disgrace', having sworn that 'none of us shall give our voices for any person whatsoever ... but only for a burgess here resident (the recorder for the time being only excepted), upon pain of degrading and expulsion'.[27] Gollop was returned with another alderman, John Major, as his senior colleague. Major died on 21 Feb. 1629, but no fresh writ was ordered, and the Parliament ended shortly thereafter.

[1] J.S. Davies, *Hist. Soton*, 152, 199. [2] *Assembly Bks. 1602-8* ed. J.W. Horrocks (Soton. Rec. Soc. xix), pp. vi-ix, xvi-xviii, xx. [3] Davies, 164, 190, 197, 208-9. [4] 'Relation of a Short Survey of the Western Counties' ed. L.G. Wickham Legg *Cam. Misc.* xvi (Cam. Soc. ser. 3, lii) pt. 3, pp. 55-7; *HMC Hatfield*, iv. 120-1. [5] *Soton City Charters* ed. E. Welch (Soton Pprs. iv), 15. [6] *VCH Hants*, iii. 517. [7] *HMC Southampton and King's Lynn Corp.*, 23; *CSP Ven.* 1603-7, p. 124. [8] *CJ*, i. 257a. [9] Ibid. 295b; *HMC Hatfield*, xxiv. 74-5. [10] *CJ*, i. 346b, 365b, 372a, 376b, 379a. [11] Soton City Archives, SC5/2/2, f. 112v. [12] *HMC Hatfield*, xix. 475-7. [13] *CJ*, i. 380a, 382a; *LJ*, ii. 523b, 526a. [14] *CJ*, i. 390a; C.C. Stopes, *Henry, 3rd Earl of Southampton*, 520. [15] Soton City Archives, SC5/2/2, f. 112v; Welch, 16. [16] *Assembly Bks. 1602-8*, pp. xxvii, 88. [17] *Assembly Bks. 1609-10* ed. J.W. Horrocks (Soton. Rec. Soc. xxi), 16; Welch, 16. [18] *Assembly Bks. 1615-16* ed. J.W. Horrocks (Soton. Rec. Soc. xxv), 13, 22, 26-7, 44; *APC*, 1625-6, p. 352. [19] *HMC Southampton and King's Lynn Corp.* 130-1; *CSP Dom.* 1619-23, p. 387. [20] SP14/84/17; *Assembly Bks. 1609-10*, pp. 4, 6; *Assembly Bks. 1615-16*, p. 33; A. Thrush, 'The Personal Rule of Jas. I, 1611-20', in *Pols., Religion and Popularity* ed. T. Cogswell *et al.* 91. [21] *CJ*, i. 555; *CD 1621*, iv. 157. [22] *HMC Var.* iv. 168-9; *CD 1621*, iii. 46, vii. 126-7, 129. [23] R.E. Ruigh, *Parl. of 1624*, p. 62. [24] J. Nichols, *Progs. of Jas. I*, iv. 966. [25] *VCH Hants*, iii. 517. [26] *HMC Cowper*, i. 344; *Procs. 1628*, vi. 165-6. [27] *Procs. 1628*, vi. 166-7.

V.C.D.M./R.C.L.S.

STOCKBRIDGE

Right of election: in the inhabitant householders

Number of voters: 30

12 Mar. 1604	SIR WILLIAM FORTESCUE	
	SIR EDWIN SANDYS	
c. 22 Mar. 1614[1]	SIR HENRY WALLOP	
	SIR WALTER COPE	8
	Sir Richard Gifford	22
	Henry St. John*	21
	Election declared void,	
	11 May 1614	
c. May 1614[2]	SIR HENRY WALLOP	28
	SIR WALTER COPE	26
	Henry St. John*	19
28 Dec. 1620	SIR RICHARD GIFFORD	
	SIR WILLIAM AYLOFFE, bt.	
Jan. 1624	SIR RICHARD GIFFORD	
	SIR HENRY HOLCROFT	
25 Apr. 1625	SIR RICHARD GIFFORD	
	SIR THOMAS BAGEHOTT	
c. Jan. 1626	SIR RICHARD GIFFORD	
	SIR THOMAS BAGEHOTT	
10 Mar. 1628	SIR RICHARD GIFFORD	
	SIR HENRY WHITHED	

Stockbridge, a small town situated where the road from Winchester to Salisbury crosses the Test, had been part of the duchy of Lancaster since the fourteenth century.[3] Though enfranchised at the instigation of the chancellor of the duchy in 1563, it was never incorporated, and consequently its municipal institutions remained primitive. The bailiff, who acted as returning officer, was elected annually by the inhabitants at the court leet, while the franchise seems to have been confined to inhabitant householders paying borough rent.[4] Throughout the period the manor and borough were leased from the duchy by Sir Richard Gifford who, through his tenantry, was able to dominate elections.[5] Further electoral influence was exercised by the St. John family of nearby Farley Chamberlayne and the Sandys family of The Vyne, near Basingstoke.[6]

Under Elizabeth the duchy had exercised little electoral patronage in Stockbridge. Indeed, the only known request for a nomination, made in 1597 by the acting chancellor (Sir) Robert Cecil†, was unsuccessful.[7] However, the chancellor in 1604, Sir John

Fortescue*, was more assertive and, presumably with Gifford's co-operation, successfully obtained a seat for his son, Sir William. The second place was taken by Sir Edwin Sandys who, though resident in Kent, was a distant cousin of William, 3rd Lord Sandys, of The Vyne. Before the 1614 election Lord Sandys again wrote to the bailiff asking for a nomination, but this time was refused.[8] Sir Richard Gifford wanted the senior seat, and the electors initially indicated that they intended to choose Henry St. John in second place, 'because his father and himself for good respects had oftentimes been burgesses in Parliament for the said borough'.[9] The support for St. John irritated the veteran official Sir Thomas Parry, who had succeeded Fortescue as chancellor of the duchy in 1607. He sent 'minatory' letters nominating Sir Walter Cope*, master of the Wards, and warned St. John that 'he should feel a greater power than he could resist, and that it would be ill taken of the state' if he did not stand down.[10] At the election the duchy was represented by its surveyor for southern England, but he seems to have allowed the initiative to pass to Gifford, styled 'a great disturber of the election' by one of the townsmen.[11] Although Gifford finished top of the poll 'for fear of revenge', the electors, 'notwithstanding that they had been much disturbed and threatened', gave St. John only one vote less. Cope, meanwhile, came a poor third.[12] Gifford, however, was now not certain that he wanted the seat, and subsequently persuaded the bailiff to delay sealing the indenture for a few days 'for himself to consider whether he would serve in it, or to have one put in his place that they should like well of'. He was presumably awaiting the outcome of the county election, in which his brother-in-law Sir Henry Wallop* was a candidate. When news came of Wallop's defeat the bailiff, allegedly assisted by a duchy pursuivant, tried to coerce the voters into electing Wallop and Cope. Indeed, one of St. John's supporters was arrested on trumped-up charges and beaten. Five electors, however, refused to vote for either Wallop or Cope, and though eight others cast their votes for St. John and Wallop they subsequently disclaimed any support for the latter in a petition to the Commons' privileges committee.[13] St. John himself also petitioned the committee, thereby fuelling a widespread suspicion at Westminster that there was a secret undertaking to manage the Commons. Although Cope tried to have St. John's complaints dismissed,[14] the case was reported on 9 May by Nicholas Fuller. Moreover, Sir Edward Hoby* produced a petition signed by 21 of St. John's supporters, one of whom had been arrested in London while two others had been threatened at the very door of Parliament. On the following day Parry's letters to the Stockbridge freemen were read out. The chancellor's conduct was clearly indefensible and he was expelled from the House. Sir Herbert Croft* subsequently moved to seat Gifford and St. John, but on 11 May the House declared the whole election void, and a fresh writ was issued.[15] At the ensuing election, held under the auspices of a new bailiff sometime later that month, Wallop and Cope were re-elected, although considerable support for St. John still existed. Neither Member had taken their seat by 31 May, when Richard Connock* moved to admit them.[16] A fresh petition from the electors against the new bailiff was referred to the privileges committee but never reported.[17] St. John subsequently sued the original bailiff for a false return in the first election, and was awarded £40 damages.[18]

Gifford's relationship with the townsmen of Stockbridge suffered a further blow in 1616 when, at the invitation of the inhabitants, a lawyer from Andover, the son of Peter Noyes*, held a court leet, claiming that Gifford's rights had lapsed through neglect.[19] The duchy upheld their principal tenant, however, and strengthened his hand by ordering that rents should be paid to him rather than the bailiff.[20] At the next election, in December 1620, Gifford re-asserted his control of the senior seat, though on the indenture the bailiff carefully stated that both Members had been chosen freely and indifferently as the law required. The second seat went to Sir William Ayloffe, an Essex gentleman whose neighbour and in-law, William Fanshawe*, was the duchy's northern auditor.[21]

In 1624 Gifford was re-elected alongside Sir Henry Holcroft, another Essex resident who may also have owed his return to Fanshawe, although he was also distantly related to the Sandys family. Following the election a petition was sent to the privileges committee claiming that the election had been held without due notice and in the absence of many electors.[22] It also complained that 'before the election [there were] two indentures, one ready sealed with Sir Richard Gifford's name for one, and a blank left for the other'. However, as only three of the borough's freemen signed the petition it is perhaps not surprising that the House upheld the election.[23] If Holcroft was indeed a nominee of Fanshawe his return was the last in which the duchy played any part. Gifford's colleague in the first two Caroline parliaments, Sir Thomas Bagehott, master of the harriers, lived in Southampton, and had various Hampshire connections that could have assisted his election. In 1628 Gifford was joined by Sir Henry Whithed, an active Hampshire magistrate who stood with the encouragement of the lord lieutenant, Lord

Conway (Sir Edward Conway I*).[24] Stockbridge was not included in the Ditchfield grant of Crown lands to the corporation of London that same year, but the alienation of the neighbouring manor of Somborne further diminished the duchy interest in the borough.[25]

[1] *Procs. 1614 (Commons)*, 195. [2] Hants RO, 44M69/G2/42. [3] *VCH Hants*, iv. 484; R. Somerville, *Hist. Duchy of Lancaster*, i. 18, 37, 313n. [4] Lansd. 256, ff. 113-16. [5] Add. 38446, ff. 1, 3, 4, 16, 20-23. [6] *VCH Hants*, iv. 444, 470, 484. [7] *HMC Hatfield*, vii. 432. [8] *Procs. 1614 (Commons)*, 195. [9] Hants RO, 44M69/G2/154. [10] *Procs. 1614 (Commons)*, 183, 195. [11] Ibid. 182. [12] Ibid. 178, 182; Hants RO, 44M69/G2/44. [13] Hants RO, 44M69/G2/154; *Procs. 1614 (Commons)*, 175. [14] *Procs. 1614 (Commons)*, 90. [15] Ibid. 177-9, 187-94, 202-205; *CD 1621*, vii. 635; T.L. Moir, *Addled Parl.* 45, 102-3; SP99/16/21; *Chamberlain Letters* ed. N.E. McClure, i. 528. [16] Hants RO, 44M69/G2/42. [17] *Procs. 1614 (Commons)*, 323, 324, 327, 390, 391, 397. [18] H. Hobart, *Reports*, (1678), p. 78. [19] Add. 38446, ff. 11, 15. [20] Ibid. f. 23. [21] C219/37/225. [22] 'Earle 1624', ff. 124, 125v; Lansd. 485, f. 21. [23] *CJ*, i. 759a. [24] *CSP Dom.* 1627-8, p. 556; *Procs. 1628*, vi. 166. [25] *VCH Hants*, iv. 471.

V.C.D.M./R.C.L.S.

WHITCHURCH

Right of election: in the freeholders

Number of voters: c.40

?7 Mar. 1604	SIR RICHARD PAULET
	THOMAS BROOKE
25 Mar. 1614[1]	SIR EDWARD BARRETT
	SIR RICHARD PAULET
8 Dec. 1620	SIR THOMAS JERVOISE
	SIR ROBERT OXENBRIDGE II
20 Jan. 1624	SIR HENRY WALLOP
	SIR THOMAS JERVOISE
28 Apr. 1625	SIR THOMAS JERVOISE
	SIR ROBERT OXENBRIDGE II
17 Jan. 1626	SIR THOMAS JERVOISE
	SIR ROBERT OXENBRIDGE II
3 Mar. 1628	SIR THOMAS JERVOISE
	SIR JOHN JEPHSON

Whitchurch was described by the antiquarian Thomas Baskerville in the later seventeenth century as a 'poor thoroughfare town' in a region devoted mainly to sheep grazing and the clothing industry.[2] The borough was owned by the dean and chapter of Winchester, but governed by a court leet presided over by an annually elected mayor and bailiff.[3] Members were first returned to Parliament in 1584, and the franchise rested in the freemen. Elections during this period were dominated by Sir Richard Paulet of nearby Freefolk and his successors. Without exception all those returned were puritan in sympathy. The freeholders seem to have expected little activity from their representatives, none of whom were either notable speechmakers or were appointed to more than a handful of committees. There is no evidence that any of the town's MPs received wages.

In 1604 Paulet was returned in first place, with Thomas Brooke, a lawyer who was the only townsman to represent Whitchurch in the period. The two had long been adversaries, quarrelling over lands and coppices which lay between Freefolk and Whitchurch, but they may both have helped the town to procure a new charter of incorporation in 1608. Brooke headed the list of 12 aldermen named in the charter, while Paulet wrote to the chancellor of the Exchequer, Sir Julius Caesar*, claiming that the town was worthy of incorporation, having 'yielded to the Crown by means of their trade of clothing great benefit yearly'.[4] The charter was granted, only to be cancelled after the dean and chapter alleged it had been obtained by deception.[5]

In the wake of this confrontation a new dean, Thomas Morton, future bishop of Chester,[6] tried to exercise influence over the borough's election in 1614, as Thomas Cheke I*, steward to the dean and chapter, secured letters of recommendation for his son and namesake. Paulet, however, was eager to consolidate his interest.[7] On 1 Mar. 1614 the vicar reported to Paulet that the voters' loyalties were divided. 'Many', he noted, 'were fearful of their landlord Mr. Dean (who wrote his letter to them for young Mr. Cheek)', but around half had promised to support Paulet regardless.[8] Probably Cheke's candidature was not pressed, as he found another opening. Consequently, Paulet was re-elected, together with Sir Edward Barrett, a courtier who owned property in Hampshire. In total Paulet had spent 20s. towards the election, including an unspecified fee for the return of the indenture.[9]

Paulet died not long after the end of the Addled Parliament, leaving Freefolk to his son-in-law Sir Thomas Jervoise. At the next election in 1620 Jervoise asserted a claim to the first seat, while the second went to Sir Robert Oxenbridge II, of Hurstbourne Priors, two miles west of the town. Jervoise was returned for the borough at every subsequent election until his death in 1654. Except in 1624, when he gave way to his wife's kinsman and fellow puritan Sir Henry Wallop,

he always took the senior seat.[10] Jervoise's accounts reveal that his electoral expenses were modest: he disbursed £5 14s. 3d. on the 'entertainment' of a score of voters in 1624.[11] Oxenbridge took second place in 1625 and 1626, but thereafter his health deteriorated, and in 1628 Jervoise was paired with another Hampshire landowner, Sir John Jephson of Froyle.

[1] Hants RO, 44M69/E4/28, f. 39v. [2] HMC Portland, ii. 286. [3] VCH Hants, iv. 299-304. [4] Hants RO, 44M69/F2/12/2, 7. [5] Brit. Bor. Charters ed. M. Weinbaum, 50; C66/1778/1. [6] Oxford DNB sub Morton, Thomas. [7] Hants RO, 44M69/F2/11/58. [8] Hants RO, 44M69/G2/41. [9] Hants RO, 44M69/E4/28, f. 39v. [10] Hants RO, 44M69/G2/47. [11] Hants RO, 44M69/G2/46, E6/140; D. Hirst, Representatives of the People?, 119.

V.C.D.M./R.C.L.S.

WINCHESTER

Right of election: in the freemen

Number of voters: unknown

9 Mar. 1604	JOHN MORE I, recorder
	EDWARD COLE, alderman
c. Mar. 1614	SIR WILLIAM SANDYS
	SIR THOMAS BILSON
14 Dec. 1620[1]	SIR RICHARD TICHBORNE
	WILLIAM SAVAGE, recorder
19 Jan. 1624	JAMES WRIOTHESLEY, Lord Wriothesley
	WILLIAM SAVAGE, recorder
17 Jan. 1625[2]	SIR RICHARD TICHBORNE vice Wriothesley, deceased
21 Apr. 1625	SIR THOMAS PHELIPS, bt.
	SIR RICHARD TICHBORNE
16 Jan. 1626	SIR RICHARD TICHBORNE
	SIR HENRY WHITHED
27 Feb. 1628	SIR RICHARD TICHBORNE
	ROBERT MASON I, recorder

Winchester, the county capital of Hampshire and seat of England's richest bishopric, received a charter in 1290 and first sent Members to Parliament seven years later. The city's clothing and leather industries, and annual fair, fell into a prolonged period of economic decline after the Black Death, and throughout the Tudor period the corporation repeatedly applied for remission of its fee farm, and for royal subsidies to repair the walls.[3] The corporation, created by charter in 1588, comprised a mayor, recorder, two bailiffs and 24 assistants or aldermen, and controlled admission to the guild merchant or roll of freemen.[4] In practice the number of aldermen fluctuated, as did that of the freemen.

By 1623 Winchester was so decayed and thinly populated that the water poet John Taylor likened it to 'a body without a soul'.[5] Its economic difficulties may explain why the borough ceased to pay parliamentary wages in this period, and why it increasingly looked to members of the local gentry, who were expected to serve without remuneration, to fill at least one of its parliamentary seats. From 1620 Sir Richard Tichborne, who lived at the castle, was able to acquire such a dominant interest that he twice succeeded in engrossing both seats, thereby squeezing out the recorder who, with the single exception of 1614, had previously always been returned.[6]

In 1604 Winchester was represented by its recorder, John More, and Alderman Edward Cole. In the Commons 'the burgesses of Winchester' were appointed in the first session of James's first Parliament to consider a bill for the charitable relief of parishes infected with the plague (18 May 1604).[7] In November the city provided the venue for a number of state trials arising out of the Bye and Main Plots. When More welcomed the king to Winchester in 1605, and presented a cup from the corporation, he pointed out the decay of the city and asked for a 'restoration' of its liberties.[8] By 1614 More was chiefly concerned with his London legal practice, which earned him advancement to the coif. Following his resignation it took the corporation another four years to find a recorder who would undertake to reside. Two country gentlemen were elected to the Addled Parliament. Sir William Sandys, though a resident and an alderman, was probably the nominee of his kinsman, Hampshire's lord lieutenant, the 3rd earl of Southampton, while the junior Member, Sir Thomas Bilson, was the bishop's son.

William Savage was appointed recorder in succession to More in 1618, and was returned to the 1621 Parliament, though in second place, with Tichborne as the senior Member. Savage was re-elected in 1624 as junior partner to the 18 year-old Lord Wriothesley, son of the earl of Southampton, who had been appointed Winchester's high steward in 1618.[9] Wriothesley died in November 1624, and in anticipation of a further session Tichborne was chosen to replace him at a by-election in January 1625. However, he had no opportunity to take his seat before the Parliament was automatically dissolved by the king's death.

In 1624 the corporation had instructed Savage to promote an Itchen navigation bill and a bill to confirm the charter.[10] His failure to do either may explain why he did not sit again. At the general election of 1625 Savage was replaced by Sir Thomas Phelips, 1st bt., a distant kinsman to Tichborne, who claimed the second seat. Phelips was also a client of the duke of Buckingham, Southampton's successor as high steward.[11] In 1626 Tichborne sat again and was probably responsible for the choice of Sir Henry Whithed, a conscientious local magistrate, for the second seat. Savage died in 1627 and his successor, Robert Mason, was elected in 1628 though forced to take second place behind Tichborne.

[1] C219/37/213. [2] Hants RO, W/B1/4, f. 39v. [3] VCH Hants, v. 4, 24, 39-40, 42-3. [4] M. Weinbaum, Brit. Bor. Charters, 50. [5] Travels Throughout Stuart Britain: the Adventures of John Taylor, the Water Poet ed. J. Chandler, 127. [6] T. Atkinson, Elizabethan Winchester, pp. 98, 101. [7] CJ, i. 213b. [8] Harl. 852, f. 5. [9] Hants RO, W/B1/4, f. 6v. [10] Ibid. f. 35v. [11] V. Hodges, 'The Electoral Influence of the Aristocracy 1604-41' (Columbia Univ. Ph.D. thesis, 1977), pp. 235-6, 453; Hants RO, W/B1/4, ff. 41v, 51v.

V.C.D.M./R.C.L.S.

YARMOUTH I.O.W

Right of election: in the corporation 1604; in the freemen 1614

Number of voters: 16 in 1625[1]

9 Mar. 1604	THOMAS CHEKE I
	ARTHUR BROMFEILD
?21 Mar. 1614	ARTHUR BROMFEILD
	THOMAS CHEKE II
3 Jan. 1621	ARTHUR BROMFEILD
	THOMAS RISLEY
20 Jan. 1624	THOMAS RISLEY
	WILLIAM BEESTON
25 Apr. 1625	SIR JOHN OGLANDER
	EDWARD CLARKE
22 July 1625	(SIR) JOHN SUCKLING vice
	Clarke, chose to sit for Hythe
23 Jan. 1626	SIR EDWARD CONWAY II
	SIR JOHN OGLANDER
18 Feb. 1628	SIR EDWARD DENNYS
	SIR JOHN OGLANDER
	Sir Fulke Greville
	Edward Reade

Yarmouth, a fortified town and harbour near the western end of the Isle of Wight, was granted a seigneurial charter about the middle of the thirteenth century, vesting town government in the mayor. Newport and Yarmouth each sent one Member to the Model Parliament of 1295, but their representation thereafter lapsed until 1584, when both towns were fully enfranchised at the instance of the captain of the Isle, Sir George Carey†.[2] He nominated both Members at Yarmouth in subsequent Elizabethan elections. In June 1603 rumours of an impending election prompted Carey, now Lord Hunsdon, to write to Yarmouth corporation asking it to send him both indentures, as it had previously done, so that he could insert the names of his unidentified candidates.[3] The request proved premature, and Hunsdon died before the Parliament was actually summoned. His replacement as captain, the 3rd earl of Southampton, nominated his servant, and later steward, Arthur Bromfeild, who was returned in 1604 together with a local gentleman, Thomas Cheke I of Mottistone, some four miles away.[4]

Cheke may have helped the town procure a charter of incorporation five years later, which reinforced his interest by appointing him steward.[5] The charter vested town government in a self-recruiting corporation consisting of a mayor and 11 aldermen, and opened the franchise to all freemen. Its cost of £86 17s.2d. had still not been fully defrayed 17 years later, and in 1611 the corporation was licensed to collect money to rebuild the church.[6] It was perhaps to augment their funds that two years later the corporation began the practice of conferring the freedom, and with it the franchise, on members of the Isle's gentry.[7]

Bromfeild was re-elected, probably at the borough assembly of 21 Mar. 1614, with Cheke's son as his junior colleague. The latter acted as returning officer at the next election in 1621, when Bromfeild was returned with Thomas Risley, another servant of the earl of Southampton. To pay his debts Cheke sold Mottistone in 1623 to the penurious Sir Robert Dillington, 1st bt.†, who does not seem to have had any parliamentary ambitions in this period.[8] At the 1624 election it was left to Southampton to allocate both seats, to Risley and William Beeston, his son's tutor. Both Members took out their freedom on this occasion.[9] The admission of the borough's MPs as freemen in accordance with electoral requirements was only haphazardly enforced during this period; there is no evidence that Bromfeild ever received the freedom, despite serving in three Parliaments, and it was conferred belatedly in the case of Thomas Cheke II, shortly after his return

from Westminster, and also Risley, whose admission had been overlooked when he was elected in 1621.

After Southampton's death his successor as captain, the unpopular Lord Conway (Sir Edward Conway I*) found it harder to exert his influence over the borough as a stranger whose duties as secretary of state precluded him from visiting the Isle for several years. He entrusted the administration of his electoral patronage to the senior deputy lieutenant, Sir John Oglander, who had himself returned in 1625 to the first Caroline Parliament. For his colleague, the borough was 'content' to elect the duke of Buckingham's servant Edward Clarke, who subsequently chose to sit for Hythe.[10] Clarke was replaced by (Sir) John Suckling, the comptroller of the Household. In 1626 Conway nominated his eldest son, also Sir Edward.[11] No details of the election survive, but Conway's name on the indenture appears to have been inserted over an erasure, and he was not made a freeman.[12] Oglander took the second seat.

According to Oglander he and his fellow deputy Sir Edward Dennys earned much ill-will by collecting the Forced Loan, but their tireless efforts to free the Isle from billeting restored their popularity.[13] On 1 Feb. 1628 Conway, now a viscount, informed Yarmouth corporation that he had nominated two candidates for the forthcoming Parliament, whose names they would receive from his deputies, undertaking 'that they are well affected to the good of your town, will study and endeavour to advance it all in their power, and will give you a good account of anything you shall commit to them'.[14] To the deputy lieutenants he wrote that his son would stand for Newport, and for Yarmouth nominated two kinsmen, Sir Fulke Greville, who had replaced Dennys as captain of Cowes Castle, and Edward Reade, who had taken out his freedom as billeting officer for the Isle. However, Oglander replied warning that 'after the delivery of your letter to Yarmouth ... the mayor told me that for my part I had not deserved so ill in my service for them as to be put out', and, following some deliberation, the townsmen 'were resolved to choose some of their own country', as a protest against both the Loan and billeting.[15] Only 11 electors had the courage to vote, but the return stated that Dennys and Oglander had been chosen 'freely and indifferently' as required by the writ of summons, which was quoted in full.[16] Conway subsequently assured Oglander that had he known he wished to stand he would have supported him.[17] Dennys appears to have regarded himself as serving for the Isle as a whole when raising the subject of billeting in the Commons.

[1] Add. 5669, f. 67v. [2] R. Warner, *Hist. I.o.W.* 129; *VCH Hants,* v. 286-90. [3] I.o.W. RO, YAR 8 (Hunsdon to Yarmouth council, June 1603). [4] *Royalist's Notebk.* ed. F. Bamford, 139-40. [5] C66/1814. [6] Add. 46501, f. 208. [7] Add. 5669, ff. 25v, 26v, 68, 73. [8] *Oglander Mems.* ed. W.H. Long, 79. [9] Add. 5669, ff. 60v. [10] R. Lockyer, *Buckingham,* 164. [11] *CSP Dom. Addenda,* 1625-49, p. 97. [12] C219/40/234. [13] L. Boynton, 'Billeting in the I.o. W.', *EHR,* lxxiv. 24, 30; *Royalist's Notebk.* 12-13. [14] *Procs. 1628,* vi. 157. [15] Ibid. 172-3. [16] Add. 5669, f. 75. [17] I.o.W. RO, OG/BB/155.

V.C.D.M./R.C.L.S.

HEREFORDSHIRE

Number of voters: unknown

3 Mar. 1604	SIR JAMES SCUDAMORE
	SIR HERBERT CROFT
c. Mar. 1614	SIR JAMES SCUDAMORE
	SIR HERBERT CROFT
18 Dec. 1620	SIR JOHN SCUDAMORE, bt.
	FITZWILLIAM CONINGSBY
7 Feb. 1624	SIR JOHN SCUDAMORE, bt.
	SIR ROBERT HARLEY
30 Apr. 1625	JOHN RUDHALE
	GILES BRIDGES
4 Feb. 1626	SIR ROBERT HARLEY
	(SIR) WALTER PYE I
c. Feb. 1628	(SIR) WALTER PYE I
	(SIR) GILES BRIDGES, (bt.)

Situated on the Welsh border, Herefordshire was described in the early seventeenth century as 'most healthful and temperate, and ... fertile for corn and cattle'. Indeed, so far as wheat, wool and water were concerned 'it yieldeth to no shire in England', and was consequently 'passing well furnished with all things necessary for man's life'.[1] However, in 1636 the sheriff complained that 'for so small a circuit of ground as this shire contains, there are not in the kingdom a greater number of poor people'. This was, perhaps, an exaggeration, as the writer was trying to explain his difficulties in collecting Ship Money, but Herefordshire certainly contained significant pockets of poverty, particularly along the Welsh border. In 1621 the county's subsidy commissioners declared that the magistrates there were 'often men of mean estate, taken for want of others', while in 1610 the south-west of the county was described as 'the plentifullest place of poor in the kingdom'.[2] Several of the county's great estates, notably the Scudamore property at Holme Lacy,

specialized in horse-breeding, and Sir John Scudamore* virtually founded the Herefordshire cider industry by developing the redstreak apple.[3]

There was widespread interest in land improvement among the Herefordshire gentry, and one squire, Rowland Vaughan, publicized his innovations in the use of water-meadows in a tract published in 1610. On 6 Feb. 1606 a bill was introduced in the Commons 'for the better maintenance of husbandry and tillage' in Herefordshire. This measure concerned half-a-dozen manors in the lower valley of the Lugg, where improvement was hindered by the intermingling of tillage with pasture and meadow. The bill, which was intended to permit freeholders to enclose up to one-third of their property, received its second reading on 17 Feb. but further debate was deferred and it was not finally committed until 20 March. Thereafter no further proceedings are recorded before the session was prorogued. In the 1606-7 session the bill was reintroduced with an amended title, and was committed on 4 Mar. 1607. Although the Herefordshire Member Sir Herbert Croft was named first, the committee was chaired by Anthony Pembrugge*, who sat for Hereford and reported the bill on 27 March. It subsequently passed both Houses and received the Royal Assent.[4]

Although Herefordshire's economy was predominantly agricultural, there was some industrial development during this period. By 1603 iron and glass production was sufficiently well developed in the county for there to be complaints that demand for fuel for those industries was denuding the area around Hereford of timber. Fuel shortages may explain why in 1628 the knights and burgesses for Herefordshire were added to the committee to consider the bill for the preservation of timber.[5] On 30 Apr. 1621 the glaziers of Herefordshire complained to the committee for grievances about the impact of the glassmaking patent on their trade, and seven days later Sir Edward Coke cited the Herefordshire industry as evidence that, contrary to the claims of the patentees, the use of coal in making glass was of long standing in England.[6] Industrial development also contributed to the construction of weirs on the River Wye, which many complained interfered with navigation and the salmon fisheries.[7] In the autumn of 1621 the Herefordshire Member Fitzwilliam Coningsby was involved in moves to raise the issue of the weirs in Parliament.[8] This ultimately proved fruitless, but a bill was introduced to remove their weirs in 1624. Herefordshire's magistrates, among them Coningsby, who no longer held a parliamentary seat, wrote to the county Members on 7 Apr. stating that they had been 'entreated' by the grand jury of the county 'to recommend unto you their grievance in point of weirs, and to join with them in request to you for your care and endeavour for the redress thereof in a parliamentary way'.[9] The bill committee was chaired by Sir Robert Harley who guided it through the Commons, but the session was prorogued before it could be sent to the Lords.[10]

Possibly because of its poverty south-west Herefordshire seems to have been relatively neglected by the Church of England, and was the centre of popular recusancy, strongest in the valley of the Monnow, which formed both the county and episcopal boundary. An attempt to arrest those responsible for the illegal burial of an excommunicated recusant in Allensmore churchyard with full Catholic ceremonies caused the 'Whitsun riot' of 1605, encouraged, according to the local bishop, by 'a lewd conceit that the king favours their course'. In the aftermath of the riot the bench was purged of justices considered sympathetic to Catholics, and by 16 Oct. the bishop claimed that 'of above 1,000 recusants in this county, the tenth part of them are now scarce left for the Pope, and most part of them women'. In the Addled Parliament, at the committee concerning recusants on 9 May 1614, it was alleged by one anonymous speaker that a messenger had been sent to the recusants of Herefordshire 'to know ... what money they would give for a toleration'. Despite the widespread evidence of recusancy in the county, the puritan Sir Robert Harley was unable to present any recusant officeholders to the Commons in 1624, and there is no evidence of Catholic influence on elections.[11] In north-west Herefordshire the inhabitants seem to have been similarly lacking in Protestant religious instruction until Harley began to promote preaching ministers after acquiring control of his family's ecclesiastical patronage in 1603.[12] However, aside from Harley's influence there is little evidence of puritanism in Herefordshire, and during the 1630s supporters of Laudianism, who included Sir John Scudamore* and Fitzwilliam Coningsby, seem to have been particularly common in the county.

In the early part of this period the major political issue in the county was the campaign against the Council in the Marches. Herefordshire was one of four English shires which, along with Wales, came under the Council's jurisdiction. Although the powers of the Council were sanctioned by statute, the 1543 Act of Union with Wales merely authorized the council to govern the 'dominion and principality of Wales and the marches of the same'. Opponents of the Council claimed that the 'marches' of Wales referred simply

to the Welsh borderlands rather than part of England. More to the point, the Herefordshire gentry resented the interference of a body over which they had little influence in the government of their county.[13]

In 1604 a ruling by King's Bench cast doubt over the legality of the Council's power over the English counties, and the following year a petition was presented to the Privy Council in the name of the four shires by four 'gentlemen protectors', one for each county, to free them from the jurisdiction of the Council in the Marches. Lord Zouche, then president of the Council, and his deputy, (Sir) Richard Lewknor[†], mounted a robust defence, and when Parliament was reconvened in January 1606 the opponents of the Council shifted the forum of their attack to the Commons. Herefordshire's 'gentleman protector' was Sir Herbert Croft, who emerged as the leader of the opposers on the floor of the House. His colleague Sir James Scudamore was active rallying support for the movement in the country. The campaign was supported by all of Herefordshire's major figures except Thomas Harley, even uniting the Coningsbys with the Crofts and the Scudamores.[14]

On 10 Feb. 1606 a bill was introduced to exempt the English shires from the jurisdiction of the Council in the Marches. It was read a second time 11 days later, when 'at first the House cried away with it'. Croft, however, defended the bill in a lengthy speech, and was seconded by the Hereford Member John Hoskins. The bill was subsequently passed by the Commons but ran into trouble in the Lords. Consequently, on 13 May Croft brought in another bill. Two days later, however, he moved that this new measure should sleep, having received assurances from James I 'that reformation shall be had in that behalf'. A new set of instructions was subsequently drafted for the Council which greatly reduced its powers, causing Lord Zouche to resign in protest.[15]

However the Council recovered most of its former powers after Parliament was prorogued in 1607, re-igniting the opposition to its jurisdiction. Although removed from the Herefordshire bench for opposing the Union, Croft attended the Michaelmas quarter sessions in 1607, at which he urged the assembled justices to resist the Council. In January 1608 Sir James Scudamore organized a letter of support for Croft's campaign signed by 27 prominent Herefordshire figures, among them the local bishop and at least 21 other magistrates. Lord Eure, the new president of the Council, complained that among the Herefordshire deputy lieutenants only Thomas Harley, the father of Sir Robert, was prepared to pay him the courtesy of a visit.[16]

When Parliament met again in 1610 Croft renewed his attack on the Council in the Marches and succeeded in getting its abolition included in the Great Contract.[17] At the Michaelmas sessions of the peace in 1610 the grand jury of Herefordshire petitioned the local magistrates to recommend the cause to the county Members. However, Eure subsequently claimed that it had been packed with relations and clients of the Scudamore, Croft and Coningsby families. In response the justices wrote a letter supporting the cause, which was presented by Sir James Scudamore to the Commons on 21 Nov. 1610.[18] Five days previously Croft took the opportunity of a meeting between the king and 30 of the most prominent Members of the Commons to press his case. When James made a last-ditch attempt to induce the Commons to vote him money he offered to allow appeals from the Council to be heard in the Westminster courts. However this concession was not put into effect after the Parliament was dissolved. By the time Parliament was summoned again, in 1614, Croft and his allies had decided to switch their tactics. Instead of bringing their case before the Commons they again lobbied the king's favourite, the earl of Somerset, but this approach proved equally unsuccessful.[19] The issue was not raised again until 1628, when a bill was introduced in the Commons on 17 May. It received a second reading two days later, when it was supported by Sir Robert Harley and committed, but it failed to progress any further.[20]

There are signs of resistance to non-parliamentary finance in Herefordshire. A request from the Privy Council for financial assistance to liberate the Palatinate was met with 'a dead silence' at a meeting of 'the country' at Hereford in May 1622. This was reported to the Privy Council by the justices, including Harley, Coningsby and John Rudhale, who were castigated for neglecting to set an example by contributing themselves.[21] Another meeting of the justices was held on 11 June, when some of those present, including Giles Bridges and James Tomkins* agreed to contribute. By the middle of the following month the magistrates had succeeded in collecting £584 15s. 11d., which in the circumstances they considered 'a great sum for so small a county'. However, they refused to return the names of those who had failed to contribute as they were unwilling 'to brand any with the disloyal mark of obstinacy or disaffection'.[22]

There was a similar reluctance to levy the Privy Seal loan demanded by Charles I in 1625. Although Sir John Scudamore* was instructed on 14 Oct. by the president of the Council in the Marches, the earl of Northampton, to certify those able to lend, John Rudhale wrote to Scudamore on 24 Nov. stating that 'in the business of the privy seals we have done nothing, but left every man to make his own excuse'. On 17 Dec. 1625 and 7 Jan. 1626 Northampton complained to Scudamore and Herefordshire's other deputy lieutenants that he had still not received a certificate. In response, on 10 Jan., presumably at the same meeting which saw Harley and Pye nominated for the 1626 Parliament, the deputy lieutenants and magistrates, including Scudamore, Harley, Fitzwilliam Coningsby, James Tomkins, Francis Smalman I* and John Hoskins, wrote to Northampton arguing that as the king's instructions to Northampton for implementing the loan had referred only to Wales, they were under no obligation to supply a certificate. Eventually, however, about £400 was collected in the county.[23]

The response of Herefordshire to the Forced Loan of 1626-7 was also disappointing, although there is little sign of outright resistance. Of the 25 commissioners summoned by Northampton to the initial meeting on 13 Feb. 1627 to execute the Loan only nine attended. However, just one commissioner – John Rudhale – refused to pay the Loan. The active commissioners included Scudamore, Coningsby and Bridges, but neither they nor their colleagues were willing to coerce Loan refusers and consequently receipts were generally lower in Herefordshire than elsewhere. Perhaps as a result of the commissioners' reluctance to execute the Loan vigorously Herefordshire's electoral politics were not disrupted, allowing Bridges to be re-elected in 1628 despite his role as a collector.[24]

Herefordshire had no resident members of the English nobility in this period. The Devereux earls of Essex owned significant estates in the county, enabling the 2nd earl to play a major role in the county's politics in the 1590s, but there is no evidence that this was emulated by the 3rd earl, who was a minor at the time of the 1604 election. It is possible that the rise to prominence of Walter Pye I was partly attributable to his close connection with the 3rd earl of Essex, but his substantial purchases of land in the county probably renders all other explanations redundant. In 1619 James I granted the manor of Leominster, Herefordshire, to the marquess (later duke) of Buckingham, whose influence on the borough of Leominster, where the electoral interest of the manor was presumably greatest, seems to have been limited to the elections of 1621 and 1624. It is therefore unlikely that the property enabled Buckingham to exercise any significant influence on the electoral politics of the county.

Although Sir Robert Harley was a major supporter of Buckingham in the parliaments of 1626 and 1628, as was Scudamore in 1628, both men were from major county families and hardly needed outside influence to secure their election. Pye was also connected to Buckingham through his brother, Sir Robert Pye*, who was one of the duke's servants, but Walter Pye seems to have felt little obligation to serve Buckingham in Parliament and anyway, as has been noted, his rise to prominence is sufficiently explained by other factors.[25]

The Coningsby, Croft and Scudamore families dominated Herefordshire's parliamentary representation for half a century between 1571 and 1621. The Scudamores and the Crofts were generally allied together, presenting a formidable political bloc, but in the 1590s Sir Thomas Coningsby†, with the backing of the 2nd earl of Essex, had been able to secure the first place for himself. Even after Essex's execution in 1601 the combined forces of Herbert Croft and Sir James Scudamore still could not defeat Coningsby. However poor health made Coningsby increasingly reluctant to make the journey to Westminster and it is likely that he refused to stand in 1604, giving Scudamore and Croft a clear run. About 21 freeholders were named on the indenture, including James Tomkins*, but few of the county magnates were present apart from the sheriff, Thomas Harley, the father of Sir Robert.[26]

Sir James Scudamore and Sir Herbert Croft were re-elected in 1614, but by 1620 the former was dead while the latter had fled abroad to escape his creditors. They were replaced by the sons of Sir James Scudamore and Sir Thomas Coningsby, but only after the county's governors had struck an agreement among themselves. In December 1620 Sir Robert Harley wrote to Sir Thomas Coningsby, Sir John Scudamore* and James Tomkins, among others, requesting a meeting before the election 'to deliberate and resolve of the fittest for that service, wherein I desire that neither faction nor affection, but discretion and true understanding, may point us out the men' to be returned.[27] On 7 Dec. a caucus of 19 members of the Herefordshire gentry, of whom at least 12 were magistrates, met at Hereford where they discussed 'what was fit to be done as well for the election of knights to serve at the next approaching Parliament as for future time'. They agreed that 'considering the great inconveniences which have heretofore happened by faction and opposition ... as well to the county in general as to particular great houses', whenever Parliament was summoned they would 'meet ... and advise who are most fit men for that service, ... to be proposed to the freeholders ... to elect if they please

to approve of them and to bend our whole endeavours ... to aid and assist those who by them and us shall be so thought fit'.[28] Those who subscribed to this agreement included Harley, Fitzwilliam Coningsby, Sir John Scudamore†, James Tomkins, Giles Bridges and John Rudhale. However several prominent Herefordshire magistrates did not attend the Hereford meeting, among them Walter Pye I.

The subsequent selection of parliamentary candidates during this period seems to have taken place at the quarter sessions. This meant that, unlike in 1620, only those who were members of the bench were involved. It is possible that this represented a conscious attempt to exclude those gentry who were not magistrates from the process of selection, but it seems more likely that it was never a long-term intention to include them in the first place. In other words, Harley only summoned a more general meeting because the parliamentary writs required the election to be held before the next quarter sessions. Whatever the truth may have been, the fact that an agreement to prevent contests was drawn up in 1620 suggests that the gentry of Herefordshire feared that the crumbling authority of the Croft, Scudamore and Coningsby families would lead to a period of political instability that would be ultimately be reflected in the county's parliamentary elections.

In 1624 the stranglehold of the three families on Herefordshire county representation was finally broken with the election of Sir Robert Harley, who was returned alongside Sir John Scudamore. As the circumstances surrounding this election are undocumented it is impossible to establish whether Fitzwilliam Coningsby chose not to stand again. By contrast, some light on the 1625 election is shed by a letter written by William Scudamore of Ballingham, one of the parties to the 1620 agreement, to his cousin Sir John Scudamore*, then in London. From this letter it is clear that Sir John Scudamore's brother-in-law Giles Bridges had declared his intention to stand. According to William Scudamore this made things complicated for Sir John, as it was thought that he was 'privy and consenting to ... Bridges standing, as a thing done of practice between you two'. This was causing 'envy' in the county, as it looked as though the Scudamore interest was trying to secure both seats. Meanwhile the sheriff, Francis Pember, had declared himself for Sir Robert Harley and John Rudhale. The latter was the brother-in-law of Sir Walter Pye, and William Scudamore had just received news from The Mynde, Pye's home, that Rudhale did indeed intend to stand. William wrote that 'many [are] promised' to

Sir John and Bridges, and despite the 1620 agreement he thought that Scudamore could appeal to the freeholders by canvassing the county, presumably in the hope that if this showed overwhelming support for Scudamore the other candidates would withdraw. But he feared that that unless Sir John had the backing of Pye the support of the freeholders would not be forthcoming, particularly as he had already lost the support of Fitzwilliam Coningsby. Without Pye, Scudamore would have to rely on 'mediation at the sessions' if he wanted a seat. This course of action was also risky and therefore William suggested a third course, which was for Sir John to voluntarily abandon his candidacy and instead use his position as *custos rotulorum* of Herefordshire to mediate between the other candidates at the sessions 'for the quiet of the country and reconcilement of other competitors'. This would 'avoid heart burning, whereof inconvenience will grow amongst your selves and hurt to the country, perhaps for many years, as it hath done in former times'. It is likely that Sir John Scudamore decided to follow the third course. He attended the Easter quarter sessions, and was a party to the subsequent return of Giles Bridges and John Rudhale, along with at least 13 others, including Fitzwilliam Coningsby.[29]

In 1626 the manoeuvrings before the election in Herefordshire are documented in an exchange of letters between Sir Robert Harley and Sir Walter Pye. On 6 Jan. Harley wrote to Pye that 'I would gladly receive your approbation of my desire to stand to be one of the knights of this shire'. Harley stated he was 'encouraged' in his hopes because he had heard from John Rudhale that Pye was also seeking election, and he asked Pye to let him know if this was true at the forthcoming Epiphany quarter sessions 'that I may be ready to return you the like love and courtesy as I entreat from you'. Pye replied from his home at The Mynde three days later, stating that Harley should 'be confident that you shall have all my power to be one of the knights of this Parliament for our county of Hereford, and I believe it will so be without any opposition'. He was more reticent about his own ambitions but said that 'if it please the gentlemen of this county to think me worthy to serve, I will not decline it'. At the meeting on 10 Jan., attended by Harley but not Pye, Sir John Scudamore nominated Pye and Harley as candidates for the county. However when Harley 'asked him in his ear' whether he was proposing Pye for the first place Scudamore 'answered, aye'. Harley then 'spoke to the hearing of the rest that were present that I, being a knight of the Bath, and Sir Walter Pye a knight bachelor, I understood it would point at my dishonour ... to have the second place,

and wished the gentlemen to nominate some other to stand ... unless I might have the first'. According to Harley, Scudamore 'stood awhile upon' this, which, curiously, he thought was 'for some other end' than to secure the first place for Pye. Rudhale acted as intermediary between the candidates, and on 14 Jan. Pye wrote to Harley agreeing to concede the first place, although he continued to argue that it was not Harley's by right.[30]

The dispute may have been part of a longstanding quarrel between Harley and Pye over precedence. When Harley had been restored to the bench in 1622 he had been placed above almost all the other knights in the list of justices. At around the same time, however, Pye, who had previously been placed last, was moved up to a position just above Harley. It would not be surprising if this had rankled Harley ever since.[31] However it seems unlikely that the quarrel over precedence ever threatened to derail the electoral peace of Herefordshire, as neither candidate showed any inclination to challenge the outcome of the selection process at the polls if they did not get their way. On the other hand, Harley's statement that he would withdraw his candidacy if he was not named first may have been made in the belief that that the majority of his fellow justices would back up his claims.

The 1628 election is much less well documented. On 16 Feb. Thomas Pierson, whom Harley had appointed minister of his home parish of Brampton Bryan, Herefordshire, informed his patron that he did not know who would be elected for the county. It is possible that Pierson was simply not up-to-date with the local news. However if the candidates had not been chosen by this date then the quarter sessions were not used to select the nominees, as the Epiphany session had already passed and the next meeting was not due until Easter. Whatever the truth may have been, Harley was already seeking a seat elsewhere by the 16th, suggesting he had no intention of standing in Herefordshire. This allowed Pye to take the first position. It is possible that an unrecorded conclusion to the 1626 dispute had been an agreement that Harley would stand aside in Pye's favour at the next election.[32]

[1] J. Speed, *Theatre of the Empire of Great Britaine* (1612), p. 49; W. Camden, *Britain* (1610) trans. P. Holland, 617. [2] Duncumb, *County of Hereford*, i. 103; R. Mathias, *Whitsun Riot*, 3-5; J. Jackson, 'Some observations upon the Herefs. Environment of the Seventeenth and Eighteenth Cents.', *Trans. Woolhope Field Club*, xxxvi. 35; *CSP Dom.* 1619-23, p. 223; R. Vaughan, *Most Approved and Long Experienced Waterworks* (1610), sig. E2. [3] J. Thirsk, 'Farming Regions of Eng.', *Agrarian Hist. of Eng. and Wales* ed. J. Thirsk, iv. 100-1, 105; Jackson, 29, 38; Vaughan, unpag. [4] *CJ*, i. 264a, 270a, 287b, 343b, 347a, 355a,

1028b; HLRO, O.A. 4 Jas. I, c.11. [5] H.C.B. Mynors, 'Iron Manufacture under Charles I', *Trans. Woolhope Field Club.* xxxiv. 3; Add. 11053, ff. 70v-1; *CD 1628*, iii. 373. [6] Nicholas, *Procs. 1621*, i. 361; *CD 1621*, iii. 195. [7] Vaughan, sigs. G2v-H4. [8] Herefs. RO, W15/2, Henry Vaughan to Fitzwilliam Coningsby, 14 Nov. 1621. [9] Add. 70086/2. [10] *CJ*, i. 711b. [11] Mathias, 2, 5, 6, 22; Vaughan, sigs. F2v, F4; *HMC Hatfield*, xvii. 235, 455-6; *Procs. 1614 (Commons)*, 185; *CJ*, i. 776a. [12] J. Eales, *Puritans and Roundheads*, 53-6; T. Froysell, *Yadidyah or, the Beloved Disciple* (1658), pp. 99-101. [13] R.E. Ham, 'Four Shire Controversy', *WHR*, viii. 382, 388. [14] *HMC Hatfield*, xvii. 552; xiii. 27; Ham, 385-6, 391; *CSP Dom. 1603-10*, p. 400. [15] *CJ*, i. 285b, 272b, 282b, 308b, 309a; *Bowyer Diary*, 49, 164; P. Williams, 'Attack on the Council in the Marches', *Trans. Hon. Soc. Cymmrodorion 1961*, p. 4. [16] Ham, 393-4; SP14/31/161; Cott. Vitellius C.I, f. 206v. [17] *CJ*, i. 393a, 451b; Ham, 396. [18] *CSP Dom. 1603-10*, p. 649; *Parl. Debates, 1610* ed. S.R. Gardiner, 138. [19] Ham, 396-7. [20] *CD 1628*, iii. 446, 464, 473-4. [21] SP14/130/34; *APC, 1621-3*, p. 229. [22] Add. 11051, f. 28; SP14/132/40. [23] Add. 11051, ff. 21, 31; Add. 11053, f. 98; C115/107/8523; *CSP Dom. 1625-6*, p. 223; SP16/18/72I; I. Atherton, *Ambition and Failure in Stuart Eng.* 105-6. [24] Add. 11051, f. 33v; SP16/54/2I; Atherton, 106-7. [25] *CSP Dom. 1619-23*, p. 64. [26] *HP Commons, 1558-1603*, i. 174-5; *HMC Hatfield*, xi. 441; C219/35/1/76. [27] *Letters of Lady Brilliana Harley* ed. T.T. Lewis (Cam. Soc. lviii), pp. xlii-xliv. [28] FSL, V.b.2(21); C66/2234. [29] Hereford City Lib., L.C. 929.2, p. 109 (we are grateful to Dr. Ian Atherton for this ref.); I. Atherton, *John, 1st Visct. Scudamore 1601-71*, p. 52; C219/39/110. [30] *Procs. 1626*, iv. 238-40. [31] C193/13/1, f. 44r-v; C66/2234. [32] Add. 70001, f. 237.

J.P.F.

HEREFORD

Right of election: in the freemen

Number of voters: 38 in 1628[1]

6 Mar. 1604	WALTER HURDMAN, alderman	
	JOHN HOSKINS	
29 Oct. 1605	ANTHONY PEMBRUGGE *vice*	
	Hurdman, deceased	
6 Nov. 1610	JOHN WARDEN *vice*	
	Pembrugge, deceased	
1614	JOHN HOSKINS	
	JOHN WARDEN	
12 Dec. 1620	JAMES RODD	
	RICHARD WEAVER	
20 Jan. 1624	JAMES CLARKE II	
	RICHARD WEAVER	
27 Apr. 1625	SIR JOHN SCUDAMORE, bt.	
	RICHARD WEAVER	
17 Jan. 1626	JAMES CLARKE II	
	RICHARD WEAVER	
26 Feb. 1628	SIR JOHN SCUDAMORE, bt.	
	JOHN HOSKINS	

Described as 'seated among most pleasant meadows and as plentiful corn fields, compassed almost round by rivers',[2] Hereford is situated on the River Wye at the point where it could be forded at two separate places.[3] The population grew from about 4,000 in the 1520s to about 5,000 in 1700, even though Speed's map suggests that by 1610 there had been little suburban development.[4] In the early sixteenth century Hereford was a moderately prosperous country town, but the cloth industry, which specialized in high quality woollens, never recovered from the destruction of the fulling mills in 1527, although the city seems still to have been counted among the 'clothing towns' in the Commons as late as 1607. The later sixteenth century was a period of economic stagnation and in 1603 the corporation complained that 'merchandise and trade is decayed amongst us and the endeavours of the greatest part and chiefest of our city are converted to husbandry, malting and other occupations unfit to sustain the ... credit of so ancient a city'.[5] However Hereford continued to benefit economically from its position as a county town and cathedral city, and acted as a significant social centre, with large numbers of gentlemen attending horse races held at the city in the early years of the seventeenth century.[6]

In 1603 the corporation of Hereford described the city as 'the ancientest and endowed with the greatest privileges of any town in the marches of Wales'.[7] It received its first charter from Henry II, and was regularly represented in Parliament from 1295. It was not incorporated until 1597, although the charter of that year seems largely to have confirmed existing practice. The government of the city was vested in a self-selecting council consisting of six aldermen and 25 common councillors. The council annually elected one of their number as mayor and also elected the high steward. The latter appointed a deputy who was required to be qualified in the law and served in practice as the city's recorder. The aldermen, deputy steward, the present and former mayors constituted the city's bench. A new charter was issued in 1619 but did not change the structure of the government.[8]

Elections were held in the guildhall with the mayor acting as returning officer. The returns were made in the name of the citizens of Hereford and subscribed by between 17 and 38 men.[9] In 1618 the corporation appealed to the lord chancellor, Sir Francis Bacon*, to avoid paying £92 demanded by one of its former Members, John Hoskins, for over 900 days parliamentary service at 2s. a day, but Bacon replied that 'he would give them no help, neither in law nor equity', and later the same year the mayor and common council had to levy a local rate to raise the money. Whether other Members were paid in this period is unknown.[10]

In 1605 the bishop of Hereford informed the 1st earl of Salisbury (Robert Cecil[†]), that the mayor and aldermen had taken 'a special oath not to choose any man but an inhabitant and member of their city', and added that even the 2nd earl of Essex 'in his best fortunes', when he was high steward, could not prevail on them to elect Sir Herbert Croft*. The bishop was probably referring to the city ordinance, said to date from 1518-19 and reaffirmed in 1559, restricting the city's representation to members of the council and threatening any citizen who voted for any other candidate with disenfranchisement. The lack of a complete list of councillors for this period makes it impossible to tell whether this ordinance was rigorously executed, but all the Members chosen were closely connected with the city government, and certainly belonged to the council at some stage in their lives.[11] The Members elected in this period consisted of three barristers (Hoskins, Pembrugge and Clarke), three mercers (Hurdman, Weaver and Rodd), a brewer (Warden) and a Herefordshire baronet (Scudamore). The prominence of lawyers and mercers reflects the importance of administration and retailing in the city's government.

After the execution of the 2nd earl of Essex in 1601, Sir John Scudamore[†], who lived five miles away at Holme Lacey, was nominated to succeed Essex as high steward. However, William Herbert, 3rd earl of Pembroke, was also put forward. Pembroke had inherited a following in the county from his father, who had been president of the Council in the Marches, but it seems likely that he was nominated because he was a prestigious but conveniently distant figure who would not threaten the independence of the corporation. Scudamore proved victorious but the libel dispersed in the city in 1608, a copy of which was affixed to the door of one of Pembroke's leading supporters, Anthony Pembrugge, suggests that the contest may have left a legacy of bitterness and political division in the city for several years.[12]

The evidence for the impact of the dispute over the stewardship on the parliamentary elections in Hereford is ambiguous. At first sight the 1604 election was a triumph for the Scudamore faction, as it witnessed the return of Walter Hurdman, who had been one of Scudamore's supporters on the corporation in 1601, and John Hoskins, Scudamore's deputy steward. However, members of the Pembroke faction, including Pembrugge, also signed the return. The first place was awarded to Hurdman, an alderman who had twice previously served as mayor, but in 1605 a fresh election

became necessary as Hurdman died.[13] In August 1605 Salisbury approached the bishop of Hereford seeking the nomination of Hurdman's replacement. The bishop subsequently 'laboured in it with all my might', but had eventually to report that the freemen, who constituted the voters, would not elect an outsider. Indeed, the opposition to outsiders was so strong that he thought it pointless even to approach Sir John Scudamore 'to have used his authority over them'. The bishop's suspicion that not even Scudamore would be able to prevail proved well-founded, for when the by-election was held in October 1605 the former Pembroke supporter Anthony Pembrugge was returned, despite the fact that he had recently been purged from the Herefordshire bench for his wife's recusancy. It seems likely that Pembrugge enjoyed the support of the mayor, James Russell, who was also a former Pembroke supporter. As in 1604, members of the two opposing faction signed the return. After Pembrugge died in 1610, he was replaced by John Warden, a former Scudamore supporter, even though Thomas Crumpe, who had backed Pembroke in 1601, then held the mayoralty.[14]

In 1614 Hoskins was re-elected along with Warden, but on this occasion the former took the first place. In the aftermath of the Parliament Hoskins was imprisoned in the Tower for his 'Sicilian Vespers' speech attacking the king's Scottish courtiers, and was removed by Sir John Scudamore from his position as deputy steward. Hoskins still retained support on the city council, however, and consequently he was elected mayor in 1616. However, the election was rescinded after an angry letter from James I was received, which stated that Hoskins had been elected 'by faction and underhand practices', and James Rodd* was elected instead. As the king's letter survives among the Scudamore papers, it seems likely that it was Sir John Scudamore, as high steward, who effected Hoskins' removal. Not long after Scudamore himself was replaced as high steward by the earl of Pembroke, possibly as an act of revenge committed by Hoskins' supporters.[15]

Pembroke's position as high steward was confirmed in the 1619 charter, which also named Sir John Scudamore and John Hoskins among the common councillors. The new charter was procured by John Clarke, who served as both town clerk and mayor, and his brother the barrister James Clarke. Their father had been one of the foremost supporters of Sir John Scudamore in 1601, but the Clarke brothers themselves were very close to Hoskins. The cost of procuring the charter came to £300, but when the Council considered how to levy the money to reimburse the Clarkes 'much opposition and tumult [was] raised' by

Philip Traherne, a common councillor and client of the Scudamores, who was thereupon disenfranchised. Eventually the Privy Council became involved, which ordered the expenses of obtaining the charter to be audited and instructed that Traherne be restored to office. The mayor and council were further ordered to 'take into their due and equal consideration without favour or partiality all such further controversies and questions as have grown by this occasion, and thereupon give such as end thereunto, ... as shall be just and equal'. Any further complaints were to be referred to the Council in the Marches. However, the dispute rumbled on. As late as 1621 James Clarke complained that he was still owed £200 for renewing the charter, even though the corporation had authorized a rate to pay the charge, and in March 1622 the corporation asked Pembroke to summon the non-payers before him. During the course of this quarrel, John Hoskins was restored to favour.[16] In addition to requesting Pembroke's aid the corporation also procured the earl's support in its conflict with Herefordshire's deputy lieutenants.[17] However Pembroke seems to have had no influence on Hereford's parliamentary elections.

In 1620 James Rodd was elected alongside Richard Weaver, a common councillor and prominent member of the Hereford Mercers' Company. Weaver was subsequently re-elected to every Parliament in the 1620s except that of 1628, when he was ineligible as he was then serving as mayor. In 1624 and 1626 Weaver was returned with James Clarke. Sir John Scudamore died in 1623 but his grandson and namesake inherited his network of clients and friends in the city, and probably his seat on the Council in the Marches. He was consequently able to secure election in 1625, although in 1626 his financial problems forced him to remain in Herefordshire.[18] Warden was an active commissioner for the Forced Loan in 1627 whereas the Clarkes tried to find excuses to avoid payment.[19] The following year Scudamore, who had been an active Forced Loan commissioner in the county, was re-elected with John Hoskins.

In the Jacobean period Hereford's principal parliamentary interest was in legislation to improve the navigability of the River Wye by removing the weirs and other obstructions, which the corporation described in 1624 as 'the great good we can ever expect to happen to this city'.[20] In 1603 the corporation argued that removing the weirs was the key to restoring the local economy, as it would improve the salmon fisheries, enable the goods of the surrounding countryside to be shipped through the city to the west country and Wales and remedy the local fuel shortage caused by the growth of iron smelting and glassworks in the county.[21] Although the corporation had support among the county's gentry, many landowners had economic interests in the weirs, including the Scudamores. Rowland Vaughan, a Herefordshire justice of the peace and opponent of the weirs, wrote in 1610 that Sir John Scudamore[†] 'hath ever said, if there were any hope that the over-throw of the weirs would make the river [Wye] navigable, portable or salmonable, he would pull down his first, to give an instance to others', but others, including the bishop of Hereford and Edward, 4th earl of Worcester, a prominent privy councillor who had a grant of weirs belonging to the Crown, were less sympathetic. In July 1603 the corporation procured a commission of sewers for the Wye, but its work was hampered by internal divisions and legal challenges. It was subsequently reported that the supporters of the weirs had appealed to lord chancellor Ellesmere (Thomas Egerton[†]), arguing that the weirs were necessary to power the watermills on the Wye, which ground the county's corn. In September 1603 Ellesmere wrote to Sir John Scudamore's son Sir James* and other members of the commission stating that he and Worcester had received complaints 'of very partial dealing, and indirect courses used by you towards some particular persons, in the execution of a commission of sewers', including a petition from the bishop and a certificate signed by the sheriff and other members of the country gentry. Faced with this opposition the work of the commission seems to have been stymied.[22]

In April 1604 a bill was introduced into the Commons 'for the abating, and to restrain, the new erection of all weirs, ... and other obstructions in great and navigable rivers'. It was supported by Hoskins at second reading on 23 June but was opposed by Robert Johnson on behalf of his patron, the earl of Worcester. The bill was committed but did not emerge again before the session was prorogued on 7 July.[23] In 1606 the bill was reintroduced, when it passed all its stages in the Commons, although at the report stage on 13 Mar. Johnson brought in a proviso, which was opposed by Hoskins.[24] However in the Lords the bill failed to emerge from committee, whose members included the earl of Worcester and the bishop of Hereford.[25]

Hoskins was a prominent supporter of a bill introduced by Sir Herbert Croft* on 6 Feb. 1606, which sought to remove the jurisdiction of the Council in the Marches over Herefordshire, Shropshire, Worcestershire and Gloucestershire. However (Sir) Richard Lewknor[†], a member of the Council, procured a certificate signed by the mayor of Hereford, James Russell, and several of the city's aldermen opposing the bill, which Hoskins was forced to acknowledge bore the mayoral seal at the third reading on 10 March. In the same debate Pembrugge attacked a similar certificate from the Ludlow corporation, suggesting that he too was an opponent of the Council, although he had only recently been returned by Russell.[26]

The shortage of fuel in Herefordshire, of which the corporation had complained in 1603, may explain why the city's burgesses were appointed to the committee for the bill 'touching assize of fuel' on 8 Apr. 1606.[27] In 1607 a proviso was added to the bill for the true making of cloth during the committee stage to enable the freemen of Hereford, Leominster, Bewdley and Coventry to enter the cloth trade without first serving an apprenticeship. The amended bill was approved when it was reported on 31 Mar. and was ordered to be engrossed, but the proviso was challenged at the bill's third reading on 11 May. Pembrugge and Hoskins argued in favour of the proviso and were supported by the county Member Sir Herbert Croft, but were unable to prevent the bill's recommitment. The following day Hoskins reported that the committee had disliked the proviso, whereupon the House ordered the proviso to be scraped out.[28]

On 6 June 1610 Hoskins introduced another bill against weirs, but it failed to proceed even to a first reading.[29] A bill against weirs was laid before the Addled Parliament on 17 May 1614, but neither of the Hereford Members were recorded as contributing to the second reading debate four days later, although both were appointed to the committee. No subsequent proceedings are recorded.[30] There were no proceedings against weirs in the first sitting of the 1621 Parliament, but in July of that year a new commission of the sewers was issued for the River Wye. Once again the proceedings of the commission rapidly became bogged down in controversy. On 10 Aug., at the request of the earl of Worcester, lord keeper Williams instructed the commissioners not to take action against the weirs granted by the Crown to Worcester before he had given a hearing to the earl's representatives. Moreover, the Duchy of Lancaster Court overturned an order of the commission to pull down a weir leased from the duchy. Faced with these obstructions the corporation and its supporters among the Herefordshire gentry seem to have decided to raise the issue in Parliament during the second sitting. On 14 Nov. it was reported that Richard Weaver* was 'retained to follow and solicit the cause' and attempts were being made to recruit the support of Sir Edward Sackville*. However there is no evidence that that matter was brought before the Commons before the dissolution. In 1622 Hereford's corporation complained

to the king that it had waited a year for the hearing of the earl of Worcester's cause, which had not yet occurred as Worcester's solicitor had refused to fix a day. It also offered to compensate the Crown for any loss of rent if the weirs were pulled down. James I's response to the petition is unknown, but the issue of the weirs was still outstanding when the 1624 Parliament met.[31]

On 25 Mar. 1624 a bill was introduced specifically to remove the weirs on the Wye, despite the fact that the bill for the preservation of salmon, which had been introduced ten days earlier, also included provisions to enable magistrates to order the destruction of weirs.[32] On 3 Apr. the bill concerning the weirs on the Wye received its second reading and was committed. Sir Robert Harley*, one of the county Members, was specifically named to the committee and the Members for Herefordshire were appointed en bloc.[33] Two days latter the corporation wrote identical letters to the county Members, stating that it had been 'given to understand by our citizens how freely it pleaseth you to afford your assistance in Parliament to the forwarding of the cause there for prostrating of the weirs'. After emphasizing the importance of the bill to the welfare of the city, the corporation requested that the county Members 'will continue your love towards us in that behalf'.[34] A two-page tract which was probably produced in response to the bill argued that it was not practicable to make the Wye navigable and that the Welsh counties upriver of Herefordshire had 'no commodities of any reckoning to be brought'. It also opposed the corporation's assertion that removing the weirs would improve the city's fuel supplies.[35] On 15 May Harley reported the bill with amendments and a proviso, but the House remained dissatisfied and the measure was recommitted after a division. He reported it again 11 days later, when it was ordered to be engrossed, but the measure was lost when the House was prorogued on the 29 May.[36] After the failure of the 1624 bill to reach the statute books, Hereford corporation made no recorded attempts to raise the issue in Parliament during this period. In 1626 a further bill for the preservation of salmon, which was also intended to improve river navigation, included provisions against weirs, but there is no evidence that it was supported by the Hereford corporation or the city's Members.[37]

[1] Herefs. RO, Hereford city misc. pprs. 4, f. 56. [2] W. Camden, *Britain* (1610) trans. P. Holland, 618. [3] M.D. Lobel, 'Hereford', in *Historic Towns*, ed. M.D. Lobel, 1. [4] A. Dyer, *Decline and Growth in English Towns*, 73; P. Corfield, 'Urban development in England and Wales', *Trade, Government and Economy in Pre-Industrial Eng.* ed. D.C. Coleman and A.H. John, p. 224; Lobel, 9. [5] Lobel, 9; E. Kerridge, *Textile Manufactures in Early Modern England*, 21; G.D. Ramsay, *English Woollen Industry*, p. 29; *CJ*, i. 372a; Add. 11053,

ff. 70v-1. [6] *Old Meg of Hereford-shire* (1609), sigs. A4-B [7] Add. 11053, ff. 70v-1. [8] I.M. Slocombe, 'Government of Hereford in the Sixteenth Cent.', *Trans. Woolhope Field Club*, xl. 367; C66/1466, mm. 7-16; Duncumb, *Co. of Hereford*, i. 355-9. [9] C219/35/1/80; Herefs. RO, Hereford city misc. pprs. 4, f. 56. [10] L.B. Osborn, *Life, Letters and Writings of John Hoskyns*, 82-3; R. Johnson, *Ancient Customs of Hereford*, 181. [11] *HMC Hatfield*, xvii. 360; *HP Commons 1558-1601*, i. 175. [12] W.J. Tighe, 'Country into Court, Court into Country: John Scudamore of Holme Lacy (c.1542-1623) and his circles', *Tudor Political Culture* ed. D. Hoak, 167, 171-3; Add. 11053, f. 67; R. Vaughan, *Most Approved, and Long Experienced Waterworkes*, (1610) sig. D4v; *HMC 13th Rep. IV*, 339. [13] C219/35/1/77; Add. 11042, f. 10. [14] *HMC Hatfield*, xvii. 360; C219/35/1/75; Add. 11042, f. 10. [15] Add. 11053, f. 77; Johnson, 229. [16] Duncumb, 356-7; *APC*, 1619-21, pp. 45, 50, 75; I. Atherton, *Ambition and Failure in Stuart Eng.* 96; *CSP Dom.* 1619-23, pp. 206, 357, 398, 401; SP14/130/116. [17] Add. 11053, f. 91. [18] Atherton, 152. [19] SP16/78/46.I. [20] C115/101/7636. [21] Add. 11053, ff. 70v-1. [22] Ibid. ff. 72, 80r-v; Vaughan, sigs. G3-H3; *River Wye (in True Examination) Very Difficult and Chargeable to be Reduced Portable Beneath Hereford* ([1624]). [23] *CD 1604-7*, p. 73; *CJ*, i. 997a. [24] Ibid. 262a, 265a, 284a, 288a, 290a. [25] *LJ*, ii. 410. [26] *Bowyer Diary*, 49; *CJ*, i. 264a, 281b; *HMC Hatfield*, xviii. 27. [27] *CJ*, i. 295b. [28] Ibid. 357b, 372a, 372b, 373a, 1043a; *Bowyer Diary*, 291-2. [29] *CJ*, i. 435b. [30] *Procs. 1614 (Commons)*, 266, 309. [31] C181/3, f. 33; C115/107/8520; R. Callis, *Reading of Famous and Learned Gentleman* (1647), 209-10; Herefs. RO, W15/2; *HMC 7th Rep.* 682; Add. 11052, f. 80r-v. [32] *CJ*, i. 737a, 749b; 'Pym 1624', f. 41. [33] *CJ*, i. 753a. [34] Add. 70086/5/4; C115/101/7636. [35] *River Wye (in True Examination) Very Difficult and Chargeable to be Reduced Portable Beneath Hereford* ([1624]). [36] *CJ*, i. 704a, 789b, 795b. [37] *Procs. 1626*, iii. 135, 139.

J.P.F./B.C.

LEOMINSTER

Right of election: in the freemen

Number of voters: 12 in 1604; 15 in 1624.[1]

6 Mar. 1604	THOMAS CONINGSBY
	JOHN POWLE
c. Mar. 1614	SIR HUMPHREY BASKERVILLE
	THOMAS CONINGSBY
c. Dec. 1620	FRANCIS SMALMAN I
	WILLIAM BEECHER
20 Jan. 1624	(SIR) WILLIAM BEECHER
	JAMES TOMKINS
25 Apr. 1625[2]	JAMES TOMKINS
	EDWARD LITTLETON II
17 Jan. 1626	JAMES TOMKINS
	EDWARD LITTLETON II
26 Feb. 1628	JAMES TOMKINS
	EDWARD LITTLETON II
aft. 27 Mar. 1628[3]	SIR THOMAS LITTLETON, bt. *vice* Edward Littleton II, chose to sit for Caernarvon Boroughs

Leominster was the market centre for a farming area famed for the quality of its wool, considered the best in the country, which was used to make high quality cloth in Worcester, Coventry, Ludlow, Gloucester, Hereford and Leominster itself.[4] Even more important was the town's position at the junction of three rivers, which powered the mills from which the local bakers produced bread of outstanding quality. The charter granted to the borough in 1605 stated that the 'town ... has in a wonderful manner been growing and flourishing, as well in wealth as in population'.[5] By 1631 Leominster had about 1,200 inhabitants.[6]

Leominster had been represented in Parliament since 1295, and was incorporated in 1554. The corporation consisted of 25 capital burgesses who annually elected one of their number bailiff.[7] Elections were held at the 'court house' with the bailiff acting as returning officer. The 1604 return does not specify the qualification to vote, but states that, in addition to the bailiff, 13 named individuals 'and others' had participated in the election. As well as the bailiff at least four of those named were probably capital burgesses, as their names correspond with those of former bailiffs.[8] Subsequent returns make it clear that the franchise lay with the freemen. In 1624 those who voted were the bailiff, 15 named individuals 'and other burgesses'. Of those named, at least six were probably capital burgesses, as men with their names had previously served as bailiffs. A further four were probably also capital burgesses, as they subsequently served as bailiffs.[9] Thereafter, only the bailiff was named in the returns, and elections were described as having been with 'the assent and consent of the rest of the burgesses'.[10]

The manor of Leominister, described as 'spacious and fertile', passed to the Crown on the Dissolution of the Monasteries.[11] On the accession of James I it was appropriated to the queen's jointure.[12] The corporation resisted without difficulty the interest of Sir Herbert Croft*, steward of the Crown manors in Herefordshire, largely with the aid of Sir Thomas Coningsby†, the tenant of the priory and high steward of the borough.[13] In 1604 Coningsby secured the re-election of his 'much beloved cousin' and agent, Thomas Coningsby,[14] and saw no reason to object to the choice of John Powle as junior Member, whose mother referred to Sir Thomas as her 'loving friend'.[15] Sir Thomas' interest at Leominster was strengthened later that year by his appointment as surveyor of the queen's jointure in Herefordshire, much to Croft's chagrin.[16] In 1605 the borough obtained a new charter at a cost of £80, most of which was disbursed by Thomas Coningsby, who had a post in the petty bag office and stood high in the favour of lord chancellor Ellesmere. The most significant innovation in the charter was a grant of an annual fair on St. Bartholomew's day, which was intended to improve the marketing and distribution of the wool produced in the area.[17]

Croft was deprived of office in 1612, and, with Powle acting as returning officer, Coningsby was re-elected to Parliament in 1614. This time, however, he took the junior seat, yielding precedence to Sir Thomas Coningsby's son-in-law, Sir Humphrey Baskerville.[18] In 1618, following the death of Thomas Coningsby two years earlier, the corporation resolved that henceforward 'no foreigner shall be admitted or elected to the office of a burgess of the Parliament by the voices of the capital burgesses, if any of the said capital burgesses will at any time take on them the said office'.[19] However, this ruling was subsequently disregarded, for after the death of Anne of Denmark the manor was transferred to the earl of Buckingham, who used his influence to bring in his client the rising official William Beecher at the next election.[20] As Baskerville was now incapacitated by debt, Beecher's colleague Francis Smalman I, another outsider, was granted the senior seat, probably with the support of Sir Thomas Coningsby, who had expressed confidence in Smalman's 'integrity and endeavour'.[21] Beecher was re-elected in 1624, accompanied by James Tomkins, probably a kinsman of the influential vicar of Leominster.[22] In 1625 Buckingham, as lord warden of the Cinque Ports, transferred Beecher to Dover, in Kent. Tomkins, however, was re-elected and moved up to the senior seat. His new partner was Edward Littleton II, who may have owed his election to Sir Thomas Coningsby's son Fitzwilliam*, who succeeded his father as steward of the borough, probably after Sir Thomas' death in May 1625.[23] Littleton was employed by Fitzwilliam's friend Sir Thomas Littleton, bt.* as steward of his estate and his first wife had been Sir Thomas' sister.[24] At the 1625 election John Powle again served as returning officer.[25]

Littleton and Tomkins were re-elected in 1626 and 1628; but in the latter Parliament Littleton opted to sit for Caernarvon Boroughs. The return for the resulting election has not survived, but his replacement was Sir Thomas Littleton, for in the Crown Office list Edward Littleton's first name was changed to 'Thomas', and 'Sir Thomas Littleton' was mentioned in the *Journal* on 7 May. A contemporary list of members of the Parliament, compiled and published towards the end of the session, confirms that Sir Thomas Littleton was Edward's replacement.[26] Sir Thomas had previously sat for Worcestershire, but in 1628 he was

replaced there by his cousin Sir Thomas Bromley. Edward Littleton therefore presumably agreed to make way for his employer. Sir Thomas Littleton may have had the support of Buckingham as well as Fitzwilliam Coningsby, as he was on close terms with Buckingham's widow in the 1630s.[27]

[1] C219/35/1/78; 219/38/91. [2] C219/29/100. [3] *CD 1628*, ii. 144. [4] M. Drayton, *Poly-Olbion* (1612), p. 105; E. Kerridge, *Textile Manufactures in Early Modern Eng.* 20-1; P.J. Bowden, *Wool Trade in Tudor and Stuart Eng.* 29. [5] G.F. Townsend, *Town and Bor. of Leominster*, 85. [6] P. Clark and J. Hosking, *Population Estimates of English Small Towns* (Cent. for Urban Hist. Working Pprs. v), 68. [7] Townsend, 105, 283-4, 288. [8] C219/35/1/78; Townsend, 293-4. [9] C219/38/91; Townsend, 294. [10] C219/39/100; 219/40/195. [11] *Sidney Letters* ed. A. Collins, ii. 306. [12] Add. 6693, f. 74. [13] *CSP Dom.* 1603-10, p. 402; *Sidney Letters*, ii. 306, 311-12, 318; *HMC Hatfield*, xi. 114. [14] Add. 70001, unfol. (Sir Thomas Coningsby to Sir Robert Harley, Dec. [1604]). [15] PROB 11/126, f. 52v. [16] *Sidney Letters*, ii. 306. [17] Herefs. RO, Leominster bailiffs accts. 1604-5; Townsend, 288. [18] *Sidney Letters*, ii. 306. [19] Townsend, 98. [20] *CSP Dom.* 1619-23, p. 64. [21] PROB 11/148, f. 292r-v. [22] Townsend, 259. [23] Ibid. 291. [24] *HMC 7th Rep.* 682; J.M.J. Tonks, 'The Lyttletons of Frankley and their estates 1530-1640' (Oxford Univ. B.Litt. thesis, 1978), p. 148. [25] C219/29/100. [26] C193/32/17, f. 5; *CD 1628*, iii. 301 n. 10; *Most Exact Catalogue of Lords Spirituall and Temporall* (1628), sig. Bv. [27] Soc. Antiq. ms 140, f. 27.

J.P.F.

WEOBLEY

Right of election: in the inhabitant householders

Number of voters: c.30 in 1628

13 May 1628	WILLIAM WALTER
	WILLIAM TOMKINS

Originally the administrative centre for the Lacy Marcher lordship, Weobley declined as Ludlow rose. Nevertheless, the borough sent Members to the Model Parliament, and continued to do so until 1306, when Bromyard, Ledbury, and Ross-on-Wye were also represented, but thereafter only Hereford and Leominster regularly returned. In 1628 Weobley formed part of the estates of the 3rd earl of Essex; but it was dominated by a local gentleman, James Tomkins* of Garnstone, who secured the borough's re-enfranchisement in alliance with Edward Littleton II*, his partner at Leominster in the Parliaments of 1625 and 1626.[1]

Littleton's researches into the legal precedents failed to uncover any returns for most of the thirteenth century, enabling him to claim that during this period Weobley and Milborne Port had 'as much proof for their sending as any borough here has'. He was doubtless the 'worthy Member of this House', who declared their status proved by the existence of suburbs and ancient burgages, and by the liability to pay tenths rather than fifteenths in parliamentary grants of taxes. With William Hakewill in the chair of the committee for privileges these arguments received a favourable hearing, and on 1 May 1628 the House endorsed his report and ordered writs to be issued.[2]

No franchise had been specified, but it was intended, on the precedent of Pontefract, Yorkshire, that it should be exercised by the inhabitant householders. The election at Weobley, 12 days later, was supervised by the sheriff of the county. No contest is likely; Tomkins's son William and Littleton's first cousin, William Walter, were returned by about 30 named 'burgesses'.

---

[1] *Trans. Woolhope Field Club*, xxxix. 105-8; C.J. Robinson, *Castles of Herefs.* 130. [2] *CD 1628*, iii. 154, 185; *Procs. 1628*, vi. 107-9.

J.P.F./S.H.

HERTFORDSHIRE

Number of voters: c.900 in 1640[1]

1 Mar. 1604	SIR HENRY CAREY I
	SIR ROWLAND LYTTON
c.Mar. 1614	(SIR) HENRY CAREY
	SIR RALPH CONINGSBY
14 Dec. 1620	SIR HENRY CAREY I, (VISCT. Falkland [I])
	SIR CHARLES MORRISON, bt.
5 Feb. 1624	SIR CHARLES MORRISON, bt.
	WILLIAM LYTTON
28 Apr. 1625	SIR JOHN BOTELER, bt.
	JOHN BOTELER
2 Feb. 1626	(SIR) JOHN BOTELER
	SIR THOMAS DACRES
c.Mar. 1628	(SIR) WILLIAM LYTTON
	SIR THOMAS DACRES

Few counties saw more of royalty than Hertfordshire, especially during the reign of James I. Royston, amid the unenclosed downlands of the north, was James's favourite centre for hunting and hawking, and to it he added Theobalds, by exchange with his chief minister the 1st earl of Salisbury (Robert Cecil[†]) in 1607, thereby acquiring a palace within easier access of Whitehall.[2]

The frequent presence of the Court had a marked effect on local food prices; purveyance was a major grievance, especially the commandeering of malt, post-horses, carts and provender, and it is probably no coincidence that the Commons' most outspoken critic of the practice, John Hare*, was a commuter from Totteridge.[3] Another unpopular consequence of the royal presence was the supersession of local courts by the newly established Court of the Verge under the knight marshal.[4] Constant reminders were issued to the local authorities for repairing the highway to Royston, which was also the principal route by which heavy wagons of Norwich-ware came to London, and the village constables were ordered to ensure that no obstacles were left in the fields after harvest to impede the royal sport.[5] Main routes to Ireland and the North also passed through the county, which was 'blessed with excellent channels of communication to London', though water transport was probably more important to its economy.[6] Barges on the rivers Colne and Lea (improved in Elizabethan times) sent hay and malt to London, returning with loads of manure to improve the fertility of 'our small and barren shire'. In this trade the corporation of London was seen as the principal enemy, with its levies of metage and portage for use of the city wharves.[7] Malt was the staple industry, and the new draperies never took root, apart from a small fustian venture at Hatfield.[8] Although from the outset of the reign it was recognized that Hertfordshire springs must be tapped if London were to secure an adequate supply of water, the county played little part in the New River project, except for the grant of way-leaves.[9]

Patronage in Hertfordshire's county elections was dominated by the Cecil earls of Salisbury.[10] Seats were shared out between the old and well-connected local families, such as the Careys – based at Aldenham, Berkhamsted, Hunsdon, and later Moor Park; the Lyttons of Knebworth; and the wealthy and prolific Botelers. The remaining Members, Sir Ralph Coningsby, Sir Charles Morrison, and Sir Thomas Dacres, all inherited competent estates in the county. Contests were not unknown under Elizabeth, but seem generally to have been avoided during the early Stuart period, and as a result the size of the electorate is unknown.

Although Hertford was the assize town, the sheriff customarily summoned the county court wherever he chose. During the Tudor period parliamentary elections were held usually, but not exclusively, at Hertford, and occasionally at various alternative locations including Waltham Cross.[11] In 1604 Sir Henry Boteler of Woodhall Lodge consulted his own convenience by summoning the electors to Hatfield, at that time still a royal manor; Sir Rowland Lytton and Sir Henry Carey I were returned. Lytton took a prominent role in the Commons' debates about the grievance of purveyance, and shortly after the dissolution of the first Jacobean Parliament, lord treasurer Salisbury, in his capacity as lord lieutenant of Hertfordshire, invited the county to agree on terms of composition. By this time, the adjoining county of Middlesex having already compounded, purveyance cast an even greater burden on Hertfordshire than before. After consulting 'the principal freeholders and yeomen of the county', the justices of the peace replied in April 1611 expressing a 'fearful doubt how they may stand secured', given the 'daily breach of the former compositions made with this county, in that the purveyors and officers do of late usually send warrants to high constables to make such takings without showing forth any commission, contrary to the law'. The delegation that presented this uncompromising document was headed by Sir Ralph Coningsby, the ranger of Enfield Chase, and also included Lytton and Hare.[12] Coningsby's local standing seems to have been enhanced by his stance against purveyance, as he won the second seat at the general election in 1614, while Henry Carey, described in a contemporary list of Members as 'son of Lord Hunsdon', was returned in first place.[13]

On 7 Dec. 1620 Sir Henry Carey I, by that time a privy councillor and courtier who had recently purchased a Scottish peerage, wrote to the 2nd earl of Salisbury (William Cecil*) announcing his intention to stand in the forthcoming election, and begging him to 'afford me your defence and favour for the place, which I am determined to pursue'. He also canvassed his kinsman Lord Hunsdon, and wrote again to Salisbury on 11 Dec. that he had heard 'some alarums ... [that] Sir Richard Lucy†, (Sir) Henry Capell†, or some of the Botelers purposed to stand, though I do not much believe it, and your declaration of affection makes me the more secure'. In a postscript Carey confided that he had joined interests with Sir Charles Morrison, 'and it is both our desires the country should not be troubled without cause'.[14] To achieve this laudable aim the sheriff held the election at St. Albans, a location almost equally convenient for Carey and Morrison, and unsuitable for the other candidates mentioned. Salisbury, perhaps wisely, did not attend in person, though the mayor erected a private enclosure for the gentry, and Carey (now Viscount Falkland, though he chose to conceal the honour from the electorate) was returned, with Morrison in second place.[15] Exception was taken against Carey in the Commons, not, it was emphasized, on personal grounds, but because Members were

wary of setting a precedent that would admit naturalized Scottish lords to sit. The privileges committee, and indeed the whole House, were unable to reach a satisfactory resolution, however, and although Carey never took his seat, no new writ was issued to replace him.[16] Morrison was briefly suspended for quarrelling violently with Clement Coke* on the Parliament stairs; after being readmitted, on 12 May he drew attention to his county's grievances over purveyance.[17]

Morrison was re-elected, again at St. Albans, as the senior Member in 1624. He was joined by Lytton's son William, who had Salisbury's full support, and was knighted later in the year, albeit apparently 'sore against his will'.[18] Morrison continued to attack purveyance in the last Jacobean Parliament, bringing complaints from the constituency against an officer of the green cloth, Sir Simon Harvey.[19] The election in 1625 was held at Baldock, in the north of the county, close to the homes of the candidates Sir John Boteler 1st bt., who was married to the duke of Buckingham's half-sister, and his cousin and namesake, John Boteler, the head of the family. On Salisbury's behalf Christopher Keightley* wrote to Coningsby's son Thomas† that the freeholders of Cashio hundred and St. Albans should be brought 'to Baldock upon Thursday come sennight ... to give their voices there for Sir John Boteler, knight and baronet, and Mr. John Boteler to be knights of the shire for Hertfordshire'.[20] Both men were duly returned. The latter was re-elected the following year, again with Salisbury's support, and received the order of the Bath at the coronation. Salisbury's choice for the second seat was Sir Thomas Dacres.[21] The election was held at Hertford, where there may have been a contest, since the indenture records that Boteler and Dacres were 'freely and indifferently elected by ... the greater part of the freeholders'.[22]

Hertfordshire was the first county to reply to demands for the Forced Loan, the commissioners (including both Botelers) writing to Secretary (Sir) John Coke* on 1 August that the unanimous answer from six Hundreds was that 'they are all most willing to contribute for the defence of the kingdom and for the supply of His Majesty's wants in that behalf by way of subsidy in a parliamentary manner even beyond their abilities'.[23] In the hundreds of Braughing and Hertford, Thomas Fanshawe II* and his fellow commissioners had little better success, where 'only some few yielded to give small sums, nothing answerable to His Majesty's occasions'.[24] Dacres and Sir John Boteler, 1st bt. were sent for by the Privy Council, and warned that they 'must look to have soldiers lodged on them' if the county maintained its long list of defaulters.[25] Resentment of arbitrary government was clearly expressed at the hustings in 1628, which saw the return of both Dacres and Sir William Lytton, who subsequently declared at 'an open assembly of the county', according to one of his tenants, that the Privy Council had no authority to compel parishes to find further funds 'for the binding out of apprentices and providing for the poor'.[26] The location of the 1628 election is unknown, as neither the indenture nor any letters of nomination survive.

[1] L. Stone, 'Electoral Influence of the 2nd earl of Salisbury', *EHR*, lxxi. 387. [2] *VCH Herts*. ii. 346-8, 363-4; *CSP Dom*. 1603-10, p. 452; 1611-18, pp. 109, 488; 1619-23, p. 416; *Illustrations of Brit. Hist.* ed. E. Lodge, iii. 108. [3] SP14/63/1; *Bowyer Diary*, 33. [4] *Procs. 1614 (Commons)*, 284. [5] C193/6/188; *CSP Dom*. 1603-10, pp. 219, 225, 624. [6] *Agrarian Hist. Eng.* ed. J. Thirsk, iv. 50-52. [7] *CJ*, i. 919b, 926b. [8] *VCH Herts*. iv. 242-3; *APC*, 1615-16, p. 464; *CSP Dom*. 1611-18, p. 525; 1619-23, p. 143. [9] *CSP Dom*. 1603-10, p. 93 [10] *CSP Dom*. 1603-10, p. 358; Stone, *EHR*, lxxi. 385-6; Clarendon, *Hist. of the Rebellion* ed. W.D. Macray, ii. 543. [11] C219/18C/50; 219/19/39, 42; 219/20/57; 219/21/74; 219/24/77. [12] SP14/63/1. [13] *Procs. 1614 (Commons)*, 451, 465. [14] *HMC Hatfield*, xxii. 136-7. [15] D. Hirst, *Representative of the People?*, 113. [16] *CJ*, i. 512b-13a. [17] *CD 1621*, iii. 235; *CJ*, i. 616b. [18] *HMC Hatfield*, xxii. 188; *Chamberlain Letters* ed. N.E. McClure, ii. 574-5. [19] *CJ*, i. 685a, 702a. [20] *HMC Hatfield*, xxii. 205. [21] Ibid. 209-10. [22] C219/40/203. [23] SP16/33/8. [24] SP16/36/41. [25] SP16/44/37; *APC*, 1627, pp. 23-24. [26] *APC*, 1630-1, pp. 386, 401-2.

J.P.F./R.C.L.S.

HERTFORD

Right of election: in the freemen

Number of voters: 244 in 1624[1]

	1st seat	2nd seat
17 May 1624 WILLIAM ASHTON I	103	
THOMAS FANSHAWE II	19	101
Richard Willows	58	87
Sir William Harington	42	48
13 May 1625 WILLIAM ASHTON I		
THOMAS FANSHAWE II		
c. Jan. 1626 SIR WILLIAM HARINGTON		
SIR CAPELL BEDDELL, bt.		
10 Mar. 1628 SIR EDWARD HOWARD II		
(SIR) THOMAS FANSHAWE II	101	
Gabriel Barbor	68	
9 May 1628 SIR CHARLES MORRISON, bt. *vice*		
Howard, called to the Upper House		
28 Jan. 1629 JOHN CAREY Visct. Rochford, *vice*		
Morrison, deceased		

Hertford was well established before the Norman Conquest, and returned Members to at least 16 medieval Parliaments. However, the town fell into severe decline as a result of the Black Death, and the franchise was allowed to lapse after 1376. During the early sixteenth century the local economy began to recover, mainly because its markets were increasingly frequented by traders from London buying grain, malt, and other staples.[2] Hertford was first incorporated in 1554, and in 1605, assisted by the borough's high steward, the 1st earl of Salisbury (Robert Cecil[†]), a new charter was granted which established a corporation consisting of a mayor, nine 'chief burgesses', 16 assistants, a steward of the borough court, and a town clerk.[3] A sign of the town's renewed prosperity was the re-endowment and enlargement of Hertford grammar school in 1617.[4] The castle, where the assizes for the county were usually held, was settled on Prince Charles in 1619, but apart from the gatehouse it was largely decayed. In its place the townsmen built 'a large and convenient house' to serve both as law court and market hall.[5] The gatehouse was leased to Salisbury's former secretary (Sir) Thomas Wilson*, keeper of records in the Tower of London, who may have helped the borough to make a case for re-enfranchisement. A survey was undertaken in 1621, presumably as a preliminary step in this process, although it defined the boundaries of the borough so tightly as to exclude some 50 poor cottagers on the waste.[6]

In Parliament, on 18 May 1621, the chairman of the privileges committee, Sir George More*, reported petitions for restoring the franchise to Hertford and three Buckinghamshire boroughs, although it was known that James I opposed the enlargement of the House of Commons. On the motion of (Sir) Robert Heath* it was immediately agreed that the privileges committee should peruse the four towns' charters and hear counsel for the Crown.[7] A further report was called for on 29 Nov., but the proposal for re-enfranchisement was lost at the abrupt dissolution of the session.[8] Ahead of the next Parliament, Prince Charles's Council decided to support the re-enfranchisement of Hertford in the expectation that they would be able to make nominations to its seats. They wrote to the corporation on 9 Feb. 1624 advising them to 'prepare a petition for reviving the said privilege this Parliament, and send it up to us', promising that 'such care shall be taken for preferring and effecting the same ... as shall be fitting, without any charge to the town'.[9] The prince's first nominees were Sir John Hobart II*, whose father was the chancellor of Charles's Household, and Christopher Vernon, who had been seconded from the Exchequer to assist the duchy of Cornwall with the recovery of lost titles.[10] In the event, Hobart was returned for Launceston, and Vernon withdrew because he, as the Prince's Council wrote on 24 Apr., 'being at this present otherwise employed for his highness's service, cannot well attend the House'. Instead the Prince's Council proposed Sir William Harington, the prince's steward at Hertingfordbury, less than two miles west of the town, 'a near neighbour unto you, who for his worth and integrity is without exception'.[11]

Once the Commons had processed the re-enfranchisement of Hertford and three other boroughs the writ was ordered on 4 May, but the sheriff did not issue his precept until 17 May, when the election itself was held at the castle.[12] By this time Thomas Fanshawe II, a nearby resident whose uncle was a senior duchy officer, had announced his intention to stand, while the 2nd earl of Salisbury (William Cecil*) put forward his man of business, William Ashton I, for the senior seat. On 15 May Salisbury was approached by lord keeper Williams, who requested a seat for his servant William Wynn*, 'the nomination whereof (I doubt not but) is very much in your lordship'. Williams added that he had been 'an earnest suitor to His Majesty for the renewing of this privilege for that town'. However, the earl was unable to oblige, replying that in addition to supporting Ashton, 'divers of the town … have desired me to give my best furtherance for Mr. Fanshawe, one whom I very well respect'.[13] An independent fourth candidate, Richard Willows, also stood, with strong local support; he was a successful lawyer from Cambridgeshire who had married the heiress of Balls Park, just outside the borough, and purchased the Priory manor in 1617.[14]

Hertford's first parliamentary election in almost 350 years gave rise to a contest in which separate ballots were held for each seat. On the first Ashton was successful with 103 votes, beating Willows with 58 and Harington with 42, while Fanshawe, who presumably did not intend to contest the senior seat, received 19 stray votes. On the second ballot Fanshawe won, with 101 votes against Willows' 87; Harington, despite the mayor's support, finished last with only 48.[15] It is possible to infer from the 244 recorded votes, and the tally of approximately 300 houses in both the 1621 survey and the 1641 Poll Tax, that the freemen comprised 'the large majority of male householders'.[16]

Ahead of the elections to Charles I's first Parliament, lord keeper Williams again asked Salisbury for a nomination, but the earl replied that considering the brevity of their service the previous year, it had already been decided that Ashton and Fanshawe should sit again, and

both were perfunctorily re-elected in 1625.[17] Harington stood once more in 1626, and was this time returned in first place; he may have anticipated another rejection, since he also secured a seat at Portsmouth in Hampshire; but he opted to represent his neighbours. Fanshawe's brother-in-law, Sir Capell Bedell, took the second seat. In 1627 Hertford castle and manor were sold to Salisbury.[18] The latter's client, Sir Edward Howard II, was returned 'by the consent of the whole borough' for the senior seat in 1628. A contest ensued for the second seat. Fanshawe stood, presumably with Salisbury's approval, but was challenged by a townsman, Gabriel Barbor, the manager of the running lotteries for the Virginia Company, who had purchased the advowson of All Saints and given it to the puritan feoffees for impropriations.[19] Unsurprisingly, Fanshawe won in the proportion of three votes out of five.[20]

A by-election was necessitated by Howard's elevation to the peerage on 12 Apr. 1628. Salisbury promised the seat to Wynn's brother Richard*, but Sir Charles Morrison bt. also put himself forward. The arrival of the writ was delayed until, on 7 May, the House ordered that it should be 'forthwith sent down for an election there to be made'.[21] Two days later Morrison was returned, presumably with Salisbury's support. In August, a month after the session was prorogued, Morrison died, whereupon Algernon, Lord Percy* reminded Salisbury, his father-in-law, of his former promise to (Sir) Richard Wynn. The earl procured a new writ, which was delivered to Wynn in October, although no election was held until the Parliament resumed.[22] On 22 Jan. 1629 the Commons, suspecting some irregularity in the way the writ had been obtained, ordered the clerk of the Crown to recover it, and by the Speaker's authority a new one was issued.[23] For reasons that are not clear Wynn at that point discreetly withdrew, and within a week John Carey, Lord Rochford, heir of the 1st earl of Dover, based at Hunsdon six miles east of the borough, was elected unopposed.[24]

---

[1] HALS, HBR 23/13, 14; D. Hirst, *Representative of the People?*, 96. [2] E. de Villiers, 'Parlty. Bors. Restored by the Commons 1621-41', *EHR*, lxvii. 180; *VCH Herts*. iii. 498-500. [3] *VCH Herts*. iii. 496; L. Turnor, *Hist. Hertford*, 77-82, 119. [4] *VCH Herts*. ii. 89-91; iii. 490. [5] Ibid. iii. 502-5; R. Clutterbuck, *Herts*. ii. 141-144; *HMC 14th Rep. VIII*, 161. [6] *VCH Herts*. iii. 493; *CSP Dom*. 1628-9, p. 41. [7] *CJ*, i. 624a; *CD 1621*, iv. 360; vi. 164. [8] *CJ*, i. 643b. [9] DCO, 'Prince Charles in Spain', ff. 37v-8; HALS, HBR 23/10. [10] DCO, 'Prince Charles in Spain', f. 38v; G.E. Aylmer, *King's Servants*, 314-15. [11] DCO, 'Prince Charles in Spain', f. 40; P.M. Hunneyball, 'Prince Charles's Council as Electoral Agent, 1620-4', *PH*, xxiii. 331. [12] *CJ*, i. 697b; HALS, HBR 23/12. [13] L. Stone, 'Electoral Influence of the 2nd earl of Salisbury', *EHR*, lxxi. 391-3; *HMC Hatfield*, xxii. 192, 205. [14] *VCH Herts*. iii. 412, 507; R. Clutterbuck, *Herts*. ii. 184. [15] HALS, HBR 23/13, 14. [16] Hirst, 96; R. Ruigh, *Parl. of*

1624, pp. 119-21. [17] HALS, HBR 23/15. [18] Stone, *EHR*, lxxi. 393. [19] *Virginia Mag. of Hist. and Biog.* lxxiv. 288; HLRO, Lords parchments, box 4. [20] HALS, HBR 23/17. [21] *CD 1628*, iii. 300. [22] *HMC Hatfield*, xxii. 245-6; *Procs. 1628*, vi. 151. [23] *CJ*, i. 921a, b. [24] HALS, HBR 23/18, 19.

J.P.F./R.C.L.S.

ST. ALBANS

Right of election: in the corporation and freemen

Number of voters: 62 in 1624[1]

7 Mar. 1604	SIR FRANCIS BACON	
	ADOLPHUS CAREY	
25 Mar. 1604[2]	TOBIE MATTHEW *vice* Bacon, chose to sit for Ipswich	
4 Jan. 1610	SIR THOMAS PARRY *vice* Carey, deceased	
	SIR HENRY HELMES *vice* Matthew, 'commanded out' Election of Helmes declared void, 14 Feb. 1610	
c.17 Feb. 1610	SIR HENRY HELMES	
c.Mar. 1614	SIR FRANCIS BACON	
	HENRY FINCH	
14 Apr. 1614	THOMAS PERIENT *vice* Bacon, chose to sit for Cambridge University	
20 Dec. 1620	THOMAS RICHARDSON	
	ROBERT SHUTE	
13 Feb. 1621	HENRY MEAUTYS *vice* Shute, deceased	
5 Feb. 1624	SIR ARTHUR CAPELL	
	SIR JOHN LUKE	
4 May 1625	SIR CHARLES MORRISON, bt.	
	SIR JOHN LUKE	
30 Jan. 1626	SIR CHARLES MORRISON, bt.	
	SIR EDWARD GORING	
c.14 Mar. 1628[3]	SIR JOHN JENNYNS	
	ROBERT KIRKHAM	

St. Albans owed its prosperity to its position as the first staging-point out of London, where the main highways to Ireland and the north-west diverged. Royal stables were maintained there, and municipal hospitality could be exercised in an enviably wide selection of well supplied inns. It was also the administrative centre of the liberty of St. Albans, comprising the former estates of the wealthy abbey scattered throughout Hertfordshire, with its own sessions of the peace and gaol. The borough received its first charter in 1253, and sent representatives to Parliament intermittently between 1301 and 1336. It was incorporated and re-enfranchised in 1553, with a mayor, a steward, and ten 'principal burgesses'.[4] The main electoral patron during the reign of James I was Sir Francis Bacon, owner of the Gorhambury estate just outside the borough, who was appointed recorder and high steward in 1613.[5] After Bacon's fall from grace in 1621, the borough deferred to the 2nd earl of Salisbury (William Cecil*), lord lieutenant of Hertfordshire.

At the general election of 1604 Bacon himself was chosen as the senior Member, while Adolphus Carey, a local gentleman who had previously represented St. Albans in Elizabeth I's last Parliament, was re-elected as his colleague. However, Bacon opted to sit for Ipswich, in Suffolk, which he had represented in two Elizabethan Parliaments, and nominated in his stead his clone Tobie Matthew. Matthew was sworn in as a freeman and undertook to serve without charge, but went abroad after the first session, and converted to Catholicism, while Carey died in 1609.[6] Consequently a double by-election was required ahead of the fourth session. Carey's cousin, Sir Thomas Vavasour*, the knight marshal, nominated Sir Thomas Parry, chancellor of the duchy of Lancaster, while Bacon put forward his favourite Sir Henry Helmes, who leased property in the county. Helmes was sworn a freeman and elected at a cost to the corporation of 4s. 10d. for wine and sugar; but because the writ had been issued on the Privy Council's orders, his return was queried by the Commons when the fourth session began.[7] Sir George More reported on 14 Feb. 1610 that the privileges committee, though it agreed that it was fitting that Matthew should be removed, was 'of opinion that the writ for a new choice was not rightly sent out'. Resolutions were passed accordingly, and Bacon paid the cost of procuring 'a warrant and writ for the second election of Sir Henry Helmes to be our burgess' himself.[8]

In 1614 Bacon, now attorney-general, was again returned in first place, and offered the second seat to Henry Finch, a distinguished lawyer from Kent. When Bacon subsequently chose to sit for Cambridge University, he recommended Thomas Perient, a student at Gray's Inn, as his replacement.[9] The admission of the attorney-general as a Member of the

Commons was highly controversial, having aroused adverse comment in 1606, when a sitting Member, Sir Henry Hobart, had been promoted to this office. After some debate it was decided on 11 Apr. to allow Bacon to remain only on condition that the situation would never be repeated.[10]

In 1619 the 2nd earl of Salisbury seems to have taken the first steps towards establishing his influence over the borough. On 5 Mar. Inigo Jones* reported from the Office of Works that the repair of the liberty gaol, kept in the gatehouse of the former abbey, devolved on the Crown, not on the county, since the building formed part of the royal stables; but the Privy Council decreed otherwise. Salisbury, in an undated letter, undertook to pay for the repairs if he were allowed to nominate the keeper. It is not clear whether this offer was at once taken up, but it certainly had no effect on the next election, which took place in December 1620.[11] Instead of awaiting a letter of nomination from Bacon, now lord chancellor, the mayor went in person 'to know the lord chancellor's pleasure who should be burgesses for this borough for the Parliament', spending 7s. 2d. in the process.[12] Bacon nominated for the first seat Thomas Richardson of Lincoln's Inn, whom he had earmarked for the Speaker's chair, and he obliged the marquess of Buckingham by offering the second to Robert Shute, a 'hangby and pettifogger' of the Villiers family.[13] Shute died soon after Parliament met, whereupon 'the messenger came down with the lord chancellor's letter for [us] to choose Mr. Henry Meautys a burgess for this borough' in his place, and the latter was duly elected by 'unanimous consent and assent'. Before his marriage Meautys, whose brother was one of Bacon's principal private secretaries, had lived in the suburbs of St. Albans. Nevertheless the mayor and chamberlains had to travel up to London to swear him in as a freeman.[14] Neither Meautys, nor even Richardson as Speaker, were able to avert the disaster which soon fell upon Bacon, which brought his long domination of the borough's elections to an end.

On the basis that certain parcels of Crown property at St. Albans belonged to the duchy of Cornwall, Prince Charles's Council wrote to both Salisbury and Bacon ahead of the next election, nominating John Maynard*, a Buckingham client. On 31 Jan. 1624 they followed this with further letters, again addressed to Salisbury and Bacon, withdrawing Maynard, who had already found a seat elsewhere, and instead proposing Sir Thomas Edmondes*, treasurer of the Household, who had been rejected at Coventry and was still 'altogether as yet unprovided for'.[15] St. Albans nevertheless returned two local men, and it may be significant

that no less than 62 electors are named on the indenture.[16] The senior Member, Sir Arthur Capell, was a younger son of a leading figure in the county administration; he was also a courtier, and the uncle of Arthur Capel†, designated as bridegroom for Salisbury's eldest daughter. His colleague Sir John Luke had resided in West Hertfordshire for 30 years.

At the general election to Charles I's first Parliament, Salisbury initially demanded both seats. However, on 30 Apr. 1625, the mayor recorded in his accounts that 'my lord of Salisbury's steward came hither about the burgesses for the Parliament, that where before he had requested to have the nomination of both of them by his letter, he was now contented to have but one'. The earl proposed Sir Charles Morrison, bt., a local landowner, who was returned together with Luke. The celebrations which followed fell heavily on corporation funds; wine, sugar, tobacco, cakes and beer were consumed to the tune of 15s. 6d., a cost which neither Luke nor his friend (Sir) John Jennyns*, the town's wealthiest inhabitant, offered to share. However, in September 1625 Luke sent the corporation a buck from his estate.[17]

Salisbury, in his capacity as Hertfordshire's *custos rotulorum*, controlled the venue for quarter sessions, and on 30 June the mayor of St. Albans was obliged to spend 8s. 4d. on a visit to Hatfield 'to speak with my lord of Salisbury that he would be pleased to keep the liberty sessions at our town'.[18] Perhaps in return for the earl's acquiescence, the corporation yielded him the nomination of both seats at the next election. Morrison was returned again in 1626, together with an outsider, Sir Edward Goring, a courtier and kinsman of Salisbury.[19]

The Forced Loan provoked widespread opposition in St. Albans. The mayor was appointed collector, but after paying three visits to every house in the borough he had received nothing (even from himself), most of the inhabitants employing the artful formula 'that they would not be the first to give nor the last'. On 4 Jan. 1627 he and seven other residents, including Jennyns, were summoned before the Privy Council, to which Salisbury had been added a few months before; whereupon their resistance soon collapsed.[20] A year later, at the next election, Jennyns was returned as senior Member, and Salisbury was informed that the other seat would be granted to him only on condition that he nominate a man 'acquainted with our town and sensible of our occasions, to whom we may have easy access and whose election may pass the common suffrages and voices'. The earl therefore chose Robert Kirkham, one of the clerks of the signet, who was perhaps slightly known in the constituency. The corporation paid 8*s.* 8*d.* for 'a gallon of sack and a gallon of claret wine bestowed upon Sir John Jennyns and Mr. Kirkham by the consent of all the burgesses when they were chosen burgesses for the Parliament'.[21]

[1] C219/38/110. [2] A.E. Gibbs, *Corp. Recs. St. Albans*, 56. [3] HALS, OFF ACC 1162/164. [4] M. Weinbaum, *British Bor. Charters*, 54; *VCH Herts.* ii. 469, 478, 482. [5] Gibbs, 62, 63. [6] Ibid. 56. [7] HALS, OFF ACC 1162/152. [8] Ibid.; Surr. Hist. Cent., LM1331/15. [9] HALS, OFF ACC 1162/155. [10] *Procs. 1614 (Commons)*, 30, 54-8. [11] *CSP Dom.* 1619-23, pp. 20, 164; *APC*, 1619-21, p. 235; L. Stone, 'Electoral Influence of the 2nd Earl of Salisbury', *EHR*, lxxi. 388-90; *HMC Hatfield*, xxii. 138. [12] HALS, OFF ACC 1162/159. [13] *Liber Famelicus of Sir J. Whitelocke* ed. J. Bruce (Cam. Soc. lxx), 58. [14] HALS, OFF ACC 1162/159; C219/37/118. [15] DCO, 'Prince Charles in Spain', f. 37; P.M. Hunneyball, 'Prince Charles's Council as Electoral Agent, 1620-4', *PH*, xxiii. 327, 329. [16] C219/38/110. [17] HALS, OFF ACC 1162/161. [18] Ibid; R. Ruigh, *Parl. of 1624*, p. 119. [19] L. Stone, *Fam. and Fortune*, 121-2. [20] SP16/44/14; *APC*, 1627, p. 5; *CSP Dom.* 1627-8, p. 9; Stone, *EHR*, lxxi. 388-9. [21] *HMC Hatfield*, xxii. 241-2; HALS, OFF ACC 1162/164.

J.P.F./R.C.L.S.

HUNTINGDONSHIRE

Number of voters: c.1,000-2,000

18 Feb. 1604	SIR OLIVER CROMWELL
	SIR ROBERT COTTON
c. Mar. 1614	SIR OLIVER CROMWELL
	SIR ROBERT PAYNE
	?Sir Robert Bevill
	Sir Robert Cotton, bt.
30 Dec. 1620	SIR ROBERT BEVILL
	SIR ROBERT PAYNE
	(Sir) Sidney Montagu*
24 Jan. 1624	EDWARD MONTAGU
	SIR OLIVER CROMWELL
c. May 1625	EDWARD MONTAGU
	SIR OLIVER CROMWELL
	Sir Robert Payne
c. Jan. 1626	EDWARD MONTAGU
	SIR ROBERT PAYNE
	?Sir Oliver Cromwell
10 June 1626	NAME ILLEGIBLE[1] *vice* Montagu, called to the Upper House
16 Feb. 1628	SIR CAPELL BEDDELL, bt.
	SIR ROBERT PAYNE

Although the second smallest county in England, seventeenth-century Huntingdonshire contained three

distinct agricultural economies: cattle fattening on the fens in the east; corn and sheep farming on the heavy clay uplands in the north and west; and a mixture of the two in the Ouse valley in the south. Most of the county's market towns lay within the last of these areas, but none achieved a position of economic dominance: Huntingdon drew a limited prosperity from its role as the county town and its position on Ermine Street, but the markets for the key local trades in livestock and corn were situated at St. Ives and St. Neots respectively.[2]

The exact size of the Huntingdonshire electorate is unknown: polls were held in 1584 and 1621, but no count is recorded. Another in 1673 was adjourned before voting was complete, but it was claimed that there were about 1,100 freeholders present.[3] A partial estimate is provided by a list of Sir Oliver Cromwell's supporters from Godmanchester at the 1625 or 1626 election. This records 107 voters from the town, whose inhabitants comprised about five per cent of the county's population, which gives a potential county electorate of about 2,000. However, this figure may be overstated, as modern research suggests that 20 of the 107 men listed were not freeholders possessed of lands worth 40*s.* p.a.[4]

Neither the knights of the shire nor their constituents showed any significant interest in sponsoring legislation to deal with local concerns during the early Stuart period. Sir Oliver Cromwell, who owned large tracts of Ramsey Fen, supported several proposals for fen drainage during the course of the 1604 Parliament, but none reached the statute books, and the work was ultimately completed by a chartered company during the 1630s.[5] Another important local project, which the Bedford corporation undertook to further by legislation in 1628, was the improvement of the navigation of the River Ouse between St. Ives and Bedford. Again, nothing was achieved, and the works were maintained by private patentees from 1617 until their inclusion in the River Navigation Act of 1665.[6] Three private bills relating to local estates – for the benefit of the Smiths of Water Newton, the Dyers of Great Staughton and the sale of Fletton manor – also came before the Commons during this period.[7]

Huntingdonshire underwent a massive upheaval at the Dissolution of the Monasteries, when the Crown acquired extensive estates in the east and north of the shire. The best were purchased by the Cromwell family, who amassed an estate of 66,000 acres in the eastern half of the county.[8] This made them the shire's largest landowners, but did not guarantee control of the parliamentary representation: in 1584 their candidate was defeated by a supporter of the then sheriff, Sir Henry Darcy[†], and in subsequent elections they had to content themselves with the junior seat. Sir Oliver Cromwell succeeded to the family estate only six weeks before the general election of 1604,[9] when he was returned for the senior county seat. There is no evidence of a contest on the day of the election, but the apparent absence of a challenge to Cromwell from Darcy's son-in-law Sir Gervase Clifton[†], senior knight in 1597 and 1601, is surprising. Moreover, the fact that the only important figures cited in the election indenture were Cromwell's brother Henry[*] and his friends Sir George Walton[†] and Christopher Hodson[*] suggests that there was some disagreement.[10] Clifton's estates were much more modest than Cromwell's,[11] but he had strong support within the county, and may only have abandoned plans to stand after interference by the king, who visited Cromwell's house at Hinchingbrooke a few days before the election. At the time of this visit, the Chancery clerk William Ravenscroft[*] reported that his clerk had prepared a patent granting Cromwell a barony for James's signature.[12] The warrant was never signed, and may only have been drafted as a ploy to help Cromwell: news of the apparent offer, which must have spread quickly, emphasized Cromwell's pre-eminence within the shire and provided justification for his claim to the senior county seat. Having yielded precedence to Cromwell, Clifton could hardly accept the junior seat, which went to Sir Robert Cotton, who had courted royal favour since the accession by playing upon his distant kinship with James.[13]

The 1614 election provides further circumstantial evidence for an abortive contest in 1604, as the field seems to have become divided between representatives of the same rival camps. Clifton was no longer eligible to stand, having been elevated to the peerage since the previous election, but he probably sponsored Sir Robert Bevill, who had become a trustee of his estates in 1613, and Sir Robert Payne, whose father had bought Midloe manor from Sir Henry Darcy in 1590. The pair may also have secured the support of the lord lieutenant, Oliver, Lord St. John[†], whose son (Sir) Oliver I[*] was another of Clifton's trustees.[14] Cromwell, by contrast, was in a weaker position than in 1604: he was mired in debt, despite recently assigning Weybridge Forest to the Crown for £16,000, and could no longer rely on James's wholehearted support, as Clifton now had his own Court contacts following his daughter's marriage to the king's cousin Lord Aubigny.[15] Bevill and Payne appear to have mounted a particularly effective canvass, and Cotton must have been alarmed when he discovered that Sir

James Wingfield, to whom he was connected through the Montagu family, declined to promise his tenants' voices to Cromwell and claimed to be unaware that Cotton was a candidate.[16] Cromwell resolved the problem by cutting a deal with his rivals at Cotton's expense, whereby Bevill stood aside in favour of Cromwell, whose followers then either supported Payne or abstained in the contest for the second seat. Payne duly trounced Cotton, whose brother protested that 'this false ploy must needs return to somebody's much discredit', and suggested a petition to the Commons against the sheriff, who was already in trouble for his conduct of the Cambridgeshire election and was later accused of conspiring with the victorious parties in both counties. However, Cotton's brother conceded that Cromwell's desertion meant that '[if] in wading in it you [Cotton] should bring it to a new election, you would come off with small amends'; there is no evidence that any formal protest was made to the Commons.[17]

The price Cromwell apparently paid for his unopposed return in 1614 was an agreement that he would not stand for the shire at the next election, when he used his membership of Prince Charles's Council to secure a nomination for the duchy of Cornwall borough of Saltash.[18] Bevill and Payne were duly returned for Huntingdonshire in December 1620, although they had to fight off a challenge from (Sir) Sidney Montagu. The latter held only a small amount of land at Little Stukeley, but must have been endorsed by his brother lord treasurer Mandeville (Sir Henry Montagu[*]), who had a much larger estate at Kimbolton, and Sir Robert Cotton, whose sister was married to his eldest brother Sir Edward Montagu[*], and on whose behalf he had apparently lobbied in 1614.[19] The 1620 contest belatedly gave rise to further controversy in May 1624, when Francis Bedell, one of Sir Sidney's supporters, prosecuted the sheriff, Thomas Maples, in Star Chamber for rejecting the voices of some of the freeholders. However, as the Parliament had long since been dissolved the allegations were of little consequence to the erstwhile candidates, and the action appears to have been brought as part of a longstanding feud between Maples and Bedell.[20]

There is no evidence of a contest in 1624, which suggests that Bevill and Payne stood aside, allowing Cromwell to be returned unopposed. However, he was obliged to yield the senior seat to Mandeville's eldest son Edward Montagu, who had recently come of age. The same pair were returned again in 1625, although on this occasion a letter from one of Cromwell's supporters indicates that Cromwell had intended to stand with Payne, who must have ceded the second seat to him when Montagu took the first.[21] Cromwell and Payne probably paired against Montagu once again in 1626, but if so, Cromwell stood aside to allow Payne the junior seat. Montagu was summoned to the Lords in May 1626, and a by-election was held on 10 June. The surviving indenture is badly damaged and consequently the result of the election is unknown, but it is likely that Cromwell was returned in his stead. If so he would only just have had time to take up his seat before the dissolution.

With Montagu in the Lords, his younger brother Walter, a diplomat, was the family's obvious candidate in 1628, but at the time of the election he was languishing in the Bastille. His brother James, who may have been considered too young for the county seat, was returned as a burgess for Huntingdon on the interest of his uncle Sir Sidney Montagu, who had recently purchased Hinchingbrooke House from Cromwell.[22] Although Cromwell retained a considerable estate at Ramsey, the sale of Hinchingbrooke delivered a heavy blow to his local prestige, and curtailed his electoral influence within the shire. Payne was returned once again, but the senior seat went to a newcomer, Sir Capell Bedell, who had recently assumed control of 5,000 acres in the west of the county after a long minority.[23]

---

[1] C219/40/68. [2] M. Carter, 'Town or Urban Society? St. Ives, Hunts. 1630-1740', *Societies, Cultures and Kinship, 1580-1850* ed. C. Pythian-Adams, 79-84, 93-8, 121-8. [3] STAC 5/A41/32; STAC 8/47/7; *HP Commons, 1660-90*, i. 272-3. [4] Hunts. RO, Godmanchester bor. recs. Box 3, bdle. 15; Carter, 81; D. Hirst, *Representative of the People?*, 40-1. [5] *CJ*, i. 207b, 277a, 382a, 413a, 1043a; SIR OLIVER CROMWELL; SIR ROBERT BEVILL. [6] D. Summers, *Gt. Ouse*, 47-50. [7] *CJ*, i. 440b, 489b, 544b, 606b. [8] M. Wickes, *Hist. Hunts.* 62-3; Add. 33462, ff. 40-3. [9] C142/283/106. [10] C219/35/1/48. [11] C142/555/83. [12] *HMC Hastings*, iv. 1. [13] K. Sharpe, *Sir Robert Cotton*, 114-15. [14] *CP sub* Clifton of Leighton Bromswold; C142/555/83; 142/281/53. [15] Hunts. RO, D/DM50/1, 3; *CSP Dom.* 1611-18, p. 190; *HMC Downshire*, iv. 231; *CP* (earl of March). [16] Harl. 7002, f. 308. [17] *Procs. 1614 (Commons)*, 38, 103, 239-41; Cott. Julius C.III, f. 115; K. Sharpe, *Sir Robert Cotton*, 161-2. [18] DCO, Letters and Patents 1620-1, f. 39v. [19] STAC 8/47/7; Harl. 7002, f. 308. [20] STAC 8/47/7. See also STAC 8/208/15; 8/285/20. [21] Add. 33461, f. 61, which can be dated to 1625 from internal evidence. [22] *CSP Dom.* 1627-8. p. 473; 1628-9, p. 81; *VCH Hunts.* ii. 136. [23] C142/337/100; 142/338/54.

S.H.

HUNTINGDON

Right of election: ?in the burgesses

Number of voters: under 100

18 Feb. 1604	HENRY CROMWELL
	THOMAS HETLEY, recorder
c. Mar. 1614	SIR CHRISTOPHER HATTON
	SIR MILES FLEETWOOD
9 Jan. 1621	SIR HENRY ST. JOHN
	SIR MILES SANDYS, bt.
28 Jan. 1624	SIR HENRY ST. JOHN
	SIR ARTHUR MAINWARING
c. May 1625	SIR HENRY ST. JOHN
	SIR ARTHUR MAINWARING
c. Jan. 1626	SIR ARTHUR MAINWARING
	JOHN GOLDSBOROUGH
11 Feb. 1628	JAMES MONTAGU
	OLIVER CROMWELL

A Saxon foundation, sited on Ermine Street where it crossed the River Ouse, Huntingdon was a thriving centre of perhaps 2,000 people in 1086. Chartered in 1205 and served by 16 churches in 1291, its prosperity was eroded by the rise of nearby St. Ives and St. Neots, which took over the local markets in livestock and grain respectively, so that by 1603, with only four churches and a population of about 750, the borough was of little consequence. However, its situation on the main route to London brought custom to its inns, and it remained the venue for quarter sessions, assizes and sewer courts. The town grew by about 50 per cent during the early Stuart period, chiefly because of improvements in the Ouse navigation, but perhaps also due to the regularity of the Court's visits to Hinchingbrooke House, just outside the town.[1]

Under its 1484 charter of incorporation, Huntingdon was governed by two bailiffs and a council of 24 burgesses.[2] Little else can be said about municipal government, as few records survive. By 1702 the parliamentary franchise was vested in the inhabitant householders, but this cannot have been the case in 1621, when three Cromwells, none of whom was a resident, were included on the indenture. This return mentioned 17 named voters and 'other burgesses of the same town'; with a population of less than 1,000 the total number of burgesses is unlikely to have exceeded 100.[3]

Although a duchy of Lancaster borough, Huntingdon is only known to have elected a duchy candidate in 1593. The town had previously returned Members at the behest of other government figures, but either in 1597 or 1601 Sir Robert Cecil's[†] request for a nomination was apparently rejected.[4] Townsmen were occasionally returned during the Elizabethan period, but representation increasingly fell into the hands of the local gentry, the most influential of whom were the Cromwells of Hinchingbrooke. A rival interest emerged in 1601 when William Beecher[†] was returned through the influence of his father-in-law Oliver, Lord St. John[†], who was both lord lieutenant and a substantial landowner at Ripton and Houghton, a few miles north of the borough.[5]

At the general election of 1604 the senior seat went to Henry Cromwell, who was returned on the family interest, while the other was bestowed upon the town's recorder, Thomas Hetley.[6] In 1614 the Cromwells focused their efforts on the hotly contested county election, and Hetley does not appear to have stood, leaving the borough open to other influences. One seat went to Lord St. John's relative Sir Miles Fleetwood, the other to Sir Christopher Hatton, whose uncle lord chancellor Sir Christopher Hatton[†] had been one of the borough's patrons during the 1580s. Most of Hatton's inheritance then lay in the hands of lord chief justice Sir Edward Coke*, who was acquainted with the Huntingdon corporation from his time as a judge on the Norfolk circuit and may have recommended him.[7] Hatton had sat for Bedford in the previous Parliament, and his move to Huntingdon may also have been encouraged by Lord St. John, who was then able to insert one of his sons, Sir Alexander St. John, at Bedford.

In 1621 Oliver St. John I*, an energetic parliamentary patron who had recently succeeded his father as both Baron St. John and lord lieutenant of Huntingdonshire, secured a seat at Huntingdon for his brother Henry. The other seat went to the Cambridgeshire landowner Sir Miles Sandys, bt., whose estates, which lay along the Ouse between St. Ives and Ely, may just have given him sufficient local influence to secure his own return. He was supported, perhaps, by his neighbour Sir Oliver Cromwell, whom he met regularly as a sewer commissioner. St. John retained his seat in the next two parliaments, but Sandys was replaced by Sir Arthur Mainwaring, a courtier whose wife was a second cousin to Cromwell.[8] In 1626 St. John's place was taken by John Goldsborough, a local man who owned Huntingdon's largest inn, the *George*. This gave him an independent interest within the borough, but he may also have been backed by Lord St. John, to whom his wife was distantly related.[9]

Huntingdon's municipal politics were irrevocably altered in the summer of 1627, when Sir Oliver Cromwell's mounting debts forced him to sell Hinchingbrooke to the Montagu family.[10] The house went to Sir Sidney Montagu*, but the electoral interest was initially used by Montagu's brother lord president Manchester (Sir Henry Montagu*), who secured the return of his son James Montagu as Huntingdon's senior burgess in 1628. The junior seat was acquired by Oliver Cromwell, who is usually assumed to have been nominated by his uncle Sir Oliver. However, Cromwell had served as one of the borough bailiffs in the previous year,[11] and while his return may have provided some comfort for the senior branch of the family, it was probably secured on the basis of his personal standing in the town.

[1] M. Wickes, *Hist. Hunts.* 35-51; M. Carter, 'Town or Urban Society? St. Ives, Hunts. 1630-1740' in *Societies, Cultures and Kinship, 1580-1850* ed. C. Pythian-Adams, 80-1, 123-5. [2] *CPR, 1476-85*, p. 443. [3] C219/37/121. [4] R. Carruthers, *Hist. Huntingdon*, 164. [5] C142/249/56. [6] C181/1, f. 87. [7] J.S. Cockburn, *Hist. Eng. Assizes*, 268-9; SIR CHRISTOPHER HATTON. [8] Vivian, *Vis. Devon*, 280; *Vis. Hunts.* ed. Ellis (Cam. Soc. xliii), 79-80. [9] C142/610/115; SIR ROBERT PAYNE. [10] Hunts. RO, D/DM50/1, 7. [11] *Ex inf.* Christopher Thompson.

S.H.

KENT

Number of voters: nearly 5,000 in 1624

6 Feb. 1604	SIR JOHN SCOTT
	SIR JOHN LEVESON
?21 Mar. 1614	SIR PETER MANWOOD
	SIR THOMAS WALSINGHAM I
	?Sir John Scott
18 Dec. 1620	SIR ROBERT SIDNEY, (LORD L'ISLE)
	SIR GEORGE FANE
12 Jan. 1624	SIR NICHOLAS TUFTON
	SIR EDWIN SANDYS
	Sir Dudley Digges
2 May 1625	MILDMAY FANE, (LORD BURGHERSH)
	SIR ALBERTUS MORTON
	Sir Edwin Sandys
	Edward Scott
9 Jan. 1626	SIR EDWARD HALES, (bt.)
	EDWARD SCOTT
	Sir Edwin Sandys
3 Mar. 1628	SIR THOMAS FINCH, bt.
	SIR DUDLEY DIGGES

A county of striking geographical diversity, Kent is bisected from west to east by the chalk ridge known as the North Downs, which provided the best agricultural land in the shire, and was used mainly to grow wheat, the county's chief crop.[1] Running parallel with the chalk ridge, sloping southwards and slightly lower, is a narrower sandstone ridge that in the early seventeenth century mainly lay wild as heath or woodland. The relatively barren soil made it ideal for hop growing, which began here on a small scale under Elizabeth and soon became widely established.[2] South of the sandstone ridge lies the Weald, a low-lying area of clay liable to winter flooding bordered by the hills and valleys of the High Weald. Unsuited to most crops, the Weald was important for cattle rearing and was the centre of the county's iron and cloth industries.[3] The area around Cranbrook was famed for its distinctive dyed broadcloths, manufactured mainly for export, while the northern parishes of the Weald produced the narrower kerseys, which were sold locally. Following the return of peace in 1604, Kent's clothiers recovered their continental markets and enjoyed a long period of prosperity, although as late as March 1610 they complained to Parliament about low sales caused, among other factors, by high wool prices and abuses in dyeing.[4] Their difficulties were exacerbated by acute competition for timber between the iron and cloth industries, and in 1607 a bill to protect the clothiers of Tenterden, one of the Weald's principal clothing towns, was considered by a Commons committee. However, it was dropped because of 'some mischief' in its wording.[5] The boom in the Kent clothing industry was interrupted by the depression of 1614-16 and the slump of the early 1620s caused by the outbreak of the Thirty Years' War and the demand for lighter cloths. Spokesmen for the Kent clothiers in February 1621 complained to the Commons, among other things, of the 'want of vent beyond sea', the increase in customs duties and the 'engrossing, mixture and falsification' of wool by the Staplers.[6] During the debate on the Merchant Adventurers' monopoly on 5 May 1624, Sir Nicholas Tufton, the senior knight of the shire, 'tendereth several petitions from the Kentish clothiers for freedom for other merchants, besides the Merchant Adventurers, to buy coloured cloths'.[7]

Around ten per cent of the county was marshland. The greatest tract lay in the south and provided the largest grazing district in the county. Here sheep were pastured to provide wool for the clothworkers of the nearby Weald. In north Kent, along the Thames estuary, lay a second area of marshland, much of it recently recovered from the sea.[8] Highly fertile, it was used mainly for growing malt and wheat, much of which was transported by water to London. By Eliza-beth's reign Kent was the capital's leading supplier of wheat by sea.[9] This lucrative business was evidently open to abuse: in 1624 the Kent carriers preferred a bill 'for suppressing extortion in meal porters', which may have been the measure misleadingly described in the Commons Journal as the London and Westminster brewhouses' bill. The bill, which did not receive a third reading, attracted the attention of two London livery companies, the Bakers and the Brewers, who employed the lawyer Thomas Malet* 'to speak before the committees of the Parliament House about the same business'.[10] During the early seventeenth century the drainage of Erith and Plumstead marshes was incomplete, and in 1607 Parliament granted statutory permission to finish the task in the hope that this would 'afford much benefit to the commonwealth and especially to the City of London being ten miles thereof'.[11] Further legislation was sought in 1624, 1625 and 1626, but none of the bills submitted progressed beyond the report stage.[12] Like the wheat grown in the reclaimed marshland of north Kent, fruit grown in the apple and cherry orchards that sprang up around Teynham after 1533 was also destined for London. The main buyers were members of the London Fruiterers' Company, who in 1624 turned to Kent's knights of the shire to petition the Commons on their behalf against Dutch imports.[13] London was probably also the main market for the paper mills that sprang up at Dartford in the 1580s. Their founder, the German-born John Spielman, was granted a royal monopoly in 1589, and royal patronage continued under James, who knighted Spielman in 1605 after visiting his mills.[14]

Kent had an estimated population of around 130,000 at the beginning of the seventeenth century. Around 15 per cent lived in the towns, a higher proportion than in most other counties. Kent was also remarkable for its number of independent towns. Canterbury was technically a county in its own right, even though it was one of the meeting places of the Kent justices, while Dover, Sandwich, Hythe, New Romney, Faversham and Tenterden all lay within the Cinque Ports. Another distinctive feature of the shire was the prevailing form of land tenure. Elsewhere in England the majority of the landowning population were copyholders, but in Kent freeholders predominated, with the result that the parliamentary electorate was abnormally large. In the spring of 1640 (Sir) Edward Dering* claimed that 10,000 freeholders turned out to vote, around eight per cent of the county's population.[15] In 1624 almost 5,000 freeholders appeared.

By the early seventeenth century Maidstone, the county town of Kent, was rivalled in administrative importance by Canterbury, the largest town in the shire. The area between Canterbury, Dover and Thanet was traditionally referred to as 'East Kent', where woodland was sparse and most of the fields were unenclosed. Ancient rivalry between east and west Kent surfaced during the economic crisis of the 1590s.[16] Easterners had further to travel to county elections, which were held on a Monday at Penenden Heath, just outside Maidstone. Consequently those living nearest to Maidstone tended to dominate parliamentary elections, particularly if the time between the announcement of the writ and the election was brief. Writing to Sir Edward Dering* at the end of January 1628, Lord Tufton (Sir Nicholas Tufton) noted that 'the time of election is so short that Maidstone will rule much'.[17] Under Elizabeth and for much of the early Stuart period, the knights of the shire were largely drawn from the western side of the county. However, in 1624 the voters of east Kent turned out in considerable numbers to capture the junior seat for Sir Edwin Sandys, who lived at Northbourne, just outside Deal. Sandys was a skilled political operator, and his description of east Kent in a letter written on election day as 'this neglected part of the shire' suggests that he exploited his neighbours' sense of grievance to the full.[18]

No single family or faction dominated Kent in this period. During the 1590s the Brookes of Cobham Hall had controlled both the lieutenancy and the wardenship of the Cinque Ports, but the fall in 1603 of Henry Brooke II *alias* Cobham†, 11th Lord Cobham, signalled the end of their dominance. His removal might have resulted in his replacement by his principal rival, Sir Robert Sidney†, but instead James I split his offices, bestowing the lieutenancy on Edward, Lord Wotton and the wardenship on Henry Howard, earl of Northampton. Neither man was capable of wielding great independent power in the county, as Wotton was a middle-ranking Kent landowner while Northampton was an outsider. Sidney, meanwhile, was placated by being raised to the peerage and appointed chamberlain to the new queen, Anne of Denmark. Sidney's neighbour at Knole, Thomas Sackville†, Lord Buckhurst, was also overlooked, but his local influence lay mainly in Sussex and in 1604 he was elevated to the earldom of Dorset. Wotton's successors as lord lieutenant were the duke of Lennox (1620-24) and Sir Philip Herbert*, earl of Montgomery (1624-42), neither of whom possessed large Kent estates. Northampton was succeeded in turn by Lord Zouche (1615-24), the duke of Buckingham (1624-28) and Theophilus Howard*, 2nd earl of Suffolk, none of whom had significant landed power in the county.[19]

The last two Elizabethan elections in Kent were dominated by faction fighting between the 11th Lord Cobham and his enemies. In 1597 Cobham's main rival, Sir Robert Sidney, took the senior seat while the junior place went to Cobham's younger brother, Sir William Brooke. Four years later the positions were reversed: Cobham's candidate, Francis Fane, was awarded the senior place, while the junior knighthood went to Sidney's friend Sir Henry Neville II. By 1604 Cobham had fallen from office, but so recently that the factional alignments remained unchanged. It was now the turn of opponents of the Cobham interest for the senior seat, which was filled by Sidney's friend, Sir John Scott. The remaining seat went to one of the Brooke family's closest allies, Sir John Leveson. Scott's claim on the senior seat may have been particularly strong, for in 1601 he had sought election with the backing of his kinsman Lord Buckhurst, who so hated Cobham that he wanted to deny him both seats. Scott had eventually agreed to withdraw, but perhaps only after being promised that he would be returned the next time round.[20]

Traces of the factional rivalry between the supporters of Lord Cobham and their enemies may have persisted well into James's reign. At the general election of 1614, Sir Peter Manwood, one of Cobham's erstwhile supporters, was returned for the first place. According to one hostile observer, Manwood was 'not ashamed to allege for himself that this is his turn', and that of Sir Thomas Walsingham I, who took the junior seat.[21] There is no evidence that Walsingham was aligned with the anti-Cobham interest under Elizabeth; indeed, shortly before the 1601 election Cobham's candidate, Sir Francis Fane, wrote asking him for his support. However, in 1608 he followed his wife into Queen Anne's Household, whose chamberlain was Sidney, now Lord L'Isle. Yet if Cobham/Sidney rivalry continued to help shape the outcome of Kent's parliamentary elections, not everyone was content to see Manwood and Walsingham returned. In September 1613 Thomas Scott* of Canterbury, anticipating that a Parliament would soon be summoned, urged his kinsman Sir John Scott to stand again, alongside Sir Edwin Sandys.[22] Sandys and Sir John Scott were natural allies as both supported free trade. By 3 Mar. 1614 it was reported that Sandys was indeed intending to contest the second seat with Walsingham,[23] and by the middle of the month Scott had also thrown his hat into the ring, thereby pitting himself as a former member of the anti-Cobham faction against the pro-Cobham Manwood. Sandys was supported by his cousin Sir Dudley Digges*, a fellow Kentish landowner, and also by the treasurer of the Navy, Sir

Robert Mansell*. Digges campaigned for Sandys in the county at large while Mansell concentrated on winning the naval bases at Chatham, Deptford and Woolwich. However, Sandys was a relative newcomer to Kent with only modest property holdings in the county, and was not a local magistrate. His presumption in seeking a county seat was clearly resented, as one of his supporters was allegedly told that 'labouring as he does for Sir Edwin Sandys he is too busy in state matters and will hear of it'.[24] On 17 Mar. Chamberlain reported that Sandys had resolved to abandon his pursuit of the county seat for lack of support.[25] Scott remained undaunted, however, coming as he did from a family long settled in the county. That same day he wrote optimistically from London to his brother-in-law and neighbour, Sir Norton Knatchbull*, to whom he had entrusted the task of mobilizing his supporters. While admitting that he had not yet achieved 'an absolute security', he claimed that 'the opposite party' had declined so much that they would cease campaigning in the area south of Ashford, where he owned his principal estate and was strongest. Indeed, Scott seems to have thought that his chief difficulty would be to maximize his advantage rather than gather votes, as he wished to call out his own supporters without alerting those of his rivals. He therefore issued detailed instructions to Knatchbull about how to manage the business secretly:

> The warning generally must be deferred to the last moment of time as with regard that the remotest parts which are those towards the sea be first sent to and Ashford which is the nearest to Rochester, but the last to whose knowledge I wish it should not come before Saturday at 6 of the clock in the evening at the soonest, and for that Saturday is market day there, you must be careful to make your dispatches elsewhere with such silence and secrecy that it be not carried thither before the appointed hour.[26]

He added that some of his supporters had already set out for Maidstone, which suggests that the election was to be held on the following Monday, 21 March. Scott's confidence ultimately proved misplaced, however, but it is uncertain whether, like Sandys, he conceded defeat before the vote.

By the next general election, in December 1620, Scott was dead and Sandys preferred to represent Sandwich. This left the way open for candidates drawn from the old Sidney and Cobham factions to divide the seats peacefully between themselves. As convention dictated, the senior knighthood went to the Sidney representative, Lord L'Isle, who was heir to the Sidney estates and whose father, the Elizabethan

Sir Robert Sidney, was now earl of Leicester. The junior place went to Sir George Fane, whose brother Sir Francis had been the pro-Cobham candidate at the county election of 1601.

In 1624 it was the turn of the Sidney candidate to occupy the junior seat. Perhaps unwilling to hold an inferior position, L'Isle turned to his brother-in-law the earl of Pembroke to secure him the sole knighthood of the shire for Monmouthshire. In his place the junior knighthood for Kent was solicited by Sir Dudley Digges, whose godfather had been Robert Dudley, earl of Leicester, brother to L'Isle's grandmother, and whose father and uncle had both shared L'Isle's enthusiam for the mathematical sciences, in which Digges himself was well versed. The sole candidate for the senior knighthood was Sir Nicholas Tufton. There is no direct evidence that Tufton was associated with the old Cobham interest, and since he was probably the wealthiest man in the county he had a good claim to the first seat in his own right. However, his father had been a close friend of Robert Cecil[†], the principal ally at Court of Cobham Hall in the final years of Elizabeth's reign. Tufton himself had cemented his family's ties with the Cecils in 1601, when he married the daughter of Thomas Cecil*, 1st earl of Exeter. Both Tufton and Digges expected their election to go unchallenged, but four days before the county court assembled some of Sir Edwin Sandys's friends urged him to stand again. Though still a relatively minor figure in local administration, Sandys was now well known on the national stage and could be expected to attract significant support among his East Kent neighbours, many of whom may have resented the dominance of the county seats by West Kent. However, the king was anxious that he should not obtain a seat, and in December 1623 he had appointed him a commissioner for reforming the administration in Ireland in the expectation that this would keep him from Westminster.[27] Sandys had no intention of being prevented from sitting, and over the coming few weeks feigned serious illness to avoid travelling to Ireland.[28] However, this charade meant that he could not attend the hustings. The day before the election more than 600 of his supporters rode without him to Maidstone, swelling the total number of voters present to almost 5,000. Alarmed, Tufton and Digges united their forces to appear stronger, 'and wheeling in very good order about, they presented themselves at their return to the sheriff'. The rest of the gathering, which reportedly outnumbered them 'by many hundreds', regarded both Tufton and Digges as unacceptable. Tufton, whose father was widely suspected of being a Catholic, was denounced as 'a papist', while Digges, who was desperate for Court office, was vilified as 'a royalist'.[29] How far Sandys himself encouraged these smear tactics is unclear, but it would not have been out of character, as in 1621 he had successfully disparaged his rival for the Sandwich seat, Sir Thomas Smythe*.[30] Sandys was returned for the junior seat, but his supporters could not prevent the election of Tufton. Lacking a leader and not all knowing one another, they were unable to agree on an alternative candidate.

Following the election, the first at county level in Kent in which religion appeared as a political issue, Digges protested that Sandys's appointment as a commissioner for Ireland made him ineligible to sit. He also claimed that Sandys had benefited from the partiality of the sheriff, Sir John Hayward*.[31] This may have been true, for in 1626 Digges counted Hayward among Sandys's chief supporters in Kent,[32] and Hayward's mother's second husband had been Sir John Scott, Sandys's ally in 1614. However, Digges did not complain to the privileges committee but instead came in for his former seat at Tewkesbury.

The 1624 election was the last in which the factional divide between the Sidneys and Brookes played a significant part. In 1625 the county seats were once again contested, but for the first time aristocratic pressure was exerted to force the return of non-residents, albeit men with a Kentish background. The royal favourite, the duke of Buckingham, wanted one seat for the newly appointed secretary of state, Sir Albertus Morton, whose family lived near Canterbury, and in mid-April he wrote to the Chatham landowner (Sir) Robert Jackson* and two senior naval officials to procure the votes of all their 'friends and tenants being freeholders, and particularly all such freeholders at or about Rochester or Chatham as have any relation to me or my office of admiral'. The other seat was coveted by Sir Francis Fane, recently ennobled as earl of Westmorland, on behalf of his 23-year old son and heir, Mildmay, Lord Burghersh, who, even before the writs of election were issued, sent letters to the Kent gentry asking for their support. Westmorland was seated at Mereworth Castle, a few miles west of Maidstone, but from at least 1617 he and his family lived increasingly on his wife's estate of Apethorpe, in Northamptonshire. In a letter addressed to the Derings on 13 Apr., Westmorland claimed that he had been 'earnestly importuned by my friends and divers of the principal gentlemen of this country' to allow Burghersh to stand. As Westmorland had entered into an alliance with Buckingham, the Derings were urged to support Morton as well as Burghersh.[33] Morton and Burghersh also received the support of another

aristocratic figure, the county's newly appointed lord lieutenant, (Sir) Philip Herbert*, earl of Montgomery. On 20 Apr. he wrote to Rochester's mayor recommending Morton for the first seat and Burghersh for the second.[34]

The aristocratic-backed candidates were not the only men with their eyes on the county seats. Before the election writs were issued, Edward Scott of Scot's Hall, brother of the late Sir John Scott, resolved to stand. Although not yet knighted, Scott had served as sheriff and was a landowner of considerable importance in south Kent, which like the eastern end of the county had reason to feel neglected. While Burghersh was sending out letters to the gentry, Scott's estate steward, Thomas Nebb, sounded out the local clergy, many of whom promised Scott their support. Nebb also contacted Lieutenant Lee of the militia, in which Scott served as a Captain, who reported that he had spoken 'to many of the band' on Scott's behalf. Moreover, Scott, through his kinsman, Edward Boys of Betteshanger, offered Sir Edwin Sandys an electoral alliance. Sandys was delighted at this overture, and through Boys replied that 'he would rather have you to be his partner in this business than any man in the county' and promised 'that all that he can prevail with shall be for you'. Boys added encouragingly that Scott already had a 'great many voices in the East part', where Sandys lived, and that he himself intended to 'tax all I can for you'.[35]

The election took place on 2 May and was attended by Sandys and 'divers thousands of freeholders' as well as those who had come to Maidstone's spring fair.[36] Unable to determine either by 'voice or view' which side had the larger vote, the sheriff, Sir Thomas Hammon*, appointed eight clerks to take a poll, 'assisted with indifferent persons to see that right were done'. Furthermore, at the voters' request, he ordered that anyone suspected of not being a freeholder should be examined upon oath 'according to the statute in that case provided'. These sensible arrangements encouraged many of those present to hope for 'a quiet and speedy election', but Hammon suddenly halted the proceedings and declared Burghersh and Morton elected, although the poll allegedly indicated that Scott and Sandys were ahead. When challenged, Hammon claimed that 'by his view' Burghersh and Morton had three times as many votes as Scott and Sandys. This was plainly absurd, for as the supporters of Sandys and Scott later pointed out,

in that party which he said was threefold the greater there were some thousands who, giving their first vote to one of those honourable persons [Burghersh and Morton] gave their second to one or other of the other two gentlemen aforesaid, which was the cause that no exact view could be taken, and notwithstanding also that there were divers hundreds of serving-men attending their masters, and others not freeholders, and mixed in that party, besides a great multitude of the townsmen of the town of Maidstone, being near adjoining, and other strangers assembled at the fair there held who, coming to see the said election, stood near unto the said party which was the cause the said party seemed greater than the other …[37]

Sandys was furious at Hammon's partisan behaviour, although he had benefited from a sympathetic sheriff himself the previous year. According to one report he 'made an oration or speech none of the wisest'.[38] Hammon remained unmoved, however, and Sandys therefore turned to Sir Robert Killigrew* for a Cornish seat, leaving Scott, who enjoyed no such connections, empty-handed. When the Commons assembled in June copies of a petition were circulated in Kent on Scott's behalf, which gathered 30 signatures in one instance and 52 in another. In addition, at least two supporting certificates were drawn up.[39] However, the Commons may never have considered Scott's complaint. Fourteen other petitions relating to different election disputes had been received before Scott's and the House resolved to deal with them in the order they had come in. Scott's agent was unable even to obtain a date for a hearing.[40]

Sandys's performance in the 1625 Parliament disappointed many of his supporters, perhaps because he was now a client of the duke of Buckingham's, who was widely perceived as an enemy of the godly. The puritan Thomas Scott, no friend of the duke, claimed that Sandys had 'deserted and even betrayed us and our freehold contrary to his own engagement and handwriting', an attitude shared by his kinsman Edward Scott. When Scott resolved to stand again early in 1626, he rebuffed Sandys's offer of an electoral pact in favour of an alliance with Sir Edward Hales, one of the richest landowners in the county. Edward Scott's supporters included his kinsman Sir Dudley Digges, who was eager to be revenged on Sandys for the humiliating defeat he had suffered in 1624. In a letter addressed (but not sent) to one of Sandys's chief supporters, the lieutenant of Dover Castle, Sir John Hippisley*, Digges revealed the extent of his animosity towards Sandys:

Believe me, Sir John, both my cousin Scott and I know Sir Edwin S[andys], and my cousin Scott found what it was to join with him when his reputation was better than it is, and I am sorry my lord duke's name, or your favour, gives him any countenance now … since there is no end of his malicious business I will everywhere now protest him to be the poor man I can prove him.

Thomas Scott, who now also detested Sandys, thought that Digges's letter was written 'more in passion than in discretion', and refused to forward it as directed. He was particularly concerned at the implied slander of Edward Scott, as the letter suggested that Edward Scott believed that Sandys had behaved dishonourably when the two men had been allied the previous year. In fact, Edward would have been prepared to ally himself with Sandys again had not Sandys deserted his constituents during the 1625 Parliament. Digges was offended at Thomas Scott's refusal to pass on his letter, creating a quarrel that threatened to undermine the unity of Edward Scott's supporters, many of whom were 'sensible of the wrong' done to Scott on the hustings the previous year.[41]

Edward Scott's refusal to join him left Sandys without a partner. Sir Albertus Morton, who had been returned with Buckingham's backing the previous year, now dead, and Lord Burghersh preferred to sit for Peterborough. The only other contender was Sir John Sedley, bt. of Aylesford, but by 7 Jan. he had given way to Scott and Hales. Sir Thomas Walsingham II also announced that he would contest the election and so mobilize west Kent, which had no candidates in the field, but his intentions seem not to have been serious. He had his eyes instead on the senior seat at Rochester, which he had occupied continuously since 1614, and was irritated that Buckingham was trying to install his nominee Sir John Smythe III* there at his expense. By declaring his intention to stand for the county, Walsingham hoped to threaten Sandys and so cause Buckingham to withdraw his support for Smythe. In fact, as Digges realized, there was a danger that his tactic would have the opposite effect by splitting the forces opposed to Sandys.

Although without a partner, Sandys was backed by one of Kent's wealthiest residents, Sir John Hayward of Hollingbourne, despite the fact that Hayward was related to Edward Scott. As sheriff at the time of the 1624 parliamentary election, Hayward had allegedly shown partiality towards Sandys. Other prominent Sandys supporters included the brothers-in-law Sir John Clerk of Ford and Sir John Howell of Wrotham. As Hayward and Howell both lived near Maidstone, it is clear that Sandys was not entirely reliant upon east Kent for support. Perhaps Sandys's most important supporter was Hippisley, Buckingham's representative in the county. At first Sandys was concerned that Hippisley was not doing enough for him, and therefore he led him to believe that Digges, the duke's enemy, was planning to stand alongside Archbishop Abbot's steward, Sir Robert Hatton*, whom Buckingham also had 'some cause to distaste'. As Sandys's hoped, Hippisley responded by sending out letters warning of the danger of a Digges/Hatton alliance. It was these same letters that so infuriated Digges and led to his quarrel with Thomas Scott. Hippisley, however, was a busy man and support for Sandys came low on his list of priorities. It was not until eight in the morning on the day before the election that he wrote from Dover warning Buckingham that Sandys might lose and urging him to send to 'those of the Navy' to turn out for Sandys. His missive did not arrive until 10 pm on the following day, by which time it was too late for Buckingham to respond.[42]

Despite the complex manoeuvrings which preceded it, the 1626 election was a relatively quiet affair. Writing to congratulate Edward Scott on his success, Thomas Brett* observed that the election had passed off with 'little noise' and only 'small trouble to the freeholders'.[43] The peacefulness of the proceedings undoubtedly owed much to Sandys who, in contrast with 1624, evidently accepted his defeat and again settled for a seat in Cornwall. The 1626 Parliament was the last in which Sandys was a Member, as he did not stand for re-election in 1628. Instead, he canvassed on behalf of Sir Thomas Finch and Sir Edward Dering for the county seats. Finch, who sought the senior position, owned the impressive Eastwell estate, just north of Ashford. His father had represented the county in 1593 and his mother was in the process of buying the earldom of Winchilsea, whereby he would enjoy the courtesy title Viscount Maidstone. Dering, whose father owned an estate at Pluckley, was Finch's near neighbour and also Buckingham's candidate, for his marriage to Anne Ashburnham linked him to the duke. In the circular he wrote on their behalf, Sandys commended Finch and Dering for 'their soundness in religion, love of their country' and their 'good discretion and moderation'. Sandys had little time for the other candidate in the field, Sir Dudley Digges, who had again decided to try for a county seat. Digges now commanded considerable respect locally, both for his resistance to the Forced Loan and for having been dismissed from the bench in July 1626 at Buckingham's behest. His popularity chiefly threatened Dering. Indeed, at the end of January Sir Nicholas, now Lord Tufton, informed Dering, his former son-in-law, that 'there is no speech but of Sir Dudley Digges'. One week later, and still almost a month before the election, Thomas Scott recorded having heard that 'our knights for Kent are, in effect, elected, Sir Thomas Finch and Sir Dudley Digges; and that Sir Edward Dering and other competitors are set down'.[44] His prediction proved entirely accurate.

[1] C.W. Chalklin, *Seventeenth-Century Kent*, 9; P. Clark, *Eng. Prov. Soc.* 6. [2] Chalklin, 9, 75, 92; J. Thirsk, 'Agriculture in Kent, 1540-1640', in *Early Modern Kent* ed. M. Zell, 84. [3] Chalklin, 10, 73; Thirsk, 89. [4] J. Andrewes, 'Industries in Kent, c.1500-1640', in *Early Modern Kent*, 110, 112, 115; Clark, 300; 'Paulet 1610', f. 3v. [5] *CJ*, i. 345b, 352b-53a, 1031a; Add. 34218, f. 94r-v. [6] *CD 1621*, iv. 96-7; Nicholas, *Procs. 1621*, i. 87. For Kent cloths lying unsold at Blackwell Hall in March 1622, see *CSP Dom.* 1619-23, p. 363. [7] *CJ*, i. 698b. [8] Chalklin, 10, 99; Andrewes, 112; Clark, 4. [9] Chalklin, 75, 81-2. For wheat production at Erith, see *CSP Dom.* 1629-31, p. 357. [10] GL, ms 5174/3, f. 354; *CJ*, i. 715b, 786b, 790a, 792a. The dates of payments in the Bakers' accounts correspond precisely with the progress of the brewhouses bill. There are no other brewing bills in the House at the time. [11] *LJ*, ii. 490a-b, 493a, 494b; *CJ*, i. 356-7, 1033; *SR*, iv. 1146-7. For the medieval and 16th cent. background, see C.J. Smith, *Erith*, 63-4. [12] *CJ*, i. 752a, 762a, 77a, 785b, 820b, 825b, 838a; *Procs. 1625*, pp. 252, 257. For further evidence of continued drainage work, however, see C106/21, 27 Nov. 1624, indenture between Lambard Cooke of North Cray and others. [13] Chalklin, 90. [14] Andrewes, 131-2. [15] D. Hirst, *Representatives of the People?*, 117. [16] Chalklin, 9; Clark, 256-7. [17] *Procs. 1628*, vi. 152. [18] Magdalene Coll. Cambridge, Ferrar Pprs. 12 Jan. 1624, Sandys to John Ferrar. [19] J. Eales, 'Rise of Ideological Pols. in Kent, 1558-1640', in *Early Mod. Kent*, 288, 291. Wotton's immediate successor as ld. lt. was Buckingham, but he surrendered his grant to Lennox after just eight days. [20] Clark, 264-5. [21] P. Clark, 'Thomas Scott', *HJ*, xxi. 10. [22] Bodl., Ballard 61, f. 88v. [23] *Chamberlain Letters* ed. N.E. McClure, i. 516. [24] T.K. Rabb, *Jacobean Gent.* 176. [25] *Chamberlain Letters*, i. 518. [26] Cent. Kent. Stud., U1115/O11, printed, but mistranscribed, in J.R. Scott, *Scott, of Scot's-Hall*, p. xx. [27] *CSP Ven.* 1623-5, pp.182-3; T. Rymer, *Foedera*, vii. pt. 4, p. 90; *APC*, 1623-5, pp. 157-8. [28] *CSP Ire.* 1615-25, pp.454, 456; *CSP Dom.* 1623-5, p. 146. [29] *Chamberlain Letters*, ii. 540. [30] Rabb, 211, 271-2. [31] *Chamberlain Letters*, ii. 540. [32] *Dorothea Scott* ed. G.D. Scull, 133. [33] *Procs. 1625*, pp. 686-7. [34] *Gent. Mag.* lxviii. pt. 1, pp. 116-17. [35] Scott, p. xxvii. [36] The annual fair was held from noon on 30 Apr. until noon on 2 May: W.E. James, *Charters of Maidstone*, 10. [37] Scott, p. xxvii. [38] *Chamberlain Letters*, ii. 615. [39] The petition is printed in Scott, xvii. but without the signatures. For the originals, see Cent. Kent. Stud., U1115/O15/1, 2, 4, 5, 6. [40] Cent. Kent. Stud., U1115/C24, printed but misdated in Scott, xxvi.-xxvii. [41] *Dorothea Scott*, 132-3, 135-43. [42] *Procs. 1626*, iv. 242. [43] Cent. Kent. Stud., U1115/C17/2, printed (but misdated 1627) in Scott, xxix. [44] *Procs. 1628*, vi. 129, 152.

A.D.T.

CANTERBURY

Right of election: in the freemen

Number of voters: c.400-500[1]

23 Feb. 1604	SIR JOHN BOYS, recorder
	MATTHEW HADDE
1614	GEORGE NEWMAN
	SIR WILLIAM LOVELACE
14 Dec. 1620	(SIR) GEORGE NEWMAN
	JOHN FINCH II, recorder
	Sir William Lovelace
	John Latham
5 Feb. 1624[2]	THOMAS DENNE
	THOMAS SCOTT
	Sir William Lovelace
	John Latham
aft. 5 Apr. 1625	JOHN FISHER
	SIR THOMAS WILSFORD
	Sir Henry Wotton*
	(Sir) George Newman
	Thomas Scott
2 Feb. 1626	(SIR) JOHN FINCH II
	JAMES PALMER
	Sir John Wilde
	Thomas Scott
13 Mar. 1628[3]	(SIR) JOHN FINCH II
	THOMAS SCOTT
	James Palmer
	?Sir John Wilde
	?John Fisher

Once the heart of the Anglo-Saxon kingdom of Kent, by the early seventeenth century Canterbury was the unofficial capital of East Kent and a staging post for princes and ambassadors travelling between London and Dover. It also boasted more lawyers than any other part of the county.[4] Successive archbishops of Canterbury preferred to reside at Lambeth, and it was five years before Archbishop Abbot even visited the city.[5] When its recorder asked Charles I in 1625 to elevate the city to a position 'in some sort proportionable' to London's, he echoed the oligarchy's frustration at its loss of importance.[6]

Incorporated under Henry I, Canterbury was granted county status by Edward IV, although its precise boundaries were disputed. In 1609 Canterbury's commissioners for the aid explained that they had not raised as much money as expected 'by reason of some differences which rest touching the bounds between the city and county of Kent'.[7] The city's boundaries had been recently eroded by the earl of Salisbury (Robert Cecil†), whose workmen had dismantled part of the city walls to provide stone for his Thames-side residence, Salisbury House, to the dismay of the citizens.[8] The lack of an agreed boundary had implications for Canterbury's parliamentary representation. In 1604 the recorder, Sir John Boys, who lived just outside the north wall in the former priory of St. Gregory's, assumed he was resident and therefore eligible for election to Parliament. However, uncertainty was expressed at the time, and therefore in about 1611 the corporation paid for an investigation of medieval records at Westminster.[9]

During the mid-1570s Canterbury's ailing economy benefited from an influx of Huguenot refugees. Most were clothworkers, but some wove silk, a craft not previously practised locally.[10] A brief period of prosperity ensued, when many of the city's buildings were repaired.[11] However, an attempt to restore its ancient river-route to the sea was thwarted in 1594 by flash floods which destroyed the works, forcing the city to sell land, pawn its plate and cut official salaries.[12] By the beginning of James's reign the city's finances had been restored, but they were dealt another devastating blow in 1608, when a Canterbury lawyer, John Denne, challenged in Star Chamber the right of all 12 of Canterbury's aldermen to serve as magistrates.[13] Denne was aggrieved that, following the indictment of his servant for murder, the corporation, sensitive of its privileges, had prevented local men from serving on a Westminster jury.[14] The city was subsequently forced to obtain a fresh charter that clarified the position, but the cost, together with that of the lawsuit, plunged it back into debt.[15] The effects of the trade depression of the early 1620s were also felt. More than half Canterbury's Walloon weavers were decayed in 1622, and by 1623 they had stopped paying 'loom money' to the corporation.[16] Severe plague outbreaks in 1605, 1608-9 and 1625 further contributed to the city's economic woes, necessitating the raising of special rates.[17] Not surprisingly, Canterbury's parliamentary representatives were unpaid during this period, although minor costs associated with elections were sometimes met. Ten shillings was paid 'for the indentures of the election of the burgesses of Parliament' in 1604, and in 1614 the city's sheriff, who served as the returning officer, was given 3s. 4d. for the writ of summons.[18]

Despite its perennial difficulties, the city was expected to provide a warm welcome to important visitors. The hospitality lavished in June 1623 on the extraordinary Spanish ambassador, the marquess of Inojosa, was said by Sir Lewis Lewknor* to have been the best he had ever seen in Kent and earned the city a royal commendation. As well as turning out in their scarlet gowns, members of the corporation greeted Inojosa with a musical band and provided a guard of honour, sweetmeats, a banquet and a guided tour of the cathedral. Such liberality may not have been entirely typical, as the corporation was eager to make amends for having arrested Prince Charles and the marquess of Buckingham four months earlier, when they had passed through the city in disguise *en route* to Madrid.[19] On the other hand, in 1613 the king had thanked the corporation for sparing no expense in entertaining Princess Elizabeth and her new husband, the Elector Palatine.[20] In 1625 the city twice played host to Charles I, who travelled to Dover to meet his new bride. According to one observer, Charles found Canterbury to be 'a very Eden or Paradise where nothing was wanting that might serve joy or delight'.[21]

From the 1590s the corporation usually returned at least one member of its standing counsel to Parliament.[22] In 1604 it elected both its recorder, Sir John Boys, and his assistant, Matthew Hadde. Canterbury nevertheless found the absence of its senior legal adviser inconvenient, and at the beginning of the 1604 session it dispatched a messenger to Boys with 'the letters touching the holding of the Lady Day quarter sessions'.[23] Boys, too, was not prepared to remain long at Westminster, returning to sit on the East Kent sewer commission at least three times while Parliament sat.[24] By the 1614 election Boys was dead, and Hadde, his successor as recorder, may have been too unwell to stand.[25] It was not the recorder but his cousin Edward Hadde who drafted a bill for the city for submission to Parliament, the contents of which remain unknown.[26] In the absence of Matthew Hadde, the city's senior seat was filled by Archbishop Abbot's commissary-general, Sir George Newman, a resident who presumably enjoyed the support of the cathedral chapter. The junior place was taken by one of the city's deputy lieutenants, the local landowner Sir William Lovelace, whose deepening financial difficulties perhaps induced him to seek parliamentary privilege as a means of escaping his creditors.

The parliamentary election of December 1620 witnessed the first contest at Canterbury since 1593.[27] Newman and Lovelace stood again, and were joined by the city's recorder, John Finch II, and John Latham, secretary to Kent's new lord lieutenant, the duke of Lennox. The latter was anxious to defend his unpopular alnage and brass farthing patents in the forthcoming Parliament, and nominated Latham by letter on 9 November. Latham, however, was disqualified by statute from serving, as he was neither resident nor a freeman when the writ of summons was issued. Furthermore, the city itself had ruled in 1581, following the controversial election of the outsider Sir George Carey, that nominees must be 'dwellers within the city and free of the same by half a year at the least'.[28] However, Lennox brushed this aside, pointing to the recent proclamation which stated that if boroughs were unable to find men well-informed about their constituencies to serve, then they were 'to make choice of other grave and discreet men'.[29] Unwilling to disappoint Lennox, the corporation made Latham a freeman three days before the election.[30] This outraged the puritan Thomas Scott, recently ejected from the city's Common Council, who characterized Latham in his diary as 'a time-server' and Catholic sympathizer. He also ridiculed Lennox's letter, as it implied that 'not a man in Canterbury knows the state of Canterbury half so well as Jack Latham, a man of mean quality', whose election would further the aims of Lennox, 'on whom he depends'. Despite the urgings of his supporters, Scott refused to stand himself 'because as yet God did not call me unto it',[31] but his views were evidently widely shared, as Latham was rejected in favour of Finch and Newman. During the Parliament the corporation sent Newman a letter regarding 'hospital business at the Parliament'.[32] This probably related to a bill that originated in the Lords on 25 May 1621 but was lost in the Commons in December.[33] Canterbury had several hospitals, including Jesus Hospital, which had been founded by Sir John Boys in the mid-1590s.

It is unclear whether Canterbury's refusal to return Latham was the cause or consequence of its loss of control of the city's militia, which seems to have occurred sometime between September 1620 and September 1621.[34] Since Henry VI's reign, the mayor had been permitted to muster the Canterbury militia, and successive lords lieutenant of Kent had accordingly appointed him one of the city's deputy lieutenants. However, sometime between September 1620 and September 1621 the mayor was omitted from the city's lieutenancy commission, despite having been previously regarded as the 'prime commissioner'. The corporation itself was partly to blame, having neglected to insert a clause in the 1608 charter confirming the mayor's automatic status as a deputy lieutenant. It appealed to Lennox, who replied, probably disingenuously, that he was powerless to act without royal permission. Thereafter Canterbury petitioned James for redress,[35] and dispatched a deputation to the king and Buckingham 'for the continuance of the mayor's authority in martial affairs'.[36] By September 1623 the issue was among a list of items for the king's consideration at Windsor.[37] A second deputation was sent to Buckingham in 1623 or 1624.[38] Canterbury's difficulties were compounded in 1623 when *quo warranto* proceedings were initiated in King's Bench to establish the extent of the city's limits.[39]

Latham was again nominated for election by Lennox in 1624. The corporation, now undoubtedly anxious to recover control over the city's militia and get the action in Kings Bench lifted, therefore campaigned on Latham's behalf 'more than before'.[40] This antagonized not only Thomas Scott but also the Canterbury lawyer Thomas Denne, the brother of the barrister who had earlier initiated Star Chamber proceedings against the corporation. Denne, who ironically had been employed by the corporation to oppose the *quo warranto*, employed 'strong arguments' to get Scott to stand, and he in turn persuaded a reluctant Denne to join him. Scott later described as 'filthy slander' an accusation that he had originally entered the lists as Latham's ally.[41] The ensuing campaign took place against a backdrop of rising religious tensions in the city. Six days before the election, a Canterbury yeoman named Simon Penny was arraigned before the mayor at the insistence of Sir William Lovelace, whose continuing financial difficulties had led him to stand again. Penny, who had been canvassing on behalf of Scott and Denne, was accused of spreading the story that Lovelace 'did cross himself before the French or Spanish ambassador', and of telling one voter 'that many of the city had popes in their bellies, and he did not know but the Captain [Lovelace] might have one in his belly'. Shortly after the election, a Lovelace supporter told the mayor that Sir Edwin Sandys* had warned Penny against voting for Lovelace because he was 'a dangerous man'.[42]

Following the election Scott claimed that he and Denne obtained 'all the lawful voices and Latham not one'. This was probably an exaggeration, but even the aldermen were not unanimously behind Latham, for according to Scott three or four of them 'did like honest men'. Those who did support Latham, who seems not to have attended the hustings in person, were evidently outnumbered and not entitled to vote.[43] Lovelace, unmentioned by Scott, may have withdrawn. Latham's supporters among the aldermen put a brave face on their candidate's defeat, spending 48s. 4d. 'at Mr. Mayor's' immediately after 'the election of the burgesses' and giving a further 30s. 'to Mr. Latham's man towards the defraying of his charges'.[44]

Lennox's reaction to his secretary's second defeat is unknown, but it was immaterial, as he died 11 days later. The triumphant Scott later complained that his presence at Westminster cost him £100 'and gained me much ill will and little thanks, even from them that laboured for me'.[45]

Lennox's successor as lord lieutenant was the earl of Montgomery (Sir Philip Herbert*), who in place of Capt. Latham (presumably a kinsman of Lennox's former secretary) appointed Capt. John Fisher as Canterbury's muster-master. In September 1624 Fisher was fêted by the mayor and aldermen, who gave him a gratuity of £4 and spent 59s. on entertaining him at the mayor's house.[46] Expectations were clearly high that Fisher would intercede with Montgomery to restore mayoral authority over the militia, and at the general election of 1625 he was the corporation's candidate for the borough's senior parliamentary seat. However, although he was a freeman, his lack of a fixed address meant that his residency was questionable. Indeed, Thomas Scott disparaged him as 'John Fisher the Rover'.[47] The corporation's choice for the second seat was the local landowner Sir Thomas Wilsford. However, Wilsford was clearly a non-resident, and was sworn a freeman only three days after the writ of summons was issued. According to Scott, his nomination infuriated many of the city's voters, who concluded that if Wilsford were permitted to stand 'they might elect as well an unfree man as a mock freeman and non-resident'. Consequently, several of them turned to the non-resident and non-freeman Sir Henry Wotton*. The half-brother of Edward, Lord Wotton, high steward of the mayoral court,[48] Wotton took his candidacy seriously, spending 'almost £50 in good drink for his followers'.[49] Others turned to the former recorder, (Sir) John Finch II, 'though not many, because of his non-residence and [Court] dependency'. Sir George Newman also put his name forward again, as did Thomas Scott at his supporters' behest.[50]

The corporation's candidates triumphed at the 1625 election. However, according to Scott, victory was obtained only by ignoring genuine voters:

> I myself was not there. If I had [been], many tell me, Sir Thomas Wilsford's unlawful voices would not have been so many as my lawful voices were. And there were some that in my behalf demanded the poll. The certain truth is, Sir George Newman and myself were lawfully chosen; but Mr. Jack Fisher (for he was the first) and Sir Thomas Wilsford unduly returned.

This was Scott's first defeat, and he may have wanted to convince both himself and others that his opponents had cheated. Had he genuinely believed it he would undoubtedly have complained to Parliament, but instead he shrugged off his defeat, recording in his diary that he had not seriously wished to serve again anyway, but had only intended 'to lend my name, as it were, unto those honest men that desired to maintain their liberty by this appeal'.[51]

The corporation's successful support of Fisher did not resolve the question of the mayor's authority over the militia, nor were the *quo warranto* proceedings brought to a successful conclusion. Indeed, as late as March 1627 Thomas Denne was paid £5 to enter a rejoinder in King's Bench.[52] Consequently, when it was announced that a new Parliament would meet in 1626 the corporation continued to cultivate Montgomery. During the election campaign the mayor told one man that he had high hopes of obtaining Montgomery's favour for the city, of which 'we have great need'.[53] On this occasion Montgomery nominated his servant James Palmer rather than Fisher, who may have stood on his own account. For the second seat the corporation decided to back (Sir) John Finch II, now a rising star at Court. At the previous election many voters had resented Finch's 'dependency', but this had now changed. The son of the puritan Sir Henry Finch*, he undoubtedly appealed to Canterbury's godly community, and his graceful speeches to the king on behalf of the city in 1625 probably increased his standing.

If the corporation's support for Finch was uncontroversial, its decision to back Palmer was deeply unpopular. Palmer lived in Buckinghamshire, and was virtually unknown in Canterbury. According to Scott, even some of his supporters were unsure who he was. 'Some say they did choose the heir of the house, being Sir Thomas Palmer†; others one Mr. Palber, or to that effect, they cannot tell whom'.[54] Those opposed to Palmer persuaded Sir John Wilde to stand against him. Wilde was a resident, and had been recommended to the duke of Lennox by two of Kent's deputy lieutenants as a possible successor to Sir William Lovelace as captain of the Canterbury militia. However, he was 'greatly hated' by many on the corporation as a friend or servant of Archbishop Abbot,[55] who had evidently been behind a commission to examine the city's alleged misappropriation of hospital funds in May 1625, to which Wilde had been named.[56] The main obstacle to Wilde's standing was that he was not a freeman. This was also true of Palmer, but whereas he was quickly sworn, Wilde's application for admission was turned down on the grounds that 'he sought it out of time, after the writ

was come forth'.[57] Many of Wilde's supporters therefore turned to Scott,[58] as did Wilde himself, who refused to accept that he was debarred from standing. On 28 Jan. he proposed a pact, but Scott replied that he still hoped that Wilde would 'take off the burden from my shoulders'. However, on 29 Jan., with just four days remaining, he announced his candidacy 'if the commons do not fall off'. Although he could not bring himself to break electoral law and vote for his new ally, he urged his followers to support Wilde, who, though not a freeman, was at least concerned for the city's welfare.[59] That same day, a Sunday, Scott spoke to two of the oldest aldermen in church. He had heard that the sheriff, an ally of the aldermen, would attempt to rig the election by refusing a poll, and warned that there would be trouble if this happened. He also remonstrated against the aldermen's refusal to make Wilde a freeman, and pointed out that Wilde 'by my l[ord] of Canterbury's means' could 'do us more good than Mr. Palmer can'. Wilde's rejection, he claimed, was done 'to affront my lord of Canterbury'. Far from denying these accusations both aldermen nervously agreed, 'especially Mr. Claggett; and Mr. Watmer blushing, and with a dejected countenance, brake out into these words, "Are we not in a hard case, Mr. Scott, that [we] must do such things?"'.[60] The sermon which followed was delivered by St. Andrew's rector, Edward Aldey, one of Wilde's supporters, who took as his theme the text: 'Awake thou that sleepest and arise from the dead'.[61] After the service Scott collared the town clerk, Ralph Groves, 'who can do much with the most and greatest citizens', and warned him that one of the city's freemen, Capt. Parker, had a letter stating that Parliament would punish the sheriff if he transgressed, which 'troubled Groves not a little'.[62] Despite his candidacy, Scott told Groves that he 'no more desired to be a Parliament citizen than to be a constable or churchwarden', and in a letter to his cousin Edward Scott* he protested that, 'if I may honestly avoid it, assuredly I will, for my health and wealth's sake'. Indeed, he offered to withdraw if two of the aldermen themselves stood, 'whether they were willing or not'.[63] Despite his contempt for the city's magistrates, Scott considered it a burden of civic office that they should seek election themselves.

Tuesday 1 February witnessed a flurry of activity, as both sides feverishly tried to gauge their strength. Wilde wrote to Scott: 'You may soon see what is like to be the success; and I desire you to be plain and real unto me in your opinion therein – George shall attend your commands, by whom be pleased to advertise me what likelihood will be of my prevailing'. Scott, however, was as much in the dark as Wilde, and told his cousin 'how it will go I cannot divine'.[64] He arranged instead to meet Wilde and several key supporters at 11 am to cement their alliance and plan tactics. On the way he encountered the city chamberlain and alderman Watson, from whom he learned that Finch, who had recently been elected dean of the Chapel at Gray's Inn, was unlikely to attend in person. Scott thereupon expressed his regret, saying that Finch's presence would have prevented the sheriff from refusing the poll. The chamberlain and Watson accused Scott of spreading the rumour that Finch had withdrawn, a charge dismissed by Scott in his diary as 'needless here to be rehearsed'. After this heated exchange, Scott met Wilde, who pledged his supporters to Scott for the first seat. In return Scott promised that his side would back Wilde in the second round.[65]

When news of this agreement reached the aldermen they were thrown into a panic. According to Scott, they laboured until nearly midnight, 'entreating, persuading, threatening' anyone suspected of supporting Scott and Wilde. Richard White, who pretended to be out when the mayor called at his house, was summoned to the *White Hart* and told that had it not been for the aldermen he would have been pressed for military service, 'and they may again do you the like friendship'.[66] Thomas Curle, victualler of the *Black Boy*, was warned that he risked losing his licence or his supply of beer (six of the aldermen were brewers). Other victuallers were instructed to use their power to give credit to put pressure on their customers. Control over the drink trade may have provided the aldermen with their most potent weapon.[67] Smear tactics were also employed, as Scott was accused of switching his support from Latham to Denne in 1624, and of not paying his taxes. This latter charge was not entirely without foundation, as Scott had not fully paid his contribution to the sick rate levied in 1625, but as Thomas Harrison, the former churchwarden of St. Alphege and a Scott supporter, pointed out, this was because he had yet been asked to pay.[68] Some of Scott's supporters, like Harrison stood firm against the aldermen, but others, such as Robert Brett, succumbed to pressure. The hatter John Lee was among those who resisted the aldermen. Summoned to the mayor's house, Lee declared that Wilde was as eligible as Palmer, as neither were freemen when the writs of summons were issued. 'Oh, I know from whom you had this', interjected the town clerk, 'you had it from Mr. Scott'. Lee responded that this was partly true, but he had heard the same claim maintained by 'others which have often times been Parliament-men', meaning, according to Scott, Sir Edwin Sandys.[69] Many of Scott's and Wilde's supporters may have

been long-standing opponents of the aldermen, for an exasperated mayor told Lee that 'there is a company of you that do always oppose the government of the city and the magistrates'.[70] An essential feature of this group of malcontents may have been a common religious outlook. Among the most active members of the Scott/Wilde faction in 1626 was Edward Aldey, rector of St. Andrew's, who owed his benefice to Archbishop Abbot.[71] Another was Richard Inge, the puritan curate of Wingham, while Scott was a self-confessed puritan.[72]

When the election was held on 2 Feb., the sheriff commenced proceedings by reading out Montgomery's letter nominating Palmer. It was not unusual for sheriffs to nominate a corporation's preferred candidates on the hustings, but the sheriff's decision to read the earl's letter before the writ was described by Scott as 'a strange and a vile insolency'.[73] The sheriff then refused to allow a poll, but instead declared Palmer and Finch elected by acclamation. Scott and his supporters were outraged, and subsequently petitioned the Commons to order a fresh election.[74] However, the committee for privileges failed to make a ruling before Parliament was dissolved. Ironically, the sheriff's refusal to permit a poll was probably unnecessary. As Scott's supporter Richard White observed, 'many that gave a softly voice for us, so as the aldermen did not perceive them', would not have dared oppose Palmer and Finch had they been required to vote openly, 'though they had formerly whispered, as it were, a Scott'.[75]

Canterbury's rulers had now returned Montgomery's candidates twice running, and consequently it was not long before the city reaped the benefit. Writing in February 1628, Scott lamented that Canterbury was now 'monstrously beholden' to John Fisher for having 'delivered us from the *quo warranto*, the commission of charitable uses, Sir John Wilde his being our captain, and the like dangers'.[76] The announcement of fresh parliamentary elections early in 1628 presented the city's aldermen with an opportunity to show their gratitude for these favours. Although Fisher had now left Montgomery's employment, they lost no time in campaigning for him with 'might and main'.[77] Few shared their enthusiasm. Popularly regarded as a 'tobacconist, swearer, scoffer, cheater and lecher',[78] Fisher offended Canterbury's puritans, who described him to his face as 'a great blasphemer'.[79] The aldermen therefore resorted to coercion again, 'so as many, for very fear, promise for him, though they mutter at it'. However, as in 1626, several freemen refused to be intimidated and spoke their mind plainly before the mayor, 'so as his ears glow at it and his breech twattles'.[80] One blunt speaker was the turner John Drought, 'an honest and stout fellow' to Scott but a puritan schismatic to the aldermen. Summoned for a dressing down, Drought accused the mayor of exceeding his authority: 'You ought not thus to send for freemen, except for the king's service'. When the mayor denied trying to force him to change his vote, Drought, being neither an alehousekeeper nor a borrower of civic funds, agreed, 'for you cannot, because I fear you not, nor look for any benefit from you'.[81]

The aldermen's enthusiasm for Fisher contrasted with their response to James Palmer's candidacy. Many of them, including the chamberlain, Avery Sabine, were disappointed with Palmer's performance in the 1626 Parliament, perceiving that he had been more interested in Court politics than the city's affairs. However, on receiving a letter from Montgomery urging them to support Palmer they reluctantly began canvassing for him.[82] Sir John Wilde also announced his intention to stand, as did (Sir) John Finch II. Since the last election, Finch had become the queen's attorney-general and an associate of the duke of Buckingham. However, Henrietta Maria was Catholic and the duke was now regarded as 'the greatest enemy to the puritans in the world'.[83] Consequently news of Finch's candidacy was widely greeted with distaste, not merely among ordinary freemen but also among the aldermen. The aldermanic leader of the anti-puritan faction, Avery Sabine, was Finch's implacable opponent and may still have suspected Finch on religious grounds. As mayor of Canterbury in 1619, Sabine had engineered Finch's brief dismissal from the city's recordership.[84] However, as Finch had been chosen to serve as Speaker of the Commons by Buckingham and the king, and Montgomery was the duke's ally, the aldermen dared not openly oppose Finch, realizing that they might soon receive a letter from Montgomery requiring them to support him.[85]

Thomas Scott shared the general dislike of Finch, considering him an 'arrant timeserver', but he also regarded him as the least unattractive of all the candidates. Fisher, though a freeman, was non-resident, while Wilde, though resident, remained a non-freeman. Scott now regretted his previous alliance with Wilde, and when asked whether he had forged a new pact with him answered that he had not and denied that he 'ever would'.[86] The least acceptable candidate to Scott was Palmer, who was not only non-resident but had taken his oath as a freeman outside the city, rendering it void in his eyes. Only Finch, a freeman

since 1617 whose principal dwelling during vacations was his house in Christ Church, Canterbury, could claim to fulfil the legal requirements of a parliamentary candidate. Finch's religious views were also agreeable, for not long since Finch had spoken 'very earnestly against the Arminians at the dean's own table'. As Scott considered anti-Arminianism 'the right strike of a rank puritan, as now puritans everywhere are defined', it followed that Finch was a puritan. Scott seems to have been crucial in persuading many of his fellow voters of Finch's continued godly leanings. When the mayor derided Finch's puritan credentials, the Scott supporter John Drought retorted that several of Finch's family had been called puritans, including one who had written a 'puritannical book' which had been condemned by Archbishop Bancroft as 'that scurrilous libel'.[87]

Scott would have preferred not to stand himself, and tried to persuade alderman James Master, captain of the city's militia, to put his name forward instead. However, he was induced to do so by 'divers preachers and citizens'.[88] Among them, perhaps, was the puritan lecturer of St. Alphege, Herbert Palmer, whom Scott had helped to install in 1625.[89] Herbert was the nephew of Scott's rival, James Palmer, but he was also distantly related to Scott. On receiving a letter from his uncle seeking his support, Herbert advised him to seek election elsewhere as the ordinary freemen were 'much against him'.[90] Sabine, Masters and their supporters were determined to ensure the return of their champion Fisher and at first planned to hold the election at the 'county' court on 14 February. However, when they realized they would lose Sabine announced that they had always intended to hold the election the following week. In fact the proceedings were postponed until 13 Mar. when, despite refusing a poll, the Sabinists were defeated by Scott and Finch.[91]

The aldermen exacted a swift revenge for their defeat. A few weeks after the election, four companies of Sir Pierce Crosby's Irish regiment were billeted on the city's inhabitants until further notice.[92] According to Scott, who received a stream of visitors from Canterbury at Westminster, his supporters suffered most from billeting, whereas 'others that were of my lord of Montgomery's faction were gently dealt with, or not at all'. Among those who joined Scott in London was his wife, Mary, who had fled after 'two lusty popish Irish soldiers' forced entry to their home. Outraged at her treatment, Scott wrote to the aldermen that billeting was 'against the liberty of a free Englishman and gentleman and of a Parliament-man'.[93] Scott subsequently spearheaded the opposition to billeting in Canterbury, encouraging others to follow his example in refusing to contribute towards its cost, but the soldiers were not withdrawn until the end of July.[94]

was probably the anti-Puritan Isaac Bargrave, dean of Canterbury: Clark, *Eng. Prov. Soc.* 326. [88] Ibid. 129, 132. [89] Ibid. 136; Clark, 'Thomas Scott', 5. [90] Ibid. 134-5. [91] *Procs. 1628*, vi. 133, 136. [92] *APC*, 1627-8, p. 370. [93] Clark, 'Thomas Scott', 21. [94] *CSP Dom.* 1628-9, pp. 78, 86, 93, 117-18, 145, 166, 197, 21, 279; *APC*, 1627-8, pp. 439-40; 1628-9, pp. 16, 29, 38-9, 57.

A.D.T.

[1] P. Clark, 'Thomas Scott and the Growth of Urban Opposition to the Early Stuart regime', *HJ*, xxi. 14. [2] Canterbury Cathedral Archives, CC/FA/23, f. 200v. [3] *Procs. 1628*, vi. 133. [4] P. Clark, *Eng. Prov. Soc.* 275, 287. [5] *CSP Dom.* 1611-18, p. 301. [6] Sloane 1455, f. 3v. [7] SP14/45/117. [8] *CSP Dom.* 1603-10, pp. 375, 450-2, 456, 458; C54/1869. [9] K.M.E. Murray, *Const. Hist. of Cinque Ports*, 99; CC/FA/22(1), f. 70. [10] F.W. Cross, *Hist. of Walloon Church at Canterbury*, 184. [11] STAC 8/115/14. [12] C21/C25/8; C3/265/51; Clark, *Eng. Prov. Soc.* 246-7. [13] STAC 8/115/14. [14] Canterbury Cathedral Archives, CC/FA/21, ff. 240v, 253; *HMC Hatfield*, xviii. 300. [15] C.R. Bunce, *A Translation of Several Charters of Canterbury* (1791), p. 171; Canterbury Cathedral Archives, CC/FA/21, f. 244v. The charter cost £379 13s. 4d.; ibid. ff. 241v-2. [16] F.W. Cross, *Hist. of Walloon and Huguenot Church at Canterbury*, 89, 187; STAC 8/115/14. [17] Canterbury Cathedral Archives CC/B/A/Q/1, 16; U66, ff. 23v-4. [18] Canterbury Cathedral Archives, CC/FA/21, f. 78v; CC/FA/22(1), f. 153. [19] *CSP Dom.* 1619-23, pp. 495-6, 597 609, 614; Canterbury Cathedral Archives, CC/FA/23, f. 150v. [20] Canterbury Cathedral Archives, CC/Woodruff/LII/25. [21] Clark, 'Thomas Scott', 12. [22] *HP Commons, 1558-1603*, sub CANTERBURY. [23] Canterbury Cathedral Archives, CC/FA/21, f. 78v. [24] Cent. Kent. Stud. S/EK/SO2, unfol. entries of 13 Apr. and 31 May 1604, and 27 May 1607. [25] *Cal. of Assize Recs. Kent Indictments, Jas. I* ed. J.S. Cockburn, 121-2; *LI Black Bks.* ii. 178. [26] Canterbury Cathedral Archives, CC/FA/22(1), f. 153. Edward Hadde's clerk was paid an additional 3s. 4d. for making a copy: ibid. f. 153v. [27] Clark, *Eng. Prov. Soc.* 253-4. [28] *HP Commons, 1558-1603*, sub CANTERBURY. [29] Cent. Kent. Stud. U951/Z17/2, unfol. item 14. [30] Canterbury Cathedral Archives, CC/FA/23, f. 7v. [31] Cent. Kent. Stud. U951/Z17/2, unfol. item 14. [32] Canterbury Cathedral Archives, CC/FA/23, f. 34. [33] HLRO, main pprs. (parchment collection), box 2B; *CJ*, i. 658b. [34] A payment of £5 was made to Latham and his servant on the city's account for that period 'for procuring and bringing down the commission for the muster': Canterbury Cathedral Archives, CC/FA/23, f. 34v. [35] Canterbury Cathedral Archives, CC/Woodruff/LII/21. [36] Canterbury Cathedral Archives, CC/FA/23, f. 151v. [37] *HMC Cowper*, i. 148. [38] Canterbury Cathedral Archives, CC/FA/23, f. 199. [39] Ibid. ff. 150r-v, 200v, 250v; *Reps. of Henry Rolle in K.B.* [40] Canterbury Cathedral Archives, U66, f. 32r-v. [41] Ibid. f. 25r-v. [42] SP14/158/67. [43] Canterbury Cathedral Archives, U66, ff. 3v-4. [44] Canterbury Cathedral Archives, CC/FA/23, f. 200v. [45] Canterbury Cathedral Archives, U66, f. 22. [46] Canterbury Cathedral Archives, CC/FA/23, f. 204. [47] Canterbury Cathedral Archives, U66, f. 51. [48] Ibid. f. 4v. For Lord Wotton's position as steward of the Mayor's Ct. see C2/Chas.I/H63/60. [49] *Chamberlain Letters* ed. N.E. McClure, ii. 615. [50] Canterbury Cathedral Archives, U66, f. 4r-v. [51] Ibid. f. 4v. [52] Canterbury Cathedral Archives, CC/FA/23, f. 337v. [53] Canterbury Cathedral Archives, U66, f. 26v. [54] Ibid. f. 33. [55] Add. 34176, f. 48; Canterbury Cathedral Archives, U66, ff. 5, 19v-20. [56] C93/10/18; Clark, 'Thomas Scott', 13. [57] Canterbury Cathedral Archives, U66, ff. 13, 14r-v. [58] Ibid., f. 13v. [59] Ibid. ff. 19v, 21r-v. [60] Ibid. f. 18r-v. [61] Clark, 'Thomas Scott', 14. [62] Canterbury Cathedral Archives, U66, ff. 16r-v, 17v. [63] Ibid. ff. 21v-2. [64] Ibid. f. 22r-v. [65] Ibid. ff. 22v-3v. [66] Ibid. ff. 23v, 26v-7. [67] Clark, 'Thomas Scott', 15. [68] Canterbury Cathedral Archives, U66, ff. 23v-4. [69] Ibid. ff. 26r-v, 28. [70] Ibid. f. 26. [71] PRO, Institution Bks. ser. A, v. f. 6. [72] Clark, 'Thomas Scott', 14. [73] *Procs. 1628*, vi. 130. [74] Clark, 'Thomas Scott', 15. [75] Canterbury Cathedral Archives, U66, f. 28. [76] *Procs. 1628*, vi. 130, 135. [77] Ibid. 129. [78] Ibid. 135. [79] Cent. Kent. Stud. U951/Z17/2. [80] *Procs. 1628*, vi. 129-30. [81] Cent. Kent. Stud. U951/Z17/2. [82] *Procs. 1628*, vi. 135. [83] Ibid. 136. [84] Clark, 'Thomas Scott', 20; Eg. 2584, f. 100. [85] Ibid. 129-30. [86] *Procs. 1628*, vi. 129, 131. [87] Ibid. 136. The dean

MAIDSTONE

Right of election: in the freemen

Number of voters: unknown

9 Mar. 1604	SIR FRANCIS FANE
	LAURENCE WASHINGTON
c. Mar. 1614	SIR FRANCIS FANE
	SIR JOHN SCOTT
13 Dec. 1620	SIR FRANCIS FANE
	SIR FRANCIS BARNHAM
28 Jan. 1624	SIR GEORGE FANE
	SIR FRANCIS BARNHAM
7 May 1625	EDWARD MAPLESDEN
	THOMAS STANLEY
	?Sir Edwin Sandys*
16 Jan. 1626	SIR GEORGE FANE
	SIR FRANCIS BARNHAM
5 Mar. 1628	SIR GEORGE FANE
	SIR FRANCIS BARNHAM

Though challenged for pre-eminence in east Kent by Canterbury,[1] Maidstone remained the official county town of Kent. A royal manor, it was also the county's principal market town,[2] and both quarter sessions and parliamentary elections were held at nearby Penenden Heath. Between 1422 and 1549 it was governed by a portreeve and 24 citizens; thereafter its affairs were controlled by a corporation comprising all the freemen, including 12 jurats, one of whom was annually elected mayor.[3] In 1559 the town obtained the right to return two burgesses to Parliament.[4] A further charter granted in December 1604 primarily aimed to remove 'certain doubts, questions and ambiguities' concerning the legal validity of the 1549 incorporation.[5] However, in 1610 the duke of Lennox, as chairman of the county bench, ordered the west Kent quarter sessions to meet at Rochester, as it was unclear from the 1604 charter whether the county's magistrates had authority to sit at Maidstone. His decision caused such uproar that the quarter sessions soon reverted to Maidstone, although Rochester continued to host occasional meetings.[6]

Lennox was not alone in exposing the weaknesses of the 1604 charter. As early as 1605 the corporation tacitly admitted its shortcomings when it limited the number of freemen sitting at 'burghmotes' to 40. Senior corporation members had become concerned that many of those who attended meetings were 'of the meanest and unfittest' sort, but their unilateral creation of a select band of freemen angered the commonalty, and in 1610 the number eligible to attend was raised to 50.[7] A further inadequacy of the 1604 charter was exposed in 1619, when some of the town's gentry who were not freemen instituted *quo warranto* proceedings after the corporation attempted to force them to undertake civic office. So determined was the corporation to win this dispute, however, that it sold the lead from its waterpipes to pay the legal costs, borrowed £160 to pay for a fresh charter, and bestowed £200 on the Howard crony Sir John Townsend* to intervene on their behalf.[8] The new charter, granted in July 1619, authorized the appointment of non-freemen as jurats provided they were inhabitants, but many of the town's gentry not only continued to refuse to serve but declined to fine as well.[9] The 1619 charter also angered the magistrates of west Kent, as it prevented them from exercising their authority in the town. Faced with the renewed threat that the sessions would be shifted to Rochester, the corporation capitulated, obtaining a supplementary charter in 1621.[10]

Maidstone's economy was heavily dependent upon the weaving industry, which had been introduced to the town in the 1570s by Dutch refugees and replaced the cloth trade, which had virtually disappeared owing to depression and increased competition from London. Flax grown in mid-Kent was dressed by the town's weavers, who turned it into thread.[11] In 1629 the corporation acknowledged that 'threadtwisting' had 'grown to be a great trade' in the town, and by 1634 as many as 50 families may have been thus employed.[12] Maidstone also boasted the second largest grain market in Kent, after Gravesend. Grain, and a ready supply of local hops and fresh water, provided the essential ingredients for a thriving brewing industry, and during the Jacobean period Maidstone produced numerous wholesale brewers, including Thomas Stanley, who represented the town in Parliament in 1625.[13] The town also benefited from a plentiful supply of fuller's earth, used to clean cloth, at nearby Boxley. During the 1590s the Medway was 'continually frequented with hoys, lighters and other boats' employed in shipping away this valuable

commodity. At least one Maidstone inhabitant was closely connected with the Boxley mine.[14]

Maidstone was the scene of an extraordinary public protest against unparliamentary taxation on 28 Sept. 1614. At a gathering of the local gentry to discuss the king's request for a benevolence, Josias Nichols, a minister formerly deprived for nonconformity, proposed that a petition be drafted to know the reason for the levy, as 'it had been the ancient custom of this land to supply the wants of their kings by Parliament, which they held to be the freehold of the subject'. For his impudence, Nichols, who also remarked upon 'the danger of this precedent',[15] was arraigned before the Council and detained for several months.[16] The impact of Nichols's protest is difficult to gauge, but Maidstone, which had previously resolved to contribute not less than £100 'if it may conveniently be received', collected only £56, substantially less than the £70 6s. contributed to the Benevolence of 1622 or the £81 10s. 8d. paid for a single subsidy in 1625.[17]

Although Maidstone's first parliamentary representatives were its recorder and ex-recorder, it generally returned members of the local gentry. Sir Francis Fane (1604, 1614, 1621) was seated at Mereworth Castle, seven miles from Maidstone, while his brother Sir George (1624, 1626, 1628), resided five miles south-west of the town at Hunton. Sir Francis Barnham (1621, 1624, 1626, 1628) lived at Boughton Monchelsea, four miles away, and also owned property in the town, as did Laurence Washington (1604). Sir John Scott (1614) dwelt at Nettlestead, five miles south of Maidstone, and was related to Washington by marriage. Only two Maidstone Members were not drawn from the gentry: the townsmen Edward Maplesden and Thomas Stanley, both of whom sat in 1625. The decision to return Maplesden and Stanley was taken by the mayor, Ambrose Beale, who resented the former Member Sir Francis Barnham because, as a deputy lieutenant, Barnham had tried to force Beale to attend musters or provide arms. Beale's revenge was calculated: he warned Sir George Fane that he would thwart Barnham at the hustings 'if there were but ten voices' against him, and apologized that this meant that Fane himself would not be re-elected. Fane objected to being wounded 'through the sides of my friend', and cautioned Beale that 'in seeking thus unduly to right himself, he did not disadvantage himself and be required to amend his indenture by the kneeling at the bar [of the House of Commons]'. Beale, however, 'cared not what he suffered'.[18] His determination created an opening for Sir Edwin Sandys, who had been defeated on 2 May at the county election, a humiliation witnessed by 'a great multitude of the townsmen of the town of Maidstone'.[19] The very next day Sandys qualified himself for the borough's forthcoming parliamentary election by getting himself sworn a freeman in the recorder's lodgings.[20] However, on 4 May he was returned for Penryn, and consequently may not have stood at Maidstone, which held its election on 7 May in the school house. There Beale nominated Maplesden and Stanley, who were returned on an unsigned indenture.[21] Fane subsequently complained to the committee for privileges, but owing to the shortness of the 1625 Parliament no action was taken against Beale. However, in 1626 Barnham exacted his revenge by having Beale imprisoned for the contempt he had shown towards his militia duties.[22]

Maidstone appears to have left its parliamentary representatives free to pursue their own interests in the Commons. Though Sir George Fane was named to the committee for the Medway navigation bill in 1628,[23] there is little evidence that Maidstone's corporation took much notice of this measure, as the Medway was theoretically already navigable as far as Yalding. Fane's interest in this bill, which was probably sponsored by the government as it offered a cheaper and quicker way of transporting iron and timber to the Chatham naval yard, was altogether more personal, as he stood to gain from an improved transport system for his timber if the river between Tonbridge and Yalding was improved.[24]

[1] P. Clark, *Eng. Prov. Soc.* 311. [2] LR2/219, f. 63; P. Clark and L. Murfin, *Hist. Maidstone*, 44. [3] J.M. Russell, *Hist. Maidstone*, 184. [4] *Maidstone Recs.* i, 8-9. [5] Ibid. 10. The charter is mis-dated 1603 by the compiler, an error reproduced in W. Roberts James, *Charters of Maidstone*, 66-86. [6] Clark, 342, 470-1. [7] *Maidstone Recs.* 60, 65. [8] Ibid. 74; *CD 1621*, v. 320. [9] Ibid. 10, 78. One even quit his lodging in protest: *APC*, 1623-5, pp. 21, 228, 233. [10] Clark and Murfin, 58-9; Cent. Kent. Stud. U274/01. [11] Clark, 301. [12] *Maidstone Recs.* 97; W. Newton, *Hist. and Antiqs. of Maidstone* (1741), pp. 100-1; Clark and Murfin, 44-5, 48. [13] Clark and Murfin, 45, 48. [14] Ibid. 47; *APC*, 1621-3, p. 313. The mine was famous in the mid-18th cent.: Newton, 103. Shipments of fuller's earth leaving Rochester in the early 17th cent. probably originated at Boxley: E190/648/11, unfol.; 190/649/20, unfol. [15] Staffs. RO, D593/S/14/60/1; *Oxford DNB sub* Josias Nichols. [16] Add. 34218, f. 148v; *APC*, 1613-14, p. 576; 1614-15, p. 52. [17] E351/1950, unfol.; SP14/156/15; E179/127/601, m. 5. [18] Surr. Hist. Cent. LM cor.4/51. [19] J.R. Scott, *Scott, of Scot's Hall*, p. xxvii. [20] *Maidstone Recs.* 85. [21] Ibid. 86; C219/39/119. [22] *APC*, 1625-6, pp. 418, 433, 448-9. [23] *CJ*, i. 895b. [24] C.W. Chalklin, 'Navigation Schemes on the Upper Medway', *Jnl. of Transport Hist.* v. 110-11.

A.D.T.

QUEENBOROUGH

Right of election: in the freemen

Number of voters: 25 in 1620[1]

20 Feb. 1604	SIR MICHAEL SONDES
	SIR EDWARD STAFFORD
21 Oct. 1605	RICHARD WRIGHT *vice*
	Stafford, deceased
	Sir John Brooke*
	Sir Moyle Finch†
31 Mar. 1614[2]	ROGER PALMER
	ROBERT HATTON
18 Dec. 1620	JAMES PALMER
	WILLIAM FROWDE
	Richard Hadsor
23 Jan. 1624	ROGER PALMER
	ROBERT POLEY
9 May 1625	SIR EDWARD HALES, (bt.)
	ROGER PALMER
	Robert Poley
23 Jan. 1626[3]	ROGER PALMER
	ROBERT POLEY
5 Mar. 1628[4]	(SIR) ROGER PALMER
	SIR JOHN HALES

Situated on the western side of the Isle of Sheppey, Queenborough was named after Philippa of Hainault, Edward III's consort, and received its first charter in 1368, which entrusted its government to a mayor, two bailiffs, and an unspecified number of freemen.[5] It owed this privilege to its castle, which however failed to generate any significant urban growth. Indeed, shortly before its enfranchisement in 1571 it consisted of only 23 inhabited houses.[6] Consequently, the constable of the castle assumed the right to nominate one of the Members. The remaining seat was, before 1604, in the gift of Lord Cobham, whose principal residence lay a few miles away. However, the fall in 1603 of the 11th Lord Cobham (Henry Brooke *alias* Cobham) meant that at the general election of 1604 the disposal of both seats fell to Sir Edward Hoby*, who had held the constableship since 1597. His choice for the senior place lighted upon Sir Michael Sondes, who lived at nearby Throwley and had represented the borough four times previously. Sondes was evidently well acquainted with Hoby, having christened one of his sons after him.[7] The second seat was bestowed upon Sir Edward Stafford who, like Hoby's father, had served as ambassador to France. Although not from Kent himself, Stafford was related by marriage to Sir John Scott*.

When Stafford died early in 1605, Hoby expressed embarrassment at the multiplicity of applications for his goodwill in the by-election; from Stafford's brother John[†], from the courtiers Sir John Brooke* and Sir William Uvedale*, and from 'sundry Kentish gentlemen, among whom Sir Moyle Finch[†] was most importunate, no whit doubting to have it without me, for so he replied unto myself'.[8] Brooke, a kinsman of Lord Cobham, must have seemed a strong candidate, as he stood to inherit an extensive Kentish estate if Cobham's attainder could be reversed. Hoby promised him 'all the kindness I could show, which has bred no small dislike towards me' among the others. In the event, however, the successful candidate was a Londoner, Richard Wright, described as 'Mr. Wright the merchant',[9] though he was by now more of an administrator and financier. Wright required a seat in Parliament to defend the Muscovy Company from attack by the free trade lobby, and may have known Hoby through the latter's close friend Sir George Carew, or as a result of a feast at Merchant Taylors' Hall, where Wright was the clerk, which Hoby had helped to organize the previous year. However, Wright also had connections in north Kent, through his daughter's marriage to Reginald Barker of Chatham. He also had a business association with Sir Philip Herbert*, who at his marriage early in 1605 obtained from the King the lease of Shurland manor. Situated near Queenborough, Shurland had previously been let to Hoby, who resented its loss.

Before the next election Herbert, now earl of Montgomery, strengthened his position in north Kent, for in 1612 he became lord of the manor and hundred of Milton.[10] By contrast, Hoby's influence continued to deteriorate, for though he remained constable of the castle he lost the stewardship of three nearby royal manors in 1606.[11] Realizing perhaps that he was now overshadowed by Montgomery, Hoby seems not to have made any recommendation to the borough in 1614. Sondes, whose finances had at any rate been severely weakened by excessive litigation, consequently proved unable to stand again. His place was taken by Roger Palmer, brother of one of Montgomery's principal servants, James Palmer, who came from a leading north Kent family. The junior seat went to Robert Hatton, steward of the household to Archbishop Abbot, a political ally of Montgomery's elder brother, the 3rd earl of Pembroke.

Montgomery's grip on the borough tightened still further in 1617, when he succeeded Hoby as constable of the castle. At the next election Hatton transferred to Sandwich, and the townsmen determined to replace him with William Frowde, a servant of Montgomery's who resided at Shurland. A gratified Montgomery proceeded to nominate James Palmer for the senior seat. However the borough was also approached by the new lord lieutenant, the duke of Lennox, who had been granted the principal Cobham estate. 'In case you shall elect some that is not of your society', he wrote, they should choose the Irish lawyer Richard Hadsor, who had defended Lennox's patent for alnage on the New Draperies before the Commons in 1606.[12] The borough council were clearly more sophisticated than their distant (and imaginary) predecessors caricatured on the stage by Middleton in *The Mayor of Queenborough*, and used Lennox's saving clause to escape offending either of these two powerful noblemen. They politely excluded Hadsor by making Palmer and Frowde of their 'society', and elected them to the third Jacobean Parliament. The indenture, containing 25 signatures, described them as freemen of the borough, a formula to be followed in all the succeeding elections of the period.[13]

By 1624 Queenborough seems to have become unhappy that outsiders always monopolized its seats. When fresh elections were announced it therefore decided to offer only one place to Montgomery and to bestow the other on one of its freemen, John Basset, who seems to have been resident as his signature appears on the election indentures of 1620 and 1624. As Basset was one of Montgomery's servants, the borough presumably expected that this arrangement would be acceptable. However, on 6 Jan. Montgomery informed them that he had already promised both seats to 'his special friends', Roger Palmer and (since Frowde was now dead) Palmer's distant kinsman, John Poley, who lived in Suffolk. He added that Basset was 'unwilling to undergo a place of that weight and trouble by reason of other employment he has in hand'.[14] The borough quickly capitulated, and during the Parliament it sent a present of lobsters to its representatives, at a cost of £1.[15] However, in 1625 the electorate rebelled against the influence of Montgomery, who had now succeeded Lennox as lord lieutenant. It is probable that they provided the initiative for the candidature of Sir Edward Hales, one of the wealthiest gentlemen in Kent who had had recently moved to Tunstall, near Sittingbourne. On 15 Apr. he and his son John were made freemen.[16] Ten days later Montgomery wrote indignantly to the borough:

I have just cause to make the worst construction of your indiscreet and uncivil carriage towards me in slighting my letters which I directed unto you for Mr. Robert Poley, a gentleman every way able to discharge a greater trust …

He was convinced that Hales, 'out of his respect to me', would be 'content to waive acceptance of that burgess-ship which you would enforce upon him'.[17] However, two weeks later Hales was elected senior burgess and Roger Palmer was relegated to the junior place. This outcome many not have been universally popular in the borough, however, as neither the mayor nor the bailiffs signed the indenture.[18]

The borough's defiance may have been responsible for persuading Montgomery to moderate his tone at the next election. Writing on 31 Dec. 1625, the earl asked merely for the right to dispose of one seat, which he desired should be conferred on Robert Poley, who is 'very able and willing to do all good offices; neither can his sufficiency and abilities be unknown to you, as being a sworn burgess of the town and one that you have had experience of already'. The voters not only demurred, but also restored Roger Palmer to the senior seat as Hales had decided to stand for the county.[19] Nevertheless, it seems that the electorate subsequently tried to lessen their dependence on their patron by seeking a grant of incorporation. The ostensible reason for the new charter was the resort to the borough of disorderly persons, both landsmen and sailors, whose misdemeanours remained unpunished for lack of resident magistrates in the neighbourhood. Montgomery may have been taken unawares, and the new charter had actually been approved by the king when the lord keeper (Sir Thomas Coventry*) intervened. A revised version passed the Great Seal on 15 Nov. 1626 with Montgomery's consent.[20] He was spared any further electoral difficulties by Poley's death on the Ile de Ré in 1627, and at the next election Hale's son was returned with Palmer, probably unopposed.

[1] C219/37/134. [2] Cent. Kent. Stud. Qb/Rpr2. [3] Cent. Kent. Stud. JMS 4, f. 76. [4] Ibid. f. 84v. [5] M. Weinbaum, *English Bor. Charters 1307-1660*, p. 63; C. Eveleigh Woodruff, 'Notes on the Municipal Recs. of Queenborough', *Arch. Cant.* xxii. 172. [6] E. Hasted, *Kent*, vi. 233-4, 237. [7] Manning and Bray, *Surr.* i. 567. [8] *HMC Hatfield*, xvii. 335. [9] SP14/18/26. [10] Hasted, vi. 175. [11] E315/310, f. 46. [12] Cent.Kent.Stud.Qb/C1/30-1; *CSPDom.* 1603-10, p.306; *CJ*, i.299a. [13] C219/37/134. [14] Cent. Kent. Stud. Qb/C1/32. For the indentures, see C219/37/134; 219/38/124. [15] Woodruff, 177. The present of lobsters is mentioned on the chamberlain's account for 1623[-4]. [16] Cent. Kent. Stud. Qb/JMS 4, f. 70v. [17] *Procs. 1625*, pp. 695-6. [18] C219/39/120; Cent. Kent. Stud. Qb/RPr4. [19] *Procs. 1626*, iv. 249. [20] Lansd. 707, f. 2; *CSP Dom.* 1625-6, pp. 471, 579.

P.J.L./A.D.T.

ROCHESTER

Right of election: in the resident freemen

Number of voters: unknown

29 Feb. 1604	SIR EDWARD HOBY SIR THOMAS WALSINGHAM I
26 Mar. 1614	SIR EDWARD HOBY SIR ANTHONY AUCHER
4 Apr. 1614[1]	SIR EDWIN SANDYS *vice* Aucher who refused to serve (Philip?) Proger
14 Dec. 1620	SIR THOMAS WALSINGHAM II HENRY CLERKE, recorder
17 Jan. 1624	SIR THOMAS WALSINGHAM II SIR MAXIMILIAN DALLISON
7 May 1625	SIR THOMAS WALSINGHAM II HENRY CLERKE, recorder
19 Jan. 1626	SIR THOMAS WALSINGHAM II HENRY CLERKE, recorder ?Sir John Smythe III*
25 Feb. 1628	SIR THOMAS WALSINGHAM II SIR WILLIAM BROOKE ?Sir Allen Apsley

Dominated by its Norman castle and cathedral, Rochester was linked to neighbouring Strood by an 11-arch stone bridge, described by one visitor in 1635 as 'fair, stately, long and strong' and 'not much inferior' to that of London.[2] The bridge and its estates were administered by two wardens and 12 assistants, who enjoyed parliamentary authority to raise taxes within a seven-mile radius of the city to help cover the costs of maintenance. The bridge Acts of 1576 and 1585 had been obtained, without payment of fees, by the bridge commissioner and judge (Sir) Roger Manwood†.[3] Under the terms of a royal charter of 1460, Rochester was governed by 12 aldermen, one of whom was annually elected mayor, and 12 common councilmen.[4] The city also had a recorder by 1616, and a high steward by 1619.[5] In 1629 the corporation complained that the names used to describe the city's boundaries in its ancient charter 'are grown obsolete and not certainly known', and was unclear whether the mayor and recorder, though city magistrates, were members of the quorum, 'whereof … a defect of justice hath ensued'. For these reasons, among others, a new charter was obtained in August 1629.[6]

Although Rochester was a seaport, it was not dependent on overseas trade or fishing. Few ships were owned or operated by local men; indeed, only two are noticed in the port book for 1604-5.[7] When the Board of Greencloth in 1617 demanded that Rochester provide 200 flounders a week for the royal Household, the corporation pointed out that, for much of the year, its fishermen were reduced to dredging for oysters.[8] Instead, the mainstay of the city's economy was brewing. In 1592 Rochester's brewers persuaded the corporation to prohibit the import of 'foreign' beer, including 1,600 tuns previously brought in annually from London. In return they agreed to sell their beer at rates set by the clerk of the market's Court, and to donate £10 to the city's coffers.[9]

The city's finances were precarious. In 1618 the corporation declared that its annual income was 'not sufficient to support the ordinary charge thereof, whereof many debts have of late grown due to such as have supplied the office of mayoralty'.[10] As late as 1630 the mayor dipped into his own pocket to help pay the costs of building 'the house on the common'.[11] As a result of its poverty, the corporation imposed a tax of 2d. on every boat which passed the bridge, but it thereby attracted the attention of the committee for grievances, which in 1624 summoned the mayor to explain.[12] The corporation was not destitute, however, and in June 1625 presented Charles I and his new queen with two cups costing £30. Sixteen months later it ordered a purchase of plate for its recorder, Henry Clerke, in recognition of his parliamentary service, the sole occasion when Rochester is known to have rewarded one of its Members.[13]

Parliamentary elections were held in the guildhall.[14] The election indentures, which were in Latin, were drawn up between the mayor, citizens and aldermen on the one hand and the sheriff of Kent on the other.[15] The right to vote was conferred by the city's freedom, which normally cost £5, provided the holder was a resident householder paying 'watch and ward, lot and scot' to the city. These restrictions may not always have been observed, however, for in September 1637 the corporation felt obliged to draw attention to them.[16] By law only those free at the time the election writs were issued were permitted to stand for Parliament, but at Rochester candidates were sometimes admitted to the freedom at the last minute. In December 1620 Sir Thomas Walsingham II was admitted on the day originally scheduled for the election. Five years later, Walsingham tried to persuade the corporation that their neighbour Sir John Smythe III could not stand as he was not a freeman, but the

aldermen simply admitted Smith the day before the election.[17]

Rochester's Members may have been required to swear a separate oath of service to the city. Among the city's fragmentary records is just such an oath, dated 1586, which reads

in consideration of your being now elected one of the two burgesses for this city and liberties you shall also swear that (in every session of this present Parliament now summoned) you shall be willing to put forth and prefer to pass, and with the other burgess of this city to the uttermost of your power to further, all and every such motions and bills as shall be thought meet and requested to be preferred by Mr. Mayor and the citizens of this city. And also that (according to the great trust in you reposed) you shall carefully and to the uttermost of your power endeavour yourself to join with the said other burgess, faithfully to stand by and maintain all the charters, grants, liberties of the said city in every session of this aforesaid Parliament. And that you shall not willingly give your assent or consent to any motion or bill therein which shall tend to the overthrow, loss or prejudice of the same charters, grants or liberties.[18]

Despite this oath, Rochester made few recorded demands on its Members. It introduced only one bill to Parliament during this period, which received a first reading in the Commons on 31 May 1610 and was committed on 22 June. It was mentioned again on 4 July, when a committee meeting appears to have been re-scheduled; thereafter it disappeared from sight. Its contents are unknown.[19]

Rochester's proximity to Chatham dockyard meant that it enjoyed a close connection to the navy. Lord admiral Nottingham (Charles Howard[†]) served as as the city's high steward, as did his successor Buckingham, and many naval personnel were admitted to the freedom, such as the surveyor Sir John Trevor I*.[20] A few naval figures also brought trade to the port, among them the sailmaker Hildebrand Prusen, who imported Norwegian deal boards, masts and spars.[21] Others furnished victuals to the king's ships, such as the brewer and former naval purser John Duling, who twice served as mayor.[22] Many of the city's leading figures found employment in the navy, including Sir Peter Buck (d.1625), clerk of the Navy, who built Eastgate House, where Christian IV of Denmark lodged in 1606 on a visit to Chatham dockyard.[23] Under Elizabeth the Navy's local importance was occasionally reflected at parliamentary elections: men responsible for victualling the queen's ships had been returned in 1559, 1563 and 1571. However, under the early Stuarts none of the navy's personnel represented Rochester, although in 1628 the victualler Sir Allen Apsley sought election, believing incorrectly that with the duke's support, 'I may not miss'.[24] The lord admiral controlled the Admiralty Court as well as the navy, and although no naval employees were returned after 1603 it might still seem that he had electoral influence at Rochester. Sir Edward Hoby, appointed vice-admiral of Milton Hundred in 1585 and Kent in 1607, represented Rochester in 1597, 1601, 1604-10 and 1614, while Sir Thomas Walsingham II, vice-admiral of Kent from August 1626, served in 1628. However, Hoby probably owed his seat to the fact that he lived at nearby Queenborough, and in 1614 he was nearly discarded as the city initially resolved to offer its places to candidates nominated by the earl of Somerset, despite the fact that Hoby had entertained the city's chamberlain during Christmas 1613.[25] It seems unlikely that Walsingham, who lived at Chislehurst in north Kent, owed his election in 1628 to the lord admiral as he had already represented Rochester on four successive occasions. In 1626, it is true, he had solicited Buckingham's support for the second seat, but he had done so only to prevent the election of the duke's nominee Sir John Smith.[26] Buckingham had subsequently endorsed Walsingham, but nevertheless told the corporation that they should elect Smith regardless of 'who[m]soever you shall make choice of [for] the other [seat]'.[27]

Smith's failure to secure a seat at Rochester in 1626 illustrated the weak electoral influence of the lord admiral. Buckingham was snubbed despite having written no less than three letters to the city in support of Smythe, including one in which he presumed upon his 'interest' as high steward 'not to be denied, nor to alter that assurance I have given him to rely upon that place and stand for no other'.[28] Possibly Buckingham exercised little influence at Rochester because he had upset several influential citizens whose naval credentials might otherwise have disposed them to support him. The suspension of the Navy Board in 1618 can hardly have endeared Buckingham to the clerk of the navy, Sir Peter Buck, while the virtual closure of Woolwich dockyard deprived the assistant master shipwright, John May, of his job. Interestingly, May was mayor of Rochester when Buckingham attempted to secure Smith's election, although since he was anxiously seeking reinstatement it should not be assumed that he was bent on revenge.[29]

Tension between the lord admiral and the city over its Admiralty jurisdiction may also help to explain why so little electoral influence appears to have been wielded by either Buckingham or Nottingham at Rochester. The city's charter of 1460 included Admiralty jurisdiction over the Medway between Hawkwood and Sheerness, but these rights were disputed by the lord admiral. At the city's request the quarrel was referred to arbitration in about 1609. Although the arbitrators subsequently ruled in Nottingham's favour, the earl complained in 1617 to Rochester's mayor, John Cobham, that 'you do daily persist in intruding upon my said jurisdiction, which I cannot but take in very ill part'.[30] Cobham responded by referring Nottingham to various royal grants confirming the city's rights and added that he hoped that, having accepted the city's high stewardship, Nottingham would 'not now be a means to question that ancient jurisdiction which His Majesty's royal progenitors have been graciously pleased to grant to this city'.[31] Nottingham subsequently ordered a fresh inquiry, which upheld the city's rights against his own officers, whom he accused of opposing Rochester's rightful liberties for their own gain.[32] This was not the end of the matter, however, as under Buckingham the Admiralty soon began to encroach upon Rochester's rights again.[33] The city was so alarmed that, shortly after the duke's death, it sought to include its claim to Admiralty jurisdiction in its new charter. Kent's vice-admiral, Sir Thomas Walsingham II, was then serving as one of Rochester's parliamentary representatives. Two days after Parliament was dissolved, in March 1629, he wrote to the Admiralty secretary Edward Nicholas* pointing out that attorney-general (Sir Robert) Heath* had only passed the new charter because its proponents had claimed that it 'is but according to their former, but in that he is deceived'. Walsingham thought that Buckingham's patent as lord admiral had kept the threat posed by Rochester's charter at bay, but now that the duke was dead 'the king's new grant will be good ... even against the said admiral and his officers, which I beseech you to make known to the lords [of the Admiralty]'. The city was naturally displeased with Walsingham's intervention, refusing to let him take a register of the port's seamen and vessels later that year. Walsingham subsequently failed to get the offending clauses removed from the new charter.[34]

As under Elizabeth, none of Rochester's aldermen are known to have put themselves forward for election, although the city's resident recorder, Henry Clerke, was returned three times. In general, Rochester preferred to choose local gentry, such as Sir Edward Hoby and the two Walsinghams. That said, Hoby and Sir Thomas Walsingham I may not have been the borough's original choice in 1604: their names on the indenture are not only written in a different ink from the rest of the text but also occupy dark patches on the parchment, which suggests that the names of previous candidates have been scraped out.[35] Sir Maximilian Dallison, who lived close by at Halling and owned property in the city, was another member of the local gentry to represent Rochester, as was Sir William Brooke, who resided at nearby Cooling. His return perhaps underlined the weakness of Buckingham's position at Rochester, for in 1618 Brooke had tried to insinuate himself into the affections of James I at the instigation of the Howards in order to oust Buckingham as favourite.

Not all of the outsiders elected for Rochester lived in north Kent. Both Sir Anthony Aucher (1614), who refused to serve, and Sir Edwin Sandys, his replacement, lived in east Kent. Aucher, then sheriff of Kent, had no known connection with the city, whereas Sandys enjoyed the support of the earl of Somerset's client, Sir Robert Mansell*, treasurer of the Navy, whose influence among Rochester's naval voters was probably considerable.

The best documented parliamentary election for the period is that of 1614. On 23 Feb. Mansell informed Somerset by letter that Rochester had been prepared to place both its seats at the earl's disposal, but having 'been importuned by several gentlemen of good quality' they were now able to offer only one.[36] Somerset accordingly nominated Sandys, but his recommendation did not reach Rochester until 27 Mar., the day after Sir Edward Hoby and Sir Anthony Aucher were elected. The mayor offered to hold another vote, but Sandys replied on 30 Mar. that he could not be 'so injurious either to your city or to the gentlemen chosen ... as to admit any thought of reversing or altering that election'.[37] There the matter might have rested had not Aucher, perhaps belatedly realizing that sheriffs were not permitted to serve in Parliament unless they were already Members of the Commons, stood down in favour of his close associate and neighbour Sir Thomas Hardres two days before Parliament was due to assemble. By that time both the mayor and two aldermen, Bartholomew Man and John Duffield, had promised Hardres their support after Aucher told them that Sandys had been elected for another constituency. This was both accurate and yet deeply duplicitous, for although Sandys was indeed elected for Hindon before Parliament opened, Aucher is unlikely to have known it. Indeed, when challenged publicly on 4 Apr. about Sandys's return for another seat, Aucher distanced himself from his messenger, whom he claimed had 'mistook him'.[38]

At first Aucher planned to hold the fresh election on the afternoon of Sunday 3 Apr., but he was prevented from doing so by an irate Sir John Leveson, who lived at Cuxton, four miles south-west of Rochester. At the previous election Leveson had canvassed on behalf of his nephew 'Proger' – possibly Philip Proger, later a groom of the privy chamber to Charles I –[39], but finding little support he had desisted at the request of Proger's father. Leveson was at church when he heard from Bartholomew Man that there was to be a fresh election in just two hours time, and was initially 'much perplexed what to do'. He was 'not willing to meddle in a business of this nature on the Sabbath day', and there was the question of whether to revive his support for Proger. 'After some further bethinking myself of the matter', he decided to forgo his lunch and hurried to Rochester where he berated the mayor and alderman Man 'for this sudden and uncouth manner of election'. After a lengthy argument the election was postponed until the following morning, though this gave Rochester less than a day to return their writ before Parliament assembled. Leveson hoped that the delay would permit his nephew to re-enter, and his hopes were raised by Aucher's message that Sandys had secured a seat elsewhere. Aucher's supporters were displeased at Leveson's intervention, however, and claimed that 'Sir Edwin Sandys's relinquishing to stand and the sheriff's resignate [sic] of the election was only to give passage to Sir Thomas Hardres'. They also objected that Proger could not stand because, unlike Hardres, he was not a freeman, and they maintained that 'it was not unusual to treat of business and conclude then on the Sabbath day'. In the event, the delay benefited Sandys rather than Proger. Overnight four of the city's leading citizens, including Sir Peter Buck and Thomas Rock, wrote to Sandys at his house in Northbourne, suspicious of the message previously sent by Aucher. They asked Sandys 'to let us understand from your own self what you resolve upon', informing him that if he arrived by 10 o'clock the next morning he would be sworn a freeman, and then 'we, altogether with the assistance of Sir John Leveson by his best power, who hath promised as much in your behalf, will stand for you'.[40] This may not have been entirely truthful, as Leveson evidently supported his nephew right up until the last moment. Sandys replied in the early hours of the morning of 4 Apr. that he was unwilling 'to disturb that which was already past and concluded'. He added that it was impossible for him to be at Rochester by ten, as it was too far from Northbourne and he had 'many business[es] to settle here before my remove hence'. He did not confirm or deny Aucher's report that he had been returned elsewhere. Sandys's reply did not reach the city until 2 pm, necessitating a further postponement of the election. Even before it was received, however, the mood had swung against Hardres. When he and Aucher arrived that morning their friends advised that 'they were in danger to lose'. In order to avoid such a humiliation, Hardres decided to give way to Sandys. Aucher, however, had other plans, and suddenly declared that he now 'stood upon his own former election and said he would return it'. In his account of these proceedings to Proger's father, Leveson diplomatically drew a veil over the reaction of the assembled electors, recording merely that 'after a better advice he waived it'. It was generally agreed that Sandys had implicitly accepted the seat by pointedly failing to refuse it. Not being a freeman, Leveson was unable to witness the election in the guildhall, but immediately afterwards he was informed that Sandys had been elected on a provisional basis: 'if Sir Edwin Sandys would serve for the town then he to have it, if he would not then your son [Proger] to have it'. Leveson thought that this was 'but a trick to cosen the ignorant multitude', but even if it were true he hoped that Proger would not 'serve for them in that kind'.[41]

One of Sandys's leading supporters in 1614 was Thomas Rock, who by the time of the next election in December 1620 was serving as mayor. Rock wanted to return Sir Thomas Walsingham II and Henry Clerke, but many of the freemen had other ideas, so that on 12 Dec. 'the mayor and his confederates, misdoubting their own strength, dissembled their int[ention of] electing burgesses at this time and so dismissed the company'. Two days later Rock and his supporters gathered together 'in a secret and clandestine manner' and elected their candidates.[42] A protest lodged with the privileges committee upheld the outcome but condemned Rock for having 'sent but half an hour's notice of the election' to the freemen, many of whom had then been at the city's market.[43]

The remaining elections of the period seem to have passed off without acrimony. However in 1626 Walsingham's claim on the senior seat was threatened by his north Kent neighbour Sir John Smith of Sutton-at-Hone. Through the intercession of Henry Rich*, earl of Holland, Smith obtained a letter of nomination from the borough's high steward, the duke of Buckingham.[44] However, after furious lobbying by Walsingham, Smith was rejected Smith, forcing Buckingham to find him a seat elsewhere.

[1] Same writ. [2] 'Relation of a short survey of the western counties, 1635' ed. L.G. Wickham Legg, in *Cam. Misc.* xvi. (Cam. Soc. ser. 3. lii), 8. [3] *Traffic and Pols.* ed. N. Yates and J.M. Gibson, 130. [4] F.F. Smith, *Hist. Rochester*, 45-6. [5] Guildhall Museum, Rochester, 'Customal', f. 79r-v; Medway Archives and Local Stud. Cent. RCA/ A5/1, f. 4v. [6] Smith, 47-50. [7] E190/648/11. [8] Medway Archives and Local Stud. Cent. RCA/A5/1, ff. 2v-3. [9] Guildhall Museum, Rochester, 'Customal', ff. 76-7. [10] Ibid. f. 80v. [11] Smith, 116. [12] *CJ*,

i. 769b; 'Nicholas 1624', f. 160v. [13] Smith, 259, 344-5. [14] Staffs. RO, D593/S4/60/13. [15] C219/35/1/61; 219/37/130. [16] Smith, 447. [17] Guildhall Museum, Rochester, 'Customal', new ff. 41, 45; Soc. Antiq. mss 199 ter, f. 7. [18] Guildhall Museum, Rochester, 'Customal', f. 72r-v. [19] *CJ*, i. 434b, 442b, 445b. [20] Guildhall Museum, Rochester, 'Customal', new f. 21. [21] E190/648/11, unfol. [22] Smith, 496; Add. 9297, f. 163; *APC*, 1630-1, p. 322; *Jacobean Commissions of Inquiry* ed. A.P. McGowan (Navy Recs. Soc. cxvi), 128, 137. For a further e.g., see Guildhall Museum, Rochester, 'Customal', f. 72r-v. [23] Guildhall Museum, Rochester, 'Customal', new ff. 12, 21; Smith, 340. [24] SP16/92/18. [25] Medway Archives and Local Stud. Cent. RCA/N1/2, unfol. payment to Hoby's servants. [26] Soc. Antiq. ms 199 ter, ff. 3, 7, 11. [27] Ibid. f. 13. [28] Ibid. ff. 5, 9, 13. [29] *CSP Dom.* 1625-6, pp. 256, 261; 1628-9, pp. 108, 144-5. [30] Medway Archives and Local Stud. Cent. RCA/A5/1, f. 1. [31] Ibid. f. 1v. [32] Ibid. ff. 2r-v, 4. [33] Ibid. f. 4. [34] SP16/132/19; 16/138/62. [35] C219/35/1/66. [36] Cott. Titus B.VII. [37] Staffs. RO, D593/S4/60/11. [38] Staffs. RO, D593/ S4/60/13. [39] E179/70/136, 146. [40] Staffs. RO, D593/S/4/60/12. [41] Staffs. RO, D593/S/4/60/13. [42] Surr. RO, Loseley 1331/28. The letters in square bracket are missing in the original, which is torn. [43] *CJ*, i. 537a. [44] Soc. Antiq. mss 199 ter, f. 7. For Walsingham's lobbying, see above.

A.D.T.

LANCASHIRE
Number of voters: unknown

13 Feb. 1604	SIR RICHARD MOLYNEUX I
	SIR RICHARD HOUGHTON
c. Mar. 1614	SIR THOMAS GERRARD I, bt.
	SIR CUTHBERT HALSALL
25 Dec. 1620	SIR JOHN RADCLIFFE
	SIR GILBERT HOUGHTON
19 Jan. 1624	SIR JOHN RADCLIFFE
	SIR THOMAS WALMESLEY
9 May 1625	SIR RICHARD MOLYNEUX II, (bt.)
	SIR JOHN RADCLIFFE
16 Jan. 1626	SIR GILBERT HOUGHTON
	ROBERT STANLEY
10 Mar. 1628	SIR RICHARD MOLYNEUX II, (bt.)
	SIR ALEXANDER RADCLIFFE

Lancashire owed its special status as a semi-autonomous palatinate to the fact that it had once been a border territory, vulnerable to invasion from Ireland or Scotland.[1] Day-to-day administration of the county was shared between the Westminster-based duchy of Lancaster, which appointed sheriffs, magistrates and assize judges, and the Stanley earls of Derby, hereditary holders of the lieutenancy of Lancashire and Cheshire.[2] There was little contact between the county's magistrates and the Privy Council, and this fact, coupled with the distance from London, gave Lancashire a sense of separateness that was heightened by differences of religion and local custom.[3] The population stood at around 95,000 in the mid-Elizabethan period, and rose to over 140,000 a century later.[4] There were no large cities and few towns of note; the county's economy was based on the grazing of livestock.[5] Industries such as woollen cloth and linen manufacturing were established around Manchester and Bolton during the sixteenth century, and 'new draperies' including fustians began to be produced in Bolton, Blackburn and Oldham under the early Stuarts.[6] Nevertheless, Lancashire remained vulnerable to subsistence crises, and in the early 1620s bad harvests and grain scarcity coincided with low prices in the wool and cloth trades.[7] Lancashire's gentry were fewer in number and poorer than their southern counterparts, a fact reflected in the low subsidy assessments for the county.[8] Some gentry households supplemented their incomes with the profits of coal extraction: collieries were opened in Wigan in the 1600s, and the coalfields around Prescot and Chorley are thought to have yielded up to 13,000 tons a year. However, costs were high and coal was yet to become a significant factor in the local economy.[9] Only one Lancashire magnate, Sir Richard Molyneux II*, was raised to the peerage during the period, confirming his status as second only to the Stanleys in terms of local power and influence.

Lancashire's parliamentary representatives played little recorded part in the Commons, perhaps because neither the county nor any of its boroughs were the subject of particular legislation during the period. Most of the committees to which the county's Members were collectively appointed concerned private measures, such as the York gaol patent bill (May 1624), which drew many comparisons with Lancaster gaol.[10] On the few occasions that Lancashire was mentioned it was as a sink of recusancy. A typical example is (Sir) Henry Spiller's report on 24 Feb. 1621, that

> there were certified out of Lancashire 1800 papists: of these there were recusants in Qu[een] El[izabeth]'s time 900; the most of the rest very poor men, and not able to pay anything. Insomuch as commissioners being sent down to value their estates, they certified that their estates in lands were but £50 and in goods but £40.[11]

Unsurprisingly, Lancashire's Members did not respond, for many of their gentry neighbours were tainted with Catholicism. The county as a whole was notorious for its Catholic survivalism, and reported recusancy rose sharply after 1603.[12] Both Sir Richard Molyneux I and Sir Richard Houghton had recusant wives and were themselves crypto-papists, though they outwardly conformed and were keen to demonstrate

their loyalty: they were listed as second and eighth respectively among those who purchased baronetcies in 1611. Sir Thomas Gerrard, another staunch Catholic and brother of the notorious Jesuit Fr. John Gerrard, also became a baronet at the same time.[13] Sir Richard Molyneux II was, like his father, known to temporize in religion. Sir Cuthbert Halsall was briefly dropped from the bench for being 'popish' early in James's reign but later conformed, while Sir Thomas Walmesley was among those who gladly compounded for recusancy during Charles's Personal Rule.

As well as Catholicism, Lancashire also had a reputation for superstition and witchcraft. Not surprisingly therefore, Sir Richard Molyneux I was one of the committeemen appointed to consider a witchcraft bill in May 1604.[14] There was a sense that the established church, under the auspices of the remote bishopric of Chester, lacked solid foundations in Lancashire.[15] In 1626 Sir Benjamin Rudyard resorted to a familiar stereotype when he deplored the example of 'two ministers in Lancashire found to be unlicensed alehouse-keepers', during a debate about the standards of the clergy (10 February).[16] Nevertheless, there were pockets of intense puritanism to be found in the clothing towns around Manchester and Bolton. It was while travelling through Lancashire in 1617 that James I issued his 'Declaration of Sports', a response to the Sabbatarian orders imposed by a few local puritan justices.[17]

Lancashire received its election writs from the chancellor of the Duchy, and elections took place at Lancaster outside the castle. The indentures were returned to the chancellor, who then passed them on to Chancery.[18] Though the chancellor claimed the right of nomination in most of Lancashire's six boroughs, and many of the personnel of the Duchy's local administration were members of the Lancashire gentry, there is no evidence of Duchy influence in county elections. The earls of Derby, by contrast, traditionally played a role in county elections, but from 1594 until his death in 1642 the 6th earl took little interest in politics and, with a few rare exceptions, kept his involvement to a minimum. This meant that, during this period, the selection of knights of the shire fell to a close circle of old gentry families. Seats were distributed between the leading gentry and their sons, and contests were avoided. In 1604 the first seat was awarded to Sir Richard Molyneux I despite his non-attendance at the election as he had already set off for London.[19] The second seat went to Sir Richard Houghton, one of the few Lancashire men who regularly attended the Court. The 1614 elections were also dominated by the heads of Lancashire's ancient families. Sir Thomas Gerrard of Bryn, another courtier, sought entry to Parliament to escape from financial problems, as did Sir Cuthbert Halsall, who took the remaining seat in the same year. Halsall was perhaps backed by the earl of Derby, to whom he was related by marriage.

In 1620 the senior seat was taken by Sir John Radcliffe, whose ancestors had long been adherents of the Stanleys. The junior place went to Sir Gilbert Houghton, a courtier who had supplanted his father Sir Richard Houghton in the Duchy offices of steward and master forester of Bowland and Quernmore, though it is unlikely that this Duchy connection was responsible for his election. Radcliffe was re-elected in 1624, together with Sir Thomas Walmesley of Dunke-halgh. Though aged only 23, Walmesley was the heir of a vast estate, and was connected to several influential families: his stepmother was Sir Richard Houghton's sister, and his father-in-law was Sir Richard Molyneux I. Radcliffe was elected for a third successive time in 1625, but conceded the senior seat to Sir Richard Molyneux II, who in 1623 had inherited not only his father's estates at Sefton and Croxteth but also the general receivership of the Duchy.

In 1626 the earl of Derby desired a seat for his second son, Robert, then aged around 18, who was paired with Sir Gilbert Houghton in first place. Molyneux II took the senior seat again in 1628, leaving the junior place to Sir Alexander Radcliffe, the 19 year-old heir of Sir John, who had died the previous year. Between the first and second sessions Molyneux was ennobled as Viscount Maryborough, but as an Irish peer he was not required to relinquish his seat in the Lower House, and so remained in the Commons until the dissolution.

[1] B. Coward, 'Lieutenancy of Lancs. and Cheshire in the 16th and early 17th Centuries', *Trans. Hist. Soc. Lancs. and Cheshire*, cxix. 39-64; J.J. Bagley, *Hist. Lancs.* [2] *30th DKR*, iii-viii; *35th DKR*, iii-xi; R. Somerville, 'Duchy and County Palatine of Lancaster', *Trans. Hist. Soc. Lancs. and Cheshire*, ciii. 59-67; B. Coward, *The Stanleys, Lords Stanley and Earls of Derby 1385-1672* (Chetham Soc. ser. 3. xxx). [3] B.W. Quintrell, 'Govt. in Perspective: Lancs. and the Privy Council 1570-1640', *Trans. Hist. Soc. Lancs. and Cheshire*, cxxxi. 35-62. [4] C.B. Phillips and J.H. Smith, *Lancs. and Cheshire from 1540*, p. 7. [5] J.K. Walton, *Lancs.: A Social Hist. 1558-1939*, pp. 12-14. [6] G. Timmins, *Made in Lancs.: A Hist. of Regional Industrialization*, 9-34; P.J. Gooderson, *Hist. Lancs.* 55-63. [7] S. Scott and C.J. Duncan, 'Mortality Crisis of 1623 in N.W. Eng.', *Local Population Studies*, lviii. 14-25. [8] P.R. Long, 'Wealth of the Magisterial Class in Lancs. 1590-1640' (Manchester Univ. M.A. thesis, 1968); B.G. Blackwood, 'Economic State of the Lancs. Gentry on the Eve of the Civil War', *NH*, xii. 53-83; O. Ashmore, 'Household Inventories of the Lancs. Gentry, 1550-1700', *Trans. Hist. Soc. Lancs. and Cheshire*, cx. 59-105. [9] Timmins, 21; J.E. Hollinshead, 'An Unexceptional Commodity: Coal in S.-W. Lancs. in the 16th Cent.', *Trans. Hist. Soc. Lancs. and Cheshire*, cxlv. 1-19. [10] *CJ*, i. 705a, 708a, 710b, 711a, 797a. [11] Nicholas, *Procs. 1621*, i. 92. [12] J.A. Hilton, *Catholic Lancs. From Reformation to Renewal*, 17-29. [13] *47th DKR*, app. 125; P. Croft, 'Catholic Gentry, the Earl of Salisbury and the Bts. of 1611',

Conformity and Orthodoxy in the Eng. Church ed. P. Lake and M. Questier, 271-2. [14] *CJ*, i. 227a; G.L. Kittredge, *Witchcraft in Old and New Eng.* 309; J.T. Swain, 'The Lancs. Witch Trials of 1612 and 1634 and the Economics of Witchcraft', *NH*, xxx. 64-85. [15] C. Haigh, *Reformation and Resistance in Tudor Lancs.* 316-32. [16] *CJ*, i. 817b. [17] L. Racaut, 'The 'Bk. of Sports' and Sabbatarian Legislation in Lancs. 1579-1616', *NH*, xxxiii. 73-87. [18] R. Somerville, *Hist. of Duchy of Lancaster*, i. 326, J.S. Roskell, *Lancs. Knights of the Shire* (Chetham Soc., xcvi.), 26-8. [19] Lancs. RO, DDM1/18.

R.C.L.S.

CLITHEROE

Right of election: in the burgage-holders

Number of voters: 25 in 1628[1]

		1st seat	2nd seat
1 Mar. 1604	SIR JOHN DORMER		
	MARTIN LISTER		
c. Mar. 1614	SIR GILBERT HOUGHTON		
	CLEMENT COKE		
3 Jan. 1621	SIR THOMAS WALMESLEY		
	WILLIAM FANSHAWE		
23 Jan. 1624	WILLIAM FANSHAWE		
	RALPH WHITFIELD		
3 May 1625	WILLIAM FANSHAWE		
	RALPH ASSHETON		
26 Jan. 1626	RALPH ASSHETON		
	GEORGE KIRKE		
c. Apr. 1626	(SIR) CHRISTOPHER HATTON *vice* Kirke, an alien Scot		
7 Mar. 1628	THOMAS JERMYN	12	-
	WILLIAM NOWELL	3	11
	Richard Shuttleworth	9	1
	Richard Aske	1	2
	William Fanshawe	-	8
	Ralph Assheton	-	2
	Thomas Carew	-	1

Clitheroe, a small and unimposing borough, was considered poor and remote even within Lancashire. Its population has been estimated at not much above 600 at the turn of the seventeenth century.[2] The castle and honour of Clitheroe, which date back to Domesday, passed into the control of the earls of Lancaster in the late thirteenth century, and so became part of the duchy of Lancaster.[3] The town's earliest extant charter, issued by Henry de Lacy in 1283, allowed the inhabitants the same liberties as Chester; this, and privileges subsequently granted by Edward III in 1346, were confirmed by James I on 11 May 1604.[4] The borough was governed by two annually elected bailiffs, one a resident, or 'in-bailiff', and the other an 'out-bailiff' selected from among the local gentry who owned freehold burgages in the town. An informal town council, made up of 12 former in-bailiffs, known as the 'brethren' or aldermen, held court leets twice a year and an annual court of inquiry, at which new bailiffs were appointed.[5]

Clitheroe first sent representatives to Parliament in 1559.[6] There is no evidence that the town paid election expenses during this period. The franchise was restricted to burgage-holders, whose tenants, the freemen of the town, were entitled to vote only if their landlords declined to do so.[7] Throughout the early Stuart period Clitheroe accepted the chancellor of the duchy of Lancaster's nominees for at least one seat, and occasionally for both. However, in 1621 the election became an arena of competition between local factions motivated by a bitter feud over the town's grammar school. The same dispute was also a significant factor in the borough's first contested election in 1628.

In 1604 the first seat went to Sir John Dormer of Dorton. Dormer was an outsider who presumably owed his election to the Duchy, either via his Buckinghamshire neighbour Sir John Fortescue*, chancellor of the duchy, or through his distant kinship with Sir Richard Molyneux I* of Sefton, the duchy's steward of Blackburn and Clitheroe since 1581. The second Member, Martin Lister, the younger son of a local family, was born within ten miles of Clitheroe, at Gisburne in the West Riding. It seems likely that he was returned through the influence of his elder brother, Lawrence Lister†, whose son-in-law, Giles Parker, then residing with him at Thornton in Craven, was Clitheroe's current in-bailiff. Neither Dormer nor Lister played any part in the progress of a duchy bill concerning the copyholders of Clitheroe in 1610, which was instead handled by Thomas Fanshawe I*, the duchy's auditor in the north.[8]

The electoral pattern in 1614 is less clear. The first seat went to Sir Gilbert Houghton, son and heir of Sir Richard Houghton* of Hoghton Tower, a powerful member of the local gentry. The allocation of the second seat to Clement Coke, the 19 year-old younger son of Sir Edward Coke*, may be attributed to the local connections of his fiancée, Sarah, daughter and heiress of Alexander Reddish (d.1613) of Reddish in Lancashire, near the Cheshire border; he perhaps also enjoyed Duchy backing as a result of his father's legal connections.[9] Coke was one of seven complete strangers to

represent Clitheroe between 1604-29 and was also one of four under-age Members to sit. Ironically, his father opposed the election of minors in later parliaments.[10]

In 1620 the duchy chancellor (Sir) Humphrey May*, seeking to muster parliamentary support for a bill concerning duchy lands that would be tabled in 1621, wrote to the bailiffs of Clitheroe 'challenging a right in the election for every corporation in his county'. His original nominee for the junior seat was reportedly 'one Mr. Shelton', perhaps Richard Shilton*, but at a late stage William Fanshawe, the duchy's auditor, also put himself forward. Fanshawe had previously sat for Lancaster in 1614, and together with other senior duchy officials had attended a meeting of Clitheroe copyholders hosted by (Sir) Ralph Assheton at Whalley in 1617.[11] Having forged useful contacts there, he invested £1,200 in property in the West Riding, and it was perhaps with Assheton's support that he finally prevailed upon May to back him ahead of Shilton. The senior seat was reserved for a wealthy local landowner, Sir Thomas Walmesley. The eldest grandson of Justice Sir Thomas Walmesley† of Dunkenhalgh, Walmesley was only 19 at the time of the election, but his family had a long history of involvement in Clitheroe politics, and upon coming of age he would inherit five burgages in the town. When Saville Radcliffe solicited a place for his West Riding neighbour Sir Richard Beaumont* of Whitley in early December 1620, he found that the first seat had been 'long ago disposed of to Sir Thomas Walmesley', and that the second was also unavailable, because 'the corporation dares not deny Mr. Chancellor'. However, he did not give up immediately. Writing to Beaumont a second time on 30 Dec. to report that Fanshawe had entered the running, Radcliffe implied that he had come close to obtaining the seat, but admitted that 'whilst I did labour to keep it in suspense Mr. Chancellor and Mr. Auditor's potency prevailed'.[12]

A week after the 1621 election, Clitheroe's court of inquiry required all resident burgage-holders to present themselves, upon pain of a £20 fine, so that their names might be listed.[13] This order suggests that Radcliffe's intervention on behalf of Beaumont had triggered disagreements about the extent of the franchise; an undated list, now torn and partly illegible, was probably the result of this exercise and originally contained about 30 names.[14] The underlying cause of the dispute was probably the continuing quarrel over the grammar school, which dated back to the 1580s and involved several local families, including the Walmesleys and Radcliffes, who were on opposing sides. A Chancery commission had been instigated by Sir Ralph Assheton of Whalley in around 1619 to investigate allegations of misappropriation of school funds by some of the governors; this was followed by a series of private suits in the duchy court and Star Chamber, and consequently the issue remained a source of local tension until the mid-1630s.[15] The influence of the school dispute on the 1621 election is implicit in Radcliffe's letter of apology to Beaumont. Radcliffe explained that his overtures on behalf of Beaumont had not succeeded because 'the burgesses of Clitheroe fail with me in the performance of that which divers of them both proffered and promised, which they are constrained by faction to fail in'.[16] John Greenacres, Radcliffe's former associate in the school dispute, was out-bailiff at the time of the election, but he was evidently not powerful enough to prevail over Walmesley, an ally of the dominant faction led by senior alderman Christopher Nowell, his kinsman.

In 1624 both places were filled by duchy candidates. The first went to Auditor Fanshawe, while the second was bestowed upon Ralph Whitfield, a Kentish lawyer. Whitfield had no formal links with either May, the duchy, or the borough, but he spoke twice in the duchy's interest in the Commons, and it seems likely that he gained his place through professional contacts in the duchy's Westminster court.[17] May nominated (Sir) Thomas Trevor*, a duchy official, as his first choice in 1625, but before the election Trevor became an Exchequer baron and was therefore disqualified from standing.[18] Auditor Fanshawe was again elected, while the second seat was taken by Ralph Assheton, the 19 year-old son and heir of Sir Ralph Assheton of Whalley, now a baronet. In 1626 Assheton was returned once more, as the first Member. His colleague was George Kirke, a groom of the Bedchamber, who had perhaps been nominated by May as a result of his Court connections. However, on 17 Feb. Fanshawe's brother, Thomas Fanshawe I, objected that Kirke, as an unnaturalized Scot, was ineligible. A new writ was issued, and at an election in April Kirke was replaced by Christopher Hatton, the Fanshawes' nephew, who although he did not come of age until June 1626, had previously sat for Peterborough. It is impossible to say why he was preferred above William Fanshawe, who had failed to find a seat. Perhaps May disliked Fanshawe, who was known to be indiscreet, for he again declined to support Fanshawe's bid for a seat at Clitheroe in 1628, advancing instead his wife's kinsman Thomas Jermyn, another member of the king's Bedchamber, as his first choice in what turned out to be a fiercely fought contest.

In 1628 the tensions that had remained beneath the surface in the 1621 election were brought into the open. May nominated Jermyn, an outsider, but

Auditor Fanshawe independently wrote to the bailiffs on 6 Feb. that he would rather 'serve for the town of Clitheroe than any other borough whatsoever', and beseeched them to continue to show him their 'accustomed respect'.[19] Five other candidates also stood. William Nowell, whose father Christopher had died only a few weeks before the parliamentary writ arrived, was motivated primarily by a private suit against the duchy's attorney, Sir Edward Mosley*. He and his father had been in conflict with Mosley for the past decade over their title to certain lands, and he wanted a seat so that he could mount a petition in the Commons accusing Mosley of corruption and malpractice.[20] Richard Shuttleworth, Nowell's cousin, stood against Jermyn for the first seat, and from the voting pattern that emerged it seems clear that he was considered to be in league with Nowell, for most of those that voted for one also voted for the other. On the other side, Ralph Assheton entered the running to oppose Nowell, who had entered a number of as yet undecided lawsuits against the baronet in relation to the maladministration of lands belonging to the grammar school.[21] The remaining candidates, Richard Aske and Thomas Carew, have not been identified, but were probably local men; Aske may have been related to the Yorkshire Askes of Aughton, in the East Riding, and would appear to have allied himself to Nowell.

The election occurred on 7 Mar. 1628 and involved 25 voters. Separate polls were taken for each seat, and the names of the voters were recorded under the names of the candidates they supported.[22] The voters were clearly divided along factional lines. One group of eight voters picked both Jermyn and Fanshawe, while a further handful of 'compromisers' paired Jermyn with Nowell or one of the other local candidates. Nowell was the only candidate who voted (for Shuttleworth and Aske in that order). The remaining 12 voters, including the in-bailiff William Herd, supported Nowell, Shuttleworth and Aske, in various combinations, the most popular being Shuttleworth and Nowell in first and second places respectively; one man even voted for Nowell in both polls. It is impossible to accept Hirst's account of 'idiosyncratic' or 'apparently random voting' in this election.[23] The support amassed by Nowell and Shuttleworth, who were both governors of the grammar school, reflects on one hand hostility towards Assheton, who received only two votes, because of his father's interference in the management of the school lands; and possibly indicates, on the other hand, local approval of Nowell's personal stand against the duchy.[24] The outcome was that Jermyn won the senior seat with 12 votes, while William Nowell took the second seat with 11, having netted 14 votes in all.

[1] Lancs. RO, MBC/78. [2] W.S. Weeks, *Clitheroe in Seventeenth Cent.* 5-6. [3] *VCH Lancs.* vi. 361-4; W.A. Abram, *Hist. Blackburn*, 48-53; R. Somerville, *Hist. of Duchy of Lancaster*, i. 19. [4] Lancs. RO PR/5013; J. Harland, *Ancient Charters and other Muniments of Bor. of Clitheroe.* unpag. [5] Lancs. RO, MBC/116-174, 351-4; Weeks, 13, 19-20. [6] *VCH Lancs.* vi. 367-9. [7] Weeks, 9-10. [8] *CJ*, i. 406b-407a. [9] Weeks, 224. [10] *CJ*, i. 649b-650a. [11] Lancs. RO, DDX/19/113; *HMC Hatfield*, xix. 86; *Jnl. of Nicholas Assheton of Downham* ed. F.R. Raines (Chetham Soc. xiv), 55. [12] Add. 24475, f. 97; Weeks, 225. [13] Weeks, 11. [14] Lancs. RO, DDX/19/152; D. Hirst, *Representative of the People?*, 97-8. [15] C.W. Stokes, *Queen Mary's G.S., Clitheroe* (Chetham Soc. n.s. xcii), 7-85; C91/5/9; C93/3/31; C93/8/2; C90/38; Weeks, 135-40; T.D. Whitaker, *Hist. Whalley* (4th edn.), ii. 93-4. [16] Add. 24475, f. 97. [17] Lancs. RO, DDX/19/167. [18] *HMC Kenyon*, 31; C218/1/19. [19] Lancs. RO, MBC/79. [20] DL1/278, 280; C2/ Chas.I/N25/35. [21] DL1/280, 281; STAC8/43/6; 8/222/22. [22] Lancs. RO, MBC/78. [23] Hirst, 127-9; Weeks, 226-30. [24] R.C.L. Sgroi, 'The Electoral Patronage of the Duchy of Lancaster, 1604-28', *PH*, xxvi. 323.

R.C.L.S.

LANCASTER

Right of election: in the freemen

Number of voters: 398 in 1664[1]

13 Feb. 1604	SIR THOMAS HESKETH, recorder
	THOMAS FANSHAWE I
4 Nov. 1605	SIR THOMAS HOWARD *vice*
	Hesketh, deceased
c.Mar. 1614	THOMAS FANSHAWE I
	WILLIAM FANSHAWE
c.Dec. 1620	(SIR) HUMPHREY MAY
	THOMAS FANSHAWE I
19 Jan. 1624	(SIR) HUMPHREY MAY
	THOMAS FANSHAWE I
2 Mar. 1624	JOHN SELDEN *vice*
	May, chose to sit for Leicester
9 May 1625	(SIR) HUMPHREY MAY
	(SIR) THOMAS FANSHAWE I
19 Jan. 1626	(SIR) HUMPHREY MAY
	(SIR) THOMAS FANSHAWE I
10 Mar. 1626	THOMAS JERMYN *vice*
	May, chose to sit for Leicester
10 Mar. 1628	(SIR) THOMAS FANSHAWE I
	SIR FRANCIS BINDLOSS

Lancaster claimed to be the most ancient borough in Lancashire. Founded on a Roman settlement, the medieval town grew up around a Norman castle erected in around 1102. It received its first known charter from John, earl of Mortain (later King John) in 1193, which granted the inhabitants the same liberties as Bristol. Between 1295 and 1331 it was represented in Parliament. In 1362 it became the official administrative capital of the county when Edward III, at the request of John of Gaunt, decreed that the assizes must be held there, establishing a monopoly of judicial process that was henceforth jealously guarded.[2] Nevertheless, the town suffered severe economic depression during the later middle ages: it lost the franchise and was gradually overtaken as a regional centre by Preston, and in the development of industry and commerce by Manchester and Liverpool.[3] Observing this sad decline, Camden remarked that Lancaster was 'not very well peopled nor much frequented, and all the inhabitants thereof are given to husbandry'.[4]

In the early sixteenth century Lancaster recovered its right to send representatives to Parliament.[5] Moreover, the castle, after major rebuilding under Elizabeth, served as the provincial headquarters of the duchy of Lancaster. A series of attempts to revive Lancaster's ailing economy, in the form of royal grants reinforcing the town's privileges, culminated in 1604 with the issue of a new charter incorporating the 'mayor, [two] bailiffs and commonalty' as a free borough.[6] This confirmed the method of appointing mayors and other officers, as laid down in a code of the borough's customs drawn up in 1572.[7] It also appointed Sir Thomas Hesketh as the town's recorder. Hesketh, a lawyer, was vice chancellor of the palatinate and a member of the Council in the North. Having already sat in four Elizabethan parliaments, he was elected on the Duchy interest at Lancaster in 1604, but died after the first session.[8] He was replaced on 4 Nov. 1605, when Sir Thomas Howard, the 18 year-old son of the lord chamberlain, Thomas, 1st earl of Suffolk, was returned, presumably through his father's influence.

The chancellor of the Duchy traditionally controlled parliamentary nominations at Lancaster, and managed throughout the period to place high-ranking Duchy officials as borough representatives, apparently without encountering opposition. The second seat in 1604 went to Thomas Fanshawe I, the Duchy's auditor in the north. Although an outsider, he evidently formed a good relationship with the corporation, particularly during an extended visit in the summer of 1611, and presented it with an engraved, silver-topped ebony mayor's staff in 1613 and a 'fine old mace' weighing 37 ounces.[9] By the time of the next general election Fanshawe was no longer an officer of the Duchy, but he was nevertheless re-elected for Lancaster in every Parliament of the period. In 1614 he was joined by his younger brother, William, who had succeeded him as Duchy auditor. In 1620 the chancellor of the Duchy, (Sir) Humphrey May, chose to sit for Lancaster himself, a sign that he considered it to be one of the safest seats within his reach.[10] The borough elected May and Thomas Fanshawe again in 1624, but this time May plumped for Leicester, another traditional Duchy seat. He was presumably responsible for putting forward a rising lawyer, John Selden, to serve at Lancaster in his stead. Together with Fanshawe, who had been knighted in 1624, May served once more for Lancaster in 1625. Both men were re-elected in 1626, but May again plumped for Leicester, whereupon he nominated his wife's distant relation, Thomas Jermyn, as his replacement.

In the final session of the period, Fanshawe was paired with Sir Francis Bindloss of Borwick Hall, the son and heir of a local magnate. Bindloss had no discernable connection with the Duchy, and it is possible that his return was indicative of worsening relations between the chancellor and the corporation. These came to a head in the 1630s, when the townsmen were sued in the Duchy court over grazing rights in Quernmore forest and nearby moorland.[11] In the absence of any borough records before 1664 it is impossible to determine whether Bindloss's return represented a challenge to Duchy control of elections.

No records of the admission of freemen survive for the period, making it difficult to estimate the number of voters in early Stuart elections. Except for Thomas Fanshawe, who was described as such in 1613, it is not known whether any of the borough's Members were enrolled as freemen, nor whether their expenses were paid by the town.

[1] J. Brownbill, *Cal. of Charters and Recs. belonging to Corp. of Lancaster*, 18. [2] T. Pape, *Charters of City of Lancaster*, 6, 33; W.O. Roper, *Materials for Hist. of Lancaster*; E. Baines, *Hist. of Palatinate and Duchy of Lancaster* ed. J. Croston, v. 461. [3] *Hist. Lancaster* ed. A. White, 54-5. [4] W. Camden, *Britannia* (1610), p. 754; T.D. Whitaker, *Hist. Richmondshire*, ii. 216-22. [5] W.D. Pink and A.B. Beavan, *Parl. Rep. of Lancs.* 103-18. [6] *CSP Dom.* 1603-10, p. 172; Pape, 36. [7] *VCH Lancs.* viii. 44. [8] *Duchy of Lancaster Office-Holders* ed. R. Somerville, 94; P.R. Long, 'Wealth of the Magisterial Class in Lancs. 1590-1640' (Manchester Univ. M.A. thesis, 1968), 134. [9] DL28/33/14A; Pape, 41. [10] R.C.L. Sgroi, 'The Electoral Patronage of the Duchy of Lancaster, 1604-28', *PH*, xxvi. 316, 322-3. [11] White, 56.

R.C.L.S.

LIVERPOOL

Right of election: in the freemen

Number of voters: 338 in 1629[1]

24 Feb. 1604	GILES BROOKE, alderman THOMAS REMCHINGE
c. Mar. 1614	THOMAS IRELAND EDWARD WYMARKE
c. May 1614	SIR HUGH BEESTON *vice* Wymarke, chose to sit for Newcastle-under-Lyme
14 Dec. 1620	THOMAS MAY WILLIAM JOHNSON
29 Jan. 1624	SIR THOMAS GERRARD, bt. GEORGE IRELAND
11 May 1625	JAMES STANLEY, LORD STRANGE EDWARD MOORE, alderman
20 Jan. 1626	EDWARD BRIDGEMAN THOMAS STANDISH
3 Mar. 1628	HENRY JERMYN JOHN NEWDIGATE

Liverpool was a small but thriving port in the early seventeenth century, a main departure point for troops and trade to Ireland, whose overseas as well as coastal commerce was steadily increasing. According to Camden it was 'very commodious for trade ... but not as eminent for its being ancient as for being neat and populous'.[2] Under the early Stuarts the corporation's annual income rose from around £130 to over £300, although this rarely produced a surplus after all expenses had been discharged of more than about £50.[3] The growth of the town engendered aspirations to independence, both from the administrative control of the port of Chester and from the feudal overlordship of the Molyneux family of Sefton.[4] The corporation's long running conflict with Sir Richard Molyneux I*, and his son, Sir Richard II*, came to a head during Charles's reign. The elder Molyneux had purchased Toxteth Park from the 6th earl of Derby in 1605, and thereafter began to extend his control over the town's commons and surrounding wasteland, claiming in 1617 that these belonged not to Liverpool but to the manor of West Derby, of which he was then steward.[5] Further disputes, for example in 1622 over wine duties, continued until 1628, when the king granted the manor of Liverpool to the corporation of London as part of the Ditchfield grant.[6]

Liverpool made a series of concerted efforts throughout the period to secure a new charter of incorporation. The town's earliest charter, granted by King John in 1207, and a further grant by Henry III in 1229, provided for a mayor and two bailiffs to be elected annually by the assembly of freemen. In 1604 an inspeximus was granted to confirm the town's previous charters, but this was found to be invalid due to a scribal error that enrolled the date as 'Anno 4 Jac.', and the town's pleas for reissue were ignored.[7] A further attempt was made in 1611, and in 1617 £70 16s. 6d. was levied upon a total of 375 freemen and women, but without success.[8] It was not until 1626 that a new charter granting exclusive rights to all freemen of the town was finally secured.[9]

The borough's electoral patronage had traditionally been shared between the duchy of Lancaster and the earls of Derby, each making a nomination for one of its two parliamentary seats. Under Elizabeth, the town had enlisted the 3rd earl's support in order to counterbalance attempts by the Duchy to control both nominations, and a cordial relationship continued between Liverpool and the 6th earl, who served as mayor in 1603-4, gave occasional gifts such as venison to the town council, and funded the construction of a new pillory.[10] Although prepared to assist the town when required, Derby showed little interest in exercising his own political influence, and this caused the previous equilibrium of Liverpool's patronage to break down during the reign of James, while the Duchy bolstered its claim to nominate at least one of the borough's members by appointing first Sir Richard Molyneux I and then his son as its receiver general.

In 1604 the chancellor of the Duchy, Sir John Fortescue*, who was perhaps preoccupied with his own election campaign in Buckinghamshire, apparently declined to name a candidate for Liverpool. In the absence of nominations from either of the usual sources two townsmen were returned: Giles Brooke, a seasoned campaigner for Liverpool's charter and independence from Chester, and Thomas Remchinge, a customs official. They are distinguished as the town's only MPs during the period to whom payment of parliamentary expenses is recorded. After the dissolution in 1611 Brooke claimed £28 14s., of which 20 marks 4s. 5d. were deducted for various reasons, and Remchinge received £25, having agreed 'willingly in respect of the town's kind dealing with him' to abate 40s. of his original claim for £27.[11]

In 1614 the first seat went to a local lawyer, Thomas Ireland of Bewsey, who had assisted the corporation in the resolution of an internal dispute two years earlier; he was an honorary freeman, and had connections to

both of the town's patrons, having been an officer of the Duchy since 1603, and the earl of Derby's trusted attorney for the previous 20 years.[12] The chancellor of the Duchy Sir Thomas Parry* was responsible for the return of an outsider, Edward Wymarke of London and Rutland, as Liverpool's second Member. In the event, Wymarke plumped for another Duchy-controlled seat, Newcastle-under-Lyme, and suggested his friend, Sir Hugh Beeston, of Beeston, Cheshire, as his replacement. Beeston was subsequently elected in May.[13] In December 1620, after 'proposition of divers gentlemen which were nominated', two non-residents were returned, namely Thomas May, brother of the new chancellor (Sir) Humphrey May*, and William Johnson, a servant of Sir Francis Bacon*.[14] Apart from the spring and summer session of 1610, the 1621 assembly was the only Parliament of the period in which the Duchy tabled legislation of its own. The bill concerned was to confirm certain decrees relating to its customary estates, which was read on 1 Dec. but disappeared after being committed.[15]

The chancellor of the Duchy played a much less prominent role in the 1624 election, when two local gentlemen were returned. The first seat went to Sir Thomas Gerrard of Bryn, brother-in-law to the younger Sir Richard Molyneux. It seems likely that the corporation offered the nomination to Molyneux, who had inherited the lordship of Liverpool in 1623, in an attempt to establish better relations with him than they had enjoyed with his predecessor, while Gerrard, seeking protection from numerous creditors, may have been pressed upon the town by Molyneux, though he later claimed to have been elected against his will. The second Member, George Ireland, was the son and legal colleague of Thomas Ireland of Bewsey. When the Catholic Gerrard ignored the summons to take the oaths at the opening of the session, Ireland, whose wife was a recusant, helped him escape the censure of the House. Liverpool was severely criticized for its choice, and was served by only one Member in this session as a result of Gerrard's aberrance; no writ for a replacement was issued.

The Duchy was denied any control over Liverpool's election in 1625, for the town instead appealed to the Stanleys, returning 18 year-old James Stanley, Lord Strange, future 7th earl of Derby, as the first Member, together with Edward Moore, a senior alderman. The choice of these candidates bolstered the town's renewed attempts to secure the charter in the first year of the new king's reign. Stanley further assisted in this objective by serving as mayor the following year; nevertheless, like his father he demonstrated very little interest in Liverpool's affairs thereafter. In 1626 the first seat was taken by Edward Bridgeman of Sankey Bridge, Warrington, brother of the bishop of Chester, after he failed to be elected for Wigan, which he represented in 1625 and 1628. The bishop, perhaps through the mediation of the chancellor of the Duchy, was presumably responsible for persuading Liverpool to return him.[16] The second seat went to a local gentleman, Thomas Standish of Duxbury, who was also the holder of a minor Duchy office. In 1628 Henry Jermyn, whose cousin was married to Sir Humphrey May, was certainly a Duchy nominee, but the election of John Newdigate, a Warwickshire squire, can only be attributed to the influence of his mother's Cheshire and Lancashire kinsmen, including Sir Charles Gerrard of Halsall, a non-resident freeman of Liverpool, and Newdigate's own passing acquaintance with Sir Richard Molyneux II, who shared an interest in horse breeding.

Some, but not all, of the borough's MPs were admitted to the freedom of Liverpool. Apart from Johnson, who was enrolled in his absence and free of charge at the time of his election, it is notable that most of the outsiders who were returned did not become freemen, nor did they receive wages. Notwithstanding the town's rising income, it was not a wealthy borough, and the corporation was apparently content to accept the return of Members with no obvious connection to or interest in Liverpool, particularly after the new charter had been granted, so long as they were willing to meet their own expenses.

[1] E.M. Hance and T.N. Morton 'The Burgess Rolls of Liverpool during the 17th century', *Trans. Hist. Soc. Lancs. and Cheshire*, xxxvi. 145-58. [2] W. Camden, *Britannia* (1610), p. 748; R. Muir and E.M. Platt, *Hist. of Municipal Govt. in Liverpool*, 87-9; M. Gregson, *Fragments relating to the Hist. and Antiquities of Liverpool*, 168. [3] G. Chandler, *Liverpool under Jas. I*, 57; G. Chandler, *Liverpool under Chas. I*, 54. [4] *HMC Hatfield*, xi. 465-7; R.C. Jarvis, 'The Head Port of Chester, and Liverpool, its Creek and Member', *Trans. Hist. Soc. of Lancs. and Cheshire*, cii. 69-84; *VCH Lancs*. iv. 17; *CSP Dom.* 1619-23, pp. 24, 34, 43, 104. [5] Liverpool RO, 352 CLE/TRA/3/8; Chandler, *Jas. I*, 187. [6] CLRO, Rentals Box 1.14; Misc. Deeds 52.14; Muir and Platt, 94-6. [7] *HMC Hatfield* xxiv, 3; *VCH Lancs*. iv. 16-19; C.F. Patterson, *Urban Patronage in Early Modern Eng.* 66. [8] Chandler, *Jas. I*, 195, 200; *VCH Lancs*. iv. 19; *Liverpool Municipal Recs.* ed. J. Picton, i. 156-7; J. Touzeau, *The Rise and Progress of Liverpool 1551-1835*, i. 156. [9] Chandler, *Chas. I*, 1-7, 44, 116, 119; Muir and Platt, 165-89. [10] R. Somerville, *Hist. of Duchy of Lancaster*, ii. 2-3; B. Coward, *The Stanleys, Lords Stanley and Earls of Derby 1385-1672* (Chetham Soc. ser. 3. xxx), 128-39. [11] Chandler, *Jas. I*, 153. [12] Ibid. 162. [13] R.C.L. Sgroi, 'The Electoral Patronage of the Duchy of Lancaster, 1604-28', *PH*, xxvi. 314. [14] Chandler, *Jas. I*, 241. [15] Somerville, ii. 19-20; R. Hoyle, 'Vain Projects: The Crown and its Copyholders in the Reign of Jas. I', *Eng. Rural Soc. 1500-1800* ed. J. Chartres and D. Hey, 86-101. [16] Sgroi, xxvi. 322.

R.C.L.S.

NEWTON

Right of election: in the freemen

Number of voters: unknown

3 Mar. 1604	SIR JOHN LUKE
	RICHARD ASHTON
c. Mar. 1614	WILLIAM ASHTON II
	ROGER CHARNOCK
4 Jan. 1621	SIR GEORGE WRIGHT
	RICHARD KIPPAX
17 Jan. 1624	THOMAS CHARNOCK
	EDMUND BRERES
6 May 1625	SIR MILES FLEETWOOD
	HENRY EDMONDES
c. Jan. 1626	SIR MILES FLEETWOOD
	HENRY EDMONDES
29 Feb. 1628	SIR HENRY HOLCROFT
	SIR FRANCIS ANNESLEY, bt.

Newton, a small market town near Wigan, appeared in the Domesday book as one of the townships in the 'fee of Makerfield', lying within Winwick parish in West Derby hundred, and was often named Newton-in-Makerfield or Newton le Willows.[1] Although it received charters for a market and a fair in 1257 and 1301, it was never incorporated.[2] Courts leet were held by the bailiff and steward, both of whom were appointees of the lord of the manor, who was formally known as the 'baron' of Newton. The bailiff, and perhaps also the steward, served as returning officers.[3] Members had first been sent to Parliament in 1559 as a result of pressure from the duchy of Lancaster. The then steward, William Fleetwood[†], a duchy official and later recorder of London, was distantly related to the 'baron' of Newton, Sir Thomas Langton (d.1569).[4] Langton's descendants sold the lordship of the manor in 1594 to another branch of the Fleetwood family, and with it the right of 'nomination, election and appointment of two burgesses to the Parliament'. However, the terms of the sale did not take effect until the death of Thomas Langton[†] on 20 Feb. 1604.[5] Langton's successor was Sir Richard Fleetwood of Colwich, Staffordshire and Penwortham in Lancashire, who served as lord of Newton throughout this period.[6] The franchise was vested in the freemen, around a dozen of whom regularly signed Newton's election indentures.[7] Despite its role in Newton's early electoral history, the duchy of Lancaster had lost all influence by the middle of Elizabeth's reign. Between 1604 and 1626 Members were chosen by Fleetwood or his cousin Sir Miles Fleetwood* without apparent reference to the chancellor of the duchy, and in 1628 the 'baron' shared his right of nomination with his son. It is unlikely that Newton was wealthy enough to pay wages to its parliamentary representatives during this period.

The election held in March 1604 took place less than three weeks before the opening of the session, and was perhaps delayed by Langton's death and his replacement by Fleetwood as lord of the manor. Sir John Luke was awarded the first seat but may not have been the first choice, as his name on the indenture appears over an erasure. A Hertfordshire man who later sat for St. Albans, Luke was connected by marriage to both the chancellor of the duchy, Sir John Fortescue*, and to Sir Miles Fleetwood.[8] The second seat went to the borough's steward, Richard Ashton, who had previously sat in 1601. It is not clear whether he returned himself, but if he did his eligibility went unquestioned.

In 1614 one seat was conferred on Ashton's younger son, William, while the other went to Roger Charnock, a local lawyer whose stepmother was Sir Richard Fleetwood's aunt. Charnock and his elder brother Thomas, who sat for Newton in 1624, were linked to the Fleetwoods both professionally and financially. They also shared with them many of the same connections, as a result of their marriages into various Lancashire families known for their adherence to Catholicism. Fleetwood himself was one of several crypto-Catholic members of the Lancashire gentry who bought baronetcies in 1611.[9]

The first seat in 1621 went to Sir George Wright, of Richmond in Surrey, the clerk of the Stables. He was possibly helped by Sir Miles Fleetwood, a client of the marquess of Buckingham, then master of the Horse. Sir Miles, who twice represented the borough himself, wielded considerable influence over his cousin, and was responsible for the selection of at least three of the five outsiders who sat for Newton during the period. The second seat went to Sir Richard Fleetwood's brother-in-law, Richard Kippax. Both Wright and Kippax spoke in the Commons on bills relating to matters of probate, which suggests that they might have been prompted to do so by their patron; certainly they had no other shared interest. Kippax also spoke on the Irish cattle bill, which was surely of interest to Fleetwood, who owned extensive lands in Munster and Cork.[10]

In 1624 two local men were elected, both of whom had close ties with Sir Richard Fleetwood and each other: Thomas Charnock of Astley, and Edmund Breres, a Gray's Inn lawyer and native of Preston. Breres had persuaded Fleetwood and Charnock to act as sureties for loans he could not repay.[11] He and Charnock therefore sought entry to Parliament as a means of obtaining protection from Breres' creditors.

In the first and second Caroline parliaments the patronage of the borough appears to have been entirely dominated by Sir Miles Fleetwood, who allocated the first seat to himself on both occasions. The second seat went twice to Henry Edmondes, son of the privy councillor and treasurer of the Household Sir Thomas Edmondes*. Sir Richard Fleetwood emigrated to Ireland in around 1626, leaving his son Thomas in control of Newton.[12] Thomas Fleetwood appeared as joint lord of the manor on the election indenture of 1628 though he was then aged only 19.[13] Two officials in the Irish administration were returned, Sir Henry Holcroft and Sir Francis Annesley. Both may have come into contact with Sir Richard Fleetwood in Ireland; Annesley was also a client of Buckingham, and may have had links with Sir Miles Fleetwood, who was also developing his Irish interests at that time.[14]

<hr>

[1] J.H. Lane, *Newton in Makerfield*, i. 3-6. [2] *CChR*, ii. 1, iii. 2; *VCH Lancs*. iv. 132-6. [3] Lane, 9, 22; E. Baines, *Hist. of Palatinate and Duchy of Lancaster* ed. J. Croston, iv. 382-3, 391. [4] R. Somerville, *Hist. of Duchy of Lancaster*, i. pp. xiv, 319, 505-6. [5] *Local Gleanings Relating to Lancs. and Cheshire* ed. J.P. Earwaker, ii. 686; *Lancs. IPMs* ed. J.P. Rylands (Lancs. and Cheshire Rec. Soc. iii), 105-6. [6] *VCH Lancs*. i. 374-5; *Wills and Inventories* ed. G.J. Piccope (Chetham Soc. li), 246-55; *Vis. Staffs.* ed. H.S. Grazebrook, 129-30; R.W. Buss, *Fleetwood Fam. of Colwich, Staffs*. 3; *Vis. Lancs.* (Chetham Soc. lxxxii), 122. [7] C219/35/53; 219/37/138; 219/38/134; 219/39/126. [8] R.C.L. Sgroi, 'The Electoral Patronage of the Duchy of Lancaster, 1604-28', *PH*, xxvi. 322-3. [9] *47th DKR*, app. 126; *CSP Dom*. 1641-43, p. 435. [10] Nicholas, *Procs. 1621*, i. 246; *CJ*, i. 615b, 650b. [11] DL1/285, 290, 291, 297, 299, 300; C2/Chas.I/F35/12; C2/Chas.I/F50/81. [12] M. MacCarthy-Morrogh, *Munster Plantation: Eng. Migration to Southern Ire. 1583-1641*, p. 195; E.T. Bewley, 'Fleetwoods of Co. Cork', *Jnl. of Royal Soc. of Antiqs. of Ire.* xxxviii. 103-25. [13] C219/41A/31. [14] E.T. Bewley, 'An Irish Branch of the Fleetwood Fam.', *The Gen.* n.s. xxiv. 217-41.

R.C.L.S.

PRESTON

Right of election: in the corporation

Number of voters: 24

c. Feb. 1604	SIR VINCENT SKINNER WILLIAM HOLT
c. Mar. 1614	EDWARD MOSLEY HENRY BANISTER
13 Dec. 1620	(SIR) EDWARD MOSLEY SIR WILLIAM POLEY
26 Jan. 1624	(SIR) EDWARD MOSLEY SIR WILLIAM POLEY
2 Mar. 1624	FRANCIS NICHOLS *vice* Poley, chose to sit for Sudbury
c. *Nov. 1624*	SIR WILLIAM HERVEY II *vice* Nichols, died 7 Sept. 1624
2 May 1625	SIR WILLIAM HERVEY II HENRY BANISTER
26 Jan. 1626	GEORGE GARRARD THOMAS FANSHAWE II
4 Mar. 1628	GEORGE GARRARD SIR ROBERT KERR

By the early seventeenth century Preston was already regarded as Lancashire's centre for local government and administration, and a focal point of county society.[1] Described by Camden as 'a great and (for these countries) a fair town, and well inhabited', the parish had a population of around 3,000 on the eve of the Civil War.[2] A new charter granted in 1566 defined Preston as 'a free corporate borough ... of one mayor, two bailiffs and the burgesses'. The mayor and bailiffs were chosen annually from among the common council of 24 principal burgesses, who constituted the borough's electorate until 1661, when the franchise was extended to all 'in-burgesses', or resident freemen.[3] Preston was renowned for its guild festival, a fair and celebrations lasting several days held only once every 20 years, at which all freemen were enrolled as guild members. In 1602 there were over 530 resident freemen, as well as many honorary 'out-burgesses' among the local gentry, who actually outnumbered the in-burgesses. In 1622 the list of out-burgesses was topped by William Stanley, 6th earl of Derby and his son and heir James Stanley*, Lord Strange, followed by Sir Richard Houghton* of Hoghton and his son Sir Gilbert*, who successively

held the fee farm of Preston rectory from 1607.[4] The king stayed at Hoghton Tower while visiting Preston in August 1617, when the corporation presented James with a bowl and held a banquet.[5] Although the surrounding region was notorious for its adherence to Catholicism, the members of Preston's corporation were inclined to puritanism. Their resolutions, recorded in a 'White Book' from 1608, demonstrate an obsession with behavioural regulations, which included a strict dress code of 'decent and comely gowns of black cloth or other black stuff', and the enforcement of decorum on Sundays.[6] When John Taylor the 'water poet' visited Preston in 1618 he declared that he 'never saw a town more wisely governed'.[7]

The borough's parliamentary patronage had traditionally been shared between the earls of Derby and the chancellor of the duchy of Lancaster. In the early seventeenth century, however, the lack of interest shown in politics by the 6th earl of Derby allowed the Duchy to dominate the borough, taking the first seat in every election and even securing both places on several occasions. None of Preston's Members in this period had strong local connections with the town, and the neighbouring gentry, such as the Houghtons of Hoghton, demonstrated very little concern either to represent the borough or promote their own candidates. In 1604 the Duchy returned for the first seat Sir Vincent Skinner, an Exchequer official and minor officeholder in his native Lincolnshire. As an outsider, Skinner was included among the 'unlawfully' elected Members in a list circulated after the opening of the session by Arthur Hall†.[8] The second seat went to William Holt, a lawyer born at Ashworth, near Rochdale, and a freeman of Preston by 1602. Holt had previously sat for Clitheroe, the borough nearest his family's estates, but it is not known whether he attempted to obtain a seat there in 1604, ahead of the Preston election.[9] An active lawyer in its court at Westminster, he probably enjoyed the backing of the Duchy.

In 1614 the Duchy gave the first seat to its recently appointed attorney-general Edward Mosley, but there is no sign that it played any part in the return of the second Member, Henry Banister. Mosley, like Holt, was the younger son of a Lancashire family, and as a successful lawyer spent most of his time in the capital. He appears in the Preston guild roll of 1622, but was probably made a freeman much earlier. Mosley's long parliamentary service for Preston – he sat again in 1621 and 1624 – owed more to his position in the Duchy than to any local ties, for despite his inheritance of some property in Manchester he never resided there. Henry Banister, a London Goldsmith, was born in

Preston and was an honorary freeman of the guild by 1622. He may have been related to Thomas Banister, a principal burgess of the town who served as a bailiff several times and as mayor in 1610, 1617 and 1625.[10]

The Duchy nominated both Members in 1621, returning both Mosley and Sir William Poley, father-in-law of the new chancellor, (Sir) Humphrey May*. In this Parliament the Duchy exerted particular efforts to fill as many seats as it could with its own nominees to ensure support for a bill to confirm decrees relating to its customary estates, which was read on 1 Dec. but disappeared after being committed.[11] In 1624 the same two men were elected, though Poley, a native of Boxted in Suffolk, chose to sit for his home constituency of Sudbury. He was consequently replaced by Francis Nichols of Ampthill, Bedfordshire, another outsider who presumably owed his return to the Duchy. Nichols died in September 1624, and at a by-election Sir William Hervey of Ickworth, Suffolk, was chosen, again at the nomination of Sir Humphrey May, who was related by marriage to Hervey's wife's cousin. In the event Hervey did not take his seat, as the session had been prorogued since May and ended automatically on the death of the king in the following March.

Hervey was re-elected to the first Caroline Parliament, this time for the first seat, along with another former Member, the elderly Henry Banister. Two outsiders were returned in 1626. The first Member, George Garrard, a courtier, had previously represented Wigan in 1621 and was perhaps a Court acquaintance of Sir Humphrey May. The second Member, Thomas Fanshawe II, an Exchequer official, was probably recommended by his uncles (Sir) Thomas and William Fanshawe, who through their ties with the Duchy had built up sufficient influence in Lancashire to represent various boroughs there in virtually every Parliament of the period.[12] In 1628 Garrard was re-elected as the first Member, and the earl of Derby's son-in-law, Sir Robert Kerr (Carr), took the second seat.

So far as is known, Preston paid little attention to either parliaments or politics under the early Stuarts, the corporation being apparently content to return complete strangers as their representatives. Only those with personal ties to the region, namely Holt, Mosley, Banister and Kerr, became honorary freemen, and of these none were closely connected to the constituency. The 'White Book' records no payments of parliamentary wages or expenses in this period.[13]

[1] VCH Lancs. vii. 73-105; A. Crosby, Hist. of Preston Guild, 34-5.
[2] W. Camden, Britannia (1610), p. 752; D. Hunt, Hist. Preston, 63.

[3] Lancs. RO, DDX/123/11; J. Lingard, Charters of Preston; A. Hewitson, Hist. of Preston, 54-5, 127; P. Whittle, Hist. of Bor. of Preston, i. 253. [4] Preston Guild Rolls ed. W.A. Abram (Lancs. and Cheshire Rec. Soc. ix), 46-53, 75-88; CSP Dom. 1603-10, p. 381. [5] H.W. Clemesha, Hist. of Preston, 117; E. Baines, Hist. of Palatinate and Duchy of Lancaster ed. J. Croston, v. 305. [6] Lancs. RO, CNP 3/1/1, pp. 9, 10, 13, 17; W.A. Abram, Memorials of Preston Guilds, 37; Clemesha, 147. [7] Travels Through Stuart Britain: The Adventures of John Taylor, the Water Poet ed. J. Chandler, 21. [8] SP14/7/82.II. [9] W.S. Weeks, Clitheroe in Seventeenth Cent. 222. [10] H. Fishwick, Hist. of Par. of Preston, 78. [11] R. Somerville, Hist. of Duchy of Lancaster, ii. 19-20; R. Hoyle, 'Vain Projects: The Crown and its Copyholders in the Reign of Jas. I', Eng. Rural Soc. 1500-1800 ed. J. Chartres and D. Hey, 86-101. [12] Duchy of Lancaster Office-Holders ed. R. Somerville, 66-7. [13] Lancs. RO, CNP 3/1/1, p. 27.

R.C.L.S.

WIGAN

Right of election: in the freemen

Number of voters: 139 in 1628[1]

2 Mar. 1604	SIR WILLIAM COOKE					
	WILLIAM BROMLEY (not returned)					
	SIR JOHN PULTENEY vice Bromley, deleted from the return by the chan. of the of duchy Lancaster					
c. Mar. 1614	SIR RICHARD MOLYNEUX II					
	GILBERT GERARD					
4 Jan. 1621	SIR THOMAS GERRARD I, bt.					
	ROGER DOWNES					
28 Feb. 1621	GEORGE GARRARD vice Gerrard, deceased					
23 Jan. 1624	SIR ANTHONY ST. JOHN					
	FRANCIS DOWNES					
10 May 1625	FRANCIS DOWNES					
	EDWARD BRIDGEMAN					
18 Jan. 1626	SIR ANTHONY ST. JOHN					
	SIR WILLIAM POLEY					

		1st seat	2nd seat
1 Mar. 1628	SIR ANTHONY ST. JOHN	65	1
	EDWARD BRIDGEMAN	7	57
	Robert Gardner	1	12
	Edward Boulton		1
	Peter Houlford		1
	?Sir William Poley		1
	William Prescott		1

Wigan's history during this period is dominated by disputes between the corporation and the rector of the local parish, who was also the lord of the manor. At issue were such matters as tithes, market tolls, corn mills, charitable uses and, by 1628, control of the borough's parliamentary elections. The background to these quarrels lay in varying interpretations of the town's original charter, granted in 1246 by the rector John Mansell and confirmed that same year by Henry III, which ordained that a mayor, two bailiffs and the burgesses would constitute a 'free borough for ever', with a merchant guild, port moot court, and other municipal arrangements.[2] Under Elizabeth this charter was confirmed twice, first in 1561 by the rector, Thomas Stanley, who was also bishop of Sodor and Man, and again by the queen in 1585.[3] However, differences remained, and from 1616 hostilities were resumed after the appointment as rector of John Bridgeman, who claimed that the townsmen had unlawfully usurped his manorial rights. Bridgeman maintained that he exercised ultimate authority over the town and its courts, since under the charter the mayor derived all his powers from the rector's grant. Indeed, he once angrily asserted that the mayor was 'his mayor, and hath not authority to whip a dog'.[4] In 1618 the town petitioned the king against Bridgeman, but the four judges appointed to review the case, Archbishop Abbot, Lancelot Andrews, then bishop of Ely, lord chief justice Sir Henry Montagu*, and Sir Henry Hobart*, ruled in the rector's favour.[5] Even after he was promoted to the bishopric of Chester in 1619, Bridgeman continued to reside at Wigan for many years, and kept a 'ledger book' that, in the absence of any surviving corporation records, is our main source for the continuing controversy between himself and the town.

Wigan first sent MPs to Westminster in 1295, and after a long pause it resumed this practice in 1547, since which time the borough's electoral patronage had generally been shared between the duchy of Lancaster and a series of local landowning interests, including the earls of Derby and the nearby Gerards of Ince. This pattern continued during the early parliaments of James's reign, but broke down in the 1620s once Bridgeman began to assert his right of nomination. The corporation, resenting Bridgeman's interference, appealed to the chancellor of the duchy in 1626, but despite this call for assistance the duchy apparently withdrew its interest in 1628. The final Parliament of the period saw Wigan's first recorded contested election. Both seats attracted multiple candidates, and the election resulted in the compilation of a poll book. It also established a new pattern for future elections, as further contests ensued in April and November 1640. On the latter occasion a dispute over who was entitled to vote was resolved by the mayor and bailiffs' ruling

that, since the 'memory of man', the franchise had encompassed all the enrolled freemen of the town.[6]

In 1604 Wigan's mayor and returning officer was Sir Thomas Holcroft*, a distant relation of Lord Cecil (Robert Cecil†). It was probably through this connection that the borough accepted Sir William Cooke, the secretary of state's kinsman, as its first Member. The nomination for the second seat was offered to the chancellor of the duchy, Sir John Fortescue*, and at the election held on 2 Mar. the corporation returned William Bromley, the duchy's vice chancellor in the palatinate of Lancaster.[7] However, when the indenture arrived in London it was altered by Fortescue, to whom the returns of all the Lancashire boroughs were sent before being passed on to Chancery.[8] He deleted Bromley's name from the indenture, which is now illegible, and substituted his son-in-law, Sir John Pulteney, who had originally been Fortescue's nominee for the borough of Leicester.[9] Pulteney had previously represented Wigan in 1601 aged only 16, and he was still a minor on his re-election in 1604. The election went unchallenged in the Commons despite being noted among a list of 'unlawful' returns circulated by Arthur Hall†.[10]

The pattern of electoral patronage remained much the same in 1614. The first seat was taken by the under-age son and heir of Sir Richard Molyneux I* of Sefton, a powerful local magnate residing 12 miles west of Wigan. The Molyneuxs were second only to the earls of Derby in terms of county influence, and as receiver general of the duchy the elder Molyneux may also have had the backing of chancellor Sir Thomas Parry* for his son's return. The second seat went to the duchy's candidate Gilbert Gerard, clerk of the duchy council, who was distantly related to the Gerards of Ince. In 1621 both seats were taken by local gentlemen, one of whom, Roger Downes of Wardley, was probably also the duchy's choice for the second seat. The first seat went to Sir Thomas Gerrard, 1st bt. of the Bryn, close to Wigan, perhaps with the help of Molyneux I, whose daughter was married to Gerrard's son and heir. Gerrard died within two weeks of the start of the session and was replaced on 28 Feb. by George Garrard, a courtier who was perhaps acquainted with the new chancellor of the duchy, (Sir) Humphrey May*. Despite the similarity in their surnames, Gerrard and Garrard were unrelated.

Bishop Bridgeman's influence is not easily discernible in the 1621 election, perhaps because he was absent from Wigan. However, in 1624 he told the townsmen that they had 'no power to elect burgesses but by my sufferance'.[11] How the borough responded is unclear, but the first seat went to Sir Anthony St. John, a gentleman of Chester, who was almost certainly nominated by the bishop since he had no known connection with either Wigan or the duchy. The second seat went to Francis Downes, the under-age second son of former Member Roger Downes, presumably through his father's connections with the town, and perhaps with the backing of the duchy. The latter furnishes a further example of Wigan's tendency to elect very young Members.

In 1625 Francis Downes was re-elected, this time taking the first seat which had been left vacant following St. John's return for Cheshire, while the second seat went to the bishop's younger brother, Edward. The first sign of resentment at the bishop's involvement in the electoral process appeared in 1626, when the election coincided with a dispute concerning the mayor, Hugh Ford, and his father William Ford, whom Bridgeman had accused of misappropriating charitable funds. A commission of inquiry was being conducted by the duchy, but in order to ensure a favourable outcome the mayor allegedly promised one of the parliamentary seats to 'one of the chancellor's friends'.[12] Although his suit against the mayor was eventually successful, the Fords being ordered to repay £100 they had taken, Bridgeman believed that the townsmen had offered the nomination to the duchy deliberately in order to thwart his brother Edward, who was instead returned for Liverpool two days later.[13] Sir Anthony St. John once again took the first seat, and the second went to Sir William Poley, the father-in-law of chancellor Sir Humphrey May.

Bishop Bridgeman was determined to claim at least one nomination for himself, but the corporation was equally determined to hold its own against his influence. Consequently there was a contest in 1628, at which votes for a total of seven candidates were recorded. The poll book of that year takes the form of a list of 139 freemen of the town, of whom at least 74 voted. Votes for the first and second seats are given alongside each name, although the document itself is partly damaged, obscuring a few entries. It was dated 1 Feb. though the actual return was not signed until 1 March. Sir Anthony St. John received almost all the votes for the first seat, leaving two other candidates, Edward Bridgeman and Robert Gardner struggling behind. The second seat was more fiercely contested. At least 17 freemen voted against the bishop's brother, who nevertheless won comfortably. These protest votes were distributed among six contestants, most notably Robert Gardner, who attracted 12 supporters.[14] Gardner, although not a freeman of Wigan,

may have been related to the Gardners of Aspull, a neighbouring minor gentry family. Despite his defeat Gardner stood again in 1640, but without success.

Of the remaining candidates who each received one vote for the second seat, all were natives of Wigan except St. John and 'milus Poley', who was almost certainly the town's former Member, Sir William Poley. Edward Boulton and William Prescott were freemen, but neither voted for himself despite the fact that they had been put forward as rival candidates. Boulton was a churchwarden and had served Bridgeman as a tithe collector in 1626.[15] Prescott was the father-in-law of the tenant of Bridgeman's corn mill, Miles Leatherbarrow, and was involved in a lengthy dispute over the tenure of the corn mill on behalf of his daughter, enlisting the support of James Stanley*, Lord Strange, via his wife, one of Lady Strange's midwives.[16] Bridgeman's response to pressure from Strange was to complain bitterly of his tenants' disrespect, in particular writing on 29 Feb. that they 'began to rebel against me and would do nothing at my motion, nor would choose a burgess for this Parliament whom I commended'.[17] However, there is more evidence that Bridgeman was behaving in a paranoid fashion than there is of a concerted movement against him. Only three of his tenants at will voted for Gardner rather than Edward Bridgeman, and the majority supported his candidate, at least for the second seat.[18] Overall the most popular combination was the pairing of St. John and Bridgeman in first and second places respectively, but a total of six voters chose St. John first and Gardner second, while another five preferred Bridgeman first and Gardner second. St. John was therefore returned as the first Member with Bridgeman as the second. This would have happened even if the votes had not been cast separately for the first and second places, as St. John received 66 votes in total, two more than Bridgeman, who got 64.[19]

[1] D. Sinclair, *Hist. Wigan*, i. 197-9. [2] *VCH Lancs*. iv. 72; G.T.O. Bridgeman, *Hist. of Church and Manor of Wigan*, i (Chetham Soc. n.s. xv), 138, 147-79. [3] C54/1200. [4] *HMC Kenyon*, 24-5. [5] Bridgeman, ii (Chetham Soc. n.s. xvi), 216-23. [6] Sinclair, i. 221-23. [7] Wigan AS, D/DX Ap.G.3; *Duchy of Lancaster Office-Holders* ed. R. Somerville, 94. [8] R. Somerville, *Hist. Duchy of Lancaster*, i. 326, J.S. Roskell, *Lancs. Knights of Shire* (Chetham Soc. xcvi), 26-8. [9] C219/35/1/58. [10] SP14/7/82.II. [11] Wigan AS, D/DZ A13/1, pp. 112, 173. [12] Bridgeman, ii. 294. [13] R.C.L. Sgroi, 'The Electoral Patronage of the Duchy of Lancaster, 1604-28', *PH*, xxvi. 322. [14] Sinclair, i. 197-9. [15] *Wigan Par. Regs. 1580-1625* (Lancs. Par. Reg. Soc. iv), 64; Wigan AS, D/DZ A13/1, p. 193; Wigan Court Leet Recs. AB/CL, Roll 2, f. 25. [16] A.J. Hawkes, 'Wigan's Part in the Civil War', in *Trans. Lancs. and Cheshire Antiq. Soc.* xlvii. 84-138. [17] Wigan AS, D/DZ A13/1, pp. 210-11. [18] D. Hirst, *Representative of the People?*, 126-7; Bridgeman, ii. 308-18. [19] Sinclair, i. 197-9; Hirst, 114-5, 124-7.

R.C.L.S.

LEICESTERSHIRE

Number of voters: c.880–1,350 in 1620

1604	SIR GEORGE VILLIERS
	SIR THOMAS BEAUMONT I[1]
6 Feb. 1606	SIR HENRY BEAUMONT I *vice*
	Villiers, deceased
28 May 1607	SIR BASIL BROOKE *vice*
	Sir Henry Beaumont, deceased

24 Mar. 1614[2] GEORGE HASTINGS
  SIR THOMAS HESILRIGE

c.Dec. 1620 SIR THOMAS BEAUMONT II, (bt.) 80[3] 100[4]
  SIR HENRY HASTINGS   800[5] 1200[6] 1250[7]
  (SIR) GEORGE HASTINGS   800[8] 1200[9] 1250[10]

  Double return of Beaumont and
  (Sir) George Hastings.
  HASTINGS declared elected 9 Feb. 1621.[11]

15 Jan. 1624 SIR THOMAS HESILRIGE, (bt.)
  SIR HENRY HASTINGS

5 May 1625[12] FERDINANDO HASTINGS, Lord
  Hastings
  SIR WOLSTAN DIXIE

12 Jan. 1626 SIR HENRY HASTINGS
  FRANCIS STARESMORE

6 Mar. 1628 FERDINANDO HASTINGS, Lord Hastings
  SIR EDWARD HARTOPP, bt.

During the Elizabethan period the electoral politics of Leicestershire were dominated by the earls of Huntingdon, heads of the powerful Hastings family. George, 4th earl of Huntingdon (Sir George Hastings[†]), who succeeded to the title in 1595, was lord lieutenant and *custos rotulorum* of the county, steward and receiver of the honour of Leicester (part of the duchy of Lancaster), and forester of the forest of Leicester.[13] It is perhaps not surprising that Thomas Fuller thought there was 'something monarchical' about the stone tower of the family seat at Ashby-de-la-Zouch, in the north-west of the county.[14] However, by the 1590s the family was heavily in debt, and in 1601 Sir John Grey* challenged the Hastings' electoral grip on the county, although he was unsuccessful.[15] Grey benefited from the accession of James I in 1603, when he was made a gentleman of the Privy Chamber and his father Sir Henry Grey[†] was raised to the peerage as Lord Grey of Groby.[16]

There is no evidence that Sir John Grey sought re-election in 1604, nor that the 4th earl of Huntingdon nominated candidates, although he probably approved of Sir Thomas Beaumont I, whom he had unsuccessfully recommended to Leicester in 1597. However, Beaumont may not have needed Huntingdon's patronage as his elder brother, Sir Henry Beaumont I*, and father, Nicholas Beaumont[†], had both been elected for the county in the Elizabethan period. His colleague Sir George Villiers, who was elected despite not being on the bench, probably owed his return to his connection with the Beaumonts. He was Sir Thomas Beaumont I's half-uncle, and his second wife came from the same family and was probably in service in Sir Henry Beaumont I's household when he met her.[17]

The 4th earl of Huntingdon died on 30 Dec. 1604 and was succeeded by his grandson Henry, who was only 18 years old. On the same day Lord Grey wrote to Viscount Cranborne (Robert Cecil[†]) requesting appointment to the 4th earl's local offices, but was opposed by the 5th earl, who hoped to succeed to these himself when he came of age. The latter, who was married to the step-daughter of lord chancellor Ellesmere (Thomas Egerton[†]), got the better of the argument as the lieutenancy was temporarily placed in abeyance, and he was appointed to his grandfather's forest and duchy of Lancaster offices the following February. The post of *custos rotulorum*, however, went to Sir Henry Beaumont I, who was apparently on good terms with the 5th earl. Despite this, local influence of the Hastings family was eroded during the minority of the 5th earl of Huntingdon.[18]

Sir George Villiers died in January 1606 and Sir Henry Beaumont I was elected in his place the following month. There were 14 parties to the indenture, of whom the most prominent was Sir Wolstan Dixie*, a newcomer to Leicestershire who was connected with the Beaumonts by marriage.[19] Sir Henry died at the end of March 1607, by which date the 4th earl of Huntingdon was within a month of his 21st birthday. Consequently it was the earl who succeeded Beaumont as *custos rotulorum*, and on 16 May he was also appointed lord lieutenant.[20] Nevertheless, there is no evidence that Huntingdon played any part in the by-election held on 28 May. The election of Sir Basil Brooke, an obscure figure with a small and desperately encumbered estate, is somewhat mysterious, but it is apparent that Brooke had some connection with the Greys.

The emergence of the 4th earl of Huntingdon as a major figure in Leicestershire local administration in 1607 led to growing political conflict in the county.

Sir Thomas Beaumont I strenuously objected to the appointment of the earl's crypto-Catholic great-uncle, Walter Hastings, to the county bench in that year. Later the same year Huntingdon and his deputy lieutenants took over the administration of the shire's composition for purveyance, whereupon they faced opposition from Sir Thomas Beaumont and the Greys, who seem to have formed a political alliance at around this time. In early 1610 Huntingdon's opponents tried to put pressure on the earl to break off the composition agreement. They also alleged corruption in the assessment of arrears against Huntingdon's cousin Sir Henry Hastings, who was one of the deputy lieutenants. In May of that year Sir John Grey and Sir Henry Hastings* went to the Netherlands to fight a duel, but in the event bloodshed seems to have been averted.[21]

The proposed abolition of purveyance was a major element in the Great Contract, which was being negotiated in Parliament in the fourth session of Parliament in early 1610, although there is no evidence that either Sir Thomas Beaumont I or Brooke then spoke about that subject in the Commons. During the recess Beaumont consulted his constituents about the Contract and on 7 Nov. he reported that he was 'charged by his country to assent to go forward with the bargain', although 'they pressed me particularly to tell them whether the impositions, which were resolved in Parliament to be unlawful, were ... to be laid down'.[22] However, Beaumont and his fellow Members rejected the contract.

In 1611 Sir Thomas Beaumont I and the Greys tried to usurp Huntingdon's position as principal intermediary between the county and Whitehall by offering to negotiate a new purveyance composition agreement themselves. In addition, in September of that year they organized a petition to Ellesmere against the appointment to the bench of John Bale, a Hastings retainer alleged to have suborned juries. However, Sir John Grey died the following month and without his Court contacts the new composition scheme collapsed. Furthermore, Huntingdon organized a petition in favour of Bale, whose appointment was confirmed at a special hearing of the assizes the following March. Although Star Chamber suits against Sir Henry Hastings continued to rumble on, Huntingdon's control over Leicestershire had been confirmed.[23]

Heartened by his victory over the Beaumont-Grey alliance, Huntingdon made his first attempt to influence Leicestershire electoral politics. On 14 Mar. 1614 Robert Heyrick†, a prominent Leicester alderman, reported that the earl hoped to secure the election of his brother, the Gray's Inn lawyer George Hastings, as knight of the shire. Nine days later he wrote that the county court was to take place the following day, between eight and nine in the morning. As the election coincided with the assizes the county justices may have taken the opportunity to meet together and agree on two nominees to be presented to the freeholders. At the subsequent election Huntingdon's choice of George Hastings was confirmed, the other successful candidate being Sir Thomas Hesilrige, who was one of the few members of the bench who appears to have been able to remain neutral in the dispute between Huntingdon and the Greys.[24]

In February 1615 the Privy Council rebuked the county justices for collecting only £400 out of the £1,000 which had been subscribed for the Benevolence launched in the aftermath of the Addled Parliament. Eventually, however, over £900 was raised while Huntingdon himself contributed a further £100.[25]

By the time of the elections to the third Jacobean Parliament both Sir Thomas Beaumont I and Lord Grey were dead. Lack of significant opposition in the county may have encouraged Huntingdon to nominate not one but two members of his family, George Hastings, who had been knighted the year before, and Sir Henry Hastings. However, another candidate also entered the ring, this being Sir Thomas Beaumont II, the son of Sir Henry Beaumont I. Although the nephew of Sir Thomas Beaumont I, there is no evidence that Sir Thomas Beaumont II had previously been on bad terms with Huntingdon. He had not joined his uncle and the Greys in opposing Bale's membership of the bench in 1611, and he had been a militia officer under Huntingdon.[26] Beaumont probably contested the election not in order to oppose Huntingdon, but to obtain protection from his increasing debts, and he may have been encouraged in this by his kinsman, the royal favourite George Villiers, marquess of Buckingham.

The election took place at the castle at Leicester, as seems to have been usual in this period. Estimates of the numbers of voters vary. The *Commons Journal* stated that 1250 men voted for the two Hastings candidates, while one diarist recorded that 'about the number of twelve hundred ... gave their voices'. Edward Nicholas says that 1200 voted for the Hastings and that not above 100 voted for Beaumont. Sir Thomas Wentworth gives the total cast for the Hastings as 800 and states that only 80 votes were given to Beaumont. Despite the differences between them, all accounts agree that an overwhelming majority voted for the two Hastings candidates. An indenture naming Sir George Hastings first and Sir Henry Hastings second was drawn up and was sealed by 17 freehold-ers. It was then delivered to the under-sheriff, who also seems to have sealed it. However, the sheriff himself, Sir Alexander Cave, had previously been a supporter of the Grey faction and he adjourned the election until two in the afternoon. Once again the two Hast-ings candidates were elected, but this time some of those present voted for both Sir Henry Hastings and Sir Thomas Beaumont, whereupon Cave drew up another indenture and returned them, thus excluding Sir George Hastings altogether.[27]

On 23 Jan. 1621 Buckingham wrote to Sir George asking him not to contest the outcome of the elec-tion. However, on 6 Feb. a petition in the name of the freeholders of the county was heard at the privi-leges committee. In defence of his election Beaumont claimed that many who had been present at the first election had been copyholders rather than freehold-ers and had therefore not been eligible to vote. He also claimed that force had been used 'to withhold some on the other part, by sound of drum, and staves, etc.', and added that, being neither a freeholder nor a resident of Leicestershire, Sir George Hastings was not eligible for election.[28]

Sir George More reported the case to the Commons the following day. The likely outcome was sufficiently evident for (Sir) George Calvert* to report to Buck-ingham that 'Sir Thomas Beaumont's election ... will not hold'.[29] Beaumont's allegations of irregularities in the election were evidently not taken seriously, and it was successfully argued that Sir George Hastings' possession of a rent charge out of the Hastings estate in the county was equivalent to freehold property. The issue of his non-residence seems to have caused more problems, but it was quickly realized that if the requirement were to be enforced a high proportion of the House would have to be unseated. It is therefore not surprising that the Commons accepted Sir Edward Coke's argument that the relevant clauses in the stat-utes were not binding. On 9 Feb. the House ruled in favour of Sir George Hastings and the sheriff was ordered to return the original indenture.[30]

The 1622 benevolence for the Palatinate seems to have aroused widespread opposition in Leicester-shire. Sir Wolstan Dixie* and Sir Thomas Hesilrige were among those called before the Privy Council for refusing to contribute and the amount collected, which totalled about £650, was significantly lower than had been raised in 1614.[31]

Despite the ultimate defeat of Sir Thomas Beau-mont II, Huntingdon seems to have been unsettled by the 1621 election dispute. In May 1623 he nominated

Sir John Grey's son, Henry, 2nd Lord Grey of Groby (Henry Grey, earl of Stamford†), who had recently come of age, to the Leicestershire bench and subse-quently appointed him one of his deputy lieutenants, presumably in the hope of neutralizing a potential source of opposition.[32] When the next Parliament was summoned in 1624 Huntingdon made careful prepara-tions. On 12 Jan. the sheriff, Sir John Bale, grandson of Huntingdon's controversial henchman, informed the earl that he had received the writ and that the elec-tion would be held on the next county day, which was the following Thursday. The same day Huntingdon wrote to the mayor of Leicester asking him to delay the borough's election until after the county day, presum-ably with the aim of adjusting his nominations for the borough should the shire election go against him. On the day itself Sir Henry Hastings was returned, as was Sir Thomas Hesilrige. Shortly thereafter Sir George Hastings was nominated for the borough of Leicester.[33]

One possible reading of the evidence is that Huntingdon, having tried to secure the return of both Sir George and Sir Henry Hastings for the county, was forced to turn to the mayor of Leicester after the election for a seat for Sir George. However, it seems implausible that Sir George Hastings, who was ulti-mately rejected by Leicester's voters, was ever put forward for the county. Hesilrige makes an unlikely anti-Huntingdon candidate, having been one of the earl's deputy lieutenants since at least 1618. True, Huntingdon had lost the right to appoint his own deputy lieutenants in June 1623, but the earl appointed Hesilrige's son captain of the county's mounted militia the following September. It is perhaps more likely that Huntingdon had decided from the outset that it was too provocative to put up two members of his own family and that it had always been his intention to nominate Sir George Hastings for Leicester.[34]

The rejection of Sir George Hastings at Leicester in 1624 may have led Huntingdon to decide to nomi-nate him for the county again the following year. On 9 Apr. 1625 Huntingdon instructed his servant, Thomas Wright, to assemble the freeholders by 7 a.m. on polling day; 'and for the other knight', his employer wrote,

at my coming home, by the grace of God, you shall know who I desire should be the other, wherein I will be very careful to nominate such a one unto them as shall be fitting for that place, both for his religion, wisdom and estate, and such a one as may be best accommodated to do the country service.[35]

Before the election took place, however, Huntingdon had changed his plans. He transferred his brother to the borough and for the county put up his 17-year old son, Ferdinando, Lord Hastings. His second candidate turned out to be Dixie, who had opposed him over the admission of Bale to the county bench, but may have switched sides after the death of Sir Thomas Beaumont I. In May 1625 Huntingdon regained his right to appoint his deputy lieutenants and seems to have taken the opportunity to make a radical change. None of the old deputies, including Hesilrige and Sir Henry Hastings, were reappointed. Their replacements included Dixie, Lord Grey and Francis Staresmore*.[36]

In 1626 Huntingdon decided that it was time to send his son to Cambridge. He therefore nominated Sir Henry Hastings again and allowed the second seat to go to Staresmore who, after the election, sent the earl regular reports of parliamentary proceedings.[37] On the day of the election the youthful sheriff, Sir Thomas Hartopp, arrested Hastings in the castle yard on a commission of rebellion, having first failed to persuade Hastings 'to disclaim his election'. However, Hastings must have been released soon thereafter, as he had taken his seat by 25 Mar. 1626, when his petition against the sheriff was read. The House found in favour of Hastings and on 4 May Hartopp was obliged to acknowledge his guilt on his knees before the House. Staresmore died on 8 May 1626, but no writ appears to have issued before the dissolution.[38] The attempt to gather a Benevolence after the 1626 Parliament was a failure. On 18 Aug. the justices, including Sir Henry Hastings and Sir Wolstan Dixie, reported that their efforts had been unavailing, 'most crying a Parliament' and 'because the denial was so general, the givers so few and the gift not fit for a supply we thought [fit] to omit the particulars'.[39]

The following November Sir William Faunte, one of the Leicestershire justices of the peace, wrote to Dixie accusing Huntingdon of overcharging the county for the militia and embezzling the surplus.[40] At the public meeting to initiate the execution of the Forced Loan at Leicester on 15 Jan. 1627, attended by two representatives of the Privy Council, (Sir) John Coke* and William, 2nd earl of Exeter (William Cecil†), these charges were reiterated by Sir Henry Shirley, a wealthy Leicestershire gentleman, who proposed that the surplus, allegedly amounting to £500, should be used towards the paying the Loan. Dixie defended the earl's conduct, but the accusations led to an investigation by the Privy Council. Huntingdon was particularly vulnerable because he was a Forced Loan refuser and, perhaps as a result, receipts initially came in slowly. However Huntingdon's most prominent

supporters in the county, including Dixie, agreed to implement the Loan, which eventually yielded over £3,000 in the county, and Huntingdon employed Sir John Skeffington*, whom he had appointed a deputy lieutenant after Staresmore's death but who also had contacts with Buckingham, to plead his cause before the Council in the following June. Despite his refusal to pay the Loan, Huntingdon was cleared of corruption and managed to retain his lieutenancy. Perhaps the king feared that to dismiss him against the backdrop of Faunte and Shirley's accusations would discourage the rigorous administration of the militia.[41]

In 1628 Shirley initially seems to have canvassed the county, although he probably withdrew before the date of the election.[42] Huntingdon felt sufficiently vulnerable to come to an agreement with Lord Grey. Together they nominated Lord Hastings and Sir Edward Hartopp of Buckminster, the cousin of the 1626 sheriff. Dixie, who was acting as go-between, wrote to Huntingdon on 2 Mar. 1628:

> The Lord Grey has not been at Bradgate since my being with your lordship, but I rest in hope he has endeavoured to procure Sir Edward Hartopp his presence at the election, ... I have carefully sounded the minds and affections of the freeholders and find them wholly your lordship's loving countrymen and servants and am persuaded none of them will be wanting at the day who are able to travel to Leicester. ... So I doubt not there will be a powerful and prevailing appearance both for my lord and Sir Edward. ... I conceive your lordship's presence at the time of election will be both acceptable and behoveful, lest any crotchet shall suddenly arise to break and sunder the forces conceived to be united.[43]

The strategy was successful, but on 26 Mar. Grey was promoted to the earldom of Stamford, and thereafter Huntingdon's primacy in the county was no longer beyond question.[44]

[1] SP14/7/82ii. [2] Cal. of Herrick Fam. Pprs. ed. P.M. Pugh (NRA 17342), 13. [3] CD 1621, v. 445. [4] Nicholas, Procs. 1621, i. 22. [5] CD 1621, v. 445. [6] Nicholas, i. 21. [7] CJ, i. 511a. [8] CD 1621, v. 445. [9] Nicholas, i. 21. [10] CJ, i. 511a. [11] CJ, i. 516a. [12] Procs. 1625, p. 691. [1] [3] HP Commons, 1558-1603, i. 192; HMC Hatfield, xvi. 387; Duchy of Lancaster Office-Holders ed. R. Somerville, 179, 182. [14] T. Fuller, Worthies, (1662), p. 126. [15] HP Commons, 1558-1603, i. 193-4; ii. 273. [16] CP, vi. 135; HMC 7th Rep. 526. [17] HP Commons, 1558-1603, i. 192-3. [18] CP, vi. 657-8; HMC Hatfield, xvi. 387; xvii. 603; HP Commons, 1558-1603, ii. 80; R. Cust, 'Honour, rhetoric and pol. culture: the earl of Huntingdon and his enemies', Pol. Culture and Culture Pols. in Early Modern Europe ed. S.D. Amussen and M.A. Kishlansky, 87-9. [19] C219/35/1/44. [20] Cust, 'Honour', 88; Sainty, Lords Lieutenants, 26. [21] R. Cust, 'Purveyance and Pols. in Jacobean Leics.', Regionalism and Revision ed. A. Gross and J.R. Lander, 152-5 [22] Parl. Debates, 1610 ed. S.R. Gardiner, 130; Procs. 1610 ed. E.R. Foster, ii. 318; Cust, 'Purveyance', 156-7. [23] HEHL, HA4327-31, 5436-8; CSP Dom. 1611-19, p. 73; STAC 8/54/13, 8/178/12; Cust, 'Purveyance', 157-9. [24] Nichols, County of Leicester,

i. 341 (see *Cal. of Herrick Fam. Pprs.* 13 for the correct dating of the second letter); Cust, 'Honour', 110. [25] *APC*, 1615-16, p. 42-3; E351/1950. [26] Cust, 'Honour', 110. [27] *CJ*, i. 511a; *CD 1621*, v. 445; vi. 360-1; Nicholas, i. 21-2; HEHL, HA4331. [28] *HMC Hastings*, iv. 204; *CD 1621*, iv. 22; *CJ*, i. 511b-12a. [29] *CJ*, i. 511b; *Fortescue Pprs.* ed. S.R. Gardiner (Cam. Soc. n.s. i), 151. [30] *CJ*, 515b-16a. [31] SP14/127/82; 14/135/62. [32] *HMC Hastings*, ii. 62; HEHL, HAM53/6, f. 129v. [33] HEHL, HA387, 1725, 5479. [34] HEHL, HAM53/6, ff. 73, 77, 88v. [35] *Procs. 1625*, pp. 691-2. [36] Sainty, 26; HAM53/6, f. 133v. [37] *Procs. 1626*, iv. 317-21. [38] Ibid. ii. 367, 369; iii. 142, 145, 155, 163; iv. 263. [39] HEHL, HAM53/6, f. 182v. [40] *CSP Dom.* 1625-6. p. 476; HEHL, HA2294. [41] *HMC Cowper*, i. 296, 298; *HMC Hastings*, iv. 209-10; HEHL, HA1676; *CSP Dom.* 1627-8, p. 193; T. Cogswell, *Home Divisions*, 142-3, 154-5, 158; Stowe, 743, f. 66. [42] Cogswell, 167. [43] *Procs. 1628*, vi. 154-5. [44] *CP*, xii. pt. 1, p. 217.

P.W.

LEICESTER

Right of election: in the corporation

Number of voters: 72

1 Mar. 1604	SIR HENRY BEAUMONT II	
	SIR WILLIAM SKIPWITH[1]	
	Sir John Pulteney*	
31 Oct. 1605	SIR WILLIAM HEYRICKE *vice*	
	Beaumont, deceased[2]	
19 May 1610	HENRY RICH *vice*	
	Skipwith, deceased	
2 Apr. 1614[3]	(SIR) HENRY RICH	
	SIR FRANCIS LEIGH I	
8 Jan. 1621	SIR RICHARD MORYSON	
	SIR WILLIAM HEYRICKE	
16 Jan. 1624	(SIR) HUMPHREY MAY	
	WILLIAM IVE, alderman	
	(Sir) George Hastings	
3 May 1625[4]	(SIR) HUMPHREY MAY	
	(SIR) GEORGE HASTINGS	36 or 37
	William Ive, alderman	20
	Arthur Hesilrige†	5[5]
22 July 1625	THOMAS JERMYN *vice*	
	May, chose to sit for Lancaster	39
	William Ive, alderman	17
	James Ellis	3[6]
13 Jan. 1626	(SIR) HUMPHREY MAY	
	(SIR) GEORGE HASTINGS	54
	James Ellis	8[7]
29 Feb. 1628	(SIR) HUMPHREY MAY	
	SIR JOHN STANHOPE II	

Leicester, the only parliamentary borough in Leicestershire, had returned Members since 1301.[8] The population at the beginning of the seventeenth century was about 3,500. In the late 1620s the corporation described the borough as 'consisting principally of manual trades ... very populous ... [with] many poor and standeth far from the sea or any navigable river is maintained chiefly by the fairs and market'. Trade in wool and textile production were important elements of the local economy.[9] Although historically part of the duchy of Lancaster, civic institutions had gradually evolved in the Middle Ages which were confirmed in the charter of 1589. This established a corporation consisting of 24 aldermen, from whom a mayor was annually elected, and 48 councilmen chosen by the aldermen from among the burgesses. Together the aldermen and councilmen constituted the common hall, whose members exercised the franchise.[10] Elections were held at the town hall. Of the six surviving indentures from this period, three were signed by the mayor alone; the others were also signed by between six and nine prominent members of the corporation.[11] Despite the 1589 charter the duchy of Lancaster remained a powerful electoral interest in this period. Another important influence was the earl of Huntingdon, head of the Hastings family, the most powerful in Leicestershire. He habitually filled the offices of the lord lieutenant and steward of the duchy lands in Leicestershire.[12] There is no evidence that any of the Members were paid in this period, although Beaumont and Skipwith were given wine and sugar after they returned from Westminster in 1604.[13]

Leicester obtained a further charter in 1599. Ostensibly it gave the corporation the right to appoint the steward and bailiff of the borough, previously duchy appointees.[14] However, in August 1603 one Christopher Tamworth presented the Leicester aldermen with a patent issued by the chancellor of the duchy of Lancaster, Sir John Fortescue*, appointing him steward of the borough. Although Tamworth was supported by the 4th earl of Huntingdon (Sir George Hastings†) the aldermen were understandably unwilling to accept his patent. This episode undoubtedly soured relations between the borough on the one hand and Huntingdon and Fortescue on the other, and helps explain why the borough refused to accept Huntingdon's nominee Christopher Cheney as recorder after John Stanford† died in December 1603. A further factor was that Cheney was 'a gentleman unknown' to the aldermen. Realizing that Cheney was unpopular, Huntingdon's kinsman, Sir Henry Hastings*, stepped in and offered himself as an alternative, but he was ignored and, on 14 Dec., the aldermen voted by

15 to eight to elect Augustine Nicholls instead. Two days earlier Tamworth initiated legal proceedings to compel the corporation to accept his patent.[15]

Given these circumstances it is hardly surprising that when Fortescue wrote to the corporation on 20 Jan. 1604 nominating his under-age son-in-law Sir John Pulteney for one of the borough's seats the reaction was unfavourable. Fortescue reminded the corporation that it had acceded to similar requests made by previous chancellors, and he assured the aldermen that Pulteney, who lived about 12 miles south of Leicester, would serve without payment.[16] However, the corporation had already promised one of its seats to Sir Henry Beaumont of Gracedieu in Leicestershire, a student at the Inner Temple who had recently emerged from the wardship of his kinsman Sir Henry Beaumont I*, one of the most influential members of the Leicestershire gentry. When it did so is uncertain, but it must have been before Michaelmas 1603, as Beaumont was made free of the borough in preparation for his election during the mayoralty of James Ellis, which finished at that date.[17] The corporation offered the remaining seat to Augustine Nicholls, its newly appointed recorder, who accepted on 25 Jan. but added that Sir William Skipwith, a Leicestershire gentleman who had a house in the town, wanted one of the borough seats for himself. Unaware of the promise made to Beaumont, Nicholls asked to 'be joined with so worthy a gentlemen' and stated that, had the borough not offered him the seat, he would have proposed Skipwith rather than himself.[18]

After the rejection of his candidate for the recordership, Huntingdon initially chose not to nominate any candidates himself. However, prompted by Fortescue, he wrote to the corporation on 31 Jan. urging it to accept Pulteney, although he added that he did 'not know how you will accept of my judgment herein, because I have found you stand off and on with me, … in other causes'. He also urged the borough to offer Fortescue the nomination of the other seat.[19] Later that day the aldermen replied that they could not proceed to the election because they had not received the writ. However, in the same letter they admitted that they had summoned a common hall regardless, which had failed to hold an election as it had been inquorate. On 14 Feb. Beaumont wrote to the corporation reminding it of its previous promise. With this confirmation of his continued interest in the seat, the borough was now unwilling to proceed with the election of Nicholls and Skipwith, and it is possible that when Nicholls came to the borough on 28 Feb. to be formally sworn in as recorder he agreed to withdraw his candidacy in Skipwith's favour. Two days later Beaumont and Skipwith

were elected, Skipwith having now become a freeman like Beaumont, for which privilege he and Beaumont paid £6 each.[20]

Huntingdon died in the following December, but relations between the corporation and his 18-year old successor, Henry, 5th earl of Huntingdon, remained poor. The 5th earl was not immediately appointed lord lieutenant because he was underage, but he did secure his predecessor's stewardship of the duchy of Lancaster properties in February 1605. Perhaps because the stewardship was his only significant office, he seems to have attached considerable importance to it. Consequently, he was alarmed to learn that the borough of Leicester was endeavouring to obtain a new charter that would rectify the defects in its earlier grant of 1599, particularly in relation to the jurisdiction of the duchy of Lancaster. In early 1605 he wrote to the attorney of the Duchy to protest that the borough's proposed new charter undermined the authority of the duchy of Lancaster and was therefore derogatory both to himself, as the Duchy's local representative, and to the king. As Huntingdon's mother-in-law was the wife of lord chancellor Ellesmere (Thomas Egerton†) he managed to block the new grant until 1609.[21]

Sir Henry Beaumont died in July 1605 and consequently a by-election was held on 31 October. Neither Fortescue nor the new earl of Huntingdon are known to have made any nominations, presumably because of continued poor relations with the borough; consequently Robert Heyrick† was able to return his brother Sir William, a wealthy London goldsmith and the king's jeweller, who had previously represented the town under Elizabeth. Relations between the borough and Huntingdon further deteriorated as a result of the Midlands Rising, the wave of anti-enclosure riots that affected several Midland counties in May and June of 1607. Huntingdon, having recently come of age and been appointed lord lieutenant of Leicestershire, ordered the corporation to erect a gibbet in Leicester, but the rioters had widespread support in the town, where the inhabitants had common rights in the surrounding fields and nearby royal forest. Consequently, the gibbet was torn down by the rioters. Huntingdon blamed the aldermen for failing to keep order and placed the mayor and Robert Heyrick (in whose ward the gibbet had been situated) under house arrest.[22]

The Midlands Rising marked the nadir of relations between Huntingdon and Leicester's corporation. However, things soon began to improve and in the autumn of 1607 a compromise over the question of the charter began to be hammered out, although agreement was not finally reached until the following year. Huntingdon promised to withdraw his objections to the new charter, and in return the corporation agreed to allow him to appoint the borough steward in alternate years. The charter was issued in April 1609 and by the end of the year the new arrangements for choosing the steward were in place.[23]

Sir William Skipwith died on 3 May 1610. That same day, capitalizing on his improved relations with the borough, Huntingdon wrote to the corporation nominating as Skipwith's replacement his kinsman Henry Rich, the younger son of Robert, 3rd Lord Rich (Robert Rich†). The aldermen replied that they were willing to elect Rich, but first they wanted him to visit the borough in order to confer the freedom on him and brief him on their affairs. Huntingdon, however, claimed that Rich was too busy to make the journey and asked for a copy of the freeman's oath to be sent to London so that the oath could be administered to him in the capital by Sir William Heyricke and the recorder. The aldermen acquiesced and consequently Rich was made free before his election but took the oath in London.[24]

When the next Parliament was summoned, in 1614, the corporation was in the process of seeking a patent to bring the hospital in the suburb of Newarke under its control. Consequently the aldermen were especially sensitive to the need to maintain good relations at Court.[25] On 21 Feb. Sir Thomas Parry*, who had succeeded Fortescue as chancellor of the duchy of Lancaster in 1607, wrote to the borough nominating Henry Felton, the grandson of the Leicestershire peer, Henry, 1st Lord Grey of Groby (Sir Henry Grey†). However, his letter was not received until 5 Mar., by which time there were other candidates on the scene.[26] Huntingdon, whose position at Leicester had been strengthened in 1612 when he successfully nominated his kinsman and counsel Francis Harvey† to succeed Nicholls as recorder,[27] felt emboldened to nominate not only his brother George Hastings* but also Henry Rich, who had now been knighted. In response Robert Heyrick, who may have remained bitter that Huntingdon had had him imprisoned seven years earlier, proposed an alternative combination, consisting of his brother, Sir William, and the recorder. This was almost certainly intended as the first step in a process of bargaining with Huntingdon, for if, as Heyrick correctly believed, Harvey refused the offer of a seat the way would be opened for a compromise arrangement, whereby Sir William Heyricke would be elected alongside one of Huntingdon's nominees. However, Robert Heyrick's plans were thwarted by the belated arrival of Parry's letter of 21 February. Acting on the

advice of Harvey, common hall agreed on 14 Mar. to offer one seat to Huntingdon and the other to Parry. This proposal was acceptable to Huntingdon because, by this stage, he was hoping to secure his brother's return for the county. On 17 Mar. the corporation notified Parry that it had decided to elect his candidate Felton, who should come up to be sworn in as a freeman, although it pointed out that previous chancellors 'have neither always written unto [us] about the choice of our burgesses neither always prevailed when they did write'. In the same letter the corporation also complained that the town was 'very much distressed by the former decay of tillage and depopulations and do see just cause to fear a daily increase of their misery'. However, before the borough's messenger reached London a further letter was received from Parry, withdrawing Felton's nomination and substituting another man in his stead, who was not named. This new nominee was presumably Sir Francis Leigh I, a Warwickshire gentleman who was elected with Rich on 2 April. Leigh was made free before his election but took his oath in London.

On 9 May 1614 the corporation wrote to Rich and Leigh at the house of Rich's father-in-law Sir Walter Cope*, requesting their support for all measures designed to prevent 'depopulation and decay of tillage' and to suppress the 'brewing of strong ale and beer'. However, there is no evidence that either Rich or Leigh displayed any interest in measures on these subjects while they were serving in the Commons.[28] With Heyricke's active assistance the following year the corporation secured the incorporation of the hospital. Heyricke also assisted the borough to become a staple for the wool trade three years later, enabling the town's wool merchants to become members of the Staplers' Company, which had recently been given a monopoly of the trade.[29]

In 1620 the borough again received two nominations from the earl of Huntingdon. Those named were Sir Richard Moryson, the lieutenant of the ordnance and one of Huntingdon deputy lieutenants, and Moryson's brother-in-law Sir William Harington*. On 17 Nov. the aldermen wrote to Huntingdon stating that they believed that the common hall would elect one of his nominees. The corporation again wrote to the earl on 16 Dec. agreeing to elect Moryson but insisting that the latter come up in person to be sworn a freeman. Huntingdon seems to have accepted that only one of his nominees would be elected but in his reply he insisted that Moryson could not be spared from his official duties and might be sworn in at London. The corporation tried to insist that it would not elect Moryson unless he appeared in person but whether it succeeded is uncertain. On 8 Jan. the common hall 'by the greater number' agreed to admit Moryson to the freedom and on the same day he was returned to Parliament.[30]

Leicester also received nominations from the countess of Devonshire, whose husband had recently purchased Leicester Abbey from Sir Henry Hastings*, on behalf of one of her sons, probably Edward Wortley*, who was made free of the borough in 1620, and from its recorder, Francis Harvey, on behalf of his son Stephen. Both were rejected in mid-December, although there is no evidence of a contest. Moryson's colleague was Sir William Heyricke, but why he should have prevailed in 1621 when he had failed in 1614 is unclear. It may be that he decided to follow the advice suggested by his brother Robert in March 1614, who wrote that 'if ever I live for to see another Parliament summoned, and that you have intention to be one of the House, we will take no other course, but have you speak to Mr. Chancellor to write but two lines to our town, that you may be one; it will be as sure as any Act of Parliament...'. Robert had died in June 1618, but in the previous March Sir William's brother-in-law (Sir) Humphrey May* had been appointed chancellor of the Duchy. Consequently it is possible that Heyricke was elected on the Duchy interest. No letters of nomination from May to the corporation survive, and when May stood for election for the borough himself in 1624 he was sufficiently unsure of his influence to seek Huntingdon's support. However, when the corporation wrote to its recorder on 16 Dec. rejecting his nomination of his son they asked him 'to give us leave to choose two burgesses' nominated by the borough's 'honourable friends'. The use of the plural here surely points to May.[31]

Heyricke's connection with the borough made it natural for the townsmen to turn to him, rather than Moryson, to conduct their business at Westminster. The corporation requested his assistance in nominating the town's commissioners to assess the subsidies granted by the 1621 Parliament.[32] In addition, on 29 Apr. a group of Leicester wool merchants wrote to Heyricke concerning the Commons' proceedings against the Staplers' Company monopoly of the wool trade. They claimed that they had been forced to purchase the freedom of the Company for £111 each in order to continue to practice their trade but were now worried that they would lose the benefits of membership without compensation. They asked Heyricke to advise them whether they should 'exhibit a bill for this grievance into the Parliament House', or if one had already been preferred then to ensure that they would be included in any concessions won.[33]

After the 1621 Parliament was adjourned on 4 June Heyricke wrote to the mayor to report the Commons' proceedings. In addition to celebrating the bellicose Protestation passed by the Commons on the last day of sitting, and claiming that there were 95 bills 'almost perfected for the good of the Commonwealth', he stated that he had delivered a petition from the borough 'concerning the abuse in the execution of the office of alnaging', the official inspection and measurement of woollen cloth, but added that 'as yet there is no time for the regulating of it'. He also acknowledged the receipt of the letter from the Leicester wool merchants, but claimed 'I cannot do them no good' because the Commons had declared the Staplers' monopoly a grievance.[34]

In 1624 May himself sought election at Leicester but was sufficiently uncertain of the Duchy interest to write to Huntingdon on 4 Jan. requesting his support. Five days later Huntingdon recommended that the borough should elect May 'for his own sake'. Interestingly, Huntingdon did not regard the chancellor as his candidate, and was waiting to see how his nominees at the county election fared before he decided who to recommend at Leicester. However, William Ive, a wealthy Leicester alderman, wanted a place, and persuaded his colleagues to try to hold the election before Huntingdon had a chance to send in his nomination. Consequently the corporation badgered the sheriff to send the writ as soon as he received it. The sheriff would have none of this, and on 10 Jan., after receiving the writ, he informed Huntingdon of the pressure he was under and of the corporation's intention to hold the election the following afternoon. On receipt of this information, Huntingdon immediately wrote to the corporation asking them to delay its election until after the county day. Faced with this direct request the aldermen were unable to refuse, and on 12 Jan. the mayor, James Ellis, agreed to the delay. However, he also stated that they would elect May on Huntingdon's recommendation, and in so doing he perhaps intended to suggest that were going to treat May as the earl's candidate. The county election was held three days later, on which day Huntingdon wrote to the corporation. He first tried to emphasize that May was not his candidate, arguing that 'in regard of the many favours the corporation hath received from him and his continual friendship to you, you could not deny to satisfy so honourable and courtly a gentleman'; he then proceeded to nominate his brother Sir George Hastings. At the election, which was held the following morning, Huntingdon's letter was read first, but it was Ive who was elected alongside May. Writing to the earl later that day the mayor stated that 'we are sorry that your honour is unsatisfied in your request', but he emphasized that Huntingdon had in fact nominated May, who had been chosen 'at your honour's request'. He also pointed out that Ive was 'a free burgess of our town, which by the laws and statutes of the realm we ought to chose'. May was made free before the election and, perhaps inadvertently, rubbed salt into Huntingdon's wounds by writing to thank the earl: 'I assure myself that I am more beholding to your favour for my election than to any interest I have of my own there'. In 1624 the corporation asked May for his aid in procuring the appointment of their nominees to the borough's subsidy commission.[35]

On 2 Apr. 1625 May wrote to Leicester announcing the summoning of Charles I's first Parliament and seeking re-election, offering to do 'any good office I may do to your corporation in general or to any particular member thereof'. Seventeen days later Sir Thomas Hesilrige, a prominent Leicestershire baronet who had sat for Leicestershire in 1624, nominated his eldest son Arthur†, claiming that this was 'the first request that I ever yet made to your society'. In fact he had written to the corporation in support of a suitor for a place at Newarke hospital seven years previously, but it seems clear from this that Hesilrige had not previously had close connections with the borough. Huntingdon initially intended that his brother Sir George Hastings should stand for the county, but in the event he substituted his heir Ferdinando, Lord Hastings, leaving Sir George free to contest the borough again, along with Ive. When the election was held on 3 May Sir Humphrey May was elected for the first seat unopposed. The record of the votes cast for the second is unclear, but Hastings seems to have garnered either 36 or 37 votes, Ive 21 and Hesilrige four. The election therefore represented a resounding victory for the Hastings interest in the borough, although this was more pronounced among the aldermen than among the common councillors.[36]

As well as securing the Leicester seat, May was elected for Lancaster. On 10 July he announced that he intended to represent the latter, a decision, he assured the members of the Leicester corporation, that 'does not proceed out of any disrespect of you, for I profess you have made me so much beholden to you that I do prefer no Duchy town in my care and affection before yours'. As his replacement he offered a kinsman, Thomas Jermyn, who was accepted by the mayor despite being 'altogether unknown to any one of us'. A substantial minority on the corporation was less compliant, but failed to agree on an alternative candidate. Ive found himself competing with a

woollen draper, James Ellis, the 1624 mayor, and was defeated two to one by Jermyn. The day after the election the mayor wrote to May announcing that Jermyn had been elected and made a freeman. Once again the Member was asked to come to the borough in person to take the freeman's oath, but there is no evidence that he ever did so.[37]

In 1626 Ive was mayor of the borough and therefore ineligible for election. On 2 Jan. May wrote to the borough again asking for a seat, promising that he would 'accept of no other place'. Huntingdon again waited until the day of the county election before nominating Sir George Hastings but was nevertheless successful. May was re-elected unopposed while Hastings secured an overwhelming victory over Ellis, by 54 votes to eight.[38]

There is no evidence that a townsman sought election in 1628. May was again returned for the first seat while the second went to Huntingdon's nominee Sir John Stanhope II, of Elvaston in Derbyshire, whose wife had been a lady-in-waiting to the earl's wife. Stanhope was made free before his election and was sworn on 8 Mar. at the town hall.[39] On 5 May the corporation agreed to send one of its number to Westminster to lobby Parliament in opposition to the deforestation of Leicester forest, which had been initiated under the supervision of Sir Miles Fleetwood* the year before. The borough chose not to take its protest to the Commons, possibly because it was counting on the support of Huntingdon, who had been the chief forester but had not been compensated for his loss of office. On 23 June petitions from the corporation and the inhabitants of the forest were submitted to the House of Lords and referred to a committee. However, when these were reported back three days later the only comfort the borough received was an order to move the king that a suit, which had been initiated in Star Chamber against the corporation after riots in opposition to the disafforestation, should cease. It is possible that the petition from the glaziers of Leicester, read in the Commons on 17 Feb. 1629, was on the same subject, as the corporation claimed that fuel from the forest was necessary for the local economy. The petition was referred to the committee for grievances but there were no further recorded proceedings. The corporation's opposition proved unavailing and the disafforestation went ahead.[40]

[1] Nichols, County of Leicester, i. 418. [2] Ibid. 417. [3] Ibid. 425. [4] Ibid. 426. [5] Leics. RO, BRII/18/15, f. 557; information from Dr. Catherine Patterson. [6] Leics. RO, BRII/18/15, f. 598; information from Dr. Catherine Patterson. [7] Leics. RO, BRII/18/16, f. 7; information from Dr. Catherine Patterson. [8] OR. [9] VCH Leics. iv. 76, 78; Recs.

of Bor. of Leicester ed. H. Stock, iv. 240. [10] *HP Commons, 1558-1603*, i. 193; C.F. Patterson, *Urban Patronage in Early Modern Eng.* 196. [11] C219/38/105; 219/39/130; 219/41A/104. [12] Sainty, *Lords Lieutenants*, 26; *Duchy of Lancaster Office-Holders* ed. R. Somerville, 179, 182. [13] *Recs. of Bor. of Leicester*, iv. 32. [14] *HP Commons, 1558-1603*, i. 193. [15] Nichols, i. 418; *Recs. of Bor. of Leicester*, iv. 5-6; Patterson, 201; J. Thompson, *Hist. Leicester*, 327; *HP Commons, 1558-1603*, iii. 435-6; Leics. RO, BRII/18/8/405. [16] Leics. RO, BRII/18/8/289. [17] Leics. RO, BRII/18/8/440; Nichols, 418. [18] Leics. RO, BRIII/18/421. [19] Leics. RO, BRII/18/8/431; Thompson, 326. [20] Leics. RO, BRII/18/8/428, 440; Nichols, 418. [21] Patterson, 202-5; *CSP Dom.* 1603-10, p. 194. [22] Nichols, i. 420; *Recs. of Bor. of Leicester*, iv. 59-64. [23] Patterson, 206-7; *Recs. of Bor. of Leicester*, iv. pp. xxxvii, 91, 240. [24] *HMC 8th Rep.* pt. 1 (1881), 435; Thompson, 342; HEHL, HA5458. [25] Nichols, i. 339-40. [26] Leics. RO, BRII/13/3; *Recs. of Bor. of Leicester*, iv. 148. [27] Nichols, i. 424; Patterson, 195; W. Prest, *Rise of the Barristers*, 367. [28] *Recs. of Bor. of Leicester*, iv. 140. [29] Ibid. 169, 171, 173; Nichols, i. 339-45, 425; Thompson, 344. [30] *HMC Hastings*, iv. 203-4; HEHL, HA5458; Leics. RO, BRII/18/14/7. [31] Leics. RO, BRII/18/14/20-1; Nichols, i. 341; *HP Commons, 1558-1603*, ii. 309-10. [32] Patterson, 188. [33] Nichols, i. 345. [34] Thompson, 347-8. [35] HEHL, HA387, 1725, 5472, 5479, 5481, 8524, 9221-2; Leics. RO, BR2/18/15, ff. 274, 279; Patterson, 188. [36] *Procs. 1625*, pp. 688-91; Leics RO, BRII/18/15, f. 557, information from Dr. Catherine Patterson. [37] *Procs. 1625*, pp. 690-1. [38] Leics. RO, BRII/18/16, f. 4; *Procs. 1626*, iv. 244. [39] *Procs. 1628*, vi. 154. [40] *Recs. of Bor. of Leicester*, iv. 240-1, 244; T. Cogswell, *Home Divisions*, 162, 206; *Lords Procs. 1628*, v. pp. 689, 704-5; *CJ*, i. 931a; Thompson, 353.

P.W.

LINCOLNSHIRE

Number of voters: at least 65 in 1604

20 Feb. 1604	THOMAS CLINTON, LORD CLINTON JOHN SHEFFIELD
6 Apr. 1610	SIR VALENTINE BROWNE *vice* Clinton called to the Upper House
c. Mar. 1614	SIR GEORGE MANNERS SIR PEREGRINE BERTIE Sir Thomas Monson, (bt.)*
1 Jan. 1621	SIR GEORGE MANNERS SIR THOMAS GRANTHAM
26 Jan. 1624	SIR MONTAGU BERTIE SIR THOMAS GRANTHAM
18 Apr. 1625	SIR JOHN WRAY, (bt.) SIR NICHOLAS SAUNDERSON, bt.
c. Jan. 1626	SIR WILLIAM ARMYNE, bt. JOHN MONSON
18 Feb. 1628	SIR JOHN WRAY, (bt.) SIR WILLIAM ARMYNE, bt.

For administrative purposes Lincolnshire was parcelled into three sub-divisions; Lindsey to the north, Kesteven to the south-west, and Holland, the area of coastal marshlands surrounding the Wash, in the south-east. Although each had separate commissions of the peace, this does not appear to have produced any regular pattern in the geographical distribution of knights of the shire during the early Stuart period. Elections were held at Lincoln Castle. By the beginning of the seventeenth century the wool trade, which had dominated the local economy during the Middle Ages, was in decline, and the county frequently complained of poverty.[1] Many of the leading landed families sought to increase their income by undertaking ambitious drainage schemes, resulting in considerable loss of common land, which at times provoked serious rioting, notably in the Isle of Ancholme, to the north-west of the Lindsey area.[2] The reclamation of extensive Holland fenlands proved less controversial, except in so far as the activities of the notorious patentees for concealed lands, Robert and William Tipper, aroused hostility to the Crown.[3] Another threat to the peace of the county was a long running feud between the 2nd earl of Lincoln (Sir Henry Clinton†) and his cousin Sir Edward Dymoke†.[4] Their rivalry found expression in the early elections of the period, but was later superseded, most notably by the influence of the Manners family, earls of Rutland, based at Belvoir Castle. James I stayed at Belvoir on his way south in 1603, and appointed the crypto-Catholic 5th and 6th earls successively to the lord lieutenancy.

In 1604, at the first general election of the new reign, the county's two previous knights of the shire, Lincoln's son Thomas, styled Lord Clinton during his father's lifetime, and John Sheffield, son of the 3rd Lord Sheffield, were returned at a well-attended county court, with some 65 freeholders named on the indenture.[5] It may have been through the agency of the Dymoke faction that Clinton, somewhat unwillingly, was summoned to the House of Lords ahead of the fourth session in 1610. If so, the vacancy seems to have been created for the benefit of Dymoke's nephew Sir Valentine Browne, who was in need of parliamentary privilege. A writ was issued on 23 Feb. 1610, but it was not until 6 Apr. that Browne was returned at what was probably a snap by-election, with only a dozen voters in attendance.[6] Despite the protests of Lord Clinton, who remained in the Commons until early June, the privileges committee eventually ordered Browne to take his seat.[7]

In 1614 the county election was contested by the 6th earl of Rutland's younger brother, Sir George

Manners, the courtier Sir Thomas Monson, who had represented the county in 1597, and Sir Peregrine Bertie, a younger son of Lord Willoughby.[8] It is not clear whether a single contest or separate polls were held for the first and second seats; the outcome was that Manners and Bertie were returned. Monson was Dymoke's brother-in-law, and his failure signals the decline of the latter faction's influence. Ahead of the next election, on 3 Dec. 1620, Manners wrote to instruct one of his servants to notify 'all my neighbours at Knaith, Bardney, Tupholme and Fulbeck that I shall desire their companies at Lincoln [on New Year's day], being the county day for choosing knights of the shire'.[9] He may have anticipated another contest, since he took the precaution of writing to Grantham's corporation in case he needed to resort to a borough seat. These preparations paid off, and he was re-elected as the senior county Member, while the second place, for the first time in the period was taken by a 'mere gentleman', Sir Thomas Grantham, a leading local puritan who had already represented Lincoln in three Parliaments. In 1624 first place in the county election was taken by Bertie's nephew, Sir Montagu, with the support of Clinton's son Theophilus, 4th earl of Lincoln. Grantham was re-elected as the junior knight of the shire.

For the first Caroline Parliament in 1625 another wealthy puritan gentleman, Sir John Wray, 2nd bt., took the senior county seat, while the second went to Sir Nicholas Saunderson, 1st bt., a social climber who had connected himself by marriage with both the Manners and Bertie families. The following year, Sir William Armyne, 1st bt., a puritan who probably enjoyed Lincoln's support, was returned in first place, together with Monson's son, John. The earl of Lincoln led widespread opposition to the Forced Loan in the county; indeed the newsmonger Sir John Scudamore, 1st bt.*, received reports that 'Lincolnshire refuseth in general, some two only excepted, and with such a fury, that my lord of Rutland was in danger to have the house where he was pulled over his ears'.[10] Unsurprisingly two prominent Loan refusers, Wray and Armyne, were returned in 1628. On 4 May complaints were presented to the Commons against one of the Lincolnshire deputy lieutenants, Sir William Welby, who was accused of imprisoning landowners for refusing to pay the rate for musters and of forcing soldiers to pay 6d. apiece at each training session. Welby was examined at the bar on 10 May, but was defended by Sir Thomas Grantham.[11] No direct action appears to have been taken against him, but in 1629 Rutland was replaced as lord lieutenant by Lord Willoughby, now 1st earl of Lindsey.

[1] VCH Lincs. ii. 279, 332; J.D. Gould, 'The Depopulation Inquisition of 1607 in Lincs', EHR, lxvii. 392-6. [2] K. Lindley, Fenland Riots, 44-6, passim; C. Holmes, 'Drainers and Fenmen', in Order and Disorder in Early Modern Eng. ed. A. Fletcher and J. Stevenson, 166-95. [3] HMC Hatfield, xii. 98; C. Holmes, Seventeenth-Cent. Lincs. 101-2. [4] STAC 8/91/18; HMC Hatfield, xii. 234, 344-5, 410-12; J. O'Connor, God's Peace and the Queen's, 108-26; HMC 3rd Rep. 57; Holmes, Seventeenth-Cent. Lincs. 98-9, 102-3. [5] C219/35/1/31-2. [6] Ibid. 36, 39. [7] CJ, i. 424b, 429a; Procs. 1610 ed. E.R. Foster, i. 94-5; ii. 5-6. [8] Chamberlain Letters ed. N.E. McClure, i. 518. [9] HMC Rutland, i. 457. [10] CSP Dom. 1627-8, p. 138; C115/107/8541. [11] CD 1628, iii. 355-60.

P.W./R.C.L.S.

BOSTON

Right of election: in the corporation bef. 1628; in the freemen from 1628

Number of voters: 30 bef. 1628; 96 from 1628

6 Mar. 1604	ANTHONY IRBY		
	FRANCIS BULLINGHAM		
18 Mar. 1614[1]	ANTHONY IRBY		
	LEONARD BAWTREE		
18 Dec. 1620	SIR THOMAS CHEKE		
	ANTHONY IRBY		
15 Feb. 1621	SIR WILLIAM ARMYNE, bt. vice		
	Cheke, chose to sit for Harwich		
23 Jan. 1624	SIR CLEMENT COTTERELL		
	WILLIAM BOSWELL		
8 Mar. 1624	SIR WILLIAM ARMYNE, bt. vice		
	Cotterell, chose to sit for Grantham		
18 Apr. 1625	SIR EDWARD BARKHAM, bt.		
	WILLIAM BOSWELL		
c. Jan. 1626	SIR EDWARD BARKHAM, bt.		
	RICHARD OAKELEY		
28 Feb. 1628	RICHARD BELLINGHAM II		
	RICHARD OAKELEY	15	15
	Sir Anthony Irby	14	81
	IRBY vice Oakeley,		
	on petition, 8 May 1628		

By the beginning of the seventeenth century the decline of the Lincolnshire cloth industry and the silting of the River Witham had reduced Boston's importance as an international port, though the town still enjoyed a modest prosperity as a centre for local trade.[2] Throughout the early modern period the repair and maintenance of the sluice and bridge over the Witham, the improvement of the harbour, and the impact of local fen drainage schemes, were issues of paramount concern to Boston's inhabitants.[3] Incorporated in 1545, the borough first sent representatives to Parliament two years later. The right of election was exercised by the corporation, which consisted of 12 aldermen (from among whom the mayor was selected annually) and 18 common councillors.[4] Under Elizabeth I the town was granted the right to hold its own Admiralty court, as a consequence of which it came into conflict with the duchy of Lancaster, which had extensive holdings in the area. Boston eventually succeeded in defending its privileges.[5] A majority of the townsmen inclined towards puritan nonconformity during this period, and this, combined with economic stagnation, resulted in the town becoming a noted point of exodus for pilgrims to the New World during the 1630s.[6]

External influence over Boston's elections had traditionally been shared between the Cecils and the earl of Lincoln, based at Tattershall, about ten miles north-west of the town. However, in 1604 neither Sir Thomas Cecil[†], who held the recordership, nor the 2nd earl of Lincoln (Henry Clinton[†]), who was steward of the borough, appears to have made any nominations. The deputy recorder Anthony Irby, a resident lawyer who represented the borough in every Parliament between 1589 and 1621, was returned for the first seat, while the second place went to Francis Bullingham, principal registrar of the diocese of Lincoln, who was admitted to the freedom without payment on the same day as the election.[7] Irby was entrusted with the town's charters of Admiralty and incorporation, and received £40 to present these to Chancery for renewal and enlargement. A new charter was accordingly granted in August 1604, whereupon Irby was paid a further £36 12s. 4d., plus £10 for parliamentary expenses. This new grant conferred upon Boston the right to purchase lands not exceeding £100 in annual value, and also the right to hold quarter sessions and a yearly fair.[8] The following year Boston appealed to Cecil, now 1st earl of Exeter, and his half-brother the 1st earl of Salisbury (Robert Cecil[†]), in a dispute over Admiralty jurisdiction concerning a beached whale.[9]

During the third session of the Parliament Boston resolved, on 23 Jan 1607, that Irby and Bullingham should be instructed to draw up a bill for repairing the sluice, which, it was hoped, would help to prevent the decline and depopulation of the town. They were also instructed to see 'that this corporation may be put amongst the decayed towns'. There is no evidence that

such a bill was ever laid before the Commons. Nevertheless, on 4 Apr. £3 6s. 8d. was granted to Irby for 'his great charges and the neglect of his own affairs ... in respect of his losses by his attendance at the Parliament'.[10] Having presumably dissuaded the corporation from proceeding by bill, Irby later enlisted the support of the earl of Exeter in a series of unsuccessful attempts to persuade the Lincolnshire sewer commissioners that the whole county should assume responsibility for building and maintaining the sluice.[11]

Irby was re-elected to the next Parliament in 1614, accompanied by Leonard Bawtree, another lawyer from a local family, who had earned the corporation's good will by supporting Boston's case over the Witham sluice, and was made a freeman without charge on the day of the election. Bawtree 'promised to do his best endeavour for the confirming of the charter by Act of Parliament and for other business for the good of this corporation', and received an advance of £30 towards anticipated expenses; however, no such bill was entered during the brief Addled Parliament, nor does it appear to have been pursued at a later date.[12] Ahead of the next general election, in November 1620, the corporation wrote to Exeter concerning the writ of election, 'whereby [it] is required that this house may make choice of two of their own freemen now dwelling amongst them'. These words have been read as an attempt by the borough to assert its independence from external influence, although the original letter itself is no longer extant and the minute book as it stands cannot support this interpretation.[13] On the contrary, it seems more likely that Boston was appealing to the earl to provide a nominee. They duly returned Exeter's kinsman, Sir Thomas Cheke, in first place, while Irby was re-elected for the last time, receiving an advance of £20 towards his expenses.[14] When Cheke, an Essex gentleman, chose to represent Harwich, for which borough he had also been elected, Exeter recommended in his stead a courtier, Sir Edward Lewis. However, the 4th earl of Lincoln, who had recently succeeded to his title, also nominated Sir Alexander Temple*.[15] Unable to please both aristocratic patrons, the corporation preferred Sir William Armyne, 1st bt., a strong puritan, whose £5 fee for the borough freedom was remitted 'in regard he is a gentleman of note in this country and likely to do good service to this house without anyways charging them'.[16] Armyne may not have been aware that he had been chosen until after the event, for immediately after the election it was resolved to write 'signifying thereby to him his said election to the end he may take upon him that place'. The corporation placated Exeter with a resolution thanking him for securing the writ from the sheriff; they furthermore agreed to defray any charges he had incurred, and paid 20s. to his footman for bringing them the writ.[17] Religious tension within Boston may have influenced the outcome of the election, for shortly afterwards Irby and Bawtree were instructed by the Privy Council to investigate the charge that the mayor, Thomas Middlecoate, a well-known puritan, had cut off the crosses from the mayoral mace. Despite Bawtree's hostility, Irby was able to bring in a report exonerating Middlecoate, a verdict subsequently upheld by the solicitor general, (Sir) Robert Heath*.[18] A minute of the corporation, mentioning 'a draft in paper of an act which should have been procured in the last Parliament', suggests that some townsmen still wished to pursue statutory confirmation of the borough's charters. These were again delivered to Irby, but, in a Parliament clogged with legislation, there is no evidence that a bill of this kind was ever presented to the Commons.[19]

In 1623 the earl of Lincoln, having failed to deliver the concessions Boston desired over the sluice, resigned the stewardship of the borough.[20] Meanwhile, the earl of Exeter died, whereupon Irby assumed the full duties of the recorder and stepped down as an alderman. He also requested licence to absent himself from Boston, which presumably explains why, for the first time in 35 years, he did not stand at the next general election.[21] A new source of patronage now emerged following the appointment as bishop of Lincoln of lord keeper John Williams. A religious moderate, Williams acquiesced in the dropping of charges of nonconformity against Boston's evangelical vicar, John Cotton, for whose learning he expressed great admiration. Perhaps in return for this favour, William Boswell, who combined the post of secretary to the lord keeper with a clerkship to the Privy Council, was elected for Boston in 1624. Boswell nevertheless had to concede the senior seat to Sir Clement Cotterell, vice-admiral of the county, who had married a Lincolnshire heiress. Cotterell, a servant of the duke of Buckingham, secured seats for himself at both Boston and Grantham, probably with the support of Armyne, who took his place at Boston when he plumped for the other constituency.[22] On 26 Apr. 1624 a bill to establish a free school and poor-house near Boston received its first reading. Engrossed the next day without referral to a committee, it was presumably the measure 'for almshouses in Lincolnshire' taken up to the Lords by Sir Edwin Sandys on 1 May.[23] During the session the inhabitants of Boston again petitioned the king concerning the maintenance of the sluice, over which they remained in dispute with the county sewer commissioners.[24]

At the 1625 general election the senior seat went to Sir Edward Barkham, whose father owned a large estate at Wainfleet, about ten miles north-east of Boston, while Boswell was re-elected in second place.[25] Barkham, who was granted the freedom of the borough gratis, was returned again in 1626, accompanied this time by the bishop's new secretary, Richard Oakeley.[26] After the dissolution Boston received an unwelcome order to provide a ship for the navy; one-third of the cost was to be borne by the town, the rest by the county. All appeals against these instructions, citing the town's poverty and the decay of trade, were unavailing.[27] In addition, quo warranto proceedings were instigated to determine upon what authority Boston's charters were founded. Having failed to carry through their intention to confirm their charters by Act of Parliament, the town was now threatened with 'very chargeable expense', if not 'ruin and overthrow', in order to protect its privileges. The king's demand for the Forced Loan later in the year produced a split within the corporation, for while the mayor and several of the more puritan-minded townsmen were in favour of resistance, a majority wished to comply in order to retain the Privy Council's favour. The latter group eventually overruled the mayor by a formal resolution assenting to the Loan.[28] Not only the mayor, but also a handful of prominent local gentry, among them Armyne, were summoned before the Council. The tactics employed by the majority evidently paid off, as the charter was confirmed by royal inspeximus on 9 June 1627.[29]

At the 1628 elections Richard Bellingham II, a strong puritan who had succeeded as Boston's recorder on Irby's death in 1625, was chosen unanimously in first place, but Oakeley's re-election to the second seat was contested by Irby's grandson and heir, Sir Anthony Irby, a noted Loan refuser.[30] Although Oakeley received 15 corporation votes to Irby's 14, Irby appealed to 'the commonalty', presumably the freemen, 67 of whom voted for him. Bellingham and Oakeley were returned; but once the Parliament opened Irby and his supporters petitioned the privileges committee. Despite the corporation's protests that Members' wages were paid by the common council out of the town treasury rather than by the commonalty, and that the franchise had been exclusive for the last 46 years, on 8 May William Hakewill reported in favour of the wider franchise, on the grounds that 'the election of burgesses in all boroughs did of common right belong to the commoners, and that nothing could take it from them but a prescription and a constant usage beyond all memory'.[31] A similar election dispute at Colchester, Essex, had been resolved in favour of Sir William

Masham* on 28 Mar., and on the basis of this precedent the House declared Irby elected without the need for a new writ, a decision which permanently enlarged the Boston electorate.[32]

[1] *Boston Corp. Mins.* ed. J.F. Bailey, i. 148. [2] *Port Bks. of Boston* ed. R.W.K. Hinton (Lincoln Rec. Soc. l), pp. xviii-xxxix; C. Holmes, *Seventeenth-Cent. Lincs.* 13-14; P. Thompson, *Hist. Boston*, 343-8. [3] Thompson, 359-64. [4] M. Weinbaum, *Brit. Bor. Charters*, 69-70; *Boston Corp. Mins.* i. app. 1. [5] *Boston Corp. Mins.* i. app. 4; ii. 134-5, 305, 308. [6] Holmes, 43, 95-6, 116; C. Brears, *Short Hist. Lincs.* 157. [7] *Boston Corp. Mins.* i. 687-8; C219/35/1/33. [8] *CSP Dom.* 1603-10, p. 130; *Boston Corp. Mins.* i. 698. [9] *CSP Dom.* 1603-10, p. 210; *HMC Hatfield*, xvii. 169, 593. [10] *Boston Corp. Mins.* i. 741-2, 745, 746. [11] Ibid. ii. 33. [12] Ibid. 148, 150-1, 155. [13] Ibid. 315; J.K. Gruenfelder, 'Boston in early Stuart elections', *Lincs. Hist. and Arch.* xiii. 47-50. [14] *Boston Corp. Mins.* ii. 318-19. [15] Ibid. 323. [16] Ibid. 322. [17] Ibid. 322-3. [18] *APC*, 1619-21, pp. 367, 381, 382, 384, 386; *CSP Dom.* 1619-23, pp. 244-5. [19] *Boston Corp. Mins.* ii. 321, 325. [20] Ibid. 435. [21] Ibid. 412, 444. [22] Ibid. 442-3. [23] *CJ*, i. 690b, 691b, 692a, 696a. [24] *HMC 7th Rep.* 251-2; *APC*, 1623-5, pp. 112, 181-3, 344, 348, 366; Holmes, 99-101. [25] *Boston Corp. Mins.* ii. 474. [26] Ibid. 490. [27] *CSP Dom.* 1625-6, p. 406; *APC*, 1627, pp. 156-61. [28] *Boston Corp. Mins.* ii. 519, 526; R. Cust, *Forced Loan*, 131-2, 172, 298-9. [29] *APC*, 1627, pp. 139, 252, 396; *CSP Dom.* 1627-8, pp. 39, 81, 138. [30] Cust, 311; *Boston Corp. Mins.* ii. 537-8. [31] *CD 1628*, iii. 325-6, 329, 331; Holmes, 107-8. [32] D. Hirst, *Representative of the People?*, 93, 234.

P.W./R.C.L.S.

GRANTHAM

Right of election: in the freemen

Number of voters: unknown

24 Feb. 1604	SIR GEORGE MANNERS
	THOMAS HORSMAN
c. Mar. 1614	SIR GEORGE REYNELL
	RICHARD TUFTON
c. Jan. 1621	SIR WILLIAM ARMYNE
	SIR CLEMENT COTTERELL
25 Jan. 1624	SIR GEORGE MANNERS
	SIR CLEMENT COTTERELL
18 Apr. 1625	SIR GEORGE MANNERS
	SIR WILLIAM ARMYNE, bt.
28 Jan. 1626	JOHN WINGFIELD
	EVERS ARMYNE
29 Feb. 1628	THOMAS HATCHER
	ALEXANDER MORE

Grantham, a market and postal town on the Great North Road, was incorporated in 1463 and first sent representatives to Parliament in 1467.[1] The corporation consisted of one annually elected alderman and 12 'comburgesses'.[2] However, the town also remained under manorial rule, and after the accession of James I it became part of Anne of Denmark's dower.[3] Influence over elections was traditionally dominated by the Manners family, earls of Rutland, seated at Belvoir Castle some seven miles distant; Roger, 5th earl of Rutland, who was both steward of the manor and lord lieutenant of the county, confirmed his interest in the borough with regular gifts of money for the poor.[4] The population of Grantham has been estimated at around 1,500 at the turn of the seventeenth century. The town had experienced a long period of stagnation due to the decline of its cloth trade during the preceding century, but nevertheless experienced, and tried to reverse, a 'great confluence and resort of poor people from foreign parts' during the early Stuart period. This arose due to the drainage and enclosure of the fens, which had displaced agricultural labour from the surrounding hinterland.[5] During the 1620s the townsmen became divided over religion, following the appointment of an unpopular Arminian vicar. The bishop of Lincoln, John Williams, overruled the latter's attempts to move the communion table and replace it with a stone altar; the majority on the corporation inclined towards puritanism, a factor which perhaps bolstered the influence of Sir William Armyne in the later elections of the period.[6] No corporation records survive prior to 1633.

In 1604 Sir George Manners, Rutland's younger brother, was returned as the senior Member, while Thomas Horsman, a local gentleman who had represented Grantham in the last three Parliaments, was re-elected in second place. Though of different generations, both had been brought up in the household of the 1st Lord Burghley (Sir William Cecil[†]), and may have been able to use their connections with the secretary of state, Sir Robert Cecil[†], to obtain a new charter for Grantham. Dated 29 May 1604, this contained substantial new privileges, notably a wool market to provide funds and employment for the poor, and a weekly court of record.[7] Horsman died on 26 Nov. 1610, during the last session of this Parliament, but no writ for a by election appears to have been issued, probably because the Parliament was prorogued prior to its dissolution just ten days later.

Rutland died in 1612 and was succeeded by his brother Francis as 6th earl. The latter was probably responsible for the return of his brother-in-law, Richard Tufton, at the next general election, although the first seat went to Queen Anne's carver, Sir George

Reynell, who had married into a Lincolnshire family. Ahead of the elections to the 1621 Parliament, Sir George Manners wrote commending himself to an eminent local barrister, (Sir) Thomas Ellis[†], who resided at Grantham, requesting 'that in regard I am a freeman and of never a corporation else, I shall take it very kindly ... if at this time they will bestow a burgess place upon me, and the more kindly for that it proceeds from my own motion'. The exact date of the election is unknown as the return does not survive, but Manners had almost certainly already been returned as knight of the shire for Lincolnshire by the time it took place. The senior seat was taken by Sir William Armyne, who had represented the borough as long ago as 1589 and whose seat of Osgodby lay some seven miles from Grantham. His political re-emergence was probably less the result of his own inclination than the desire of his son to establish an interest by appealing to the growing number of puritans within the town and among the corporation. Sir Clement Cotterell, vice admiral of Lincolnshire and the owner of a small estate at nearby Wilsford, was returned in second place, perhaps having been recommended to Rutland by his patron, Buckingham, the earl's son-in-law. Sir George Manners claimed the senior seat at Grantham in 1624, with Cotterell re-elected in second place. Cotterell had also been returned for Boston two days previously, and when he plumped for Grantham it was presumably as part of a deal whereby his place at Boston was taken by Armyne's son and successor, the first baronet.

Manners and the younger Armyne were returned together to Charles I's first Parliament in 1625. The senior seat in 1626 went to an outsider, John Wingfield, while the second seat went to the baronet's younger brother, Evers Armyne. Wingfield may have been recommended by his kinsman, the 2nd earl of Exeter (William Cecil[†]), Rutland's brother-in-law. Aristocratic influence seems to have been absent from the elections to the 1628 Parliament, when a local gentleman who shared the Armynes' radical puritan views, Thomas Hatcher of Careby, was returned in first place, and the second seat went to a townsman, Alexander More junior. After the dissolution the corporation petitioned for a new charter in order to resolve ambiguities that had arisen following the grant of the manor to Queen Henrietta Maria. Their request was finally granted in 1631.[8]

[1] E. Turnor, *Colls. for Hist. Grantham*, 56. [2] G.H. Martin, *Charters of Grantham*, 14-16, 24-47; C. Holmes, *Seventeenth-Cent. Lincs.* 32-3. [3] B. Street, *Notes on Grantham*, 28 [4] *HMC Rutland*, i. 454; *HMC Hatfield*, xvi. 318. [5] J.B. Manterfield, 'Top. development of Grantham, Lincs. 1535-1835' (Exeter Univ. Ph.D. thesis, 1981), p. 140; Holmes, 20, 37. [6] Holmes, 114-16; Street, 82-3, 85; *HMC 3rd Rep.* 214. [7] Martin, 109-19; *CSP Dom.* 1603-10, p. 115. [8] *CSP Dom.* 1628-9, p. 545; 1629-31, p. 37; S. Bond and N. Evans, 'The process of granting charters to Eng. bors. 1547-1649', *EHR*, xci. 105-6, 110.

P.W./R.C.L.S.

GREAT GRIMSBY

Right of election: in the freemen

Number of voters: 64 in 1640[1]

17 Feb. 1604	SIR GEORGE ST. PAUL
	SIR WILLIAM WRAY
22 Mar. 1614[2]	SIR JOHN WRAY
	RICHARD TOWTHBY
26 Dec. 1620	CHRISTOPHER WRAY
	HENRY PELHAM
22 Jan. 1624	(SIR) CHRISTOPHER WRAY
	HENRY PELHAM
26 Apr. 1625	(SIR) CHRISTOPHER WRAY
	HENRY PELHAM
26 Jan. 1626	HENRY PELHAM
	THOMAS BRETT
2 Mar. 1626	WILLIAM SKINNER *vice* Brett, chose to sit for New Romney
c. Feb. 1628	(SIR) CHRISTOPHER WRAY
	HENRY PELHAM

By the early seventeenth century Grimsby, long in decline as a port, had been eclipsed by Hull, across the Humber, in both commercial and political importance. Gervase Holles[†], who was born in the town in 1607, observed that 'the haven hath been heretofore commodious, [but] now decayed; the traffic good, now gone'. He described Grimsby as 'mean and straggling by reason of depopulation, and the town very poor'.[3] Throughout the early Stuart period the borough council divided its resources between futile attempts to dredge the harbour, and evasion of the jurisdiction of the custom house at Hull; they also tried to take advantage of changes in the coastline by draining and improving salt marshes in the surrounding area. The borough owned 80 acres in 1599, of which half was leased to the freemen, while the commoners, who had once exercised their rights over the whole, had to be content with the remainder until the leases fell in.

Private landlords, notably Sir William Wray*, were engaged in similar activities in the neighbourhood, leading to complaints of encroachments on commons and destruction of farmsteads.[4]

The borough received its first charter from King John in 1201 and had regularly returned Members to Parliament since 1295. The corporation was ruled by a council of 24, of whom 12 were aldermen, headed by an annually elected mayor.[5] Due to the poverty of the town, its MPs were required to enter into bonds of indemnity guaranteeing that they would serve at their own charge, and as a result all but one of those returned during the period were drawn from the local gentry, notably the Wrays of Glentworth, and Pelhams of Brocklesby.[6] Neither the recorder Edward Skipwith†, nor the high steward Sir Thomas Heneage, nor their successors appear to have exercised any electoral influence.[7] Most of the surviving indentures record the 'mutual and common consent' of the mayor and 'burgesses'; and none of the elections between 1604-28 seems to have been contested.

In 1604 Sir William Wray was 'freely elected' with his brother-in-law, Sir George St. Paul, who owned property in Grimsby.[8] Both men were both noted for their patronage of puritan preachers, although there is little sign that the inhabitants of Grimsby shared their enthusiasm. Shortly after the election the town received a new charter confirming all its rights and privileges and allowing the mayor and two 'burgesses' to be chosen annually to serve as justices of the peace.[9] Wray may have helped to secure this grant and he was also probably involved in an attempt in 1606 to raise funds to clear the haven. A royal letter was obtained recommending the sheriffs and magistrates of Lincolnshire, Nottinghamshire, Derbyshire and West Riding to render assistance.[10] Some disaffected inhabitants, blaming the enclosure of the marshes for the silting of the harbour, brought an Exchequer action in 1607 against the mayor and freemen for enclosing common land and re-letting it to themselves at low rents.[11] An inquiry team, headed by Leonard Bawtree*, failed to make a recommendation because the council refused to co-operate. The matter was finally settled after further litigation, when an Exchequer verdict confirmed the freemen's right to the marshes.[12]

At the next election the first seat went to Wray's eldest son, Sir John, while second place was taken by Richard Towthby, the head of a minor gentry family. In 1620 Sir John Wray's younger half-brother, Christopher, was returned for the first seat, while still a minor. The junior Member, Henry Pelham of Gray's

Inn, was only a few years older, and moreover out of the country at the time. The validity of his election was questioned in the House because he was overseas by his own volition, but on his return six weeks later he was allowed to take his seat.[13]

(Sir) Christopher Wray and Pelham were re-elected at the next two elections, in 1624 and 1625. By this time the commoners had revived their claim to the marshes; but Wray, who had been knighted in 1623, persuaded the attorney-general Sir Thomas Coventry*, after perusing the charters, to refuse to intervene.[14] At the next election Pelham was returned as the senior Member, and the second seat went to Capt. Thomas Brett, a Kentish soldier whose only connection with the town was via Wray's father-in-law Viscount Wimbledon (Sir Edward Cecil*), with whom he had served in several military expeditions.[15] In the event Brett was also returned for New Romney, and at the ensuing election in March 1626 William Skinner, of nearby Thornton College took his place. Sir Christopher Wray and Pelham served again in 1628.

[1] NE Lincs. Archives, Grimsby Bor. Recs. 1/102/7, f. 71. [2] HMC 14th Rep. VIII, 279. [3] G. Holles, Lincs. Church Notes (Lincoln Rec. Soc. i), 2. [4] NE Lincs. Archives, Grimsby Bor. Recs. 1/102/6, f. 526; E. Gillett, Grimsby, 98-117; J.D. Gould, 'The Depopulation Inquisition of 1607 in Lincs', EHR, lxvii. 392-6. [5] G. Oliver, Mon. Antiqs. of Grimsby, 79, 80, 119; L. Greenfield, Grimsby's Freemen, 9, 39-40, 53. [6] C. Holmes, Seventeenth-Cent. Lincs. 15, 35. [7] Oliver, 122-3. [8] C219/35/1/34; NE Lincs. Archives, Grimsby Bor. Recs. 1/560/109. [9] NE Lincs. Archives, Grimsby Bor. Recs. 1/22/1; CSP Dom. 1603-10, p. 129. [10] Gillett, 120. [11] NE Lincs. Archives, Grimsby Bor. Recs. 1/721. [12] HMC 14th Rep. VIII, 261-2. [13] CJ, i. 511b, 513b; Nicholas, Procs. 1621, i. 26-7. [14] HMC 14th Rep. VIII, 257. [15] C. Dalton, Life and Times of Gen. Sir Edward Cecil, i. 180, ii. 304, 353.

P.W./R.C.L.S.

LINCOLN

Right of election: in the freemen

Number of voters: unknown

c. Feb. 1604	SIR THOMAS GRANTHAM
	SIR EDWARD TYRWHITT
c. Mar. 1614	SIR THOMAS GRANTHAM
	EDWARD BAESHE
	?Sir Robert Monson
8 Jan. 1621	SIR LEWIS WATSON
	SIR EDWARD AYSCOUGH
2 Feb. 1624	SIR LEWIS WATSON, (bt.)
	THOMAS HATCHER
25 Apr. 1625	SIR THOMAS GRANTHAM
	JOHN MONSON
30 Jan. 1626	SIR THOMAS GRANTHAM
	SIR ROBERT MONSON
25 Feb. 1628	SIR THOMAS GRANTHAM
	SIR EDWARD AYSCOUGH

Lincoln's first extant charter dates back to 1157, and the town first returned MPs to Parliament in 1265. The borough was governed by a mayor, 12 aldermen, and a common council varying in size from about 30 to 48.[1] By the early seventeenth century the decay of the wool trade had left the city in economic decline despite its role as the county's administrative centre.[2] Religious issues were particularly divisive among the corporation: in 1600 a furious quarrel erupted over the election by one vote of the puritan John Smith as preacher of the city. Two years later Smith's supporters obtained a life patent for him, but the incoming mayor rallied the opposition to dismiss him, cancel the grant and remove two of his supporters from the aldermanic bench. Smith began legal proceedings and by the summer of 1603 the corporation was in such confusion that the dispute was referred to Sir William Wray*, Sir Philip Tyrwhitt, Edward King, and the dean of Lincoln. No agreement could be reached, until Edmund, 3rd Baron Sheffield was called in as arbitrator.[3] The dispute forms the backdrop to the parliamentary election of 1604, in which a leading local puritan, Sir Thomas Grantham, and Tyrwhitt's son Sir Edward were returned. Although it had previously been traditional for at least one of the Members to be the town's recorder, this practice seems to have been discontinued by 1604, from which point onwards seats were generally shared out between members of the local gentry who were

willing to serve without wages; there is no evidence of a cathedral influence in the borough. The dispute in the corporation flared up again in 1608, and had to be resolved by the Privy Council.[4]

In 1614 Grantham was re-elected in first place. On 9 Mar. two strangers bought the freedom of the borough, namely Sir Robert Monson, who owned property in north Lincolnshire but resided mainly in Yorkshire, and Edward Baeshe, the under-age stepson of the local magnate, Sir George Manners*.[5] Monson may have been dissuaded from standing once he became aware of Baeshe's candidacy; the latter was returned and we have no evidence that a contest actually occurred. James I visited Lincoln in March 1617, and appointed it a staple town, in a bid to reverse the dislocation of the cloth trade caused by the Cockayne Project.[6] The more enterprising members of the corporation, desirous to re-establish the city's position as a principal outlet for the West Riding of Yorkshire, put together proposals to clean and improve the Fosse Dyke, which joined Lincoln to the Trent.[7] Manners' elder brother, the 6th earl of Rutland, promised £100 towards the expenses, and after some misgivings the local gentry offered £300 if the city could raise a like sum, which was achieved by deducting £50 a year for six years from the mayor's allowance.[8] At the next election Sir Lewis Watson of Rockingham in Northamptonshire, who had recently married into the Manners family, was presented to the borough, presumably either by Rutland or Sir George Manners. The second seat went to Grantham's protégé, Sir Edward Ayscough.

By the early 1620s the English cloth trade remained in recession. The Fosse Dyke project was abandoned, and its promoters fell into dispute with the Merchant Staplers over Lincoln's position as a staple town. However, none of this is reflected in the town's elections, which continued to be dominated by the gentry. In 1624 Watson, having failed to obtain a seat in his native county was re-elected for Lincoln, together with Ayscough's brother-in-law Thomas Hatcher, of Careby. Sir Thomas Grantham was re-elected as the senior Member in 1625, while the second seat went to John Monson, who lived just outside the town. The following year Grantham was returned again, with Monson's uncle Sir Robert, who continued to reside in Yorkshire. In April 1626 a writ of *quo warranto* obliged the corporation to seek either a confirmation or a renewal of their charter, and they mortgaged various property to raise £200 for the purpose.[9] Lincolnshire as a whole was much opposed to the Forced Loan, and at the general election of 1628 Lincoln returned Grantham and Ayscough, both of whom were prominent Loan refusers.[10] During the recess the new charter was issued, under which the common council was to consist of between 40 and 45 members, of whom 13 would be styled aldermen.[11]

[1] W. de Gray Birch, *Royal Charters of Lincoln*, 1-2, 74; Lincs. AO, L1/1/1/4, f. 214. [2] J.W.F. Hill, *Tudor and Stuart Lincoln*, 18-22, 69-73. [3] *HMC 14th Rep. VIII*, 76-9. [4] Ibid. 82; Lincs. AO, Cor/B/2, 6, 7, 8. [5] Hill, 117; Lincs. AO, L1/1/1/4, f. 114. [6] *APC*, 1616-17, pp. 178-81; *HMC 14th Rep. VIII*, 91-5. [7] Hill, 128-34. [8] *HMC 14th Rep. VIII*, 97. [9] Ibid. 98; Hill, 120. [10] R. Cust, *Forced Loan*, 117-8, 286-8, 298-9. [11] Birch, 200; *HMC 14th Rep. VIII*, 13, 99.

P.W./R.C.L.S.

STAMFORD

Right of election: in the corporation

Number of voters: 25 in 1604; 37 in 1605

21 Feb. 1604[1]	SIR ROBERT WINGFIELD
	HENRY HALL
7 Dec. 1609	SIR EDWARD CECIL *vice*
	Wingfield, deceased
21 Mar. 1614[2]	RICHARD CECIL
	JOHN JAY
19 Dec. 1620	(SIR) RICHARD CECIL
	JOHN WINGFIELD
20 Jan. 1624	SIR GEORGE GORING
	EDWARD AYSCOUGH
1 Mar. 1624	JOHN ST. AMAND *vice*
	Goring, chose to sit for Lewes
23 Apr. 1625	SIR MONTAGU BERTIE
	JOHN ST. AMAND
26 Jan. 1626[3]	SIR MONTAGU BERTIE
	BRIAN PALMES
23 Feb. 1628	SIR THOMAS HATTON
	(SIR) EDWARD BAESHE

Positioned astride the River Welland, Stamford occupied an anomalous geographical position, as it was situated where the counties of Lincolnshire, Northamptonshire and Rutland met. The borough was incorporated in 1462, with a council consisting of an annually elected 'alderman', 12 other 'comburgesses', and 12 'capital burgesses'. Its record of regular representation in Parliament began five years later.[4] In this period its diocesan, lord keeper Williams, described it as 'much decayed', as it suffered from the decline of the weaving industry and the silting up of the Welland, which barred it from participating in the corn trade. Between 1620 and 1623 an attempt to make the Welland navigable by building a new cut served merely to plunge the town into financial difficulties.[5] Nevertheless, Stamford remained a market town and a staging point on the Great North Road, with some flourishing local industries, notably leather, and its easy access to several of the finest building stones in England must already have given it a dignified air. The chief interest lay with the Cecil family, whose great mansion at Burghley was only two miles away. The Cecils owned extensive property in and around the town and dominated the corporation through their tenure of the recordership. Moreover, in 1597 the 1st Lord Burghley (Sir William Cecil[†]) founded a hospital by the bridge.[6] None of the early Stuart parliamentary elections seem to have been contested: all the returns contain words such as 'with one voice and assent', and the entries in the hall book show no signs of dissension.[7]

In 1604 Sir Robert Wingfield, a native of the town and the senior 'comburgess', was re-elected for the sixth consecutive time, no doubt with the approval of his first cousin, the 2nd Lord Burghley (Thomas Cecil[†]). Corporation interest also accounted for the election of the junior Member, Henry Hall, another gentleman of the neighbourhood. In March 1605 Wingfield, no doubt with the assistance of Burghley's brother, Viscount Cranborne (Robert Cecil[†]), secured the remission of almost a quarter of the sum required as fifteenths and tenths from the borough and its Northamptonshire suburbs under the 1601 subsidy, 'in regard that the town hath been much visited with sickness'.[8] Disputes over municipal elections obliged the corporation, through the good offices of Burghley (now 1st earl of Exeter), to obtain a new charter four months later, increasing the number of capital burgesses to 24.[9] Exeter placed the town under further obligation in 1609, when he donated a perpetual annuity of £41 1s. 8d. to provide apprenticeships for poor children.[10] On Wingfield's death that same year, Exeter's son, Sir Edward Cecil, a professional soldier in the service of the States General, took over the senior seat.

Cecil's absences abroad possibly deterred him from standing again in 1614; at any rate his place as the borough's senior Member was taken by his brother, Richard. Hall was by now a septuagenarian and is not likely to have considered enlarging his parliamentary experience. Instead the corporation interest went to a Norfolk gentleman, John Jay, who had family connections in the neighbourhood and was brother to a leading member of the Drapers' Company of London. Jay died before the next election, which saw the earl of Exeter apply to the borough for permission to nominate both Members. On 14 Nov. 1620 the corporation considered the matter, and 'with a general consent' decided to grant the earl's request. Richard Cecil was subsequently re-elected, together with John Wingfield, [11] the brother of Sir Robert, who advanced £60 to the corporation for dredging the Welland.[12]

In 1624 the 2nd earl of Exeter gave one seat to Sir George Goring, a trustee of his marriage settlement, who had acted as intermediary between himself and the duke of Buckingham.[13] The identity of the other Member, Edward Ayscough, is obscure. He may have been the Edward Ayscough who lived just outside Nottingham at Nuthall, or he may have been a minor government servant from central Lincolnshire; if the latter he was presumably nominated by Williams. The hall book records that 'Mr. Alderman, with the rest of the comburgesses and capital burgesses ... made a free election'.[14] When Goring subsequently chose to sit for Lewes, his seat was filled by Williams's secretary, John St. Amand, who also boasted Nottinghamshire descent. The corporation, being hard pressed to repay the loans raised for the Welland project, was rewarded later that year with another remission of taxes, obtained for it by Williams. In return it supported Williams against one of the Stamford incumbents, John Vicars, who was accused of holding conventicles and propounding dangerous doctrines, which caused discord and 'great contempt' of authority. He was eventually disciplined by High Commission.[15]

For the election to the first Caroline Parliament St. Amand was again chosen, but a new interest appeared in the borough with the return of Sir Montagu Bertie, the youthful heir of Lord Willoughby of Eresby. Bertie was re-elected in 1626, but by then Williams had fallen from office, leaving St. Amand without a patron. St. Amand's replacement was another young heir from the vicinity, Brian Palmes, whose father's long service as knight of the shire for Rutland had been (no doubt deliberately) interrupted by pricking him as sheriff. In this Parliament John Wingfield served for Grantham, probably on the interest of Sir George Manners*; at the next election the earl of Exeter seems to have returned the compliment, as Manners' stepson, Sir Edward Baeshe, was returned at Stamford. The other seat in the third Caroline Parliament was also taken by a Cecil candidate, Sir Thomas Hatton, whose cousin, Lady Hatton (the estranged wife of Sir Edward Coke*) was Exeter's sister.[16]

[1] Stamford Town Hall, hall bk. 1, f. 276. [2] Ibid. f. 309. [3] Ibid. f. 345. [4] HP Commons 1558-1603, i. 199; OR. [5] SP14/170/81; The Making of Stamford ed. A. Rogers, 59-64, 70-1. [6] Making of Stamford, 73, 82. [7] Stamford Town Hall, hall bk. 1, ff. 276, 309. [8] CSP Dom. 1603-10, p. 202; SO3/2, unfol., 5 Mar. 1605. The town had been seeking this remission ever since June 1603: Stamford Town Hall, hall bk. 1, f. 274. [9] J. Drakard, Stamford, 102; Stamford Town Hall, charters 1B/3, pp. 83-90. [10] Drakard, 352. [11] Stamford Town Hall, hall bk. 1, ff. 331-2. The entry in the hall book relating to the election is printed, but incorrectly dated 1619, in The Gen. ii. 154. [12] Stamford Town Hall, hall bk. 1, f. 342. [13] C.M. Borough, 'Cal. North Pprs. in Bodl.', 18; Harl. 1580, f. 424. [14] Stamford Town Hall, hall bk. 1, f. 341. [15] CSP Dom. 1623-5, pp. 317, 319, 343, 426; 1628-9, p. 363. [16] Stamford Town Hall, hall bk. 1, ff. 343, 345, 349.

P.W./A.D.T.

MIDDLESEX

Number of voters: unknown

23 Feb. 1604	SIR ROBERT WROTH I
	SIR WILLIAM FLEETWOOD I
20 Feb. 1606	SIR JOHN FORTESCUE vice Wroth, deceased
aft. 23 Dec. 1607	SIR ROBERT WROTH II vice Fortescue, deceased
10 Mar. 1614	SIR JULIUS CAESAR
	SIR THOMAS LAKE I
7 Dec. 1620	SIR FRANCIS DARCY
	(SIR) GILBERT GERARD, (bt.)
	Sir Julius Caesar
	Sir Thomas Edmondes*
29 Jan. 1624	(SIR) GILBERT GERARD, (bt.)
	(SIR) JOHN SUCKLING
	Sir John Hippisley*
	Sir John Franklin
21 Apr. 1625	SIR JOHN FRANKLIN
	(SIR) GILBERT GERARD, (bt.)
	(Sir) John Suckling
1626	(SIR) EDWARD SPENCER
	(SIR) GILBERT GERARD, (bt.)
by 22 Feb. 1628[1]	(SIR) HENRY SPILLER
	SIR FRANCIS DARCY

Described by Thomas Fuller in the early 1660s as 'but the suburbs at large of London', Middlesex was a small county, 'scarce extending east and west to eighteen miles in length, and not exceeding twelve north and south in the breadth thereof'. Except near the Thames, where livings were made either by ferrying or fishing, the county's inhabitants were mainly farmers for, despite its size, Middlesex boasted some of the most fertile soil anywhere in the country. Writing in 1592, the surveyor John Norden commented not only on the abundance and excellence of its wheat (which Fuller later reckoned to be 'the best in England') but also on the plentiful dairy produce, poultry 'and a thousand other country drugs'. The fruits of Middlesex's bountiful harvests found a ready market among London's large and rapidly expanding population, but such easy pickings undoubtedly bred contempt for improved farming methods. 'Things are more confounded by ignorance and evil husbandry in this shire than in any other shire that I know', wrote Norden, a lament which was to be echoed many times over the following three centuries.[2] Just as the county's rich soil provided the key to agricultural abundance and prosperity, so too it formed the basis for the shire's principal industry, the manufacture of tiles and bricks.[3] At least one of Middlesex's early Stuart parliamentary representatives was involved in this trade. This was Sir Gilbert Gerard who, in the mid-1630s, was accused by the lord of the manor of Sudbury and Harrow of stealing his sand, whereby Gerard 'became a brickmaker and, by underselling my brick at 6d. in the thousand, had the custom of the country'.[4]

The abundance of its harvests and its proximity to London naturally made Middlesex a prime source of foodstuffs and fuel for the purveyors of the royal Household. During the 1589 Parliament the Middlesex Member Sir Robert Wroth I joined the chorus of objections to the abuses perpetrated by purveyors and cart-takers, but in the 1590s the county resisted entering into a general agreement for composition with the board of Green Cloth, preferring instead to compound for wheat alone. Returned once again for Middlesex in 1604, Wroth raised the issue of purveyance in the Commons, probably with the encouragement of his patron, Lord Cecil (Robert Cecil[†]), who hoped to sell this fiscal prerogative in return for a fixed annual revenue rather than extend the county compositions. Nothing came of this intervention, and on 18 Mar. 1606 Sir Oliver St. John, a commissioner of the Verge and Member for Bedfordshire, suggested that Middlesex should enter a general agreement for composition. However, it was probably not until after the failure of the Great Contract that Middlesex's justices finally consented to broadening the existing arrangements for composition.[5]

On the face of it, the new agreement, which entitled the justices to appoint undertakers for the composition, gave the Middlesex bench considerable scope for curtailing the abuses of purveyors, as these were now

their employees. In April 1613 a committee of magistrates dismissed the undertakers for having raised their rates and stripped the county bare to provide foodstuffs for other shires which had compounded. However, in the following September the board of Green Cloth responded by insisting that one of the undertakers, Thomas Gawen, remain in post. The composition scheme was further undermined by the exemptions claimed by many of Middlesex's inhabitants, and by Green Cloth's dithering over whether it wished to receive payment in money or in kind. By October 1614 the county's magistrates were so irritated by the Board's indecision that they threatened to terminate the composition arrangements altogether.[6] Though this threat was never carried out, purveyance remained a grievance. On 26 Mar. 1621 a bill to regulate the purveyance of carts was brought into the Commons 'by Middlesex men'. One of the bill's principal complaints was that the ancient verge of the Court, which established the area within which purveyors were entitled to take up carriages, had been extended from 12 miles for horse-drawn carts and eight miles for ox-drawn wains to 30 miles. It was also alleged that those who refused to allow their carts to be employed for the use of the royal Household were often forced to compound at rates greater than the value of the load to be carried. Though this measure failed to clear the Lords after successfully completing all its Commons' stages,[7] it served to spur the Privy Council into action, for in April 1622 Middlesex entered into a fresh composition agreement with the whitestaves.[8] Unfortunately, the new arrangements proved unpopular with Middlesex's neighbours. In March 1624 Sir Charles Morrison, Member for Hertfordshire, complained of 'the excessive pressing upon his county by carriages, especially sithence Middlesex hath compounded'.[9] According to Morrison, the burden previously borne by Middlesex of carrying goods for the royal Household had been transferred to Hertfordshire, which was now forced to provide 500 carts each year rather than 200.[10] His complaint was taken up by the committee for grievances, which found in favour of Morrison on 11 May.[11] However, the committee was powerless to act.

There was no settled venue for the county's parliamentary elections, which were held at Uxbridge in 1614, at Brentford in 1624, and at Hickes' Hall, the recently acquired sessions' house of the Middlesex bench at Clerkenwell, in 1625.[12] Though the county always returned residents, its freedom of choice was restricted by the demand for seats of senior government officials, at least before 1620. Of the four Members who represented Middlesex during the first Jacobean Parliament, one was a privy councillor

(Sir John Fortescue), two were employees of Robert Cecil as master of the Game and Forests (Sir Robert Wroth I and Sir Robert Wroth II) and one held office in the Court of Wards (Sir William Fleetwood I), a department also headed by Cecil. The same pattern was repeated in 1614, as three of the four candidates were senior government officials. Sir Julius Caesar was chancellor of the Exchequer, Sir Thomas Lake I was a privy councillor and Sir Walter Cope, who withdrew his candidacy before the election, was Cecil's successor as master of the Wards. Only Sir Francis Darcy, who may still have been an equerry in the king's stables, was without government office. Under pressure from the Privy Council and the king, Darcy was forced to withdraw. However, his bitterness at being forced to step aside was communicated to the freeholders by one of his servants who, 'getting up upon a table, told the assembly that his master meant to have stood, but was forbidden by the king'. He then added that Darcy 'desired all his well-willers to give their voices to master chancellor, and for the second place to do as God should put in their minds'. Not surprisingly, the servant was arrested for insulting Lake, and Darcy himself was 'called in question for the message'.[13] The latter obtained his revenge in December 1620, however, when the freeholders rejected the privy councillors Caesar and Sir Thomas Edmondes, the treasurer of the Household, in favour of Darcy and Sir Gilbert Gerard, clerk to the council of the duchy of Lancaster. Though Caesar and Edmondes 'made all the means they could', Middlesex's voters were no longer persuaded that their interests would be best served by privy councillors.[14] Already, perhaps, there were moves afoot to present a bill to Parliament against the purveyance of carts, and it was realized that Edmondes in particular, as a Household official, would oppose rather than support this measure.

It has been argued that the 1620 election 'was the last sign of Council intervention in Middlesex'. However, in 1624 the privy councillor Sir John Suckling secured the county's second seat, albeit only after a hotly contested election. Suckling was a client of Middlesex's new lord lieutenant, the duke of Buckingham, and it is therefore ironic that his nearest rival was evidently his fellow Buckingham client Sir John Hippisley. Though recently admitted to the Middlesex bench and the rangership of Bushey Park, Hippisley was an outsider, who used his influence in the royal stables, where he was an equerry, and with the lieutenant of the Tower, Sir Allen Apsley (another Buckingham supporter), to pack the assembled voters with 'stable and Mint men', who were not freeholders. At first it seemed that Hippisley had carried the seat, but

on closer inspection Hippisley's ploy was discovered, and after a count of the legitimate voters it was found that Hippisley came short of Suckling 'ten or twelve voices'. Suckling's challengers also included the youthful Sir John Franklin who, though permanently resident at Willesden, had not yet obtained admission to the Middlesex bench. A petition by several of the county's freeholders drawn up on Franklin's behalf later claimed that Suckling had been 'unduly returned in his stead', and was submitted to the Commons by Franklin's uncle Edward Roberts, Member for Penryn. However, it was subsequently withdrawn by the petitioners, who declared that they were 'better informed and advised now than when their petition was first preferred'. In view of this change of heart, the committee for privileges and returns cleared Suckling of any suspicion of fraud. Suckling's fellow knight of the shire was Sir Gilbert Gerard, who, though he took the first seat with ease,[15] may not have been confident of success, as he absented himself from the hustings and hedged his bets by also standing in the Isle of Wight. This was ironic, as Gerard's candidacy seems to have worried the Privy Council as it meant that all the other candidates would have to fight over the second seat. Three weeks before the election it restored Gerard to the bench, from which he had been removed in 1621 for lessening his subsidy assessment without proper authorization, perhaps in the hope that this concession might induce him not to stand.[16]

Undeterred by the defeat he had suffered in 1624, Sir John Franklin resolved to stand for the senior knighthood of the shire in 1625. However, he also secured Buckingham's nomination for a place at Rye, whose jurats were assured by the duke that Franklin was his 'deserving friend'.[17] On the day of the Middlesex election, Franklin spent £7 5s.10d. in buying the votes of freeholders at Hickes' Hall.[18] This relatively modest sum was sufficient to allow him and Gerard to inflict a humiliating reverse on Suckling, who unwisely attended the hustings in person.[19]

Neither Suckling nor any other government minister appears to have put his head above the parapet in 1626. That year Gerard was again returned, alongside a newcomer to the county, (Sir) Edward Spencer, who had recently married a widow from Middlesex. No government ministers are certainly known to have stood in 1628 either, an election which, like so many others that year, was dominated by hostility to the Forced Loan. At least one of the successful candidates, (Sir) Henry Spiller, had been summoned before the Privy Council in 1627 as a Loan defaulter. Spiller's supporters undoubtedly included the 'plain countryman' who, on being asked by Sir Thomas Edmondes who he would support, declared that he would vote 'for those who have suffered for their country'.[20] Apart from Spiller and Sir Francis Darcy, who took the second seat, there must have been at least one additional candidate, as Edmondes' question clearly implies. Possibly Sir Gilbert Gerard cast his hat into the ring again. Gerard later feigned indifference to the affairs of the 1628-9 Parliament, but it is clear from the fact that he obtained a large folio book of its proceedings that he was actually deeply interested in its activities.[21] However, for the first time in the 1620s he would have been considered unacceptable, as he had paid his contribution to the Loan.[22]

Several of Middlesex's Members were attuned to the concerns of their constituents. Apart from raising the issue of purveyance in 1604, Sir Robert Wroth I was probably responsible for introducing a bill to ban the use of barges on the River Lea. His hostility to the 1571 Lea Navigation Act, which threatened the livelihood of the carters of Enfield, where he lived, is well-documented, and in all likelihood he was in the House on the day that the bill was introduced (14 May 1604) as he was subsequently named to two committees.[23] In 1621 Sir Francis Darcy was named to the committee for the bill concerning the purveyance of carts. Darcy's concern for the welfare of his constituents was expressed on 2 May, when he requested that a bill concerning the provision of poor relief in London and its hinterland be made 'general for Middlesex at least'.[24] When the purveyance of carts bill was revived in 1624, Sir Gilbert Gerard was appointed to the committee, as was Sir John Suckling, though he may have been more concerned to protect the interests of the royal Household than those of his constituents.[25] It is striking that Gerard and Suckling were almost the only Members to attend the committee's meeting.[26] Both Gerard and Sir John Franklin were named in March 1626 to the bill to enable the sale of the Hertfordshire and Middlesex lands of the late Sir James Altham the younger.[27]

[1] OR. [2] Fuller's Worthies ed. R. Barber, 241; M. Robbins, Mdx. 32-3. [3] Robbins, 49. [4] LMA, Acc.76/827; DL1/340, unnumb. item. [5] A. Woodworth, Purveyance in Reign of Queen Eliz. (Trans. Am. Phil. Soc. n.s. xxxv. pt. i), 80-3; CJ, i. 286a. [6] Mdx. Sessions Recs. (n.s.) ed. W. le Hardy, i. 254-5, 459; ii. 117, 292-3; iii. 341-2; iv. 102-3, 335. [7] CD 1621, iii. 417, n. 25; iv. 243, 372; v. 322; vii. 301. [8] CSP Dom. 1619-23, p. 373; Som. RO, DD/MI/Box 18, OBI/39, 40. [9] CJ, i. 685a. [10] 'Holland 1624', i. f. 50v. [11] CJ, i. 702a. [12] Chamberlain Letters ed. N.E. McClure, i. 517; ii. 543; Archaeologia, xv. 160. [13] Chamberlain Letters, i. 517. [14] CSP Dom. 1619-23, p. 200; HMC Buccleuch, i. 256; J.K. Gruenfelder, Influence in Early Stuart Elections, 108. [15] Chamberlain Letters, ii. 243; Lansd. 485, ff. 25v-6; CJ, i. 783a. [16] APC, 1621-3, p. 52; C231/4, f. 160. [17] Procs. 1625, p. 698. [18] Archaeologia, xv. 160. [19] Chamberlain Letters, ii. 614. [20] Letters of John Holles ed. P.R. Seddon (Thoroton Soc. xxv), 377. Seddon's identification of Sir James Ley* rather than Edmondes as 'Mr. Treasurer' is incorrect. [21] Barrington Fam. Letters ed. A. Searle (Cam. Soc. ser. 4. xxviii), 50; CD 1628, i. 7. [22] T. Birch, Ct. and Times of Chas. I, i. 197. [23] CJ, i. 208b, 209b, 971a-b. [24] Ibid. 602b. [25] Ibid. 585b, 679a. [26] HLRO, main pprs. 20 Mar.-8 Apr. 1624. [27] Procs. 1626, ii. 312.

A.D.T.

LONDON

Right of election: in the freemen

Number of voters: c.2,500[1]

14 Feb. 1604	SIR HENRY BILLINGSLEY, alderman and Haberdasher
	SIR HENRY MONTAGU, recorder
	NICHOLAS FULLER
	RICHARD GORE, Merchant Taylor
2 Dec. 1606	SIR THOMAS LOWE vice Billingsley, deceased
1 Mar. 1614[2]	SIR THOMAS LOWE, alderman and Haberdasher
	SIR HENRY MONTAGU, recorder
	NICHOLAS FULLER
	ROBERT MYDDELTON, Skinner
20 Nov. 1620	SIR THOMAS LOWE, alderman and Haberdasher
	ROBERT HEATH, recorder
	ROBERT BATEMAN, Skinner
	WILLIAM TOWERSON I, Skinner
13 Jan. 1624	SIR THOMAS MYDDELTON I, alderman and Grocer
	(SIR) HENEAGE FINCH, recorder
	ROBERT BATEMAN, Skinner
	MARTIN BOND, Haberdasher
26 Apr. 1625[3]	SIR THOMAS MYDDELTON I, alderman and Grocer
	(SIR) HENEAGE FINCH, recorder
	ROBERT BATEMAN, Skinner
	MARTIN BOND, Haberdasher
11 Jan. 1626[4]	SIR THOMAS MYDDELTON I, alderman
	(SIR) HENEAGE FINCH, Recorder
	(SIR) MAURICE ABBOT, Draper
	ROBERT BATEMAN, Skinner
19 Feb. 1628	THOMAS MOULSON, alderman and Grocer
	CHRISTOPHER CLITHEROW, alderman and Ironmonger
	HENRY WALLER, Draper
	JAMES BUNCE, Leatherseller

The 'great beehive of Christendom', London in the early seventeenth century was the largest city in England, home to more than 200,000 souls. Its population growth, more rapid than that of the rest of the country, was not halted even by severe plague outbreaks like that of 1603, which claimed the lives of around a fifth of its inhabitants. As the population rose, so the demand for additional housing increased, and by the early seventeenth century London was no longer defined by the area within its medieval walls, though it was administratively separate from nearby Westminster, to which it was physically joined. Many contemporaries lamented the capital's expansion, among them James I, who commented that 'soon, London will be all England'.[5]

London's rapid growth was driven by its economic prosperity. The City had long been the financial centre of the kingdom, and its banking facilities were used by successive monarchs, though the early Stuarts kings found it harder to extract loans from the City than many of their predecessors.[6] During the first half of the seventeenth century perhaps the most prominent feature of London's trade was the new draperies, light-weight fabrics that were exported mainly to south and eastern Europe. The trade in shortcloths continued to form the backbone of the City's economy, but by 1640 the volume of exports of the newer fabrics almost equalled the old.[7] Seasonal tourism, too, remained important. Starting in the autumn and ending in June, a steady flow of visitors arrived in the capital, their numbers tending to peak around Christmas. They came to shop and socialize, and their spending on goods, services and entertainment contributed greatly to the capital's prosperity.[8] The summons of a Parliament helped to swell this influx, there being more than 600 members of the Lords and Commons, many of whom were accompanied by wives and dependants.[9] When James I considered reconvening Parliament at York in 1607 if the Commons did not hasten its consideration of the Union, he was in part threatening the economic interests of the capital.[10]

By the early seventeenth century, London had pretensions to being regarded as the first city in Europe. Not long after James's accession Dekker described the capital as 'Europe's jewel', and in 1628 he characterized it as a new Troy or new Rome.[11] Civic improvements, such as the New River project, which brought an important new supply of fresh water to London during James's reign, undoubtedly enhanced the City's reputation. Yet prosperity brought with it severe social problems: dirt, noise and overcrowding appalled visitors and residents alike, especially those used to small-town or rural life. After spending just three days in London in December 1604, John Packer* complained that he felt as if he had been there three years, 'so unpleasant a thing it is to live here for him which hath tasted the quiet pleasure of the country'. Conditions were considerably worse in the summer, when plague was rife and the stench unbearable. Writing from London in August 1617, Sir John Holles* bluntly referred to 'this stinking town'.[12] Environmental corruption was accompanied with moral decay too, as those who admired the city for its virtues were ready to admit. 'Thou hast all things in thee to make thee fairest', Dekker wrote, 'and all things in thee to make thee foulest'.[13] Then, as now, it was perfectly possible to love and loathe London simultaneously.

London's government was in the hands of the City Corporation, which comprised the Courts of Aldermen and Common Council. Its executive functions were discharged by the aldermanic court, whose chairman was the lord mayor. The aldermen, of whom there were 26 (one for each ward) were appointed for life, and took turns to serve as mayor. Legislative functions were in the hands of Common Council, whose membership numbered 196 at the start of the century. This body has been likened to the contemporary House of Commons, as it enjoyed the power of taxation and its members were elected by the freemen of each of ward, the municipal equivalent of a parliamentary constituency. However, the comparison is not exact. Unlike Members of the Commons, councilmen were required to submit themselves for re-election each year. Moreover, whereas the Commons determined to a considerable degree its own business, Common Council was more strictly circumscribed, as the aldermen could veto its bills while the lord mayor controlled its sittings.[14]

I. Representation and Elections

London was the only borough apart from the combined borough of Weymouth and Melcombe Regis, to send four representatives to Westminster. Nevertheless, considering its immense population, the capital was severely under-represented. To some extent this problem was more apparent than real, for in most parliaments there were several leading Londoners who, unable to secure seats in the capital, found places elsewhere. In the first Jacobean Parliament London's honorary Members included the alderman and Vintner Sir John Swinarton, who sat for East Grinstead. A member of London's committee for parliamentary legislation, Swinarton was instructed by the Corporation in February 1606 to help lobby the

House regarding one of its bills.[15] The prominent City merchant Sir Thomas Smythe also sat in the same Parliament; he served for Dunwich, and went on to represent Sandwich in 1614 and Saltash in 1621. Other leading Londoners to serve in the Commons during this period for constituencies outside the capital included the Goldsmith Sir William Heyricke, who served for Leicester between 1605 and 1610, and again in 1621; the Skinner Robert Bateman, who represented Weymouth and Melcombe Regis in 1614; the Draper Maurice Abbot, who sat for Hull in 1621 and 1624; the Mercer Sir Baptist Hicks, who represented Tavistock in 1621 and Tewkesbury thereafter; the Muscovy merchant and City financier Sir William Russell, who sat for New Windsor in 1626; and the Draper George Lowe, who sat for Calne in 1625, 1626 and 1628. In 1610 the former remembrancer, Clement Edmondes, came in for Caernarvon Boroughs at a by-election, and in 1621 the City's serving remembrancer, Robert Bacon, was elected for St. Ives. An expectation that Bacon would serve London interests was stated explicitly in January 1621, when the Court of Aldermen ordered that he be paid 100 marks in view of 'the great and extraordinary pains' that he 'must necessarily take for the City's service, especially against the Parliament now approaching'.[16] In 1624 and 1625 the City's fee'd counsel, Thomas Crewe, served as Speaker and sat for Aylesbury and Gatton respectively. Shortly before the 1624 Parliament was prorogued, the Court of Aldermen ordered that Crewe be paid £10 as thanks for 'the favours and respect shown unto this City by him'.[17] Alongside these unofficial London Members, there were many others who could be relied upon in matters of interest to the City. Some invested in the London trading companies, while others had townhouses or regular lodgings in and around the capital.

The two senior London Members were considered knights of the shire, a distinction not accorded to the parliamentary representatives of other county boroughs. In May 1628 the Commons queried whether the City's senior Members were entitled to be regarded as knights, and ordered London's writ to be examined,[18] but nothing came of its investigation. In 1571 London's Members, like those of York, had sat on the right of the Speaker, below the privy councillors.[19] Whether they continued to enjoy this privilege under the early Stuarts is unknown, though they probably sat together: in March 1624 Edward Alford moved to have Martin Bond summoned to the bar 'for whispering his partner Bateman in the ear'.[20]

All four Members received wages. In 1584 the junior Members had each been paid the statutory rate of 2s.

per day, and their senior colleagues received twice that amount. Every Member also received a clothing allowance of £6 13s. 4d. to purchase a scarlet gown.[21] In the early seventeenth century the remuneration was unchanged, for in July 1604 Common Council ordered that the City's Members be paid 'all such duties and allowances as are due unto them for their robes, service and attendance as in former times hath been accustomed'.[22] Travelling expenses to Westminster were not paid after 1587, but in December 1625 London's representatives were reimbursed for 'their extraordinary charges and expenses for the time the Parliament was kept at Oxford'.[23] As well as their remuneration, the City's Members were accorded the right, by the Corporation, to nominate collectors for the subsidy whenever Parliament voted the king money.[24]

London's parliamentary elections during this period are poorly documented, for while the Common Council minute books for the years 1604-28 survive intact, they record only the election of 1604.[25] Nevertheless, the general procedure governing elections is clear. The returns indicate that elections were held at the Guildhall, and were presided over by the City's two sheriffs. The law required that they be held in the Court of Husting, London's equivalent of the county court, but ever since the mid-fifteenth century they were actually held in the Court of Common Council, which was restyled a meeting of the Court of Husting for the purposes of the return. The decision to hold elections in Common Council rather than the Court of Husting may have reflected purely practical considerations. By the mid-fifteenth century the Husting Court, unlike Common Council, was primarily a court of law rather than an arena for debate. Moreover, by transferring elections to Common Council London's oligarchs perhaps hoped to deter the freemen from attending.[26] One reason for this was to avoid overcrowding, for by the early seventeenth century there were around 2,500 freemen, far too many to squeeze into the Guildhall, whereas there were only about 200 common councilmen and just 26 aldermen, including the mayor. However, it was probably also the case that the Corporation thereby hoped to increase its own influence. If so it was unsuccessful, as both the medieval and early modern evidence indicates that considerable numbers of ordinary freemen regularly continued to vote. Indeed, the financial records of the livery companies for the early seventeenth century are certainly telling. In 1614 the Carpenters spent 11s. 'when we came from Guildhall for election of knights and burgesses for the Parliament for dinner at the King's Arms at Bassishaw', and following the 1621 election 'some of the Company [of Turners], meeting at the choice of the burgesses for the Parliament', paid 'for a supper at Mr. Pike's'.[27] Similar payments are among the Mercers' accounts for 1606, 1614 and 1625.[28] Dinners like these demonstrate the continuing involvement of the rank and file freemen, as well as showing that elections were as much social occasions as political events.

Although ordinary freemen were permitted to vote, the right of nomination was more narrowly controlled. The aldermen alone selected the candidates for the two senior seats. For the prime place they chose from their own number someone who had recently held the mayoralty and was of knightly status. Often the man picked was a Merchant Adventurer, and he usually belonged to one of the Great Twelve livery companies.[29] The choice for the second seat traditionally fell upon the recorder. In both cases the electors were expected merely to ratify the aldermen's decision. For the two junior seats the aldermen presented a slate of up to 12 men to the rest of the assembly. Successful candidates were drawn from outside the aldermanic circle but were usually senior members of one of the Great Twelve. Robert Bateman was master of the Skinners when he represented London for the first time in 1621, while Maurice Abbot was master of the Drapers when he sat in 1626. Martin Bond was a former first warden of the Haberdashers when he took his seat in 1624, and was master by the time he sat again in 1625. Richard Gore and William Towerson, who sat in 1604-10 and 1621 respectively, were former masters of their companies, and Robert Myddelton had recently served as warden of the Skinners when he was elected in 1614. These men also tended to be leading members of London's powerful trading companies. Abbot was governor of the East India Company when he sat, while Gore and Towerson were senior Merchant Adventurers. Bond and Robert Myddelton, too, were Merchant Adventurers, as was Bateman, who was also an officer of the Levant Company. The sole exception to this pattern was Nicholas Fuller, the City's common pleader, who neither belonged to a trading company nor was a member of a livery company. However, his father had been a Mercer, and by 1604 he himself had forged close links with several of the livery companies, inspecting proposed legislation and accepting a retainer from the Vintners to keep a watchful eye out for them in Parliament.

A third characteristic which distinguished many of the men elected to the junior seats was their association with the City government. Fuller was a Corporation lawyer; Gore was a deputy alderman and a former City auditor; and Bond was a serving auditor, as was Abbot, who may also have been a deputy alderman. Robert

Myddelton's electoral prospects were undoubtedly improved by the fact that, at the time of his election, his brother, Sir Thomas Myddelton I, was lord mayor.

London elections rarely gave rise to controversy, let alone contests, but in 1614 there may have been a tussle for one of the junior seats, as one observer reported that the Skinner William Towerson had been returned, whereas the successful candidate was actually Robert Myddelton. Confusion also surrounded the election to the second of the two senior seats, which was customarily bestowed upon the recorder. It appears that the City initially declined to choose its recorder, Sir Henry Montagu, because it was feared that the king had selected Sir Thomas Lowe, the City's choice for the first seat, as Speaker of the forthcoming Parliament. Under normal circumstances Lowe's selection as Speaker would not have posed any difficulty; after all, a London Member had served as Speaker in 1601. However, in this instance the matter was complicated by the fact that Montagu had recently been promoted to king's serjeant. London's ordinary voters, and perhaps also many in Common Council, realized that, were they to return both men, the king rather than the City would have first claim on the loyalty and service of both its senior Members. Consequently, at the election on 1 Mar. the City endorsed the return of Lowe, but would 'in no wise ... admit master recorder, alleging only that he is the king's serjeant'. As no alternative candidate was offered, the seat remained vacant for several days.[30] However, sometime before 12 Mar. the City relented and agreed to return Montagu.[31] The reason for this change of heart is unclear, but it seems likely that London had discovered that Ranulphe Crewe would be Speaker rather than Lowe.

Technically speaking London managed to avoid a contest in 1628, when hostility to the Forced Loan spilled over into the parliamentary election. London was incensed at the demand for a Loan, as it had not yet been repaid the money it had lent the king in 1617 and 1625 and was in the middle of raising money to pay for a fleet of 20 ships for the Navy. In April 1627 individual members of the Privy Council went to the Guildhall to persuade the citizenry to contribute, but though the City's officers said they would oblige it was 'generally refused by the commons'.[32] The aldermen's unwillingness to oppose the Loan cost them dear. The most notable casualty was the recorder, Sir Heneage Finch, who had served as a Loan commissioner, paid his own contribution with alacrity, and was closely connected to the royal favourite, the duke of Buckingham.[33] As the electors would not hear of him, Finch, whose name appears on the indenture as one of the voters, evidently stood aside in favour of one of the aldermen, Christopher Clitherow.[34]

City anger over the Forced Loan may have also played a part in the election of Thomas Moulson for the first seat. Moulson is unlikely to have been the aldermen's preferred choice, for though an alderman, Grocer and governor of the Merchant Adventurers, he had never served as mayor nor had he been knighted. City-wide anger certainly lay behind the election of the Loan refusers James Bunce and Henry Waller to the junior seats. Both were common councilmen, but Waller had never been an officer of his Company and Bunce, though a prominent Leatherseller, was not a member of one of the Great Twelve. The electoral upset of 1628, in particular the rejection of the recorder, was deeply humiliating to the Court of Aldermen and caused 'great heart-burning in the City'. Indeed, one Jesuit observer noted with relish that London was 'as much distempered as ever Florence was'.[35]

II. Purveyance and Parliament

Criticism of the abuses associated with purveyance was acute in later Elizabethan parliaments, and following James's accession this resentment increased. Whereas Elizabeth had remained unmarried, James had a wife and children, thereby multiplying the number of servants requiring to be fed. London, being the seat of royal government, suffered particularly badly from the purveyors, who frequently exceeded their commissions, and grievances quickly surfaced. In July 1603 the City instructed its common pleader, Nicholas Fuller, to seek a legal remedy for the Poulterers, who complained that their stock had been impounded by the purveyors.[36] An alternative source of redress became available at the beginning of 1604, when Parliament was summoned. On 7 Feb., eight days after the writs were issued, the corporation sent a deputation to secretary of state Sir Robert Cecil, and another to the king's cousin, the duke of Lennox, 'about the special affairs of this City'.[37] Both bodies included Alderman Sir Thomas Lowe, soon to be returned as the City's senior knight. Shortly before Parliament assembled, the City also forwarded a petition from the Poulterers complaining of the abuses of purveyance to Sir John Fortescue, one of the two privy councillors elected to the Commons. These overtures were received favourably, for on the first day of Commons' business (23 Mar.) Cecil's client, Sir Robert Wroth I, included purveyance among the list of topics he wished to be considered. The House accordingly established a small committee that included the London Member Nicholas Fuller to draft a bill to restrain the purveyors.[38]

The 1604 session ended without resolving the problem. When Parliament reassembled in November 1605, London's attitude towards the demands of the board of Green Cloth had begun to harden. Until then the Corporation had sought merely to reform purveyance, but on 6 Nov. the London-based Spanish Company declared that the capital's ancient charters freed the City 'from all such purveyance, exactions and charges'.[39] The Corporation, aggrieved that these immunities had been excluded from the new charter recently granted by the king, responded six days later by establishing a committee to consider its charters 'in that point', whose members included two of its parliamentary representatives, Sir Henry Montagu and Nicholas Fuller. It also resolved to bear the cost of any resultant lawsuits itself. Two days later, it dispatched a four-man deputation, including Montagu, to speak with the lord chancellor regarding 'the affairs of this City'.[40] This meeting evidently achieved nothing, for though the Privy Council had recently discussed the importance of reforming purveyance in the forthcoming parliamentary session,[41] there was no appetite for granting London the immunity it sought. A legal challenge was therefore mounted, but was presumably interrupted when the law term ended on 28 November.[42]

Why had the Spanish Company suggested a radical solution to the problem of purveyance? Pauline Croft argues that one reason must lie in the strained relations between those of its members who traded with the Levant and the board of Green Cloth. In 1597 the Levant merchants had entered into a composition agreement with the Green Cloth, but they objected to the size of the sums demanded and fell into arrears. In June 1604 the king's Grocer summoned them to complain, and by November 1605 continued non-payment had led the purveyors to seize several cargoes of imported currants, including those belonging to the influential Levant merchant, John Bate, whom the Spanish Company named to the small committee set up on 6 Nov. to resist the demands of the royal Household.[43] Nevertheless, the grievances of the Levant merchants were probably not the only reason why the Spanish Company adopted an uncompromising stance. It is striking that the latter was following the example recently set by Bristol's merchants. In January 1604 Bristol had complained at being forced to provide wine and other provisions for the royal Household, 'being a matter never heretofore taken in this city until now of late by Simon Harvey, His Majesty's Grocer'.[44] After failing to persuade the Green Cloth of its case, Bristol had taken its claim of immunity to the Exchequer and King's Bench during the first half of 1605.[45] These developments cannot have gone unnoticed by the Spanish Company, among whom were several leading Bristolians, including Alderman John Whitson, who helped pursue Bristol's suits at Westminster.

London now appeared determined to fight for complete immunity based on its charter. Many in the capital may have believed that the chances of success were high, as two years earlier the City had successfully stood on its charter rights to help strike down in Queen's Bench the patent for the import, manufacture and distribution of playing cards.[46] However, London was not a unified entity, and while many merchants, angry at the greed of the purveyors, doubtless wished to fight for immunity it is doubtful whether the Corporation seriously believed that the Crown would agree to relinquish its right of purveyance in the capital. Its earlier success was misleading, for the loss of the card monopoly had not seriously dented the royal finances, whereas London's claimed exemption from purveyance posed a far more serious threat to the Exchequer. Perhaps the Corporation's real object remained the same as ever – to reform purveyance – and the adoption of radical demands was merely a tactic designed to achieve this end. Evidence that the Corporation remained committed to reform is to be found in a letter from the City's mayor to the Privy Council in December 1605. The City had seized control of the warehouses containing the currants impounded by the purveyors, and the Council naturally wished to regain possession for the king. The mayor refused, but rather than argue the case for London's immunity he merely stated that the merchants wished that no more should be taken from them than was needed for the king's service.[47]

The Corporation's essentially moderate position is also discernable in the Commons' debates of 1606. These revolved mainly around the bill preferred by John Hare which, in effect, aimed to abolish purveyance on the grounds that it was illegal. While the king would retain the right of pre-emption he would no longer be able to pay less than the market price for goods taken up, nor would he be compensated for the additional cost to the Exchequer. However, Recorder Montagu, who seems to have acted as London's chief spokesman in the Commons on this issue, threw his weight behind the more moderate measure preferred by Sir Robert Johnson, which advocated composition.[48] On 26 Feb. Montagu criticized the preamble of Hare's bill, and on 12 Mar. he 'taketh some exception to a clause against London'. The previous day he made an important concession when he stated that the fourteenth century charter granting London immunity

from purveyance should not impede a nationwide composition if that was thought convenient. However, cracks in London's position can also be discerned. Nicholas Fuller, who was well known for speaking his mind, was not prepared to support composition, fearing that in time it would become little more than an extra source of royal income, and that the king would continue to demand provisions regardless.[49] Indeed, like most of the Commons, Fuller seems to have preferred Hare's bill to Johnson's. By April 1606 London had begun to lose interest in the issue of purveyance, probably because, as Croft suggests, it now faced the more urgent matter of impositions. It was Fuller who represented the complaints of the merchants, just as he had spoken up for them over purveyance. On 7 Apr. he declared that the recent increase in the impost on currants 'is so heavy that men have given over to build ships. Yea, the best merchant of London is determined to sell four great ships, and doth offer in them to lose diverse thousand pounds'. One month later, he brought in from committee the bill to outlaw impositions.[50]

Following the end of the second session, purveyance largely vanished from the Commons' agenda. When one of the Members for Gatton, Sir Nicholas Saunders, proposed that a fresh bill against purveyors and cart-takers be drafted he found no support, not even among the London Members despite the fact that abuses by purveyors continued to antagonize the City's government.[51] However, in 1621 the issue resurfaced, albeit on a smaller scale, when the Brewers' Company complained to the Commons about a composition agreement of 1614. By the terms of this agreement, each Brewer was meant to pay 4d. for every quarter of malt that he brewed to a royal farmer, who provided the royal Household with beer worth £3,000 p.a. In return, the Brewers were no longer troubled by the purveyors. Although only a handful of Brewers had actually entered into this agreement, the Green Cloth insisted that it bound them all. When Christopher Smyth took over the farm in 1617 he encountered widespread refusal to pay the 'composition groats', and responded by prosecuting offenders in the Court of Requests, many of whom were imprisoned.[52] The matter came before the Commons on 25 May 1621,[53] and the matter was fully debated on 30 Nov., when the Brewers' case was argued by Thomas Malet, one of the Members for Tregony, who had represented individual Brewers in the preceding lawsuits. Malet argued that the king had no right to purvey beer because it was manufactured and that consequently he was not entitled to demand composition. His fellow lawyer William Noye concurred, for if the king's officers could purvey beer 'they may purvey bread and at last purvey in cook's shops'. Questions were also raised about the nature of the composition agreement, for as only a handful of Brewers were involved it could hardly be considered binding on the rest. However, not all were convinced. Sir Edward Coke and the solicitor general argued that the Crown's rights certainly extended to beer, and indeed beer had always been taken up for as long as anyone could remember.[54] The inconclusive nature of the debate meant that the Brewers renewed their complaint in 1624, 1626 and 1628.[55] On the last of these occasions they also distributed a printed broadside which maintained that the groats were 'more grievous and burthensome unto them than if they paid ten subsidies a year'.[56] Moreover, they revived the claim, last heard in 1606, that London was exempt from purveyance. The Commons, then engaged in a wider battle with the Crown over arbitrary taxation and imprisonment, now took pity on those Brewers who had been imprisoned for refusing to compound, and on 19 June the composition was condemned as 'a grievance both in creation and execution'. At last it seemed as if the Brewers would obtain redress, but when Parliament was dissolved one week later they were no further forward. In December the exasperated Company, perhaps taking their cue from the Levant merchants who now withheld Tunnage and Poundage, resolved to pay no further composition. The following month, it ordered legislation to be drafted for the forthcoming session 'with all expedition'. However, if a bill was ever drawn up it was not read before the Parliament broke up in March.[57]

III. Free Trade and Parliament

As the greatest port in England, London handled a large share of the country's overseas trade. Much of this commerce was in the hands of a small number of chartered trading companies, of which the most important at the beginning of James's reign was the Merchant Adventurers, who dominated cloth exports to the Continent. Trade with the Indies was controlled by the newly formed East India Company, while the route to Russia was monopolized by the Muscovy Company. Of the major London trading companies, only the Eastland Company, which traded with the Baltic, did not enjoy a monopoly. London-based trading companies were in theory national ventures, open to anyone who had the money to invest in their stock, but in practice they were dominated by a small number of wealthy London merchants, who jealously guarded their monopoly rights at the expense of the outports. Their extensive trading privileges were a source of envy outside the capital, particularly during the final years of Elizabeth's reign, when there was general hostility to all forms of monopoly.

London's dominant position came under attack at the beginning of James's reign. On 18 Apr. 1604 a bill to grant free trade to all merchants was given a first reading in the Commons. The Venetian ambassador believed that this bill, which threatened to dissolve the London trading companies, was drawn up in response to a petition 'signed by many merchants'.[58] By 24 Apr. the bill had been joined by a second, and the two measures were entrusted to the same committee, which pursued only one of them. A period of intensive lobbying followed. Large numbers of merchants 'from all parts of the realm', but 'especially' from London, besieged the committee. The Trinity House of Deptford sided with the Merchant Adventurers, whose dissolution, it claimed, would weaken the kingdom's naval power and diminish the standing of English merchants abroad, as trade would henceforward be carried on by 'peddlers and not with merchants'. However, the committee was not susceptible to these arguments, being dominated by the outports, whose representatives had been granted membership of the committee en bloc. On 21 May it announced, through its spokesman Sir Edwin Sandys, that London's joint stock companies 'cannot be otherwise counted than a monopoly'. A mere 200 Merchant Adventurers enjoyed 'the managing of the two thirds parts of the clothing of this realm', and yet the trade might 'well maintain many thousand merchants more'. The Muscovy Company, whose recent whaling expeditions to Spitzbergen aroused the hostility of the outports, particularly Hull and King's Lynn, was even more objectionable as it was 'a monopoly in a monopoly', for though there were 160 investors it was controlled by just 15 directors. The Muscovy merchants did not deny this accusation, but argued that 'the state of the country [Russia] cannot bear any other kind of managing of the trade'. The Commons concurred with the committee, however, and the first of the free trade bills was permitted to continue.[59] London's Members subsequently did their best to hinder its progress. On 31 May Montagu, supported by the Merchant Adventurer Gore, made such a powerful case that on 4 June Sandys was obliged to rebut his speech 'point by point'. Five days later the bill was sent up to the Lords, where it encountered considerable hostility.[60] However, the bill's fate was probably sealed when it was learned that James had urged the Muscovy Company to dispatch an embassy to Russia, which the Company had delayed sending for fear that it was about to be dissolved. James needed the Muscovy Company to continue in order to maintain diplomatic relations with Russia, and his intervention gave a clear signal that the free trade bill would never receive the Royal Assent.[61]

The failure of the free trade bill did not deter the opponents of London's trading companies from mounting fresh attacks. When Parliament reassembled in November 1605, the attentions of the free-traders focused on the Spanish Company, which had been recently revived after a long period of inactivity caused by the Elizabethan war with Spain. The Company was aware of its vulnerability, and in order to avoid parliamentary opposition it had obtained a fresh charter in June 1605 that widened its membership. As a result, almost half the governing assistants were drawn from the outports.[62] However, the free-traders in the Commons ignored the new charter, and on the first day of the second session Sir George Somers, sitting for Lyme Regis, complained of 'inconveniences' arising from the revived Company. Consequently a committee was appointed which drafted a bill throwing open the Spanish trade to all-comers. Faced with this assault, and without the assistance of the king, who did not need it for his diplomacy, the Company began to melt away. Its meetings ceased and the Bristol members seceded, leaving those who remained to argue that free trade would 'discourage the expert and skilful merchant from trading' and cause confusion that would 'utterly overthrow the whole trade'.[63] By the time the bill was enacted in June 1606 the Spanish Company was already defunct.

The overthrow of the Spanish Company was not quite the final act in the free trade dramas of 1604-6, as it put fresh heart into the opponents of the London trading companies. On 17 Mar. 1606, five days after the bill condemning the Spanish Company was sent up to the Lords, a measure to throw open the Muscovy trade received a second reading and was committed.[64] A few weeks later, on 3 Apr., a bill 'for the liberty of free trade into all countries', received a second reading and was committed.[65] Although neither bill progressed any further,[66] the renewed attacks of the free trade lobby were bolstered by separate legislative assaults on the Eastland Company and Merchant Adventurers. These related attacks repay close attention.

The free trade debates of 1604-6 underlined sharp differences between London's economic interests and those of the rest of the country, particularly the outports. However, opposition to the London trading companies was not confined to lobby groups outside the capital. In his report on free trade in May 1604, Sir Edwin Sandys observed that London was not a single economic entity but a city of competing commercial interests. All the merchants who had come before the committee had

> complained grievously of the engrossing and restraint of trade by the rich merchants of London, as being to the undoing or great hindrance of all the rest; and of London merchants, three parts joined in the same complaint against a fourth part; and of that fourth part, some standing stiffly for their own Company, yet repined at other companies.[67]

The truth of Sandys's observation is borne out by the hostility expressed by the Clothworkers towards the Merchant Adventurers in 1604 and 1606. Longstanding enemies of the Merchant Adventurers, the Clothworkers existed to dress cloth whereas the Merchant Adventurers wanted to export cloth in an unfinished condition. In 1566 a bill protecting the Clothworkers' interests was enacted but was widely disregarded, not least by the Crown, which had recently granted several licences allowing unfinished cloth to be exported. Consequently, soon after Parliament met in March 1604, the Clothworkers agreed to finance a bill drawn up by their yeomanry concerned with 'work'. Ten days later, on 31 Mar., a bill 'against transporting of woollen cloths and for setting on work the poor commons of this realm' was given a first reading. However, the Merchant Adventurers, not yet under fire by the free trade lobby, were prepared. When the bill was given a second reading on 4 Apr. another measure, to permit the export of unfinished cloths, was also read. The Clothworkers failed to make headway, and not until the Spanish Company was mired in difficulties, in early 1606, was the climate right to try again. In February 1606 a bill to prevent the export of undressed cloth received two readings in the Commons. The following month a bill forbidding the export of undressed coloured cloths received a second reading and was opposed by the Merchant Adventurer Richard Gore 'as against the common conditions of peace with our neighbours'. Sent up to the Lords in April, it was rejected as unfit, although the Clothworkers had tried to enlist the aid of the earl of Salisbury (Robert Cecil[†]).

The Clothworkers were not the only livery company to throw in their lot with the free trade lobby in 1604 and 1606. The artisan skinners, reluctant members of the Skinners' Company, were restricted to dressing furs as they were barred from the export trade by the Eastland Company's charter. This limited trade was jeopardized altogether by the Eastland merchants, who by 1604 had begun buying up undressed skins from petty chapmen.[68] The artisan skinners, with the blessing of their Company, consequently preferred to the Commons a measure 'for the relief of such as use the handicraft of skinners'. Laid twice before the House, the bill failed to gain support and was rejected.[69] However, like the Clothworkers, the artisan skinners were encouraged to try again by the attack on the Spanish Company, and on 6 Mar. 1606 their bill was read in the Lords. This renewed assault so alarmed the Eastland Company that it turned to the Court of Aldermen, who referred the matter 'to the consideration of the knights and burgesses for this City' and ordered its counsel to act for the merchants at its own charge.[70] Despite this powerful opposition, the bill was enacted as 'An Act for the Relief of such as lawfully use the Trade and Handicraft of Skinners'. It obliged the Eastland merchants to buy their furs from the skinners, and only to export black rabbit skins that they had dressed.[71]

The acts to relieve the artisan skinners and dissolve the Spanish Company dealt a significant blow to the London joint stock companies. Although the assault was not renewed in the 1606-7 session widespread resentment at London's privileges remained, and resurfaced as a result of the Southampton charter bill. Towards the end of Elizabeth's reign, a London merchant named John Davies had set up shop in Southampton, even though Southampton's charter of 1445 prohibited merchants not free of the town from buying or selling merchandize within its precincts upon pain of forfeiture of the goods. After the mayor seized Davies' goods as 'foreign bought and sold', Davies bought back his property for £40, but subsequently sued in King's Bench for the return of this money, arguing that London's charters entitled him, as a London merchant, to buy and sell freely anywhere in England.[72] By the beginning of 1607 the case had dragged on for six or seven years, and had cost Southampton more than £200 in legal fees. As no resolution seemed to be in sight, Southampton's corporation ordered that a bill be laid before the Commons, and on 29 Apr. a measure confirming the town's fifteenth century charter received a first reading.[73] This was not a threat that London could safely ignore. At the second reading on 1 May, three of its Members secured places on the committee; the fourth gained a place soon afterwards, as did the London Skinner Robert Myddelton. On 7 May the Court of Aldermen instructed an eight-man deputation to lobby the committee.[74] These efforts to smother the bill were not well received in the Commons. Indeed, according to Southampton, the bill received no opposition except from 'the citizens of London, who have the like grant themselves but cannot be content that any other town besides themselves should enjoy any liberty'. In early June the bill

was sent up to the Lords, when London again tried to stifle it. A City deputation was ordered to attend the Lords' committee, and a hearing for counsel was sought, even though London's lawyers had previously addressed the Commons for two hours. The Southampton side responded by accusing London of dragging out the bill in the hope that Parliament would be prorogued before the matter could be resolved, and indeed the bill was only just enacted, completing its passage the day before both Houses rose.[75]

When Parliament reassembled in 1610, London's privileges were largely forgotten amid concern for impositions and the Great Contract. By 1614, however, there was renewed interest in London's trading companies. A quarrel between the Muscovy Company and Hull over whaling off Greenland saw the establishment of a Commons' committee of inquiry, and when the House learned of plans to replace the Merchant Adventurers with a rival consortium of London merchants led by Alderman Cockayne it responded by summoning representatives of both groups.[76] The Commons' main interest, however, focused on the newly incorporated French Company, which enjoyed a monopoly of the export trade to France in defiance of the 1606 Free Trade Act, which had dissolved not only the Spanish Company but opened up trade to France to all-comers.

Like the ill-fated Spanish Company, the French Company was not entirely composed of London merchants but it was clearly dominated by them. Many Members of the Commons, particularly those from Devon and Bristol, saw the establishment of the Company as yet another sign that greedy London merchants were trying to monopolize trade at the expense of the rest of the country, and they reacted accordingly. The Plymouth Member, Sir William Strode, complained that 'the Londoners' had obtained the patent in an underhand fashion, and tried to whip up support for a new free trade bill.[77] The Navy treasurer and Harwich Member Sir Robert Mansell declared that 'the reducing of commerce into companies, especially of the French, is the cause that the western parts are altogether barren of sailors'. Those who 'would have all trade brought to London', he added, could show 'no reason why every port town should not govern themselves as well as London govern the whole kingdom'. The Commons' investigating committee shared these concerns at the exclusion of the West Country merchants, and observed that 'the western men can go and return twice before the Londoners can go once'.[78] However, the French Company offended certain vested London interests almost as much as those of the West Country. The Company's chief opponents in London were the Vintners. In 1610 they had closely monitored the French merchants' bill to prevent wine from being imported at certain times of the year.[79] After the French merchants were incorporated in 1611, the Vintners had fought a running battle with them with the assistance of London's recorder, Sir Henry Montagu. When the Commons called in the French Company's charter for inspection in April 1614, the Vintners joined in the attack, spending £4 8s. on legal fees in the process.[80] Montagu, then sitting in the Commons for London, naturally supported his clients, as did his London colleague Nicholas Fuller, who suggested that the patent be 'made convenient'. The open hostility of Montagu and Fuller, and the silence of London's other parliamentary representatives, may have taken the free trade lobby in the Commons by surprise. It certainly prevented the debate from becoming polarized along the usual lines, and perhaps explains why, despite Strode's suggestion, a free trade bill was not introduced. The unlikely alliance of London's Members with the representatives of the outports may actually have helped save the French Company from dissolution, especially as attention was soon diverted by impositions. Lacking friends, the French merchants confessed their fault and offered to surrender their objectionable patent in exchange for an Act that would place its government on an acceptable footing.[81]

The 1614 Parliament was dissolved before the matter could be resolved to the Commons' satisfaction. By the time Parliament reassembled in 1621, attitudes towards the London trading companies had hardened owing to the trade depression and the general unpopularity of monopolies. Indeed, so numerous were the complaints that one historian has rightly observed that 'the Parliament of 1621 represents the high point of the hostility of the Commons to the national chartered companies'.[82] The Merchant Adventurers, blamed for the cloth depression, were subjected to a series of attacks, including a bill to undermine their monopoly by restoring the free trade of the Merchants of the Staple, which received two readings. Feelings ran so high that, when the Cinque Ports petitioned against them, Sir Edward Coke remarked that there was 'no greater cause in all this Parliament'.[83] The French Company, too, came in for renewed criticism. This time there was no question of putting the Company on a statutory footing, as the years before 1621 had seen fresh disputes arise between the Company and its opponents, among them Shrewsbury's drapers. Moreover, while London's Members were no longer critical of the Company, the Vintners continued to

side with the free trade lobby, spending money on 'the general bill of grievance exhibited against the French patent'.[84] Hostility towards the French Company resulted in the Commons twice ordering the French merchants to submit their charter for examination, and in May a bill to permit free trade into France received a first reading.[85] Another London trading company to feel the wrath of the Commons was the East India Company, which had previously escaped criticism. In February it was accused of contributing to the general shortage of coin by its export of bullion to the Orient, a charge it denied, and had to be defended by its allies in the House, including the London Members William Towerson and Robert Bateman, both of whom were members of the Company.[86] It was against this backdrop of general hostility towards the trading companies that in May the Eastland Company preferred a navigation bill to the Commons aimed at prohibiting Dutch imports. Perhaps the most striking feature of this ill-judged piece of legislation is that it actually received a second reading, albeit not until November.[87]

The wave of hostility against London's merchants emanated mainly from the outports, but there were also elements within the City which sought to capitalize on the discomfiture of the trading companies. As well as the Vintners, the Grocers' Company exploited the situation to its advantage. After refusing to pay the Levant Company for currants they had received, complaining of high prices, they appealed to the Commons for redress. They did so at the suggestion of the Venetian ambassador, who explained to his political masters that this was 'the best way to unsettle the [Levant] merchants, since they know that there are many in the assembly [i.e. the Commons] who intend to destroy all the companies, the roots of a thousand disorders, and to make free trade'.[88]

When Parliament reassembled in 1624 the Commons' antipathy towards the London trading companies had begun to soften. There was now some sympathy for their grievances where these coincided with the interests of the commonweal. Indeed, the House endorsed the complaint of the Levant Company, which petitioned to have an increase of 2s. 2d. in the impost upon currants removed, although it refused to condemn an even higher rise in the levy on raw silk, regarding this as 'but an increase in subsidy'. It also supported the Merchant Adventurers when they complained of the pretermitted customs, undue levies by the Customs house, and exactions by the Dutch and the archduchess.[89] However, broad hostility to the London trading companies remained. Five days after the session opened, the Dartmouth Member,

William Nyell, denounced the patents of the London trading companies as 'the principal means of decay of trade' and called for the charters of both the Eastland Company and Merchant Adventurers to be brought in.[90] He was especially aggrieved that the Eastland Company compelled West Country shipowners to buy their masts, cordage and pitch from London. He later observed that before the mid-1560s the Merchant Adventurers had been known as the Merchant Adventurers of England but they were referred to simply as being 'of London'. The Commons shared Nyell's anger, and took up his grievances in the committee for trade. However, Nyell undermined his own case against the Eastland Company when he argued that shipowners should be free to buy their supplies from the Dutch. The Commons was unwilling that this trade should pass into foreign hands, particularly in the midst of a trade depression, and consequently refused to condemn the Eastland charter as a monopoly 'for the present'. Greater sympathy was expressed for the outport merchants, who complained of being forced to join the Company against their will. Shortly before Parliament rose the Commons agreed to include their grievance in its petition to the king.[91] Nyell's complaint against the Merchant Adventurers was also endorsed; an impost laid on cloth by the Company was ordered to be removed, being 'unlawful, unjust and a grievance to the people', and the Company's charter was denounced as 'a grievance, both in the creation and execution'. A new charter was to be sought for the Company, which would no longer give it the exclusive right to export dyed or dressed cloths to Germany and the Low Countries. The House also contemplated opening up the export trade in white cloths, 'the rich commodity of this kingdom', but it preferred to recommend that if the Merchant Adventurers failed to buy any white cloths within a month of their being put on sale in Blackwell Hall the owners should be free to export them themselves.[92] The enthusiasm with which the Commons pursued the Merchant Adventurers served to encourage the latter's old antagonists, the Clothworkers, who revived their earlier parliamentary campaign to be permitted to export a limited number of dressed cloths in accordance with the 1566 Act.[93] During the course of the free trade debates of 1624, which closely resembled those of 1604 in their focus on the Merchant Adventurers and Eastland Company, the Merchant Adventurers were defended unsuccessfully by London's recorder, Sir Heneage Finch.

The parliaments of 1625-9 saw an end to the Commons' criticism of the London trading companies. The single exception was that of 1628, when the Greenland Company, an offshoot of the Muscovy Company, was condemned for aggressively monopolizing the North American whaling trade.[94] The absence of criticism was partly due to the outbreak of war with Spain, which made allies of London and the outports, all of whom suffered heavy losses at the hands of the Dunkirkers. Instead of quarrelling over free trade, the two sides were united in complaining about the disruption to trade and the inadequate protection afforded to shipping by the Navy. Another factor was the growing convergence between City merchants and the Commons over unparliamentary customs duties. The Commons had long opposed impositions, and in 1624 had supported the Levant Company after it complained about an additional duty laid on imported currants. However, in March 1628 the issue came to a head when the wine merchants trading to France complained that some of their members had been impounded for refusing to pay a new imposition that had been laid on wines in December 1627. Their petition was shortly followed by another from the Levant merchants, protesting that the Customs' officers had impounded currants belonging to several merchants who were refusing to pay the additional 2s. 2d. impost laid upon currants. The Commons, already deeply critical of the king's continued levy of Tunnage and Poundage without parliamentary approval, sympathized with both sets of grievances, but despite its representations the king refused to lift the offending imposts or release the imprisoned merchants and impounded currants.[95]

The failure of London's merchants to obtain redress in 1628 caused some of them to take radical action. In September 1628 14 Levant Company merchants broke into the Customs house to take back their currants, among them the governor of the East India Company and former London Member, Sir Maurice Abbot. By the beginning of 1629 some radical merchants, among them the Levant Company merchant-MP John Rolle, were refusing to pay any customs duties not specifically sanctioned by Parliament, including Tunnage and Poundage, thereby linking their cause with that of the Commons, which had explicitly condemned the king's continued levy of this duty in June 1628. When Parliament reassembled in January 1629, the Commons took up their cause, though without success. Following the dissolution, however, both the Levant Company and the Merchant Adventurers cited the Commons' Protestation of March 1629 as the reason for their continued refusal to pay.[96]

The period between the accession of Charles I and the dissolution of 1629 clearly witnessed a major political realignment. Whereas before 1625 the London trading companies and the Commons had seemed natural enemies, by 1629 they were natural allies. As relations between the two sides thawed the trading companies turned to the Commons for support, and not just in matters connected with unparliamentary customs duties. In 1626, for example, the Levant Company appealed to the Commons for help in its fight to retain Sir Thomas Roe as ambassador to Constantinople.[97] In April 1628 the London Member and Eastland merchant Christopher Clitherow seconded secretary of state (Sir) John Coke, who appealed for a generous vote of supply to pay for a naval squadron for the Baltic and troops to assist the Danes. Commenting on the strategic importance of the Baltic, Clitherow pointed out that the fortunes of the whole country were bound up with the continuation of his Company's trade:

> There we vent our cloths and wool, and from thence we bring tar, pitch, etc.by which the kingdom is provided with the Navy, and if the emperor take it [the Baltic] he will master us all, and that he will easily do if we take not part in defence of it.[98]

The East India Company also took advantage of the improved relations between the trading companies and the Commons by drafting a petition to the Lower House pointing out the benefits to the kingdom of the East India trade and asking for a public declaration of encouragement. In 1626 the Company had evidently been widely criticized for failing to stand up to Buckingham, who had extorted £22,000 from them. Responsibility for the petition was handed to its deputy governor, Clitherow. Soon after he appealed to the Commons on behalf of the Eastland Company, Clitherow privately approached the chairman of the committee for trade, Sir Dudley Digges, to learn whether the petition would be well received. Digges, himself a member of the East India Company, assured him that it would, for 'though two years ago there was a little imputation on the Company by the gentry of the kingdom, they were now better affected towards them'. However, despite repeated attempts, Clitherow failed to get the petition read, probably because other issues were more pressing.[99]

IV. Corporation Legislation

As the largest city in England, London had a tremendous appetite for legislation. Indeed, during Elizabeth's reign, as David Dean has remarked, 'more bills pertained to London than to any other locality'.[100] Under James London continued to generate more legislation than any other constituency, much of it drafted by the Corporation.

The business of determining the City's legislative agenda was usually entrusted to a committee appointed by the Court of Aldermen. Consisting mainly of aldermen and common councilmen, it was normally established shortly before Parliament met. However, in 1614 this committee was not appointed until the first day of the session, and for the first Jacobean Parliament it was not appointed until October 1605.[101] Once established, the committee usually continued for the duration of the Parliament, although the committee of 1605 was replaced in January 1610, presumably because so much time had elapsed since its appointment.[102] The committee tended to vary in size: the largest, that of 1605, consisted of 23 members, while the smallest, appointed in 1624, was only nine strong.[103] All four London Members usually belonged to the committee, ensuring that they were acquainted with the legislation they were expected to promote, and in 1605 the committee also included one of the Members for East Grinstead, Sir John Swinarton. However, in 1610 and 1614 London's Members were inexplicably omitted.

Although the City's parliamentary committee largely determined the legislative agenda, the Court of Aldermen continued to take a close interest in parliamentary business. The committee kept the aldermanic council informed of its proceedings, and from time to time the aldermen intervened directly to order particular bills to be drafted or followed. In April 1606, for example, the aldermen instructed that bills for weighing seacoal and prohibiting the sale of 'unsized' loaves within the City be preferred.[104] The aldermen also co-ordinated opposition to hostile bills. In May 1604, for example, London's Members, two lawyers and four merchants were ordered to attend the Commons' committee for the London tithes bill, 'and in the meantime to meet and confer together touching the same'. In April 1624 the Court of Aldermen instructed the City's Members to 'use their best endeavours' to kill off a bill hostile to the interests of the London Butchers' Company.[105] Aldermanic control of parliamentary business left little scope for Common Council to become involved, and indeed the only legislation to which it gave rise were the New River bill of 1606 and the Leadenhall market bill of 1610.[106]

Corporation bills were usually drafted by the City solicitor, who attended the City's parliamentary committee and took advice from the recorder and the City's other law officers.[107] He was also responsible for preferring completed bills to the Speaker, paying the appropriate fees and lobbying behind the scenes. During the first three sessions of the first Jacobean

Parliament the office of solicitor was held by William Dyos, who frequently requested reimbursement for prosecuting the City's legislative business.[108] In July 1609 Dyos was appointed remembrancer, but he continued to be valued for his lobbying skills. Indeed, in 1610 it was Dyos who followed the City's legislative business rather than the new solicitor, Clement Mosse, who was merely granted membership of the 1610 parliamentary committee.[109] Dyos's successor as remembrancer was Robert Bacon, who in 1621 sat for St. Ives and in 1624 helped Mosse lobby on behalf of the corporation.[110] As well as the solicitor and remembrancer, who were chiefly responsible for prosecuting the City's legislative agenda, other lobbyists were sometimes employed to pursue individual measures. In 1610 a bill to prevent the abuses of brewers, paid for out of corporation funds, was 'solicited by Mr. Stanley, scrivener, by my lord mayor's directions'.[111]

The precise volume of legislation pursued by the Corporation is difficult to establish. Decisions regarding the legislative programme were mainly taken in committee, whose proceedings went unrecorded, while the accounts of the City chamberlain, which doubtless indicated the exact number of bills preferred each session, no longer exist for this period. Nevertheless, the City's legislative programme can partially be reconstructed from the minutes of the Court of Aldermen, which often mention bills, and from the parliamentary records themselves.

In 1604 the Corporation, despite neglecting to appoint a committee to determine its parliamentary business, may have preferred or sponsored as many as eight bills. Four were certainly drawn up or paid for by the City: the bill to relieve debtors and recover small debts in London (which concerned the City's Court of Requests, also known as the Court of Conscience);[112] a measure for the better execution and explanation of the Statute of Bankrupts (which was paid for, in whole or in part, by the Grocers' and Merchant Taylors' companies);[113] a bill prosecuted by the searchers and sealer of tanned leather;[114] and a bill to modify the 1529 Act on seacoal.[115] The contents of four other bills suggest that they were City measures. One addressed the problem of overcrowding, a perennial concern of London's governors, by seeking to restrict new building in and around the capital and prevent the subdividing of existing buildings into tenements;[116] another sought to suppress unauthorized quays and wharves in the City and ratify those properly established by statute.[117] A third aimed to establish a Court of Merchants in London along the lines of those in Scotland and France, and was perhaps a revamped version of the 1601 bill 'for policy of assurances used among merchants'.[118] The fourth bill concerned the garbling of spices, and the evidence to suggest that it originated with the City is particularly strong. On 9 May 1604 the king, responding to complaints against the City's garblers and knowing that the matter had been disputed in Elizabeth's reign, ordered an investigation to determine whether the right to appoint the garblers belonged to the City or the Crown. James's action led the Court of Aldermen nine days later to order several of its members to confer with the wardens of the Grocers' Company and two of its lawyers, Sir Henry Montagu and Nicholas Fuller, both of whom also represented London in Parliament.[119] The outcome of this meeting is not certain, but on 22 May a bill concerning spice garbling in London received a first reading in the Commons.[120]

The City's legislative programme for the 1605-6 session was just as extensive as it had been in 1604. As well as the New River bill and measures concerning seacoal and 'unsized' loaves, London's governors preferred a bill regarding the manufacture, finishing and searching of cloth, which was drafted in consultation with the appropriate livery companies.[121] They also reintroduced the bill to curb new building and overcrowding[122] and submitted a measure to supplement the 1604 bill for relieving poor debtors in London, which had been enacted.[123] A further measure, to bring London under the jurisdiction of the commissioners of sewers, must surely have been drafted by the corporation's lawyers.[124] Common Council authorized the introduction of an eighth bill, to give statutory authority to Leadenhall market as the venue for selling new drapery, but it was evidently not preferred until 1610.[125]

During the third session, the City's legislative programme was only slightly less ambitious. Shortly before Parliament reassembled, William Dyos was told to prefer a bill 'concerning new buildings and divided houses in and about London, and to follow the same in such manner as it may best take effect', previous attempts to secure legislation having failed.[126] In the event three separate bills were drafted, two of which began in the Lords.[127] Another bill preferred by the Corporation was designed to supplement the New River bill of 1606, which had been enacted.[128] However, the City's main focus was undoubtedly on the London estates' bill, which sought to give London's various corporations, including the livery companies and London hospitals, secure title for their lands. The City government not only contributed towards the cost of enacting this bill, but also charged its recorder, Sir Henry Montagu, with raising contributions from the livery companies. Prosecution of the bill fell to Dyos, aided by the clerk of the Vintners' Company.[129]

The records relating to the fourth session in 1610 are more helpful than those for the period 1604-7. On 14 June 1610 the Court of Aldermen recorded that six bills had been drawn up on their behalf.[130] Three were certainly presented to the Commons, and can be traced in its records. They concerned those who cheated their creditors by assigning their debts to the king, 'contentious' suits against constables and magistrates, and overcrowding (the bill 'against inmates and new buildings').[131] It is unclear whether a fourth bill, concerning brewers' malpractices, was the same as the measure to prevent brewing in victualling houses that was rejected at its first reading on 21 March.[132] A bill to suppress 'the infinite number of alehouses' was penned by counsel 'but upon the reading stayed by order of this court'. The sixth bill, concerning the employment of merchant strangers, left no mark on the records of either House. The Corporation must also have been behind a bill concerning Leadenhall market, which was probably identical to the one drafted by Common Council in 1606. While the 1610 bill was going through the Commons, the Corporation was busily negotiating to lease part of the market for the new draperies to a consortium of clothworkers.[133]

The City submitted no legislation to the fifth session, although it did give Hugh Myddelton leave to petition the Commons to inspect the New River works.[134] When Parliament reassembled in 1614 the Corporation rediscovered its enthusiasm for legislation, although it delayed appointing the customary committee until 5 Apr., the first day of the session. On 14 Apr. the City Solicitor, Mosse, was instructed to follow a bill for preventing the removal of small claims of £10 or less from the City's Court of Requests. It is unclear whether the measure was ever heard, as it seems not to have been the twice-read bill for the speedy recovery of small debts, whose author was apparently the Bristol Member John Whitson.[135] On 19 Apr. the Court of Aldermen ordered a bill concerning overcrowding to be drawn up. This was presented to the court on 4 May, together with three more bills that presumably originated in the Corporation's parliamentary committee. These additional measures aimed to prevent the fraudulent dyeing of silk, drunkenness, the inordinate consumption of corn and deceits in the use of weights and measures.[136] All four bills were subsequently laid before the Commons,[137] as was a measure to exempt London's cheesemongers

and butter traders from the penalties imposed under an Edwardian Act for selling butter and cheese in bulk. This latter bill was drawn up by the cheesemongers themselves, and was not, strictly speaking, a piece of Corporation legislation. However, the cheesemongers lacked formal organization and could not easily pursue legislation on their own. Consequently, the Corporation agreed to sponsor the bill, although the cheesemongers were to bear the cost themselves.[138]

The cheesemongers' bill made little progress before the Parliament was dissolved. It was resubmitted with Corporation sponsorship in 1621, when the Corporation promoted little legislation of its own. In April the Court of Aldermen ordered another bill to be drafted concerning new buildings and the subdivision of existing properties. London's governors may also have been behind bills for relief of the poor in and around London and for the recovery of small debts in the capital.[139] The decline in City legislation continued in 1624. Apart from again sponsoring the cheesemongers' bill, which was finally enacted, the Corporation laid no bills before Parliament apart, perhaps, from a bill on poor relief, which was described as a London bill during the second reading debate on 8 May.[140] The Corporation did contemplate introducing a bill to put a stop to 'corrupt and heavy dyed silk throughout the realm', but the measure was probably not drafted, as four days later the Commons ordered the mayor to deal with the abuses of dyeing heavy silks himself.[141]

In 1625 the Corporation did not tender a single bill to Parliament. The severe outbreak of plague may have been largely responsible, but the previous two assemblies showed that its enthusiasm for legislation was waning. In 1626 the Corporation made clear to the City Members and its committee for parliamentary affairs that its main concern in Parliament was with 'the monies disbursed by the City about levying of the soldiers' for the war against Spain.[142] Consequently, the only bill that seems to have been introduced by the Corporation was the routine measure to restrict the number of inhabitants per building, which received two readings.[143] On 6 June the Court of Aldermen also referred the preservation of London bridge to its committee for parliamentary affairs, but as the Parliament was dissolved nine days later there was insufficient time to prepare a bill.[144] The absence of legislation in 1626 is especially remarkable as the Speakership was then occupied by the City's recorder, Sir Heneage Finch. Since the Speaker controlled which bills were read, any City measures would inevitably have been guaranteed a hearing. No bills at all were submitted by the Corporation in 1628/9, when the Court of Aldermen seems not to have appointed the usual committee to manage its parliamentary business.

The striking collapse in the Corporation's appetite for legislation was mirrored by a similar decline in the legislative interests of London's companies.[145] So far as the Corporation is concerned, the reasons for the collapse are obscure, but they may lie in a dramatic alteration in its legislative fortunes. During the first Jacobean Parliament the Corporation had enjoyed a degree of legislative success. In 1604 four bills (out of the seven or eight promoted) were enacted: those concerned with the Court of Conscience, bankruptcy, spice garbling and leather. Following the second session three more, out of the six or seven preferred, became law: those concerned with the New River, small debts and sewers. Lastly, the third session produced the London estates Act and the second New River Act, and in 1610 bills were enacted to prevent the harassment of magistrates and constables and the assigning of private debts to the king. This picture of broad success altered dramatically in 1614. The premature dissolution caused the Corporation to lose all four of its bills plus the cheesemongers' measure which it sponsored. In 1621 it scaled back its legislative programme, but again came away empty-handed. These setbacks proved so discouraging that in 1624 the Corporation scarcely bothered to prefer bills, and during the first three assemblies of Charles's reign it offered just one.

An important factor in the Corporation's abandonment of its customary legislative programme was undoubtedly the money wasted on the fruitless pursuit of bills. The financial losses incurred in 1614 and 1621 are unknown, but spending on bills in previous sessions was certainly heavy. In 1604 around £100 was spent, and in addition, as tradition demanded, a gratuity of £10 was given to the Speaker at the beginning of the session.[146] The 1605/6 session saw no less than £238 17s. laid out.[147] In 1610 Dyos received £131 15s. 10d. to offset the cost of the City's legislative programme, and a further £10 was given to the Speaker.[148] Sums of this magnitude could only be justified if there was a realistic prospect of success. As this dwindled, the Corporation's attitude to parliamentary spending changed. After 1610 the only Speakers to receive a gratuity were Thomas Crewe in 1624 and Sir John Finch in 1629.[149] London's governors must also have been swayed by the emptiness of their coffers, though, for early in Charles's reign the City's chamber calculated that its annual expenditure exceeded its income by almost £2,900.[150]

The Corporation's abandonment of parliamentary legislation meant that it was compelled to explore other avenues to solve its problems. Royal Proclamations had long been regarded as an alternative to legislation, even before the 1620s, especially in relation to the problems posed by overcrowding and new buildings. After the parliamentary sessions of 1604-7, which witnessed the loss of five bills on these subjects, the king stepped in and issued two Proclamations. Another, designed to close various loopholes, was issued in July 1620. Proclamations lacked the authority of statute law, however, and consequently in 1614 and 1621 the Corporation again tried to persuade the Commons to pass legislation. Far from lending a sympathetic ear, in 1621 and 1624 the House took up the complaint of the Carpenters' Company which, along with various builders, protested at the Crown's establishment of commissions restricting building activity in and around the capital. In May 1624 the Commons found for the Carpenters, and included their complaint in the grievances presented to the king. However, James was fully behind the City's governors, and expressed surprise that the Commons had made 'a matter of building about London a grievance'.[151] Another alternative to parliamentary legislation was the City's own ordinances. After the Corporation failed to obtain statutory authority to set up a cloth market specifically for the new draperies in 1610, it decided to press ahead regardless, and by 1622 at the latest a new market at Leadenhall had been established.[152]

Despite abandoning its customary legislative agenda in the 1620s, the Corporation continued to take an interest in others' bills, particularly those it deemed harmful to the City's interests. After the artisan Clothworkers submitted a bill to the 1624 Parliament seeking to prohibit freemen belonging to other London livery companies from employing apprentices to row, shear and dress cloth, the aldermen instructed the City's Members 'to use their endeavour and best intents to suppress the said Act [sic]'. The aldermen also intervened on behalf of the Butchers' Company, which complained that a bill to prevent butchers from grazing their cattle disadvantaged its members. Indeed, they instructed London's representatives to 'use their best endeavours for stay of the same Act [sic], which is conceived by this court to be hurtful unto this City'.[153] Even if it was only suspected that a bill was hostile, it was essential to monitor it. After Sir Henry Poole introduced a measure for the better sale of home-produced white woollen cloths, several aldermen were instructed to attend the bill committee, 'to the end that they may maintain and preserve as much as in them lieth the privileges and freedoms of this

City'.[154] In April 1621 the Court of Aldermen established a committee to take notice of a bill preferred by the Fishmongers' Company to the Commons 'against the use of the trawl net' and advise them what to do.[155]

V. London's Companies and Hospitals

The Corporation of London was the major interest group in the City, but it was not the only one. Most of the capital's livery or trading companies approached Parliament at one time or another, either to extend their authority or defend their interests. The almost complete absence of any reference to Parliament in the highly detailed accounts of the Turners' Company is striking precisely because it is so untypical.[156] Even if they did not have business of their own to pursue, the London companies often found it prudent to watch for hostile bills or petitions. In 1606 the Cordwainers paid the clerk of the Commons 16s. 4d. 'to give notice of any bill that should pass this Parliament concerning the Company', and in 1621 the Grocers gave him 22s. so that he would 'give this Company notice of the Apothecaries' proceedings'.[157] Payments included among the parliamentary expenses of the Vintners' Company in March 1604 may have had a similar purpose. The recipients, a Mr. Moore and a Mr. Fuller, were presumably the Reading Member Francis Moore and the London Member Nicholas Fuller.[158] An alternative method of keeping a watch on Parliament was adopted in April 1614 by the Vintners, who established a committee to 'give directions touching all such bills or other matters as shall be preferred to the Parliament House and may concern this corporation to prevent as much as may be such dangers or hindrances as may fall to this Company for want of due care'.[159]

Unlike the Corporation, London's companies were not automatically entitled to instruct the City's parliamentary representatives. However, as we have seen, the Court of Aldermen sometimes required London's Members to further a particular Company's parliamentary interests. Moreover, the companies often employed London's lawyer-Members when they had business in Parliament. In 1604, for example, Nicholas Fuller seems to have been active on behalf of five livery companies, as well as Bridewell Hospital, whose bill he may have helped to draft. Fuller's fellow London lawyer and Member, Sir Henry Montagu, provided the Vintners with legal advice on an alehouse bill, and in 1614 both he and Fuller advised the Bakers over their legislation. The companies also approached those London Members with no legal expertise. In 1621 the Plaisterers evidently lobbied Sir Thomas Lowe to oppose the Bricklayers' bill, as they bestowed 3s. 8d. upon his servant.[160] That same year the Grocers

paid 2s. 6d. to a coachman 'for carrying Sir Thomas Myddelton to Westminster' in connection with their continuing battle with the Apothecaries.[161]

Many livery companies looked beyond London's own parliamentary representatives for assistance in the Commons, particularly to those barrister-Members who counted them among their clients. In 1604 the Vintners turned to the Berkshire lawyer Francis Moore, who had been giving the Company legal advice since about 1599.[162] In 1621 the Brewers' advocate in the Commons was the Cornish lawyer Thomas Malet, who had defended several of their members in the Court of Requests.[163] It was not unknown for a Company with interests outside London to seek help from the parliamentary representatives of the area concerned. In May 1624 the Fruiterers asked Kent's knights of the shire to lobby on their behalf for 'some good law' to curb Dutch imports, as they represented the county 'in which is the greatest plantation' of fruit.[164] Many companies also had friends among the gentry sitting for other constituencies. In 1610 the Salters evidently depended upon the Warwickshire Member Sir Edward Greville, who reported their bill against logwood and belonged to the bill committee for confirming them in possession of their lands. The source of the connection is unclear, but whenever he visited London Greville stayed at *The Swan with Two Necks* in Milk Street, thereby making him a close neighbour to the Salters, whose hall lay in nearby Bread Street. The Woodmongers had an astonishing range of friends at Westminster. In 1621, having discovered that the wharfingers had introduced a hostile bill to the Commons, they appealed for assistance to the Hampshire squire Sir Thomas Jervoise (Whitchurch), asking him to nominate several named individuals if the bill was committed. As well as the London Members and two of the City's honorary representatives, Sir Baptist Hickes and Robert Bacon, the list included Sir Robert Knollys II (Berkshire), Sir Dudley Digges (Tewkesbury), John Angell (Rye), Richard Digges (Marlborough) and John Pym (Calne).[165]

Although many London companies enjoyed an enviable range of contacts in the Commons, they did not neglect to lobby the vast mass of Members with whom they were unconnected. In 1610 the Grocers paid their clerk 10s. for making copies of a summary of the Apothecaries' bill, which they opposed, 'and other instructions for the knights of Parliament to speak to [sic] the bill for this Company'.[166] In 1621 the Plaisterers' clerk received 15s. for 'writing several things for the burgesses in the Parliament House', while in 1624 the Apothecaries ordered breviates detailing their dispute with the Grocers to be drafted quickly so that 'some may be delivered to as many Parliament men as shall be thought fit'.[167] During the first Jacobean Parliament a few companies used the printing press to generate lobby documents in bulk, such as the Clothworkers, whose 1604 petition was printed, and the Carpenters, who in 1607 printed three quires of breviates of their bill at a cost of 14s. 4d.[168] By the 1620s the use of print had become widespread. In 1621, for example, the Apothecaries were anxious to lay their hands on 'bills and printed briefs preferred to the House by the Physicians, Chirurgeons [Barber-Surgeons] and Distillers'.[169] That same year the Woodmongers printed their petition against the wharfingers, and the Tylers and Bricklayers produced 'printed breviates' costing 11s.[170] Many other examples could be given.[171]

While print made for more effective distribution of information, there was no substitute for lobbying in person. In 1604 a delegation from the Cordwainers visited Sir John Savile, the chairman of the committee for the tanners' bill, to put their case.[172] Ten years later, the clerk of the Bakers' Company and another man travelled to Westminster 'to speak with Mr. [John] Hoskins, one of the burgesses' about their bill. The clerk subsequently made several more journeys to Westminster in the hope of hearing the bill read, and also 'to deliver briefs ... to divers other of the burgesses'.[173] Direct lobbying of individual Members of the Commons is not always so well recorded, though it can sometimes be inferred from Company accounts. A case in point concerns the Brewers, who in 1614 succeeded in getting their bill committed. As they did not know the identities of the Welsh Members, who had been appointed to the committee *en masse*, they spent 5s. in 'going to Westminster to fetch out the names of the knights of Wales'.[174] Clearly they intended to lobby the Welsh Members individually once they had learned who they were. Lobbying Members of the Commons in person was not necessarily guaranteed to succeed. In February 1621 the Physicians, learning that the Barber-Surgeons were about to seek parliamentary permission to encroach upon their privileges, instructed its fellows to 'visit as soon as possible those friends whom they had among the burgesses of Parliament and win them over, particularly those representing the universities'. However, the Physicians' easy assumption that the university Members would sympathize with their cause proved ill founded. At a meeting between the college's representatives and the Members for Cambridge University, the Physicians were accused, *inter alia*, of admitting to their ranks too many doctors from other universities.[175]

Under Elizabeth, London companies sometimes dined or bought drinks for Members of the Commons whose views they wished to influence. In 1566, for instance, the Clothworkers spent £4 10s. on 'fish sent to Sir Ambrose Cave's [sitting for Warwickshire] for dinners at two several times when the committees of our bill met there'.[176] By the beginning of James's reign, however, this practice had largely ended or was no longer being recorded. When Company officers travelled to Westminster to pursue parliamentary business they certainly dined at their Company's expense, as did key witnesses and the Company lawyers, but Members of the Commons were not accorded the same hospitality. Nor was it usual for the companies to bestow gifts or food on individual Members, although in 1604 the Coopers gave 'a runlet of Rhenish wine' costing 23s. 6d. to 'one of the Parliament House'.[177]

Unlike the Corporation, London's companies were not entitled to use the City solicitor to prosecute their business unless they hired his services. In 1614 the Bakers paid him 20s. 'for his pains' in preferring their bill, and in 1621 the Plaisterers gave him 11s. for helping them to oppose the Bricklayers.[178] From time to time the companies roped other City officials into lobbying for them. In March 1621 the Carpenters gave 5s. to Mr. Bayard, one of the mayor's officers, 'when the committees met for buildings', and they gave another of the Mayor's men 20s. 'towards an offering for his maid'. How far Bayard and his colleague were acting with the mayor's authority is uncertain, as the Carpenters were opposing City legislation to control the amount of new building in and around the capital. City officers were not the only lobbyists for hire. In 1604 the Brewers gave £5 'to one George Whitton to help us to prefer our bill in the Parliament House'. Whitton, a minor Oxfordshire gentleman, had sat in the Commons during the 1570s and 1580s, and seems to have been the first former Member of the Commons to become a lobbyist.[179] In 1626 the Bakers paid £15 to Thomas Reading, 'a solicitor', to prefer their petition against Sir Abraham Williams' patent for a machine to sieve and dress meal.[180] Many London companies with business in Parliament, however, preferred to use their own officers to lobby the Commons, as did the Carpenters in 1621 and the Brewers in 1624 and 1626.[181] The Charterhouse Hospital, too, employed its solicitor and auditor to prosecute its bill in 1624 and 1628.[182]

Legislation was expensive, and for most companies it represented a major drain on their resources. In the financial year 1586/7 half the Curriers' spending went on a single piece of legislation.[183] Not everyone could afford this sort of outlay. Indeed, in 1624 the Fruiterers' claimed that they were 'not able to be at the charge to prefer a bill'.[184] The most costly piece of Company legislation during the early Stuart period was the London estates Act of 1607. As well as the usual fees payable to the officers of both Houses, the companies who contributed were forced to find £2,500 between them to buy off the king's chief ministers.[185] Each Company paid in proportion to their size and importance. At one end of the spectrum were the Goldsmiths, who forked out £300, while at the other were the Barber-Surgeons, who paid just £10.[186] The London estates Act was exceptional, however, as bills were not normally this expensive. Nevertheless, statutory confirmation of the Charterhouse Hospital in 1628 cost £100 1s. 9d., an astonishing sum.[187] Failed legislation was not as costly as enacted bills, of course, and the amounts spent tended to vary wildly. This was partly because spending depended on how far a bill had progressed. For example, the Tallowchandlers' bill of 1621, which was read just once, cost £5 12s., whereas the Carpenters' bill of 1607, which was read twice, cost £16 13s. 3d.[188] Another important factor in determining cost was the House of origin, as a bill preferred to the Lords would immediately incur the higher fees charged there. Not surprisingly, few London companies initiated their legislation in the Upper House. Cost was also partly determined by experience. Companies versed in lobbying Parliament often declined to disburse money until they had received some service in return. In 1589, for instance, the Coopers, veteran lobbyists, withheld paying fees to the officers of the Commons until after it was ordered that their bill be engrossed.[189] However, a Company inexperienced in the art of lobbying was sometimes less wary about paying fees in advance. In 1614 the Bakers, who had no recent experience of approaching Parliament, spent £20 17s. 8d. on parliamentary and legal fees, drinks, dinners and travelling costs, but failed to obtain even a first reading of their bill.[190]

Most livery company legislation was drawn up on the orders of the Company officers, but ordinary members might also offer up their own bills for approval. In May 1604 the Fishmongers were asked by one of their members, Thomas Fuller, to help pay for a bill to enforce the observation of fish days, which he and another man had already introduced to the Commons. The Company agreed, and though the bill failed to proceed beyond a second reading Fuller was repaid all the money he had laid out, amounting to £11 13s. 4d.[191] Companies naturally liked to be asked before any of their members approached Parliament in their name. In 1624 two Leathersellers cheekily requested the wardens

of their Company to attend the committee for grievances that afternoon after they petitioned the committee in the Company's name against Sir Thomas Glover's patent for searching tanned leather. The Company was naturally annoyed at these unauthorized proceedings, and though it agreed to the request it declared that it would not be put 'to any charge about the same'.[192]

In theory, the livery companies were expected to obtain the approval of the Court of Aldermen before preferring legislation to Parliament. In practice, however, this requirement was widely disregarded: between 1571 and 1601 only the Bakers, in 1589, are known to have sought permission to submit a bill.[193] After 1603 most livery companies continued to act without reference to the aldermen, although the Painters' bill of 1604 seems to have been drafted with the assistance of a committee appointed by the Corporation. Moreover, in 1621 some of the Dyers asked the City's permission to present a bill to reform abuses in the dyeing of black silk.[194] The independent outlook of the livery companies contrasts with the deference of London's unincorporated workers, who also occasionally looked to Parliament for redress. Lacking the lobbying and organizational skills of the companies, they tended to seek aldermanic approval before approaching Parliament, perhaps in the hope that the City would aid their cause. In 1614, and again in 1621 and 1624, the cheesemongers, who had never been incorporated, requested and obtained aldermanic approval of their bill. In each case the aldermen agreed to support the measure, and ordered the City solicitor to follow it through Parliament, but added that the cost was to be borne by the cheesemongers themselves.[195] In 1621 the Court of Aldermen were approached by the 'poor flaxdressers, shopkeepers and traders in undressed flax within London', who desired to approach Parliament by petition rather than by bill. After ordering the petition to be redrafted by its committee for parliamentary affairs, the aldermen promised that the City solicitor would follow the matter at the charge of the petitioners.[196] London's unincorporated workers were not alone in seeking aldermanic approval before taking their grievances to Westminster. In 1626 several tanners living outside the capital asked to petition Parliament to alter the weekly meat market at Leadenhall from Monday to Tuesday, because many tanners refused to bring their meat to market for Monday for fear of transporting it on the Sabbath contrary to Proclamation. As the resultant shortage of meat had meant high prices, the aldermen readily agreed.[197]

Livery companies generally preferred bills to Parliament on their own, but where the interests of more than one Company coincided it made sense for those concerned to pool their resources. In 1606 the Great Twelve jointly preferred a bill to clarify an Act of 1504 regarding the execution of Company ordinances. Each Company paid a share of the cost, and the responsibility for following the bill settled upon William Dyos, the clerk to the Goldsmiths' Company and City solicitor.[198] This bill disappeared after it was engrossed, but an even more ambitious collaborative venture was undertaken soon afterwards. In December 1606 the livery companies complained to the Privy Council that they were required to compound for lands bequeathed to them, despite having already done so several times.[199] The matter was referred to Parliament, and in February 1607 a bill was laid before the Lords.[200] The measure, enacted at the end of the session, was supported by the Corporation, which sought security of title for its own lands and those belonging to the London hospitals. Responsibility for collecting financial contributions fell to the City's recorder, Sir Henry Montagu, while the task of lobbying was entrusted to Dyos and the clerk of the Vintners' Company. From the outset the chief obstacle to progress was money, as the king's ministers demanded £2,500 in return for allowing the bill to pass, and there were also the fees payable to the officers of both Houses.[201] While most companies were anxious to benefit from the bill, few were willing to part with the large sums required. During the Easter recess the Court of Aldermen, learning of this, summoned the wardens of the companies and demanded to know whether to proceed further.[202] The assurances they received over the next few days inclined them to continue,[203] but many companies remained cautious, disbursing only what was needed until they were sure that the bill would pass. The Mercers, for instance, voted £200, but only 'provided that the Royal Assent be absolutely procured'. Even after the bill was enacted, some foot-dragging continued. The Goldsmiths delayed making arrangements to pay their contribution until 17 July, while the Barber-Surgeons ordered no payment until 20 July.[204] The Tallowchandlers' contribution of £15 was not paid until 1609 at the earliest.[205] Many companies probably also prevaricated because they feared being charged more heavily than others of comparable wealth and status. None were more worried about favouritism than the Merchant Taylors who, on 18 Apr., ordered £5 to be paid to Recorder Montagu 'to have special care that the Company may be reasonably charged'.[206]

The ordinances bill of 1606 and the London estates bill of 1607 were notable examples of co-operation between the livery companies, but they were far from unique. In 1604 the Blacksmiths and the Girdlers jointly

presented a bill to Parliament, which failed to gain a first reading.[207] That same year the Cordwainers spent £5 11s. 8d. 'in joining with the other companies about the tanners' bill', and in 1607 they laid out a further £5 10s. 'in defending the Curriers' bill'.[208] In 1610 the Salters not only collaborated with the Dyers to promote a bill against logwood,[209] they also allied themselves with the Brewers to plug a gap in the London estates Act of 1607 regarding some properties they owned in Fleet Street.[210] On the latter occasion the Brewers paid their share of the costs to the Salters, who presumably prosecuted the bill on their behalf.[211] In 1624 the Bakers and Brewers acted jointly to oppose 'a bill preferred by the Kentishmen for suppressing extortion in meal porters and other such like' by hiring a barrister to represent them at the Commons' committee.[212]

Co-operation between the livery companies was less common, however, than conflict. Many companies had overlapping economic interests, and regarded legislation as a useful means of improving their position at the expense of their rivals or those in associated trades. For example, in 1593 and 1604 the Coopers preferred legislation to force individual Brewers to limit the number of coopers they retained.[213] Over the course of three successive parliaments the Painters introduced legislation to prevent other workers engaged in the building trade from practising their art, to the dismay of the Plaisterers, who put up a dogged resistance. The Painters' persistence paid off in 1604, when their bill was finally enacted.[214] In 1621 the Distillers preferred a bill to benefit their members, only to run into the opposition of the Apothecaries, who resolved 'to set down their several reasons to induce the Parliament not to allow of the Distillers' bill'.[215] Many other examples of conflict based on competing economic interests could be given.

Companies with overlapping interests were often reluctant to consult each other before introducing legislation, with predictable results. In 1607 the Carpenters preferred a bill for the proper measuring and marking of timber. After a first reading in the Commons on 10 Mar., the bill encountered opposition from the Shipwrights. The Carpenters responded by belatedly conferring with the Shipwrights, paying them for copies of their objections and bestowing 20s. upon their clerk. Despite these conciliatory gestures, the bill was rejected at its second reading in May.[216] Another Company which listened too late to its opponents' objections were the Barber-Surgeons, who in March 1607 laid before the Lords a bill 'for the more convenient examination and approbation of surgeons in and about the City of London by men expert and skilful in that science and faculty'. Intended to permit the Surgeons to administer internal as well as external medicaments, it was rejected at its second reading.[217] The Surgeons were bitterly disappointed and blamed their failure on hostile lobbying by the Royal College of Physicians. At first they considered reintroducing the bill 'with considerably more favourable conditions', but on reflection they arranged to meet the Physicians in early April. At this meeting they admitted that their bill had been 'extremely unjust and unreasonable', but denied that they had sought to undermine the Physicians' privileges, instead blaming the lawyers who had drafted the bill for giving it 'excessive clarity', which had 'distorted the sense'. The Physicians replied that it would have been prudent had the Surgeons consulted them first, 'for everyone agreed that they had tried to achieve their purpose secretly and treacherously'.[218] Chastened, the Surgeons ordered their bill to be redrafted, 'and that part ... which concerneth the practice of physic is to be showed to the Physicians'.[219] However, there is no evidence that the redrawn bill was submitted before Parliament was prorogued in July.

While some companies were at odds with each other, others were at war with themselves, and these internecine conflicts sometimes spilled over into Parliament. In 1624 the Goldsmiths presented a bill to the Lords to force its members to reoccupy the shops along Cheapside and Lombard Street, many of which were closed or occupied by 'mean traders'. However, those Company members who lived outside London were unwilling to move their premises, and in April more than 100 of them descended upon the Lords' committee for the bill 'in a tumultuous fashion' to protest. Their noisy intervention effectively scuppered the bill.[220] Internal divisions also appeared in the Grocers' Company in 1610. The Grocers were a broad church, and before 1617 their ranks included London's apothecaries and druggists. However, the vast increase in the number of imported drugs between 1567 and 1609 opened up the possibility of large profits for the apothecaries if they could secure independence from the Grocers. In June 1610 a wealthy foreign apothecary named Gilbert de Laune, who was not himself a member of the Grocers, preferred a bill to the Commons granting independence to the apothecaries, which secured a first reading. When the Grocers learned of this they rounded up those of their members whom they suspected of involvement and forced them to distance themselves from the bill, which failed to progress any further.[221] Another Company threatened with secession by part of its membership was the Leathersellers. In January 1620 the glovers in their ranks petitioned the Privy

Council for the right to form their own Company, but were opposed by the City government. When Parliament assembled the following year the glovers drafted a bill, which failed to gain even a first reading.[222] The wharfingers, too, sought permission to break free of the Woodmongers.[223]

Unlike the capital's trading companies, none of London's livery companies found their right to exist explicitly questioned by Parliament before the early 1620s, with the possible exception of the Pinmakers in 1606.[224] However, the general antipathy towards monopolies in the Commons in 1621 and 1624, and the concurrent revival of the free trade debates, meant that hostility towards the London companies, particularly those which had been newly created and therefore seemed vulnerable, quickly surfaced. In 1621 the shipwrights of Ipswich tried to persuade the House to order the dissolution of the Shipwrights' Company, which had been founded in 1605, as it was said to 'impose exceedingly upon builders of ships'. The master of the Company, William Burrell, was so alarmed that he appealed for assistance to his fellow Navy Commissioner John Coke, then sitting for Warwick.[225] The Shipwrights were not alone in being threatened with dissolution. In 1621 and 1624 the Grocers asked the Commons to suppress the Apothecaries, who had been incorporated in 1617. A sympathetic Commons denounced the offending patent as a grievance in May 1624 because it forced merchants to sell only to the Apothecaries. However, James rejected their criticism, declaring that the patent had been granted at his express wish 'for the health of his people, knowing that grocers are not competent judges of the practice of medicine'.[226]

The agitation against monopolies, which resulted in attacks on two of the livery companies, also blighted attempts by several companies to pass legislation. In March 1621 a bill to confirm the Gardeners' Company was rejected after a first reading 'without one negative', and the Company's patent was called in to be examined.[227] The fate of the bill may explain why the Apothecaries, who early in the Parliament drafted legislation to confirm their own charter, had still not introduced their own bill in December.[228] In 1624 the Goldwiredrawers introduced a bill to confirm their letters patent, but this too fell at the first reading after Sir William Strode declared that to pass it would be 'to confirm a monopoly by Act of Parliament'.[229] The Apothecaries fared slightly better as their bill was committed, but there was never any realistic prospect that the House would endorse a measure confirming the Company's charter when it condemned the charter itself.[230] There were further legislative casualties in 1621. A bill preferred by the Bricklayers' and Tylers' Company to reform abuses in the making and selling of bricks, tiles, lime and sand in the London area was rejected at the first reading 'because it was generally conceived to be a monopoly'.[231] Soon afterwards the Pewterers' bill 'touching divers inconveniences in our trade' was also cast out at the first reading after it was described as a monopoly.[232]

The volume of legislation laid before Parliament by London's companies and hospitals is difficult to gauge accurately because of gaps in the records, but it is clear that between them they were responsible for generating more bills than the Corporation. During the 1604 session the Corporation promoted seven or eight bills at most, whereas London's other lobby groups introduced at least ten: the Blacksmiths, Brewers, Clothworkers, Coopers, Painters, Skinners and Watermen all introduced bills;[233] the Fishmongers paid for a bill drafted by one of its members to preserve small fry;[234] the Leathersellers contributed £15 towards the cost of a bill 'for pelts';[235] and Bridewell Hospital twice introduced legislation to confirm its charter. The Barber-Surgeons also drafted a bill which seems not have been presented.[236] The Merchant Taylors may have introduced a bill regarding woollen cloth, but the recorded expenditure implies that they actually paid to have their views on someone else's bill represented in the Commons.[237]

After 1604 the companies' initial burst of legislative enthusiasm began to subside. Nevertheless, in 1605/6 the Great Twelve jointly sought to confirm their ordinances, and measures were also preferred by the Brewers, Clothworkers, Plaisterers, Pinmakers and Skinners, though the Brewers' seems never to have been read.[238] In addition, the City's unincorporated cheesemongers were probably behind a bill concerning London's traders in butter and cheese, which was twice laid before the Commons.[239] In the 1606/7 session most of the livery companies were involved in the London estates bill, and separate measures were presented by the Barber-Surgeons, Carpenters, Curriers, and (perhaps) the Leathersellers. The Curriers may actually have been behind two separate pieces of legislation, one to relieve poor members of their craft and the other to prevent leather being made from horse-hides and pigskins.[240] The spring session of 1610 also gave rise to a clutch of Company bills. The Salters and Brewers combined to confirm their title to their Fleet Street properties; the Horners attempted to revive a fifteenth-century statute to stop aliens from buying unfinished English horns;[241] the Dyers and Salters combined to outlaw the use of logwood; and

a splinter group of Grocers evidently supported de Laune's bid for independence for the Apothecaries. In addition, the butter and cheese bill resurfaced, and a measure to bring water to the college at Chelsea from Hackney marsh was introduced.[242]

Only one of the London companies preferred legislation to the winter session of 1610. This was the Fishmongers, who agreed to pay the charges of a bill to repeal an Act against barrelled fish.[243] The absence of legislation suggests that it was widely believed that the session's main purpose was to consider the Great Contract rather than bills. Interest in legislation revived in 1614, when five companies (the Bakers; Brewers; Haberdashers; Plaisterers; and Tylers and Bricklayers)[244] all preferred bills, as did the newly founded Charterhouse Hospital.[245] This enthusiasm for bills continued into 1621. The Blacksmiths, Carpenters, Coopers, Dyers, Gardeners, Pewterers, Tallowchandlers and Watermen all put in bills, as did the Eastland Company and the Tylers' and Bricklayers' Company.[246] The Fishmongers, too, gave financial backing to several fish traders who laid two or three measures before the Commons;[247] the Apothecaries, Grocers and Saddlers ordered legislation to be drawn up;[248] the Charterhouse Hospital and New River Company sought statutory confirmation of their charters; the Merchants of the Staple asked for the legal right to trade freely;[249] and the glovers and wharfingers tried to break free of the Leathersellers and Woodmongers respectively.[250] By 1624, however, the appetite for legislation was considerably reduced. Only eight bodies – the Apothecaries, artisan Clothworkers, Feltmakers, Goldsmiths, Goldwiredrawers, Charterhouse Hospital, New River Company and cheesemongers – put in bills.[251]

Like the Corporation, none of the London companies preferred legislation to the 1625 Parliament, presumably because of the plague epidemic. However, when Parliament reconvened in 1626 very few companies submitted bills, even though Parliament sat for more than four months and the threat of plague had lifted. The New River Company and Apothecaries offered one each, and London's clothworkers and dyers were probably behind a measure to relieve those in their trades who were suffering as a result of the Spanish war and the trade depression, but that was all. By 1628 the picture had worsened. None of the livery companies submitted legislation in 1628, and in 1629 only the Brewers contemplated doing so.[252] The sole London body to submit legislation in 1628 was the Charterhouse Hospital, which finally secured statutory confirmation of its patent.[253]

The sharp decline in Company legislation in the 1620s broadly mirrors the Corporation's abandonment of its customary legislative programme. In both cases, the main reason for the decline undoubtedly lay in falling success rates. Seven of the 29 or so Company measures laid before the first Jacobean Parliament were enacted, these being the Watermen's (1604), Painters' (1604), Skinners' (1606), Leathersellers' (1607), Salters' and Brewers' (1610), Horners' (1610), and London estates' bills (1607). However, the Parliaments of 1614 and 1621 were entirely sterile, enacting no private legislation at all. At first several companies regarded this as an aberration, and in 1624 eight of them preferred legislation. However, they soon discovered their mistake, as only the Cheesemongers saw their bill pass into law. Thereafter only a handful of companies were prepared to finance legislation that had little or no chance of success. The persistence of the Charterhouse Hospital was almost certainly down to the fact that its parliamentary costs were funded, not from its own limited resources, but from the personal estate of its late founder, Thomas Sutton, who had died the wealthiest commoner in England.[254]

Another factor which helps to explain the decline in volume of Company legislation was the development of an alternative method of bringing business to Parliament's attention. In 1621 many companies chose to petition the Commons rather than prefer bills, especially when their intention was to seek redress of their grievances rather than extend their authority. Petitioning the Commons was not entirely new, of course, but the emergence of the committee of the whole House, which dealt exclusively in non-legislative business, resulted in a vast increase in petitioning. One of the main advantages of proceeding by petition was that it obviated the need to pay fees in the Lords, thereby reducing the cost of parliamentary lobbying. Petitioning was also regarded as an attractive option because there was a good chance that any grievances taken to the Commons would be presented to the king, whereas a bill had to succeed for it to have any effect.[255] Among the livery companies to petition the Commons in 1621 were the Barber-Surgeons, Bookbinders, Brewers, Dyers, Stationers and Grocers, who petitioned against both the Apothecaries and the Levant Company, and perhaps also the starch monopolists, although they originally intended to attack them by bill. Evidence that petitions displaced bills as the preferred means of approaching the Commons is provided by examination of the Brewers' approaches to Parliament. Between 1601 and 1614 the Brewers laid bills before the Commons on five separate occasions, but only

one entered the statute book, the measure promoted jointly with the Salters to secure the title of their Fleet Street lands in 1610. Given this poor success rate it is not surprising that during the 1620s, when they tried to get the groats on malt lifted, the Brewers abandoned legislation in favour of petitioning. Only after exhausting this new method, at the beginning of 1629, did the Company began to contemplate legislation once more.

The plague outbreak of 1625 meant that none of the London companies petitioned the Commons that year, although a petition from the London merchants trading to France was warmly entertained.[256] However, during the parliamentary sessions of 1626 and 1628 a steady stream of petitions reached the Lower House. In 1626 the Bakers, Brewers, Goldwiredrawers and Levant Company, plus the London merchants trading to France, all tendered petitions. In 1628 the Apothecaries, Brewers, Goldsmiths, artisan Clothworkers, Levant Company and merchants trading to France all lobbied in this way,[257] as did the East India Company, although its petition calling for its trade to be defended may never have been formally presented.[258] It was probably because of the shortness of the session that in 1629 none of the London lobbies petitioned the Commons, with the possible exception of the Leathersellers.[259]

Petitioning helps to explain the reduction in the volume of legislation preferred by London companies during the 1620s. Even so, the number of petitions was smaller than the shortfall in bills. Indeed, the overall volume of Company business before the parliaments of the later 1620s was markedly less than it had been at the beginning of James's reign. When the Corporation's abandonment of its legislative programme is also taken into account, it is clear that the 1620s witnessed a general collapse in the volume of London's parliamentary business. This was ironic, for the 1620s were a time when fears for the survival of Parliament were widespread. At the very moment when many Englishmen were desperate to preserve the nation's representative body, London's institutions evidently lost confidence in Parliament, and in particular its role as a legislative assembly.

[1] I. Archer, *Pursuit of Stability*, 19. [2] *Recs. of Carpenters' Co. VII* ed. A.M. Millard, 490. [3] GL, ms 4326/7, f. 119. [4] Ibid. f. 128v. [5] *Harl. Misc.* ix. 312; C. Creighton, *Hist. of Epidemics in Britain*, ii. 473-4, 519 – 20; F.J. Fisher, 'Development of London as a Centre of Conspicuous Consumption in the 16th and 17th Centuries', *TRHS* (ser. 4), xxx. 41. In Apr. 1621 Sir Edward Coke claimed that London's population at the time of the Armada had been 900,000, 'and there are not fewer mouths now': *CD 1621*, v. 97, 349; vi. 99. [6] R. Ashton, *Crown and the Money Market, passim.* [7] F.J. Fisher, 'London's Export Trade in the Early 17th Century', *EcHR* (ser. 2), iii. 154. [8] Fisher, 'Development of London', 43, 46. [9] P. Croft,

'Capital Life: Members of Parl. outside the House', in *Pols., Religion and Popularity* ed. T. Cogswell, R. Cust and P. Lake, 66-7. [10] *CSP Ven.* 1603-7, p. 488. [11] J.F. Merrit, 'Perceptions and Portrayals of London', *Imagining Early Modern London* ed. J.F. Merritt, 16; P. Lake, 'From Troynouvant to Heliogabulus Rome and back', *Imagining Early Modern London*, 220-1. [12] *Winwood's Memorials* ed. E. Sawyer, ii. 39; *Holles Letters* ed. P. Seddon (Thoroton Soc. Rec. ser. xxxv), 193. [13] Merritt, 16; Lake, 222. [14] R. Ashton, *City and the Ct.* 6-8; Archer, 18-19. [15] CLRO, Reps. 27, ff. 104v, 156v. [16] CLRO, Reps. 35, f. 63. [17] CLRO, Reps. 38, f. 129v. [18] *CD 1628*, iii. 354, 358. [19] J. Hooker, *Order and Usage* ed. V.F. Snow, 164. For a detailed discussion of seating arrangements, see the SURVEY. [20] *Holles 1624*, p. 24. [21] *Chamber Accts. of Sixteenth Cent.* ed. B.R. Masters (London Rec. Soc. xx), 39-40. [22] CLRO, Letter Bk. CC, f. 1v. [23] CLRO, Reps. 40, f. 53. [24] CLRO, Jors. 28, ff. 42v, 158v. [25] CLRO, Jors. 26, f. 172v. [26] C. Barron, 'London and Parl. in the Lancastrian Period', *PH*, ix. 345. [27] *Recs. of Carpenters' Co. VII*, 490; GL, ms 3297/1, unfol. The Turners also spent 9s. 6d. on a dinner following the 1624 election. [28] Mercers' Hall, London, renter warden's accts. 1603-24, unfol.; second warden's accts. 1617-29, f. 205. [29] The exception was Sir Stephen Soame in 1601: his Co. was the Girdlers, which ranked 31 in the pecking order. [30] *Chamberlain Letters* ed. N.E. McClure, i. 515-16; *HMC Downshire*, iv. 325. [31] *HMC Downshire*, iv. 333. [32] Harl. 7010, ff. 5r-v, 8. [33] Ibid. f. 75v; *Fairfax Corresp.* ed. G.W. Johnson, i. 89. [34] C219/41A/130. [35] Lansd. 494, f. 41 (intercepted letter addressed to the rector of Brussells). [36] P. Croft, 'Purveyance and the City of London, 1589-1608', *PH*, iv. 14. [37] CLRO, Reps. 26/1, f. 275. [38] *CJ*, i. 153b. [39] P. Croft, 'Free Trade and the House of Commons, 1605-6', *Ec.HR* (ser. 2), xxviii. 64. [40] CLRO, Reps. 27, ff.112, 114v. [41] Croft, 'Purveyance', 19-20. [42] For payments associated with the lawsuit, see CLRO, Reps. 27, f. 131. [43] Croft, 'Spanish Co.', 20-1. [44] LS13/280, f. 158. [45] Ibid. ff. 166, 168; Bristol RO, Common Council Procs. 1598-1608, pp. 91, 93. [46] Darcy v. Allen: Croft, 'Purveyance', 22. [47] Croft, 'Purveyance', 22. [48] Ibid. 28. [49] *CJ*, i. 261b. See also Fuller's speech of 5 Mar. 1606: ibid. 278a. [50] *Bowyer Diary*, 105; *CJ*, i. 307b. [51] *CJ*, i. 1005a; CLRO, Remembrancia, ii. no.281. [52] REQ2/393/118; 2/400/68; 2/402/67; 2/420/133. [53] *CD 1621*, ii. 390. [54] Ibid. 480-1; vi. 215-17. [55] GL, ms 5445/14, unfol., entries of 20 Feb. 1624, 17 Jan. and 27 June 1626; *Procs. 1626*, iii. 344-5. [56] GL, Bsides 24.20. In 1626, counsel for the Brewers had claimed that the groats were 'heavier than 40 subsidies upon each particular man *per annum*': *Procs. 1626*, iii. 344-5. [57] GL, ms 5445/15, unfol. entries of 23 Dec. 1628, 27 Jan. and 12 Feb. 1629. The Brewers had contemplated a tax strike in June 1626: GL, ms 5445/14, unfol. entry of 27 June 1626. [58] *CJ*, i. 176a; *CSP Ven.* 1603-7, p. 163. [59] Ashton, *City*, 89; *CJ*, i. 218a-21b; SP14/8/59. [60] *CJ*, i. 229b, 232a, 236a. [61] *CSP Ven.* 1603-7, p. 164. [62] Croft, 'Free Trade', 18-19. [63] SP14/19/97. [64] *Bowyer Diary*, 81-2. It is not known when the Muscovy bill was first read, but it is unlikely to have been before 9 Mar., when one Company member wrote: 'though much hath been attempted against us in Parliament, yet nothing is done harder than of old nor as I hope will be': SP14/19/26. [65] *CJ*, i. 292b. No first reading is recorded in the Journal. [66] The Muscovy bill was reported as fit to sleep: ibid. 301a. [67] *CJ*, i. 218a. [68] *LJ*, ii. 388b, 389b; Cott. Titus B.V, ff. 303-7. The artisan skinners came close to establishing their own Company in 1607: CLRO, Remembrancia, ii. no. 282; Add. 11402, f. 123. [69] GL, ms 30708/2, ff. 351v, 356v, 370; *CJ*, i. 189a, 214b, 233b, 235b, 237b. [70] CLRO, Reps. 27, f. 172. The City's order perhaps placed Nicholas Fuller, counsel for the corporation and one of the Members for London, in a difficult position, as he probably sympathized with the Skinners, having reported their bill in 1604. [71] *SR*, iv. 1084-5. [72] *HMC Hatfield*, xix. 476-7. [73] *Soton's Mayor's Bk. 1606-8* ed. W.J. Connor (Soton Rec. Ser. xxi), 70-1; *CJ*, i. 364b. [74] *CJ*, i. 365b, 372a; CLRO, Reps. 27, f. 19v. [75] *LJ*, ii. 523b, 526a, 530a, 531a, 532a, 535b; CLRO, Reps. 27, f. 43v; *HMC Hatfield*, xix. 475-7; *CJ*, i. 380a-b, 1056b. For the Act, see *SR*, iv. 1148-9. [76] *CJ*, i. 488b, 491a-92a, 502a, 504. [77] Ashton, *City*, 97; *CJ*, i. 461a. [78] *HMC De L'Isle and Dudley*, v. 176. [79] The bill was rejected: ibid. 412b, 414a, 437a; GL, ms 15201/1, p. 133. [80] GL, ms 15333/2,

p. 606. [81] *CJ*, i. 469b-70a, 471b; Ashton, *City*, 100-1. [82] Ashton, *City*, 108. [83] *CJ*, i. 592a, 594a 598b, 612a, 613a, 618b, 620b, 630a. [84] GL, ms 15333/3, unfol. [85] Ibid. 563b, 609a, 605b. [86] *CJ*, i. 510b-11a, 527a-8a, 552a; *CSP Col. E.I.* 1617-21, pp. 431-2; Ashton, *City*, 107-8. [87] *CJ*, i. 615a, 642a; Ashton, *City*, 107. [88] *CSP Ven.* 1621-3, pp. 22-3. The Grocers originally planned to proceed by bill: GL, ms 11588/3, pp. 165-6. For the Levant Co.'s response, see SP105/148, ff. 52, 53v-5. [89] *CJ*, i. 710b; Harl. 4289, ff. 183-4v. [90] *CJ*, i. 672b; 'Earle 1624', f. 15. [91] *CJ*, i. 681a, 710a-b, 712b. [92] Ibid. 689a-b, 695b, 698b, 699a, 702a-b, 706b; Harl. 4289, ff. 180v-2v. [93] *CJ*, i. 711a, 712b. [94] *CD 1628*, iv. 467. For the complaint against the Company by Hull's merchants, see KINGSTON-UPON-HULL, and *CD 1628*, iii. 122, 344, 437, 620. [95] R. Brenner, *Merchants and Rev.* 228-30; *CJ*, i. 877a, 882a, 885b, 890b, 899a, 900a, 904a, 915b. [96] Brenner, 232-6; Ashton, *City*, 129-30. [97] *Procs. 1626*, ii. 271-2, 329-30; SP105/148, ff. 145-6. [98] *CD 1628*, ii. 300, 305. [99] *CSP Col. E.I.* 1625-9, pp. 489-90, 493, 507. [100] D.M. Dean, 'Public or Private? London, Leather and Legislation in Elizabethan Eng.', *HJ*, xxxi. 529. [101] CLRO, Reps. 27, f. 104v; Reps. 31/2, f. 290. For the late Elizabethan committee, see Dean, 529. [102] CLRO, Reps. 29, f. 165v. [103] CLRO, Reps. 38, f. 61. [104] CLRO, Reps. 27, ff. 176, 178. [105] CLRO, Reps. 26/2, f. 360; 38, f. 61. [106] CLRO, Jors. 26, f. 384. For the 1610 bill, which originated in 1606, see below. [107] E.g. CLRO, Reps. 27, f. 295v; 38, f. 108v. [108] CLRO, Reps. 26/2, f. 405r-v; 27, ff. 135v, 143v, 168, 191, 196v, 178r-v, 295v, 363v; 28, ff. 38, 44, 55. [109] For Dyos's activity in 1610, see CLRO, Reps. 29, f. 185v, 238v. For Mosse's role in 1614, see ibid. 31, f. 292v. For Dyos's appointment as remembrancer, see *Remembrancia* ed. W.H. and H.C. Overall, 188, n. 2. [110] CLRO, Reps. 35, f. 63; 38, ff. 114, 135v. [111] CLRO, Reps. 29, f. 238v. [112] CLRO, Reps. 26/2, ff. 378, 405. For the bill's progress, see *CJ*, i. 178a, 209a, 229b, 236a; *LJ*, ii. 316b, 317b, 320a, 322a. [113] GL, ms 11571/9, f. 146v; GL, Merchant Taylors' accts., unfol., acct. for 1604/5. For the bill's progress, see *CJ*, i. 965b, 208b-9a, 236b, 239a. [114] CLRO, Letter Bk. CC, f. 1v. [115] *CJ*, i. 182b, 228b; CLRO, Reps. 26/2, f. 340. [116] *CJ*, i. 181a, 188a; *LJ*, ii. 318a, 333b. [117] *CJ*, i. 178b, 243b. [118] The 1604 bill was introduced twice: *CJ*, i. 165a, 178b, 190a. For the bill breviate, see Soc. Antiqs., ms 552/5, which includes a list of the names of the merchants who supported it. For the 1601 measure, which sought to bypass Chancery because 'the merchant cannot endure delays', see *Procs. in Parls. of Eliz. I* ed. T.E. Hartley, iii. 439-40. [119] *CSP Dom.* 1603-10, p. 107; CLRO, Reps. 26/2, f. 365. For the Elizabethan dispute, see Archer, 35-7. [120] *CJ*, i. 221b. For the progress of this bill, which was enacted, see ibid. 228b, 232b, 251b; HLRO, ms Jnl. 4, f. 268v (the 3rd reading, unrecorded in the printed Journal); *LJ*, ii. 318a, 320a-b. The Crown responded to the City's bill by preferring to the Commons a measure to resume the office of garbler into the king's hands, but it was rejected after a 1st reading: *CJ*, i. 237a. [121] *CJ*, i. 267a, 270b; *Bowyer Diary*, 33-4, 47; CLRO, Reps. 27, ff. 161v, 351v. [122] *CJ*, i. 258b, 259b, 273b, 277a, 292a. [123] The first three Members named to the cttee. sat for London: *CJ*, i. 259a, 260b, 269b, 277a, 278b. [124] *CJ*, i. 261b, 262a, 265b [125] CLRO, Jors. 27, ff. 26, 30. For the 1610 bill, see below. [126] CLRO, Reps. 27, f. 295v. [127] *CJ*, i. 328b, 349b, 351a, 364a, 374a, 386a, 1008a, 1029a-b, 1035b, 1038a, 1941a; *LJ*, ii. 456b, 457b, 460b, 461a, 469b, 481b. [128] CLRO, Reps. 28, f. 6. For the bill's progress, see *CJ*, i. 346b, 1038b, 371a, 372b, 312b. [129] CLRO, Reps. 27, f. 56v. For a more detailed discussion of this bill, see the section on the livery companies and hospitals below. [130] CLRO, Reps. 29, f. 238v. [131] Debtors: *CJ*, i. 407b, 411b, 419b, 429b, 430a, 434a, 445a-b, 447a, 449a; suits: ibid. 408b, 415b, 429a, 441a; overcrowding: ibid. 425a, 426a, 429a, 436b, 441b, 445a, 448a. [132] Ibid. 413a-b. [133] For the bill's progress, see *CJ*, i. 415a, 419a, 423a. For the negotiations, see CLRO, Reps. 29, ff. 165v, 276r-v. [134] CLRO, Reps. 30, ff. 24v-5. [135] CLRO Reps. 31/2, f. 292v; *CJ*, i. 474b, 481a, 490a. [136] CLRO, Reps. 31/2, f. 302v. [137] *CJ*, i. 476b, 481a, 483a, 489a, 492a, 495a, 504a. [138] CLRO, Reps. 31/2, f. 322. The bill received a 1st reading in the Commons: *CJ*, i. 502a. It was not enacted until 1624: *SR*, iv. 1231. On the cheesemongers' failure to form a company, see W.M. Stern, 'Where, oh where, are the Cheesemongers of London', *London Jnl.* v. 228-9. [139] *CJ*, i.

521b, 568a, 602b. [140] 'Pym 1624', iii. f. 33. [141] CLRO, Reps. 38, f. 108v; *CJ*, i. 771a-b. [142] CLRO, Reps. 40, ff. 94-5. [143] *CJ*, i. 824b, 830b. [144] CLRO, Reps. 40, f. 233. [145] For a discussion of the livery companies, see below. [146] Payments to Dyos amounting to £125 6s. 10d. are recorded, but they include unspecified sums for lawsuits: CLRO, Reps. 26/2, ff. 320, 405. [147] CLRO, Reps. 27, ff. 135v, 143v, 168, 178v, 191, 196v. Croft estimates that the City spent £284 18s. on legislation between 1604 and 1606, but the total expenditure for the 1st and 2nd sessions alone amounted to around £340, not including the fees payable to the recorder and Nicholas Fuller: Croft, 'Purveyance', 34, n. 40. [148] CLRO, Reps. 29, ff. 168, 238v. [149] CLRO, Reps. 38, 129v; 43, f. 36. [150] CLRO, Misc. MSS/166/1. [151] *Stuart Royal Procs.* ed. J.F. Larkin and P.L. Hughes, 171-5, 193, 485-6, 597-8; *CJ*, i. 711a, 796a. For the Carpenters' lobbying, see Ms 4329/4, ff. 43v, 46; 4326/7, ff. 85v-6. [152] *CSP Dom.* 1619-23, p. 363. See also GL, ms 12806/3, ff. 122-3; CLRO, Jors. 28, f. 239v. Jones claims incorrectly that Leadenhall was not in use as a cloth market before 1631: D.W. Jones, 'The "Hallage" Receipts of the London Cloth Markets, 1562-c.1720', *Ec.HR* (ser. 2), xxv. 576. [153] CLRO, Reps. 38, ff. 115, 117v. [154] CLRO, Reps. 40, f. 239v. Curiously, none of London's Members were named to the cttee.: *CJ*, i. 866b. [155] CLRO, Reps. 35, f. 155. [156] GL, ms 3297/1. The only mentions of Parliament relate to dinners following London's parliamentary elections in 1621 and 1624, for which see above. [157] GL, ms 7351/1, unfol. (1605/6 acct.); ms 11571/10, f. 445. [158] GL, ms 15333/2, p. 359. [159] GL, ms 15201/2, pp. 136-7. [160] GL, ms 6122/1, unfol. entry for 21 Apr. 1621. [161] GL, ms 11571/10, f. 445. [162] GL, ms 15333/2, pp. 279-80, 298, 320, 338. [163] For Malet and the Brewers, see above, *sub* 'Purveyance'. [164] Add. 33924, f. 32. [165] Hants RO, TD540/Scrapbook, note appended to the foot of the Woodmongers' petition. We are grateful to Chris Kyle for this ref. [166] GL, ms 11571/9, f. 356. For an Elizabethan e.g. of the same, see Dean, 546. [167] GL, ms 6122/1, unfol. 1621 acct.; ms 8200/1, p. 130. [168] SP14/6/109; *Recs. of Carpenters' Co. VII*, 287. [169] GL, ms 8200/1, pp. 55-6. For the Surgeons' petition, which was copied out by the Physicians, London, see Royal Coll. of Physicians, ms 2288, Annals III, pt. 1, pp. 144-6. [170] GL, ms 3054, unfol. 1620/1 acct. For a copy of the Tylers' petition, see Soc. Antiqs., Broadsides no. 138. [171] For some other companies which ordered documents to be printed, see GL, ms 6440/2 (Butchers), f. 322; 5257/5 (Surgeons), p. 28. For some examples of petitions printed by the companies, see GL, Bsides 24.20 (Brewers), 24.31 (artisan Clothworkers). [172] GL, ms 7351, unfol. [173] GL, ms 5174/3, f. 250. [174] GL, ms 5442/4, unfol. (1613-14 acct.). [175] Royal Coll. of Physicians, London, ms 2287, p. 142. [176] Clothworkers' Hall, London, renter warden's acct. 1566-7, f. 4v. For other e.g.s, see Dean, 533. [177] GL, ms 5606/2, f. 298v. [178] GL, ms 5174/3, f. 249v; 6122/1, unfol. [179] GL, ms 5442/5, unfol. [180] GL, ms 5174/4, ff. 6v, 7v. [181] Carpenters: GL, ms 4329/4, ff. 43v, 46; Brewers: GL, ms 5445/14, unfol. entries of 20 Feb. 1624 and 27 June 1627. [182] LMA, Acc/1876/01/10/2-5. [183] Dean, 537. [184] Add. 33924, f. 32. [185] GL, ms 5570/1, p. 492. [186] Goldsmiths' Hall, London, min. bk. 1605-11, p. 536; GL, ms 5255/1, unfol.(1606/7 acct.) For further discussion of this bill, see below. [187] LMA, Acc/1876/G/01/10/5. [188] GL, ms 6152/2, f. 164v; *Recs. of Carpenters' Co. VII*, 287. [189] GL, ms 5606/2, f. 152v; S. D'Ewes, *Jnls. of all Parls. of Queen Eliz.* (1682), p. 452. [190] GL, ms 5174/3, f. 249v-50v. [191] GL, ms 5570/1, pp. 379, 384. [192] Leathersellers' Hall, London, min. bk. 1623-32, f. 5. [193] Dean, 527-8. [194] Cott. Titus F.IV; CLRO, Reps. 35, f. 121. [195] CLRO, Reps. 31/2, f. 322; 35, ff. 121, 133; Reps. 38, f. 92v. There is no evidence that the bill was read by Parliament in 1621. [196] CLRO, Reps. 35, ff. 129v-30. [197] CLRO, Reps. 40, f. 142. The bill subsequently received one reading in the Commons: *CJ*, i. 830b. For a summary of its contents, see Add. 34218, f. 99v. The Ct. of Aldermen had themselves consented to the change of day in May 1621: Reps. 35, f. 165. CLRO, Reps. 35, ff. 129v-30. [198] Drapers' Hall, London, WA6/3, p. 47; Mercers' Hall, London, Acts of Court 1595-1629, f. 69; GL, ms 30708/2 (Skinners' mins.), f. 381; ms 30727/5, unfol. Skinners' accts. 1605-6; ms 11571/9 (Grocers' mins.) f. 191; GL, microfilm Merchant Taylors' accts. vol.9, unfol. For the

progress of the bill, see *CJ*, i. 272a, 275b, 282a. [199] *CJ*, i. 372a. [200] For the progress of the bill, see *LJ*, ii. 474b, 479a, 496b-97a, 498a-b, 499b, 507b; *CJ*, i. 364a, 365a, 368b, 370b, 372a-b, 521a, 1037a, 1040a; *Bowyer Diary*, 254. [201] GL, ms 5570/1, p. 492. It is not known which ministers demanded payment, but the most likely candidates are Dorset, Salisbury and Northampton, to whom the king initially referred the matter: Cott. Titus B.V, f. 349. [202] GL, ms 5570/1, p. 494. [203] Companies which responded to this prodding included the Drapers and the Saddlers: Drapers' Hall, London, ct. of assts. min. bk. 1604-40, f.46v; GL, ms 5385, f. 10v. [204] Goldsmiths' Hall, London, min. bk. 1604-11, pp. 352, 356; GL, ms 5257, p. 246. [205] GL, ms 6152/2, f. 99. [206] GL, microfilm, Merchant Taylors' accts. vol. 9, unfol. [207] GL, ms 2883/3, p. 92. The contents of the bill are unknown. [208] GL, ms 7351/1, unfol., 1603-4 and 1606-7 accts. The 1604 bill may have been the one promoted by the searchers and sealer of tanned leather mentioned above. [209] *CD 1621*, vii. 407-8. For the bill's progress, see *CJ*, i. 409a, 416b. [210] For a breviate of the bill, see Cott. Titus B.V, f. 349. For its progress, see *CJ*, i. 396a, 397b, 398b, 403b, 404b, 411b, 419b, 421a, 422b ; Procs. 1610, i. 84, 90, 94. The bill was enacted: HLRO, O.A. 7 Jas. I, c.49. [211] GL, ms 5442/5, Brewers' accts. 1609-10, unfol. [212] GL, ms 5174/3, f. 354. The bill was probably the one concerning London and Westminster brewhouses, which was introduced in the Lords: see *CJ*, i. 715b, 786b, 790a, 792a. [213] Dean, 544; GL, ms 5602/2, f. 48. The bill received 2 readings: *CJ*, i. 178b, 183b. [214] *Procs. in Parls. of Eliz. I*, iii. 418-19, 467; Cott. Titus F.IV, f.328 (undated breviate printed in late May 1604). For the bill's progress in 1604, see *LJ*, ii. 292b, 294b, 295b, 305a, 338b; *CJ*, 228a, 239b, 246a, 996a. For the Plaisterers' lobbying, see *HMC Hatfield*, xvi. 454; GL, ms 6222/1, unfol. 6 July 1604. For the 1604 Act, see *SR*, iv. 1037-8. [215] GL, ms 8200/1, pp. 55-6, 59. The bill received one reading only: *CJ*, i. 529a. [216] *Recs. of Carpenters' Co. VII*, 287; *CJ*, i. 351a, 373a. [217] GL, ms 5257/3, p. 234; *LJ*, ii. 495a-b. [218] Roy. Coll. of Physicians, ms 2287, pp. 192-3. [219] GL, ms 5257/3, p. 238. [220] P. Griffiths, 'Pols. made visible: Order, Residence and Uniformity in Cheapside, 1600-45', *Londinopolis* ed. P. Griffith and M.S.R. Jenner, 179, 181; Goldsmiths' Hall, London, min. bk. 1618-24, pp. 702, 707. The Goldsmiths' had contemplated petitioning Parl. about the same matter in 1621: min. bk. 1618-24, pp. 484, 494, 496. [221] P. Hunting, *Hist. of Soc. of Apothecaries*, 29-30; GL, ms 11588/2, pp. 586-7; *CJ*, i. 436b. [222] *CD 1621*, vii. 144-56, 363. [223] Hants RO, TD540/Scrapbook; *CJ*, i. 533b. [224] Cott. Titus B.V, ff. 287, 314; *CJ*, i. 264b, 291b. [225] *CJ*, i. 563a; *HMC Cowper*, i. 111. [226] GL, ms 11588/3, p. 172; 11571/10, f. 445; 11571/11, ff. 74, 117; *CD 1621*, vii. 80-5; GL, ms 8200/1, p. 130; *CJ*, i. 756a; C.R.B. Barrett, *Hist. of Soc. of Apothecaries of London*, 23-4. [227] *CJ*, i. 544b. The Gardeners were incorporated in 1605, and obtained fresh letters patent in 1616: *CD 1621*, vii. 361. For the bill see ibid. 119-21. [228] GL, ms 8200/1, pp. 55-6, 59, 67. [229] *CJ*, i. 726b. [230] Ibid. 770a, 772a-b, 696b, 785b, 704a, 715b. [231] *CD 1621*, ii. 97. Nicholas alleges that the bill was thrown away because the bill would have given the Company power to impose fines on offenders. For the bill, see Soc. Antiqs., Broadsides no.138; GL, ms 3054/1 (Tylers' and Bricklayers' accts.), unfol., 1620/1 acct. [232] GL, ms 7090/4, f. 148; *CJ*, i. 619b-20a. For the bill and its breviate, see *CD 1621*, vii. 287-93. [233] Blacksmiths: GL, ms 2883/3, p. 92; Brewers: GL, ms 5442/5, unfol. (1603/4 acct.); *CJ*, i. 156b; Clothworkers: Clothworkers' Hall, London, Bk. of courts 1581-1605, f. 232; quarter warden's acct. 1603-4, f. 8v; Coopers: GL, ms 5606/2, f. 188; ms 5602/2, f.48; *CJ*, i. 178b, 183b; Painters: GL, ms 6122/1, unfol.; Cott. Titus F.IV (undated breviate, but late May 1604); *LJ*, ii. 292b, 294b, 295a, 305a, 338b; *CJ*, i. 228a, 239b, 996a, 246a; Skinners: GL, ms 30708/2, ff. 351v, 356v, 370; *CJ*, i. 189a, 214b, 233b, 235b, 237b, Watermen: *CJ*, i. 194b, 204a, 212a, 215a, 224b. [234] GL, ms 5570/1, pp.379, 384. For the bill's progress, see *CJ*, i. 194b, 209a, 243a. [235] Leathersellers' Hall, London, ACC/1/2, f. 112v. The bill was presumably the one described as 'concerning tanners of leather' which received a first reading on 2 Apr. The relationship of this bill with the one promoted by the searcher and sealers of leather (see above) is unclear. [236] GL, ms

33022/4, f. 441v; J.F. South, *Memorials of the Craft of Surgery in Eng.* ed. D'Arcy Power, 197. For the progress of the Bridewell Hosp. bills, see *CJ*, i. 173a, 187b, 228a, 235b, 996a, 999a. [237] GL, microfilm of Merchant Taylors' accts. vol. 8, unfol. [238] The Great Twelve may also have been behind the corporations bill of 1606, which looks like a precursor of the 1607 measure to secure the companies' lands: *CJ*, i. 287a. For the ordinances' bill and those of the Clothworkers and artisan Skinners, see above. For the Brewers' bill, see GL, ms 5445/12, unfol. entry of 1 May. For the Plaisterers' bill, which was committed by the Commons but has not been traced in the *CJ*, see GL, ms 6122/1, unfol., entries of 31 Jan. and 25 Apr. 1606. For the Pinmakers' bill, see Cott. Titus B. V, f. 314; *CJ*, i. 264b, 291b. [239] *CJ*, i. 259a, 260b, 273b, 286a, 292a, 293b; *Bowyer Diary*, 82. [240] For the Barber-Surgeons' and Carpenters' bills, see GL, ms 5257/3, p. 234; *Recs. of the Carpenters' Co. VII*, 287, and also above. The Curriers' records for this period are missing, but for the poor curriers' bill see GL, ms 7351/1, unfol. (Cordwainers' accts. 1606-7); *CJ*, i. 352b, 355a, 357b, 1038a, 373b, 1045a, 1056b, 390a-b. For the bill to prevent the use horsehides and pigskins, see *CJ*, i. 389a, 389b, 390a; SP14/7/88. The Leathersellers' do not mention that the company was behind a bill, but see *CJ*, i. 328a, 329a, 1029b, 352b, 355a, 357b, 1035b, 1039b, 1045a. [241] *CJ*, i. 398b, 399a, 403b, 408a, 409b; *SR*, iv. 1170-1. No Company records for this period survive. [242] For the butter and cheese bill, see *CJ*, i. 419b, 428a, 433a, 434a; *LJ*, ii. 605a, 629a. For the Chelsea College bill, see *CJ*, i. 436b, 442b, 446b, 448a; *SR*, iv. 1165-7. [243] GL, ms 5570/2, p. 1. [244] Bakers: GL, ms 5174/3, ff. 249v-50; Brewers: GL, ms 5445/13, unfol. (1613 – 14 acct.); Haberdashers: *CJ*, i. 465b; Plaisterers: *CJ*, i. 457a, 465b; Soc. Antiq., Broadsides, no. 138; Tylers and Bricklayers: GL, ms 3054/1, unfol.; *CJ*, i. 495a. The Brewers' bill was probably the measure to prevent brewers from becoming magistrates: *CJ*, i. 495a, 503b. [245] LMA, Acc/1876/G/01/16/1-3. [246] Blacksmiths: GL, ms 2883/3, pp. 311-12; Carpenters: GL, ms 4329/4, ff. 43v, 46; ms 4326/6, f. 567r-v; ms 4326/7, ff. 85v-6; *CJ*, i. 619a; Coopers: GL, ms 5606/3, f. 188; *CJ*, i. 546a; Dyers (there were two bills): Soc. Antiqs. Broadsides no. 181; *CD 1621*, vii. 132-8; *CJ*, i. 546a, 549. Gardeners: *CJ*, i. 544b; *CD 1621*, vii. 119-21; Pewterers: GL, ms 7090/4, f. 148; *CJ*, i. 619b-20b; *CD 1621*, vii. 287-93; Tallowchandlers: GL, ms 6152/2, f. 164v; *CD 1621*, v. 285; Tylers: GL, ms 3054/1, unfol. (1620/1 acct.); Soc. Antiqs., Broadsides no. 138; *CJ*, i. 525a; Watermen: *CJ*, i. 609a; GL, Bside 24.41; C. Kyle, 'Parl. and the Palace of Westminster', in *Housing Parliaments. Dublin, Edinburgh and Westminster* ed. C. Jones and S. Kelsey, 94. For the Eastland Company's navigation bill, see the section on free trade above. [247] GL, ms 5570/2, pp. 408, 413; CLRO, Reps. 35, f. 155. [248] GL, ms 8200/1, pp. 55-6, 67; ms 11588/3, pp. 165-6; ms 5385, f. 93. The Grocers may have abandoned proceeding by bill in favour of petition: see below. [249] *CJ*, i. 568b, 611a, 612a-b, 592a, 612a. [250] See above. [251] Apothecaries: GL, ms 8200/1, p. 130; artisan Clothworkers: CLRO, Reps. 38, f. 117v; Feltmakers: Kyle thesis, 454; Goldsmiths: Goldsmiths' Hall, London, min. bk. 1618-24,, pp. 702, 707; Goldwiredrawers: *CJ*, i. 726b; Charterhouse Hosp.: *CJ*, i. 877a, 880a, 880b, 887a, 894b; New River Co.: *CJ*, i. 727a, 745a, 749b, 755b; cheesemongers: CLRO, Reps. 38, f. 92v. [252] GL, ms 5445/15, unfol., entries of 27 Jan. and 12 Feb. 1629. Parliament's dissolution prevented the company from introducing the bill. [253] *CJ*, i. 877a, 880a-b, 887a, 894b; LMA, Acc/1876/G/01/10/5. [254] LMA, Acc/1876/G/01/10/1-2. [255] For a more detailed discussion of the legislative crisis of the 1620s and the concomitant growth in petitioning, see the SURVEY. [256] *Procs. 1625*, pp. 268, 284-5, 287, 323, 335, 326-7. [257] For 'Purveyance'. For the Apothecaries: GL, ms 8292; ms 11588/3, p. 368; Bakers: GL, ms 5174/4, ff. 6v-7v; Clothworkers: *CJ*, i. 887a; GL, Bsides 24.31; Goldsmiths: Goldsmiths' Hall, London, min. bk. min. bk. 1624-9, pp.161-2; *CJ*, i. 899a, 912a, 913b, 917b; Goldwiredrawers: *CJ*, i. 850a, 850b; Levant Co.: SP105/148, ff. 145-6; *Procs. 1626*, ii. 271-2, 329-30; Brenner, 228-9; merchants trading to France: *CJ*, i. 865b, 877a, 882a, 882b, 885b. [258] See above, *sub* 'Free trade'. [259] C. Kyle, 'Parl. and the Palace of Westminster', 96. There is no mention of

this petition, which took the form of a book cataloguing the ills of their trade, in the Company's records.

A.D.T.

WESTMINSTER

Right of election: ?in the inhabitant householders

Number of voters: over 1,000

21 Feb. 1604	SIR THOMAS KNYVETT SIR WALTER COPE
c.4 July 1607	SIR JULIUS CAESAR *vice* Knyvett, called to the Upper House
c. Mar. 1614	(SIR) HUMPHREY MAY EDMUND DOUBLEDAY
11 Dec. 1620[1]	SIR EDWARD VILLIERS SIR EDMUND DOUBLEDAY
30 Dec. 1620	WILLIAM MAN *vice* Doubleday, deceased Edward Forsett*
22 Jan. 1624	SIR EDWARD VILLIERS WILLIAM MAN
25 Apr. 1625	SIR EDWARD VILLIERS WILLIAM MAN
1626	(SIR) ROBERT PYE PETER HEYWOOD
c. Mar. 1628	THOMAS MORICE JOSEPH BRADSHAW (Sir) Robert Pye ?Sir Robert Cotton*

Westminster's economy revolved largely around the retail trades, beer-brewing and the letting of residential property.[2] The law courts in Westminster Hall, and the king's Court at Whitehall, brought a steady stream of people to the city. Whenever Parliament met business also boomed, as Members of both Houses, along with their wives and servants, descended on Westminster's numerous inns and hostelries,[3] as did lobbyists and petitioners, many of them from the London livery companies. In 1621 the officers of the Tylers and Bricklayers' Company spent 5s. 5d. 'about the Parliament business and certain other days going by water and at the *Dog* at Westminster', while in April 1624 the Barber-Surgeons, having determined to submit a petition to the committee for grievances, instructed its representatives to meet 'at the *Three Tuns* at Westminster on Friday next by eleven of the clock in the foreoon and dine there at the charge of this house'.[4]

Much of Westminster's rented property was owned by the dean and chapter of the former abbey (then officially known as the Collegiate Church of St. Peter). Consequently the dean wielded enormous local influence, a fact which, before the mid-1580s, obviated the need for a municipal corporation. However, the enormous growth in the city's population caused by immigration from the surrounding areas, and the attendant problems of poverty and disorder, exposed the weakness of the city's government and prompted some of the townsmen, led by members of St. Margaret's vestry, to present a bill to Parliament in 1585 for the creation of a corporate government comparable to London's.[5] This posed a threat to the abbey authorities, and as a result of pressure exerted by the dean and chapter 'for the preserving of our liberties and privileges' the bill was so watered down that most of the changes wrought by the subsequent legislation have been described as largely 'cosmetic'.[6]

The 1585 Act divided the city's four parishes into 12 wards and created a court of 12 burgesses and 12 assistants. It also likened the burgesses to London's deputy aldermen. Such a comparison was inappropriate, however, for whereas the Court of Aldermen owned property and exercised the right to impose taxes on London's citizens, Westminster's Court of Burgesses lacked revenue-raising powers and was therefore unable to fund civic projects or pay for its own bureaucracy. Moreover, while London's aldermen and common councilmen enjoyed a local legislative power, Westminster's Court of Burgesses was largely restricted to the enforcement of ordinances drawn up in 1585. The 1585 Act did nothing to curb the powers of the dean and chapter, which if anything were enhanced by the new legislation. Not only were the dean and chapter excluded from its provisions, the Act vested the right to appoint the burgesses and their assistants both in the dean and the city's high steward. Thus the efforts of St. Margaret's vestry to create a powerful city corporation independent of the abbey were largely thwarted.[7]

At the start of each Parliament the Commons held a collective communion service. Before 1614 the normal venue was the former abbey of Westminster. However, in April 1614 the House resolved to switch to the parish church of St. Margaret's, opposite Westminster Hall, since the abbey's clergy 'administer

not with common bread'.[8] When Parliament reassembled in 1621, the dean, John Williams, attempted to prevent the Commons from again resorting to St. Margaret's, over which he claimed jurisdiction. However, he was eventually thwarted as the Commons obtained a licence from the king instead.[9] Thereafter the undisputed venue for the communion service was St. Margaret's, whose churchwardens were responsible for distributing the money collected from each Member to the poor of the city.[10]

The borough's parliamentary elections were held in Westminster Hall, and were presided over by the city's bailiff. In March 1621 this practice was challenged on the grounds that by a statute of 1445 only sheriffs were legally entitled to act as returning officers. However, by 168 votes to 155 the Commons ruled in favour of the bailiff's right to discharge this duty, an outcome which one diarist described as 'the upholding of a custom against the Common Law'.[11] It is unclear who was entitled to vote at elections, but it seems likely that, as in the second half of the seventeenth century, the franchise resided in the inhabitant householders, as Sir Robert Pye was defeated in 1628 'by above a thousand voices'.

Nomination to the borough's senior parliamentary seat was in theory the preserve of the dean, but in practice this privilege was exercised by the high steward. In February 1628 Dean Williams wrote to Sir Robert Cotton that his choice was 'none other than was recommended unto me by my lord duke of Buckingham, our high steward'.[12] The office of high steward was a Crown appointment, whose functions included the right to nominate the city's bailiff. Between 1561 and 1598 the stewardship was held by William Cecil[†], Lord Burghley. Throughout Elizabeth's reign, Gabriel Goodman, then dean of Westminster and Burghley's friend, secured the return of numerous Cecil candidates to Parliament. Following Burghley's death in 1598 the stewardship passed to Burghley's son, Robert Cecil[†], later 1st earl of Salisbury, who by 1604 was also the borough's bailiff.[13] During James's reign two members of Cecil's circle were returned to Parliament for Westminster: Sir Walter Cope (1604) and Sir Julius Caesar (1607). Sir Thomas Knyvett, who served as a Westminster burgess from 1604 until his elevation to the peerage in July 1607 and whose niece, the countess of Suffolk, acted as one of Cecil's informal contacts with the Spanish embassy, was probably also a Cecil dependent. Knyvett, too, was one of three officers of the Mint who represented Westminster during this period – the others were Edmund Doubleday and Sir Edward Villiers

– but given that many government officials lived and worked in Westminster this may have been merely coincidental.

Salisbury's successor as high steward was the royal favourite Robert Carr, earl of Somerset, through whose influence, no doubt, Sir Humphrey May, the remembrancer for Irish affairs, was elected to the Addled Parliament. Following Somerset's disgrace the stewardship was conferred on the earl (later duke) of Buckingham, who procured the post of bailiff for his servant Thomas Fotherley* in 1622.[14] Through his patronage, and with the co-operation of Dean Williams, seats were found for the duke's half-brother, Sir Edward Villiers in 1621, 1624 and 1625 and Buckingham's servant Sir Robert Pye in 1626.[15] Interestingly, Pye was elected in 1626 even though Buckingham had obtained Williams' dismissal as lord keeper in October 1625. Although Pye was subsequently heavily defeated in the 1628 Westminster election following a campaign lasting three days, this was largely the result of popular hostility to the Forced Loan rather than Williams' attempt to persuade Sir Robert Cotton to stand.[16]

St. Margaret's vestry traditionally enjoyed the right to nominate the borough's junior Member. Three of its number were elected to the borough's second parliamentary seat between 1604 and 1628: Edmund Doubleday (1614), William Man (1621, 1624, 1625) and Peter Heywood (1626). A fourth member of the vestry, Thomas Morice, took the senior seat in 1628 after the high steward's candidate, Sir Robert Pye, was rejected by the voters. All four vestrymen-MPs were also members of Westminster's Court of Burgesses. Only in 1604 did the vestry fail to secure the return of one of its own number, both seats being occupied instead by clients of Robert Cecil, the borough's high steward. To some extent this failure may have been offset in November 1606, when Edward Forsett, a member of the Court of Burgesses and a resident of St. Margaret's, was returned at a by-election for Wells. On the other hand, Forsett was not a member of St. Margaret's vestry and, like the two Westminster Members, was a Cecil client. Forsett's committee appointments included a bill designed to curb the number of buildings in and around London (8 Dec. 1606).[17]

Although St. Margaret's vestry customarily controlled the borough's junior seat, it was expected to seek the approval of the dean of Westminster for its nominee. However, the vestry jealously guarded its right of nomination. Writing to Sir Robert Cotton in February 1628, Dean Williams observed that whenever St. Margaret's vestry 'pitch upon any neighbour of their own, especially upon any one of the 12 burgesses, they are like that little God Terminus, that will not be removed from their opinions'.[18] Yet while Williams realized that there was little point in trying to impose his own nominee on the borough for the second seat, he thought that the vestry might be capable of manipulation. He advised Cotton, who wished to secure the junior seat for himself, to seek the backing of the vestry on his own. Once this had been obtained, Williams promised to let the vestry know that he approved of its choice – provided that Cotton donated his printed books to the abbey library. However, this elaborate attempt at manipulation proved unsuccessful.

The vestry and the dean were not always at loggerheads in determining a candidate for the junior seat. Peter Heywood was elected in 1626 because he was a town burgess and a vestryman of St. Margaret's, but he was may also have been acceptable to the dean, as he lived in property rented from the abbey. It is also noteworthy that the only committee to which Heywood was ever appointed was established to amend a bill prohibiting clergymen from becoming magistrates to exclude deans.[19] The interests of vestry and dean coincided most clearly, however, in the form of William Man, who represented Westminster on three occasions. Like Heywood, Man was both a member of the Court of Burgesses and a vestryman but he was also a senior abbey administrator and its principal rent-collector. The circumstances of his election to Parliament in December 1620, following the death of Edmund Doubleday, who had been elected but not returned, indicates the degree of influence which, on one occasion at least, the dean was able to exercise over the electoral process.

According to a petition drawn up by 60 disgruntled voters living in the parishes of St. Martin-in-the-Fields, St. Clement Danes and St. Mary-le-Strand, it was the dean who nominated Man and set the date for the fresh election.[20] In order to be sure of securing Man's return, the dean also allegedly failed to notify the voters of these three parishes of the impending election, 'but only private notice was given the night before about 7 or 8 of the clock to every particular home in the parish of St. Margaret's'. The news that there was to be a fresh election nevertheless leaked out, and many of those who had not received official notification turned out to support their rival candidate, Edward Forsett, 'though he never made suit nor stood for the same'. Forsett posed a threat not only to the dean but also to St. Margaret's vestry, whose monopoly of the right to nominate the borough's townsman Member was jeopardized by his candidature. According to the account of the election presented to the Commons by the aggrieved voters, Forsett was subsequently defeated because the dean permitted the voices of 'serving men, apprentices, women, children, watermen [and] porters' to carry the vote. However, when the matter came to be debated in Parliament, the main objection to Man's election was held by some to be that he had been returned on the same writ that had been used to elect Doubleday.[21]

Apart from those hardy perennials, the oft-introduced bills to curb new buildings and overcrowding in and around London, the only measure of specific interest to the city of Westminster laid before the Commons during this period concerned the paving of Drury Lane. After receiving a first reading in March 1606, the bill cleared all its Commons' stages in just two months and was subsequently enacted.[22] Its sponsor is unknown, but its swift progress undoubtedly owed something to the fact that Boswell House – the London address of the then Speaker, Sir Edward Phelips – was situated in Drury Lane.

[1] On 14 Dec. 1620 John Williams, dean of Westminster, stated that the election had been held on 'Monday last': NLW, ms 9057E/926. For the other dates of election given here, see *OR*. [2] Cf. G. Rosser, *Medieval Westminster*, 43-165. [3] Croft estimates the number to have been at least 1,000: P. Croft 'Capital Life: Members of Parliament Outside the House', in *Pols. Religion and Popularity* ed. T. Cogswell, R. Cust and P. Lake, 66. [4] GL, ms 3054/1, unfol. 1620/1 acct.; ms 5257/5, p. 30. [5] J.F. Merritt, 'Religion, Govt. and Soc. in Early Mod. Westminster, c.1525-1625' (London Ph.D. thesis, 1992), p. 106. [6] WAM, Chapter Act Bk. I. f. 200; Merritt, 102. [7] Merritt, 108-16. [8] *CJ*, i. 463b. [9] Ibid. 510b, 515b, 516b; *CD 1621*, ii. 49, n. 16; Nicholas, *Procs. 1621*, i. 14. [10] H.F. Westlake, *St. Margaret's, Westminster*, 99-100. [11] *CD 1621*, ii. 256-7; v. 62, 317. [12] *Procs. 1628*, vi. 1713. [13] C 219/35/1/28. [14] Merritt, 148-9. [15] For direct evidence that Williams secured Villiers' election in 1620, see NLW, ms 9057E/926. [16] T. Birch, *Ct. and Times of Chas. I*, i. 327. For Williams' approach to Cotton, see below. [17] *CJ*, i. 328b. [18] *CD 1628*, vi. 171. [19] *CJ*, i. 834a. [20] Surr. Hist. Cent. LM 1989. See also ibid. 1331/27. [21] *CD 1621*, ii. 126-7, 141-3; vi. 430-1. [22] *CJ*, i. 279a, 287a, 303a, 306a, 307b.

A.D.T.

MONMOUTHSHIRE

Number of voters: c.1000 in 1572[1]

23 Feb. 1604	SIR JOHN HERBERT THOMAS SOMERSET
c.Feb. 1614	WILLIAM JONES II SIR WALTER MONTAGU
4 Jan. 1621	SIR EDMUND MORGAN CHARLES WILLIAMS
c.Jan. 1624	SIR WILLIAM MORGAN SIR ROBERT SIDNEY, (LORD L'ISLE)
c.May 1625	SIR WILLIAM MORGAN SIR ROBERT SIDNEY, (LORD L'ISLE)
c.Jan. 1626	NICHOLAS ARNOLD WILLIAM HERBERT II
21 Feb. 1628	NICHOLAS ARNOLD NICHOLAS KEMEYS

Monmouthshire was created in 1536 by joining the ancient kingdom of Gwent with the cantref of Gwynllŵg. The new shire had an anomalous position, however, for although omitted from the jurisdiction of the Welsh Great sessions courts, placed in the Oxford assize circuit and given two county Members in Parliament like other English counties, it was culturally and linguistically still very much Welsh in character, and many contemporaries continued to consider it part of Wales.[2] The special provisions accorded to Monmouthshire in the Union legislation were a reflection of the county's relative prosperity compared with the rest of Wales, and its comparative proximity to London.[3] Physically it was divided into three main regions: a flat, marshy coastal plain; mountains in the north and west; and the lower hills and fertile valleys, which covered most of the remainder of the shire.[4] Dairy farming in the more mountainous regions had become increasingly important since the fourteenth century, one seventeenth-century gentleman described his tenants as having 'little or no other subsistence' than their cattle.[5] Sheep-rearing was also significant in these pastoral regions and sustained a textile industry upon which the prosperity of towns such as Abergavenny rested. The wool was also used to make Monmouth caps: 6,000 were purchased to outfit soldiers in 1627, an order which must have provided a considerable boost to the local economy.[6] The lowlands of the coastal plain and the region between Monmouth, Usk and Abergavenny supported mixed farming. The Bristol Channel, meanwhile, allowed for a coasting trade in commodities such as butter, timber and grain, which were exported to south-west England and Ireland.[7] There was also a tradition of metalworking, especially in the wireworks established at Tintern, where some 600 men were employed by 1603, and also at several other forges maintained by county gentlemen.[8]

The only resident peer, Edward Somerset, 4th earl of Worcester, owned vast estates in Monmouthshire and from the opening of the period was also the county's lord lieutenant. Although himself a conformist, he was the main patron of the county's substantial Catholic community, whose very visible adherence to the old faith engendered alarm in Protestant gentry like the powerful Morgans of Tredegar. These Protestant families often looked to the patronage of William Herbert, 3rd earl of Pembroke, who owned the lordships of Usk, Caerleon and Trelleck, although Pembroke resided in Wiltshire. In 1609 Ralph, Lord Eure[†], then lord president of Wales, wrote that 'few causes arise in the shire which are not made a question betwixt the Protestant and the recusant',[9] but it is difficult to reduce the county's electoral politics in the early seventeenth century to confessional antagonism. Besides, there is no evidence of any contest for the county seats in this period, nor of any rivalry between Worcester and Pembroke that might have translated into electoral conflict, although this may merely reflect the paucity of the source material. Only the return of Sir William Morgan of Tredegar in 1624 and 1625 provides any evidence for the existence of the religious rivalries which bubbled beneath the surface of Monmouthshire society. Determined to confront the Catholic threat in the shire, Morgan used the 1624 Parliament to highlight the prevalence of recusants, and to present some of Worcester's family and dependants as recusant officeholders, although he avoided naming Worcester in person.

Worcester undoubtedly facilitated the return of his son, Thomas Somerset, in 1604, and probably also sponsored the election of his steward, William Jones II, in 1614. Thereafter, however, his electoral influence seems to have waned. In 1616 he surrendered his position as master of the horse to King James's new favourite, George Villiers, earl of Buckingham. At around the same time, Pembroke achieved high office, becoming lord steward. During the 1620s, many of Monmouthshire's Members were connected with Pembroke, who evidently supplanted Worcester as an electoral patron. William Herbert II was a distant relation of the 3rd earl, while Nicholas Arnold was a former ward of Pembroke's. Charles Williams's family, too, had long-standing ties with the house of Herbert. How far Worcester acquiesced in his own replacement by Pembroke is unclear, but it may be telling that his steward, William Jones II, endorsed the 1628 election return alongside William Herbert II.[10]

None of the men returned for the county were prominent figures on the parliamentary stage. Nevertheless, Monmouthshire business did occasionally come before Parliament. On 3 Mar. 1607 a committee which included the Monmouthshire knights and burgess was appointed by the Commons to consider possible remedies in the wake of the flooding which had recently devastated south Wales and south-west England. Monmouthshire had been particularly badly hit, for in addition to many deaths, there was such widespread damage to crops and livestock in 26 southern parishes that one pamphlet noted 'there is no probability that that part of the county will ever be so inhabited again in our age as it was before this flood'.[11] In 1614 the senior Member, William Jones II, may have helped promote a bill for establishing a school and almshouses in Monmouth.[12] He may also have been involved in promoting the bill to incorporate a hospital in Llangview and erect a grammar school in Usk. In 1624 the town of Chepstow, in Monmouthshire, petitioned Parliament regarding the foundation of an almshouse from the legacy of a former county Member, Sir Walter Montagu, which had been obstructed by disputes over his will.[13] The 1628 Parliament saw a Monmouthshire native, Edward Morgan of Penrose, use private legislation to resolve a dispute with Thomas Somerset, now knighted, and Edward, 4th earl of Worcester. Morgan's father, William, had married one of the earl's daughters, but became indebted and wished to sell lands in Somerset which Worcester maintained had been reserved for his daughter's jointure. The successful legislation allowed for these properties to be conveyed to Edward Morgan under an assurance made by his deceased father.[14]

[1] STAC 5/M31/39, f. 3. [2] A. Clark, *Story of Mon.* i. 133-4; *Law and Disorder in Tudor Mon.* ed. B. Howell, pp. xix-xxiii; G. Owen, *Description of Penbrokshire* ed. H. Owen (Cymmrodorion Rec. Ser. i.), iii. 39-40; E.E. Havill, 'Parlty. Representation of Mon. and Monmouth Bors.' (Univ. Wales, M.A. thesis, 1949), pp. 6-11. [3] *Memorials of Father Augustine Baker* ed. D.J. McCann and D.H. Connolly (Cath. Rec. Soc. xxxiii), 11-12. [4] D. Sylvester, *Rural Landscape of the Welsh Borderland*, 379-81. [5] C3/454/60. [6] *APC*, 1627-8, p. 125; K. Buckland, 'Monmouth Cap', *Costume*, xiii. 23-37. [7] *APC*, 1581-2, p. 205; 1596-7, pp. 339-40; Clark, i. 137-42; M. Gray, 'Dispersal of Crown Property in Mon. 1500-1603' (Univ. Cardiff Ph.D. thesis, 1984), pp. 6-9; *Agrarian Hist. of Eng. and Wales* ed. J. Thirsk, iv. 132-4; *Acct. of the Official Progress of ... The First Duke of Beaufort* ed. T. Dinley, 368. [8] G. Williams, *Renewal and Reformation*, 399; NLW, Milborne 4930; STAC 8/218/16; DL4/83/41, f. 2; P. Courtney, 'Some New Light on the Gwent Iron Industry in the 17th Century', *Mon. Antiquary*, vii. 65. [9] SP14/48/121. [10] C219/41B/97. [11] *CJ*, i. 346a; *Lamentable Newes Out of Mon. in Wales* (1607), sig. C4v. [12] NLW, Kyrle-Fletcher A(39); *CJ*, i. 486a. [13] HLRO, main pprs. 14 May 1624. [14] HLRO, O.A. 3 Chas. I, c.14; SP16/124/31; C2/Chas.I/W103/54; 2/Chas.I/W117/35; 2/Chas.I/M14/10.

L.B.

MONMOUTH BOROUGHS

Right of election: in the freemen of Monmouth, Abergavenny, Caerleon, Chepstow, Newport, Trelleck and Usk

Number of voters: unknown

c. Jan. 1604	ROBERT JOHNSON
c. Feb. 1614	ROBERT JOHNSON
c. Dec. 1620	THOMAS RAVENSCROFT
26 Jan. 1624	WALTER STEWARD Election declared void, 28 May 1624.
c. May 1625	WALTER STEWARD
c. Jan. 1626	WILLIAM FORTUNE
21 Feb. 1628	WILLIAM MORGAN

Monmouth was established around a Norman castle situated at the confluence of the rivers Monnow and Wye. It thus occupied a significant strategic and cultural position on the boundary between Wales and England. In the thirteenth century the borough passed into the hands of the house of Lancaster, and thereafter it remained a duchy possession down to 1631. The town enjoyed good trading contacts by river and land, and possessed a market by the end of the eleventh century, but suffered severely in the Glyndŵr rebellion and struggled to recover economically.[1] In the 1590s it was described as 'somewhat decayed' and a common stock was provided to stimulate the manufacture and dressing of Welsh freizes.[2] Despite these difficulties, by the early seventeenth century Monmouth possessed guilds of mercers, drapers, grocers, tanners and glovers.[3] A major cottage industry in the town had been the manufacture of knitted Monmouth caps, although production ultimately migrated to Bewdley, Worcestershire.[4] Trade in commodities such as wine and timber along the Wye had been impeded since Marian times by the nearby Monmouth weir, but in the early 1620s orders were given to level the weir by the local sewer commissioners.[5]

Monmouth was incorporated in 1549, under a charter which provided for the election of a mayor and two bailiffs from the burgesses. A fresh charter 'for the better government, regulation and bettering of the town' was granted in December 1605. This created a common council of 15 chief burgesses, from among whom the mayor and bailiffs were chosen, which was empowered to make ordinances for the town.[6] This charter may have been the product of internal divisions, as Thomas Sadler, mayor in 1604-5, had been accused of corruption in office by a burgess and glover, James Gwillim. The new charter named Sadler and his bailiffs as common councillors and omitted Gwillim, suggesting that the purpose of the grant was to confirm Sadler's position.[7] Indications of continued division may be seen in ordinances passed in 1611, which recounted that the borough was liable to 'fall to utter ruin' on account of the multiplicity of suits brought against townsmen by their fellow inhabitants. Provisions were also made to disenfranchise any who attempted to overthrow the charter.[8] Municipal unrest seems not to have affected Monmouth's parliamentary elections, however, as the borough generally returned outsiders.

Although Monmouthshire had been created (in 1536) as an essentially English county, Monmouth itself was treated like a Welsh borough, being given the right to return only one Member. Furthermore, several other towns within the shire were entitled to vote in the borough election, an arrangement which was uniquely Welsh. Of these, four were controlled by the earls of Pembroke (Caerleon, Newport, Trellech and Usk), Chepstow belonged to the earls of Worcester, and Abergavenny was subject to the influence of the Neville family. It is unclear, however, how far these contributory boroughs were involved in practice in Monmouth's elections, as many of the election indentures have been lost. Although the return of 1628 refers to the 'full assents and consents of the burgesses and commonalty of all other borough towns' within the county, the contracting parties can generally be identified as townsmen of Monmouth.[9] The 1624 indenture, meanwhile, acknowledges only the assent of the 'mayor, bailiffs and the whole burgesses and commonalty' of Monmouth.[10]

Even though the duchy of Lancaster owned the borough until 1631, there is no indication that successive chancellors attempted to exert any patronage there; nor does Pembroke's influence in several of the contributory boroughs appear to have had any impact on electoral politics in this period.[11] However, Monmouth was amenable to the influence of the earls of Worcester, stewards of the manor, who resided at nearby Raglan. The family owned several burgages within the town, most of them held by the sons of the 4th earl of Worcester, which would have afforded significant electoral influence.[12] Many of those elected can be identified with the Worcester interest. The Member in 1604 and 1614, Robert Johnson, was an associate of the 1st earl of Salisbury (Robert Cecil[†]), but his interest at Monmouth almost certainly stemmed from his earlier employment as an auditor for the earls of Worcester. The 1621 Member, Thomas Ravenscroft, owned burgages in Monmouth, but more importantly he married into a closely linked circle of families with ties to Worcester. Similarly William Fortune, although a prominent burgess with properties in the borough, had links with townsmen described as Worcester's retainers.[13] The election of the courtier Walter Steward in 1624 and 1625 was doubtless engineered by Worcester, who held the office of lord privy seal. Only William Morgan, Member in 1628, appears to have had no ties to the earl, although the presence of men like William Fortune on his election return suggests that he was not distasteful to the Raglan interest.

Borough business occasionally came before Parliament in the early Stuart period. The Chepstow bridge over the Wye collapsed in 1603, and a bill was promoted in 1606 to provide for the building and maintenance of a new structure. Robert Johnson offered a proviso for Monmouth exempting it from contributing to the costs of construction and repair, but was successfully countered by John Hoskins, Member for Hereford.[14] Johnson also moved for a similar exemption for the town during a debate over a bill concerning the repair of bridges in 1614.[15] Also in 1614, a bill was introduced for the provision of a school and almshouses in the town as part of the bequest of William Jones, a wealthy Haberdasher and Monmouthshire native. The bill was sponsored by the Member for Gatton, Sir John Brooke, who had sold the Haberdashers' part of the manor of Hatcham Barnes to provide the bequest. Brooke assured the Company that the bill would exempt the purchase of the remainder from mortmain legislation, but though it passed both Houses it was lost at the acrimonious dissolution.[16]

[1] K. Kissack, *Monmouth*, 1-2. [2] DL1/166/420. [3] Monmouth Mus., Monmouth bor. mss, Miscellanea 3. [4] Kissack, 15-17. [5] NLW, Tredegar Park 59/5-6; Add. 21567, f. 3; DL4/72/26; 1/161/196; 1/175/329-30. [6] *Charters of Town and Bor. of Monmouth*, 14-30; C66/1674. [7] STAC 8/152/21. [8] NLW, Arnott 49. [9] C219/41B/98. [10] C219/38/165. A survey of 1609, stated that Monmouth's franchise was reserved to all free and customary tenants in the town: *Survey Duchy of Lancaster Lordships* ed. W. Rees (Univ. of Wales, Bd. of Celtic Studies, Hist. and Law ser. xii), 4. [11] Cf. J.K. Gruenfelder, *Influence in Early Stuart Elections*, 45, 80, 83. [12] *Survey*, xxix. [13] DL1/166/419-20. [14] L. Bowen, 'Wales in British Pols. c.1603-42' (Cardiff Univ. Ph.D. thesis, 1999), pp. 134-8; *CJ*, i. 296b-7a. [15] *Procs. 1614 (Commons)*, 174. [16] GL, ms 15842/1 ff. 184v-88; I. Archer, *Haberdashers' Co.* 72-82; *CJ*, i. 478a, 486a, 492a, 493b; HLRO, main pprs. 23 May 1614; Bowen, 140-2.

L.B.

NORFOLK

Number of voters: c.3,000-7,000

20 Feb. 1604	NATHANIEL BACON
	SIR CHARLES CORNWALLIS
	Sir Miles Corbet
	Sir Arthur Heveningham
7 Mar. 1614	SIR HENRY BEDINGFIELD
	SIR HAMON L'ESTRANGE
	(Sir) Henry Rich*
4 Dec. 1620	SIR HAMON L'ESTRANGE
	DRU DRURY
	(Sir) Nathaniel Bacon
	Mr. Jenkinson
26 Jan. 1624	SIR THOMAS HOLLAND
	SIR JOHN CORBET, bt.
	Sir Robert Gawdy[†]
	Sir Roger Townshend, bt.
	(proxies: Robert Catelyn and Henry Gawdy)
18 Apr. 1625	SIR EDWARD COKE
	SIR ANTHONY DRURY
	Sir Robert Gawdy
	Sir Charles Le Gros*
	Sir John Corbet, bt.
23 Jan. 1626	SIR EDWARD COKE
	SIR ROBERT BELL
	Sir Roger Townshend, bt.
	(proxy: Rice Gwyn*)
18 Feb. 1628	SIR ROGER TOWNSHEND, bt.
	SIR JOHN HEVENINGHAM

Norfolk in the early seventeenth century boasted the second largest city in England (Norwich) as well as two major seaports (Great Yarmouth and King's Lynn). It was also the centre of the new drapery trade, with a large, fertile hinterland criss-crossed with navigable waterways.[1] Thomas Fuller noted that 'all England may be carved out of Norfolk',[2] and certainly the county possessed three distinct regions: the Fenlands of the western and northern borders; the sheep-grazing and corn-growing area of the north; and a southern wooded region, where cattle raising and dairy farming predominated. The foldcourse system of sheep grazing, developed in Norfolk, allowed large flocks to be efficiently managed, and consequently wool production formed an important part of Norfolk industry, especially in the manufacture of worsted cloth and the new draperies.[3]

Norfolk's inhabitants, noted Aubrey, were 'the most litigious of all England: they carry Littleton's tenures at the plough-tail';[4] while Fuller considered that he if had to go to law, 'I wish them rather my counsel than my adversaries'.[5] Many of the county's senior gentry built their fortunes on the law, including the Bacons, Bells, Cokes, Gawdys, Hobarts and Yelvertons. There were so many lawyers in Norfolk that in the 1580s several bills to limit their number were laid before Parliament.[6] As well as enjoying a reputation for being litigious, Norfolk's inhabitants were known for their puritan tendencies, an image reinforced by an influx of refugees from the Low Countries under Elizabeth and bolstered by a number of home-grown Protestant sects, especially the Brownists. However, a handful of Catholic families, such as the Bedingfields and Pastons, continued to flourish.[7] Adherence to Catholicism seems to have had little effect on personal relationships within the gentry; nor did it prevent Sir Henry Bedingfield's election to Parliament in 1614.

Before 1572 the largest landowners in the county were the Howard dukes of Norfolk, who presided over county affairs from houses at Kenninghall, Norwich, Castle Rising and Framlingham. However, following the execution of the fourth duke in 1572, Howard influence waned, giving rise to increasingly bitter divisions within the gentry. In the second half of Elizabeth's reign, shire elections were strongly contested by two rival factions, one led by Sir Arthur Heveningham of Heveningham, Suffolk and Ketteringham, Norfolk, and the other by Nathaniel Bacon of Stiffkey, in Norfolk, and his brother Sir Nicholas of Redgrave, Suffolk. The Bacons' main allies were Sir Edward Coke* of Mileham and their cousins the Gawdys. This factional division continued into James's reign. Shortly after the king ascended the throne, canvassing started in anticipation of a Parliament. Nathaniel Bacon and Henry Gawdy[†] of Claxton both announced their intention to stand, but as neither would accept the junior seat Gawdy withdrew by July 1603, leaving Bacon to pair up with Sir Charles Cornwallis, who had recently purchased the estate of Horsham St. Faith's, near Norwich, and agreed to accept the junior place.[8] Heveningham was unable to stand against them as he was then serving as sheriff, and therefore he proposed that his place be taken by his son John. He also suggested that Thomas Knyvett, son of Sir Thomas Knyvett[†] of Ashwellthorpe, Norfolk, should put himself forward for the other seat. On the surface, this proposal looked unpromising as both sons were young and neither of them held county office. Moreover, Knyvett was closely allied with the Bacons, and neither Heveningham nor Knyvett could muster the

freeholder support needed to defeat the Bacon/Gawdy/Coke alliance. Heveningham hoped to prevail by a 'trick of office', which probably meant that he intended to exploit his position as sheriff to move the election at the last minute to the south of the county, where his support was strongest.[9] An early election did not materialize, however, and by the time that writs were actually issued, in late January 1604, Heveningham was no longer sheriff and thus able to stand. He paired himself with an ally among the south-Norfolk gentry, Sir Miles Corbet of Sprowston, the grandfather of Sir John* and Miles Corbet*. Meanwhile, the Bacon/Cornwallis partnership was in danger of collapsing, as Cornwallis demanded the first seat. Bacon was so alarmed at his colleague's behaviour that he considered asking for the election to be moved to Dereham, where his freeholder supporters were most numerous, but at the last minute Cornwallis seems to have agreed to accept the second position. At the subsequent election, held in Norwich, Heveningham and Corbet were defeated.[10]

The 1604 election was the only occasion during the period when the factional divisions that had dominated Elizabethan elections are evident.[11] By 1614 Bacon was elderly and feared he was dying, while Heveningham, who was perhaps disillusioned by his failure at previous Norfolk elections dating back to 1593, had retired from the political scene. Despite the demise of these dominant factions, fierce rivalry between the leading members of the gentry remained the norm. On the day of the 1614 election a contest was subverted by the last minute re-location of the hustings. An outsider, (Sir) Henry Rich*, armed with a letter of nomination from the lord chamberlain, the earl of Suffolk (Thomas Howard), had assembled the support of up to 4,000 freeholders in Norwich. The under-sheriff opened the sheriff's court there but adjourned it half an hour later to Swaffham, 20 miles to the west, where the sheriff, Sir James Calthorpe, was waiting to preside over an election held before 8 am at which his nephew Sir Hamon L'Estrange of Hunstanton and Sir Henry Bedingfield of Oxburgh were returned. Both L'Estrange and Bedingfield had connections with the Howard earls of Northampton and Arundel, though there is no evidence that the earls were directly involved in sponsoring them on this occasion. The decision to switch venue benefited both candidates, as Swaffham lay near Bedingfield's residence and was conveniently located for L'Estrange's allies and freeholders from the north of the county. A petition from various freeholders to Parliament, disputing the legality of shifting the venue and pointing out the impossibility of covering the 20 miles from Norwich to Swaffham on bad roads in less than half an hour, was referred to the privileges committee. As it was illegal to hold elections before 8 am, the committee may have sympathized with the complainants, but in the event it never reported its findings to the House, possibly because it was too busy investigating several other cases of electoral malpractice, such as those at Northumberland and Stockbridge.[12]

The next election, in December 1620, was held in the county town but was again contested. Sir Hamon L'Estrange stood once more, and paired himself with his kinsman, Dru Drury. L'Estrange probably enjoyed Arundel's backing, and Drury mobilized the support of his wife's relatives the de Greys of Merton and the Calthorpes of Hempstead.[13] Ranged against him and Drury was the powerful but now ageing Sir Nathaniel Bacon and a certain Mr. Jenkinson, possibly Richard Jenkinson of Tunstall. According to Philip Calthorpe, Bacon tried to upset L'Estrange's plans by concealing the writ, 'so that he hath had little warning of it, as I think verily the fift[h] p[ar]t of those that would have been with him must now fail him because they know not the day'.[14] This tactic did not succeed however, as L'Estrange won the first place and Drury took the second.

The 1624 election saw the most protracted and bitter contest of the period. Strenuous efforts were made to persuade Bacon's grandson and successor, Sir Roger Townshend to put himself forward. Indeed, he received letters urging him to stand from such prominent members of the East Anglian gentry as Sir Henry Spelman* of Congham; Sir John Hare* of Stow Bardolph; and the sheriff, Sir L'Estrange Mordaunt of King's Lynn.[15] Sir Hamon L'Estrange also approached Townshend after learning that Sir John Hobart II*, the son of L'Estrange's kinsman, Sir Henry Hobart*, could secure a seat elsewhere. L'Estrange believed that Townshend and Sir John Corbet of Sprowston would be elected by the 'acclamation of the county without exception'. Although he had heard that Sir Thomas Holland had considered standing, he thought that Holland would prefer to serve 'his lord [the earl of Arundel] in the country [rather] than in Parliament'.[16] However, Townshend preferred to remain aloof from national politics and instead supported the candidature of his two close friends, Corbet and Holland, who put himself forward despite L'Estrange's doubts. Townshend's reluctance to be nominated was disregarded by his uncle, Sir Robert Gawdy, who intended to stand himself. As well as canvassing ministers in Norfolk to support his own nomination from the pulpit, he sought a proxy to act on Townshend's behalf.[17] This did not meet with the approval of Townshend, who considered it

'an insufferable wrong' to have his name made 'the instrument of Sir John Corbet's disgrace'.[18]

Election day witnessed great confusion and much tactical manoeuvring. After the writ was read, Holland and Corbet waited until Gawdy declared his candidature before announcing their intentions to stand as a pair. In response Gawdy's supporters attempted unsuccessfully to persuade L'Estrange to stand as Gawdy's ally, and then in desperation sought a proxy for Townshend. Sir Henry Hungate*, Thomas Knyvett, Sir Charles Le Gros, John Potts and one Mr. Rennell, all refused before Robert Catelyn was finally drafted in to stand as Townshend's proxy. The polls for both seats were then held, amid much confusion. It took the sheriff and magistrates over an hour to count the votes. Once this was done, they adjourned to the Shirehall with the four candidates, where it was determined that Holland had secured the first place. Catelyn, in Townshend's name, objected to the outcome and demanded a recount based on the total number of votes that each candidate had received. The sheriff refused, and reiterated that Holland was duly elected, but did agree to a fresh poll for the second place.

Catelyn and Gawdy continued to protest, whereupon the sheriff asked the magistrates to determine collectively who should serve for the second seat. With the exception of Framlingham Gawdy and a Mr. Shepherd, all of them decided that Corbet had the most support. Again Sir Robert Gawdy and Catelyn objected, and pressed for a vote of all the freeholders. Their supporters, among whom were some described by Corbet as 'papists', had in the meantime informed Holland's company that they could disperse as they were no longer needed. When Holland learned this, he chased after them, and, aided by Dru Drury and John Potts, managed to persuade many to return and support Corbet. Meanwhile, Gawdy urged Hungate to replace Catelyn as Townshend's proxy, hoping thereby that Hungate's standing would draw more voters. However, Hungate remained loyal to Townshend's wishes. Catelyn then withdrew, and Gawdy's son, Henry, was drafted in as his replacement. By now the sheriff had lost control of the election, for when he tried to call for another poll he was overruled by the magistrates, who had already decided that Corbet would serve as the junior knight. While Holland and Corbet were carried to the *King's Head*, the Gawdys went 'in triumph' to the marketplace, where the assembled multitude chanted Townshend's name. Sir Robert Gawdy invited all those who had supported himself and Townshend to the *Maid's Head* for free food and drink, an offer which, as Corbet noted, 'did draw many of our side'.

Following these chaotic scenes a petition was drafted to the king challenging the outcome of the election. Although it contained between 500 and 600 names, L'Estrange informed Townshend that only one of the signatories was a gentleman, the rest being 'the dregs of the people'.[19] Shortly after Parliament assembled, Sir Robert Gawdy complained to the privileges committee that the poll had been peremptorily conducted and no proper count had taken place. Witnesses, counsel and proofs were heard for two days, as were Holland, Corbet, Drury and Sir Robert Gawdy. The chairman, John Glanville, argued that a new writ should be dispatched, but by a majority vote the committee ultimately decided that the election should stand. The Commons, however, proved unhappy with the committee's report, which failed to outline its reasons, and consequently the committee was obliged to re-examine the entire case. It was therefore not until 24 Mar., after witnesses had been heard again, that Glanville reported back. Once more, the committee decided to allow the election to stand. In the ensuing debate, Glanville and Christopher Wandesford argued for a new writ but were opposed by Drury, William Coryton and Sir George More. The subject was further complicated by Sir Henry Poole, who doubted the validity of Corbet's election but not Holland's. This raised the question whether it was possible to nullify the election of one candidate without declaring the entire election invalid. The House determined that the election must be considered as a whole, and after further procedural wranglings it was finally decided, by 200 votes to 129, that the election was valid.[20]

The opening Parliament of a new reign did not dull the appetite of Norfolk's gentry for contested elections. In 1625 Sir Edward Coke and Sir Anthony Drury stood together, apparently against Sir Robert Gawdy and Sir Charles Le Gros.[21] Sir John Corbet again offered himself as a candidate but managed to attract only about 100 votes. Coke and Drury defeated their rivals, although by what margin is unclear. Katherine Paston of Oxnead reported that 'he that had the least had 1,100 and he that had most had 1,610', but her observation, which took no account of Corbet's poor showing, is not entirely helpful.[22] Coke evidently expected his return to be challenged, for a week after the election he unsuccessfully appealed to the bailiffs of Scarborough for one of the borough's seats, and subsequently secured a place at Coventry, where he was recorder. When Parliament opened, on 22 June, he asked for time to decide which seat he would represent, and did not finally plump for the county until 4 July, by which time it was apparent that no petition from Norfolk was forthcoming.[23]

On 6 Dec. 1625, prior to the next general election, Sir John Spelman* informed his father that John Hobart II was already canvassing for a Norfolk seat. However, Hobart's father died on 26 Dec., the date on which the election writs were actually issued, and was presumably persuaded to stand down, as he was eventually returned as a borough Member for both Thetford and Brackley, plumping for the latter. Coke stood again and was returned as the senior knight of the shire alongside Sir Robert Bell of Beaupré Hall, Outwell, the grandson of Coke's predecessor as Speaker of the Elizabethan House of Commons. The election was contested by Rice Gwyn* of Little Snoring, who put himself forward as a proxy for Townshend. Following the poll, John Yates informed Townshend, who was again uninterested in standing, that he had been elected, but although he certainly gathered 600 votes from among those described as the 'most substantial freeholders', he seems to have been easily defeated by Coke and Bell, who were supported by Sir John Corbet and Sir Hamon L'Estrange.[24] Unfortunately for Coke, however, the king had earlier pricked him as sheriff of Buckinghamshire in order to exclude him from the Parliament. Charles expected the Commons to order a fresh election, but Coke's son, Clement, made an impassioned plea on behalf of his father, arguing that the king was trying to usurp the privileges of the House. Many Members clearly found this claim persuasive, for although the Commons' rules clearly prohibited the election of sheriffs the House declined to resolve the issue one way or another.[25]

The election held in 1628 was the first to be uncontested in Norfolk since 1588. Widespread anger and resentment against the Forced Loan persuaded former rivals to bury their differences. The first seat was taken by Townshend, who was finally convinced to stand. Townshend was disturbed by the death of his close friend, Sir John Corbet, who had been imprisoned for refusing to contribute to the Loan. The second seat was occupied by Sir John Heveningham, another of the 'Five Knights' who had steadfastly opposed the Loan.

Norfolk's elections are characterized by several unusual features, namely the large size of the electorate, the absence of external influence, the existence of factions among the gentry, the independence and political awareness of the freeholders, the frequency with which seats were contested, and the necessity for pre-election campaigning.[26] The exact size of the electorate is difficult to determine, but in 1593 Coke claimed to have been elected by more than 7,000 supporters, while in 1614 Rich marshalled around 4,000.[27] The absence of outside interference stemmed largely from the fact that no member of the peerage lived in Norfolk. Of course, many of the gentry, such as L'Estrange and Holland, were closely connected with the Howards, but neither the earl of Northampton nor the earl of Arundel were usually active in shire elections, perhaps realizing that their influence only extended to boroughs such as Castle Rising and Thetford. An attempted intervention by the earl of Suffolk in 1614 ended in humiliating failure. Although Norfolk was a predominantly puritan county, its gentry preferred to acquiesce in the election of Bedingfield, a known Catholic, rather than return Suffolk's nominee. The gentry were divided along regional lines, for in most elections one Member was elected from the north of the county and the other from the south. Only in 1624, when both successful candidates came from the south, was this pattern interrupted. Gawdy's intervention that year was perhaps motivated in part by a desire to achieve 'a better-balanced ticket'.[28]

Throughout the period, Norfolk's representatives paid particular attention to matters regarding agriculture and the cloth trade, especially the Act of 1607 which regulated the making of cloths, including East Anglian new draperies, and the 1621 and 1624 bills for the regulation of Norfolk and Norwich weavers.[29] In 1606 Norfolk's Members were appointed to consider bills for the relief of the poor (23 Jan.) and for the better maintenance of ministers in Norwich (13 February).[30] In 1610 Norfolk's Members were appointed to consider bills concerning the continuing fishing dispute between Lowestoft and Great Yarmouth (13 Mar.), fen drainage (20 Mar.), the sale of lands by Charles Waldegrave (14 June) and Thetford school (15 June).[31] In 1621 they were eligible to attend committees to consider the sale of the estate of Martin Calthorpe (17 Mar.), cart-taking (21 Apr.) and the sale of Peyton Hall manor (27 April).[32] Three years later, Norfolk's Members were named to bill committees on the transportation of butter and cheese (3 Apr.), the naturalization of a Norwich grain merchant, Peter Verbeake (12 Apr.), Calthorpe's bill (14 Apr.), the repair of Colchester haven (14 Apr.) and improvement to the two new drapery cloths, serges and perpetuanas (20 April). In 1626 they were appointed to consider bills concerned with citations from ecclesiastical courts (1 Mar.), the sale of Sir Henry Clere's land (4 May) and confirmation of a Chancery decree for Feltwell manor (6 May).[33] In the last Parliament of the decade the Norfolk knights were eligible to sit on the bill committee for the preservation of timber (21 May).[34]

[1] A.H. Smith, *County and Ct.* 1-20; R.W. Ketton-Cremer, *Norf. in Civil War*, ch. 1. [2] T. Fuller, *Worthies*, ii. 444. [3] K.J. Allison, 'Flock Management', *EcHR*, xi. 98-112; K.J. Allison, 'Norf. Worsted Industry', *Yorks. Bull. Ec. and Social Res.* xii. 73-83; K.J. Allison, 'Sheep-corn Husbandry of Norf.', *Agric. Hist. Rev.* v. 12-30; J. Thirsk, *Agrarian Hist. of Eng. and Wales*, iv. 40-9. [4] J. Aubrey, *Hist. Wilts.* 12; Ketton-Cremer, 21. [5] Fuller, ii. 446. [6] D.M. Dean, *Law-Making and Soc. in Late Eliz. Eng.: Parl. 1584-1601*, p. 214. [7] Ketton-Cremer, 21-6. [8] Norf. RO, NNAS C3/1/9/5; FSL, L.d.102, 105. [9] Norf. RO, NNAS C3/1/9/5. [10] Smith, 330: FSL, L.d.107. [11] G.L. Owens, 'Norf. Local Govt. 1620-41' (Univ. of Wisconsin Ph.D. thesis, 1970), pp. 33-5. [12] *Procs. 1614 (Commons)*, 38, 46-7; *Chamberlain Letters* ed. N.E. McClure, i. 518; Eg. 2804, f. 208. [13] Norf. RO, WLS XVII/2, ff. 30-1v. [14] Ibid. f. 31. [15] Norf. RO, RAY 429; FSL, L.d.543. [16] *Off. Pprs. of Sir Nathaniel Bacon* ed. H.E. Saunders (Cam. Soc. xxvi), 38-9. [17] FSL, L.d.238. [18] L. Campbell, 'Sir Roger Townshend and his Fam.' (Univ. E. Anglia Ph.D. thesis, 1990), p. 82. [19] FSL, L.d.215, 238, 418, 543; *HMC Townshend*, 21; *Off. Pprs. of Sir Nathaniel Bacon*, 38-41; Add. 63082, f. 31; Norf. RO, RAY 429, 484. [20] 'Earle 1624', ff. 65v-6, 110; 'Pym 1624', i. ff. 40v-1; *CJ*, i. 749a-b; J. Glanville, *Reps.* 3-6. [21] *HMC Gawdy*, 122. [22] FSL, L.d.418; *Corresp. Lady Katherine Paston* ed. R. Haughey (Norf. Rec. Soc. xiv), 82, 126. [23] *Procs. 1625*, pp. 216, 297, 701. [24] Norf. RO, RAY 484; W. Prest, 'Bacon-Townshend Pprs. at the Univ. of Adelaide', *Norf. Arch.* xxxvii. 121-2; *HMC Townshend*, 23. [25] *Procs. 1626*, ii. 34, 39; iii. 407. See also SURVEY, *sub* 'Rules of Membership'. [26] Smith, 314. [27] J.E. Neale, *Elizabethan House of Commons*, 78; Harl. 6687, i. f.14. [28] Campbell, 86. [29] *SR*, iv. 1137-40 Kyle, thesis, 108-20. [30] *CJ*, i. 258b, 267b. [31] Ibid. 410a, 413a, 438b, 440a; *Procs. 1610* ed. E.R. Foster, i. 10 n. 1. [32] *CJ*, i. 559b, 585b, 593b. [33] *Procs. 1626*, ii. 158; iii. 155, 180. [34] *CD 1628*, iii. 512.

C.R.K.

CASTLE RISING

Right of election: in the freemen

Number of voters: unknown

24 Feb. 1604	SIR THOMAS MONSON
	SIR ROBERT TOWNSHEND
c. Mar. 1614	SIR ROBERT WYNDE
	THOMAS BYNG
19 Dec. 1620	JOHN WILSON
	ROBERT SPILLER
1 Feb. 1624	(SIR) ROBERT SPILLER
	THOMAS BANCROFT
c. Apr. 1625	SIR HAMON L'ESTRANGE
	THOMAS BANCROFT
c. Feb. 1626	THOMAS BANCROFT
	NATHANIEL GURLYN
26 Feb. 1628	THOMAS BANCROFT
	SIR ROBERT COTTON, (bt.)

Four miles north-east of King's Lynn, Rising had during the Middle Ages been an important and prosperous coastal town, dominated by an enormous castle (from which it took its name).[1] However, it fell into decay as gradual silting caused the sea to retreat. By the mid-sixteenth century the castle was in ruins and the town had been eclipsed by King's Lynn.[2] Nevertheless the traditional 15-day fair (1-14 May) continued, and Rising Chase was still considered one of the best deer hunting regions in England.[3]

In the mid-sixteenth century the lordship of the manor was the property of the 4th duke of Norfolk, whose influence brought about the borough's enfranchisement in 1559.[4] Howard patronage waned after the duke's attainder and execution in 1572, but had recovered by 1604, when the manor was jointly owned by Henry Howard, created earl of Northampton in March 1604, and his great-nephew Thomas Howard. Henry provided the town with an almshouse which abutted the church of St. Lawrence, at a cost of £451 14s. 2d. Endowed with lands worth £100 p.a., it housed 12 poor women and a governess.[5] The franchise rested in the freemen of the borough, and election indentures were signed by the mayor and townsmen; in 1604 the return was decorated with six of their seals.[6] At the parliamentary election of 1604, Henry had his client Sir Thomas Monson returned for the first seat. The second place went to Sir Robert Townshend who, though closely connected with the Howards, also enjoyed local influence and had been returned for the borough in 1601. During the 1604 session Thomas Howard was restored in blood as earl of Arundel, and Townshend was named to the bill committee.[7]

In 1614 the first seat went to Sir Robert Wynde, a gentleman of some standing in Norfolk, who shortly beforehand had sold land near Castle Rising to Northampton. His fellow Member, Thomas Byng, has not been clearly identified, but the Byng family was certainly closely linked with the Howards. After Northampton's death, parliamentary elections were controlled by Arundel, as a letter written by the earl addressed to the 'mayor and inhabitants' of Rising makes clear:

> whereas at the last summons for a Parliament you did willingly and freely make choice of R[obert] S[piller] and J[ohn] W[ilson] for your burgesses upon my recommendation ... I do now again recommend and nominate unto you R[obert] S[piller] and A.D., who are able and worthy to undergo that service.[8]

Wilson's identity is uncertain, but Spiller was one of Arundel's clients, his uncle having been steward to the dowager countess of Arundel. 'A.D.' was perhaps Sir Anthony Drury*, another Arundel client, who entered Parliament in 1625 as knight of the shire for Norfolk.[9] In the event 'A.D.' was not elected, but was replaced by Thomas Bancroft, a minor Exchequer official who had recently purchased Santon manor from Arundel. Bancroft subsequently served for Castle Rising in the next three parliaments. In 1625 he was joined by Sir Hamon L'Estrange, the head of the dominant gentry family in north Norfolk. L'Estrange was sufficiently influential to be elected on his own account, as the family had longstanding connections with the borough, where one of the castle's towers was called 'Strange Tower'.[10] In 1626 the borough returned another Member not known to have been connected with Arundel – Nathaniel Gurlyn, the son of a prosperous King's Lynn brewer. However, by 1628 the earl had regained control over both seats, for he had his client and close friend Sir Robert Cotton returned alongside Bancroft.

[1] J.M. Wilson, *Imperial Gazetteer of Eng. and Wales*, i. 380; *National Gazetteer of Eng. and Wales*, iii. 514-15. [2] W. Camden, *Britannia*, i. 383. [3] F. Blomefield, *Hist. Norf.* ix. 52, 56. [4] A.D. Hawkyard, 'Enfranchisement of Constituencies', *PH*, x. 20. [5] Blomefield, ix. 55. [6] C219/35/1/17. [7] *CJ*, i. 162a; HLRO, HL/PO/PB/I/1603/1J1n38; R.H. Mason, *Hist. Norf.* 233 n. 2. [8] He also noted that they were willing to serve without wages. SP14/135/42. [9] J.K. Gruenfelder, *Influence in early Stuart Elections*, 134-5. [10] H. Bradfer-Lawrence, *Castle Rising*, 30-1.

C.R.K.

GREAT YARMOUTH

Right of election: in the corporation

Number of voters: 72

1 Mar. 1604[1]	THOMAS DAMET, alderman	
	JOHN WHEELER, alderman	
18 Mar. 1614[2]	GEORGE HARDWARE, alderman	
	SIR THEOPHILUS FINCH	
12 Dec. 1620[3]	BENJAMIN COOPER, alderman	
	EDWARD OWNER, alderman	
28 Jan. 1624[4]	GEORGE HARDWARE, alderman	
	BENJAMIN COOPER, alderman	
27 Apr. 1625[5]	SIR JOHN CORBET, bt.	
	EDWARD OWNER, alderman	
26 Jan. 1626[6]	SIR JOHN CORBET, bt.	
	THOMAS JOHNSON, alderman	
29 Feb. 1628[7]	SIR JOHN WENTWORTH	
	MILES CORBET, recorder	

Situated at the mouth of the Yare on the southern border of Norfolk, Yarmouth had been an important fortified town and a major fishing port since Saxon times. The epithet 'Great' was added during Edward I's reign, probably to distinguish it from Little Yarmouth, in Suffolk.[8] Built around a large central marketplace, the town's most unusual feature was that it comprised a single parish.[9] In the nineteenth century the huge church of St. Nicholas was the 26th largest in England, making it bigger than some cathedrals.[10]

By the beginning of the seventeenth century, Yarmouth supported a population of 6,000-7,000, and was governed by two bailiffs, an inner council known as the Twenty-Four, and a common council referred to as the Forty-Eight, assisted by an under-steward and various minor officials. The office of high steward was filled by Charles Howard[†], 1st earl of Nottingham (1601-24), and later by Sir James Ley*, 1st earl of Marlborough (1625-9). Yarmouth also retained numerous lawyers. In 1603 there were five, including Sir Edward Coke* and Sir Henry Hobart*, and by 1624 there were nine, each one retained at a cost of 40s.[11] In 1608 Yarmouth obtained a new charter, which replaced the under-steward with a recorder and renamed the members of the inner and common councils as aldermen and councillors respectively.[12] This form of government went unchallenged until 1627, when aldermen Benjamin Cooper* and George Hardware* asked the king to replace the bailiffs with a single mayor. Many of their colleagues were furious at this unauthorized action, and consequently both men were removed from the aldermanic bench. The king, concerned at this dissension in a major town, ordered that they be restored, and instructed that Yarmouth's charters be brought to London for examination. However, the displaced aldermen were only reinstated after the direct intervention of attorney-general (Sir) Robert Heath* and Secretary Dorchester (Dudley Carleton*). Although a new charter was drafted, which would have installed a mayor and halved the size of the town's governing body, it was held in abeyance by the Privy Council as its provisions were contrary to the wishes of the vast majority of the corporation.[13]

Yarmouth's corporation during this period enjoyed an annual income of more than £1,500 p.a., and was able to contribute £120 to a royal aid in 1611 and more than £270 towards the Benevolence of 1614.[14] However, more than £500 was needed every year to maintain the haven.[15] In 1622, following an inquiry, the town was granted the right to export 4,000 tons of beer duty free to raise funds for repairs. This produced a windfall of £1,800, and in 1626 a second licence, to export 1,000 tons, was issued with the help of the town's steward, lord treasurer Marlborough.[16] The additional revenue was undoubtedly welcome, for in the mid-1620s, when fears of invasion were rife, the corporation was forced to spend £300 a year to keep its fortifications in good repair. This was not enough, but the town pleaded poverty, claiming that its merchants had lost goods and shipping to the Dunkirkers worth £25,000 in the space of two years.[17]

Yarmouth's prosperity was based largely upon the herring industry. The annual herring free-fair, held between Michaelmas and Martinmas and administered jointly with two representatives of the Cinque Ports, attracted huge numbers of vessels.[18] The tolls and customs collected during the fair were vital to the town's economy, as was the money spent by the influx of mariners.[19] However, for many years Yarmouth had been engaged in a bitter dispute with nearby Lowestoft over fishing rights. The history of the conflict is well documented and illustrates how the outports could utilize the forum of Parliament to gain superiority.[20]

The quarrel with Lowestoft was re-ignited in 1608 by Yarmouth's new charter. As well as modifying its form of government, the new charter granted Yarmouth Admiralty rights between Easton Ness and Winton Ness, a distance of over 14 leagues, placing Lowestoft firmly under its jurisdiction. Yarmouth's high steward, lord admiral Nottingham, appears to have been instrumental in obtaining the charter. In return for 40 barrels of herring and 100 lings a year for life, he surrendered his Admiralty rights to the king, who then transferred them to Yarmouth.[21] Lowestoft was horrified, and drafted a bill to be laid before Parliament, which attracted support from fishermen as far away as Brighton.[22] The measure, a copy of which survives among Yarmouth's records, was similar to a bill introduced by Lowestoft in 1597-8, which sought to limit Yarmouth's jurisdiction to a radius of seven miles.[23] Following the bill's first reading, on 26 Feb. 1610,[24] the corporation dispatched two aldermen to London to assist its Members and prepare documents illustrating the bill's faults.[25] One of Yarmouth's Members, Thomas Damet, who had led the opposition to Lowestoft under Elizabeth, subsequently denigrated Lowestoft as 'a town of small importance to [the] state', whose inhabitants were poor 'by their idleness'.[26] These tactics ensured that the bill did not return from committee after its second reading on 13 March.[27] Lowestoft may have introduced another bill to the same effect in 1621, but if so it failed to receive even a first reading.[28]

Yarmouth not only had to contend with legislative attacks from Lowestoft but also from its other perennial opponent, the London Fishmongers' Company. In 1604 the Fishmongers supported a bill against the drying of summer herrings – a method used in Yarmouth – by sending some of its members to the parliamentary committee meeting.[29] In 1610 they also sponsored a bill designed to overturn an Elizabethan statute on barrelled fish.[30] The main dispute between Yarmouth and the Fishmongers, however, was over the granting of the annual herring licence to Yarmouth by the Privy Council. This licence enabled Yarmouth to transport 600 lasts of herrings in strangers' bottoms, and was of considerable importance because of the foreign shipping and customs it brought to the port. In 1613 the licence came under attack from a combination of the Fishmongers, Deptford's Trinity House, and London merchants and shipowners. They claimed that Yarmouth's export of herrings in foreign ships was contrary to statute, led to the decay of English trade, and left many English mariners unemployed. After much wrangling, the licence was renewed, but another sustained attack in 1615 not only persuaded the Board to revoke it, but to forbid the town from seeking a further renewal, 'it being resolved ... that none at all shall be hereafter granted, as a thing every way prejudicial and inconvenient'.[31]

This state of affairs lasted only until 1617, when the Privy Council, alarmed that 'such strangers as were accustomed to buy their herrings do now altogether forbear to buy and provide herrings at that town as heretofore', restored the licence.[32] It was again revoked in 1624, however, despite the support of (Sir) John Suckling* and the duke of Buckingham, after the Fishmongers and merchants said they were prepared to buy the 600 lasts at the same price as foreign merchants paid.[33] Despite these assurances, the Londoners failed to fulfil their part of the agreement, and in 1627 Yarmouth's right to ship herrings in strangers' bottoms was, with some difficulty, restored.[34]

Writs for parliamentary elections in Great Yarmouth were directed to the sheriff of Norfolk, who issued a precept to the bailiffs. The franchise was vested in the corporation, and an oral vote was taken during the meeting. After the election, a committee of aldermen was appointed to consider what instructions to give the burgesses before they departed for Westminster.[35] Yarmouth's Members seem to have been expected to report events at Westminster to their constituents, both verbally and by letter, and indeed they often supplied copies of speeches and other proceedings.[36]

From about 1584 Yarmouth had generally returned aldermen as its representatives. This pattern continued into James's reign, for before 1625 the only outsider to be returned was Sir Theophilus Finch, who was chosen for the junior seat in 1614. Finch, though not resident in Norfolk, had married into the Heydon family of Baconsthorpe, and his mother-in-law was the widow of Sir Edward Clere of Ormesby, four miles north of Yarmouth. Interest in Yarmouth's seats rose sharply in 1624, however, when the borough received several letters from outsiders. The corporation resolved that only aldermen should be elected,[37] but in 1625 it gave way after four outsiders, all of them knights, approached the borough. At the election on 27 Apr. it was decided, by a majority vote, to return Sir John Corbet of Sprowston as senior burgess. Corbet's manor lay close to Norwich, and his brother, Miles, was Yarmouth's recorder.[38] Corbet was returned again in 1626, but this time 'without any opposition or contradiction'.[39] At the 1628 election the corporation decided to confer both its seats on outsiders. Sir John Wentworth, who lived at nearby Somerleyton in Suffolk, was awarded the senior place, while Miles Corbet, the recorder, was returned as junior burgess. It is unclear why the borough was prepared to elect outsiders on a regular basis from 1625, but losses suffered during the wars with Spain and France, and the expense of maintaining the town's fortifications, may have made it willing to look more kindly on men prepared to serve in Parliament without wages. Townsmen who were elected received 10s. per day in travelling costs, and 6s. 8d. for every day they were in London.[40]

[1] Norf. RO, Y/C19/5. f. 39. [2] Ibid. f. 125. [3] Ibid. f. 228. [4] Ibid. f. 292v. [5] Ibid. f. 323. [6] Ibid. Y/C19/6, f. 10. [7] Ibid. f. 89v. [8] F. Blomefield, *Hist. Norf.* xi. 255. [9] Cott. Augustus I (i), no. 74. [10] E.J. Lupson, *St. Nicholas*, 8. [11] Norf. RO, Y/C21/1, f. 260v; C21/1, unfol. [12] Norf. RO, Y/C2/12; Y/C18/4, ff. 67-76v. [13] Blomefield, xi. 302-7; H. Swinden, *Hist. Gt. Yarmouth*, 477-514; SP14/180/45; SP16/147/56-9; 16/148/58, 60-1, 74, 88; Norf. RO, Y/C19/6, ff. 126, 127, 129, 161v. [14] Norf. RO, Y/C19/5, f. 93; E351/1950. [15] Norf. RO, Y/C18/4, f. 66v. [16] Norf. RO, Y/C19/6, f. 124. [17] Blomefield, xi. 359. [18] W.F. Crisp, *Chronological Hist. Gt. Yarmouth*, unpag.; D.M. Dean, 'Yarmouth-Lowestoft Fishing Dispute', *Albion*, xxii. 41. [19] A.R. Michell, 'Herring Fishing', *Camb. Economic Hist. of Europe* ed. E.E. Rich and C.H. Wilson, v. 143-7; A.R. Michell, 'Port and Town of Gt. Yarmouth' (Univ. Camb. Ph.D. thesis, 1978), esp. pp. 387-8. [20] Dean, 39-64; R. Tittler, 'Eng. Fishing Industry – Gt. Yarmouth', *Albion*, ix. 40-60; A. Saul, 'Herring Industry – Gt. Yarmouth', *Norf. Arch.*, xxxviii. 33-43. [21] Norf. RO, Y/C19/5, f. 66r-v. [22] Harl. 6838, ff. 215v-16, 219, 221. [23] Norf. RO, Y/C36/7/2. [24] *CJ*, i. 400a. [25] Norf. RO, Y/C19/5, f. 77. [26] Ibid. Y/C36/7/2, 21, 25; Harl. 6838, ff. 230v-1, 243; Suff. RO (Lowestoft), M18/06/1, ff. 42v-54v, f. 68v. [27] *CJ*, i. 410a. [28] Norf. RO, Y/C20/1, f. 12v. [29] GL, ms 5570/1, p. 376. [30] Ibid. 5570/2, p. 1. [31] *APC*, 1613-14, pp. 594-5; 1615-16, pp. 327-9; GL, ms 5570/2, pp. 94-5, 123; Norf. RO, Y/C19/5, ff. 116, 119-20. [32] *APC*, 1616-17, p. 350. [33] Ibid. 1623-5,

pp. 317, 321-2, 367-8; Add. 12496, ff. 375-6v, 377, 379-82v; Norf. RO, Y/C19/5, ff. 299, 304, 308, 312v; D.R. Butcher, 'Development of Lowestoft' (Univ. E. Anglia M.Phil. thesis, 1991), p. 261. [34] Norf. RO, Y/C19/6, f. 78v; *APC*, 1627-8, pp. 53-4. [35] Norf. RO, Y/C19/5, ff. 231, 293. [36] Ibid. ff. 132v, 234, 296, 331v; C19/6, ff. 20, 24v, 95. [37] Ibid. f. 292v. [38] Ibid. ff. 228, 323. [39] Ibid. Y/C19/6, f. 10. [40] Ibid. Y/C19/5, f. 292v.

C.R.K.

KING'S LYNN

Right of election: in the corporation

Number of voters: 31

18 Feb. 1604	THOMAS OXBOROUGH, recorder ROBERT HITCHAM
11 Mar. 1614[1]	MATTHEW CLARKE, mayor THOMAS OXBOROUGH, recorder
15 Dec. 1620	MATTHEW CLARKE, alderman JOHN WALLIS, alderman
22 Jan. 1624	JOHN WALLIS, alderman WILLIAM DOUGHTY, alderman
25 Apr. 1625	THOMAS GURLYN, alderman JOHN COOKE, alderman
16 Jan. 1626	THOMAS GURLYN, alderman JOHN COOKE, alderman
25 Feb. 1628	SIR JOHN HARE WILLIAM DOUGHTY, alderman

Situated on the south-east corner of the Wash, King's Lynn is 'flanked to the east by the dry sandy loams of Norfolk, and bounded to the south and west by marsh and fen'.[2] Lynn derives the second part of its name from 'Lun' or 'Lena', an ancient British word meaning lake.[3] The town was principally founded by the bishop of Norwich in the eleventh century,[4] when it was known as Bishop's Lynn. It continued under episcopal control until 1536, when Henry VIII seized control, and in July 1537 the town was formally renamed King's Lynn.[5] Despite the change of name, Lynn's form of government, by a mayor, 12 aldermen, and 18 common councillors, remained unaltered. The mayor was chosen annually by those aldermen who had not served as mayor themselves in the last five years, while the aldermen were appointed by the councillors, and *vice versa*. The corporation also had a recorder, town clerk, and various other officials.[6]

In the early seventeenth century Lynn may have had as many as 6,000 inhabitants.[7] Its economy was dominated by trade, and in particular the import of coal from Newcastle and the export of corn, mainly to London. Traffic with Scotland increased dramatically during James's reign,[8] and following the peace with Spain, Lynn joined the reconstituted Spanish Company, which enjoyed only a brief existence. However, intercourse with southern Europe formed only a minor part of Lynn's trade.[9] Lynn owed its prosperity to the fact that its hinterland was 'opened up by the most extensive system of navigable rivers in England'.[10] It sent its goods into ten counties, and acted as an important conduit for goods travelling to Stourbridge, which hosted one of England's largest annual fairs.[11]

Lynn's corporation boasted an annual income of over £1,000 from its lands alone.[12] Mayors received the town plate, an allowance of 200 marks, and the lease of the dovecote at Whitefriars.[13] The corporation was the guardian of the town's prosperity, and often sent its members to London, Norwich, and the Norfolk assizes to watch over the borough's interests. It also actively encouraged Dutch manufacturers of the new draperies to settle in Lynn,[14] and had water piped into many houses for use in brewing.[15] It was alarmed by the levy of 2d. per chaldron of coal imposed upon Lynn merchants by the Newcastle Hostmen, but in 1609 after much legal wrangling the Hostmen agreed to drop the charges.[16] Lynn readily contributed £100 towards the Palatinate cause in 1622, but four years later pleaded poverty when it was required to provide two ships for the war effort, claiming that it had spent heavily on its defences against the Dunkirkers.[17]

Lynn elected its Members by vote of the corporation. Election indentures were signed by the mayor and various other corporation members. Those chosen were usually selected from within the corporation itself. Indeed, only two outsiders, Robert Hitcham in 1604 and Sir John Hare in 1628, were elected during this period. Hitcham, Anne of Denmark's attorney-general, was probably returned on the recommendation of Lynn's high steward, Lord Ellesmere (Sir Thomas Egerton I†). Hitcham was required to travel to Lynn to take the oath of a freeman, as previously, only residents of the town had served as Members.[18] The second seat in 1604 went to the town's recorder, Thomas Oxborough. Hitcham applied to the corporation again in 1614, as did Sir Henry Spelman*. Faced with a difficult choice, the corporation decided to reject both candidates on the grounds of non-residence, and stood resolute despite a second appeal from

Hitcham.[19] Instead, the first seat was bestowed upon the mayor, Matthew Clarke, while the seat went once again to Oxborough. When the Parliament assembled, Sir Robert Cotton*, hoping belatedly to find a seat for himself, tried to challenge the validity of Clarke's election, as mayors were not permitted to sit. He arranged with a Member named Byng (there were three then sitting) to raise the issue, but the Commons was swayed by 'an eloquent oration' made by Clarke, who protested that he would 'rather continue to be a scholar in this school of wisdom than governor of the best town in the realm'.[20]

During the 1620s Lynn continued to return townsmen. In 1621 Clarke was joined by the borough's largest merchant trader, John Wallis. The latter served again in 1624 with his fellow alderman, William Doughty. In the first Parliament of Charles's reign, Lynn was served by Thomas Gurlyn and John Cooke, both of whom were aldermen, and the same pair sat again in 1626. It was not until 1628 that Lynn once again broke with tradition, by electing the non-resident Sir John Hare to the first seat. Hare, an influential wealthy landowner whose estates at Stow Bardolph lay about seven miles south of Lynn, was sworn a freeman four days after his election.[21] Hare's partner, however, was alderman William Doughty.

Lynn corporation usually contributed to its Members' daily expenses, and also paid the costs of travelling to and fro.[22] Rates of payment were apparently negotiable. Hitcham agreed to serve without wages, but received a gratuity of £20 in July 1610 in recognition of the length of the Parliament.[23] In 1614 and 1621 the corporation paid 10s. a day, but in the following three parliaments cut the rate back to 5s. a day.[24] The Hall Book also records instances of Members being paid for 'parliament writings'.[25] Sir John Hare was the only Member not to have received payment at all.

Lynn is not known to have promoted any particular objectives in Parliament during this period. However, in November 1605 its Members were invited to give evidence to a committee concerning the newly reconstituted Spanish Company (to which Lynn was affiliated), before being added to the committee when Parliament reconvened the following year.[26] Neither Hitcham nor Oxborough are recorded as having spoken against the free trade bill, which ultimately abolished the Company, and indeed Hitcham supported the cause of free trade in 1604. This cannot have endeared him to his constituents, and may help to explain why the borough decided not to elect him again in 1614.[27] In February 1606 Lynn's Members

were named to consider a bill to prevent the erecting of cottages, and in May 1614 they were appointed to examine a measure to restrain brewers from serving as magistrates.[28]

[1] Norf. RO (King's Lynn), KL/C7/9, f. 54. [2] V. Parker, *Making of King's Lynn*, 3. [3] F. Blomefield, *Hist. Norf.* viii. 476. [4] Parker, 1. [5] *SR* iii. 608-9, Norf. RO (King's Lynn), KL/C2/48. [6] Norf. RO (King's Lynn), KL/C2/46. [7] H. Clarke and A. Carter, *Excavations in King's Lynn*, 431-2. [8] G.A. Metters, 'Rulers and Merchants of King's Lynn' (Univ. E. Anglia Ph.D. thesis, 1982), 122-4, 129-35, 198; E190/434/7-13. [9] P. Croft, *Spanish Co.* (London Rec. Soc. ix), 24, 28. [10] T.S. Willan, *Eng. Coasting Trade*, 125. [11] Norf. RO (King's Lynn), Mart Bk. 1618; Parker, 9, 12; F.W.B. Gras, *Corn Market*, 62-3; *HMC Ancaster*, 350. [12] Norf. RO (King's Lynn), KL/C39/97-101. [13] Ibid. KL/C7/9, ff. 41v, 348. [14] Ibid. KL/C7/8, f. 456v; C7/9, f. 55. [15] Ibid. KL/C44/8, C39/97, ff. 42, 56. [16] Ibid. KL/C4/17; J. Hatcher, *Hist. of Brit. Coal Industry*, 509-25. [17] Norf. RO (King's Lynn), KL/C7/9, ff. 173, 249v, 255, 260v; *APC*, 1626, pp. 48, 137-8, 177; SP16/61/81, 50/46, 58/14. [18] Norf. RO (King's Lynn), KL/C7/8, ff. 295, 300v, 301v. [19] Ibid. KL/C7/9, ff. 52, 53v. [20] *Procs. 1614 (Commons)*, 103, 107. [21] Norf. RO (King's Lynn), KL/C7/9, f. 282. [22] Ibid. ff. 214v, 249. [23] Ibid. KL/C7/8, f. 465. [24] *HMC Southampton and King's Lynn Corp.* 177. [25] Norf. RO (King's Lynn), KL/C7/9, f. 260v, C39/100, unfol. [26] *CJ*, i. 257a, 261a. [27] Ibid. 985b. [28] Ibid. 269b; *Procs. 1614 (Commons)*, 394.

C.R.K.

NORWICH

Right of election: in the freemen

Number of voters: c.1,500

27 Feb. 1604	SIR HENRY HOBART
	JOHN PETTUS
1614	SIR THOMAS HYRNE
	RICE GWYN
16 Dec. 1620	RICHARD ROSS
	WILLIAM DENNY
2 Feb. 1624	SIR THOMAS HYRNE
	WILLIAM DENNY
1625	SIR THOMAS HYRNE
	WILLIAM DENNY
30 Jan. 1626	SIR THOMAS HYRNE
	(SIR) JOHN SUCKLING
25 Feb. 1628	SIR PETER GLEANE
	ROBERT DEBNEY

Dominated by its Norman keep and cathedral, and bounded by medieval walls and the meandering River Wensum, Norwich was the second largest city after London, and one of the major provincial capitals of

England. It boasted over 30 churches, and supported a growing population, which rose from about 12,000 in the 1580s to approximately 20,000 in 1620.[1] One reason for this remarkable increase was the economic boom of Elizabeth's reign, which continued into the seventeenth century, especially in the cloth trade. Another factor was the city's stranger community, which grew rapidly after 1565, when Elizabeth allowed 30 families from the Low Countries to settle in Norwich in order to introduce the manufacture of new drapery cloth. By 1583 the community exceeded 4,000 people,[2] and by the early seventeenth century Norwich, helped by a fertile hinterland and the foldcourse method of sheep farming, had become the centre of England's new drapery trade. Indeed, some new types of cloth even came to be known as 'Norwich stuffs'.[3]

Described by Sir John Harington[†] as 'another Utopia',[4] Norwich was incorporated under Henry II, when it was also granted county status.[5] A charter of 1417 established the form for civic elections and declared that the city was to be governed by a mayor, two sheriffs, 24 aldermen and 60 common councillors.[6] The mayor was chosen annually by the aldermen from two of their number nominated by the commonalty. The latter enjoyed unique powers in English city government, as they also nominated the aldermen and both nominated and elected the common councillors and one of the sheriffs. The city was divided into four great wards, each of which were subdivided into three lesser wards. The sub-wards elected aldermen for life, while the great wards chose the common council each year, based upon a proportional system which reflected the demographic situation of early fifteenth century Norwich.[7] Various town officials, such as the recorder, town clerk, steward, and legal officers on retainer, were chosen at meetings of the mayor, sheriffs, aldermen and councillors. Elections to the mayoralty occurred in the Guildhall on May Day. Problems in 1618 arose when the citizens nominated two junior aldermen, Richard Rosse* and Henry Fawcett.[8] Fawcett was senior to Rosse, but the aldermen ignored custom and picked Rosse instead. The following year three sub-wards elected aldermen who were young and inexperienced.[9] The city was subsequently rebuked by the king for elevating men above their status, and was ordered to adopt the practice followed in London, where the senior alderman was automatically elected as mayor.[10] However, there was some resistance to this demand, and the chief justice of the Common Pleas, Sir Henry Montagu*, and two of Norfolk circuit judges were ordered to investigate.[11] Their solution effectively rode roughshod over the town's charter, for they abolished elections entirely and ordered that from henceforth nominations could only be of 'two of the ancientest aldermen in rank as have been sheriffs of the said city and have not before that time borne the office of mayoralty'.[12] There were further disturbances in 1627, when the freemen attempted to elect John Kettle as sheriff, 'a basketmaker, a man so unworthy of a place of magistracy [and] so rude and uncivil as he is not fit for common society, a man so addicted to railing and drunkenness as he hath been bound to his good behaviour, and yet never reformed'.[13]

The wealth of the city was reflected in the grandeur of the houses and fortunes of its leading merchants. According to Sir Thomas Wilson*, the aldermen were 'esteemed to be worth £20,000 apiece, some much more'.[14] However, despite the generosity of the mayor's salary (£100 p.a.), the corporation enjoyed only a modest income. This stood at £419 in 1605, and £750 in 1622.[15] By comparison, King's Lynn, a town with one quarter of the population of Norwich, generated an annual income of over £1,000.[16] Norwich often protested its 'poverty', and in 1615 the city was rebuked by the 1st earl of Suffolk for its meagre contribution towards the Benevolence.[17] On the other hand, the collectors' accounts demonstrate that the city eventually paid £488, more than any other city apart from London.[18] Norwich contributed a further £270 towards the Palatine Benevolence in 1620,[19] but throughout the 1620s and 1630s it continually complained of its inability to raise money for the Crown, pleading the high charge to which it was continually put in maintaining and repairing Yarmouth haven.[20] In 1626 Norwich flatly refused to provide two warships for the Navy,[21] and in the following year asserted that the Forced Loan could not be collected unless the earlier requirement for ships was lifted.[22] As only a third of the money for the ships was collected, and almost nothing of the Loan, two writs of *quo warranto* were brought against the mayor, but in 1629 the courts ruled in Norwich's favour.[23] Relations between the government and Norwich deteriorated even further in late 1627, when 200 Irish soldiers were billeted there. By March 1628, the corporation, fed up with their behaviour, ordered them to be disarmed and only given weapons during exercises.[24] This order was later repealed, but the corporation feared that more 'outrages and disorders' would ensue.[25] The city fell further out of favour in October 1629, when the 3rd earl of Pembroke complained that the herring pies sent as the city's annual fee-farm rent were baked in a thin pastry. Many were also broken on arrival, too few had been sent and many contained only four herrings instead of five![26]

During the sixteenth century Norwich was a nonconformist stronghold.[27] Its two most important lectureships were at St. Andrew's, where the advowson was held by the corporation.[28] In 1619 the anti-Calvinist, Samuel Harsnett, became bishop of Norwich and attempted to suppress the lectureships. Instead, he required the population to attend sermons at the cathedral.[29] In response, a petition was presented to Parliament in 1624 in the name of the 'citizens of Norwich'. Advocated in the Commons by Sir Edward Coke, the petition was a clear attack on Harsnett's suspected Arminianism.[30] The Commons requested a joint conference, and after the meeting Archbishop Abbot summed up the charges against Harsnett to the Lords.[31] The matter was referred to the High Commission,[32] but no further action seems to have been taken and preaching did not increase in Norwich until after Harsnett was translated to York in 1629.[33]

The attack on Harsnett was not the only business pursued by Norwich in Parliament. An Act of 1610 for new draperies or 'Norwich stuffs', sought to remedy the embezzlement of wool and yarn, but had little effect in East Anglia, so that in 1616 Norwich's worsted weavers complained to the Privy Council about the quality of wool and yarn they received. The weavers claimed that they were forced to falsify the cloth and 'afterwards to sell the same privately, unsealed, to the prejudice of His Majesty in the duties and subsidies due for the same stuffs'.[34] Another petition by the weavers in 1618 led to an investigation by Sir Edward Coke and Sir Julius Caesar*.[35] The problem remained, however, and in 1621 the corporation of Norwich resolved to introduce a bill in Parliament to regulate the trade:

> One inconvenience is that the Norw[i]ch commodities are made in Canterbury [and] other places of less length and breadth whereby they undersell the city. Another inconvenience is the yarn-men who do buy up false wares [and] carry them into the country for sale. It is moved that the weavers of the city and country and the merchants may meet [and] confer of some courses to be taken for a law to be sued for at the Parliament for reforma[ti]on of abuses.[36]

However, the matter then seems to have lapsed until 1628, when Coke introduced a bill 'for the sealing and searching of divers new stuffs called new draperies' (21 March). This received a second reading and was committed (1 Apr.), but was never reported.[37]

In 1624 the weavers and merchants, probably reluctant to involve the corporation after it failed to take action in 1621, drafted their own regulatory bill based upon a mid-fifteenth century statute, which controlled the worsted industry in Norwich. This sought to reorganize the Company of Norfolk Worsted Weavers and place the manufacture of all new draperies under their aegis.[38] The corporation wrote to their Members at Westminster informing them that the bill had been exhibited and enclosing a copy of the measure.[39] The bill received only one reading, however, and did not appear again in the Commons.[40]

The Norwich weavers were themselves the subject of a hostile bill introduced by the Norfolk woolgrowers. The woolgrowers complained that foreign (non-Norfolk) wool was unsuitable for the manufacture of worsted, and that it was the use of such wool which partly accounted for the deceits complained of by the weavers. They also noted that, as Norfolk woolgrowers, they were prohibited by statute from selling their wool outside the county. The bill therefore sought to forbid the Norwich weavers from using any foreign wool.[41] However, in the anti-monopolistic atmosphere of 1624, the weavers had little to fear, and at the second reading in the Commons (23 Apr.) the bill was 'wholly [and] unmindfully rejected and cast out of the House as a monopoly'.[42]

The Norwich Company of Dornicks Weavers laid a bill before the Commons in 1610. The measure, which sought to incorporate the Company, was sponsored by the Norwich Member (Sir) John Pettus, but failed to proceed even to a first reading.[43] The Company tried once more in 1621, when the bill received one reading, and again in 1624, when the measure was committed.[44] Although the committee included both Norwich Members, the bill subsequently failed to return to the Commons. The reason for the bill's repeated failure to progress is unclear, but the Norwich Dornick Weavers had never exceeded more than 20 members, and there must be some question as to whether a small provincial company needed to be incorporated by Parliament to remedy the problems in their trade.[45] It may also be significant that the bill, which was termed a private measure by John Pym*, does not seem to have received active backing from the Norwich corporation.[46]

The Norwich Members, often incorrectly referred to in the Commons Journal as the 'knights and burgesses of Norwich', were appointed to three bill committees in 1604, all of which reflected the city's interests.[47] The True Making of Hats and Felts (31 Mar.) concerned a type of cloth manufacture practised in Norwich, while Edward Downes's land sales' measure (2 May) dealt with lands in which the corporation had an interest.[48] The third bill sought to establish that children born in England to foreign parents were denizens and not citizens. This was a matter of interest to Norwich because of its large stranger population, although the bill was probably aimed at Scots rather than foreign artisans.[49] In 1605-6, ministers in Norwich petitioned Parliament to increase their stipend, and then introduced a bill to that end, which rated every rented house, shop and stall at 2s. per pound.[50] One of the city's Members, John Pettus, was thoroughly alarmed, and wrote to the mayor on 6 Mar. 1606 that 'there have not been so many committees together on any private bill since the beginning of the Parliament, and the more part were for passing the bill, had not Sir Henry Hobart* [Norwich's steward] given them to understand the inconveniences that might grow thereupon'.[51] The committee agreed to draft a new bill, but Pettus intervened, and with the assistance of one of Norwich's legal counsel he persuaded the ministers to accept a city ordinance. This was subsequently drafted, but only after pressure was applied by the Privy Council.[52]

The Norwich Members' committee appointments in 1610 all concerned Norfolk bills, apart from a general measure for the suppressing of idleness (19 Apr.), which was of interest to all corporate towns.[53] They were also eligible to sit on the committees concerned with the perennial dispute between Lowestoft and Great Yarmouth (13 Mar.), fen drainage in Norfolk and Suffolk (20 Mar.), the sale of lands of Charles Waldegrave (14 June) and the bill to establish Thetford school (15 June).[54] In the Parliament of 1614, the Norwich MPs were included on measures to repair the highways (7 May) and the false dyeing of silk (24 May).[55] In 1621 the Norwich Members were not named as a group to any bill committees, but as representatives of Norfolk constituencies they could attend committees for the sale of the estate of Martin Calthorpe (17 Mar.), cart-taking (21 Apr.) and confirmation of the sale of Peyton Hall manor (27 April).[56] Three years later they were eligible to attend committees on the transportation of butter and cheese (3 Apr.), the naturalization of a Norwich grain merchant named Peter Verbeake (12 Apr.), Calthorpe's bill (14 Apr.), the repair of Colchester haven (14 Apr.) and the better making of two types of new draperies, serges and perpetuanas (20 April).[57] Indeed, as a principal clothing town, Norwich would have had an interest in all bills throughout the period which concerned wool or cloth.

Norwich had sent Members to Parliament since at least 1298. Writs for parliamentary elections were directed to the sheriffs of Norwich, and the indenture was drawn between the sheriffs and around 20 or 30 citizens. The elections followed the form in the city's *Liber Albus*:

That burgesses ... shall be chosen by the common assembly, and the persons so chosen their names shall be

presented and published in plain shire and within the city to the mayor [and] sheriffs and to the council being in the Guildhall.[58]

This meant that the Norwich electorate comprised the freemen, who numbered approximately 1,500 in the early 1620s.[59] It is not known whether any elections were contested, but given the volatility of both civic and county elections it would be surprising if only two candidates were presented at each election. Norwich usually returned its own citizens to Parliament, and eight of the nine Members who represented the city during the period were freemen – the steward William Denny being the exception. Of these nine, only three were not aldermen: Sir Henry Hobart, whom Denny succeeded as steward; Denny himself; and the comptroller of the Household, Sir John Suckling. The latter, elected in 1626, had been born in Norwich, and his father had twice represented Norwich under Elizabeth. Although he no longer resided in Norwich, Suckling claimed the freedom as his birthright on 28 Jan. 1626, just two days before the election.[60]

---

[1] J.T. Evans, *Seventeenth Cent. Norwich*, 4-5; P. Corfield, 'Provincial Capital of Norwich', *Crisis and Order in Eng. Towns* ed. P. Clark and P. Slack, 265. [2] A.H. Smith, *County and Court*, 9. [3] D.C. Coleman, 'New Draperies', *EcHR*, (ser. 2), xxii, no. 3, pp. 417-29; K.J. Allison, 'Norf. Worsted Industry', *Yorks. Bull. Ec. and Social Res.*, xxii, no. 2, pp. 73-83; E. Kerridge, *Textile Manufacture*, 42-59, 66-88. [4] J. Harrington, *Nugae Antiquae* ed. T. Clark, ii. 170. [5] *Recs. Norwich* ed. W. Hudson and J.C. Tingey, i. 31-6; *CCR*, v. 421. [6] *Recs. Norwich*, i. 36-7. [7] Evans, 34. [8] Ibid. 66-73. [9] Ibid. 68. [10] SP14/108/80; Norf. RO, NCR case 16/A/15, f. 234. [11] *APC*, 1618-19, p. 484. [12] Norf. RO, NCR case 16/D/5, f. 119. [13] Evans, 75. [14] T. Wilson, 'State of Eng. 1600' ed. F.J. Fisher in *Cam. Misc. XVI* (Cam. Soc. ser. 3, lii), 20. [15] Norf. RO, NCR Press E, case 18/A (1603-25), ff. 40-7v, 346-55v. [16] Norf. RO (King's Lynn), KL/C39/97-101. [17] F. Blomefield, *Hist. Norf.* iii. 366. [18] E351/1950. [19] Norf. RO, NCR case 16/A/15, f. 319. [20] Ibid. NCR case 16/D/5, ff. 138, 144v, 145, 214. [21] Ibid. NCR case 16/A/16, f. 63; case 16/D/5, ff. 225v, 228; SP16/24/44; 16/35/1; 16/51/1; *APC*, 1625-6, pp. 150-1. [22] SP16/61/83. [23] *VCH Norf.* ii. 505-6; Blomefield, iii. 374. [24] Norf. RO, case 16/D/5, f. 229v. [25] Ibid. f. 238v. [26] Blomefield, iii. 375-6. [27] P. Collinson, *Eliz. Puritan Movement*, 172, 174, 176, 188. [28] Evans, 85. [29] N. Tyacke, *Anti-Calvinists*, 164-5. [30] *CJ*, i. 699b; *LJ*, iii. 388. [31] *CJ*, i. 699b, 705a. [32] *LJ*, iii. 388-90. [33] Evans, 86-7. [34] 7 Jas. I c. 7; *APC*, 1616-17, p. 35. [35] *APC*, 1616-17, pp. 252-3; 1618-19, p. 316. [36] Norf. RO, NCR case 16/A/15, f. 327. [37] *CD 1628*, ii. 42, 47, 227, 510. [38] Kyle, thesis, 117; HLRO, main pprs. 26 Apr. 1624. [39] Norf. RO, NCR case 16/A/15, f. 526v. [40] *CJ*, i. 775a. [41] Kyle, 117; HLRO, main pprs. 17 Apr. 1624. [42] 'D'Ewes 1624', f. 111v; *CJ*, i. 689a. [43] *CJ*, i. 424b. [44] Ibid. 619b, 768a, 769b. [45] Kyle, 119-20. [46] 'Pym 1624', i. f. 69. [47] Under the terms of the town's charter, they were 'knights of the shire for Norwich'. [48] *CJ*, i. 160b, 195a. [49] Ibid. 197b. [50] Bodl. Tanner 290, f. 102; *CJ*, i. 261b, 267b; M. Wren, *Parentilia*, 112; K. Sharpe, *Personal Rule*, 315. [51] Blomefield, iii. 361. [52] Ibid. 361-2. [53] *CJ*, i. 419a. [54] Ibid. 410a, 413a, 438b, 440a. [55] *Procs. 1614 (Commons)*, 170, 330. [56] *CJ*, i. 559b, 585b, 593b. [57] Ibid. 753a, 757a, 762b, 766a, 766b, 769a, 771b. [58] Norf. RO, *Liber Albus*, unfol. [59] Evans, 10-11. [60] Blomefield, iii. 373.

C.R.K.

THETFORD

Right of election: in the corporation

Number of voters: 31

		1st seat	2nd seat
5 Mar. 1604	SIR BASSINGBOURNE GAWDY	24	
	SIR WILLIAM PADDY	2	13
	Edward Clere	1	4
	Sir Henry Warner		4
	Mr. Whettle		3

29 Oct. 1606[1] SIR WILLIAM TWYSDEN *vice* Gawdy, deceased

		1st seat	2nd seat
11 Mar. 1614[2]	SIR WILLIAM TWYSDEN	24	
	FRAMLINGHAM GAWDY		16
	Sir William Barwicke		7
	Rice Gwyn*, recorder		1

11 Dec. 1620[3] SIR THOMAS HOLLAND
FRAMLINGHAM GAWDY

		1st seat	2nd seat
21 Jan. 1624	FRAMLINGHAM GAWDY	23	1
	DRU DRURY	2	17
	Sir Charles Le Gros*	3	11
	Sir Robert Cotton, (bt.)		1

		1st seat	2nd seat
25 Apr. 1625[4]	SIR ROBERT COTTON, (bt.)	28	
	FRAMLINGHAM GAWDY		15
	Sir Charles Le Gros*		13

		1st seat	2nd seat
17 Jan. 1626	SIR JOHN HOBART II	21	
	FRAMLINGHAM GAWDY		21

c. Feb. 1626[5] NATHANIEL HOBART *vice* Hobart, chose to sit for Brackley

		1st seat	2nd seat
20 Feb. 1628	(SIR) HENRY SPILLER	26	
	EDMUND MOUNDEFORD		23
	Sir Charles Gawdy		3

24 Mar. 1628[6] SIR HENRY VANE *vice* Spiller, chose to sit for Middlesex

Situated at the confluence of the rivers Thet and Little Ouse, and straddling the Norfolk/Suffolk border, Thetford existed as a market town before Roman times, when it was known as Sitomagus. During the early Middle Ages it flourished, but by the late sixteenth century, having ceased to be an important staging post, it was chronically poor and 'ruinated', its income barely exceeding £60 p.a.[7] It nevertheless boasted a royal hunting lodge, and continued to enjoy the right to stage the assizes, much to the annoyance of Norwich and many of the Norfolk gentry. However, the assizes placed a heavy strain on the borough's slender resources,[8] while James I sold the hunting lodge.[9] Thetford's fortunes were not helped by a serious fire in 1616, nor by the cancellation of its annual horse races in 1620, following a riot in which 'divers persons have been hurt and some killed'.[10]

A borough by prescription, Thetford was not incorporated until 1573, when its government was placed in the hands of a mayor, ten burgesses and 20 commoners, all of whom were constituted as the voters in parliamentary elections. The 1573 charter, which was probably obtained through the influence of the Howards, also provided for the appointment of a recorder for life.[11] During the sixteenth century, electoral patronage was divided between the local gentry, the Howard family and the duchy of Lancaster, which had previously owned Thetford manor.[12] By 1604 duchy influence had waned, but that of Henry Howard, who was created earl of Northampton in March 1604, and the pre-eminent gentry family, the Gawdys, continued.

Thetford's elections were often contested. In 1604 five candidates presented themselves to the corporation. Sir Bassingborne Gawdy, who had previously represented the borough in 1593 and was the largest local landowner, had no difficulty in achieving the first place, although his brother Philip had hoped to stand in his stead or to use his influence with Sir Nicholas Bacon† to secure him a place at Eye, in Suffolk.[13] Sir Bassingborne had previously secured the support of the attorney-general and influential Norfolk-man, Sir Edward Coke*, as Philip informed him: 'I was with Mr. Attorney when Sir Henry Warner† did ask his counsel about Thetford for you. I heard him make this answer, that if they would choose you there would be no exception taken, nor any refusal made'.[14] Warner, a Suffolk gentleman who had represented the borough in 1601, also stood but achieved fourth place with only four votes. The junior burgess was Sir William Paddy, physician to both King James and the borough's patron Henry Howard. Paddy, with 15 votes, easily defeated his closest rival, Edward Clere, whose father had represented the town in 1558 and 1563. The fifth candidate, one Mr. Whettle, gained the support of four commoners only.[15]

The death of Gawdy on 17 May 1606 necessitated a by-election, at which the successful, and perhaps sole candidate, was Sir William Twysden. A Kentishman, learned in theology, astronomy and mathematics, Twysden had long been a client of the earl of Northampton. On 15 July 1606 the corporation agreed, 'upon my lord of Northampton's letters, then showed and read, [that] his lordship should have the nomination of a burgess for the Parliament'.[16] Towards the end of October, with the new parliamentary session close at hand, the 17 corporation members present unanimously elected Twysden.[17] Twysden was also returned in 1614, when he again secured all the available votes. The second place was taken by Framlingham Gawdy, who received the support of 13 of the 16 burgesses present but only three of the ten commoners. Sir William Barwicke, a minor Suffolk gentleman who lived near the town, managed five votes from the commoners but just two from the senior corporation officials. The recorder, Rice Gwyn, gained a solitary vote and was returned instead for Norwich.[18]

Following Northampton's death the patronage of the borough was assumed by his great-nephew, the earl of Arundel. The 1620 election, held on 11 Dec. but dated three days later on the return, saw no need for a poll as Arundel's client, Sir Thomas Holland, and Framlingham Gawdy were elected unopposed.[19] However, the 1624 election witnessed a return to the usual rivalry for seats, although Gawdy, who stood for the first place, met little opposition, receiving 23 of the 30 available votes. The second seat went to an Arundel client, Dru Drury, who defeated his nearest rival, Sir Charles Le Gros* of Crostwight, Norfolk, by 17 votes to 11. The last candidate was Sir Robert Cotton*, but though a Howard client he seems not to have enjoyed Arundel's support on this occasion, as he received only one vote.[20]

When a new Parliament was summoned in 1625, Holland wrote to Gawdy on 9 Apr. informing him that Arundel was committed to backing Cotton for the first seat at Thetford, and therefore requesting that Gawdy should allow the second seat to go to Le Gros.[21] Cotton was indeed informed by the corporation that he had been chosen for the first place 'with not one voice against him ... upon the commendation of the Right Honourable the earl of Arundel'.[22] However, the junior seat was again contested, with Gawdy emerging the narrow victor over Le Gros, who thereafter switched his electoral attention to Orford, in Suffolk.[23] In 1626 the only candidates to stand for election were Framlingham Gawdy and another local gentleman, Sir John Hobart II. However, Hobart was also returned for Brackley, and his younger brother, Nathaniel, was subsequently elected in his stead.[24]

In 1628 Framlingham Gawdy was sheriff of Norfolk and thus ineligible for election. His brother, Sir Charles Gawdy, seeing an opportunity to escape his creditors, therefore wrote to him for his help in gaining a seat, professing that he had 'a great desire' to be a Member of the Commons: 'I know nobody that can make better means to Thetford than yourself'.[25] As Framlingham did not stir himself, he wrote again from London:

> I am bold once more to solicit you that you would be pleased to go instantly about it yourself in person or else it will be gone, for Dru Drury* was here in this town and do[es] purpose to send to Thetford tomorrow, not for himself but for a friend. And I am sure you have as much interest as he and therefore I beseech you make no delays but go about the business with all possible speed. The day is certain for the Parliament, 17 March. There is such a stir for places that they are all gone or promised by this time.[26]

However, Framlingham made no effort to assist his brother, and instead probably supported his close friend, Edmund Moundeford, who defeated Sir Charles by 23 votes to three.[27] At Arundel's request the first seat went to Sir Henry Spiller, who subsequently chose to sit for Middlesex. He was replaced by Sir Henry Vane, another Arundel client.[28]

Only one matter of parliamentary business directly concerned Thetford in this period. In 1567 Sir Richard Fulmerston†, a native of Thetford, left lands in Croxton valued at £35 p.a. to the town for the benefit of the grammar school, to be administered by his son-in-law and heir, (Sir) Edward Clere†. By the turn of the seventeenth century, however, the Croxton lands generated £100 in rent, but Clere continued to pay only the £35 mentioned in the will. In 1606 a bill concerning the school was submitted to the Commons, presumably by Clere, as the corporation's Hall Books fail to mention any payment for drafting it or for overseeing its progress through Parliament. This may explain why Clere's son stood at Thetford in 1604, and also why he suffered such a resounding defeat at the poll. In March 1606 the younger Clere pleaded with the earl of Salisbury (Robert Cecil†), for his release from prison in order to 'attend his causes in Parliament'.[29] However, a committee mainly comprised of Norfolk men, including the Thetford Members Sir Bassingborne Gawdy and Sir William Paddy, recommended that the bill was 'fit to sleep'.[30] The situation was reversed in 1610 when Thetford corporation submitted its own bill to Parliament. By this time Sir Edward Clere was dead and his son, Edward, was in prison accused of sheltering a seminary priest.[31] It was entered in the Lords, where the town's patron the earl of Northampton spoke in favour of its committal. Clere was allowed to be present at the committee meeting, as a note from the clerk of Parliaments, Robert Bowyer*, requested that his prison-keeper have him escorted to the Painted Chamber to answer questions.[32] The matter was referred by the Lords' committee to three of their legal assistants, and after hearing the case for two days at Serjeants' Inn, the judges recommended that all the revenue and profits from the lands should be employed as directed in Fulmerston's will.[33] The bill gained the approval of the Lords on 30 May, and passed the Commons on 26 June with only minor opposition.[34] The passage of the bill cost Thetford dear, as the corporation agreed on 3 Mar. that the town should meet all the expenses. One of the burgesses, Robert Abraham, was dispatched to London with £3 'about the Parliament business', while the town counsel and schoolmaster William Jenkinson was paid £6 15s. 6d. for his efforts in ensuring the success of the enterprise.[35]

[1] Norf. RO, T/C1/3, p. 16. [2] Ibid. 38. [3] Ibid. 72. [4] Ibid. T/C1/4, p. 17. [5] Ibid. 28. [6] Ibid. 55. [7] F. Blomefield, *Hist. Thetford*, 2, 61; F. Blomefield, *Hist. Norf.* 42-3; Norf. RO, T/C1/3, p. 40. [8] Norf. RO, T/C1/3, p. 34; T/C1/4, p. 62. [9] A.L. Hunt, *Capital Ancient Kingdom of East Anglia*, 148. [10] *APC*, 1619-20, p. 180. [11] Norf. RO, T/C1/6, ff. 22v-24. [12] Norf. RO, T/NS1/33; G. Burrell, *Acct. Gifts and Legacies to Thetford*, 64-5. [13] Eg. 2804, f. 176. [14] Ibid. f. 177. [15] Norf. RO, T/C1/3, pp. 2-3. [16] Ibid. 14. [17] Ibid. 16. [18] Ibid. 38. W. Blomefield, *Norf.* iii. 71. [19] Norf. RO, T/C1/3, p. 72. [20] Ibid. T/C1/4, p. 1. [21] Norf. RO, MC 2208/1, 938X8. [22] Cott. Julius C.III, f. 284. [23] Norf. RO, T/C1/4, p. 17. [24] Ibid. 27-8. [25] *CD 1628*, vi. 167-8. [26] Ibid. 168; Eg. 2715, ff. 240, 366. [27] Norf. RO, T/C1/4, pp. 54-5. [28] *Procs. 1628*, vi. 168. [29] SP14/19/107; *HMC Hatfield*, xviii. 386-7. [30] *CJ*, i. 258a, 259a, 278a. [31] *HMC Hatfield*, xvii. 531-2. [32] HLRO, main pprs. 22 Mar. 1610. [33] Coke, *8th Rep.* Thetford sch. case (1610); 1 Equity Case Abridged 100 in, *Eng. Rep.* 21, pp. 909-10. [34] *LJ*, ii. 598, 600, 603, 604; *CJ*, i. 435b, 438b, 440a, 442a, 443a, 443b. [35] Norf. RO, T/C1/3, pp. 29, 30.

C.R.K.

NORTHAMPTONSHIRE

Number of voters: unknown

8 Mar. 1604	SIR EDWARD MONTAGU
	SIR VALENTINE KNIGHTLEY
c.Apr. 1614	SIR EDWARD MONTAGU
	SIR WILLIAM TATE
23 Nov. 1620	(SIR) WILLIAM SPENCER
	SIR EDWARD MONTAGU
22 Nov. 1621	RICHARD KNIGHTLEY *vice* Montagu, called to the Upper House
15 Jan. 1624	(SIR) WILLIAM SPENCER
	RICHARD KNIGHTLEY
c.Apr. 1625	(SIR) WILLIAM SPENCER
	RICHARD KNIGHTLEY
12 Jan. 1626	(SIR) WILLIAM SPENCER
	SIR JOHN PICKERING
	Sir Lewis Watson, bt.*
6 Mar. 1628	RICHARD KNIGHTLEY
	FRANCIS NICOLLS

Northamptonshire, situated according to Camden 'in the very middle, and heart, as it were, of England', was divided by the River Nene into eastern and western divisions. To the east lay the soke of Peterborough, much of it fenland, and the royal forest of Rockingham; to the west rich farming country 'beset with sheep'.[1] Traditionally one Member was elected from each division, although exceptions occurred.[2] The eastern division was dominated during Elizabeth's reign by Sir Walter Mildmay[†], chancellor of the Exchequer, and the Cecils; in the west the Knightleys of Fawlsey were the most influential family. However, a new pattern emerged in 1604, when Sir Robert Spencer[†] of Althorp began to assert electoral influence in the west, and Sir Edward Montagu, keeper of Rockingham forest, was able to revive an interest formerly exercised by his ancestors in the east. Lord Mordaunt, a suspected Catholic, may have hoped that he too could establish a claim to patronage, but he failed to impress the predominantly puritan gentry.[3] The 1st earl of Exeter (Sir Thomas Cecil[†]), lord lieutenant of the county, is conspicuous by his absence as an electoral patron in the early Stuart period, perhaps because he was content to allow Montagu a dominant role. Generally, Spencer and Montagu worked well together with the aim of avoiding contests. Elections were held at Northampton, and during the 1620s some candidates openly canvassed the townsmen. The evidence suggests that candidates were endorsed at gentry meetings, at least at the beginning of the period, thus avoiding the expense and possible disorder of a poll.

Shortly after James's accession an election was rumoured to be imminent, whereupon Spencer and Montagu decided to stand together. On 18 Apr. 1603 Montagu warned Spencer that Lord Mordaunt desired a seat for Sir Anthony Mildmay[†], but in fact he need not have worried, as he and Spencer were nevertheless endorsed at a gentry meeting on the following day.[4] Moreover, the bishop of Peterborough promised them his support.[5] Thereafter neither Mordaunt nor Mildmay tried to intervene in county elections again. The rumour of an election turned out to be premature, as writs were not dispatched until January 1604, by which time Spencer had been raised to the peerage. Spencer's neighbour Sir Richard Knightley[†] therefore wrote to Montagu to propose his son Sir Valentine for the junior seat. Montagu remained non-committal until he was sure of Lord Spencer's approval, so the younger Knightley took the precaution of getting himself elected at Dunwich, Suffolk.[6] This proved unnecessary, however, as Spencer wrote to Montagu on 6 Feb. assuring him that Knightley had his 'absolute voices and furtherance', and advising them to 'raise as small numbers as may be for your elections, perceiving none to oppose you'.[7]

After they were returned, Montagu and Sir Valentine Knightley were charged by the freeholders to put the county's grievances before Parliament, which Montagu did on the first day of business, 23 Mar. 1604.[8] The main complaints were the oppression of the commissaries' courts, the plight of deprived or suspended ministers, and depopulation caused by enclosures. A committee of grievances was appointed, but little progress was achieved before the end of the first session.[9] During the prorogation, in February 1605, the two Members presented the king with a petition signed by dozens of Northamptonshire gentlemen, on behalf of deprived ministers.[10] This alarmed and angered James, and the petition was denounced by Bishop Ussher as 'the most ill-advised and rash act' by the puritans in 20 years. Montagu and Knightley were both sent home in disgrace and dismissed from county office. In 1607 agrarian grievances erupted in enclosure riots across the Midlands and, as a largely pastoral county, Northamptonshire was particularly badly hit. Montagu, who had by this time been restored to the magistracy, helped to restore order and sat on the subsequent commission to inquire into illegal enclosures.[11]

Montagu was informed on 8 Feb. 1614 by his brother Sir Charles Montagu* that a Parliament would be summoned shortly.[12] At the general election Montagu was returned again, together with Sir William Tate who, as sheriff, had been ineligible in 1604. Tate was among those who had signed the petition for the deprived ministers; his residence just outside Northampton gave him a great advantage in case of a poll, although on this occasion there was no contest, and as a westerner he balanced Montagu. In July 1620 a group of Northamptonshire gentlemen including Montagu petitioned the king again concerning ecclesiastical grievances, especially the deprivation of nonconformist preachers, and the leniency being shown towards recusants; unsurprisingly this incurred James's 'heavy displeasure', but the petitioners refused to accept the Privy Council's attempts to dilute their protests.[13] At the general election later that year Spencer's heir, (Sir) William was returned as the senior Member, with Montagu taking second place. During the summer recess Montagu was elevated to the peerage, and at the ensuing by-election Knightley's nephew and heir, Richard, was returned, even though this broke the convention whereby the eastern and western sides of the shire shared the county's representation.

Before the next election Lords Montagu and Spencer seem to have agreed that the same knights would be re-elected to the 1624 Parliament. However, the plan went awry when Montagu's kinsman and neighbour Sir Lewis Watson*, a client of the royal favourite, the duke of Buckingham, expressed a desire to sit. Montagu wrote to Lord Spencer proposing that Watson might fulfil 'the ancient course observed to have a knight on each side for the better service of the country, without any opposition'. Assuming that Sir William Spencer would take the senior seat, he asked Lord Spencer to 'prevail so much with my cousin Knightley ... that having had the honour already of it, he would now give way to Sir Lewis Watson, and so the business may be carried fairly without offence'.[14] However, Spencer responded sharply on 7 Jan. that Knightley was 'the far the fitter man for that place than the other', and warned that 'the opposition [to Watson] will be great, for we on this part will not sit down, except you can force us to lie down'. He termed Montagu's assertion that each side of the shire should choose a Member 'your new-erected custom', pointing out earlier instances when it had not been observed. Nevertheless his real objection seems to have been to Watson personally, whom he disparaged as 'the unfittest of any man on that part of the shire', somewhat unfairly since Watson's family had been seated at Rockingham for two generations. Watson seems to have also secured the backing of Sir Francis Fane*, who had succeeded to the Mildmay estate and interest. Normally Fane was at odds with Montagu over the forest of Rockingham, and Spencer sarcastically hoped that their 'close combining' over the election might reconcile them.[15] In the event Watson found a seat elsewhere, and Spencer and Knightley were returned without a contest.

The same Members were re-elected in 1625. It is not known whether Montagu, who was suffering from ill health, attempted to intervene; he was probably unwilling to court another rebuff from Spencer. He may also have been reluctant to do anything that might weaken the opposition to Fane, now earl of Westmorland who, as *custos rotulorum*, had stirred up great hostility by attempting to move the quarter sessions from Northampton to Kettering.[16] Any advantage such a move might have in strengthening the influence of the eastern part of the shire was outweighed in Montagu's mind by the prestige it would give to his hated rival, and in conjunction with the Spencers and Knightley, he took the lead in opposing it. Despite their efforts, in December 1625 Westmorland managed to obtained the Privy Council's authorization to hold the sessions at Kettering.[17]

It was against this background of east-west rivalry and conflicting interests that the election to the second Caroline Parliament took place. Knightley had been pricked as sheriff and was therefore ruled out. On 21 Dec. Montagu wrote to Lord Spencer, asking him to endorse Watson's candidature and expressing the hope that the election might be 'carried in love and with small charge, which otherwise may breed new distractions'.[18] On the following day Sir William Spencer informed Montagu that 'I intend not to stir or stand to be knight of the shire if there shall be a Parliament. I have had labour and travail enough in that kind'. Although he expressed no objection to Watson, he added that 'I could wish that Sir John Pickering might not be forgot, who, I am sure, is equivalent in merit to the other'.[19] Pickering, the son-in-law of Sir Erasmus Dryden*, lived at Titchmarsh on the eastern border of the county, and despite having no parliamentary background had been mentioned as a possible alternative to Watson in 1624. Now keen to stand, on 27 Dec. he wrote to Montagu, assuming that he would be elected unopposed with Spencer and Montagu's blessing, to request that Montagu take care to 'conceal the conclusion your lordships have made, lest the freeholders, whose birthright it is to elect, should take it ill, conceiving themselves to be concluded thereby'.[20] This seems to have irritated Montagu, who noted that the letter contained 'neither thanks for my goodwill proffered, nor request for anything'.[21] Furthermore, he may have had misgivings about the pairing of Watson and Pickering, since both hailed from the east of Northamptonshire, and Lord Spencer had shown such great hostility to Watson in 1624.

The attitude of Westmorland is not known, although if his manoeuvrings two years previously are anything to go by, his preference was probably for Watson; but rumours were reported by Lord Spencer that the earl wanted a seat for his son, Mildmay Fane*, Lord Burghersh.[22] On 30 Dec. 1625 Pickering informed Montagu that Sir William Spencer had apparently changed his mind and decided to stand after all. He asked if this were true, adding that he himself, 'having by your lordship's means and relation the more deeply engaged myself to stand ... I cannot go back'.[23] He wrote again on 2 Jan. 1626, denying that he had canvassed for himself alone, or that he had 'preoccupated' the town of Northampton; neither, he claimed, had he 'dissuaded any from giving voice to Sir Lewis Watson, but rather, where I might be bold, have showed what my Lord Spencer and your lordship have agreed for the peace of the county'.[24] On the same day a letter from Montagu's agent, Thomas Jenyson, reveals that he was canvassing for Watson alone.[25] Lord Spencer informed Montagu on 6 Jan. that his rival Westmorland was confident of winning the junior seat for his son, with Watson as his senior colleague. He therefore proposed to 'let Sir John Pickering have the first place, then we are all secured that Burghersh cannot come in', but omitted to say who, in this case, would take the second seat.[26] Montagu may well have agreed that Fane had to be excluded at all cost; he was by this time entrenched in a Star Chamber suit against the earl, in which he had appealed to Buckingham for furtherance.[27] Nevertheless, he could not bring himself to favour Pickering above Watson. Montagu therefore wrote on 7 Jan. to the corporation of Northampton informing them that the Spencers supported the joint candidature of Watson and Pickering;[28] but two days later Jenyson reported to Montagu that 'there is extraordinary labouring, and that very seriously, for Sir William Spencer openly, and privately for him whom Mr. High Sheriff [Knightley] shall nominate [Sir John Pickering], which is kept secret'. While canvassing hard for Watson, he added, he was caught in the act by Pickering, who was outraged to find himself without the backing he had taken for granted.[29]

The corporation of Northampton informed Montagu on 10 Jan. that they could not endorse Watson, having already resolved on Sir John Pickering for the east side and Spencer for the west, whose record as MP, 'though his honoured father and himself should oppose, do much bind us to give our voices for him'.[30] Richard Spencer*, who had represented Northampton in the last three parliaments, also wrote from the town to Montagu that same day. In his letter he observed that he had failed to persuade the corporation to support Watson, claiming that there would not have been 'the least rub in this business if there had not been canvassing for voices ... for Sir Lewis Watson against Sir John Pickering, and warrants sent to constables to get voices for Sir Lewis Watson and none other'.[31] Sir William Spencer's motives can only be conjectured. If his unwillingness to stand was genuine, he must have been put up to exclude either Burghersh or Watson. As Lord Spencer is the only authority for Burghersh's candidature, it is possible the Spencers used the ruse that Burghersh intended to stand as an excuse for breaking their agreement with Montagu. It is not known whether there was a poll. In an outcome which represented a serious rebuff to Montagu, both Spencer and Pickering were elected. Writing to his brother after the event, Montagu attributed the debacle to 'the potency of the west [division] by their strength of the town of Northampton, together with their distaste about the sessions'.[32]

The Forced Loan was bitterly opposed in Northamptonshire, even by such loyalists as Watson at first.[33] Despite a visitation from privy councillors intent upon overseeing the collection of the Loan, 'a strong combination of two and twenty principal gentlemen ... drew after them near half the shire' in flat defiance of the Loan commissioners. At a meeting on 12 Jan. 1627 Knightley, supported by no less than 205 freeholders, even presented them with a petition against it. Montagu's compliance with the Loan 'lost him the love of the country', which, together with his humiliation in 1626 perhaps explain why he seems to have kept a low profile at the general election for Charles's third Parliament.[34] Sir William Spencer succeeded his father as the 2nd Baron Spencer in 1627, leaving the way open for Knightley to be returned as senior knight of the shire in the 1628 Parliament. The second seat went to a friend of Montagu, Francis Nicolls of Faxton, whose estate lay to the south-west of Kettering. Although Nicolls lacked the status usually expected of a county Member, he gained popularity as an open opponent of the Forced Loan, and was apparently returned without needing any public endorsement from Montagu.

[1] W. Camden, *Britannia* (1772), i. 402. [2] J.E. Neale, *Eliz. House of Commons*, 34. [3] Sloane 271, f. 20v. [4] *HMC Buccleuch*, iii. 73-4. [5] Ibid. 74-5. [6] *HMC Montagu*, 32; *HMC Buccleuch*, iii. 77-8. [7] *HMC Buccleuch*, i. 237. [8] Ibid. iii. 91. [9] *CJ*, i. 151a. [10] B.W. Quintrell, 'Royal Hunt and the Puritans', *JEH*, xxxi, 53-6; E.S. Cope, *Edward Montagu* (Amer. Phil. Soc. cxlii), 37-40. [11] C205/5/5; Cope, 50-52; G. Clark, 'Jacobean Northants.', *Northants. P and P*, ii. 212-16. [12] *HMC Montagu*, 90. [13] *HMC Buccleuch*, iii. 220-1. [14] Ibid. i. 259-60. [15] *HMC Montagu*, 105-6. [16] *HMC Buccleuch*, iii. 253-6. [17] Ibid. [18] Ibid. 257. [19] *HMC Montagu*, 109. [20] *HMC Buccleuch*, iii. 258-9. [21] Ibid. [22] J.K. Gruenfelder, 'Northants. election 1626', *Northants. P and P*, iv. 159-65. [23] *HMC Buccleuch*, iii. 259. [24] Ibid. 260-1. [25] Ibid. 261. [26] *HMC Montagu*, 110. [27] *HMC Buccleuch*, iii. 264-5. [28] Ibid. i. 259. [29] Ibid. iii. 262. [30] Ibid. iii. 262-3. [31] Ibid. i. 259. [32] Ibid. iii. 263. [33] E407/123. [34] R. Cust, *Forced Loan*, 111, 117-18, 168, 225.

V.C.D.M./R.C.L.S.

BRACKLEY

Right of election: in the corporation

Number of voters: 33

6 Mar. 1604	SIR RICHARD SPENCER
	WILLIAM LISLE
c. Mar. 1614	WILLIAM SPENCER
	ARTHUR TYRINGHAM
11 Dec. 1620	EDWARD SPENCER
	SIR THOMAS WENMAN
17 Jan. 1624	EDWARD SPENCER
	SIR THOMAS WENMAN
29 Apr. 1625	SIR THOMAS WENMAN
	EDWARD SPENCER
	Sir Richard Anderson
17 Jan. 1626	SIR JOHN HOBART II
	JOHN CREWE
3 Mar. 1628	SIR THOMAS WENMAN
	JOHN CURZON

Located at the southernmost point of Northamptonshire, about half way between Banbury and Buckingham, Brackley was a small agricultural town that in its medieval heyday had served as 'a famous staple for wool'. However, by the turn of the seventeenth century, as William Camden noted, it could 'only boast how great and wealthy it once was by its ruins'.[1] The town was governed under a seigneurial charter granted in 1260 by the earl of Winchester to the mayor and around 32 'burgesses'.[2] Members were first sent to Parliament in 1547. Brackley had long suffered from absentee landlords, and throughout this period the principal manor was held in dower by the countess of Derby, with remainder to her daughter Frances.[3] She nominated her nephew Robert Spencer† (later the 1st Baron Spencer) in 1597 and her brother Sir Richard Spencer in 1604. Several months before the general election of 1604 Lady Derby wrote to the corporation on the latter's behalf. Returned in his absence as senior Member, he wrote on 8 Mar. to William Clarke, one of the corporation, promising 'to acquaint my honourable sister, the countess of Derby, how ready yourself and the rest have been to effect her letter'.[4] The second seat went to William Lisle, who owned the rectory and advowson, and resided at the Tithe House in the town until he sold it to Sir Richard Wenman* in 1606, and moved to Evenley.[5]

After the double marriage of the countess to lord chancellor Ellesmere (Thomas Egerton[†]) in 1600 and the countess's daughter to Ellesmere's son John a year later, John Egerton[†] attempted to assume control of the borough's patronage, though he had no residence in the neighbourhood. However, this brought him into conflict with both the Spencers and the Wenmans. Ahead of the next general election, on 23 Dec. 1613, Lord Spencer, who wanted a seat for his son William, thanked Clarke for a warning about an attempt to set up a rival interest by 'the blind baronet', an unidentified figure of whom no more is heard. On the arrival of the writ he politely offered to withdraw in the unlikely event of two townsmen being nominated, but undertook that his son, if elected, would 'no way be either troublesome or chargeable to you'.[6] The corporation were agreeable, and (in a letter which has not survived) informed Egerton of their choice and asked him to nominate a second candidate. Egerton replied on 13 Mar. proposing his 'loving and well esteemed friend', Arthur Tyringham, to serve with Spencer. However, he warned the corporation 'both in respect of your own and my right in that place, being as you know lord ... thereof, that you admit not any continued prescription in such election, wherein I purpose not to give way to equal any man's interest with my own'.[7]

Egerton's attempt to dominate the borough's patronage was evidently resented by the townsmen, for on 11 Jan. 1616, against the backdrop of rumours that a fresh Parliament was imminent, he was informed that they 'had given all their hands at Whitsuntide last for Sir R[ichard] W[enman's] son and are resolved to stand therein. The other, although several means are made, yet stay is made till your pleasure be known'.[8] Egerton therefore appealed to Ellesmere, who issued a writ of *quo warranto* challenging Brackley's right to send Members to Parliament.[9] To this the corporation replied that 'they hold their mayoralty and places of burgesses together with other privileges by prescription; and ever to this day have had the election and nomination of two burgesses for every Parliament'. They nevertheless capitulated under pressure and on 4 June wrote to Egerton, fulsomely apologizing for their previous disobedience to him and begging him to procure a charter for the town. They renewed their request in November, pointing out that 'some other things for which they are questioned concern your honour's right', and adding that 'howbeit the body of the said corporation is very poor, yet it is not doubted but that there will be raised such contribution for part of the charge therein amongst them as their estate may afford'.[10]

No charter was forthcoming, and for the election of 1620 Egerton (now earl of Bridgewater) nominated

Spencer's brother Edward. He was returned 'by general assent', with the name of Sir Thomas Wenman inserted in the indenture for the second seat, possibly over an erasure. Brackley's troubled relations with Bridgewater continued, and on 29 Apr. 1621 the mayor and nine other 'burgesses' wrote to the earl again appealing for help with the 'rem[ed]ying of our charter'. The signatories, 'being desirous ever to be reputed, or rather actually to be, your lordship's obedient servants and tenants' promised to contribute £50 towards the charter and begged Bridgewater to make up the rest of the charge, otherwise they would 'unwillingly be enforced to disclaim our corporation'.[11] However, nothing came of their plea. Spencer and Wenman were re-elected in 1624.

In 1625 Bridgewater nominated Spencer and Sir Richard Anderson, his brother-in-law, and on 26 Apr. was confidently informed by a member of the corporation, George Smalman, that 'there will be no opposition ... only two or three desire to be freed of their promises, which upon your lordship's first letter they had passed, as Mr. Clarke and Mr. Mayor'.[12] He added that Thomas Loveday, the previous mayor, and his brother George were trying to assess Bridgewater's property for church and poor rate. He had evidently reckoned without a challenge from another candidate, and in the event Wenman defeated Anderson for the first place, while Spencer was re-elected in second.

In 1626 Bridgewater nominated his son-in-law, Sir John Hobart II, while the second seat was taken by John Crewe, son of the former Speaker Thomas Crewe, whose estate was situated two miles away at Steane. Hobart does not seem to have been entirely confident of his election, since he also had himself returned for Thetford. Wenman was again returned for Brackley in 1628, but the choice of Crewe's brother-in-law, John Curzon, for the second seat perhaps signals the withdrawal of, or resistance to, Bridgewater's influence. It is notable that four of the nine Members elected in the period (Sir Richard Spencer, Tyringham, Crewe and Curzon) matriculated at Magdalen College, Oxford, an institution connected with Brackley's free school and endowed by its founder with considerable property in the town.[13] In 1629 Bridgewater had to defend his seignorial rights against Magdalen; but William Noye* assured him that the college had no case that would stand up in court.[14] There is no evidence that Brackley paid wages to any of its representatives, or pursued legislation in any of the parliaments of the period.

[1] Baker, *Northants*. i. 567, 573-4. [2] *Northants. P and P*, iii. 3. [3] Ibid. 564. [4] Northants. RO, E(B) 566, (Sir Richard Spencer to Clarke, 8 Mar. 1604). [5] Harl. 158, f. 167; Add. 38139, f. 94; Baker, *Northants*. i. 574. [6] Northants. RO, E(B) 572-3 (Lord Spencer to Clarke, 23 Dec.

1613, 28 Feb. 1614). [7] Northants. RO, E(B) 574 (Egerton to Brackley corp. 13 Mar. 1614). [8] Northants. RO, E(B) 576 (Cartwright to Sir John Egerton, 11 Jan. 1616). For the rumours that a Parliament would soon meet, see A. Thrush, 'The Personal Rule of Jas. I, 1611–20', *Pols. Religion and Popularity* ed. T. Cogswell, R. Cust and P. Lake, 91–2. [9] Northants. RO, E(B) 510, 512-14 (Brackley corp. to Egerton, 4 June 1616). [10] Northants. RO, E(B) 515 (Brackley corp. to Egerton, 16 Nov. 1616). [11] Northants. RO, E(B) 516 (mayor of Brackley to Bridgewater, 29 Apr. 1621). [12] Northants. RO, E(B) 585 (Smalman to Bridgewater, 26 Apr. 1625). [13] Baker, *Northants.* i. 581. [14] Northants. RO, E(B) 517, 518, 587 (Noye to Bridgewater, 29 Oct. 1629; Kent to Bridgewater, 11 Dec. 1629).

V.C.D.M./R.C.L.S.

HIGHAM FERRERS

Right of election: in the corporation

Number of voters: 21

c. Mar. 1604	SIR GODDARD PEMBERTON
c. Mar. 1614	ROWLAND ST. JOHN
20 Nov. 1620	SIR CHARLES MONTAGU
15 Jan. 1624	SIR CHARLES MONTAGU
3 May 1625	SIR CHARLES MONTAGU
c. Jan. 1626	SIR THOMAS DACRES
14 Feb. 1626	SIR GEORGE SONDES *vice* Dacres, chose to sit for Hertfordshire
13 Feb. 1628	SIR GEORGE SONDES

A small market town on the east bank of the River Nene, Higham Ferrers received a charter in 1556 which vested government of the town in a corporation consisting of a mayor, seven aldermen and 13 'capital burgesses'; it also conferred upon the borough the right to send one Member to Parliament.[1] Before 1640 the franchise rested exclusively with the corporation.[2] The borough was technically part of the duchy of Lancaster, but the duchy showed no interest in its elections during the early Stuart period. Patronage was shared between various local gentry interests, but from 1620 was dominated by the Montagu family of Boughton.

Sir Goddard Pemberton, whose family owned the nearby estate of Rushden, was a kinsman by marriage of the steward of the manor of Higham Ferrers, Sir John Stanhope I*. Following his election to James's first Parliament, Pemberton may have helped the borough to obtain a new charter, which passed the seal on 6 July 1604.[3] This authorized the corporation to hold two weekly markets and four annual fairs, but these additional privileges seem to have done little to increase either the town's population or its prosperity. Higham Ferrers was represented in the Addled Parliament by Rowland St. John, who lived eight miles away at Bletsoe, in Bedfordshire.

In the next three elections the Northamptonshire magnate, Sir Edward Montagu*, secured the return of his brother and London agent, Sir Charles, 'by common assent and consent'. Following the latter's death, in 1626 Lord Montagu (as Sir Edward had now become) requested the seat for his nephew, Sir George Sondes, but he failed to give the corporation sufficient notice.[4] Consequently, Sir Thomas Dacres, a Hertfordshire gentleman whose family had owned the college of Higham Ferrers and its appurtenances since 1543, was elected with the support of the corporation.[5] However, Dacres subsequently chose to sit for Hertfordshire, and was replaced by Sondes, who was re-elected in 1628.

[1] *VCH Northants.* iii. 269-71. [2] Northants. RO, FH3467; A.N. Groome, 'Higham Ferrers Election in 1640', *Northants. P and P* (1958), pp. 243-51. [3] *CSP Dom.* 1603-10, p. 129. [4] V. Hodges, 'The Electoral Influence of the Aristocracy 1604-41' (Columbia Univ. Ph.D. thesis, 1977), p. 311. [5] C2/Jas. I/D13/25.

V.C.D.M./R.C.L.S.

NORTHAMPTON

Right of election: in the corporation

Number of voters: c. 63

16 Feb. 1604[1]	HENRY YELVERTON, recorder EDWARD MERCER, alderman
11 Mar. 1614[2]	HENRY YELVERTON, recorder FRANCIS BEALE
18 Dec. 1620	RICHARD SPENCER THOMAS CREWE (Sir) HENRY YELVERTON JOHN LAMBE
16 Jan. 1624	CHRISTOPHER SHERLAND, recorder RICHARD SPENCER
28 Apr. 1625	CHRISTOPHER SHERLAND, recorder RICHARD SPENCER
5 Jan. 1626	CHRISTOPHER SHERLAND, recorder RICHARD SPENCER
20 Feb. 1628[3]	CHRISTOPHER SHERLAND, recorder RICHARD SPENCER

A staple town, Northampton received its first charter in 1189, and sent Members to Parliament in 1283.[4] Elections were originally popular, but an Act of 1489 vested the government of the town in a mayor, two bailiffs, the ex-bailiffs (usually numbering about 12) and 48 'burgesses' chosen by the mayor and his brethren, and confined the franchise to this assembly.[5] By the mid-sixteenth century it was usual for the recorder to be chosen as one Member, and this tradition continued with only one exception under the early Stuarts, being the 1620 election, when (Sir) Henry Yelverton was in the Tower.[6] The second seat was normally occupied by members of the local gentry who were, as the borough typically stipulated, willing to serve without wages. Elections took place in the guildhall. The town was a stronghold of puritanism, and when Sir Thomas Tresham entered the town on 25 Mar. 1603 to proclaim James I and called on the inhabitants to pray for the new king, the vicar of All Saints, Robert Catelyn, added: 'let us pray that the king prove sound in religion'.[7] Catelyn was subsequently suspended for refusing to adhere to the Canons of 1604, but was eventually reinstated as a result of pressure from the corporation and the local gentry.[8] Northampton was badly affected by the 1603 plague epidemic, and levied £20 a month to deal with its consequences, which must have proved a severe drain on its resources.[9]

In 1604 Yelverton and the former mayor Edward Mercer were elected 'by and with the whole consent and assent of the said assembly'. However, the usual requirement that they should pay their own expenses was omitted, perhaps out of particular regard for Mercer, a draper, and the only townsman elected during this period.[10] Both Mercer and his father signed the petition from the corporation in January 1605 for Catelyn's reinstatement.[11] In 1607 the town voted Yelverton £5 on his appointment as reader of Gray's Inn. He had offended the king during the first three sessions of the Parliament, especially by his opposition to the Union with Scotland, increased taxation, and purveyance; but after a grovelling apology he was restored to favour at Court in 1609, at which point Northampton resolved that no more money should be allowed for his entertainment.[12]

The corporation refused to pay the aid for Princess Elizabeth in 1613, during Mercer's third term as mayor, until it was informed of the reason for the levy.[13] In February 1614 it unsuccessfully petitioned Sir Henry Carey I*, who owned the advowson of All Saints, to reinstate Catelyn, who had once more been threatened with deprivation.[14] At the general election two months

later, Yelverton not only had himself re-elected but persuaded the corporation to accept his brother-in-law Francis Beale, the obscure son of an Elizabethan official, as the second Member in 1614, although Beale had no other connection with the constituency. It was stipulated that both Members should defray their own charges.[15] A new charter granted to the town in 1618 gave former bailiffs the title of aldermen, extended the borough boundaries, and increased its immunity from outside interference. Yelverton, who had procured it, was nominated recorder for life, and the corporation was empowered to choose his successors.[16]

There was evidently a contest in 1620, though it may not have been carried to a poll. It was incorrectly reported that Yelverton had been re-elected, despite his incarceration in the Tower on a trumped-up charge of corruption after he had offended the marquess of Buckingham.[17] With the recorder absent, a contest ensued between three candidates. One contender was Dr. John Lambe, the unpopular chancellor of the diocese of Peterborough, who perhaps stood in an attempt to prevent the corporation from protesting against his treatment of puritans in the town. However, the successful candidates were Richard Spencer, a younger son of Lord Spencer (Sir Robert Spencer†), of Althorp, and Thomas Crewe of Steane, both Northamptonshire gentlemen 'of good descent and efficiency', who were returned on condition that they took out their freedom and served without charge.[18] The corporation resolved on 26 Jan. 1621 to exhibit a bill in the Parliament concerning the River Nene from Northampton to Peterborough, which they desired to be made navigable; however, there is no record that such a bill was ever read in the Commons.[19] On 11 May 1621 the corporation presented a petition to Parliament accusing Lambe of oppression and extortion. After giving specific instances, the petition went on to allege that 'because ... divers townsmen refused to give him their voices to be one of the burgesses of Parliament for Northampton (which he would fain have obtained by both fair means and threatenings) he presently cited many to the court, and there threatened them'.[20] The Speaker issued warrants for the examination of witnesses; but the king stopped the proceedings and Lambe was knighted shortly after the adjournment of the first sitting.[21]

Northampton again resisted pressure to yield a Benevolence for the Palatinate in 1622, protesting to the Privy Council that 'the decay of the town prevents the general contribution from being good'.[22] On 19 June 1623 Yelverton, who had again been restored to royal favour, resigned the recordership in anticipation of his promotion to judicial office, and recommended as his successor his nephew Christopher Sherland, a puritan lawyer. Sherland was duly appointed on condition of taking out his freedom, and was returned to every subsequent Parliament of the period as the town's first Member, together with Richard Spencer.[23] On 3 May 1624 Spencer preferred another petition against Lambe on behalf of the constituency.[24] It was referred to the committee of courts of justice and reported by Sir Robert Phelips* three weeks later. The charges were the same but again no action was taken. It may also have been Spencer who preferred a petition from Northampton against the alnage, which was reported by Sir Edwin Sandys* on the same day.[25]

Quarter sessions had hitherto been held at Northampton, the county capital, but after protests from gentry in the east of Northamptonshire (including the *custos rotulorum* the 6th earl of Rutland) the Privy Council ruled in 1624 that the sessions should be re-located to Kettering. This had not been effected a year later, when it was again ordered that the post-Christmas quarter sessions should be held at Kettering.[26] As a result of this snub to their town the corporation politely refused a request from Lord Montagu (Sir Edward Montagu*) to endorse Sir Lewis Watson* as one of the knights of the shire in 1626, and instead gave their votes to Spencer's brother William and Sir John Pickering*. Montagu attributed the victory of the rival faction largely to 'the strength of the town of Northampton, together with their distaste about the sessions'.[27] The corporation was nevertheless in agreement with many of the local gentry against the Forced Loan in 1627, which met with particularly entrenched resistance in Northamptonshire; the Privy Council clearly disbelieved the excuses offered by the mayor, who had managed to collect less than half of the first instalment due from the town.[28] Spencer, as a Loan collector, an Arminian, and a supporter of Buckingham, now a duke, had lost the support of most of Northampton's electorate by the time of the next general election, and he was further disadvantaged by leaving the county on his marriage in early 1628. On 1 Mar. it was reported that the corporation were determined to elect Sir Erasmus Dryden* in second place; however, Spencer was able to secure the seat, probably as a result of his family's influence.[29] During the debates that preceded the Petition of Right, Sherland protested against the billeting in Northampton of troops commanded by a Catholic, which he declared had been taken by the townsmen 'to frustrate the hope of this Parliament'.[30]

[1] Northants. RO, Northampton bor. 3/1, p. 590.   [2] Ibid. 685-6.   [3] Ibid. 809.   [4] *Northampton Bor. Recs.* ed. C.A. Markham, i. 25.   [5] *VCH Northants.* iii. 9-13; *Northampton Bor. Recs.* ed. J.C. Cox, ii. 16-17.   [6] *VCH Northants.* iii. 17.   [7] *HMC Var.* iii. 118-23.   [8] W.J. Shiels, *Puritans in Dioc. Peterborough* (Northants. Rec. Soc. xxx), 80-1; B.W. Quintrell, 'Royal Hunt and the Puritans', *JEH*, xxxi. 53-4.   [9] *Northampton Bor. Recs.* ii. 234-6.   [10] Northants. RO, Northampton bor. 3/1, p. 590.   [11] *HMC Hatfield*, xvii. 26.   [12] *Northampton Bor. Recs.* ii. 105.   [13] *HMC Buccleuch*, iii. 162.   [14] Sloane 3827, f. 10; *CSP Dom. 1611-18*, p. 254.   [15] *Northampton Bor. Recs.* ii. 495.   [16] Ibid. i. 125-37.   [17] *CSP Dom. 1619-23*, p. 200.   [18] *Northampton Bor. Recs.* ii. 495; Northants. RO, Northampton bor. 3/1, p. 758.   [19] Northants. RO, Northampton bor. 3/1, p. 760.   [20] *CD 1621*, vi. 475-6; Nicholas, *Procs. 1621*, ii. 59.   [21] *CSP Dom. 1619-23*, pp. 280-1.   [22] *CSP Dom. 1619-23*, p. 397.   [23] *Northampton Bor. Recs.* ii. 105; Northants. RO, Northampton bor. 3/1, pp. 780, 792, 796.   [24] 'Earle 1624', f. 166v.   [25] *CJ*, i. 709, 774a.   [26] *APC*, 1623-5, p. 365; 1625-6, p. 293.   [27] *HMC Buccleuch* i. 258-9, iii. 262-3.   [28] *CSP Dom. 1627-8*, pp. 15, 317, 254; R. Cust, *Forced Loan*, 111, 117.   [29] *Procs. 1628*, vi. 122-3.   [30] *CD 1628*, ii. 361-2, *Procs. 1628*, vi. 64-5.

V.C.D.M./R.C.L.S.

PETERBOROUGH

Right of election: in the inhabitant ratepayers[1]

Population: c.280 in 1561[2]

12 Mar. 1604	RICHARD CECIL
	EDWARD WYMARKE
c.Mar. 1614	SIR WILLIAM WALTER
	EDWARD WYMARKE
c.May 1614	ROGER MANWOOD *vice*
	Wymarke, chose to sit for
	Newcastle-under-Lyme
22 Nov. 1620	MILDMAY FANE
	WALTER FITZWILLIAM
15 Jan. 1624	SIR FRANCIS FANE
	LAURENCE WHITAKER
18 Jan. 1625	CHRISTOPHER HATTON *vice*
	Fane, called to the Upper House
23 Apr. 1625	LAURENCE WHITAKER
	CHRISTOPHER HATTON
c.Jan. 1626	MILDMAY FANE, (Lord Burghersh)
	LAURENCE WHITAKER
18 Feb. 1628	MILDMAY FANE,(Lord le Despenser)
	LAURENCE WHITAKER

Situated near Northamptonshire's boundary with Huntingdonshire and Cambridgeshire, Peterborough became enfranchised shortly after its former

Benedictine monastery was reconstituted as a cathedral in 1541. The small town had no municipal authorities, and was run by the dean and chapter; it received no charter of incorporation until 1874, until which time the dean served as a quasi-mayor. Accordingly, it was the dean's bailiff who received the sheriff's precept for parliamentary elections.[3] In theory the cathedral interest in elections should have been strong, but it seems to have been in abeyance during the long episcopate of Thomas Dove (1601-30). One seat was controlled throughout this period by the Apethorpe interest, which passed from Sir Anthony Mildmay† in 1617 to his son-in-law Sir Francis Fane, an ambitious courtier.[4] The other seat was claimed by the Cecils of Burghley, who owned the liberty of Peterborough.[5]

The two Members returned to the first Stuart Parliament were Richard Cecil, the younger son of the 1st earl of Exeter (Sir Thomas Cecil†), and Edward Wymarke, elected on Mildmay's recommendation although 'hardly known to the town of Peterborough'.[6] In 1614 Exeter nominated an outspoken puritan, Sir William Walter of Wimbledon, whose family had a long-standing connection with the Cecils. Wymarke was re-elected, but chose to sit for Newcastle-under-Lyme. His place was taken by Roger Manwood, the son of Mildmay's neighbour in London, who, as a Kentish squire, was doubtless recommended by Fane, who was sitting for Maidstone. At the next election in 1620 Fane's eldest son Mildmay was returned with his cousin, Walter Fitzwilliam, a bankrupt courtier. The fact that Fane seems to have taken control of both seats perhaps indicates a wane in Cecil influence in the borough from this point onwards.

In 1624 Fane himself took the first seat, together with Laurence Whitaker, a government clerk of obscure origins but pronounced puritan views. The latter's connection with the constituency is unclear; his mother was from Peterborough, and he may have been recommended to the 2nd earl of Exeter (William Cecil†) by his in-laws, the Egerton family. After the prorogation Fane was raised to the peerage as the earl of Westmorland, and at the ensuing by-election it was presumably he who nominated as his replacement Christopher Hatton of Kirby, aged only 19 at the time. Hatton had no opportunity to take up his seat before the death of James I automatically dissolved the Parliament, but he was re-elected to the first Parliament of Charles I, together with Whitaker. The same pair were again elected together in both 1626 and 1628. There is no evidence that the borough paid wages to its Members or pursued any legislation during the period.

[1] Bridges, *Northants.* ii. 539. [2] W.T. Mellows and D.H. Gifford, *Eliz. Peterborough* (Northants. Rec. Soc. xviii), 26. [3] W.T. Mellows, *Foundation of Peterborough Cathedral* (Northants. Rec. Soc. xiii), p. xxiv. [4] E.A. Webb, *Recs. St. Bartholomew Smithfield*, ii. 265-7. [5] *VCH Northants.* ii. 421-3. [6] Mellows and Gifford, 33.

V.C.D.M./R.C.L.S.

NORTHUMBERLAND

Number of voters: at least 324 in 1614

c. Mar. 1604[1]	SIR RALPH GREY
	SIR HENRY WIDDRINGTON
c. Mar. 1614	SIR HENRY WIDDRINGTON
	SIR GEORGE SELBY
	Sir Ralph Grey
?12 May 1614	SIR WILLIAM SELBY II *vice*
	Selby, ineligible to sit
14 Dec. 1621	SIR WILLIAM GREY, bt.
	SIR HENRY WIDDRINGTON
12 Feb. 1624	SIR WILLIAM GREY, 1st bt.
	SIR FRANCIS BRANDLING
c. Mar. 1624	SIR JOHN FENWICK *vice*
	Grey, called to the
	Upper House
c. Apr. 1625	SIR JOHN FENWICK
	SIR FRANCIS BRANDLING
9 Feb. 1626	SIR JOHN FENWICK
	SIR JOHN DELAVAL
4/6 March 1628[2]	SIR JOHN FENWICK
	SIR WILLIAM CARNABY

Prior to James I's accession in 1603, Northumberland's history was dominated by its location on England's northern border. Following centuries of intermittent war with Scotland, the county was run effectively as a military zone, divided into Marches, and exempted from national taxation so that local resources could be utilized for defence purposes. Under the early Stuarts, with peace now supposedly assured, serious efforts were made to develop a more conventional administrative framework. However, although James appointed a lord lieutenant, the earl of Cumberland, in the opening months of his reign, the local militia was not brought into line with the national model until the late 1620s, and the Crown relied on special Border commissions to enforce law and order until 1625.[3] The routine processes of government were further hampered by the fact that Northumberland's two biggest towns, Berwick-upon-Tweed and Newcastle-upon-Tyne, were independent jurisdictions, while the north-east of the county was officially part of the palatinate of Durham.[4]

Northumberland was also fragmented socially and economically. The sparse population of around 85,000 was unevenly distributed, the eastern lowland region being more densely inhabited, while the poorer highland zone was widely considered to be a hotbed of crime.[5] Local recusancy levels were habitually exaggerated during this period, but several of the most important gentry families, such as the Greys and Widdringtons, displayed strong Catholic leanings. This naturally caused tensions within the county elite, particularly at such times of crisis as the Gunpowder Plot.[6] Northumberland's economy was still primarily agricultural, but food production scarcely met local needs, while the wool from the region's sheep was so coarse that it was unsuitable for cloth, and had to be exported in its raw state.[7] The burgeoning coal industry, an isolated success story, was virtually monopolized by Newcastle's merchants, and competition elsewhere in the county was severely restricted by the heavy capital outlay required for mining.[8] Despite these difficulties, Northumberland's tax exemption was ended in 1610, and Parliament rejected efforts to protect the wool trade in the 1620s.[9] The struggling population could expect little leadership from its aristocratic landlords, who were almost exclusively non-resident, and whose rent demands drained the county of coin. Instead, the key figures were the major gentry, whose continuing hold over their own extended kinship groups perpetuated clan-like local rivalries. For example, the effects of Ralph Grey's bitter disputes during the 1590s with Henry Widdrington and Ralph Selby were still being felt in the county's parliamentary contests several decades later.[10]

Northumberland's elections were held at Alnwick, the official county town. The average number of voters is unclear, for the surviving indentures ordinarily just list the principal gentlemen present, then add a phrase such as 'many other electors'. However, more than 300 people attended the first election of 1614, and the turnout was probably even higher at the second. On that occasion there was a serious attempt to record all the voters. Although the indenture has faded badly, nearly 200 names can still be identified, while those that are now illegible probably amounted to a similar total. This indenture is also untypical in that it was written in English, rather than the customary Latin.[11]

During Elizabeth's reign, Northumberland's electors routinely awarded at least one seat to an outsider linked to the county's military establishment or the Council in the North.[12] However, with the accession of James I, and the formal end to hostilities with Scotland, this pattern changed. The 1604 election saw the returning of those two prominent gentlemen, Sir Ralph Grey and Sir Henry Widdrington, both of whom had been knighted in the early days of the new reign.[13] The same result seemed likely in 1614, but while Widdrington was safely re-elected, Grey was unexpectedly defeated, apparently through malpractice by the sheriff, Sir Ralph Selby, with whom Grey had quarrelled in the 1590s. According to subsequent complaints in the Commons, Selby failed to announce the choice of candidates until half-an-hour before the election, and ignored around 300 voters who had turned up to support Grey. He then extended the election by another half-hour, until he had counted 24 votes for his own brother-in-law, Sir George Selby, a wealthy Newcastle gentleman, whom he duly returned. In the event, this stratagem foundered because Sir George was currently sheriff of county Durham, and therefore deemed ineligible by the Commons. Nevertheless, in the subsequent election in early May Sir George's brother, Sir William Selby of Shortflatt, was chosen to replace him. Grey's complaints about the management of the original election were not discussed at Westminster until 24 May, and even then Sir Ralph Selby's alleged fraud in discounting legitimate voters excited Members less than his indisputable offence in returning a fellow sheriff. Although Widdrington, a kinsman of the Selbys, distanced himself in the Commons from the whole affair, he was probably not sorry to see Grey defeated, and may well have helped to muster the opposition to him. It was noted in the House that a certificate defending Sir Ralph Selby's conduct was signed mainly by the electors whom he had counted, and that around a third of these belonged to the Selby and Widdrington families.[14]

These rivalries continued in December 1620, when Widdrington was elected for a third time, but had to yield the senior seat to Grey's son, Sir William, who was a baronet. Widdrington felt this indignity very strongly, and on 27 Apr. 1621 he pointedly complained in the House about people who achieved higher social status by purchasing honours.[15] By 1624 Widdrington was dead, clearing the way for Sir William Grey to be returned again, alongside his own brother-in-law, Sir Francis Brandling. However, this double triumph was short-lived. Grey was created an English peer one day before the election, which rendered him ineligible to sit in the Commons, and he was replaced by Sir John

Fenwick, another prominent local gentleman who had formerly been one of Widdrington's closest associates.[16] Fenwick retained his seat for the remainder of this period. He was again partnered by Brandling in 1625, but the new Lord Grey was now spending increasing amounts of time in London, and his electoral influence apparently ended at this point. The junior knights of the shire in 1626 and 1628 were Sir John Delaval and Sir William Carnaby, minor Northumberland gentry who were active figures in local government.[17]

Of the eight legitimate Members, only Widdrington proved to be an effective spokesman for his county. Appointed a commissioner for the Anglo-Scottish Union treaty in 1604, he campaigned successfully in the Commons in 1607 against the practice of remanding, whereby an Englishman accused of committing a crime in Scotland could be tried under Scottish law.[18] By comparison, Sir Ralph Grey's principal initiative in 1604 was a short-lived bill to ease the financial pressure on recusants, which would primarily have benefited his own circle, while in 1610 he failed to convince the House that Northumberland should continue to be exempted from paying subsidies.[19] In 1621 both Widdrington and Sir William Grey opposed a ban on the export of local wool, but they were merely supporting a motion by a Berwick-upon-Tweed Member, Sir Robert Jackson, which was in any case rejected.[20] Thereafter, Northumberland's knights rarely contributed to the Commons' proceedings except in connection with the presentment of local recusant office-holders.[21]

[1] SP14/7/82.II. [2] OR. [3] S.J. and S.J. Watts, From Border to Middle Shire: Northumb. 1586-1625, pp. 14-15, 30, 136, 201; CSP Dom. 1625-6, p. 102; 1627-8, p. 214. [4] Watts, 15; CSP Dom. 1611-18, p. 113; 1625-6, p. 165. [5] Watts, 23-4, 40-1. [6] Ibid. 84-6; HMC Hatfield, xviii. 457-9; xix. 3-5; CSP Dom. 1603-10, pp. 313, 543. [7] Watts, 49-51; CJ, i. 653a; CD 1621, ii. 478; APC, 1618-19, p. 137. [8] Watts, 51-4. [9] CJ, i. 449b, 628a, 653a. [10] Watts, 59; W. Brereton, Travels in Holland, Eng., Scotland and Ireland ed. E. Hawkins (Chetham Soc. i), 89; CBP, 1560-94, p. 463; 1595-1603, pp. 250-1, 278, 286-7. [11] C219/36/7; 219/37/177; 219/38/186; 219/40/2; 219/41B/182; Procs. 1614 (Commons), 337. [12] HP Commons, 1558-1603, i. 219. [13] WARD 7/70/192; C142/242/95; Shaw, Knights of Eng. ii. 100. [1] [14] Som. RO, DD.SF1076; Procs. 1614 (Commons), 30, 37-40, 74, 78, 332-4, 336-7; Watts, 263-5. [15] CD 1621, v. 109. [16] WARD 7/70/187; Hist. Northumb. (Northumb. Co. Hist. Cttee.), xiv. 328; CSP Dom. 1611-18, p. 465; 1623-5, p. 161. [17] C142/300/185; Hist. Northumb. xiii. 181; Recs. of Cttees. for Compounding in Durham and Northumb. ed. R. Welford (Surtees Soc. cxi), 144. [18] CJ, i. 208b, 1047b-8b; HMC Hatfield, xix. 155. [19] CJ, i. 449b; 948b. [20] Ibid. 653a; CD 1621, vi. 214. [21] CJ, i. 776b; Procs. 1626, ii. 81; CD 1628, ii. 41.

P.M.H.

BERWICK-UPON-TWEED

Right of election: in the freemen

Number of voters: 64 in Mar. 1628

5 Mar. 1604	SIR WILLIAM SELBY I CHRISTOPHER PARKINSON, recorder
1614	SIR JOHN SELBY MEREDITH MORGAN
21 Dec. 1620[1]	SIR JOHN SELBY SIR ROBERT JACKSON, alderman
23 Jan. 1624[2]	SIR ROBERT JACKSON, alderman EDWARD LIVELEY
29 Apr. 1625	SIR JOHN SELBY SIR ROBERT JACKSON, alderman
23 Jan. 1626[3] by 6 Feb. 1626[4]	SIR ROBERT JACKSON, alderman RICHARD LOWTHER
29 Feb. 1628[5]	(SIR) EDMUND SAWYER EDWARD LIVELEY
1 Oct. 1628	SIR ROBERT JACKSON, alderman vice Sawyer, expelled the House

Originally a Scottish burgh, Berwick was a key border fortress during the medieval Anglo-Scottish wars, changing hands nine times in barely 300 years. Under permanent English control from 1482, it achieved parliamentary representation at Westminster by 1512, but was not formally incorporated into England until the nineteenth century.[6] Berwick's status as a principal customs post for trade with Scotland was confirmed by Parliament in 1483, when its merchants were also granted the privilege of unrestricted overseas exports. However, successive sieges, sacks and occupations had permanently damaged the local economy, and by the late Tudor period the town depended heavily on the Tweed salmon fisheries and the trade generated by the substantial garrison. Thus, while James I's accession brought with it the prospect of a lasting and beneficial peace in the Borders, the king's decision to reduce the garrison in 1603 and then dissolve it eight years later had serious repercussions. With the soldiers either relocated or downgraded to pensioners, the government's financial input fell from around £15,000 p.a. at the end of Elizabeth's reign, to £4,925 in 1610, £1,905 a decade later, and just £928 in 1630.[7] Simultaneously, the borough found itself responsible for up to 7,000 extra people, formerly dependant on the garrison, and now without a livelihood; in 1622, the corporation informed the Privy Council that Berwick's population now largely consisted of the widows and orphans of dead soldiers. Already in 1607 the town was reported to be 'much decayed since the discharge of the garrison', and the situation continued to deteriorate. Berwick was hit hard by the 1614 ban on wool exports, and an attempt to compensate by introducing cloth manufacture during the following decade failed. The local fishing and coal industries also experienced difficulties during the early seventeenth century.[8]

Although Berwick's merchants traded as far afield as Spain and the Baltic, the volume of cargoes from overseas was relatively small, the Crown's customs revenues coming mainly from the goods which crossed the wooden bridge over the Tweed. When this structure partially collapsed in 1607, the town was unable to fund even temporary repairs, and the government was persuaded to pay for a stone replacement. Construction finally began four years later, on an estimate of around £8,500, but by 1620 nearly £10,000 had been spent, and the bridge was still unfinished. A Privy Council inquiry cleared the builders of malpractice, but the project was placed under the supervision of the bishop of Durham, Richard Neile, before further funds were released. The bridge finally opened to traffic in 1624, having by now cost the Exchequer £13,000, though minor works continued for another decade.[9]

Until 1603 Berwick was run by the governor's council, primarily a military body, though with a small civilian presence. However, the management of local trade was entrusted to the guild of burgesses, the origins of which lay in the Scottish burgh more than three centuries earlier. The guild, which considered itself to be a corporation, already possessed most of the features associated with conventional English boroughs, including a mayor, recorder, bailiffs, aldermen, and an inner council known variously as the Twelve, the 'fering men' or the 'private guild'.[10] These officials received around £50 p.a. from the Exchequer towards their expenses, but this subsidy was withdrawn when the garrison was dissolved. The guild's other principal source of income was the rent from roughly two-thirds of the land in and around Berwick, to which the town's burgesses enjoyed a customary claim. As a precaution the guild began lobbying the government in September 1603 for confirmation of its title to this property. The situation became more urgent in January 1604, when the king granted Berwick castle and the other remaining lands to Sir George Home (later earl of Dunbar), the lord treasurer of

Scotland. Fortunately Home, who shortly afterwards became the new governor, proved to be a generous benefactor of the town, and helped to procure a new borough charter in the following April.[11] Under its provisions the guild's corporate status and structures were confirmed, as were its trading privileges, and its ownership of the lands not already granted to Home. The charter also guaranteed the borough's exemption from payment of subsidies, tenths and fifteenths, and awarded the mayor the custody of the town gates. The corporation took formal possession of its new property a few months later, though it finally secured the town keys only in 1611, when the residue of the garrison was absorbed into the borough, and full civilian rule was finally achieved. The land grant brought the borough a welcome financial boost, as it included some property formerly occupied by the garrison, but without the supplementary Exchequer funding the corporation's expenses generally outstripped its revenues. In 1624 Sir Robert Jackson was offered a gift of £10 for services to the borough, possibly in Parliament, but three years later he was still awaiting payment.[12]

Berwick's parliamentary franchise was vested in the freemen. In February 1628 almost half of the eligible voters definitely participated in the borough's election of Members to the third Caroline Parliament.[13] The 1604 election, unmentioned in the guild's records, was presumably managed by the governor's council, as the return described the voters simply as 'burgesses' and 'freemen'. However, by 1614 the corporation had taken full control of the borough, and subsequent returns referred to the 'mayor, bailiffs and burgesses'. Berwick's unique administrative status as a territory independent of any English county ruled out the standard format for parliamentary returns, this being an indenture made between the borough and the local sheriff. Instead, during James's reign a declaration of the election result was sent to Westminster, bearing the town's common seal and, in 1604, the mayor's signature. In 1625 a new approach was adopted, and thereafter the returns took the form of indentures, with the mayor and bailiffs as one party, and 'those burgesses of the said borough who were present at the election' as the other. These indentures were signed and sealed by the returning officers, the mayor and bailiffs, and, at the two 1628 elections, also signed by the other participating freemen. The change of style probably reflected a desire for greater formality, since the indentures in 1625 and October 1628 were in Latin rather than English.[14] Such concern with presentation did not, however, reflect a punctilious observance of electoral law. A draft text for the 1625 return, complete except for the days on which the election was proclaimed and held, was entered in the corporation minutes, with marginal instructions for the clerk: 'put in the day of election' and 'put in the day that Proclamation was made if there were as many days between the Proclamation and the day of election as the statute requires, otherwise antedate'.[15]

On the grounds of the corporation's poverty, Berwick looked to its representatives in the Commons to cover their own expenses. Specific assurances on this point were sought in 1620, 1624 and 1625, and no record of parliamentary wages has been found. Surprisingly, there is little evidence that external patrons sought to exploit this situation by offering to supply the borough with candidates free of charge.[16] In the late Elizabethan era the borough normally returned one soldier and one civilian. This pattern continued in 1604, with the fifth consecutive election of Sir William Selby I, the recently retired gentleman porter of Berwick garrison, alongside the town's recorder, Christopher Parkinson. A decade later, military government had ended, though a few former garrison members found places in the corporation. These included Sir John Selby, Sir William's nephew, a local landowner with a house in Berwick, who served briefly on the council of Twelve, and represented the borough in 1614, 1621, and 1625. His partner in the Addled Parliament was Meredith Morgan, secretary to the 1st earl of Suffolk. A complete outsider, Morgan probably owed his election to the fact that Suffolk's eldest son, Theophilus Howard*, had married Sir George Home's daughter and coheir, and obtained his Berwick estates.[17]

For much of the 1620s the construction of the new Tweed bridge was one of the town's most pressing concerns, and not surprisingly it seems to have influenced the choice of Members. Sir Robert Jackson, a senior alderman who was regularly employed to receive the Exchequer's disbursements towards the bridge, sat in every parliamentary session during this decade except for 1628, when his status as mayor of Berwick rendered him ineligible. His partner in 1624, Edward Liveley, was secretary to Bishop Neile, the bridge project's supervisor, and the borough employed him several times between 1622 and 1625 to help Jackson collect money from London. As Neile was also acting as Berwick's patron at Court, it is possible that Liveley's election was intended as a favour to the bishop, though it is equally likely that the borough opted for a man it felt it could trust to represent its interests at Westminster. There was apparently some confusion over the nomination process in 1624, probably linked to the fact that neither Jackson nor Liveley was actually in Berwick. Although the election was held on 23 Jan., an instruction for Liveley to be sworn in as a freeman by proxy was not issued until 2 Feb., and the election return was dated to 7 February.[18]

A similar situation in 1626 was more fully recorded. Jackson was elected as senior Member on 23 Jan., with the second place falling to Sir Edmund Sawyer, 'if he be pleased to accept thereof'. Sawyer, an Exchequer auditor, was probably known to the borough due to the annual ritual of passing the bridge accounts. He had apparently not requested a seat, and, as some voters observed: 'it might be Sir Edmund was already chosen a burgess for the Parliament in some other place, and in that respect could not stand to the election of this borough'. Accordingly, a letter was sent to Jackson, asking him to inform Sawyer that a seat was available if he wanted it; if not, then Edward Liveley was to be approached instead. In the event, neither man entered the Commons that year. By 6 Feb. the borough finally settled on Richard Lowther, an obscure Yorkshire gentleman with no obvious ties to Berwick, possibly nominated by his kinsman, Henry Clifford, Lord Clifford*, lord lieutenant of Northumberland. The corporation assumed that Lowther would head straight to London, and made plans for him to take his oath as a freeman there, but on 8 Feb. he unexpectedly arrived in the town to thank his electors in person. For the sake of appearances, he was recorded in the corporation minutes as having been elected with Jackson 16 days earlier. Regrettably, that year's election return, which Lowther delivered to London, does not survive.[19] In 1628 the nomination process ran more smoothly. With Jackson unavailable, the borough secured the services of both Sawyer and Liveley, the latter being deputed to admit the former as a freeman, and the parliamentary indenture was dated only three days after the actual election. Unfortunately, Sawyer was then expelled from the Commons on 21 June for attempting to subvert the inquiry into the new books of rates. By the time the by-election writ reached Berwick, Jackson's term as mayor had expired, and he was promptly chosen to fill the vacancy.[20]

Until February 1628 the borough always returned at least one senior member of the corporation, no doubt to ensure that Berwick's interests were being properly represented in the Commons. The instructions drawn up when two outsiders, Sawyer and Liveley, were elected in 1628, give a good sense of the borough's priorities:

1. Get your appearance recorded.

2. It will not be amiss to make your acquaintance with the Speaker and with the clerk of the Parliament House.

3. Then not only to be acquainted, but also associate yourselves with the burgesses of other boroughs, and to have often mutual conference with them, or as many of them as conveniently can, about the bills preferred; and whether the passing of any bill may be prejudicial to this borough or not, as if [by] any bill preferred to be read any staple ware, as well skins, as wool fells, hides or like [is] to be prohibited to be transported.

4. Or the transporting of white cloths out of this country be forbidden.

5. Or any tenths, subsidies, or fifteenths granted.

6. Or privy seals, or any other things in your judgments that may be prejudicial to the good of this place or against our ancient liberties, that you speak yourselves, and procure other burgesses to speak, for a proviso for this place, as ever hath been accustomed, requesting their kindness with a like return on any their like occasions.[21]

The frequency with which Berwick features in the Commons' records during this period suggests that its Members took their responsibilities seriously. Following the grant of the 1604 charter, the borough moved swiftly to have the charter confirmed by statute. A bill was introduced into the Lower House on 11 May, and Selby and Parkinson were both named to the committee on 16 May. The measure proceeded smoothly through both Houses, and became law at the end of the session. Simultaneously, bills to naturalize Sir George Home and confirm his grant of Berwick lands were also going through Parliament. It is not known whether the Berwick Members were asked to help out, but both were nominated to the committees for each bill (18 and 30 May). Some disquiet was voiced in the Commons on 4 June at Berwick Castle being granted to a Scot, but with minor amendments this measure also successfully completed its passage, as did the naturalization bill.[22]

On the wider aspects of Anglo-Scottish relations, only one speech by Christopher Parkinson on cross-border law enforcement survives (28 May 1607), but Berwick naturally featured in discussions of the Union. On 19 Feb. 1606, lord treasurer Dorset (Thomas Sackville†) reminded both Houses that the king's accession had made significant economies possible through the reduction of the garrison there. However, as Nicholas Fuller observed on 7 May 1607, the town's peculiar status as an adjunct to England would complicate any formal dismantling of the border, while the next day an anonymous speaker complained that the Scots would benefit unfairly from the abolition of hostile laws, since, among other things, they would now be allowed to victual Berwick.[23]

Although the 1604 charter and its confirmatory Act enshrined the principle that Berwick was exempt from extraordinary taxation, the accession of a Scottish king effectively removed the justification for this privilege. When the 1606 subsidy bill included the customary exemption for the four northern counties and for Berwick and Newcastle, Sir Edwin Sandys tried on 9 May to insert a proviso which stated that no precedent was being set for the future. This manoeuvre failed, but the 1610 subsidy bill reduced the exemption specifically to Berwick, and then only after a proviso was successfully moved on the town's behalf (14 July). The battle resumed in 1621, when the draft subsidy bill again scrapped the town's exemption, and Sir Robert Jackson had to plead the borough charter in order to get it reinstated (12 March).[24] The issue appears not to have generated debate in the next three parliaments, and the usual proviso appeared in the 1624 and 1625 subsidy Acts. However, in 1628 Sir Robert Pye's complaint that Berwick's exemption had been rendered obsolete by the garrison's dissolution carried more weight than Sir Edmund Sawyer's trumpeting of the borough charter (10 June). That year's subsidy Act finally scrapped the proviso, albeit by arguing that the current financial crisis justified the temporary waiving of charter privileges. Nevertheless, the borough apparently continued the fight outside Parliament, since on 17 July Berwick was discharged from paying the newly granted taxes.[25]

The corporation was less successful at protecting its trading privileges. The 1614 ban on wool exports badly affected Berwick, prompting strenuous efforts to get it lifted. In 1621 Sir Robert Jackson collaborated with his Newcastle counterparts in a bid to get both towns exempted from the bill against wool exports, but this manoeuvre was defeated on 26 May, while a proviso for Berwick alone, tendered by Jackson on 30 Nov., was also rejected.[26] The ban was renewed by Proclamation in the following year, and in December 1623 the corporation agreed on a two-pronged response, namely that a delegation would be sent to London and a bill introduced in the next Parliament to restore Berwick's privileges. However, neither tactic seems to have been carried through, and a petition to the government in September 1624, requesting permission for the town to resume wool exports, also failed to find favour.[27] A final attempt was made to resolve the issue when a new bill against transportation of wool was debated in the 1626 Parliament. A proviso for Berwick was tendered and rejected in the Commons on 14 March. Jackson then wrote to the corporation, requesting that its members draft a petition, presumably on the same subject. At about this juncture the borough borrowed £10, which was spent on 'some business ... nearly concerning this town' in Parliament. The outcome of this activity was probably the proviso submitted when the wool exports bill reached the Lords, but this too was thrown out on 20 April.[28]

[1] Berwick RO, B1/8, p. 109. [2] Ibid. B1/8, p. 162. [3] Berwick RO, B1/8, p. 198. [4] Ibid. B1/8, p. 201. [5] Ibid. B1/9, f. 24v. [6] J. Scott, *Berwick-upon-Tweed*, 6, 9-10, 25, 43, 56, 78-9, 84, 94-5, 99; *HP Commons, 1509-58*, i. 162; S.J. and S.J. Watts, *From Border to Middle Shire*, 15. [7] *SR*, ii. 475; Scott, 101; *CSP Dom.* 1603-10, p. 56; 1611-18, p. 21; Watts, 159; F.C. Dietz, *English Public Finance 1558-1641*, 109, 429. [8] *HMC Hatfield*, xv. 351; xix. 146; *CSP Dom.* 1611-18, p. 381; 1619-23, pp. 384, 419; *Stuart Royal Procs.* ed. J.F. Larkin and P.L. Hughes, i. 317-19; Bodl. Add. C.259, f. 140; Scott, 194-5; Watts, 52. [9] E190/161/1, 3-4, 12-13; *HMC Hatfield*, xix. 137, 146, 153-4; *CSP Dom.* 1603-10, pp. 358, 431; 1611-18, pp. 24, 33; 1619-23, pp. 127-8; *APC*, 1619-21, pp. 123-4, 170-2, 254; Dietz, 429; Scott, 415. [10] Scott, 245, 257; Berwick RO, B1/7, ff. 17-18v, 24v; B1/9, f.134. [11] Scott, 189-90, 195, 256, 312-13; Berwick RO, B1/7, ff. 9v, 16, 21; *CSP Dom.* 1603-10, pp. 64, 87. [12] Scott, 192, 267-8, 314-27; Berwick RO, B1/7, f. 28; B1/8, p. 246; *CSP Dom.* 1611-18, p. 36. [13] Out of around 140 freemen, 64 signed the indenture: C219/41B/114; Berwick RO, B1/9, f. 7. [14] C219/35/1/19; 219/38/181; 219/38/179; 219/39/151; 219/41B/114, 125. The returns for 1614 and 1626 are lost. [15] Berwick RO, B1/8, p. 183. [16] Ibid. 109, 162, 184. [17] *HP Commons, 1558-1603*, i. 220; *CSP Dom.* 1603-10, p. 125; Watts, 66, 183, 252, 262; Scott, 190; Berwick RO, B1/8, pp. 9, 96. [18] Berwick RO, B1/8, pp. 133, 146, 162-3, 166-7, 185; B1/9, f. 11v; C219/38/179. [19] Berwick RO, B1/8, pp. 198, 201-2; *Vis. Cumb. and Westmld.* ed. Foster, 83-4; T.D. Whitaker, *Hist. Craven Deanery*, 311. [20] Ibid. B1/9, ff. 24v-5, 36v; C219/41B/114; *CD 1628*, iv. 404. [21] Scott, 473 (the original ms appears to be lost). [22] *CJ*, i. 207b, 211b-212a, 213b, 217b, 224b, 228b, 231b, 985a; *LJ*, ii. 306a, 308b-9a, 311b; *SR*, iv. 1057-8; HLRO, 1 Jas. I, c.46-7. [23] *CJ*, i. 1047b; *Bowyer Diary*, 374, 380, 382. [24] *CJ*, i. 307a, 450a, 550b; *SR*, iv. 1124-5, 1201; *CD 1621*, v. 23; *Anno XVIII Jacobi Regis. An Act for the Grant of two entire Subsidies, granted by the Temporality* (1621). [25] *SR*, iv. 1260; v. 20-1, 51; *CD 1628*, iv. 221, 231; *CSP Dom.* 1628-9, p. 216. [26] *CD 1621*, ii. 394-5, 478; iv. 380; *CJ*, i. 628a, 653a. [27] *Stuart Royal Procs.* i. 545-9; Berwick RO, B1/8, p. 161; *HMC Cowper*, i. 171. [28] *Procs. 1626*, i. 292; ii. 278; Berwick RO, B1/8, pp. 204, 211.

P.M.H.

MORPETH

Right of election: in the freemen

Number of voters: 33 in 1621

1604	SIR CHRISTOPHER PARKINS JOHN HARE
1614	SIR WILLIAM BUTTON ARNOLD HERBERT
22 Dec. 1620	ROBERT BRANDLING JOHN ROBSON
26 Feb. 1621	RALPH FETHERSTONHAUGH *vice* Robson, ineligible
10 Feb. 1624	SIR WILLIAM CARNABY THOMAS REYNELL
1625	THOMAS COTTON THOMAS REYNELL
19 July 1625	(SIR) ARNOLD HERBERT *vice* Cotton, chose to sit for Great Marlow
26 Jan. 1626	(SIR) THOMAS REYNELL JOHN BANKES
28 Feb. 1628[1]	(SIR) THOMAS REYNELL JOHN BANKES

Morpeth grew up in the shadow of the Norman castle constructed to guard the Great North Road's crossing over the River Wansbeck. The town was granted a fair and market in 1199, and achieved borough status by 1382. In the early seventeenth century Morpeth boasted a tollbooth, a moot-hall and a grammar school. A post-town on the main route from the Scottish border to London, it was a regular meeting-place for Northumberland's magistrates and deputy lieutenants. Nevertheless, it was far from flourishing: the parish church was reportedly decayed in 1605, and Morpeth market, despite being one of only seven regular venues in the county, typically generated tolls of just £11 or £12 a year in the early 1610s. Only 17 inhabitants were assessed for subsidy in 1628, with £3 being the highest rating. Physically and politically, the town was still dominated by the castle, the administrative centre of Morpeth barony.[2]

Devoid of a royal charter until 1682, Morpeth remained a borough by prescription only, presided over by two bailiffs and seven aldermen, the latter representing the interests of the town's seven trading guilds. This body, which termed itself a corporation, was further dignified by a serjeant-at-mace.[3] Morpeth first sent representatives to Parliament in 1553. Elections were announced at the tollbooth, and presumably also held there, with the bailiffs acting as returning officers. Early Stuart election indentures were invariably made out in the name of the bailiffs and the burgesses. Five of the surviving six from this period carried the borough's seal, but were not signed. The exception was the 1621 return, which followed a markedly different format, listing by name all the participating voters, the bulk of whom also signed or sealed the indenture.[4]

Almost all of the borough's Members during the early seventeenth century were nominated by Lord William Howard of Naworth Castle, lord of the manor and barony of Morpeth, who acquired the title to these properties by marriage, and finally secured absolute possession of them in 1601. Although he was an absentee landlord, resident in Cumberland, the presence of his constable in Morpeth castle served as a constant reminder of his local power. Howard presented the borough with a new mace in 1604, but he was an aggressive landlord, who repeatedly sued the corporation to confirm his authority over the town.[5]

Morpeth was represented in the first Jacobean Parliament by Sir Christopher Parkins, master of Requests, and John Hare, attorney in the Court of Wards. Both men were nominated by Howard, on the recommendation of the secretary of state, Lord (Robert) Cecil[†].[6] In 1614, the borough returned Sir William Button and Arnold Herbert, two servants of Howard's brother, the 1st earl of Suffolk.[7] Howard was doubtless also responsible for the repeated elections from 1624 to 1628 of the courtier Thomas Reynell, a client of his nephew, the 21st earl of Arundel. Reynell was initially accompanied in 1625 by Howard's son-in-law, Thomas Cotton, and when the latter opted to sit for Great Marlow instead he was replaced by Arnold Herbert. John Bankes, one of Howard's lawyers, served as the junior Member in 1626 and 1628.[8]

Despite Howard's virtual monopoly of electoral patronage, Morpeth's voters rejected his authority in 1620-1. The cause of this surprising development was apparently mounting local resentment at his heavy-handed enforcement of his tenurial rights. In November 1619, after losing the latest of their intermittent legal battles with Howard, the bailiffs were forced to issue a humiliating declaration that the corporation would no longer claim title to the town's courts, markets or tolls. Another major grievance concerned a 200-acre pasture near Morpeth, which the burgesses had been leasing from Howard at the steep annual rent of £500. Believing that this land rightly belonged to them by custom, the burgesses refused to renew the lease when it expired in 1619. While it cannot be proved that such events determined the course of the election in December 1620, the customary bonds of loyalty between the borough and its lord had clearly now broken down, and the voters pointedly opted for prominent figures within their own community: Robert Brandling, a gentleman from county Durham who owned the Newminster Abbey estate just outside Morpeth; and the local rector, John Robson. However, the latter proved unacceptable to the Commons on account of his clerical status, and his election was ruled invalid on 8 February. Indeed, the borough was almost fined for returning him, but was spared on account of its poverty. The corporation, apparently uncertain how to replace Robson, eventually turned to another county Durham man, Ralph Fetherstonhaugh, who was already in London to lobby for the enfranchisement of his county, and doubtless welcomed the opportunity of a platform inside the Commons. Unusually, the voters' names were listed on the election indenture, a decision which may, perhaps, be seen as an act of continuing defiance towards Howard.[9]

The acrimony between Howard and the borough lasted until at least 1622, when the peer sought legal advice from John Bankes over the refusal of some tenants to use his corn mill at Morpeth. Although Howard's nominee, Thomas Reynell, took the second seat in 1624, the senior place went to Sir William Carnaby, who owned a seat nearby at Bothal, and then had no discernible ties with Howard. It is therefore possible that on this occasion the borough again asserted itself, and accepted only one nomination from its irascible patron.[10]

[1] OR. [2] J. Hodgson, Hist. Northumb. pt. 2, ii. 371, 384-5, 400, 419-21, 423, 441, 454, 516; N. Pevsner, I. Richmond et al., Northumb. (2002), pp. 396-7; CSP Dom. 1619-23, pp. 384, 405, 419; 1627-8, pp. 126, 214; 1628-9, p. 374; Addenda, 1580-1625, p. 209; APC, 1619-21, p. 219; S.J. and S.J. Watts, From Border to Middle Shire, 51; E179/158/95. [3] Hodgson, pt. 2, ii. 428-30, 432, 517; CSP Dom. Addenda, 1580-1625, p. 209. [4] Hodgson, pt. 2, ii. 531; C219/37/182-4; 219/38/187; 219/39/153; 219/40/41; 219/41B/183. [5] Hodgson, pt. 2, ii. 381, 432-3, 516-17; Household Bks. of Lord William Howard of Naworth Castle ed. G. Ornsby (Surtees Soc. lxviii), pp. xviii, xxii; Watts, 58. [6] APC, 1601-4, p. 499; H.E. Bell, Ct. of Wards, 26-7; H.V. Jones, 'Jnl. of Levinus Munck', EHR, lxviii. 250. [7] J.K. Gruenfelder, Influence in Early Stuart Elections, 138; CSP Dom. 1611-18, p. 190; Hodgson, pt. 2, ii. 381. [8] CSP Dom. 1623-5, p. 54; CP, i. 46; Household Bks. of Lord William Howard, 114-15, 200, 209. [9] Hodgson, pt. 2, ii. 414, 516-17; Watts, 174; CJ, i. 513a-b; CD 1621, ii. 41; v. 442; Vis. Durham ed. Foster, 119; R. Surtees, Hist. and Antiqs. of Co. Dur. iv. 157-8; C219/37/183. [10] Household Bks. of Lord William Howard, 200; Hist. Northumb. (Northumb. Co. Hist. Cttee.), x. 408.

P.M.H.

NEWCASTLE-UPON-TYNE

Right of election: in the freemen

Number of voters: several hundred

c. Mar. 1604	SIR GEORGE SELBY, alderman
	HENRY CHAPMAN, alderman
c. Mar. 1614	SIR HENRY ANDERSON, alderman
	WILLIAM JENISON, alderman
13 Dec. 1620	SIR HENRY ANDERSON, alderman
	SIR THOMAS RIDDELL, alderman
21 Jan. 1624	SIR HENRY ANDERSON, alderman
	SIR PETER RIDDELL, alderman
c. Apr. 1625	SIR HENRY ANDERSON, alderman
	SIR THOMAS RIDDELL, alderman
18 Jan. 1626	SIR HENRY ANDERSON, alderman
	SIR PETER RIDDELL, alderman
c. Mar. 1628	SIR THOMAS RIDDELL, alderman
	SIR PETER RIDDELL, alderman

Named after the Norman keep built on the site of one of the forts of Hadrian's Wall, Newcastle-upon-Tyne was the chief bulwark of north-eastern England's defences against the Scots until 1482. It was also the region's most important port town, dealing in wool and hides, and increasingly in coal, abundant reserves of which lay close to the surface on both banks of the Tyne; in 1560 perhaps 40 per cent of national production came from coal pits near the Tyne and Wear rivers, a proportion which increased substantially over the next century. Economic success brought a rapidly expanding population, probably in excess of 15,000 under the early Stuarts, although 5,000 died in a plague epidemic in 1635-6. Chartered by 1135, the borough expanded its limits and its powers during the Middle Ages, acquiring county status separate from Northumberland in 1400. Under James I it was governed by a corporation comprising a mayor, sheriff and ten aldermen, who were elected by an oligarchic system based on the 12 most important town guilds; the 1604 charter also recognized the existence of a common council of 24 members.[1]

Tyneside coal was sold along the east coast, and across the North Sea in the Low Countries and the Baltic, but its main market lay in London, where consumption rose voraciously after 1580. Shipments of Newcastle 'seacoal' doubled between 1580 and 1600, and doubled again (to over 400,000 tons annually) by

the 1630s.[2] Two developments of the later Elizabethan period ensured that control of the industry was delivered to a cartel of northern mineowners: the so-called Grand Lease and the incorporation of the Hostmen's Company.[3] In 1577 the bishop of Durham was prevailed upon to assign a 79-year lease of his manors of Wickham and Gateshead to the Crown at a rent of £117 a year. This 'Grand Lease', comprising many of the most easily worked coal deposits, was initially operated by the London financier Thomas Sutton, but his trade was hindered by a statute of 1529 requiring all goods shipped to and from the Tyne to be loaded at Newcastle, which effectively reserved the trade for Newcastle burgesses. In 1583 the corporation's refusal to make him a freeman induced Sutton to sell his lease to two Newcastle aldermen, Henry Anderson[†] and William Selby[†]. The original intention may have been to assign this lease to the corporation, but instead, the lessees went into partnership with a number of other Hostmen, many of whom were already mineowners.[4]

As the profits from coalmining accrued to this close-knit group, complaints were made by both Londoners, who complained about excessive price rises, and by other Newcastle men who were excluded from the cartel. The Privy Council ordered investigations during the later 1590s, but in 1600 the Hostmen outflanked their critics with a guild charter which confirmed their monopoly of the coal trade and exempted them from the 1529 Newcastle Act, which meant they were able to load coals directly from the wharves nearest to their pits. In return for these concessions, the Crown secured a duty of 12d. upon every chaldron[5] of coal shipped from the Tyne for domestic use, a levy which initially yielded around £5,000 a year, far more than the 5s. per chaldron custom on coal exports.[6] Not surprisingly, the Hostmen's economic power had a major impact on municipal politics: from the inception of the Grand Lease, most Newcastle aldermen and all but one of the borough's MPs were Hostmen; and any threat to their interests was assured of a vigorous response.

The parliamentary election of 1604 saw the return of Sir George Selby, heir to one of the 1583 lessees, and Henry Chapman, a more senior figure who had played a key role in securing the Hostmen's charter, and who had resolved a dispute with freemen pressing to join the Company only a few weeks before the election. Chapman probably managed the opposition to a bill to modify the 1529 Newcastle Act, promoted by the London corporation, which was rejected at its second reading on 30 May 1604.[7] During the 1605-6 session, the Members for Newcastle, Hull and York collaborated over a bill to reinstate a 20 per cent discount on the customs on northern cloth originally granted in 1591, which the farmers of the new customs lease inaugurated in December 1604 refused to acknowledge; this failed in the Lords, but a private approach to secretary of state Salisbury (Robert Cecil[†]) secured the discount after the end of the session.[8]

For the Newcastle men, however, the main business of the 1606 session was the repulse of another attempt to repeal the 1529 Newcastle Act. Complaints about the price of Newcastle coal rose steadily during 1605: the Londoners boycotted the Tyneside collieries for two months in the spring, in protest at a new cartel agreement among the Hostmen; and while the cartel was suppressed under orders from the Privy Council in July, the issue was still being contested on the eve of the new session.[9] In February 1606 the Londoners revived their 1604 bill, this time in the Lords, but Selby and Chapman appealed to Salisbury, and succeeded in having the bill laid aside on 10 March. The Lords called for a fresh draft to reform unspecified 'abuses in the sale of those coals', but none reached the floor of the House before the prorogation; nor did another bill mooted by the London corporation for measurage of coals landed at the City's wharves.[10] Frustrations with the Tyneside cartel led the Londoners to open negotiations with mineowners on Wearside, where shipments quickly began to rise. In 1610, doubtless prompted by the Londoners, the Commons complained about the application of the 12d. seacoal levy to shipments from the River Wear and the Northumberland coast, neither of which was covered by the Hostmen's agreement of 1600. The Crown agreed to waive this charge, and following the failure of an attempt by the Hostmen to have the levy reinstated in the autumn of 1610, shipments from Sunderland more than doubled, to 35,000 tons a year.[11]

At the 1614 general election Selby was returned for Northumberland, while Chapman, about to hand control of his business to a nephew, apparently had no interest in re-election. They were replaced at Newcastle by Sir Henry Anderson, son of the 1583 lessee, and William Jenison, founding governor of the Hostmen's Company, who had previously represented the town in the 1601 Parliament. Both Members were involved in promoting the bill for the enfranchisement of county Durham, but no other local business featured on the parliamentary agenda during the brief session.[12] Shortly after the dissolution a fresh threat to the Hostmen emerged with the erection of a new office for the survey of Newcastle coals. Complaints

about the quality of Tyneside coals were a commonplace among customers, partly because seams varied widely in both purity and calorific content, but also because of sharp practices by mineowners. In February 1616 Andrew Boyd, a client of the 3rd duke of Lennox, was granted a patent to survey the quality of north-eastern coal, charging shippers 4d. per Newcastle chaldron for the privilege. A storm of protest was raised by both the Hostmen and the shippers, and after a year of vigorous debate the Privy Council referred the case to trial at law.[13] During the resulting Star Chamber suit the claims of the Hostmen and mariners as to the fineness of Tyneside coal were refuted by the London coal merchants, and the defendants (including Jenison) were fined £20 apiece, committed to the Fleet prison and publicly humiliated by having the decree against their abuses read out in public at Newcastle in August 1618. However, mariners continued to boycott Boyd's officials, and in October 1618 the Privy Council, besieged by angry coal shippers, suspended the patent.[14]

At the general election of December 1620, Anderson was again returned as senior Member for Newcastle, but Jenison stood aside, and was replaced by one of Boyd's most energetic opponents, Sir Thomas Riddell. These two men and the latter's half-brother, Sir Peter Riddell, represented the borough in Parliament throughout the 1620s, when the Hostmen's monopoly came under attack from several different interests. In 1621 the main challenge came from a local man, Robert Brandling of Felling, co. Durham, who was returned as MP for Morpeth. While he had paid the unusually large sum of £10 to join the Hostmen's Company in 1601, Brandling did not belong to the trading cartel which formed the Company's inner clique. In August 1620 he petitioned against the duties levied upon coal shipments by the Newcastle corporation, objected to the Hostmen's exemption from the 1529 Newcastle Act, and protested against the fact that the Grand Lease allowed the oligarchs to acquire control of lucrative mines at negligible rents. It was doubtless Brandling who secured the reading of a bill to abolish the corporation's coal duties and overturn the 1529 Newcastle Act (27 Feb.), which proceeded no further, presumably because of intervention by the Newcastle Members and Exchequer officials. Brandling offered his response on 26 Mar., the day before the Easter recess, by which time the Newcastle MPs had already departed for the north. Moving 'that the [Hostmen's] patent for Newcastle coals may be brought in', Brandling attacked the duty of 12d. per chaldron, and while solicitor general Heath warned against meddling with Crown revenues, and the York MP Christopher Brooke urged to leave the matter until the session reconvened, an investigation was ordered. This never reported to the House, and while the contribution the Newcastle Members made towards the stifling of this complaint can only be conjectured, Sir Thomas Riddell later opposed another bill seeking to impose a levy on Newcastle coal, for the maintenance of Dunwich harbour in Suffolk (3 December).[15]

As well as defending their own interests, the 1621 MPs also played a part in the wider debate about the decay of trade, which centred on two other commodities traded at Newcastle, corn and wool. A bumper harvest in 1620 led to calls for an embargo on grain imports, but at the second reading of a bill to this end on 8 Mar. 1621 John Lister of Hull and Sir Thomas Riddell both warned that Baltic merchants were often unable to find anything but Polish rye in exchange for their northern cloths. Riddell also observed that if an import ban was fixed at a particular price level, a merchant might buy in good faith, only to find the price of grain had fallen by the time his cargo reached England. He repeated the same arguments when the bill was reported on 17 May, and a host of similar objections from other merchants ensured that the measure was sent back to the committee, never to return.[16] Meanwhile, it was proposed to revive the ailing cloth trade by banning the export of wool, a bill widely supported by clothing interests. However, at its second reading on 30 Apr., Riddell tabled a proviso to exempt the coarse wool grown in the borders, and was supported by Anderson. This was apparently rejected in committee, as Riddell renewed his motion at the report stage (26 May), observing that Scottish wool grown on the other side of the Tweed would not be subject to the ban. Although he was backed by Anderson, the Northumberland MP Sir William Grey, and Sir Robert Jackson of Berwick, the bill was engrossed without alteration. At the third reading on 30 Nov., Jackson argued for exemption for Berwick alone, but despite support from Riddell, Grey and Sir Henry Widdrington, the proviso was rejected. The bill was lost at the dissolution, but revived in 1624, when it passed the Commons with very little debate, only to be frustrated in the Lords' committee, probably by Grey, who had by then been ennobled as Lord Grey of Warke.[17]

The Hostmen's dispute with Brandling was settled in April 1622, when his son Sir Francis* was co-opted into the Company's new cartel arrangements, but the family still refused to pay the 12d. per chaldron duty, and their factor, John Brandling, was prosecuted in the Exchequer. He quickly settled the arrears owed to the Crown, but declined to join the Hostmen's Company, and his stand probably explains why his brother Sir Francis, MP for Northumberland in 1624, unsuccessfully called for all northern mineowners to gain admission as Hostmen in the Commons (19 May). The same session saw a fresh petition against the Hostmen's monopoly (9 Apr. 1624), and the Company was sufficiently concerned to recruit the services of attorney-general Coventry to ensure that their charter was exempted from the provisions of the Monopolies' Act, which passed into law at the end of the session. Under pressure, the Brandling family subsequently withdrew from the coal trade, and an Exchequer decree of June 1625 upheld the Hostmen's monopoly.[18]

During the 1624 session a further dispute over coal duties erupted over the countess of Bedford's 1619 patent for the levying of a duty of 2d. per chaldron of coal imposed by a statute of 9 Henry V.[19] The Hostmen claimed that this duty had never been collected, and an extensive search by the patentees failed to find any evidence to the contrary, so in 1624 the patentees tabled a parliamentary bill to secure its enforcement. At the second reading on 29 Apr., Sir Peter Riddell insisted that the duty specified in the original Act had been assigned to the corporation to assist in the payment of the borough fee-farm. He also maligned the proposed duty as 'another pretermitted custom' – a cloth duty then under attack in the Commons – and the Newcastle men ensured that the bill never emerged from committee, whereafter the patent proved unenforceable.[20]

Finally, the dispute over Boyd's coal survey patent simmered throughout the 1620s. On 5 May 1621 Robert Snelling of Ipswich – the mariners of which port handled much of the London coal trade – warned that Boyd's surveyorship had been assigned to Roger Langford, another of Lennox's clients; this protest was referred to the committee of grievances, which apparently quashed the new grant.[21] Trouble broke out anew in April 1622, when the Hostmen reached a new cartel agreement, which required colliers to negotiate with a consortium of seven Hostmen, led by Sir Peter Riddell, for the purchase of coals. At the same time, the London Woodmongers' Company complained to the Privy Council about the Hostmen's deliberate adulteration of their fuel with poorer grades of coal. Surveyors sent from London confirmed these allegations, and in February 1623 Langford was again appointed surveyor.[22] A summer of recriminations followed, with the Londoners complaining about poor quality and rising prices, while the shippers were alarmed to discover that payment of the survey fee of 4*d*. per chaldron was to fall exclusively on their shoulders. The shippers' chief grievance, however, was the Hostmen's abolition of 'gift-coal', a custom under which colliers received up to 20 per cent more coal than they officially paid for, which served both as compensation for poor quality coal, and as a means of evading customs duty. Langford quickly resigned his patent, and in September 1623 Lennox nominated the Exchequer official Sir Robert Sharpeigh and Alexander Haitley as his replacements.[23] Lennox's death, just before the opening of the 1624 Parliament, opened the way for further complaints, and on 13 Mar. Sir Edward Coke reported from the grievances' committee that 'there are 40 surveyors for this business, who are as so many flies to afflict the poor subjects'. The patent was suspended pending further investigation, and despite Sharpeigh's robust defence it was condemned as a grievance at the end of the session, when the king agreed to revoke it.[24] However, in February 1625, only days after the next parliamentary session had been postponed, Sharpeigh's patent was confirmed by Proclamation.

Nothing more was done during the brief parliamentary session of 1625, but in the following year two bills were tabled in the Commons. The first, to prevent the use of false measures for seacoals – presumably intended to confirm Sharpeigh's patent – received two readings (16, 20 Feb. 1626), but proceeded no further. The other, to punish Sharpeigh for reviving his patent, was first read on 27 Mar., but its progress was delayed by Buckingham's impeachment, and it was not committed until 1 June, too late to progress any further before the dissolution. In the meantime, the grievances' committee was prompted to seek belated cancellation of 1,200 bonds Boyd had taken for payment of the survey duty in 1616-18, although these efforts were presumably also frustrated by the dissolution.[25]

By 1626 factional squabbles over the technicalities of the coal trade were overshadowed by the stresses of war, particularly the depredations visited upon the coal trade by enemy privateers. A sortie of Spanish privateers from Dunkirk in October 1625, while primarily aimed at the Dutch herring fleet, also wrought havoc upon the east coast coal trade, and shortly before Parliament met in January 1626 the Deptford Trinity House recommended the arming of Newcastle colliers. Edward Whitby of Chester raised the subject in the Commons on 16 Feb., when Sir Peter Riddell moved to consult Elizabethan precedents.[26] These included a wartime levy of 12*d*. per chaldron of coal to maintain a coastal protection squadron, but when secretary of state (Sir) John Coke urged a revival of this scheme

on 25 Feb., it was quickly attacked as an imposition on trade. Sir Henry Anderson despaired of any solution to the problem; while Sir Peter Riddell complained 'that there is 8,000 persons at least set a-work in that work who are now idle', but argued against any increase in the £16,000 duty already charged upon the coal trade. On the following day both Newcastle MPs highlighted the plight of their constituents and appealed for a swift government response: 'those countries poor, and the recusants planted on the river; all along the people apt to stir'. Two weeks later Anderson and William Cage of Ipswich relayed news of further enemy depredations on the coal trade, and on 22 Mar. a petition from the Newcastle mariners protested at arrears of wages due to the crews of colliers pressed into royal service.[27]

Parliamentary complaints were designed to ensure that the Crown paid for coastal protection from existing revenues, but as Buckingham, the lord admiral, protested when confronted in the Lords on 1 Apr., the Navy's budget allowed only £22,000 for coastal defence; he recommended the appropriation of the duty charged for measuring of coal by the London corporation. This suggestion was ignored, but the Navy, stung into action by these criticisms, assigned a squadron of six ships to coastal defence at Easter 1626. The loss of £300,000 worth of subsidies at the dissolution of June 1626 meant that funds quickly ran short, and coal shipments declined to a new low during the winter of 1626-7, but from May 1627 Sir John Savile* encountered more success in raising funds by a levy of 6*d*. per chaldron on northern coal. This duty raised £953 over six months, but was unpopular with the colliers, who had armed themselves and organized their own convoys, and was dropped shortly before a new Parliament convened in March 1628.[28]

Disputes over the Forced Loan, arbitrary imprisonment and billeting left little room on the parliamentary agenda for other complaints, but on 7 May 1628, with an angry dissolution seemingly imminent, alderman Thomas Hoyle of York protested about the lack of coastal defences, and Sir Thomas Riddell raised the questions of shipping losses, and alleged plans for a further 2*s*. per chaldron imposition on coal. On 4 June, just after the king's first, unsatisfactory answer to the Petition of Right, an account of English shipping losses included 26 from Newcastle, and when Buckingham's failure to protect merchantmen was raised as part of the Remonstrance debate of 9 June, Sir Peter Riddell renewed complaints about Dunkirkers and the recently abandoned 6*d*. per chaldron Imposition. These complaints had some impact: after the end of the session, Savile's squadron was assigned Yorkshire subsidy revenues for its maintenance; and the colliers were forbidden to sail without naval escort. However, until the end of the war, the shipowners remained unenthusiastic about any new levy on coal for coastal defence.[29]

[1] W. Gray, *Chorographia* (1649); R. Howell, *Newcastle-upon-Tyne and the Puritan Rev.* 1-7; J. Hatcher, *Hist. of Brit. Coal Industry*, 68, 72-7; *HP Commons, 1386-1421*, i. 545-9. [2] Around 10 per cent of this total was exported. For the most credible analysis of shipments, see Hatcher, 483-504. [3] Originally innkeepers, Hostmen became middlemen, and later often mineowners. [4] *SR*, iii. 302-3; C54/1046, 1142; *CPR*, 1575-8, p. 433; 1582-3, p. 67; J.U. Nef, *Rise of Brit. Coal Industry*, i. 151-4; Hatcher, 512-14. [5] A Newcastle chaldron of coal was 53 cwt., twice the weight of a London chaldron: Hatcher, 559-69. [6] *Recs. Co. Hostmen* ed. F.W. Dendy (Surtees Soc. cv), 2-19; *CSP Dom.* 1595-7, pp. 501-2; *HMC Hatfield*, viii. 373-5, 384, 397, 413, 419; ix. 34; E. Suss. RO, GLY/447-8. [7] *Recs. Co. Hostmen*, 19-27, 49, 243; Hatcher, 517-18; CLRO, Reps. 26/2, f. 343; *CJ*, i. 228b. [8] *Newcastle Merchant Adventurers* ed. F.W. Dendy (Surtees soc. xciii), 115; *LJ*, ii. 394a, 396b; *HMC Hatfield*, xxiii. 220-1; xxiv. 52-3; Hull RO, L.159-60. [9] CLRO, Reps. 26/2, f. 546v; Reps. 27, ff. 10, 18, 30, 36v, 38v, 108, 110, 117; SP14/18/60; *Recs. Co. Hostmen*, 50-6. [10] CLRO, Reps. 27, ff. 150v, 160v, 176v, 180, 182v; *LJ*, ii. 368b, 370a, 392a. [11] CLRO, Reps. 27, f. 120v; *Procs. 1610* ed. Foster, i. 133; ii. 267-8; *Recs. Co. Hostmen*, 61; Hatcher, 493. See also E112/112/154. [12] *Procs. 1614 (Commons)*, 40, 236-7, 244, 307, 389, 397. [13] *Trinity House Trans.* ed. G.G. Harris (London Rec. Soc. xix), 18-19, 25-7; C66/2076/11; *Recs. Co. Hostmen*, 62; *APC*, 1615-16, pp. 519-20; 1616-17, pp. 135-6, 138-9, 165-7; SP14/87/61, 66. [14] STAC 8/21/2, 8/56/10; E159/454; SP14/98/29; *APC*, 1618-19, pp. 272-6, 373. [15] *Recs. Co. Hostmen*, 242, 267; *CD 1621*, iv. 196; *CSP Dom*. i. 529a, 575a, 655a; Nef, ii. 128-9. [16] *CJ*, i. 544b, 624a; *CD 1621*, ii. 378-9; iii. 281. [17] *CJ*, i. 597a, 628a, 653a; *CD 1621*, ii. 394-6, 478-9; iv. 276; vi. 214-15; Kyle thesis, 80-6. [18] *Recs. Co. Hostmen*, 69-70, 73-4; 'Pym 1624', i. f. 57; 'Nicholas 1624', f. 132v; *CJ*, i. 703b, 706a, 790b; E112/113/234; 112/113/236; E126/3, ff. 58-60. [19] C66/2180/5; *CSP Dom.* 1619-23, p. 61; E112/113/215; *Chamberlain Letters* ed. N.E. McClure, ii. 275. [20] SP46/164, f. 92; E126/2, ff. 244v-5, 248v; *CJ*, i. 693b, 769b; 'Pym 1624', i. f. 83; Nef, ii. 267-8. [21] *CSP Dom.* 1619-23, p. 58; *CJ*, i. 609a. Langford's 1623 patent (C66/2270/17) was apparently a poor redrafting of this grant. [22] *Recs. Co. Hostmen*, 67-70; *CSP Dom.* 1619-23, pp. 189, 406, 412, 538, 563; *APC*, 1621-3, pp. 318-19, 390; C66/2270/17. [23] *APC*, 1621-3, pp. 471-2, 503-4; 1623-5, pp. 49-50; *CSP Dom.* 1619-23, pp. 566, 587; C66/2310/11; SP14/162/20. [24] 'Nicholas 1624', f. 79v; *CJ*, i. 685b, 711-12, 794-6; 'Holland 1624', i. f. 52; SP14/162/20. [25] *Stuart Roy. Procs.* ed. J.P. Larkin and P.L. Hughes, i. 619-25; *Procs. 1626*, ii. 53, 72, 374; iii. 319, 312-3, 340-2. [26] R.A. Stradling, *Armada of Flanders*, 39-45; *Trin. House Trans.* 67-8; *Procs. 1626*, ii. 56. [27] *CSP Dom. Addenda*, 1580-1625, pp. 418-19; *Procs.1626*, ii. 130-1, 137-8, 141-2, 298, 313. [28] *Procs. 1626*, i. 239-42; *CSP Dom.* 1625-6, pp. 306, 350; *Trin. House Trans.* 83-4, 89-90; T. and W. RO, GU/TH/21; E351/2595. [29] C. Russell, *PEP*, 368-72; *CD 1628*, iii. 310-11, 319; iv. 91-9, 203, 211, 216; *APC*, 1628-9, pp. 6-7, 16, 101-2; 1629-30, pp. 394-5; SP16/133/5; *Trin. House Trans.* 107-10.

S.H.

NOTTINGHAMSHIRE

Number of voters: unknown

c. Mar. 1604	SIR JOHN HOLLES
	SIR PERCIVAL WILLOUGHBY
c. Mar. 1614	SIR GERVASE CLIFTON, bt.
	SIR JOHN HOLLES
27 Nov. 1620	SIR GERVASE CLIFTON, bt.
	SIR GEORGE CHAWORTH
19 Jan. 1624	SIR GERVASE CLIFTON, bt.
	ROBERT SUTTON
9 May 1625	SIR GERVASE CLIFTON, bt.
	HENRY STANHOPE
c. Jan. 1626	HENRY STANHOPE
	SIR THOMAS HUTCHINSON
c. Feb. 1628	SIR GERVASE CLIFTON, bt.
	(SIR) JOHN BYRON

Writing in response to the Crown's demand for Privy Seal loans, the Nottinghamshire commissioners for musters wrote in November 1625 of the 'smallness of this county ... and vastness of a forest running quite through it'. Their county was 'without trade or manufacture, without lead, iron or hidden treasurer, merely subsisting on the benefits common to it with all others', and it was afflicted by floods of the River Trent, of which 'they have of late lamentable experience'.[1] However, others viewed the county in a more favourable light. In Speed's *Theatre of the Empire of Great Britaine*, published in 1611, Nottinghamshire is described as possessing rich soil, 'good, wholesome and delectable' air, and 'corn and grass so fruitful, that it secondeth any other in the realm: and for water, woods and ... coals [it is] abundantly stored'.[2] Camden divided the county into two regions: a western part, dominated by Sherwood Forest, where the soil was predominantly sandy; and a more fertile region in the south and east, watered by the Trent, where the soil was more clayey. These two areas were referred to by the county's inhabitants as the sand and the clay.[3] The county town, Nottingham, is situated in the south. The gentry of the south exercised an almost complete stranglehold on the county's electoral politics, for of the men returned for the shire in this period only Holles lived in the north.

Although Nottinghamshire was notorious for its factionalism, there is no evidence that elections were contested in this period. Nottinghamshire's gentry, seeking to avoid a recurrence of the 1593 contest, which had split the county from top to bottom, evidently negotiated among themselves to ensure that the different interests had been accommodated prior to each election. This was apparently done informally, for when the 1st earl of Kingston (Sir Robert Pierrepont[†]) proposed a meeting of Nottinghamshire's great and the good to decide on nominations for the Short Parliament in 1640 he seems to have been suggesting an innovation.[4] Despite the absence of contests in this period, an understanding of the factions is essential to understanding how the parliamentary candidates were selected.

The rise in factionalism in the county was due to the collapse in influence of the Manners family in the late 1580s and the subsequent resistance by the local gentry to attempts by the Talbots to establish themselves as the dominant force in the county's politics. In the middle years of Elizabeth's reign Nottinghamshire's electoral politics were dominated by Edward Manners, 3rd earl of Rutland,[5] who died without leaving a son in 1587, whereupon the earldom passed to his brother John. However, Edward bequeathed a substantial part of his estates, perhaps a quarter or a third of the total, to his daughter, Elizabeth, who inherited the barony of Ros. The fourth earl died a year after his brother, leaving behind an 11-year-old son. Even after he came of age, the 5th earl seems to have made little impact on the politics of Nottinghamshire.[6]

After the death of the 4th earl of Rutland in 1588, George Talbot, 6th earl of Shrewsbury was appointed lord lieutenant of Nottinghamshire.[7] However, after Shrewsbury's death two years later an alliance of Nottinghamshire gentlemen led by Sir Thomas Stanhope[†], who had previously sat for the county at the 3rd earl of Rutland's nomination, and Stanhope's son-in-law, (Sir) John Holles, challenged the attempts of Gilbert Talbot[†], 7th earl of Shrewsbury, to control the politics of the county. This led to a bitterly fought election in 1593, in which Shrewsbury triumphed. The election of Richard Whalley in 1597, a member of the Stanhope faction whose family had been closely connected with the earls of Rutland, suggests a revival of the Manners interest. He took second place to John Byron, whose father, in addition to being sheriff, had attached himself to Shrewsbury in the 1590s. This arrangement may indicate that an accommodation had been reached between the two factions, with representatives of each taking one seat. If so this accord had broken down by 1601, possibly because of the 5th earl of Rutland's involvement in the 2nd earl of Essex's rising earlier that year. This enabled Shrewsbury to secure the return of his brother-in-law Sir Charles Cavendish and his nephew Robert Pierrepont, who was also married to his niece Gertrude Talbot.

Nevertheless, Stanhope and his allies managed to prevent Shrewsbury from succeeding his father as lord lieutenant. The county's military affairs were instead managed by a commission of musters, from which Shrewsbury was excluded.[8] Shrewsbury entertained James I lavishly at his home at Worksop in Nottinghamshire when the latter journeyed south on his accession in 1603. However, despite summoning his followers to attend him, no doubt to impress the new king with his regional power base,[9] he failed to persuade James to appoint him lord lieutenant.[10]

Shrewsbury may have been unable to consolidate his control over Nottinghamshire because of the emergence of (Sir) William Cecil[†] as a significant forced in the county's politics. Cecil was the son of Thomas, 2nd Lord Burghley (Thomas Cecil[†]) and nephew of James I's chief minister Robert Cecil[†], subsequently 1st earl of Salisbury. In 1589 William married Elizabeth the daughter of 3rd earl of Rutland and subsequently established himself at Newark-upon-Trent in Nottinghamshire, acquiring the lease of the castle and purchasing property nearby. In 1600 he was also appointed *custos rotulorum*. However, Cecil's power base in the county was limited, as his wife's share of the Manners estate lay mainly outside Nottinghamshire. Moreover, it is unlikely that he could count on the support of the earls of Rutland. In addition to the 5th earl's support for Essex, the Cecils' great rival, Thomas Cecil was in dispute with the Manners family over his wife's property and his son's title to the barony of Ros. William's influence in the county, such as it was, was therefore almost certainly derived from his connections at Court.[11] Despite this, it seems likely that Sir John Holles owed his return to Cecil; by 1604 the two men had struck up a close friendship, with the former keeping the latter informed of proceedings in the Commons during the parliamentary session of that year.[12]

Holles' colleague Sir Percival Willoughby was a newcomer to the county, who had acquired its grandest house, Wollaton, by marriage, together with a load of debt. He was sufficiently uncertain of success to stand for a second seat, at Tamworth, Staffordshire, which of course he waived after his return for the county. Willoughby was among those who had been knighted when James I visited Worksop in 1603 and may therefore have been more acceptable to Shrewsbury. This suggests that, as in 1597, the two factions agreed to divide the seats between them, but in 1604 the anti Talbot candidate took the first seat, whereas in 1597 the anti Talbot candidate had been returned second.[13]

Holles made a serious effort to gauge the attitude of his constituency to the Great Contract during the recess of 1610, though he did not miss the chance to complain of the misconduct of Shrewsbury's kinsmen, the Pierreponts. On 22 Sept. he reported to lord treasurer Salisbury that he had 'preached from region to region of this country' and found:

> in the better sort a very sharp appetite; but in these plebs ... a very uncertain temper. Yet methought they bit somewhat eagerly at the taking away all manner of purveyance. ... For though the king's person shines not so far northward, yet his castle and parks ... covet yearly many loadings forth of the king's woods. Likewise in tenures they tasted best the removing of escheators and feodaries, who, as they said, troubled them most of all upon supposed tenures, and that for small patches of land. So, as I think, out of this great magazine every one will find stuff to his fancy, though of much they suppose they have no use, and consequently not to be bargained for by them.[14]

Holles was re-elected to Parliament in 1614, but on this occasion the gentry of Nottinghamshire decided to give the Talbot interest primacy in the return. Consequently Holles had to take second place to Sir Gervase Clifton. The latter was head of the oldest family in the county, who had come of age since the last election and accepted one of the original baronetcies. As a kinsman of the Pierreponts he was connected to the earl of Shrewsbury, who had had taken an interest in his education, describing Clifton, while still a teenager, as 'of a rare and excellent wit'.[15]

Holles reluctantly agreed to support the Benevolence levied by James I after the 1614 Parliament failed to vote subsidies. Writing on 20 Oct. 1614 to John Wood, a Nottinghamshire commissioner of the musters, he argued that it was 'expedient ... to give as our fellows do, than to offer with one finger to stay a falling house'. He was particularly concerned that Shrewsbury might persuade James I to attribute resistance to the Benevolence to the lack of a lord lieutenant, and 'translate our aristocratical commission into a monarchical lieutenancy', because 'if only Nottingham[shire] look upon the commonwealth ... our obstinacy and stoutness [will] be attributed to the commissioners' ill affection or ill government'. He apparently believed that Shrewsbury was trying to put additional pressure on the Nottinghamshire gentry to respond quickly to the Benevolence in a covert attempt to foment resistance. Holles therefore suggested that it was better to raise the equivalent of a subsidy.[16] Holles' suspicions may have been well-founded, for in mid-November several of the earl's supporters – (Sir) George Parkins[†], who had been the previous year's sheriff, Sir Gervase Clifton, Robert Pierrepont[†], and John Hacker, a servant of Shrewsbury's – were summoned by the Privy Council to Whitehall, presumably in connection with the Benevolence.

Publicly, however, Shrewsbury acted beyond reproach, contributing over £160 in cash and a quantity of gilt plate. Perhaps as a result of the summons issued to his allies, Shrewsbury and his allies subsequently abandoned their obstructionism. Indeed, four years later Pierrepont informed Sir Thomas Lake I* that a third of the receipts from the Benevolence in Nottinghamshire had been raised by him. In total over £580 was collected in Nottinghamshire, of which Holles provided £30, Clifton £26 13s. 4d., and Shrewsbury's brother-in-law, Sir Charles Cavendish[†], £50.[17]

In July 1616 Holles was raised to the peerage, thereby rendering him ineligible for further election. He evidently failed to influence subsequent Nottinghamshire elections as he fell out with his nephew Philip, 1st Lord Stanhope, the grandson of Sir Thomas. Moreover, his relations with Thomas Cecil seem to have cooled after the latter succeeded as 2nd earl of Exeter in 1623, possibly because Exeter became an adherent of the duke of Buckingham, whom Holles opposed.[18]

On the death of Shrewsbury in May 1616 the earl's title was divided from his estates. The former went to his brother Edward, while the lands were divided between his three daughters, the wives of William, 3rd earl of Pembroke, Thomas Howard, 21st or 14th earl of Arundel, and Sir Henry Grey*. Shrewsbury appointed Sir William Cavendish II*, the son of Sir Charles, as his executor. Cavendish proceeded to lay claim to part of the Talbot estate in lieu of the money that his father had lent Shrewsbury. The dispute continued until 1620 when, shortly before the elections, Pembroke procured a peerage for Cavendish, who became Viscount Mansfield, in return for which Cavendish withdrew his claims.[19]

The principal figures who had been allied to the earl of Shrewsbury – Cavendish, Clifton and Pierrepont – were powerful in their own right and were closely tied by bonds of friendship and family. They therefore remained important in Nottinghamshire electoral politics, and may have been more influential now that their neighbours no longer feared that Shrewsbury would dominate the shire. However, only Clifton was capable of standing for election, as Cavendish was a peer and Robert Pierrepont was widely suspected of Catholicism. Consequently, it was Clifton who was re-elected in 1620, when he took the first place.[20] The second seat went to the courtier Sir George Chaworth, a member of an old Nottinghamshire family. Chaworth had previously been connected with the earl of Shrewsbury, and probably had the support of Clifton and Pierrepont, having in June 1620 appointed them trustees for his wife. Moreover, he may also have been supported by one or more of Shrewsbury's coheirs. By 1624 he had attached himself to the earl of Arundel, and his sister married Pembroke's secretary Edward Leech*, although at what date cannot be established.[21]

Clifton was again returned for the senior seat in 1624. It is not known if Chaworth also sought re-election, but the second place went to Robert Sutton, scion of another long-established family. Sutton may have been nominated the earl of Exeter, as two years later Exeter recommended Sutton for inclusion in the commission for musters.[22] There were at least 29 parties to the election indenture, including five members of the county bench and Sutton's uncle, John Odingsells†.[23] It was Sutton who, on 27 Apr. 1624, presented the names of Nottinghamshire's suspected recusant officeholders to the Commons, among them three Nottinghamshire justices who were married to recusants – Robert Pierrepont; Pierrepont's brother-in-law Fulke Cartwright; and Sir George Parkins. This rather suggests that Sutton was no friend of Pierrepont and his allies.[24]

The 1625 election saw the re-emergence of the Stanhope family in Nottinghamshire electoral politics with the election of Lord Stanhope's son Henry, who was still under-age. The indenture was signed by Sir Matthew Palmer, who had conducted the previous election, William Stanhope† (the candidate's uncle) and 26 others, of whom only two appear to have been Nottinghamshire justices.[25] However, this does not mean that the Nottinghamshire bench was uninterested in Parliament, as its members clearly followed proceedings in the Commons closely. On 1 Aug. they wrote to their MPs asking them to amend the bill to regulate clerks of the market, which had received its first reading on 27 June, by introducing a clause 'to remedy the use of unreasonable and variable measures in market towns'. However, Parliament was dissolved eleven days later before the bill could be committed.[26]

In the absence of deputy lieutenants the Nottinghamshire commissioners of musters were charged with levying the Privy Seal loan initiated by Charles I after the 1625 Parliament. In the letter to the Privy Council quoted above the commissioners admitted that the total sum they had assessed on their neighbours was low, which they justified by arguing that Nottinghamshire was too poor to yield more. Possibly as a result, a high proportion of the £720 demanded from the lenders of Nottinghamshire was collected. In January 1626 Clifton, who had been appointed collector, reported to the Privy Council that he had received payments from 34 of the 45 men to whom he had issued demands, and in the following month he paid £530 into the Exchequer.[27]

On 4 Jan. 1626 Holles, by now earl of Clare, wrote to the earl of Exeter that 'a prophetical spirit of a Parliament walks for voices, up and down the country'. This suggests that at least one potential candidate had already begun canvassing in Nottinghamshire, although Clare himself was evidently uninvolved, as he complained that 'this country [is] barren of fit instruments for such a work'.[28] For the first time since he came of age, Sir Gervase Clifton failed to secure one of the county seats. Perhaps his activities as collector of the Privy Seal loan had impaired his standing in the county. Alternatively, he may have been reluctant to take the second seat after Stanhope secured the first. The junior place went instead to Sir Thomas Hutchinson, who may have been acceptable to Clifton, having been the sheriff who returned him and Chaworth in 1620.[29]

A week after the dissolution the attorney-general was ordered to prepare a commission appointing Mansfield lord lieutenant of Nottinghamshire, thereby dissolving the commission of musters.[30] On 17 Aug. Mansfield, an ally of Buckingham's, wrote to Secretary Conway (Sir Edward Conway I*) assuring him that he would do his best to levy the Benevolence demanded in the wake of the 1626 Parliament's failure to vote subsidies, but he feared that his neighbours were 'governed by ill precedents, and … the dregs of the last Parliament'. His fears were well founded, for on 22 Sept. the Nottinghamshire justices reported to the Council that 'the generality, save very few whose offers in the whole county came to about £70, refused to give otherwise than by Parliament, the ordinary and usual way as they alleged'.[31] Early the following year the commissioners for the Forced Loan found 'the country …, not a little perplexed with the height of the demand, and the manner of it, as not being moulded and concluded in Parliament'. Clare and Lord Stanhope refused to pay, and were subsequently purged from the bench, while Hutchinson absented himself from the county, although he subsequently submitted after being summoned before the Privy Council. Moreover, a servant belonging to Theophilus, 4th earl of Lincoln, scattered a manuscript tract against the Loan in the highway leading to Nottingham at the same time that the commissioners met. However, led by Mansfield, the commissioners succeeded in allaying local anxieties, in particular by emphasizing Charles I's promises that the Loan would not become a precedent and payment would not deter him from summoning parliaments in the future. As a result, in August 1627 the commissioners reported that all but £27 had long since been paid into the Exchequer.[32]

With Stanhope's father no longer on the bench, Clifton was again returned first for the county when a fresh Parliament was summoned at the beginning of 1628. However, Clifton took care not to ride rough-shod over Stanhope by ensuring that the latter was returned for East Retford, where Clifton was high steward. The second place was taken by Sir John Byron, the grandson of the 1597 member, the head of an important but highly indebted Nottinghamshire family, and brother-in-law of Sir Thomas Hutchinson. It is unlikely that Byron had the support of Mansfield, who had not appointed him a deputy lieutenant even though Byron had been added to the commission of musters on the earl of Exeter's nomination in May 1626.[33] The Nottinghamshire members reported that there were no recusant officeholders in their county on 24 Apr. 1628, perhaps because Robert Pierrepont's son Henry sat for Nottingham, but when Sir Thomas Hoby reported the full list on 14 June Pierrepont, by now Viscount Newark, had his accustomed place.[34]

[1] SP16/10/61. [2] J. Speed, *Theatre of the Empire of Great Britaine* (1611), p. 65. [3] W. Camden, *Britain* trans. P. Holland (1610), p. 547. [4] A. Wall, 'Patterns of pols. in Eng., 1558-1625' *HJ*, xxxi. 950; *HP Commons, 1558-1603*, i. 233; M.A. Kishlanksy, *Parlty. Selection*, 56. [5] *HP Commons, 1558-1603*, i. 222. [6] L. Stone, *Fam. and Fortune*, 174-6, 201; *CP*, xi. 259. [7] *CPR*, 1588-9 (L. and I. Soc. ccc), 62. [8] *HP Commons, 1558-1603*, i. 222-3, 525; iii. 607; *Cal. Talbot Pprs.* ed. G.R. Batho (Derbys. Recs. ser. iv), 177, 316; *Illustrations of Brit. Hist.* ed. E. Lodge, iii. 2-6; *Cal. of Shrewsbury Pprs. in LPL* ed. E.G.W. Bill (Derbys. Arch. Rec. Soc. i), 157; W.T. MacCaffrey, 'Talbot and Stanhope: an Episode in Elizabethan Pols.', *BIHR*, xxxiii. 76, 81. [9] *True Narration of the Entertainment of his Royall Majestie* (1603), unpag.; J. Hunter, *Hallamshire*, 121. [10] *Cal. of Shrewsbury Pprs. in LPL*, 166. [11] C. Brown, *Hist. Newark-on-Trent*, 16-17, 24; Stone, 175, 177, 196; *CP*, xi. 109; C231/1, p. 180. [12] *HMC Portland*, ix. 11-13, 153. [13] Nichols, *Progs. Jas. I*, i. 88. [14] *Letters of John Holles* ed. P.R. Seddon (Thoroton Soc. Rec. ser. xxxvi), 513-15. [15] *HMC Hatfield*, xii. 276, 540; Thoroton, *Notts.* (1790), i. 105. [16] *HMC Portland*, ix. 139. [17] *APC*, 1613-14, pp. 625-6; *List of Sheriffs* comp. A. Hughes (PRO, L. and I. ix), 104; *Cal. Talbot Pprs.* 269; D. Hirst, 'Privy Council and Problems of Enforcement in the 1620s', *JBS*, xviii. 62, n. 62; *CSP Dom.* 1611-18, pp. 260, 538; E351/1950. Parkins may have deputized for Robert Pierrepont's father as recorder of Nottingham. *HP Commons, 1558-1603*, iii. 176, 222. [18] *Letters of John Holles* (xxxi), 141-2; Ibid. (xxxv), 317; *CSP Dom.* 1625-6, p. 230. [19] C.R. Mayes, 'Sale of Peerages in Early Stuart Eng.', *JMH*, xxix. 23-7; C142/444/87; PROB 11/128, ff. 307v-8; [20] Thoroton, i. 176; *HMC Var.* vii. 402, 411; *Oxford DNB sub* Pierrepont, Robert. [21] PROB 11/181, f. 310v; Add. 72368, f. 11; *Vis. Notts.* (Harl. Soc. iv), 128. [22] *CSP Dom.* 1625-6, p. 231. [23] C219/38/180; T. Rymer, *Foedera*, viii. pt. 2, p. 13. [24] *CJ*, i. 776b; *Parlty. or Constitutional Hist. of Eng.* (1751-61), vi. 328; Thoroton, i. 176; C219/38/180. [25] C219/39/148; Rymer, viii. pt. 2, p. 13. [26] Nottingham UL, Cl/C 360; *Procs. 1625*, p. 252. [27] SP16/10/61; *CSP Dom.* 1625-6, pp. 165, 231; E401/2586 pp. 203-5; E401/1912. [28] *Letters of John Holles* (xxxv), 317. [29] *List of Sheriffs*, 104. [30] *CSP Dom.* 1625-6, p. 359. [31] *CSP Dom.* 1625-6, pp. 406, 434; R. Cust, *Forced Loan and English Pols.* 95, 159. [32] *Notts. County Recs.* comp. H.H. Copnall, 110-11; *APC*, 1627, p. 74; Add. 12496, f. 125; *Historical Collections* ed. J. Rushworth, iii. app. 8; Cust, 102, 104-5, 118, 170-1, 228-9; *Oxford DNB sub* Stanhope, Philip. [33] *APC*, 1625-6, p. 476. [34] *CD 1628*, iii. 63; iv. 319.

J.P.F.

EAST RETFORD

Right of election: in the freemen

Number of voters: 83 in 1624

1 Mar. 1604	SIR JOHN THORNHAUGH	
	SIR THOMAS DARRELL	
c. Mar. 1614	SIR WILLIAM CAVENDISH II	
	SIR WALTER CHUTE	
c. Dec. 1620	(SIR) NATHANIEL RICH	
	EDWARD WORTLEY	
	?George Lassells*	
20 Jan. 1624	JOHN HOLLES	
	(SIR) NATHANIEL RICH	
	?(Sir) Edward Wortley	
9 Mar. 1624	JOHN DARCY *vice* Rich,	
	chose to sit for Harwich	47
	(Sir) Edward Wortley	36[1]
c. *May 1624*	SIR FRANCIS WORTLEY, bt. *vice*	
	Darcy, deceased	
3 May 1625	JOHN HOLLES, (Lord Houghton)	
	SIR FRANCIS WORTLEY, bt.	
20 Jan. 1626	JOHN HOLLES, (Lord Houghton)	
	(SIR) EDWARD WORTLEY	
c. Feb. 1628	(SIR) HENRY STANHOPE	
	SIR EDWARD OSBORNE, bt.	

Situated on the River Idle in the north-eastern Nottinghamshire hundred of Bassetlaw, 32 miles from Nottingham, East Retford was an important market town and administrative centre, whose suburbs stretched into the neighbouring parishes of West Retford, Clarborough and Ordsall, though these lay outside the corporation's jurisdiction. A regular location for meetings of the county magistrates, and the centre of the local deanery, East Retford also boasted a significant textile industry, although this declined during this period, as a result of which the urban population contracted from about 1,150 in 1603 to about 850 in the late 1620s.[2]

East Retford was not incorporated until 1607, when it received a charter which confirmed the previous structure of a common council comprising two bailiffs, who each served for a year, and 12 aldermen, who served for life. However, the charter also restricted the previously untrammelled power of the freemen over the election of borough officers. When vacancies occurred among the aldermen, the freemen's choice of replacements was restricted to nominees chosen by the council. The same was true in respect of the office of junior bailiff, and in the case of the senior bailiff the council alone determined the matter. It also appointed a steward 'instructed in the law of England' to preside over the borough court, who became known as the 'learned steward', and a high steward, who was described in 1624 as the borough's 'protector'.[3]

East Retford was represented in Parliament once in the early fourteenth century but did not subsequently return Members until 1571.[4] The franchise rested with the freemen, the two bailiffs acted as returning officers and elections were held at the Moothall. Returns were made in the name of the bailiffs and burgesses, and were signed by the bailiffs.[5] There is no evidence that the corporation tried to promote any legislation in Parliament or that its Members were ever paid.

Of the 11 Members elected in this period, none were townsmen and only four – Cavendish, Holles, Stanhope and Thornhaugh – were Nottinghamshire residents. Of these four, Stanhope lived in the south of the county. As many Members came from the West Riding of Yorkshire (John Darcy, the Wortleys and Sir Edward Osborne) as from Nottinghamshire, which was probably attributable to East Retford's location close to the Yorkshire border. In 1624 Darcy was described as 'a neighbour'.[6] Of the remaining three Members, Darrell lived in Gainsborough, just across the border in northern Lincolnshire. Only Sir Nathaniel Rich and Sir Walter Chute were not in any sense local men.

In an account of the second 1624 election among the Clifton manuscripts it is stated that the borough's high steward had 'always at every parliament recommended to the town some gentleman of worth for one of the burgesses'. This recommendation, 'being all the courtesy the town hath been able to afford' the high steward, had 'always been yielded to without contradiction'.[7] For most of the Jacobean period this claim appears to have been accurate, as one Member at each election can be identified as the known or probable nominee of the high steward, while the other was usually drawn from the local gentry. At the beginning of James's reign the office of high steward was held by Roger Manners, 5th earl of Rutland, whose family had secured the borough's enfranchisement in 1571.[8] He almost certainly secured the return in 1604 of Sir John Thornhaugh, whose father was his deputy warden of Sherwood Forest.[9] Thornhaugh's junior colleague was Sir Thomas Darrell, whose son had acquired

the manor of West Retford, situated across the river from the borough, by marriage. When the 5th earl of Rutland died in 1612 the title passed to his younger brother, Francis Manners. As he was suspected of recusancy,[10] the common council preferred to elect as the new high steward the 7th earl of Shrewsbury (Gilbert Talbot[†]), who in 1614 nominated his underage nephew Sir William Cavendish II, assuring the council that:

> what he shall want in the gravity of grey hairs to do your town any good or to defend it from any prejudice I dare undertake will be supplied in the love and good affection that he beareth unto the welfare thereof and unto all you his good neighbours the inhabitants there, wherein he shall be most assured of my best help and assistance.

In March 1614 Sir Richard Williamson*, the borough's learned steward, wrote to the council requesting the other seat, arguing that if the borough elected a stranger it might be thought that he was 'either unwilling or unworthy to be employed ... which may be some disreputation to myself but (which I more regard) some disgrace to the body of your incorporation'.[11] In the event the remaining seat went to a Kentish courtier, Sir Walter Chute, the son of an old friend of Sir John Holles*. A wealthy local landowner, Holles was elected for the county in 1614.

On Shrewsbury's death in 1616 the Talbot estates were divided up between the earl's three daughters. East Retford's next high steward was thus not a peer but Sir Gervase Clifton* who, 'being a near neighbour', was someone 'from whom the town had received many favours'.[12] However, despite a promising beginning, Clifton subsequently found it difficult to maintain the high steward's parliamentary patronage in the borough, perhaps because of his lower social status. In 1620 he almost certainly nominated the Essex gentleman Sir Nathaniel Rich, a connection of his first wife, who took the senior seat. Sir John Holles, by now Lord Houghton, sought the remaining place for his eldest son, John, but warned the latter on 16 Nov. 1620 that William, 3rd earl of Pembroke, whose wife was one of Shrewsbury's heirs, and Pembroke's principal local agent George Lassells, had already 'spoken to those of Retford for their burgess before I sent to them'.[13] This strongly suggests that Pembroke had nominated Lassells for the seat, but if he did so then Lassells was either rejected or was defeated after a contest, as the place went to Edward Wortley, whose mother held considerable property in the neighbourhood in jointure and whose second husband, William Cavendish[†], 1st earl of Devonshire, owned the advowson of the East Retford parish church.

In 1624 Clifton again nominated Rich, who was elected, according to the town clerk Robert Browne, with 'not one voice dissenting'. However there was 'great opposition' for the other seat, indicating that John Holles was only chosen after a contest.[14] The other candidate or candidates were not named in Browne's account, but it is likely that Edward Wortley, now knighted, also stood. Following the election Rich agreed to serve for Harwich, where he had also been returned, at the request of the countess of Devonshire to make way for Sir Edward Wortley.[15] However this private agreement cut across the rights of Clifton as high steward and consequently on 23 Feb., the day after Rich formally plumped for Harwich, Clifton's messenger, a Mr. Saunderson, arrived in East Retford. Having determined that the bailiffs, who were unaware that Rich had been returned twice, had not already promised the vacant seat to someone else, Saunderson presented Clifton's letter recommending John Darcy, the son of the 3rd Lord Darcy and nephew of Clifton's close friend Sir Peter Frescheville*. The bailiffs thereupon convened a meeting of the aldermen and freemen for the following day, at which Clifton's letter was read out. According to Robert Browne, the assembly 'generally approved' of its contents, 'not one burgess gainsaying' the choice of Darcy. The next day, however, saw the arrival of the countess of Devonshire's messenger, Philip Spurling, with her nomination of Sir Edward Wortley. On learning that the corporation had already committed itself to Darcy, Spurling refused to withdraw and 'requested a fair election'. In order to accomplish this, however, he needed time in which to build up a party in the town for Wortley. Fortunately for him he possessed the means to delay the election as, before leaving Westminster, he had obtained the writ for the election which, naturally, he refused to hand over to the bailiffs, claiming that he was first owed a fee for its carriage. When the bailiffs refused payment, on the ground that no fee was due for writs conveyed on the king's business, Spurling delivered the writ to the sheriff, whose precept did not reach the borough until 5 March. Consequently, the election was not held until 9 March.[16]

Between his arrival in East Retford on 26 Feb. and the date of the election Spurling succeeded in building up an impressive political machine which, if not successful in securing the election for Wortley, did seriously alarm Clifton's supporters. The core of Wortley's support came from townsmen connected to the countess of Devonshire and those disaffected with the corporation. The former group included the bailiff of the countess' nearby property and the vicar, who used his Sunday sermon to sing the praises

of his patroness, 'naming the countess divers times ..., pressing what good her honour had done to him and intended to the town'. In addition the family of Richard Elsam, a prominent supporter of Wortley, came from the manor of Ordsall, part of the countess' property near the town. Wortley supporters also included Thomas Draper, who had been dismissed as alderman 'for his miscarriage and evil government' in 1622, and Richard Welch, a butcher who had long been in dispute with the corporation about commercial premises in the borough.

Spurling used various forms of persuasion to reach beyond his core support. He argued that Darcy was too young to be elected, claiming that he was only 16, whereas he was probably 22. He also alleged that Clifton was actually indifferent to the outcome of the election, said that Clifton was not 'great enough' to act as patron for the borough, 'for he could not speak to the king for the town if need be', and questioned the legality of Clifton's office, arguing that 'the town had no power to make a high steward'. This was presumably a reference to the fact that the office of high steward was not actually mentioned in the 1607 charter. Furthermore, Spurling made various threats and promises on behalf of the countess of Devonshire. She would, he declared, establish a workhouse in the town to relieve the poor if Wortley were elected, but if she did not get her way any enclosures on property leased by freemen from the earl or countess of Devonshire would be levelled and actions brought for trespass. Moreover, the poor would lose their rights to glean in her fields and gather fuel in her woods. Although the poor had no vote, Spurling was clearly hoping to intimidate them into coercing the freemen. Spurling also used more direct inducements to influence the voters. According to Browne, the town clerk, Spurling's faction 'spent bravely and entertained their burgesses that they won with brave merriments at the tavern', inviting their wives as well 'to make their husbands faster', and running up a bar bill of £40. Direct bribery was also used to buy the votes of the 'poorer burgesses', the going rating varying between £2 and £4 a vote, so that by the eve of the election the 'common speech through the town' was 'ten pounds for three voices'. To prevent any backsliding, those whose votes were purchased were forced to sign an agreement and threatened with prosecution in Star Chamber if they broke their promise. Naturally, Wortley's supporters subsequently cast doubt on the charge that they had bought votes, claiming that the allegation was 'slenderly proved by persons of mean condition', and that there was only one witness per each incident.

To counteract Spurling's threats and rumours the bailiffs convened a meeting on 1 Mar., at which Clifton's messenger, Saunderson, reassured the freemen that Clifton was serious in his support for Darcy, and how 'fearful Sir Gervase was to hazard my Lord Darcy's honour and his son's upon the strength of his letter now in absence'. In addition, the bailiffs and aldermen, 'fearing that ... the town should receive an incurable blemish to have a burgess place thus bought and sold', tried to pack the electorate at this meeting by enrolling new freemen sympathetic to Clifton. The town clerk Browne claimed that all the new freemen were legitimately enfranchised, being the sons of aldermen, but in a paper apparently drawn up for the Commons' privileges committee, Wortley's supporters claimed that only one of the 11 new freemen created was a householder and thus eligible to vote: the rest were 'foreigners and sojourners'. When Wortley's supporters presented their own sons to be made free, they were rejected on the grounds that they had not given prior notice and had not brought proof of their sons' dates of birth. The meeting ended in 'a great uproar' and the 'bailiffs were enforced in all haste to adjourn the court and speed themselves away for fear of some mischief'.[17]

On the day of the election the town authorities took steps to maintain order and overawe Wortley's supporters. The bailiffs posted a guard of 10 or 12 armed men to stand at the door of the Moothall. Sir George Lassells 'and other gentlemen that were comed [sic] to the town as well wishers to Mr. Darcy' were asked to patrol the market place during the election to 'stay the multitude'. Lassells, presumably a relation of George Lassells*, was a Nottinghamshire j.p. and friend of Clifton's, who had been sued by Wortley's elder brother Sir Francis in Star Chamber in 1620 for beating his servant. In addition the bailiffs and town clerk had the serjeant-at-mace arrest two prominent members of the Wortley party. Only the freemen were allowed into the hall, but then, according to Browne:

> just as it was plotted beforehand, all the poor of the town, with some others of the commons were brought into the market place accompanied with Vicar Watt and Welch his wife, who emboldened and encouraged them to cry 'a Wortley, a Wortley', telling them, that if were not 'a Wortley' they and all the town were undone. There upon begun a great cry and noise, with whooping and shouting so loud that we in the hall could not hear one word when the king's writ was read.

Indeed, the disturbance was so great that Browne was forced to stop reading the writ until the noise had died down. When he finally resumed he was again interrupted, this time by the noise from the market place. Nevertheless the bailiffs were eventually able to proceed to the election, and Darcy was returned, winning the seat by a margin precisely equal to the number of new freemen created by the corporation.[18]

In his account of the election, Browne constantly emphasized the poverty of Wortley's supporters. This allowed him to emphasize the use of bribery and threats in Spurling's campaign, which would have had more influence on the poor freemen, and to portray the Wortley campaign as socially subversive. However, while it is true that only two of the 12 aldermen voted for Wortley, the latter's supporters included other prominent townsmen, among them at least three former bailiffs.[19]

In the aftermath of the election both factions considered how to continue their struggle. During the Easter recess Clifton wrote to the corporation thanking it for 'preserving my reputation withal which hath ever been of more esteem with me then all I possess'. He also supported a proposal by Browne to have 'some exemplary punishment ... mediated, for avoiding this tumultuous and corrupt carriages of elections hereafter, and to reduce the inferior sort to terms of better conformity'. Browne seems to have been thinking along the lines of a prosecution in Star Chamber, probably because he considered that Wortley's supporters were essentially guilty of riot. However, Clifton advised a petition to Parliament 'because it is the proper court for complaints of that nature'. He may also have heard that Wortley's supporters were preparing to petition the committee for privileges, and consequently wanted to bring a counter suit. The corporation agreed with Clifton, and borrowed £60 to fund their own petition, which was subsequently termed 'the second or cross petition' by Wortley's supporters.[20]

One of the most interesting features of the Wortley petition is that its authors never claimed that their candidate had been rightfully elected. Instead they charged Browne with 'divers misdemeanours' and sought a new writ. Clifton himself acknowledged the importance of Browne's 'endeavours throughout the whole passage', praising him as not merely 'firm and cordial' but also 'ingenious'. Before the case could be heard, however, Darcy unexpectedly died. The committee nevertheless considered that 'the misdemeanours, on either side, touching the undue preparation or disturbance of the election remained fully examinable', and consequently it proceeded to a hearing. As well as complaining of the creation of the new freemen, Wortley's supporters protested against the arrest of prominent members of their faction by the town serjeant, who apparently told one voter that 'he would pull the flesh from his bones if he gave his voice for Sir Edward Wortley'. They also argued that the bailiffs had been openly opposed to Wortley and that the security measures adopted on election day had been unnecessary. The committee decided that offences had committed by both sides, but that three Wortley supporters, Spurling, Watt and Welch, were particularly culpable, as was the serjeant. This finding was reported by John Glanville* to the Commons on 28 May, but he also recommended that as Darcy was dead, the session was drawing to an end and 'the offences committed were not very enormous, nor proved for the most part, other than by single testimony', it would be advisable to 'pass by the matter'. According to Glanville's own account the House agreed to these suggestions, but the evidence of the Commons Journal suggests rather that it was decided to let the matter sleep until the next session which, in the event, never transpired.[21]

The election of Darcy proved to be a pyrrhic victory for Clifton. At the by-election held to choose Darcy's replacement Sir Edward Wortley's elder brother Sir Francis was returned. Sir Francis was re-elected in 1625, and Sir Edward himself was returned again in 1626, when Sir Francis was a candidate in the Yorkshire county election. As Holles was returned for the other seat on both occasions it would seem that Clifton had lost his influence over the borough. He did not recover it until 1628, at which time Holles was abroad and the influence of the countess of Devonshire may have been diminished by the death of her husband. Clifton brought in Sir Peter Frescheville's son-in-law, Sir Edward Osborne, bt., and probably supported Sir Henry Stanhope in return for his father's interest in the county election.[22]

[1] P.R. Seddon, 'Parlty. Election at East Retford, 1624', *Trans. Thoroton Soc.* lxxvi. 31. [2] D. Marcombe, *English Small Town Life*, 10-11, 26-7, 112-13. [3] Ibid. 47-51; J.S. Piercy, *Hist. Retford* (1828), pp. 31-49; Nottingham UL, CL/LP51. [4] *OR.* [5] C219/39/149. [6] Nottingham UL, CL/LP51. [7] Ibid. [8] *HP Commons, 1558-1603*, i. 224. [9] Marcombe, 74 [10] *Oxford DNB sub* Manners, Francis, sixth earl of Rutland. [11] Marcombe, 75. [12] Nottingham UL, CL/LP51. [13] *Letters of John Holles* ed. P.R. Seddon (Thoroton Soc. Rec. ser. xxxv), 247-8. [14] Nottingham UL, CL/LP51. [15] *HMC 8th Rep.* pt. 2 (1881), p. 29. [16] Nottingham UL, CL/LP51; PROB 11/165, f. 333v. [17] Ibid.; Seddon, 31. [18] Nottingham UL, CL/LP51; Harl. 6806, ff. 253v-4; Marcombe, 77; Seddon, 31; STAC 8/303/17. [19] Marcombe, 84-6. [20] Nottingham UL, CL/C378; Marcombe, 82; Harl. 6806, ff. 253v-4. [21] J. Glanville, *Reps. of Certain Cases Determined and Adjudged by the Commons in Parl.* (1775), pp. 128-32; Nottingham UL, CL/C378; Harl. 6806, ff. 253v-4; Seddon, 32-3; *CJ*, i. 797b. [22] *Letters of John Holles*, 373; *HP Commons, 1558-1603*, i. 569.

J.P.F./B.C.

NOTTINGHAM

Right of election: in the freemen

Number of voters: 44 in 1624[1]

c. Mar. 1604	RICHARD HURT, alderman
	ANKER JACKSON, alderman
	Robert Pierrepont†
c. Mar. 1614	WILLIAM GREGORY, town clerk
	ROBERT STAPLES, alderman
4 Dec. 1620	MICHAEL PUREFOY
	GEORGE LASSELLS
26 Jan. 1624	JOHN BYRON
	SIR CHARLES CAVENDISH
c. May 1625	ROBERT GREAVES
	JOHN MARTYN
c. Jan. 1626	SIR GERVASE CLIFTON, bt.
	JOHN BYRON
18 Feb. 1628	SIR CHARLES CAVENDISH
	HENRY PIERREPONT

Situated in south Nottinghamshire, a mile north of the river Trent, Nottingham was dominated by its castle perched on a rock.[2] During the late Elizabethan period the borough grew rapidly, so that by the beginning of the seventeenth century it was a medium-sized town of about 3,500 people, but thereafter successive outbreaks of plague served to halt the population increase.[3] The mainstay of the local economy was the leather trade which, though in decline, nevertheless employed the largest proportion of the town's workforce in 1625. Nottingham was also a major centre for the coal trade, which was shipped up the Trent to the ports on the Humber. This trade was dominated by the local gentry, many of whom had houses in the borough, including Sir John Holles* and Sir Thomas Hutchinson*. The decline in the leather industry, coupled with the economic importance of the gentry, may explain the difficulties the town faced in maintaining its electoral independence in this period.[4]

Early seventeenth-century Nottingham was governed in accordance with the charter granted in 1448, which established the town as a county borough. Under this charter, Nottingham was governed by a council or 'hall' composed of the mayor, six other aldermen and several select 'burgesses'. Officials were originally chosen by the freemen, but these rights had been engrossed by the council. There was, however, a significant broadening of the governing body during the early Jacobean period. Since 1577 the hall had consisted of seven aldermen and 12 common councilmen, all of whom were of the 'clothing' (previous officeholders). In 1606, however, after a protracted dispute, the number was expanded from 19 to 31, and was henceforth to include six ordinary freemen not of the clothing, who were to be chosen by the commonalty.[5]

Nottingham was first represented in Parliament in 1295.[6] As a county borough it had its own sheriffs, who conducted the parliamentary elections, which were held at the county court, in the guildhall. The returns were made between the sheriffs and the freemen, of whom there were 516 in 1625. Under Elizabeth only members of the corporation participated in elections. However, in 1624, as is clear from the return, elements outside the hall played a part in the formal election. Forty-four freemen were party to the indenture, of whom just over one-third are identifiable as members of the governing body or as past officeholders. The others were evidently ordinary freemen, plus a few eminent men closely associated with the corporation but not actually part of it. Two men who fell into this latter category were the archdeaconry official Michael Purefoy and the lawyer John Martyn, both of whom represented the town in Parliament on other occasions.

The participation of ordinary freemen in the electoral process in the early Stuart period does not mean that they had much power to affect the outcome. Normally the hall seems to have sewn up elections in advance by itself. The corporation records include a list of the 'suitors' for election in 1624, presumably those who had applied to the Hall for a seat. The Hall seems to have selected two men from the list, who were then presented to a general meeting of the freemen for formal election. In 1620 a meeting of the Hall took place three days before the date of the return, at which it was decided to open up the election to outsiders. A similar meeting was also recorded in 1625, when it was decided to restrict the election to townsmen. These gatherings show that the Hall did discuss elections on its own, and make decisions concerning their outcome. Although only the 1628 Members were recorded as having been approved by the Hall before their election, it therefore seems likely that it was the normal practice for the Hall to present two nominees to a general meeting of the freemen for formal election.[7]

During the early Elizabethan period the earls of Rutland, the traditional custodians of Nottingham castle, were usually able to secure one seat for their own candidate. However, the influence of the Manners family lapsed with the death of the 4th earl in 1588. The 5th earl, Roger Manners, seems to have been unable or unwilling to influence the borough, even after he came of age, despite being appointed constable of Nottingham castle in 1600. Moreover, his brother, who succeeded him as both earl and constable in 1612, was a recusant.[8] The obvious candidate to fill the void created by the absence of a Manners interest was Gilbert Talbot[†], 7th earl of Shrewsbury, a powerful figure in the Midlands, who made Worksop manor in Nottinghamshire his principal seat. In July 1603 Shrewsbury secured the election of his brother-in-law, (Sir) Henry Pierrepont[†], as recorder of Nottingham, despite the latter's lack of legal qualifications. However Shrewsbury was unable to persuade the borough to return Pierrepont's son, Robert[†], to Parliament in 1604. Instead, the borough elected two aldermen, Richard Hurt and Anker Jackson, both of whom were mercers and former mayors. Hurt was the more senior figure, having been elected mayor three years earlier than Jackson, and consequently was named first in the return, although Jackson had previously sat for the borough in 1597.[9]

The corporation may have subsequently regretted its rebuff to Shrewsbury, for not long after the 1604 election its dispute with the freemen over the size of the Hall was referred to the Privy Council, of which Shrewsbury was a member. To rectify the situation, Shrewsbury was appointed high steward of the borough in January 1606, the only occasion when this position was filled during this period. Another reason the corporation may have regretted its decision to elect townsmen was that it fell into dispute with Hurt and Jackson over the payment of parliamentary wages for the first session. In January 1606 it reluctantly agreed to pay up after Hurt and Jackson initiated legal proceedings against the borough sheriffs. For the rest of the Parliament the corporation made no difficulty about paying parliamentary wages.

There is no evidence that Shrewsbury sought to influence the election for the Addled Parliament. Instead, the borough returned its town clerk, William Gregory, the son of an alderman, and Alderman Robert Staples, a cordwainer. Having previously sat in 1601 Gregory was returned first. Two months after the Parliament ended, on 8 Aug. 1614, the corporation ordered that Robert Staples be paid £3, which sum was issued three days later. His colleague, William Gregory, received £3 12s., but it is not clear how long he had to wait nor why his payment was larger.[10]

On the death of Sir Henry Pierrepont in 1616 the corporation agreed to appoint a qualified barrister as his successor. It therefore elected William Fletcher, a bencher of the Inner Temple, who defeated Sir Philip Stanhope, a major Nottinghamshire landowner and father of Henry Stanhope*, by 35 votes to 9. Fletcher served as the borough's recorder until 1642 but appears to have shown no desire to be elected to Parliament.[11] Pierrepont's death occurred in the same year as that of the earl of Shrewsbury, whose estates were divided between his three daughters, the wives of William Herbert, 3rd earl of Pembroke, Thomas Howard, 14th earl of Arundel, and Sir Henry Grey*. In the first instance it seems to have been Pembroke, who had married the eldest daughter, who acquired the bulk of the Talbot political influence, which he sought to use in the elections for the 1621 parliament. In November 1620 Pembroke and his agent George Lassells approached the corporation of East Retford, where Shrewsbury had been high steward, for a seat. They were apparently rebuffed, but Lassells was subsequently successful at Nottingham, presumably with Pembroke's backing.[12]

Pembroke succeeded in 1620 where Shrewsbury had failed in 1604 because the corporation decided, on 1 Dec., to abandon its practice of electing only townsmen. As indicated above, the reason for this change was financial, 'for the easing of the towns charges', as outsiders would not expect to be paid for their service. However, it was not uncontroversial, for of the 26 members of the hall present on the 1st, six wanted to elect two townsmen and three wanted one townsman and one outsider.[13]

A note in the corporation minutes indicates that there were five candidates who 'stand to be burgesses of the Parliament'. This list is not dated and in itself it does not mean that the election was contested. On the contrary, it may simply be a list of those strangers who had approached the corporation for a seat. None of the candidates were drawn from the top of Nottinghamshire's hierarchy, possibly because the leading figures of the county did not wish to risk the disgrace which a rebuff would bring. In addition to Lassells, the candidates were 'Mr. Wood, Mr. Purefoy, Mr. Zouche and Mr. Bowne'.[14] Aside from that of Michael Purefoy, the other successful candidate, the identity of these men is uncertain. Bowne was probably Gilbert Boune, a Lincoln's Inn barrister from Nottinghamshire whose grandfather sat for Nottingham in 1558 and who himself represented the borough in April 1640.[15] Wood was probably John Wood of Lambley in Nottinghamshire, a member of the county bench and commissioner of musters, or one of his numerous brothers.[16] Zouche may have been John Zouche of

Codnor in Derbyshire, which is situated close to the border with Nottinghamshire.[17]

Although Purefoy was elected as a 'stranger', he was in fact a resident of Nottingham, where he was the judge of the Archdeaconry Court. His election may have been the result of faction fighting on the corporation between puritans and their enemies. In 1617 a group of Nottingham residents, including the mayor, Thomas Nix, a friend of Purefoy's, were prosecuted in Star Chamber for spreading libels alleging that Anker Jackson and some other Nottingham inhabitants attended conventicles and engaged in other puritan practices. Jackson and his co-defendants were in turn alleged to have themselves libelled Purefoy. In 1620 Star Chamber ordered the removal of Nix from the corporation, which occurred on 4 September. According to the official minutes, the town council was delighted with this outcome, as there had been 'much disliking of Master Nix's carriage, as well in the time of mayoralty as since'. However, Jackson had only recently been re-elected mayor and the official record may actually represent his view, and that of his friends, than the opinion of the rest of the council. The election of Purefoy to Parliament three months later suggests that Jackson's control of the corporation was far from complete and perhaps represents the revenge of Nix and his allies.[18]

In 1624 the Nottingham corporation records contain a note of the names of ten 'suitors for the burgesses places', but there is no evidence that those mentioned did anything more than express an interest in representing the borough.[19] Lassells and Boune were the only candidates from 1620 who sought re-election in 1624, but were both rejected. The other candidates included John Darcy, the 22-year-old son of John, 3rd Lord Darcy, a south Yorkshire peer who was a friend of the Nottinghamshire magnate Sir Gervase Clifton. It seems likely that Clifton was behind Darcy's nomination, as he subsequently nominated Darcy for East Retford the following April.[20] Of the other candidates, Henry Willoughby was a younger son of Sir Percival Willoughby* of Wollaton, three miles west of Nottingham. Sir Percival had sat for Nottinghamshire in 1604 but was repeatedly outlawed for debt in the early 1620s. Edward Ayscough was probably the son of Sir Roger Ayscough of Nuthall, Nottinghamshire, although he may instead have been a Lincolnshire namesake. Either way, Ayscough probably did not contest the Nottingham election, for a man of this name was returned for Stanford six days earlier.[21] 'Mr. Teverey' was almost certainly Gervase Teverey of Stapleford, six miles west of Nottingham, who was a member of the Nottinghamshire bench.[22] Sir George Chaworth was a more prominent member of the Nottinghamshire bench who sat for the county in 1621. He too probably also dropped out by the time of the election, having been returned for Arundel at the nomination of the earl of Arundel on 23 January. It seems likely that Chaworth was one of four competitors for the Talbot interest in Nottingham, as the countess of Arundel was one of the co-heirs of the earl of Shrewsbury. The other competitors were Lassells, who was connected with the earl of Pembroke; John Selden*, who had recently entered the service of the earl of Kent, the husband of Shrewsbury's third daughter; and Sir Charles Cavendish, who succeeded where his rivals failed. Cavendish was the younger brother of Sir William Cavendish II* of Welbeck Abbey, who in 1620 had been raised to the peerage as Viscount Mansfield. Cavendish and his brother had been closely connected with the 7th earl of Shrewsbury, whose widow was their aunt. They were brought up in Shrewsbury's household and the earl had appointed Sir William Cavendish his executor.[23] Apart from Sir Charles Cavendish, Nottingham also returned John Byron, the eldest son of Sir John Byron of Newstead Abbey, 12 miles north of Nottingham. The Byrons were severely indebted but were a well-established and prominent county family, and Byron's father had recently inherited the family estate on the death in 1623 of Byron's grandfather and namesake, who had represented the county in 1597. Despite Cavendish's knighthood Byron was named first in the return.[24]

In 1625 there were five 'suitors for burgesses places', of whom four had appeared on the previous year's list: Cavendish, Chaworth, Byron and Lassells. The only newcomer was Sir Francis Foljambe, a baronet with estates in Derbyshire and Yorkshire.[25] However, at a meeting of the mayor, recorder, aldermen, council and clothing on 15 Apr. it was agreed, 'and none other in any wise', to revert to electing townsmen. Consequently the five suitors were rejected. Rather than elect two aldermen, however, it was decided to return two lawyers – Robert Greaves, the town clerk, and John Martyn, an attorney. Both were probably selected at the 15 Apr. meeting. No explanation was recorded for the decision to revert to electing townsmen, but as there is no evidence that either Greaves or Martyn were paid it is possible that they secured their election by offering to serve without wages. In subsequent elections, however, the borough reverted to returning outsiders, which perhaps suggests that none of the other townsmen were prepared to follow the example set by Greaves and Martyn.[26]

The 1626 election is almost entirely undocumented, as it is unmentioned in the corporation records and no indenture survives. However, on this occasion Sir Gervase Clifton, who had previously sat four times for the county, was returned alongside Byron, who by now had succeeded to his father's estate. Following the Parliament it was decided to continue returning outsiders, for on 20 Nov. 1627, as rumours of an approaching Parliament circulated, the corporation agreed by 24 votes to one to elect 'two gentlemen of the country … for easing the town's charges'. It was also agreed, by 23 votes to two, to re-elect Sir Charles Cavendish, together with Henry Pierrepont, the son of the unsuccessful 1604 candidate. The decision may have been prompted by an approach from Cavendish and Pierrepont and was intended to 'gain the friendship and favour of those two noble families, and have their assistance to the town when any occasion shall [be] offered'. Cavendish's elder brother, Viscount Mansfield, had been appointed lord lieutenant of Nottinghamshire in July 1626. Pierrepont's father, who lived at Holme Pierrepont, four-and-a-half miles from Nottingham, had accumulated the largest landed estate in the county and, with Mansfield's assistance, had recently purchased the title of Viscount Newark.[27] When a Parliament was summoned early in 1628, Cavendish and Pierrepont were duly returned, with Cavendish on this occasion taking the first place.

There is no evidence that the corporation sought to promote any legislation in this period. The only occasion on which the borough's Members were specifically appointed to a committee was in 1606, when they were among those appointed to consider the bill concerning navigable rivers (7 Feb.), an issue of obvious concern considering the importance of the Trent to the local economy.[28] Nevertheless in the Jacobean period the borough's Members performed a variety tasks both inside and outside the Commons for their constituency. In March 1608 Jackson presented a bill for his expenses which totalled £7 13s. 4d. and included 16s. 8d. for copying the will of Sir Thomas White, a sixteenth-century London aldermen who had bequeathed money for charitable purposes in Nottingham.[29]

Although the corporation largely elected strangers in the 1620s, it still expected Members to perform some service on behalf of the borough. Shortly after the election of Lassells and Purefoy in December 1620, the corporation sent its town clerk, Robert Greaves, to London to obtain the assistance of Lassells regarding a decree in the duchy of Lancaster Court concerning the town's tolls.[30] Purefoy was probably speaking on behalf of the Nottingham corporation when he attacked the execution of the alehouse patent on 25 Apr. 1621, stating that the patentees' representatives 'took the upper hand of the mayor'.[31] On 30 Jan. 1624 the corporation agreed to write to the recorder, who was presumably then in London, to consult the borough's recently elected Members concerning the repair of the Leen bridge, which connected the borough to Trent bridge, and also about the fees payable in the Exchequer for passing the accounts of the mayor as the *ex officio* escheator of Nottingham, 'in case occasion shall be offered this Parliament or otherwise'. However nothing seems to have been done in either case.[32]

Initially Nottingham seems to have resisted prerogative finance. It contributed only £30 towards the Benevolence levied after the 1614 Parliament, about five per cent of the total raised by the county and significantly less than the £50 contributed by Cavendish's father.[33] When the Benevolence for the Palatinate was collected after the 1621 Parliament the grand jury of the borough sessions protested that 'the poor burgesses thinks themselves not well dealt withall' and asked for the money to be refunded.[34] However the Forced Loan of 1626-7 seems to have aroused little opposition. The mayor and aldermen were appointed commissioners of the Loan, and Robert Staples, who had sat in Parliament in 1614, was active in its enforcement. On 12 Feb. 1627 the corporation reported to the Privy Council that the subsidy-payers had consented to the levy, and the first receipts were paid in by the collectors eight days later. By the following September £129 had been received by the Exchequer, probably over 90 per cent of the total expected from the borough.[35]

[1] C219/38/178. [2] A. Henstock, 'Changing Fabric of the Town, 1550-1750', in *Centenary Hist. of Nottingham* ed. J. Beckett, 107. [3] S. Wallwork, 'Population Estimates before the Census: Nottingham, 1570-1801', *East Midland Historian*, ix. 38, 41. [4] D. Palliser, *Age of Eliz.* 217-18, 243, 246; A. Henstock, S. Dunster, and S. Wallwork, 'Decline and Regeneration: Social and Economic Life', *Centenary Hist. of Nottingham*, 132, 141-2, 145-7; Henstock, 110-11. [5] A.C. Wood, *Hist. Notts.* 113; J. Blackner, *Hist. Nottingham*, 263, 266, 275; D. Gray, *Nottingham Through 500 years*, 30, 32, 36-37, 39, 55, 58-59, 61. [6] *OR*. [7] C219/38/178; Henstock, Dunster, and Wallwork, 149; *Recs. of Bor. of Nottingham* ed. W.H. Stevenson, iv. 373, 387; *Recs. of Bor. of Nottingham* ed. W.T. Baker, v. 102, 129. [8] *HP Commons, 1558-1603*, i. 225; M. Bennett, 'Turbulent Centuries: the Political Hist. of Nottingham, 1550-1750', *Centenary Hist. of Nottingham*, 167; *CP*, xi 260-1; *Oxford DNB sub* Manners, Francis, 6th earl of Rutland. [9] G.R. Batho, 'Gilbert Talbot, 7th Earl of Shrewsbury (1553-1616): the "Great and Glorious Earl"?', *Derbys. Arch. Jnl.* xciii. 29; *Recs. of Bor. of Nottingham*, iv. 426; *HP Commons, 1558-1603*, iii. 176, 221-2; *Vis. Notts.* (Harl. Soc. n.s. v), 2; *Cal. Talbot Pprs.* ed. G.R. Batho (Derbys. Recs. ser. iv), 269, 272. [10] *Recs. of Bor. of Nottingham*, iv. 317, 326. [11] *Recs. of Bor. of*

Nottingham, iv. 342, 429; W. Prest, *Rise of the Barristers*, 362; Blackner, 287. [12] C142/444/87; *Letters of John Holles* ed. P.R. Seddon (Thoroton Soc. Rec. ser. xxxv), 247-8; *Strafforde Letters* (1739) ed. W. Knowler, i. 11. [13] *Recs. of Bor. of Nottingham*, iv. 373; T. Bailey, *Annals of Notts.* ii. 600. [14] *Recs. of Bor. of Nottingham*, iv. 375. [15] *LI Black Bks.* ii. 202; *HP Commons, 1509-58*, i. 464-5; *OR*. [16] *Vis. Notts.* (Harl. Soc. iv), 87-8; C193/13/1, f. 77v; SP14/72/92; V.J. Hodges, 'Electoral Influence of the Aristocracy, 1604-41' (Columbia Univ. Ph.D. thesis, 1977), 298. [17] *The Gen.* n.s. viii. 180. [18] STAC 8/303/8; C.J. Sission, *Lost Plays of Shakespeare's Age*, 196-203; PROB 11/152, f. 273v; *Recs. of Bor. of Nottingham*, iv. 365. [19] *Recs. of Bor. of Nottingham*, iv. 387, [20] *CP*, iv. 76-7; Nottingham UL, CL/LP51; PROB 11/165, f. 333v. [21] Thoroton, *Notts.* (1790), ii. 213. [22] Ibid. 193; C193/13/1, f. 77v. [23] M. Cavendish, *Life of William Cavendish Duke of Newcastle*, 1-3; *CP*, xi. 716. [24] *HP Commons, 1558-1603*, i. 525. [25] Notts. RO, CA3399, f. 60. This list in printed in Bailey, ii. 612, where it is assigned to the 1626 election. However it is at the back of the hall book for the year ending September 1625. [26] *Recs. of Bor. of Nottingham*, v. 102. [27] Notts. RO, CA3402, f. 57. [28] *CJ*, i. 265a. [29] Ibid. 288. [30] Notts. RO, CA 3395, f. 21. [31] *CD 1621*, iii. 83. [32] *Recs. of Bor. of Nottingham*, iv. 385. [33] E351/1950. [34] *Recs. of Bor. of Nottingham*, iv. 380-1, 382. [35] Ibid. v. 116-18; SP16/53/86; *CSP Dom.* 1627-8, pp. 53, 338; E401/1386, m. 60. The Forced Loan was expected to raise the equivalent of five subsidies, £29 2s. had been collected in Nottingham for the second subsidy voted by the 1625 Parliament, but 14s. 6d. was deducted for collectors fees. SP16/84/89; E359/68.

G.Y.

OXFORDSHIRE

Number of voters: unknown

7 Mar. 1604	LAWRENCE TANFIELD JOHN DOYLEY
c.*Feb.* 1606	SIR ANTHONY COPE *vice* Tanfield, appointed to office
c.Mar. 1614	SIR ANTHONY COPE, (bt.) SIR JOHN CROKE
20 Dec. 1620	SIR RICHARD WENMAN SIR WILLIAM POPE
14 Jan. 1624	SIR WILLIAM COPE, (bt.) SIR HENRY POOLE Sir William Pope
c.Apr. 1625	EDWARD WRAY SIR RICHARD WENMAN
c.Jan. 1626	JAMES FIENNES SIR THOMAS WENMAN
5 Mar. 1628	JAMES FIENNES SIR FRANCIS WENMAN

Oxfordshire was described by William Camden as a 'rich and fertile county'; but it had been troubled by a recent history of agrarian protest against enclosures.[1] The armed uprising of 1596 was targeted against the modernizing activities of landlords such as Sir William Spencer†; a decade later rumours that Oxfordshire labourers intended to join the Northamptonshire 'Diggers' came to nothing, perhaps because the preceding episode had been harshly suppressed.[2] Special measures were again needed in 1621-2 to deal with unemployed clothiers when the county was hit hard by the recession in the cloth trade. By 1636 Oxfordshire, which had previously been considered second only to Middlesex in terms of wealth, was only ranked England's seventeenth richest county in the Ship Money assessments.[3]

Elections continued to be held at Oxford castle, which served as the county gaol. The original Norman fortifications were by this time badly dilapidated, and most of the castle's former administrative functions, such as the holding of quarter sessions, had been relocated to the town hall in St. Aldates following the plague-stricken 'black assizes' of 1577.[4] Throughout the Elizabethan period the county's parliamentary elections had been dominated by the Knollys family, but this ceased under James, when Lord (Sir William†) Knollys, later 1st earl of Banbury, transferred his interest to Berkshire, where he also owned estates. Instead, seats were shared between the county's Protestant gentry. (Around a quarter or a third of the gentry were Catholic, and therefore incapable of election).[5] It is notable that Sir Richard Wenman, who had represented the county in 1597, did not sit in any Jacobean Parliament until the death of his recusant first wife. In 1604 Sir Anthony Cope of Hanwell would doubtless have been elected had he not been serving as sheriff, but he was able to secure the return of his brother-in-law, John Doyley, who shared his puritan views. The senior knight of the shire was Lawrence Tanfield, a lawyer from Burford who had already received conspicuous marks of favour from the new king. When he was raised to the bench in January 1606 he was replaced by Cope, although the by-election return does not survive.

Cope was re-elected in 1614 with young Sir John Croke, whose father was ineligible to serve as he, like Tanfield, was a judge. In 1621 Sir Richard Wenman stood again after a lapse of four parliaments. The junior seat went to Sir William Pope, the eldest son of the future 1st earl of Downe. The contested election of 1624 is the only instance of the exercise of interest by a local magnate, Lord Danvers. Pope stood again, but Danvers backed Sir Henry Poole to defeat him.[6] Poole, an industrious and experienced candidate

whose main estates lay in Wiltshire, could lay claim to a seat in Oxfordshire through the property that his second wife had brought him ten years earlier. The second seat went to Cope's heir, Sir William Cope, who was heavily indebted and sought the protection of parliamentary privilege. The return was accompanied by a certificate bearing at least thirty signatures, which stated that the election had been witnessed by, among others, Sir Richard Wenman and two senior members of the university, Dr. Robert Clay, who held several benefices in the county, and the principal of Gloucester Hall.[7]

The Wenman family filled one of the county seats throughout the reign of Charles I. In 1625 Sir Richard Wenman sat again but gave precedence to Edward Wray, a newcomer to the county who had become a kinsman by marriage into the Norreys family. This was the only occasion on which both candidates hailed from the same part of the county; in all the other elections of the period it is conspicuous that the geographical distribution of seats followed a pattern of one knight from the north or the west of the county serving with another from the east or the south. In 1626 two young men of puritan connections were elected: Wenman's son Sir Thomas and James Fiennes, the heir of 'Old Sublety', Lord Say and Sele, of Broughton Castle. Fiennes was re-elected as knight of the shire in every Parliament until the Restoration. In 1628 Sir Francis Wenman, from a cadet branch of the family, was initially recommended to the corporation of Oxford by the fifth earl of Huntingdon. However, the townsmen already faced a heated contest for their seats, and to appease the earl promised to support Wenman as a knight of the shire: 'both ourselves and all our freeholders within our city ... will be most ready and willing to confer all our voices upon him'. Wenman was thereupon returned with Fiennes.[8]

[1] W. Camden, *Britannia* (1772), i. 291. [2] STAC 8/297/4; J. Walter, 'The Oxon. Rising of 1596', *P and P*, clxx. 143. [3] *VCH Oxon.* ii. 190-97; T. Rogers, *Hist. of Agriculture and Prices in Eng.* v. 69, 104. [4] *VCH Oxon.* iv. 296-300; M.S. Gretton, *Oxon. JPs in Seventeenth Cent.* (Oxf. Rec. Soc. xvi), p. lxxxvi. [5] *VCH Oxon.* ii. 43; A. Davidson, 'Catholicism in Oxon. c.1580-c.1640' (Bristol Univ. Ph.D. thesis, 1970), pp. 2-9. [6] *Chamberlain Letters* ed. N.E. McClure, ii. 543. [7] C219/38/167-8. [8] *Procs. 1628*, vi. 158-9.

A.D./R.C.L.S.

BANBURY

Right of election: in the corporation

Number of voters: 24 in 1608; 18 from 1608

1 Mar. 1604	SIR WILLIAM COPE
c. Mar. 1614	SIR WILLIAM COPE
22 Dec. 1620	SIR WILLIAM COPE, (bt.)
24 Jan. 1624	SIR ERASMUS DRYDEN, bt.
30 Apr. 1625	SIR WILLIAM COPE, (bt.)
19 July 1625	JAMES FIENNES *vice* Cope, election declared void
c. Jan. 1626	CALCOT CHAMBRE
10 Mar. 1628	JOHN CREWE

Banbury, a small market town, was enfranchised as a single member constituency and incorporated by a charter of 1554.[1] Twelve aldermen, one of whom served as bailiff, and 12 capital burgesses together constituted both the common council and the electorate.[2] A 'Banbury man' on the Jacobean stage and in common parlance signified a puritan, and all the five Members who represented the borough were associated with local puritan ministers, notably John Dod and William Whately, whose father acted as returning officer in 1624.[3] Sir William Cope of Hardwick, a mile north of Banbury, whose father Sir Anthony* was sheriff of Oxfordshire in 1604 and had sat for the borough seven times under Elizabeth, represented the borough in the first three Parliaments of James I. Thereafter the borough's electoral patronage was shared between Cope, who succeeded to his ancestral estate of nearby Hanwell in 1614, and the Fiennes family of Broughton, three miles away. All of Banbury's Members were related to each other by ties of blood and friendship, and no contests are known to have occurred. No payment of wages to representatives is recorded in the town's accounts for any of the early Stuart Parliaments.[4]

A new charter dated 28 June 1608 substituted a mayor for the bailiff, reduced the number of capital burgesses to six, and added 30 'assistants' to the corporation, though the latter had no share in parliamentary elections.[5] Lord (Sir William†) Knollys, later 1st earl of Banbury, was named high steward, but appears to have exercised no interest in this borough.[6] In 1624 Cope moved up to sit for the county, and Banbury was represented by his cousin Sir Erasmus Dryden, the only Member in this period who cannot be considered a local resident.[7] Shortly after the prorogation in 1624 Cope was arrested and imprisoned in the Fleet for a debt of £3,000. He had been released on bail when Charles I's first Parliament was summoned, and tried to regain his seat with the support of the mayor, John Nicholas, who had acted as one of his sureties. However, his creditor, Lady Coppin, was quick to enter a petition against him in the Commons, and after it was referred to the privileges committee at Cope's own motion, he was ruled ineligible on 23 June.[8] He was replaced by a more radical puritan, James Fiennes, the eldest son of the 1st Viscount Saye and Sele of Broughton. Fiennes in his turn moved up to the county for the second and third Parliaments of Charles I. In 1626 Banbury was represented by a local gentleman, Calcot Chambre, one of the corporation's 30 assistants, and a business associate of both Cope and Fiennes. There was strong resistance to the Forced Loan in Banbury, led by Saye and Sele, and also resentment at the billeting of soldiers, which was imposed in part as a punishment for non-payment; however, this seems to have had no direct impact on the result of the next general election.[9] Cope's continuing financial difficulties had forced him to sell some of his estates in the area by this time, transactions in which the king's serjeant (Sir) Thomas Crewe* became involved. It was probably through this connection that Crewe's eldest son, John, was returned for Banbury in 1628, and became a trustee of Chambre's Irish estates together with Fiennes in the following year.

[1] A. Beesley, *Banbury*, 219-22. [2] *VCH Oxon*. x. 73-4. R.K. Gilkes 'Banbury: the Pattern of Local Govt.', *Cake and Cockhorse*, v. 3. [3] *VCH Oxon*. x. 7. [4] *Banbury Corp. Recs*. ed. J.S.W. Gibson and E.R.C. Brinkworth (Banbury Hist. Soc. xv), p. xiii. [5] Beesley, 254-8. [6] Gilkes, 6. [7] C78/199/4. [8] C2/Jas.I/W26/22; *Procs 1625*, pp. 206, 207, 215, 222-3, 227. [9] J.B. Blankenfeld, 'Puritans in Banbury 1554-1660' (Yale Univ. Ph.D. thesis, 1985), pp. 213-35.

A.D./R.C.L.S.

NEW WOODSTOCK

Right of election: in the freemen

Number of voters: about 65[1]

1 Mar. 1604	SIR RICHARD LEE THOMAS SPENCER
6 Dec. 1609	JAMES WHITELOCKE, recorder *vice* Lee, deceased
c. Mar. 1614	SIR PHILIP CAREY JAMES WHITELOCKE, recorder
7 Dec. 1620	(SIR) JAMES WHITELOCKE, recorder SIR PHILIP CAREY
14 Jan. 1624	SIR PHILIP CAREY WILLIAM LENTHALL, recorder
20 Apr. 1625	SIR PHILIP CAREY SIR GERRARD FLEETWOOD
14 Jan. 1626	SIR GERRARD FLEETWOOD EDMUND TAVERNER
c. Mar. 1628	SIR MILES FLEETWOOD EDMUND TAVERNER

New Woodstock, a small market town that had grown up near the royal manor and park, was incorporated in 1453, but did not return Members to Parliament until a century later. In this period it was governed by a mayor, four aldermen, and 20 common councillors, who together with a slightly larger body of freemen formed the electorate.[2] Returns were made by the mayor and commonalty. It had become 'ever usual with them' to reserve one seat for the recorder and to prove amenable to the wishes of the high steward for the other.[3] However, by the reign of Charles I the corporation's control over one of its seats declined before the interest exercised by two royal officials, the steward of the manor and the ranger of Woodstock Park.

In 1604 Sir Henry Lee† was both high steward of the borough and steward of the manor. Since the recorder, Sir Lawrence Tanfield*, had secured election for the county, Lee nominated his younger half-brother Sir Richard Lee in the senior place, and the junior seat went to Thomas Spencer, the 18-year old son of a neighbouring gentleman. Lee died after the third session of the Parliament, and was replaced by the new recorder, James Whitelocke; the chamberlains' accounts show payments of 6s. 8d. to the under-sheriff and 12s. 6d. for a mayoral dinner at the by-election.[4] When Sir Henry Lee died in 1611 he was succeeded by Spencer as high steward, while the 1st earl of Montgomery (Sir Philip Herbert*) became

steward of the manor.[5] The borough paid the sheriff 3s. in 1614 'for the warrant to choose our burgesses'.[6] Spencer 'refused to serve himself', but 'commended' Sir Philip Carey, a well-connected courtier and a relative by marriage of Tanfield, who maintained his link with the borough and was occasionally the recipient of gifts of cake from the corporation.[7] Montgomery tried to nominate the other Member, probably Sir Thomas Tracy*, but recorder Whitelocke was re-elected.[8] In 1617 the manor was settled on Prince Charles, from whom the borough received 'a letter about the election of a burgess' before the 1620 election, but in the event Whitelocke and Carey were re-elected.[9] Montgomery succeeded Spencer as high steward of the borough in 1622, but is not known to have exercised any influence over the next two elections.[10] Carey was re-elected in 1624, together with William Lenthall, a young lawyer and Tanfield's kinsman who had replaced Whitelocke as recorder in 1621.[11]

Charles's first Parliament saw a break with the traditional pattern of Woodstock's elections, as the recorder now found himself excluded. Carey again took the first seat, but the second went to Sir Gerrard Fleetwood, ranger of Woodstock Park. Lenthall, who did not manage to find a place elsewhere, described his failure to gain the seat as 'a disgrace'.[12] The chamberlains' accounts record the payment of 8s. to the 'clerk of the Parliament [sic] for the filing of the indenture', a procedure which was repeated in the following two elections.[13] Fleetwood sat again as the senior member in 1626, and was joined by Montgomery's secretary Edmund Taverner, who had the advantage of being a local man by birth and was related to the Fleetwoods.[14] In 1628 Fleetwood yielded his seat to his elder brother, Sir Miles, while Taverner was re-elected in second place. Members do not appear to have been paid wages during this period. It is not known whether the town was interested in any particular bills, though the town clerk bought 'a statute book of the last Parliament' in 1624 and again in 1628.[15]

[1] A. Ballard, *Chrons. Woodstock*, 60; Oxon. RO, Woodstock Bor. mss B78/2, ff. 44-46v, B78/3, ff. 258v-259. [2] Ballard, 26-7, 35, 37, 61. [3] *Liber Famelicus of Sir J. Whitlocke* ed. J. Bruce (Cam. Soc. lxx), 19. [4] *Woodstock Chamberlain's Accts. 1609-50* ed. M. Maslen (Oxon. Rec. Soc. lviii), 6. [5] *CSP Dom.* 1603-10, p. 152. [6] *Woodstock Chamberlain's Accts. 1609-50* (Oxon. Rec. Soc. lviii), 51. [7] *Liber Famelicus*, 41; *Woodstock Chamberlain's Accts. 1609-50*, pp. 94, 99. [8] *Liber Famelicus*, 40. [9] *Woodstock Chamberlain's Accts. 1609-50*, p. 80; E. Marshall, *Woodstock Manor*, 177, 183, 184. [10] *Woodstock Chamberlain's Accts. 1609-50*, p. 89. [11] Ibid. 86. [12] Berks. RO, D/ELL/o.5/12. [13] *Woodstock Chamberlain's Accts. 1609-50*, pp. 104, 106, 116. The payment was probably actually made to the clerk of the crown in Chancery, who customarily received a fee for the filing of indentures. [14] *The Gen.* n.s. x. 76. [15] *Woodstock Chamberlain's Accts. 1609-50*, pp. 99, 116.

A.D./R.C.L.S.

OXFORD

Right of election: in the freemen

Number of voters: c.700 in 1626[1]

1 Mar. 1604	SIR FRANCIS LEIGH I
	THOMAS WENTWORTH I
c. Mar. 1614	SIR JOHN ASTLEY
	THOMAS WENTWORTH I
c. Dec. 1620	SIR JOHN BROOKE
	SIR FRANCIS BLUNDELL, bt.
	Thomas Wentworth I
	THOMAS WENTWORTH I *vice*
	Blundell, on petition, 9 Feb. 1621
19 Jan. 1624	THOMAS WENTWORTH I
	JOHN WHISTLER
c. Apr. 1625	THOMAS WENTWORTH I
	JOHN WHISTLER
23 Jan. 1626	THOMAS WENTWORTH I
	JOHN WHISTLER
3 Mar. 1628	JOHN WHISTLER
	THOMAS WENTWORTH II 204
	(Sir) Henry Croke* 106

Although dominated by its university, Oxford was a thriving city under the early Stuarts, and hosted royal visits in 1605 and 1629 as well as the Parliament of 1625.[2] It was governed by a mayoral council known as the Thirteen, but was aided by a common council. A new charter of incorporation, granted in 1605, added two bailiffs to the mayor's council and limited the size of the common council to 24.[3] Despite these formal arrangements, decisions seem to have been made by a larger body, as most reporters of the disputed election to the 1621 Parliament refer to a council of 48.[4] The right of election lay in the freemen, but the method adopted throughout this period was for the common council to choose the candidates and present them for approval to the freemen assembled in the guildhall or courtyard.[5] However, since 1571 the city's high steward had enjoyed the right to nominate one Member, while from 1586 the borough had returned its junior counsel for the other seat. (The recorder, Robert Atkinson[†], who held office between 1566 and 1607, had disqualified himself as a convicted recusant).[6] Catholics maintained a strong presence in the city, as in the university, for in 1612 Thomas Chamberlain complained to lord chancellor Ellesmere

(Thomas Egerton[†]) that the borough was 'the only receptacle and harbour of all Jesuits and priests' in the county, a situation for which he blamed 'the mayor and his company, who want both courage and discretion'.[7] Oxford petitioned unsuccessfully in 1617-20 for a new charter to accord a greater role to the town's bailiffs and chamberlain, but this provoked a conflict with the university, and eventually the matter was dropped.[8]

In 1604 Ellesmere, as high steward, nominated his son-in-law Sir Francis Leigh I, who had represented the borough in 1601, as Oxford's senior Member. The second seat went to the newly appointed counsel, Thomas Wentworth I. The corporation hoped to secure legislation that would make the Thames navigable and prevent the erection of cottages within the city and its suburbs. The river bill was needed because of a prosperous local trade in Cotswold stone, which was exported to London, and because of the water traffic required to supply the city and colleges with food and fuel.[9] Wentworth duly chaired the committee for the navigation bill, which was passed in 1606; but he seems to have been unable to do anything to promote the other measure, even though it enjoyed the support of the university.[10] Oxford did not pay its Members wages, but in 1610 and on at least one later occasion, Wentworth was voted small sums 'in respect of his pains and attendance at the Parliament'.[11] Wentworth succeeded Atkinson as recorder in 1607, and consequently in 1614 he laid claim to the city's second parliamentary seat. Lord (William[†]) Knollys, who had become high steward in 1611, nominated the courtier Sir John Astley for the second seat.[12] During the Parliament the University's Members attempted to obtain amendments to the Thames Navigation Act of 1606, and were supported by the city, which offered to share in the expense. However, there is no mention of the subject in the records of the Addled Parliament.[13] Although relations between town and gown were not always harmonious, the corporation often joined with the university in lobbying Parliament over the Thames navigation and cottages for the poor.[14]

In 1620 Knollys, now Viscount Wallingford, not only nominated another courtier, Sir John Brooke, but also asked to supply the second Member, 'if you do not nominate one of your own body'.[15] This was almost certainly a broad hint that Wentworth would not be regarded as acceptable by the king, who had been offended by his speeches in 1610 and 1614 and clearly regarded him as one of the 'curious and wrangling lawyers' referred to in his recent Proclamation (6 Nov. 1620) concerning the forthcoming elections. Indeed, according to Wentworth's counsel, both these points were brought to the attention of the freemen.[16] In his stead Wallingford nominated Sir Francis Blundell, an Anglo-Irish official. At the pre-election held on 22 Dec. the common council decided in favour of Blundell, but the freemen refused to accept anyone but Wentworth, even when other citizens were suggested to them; accounts differ as to the number of votes cast and in what proportion.[17] The mayor nonetheless returned Brooke and Blundell. Wentworth naturally challenged the return, and on 9 Feb. 1621 the House unseated Blundell in his favour. The mayor was subsequently called to the bar of the Commons to make a kneeling submission of apology.[18] In January 1621 the corporation, having consulted Wentworth, instructed Brooke and Blundell to propose amendments to the 1606 Thames Navigation Act, and again joined with the university to share the expense. However, as in 1614 its efforts came to nothing.[19]

Wentworth took the senior seat in the next three Parliaments, together with his deputy John Whistler. In 1624 they were once again instructed to promote the Thames navigation bill 'as they should in their wisdoms order', and Whistler accordingly steered it through committee; this time it passed and finally replaced the 1606 Act.[20] The city's special contribution to the 1625 Parliament, which adjourned to Oxford in August in order to escape the plague in London, was to remove some of the windows from St. Martin's church to provide fresh air for the expected 'excess of citizens and Parliament men'.[21] In 1626 Whistler took the chair in committee for a general bill to prevent the erection of cottages, but without success; the city also joined with the University to petition the Privy Council about the burden of poor relief, which remained a problem throughout the period.[22] Wentworth died in 1627, and was succeeded as recorder by Whistler, who was returned as Oxford's senior Member in 1628.[23] A contest for the second seat was won by Wentworth's son, who garnered almost twice as many votes as his rival (Sir) Henry Croke, a local gentleman and magistrate.[24] Croke may have been backed by Wallingford, who had been created 1st earl of Banbury in 1626. Henry, 5th earl of Huntingdon, who was helping the city in a lawsuit over a charity with Brasenose College, recommended a fourth candidate, Sir Francis Wenman*, apparently unaware that Wenman had already declared that he wanted a county seat. Oxford, which knew of this, therefore replied that it would only support Wenman in the county election.[25]

[1] Oxf. Council Acts ed. H.E. Salter (Oxf. Hist. Soc. lxxxvii), xi. [2] R. Fasnacht, Hist. City of Oxf. 92-3. [3] Royal Letters to Oxf. ed. O. Ogle, 229. [4] VCH Oxon. iv. 131; Nicholas, Procs. 1621, i. 28-29. [5] VCH Oxon. iv. 150. [6] Ibid. iv. 148. [7] Ellesmere MSS ed. A.G. Petti (Cath. Rec. Soc. lx), 208. [8] VCH Oxon. iv. 131; Oxf. Council Acts, lix. [9] Fasnacht, 97-8. [10] Oxf. Council Acts, 159, 164-5, 173; CJ, i. 308b; 3 Jas. I. c.20. [11] Oxf. Council Acts, 204, 234, 395. [12] Ibid. 205, 232. [13] Oxf. Council Acts, 233-4. [14] VCH Oxon. iv. 155-9. [15] Ibid. iv. 151. [16] Stuart Royal Procs. ed. P.L. Hughes and J.F. Larkin, i. 493. [17] Oxf. Council Acts, 297. [18] CJ, i. 515a-b; CD 1621, ii. 47-49; iv. 32, 34; v. 250, 444; vi. 361. [19] Oxf. Council Acts, 297-8. [20] Oxf. Council Acts, 323; 21 Jas. I. c.32; VCH Oxon. iv. 291-2. [21] Oxf. Council Acts, 331. [22] APC 1625-6, p. 303. [23] Oxf. Council Acts ed. M.G. Hobson and H.E. Salter (Oxf. Hist. Soc. xcv), 6. [24] Oxf. Council Acts ed. Hobson and Salter, 9, 10. [25] Procs. 1628, vi. 158-9.

A.D./R.C.L.S.

OXFORD UNIVERSITY

Right of election: in the masters and scholars

Number of voters: unknown

16 Mar. 1604	SIR DANIEL DUNNE SIR THOMAS CROMPTON
21 Oct. 1609[1]	WILLIAM BYRD *vice* Crompton, deceased
28 Mar. 1614[2]	SIR DANIEL DUNNE SIR JOHN BENNET Francis James*
20 Dec. 1620	SIR JOHN BENNET (SIR) CLEMENT EDMONDES
29 May 1621	SIR JOHN DANVERS *vice* Bennett, expelled the House
8 Jan. 1624	(SIR) GEORGE CALVERT SIR ISAAC WAKE
16 Apr. 1625	SIR THOMAS EDMONDES SIR JOHN DANVERS
17 Jan. 1626	SIR THOMAS EDMONDES SIR JOHN DANVERS Sir Francis Stewart
23 Mar. 1626	SIR FRANCIS STEWART *vice* Edmondes, election declared void
20 Feb. 1628	SIR HENRY MARTEN SIR JOHN DANVERS Michael Oldisworth*

Writs were issued to the universities of Oxford and Cambridge for the Parliament of 1301, and after the failure of several petitions during the reign of Elizabeth they were re-enfranchised by letters patent on 12 Mar. 1604, exactly a week before the meeting of the first Parliament called by James I.[3] The reason given was the need to protect the colleges against legislation, such as the frequent bills against pluralism, since benefices provided the only means of support for married scholars, the majority of whom were in orders.[4] Another motive may have been the need for protection against their neighbours, the city of Oxford and the town of Cambridge. Significantly, the only voice known to have been raised in protest against the enfranchisement came from one of Oxford's borough Members, Thomas Wentworth I*.[5] The election of Members was entrusted to 'the chancellor, masters and scholars', the customary legal description of the universities, as employed in their Act of Incorporation in 1571.[6] In practice, the right of election at Oxford lay in convocation, with the doctors and masters of arts, with the addition, as the election petition of 1626 shows, of at least the bachelors of divinity. Since the fifteenth century the chancellor had almost always been a non-resident magnate, chosen for life in convocation to protect the university's interest at Court; the executive head or 'governor' of the university was the vice-chancellor, nominated annually by the chancellor from the heads of colleges and confirmed in convocation. Provision was made for the university to bear the 'charges or costs' of its Members, but no payments are known to have been made in this period, when all those returned had private or official residences in the London area.[7]

Sir Edward Coke*, the prime mover in obtaining the enfranchisement, transmitted the letters patent to Oxford (as to Cambridge), enclosing a letter of explanation and advice to the vice-chancellor. He acknowledged the assistance of Sir Daniel Dunne, dean of Arches, in preparing the petition at a time 'when His Majesty, exceeding all his progenitors in learning and knowledge, so favoureth and respecteth the universities', and also urged the university to thank its own chancellor, Lord Buckhurst (Sir Thomas Sackville†), and lord chancellor Ellesmere (Sir Thomas Egerton†) for furthering the petition at Court. Coke recommended the election of 'some professor of the Civil Law, or some other that is not of the convocation house', a suggestion which Wood and later writers interpreted to mean that the enfranchisement itself had been designed to encourage the faculty of Civil Law.[8] There was no stipulation that the university's representatives must be resident members, and in practice none were, not least because most of those who would have been of sufficient standing were clerics.

In 1604 the university, following Coke's advice, chose two leading civilians, Dunne and Sir Thomas

Crompton, the advocate-general. There is no evidence of any outside influence being brought to bear. Measures passed during the Parliament included an Act of 1606 against recusancy (3 Jas. I, c.5), which disabled convicted recusants from being presented to livings, and divided their rights between the two universities. Another Act of the same year (3 Jas. I, c.20) was intended to facilitate the navigation of the Thames between Oxford and London, 'to the great commodity, ease, benefit and enrichment ... of the university and city of Oxford'. Furthermore two colleges, Corpus Christi and Oriel, secured private Acts confirming their incorporation.[9] Crompton died in 1609, and was replaced by another civilian, William Byrd, who was distantly related to Dunne and may have been recommended by him.

In 1614 the civil lawyer Sir John Bennet, judge of the Prerogative Court of Canterbury, was elected in the senior place, presumably in recognition of his benefactions to the university made in association with Sir Thomas Bodley†. There was a contest for the other seat between Dunne and yet another civilian, Francis James*, who was probably more prominent in Parliament than in his profession. When it became clear that Dunne could not count upon re-election, Ellesmere, now chancellor of the university, wrote in his favour to the vice-chancellor, but there is nothing to show that this recommendation was formally communicated to convocation.[10] Its records do show that the vice-chancellor was at first doubtful whether the greater part of the voters were crying for Dunne or James, but that a division gave Dunne the election.[11] The newsletter writer John Chamberlain nonetheless heard that he won it more through the favour and partiality of the senior members of convocation than 'by multitude of voices'.[12] This favouritism accounts for the placing of Dunne's name before Bennet's on the return.

In 1620 Bennet was re-elected in first place. His colleague Sir Clement Edmondes, a clerk of the Privy Council, may have had the support of the new chancellor, the 3rd earl of Pembroke. Although his return broke with the pattern of civilian representation, Edmondes was a former fellow of All Souls and had a reputation for learning. When Bennet was expelled from the House for corruption in May 1621, he was replaced by Sir John Danvers, whose elder brother founded the Physic Garden for the university and who eventually made his chief residence at Cornbury Park, only a dozen miles away. Danvers had matriculated from Brasenose, but never took a degree. His wife, however, had resided at Oxford with her son

Sir Edward Herbert*, and was much esteemed in the university. A bill to confirm the new foundation of Wadham College passed both Houses in 1621, under the charge of William Hakewill in the Commons, but failed to receive the Royal Assent at the abrupt dissolution.[13]

Both Members elected in 1624, Sir George Calvert, secretary of state, and Sir Isaac Wake, a diplomat, were Oxford alumni, and Wake had two years earlier been a candidate for the wardenship of Merton college. During the Parliament Calvert wrote to the university about a further Thames navigation bill, successfully promoted by the university and the city.[14] The revived bill for Wadham College was steered through committee by Arthur Duck*, and finally enacted.[15] A bill against simony, intended to restrict Crown patronage in the universities, was sponsored by Sir Walter Earle*, but did not pass into law, and met with an equal lack of success when reintroduced in 1625, 1628 and 1629.[16] The 1624 Parliament also considered charges of financial irregularity and moral turpitude brought against Dr. Anyan, president of Corpus Christi College, and these likewise became a perennial source of concern.[17]

In the elections to the first Parliament of Charles I the chancellor, for the first time on record, claimed the right to nominate at least the senior Member. Pembroke's nominee, Sir Thomas Edmondes, treasurer of the Household, also had the support of Archbishop Abbot, expressed in a private letter to the vice-chancellor. Pembroke drew attention to the 'affectation' that Edmondes had shown Oxford in sending his son there, a somewhat maladroit attempt to gloss over the candidate's own lack of a university education.[18] He was nonetheless returned, and Danvers was re-elected in second place. Oxford was chosen as a place of refuge when the Parliament adjourned to escape the plague in London in August 1625; the university's public buildings provided adequate accommodation for the session to continue, although the services of Dr. Anyan as preacher, on the appointment of the university, were firmly refused.[19] According to Wood, it was observed by some that the meeting of the Commons in the divinity school 'did first put them into a conceit that the determining of all points and controversies in divinity did belong to them'.[20]

In 1626 Sir Thomas Edmondes again presented himself to convocation on the nomination of Pembroke, who was now able to describe him as one 'of whose integrity and care to advance the affairs of the university you have had experience this last Parliament'. Abbot likewise sent a letter of support, which was read out in convocation.[21] According to its record, Edmondes was elected to the senior seat without any other nomination being made, although some masters shouted 'non'.[22] In fact there was another candidate, Sir Francis Stewart, a Christ Church graduate who had become a courtier and naval officer. On the 'division' or view, it was claimed, 'a greater part by much went on Sir Francis Stewart's part or side', but the vice-chancellor twice refused a 'scrutiny' or poll, and returned Edmondes and Danvers.[23] A petition was subsequently lodged in the Commons by some of the masters and bachelors of divinity, and on 17 Mar. Edmondes's election was declared void.[24] Stewart, who had in any case been returned as Pembroke's nominee at Liskeard in Cornwall, was chosen at the Oxford ensuing election, and on 4 Apr. he asked for the 'direction' of the House. On 19 Apr. the university election was again referred to the privileges committee, but no action seems to have been taken to clarify the situation. Stewart continued to occupy both seats while Edmondes remained in the House and was named with Stewart, but not Danvers, to consider an unsuccessful bill to void a lease made by Merton College.[25]

In the 1628 election Pembroke nominated the elderly civilian Sir Henry Marten, indicating a reversion to the earlier tradition. To the other points in his favour, Pembroke added that he would not 'put the university to any charge for his attendance upon the service', being 'tied to a necessary abode in these parts' as an Admiralty judge. Pembroke ventured in a later letter to make a second nomination, of his own secretary, Michael Oldisworth*.[26] However, the poll, by scrutiny, went in favour of Marten and Danvers; as in the earlier contests the voting figures are unknown. During the 1629 session, on the motion of Sir Benjamin Rudyard*, the Speaker was instructed on 10 Feb. to write to both universities for details of their proceedings against 'popery or Arminianism'.[27] It was not until Laud succeeded the Calvinist Pembroke as chancellor in 1630 that Oxford itself became a hotbed of Arminianism.[28]

[1] R.L. Poole, *Univ. Archives*, 34. [2] Oxf. Univ. Arch. Reg. Convoc. K. (22), f. 139v. [3] *OR*; K. Fincham, 'Oxf. and the Early Stuart Polity', *Hist. Oxf. Univ. iv: Seventeenth-Cent. Oxf.* ed. N. Tyacke, 196-9; M.B. Rex, *Univ. Representation in Eng. 1604-90*, pp. 22-36. [4] A. Wood, *Univ. Oxf.* ii. 281. [5] *HMC Buccleuch*, iii. 81; *CJ*, i. 151a. [6] *VCH Oxon*. iii. 22. [7] T.L. Humberstone, *Univ. Representation*, 25. [8] Ibid. 21. [9] *Enactments in Parl.* ed. L.L. Shadwell (Oxf. Hist. Soc. lviii), 225-41. [10] Bodl. Tanner 74, f. 34. [11] Oxf. Univ. Arch. Reg. Convoc. K. (22), f. 139v. [12] *Chamberlain Letters* ed. N.E. McClure, i. 525. [13] *CJ*, i. 576b, 626a, 631a. [14] Oxf. Univ. Arch. Reg. Convoc. N.(23), f. 177v; *Oxf. Council Acts* ed. H.E. Salter (Oxf. Hist. Soc. lxxxvii), 325; C. Russell, *PEP*, 194. [15] *CJ*, i. 677b,

686b. [16] Ibid. 735b; Russell, 198, 234, 406. [17] *CJ*, i. 693b, 707a, 777a; Shadwell, 245-57. [18] Oxf. Univ. Arch. Reg. Convoc. N. (23), f. 203v. [19] *Procs. 1625*, p. 380. [20] Wood, ii. 355. [21] Oxf. Univ. Arch. Reg. Convoc. N. (23), f. 214v; *Procs. 1626*, iv. 247-8. [22] Oxf. Univ. Arch. Reg. Convoc. N. (23), f. 215; Wood, ii. 356-7. [23] Bodl. ms 594, ff. 133-5; Rex, 356-9. [24] *Procs. 1626*, ii. 55, 305-7. [25] Ibid. ii. 427. [26] Oxf. Univ. Arch. Reg. Convoc. N. (23), ff. 251-2v. [27] Russell, 410; *CD 1629*, p. 137. [28] *Origins of the Eng. Civil War* ed. C. Russell, 120, 133.

A.D./R.C.L.S.

RUTLAND

Number of voters: perhaps 500 in 1601

c. Mar. 1604	SIR JAMES HARINGTON
	SIR WILLIAM BULSTRODE
	?Sir Andrew Noell[†]
	?Sir Edward Noell[†]
c. Mar. 1614	SIR GUY PALMES
	BASIL FEILDING
	?Sir Edward Noell[†], 1st bt.
	?Sir William Bulstrode
c. Dec. 1620	SIR GUY PALMES
	SIR WILLIAM BULSTRODE
15 Jan. 1624	SIR GUY PALMES
	SIR WILLIAM BULSTRODE
5 May 1625	SIR GUY PALMES
	SIR WILLIAM BULSTRODE
c. Jan. 1626	SIR WILLIAM BULSTRODE
	SIR FRANCIS BODENHAM
6 Mar. 1628	SIR GUY PALMES
	SIR WILLIAM BULSTRODE

Rutland is, by a considerable margin, the smallest county in England. Part of the jointure estate of three late Saxon queens, it acquired shire status only after the Conquest, and returned two knights to Parliament from 1295.[1] While the county contains two small market towns, Oakham and Uppingham, neither was ever represented in the Commons, and lesser residents who sought a place in Parliament, such as John Wingfield*, Brian Palmes* and Edward Wymarke*, were obliged to migrate to the neighbouring boroughs of Grantham, Stamford and Peterborough. The pollbooks which were prepared for the 1601 by-election do not survive,[2] but contemporary testimony indicates that the assembled freeholders were crammed into the castle hall at Oakham, which would suggest an electorate of perhaps 500;[3] attendance was almost certainly lower at uncontested elections.

From 1529 the county's parliamentary representation was dominated by its largest landowners, the Haringtons of Exton and Burley-on-the-Hill. At the end of the century Sir John Harington[†] habitually shared the county seats with his brother-in-law, Sir Andrew Noell[†] of Brooke. This amicable arrangement broke down in 1601, when Noell, whose shrievalty disqualified him from standing, nominated his 19-year-old son Edward for the second seat. Harington, who apparently assumed that Noell would propose his son-in-law, Sir Edward Cecil*, publicly spurned this proposal, and the stalemate was only resolved by the temporary expedient of returning Noell himself.[4] While Noell was certain to be rejected, the return was probably made on the assumption that he would have been replaced as sheriff by the time a new writ arrived, and thus be eligible for re-election. However, while a fresh writ was moved in the Commons on 4 Nov. 1601, the annual pricking of sheriffs was delayed until 2 December.[5] Consequently, Noell revived his son's candidature and began canvassing the freeholders,[6] whereupon Harington put up his brother James and hastily began a rival canvass[7] led by his cousin Sir William Bulstrode.[8] At the ensuing by-election James Harington was defeated, although he claimed to have received a majority of voices and accused Noell of rejecting Harington supporters at the poll in order to give his own son victory. These allegations may have been true, as one of Noell's supporters certainly advised Noell to return his son on the cry regardless of numbers.[9]

The controversy begun at this election far outlasted the Parliament with which it was ostensibly concerned: the Haringtons prosecuted Noell in Star Chamber for electoral malpractice, and the latter responded by accusing his opponents of soliciting for voices, which, though commonplace, was technically illegal.[10] Both suits lapsed at the end of 1602, but Noell took depositions from three dozen local witnesses in January 1604,[11] which suggests that the two sides were jockeying for position in the forthcoming parliamentary election. No contest is known to have taken place in 1604, but it is unlikely that Noell welcomed the return of Bulstrode and Sir James Harington, his son's chief opponents in 1601. He remained unhappy with his relatives shortly before his death in 1607, when he declined to serve as deputy lieutenant under Sir John (now Lord) Harington.[12]

The political situation within the county changed completely in the year before the 1614 general election: Lord Harington died in August 1613, his brother Sir James expired on 4 Feb. 1614,[13] and John, 2nd Baron

Harington* died of smallpox at the end of February 1614, leaving the bulk of his estates to his mother, who was to pay off his father's debts of £40,000 and then pass the remaining lands to his sisters Lucy, countess of Bedford and Frances, Lady Chichester.[14] By the time of the election the only male member of the family who still held lands in the county was Sir James's eldest son Sir Edward Harington, who had no known parliamentary ambitions. The most remarkable aspect of the 1614 election was the absence of any contest between the two surviving antagonists of 1601, Bulstrode and (Sir) Edward Noell. This is surprising, as the latter, by then immune from the charges of youth and inexperience levelled at him by the Haringtons in 1601,[15] must have been tempted to reverse the result of 1604. Bulstrode too may have considered standing, as he sat for the county throughout the 1620s, but it seems as though his interests had been temporarily diverted to Essex, where his second wife held a substantial jointure estate from her first husband.[16] Rather than stand against each other, Bulstrode and Noell may have decided to bury their differences by giving way to their respective supporters, Sir Guy Palmes and Basil Feilding, both of whom were political novices who had only recently succeeded to their estates. Palmes had been a Harington supporter in 1601, and was recommended as a deputy lieutenant by Lord Harington in 1607,[17] while Feilding was an executor of Sir Andrew Noell's will.[18]

Sir Edward Noell was ruled out of contention in subsequent elections following his acquisition of a peerage in 1617, and it was not until 1640 that his son, Baptist Noell, was old enough to stand for election. The unexpected inheritor of the Haringtons' electoral interest was their cousin, Henry, 5th earl of Huntingdon, appointed lord lieutenant of Rutland a few months after the death of the 2nd Baron Harington.[19] However, his political authority was diminished by the fact that he did not hold any significant estates within the shire. Although he recommended Bulstrode and Palmes, two of his deputy lieutenants, to the freeholders at the 1624 election,[20] their background as local residents, Harington associates and former Members makes it likely that Huntingdon was merely reinforcing their natural claim to the seats. The repeated election of the pair probably also owed much to the influence of Huntingdon's mother, a sister of the 1st Baron Harington. She certainly interceded with her third husband, lord warden Zouche, to secure Palmes a second nomination at Hythe in December 1620.[21]

If Huntingdon's electoral influence within the shire was limited, that of the king's favourite, the marquess of Buckingham, who purchased the Harington manor of Burley in 1621, was negligible.[22] One of the few actions of his which had any repercussions within the county was his procurement of a viscountcy for his brother-in-law, William Feilding, on the eve of the 1621 Parliament. The latter's father, the 1614 MP, did not stand for election again: without Noell's active support his return for the shire was unlikely, but his unusual status as the father of a peer may also have helped to rule him out of contention.[23] The only occasion on which Buckingham intervened directly in county politics was in November 1625, when he had Palmes pricked as sheriff to exclude him from Parliament in the following spring.[24]

Palmes may have wished to see his son Brian* elected in his stead in 1626, but the uproar caused by the election of Edward Noell in 1601 probably dissuaded him from attempting the substitution. Instead, he arranged a deal with Sir Francis Bodenham, a minor landowner whose mother had been a Harington, and whose father had been spoken of as an alternative candidate to Sir James Harington at the 1601 by-election.[25] Thus in 1626 Palmes backed Bodenham for the knighthood of the shire, in return for which the latter's cousin John Balguy used his influence at Stamford, where he was deputy recorder, to secure the return of Brian Palmes.[26]

Rutland's Members were generally not very active on their constituents' behalf, but the notion that they should represent local interests retained some significance. Sir James Harington appealed to this theory at the 1601 by-election, when he advised the freeholders that his brother, then their sole representative at Westminster, 'was [advanced] in years, and then so sickly as by means thereof yet [sic it] might so happen he could not come to speak and do that good for his country in the said Parliament House as he desired'.[27] This invited the freeholders to make the inference that Edward Noell, if elected, would not be sufficiently experienced to raise local issues in the House. The only specific item of legislation which owed something to the shire's MPs was the 1625 bill to naturalize the nearby landowner Sir Daniel Deligne of Harlaxton, Lincolnshire. Apparently sponsored by Palmes and Bulstrode, who were the first Members named to the committee on 11 Aug., this bill eventually found its way onto the statute book in 1628 without further help from the pair.[28] At a less formal level, Palmes's support for bills to increase the price of corn and wool in 1621 was undoubtedly welcomed by the shire's gentry farmers,[29] and Bulstrode considered the needs of poorer taxpayers in the supply debates of 1626, when he proposed that the final subsidy should fall due in September 1627, as 'the husbandman then has his corn and wool come in'.[30] Harington, Bulstrode and Palmes also took an interest in religious affairs which reflected the godly ethos of their county. Bulstrode, for instance, presented a petition against the chancellor of Peterborough diocese in May 1621. This reportedly originated in Northamptonshire but it probably also included signatures from Rutland, which was part of the same see.[31] He also presented the Rutland j.p. Sir Henry Mynne as a recusant during the compilation of the petition against Catholic officials in April 1624, and was presumably responsible for Mynne's inclusion in a similar petition in 1626.[32]

---

[1] VCH Rutland, i. 134-6; ii. p. xxviii. [2] STAC 5/H9/34, depositions of Walter Nebon, Peter Martin, John Barnes and Thomas Conande, answer 8; STAC 5/H46/9, deposition of Sir Andrew Noell, answer 10; STAC 5/N6/11, depositions of Thomas Exton, Edward Harbottle and John Campion, answer 7. [3] STAC 8/220/32, depositions of Clement Smith, John Butler, William Dalby, Sir Guy Palmes and William Shortred, answer 13. [4] STAC 5/H57/26, H46/9; J.E. Neale, 'Rutland election of 1601', EHR, lxi. 29-41. [5] Neale, 37; C227/20B. [6] For which STAC 5/H2/7 and 5/H9/34 provide ample evidence. [7] STAC 5/N1/32, f. 3; 5/N6/11, deposition of George Botelar, and Thomas Exton, answers 6-7; 5/N12/25, deposition of James Harington, answer 5; STAC 8/220/32, deposition of Thomas Hunte and Jasper Burneby, answer 4. [8] Vis. Bucks. (Harl. Soc. lviii), 13, 148-9, as corrected by Liber Famelicus of Sir J. Whitelocke ed. J. Bruce (Cam. Soc. lxx), 26-7. [9] STAC 5/H57/26, f. 3; STAC 8/220/32, depositions of Clement Smith, William Dalby and John Butler, answer 12. For a denial, see STAC 5/H9/34, deposition of Walter Nebon, answer 17. [10] STAC 5/H57/26; 5/N1/32. [11] STAC 8/220/32. [12] HMC Hatfield, xix. 124. [13] C142/342/105; 142/356/116. [14] C142/356/117; PROB 11/123, ff. 257-8; Chamberlain Letters ed. N.E. McClure, i. 516. [15] STAC 5/N12/25, deposition of (Sir) James Harington, answer 9. [16] PROB 11/96, ff. 24v-26v; Liber Famelicus, 26-7. [17] STAC 5/N12/25, deposition of James Harington, answer 11; STAC 8/220/32, deposition of Sir Guy Palmes; HMC Hatfield, xix. 124. [18] PROB 11/111, f. 356. [19] HMC Hastings, iv. 201; CSP Dom. 1611-18, p. 242. [20] HEHL, HA5480. [21] Vis. Rutland (Harl. Soc. iii), 38-9; SP14/118/26. [22] I. Grimble, Harington Fam. 169-70; R. Lockyer, Buckingham, 63. [23] CP sub Baron Noel; Viscount Feilding; earl of Denbigh. [24] Wentworth Pprs. ed. J.P. Cooper (Cam. Soc. ser. 4. xii), 240; Procs. 1625, p. 451; J.J. Scarisbrick, Henry VIII, 11-12. [25] Lincs. Peds. (Harl. Soc. li), 461-3; Vis. Rutland (Harl. Soc. iii), 38-9; STAC 5/N6/11, deposition of Thomas Exton, answer 7; STAC 8/220/32, depositions of Richard Tampion and Thomas Hunte, answers 30-31. [26] CSP Dom. 1631-3, p. 321; Lincs. Peds. (Harl. Soc. l), 72-3; PROB 11/110, f. 396v. [27] STAC 5/N12/25, deposition of (Sir) James Harington, answer 9. [28] Procs. 1625, p. 457; Lords Procs. 1628, v. 531. [29] CJ, i. 545a, 583b, 625a; CD 1621, iii. 29, 289; iv. 362; v. 83, 340; Nicholas, Procs. 1621, ii. 91. [30] Procs. 1626, iii. 147. [31] CD 1621, ii. 370; iii. 264; iv. 348. [32] CJ, i. 776b; DCO, 'Parl. Procs. Charles I, 1625-6', unfol. (June 1626).

S.H.

SHROPSHIRE

Number of voters: about 1,100 in 1677[1]

Feb. 1604	SIR RICHARD LEVESON
	SIR ROBERT NEEDHAM
by 22 Jan. 1606	SIR ROGER OWEN vice
	Leveson, deceased
c. Mar. 1614	SIR ROGER OWEN
	RICHARD NEWPORT
21 Dec. 1620	SIR ROBERT VERNON
	SIR FRANCIS KYNASTON
c. Jan. 1624	(SIR) RICHARD NEWPORT
	SIR ANDREW CORBET
5 May 1625	(SIR) RICHARD NEWPORT
	SIR ANDREW CORBET
12 Jan. 1626	(SIR) ROWLAND COTTON
	RICHARD LEVESON
c. Mar. 1628	(SIR) RICHARD NEWPORT
	SIR ANDREW CORBET

Early Stuart Shropshire enjoyed a rapidly expanding agricultural economy: the lowland plains in the north produced beef and cheese, while the southern hills specialized in high-grade wool. Meanwhile, Ludlow's dwindling broadcloth industry was surpassed by Shrewsbury's booming trade in the finishing of Welsh cottons; the coal measures at Broseley began to be exploited on an industrial scale; and the iron industry on Cannock Chase, Staffordshire spilled over into the eastern fringes of the shire. The benefits of this prosperity accrued to the county's elites, both the old gentry families and those who had made their fortune as merchants in Shrewsbury and London; all invested heavily in the shire's ex-monastic estates.[2]

Shropshire lacked a dominant political interest in this period. There were no resident peers: the Howards regained their ancient lordships of Clun and Oswestry in 1603, but their positions at Court meant that they were absentee landlords, using their estates as a financial rather than a political asset; Sir Thomas Egerton† (Lord Ellesmere from 1603) owned lands in the north of the county, but was similarly confined to the metropolis as lord chancellor; and while the Shropshire Talbots inherited the earldom of Shrewsbury in 1618, their Catholicism disqualified them from office.[3] The most influential institution within the county was the Council in the Marches, based at Ludlow, which numbered several county families among its member-ship, but had little influence over local administrative affairs. Successive lords president and justices wielded some electoral influence at Bishop's Castle, Bridgnorth and (from 1614) Ludlow, but there is no evidence of any official involvement in the shire elections.

In the absence of aristocratic influence the county seats were shared among the local gentry by mutual consensus prior to the election, apparently with an informal agreement that no shire knight should be returned for two consecutive parliaments. There were exceptions to this rule, but it ensured that no single interest predominated. In practice, a loosely related caucus of landowners from the northern half of the county (lying nearest to the county court at Shrews-bury) controlled the shire elections. This does not appear to have created any significant tensions, partly because the gentry from the southern parts could apply to four local boroughs for parliamentary seats, and also because their estates were generally smaller than those of their northern counterparts. In the few instances where southern families did hold large estates, other circumstances kept them from stand-ing: the Foxe estates around Ludlow were partitioned between three separate families; while the Lacons of Kinlet were denied influence through a combina-tion of Catholicism and mounting debts. The county (unlike several of its parliamentary boroughs) had no substantial legislative agenda, though the knights of the shire were happy to support the Shrewsbury drapers in their dispute with the Welsh clothiers in 1621.[4]

In the second half of Elizabeth's reign the Shrop-shire county seats were shared among eight local fami-lies: the Egertons, whose estates lay around Ellesmere; the Owens of Condover; the Leightons of Wattles-borough; the Bromleys of Shrawardine, whose main estates lay in Worcestershire; the Newports of High Ercall; the Corbets of Moreton Corbet and Child's Ercall; the Levesons of Lilleshall, who also held lands in Staffordshire; and the Needhams of Shavington, whose chief estates lay in Cheshire but who were connected to many of Shropshire's most prominent families by marriage. Several of these families were not available for election in 1604: John Egerton, knight of the shire in 1601, who was required to stand aside by tradition, was also preoccupied by a protracted dispute with the Stanley family; Sir Roger Owen of Condover (the other 1601 MP) was serving as sheriff; Robert Leighton of Wattlesborough, who had just succeeded to his estates, was under-age; while Sir Henry Bromley* fought and won a bruising contest for

the Worcestershire seats. Among the available alterna-tives, Sir Richard Leveson, fresh from his capture of a Portuguese carrack in 1602, was an obvious choice for the senior seat, while his junior partner Sir Robert Needham (previously knight of the shire in 1593) had inherited his estates two months earlier. Sir Francis Newport[†] of High Ercall and Sir Vincent Corbet of Moreton Corbet both recorded their assent to this choice by signing the election return.[5]

Leveson died on 2 Aug. 1605, and was replaced at a by-election by Sir Roger Owen, an influential figure within the Commons who was (unusually) re-elected in 1614. Needham, a much less prominent Member, never stood for election again. He was replaced in 1614 by Richard Newport, heir to the High Ercall estate, who cemented his electoral prospects by marrying a daughter of Sir John Leveson* only a few weeks before his return. Owen died before the next general elec-tion in December 1620, while Newport, in deference to local custom, transferred to Shrewsbury, presum-ably voluntarily, as he and his father both signed the return for Sir Robert Vernon and Sir Francis Kynas-ton. Vernon was doubtless backed by Needham, his brother-in-law, another signatory of the return, while Kynaston, a courtier, was promoted by his father, one of the county's most active magistrates.[6]

In 1624 Vernon and Kynaston were succeeded by Newport and Sir Andrew Corbet, both of whom had recently inherited large estates in the north of the county. In April 1624 Newport presented Sir Francis Lacon as a recusant officeholder, who became one of the few men to be removed from office in the aftermath of the session.[7] Newport and Corbet were re-elected in 1625, an unusual occurrence probably explained by the new king's wish that those returned in 1624 should have their mandate renewed. The county reverted to a normal rotation in 1626, when Sir Rowland Cotton (whose late wife was another of Sir Robert Needham's sisters) and Richard Leveson were elected, appar-ently upon a broad consensus, as Corbet, Kynas-ton, Newport and Vernon all signed the return. The gentry were reported to have petitioned against either the Benevolence or the Forced Loan in the autumn of 1626, warning 'how dangerous this course might prove to stir up an insurrection'. However, lord presi-dent Northampton encountered no overt resistance to the Forced Loan, and any early problems were over-come by allocating some of the Loan money to pay off outstanding debts for coat and conduct money. After a hesitant start the county returned £2,997 to the Exchequer, a figure which represented 82 per cent of its original quota, and exceeded the national average of 72 per cent by a comfortable margin.[8] There is no evidence of a contest in 1628, when Cotton transferred to Newcastle-under-Lyme, allowing Newport and Corbet to be returned for the shire. During the 1628 session Corbet made his views about recent events clear by moving for a vote of four subsidies rather than five in return for a royal undertaking not to levy another Forced Loan, while he joined in the widespread attacks on the duke of Buckingham in June.[9]

[1] Salop RO, 6001/286. [2] P.J. Bowden, *Wool Trade in Tudor and Stuart Eng.* 30-1, 58, 81, 92; P. Edwards, 'Cattle trade of Salop', *Midland Hist.* vi. 72-94; SHREWSBURY; E. Kerridge, *Textile Manufactures in Early Mod. Eng.* 19, 177-9; B. Trinder, *Industrial Rev. in Salop*, 7-15. [3] SIR ROBERT HOWARD; C142/345/146; 142/396/151. [4] C142/235/111; 142/312/147; 142/448/89; *CJ*, i. 534b, 364b, 588-9; *CD 1621*, iii. 65-7; SHREWSBURY. [5] C142/261/25; 142/290/101; C219/35/2/37; B. Coward, 'Disputed Inheritances', *BIHR*, xliv. 204-11. [6] C142/312/158; 142/402/146; C219/37/195. [7] C142/399/154; 142/402/146; *CJ*, i. 776b. [8] C219/40/224; NLW, 9061E/1442; SP16/54/28; 16/78/42; PRO 30/53/11, f. 21. [9] *CD 1628*, ii. 308; iv. 128, 268.

S.H.

BISHOP'S CASTLE

Right of election: in the resident freemen

Number of voters: several dozen

c. Feb. 1604	SAMUEL LEWKNOR WILLIAM TWYNEHO
24 Oct. 1610	SIR WILLIAM CAVENDISH I *vice* Twyneho, deceased
c. Mar. 1614	THOMAS HITCHCOCK EDWARD LITTLETON I or II
3 Jan. 1621	FRANCIS NICHOLS SIR GILBERT CORNEWALL
c. Jan. 1624	SIR ROBERT HOWARD RICHARD OAKELEY
25 Apr. 1625	SIR ROBERT HOWARD WILLIAM BLUNDEN
20 Jan. 1626	SIR ROBERT HOWARD WILLIAM BLUNDEN
8 Mar. 1628	SIR ROBERT HOWARD SIR EDWARD FOXE

Founded in the early twelfth century, Bishop's Castle failed to prosper due to its distance from the Severn valley, the key communications route in the region; under the Stuarts it was a local market town with a population of little more than 500. The manor belonged to the bishops of Hereford until 1559, when it was sequestrated by the Crown, and in 1573, amid protests that episcopal charters were being disregarded, a royal charter appointed a corporation comprising a bailiff and 14 capital burgesses. No right of parliamentary representation was mentioned, but several boroughs chartered by the early Tudors had made returns under similar circumstances: at the 1584 general election two relatives of the local lawyer Edmund Plowden[†] were elected, and their return went unchallenged in the Commons.[1]

With few local gentry families of any standing, electoral patronage at Bishop's Castle remained fluid until the 1620s. At the end of Elizabeth's reign the chief influences were Sir Henry Townshend*, the town's recorder and one of the justices at Ludlow, whose eldest son was returned in 1597 and 1601, and Alexander King[†], the Exchequer auditor whose circuit included Shropshire. Townshend's son probably died shortly before the 1604 election, when the senior seat went to Samuel Lewknor, Townshend's son-in-law and a nephew of Sir Richard Lewknor[†], chief justice of Chester. King is not known to have stood again, and in 1604 the second seat at Bishop's Castle was filled by William Twyneho, an associate of Robert Sackville*, presumably on the Lewkenor interest, which also secured his return for Midhurst, Sussex.

Twyneho's death in the summer of 1610 created a vacancy at Bishop's Castle, which was filled by Henry Howard, earl of Northampton, owner of the neighbouring lordship of Clun. This property had been seized by the Crown in 1572, but restored to the earl in February 1604. Northampton reinforced his local interest in 1608 with the appointment of his secretary John Griffith II* as bailiff of the Crown manor of Bishop's Castle, while a year later Arthur Ingram* purchased the manor on his behalf. The earl quickly earned the townsmen's gratitude by helping to quash a potentially damaging grant for a rival market at Church Stretton, Shropshire, and upon his recommendation the borough returned Sir William Cavendish I on 24 Oct. 1610.[2]

Neither of the 1610 MPs was returned at the 1614 general election, when Northampton nominated the London lawyer Thomas Hitchcock, and the other seat went to Edward Littleton, whose identity remains uncertain. The most likely candidates were two men with strong local connections: Edward Littleton I*, a senior lawyer in the Marches court at Ludlow, whose estates lay in south-eastern Shropshire, and his son

Edward II*, then a student at the Inner Temple; both were ideally placed to secure the backing of Lewknor and Townshend.[3]

Cavendish helped the corporation secure a new charter in 1617, and in return he was granted a nomination at the next election, which he exercised on behalf of Francis Nichols, a relation of his wife by marriage. The second seat in 1621 went to Sir Gilbert Cornewall, whose estates lay some 20 miles east of Bishop's Castle; his father was a member of the Council in the Marches, and he was presumably elected on Townshend's interest. After Northampton's death in June 1614 the Clun lordship passed to his great-nephew Henry Howard*, who died two years later, and thereafter to the latter's brother Sir Charles Howard, the only one of lord treasurer Suffolk's sons never to sit in the Commons. At Sir Charles's death in 1622 these estates devolved upon his younger brother Sir Robert Howard, who represented the borough for the remainder of the decade.[4]

Sir James Whitelocke* was appointed recorder of Bishop's Castle after Townshend's death in 1621, and it was doubtless upon his recommendation that his former secretary, Richard Oakeley, whose own lands lay just outside the borough, was returned in 1624. Whitelocke removed to King's Bench in October 1624, and the next two elections saw the return of one of the town's chief landowners, William Blunden. In 1628 Blunden was replaced by Sir Edward Foxe, another member of the Council in the Marches, who held estates worth £300 a year a few miles west of the borough, in Montgomeryshire.[5]

[1] M. Beresford, *New Towns of Middle Ages*, 479; *CPR*, 1572-5, pp. 14-5; A.D.K. Hawkyard, 'The enfranchisement of constituencies, 1504-58', *PH*, x. 11. [2] *Exchequer Officeholders* comp. J.C. Sainty (L. and I. soc. spec. ser. xviii), 123; *CSP Dom.* 1603-10, p. 77; E315/310, f. 52; E401/2412; C54/1995/1; *HMC 10th Rep.* iv. 401, 406. [3] SP14/77/42; Shaw, *Knights of Eng.* ii. 103; *Vis. Worcs.* (Harl. Soc. xc), 62-4; NLW, 9056E/780. [4] C66/2149/4; *HMC 10th Rep.* iv. 402; *Vis. Salop* (Harl. Soc. xxviii), 147-8; C142/384/161; 142/475/130; 142/559/145. [5] *Liber Famelicus of Sir J. Whitelocke* ed. J. Bruce (Cam. Soc. lxx), 90, 95-7.

S.H.

BRIDGNORTH

Right of election: in the freemen

Number of voters: c.300 in 1640

1 Mar. 1604	SIR LEWIS LEWKNOR
	EDWARD BROMLEY
14 Feb. 1610	SIR FRANCIS LACON
	Sir George Hayward *vice* Bromley, appointed to office
c.Mar. 1614	JOHN PIERSE, alderman
	RICHARD SYNGE, alderman
3 Jan. 1621	SIR JOHN HAYWARD
	WILLIAM WHITMORE
23 Jan. 1624	(SIR) WILLIAM WHITMORE
	GEORGE SMYTH
26 Apr. 1625	(SIR) WILLIAM WHITMORE
	GEORGE VERNON
	SIR GEORGE PAULE
	Double return of Vernon and Paule
17 Jan. 1626	SIR RICHARD SHILTON
	GEORGE VERNON
?1 Mar. 1628	SIR GEORGE PAULE
	SIR RICHARD SHILTON

Situated on a promontory overlooking the Severn, Bridgnorth was chartered in 1157 and returned two Members to the Commons from 1295. While regarded as 'the second town of Shropshire', its economic base was surprisingly modest: the medieval cloth industry declined under the Tudors, particularly after knitted caps, a local speciality, fell out of fashion, and in the 1630s the town's Ship Money assessment of £50 was only half that of the comparably sized borough of Ludlow.[1] The key to the town's survival lay in its role as a service centre: the only bridging point on the Severn for ten miles in either direction, it was the premier market town in south-eastern Shropshire, particularly for horses and cattle, while the rise of coal mining at Broseley increased the river traffic passing through the town, and its large number of alehouses occasioned adverse comment.[2] The corporation bolstered this role by ensuring that the town remained the regular venue for Shropshire's Lent assizes, despite a challenge from Shrewsbury in 1621, and also received occasional visits from the Council in the Marches.[3]

The population of early Stuart Bridgnorth was probably not far short of the 2,940 recorded in a census of 1688; thus the 300 freemen who voted in the parliamentary election of March 1640 must have represented nearly half the town's heads of household.[4] Governed by two annually elected bailiffs, 24 aldermen and a recorder, in 1547 the borough also inherited the secular jurisdiction which the collegiate church of St. Mary Magdalen had hitherto held over the town and parts of four adjacent rural parishes.[5] Yet this administrative autonomy was deceptive, as the corporation's modest income, around £100 a year under the early Stuarts,[6] meant that it was always susceptible to outside influences, and under the Tudors the retailers and craftsmen who dominated municipal life shared power with several neighbouring gentry families.

In the latter half of Elizabeth's reign the parliamentary representation of Bridgnorth was monopolized by local lawyers. Edward Bromley of the Inner Temple was returned in 1586 on his father's interest as recorder; the latter was dead by the next election, but in 1591 the family estates devolved upon Bromley's infant nephew, leaving the MP as the effective head of the family. This ensured the continuance of his electoral interest until his appointment as Exchequer baron removed him to the Lords as a legal assistant in 1610. Until 1597 he was partnered with John Lutwich, a Lincoln's Inn man from a Shropshire family who ceased to sit after his retirement to the 3,000-acre estate he purchased at Shipton, ten miles west of Bridgnorth.[7] Thomas Horde, then recorder, was returned in 1601, but his service as bailiff rendered him ineligible at the next election, and in 1604 a complete outsider, Sir Lewis Lewknor, who had just been appointed to the newly created post of master of ceremonies at Court, was chosen in his stead. The latter was almost certainly recommended by his uncle Sir Richard Lewknor[†], chief justice of Chester, upon whom the corporation bestowed a sugarloaf at around the time of the election, and from whom they sought assistance in establishing the town as a regular venue for the sittings of the Council in the Marches.[8]

Bromley's promotion occasioned a contentious by-election in February 1610, the origins of which lie in the municipal politics of the intervening years. In 1604 the corporation confronted their neighbour Sir John Whitbrooke over the nuisance the latter's weir on the Severn was allegedly causing to both the town's bridge and river-borne traffic. Bailiff Horde, though accused of provoking this confrontation to facilitate the construction of a weir on his own estates a mile upstream, headed an inquiry which concluded that

Whitbrooke's weir should be demolished, a ruling endorsed by the Exchequer court. Three years later, Whitbrooke was prosecuted in Star Chamber for procuring the undue imprisonment of John Hayward in 1602 for non-payment of a debt of £50. Having originally loaned the money at the behest of Sir John Thynne* to save Hayward from debtor's prison, Whitbrooke had ultimately been vigorous in his pursuit of repayment. Such behaviour was hardly uncommon among creditors, but Whitbrooke's enemies combined this with other accusations concerning the demolition of the Horde family pew in St. Mary's church, and a forcible entry instigated by him. None of these accusations was particularly damning on its own, but taken together they earned Whitbrooke fines totalling £200.[9] This dispute clearly began as a family rift: the protagonists were related through the London alderman Sir Rowland Hayward[†], and John Hayward had carried the order for the destruction of Whitbrooke's weir down to Bridgnorth in 1605. Yet by 1607 a significant proportion of the town's elite was prepared to take sides over the Star Chamber suits, partly thanks to Whitbrooke's intemperate behaviour, but perhaps also because of underlying religious differences, as Whitbrooke was convicted of recusancy in 1609/10.[10]

With these tensions in the air, the by-election to replace Bromley was held on 14 Feb. 1610. As reported in the Commons on 7-14 Mar., the case ostensibly revolved around the borough franchise, with Bailiff William Capper returning Sir Francis Lacon on a freeman franchise, and bailiff Richard Sotherne backing Sir George Hayward's return by a majority of the inhabitant householders. The parliamentary franchise had never previously been an issue of contention, and, perhaps because of the weakness of this charge, the debate shifted onto the inadequacy of the return, which Capper had sealed with the town's ale seal, reinforced by the signatures of five aldermen; Sotherne complained that indentures were usually sealed with the town seal and signed by the two bailiffs. After a week's examination the bailiffs were allowed to return home for the assizes, and while they returned to Westminster in May, no definitive decision was reached, allowing Lacon to keep his seat by default.[11] Intriguingly, the battle lines in this quarrel echo the factional divides of the previous six years: Capper (or his father) had been tenant of Whitbrooke's weir in 1604, while Lacon was another notorious Catholic. Hayward, meanwhile, was doubtless backed by his brother-in-law Sir Henry Townshend*, who succeeded Horde as recorder shortly thereafter.[12]

Echoes of these factional divisions can be detected in 1614, when two townsmen, Richard Synge and John

Pierse, were returned, as Synge's relative Humphrey Synge was Whitbrooke's servant. However, it was clearly of more significance that Humphrey was then serving as one of the bailiffs, as was Rowland Pierse, brother of the other MP. During the parliamentary session another of Whitbrooke's associates filed a Chancery suit accusing Sir Henry Townshend of malpractice, but the plaintiff failed to find anyone to corroborate the accusations he made in a subsequent Star Chamber suit, perhaps an indication that local tensions were declining. The dispute, which had probably always centred around the ambitions of Horde and Whitbrooke, was ultimately defused once Horde first mortgaged and then sold his patrimony to the Crown land speculator Sir William Whitmore between 1609 and 1620, while Whitbrooke's local influence was neutralized after his estates were extended by his creditors in 1615.[13]

The demise of the Horde and Whitbrooke interests lent a very different complexion to the elections of the following decade. In 1621 (Sir) William Whitmore acquired one seat following his purchase of the Horde property, while the other went to Sir John Hayward, younger brother of the recently deceased Sir George. Shortly thereafter Hayward married a widow with jointure estates in Kent, and began selling his Shropshire lands. In 1624 the parliamentary seat thus vacated went to George Smyth, whose father had been one of Hayward's bailiffs. Yet Smyth's father did not lack an interest of his own: a substantial landlord within the borough, at the time of the election he was also serving as both master of the Mercers' Company and town bailiff. As he was concurrently in dispute with Hayward over the settlement of his accounts as manorial bailiff, it is possible that he intended his son's return to be seen as a snub to Hayward.[14]

In 1625 a fresh interest emerged in the shape of Sir George Paule, a courtier whose brother was a townsman. He challenged Smyth's nomination of the lawyer George Vernon, uncle of the 1624 MP. The indenture recorded the return of Whitmore and Vernon, but the official Crown Office list noted a double return, which was never resolved. Vernon sat unopposed in 1626, while his preferment as Exchequer baron in November 1627 allowed Paule to take his place in 1628.[15] Meanwhile, in 1626 and 1628 Whitmore gave way to solicitor-general Richard Shilton, a Buckingham appointee whom he doubtless found convenient to cultivate for professional purposes.

---

[1] J.F.A. Mason, *Bridgnorth*, 10-17; T. Rowley, *Salop Landscape*, 187-91; J. Leland, *Itinerary* ed. L. Toulmin Smith, ii. 85; G. Bellett, *Antiq. Bridgnorth*, 114-15, 220-1; *CSP Dom.* 1635, pp. 364, 503. [2] P.R. Edwards, 'Cattle Trade of Salop', *Midland Hist.* vi. 72-94; P.R. Edwards, *Horse Trade of Tudor and Stuart Eng.*; STAC 8/173/19;

Trans. Salop Arch. Soc. x. 144; R. Baxter, *Autobiog.* ed. N.H. Keeble, ch. 2; T.S. Willan, *Inland Trade*, 19-20; J. Hatcher, *Hist. of Brit. Coal Industry*, 141-8. [3] *Trans. Salop Arch. Soc.* iii. 282-350; Nicholas, *Procs. 1621*, ii. 151. [4] Bodl. Blakeway 18, f. 110; Salop RO, BB/B6/4/1/1. [5] Bodl. Blakeway 18, ff. 6, 68. [6] Including the accts. of the chamberlains, bridgemasters and millmasters in Salop RO, BB/D1/2/1. [7] C142/232/62, 142/354/95; PROB 11/125, ff. 325v-7. [8] Bodl. Blakeway 18, f. 40; C219/35/2/38; *Trans. Salop Arch. Soc.* x. 150. [9] E112/116/151; E124/1, f. 320; E134/2Jas.I/Mich.30; E178/4423, 4436; STAC 8/166/5, 8/173/19, 8/176/22; Barnes, *STAC Fines.* [10] PROB 11/83, ff. 178-80; C142/241/125; 142/381/158; *CSP Dom.* 1603-10, p. 592. [11] *CJ*, i. 407-10; *Procs. 1610* ed. E.R. Foster, ii. 361 n. 6; C219/35/2/29. For the normal indenture format, see 38. [12] E134/2Jas.I/Mich.30; Bodl. Blakeway 18, f. 40. [13] STAC 8/56/3; Salop RO, 5586/5/5/1; Mason, 17-18; C142/381/158. [14] C142/363/194; Mercers' Hall, London, Bridgnorth Mercers' Order Bk. ff. 12v-13v; Salop RO, BB/B6/3/1/4; C2/Jas.I/S37/2. [15] *Vis. Surr.* (Harl. Soc. xliii), 205; *Vis. Cheshire* (Harl. Soc. lix), 243-4; C219/39/167; *Procs. 1625*, p. 598; *VCH Salop*, iii. 244; Sainty, *Judges*, 32.

S.H.

LUDLOW

Right of election: in the corporation

Number of voters: 37

27 Feb. 1604	ROBERT BERRY, alderman RICHARD BENSON, high bailiff
7 Dec. 1609	RICHARD FISHER, high bailiff *vice* Benson, deceased (Sir) Francis Eure* John Leveson
26 Mar. 1614[1]	SIR HENRY TOWNSHEND, recorder ROBERT BERRY, high bailiff ?Richard Tomlyns ?Sir Edward Foxe*
11 May 1614[2]	ROBERT LLOYD *vice* Berry, unseated on petition ?Sir Edward Foxe* ?Richard Tomlyns
2 Jan. 1621	SPENCER COMPTON, LORD COMPTON RICHARD TOMLYNS
3 Feb. 1624[3]	RICHARD TOMLYNS RALPH GOODWIN
2 May 1625[4]	RICHARD TOMLYNS RALPH GOODWIN
21 Jan. 1626	RICHARD TOMLYNS RALPH GOODWIN
8 Mar. 1628	RICHARD TOMLYNS RALPH GOODWIN ?Sir Robert Harley*

Ludlow Castle was built at the end of the eleventh century on high ground by a crossing of the River Teme, and the town first appears in Exchequer records in 1169. A borough by prescription, municipal government was established over 150 years before the first surviving charter, of 1449, which confirmed the existing structure of two bailiffs, drawn from a corporation of 12 aldermen and 25 common councillors. Edward IV, who inherited a moiety of the borough, granted the townsmen parliamentary representation in 1461, and a Council of the Marches decree of 1553 settled the franchise in the corporation, although election returns habitually defined the franchise in more evasive terms as 'all the burgesses of the said town to whom the said election doth appertain'.[5]

Ludlow probably reached the peak of its prosperity in about 1580, with much new building, a population approaching 3,000 and a flourishing economy. Good connections to Wales and the Severn along the Teme valley offered it a substantial natural hinterland, and its cattle and horse trades acquired a regional significance by the early modern period. However, the town's chief economic asset was its easy access to the local fine quality wools, from which 400-800 'Ludlow white' broadcloths were produced annually by the mid-sixteenth century.[6] Ludlow's success was boosted by the presence of the Council in the Marches at Ludlow Castle, which served as its main base. Law terms in the Marches Court were only a few weeks long, but they attracted several hundred officials, lawyers and litigants, and the Ludlow corporation lobbied hard and spent around £20 a year on gratuities to Council officials (far more than any of its rivals) to ensure that their town reaped the benefit of these sessions. The corporation also co-opted a number of Council officials onto the town corporation.[7]

For all its success, Ludlow was not without its problems. In the 1590s the corporation was riven by a feud between an 'inner circle' accused of monopolizing access to municipal office and lands, and a loose coterie of those excluded from power. This dispute was only resolved after a decade of litigation, a new and controversial charter in 1596, a rigged parliamentary election return in 1597 and several expulsions from the corporation. One of the first signs of settlement came in October 1602 when Robert Berry, newly elected high bailiff, and one of his erstwhile enemies, Alderman Edward Crowther, were delegated to seek advice about the town charter. In January 1604 Berry, Crowther, the then high bailiff Richard Benson and coroner Richard Bayly were ordered to petition the king for a new charter. Plans changed upon the arrival of the writ

for a parliamentary election: Berry and Benson were returned to the Commons and instructed to secure a new charter while at Westminster, thus enabling the corporation to secure both its aims for minimal expenditure. Berry had served as MP six times previously, but Benson, who had never sat before, presumably owed his election to his office. Neither man left any trace on the Commons' proceedings, although the corporation did later acquire a copy of the Act for settling the Queen's jointure, to which the Ludlow fee-farm had been assigned. The new charter was acquired at a cost of £66 9s. 1d., while both MPs were allowed parliamentary wages of 2s. a day.[8]

Benson died of the plague in November 1609, and a number of rival candidates were nominated in anticipation of the ensuing by-election. Before the writ was issued the corporation resolved to follow the precedent of 1604 in returning their high bailiff, Richard Fisher, but matters were complicated by lord president [Ralph] Eure†, who put forward his brother Sir Francis*. The latter, who had been returned for Scarborough in 1604, had no need of another seat, so it is possible that the president was merely aiming to establish the Council's electoral influence in principle while allowing the corporation to prevail on this occasion. The townsmen certainly went out of their way to placate him, sending a delegation to Bewdley to explain their decision, and giving him a sugarloaf shortly after the start of the parliamentary session. Lord treasurer Salisbury (Robert Cecil†), who was attempting to bolster his own following in the Commons in anticipation of the Great Contract negotiations, accompanied the election writ with another letter of nomination, for John Leveson, heir to Sir John Leveson*, a Cecil client with substantial estates at Lilleshall, Shropshire. This request was similarly rejected, and Fisher was returned on 7 December.[9]

The sudden invasion of outside influences in 1609 was probably linked to the town's declining economic fortunes. Whereas peace with Spain had led to a nationwide boom in the cloth trade in 1604, Ludlow's industry faltered and then collapsed: in 1609-10 only 61 cloths were sealed by the town's alnager, representing less than ten per cent of pre-war production. While Salisbury nominated to every vacant seat in the autumn of 1609 regardless of local circumstances, Eure timed his bid at Ludlow to coincide with the precise moment at which the town was most dependent economically upon the continuation of Council patronage. He may even have been offered some influence at the next election in return for waiving his nomination in 1609. This would explain the corporation's unusual behaviour on 26 Mar. 1614, when recorder Sir Henry Townshend, one of the justices in the Marches, was elected a common councillor and returned as MP together with Berry, while a resolution was then passed barring non-members of the corporation from election. This allowed the townsmen to rebuff an overture from the Ludlow-born Richard Tomlyns, and, more significantly, to reject Sir Edward Foxe*, another Council member who was probably Eure's nominee, who owned property in the town, and whose forbears had been MPs in the early sixteenth century.[10]

If Eure was annoyed by the corporation's behaviour, a means of retribution lay ready to hand: Berry, then high bailiff, had committed a technical offence in returning himself at the election, as was quickly pointed out to the Commons' privileges' committee. When this was reported to the House on 9 Apr., the London lawyer Nicholas Fuller* called for Berry's expulsion, citing precedents for the removal of mayors who had returned themselves. The parallel was not exact, as Ludlow had two bailiffs rather than one mayor, and was thus able to continue its business in Berry's absence, while the fact that Ludlow had returned its high bailiffs in 1593, 1604 and 1609 without demur was ignored. Yet at Fuller's insistence Berry, who had admitted the circumstances of his return, was ejected on 14 April. Foxe's family, perhaps lobbying in anticipation of the ensuing election, were entertained at Ludlow in the same month, and Foxe himself was admitted a freeman on 28 April. However, the corporation bestowed the seat upon Robert Lloyd, a member of the queen's Household. Anne's influence stemmed from the fee-farm of £33 6s. 8d. she received from the town, a sum which represented approximately one-quarter of the town's annual expenditure. Nevertheless, in choosing Lloyd the corporation delivered a second snub to Eure's nominee.[11]

At the time of the next parliamentary election in January 1621 only three of the town's former MPs were still alive. Of these Townshend, although still active as justice and recorder, was over 80; Lloyd's patronage had lapsed with the death of Queen Anne; and Alderman Fisher showed no signs of wishing to stand again. The shortage of candidates was exacerbated by the fact that the election of a serving bailiff was now out of the question. Furthermore, the town's economic dependence on the Council in the Marches remained acute, as its cloth industry showed no signs of revival. Yet with the demise of both Berry and Eure minimizing any lingering animosity from 1614, the townsmen suspended their ban on the election of non-corporation members in order to return Spencer, Lord

Compton, son of lord president Northampton. The second seat went to Richard Tomlyns, who had been rejected at the previous election, but had gained his freedom in July 1614. He renewed his suit in November 1620 with the support of the town's London attorney, George Holland. Tomlyns' residence at Westminster Abbey allowed him to serve without expenses, and even more attractively, he offered to assist with the purchase of the town's fee-farm, recently put up for sale by the Crown at over £400. This sum, representing about three times the town's annual income, was way beyond the corporation's means, and Tomlyns, having no family, undertook to bequeath the fee-farm to charitable uses within the town after his death.[12]

Tomlyns initially aspired to be a diligent MP, sending the Ludlow bailiffs a lengthy account of proceedings during the Easter recess, promising to give the corporation a gold cup, and undertaking to ask Lord Compton to speak with his father about an unidentified dispute, perhaps the town's claim to jurisdiction over Ludford, south of the Teme. During the summer he completed his purchase of the fee-farm, but quickly found himself frustrated by his inability to collect his dues from the corporation. Tomlyns had originally told the corporation that he might assign the fee-farm to them 'in part while I live, but sure after my decease, if it please God', an undertaking the townsmen had clearly interpreted in an over-optimistic light. The discovery that Tomlyns intended to enjoy a lifetime's income from his purchase helps to explain their hesitation, as does the Exchequer's incompetence in failing to forward the necessary paperwork to its local officials, who continued to harrass the town for payment of the fee-farm for at least a year after the sale had taken place.[13]

Tomlyns and the corporation grudgingly resolved their differences shortly before the 1624 election, which explains the peremptory tone in which he canvassed the corporation:

> I do hear it is with you as with most towns of this kingdom (the more to be lamented) that Ludlow grows very poor, partly occasioned by reason of the Council's uncertain and seldom abode there. I could wish with all my heart that you could subsist without them and that you would settle yourselves to your old trade of clothin[g] or some such profitable trade, that so you might not depend upon them, and leave this victualling and tippling whereon the inhabitants now chiefly liveth.

This was hardly diplomatic language, and Holland was forced to step into the breach to quash rumours that Tomlyns 'is inclinable to popery, and will (if he be chosen) expect or sue for his charges of attendance in Parliament', which sufficed to secure his election. Lord Compton did not stand again, and was replaced by his father's secretary, Ralph Goodwin, who was admitted as a burgess and, like Compton, had the rule barring election of non-corporation members suspended in his favour.[14]

Relations between Tomlyns and the corporation improved considerably once the fee-farm issue was resolved: he assisted Holland in securing an Exchequer decree waiving Ludlow's liability to parliamentary fifteenths at Easter 1625; and in the following year he assisted the town clerk in lobbying for a new charter. Both Tomlyns and Goodwin were re-elected in 1625, 1626 and 1628, although in 1628 Tomlyns, then 64 years old, confessed,

> I had resolved with myself, being now grown into years and sickly, not to have been in any more Parliaments, nevertheless some gentlemen of worth and others my familiar friends have persuaded me once more to be of this Parliament in hope of better success, which God grant that the king and his people may accord to the glory of the Almighty and the public welfare and good of the Commonwealth.

This was unfortunate for Sir Robert Harley, who, being doubtful of a seat in Herefordshire, appealed to Ludlow for succour in February 1628. After some debate the corporation decided that Northampton's institutional influence and Tomlyns's ownership of their fee-farm trumped Harley's reputation as a godly commonwealthsman, obliging him to seek relief at Evesham.[15]

[1] Salop RO, LB2/1/1, f. 103v. [2] Ibid. f. 104. [3] Ibid. f. 142. [4] Ibid. f. 147. [5] M. Faraday, *Ludlow 1085-1660*, pp. 1-31, 44; *Ludlow Castle* ed. R. Shoesmith and A. Johnson, 5-35; C219/35/2/31. [6] Faraday, 103-8, 114-27, 157-63; P.J. Bowden, *Wool Trade in Tudor and Stuart Eng.* 29-30; E. Kerridge, *Textile Manufactures in Early Modern Eng.* 20-1; P. Edwards, *Horse Trade of Tudor and Stuart Eng.* 30-5, 62; P. Edwards, 'Cattle Trade of Salop', *Midland Hist.* vi. 72-94. [7] Faraday, 96-102; *Ludlow Castle* ed. Shoesmith and Johnson, 68-82; P. Williams, *Council in Marches of Wales under Eliz.* 187-9. [8] Faraday, 31-7; Salop RO, LB2/1/1, ff. 43, 45, 49v-51; LB8/1/128/3; LB8/1/129/4. [9] Salop RO, LB2/1/1, ff. 80v-2v; *CSP Dom.* 1603-10, p. 566. [10] Faraday, 124-5; Salop RO, LB2/1/1, f. 103v. [11] *Procs. 1614 (Commons)*, 38-9, 80; Salop RO, LB2/1/1, f. 104; LB8/1/136/4-7; LB8/2/57-74. [12] Salop RO, LB2/1/1, f.131; LB7/1677; LB8/2/89. [13] Salop RO, LB2/1/1, f. 131v; LB7/1677-8, 1680-91; LB8/2/87-8. [14] Salop RO, LB2/1/1, f. 142; LB7/1692; LB8/2/94. [15] Salop RO, LB2/1/1, ff. 151v-2, 157v; LB7/1693-5; LB8/2/93.

S.H.

MUCH WENLOCK

Right of election: in the freemen of Wenlock liberty

Number of voters: 152 in 1599

6 Mar. 1604	GEORGE LAWLEY
	ROBERT LAWLEY
c. Mar. 1614	EDWARD LAWLEY
	ROWLAND LACON
2 Jan. 1621	(SIR) EDWARD LAWLEY
	THOMAS WOLRYCHE
22 Jan. 1624[1]	THOMAS WOLRYCHE
	HENRY MYTTON
2 May 1625	THOMAS WOLRYCHE
	THOMAS LAWLEY
	?Henry Mytton
25 Jan. 1626	THOMAS LAWLEY
	FRANCIS SMALMAN II
4 Mar. 1628	THOMAS LAWLEY
	GEORGE BRIDGEMAN

Sited on a ridge west of the Severn, Much Wenlock's prosperity was founded upon the sale of March wool from sheep grazed on Wenlock Edge. However, the town itself, with a population of no more than 600-700 in the early Stuart period, was in decline: the prosperity which had built its magnificent market hall in the fifteenth century was but a memory, while the borough was not even designated a staple market for the wool trade in 1617. Meanwhile, such industry as the town did possess was being eclipsed by the growth of coalmining at nearby Broseley.[2]

Wenlock secured parliamentary representation under its charter of 1468, which granted the borough civil authority over the parish of Holy Trinity. As this church had originally served all the priory's estates, the municipal jurisdiction was tacitly extended to cover the entire monastic liberty, comprising several dozen manors on both sides of the Severn. This broad interpretation of the charter opened the borough to the gentry of a substantial swathe of south-eastern Shropshire: a burgess list from 1599 shows only one-third of the 152 burgesses as residents of Wenlock proper.[3] Thus gentry families who had invested in ex-monastic estates in the liberty were easily able to intervene in municipal politics. Many of the borough's bailiffs were drawn from the gentry of the liberty, while parliamentary election indentures include a cross-section of the liberty's elites as attestors, and habitually describe the electorate as the burgesses of the 'town, borough and liberty'.[4]

Almost all of Wenlock's early modern MPs can be linked to the liberty, particularly the Lawleys, who acquired the site of the priory and several manors in the immediate vicinity of the borough in the 1540s.[5] The head of the most influential branch, Thomas Lawley[†], augmented his local influence through the purchase of Wenlock manor and ex-chantry lands within the borough in 1600, and at the general election of 1604 he secured the return of two of his brothers. This was the only occasion on which the family took both seats, and there may have been some dissent, as the bailiff, John Lutwich[†], departed from usual practice in neglecting to include the names of any attestors upon the indenture. It is unlikely there was a contest, as the only credible alternative was Lawley's 18-year-old heir, Edward, who was admitted a freeman at around the time of the election. However, his father ultimately decided to send him to Oxford rather than Westminster.[6]

Edward Lawley subsequently represented his home town in the Parliaments of 1614 and 1621. The other seat in 1614 went to Rowland Lacon, heir to Sir Francis Lacon* of Kinlet, whose ancestral home at Willey lay within the borough's liberty. In 1618 Lacon sold this property to the Worcestershire lawyer John Wylde*, whose influence at Droitwich meant that he had no need of a parliamentary seat elsewhere.[7] Thus the junior seat at Wenlock in 1621 fell to a comparative outsider, Thomas Wolryche, whose main seat at Dudmaston lay on the other side of Bridgnorth. However, Wolryche had recently acquired the liberty's manor of Hughley as part of an agreement to restructure the debts of his uncle William Gatacre, and he was admitted burgess on the day of his election. His return was doubtless arranged by the town's recorder, (Sir) Edward Bromley*, a trustee of Wolryche's estates under the terms of his father's will.[8]

The Lawleys' electoral interest at Wenlock underwent a major upheaval during the 1620s. Thomas and Sir Edward Lawley died in quick succession in 1622-3, and their estates passed to Sir Edward's under-age daughter, Ursula. Sir Edward's widow also died in December 1623, leaving Ursula to the custody of her mother and Henry Mytton, a gentleman of the privy chamber and uncle of the local man Henry Mytton of Shipton, who had been borough bailiff in 1622-3.[9] Within a month, the courtier had become a freeman and MP for Wenlock, but his subsequent decision to carry Ursula off to his Leicestershire home alienated her grandmother, while he apparently upset the Wenlock corporation with a ham-fisted attempt to influence the election of the borough bailiff in September 1624.[10] The corporation revenged themselves upon Mytton at the next parliamentary election in May 1625, when they returned Thomas Lawley, a London Draper descended from another branch of the local family, who had recently inherited the Spoonhill estate just south of Wenlock. Mytton may have put himself forward as a candidate, but, probably to quash any notion of a challenge, the bailiff endorsed Lawley's return with the words 'nemine contradicente'.[11]

Although he remained a London resident, Lawley was re-elected at Wenlock in both 1626 and 1628. However, Wolryche, having served in three Parliaments, was replaced by Francis Smalman II in 1626. It is possible that Wolryche contested the election, but the most straightforward explanation for his disappearance from the hustings is the failure of Recorder Bromley, who died only months later, to nominate his protégé. Smalman's family had estates at Wilderhope, which abutted the liberty's manor of Shipton, while he and his father were both burgesses of Wenlock, and had formerly lived with the Lawleys at Spoonhill.[12] In August 1626 the corporation appointed the Gloucestershire lawyer Sir John Bridgeman as recorder in succession to Bromley. His eldest son George was made a freeman in the following month, and succeeded Smalman as MP in 1628.[13]

[1] Trans. Salop Arch. Soc. (ser. 2), vi. 275. [2] VCH Salop, x. 429-30; J.U. Nef, Rise of the Brit. Coal Industry, i. 64-5, 96-7; Stuart Royal Procs. ed. J.F. Larkin and P.L. Hughes, i. 367. [3] P.J. Bowden, Wool Trade in Early Modern Eng.; VCH Salop, x. 195-6, 203-5; Trans. Salop Arch. Soc. (ser. 2), vi. 270-3. [4] Trans. Salop Arch. Soc. (ser. 2), vi. 263-79; C219/35/2/39; 219/40/228; 219/41A/51. [5] VCH Salop, x. 416-17, 420-1; HP (Commons) 1558-1603, i. 232-3. [6] C219/35/2/38; Trans. Salop Arch. Soc. (ser. 2), vi. 273. [7] Vis. Salop (Harl. Soc. xxix), 308; VCH Salop, x. 450. [8] C142/345/135; C3/389/9; Trans. Salop Arch. Soc. vi. 274-5, 277. [9] C142/393/142; 142/401/105; PROB 11/142, f. 502. [10] Trans. Salop Arch. Soc. vi. 275-6; WARD 10/43/1. [11] C142/431/98; C219/39/166. [12] Trans. Salop Arch. Soc. xi. 12; ibid. (ser. 2), vi. 276. [13] Vis. Glos. (Harl. Soc. xxi), 27; Trans. Salop Arch. Soc. (ser. 2), vi. 277.

S.H.

SHREWSBURY[1]

Right of election: in the freemen

Number of voters: 475 in 1584[2]

8 Mar. 1604	THOMAS HARRIS RICHARD BARKER, recorder FRANCIS TATE
	Double return of Harris and Barker. Election declared void, 13 Apr. 1604
28 Apr. 1604	RICHARD BARKER, recorder FRANCIS TATE Thomas Harris
c. Mar. 1614	FRANCIS BERKELEY LEWIS PROWDE
23 Dec. 1620	(SIR) RICHARD NEWPORT FRANCIS BERKELEY
c. Jan. 1624	FRANCIS BERKELEY THOMAS OWEN, town clerk
6 May 1625	SIR WILLIAM OWEN THOMAS OWEN, town clerk
24 Jan. 1626	SIR WILLIAM OWEN THOMAS OWEN, town clerk
8 Mar. 1628	SIR WILLIAM OWEN THOMAS OWEN, town clerk

The 'proud Salopians' of Shrewsbury, as their rivals termed them, achieved the high-water mark of their prosperity in the century before the Civil War: the town's population rose from 3,000 to 7,000, the urban area was largely rebuilt, and the borough evolved from a county seat into the economic and social focus of an area stretching from the Wrekin to Cardigan Bay. Shrewsbury's urban growth mirrored developments at neighbouring Chester and Worcester, but the simultaneous expansion of its hinterland gave it a regional significance comparable to that of much larger centres such as York, Norwich, Bristol or Exeter.[3] This expansion was partly due to Shrewsbury's location at the head of the Severn navigation, which facilitated communications to Gloucester, Bristol and beyond, while the town's proximity to the upland pastures of southern Shropshire made it the entrepôt for top-quality March wool coveted by broadcloth weavers from Gloucestershire to the Low Countries.[4] Westwards, the river allowed easy access to much of Wales – the borough was an important mart for the Welsh livestock trade, and provided

both manufactures and credit in return – while a rising proportion of townsmen and many of the 300 pupils at Shrewsbury School were Welsh.[5] Yet if this topographical advantage had sufficed, the town's heyday would have occurred during the wool boom of 1250-1350. What made the difference three centuries later was the winning of a key role within the regional cloth trade.

Shrewsbury's medieval prosperity was founded upon the sorting and packing of wool; cloth-making only developed there in the fifteenth century. By 1588 the 125-strong Weavers' Company specialized in the production of bays and says,[6] though it was not manufacture, but the finishing of coarse but soft Welsh cottons, frises and flannels – chiefly used as linings in tailored garments – which became the mainstay of Shrewsbury's economy during the sixteenth century. Bought from Welsh clothiers at Oswestry, then rowed, sheared and occasionally dyed at Shrewsbury, the cotton finishing trade provided employment for up to 800 men.[7] Some of this cloth was marketed in the Midlands, but much was shipped to France via London, where exports of Welsh cottons were worth £15,000 to £30,000 a year by the early seventeenth century.[8]

Shrewsbury's growing reliance on Welsh cloth, reflected in the town's rapid growth during the sixteenth century, fostered tensions between the town's most important trades. The shearmen, numerically the largest guild, had little political power, as their business depended upon capital provided by the merchants, most of whom originally belonged to the Mercers' Company. However, the mercers' preeminence was overthrown by the statutory monopoly of the Welsh cloth trade secured by the Drapers' Company in 1566. This Act was revoked only six years later, but during that brief interval the balance of power within the town was irrevocably altered, and four of the wealthiest mercers subsequently defected to the drapers, leaving a legacy of resentment between the two guilds.[9] Having won their domestic power struggle, the drapers faced governmental attempts to regulate the quality of their product, Welsh resentment at the Company's stranglehold on their industry, and interlopers who clamoured to redirect the flow of Welsh cloth through Chester, Aberdovey or London. Their tenacity in defending their privileges welded the Company into one of the best-organized lobby groups in England, and their successful efforts secured the town's prosperity for the better part of two centuries.

I. Electoral Politics, 1604-29

In 1603 the Shrewsbury corporation resolved that the town's parliamentary representatives should henceforth be 'then inhabiting within this town or suburbs, being burgesses of the town and known to be men fearing God, of sound religion, lovers of the estate of the town and able to speak in that place as occasion may require'. However, since 1581 the borough had returned only lawyers and gentry, eschewing its tradesmen, probably to avoid a repetition of the controversies of 1566-72, when townsmen MPs had echoed the corporation's divisions over the merits of the drapers' statutory monopoly of the Welsh cloth trade. This policy had not entirely succeeded in eliminating electoral controversies due to the rival ambitions of various local candidates and the fractious nature of the commons, who regarded election eve as a time of misrule. The 1584 election was contested by three local lawyers, Thomas Owen[†], Richard Barker and Thomas Harris, and although Harris, the unsuccessful candidate, was returned unopposed in 1586, the experience may have left a residue of ill-feeling, for when Barker's nephew stood in 1601 he was elected only with 'much ado'.[10]

These latent tensions notwithstanding, the corporation was clearly surprised by the eruption of strife at the general election of 1604, as the field of potential candidates was unusually narrow. Reginald Scriven, having represented the borough in five Elizabethan parliaments, stood aside, and Sir Francis Prince, who had lately inherited a substantial estate in the town's Abbey Foregate suburb, apparently had no parliamentary ambitions. Another potential candidate, Sir Roger Owen* (son of the 1584 MP), was ineligible since he was sheriff of Shropshire.[11] The corporation earmarked one seat for Richard Barker, recently appointed recorder, and offered the second to lord president Zouche, perhaps to induce him to hold occasional sessions of the Council in the Marches at Shrewsbury. On 7 Feb. Zouche nominated his daughter's brother-in-law, the newly appointed Welsh judge Francis Tate, vouching for his readiness 'to be employed in any of your affairs' and assuring the bailiffs that his election would not contravene the recent Proclamation against electing nominees or the relatives of great men. In deference to the corporation's resolution to restrict their choice to resident townsmen, he undertook 'to do my endeavour that he [Tate] shall make his choice to be resident amongst you before any place', a condition the corporation had insisted upon when they awarded Tate his freedom on 29 January.[12] This careful arrangement was upset by Sheriff Owen, who proposed Serjeant Thomas Harris instead of Barker, threatening a re-run of the 1584 contest. Now doubtful of Tate's chances, on the eve of the election Zouche conceded that Barker's return

must take priority over that of his own candidate, but he had misunderstood Owen's intention, which was to block Barker by returning the other two candidates. Exploiting his office to the full, Owen delayed publishing the writ, and then, after the corporation elected Barker and Tate, he rejected the return on the spurious grounds that Barker was not a freeman, procuring signatures to a rival indenture naming Tate and Harris instead.

It was Tate, effectively the disinterested party in this dispute, who brought the matter to the Commons' attention. On 13 Apr. both returns were declared void and a fresh election was ordered.[13] In the intervening weeks Owen moved to his town-house at Shrewsbury, the better to intimidate the corporation, while the under sheriff, charged with supervising this election, delayed announcing the new writ; it was also later claimed that Owen attempted to start a brawl at the hustings. Despite these tactics, Barker and Tate were returned on 28 April. Further complaints were made, but since the return was not irregular the Commons lost interest in the issue, and so Owen was never brought to account for his unseemly conduct.[14]

By 1614, Barker was on the verge of retirement from public life. His decision not to stand again meant that Owen, who was returned for the county, felt no need to put up a rival candidate. Tate was still a Welsh judge, but his patron, Zouche, had long since been replaced as lord president by Ralph, Lord Eure[†]. Eure was probably responsible for nominating another Welsh justice, Lewis Prowde, but even without his endorsement the corporation had sufficient grounds for choosing Prowde: a Shrewsbury man by birth, he was in 1613 one of the authors of an important series of reports to the Privy Council upholding the town's claim to maintain the staple market for Welsh cloth at Oswestry.[15] With Barker and Harris out of the running, the other seat might have gone to the local lawyer Roger Pope, had he not spent much of the previous decade troubling the burgesses with a vexatious lawsuit.[16] The corporation therefore selected a less prominent lawyer, Francis Berkeley, who carefully followed the town's brief during the next three parliaments.

Prowde was dead by the next election in December 1620, and although Pope had settled his differences and been co-opted onto the corporation, he was, as bailiff, not permitted to stand. Yet with Berkeley assured of re-election there was no pressing need for a second lawyer, and the corporation therefore chose Richard Newport, heir to a large estate at nearby Wroxeter and Owen's fellow knight of the shire in 1614. Perhaps nominated by Sheriff Walter Barker, to whom he was related by marriage, Newport probably agreed not to seek re-election, because in 1624, when he sat for the county, he sought to insure himself against defeat by securing a burgess-ship at Much Wenlock rather than Shrewsbury.[17]

The Thomas Owen who was elected alongside Berkeley in January 1624 was undoubtedly the man who succeeded Thomas Dyos as town clerk that month. Owen's father, a draper, had been bailiff four times. He himself was entirely familiar with municipal politics, having deputized for Dyos as clerk of the town courts since 1610.[18] His re-election to the next four parliaments therefore proceeded without incident. Berkeley, however, did not stand again, apparently out of choice, and at the next three elections his seat went to Sir William Owen, brother of the late Sir Roger, resident since 1611 and senior bailiff in 1621-2.[19]

II. The Alnage Dispute and Parliament, 1602-9

At the end of Elizabeth's reign the Shrewsbury Drapers' chief concern was a dispute over quality control in the cloth industry, which arose from a French edict of 1600 banning the importation of tentered cloth. As tentering was necessary to correct uneven shrinkage during fulling, the decree was tantamount to a total boycott and threatened Shrewsbury's trade with Rouen, which had boomed since 1594. Although the English Privy Council immediately banned tentering, an Act of 1601 recognized that it was an essential part of the finishing process and also specified the precise length, breadth and weight for various kinds of cloth, which were to be inspected by the London alnager at Blackwell Hall.[20] The Cloth Act's primary aim was to persuade the French to lift their embargo, but the Exchequer soon realized that it could be used as a revenue raising device, as it brought many kinds of cloth, including Welsh cottons, under the purview of the London alnager for the first time since the 1550s.[21] Defective cloths were to be forfeited, and the proceeds divided equally between the informer and the Crown.[22] All that the Exchequer required to exploit this situation was a man willing to enforce the legislation with vigour.

In 1602 'a man of very good credit' warned the Shrewsbury drapers' London partners of impending disaster, urging an embargo on all consignments of cloth which failed to meet the standards laid down in the recent Act. Consequently, the Drapers' Company, with the advice of Thomas Harris and Roger Pope, tried to persuade lord president Zouche of the necessity of improving the quality of Welsh clothmaking. Before any remedial action could be taken, however,

the London alnager, John Tey*, laid informations in the Exchequer against a wide range of clothiers, including 12 Shrewsbury drapers.[23] The Company feared an unfavourable verdict, and therefore in 1604 it sent two of its members to lobby in Parliament for alterations to the 1601 statute, which, as a probationer, required renewal. Their behind-the-scenes manoeuvres paid off, for at the second reading of the expiring laws' continuance bill on 5 June, Francis Moore, parliamentary spokesman for lord chancellor Ellesmere (Thomas Egerton†), offered a proviso which exempted Welsh cloth priced at under 15d. a yard from the 1601 Act, and relaxed the quality threshold for the more expensive cottons. His speech bore all the hallmarks of a pre-arranged compromise: Tate and Barker were named to the committee, and the amendment passed into law without incident.[24]

The enactment of this proviso undermined Tey's case and helped reduce the profits from his lease, which yielded only £224 to the Exchequer in the two-and-a-half years to Michaelmas 1604. However, Tey quickly found another legal loophole to exploit: while the 1604 proviso exempted cheap Welsh cottons from the requirement for an alnage seal, it overlooked a clause in the 1552 Cloth Act stipulating that each cloth should include a second seal from the maker specifying its dimensions and weight. A contentious issue in Mary's reign, this measure had not been enforced since 1558, but seizures began anew at Bartholomew Fair in August 1604, and a year later the drapers were warned by their London partners that an Exchequer decree in Tey's favour could cost them £150 a year in forfeitures. The question of how to pay for this lawsuit dominated half a dozen indecisive Company meetings, during which time Tey won his Exchequer case. The drapers responded in February 1606 by voting to raise a fighting fund by means of a weekly levy on cloth sales at the Oswestry market, and to send a man to join their London partners in lobbying for a fresh statute at the new parliamentary session.[25]

The drapers initially hoped to insert a clause in the general cloth bill promoted by London interests, but the measure was delayed in committee for three months while amendments proposed by other interested parties were scrutinized.[26] The Company therefore tabled a separate bill, which received two readings (28 Feb. and 10 March). Barker and Tate were named to the committee along with the shire knights, Sir Roger Owen and Sir Robert Needham, but Tey was also included, and displayed samples of defective cloth to convince the committee that his activities were necessary. The drapers, enjoined to show more concern for quality, drafted a bill to this effect and sent it to Shrewsbury for the Company's approval. It was thereafter conveniently forgotten, but this co-operative attitude placated the committee sufficiently to allow the bill to be reported on 17 Mar.; the drapers later credited Owen with this achievement, sending him a tun of wine in recognition of his efforts.

Though frustrated in the Commons, Tey now applied pressure upon the drapers by implementing his Exchequer decree. At the Welsh cloth market at Blackwell Hall, he prowled menacingly among the stalls in the company of a pursuivant, who had orders to haul anyone who opposed his seizures before lord treasurer Dorset (Thomas Sackville[†]).[27] With resistance guaranteed to play into their enemies' hands, the London partners closed their market and asked the Privy Council to suspend all further seizures until the writ of error brought against Tey's Exchequer judgment was decided. Meanwhile, in the Lords, the drapers' bill was hotly disputed in committee, both by Dorset and by London merchants trading with France, who objected to the 1604 dispensation in favour of tentering which was to be confirmed by the new bill. One of the London partners, William Spurstowe[†], successfully defended the tentering proviso before the Lords' committee, while Dorset's hostility was probably neutralized by his fellow committee member, lord chamberlain Suffolk (Thomas Howard[†]), who had been petitioned by the corporation of Oswestry, where he was lord of the manor. Although Dorset threatened to mount another attack at the third reading, the Welsh cottons' bill was enacted.[28]

Freedom from Tey's attentions came at a heavy price, as the drapers' London partners incurred costs amounting to £237 14s. 4d. Aware that paying this bill would prove unpopular, the partners, who submitted their accounts in November 1606, reminded the Company of the alternative to such prodigious expense:

> there is not any country that tradeth cloth to London, but one way or other it hath cost them more than our disbursements, besides they are still subject to seizures and impositions and much servitude by that implacable monster of men, that wolf Tey and his ministers, whose taxations are yearly increased and the poor country then grievously polled and vexed, and are remediless.

Such arguments left some unmoved: one Richard Jones refused to pay the cloth levy three months later, and there were damaging (though unfounded) rumours that Spurstowe was secretly assisting the London merchants in their opposition to the tentering clause of the drapers' bill. In April 1607 an attempt to collect arrears of the levy on cloth provoked a heated exchange in the Drapers' Hall, and in the following year two of the London factors, despairing of payment, sued the Company for restitution. The case was settled by arbitration in 1609, but it was another nine years before the debt was paid in full.[29]

III. The Drapers' Quest for a Monopoly, 1609-10

The alnage dispute highlighted the shortcomings of the drapers' dependence on the London market, and efforts to diversify the trade over the next few years were almost certainly prompted by this unpleasant experience. The possibility of using Bristol as an alternative had been explored as early as 1582, but the port's Merchant Venturers found no market except at Rouen, where the Londoners were already well established. Trade down the Severn was sustained at a low level until the peace of 1603 opened up new outlets in the Iberian peninsula. The subsequent boom was facilitated by the Shrewsbury corporation's decision to allow the draper Rowland Jenks to rebuild the town's river quays in 1606, and over the next decade the value of exports through Bristol rose to about £5,000 a year, a volume which was sustained until the Civil War.[30]

In 1609 Sir Roger Owen procured a fresh charter giving Shrewsbury's drapers a monopoly of sales of Welsh cloth within Shrewsbury. A few hapless retailers were subsequently prosecuted for infringement of this right, but since the charter cost £80 this was seemingly an expensive gesture to reinforce a privilege which had remained uncontested for almost 50 years. However, the Company's reasoning becomes clearer when viewed in the light of the ambitious legislation it laid before Parliament in February 1610.[31] The drapers proposed an Act 'for cutting off of all interlopers in our trade of drapery', not simply in Shrewsbury, but nationally. The bill's general nature was doubtless partly designed to attract contributions from other towns to bolster the Company's modest fighting fund of £30, but it was also influenced by contacts with the Coventry drapers, whose role in the finishing of Gloucestershire broadcloth mirrored its own in the Welsh industry and with whom it proposed to act in concert.[32]

The drapers' hopes were quickly dashed. A general meeting of the bill's backers was arranged for the afternoon of 14 Feb., the first full day of Commons' business, but apart from John Niccolls, the Shrewsbury lobbyist, the Coventry men were the only others present. Prospects for effective co-operation dimmed even further when Coventry decided to abandon Shrewsbury's agenda in favour of a bill to restrict the sale of cloth by chapmen and pedlars to towns with a resident alnager. Niccolls reminded them of their earlier undertaking but was told that 'their counsel ... did confirm it was in vain to make such a suit, for it could not be granted'. He declined to contribute towards the cost of their new bill, although he promised 'I would further them all I could in their suit, both in London and with our knights and burgesses'. Over the next five days he solicited some small donations at Blackwell Hall, but his enthusiasm waned after the Derby draper Peter Geary also refused to part with any cash, and he made plans to return to Shrewsbury even before the Coventry bill was rejected at its first reading on 24 February.[33]

IV. London Interlopers, 1611-21

The drapers' quest for statutory confirmation of a monopoly of the cloth trade at Shrewsbury highlighted its fear of interlopers. Apart from a minor incident in 1602, there was no sign of trouble with interlopers until the French Company was chartered in 1611. A large group of merchants from London and the outports were granted a monopoly of the export trade to France; but clothiers and Blackwell Hall factors were specifically excluded from Company membership. Naturally, the drapers petitioned the Privy Council either to have the grant rescinded or to be allowed a compensatory right of export themselves, but nothing was achieved, despite private appeals to lord treasurer Salisbury (Robert Cecil[†]), the earls of Northampton and Suffolk, Lord Zouche, and even the Shrewsbury native Clement Edmondes*, one of the Privy Council clerks.[34]

On the face of it, the French Company's charter merely denied the drapers export rights in which they had never previously been interested. However, there was a very real danger that it would ultimately allow London merchants to intrude into the drapers' monopoly of the inland trade. This was indeed what happened, for in March 1613 the Shrewsbury draper Robert Charlton and the London merchant Job Harby began buying cloth at Machynlleth, Montgomeryshire for direct export to the Continent from nearby Aberdovey.[35] Further petitions were now sent to the Privy Council, and this time the complaints were taken seriously: the case was referred to legal counsel including the Salopians Barker and Prowde, whose report endorsed both the Oswestry staple and the Shrewsbury drapers' monopoly of the inland trade. Charlton and Harby returned to Wales a few months later, but were swiftly convented before the Council and obliged to give bonds to cease their activities.[36]

By 1621 the drapers had developed a lasting grudge against the French Company after London's corporation, swayed by a petition from a host of City luminaries including Sir Thomas Smythe*, William Towerson*, Sir Maurice Abbot*, Robert Bateman* and Hugh Myddelton* – and also (more curiously) by two Shrewsbury drapers, John Prowde and Peter Mytton – complained in November 1619 to the Privy Council about the Shrewsbury drapers' manipulation of prices at Oswestry and Blackwell Hall. Although the drapers' monopoly was upheld, their trade was almost certainly boycotted briefly by the French Company.[37] Consequently, in the 1621 Parliament Shrewsbury promoted a petition against their enemies' patent, which was filed by Sir Richard Newport on 26 April. The sheer press of business after the Easter recess meant that it was not until 5 May that the drapers' lobbyist managed to have the patent called into the House, although in the meantime other opponents of the French Company secured a single reading for a bill designed to dash the same patent by confirming the 1606 Act for free trade with France and Spain. The drapers' cause was eventually timetabled for debate at the grievances' committee on the afternoon of 28 May, but that day Secretary Calvert informed the House that Parliament would be adjourned a week later. Newport's motion to have the patent read was therefore brushed aside in the rush to get the grievances ready for presentation to the king.[38]

V. Welsh Attempts at Interloping, 1604-24

Although the drapers had succeeded in upholding their privileges at the Council board, they had done so only with considerable difficulty. Emboldened by this knowledge, the Welsh clothiers, who resented having to deal exclusively with Shrewsbury, complained against the Drapers' Company. This posed a significant threat, as the Welsh clothiers provided the raw material upon which the drapers' trade was founded. Moreover, they were a far larger and potentially better organized group than any of the drapers' other rivals, particularly in Parliament, where Salopian interests could easily be drowned out by the voices of the more numerous Welsh MPs.

Welsh objections to the drapers' monopoly first received a serious hearing in the Commons in 1604. In a poorly reported speech during the free trade debate of 6 June, Sir William Maurice apparently complained that in 1583 the Privy Council had used the royal prerogative to revive the repealed statute of 1566, which had granted the Shrewsbury drapers their monopoly of the Welsh cloth trade. The timing of his speech, which was delivered the day after the drapers had secured the proviso freeing them from the alnage, is intriguing, but in a debate which focused on the export trade his intervention was poorly judged, and he received no support.[39] Ten years later, with the disputes of 1613 still ringing in the Privy Council's ears, the Welsh missed another opportunity to reorder their relationship with the Shrewsbury drapers. Richard Wynn* observed that at the committee for petitions and grievances 'there might some good be done touching our Welsh cottons if there were anybody to follow it', but nothing seems to have been done before the dissolution.[40]

In 1621, by contrast, the Welsh called the drapers' monopoly into question from the start of the session. In a poorly recorded debate at the grievances' committee on 23 Feb., its defenders (presumably the Shrewsbury MPs Berkeley and Newport) stated that the drapers' privileges were founded upon the Company charter of 1609 and the Privy Council order of 1613, and claimed 'that this opposition is by the Londoners and Jersey men for their own ends'. This assumption was probably wrong, as the protestors called for free trade in Welsh cottons, a demand unlikely to have originated with the French Company, which had its own problems with the free trade lobby. Moreover, it was said 'that in making the order [of 1613] the Welshmen were not heard', an oversight unlikely to have been of significance to any but the Welsh clothiers. On the same day, the Drapers' Company met at Shrewsbury, having only just received warning of the impending attack, and voted to send John Prowde to lobby at Westminster on their behalf. He clearly missed the first reading of the Welsh cottons' bill three days later, as it met no opposition even though it constituted a full-scale assault on the drapers' privileges. It painted the Privy Council orders of 1613 and 1619-20 as undesirable innovations rather than confirmations of existing practice, and proposed to open both inland and export trades to all comers, a move clearly intended to destroy Shrewsbury's monopoly.[41]

Prowde worked hard to galvanise his countrymen into action at the bill's second reading on 2 Mar., when both sides in the debate showed every sign of have carefully choreographed their moves in advance. Before the bill was even read, Francis Berkeley proposed to defer it on the grounds that 'it concerneth but the moiety of two shires, and that they have put in a petition of grievance for which counsel appointed to be heard, and that time not yet come'. This motion was ignored, the bill read, and the London Welshman (Sir) Thomas Trevor promptly moved for committal, whereupon John Whitson of Bristol denied that the

drapers' privileges constituted a monopoly, citing the considerable export trade through his town. Berkeley reinforced this point by observing that the drapers of Chester, Coventry and Whitchurch were also allowed access to the Oswestry staple. He also warned that the bill would ruin Shrewsbury's economy and offered a rather desperate motion to exclude Welsh and Shropshire MPs from the bill committee. Sir James Perrot of Pembrokeshire and John Ratcliffe of Chester both pressed for committal, and all Sir Richard Newport was able to achieve was an order allowing counsel to be heard at the committee, to which all Welsh and Shropshire MPs were named.[42] Although well marshalled, the Salopians' arguments had done little to shift opinion within the House: William Wynn* remained confident that the bill 'is like to overthrow the Shropshire men', while one diarist recorded that 'Mr. Berkeley spoke *multa* but not *multum*'.[43]

With the Welsh loudly insisting that the drapers' monopoly was the prime cause of the recent slump in their trade, the Salopians were able to achieve little in committee, except to delete the erroneous claim made in the bill's preamble that the drapers had restricted the export trade to London. They also managed to have the right of sale restricted to inhabitants of Wales, and had the bill made a probationer. Yet no sooner was the bill reported on 20 Mar. than Sir Robert Vernon of Shropshire and Sir Fulke Greville – chancellor of the Exchequer and one of the referees who had scrutinized the case against an interloper named Davies in 1619-20 – moved to protect the livelihood of the Shrewsbury shearmen with a proviso banning the export of undressed cloth from Welsh ports. The West Country men Sir William Strode and Sir Walter Earle retorted that the committee had been content to allow the export clause, whereupon Newport declared that he was 'of the committee and yet not satisfied'. Carrying on where Vernon had left off, Newport outlined the damaging effects of this clause, not only on Shrewsbury, but also on carriers, innkeepers and the inmates of Christ's Hospital, London, which received a fee for each cloth sold at Blackwell Hall. One of the Caernarvonshire MPs tentatively conceded that the Welsh did not seek a right of exportation for themselves, and solicitor general Heath proposed a general amendment to bar the export of unfinished cloth.[44] The bill was recommitted for this purpose, returning to the floor of the House six days later, when Berkeley and recorder Heneage Finch of London insisted that the proviso be given teeth by allowing for the forfeiture of any cloth exported in defiance of the Act. Consequently, the text was amended and the bill engrossed.[45]

Having achieved some success over the export clause, the Shrewsbury men aimed to neuter the proposal to free the inland trade at the third reading on 24 April. Newport opened the debate with a general warning against the ways in which 'this bill crosses corporations by charter erected and overthrows them, gives way to forestallers, lets every man sell by retail to sell where they will, crosses former Acts of Parliament'. Perrot insisted that the bill offered no encouragement to forestallers, and was followed by Sir Robert Phelips, who endorsed the measure as part of the House's general attack on monopolies. Berkeley then deployed a series of precedents against Perrot's arguments, and Edward Alford conceded that free trade should be denied to retailers. However, any hopes that the House might come to see the merits of Shrewsbury's case were crushed by the intervention of Sir Edward Coke, who tartly observed that 'he that likes not the body of the bill will find many exceptions' and delivered a ringing endorsement of free trade, which carried the day for the Welshmen.[46]

During the Easter recess Prowde apparently persuaded the drapers to rack up the pressure on the Welsh clothiers with a boycott of the Oswestry staple, aiming to remove the marketplace to Shrewsbury itself. On his return to Westminster he received a complaint about this tactic from Sir William Herbert*, the leading promoter of the bill. Prowde made a conciliatory reply, but privately advised the drapers 'that if you forbear buying but a while they will wish they had not stirred in this business'. He added that, as France was teetering on the brink of civil war, a pretext for not buying was readily to hand.[47]

Despite Prowde's efforts, the cloth bill cleared the House of Lords largely unscathed in a mere three weeks. At the Lords' second reading on 30 Apr. a lengthy petition claimed that the bill would destroy the economies of both Shrewsbury and Oswestry, allow aliens to monopolize the trade, and facilitate the smuggling of cloth, wool, fuller's earth and hides from obscure Welsh ports.[48] Summoned to the Lords' committee on 8 May, Prowde managed to secure a proviso upholding the monopoly of retail sales at Shrewsbury granted in the drapers' 1609 charter, but failed to block the export of dressed cloth from Welsh ports. This raised the spectre of a mass exodus of shearmen from Shrewsbury to process the cloth which, thereafter, would make its way to the Welsh coast rather than eastwards. In these circumstances, and with the situation in France still deteriorating, Prowde advised the drapers to keep calm:

whereas you may fear the coming down of drapers or merchants of London or transportation out of Wales by Flemings, let this assure you that your fear is causeless, for those that perhaps have a will that way want money, and those that are provided of money will find better commodities to bestow it in than Welsh cloth; neither is there any danger in abstaining since all is set at liberty.[49]

The bill returned to the Commons on 16 May, when Perrot attempted to scupper the Lords' proviso by claiming that the Upper House could not amend a bill without a joint conference. This objection was brushed aside by Alford, the amendment incorporated, and the bill thereafter awaited royal approval.[50]

The Commons' decision not to press for a legislative session at the adjournment of 4 June meant that the Welsh cottons' bill was lost at the dissolution eight months later. However, by then the Welsh clothiers had won a grant of similar privileges from the Privy Council after they submitted a petition which, in effect, reiterated the terms of the cloth bill. On 13 June the orders of 1613-14 and 1619 which underpinned the drapers' monopoly were rescinded, and four weeks later a Proclamation was issued specifying that Welsh cloth 'may from henceforth be freely bought and sold in all places and to all persons where and to whom the same by the laws of the realm may be sold'. In stark contrast, the drapers' request for permission to export the stocks of cloth remaining on their hands was ignored.[51]

Over the next few years the boycott of Oswestry by the Shrewsbury drapers began to have an effect, aided by the slump in the cloth market generally. In November 1621 the Welsh clothiers and Oswestry burgesses petitioned the Privy Council to end the drapers' boycott, and in June 1622 the protests of the Welsh clothiers were referred to attorney-general Sir Thomas Coventry*.[52] Eventually, the Welsh clothiers lost confidence in the Oswestry men, who failed to devise any workable guarantee for minimum weekly sales at their market, and consequently they came to terms with the Shrewsbury drapers, and were rewarded with record export figures in 1624. In April 1623 the Shrewsbury corporation awarded honorary freedoms to those who had helped to resolve the crisis, including lord treasurer Middlesex (Sir Lionel Cranfield*), Sir Fulke Greville (now Lord Brooke), and their erstwhile opponents, Sir William and Sir Percy Herbert*. This rapprochement made all the difference in the 1624 Parliament, when the same Welsh cloth bill which had been so keenly fought over in the previous session was enacted after passing both Houses without a murmur of dissent.[53]

VI. Other Municipal Interests

While Shrewsbury's parliamentary agenda was dominated by the cloth trade, other groups within the town aspired to further or defend their interests in the Commons, and it is worth comparing their achievements with those of the drapers. The mid-Jacobean period saw an upheaval in the wool trade which threatened Shrewsbury's pivotal role as a distribution centre. The courtier Viscount Fentoun took over Sir Edward Hoby's* patent for regulation of the wool trade in 1615, which he vigorously enforced to maximize revenue. The resulting outcry led to a Privy Council order of 1616 barring all except clothiers from purchasing wool before Michaelmas, which was widely evaded: the Worcester clothiers complained that Shrewsbury staplers had engrossed that year's clip of wool throughout the Marches. There were threats of prosecution in Star Chamber, but in March 1617 the contentious order was revoked and 23 towns, including Shrewsbury and Oswestry, were designated as staples for the domestic wool trade. In 1621 the Worcester MPs Robert Berkeley and Thomas Chettle attempted unsuccessfully to revive the clothiers' claim to pre-emption with an amendment to the bill for free trade in wool. Newport and Francis Berkeley evidently played no part in opposing the bill's passage, a silent rebuke, perhaps, to Arthur Kynaston, wealthiest of the Shrewsbury wool staplers, who in 1621 had betrayed the Drapers' Company by siding with Oswestry.[54]

In a municipality dominated by powerful economic interests, Shrewsbury's corporation occupied a peculiarly subordinate position. Nevertheless, it promoted a small number of schemes for the general good, albeit with a conspicuous lack of success. One longstanding aspiration concerned the borough's status as a shire town: Shropshire's Epiphany quarter sessions was invariably held at Shrewsbury, and in 1579 the town wrested the right to hold the summer assizes from Bridgnorth, but its position was eroded from 1601, when the Council in the Marches discontinued its practice of holding intermittent sittings at Shrewsbury. The offer of a parliamentary seat to Tate in 1603 failed to convince Zouche to transfer any business from Ludlow, and his successor paid only a few ceremonial visits to the town, despite a Privy Council order of 1612 requiring the Council in the Marches to meet there occasionally during the law terms. On 2 June 1621, at the corporation's behest, Newport tabled a parliamentary bill to settle the assizes at county towns, which would have benefited Shrewsbury at the expense of Bridgnorth, but this failed to receive a

reading, and the corporation thereafter abandoned its quest.[55]

The corporation also looked to Parliament to confirm its charter rights. Between 1584 and 1638, when charters were granted, reform of the municipal constitution was frequently mooted to deal with problems such as the legal status of the town's suburbs, the monopoly of the retail trade in cloth granted to the drapers in 1609, and the borough's liability for purveyance. On three of these occasions – 1601, 1604 and 1610 – it was resolved to seek statutory confirmation of the charter, although no legislation is known to have resulted. One source of pressure for change arose from the grammar school, of which the corporation were trustees. As most of the school's income was derived from impropriated tithes, it was approached by the ecclesiastical authorities to increase the stipends of the curates it hired to serve the benefices. The school declined this request, and consequently in 1610 and 1629 there were proposals to resolve this issue by a fresh charter, to be backed by statutory approval. This plan failed to bear fruit, and the dispute continued, later becoming one of the major factors behind the town's charter renewal of 1638.[56] The failure of this scheme, and indeed of all the corporation-backed plans for legislation, can probably be ascribed to an understandable lack of determination. The cost of the lengthy lobbying process needed in order to achieve a fresh charter was simply not worth the potential benefits.

---

[1] This article has benefited from the advice and assistance of Mr. James Lawson and Dr. William Champion. [2] *Trans. Salop Arch. Soc.* iii. 300. [3] A.D. Dyer, *Worcester in Sixteenth-Cent.*; D.M. Woodward, *Trade of Elizabethan Chester*; D.H. Sacks, *The Widening Gate: Bristol and the Atlantic Economy 1450-1700*; C. Pythian-Adams, 'An agenda for Eng. Local Hist.', in *Societies, Cultures and Kinship, 1580-1850*, pp. 1-23. [4] *VCH Salop* v. (forthcoming); P.J. Bowden, *Wool Trade in Tudor and Stuart Eng.* [5] C. Skeel, 'Cattle Trade bet. Wales and Eng.', *TRHS* (ser. 4), ix. 135-58; P. Edwards, 'Cattle Trade of Salop', *Midland Hist.* vi. 72-94; P. Edwards, *Horse Trade of Tudor and Stuart Eng.*; *VCH Salop* v. (forthcoming). [6] *Trans. Salop Arch. Soc.* (ser. 2), ii. 281; Salop RO, 6001/3359, ff. 3-4; E112/37/84. [7] T.C. Mendenhall, *Shrewsbury Drapers and Welsh Wool Trade*; J.G. Jenkins, *Welsh Woollen Industry*; E. Kerridge, *Textile Manufactures in Early Mod. Eng.* 19. [8] REQ 2/301/102. London exports are calculated from Mendenhall, 13-14, 53-62, and represent a minimum, as customs officials did not always distinguish between Welsh and Manchester cottons. [9] Mendenhall, 120-32; *Trans. Salop Arch. Soc.* iii. 270. [10] *Trans. Salop Arch. Soc.* iii. 295, 300, 315, 320-2, 331-2, 347; Salop RO, 6001/290. [11] C142/252/41; *List of Sheriffs* comp. A. Hughes (PRO, L. and I. ix), 119. [12] H. Owen and J.B. Blakeway, *Hist. Shrewsbury*, i. 538, 568; Salop RO, 3365/2617/108; *Stuart Royal Procs.* ed. J.F. Larkin and P.L. Hughes, i. 67-8; *Trans. Salop Arch. Soc.* (ser. 2), x. 306; Salop RO, 6001/290. [13] Salop RO, 3365/2617/108; *CJ*, i. 154a, 170b-1a, 201a-b, 936a. Barker's return is in C219/35/2/35; Harris's does not survive. [14] *CJ*, i. 195a, 201; C219/35/2/36. [15] *APC*, 1613-14, pp. 9-10, 34-40, 310-11, 351-5. [16] Salop RO, 3365/2502; decree in *Trans. Salop Arch. Soc.* xlvii. 70-1. [17] *Vis. Salop* (Harl. Soc. xxviii), 27-8;

Trans. Salop Arch. Soc. (ser. 2), vi. 276. [18] Trans. Salop Arch. Soc (ser. 3), v. 128; Owen and Blakeway, i. 543; St. Chad's, Shrewsbury, 33; THOMAS OWEN. [19] C142/374/86; Salop RO, 946/B/752, 755-6; Owen and Blakeway, i. 532. [20] Mendenhall, 138-40; APC, 1600-1, pp. 387-9; D. Dean, Law-making and Soc. in late Elizabethan Eng. 138-40. [21] Mendenhall, 140. For the Elizabethan background of the London alnage, see G.D. Ramsay, Wilts. Woollen Industry, 54-8. [22] E112/37/84, 109. [23] E112/94/475; E124/1, f. 258; Salop RO, 1831/14, letter of 30 Apr. 1602; 1831/6/1, pp. 347-8; 1831/2/1, f. 19v. [24] Salop RO, 1831/6/1, p. 352; CJ, i. 232b, 986a; SR, iv. 1051. [25] AO1/594/1; C2/Jas.I/U4/8; C8/10/102; Mendenhall, 140-2; Salop RO, 1831/6/1, pp. 356-7; 1831/14, letter of 20 Sept. 1605. [26] Salop RO, 1831/14, letter of 1 Mar. 1605/6; CJ, i. 270b; CLRO, Rep. 27, f. 165v; Bowyer Diary, 47, 290-1. [27] CJ, i. 275b, 281b; Salop RO, 1831/6/1, p. 358; 1831/14, letters of 1 Mar., 8 Mar., 18 Mar. 1605/6. [28] Salop RO, 1831/14, letters of 1 Mar. 1605/6, 13 Apr., 1 Nov. 1606; LJ, ii. 402a, 408-9, 412a, 423a; SR, iv. 1092. [29] Salop RO, 1831/6/1, pp. 358, 362; 1831/6/2, ff. 1v-5, 26-27v; 1831/14, letter of 1 Nov. 1606 and enclosure; C8/10/102; C2/Jas.I/ U4/8. [30] Mendenhall, 68-74; Salop RO, 6001/290. Export values are calculated at 2s. per goad. [31] Salop RO, 1831/2/1, ff. 22v-23v; 1831/6/2, ff. 1, 3v-5v; 1831/14, letter of 6 May 1609; C66/1799/2. [32] Salop RO, 1831/6/2, f. 9; Coventry Archives, PA 100/12/1-35. [33] Salop RO, 1831/14, letter of 19 Feb. 1609/10; CJ, i. 399a. [34] Select Charters of Trading Cos. ed. C.T. Carr (Selden Soc. xxviii), 62-78; Salop RO, 1831/2/1, f. 24v; 1831/6, resolution of 11 Aug. [1611]; 1831/6/2, f. 13; 1831/14, letter of 24 June 1611. [35] Salop RO, 1831/6/2, f. 16; 1831/14/26-8; 3365/2617/164. [36] Mendenhall, 147-8; Salop RO, 1831/2/1, ff. 26-7; 1831/6/2, ff. 17-18; APC, 1613-14, pp. 9-10, 34-40, 51-3, 191-2; SP14/112/40 (misdated to 1620 in CSP Dom. 1619-23, p. 117). [37] CSP Dom. 1619-23, pp. 116-17; APC, 1619-21, pp. 63, 115, 122, 129-30, 135, 138; SP14/112/41-2, 14/113/57. [38] CJ, i. 592b, 605b, 626a, 629a; Nicholas, Procs. 1621, ii. 10; SR, iv. 1083; CD 1621, iii. 330-1; C. Russell, PEP, 118. [39] CJ, i. 987b. [40] Procs. 1614 (Commons), 35; NLW, 9055E/651. [41] CD 1621, iv. 95; Salop RO, 1831/6/2, f. 35v; CJ, i. 526b; Mendenhall, 237-8. [42] CJ, i. 534b; Mendenhall, 171-3. [43] NLW, 9057E/939; CD 1621, v. 268. [44] CD 1621, ii. 214; CJ, i. 564; D.W. Jones, '"Hallage" receipts of the London cloth markets', EcHR, xxv. 567-87; Mendenhall, 174-5. [45] CJ, i. 575a; CD1621, iv. 198; Mendenhall, 175-6. The evolution of the draft bill can be seen in Mendenhall, 237-8; SR, iv. 1218-19. [46] CJ, i. 588-9; CD 1621, iii. 65-7; Mendenhall, 176-80. [47] V.-L. Tapié, France in Age of Louis XIII and Richelieu, 120-3; M.P. Holt, French Wars of Religion, 178-80. [48] Salop RO, 1831/14, letters of 25 Apr., 30 Apr., 2 May 1621; LJ, iii. 96, 101. [49] Salop RO, 1831/14, letter of 8 May 1621; LJ, iii. 117, 124. [50] CJ, i. 622b; CD 1621, ii. 372; iii. 271-2; Nicholas, ii. 79-80; Kyle thesis, 126. Pym wrongly claimed that the bill was recommitted. CD 1621, iv. 352. [51] NLW, 9057E/957; SP14/121/58; APC, 1619-21, pp. 396-7; Stuart Royal Procs. i. 511-19; CSP Dom. 1619-23, p. 329. [52] B.E. Supple, Commercial Crisis and Change in Eng. 53-8, 68-70, 239-42; SP14/129/60; 14/131/22; APC, 1621-3, pp. 131-3; Salop RO, 1831/6/2, f. 37v; CSP Dom. 1619-23, pp. 403-4, 407. [53] APC, 1621-3, p. 447; Salop RO, 6001/290; Mendenhall, 54; Kyle thesis, 127. [54] Bowden, 164-74; APC, 1616-17, pp. 35, 178-81; Stuart Royal Procs. i. 365-9; Kyle thesis, 89-91; ROBERT BERKELEY. [55] Trans. Salop Arch. Soc. iii. 282-350; CSP Dom. 1611-18, p. 62; Salop RO, 6001/290; Nicholas, ii. 151. [56] Salop RO, 6001/290; THOMAS OWEN; VCH Salop v. (forthcoming).

S.H.

SOMERSET

Number of voters: over 2,600 in 1614

20 Feb. 1604	SIR FRANCIS HASTINGS SIR EDWARD PHELIPS	
22 Oct. 1610	JOHN POULETT vice Hastings, deceased	
4 Apr. 1614	SIR MAURICE BERKELEY JOHN POULETT Sir Robert Phelips*	c.1150
1 Jan. 1621	SIR HENRY PORTMAN, bt. ROBERT HOPTON ?William Seymour*, Lord Beauchamp	
26 Mar. 1621	CHARLES BERKELEY vice Portman, deceased	
26 Jan. 1624	SIR ROBERT PHELIPS JOHN SYMES	
c. May 1625	JOHN STAWELL SIR ROBERT PHELIPS	
23 Jan. 1626	SIR HENRY BERKELEY SIR JOHN HORNER	
12 Feb. 1628	SIR ROBERT PHELIPS SIR EDWARD RODNEY ?Sir Henry Berkeley	

Somerset was a wealthy and exceptionally populous county with a wide range of economic interests. The vale of Taunton Deane was well known for its cattle; and inferior Irish imports were resented less as competition than as a threat to the breed. The shire's most celebrated product, Cheddar cheese, was used by local politicians to gratify their metropolitan contacts. Much arable land was already enclosed, but large-scale improvements were still possible on Crown estates, where Charles I promoted the drainage of the Sedgemoor levels and the disafforestation of Neroche and Selwood, with varied success. During this period, coal and lead mining reached its peak in the Mendips, though among the magnates Robert Hopton* is the only ironmaster to be identified. There were two areas of cloth manufacture of more than local importance, one in the south-west and the other along the eastern border, where the demand for labour occasioned the building of many cottages and a loosening of control by the traditional ruling class. 'Somerset's yeomanry were many in number, fairly prosperous, and decidedly ambitious', and adept politicians like Sir Robert Phelips* and Hugh Pyne* did not neglect even non-voting copyholders, who could be used to swell the 'cry' for a popular candidate on election day.[1]

It has been reckoned that some 25 major gentry families effectively governed the county, from whose ranks came those who aspired to the coveted honour of knight of the shire. There was no resident peer until John Poulett* of Hinton St. George was ennobled in 1627, and throughout the period the lieutenancy was combined with Wiltshire. Both the 1st earl of Hertford, who held office until his death on 4 Apr. 1621, and his successor, William Herbert, 3rd earl of Pembroke, were Wiltshire residents, and neither seems to have been popular in Somerset. Possibly the most influential landlord in the county was the bishop of Bath and Wells, who could muster 300 freeholders 'besides the vestry'.[2]

The absence of contests between 1571 and 1614 was probably the result of preliminary meetings held among members of the gentry at which the names of two candidates to be presented to the freeholders would have been agreed. In 1604 Sir Edward Phelips of Montacute was elected for the second time in a row, but Sir Maurice Berkeley of Bruton, his colleague in 1601, was obliged to find a seat at Minehead, the least respectable of the Somerset boroughs, in order to make way for Sir Francis Hastings, an ardent puritan of high birth but inconsiderable estate. Phelips, appointed king's serjeant at the outset of the reign, was probably already identified as Speaker-designate, in which capacity he was able to draw the attention of the Commons to such local matters as the disastrous floods of March 1607. Hastings' death in September 1610 caused a by-election, his place being taken by John Poulett, who came from a similarly godly background but was very young. He claimed to revere Speaker Phelips as a father, but had scarcely time to familiarize himself with the Commons before the dissolution.[3]

By convention, a former Speaker never sat as an ordinary Member in the House over which he had presided – and Phelips, as master of the Rolls, may also have expected a summons to the Lords as a legal assistant. Therefore, when a fresh Parliament was called in February 1614, he was prepared to listen to the overtures of Sir Maurice Berkeley, who had been approached to stand for the senior seat (which he had held in 1601). Phelips politely declined Berkeley's offer to pair with him – which must have been *pro forma* – and stated that he had no intention of promoting the candidacy of his son Sir Robert, who swiftly confirmed that 'at that present I did not intend to have been of the House at all'. However, Berkeley's news that Poulett, Sir Robert Phelips's exact contemporary, intended to stand again, prompted a change of heart, as Sir Robert now accepted the offer to pair with Berkeley. This deliberate misconstruction of a courtesy placed Berkeley in an awkward position, from which he attempted to extricate himself by asking Sir Robert or his father to write to Poulett 'to entreat his furtherance' – in other words, to stand aside. However, Berkeley made it clear that Poulett, having asked first, had the prime claim to his support: 'though to be a knight of the shire be a thing I desire, and even the highest mark of my ambition, yet I would be loath to purchase it with the unnecessary loss of such a friend'. Following this exchange, Sir Robert persuaded his father that Berkeley's offer of a pairing had been more than a courtesy. Thus satisfied, Sir Edward, who warned that business would keep him in London, allowed his son to stand, provided that he notified Berkeley and Poulett in writing of his intentions.[4]

After spending some time on his Wiltshire estates, Berkeley arrived in Somerset to find Phelips' canvassing in full swing, under the direction of Thomas Hughes† and Francis James*, the chancellor of Bath and Wells diocese. Meanwhile, Poulett, returning from a visit to Devon, was approached by Sir Edward Phelips' servant John Seward, who assumed that Sir Robert had contacted him to ask him to stand down. Poulett insisted that he had received no such letter, but to avoid giving offence declared that he was happy to see Sir Robert Phelips and Berkeley paired for the county. However, he added that if Sir Edward and Sir Robert decided not to stand he would do so himself, in accordance with his former promise to Sir Maurice Berkeley. He also urged Seward to procure a letter from Sir Robert confirming the tenor of this conversation.[5]

Matters turned sour at the county court at Ilchester on 7 Mar., when Poulett and Berkeley appeared with their supporters only to find that the writ had not yet arrived, Phelips was still absent in London, and no election was to be held. Poulett, who had carefully avoided declaring himself a candidate beforehand, later indignantly declared to Sir Edward Phelips that if he 'had met Sir Robert or any letter from him' he would have 'entreated all my voices to cry out for him'. Berkeley, for one, clearly suspected that the writ had been detained in Chancery by Sir Edward Phelips' means; and he and Poulett promptly agreed to join forces against Sir Robert.[6] The angry exchange of letters which ensued finally persuaded Sir Edward

Phelips to throw his weight wholeheartedly behind his son in order to avert an electoral humiliation. Sir Edward wrote to 'the knights, justices of peace, and gentlemen of the county of Somerset' meeting at the Chard assizes, asking them to exercise their 'worthy and discreet moderation ... without dividing the country or putting it to the public question; whereby love may continue, and sedition be prevented'. This letter proved so efficacious that none of the magistrates except Robert Hopton* and John Symes* ultimately voted against Phelips' son. Sir Edward also approached the Scottish favourite, Robert Carr, earl of Somerset, but through Viscount L'Isle (Robert Sidney†) he received only advice to desist. Bishop James Montagu of Bath and Wells, however, pledged his support: detained in London by his duties as dean of the Chapel Royal, he urged his chancellor to redouble his efforts in the constituency, and undertook that if any of his tenants went the wrong way 'they shall smart for it'. Other non-resident landlords, such as Sir Mervyn Audley*, were successfully approached, though the earl of Hertford and Sir Nicholas Halswell* would only promise the 'second voice' of their tenants – in other words, they would back Phelips against Poulett, but not Berkeley.[7]

Sir Robert Phelips went down to Somerset to make careful preparations for the hustings, which were conveniently located near the family seat at Montacute. Early on the morning of the election his supporters, efficiently marshalled by Thomas Warre*, took possession of almost the whole town of Ilchester, so that the sheriff and the other candidates had to struggle through them to reach the market place. 'The cry "A Phelips! a Phelips!" was so great and violent for three-quarters of an hour at least that at the cross and all about it I heard no other voice nor sound'. Much to the credit of Sheriff Still, the candidates, and the voters, there was no disorder; but in other respects, after six weeks' campaigning, no holds were barred. The sheriff was momentarily 'staggered' by Berkeley's assertion that Phelips was ineligible because he was not resident in the county at the date of the writ; while on the other side six lawyers gave their opinion that Poulett, as a mere esquire, could not be allowed to challenge a genuine knight like Phelips. Yet the sheriff proved fully equal to the occasion – when the poll was demanded he adjourned the court from the overcrowded market place to a field on the outskirts of the little town. Phelips, at the suggestion of his father, now played his last card, proposing that the voters should be separated into three groups, one for each candidate, thereby nullifying the Berkeley-Poulett alliance and eliminating second choices. But the sheriff would

have none of it, and Phelips left the scene, accompanied by many of his supporters. Some, like Halswell, were no doubt reluctant to commit themselves further, while others were deterred by the requirement that they should be sworn to a 40s. freehold. Sir Francis Popham* and Sir John Malet remained, however, to supervise the poll on Phelips' behalf, while Symes and his brother-in-law Sir John Horner* performed the same service for the confederates. The exact figures do not survive, but Still's under-sheriff estimated that only about 1,150 voters were sworn for the victors, and it was claimed that 'Sir Robert Phelips had at the time of the election 1,500 votes more'.[8]

Upon his defeat, Phelips immediately drafted a petition to his father's immediate superior, lord chancellor Ellesmere (Thomas Egerton†), which was signed by his closest allies: Sir Francis Popham and his uncle Edward Popham*, (Sir) Thomas Thynne*, Thomas Southworth*, Francis James, Thomas Hughes and Thomas Warre. Lists of freeholders who had attended at Ilchester to vote for Phelips, to the number of 500, were obtained from their landlords. However, Ellesmere was unwilling to risk a confrontation with the Commons by quashing the election return, as this would have reopened the controversy over the Commons' right to judge of returns without reference to Chancery. On 26 Apr. the Privy Council ordered a general reconciliation, to which Phelips replying on behalf of the county bench, complained of Berkeley, 'who is reported to have affirmed to divers men in public places that those who say the election was not duly made are knaves, and such as believe it are fools'. By this time Phelips had been returned for a Cornish borough, and his behaviour in the House gave such offence (not least to his father) that no one felt any inclination to protect him.[9]

The temporary eclipse of the Phelips interest did not render the Somerset gentry more amenable: the demand for a Benevolence which followed the angry dissolution of the Parliament was opposed by Berkeley, Halswell and Poulett, who were summoned before the Privy Council on 2 Nov. 1614, when Sir Edward Coke* bludgeoned them with precedents. The seditious writings discovered on the unfortunate clergyman Peacham, who held a Poulett family living, were supposed for a time to be evidence of a conspiracy, in which Berkeley was implicated.[10] Berkeley died in 1617, scarcely 40 years of age, shortly after Sir Robert Phelips had been restored to local office. There seems to have been no difficulty in restoring cordial relations between the two families; but Poulett and Phelips remained estranged.

At the 1621 election Poulett found a borough seat at Lyme Regis, Dorset, but prevailed on the gentry to nominate his ally Robert Hopton as junior colleague to Sir Henry Portman. Phelips may be suspected as the architect of the earl of Hertford's unprecedented attempt to secure the return of his grandson and heir William Seymour*, Lord Beauchamp, as a counterpart to the election of his younger grandson, Sir Francis Seymour*, as knight for Wiltshire. Poulett and his allies Sir John Horner and John Stawell*, having conferred with Sir Francis Seymour at Wells, firmly rejected this proposal: 'we are persuaded that every gentleman that hath not fear nor faction in his heart will join with us', they wrote, and the gentry candidates carried the day. Phelips may have gained some consolation from the fact that when Portman died of smallpox a few weeks later, the by-election saw the return of Sir Maurice Berkeley's son Charles, one of his most loyal supporters. Phelips himself sat for Bath, which enabled him to speak for the county on such subjects as charitable briefs, alehouses, common lands, and Irish cattle. But his role in galvanizing the Commons over the freedom of speech debate with which the session ended in December brought him eight months imprisonment in the Tower.[11]

Before the 1624 election Phelips, having reconciled himself with Buckingham and the anti-Spanish party at Court, felt sufficiently rehabilitated to stand for the county again. Poulett's steward, Hackshaw, wrote to Sir Edward Hext*, Stawell's father-in-law:

> I hear of a secret labouring about Petherton, Martock, and the adjacent parts to Ilchester for the election of Sir Robert Phelips for one of the knights. ... I also hear the country is well inclined to join my master with him for the second, which I know my master will utterly mislike, and so much he hath signified to me by his letters. ... I have heard some speech that Sir John Sydenham hath laboured about Yeovil for voices from Mr. Stawell, who I doubt not is able to carry it if it please him to stand for the place, and he shall not want the best help Mr. Amyas Poulett and my poor endeavours can afford.

Hext immediately transmitted this letter to Phelips, commenting:

> I hope there will be no opposition to you. I once heard that it was intended to be laid upon my son[-in-law] and young Mr. [Ralph] Hopton*, but Mr. Hopton in great modesty refused it. ... My cousin [John] Malet* piddles for freeholders about Taunton, who will all go from him to my son if he will stand.

Montagu's successor, Bishop Lake, found 'such silence among the gentlemen that I cannot tell whether they purpose at all to meddle, or leave the country to do as they will'. Stawell was apparently indisposed before the election, and the Poulett interest went to John Symes instead, who protested to Phelips that he had been much importuned to stand.[12] There were about 20 signatures on the election indenture, including those of Sir George Speke, who had originally proposed Symes, Phelips' loyal henchman Charles Berkeley, and Phelips' uncle Sir Henry. Phelips' attempts to support the 'patriot' cause in the Commons were not always productive; but he was able to attack the heralds who had visited Somerset in the previous year under the authority of Buckingham's rival, Thomas Howard, 21st or 14th earl of Arundel.[13]

The 1625 election produced the most unruly scenes of the period, though it is not clear whether there was a contest. On 14 May 1625 the Privy Council issued a warrant for the arrest of Poulett's kinsman, Edmund Kenn, for his 'unadvised behaviour' at the hustings, and for 'giving out scandalous speeches' against Phelips 'to hinder his election'. Kenn was committed to the Fleet, and released only after undertaking to make a public acknowledgment of his offences in Phelips's presence. Perhaps it was as well for him that Phelips again disdained the elections committee, and had offended Buckingham over his conduct in Parliament. Stawell, also implicated, could not be charged, for he had been elected senior knight of the shire, taking precedence of Phelips, though a mere esquire. In Hilary term 1626 Phelips and Thomas Wyndham, who had presided over the election as sheriff, travelled to London 'to take advice by their learned counsel for framing the information', and attorney-general (Sir) Robert Heath* commenced a Star Chamber suit against Stawell 'for giving the lie to the plaintiffs sitting on the bench'. Stawell was ultimately convicted and fined £200, a Pyrrhic victory for the plaintiffs, whose costs totalled £243 9s.10d.[14] This suit may have deterred Stawell from standing again in 1626; while on this occasion Phelips was one of several troublesome MPs deliberately rendered ineligible by being pricked as sheriff of Somerset. In this capacity, Phelips had the satisfaction of returning his devoted supporter Sir Henry Berkeley for the senior seat. The second place was bestowed upon Sir John Horner, who was presumably a Poulett candidate, though among those who signed the return only Hopton can be identified with this faction.[15]

At Court Poulett was now in the ascendant: he was raised to the peerage in the following year, while Phelips, again stripped of local office, ignominiously sneaked out of the county to avoid committing himself for or against the Forced Loan. By contrast,

Poulett and his allies did not equivocate, denouncing the seekers after 'popularity' who obstructed the king's wishes.[16] By 1628 Phelips had recovered his confidence, writing from London about his concerns

for the prevention of any tumultuous combustion which might happen in our country by reason of the election of knights for this Parliament. It is true I have declared myself to stand for one of those places in case the gentlemen of the county should think me fit for it, and [provided] that I might obtain it with peace and without noise; and for that purpose (not knowing of any other that did stand) I offered myself to Sir Hugh Portman*, from whom as yet I have received no direct answer. And now from the country I am advertised that there is a party made to oppose me.

On his return to Somerset he wrote to a more committed supporter:

The people we have to deal with are a subtle generation; and all the east and northerly parts are laboured for double voices, and all about me for one, so to weaken me that if [Sir John] Stawell or Sir Ralph Hopton shall appear upon the place they will hazard me. And being thus spitefully bent as they are, to whisper it in your ear, if I find our party strong enough to carry both, we will (if you like it) exclude a deputy lieutenant, and choose an honest, faithful countryman and your servant, Sir Henry Berkeley. But this reserve to yourself, and come as strong as you may for my purpose; and for voices that will give but one, give them leave to save their journey. Only if another move them therein, that then they will be also for me.

Stawell's agents had been so active, not to say abusive, in soliciting 'double voices' among the Taunton freeholders that it was clearly his intention to join with another of the deputy lieutenants whom Phelips had consistently obstructed. But it was not until three days before the election that the other candidate was identified as Sir John Rodney, who offered Hopton his seat at Wells in return. Rodney was apparently too strong for Berkeley, for whom Phelips found a seat in his pocket borough of Ilchester. Stawell, on the other hand, was no match for Phelips, and it is not surprising that he seized the opportunity of revenge by billeting soldiers on the wealthier inhabitants of Taunton, who had rejected him. The matter was raised in the Commons, provoking angry exchanges between Phelips and Rodney; but Stawell, having done no more than follow the orders of the Privy Council, was discharged without penalty.[17]

[1] *Agrarian Hist. Eng. and Wales* ed. J. Thirsk, iv. 72-80; T.G. Barnes, *Somerset 1625-40*, pp. 2-6, 11, 13, 22; D. Underdown, *Revel, Riot and Rebellion*, 7-8, 113, 122-3. [2] *Som. and Dorset N and Q*, xxxi.

351; E. Farnham, 'Somerset Election of 1614', *EHR*, xlvi. 590, 597; SP16/40/58. [3] Som. RO, DD/PH224/8; *CJ*, i. 346a; M. Kishlansky, *Parlty. Selection*, 91. [4] Kishlansky, 85-7; Som. RO, DD/PH216/84, 87-8. [5] Kishlansky, 88-9; Som. RO, DD/PH216/82-4, 87-9. [6] Kishlansky, 89-90; Som. RO, DD/PH216/86, 89. [7] Kishlansky, 90-8; Som. RO, DD/PH216/81, 83-4, 86-9; *Chamberlain Letters* ed. N.E. McClure, i. 518, 524. [8] Kishlansky, 98-100; Som. RO, DD/PH216/95, 115; DD/PH224/8-9; Farnham, 595. [9] Kishlansky, 99-101; Som. RO, DD/PH216/116; DD/PH228/19. [10] *APC*, 1613-14, p. 611; S.R. Gardiner, *Hist. Eng. from Accession of Jas. I*. ii. 266, 274. [11] HLRO, HC/LB/1/19; *CD 1621*, ii. 109; iii. 186, 214; v. 95; SIR ROBERT PHELIPS. [12] T. Cogswell, *Blessed Revolution*, 157-8; Som. RO, DD/PH219/32; DD/PH224/12; DD/PH227/16. [13] C219/38/205; *CJ*, i. 701b. [14] *APC*, 1625-6, pp. 53, 75, 104; Som. RO, DD/PH198, DD/PH216/12; *Historical Collections* ed. J. Rushworth, iii. (app.), 26-7. [15] C219/40/129. [16] *CSP Dom*. 1629-31, p. 120; R. Cust, *Forced Loan*, 107-8, 210. [17] Som. RO, DD/PH216/108, DD/PH221/2-3; *CD 1628*, iii. 419-20.

J.P.F./S.H.

BATH

Right of election: in the corporation

Number of voters: 31[1]

26 Feb. 1604	WILLIAM SHERSTON, alderman	
	CHRISTOPHER STONE, town clerk[2]	
28 Mar. 1614[3]	SIR JAMES LEY	
	NICHOLAS HYDE, recorder	
5 Jan. 1621	SIR ROBERT PHELIPS	
	ROBERT PYE[4]	
30 Jan. 1624	(SIR) ROBERT PYE	
	JOHN MALET	
1625	NICHOLAS HYDE, recorder	
	EDWARD HUNGERFORD	
c. June/July 1625	RALPH HOPTON *vice*	
	Hyde, chose to sit for Bristol	
20 Jan. 1626	RICHARD GAY, alderman	
	WILLIAM CHAPMAN, ?alderman	
3 Mar. 1628	JOHN POPHAM	
	WALTER LONG II	

Situated on the Avon 12 miles south-east of Bristol, and described by a local doctor in 1628 as 'a well compacted city, ... beautified with very fair and goodly buildings for the receipt of strangers', Bath was already famous for the healing powers of its waters, which were visited by Anne of Denmark in 1613 and 1615, and by Charles I in 1628.[5] Under the terms of a charter granted in 1590, a mayor, between four and ten aldermen and a council of 20 governed Bath.[6] Little can be said about the town's activities for, other than the chamberlains' accounts, few municipal records survive for this period. The parliamentary franchise was vested in the corporation, although this only becomes clear from post-Restoration evidence noted by William Prynne[†], when various inhabitants who witnessed Jacobean parliamentary elections testified to this effect.[7] The indentures made in the name of the (unnamed) mayor, aldermen and citizens were not signed.[8] Throughout the period Bath paid 2s. per day in parliamentary wages, although it appears that payments were made to townsmen only, and not to gentry Members. Some of the latter were made free: in the case of Sir James Ley, the taking of the oath of a freeman occurred at the election, but Sir Robert Phelips' enfranchisement seems to have been delayed until the year after his return.[9]

In the sixteenth century the majority of Bath's Members were local townsmen and/or borough officials. This pattern was repeated in 1604, when Alderman William Sherston, then approaching his sixth Parliament, was joined by the town clerk, Christopher Stone. Ten years later the town elected its recorder, Nicholas Hyde, and Sir James Ley, a prominent lawyer and future lord treasurer. Ley had no apparent connection with Bath and the town's reason for electing him in preference to a local man is unknown. During the 1620s a strong puritan faction dominated Bath, and the neighbouring godly gentry families of Popham, Horner, Harrington, and Hungerford generally influenced elections.[10] In 1621 Sir Robert Phelips, a leading member of the Somerset gentry, took the first seat while Robert Pye, an Exchequer official and client of George Villiers, marquess of Buckingham, sat as the junior Member. Pye occupied the senior position in 1624, and was joined by John Malet, whose mother was a Popham. Ahead of the first Caroline Parliament, Bath re-elected its recorder, Hyde, but the latter chose to sit for Bristol, whereupon Ralph Hopton took his place. It is not known why Hopton was elected, nor is it clear when he was chosen. Serving overseas with Mansfeld's expedition, he only returned to England on 20 July 1625, eight days after the Westminster sitting of Parliament had ended.[11] The puritan Edward Hungerford, who owned a house and messuage in the town, took the junior place.[12] In 1626 Bath reverted to electing townsmen, choosing Richard Gay for the first and William Chapman for the second seat. However, in a reversal of policy, the corporation elected two members of the local puritan gentry in 1628, John Popham and Walter Long II. Poham lived on his father's estate in Hunstrete, five miles west of Bath, while Long resided

nine miles west of Bath.[13] The town does not appear to have introduced any legislation during the period but the corporation complained to the Commons in 1621 that Giles Mompesson's abuses of his patent for licensing inns had led to a three-fold increase of inns in Bath, many of which were unsuitable to be licensed.[14]

[1] A.J King and B.H. Watts, *Municipal Recs. of Bath*, 43; W. Prynne, *Brevia Parliamentaria Rediviva* (1662), 317-19.   [2] Prynne, 310.   [3] Bath RO, Transcript of Council Mins. i. p. 6. Hyde was named first in the corp. records.   [4] Prynne, 311, where Phelips' knighthood is omitted.   [5] T. Vennner, *Baths of Bathe* (1628), 1; Bath RO, 'Elevation of the status of the mayor of Bath'.   [6] J. Collinson, *Hist. and Antiqs. of Co. of Som.* (1791), i. pt. 2, pp. 22-3.   [7] Prynne, 317-19.   [8] Ibid. 310-13; C219/38/207; 219/41A/61.   [9] Bath RO, chamberlains' accts. transcripts, nos. 45, 64; council mins. i. 6.   [10] D. Underdown, *Som. in Civil War and Interregnum*, 143; J. Wroughton, 'Puritanism and Traditionalism: Cultural and Political Divisions in Bath', *Bath Hist.* iv. 53.   [11] *CSP Dom.* 1625-6, p. 71.   [12] J.F. Meecham, *Famous Houses of Bath*, 5.   [13] C2/Chas.I/P63/62.   [14] Nicholas, *Procs. 1621*, i. 66, 71.

C.R.K.

BRIDGWATER

Right of election: in the burgesses

Number of voters: 13 in 1605

27 Feb. 1604	SIR NICHOLAS HALSWELL ROBERT BUCKING
5 Nov. 1605	JOHN PORY *vice* Bucking, deceased
c. Mar. 1614	THOMAS WARRE, recorder ROBERT HALSWELL
c. Dec. 1620	EDWARD POPHAM ROGER WARRE, recorder
27 Jan. 1624	EDWARD POPHAM ROGER WARRE, recorder
6 May 1625	SIR ARTHUR LAKE EDWARD POPHAM
19 Jan. 1626	SIR ARTHUR LAKE EDWARD POPHAM
5 Mar. 1628	SIR THOMAS WROTHE THOMAS SMYTH

Located five miles inland on the River Parrett, Bridgwater owed its early prosperity to the manufacture and export of cloth, principally lightweight broad cloths known as Bridgwaters, but also coarser, narrow cloths, or kerseys, which were exported to France, Spain and Ireland. While its volume of trade was much smaller than that of Bristol, Gloucestershire, or the major Devon towns, Bridgwater was reportedly Somerset's busiest port in the third quarter of the sixteenth century, and recovered strongly in the early 1600s after the disruption of the Elizabethan war years.[1] However, by now cloth exports were dwindling, and the local economy was much more reliant on other commodities, notably beans and coal. Indeed, in 1622 the corporation claimed that 'no merchant vessels are now employed in the town except to carry coal'.[2] Trade was inevitably disrupted by the wars of the later 1620s, and when the Commons in June 1628 compiled a list of shipping lost at sea, Bridgwater was among a group of 20 towns noted as having suffered 'great loss, whereof there is as yet no particular'.[3]

Early seventeenth-century Bridgwater was governed by a charter of 1587, which provided for a corporation consisting of a mayor, two aldermen, and 18 principal burgesses. A further charter was granted in March 1628, which extended the corporation's jurisdiction to cover the whole parish of Bridgwater, and increased the number of principal burgesses to 24.[4] The borough first sent representatives to Parliament since 1295. Early Stuart election indentures were made out in the name of the mayor, aldermen and burgesses, with 13 individual voters identified in 1605. Although it has been argued that the franchise was exercised solely by the corporation during this period, subsequent lawsuits on this issue suggest that a much larger number of the inhabitants were actually entitled to vote, even if in practice the corporation controlled the choice of candidates.[5]

For much of Elizabeth's reign Bridgwater routinely returned its recorder, usually a local gentleman, along with a prominent townsman, both Members receiving parliamentary wages.[6] However, in the early Stuart period the neighbouring gentry tightened their grip over the borough. Sir Nicholas Halswell of Goathurst, three miles from Bridgwater, took the senior seat in 1604, while his son Robert was elected ten years later.[7] Sir Nicholas was partnered initially by Robert Bucking, the only townsman to serve during this period, who had also sat in 1593. He received wages of £16 for the first session, but died before the Parliament resumed in 1605.[8] Bucking was replaced by a complete outsider, John Pory, who probably owed his nomination to the Pophams of Huntsworth, another gentry family resident just outside the town; the Pophams had frequently held the recordership in the late Tudor

period. Robert Halswell was accompanied in 1614 by the then recorder, Thomas Warre.[9]

During the 1620s the Halswells gradually lost their local standing due to financial difficulties, and Edward Popham was able to secure a Bridgwater seat for himself in every Parliament between 1621 and 1626. On the first two occasions Popham was joined by Roger Warre, who had become recorder after the death of his brother Thomas.[10] The first seat in 1625 and 1626 went to another outsider, Sir Arthur Lake, who was probably recommended either by his uncle, the bishop of Bath and Wells, or by his brother-in-law, Sir Edward Rodney*, an important Somerset gentleman.[11] By 1628 Popham had himself succumbed to financial troubles, and consequently his role as the borough's principal gentry patron passed to Sir Thomas Wrothe of Petherton Park, five miles from Bridgwater, who became recorder under the new charter of March 1628.[12] Wrothe took the senior seat in 1628, while the junior place went to the 18-year-old Thomas Smyth on the nomination of the latter's father-in-law, John (Lord) Poulett*, one of the county's most powerful figures. It appears that the borough had been approached by other local gentlemen, possibly political rivals of Poulett, for on the day of the election the corporation wrote to the peer:

> May it please your lordship that this morning we have elected Mr. Thomas Smythe ... to be one of our burgesses for this next Parliament, and we shall entreat your lordship's favour to further him and the town on those occasions that shall be needful. And we have some doubt that some may be offended at that which is done. If therefore it would please your lordship to afford us a word or two to Sir John Stawell*, that he may be pleased (if occasions require) to stead the town the best he may, we shall account ourselves bound unto your lordship.

Stawell, another leading Somerset gentleman, was Poulett's close ally, and currently engaged in billeting soldiers around the county.[13]

The surviving records indicate that relations between the borough and its Members were generally cordial. Both Sir Nicholas Halswell and Roger Warre are known to have received regular gifts during their periods of service, typically wine or sugar loaves.[14] Similarly, Thomas Smyth wrote to the corporation in September 1628, offering to provide a buck if the corporation held a dinner for its two Members. In response, the mayor suggested a gathering at Michaelmas, at which the borough might thank them both for their 'worthy pains taken for this corporation in the late session of Parliament'.[15]

Little evidence has emerged about the specific tasks performed by Bridgwater's Members, none of whom spoke directly on their constituency's behalf in the Commons. However, in 1606 Sir Nicholas Halswell probably supplied the borough with its copy of the 1604 Act clarifing the power of local magistrates to set labourers' wages, while in 1621 Roger Warre may have arranged for the town to obtain the Proclamation for the arrest of the fugitive monopolist, Sir Giles Mompesson*.[16] One entry in the borough's accounts, dated 13 Nov. 1621, indicates that the corporation sought to introduce legislation that year. Warre was paid 16s. for 'drawing the books for a bill to be exhibited in the Parliament for the long casey'. Assuming that 'casey' was a mis-spelling of carsey or kersey, the borough was probably responding to a bill on cloth manufacture introduced in the first sitting of 1621. This measure, which would have restricted the types of wool that could be employed in the making of longer cloths, threatened the future of Bridgwater's kersey industry, which routinely used inferior oddments known as 'noiles'. If this reading is correct, Bridgwater was clearly seeking to defend its economic interests in Parliament. In the event, though, the measure on cloth manufacture failed to make further progress in the Commons, and the intended Bridgwater bill was never introduced, presumably because there was now no need for it.[17]

[1] VCH Som. vi. 218-19; E. Kerridge, Textile Manufactures in Early Modern Eng. 5, 18. [2] E190/1084/12, 21; 190/1085/4; 190/1086/4, 14; A. Friis, Alderman Cockayne's Project and the Cloth Trade, 454-5; VCH Som. vi. 219; CSP Dom. 1619-23, pp. 388, 578-9. [3] HMC Var. viii. 199. [4] Som. RO, D/B/bw 2409, ff. 34-9; CSP Dom. 1628-9, p. 41. [5] C219/35/2/10; D. Hirst, Representative of the People?, 213; Som. RO, DD/X/ME5. [6] HP Commons, 1558-1603, i. 235. [7] Vis. Som. (Harl. Soc. xi), 45. [8] Som. RO, D/B/bw 1589. [9] A. Brown, Genesis of US, ii. 969; Vis. Som. 87-8; HP Commons, 1558-1603, i. 235. [10] CSP Dom. 1628-9, p. 361; Sales of Wards 1603-41 ed. M.J. Hawkins (Som. Rec. Soc. lxvii), p. xix. [11] Oxford DNB (Arthur Lake); The Gen. n.s. xvii. 101-2. [12] E115/426/23; Som. RO, D/B/bw 2409, f. 38. [13] Procs. 1628, vi. 125. [14] Som. RO, D/B/bw 1589, 1592, 1598, 1609. [15] Procs. 1628, vi. 215-16. [16] Som. RO, D/B/bw 1591, 1609; SR, iv. 1022-4. [17] Som. RO, D/B/bw 1609; SR, iv. 1137-9; CD 1621, vii. 123-8; Kerridge, 26-7.

G.Y.

ILCHESTER

Right of election: in the ratepayers

Number of voters: 140 in 1688

10 Apr. 1621	SIR RICHARD WYNN
	ARTHUR JARVIS
26 Jan. 1624	(SIR) RICHARD WYNN
	NATHANIEL TOMKINS
c. Feb. 1624	EDMUND WALLER vice Tomkins, chose to sit for Christchurch
27 Apr. 1625	(SIR) RICHARD WYNN
	SIR ROBERT GORGES
2 Feb. 1626	EDWARD KIRTON
	JOHN SELDEN
c. Mar. 1626	(SIR) WILLIAM BEECHER vice Kirton, chose to sit for Marlborough
	ROBERT CAESAR vice Seldon, chose to sit for Great Bedwyn
4 Mar. 1628	SIR HENRY BERKELEY
	SIR ROBERT GORGES

Ilchester was the county town of Somerset, having not only the county gaol but also hosting regular meetings of the shire and circuit courts.[1] However, it failed to develop an economic base to match its administrative importance: under Henry VIII, John Leland observed that the town 'hath been a very large thing', but 'at this time it is in wonderful decay, as a thing in a manner razed with men of war'.[2] The borough's charter of incorporation, granted in 1556, was intended to restore ancient rights, the lapsing of which had brought the borough 'near to ruin'; to raise funds for the county gaol; and perhaps to pre-empt a proposal to make Glastonbury the county town.[3] Few signs of revival were detectable under the early Stuarts, when it was still a 'decayed town'.[4] It retained the county gaol and remained the venue for the spring quarter sessions and the shire court, in which the county elections were held.[5] Yet brewing was said to be the town's only notable economic activity, serving those who attended the prison and the courts;[6] visiting magistrates complained of the town's lack of facilities.[7] As the local proverb went, 'all Ilchester is gaol, say prisoners there'.[8]

Ilchester had returned Members to Parliament from 1298 to 1361, but thenceforth its representation lapsed, doubtless as a consequence of the town's decline.[9] The 1556 charter established an oligarchic government by a bailiff and 12 capital burgesses, but made no reference to parliamentary representation.[10] The town owed its revival as a parliamentary borough to the influence and ambitions of Sir Robert Phelips*, of nearby Montacute, who served as Ilchester's high steward from 1615. Having been defeated by John Powlett in a bruising contest for the county election

1614, he apparently thought that a pocket borough at Ilchester would be an effective safety net, as well as a valuable addition to his patronage.[11] However, his petition for Ilchester's re-enfranchisement, submitted to the Commons on 26 Mar. 1621, struggled to present a logical case.[12] It stated that Ilchester had returned Members in the distant past, but 'being grown poor', the town had 'forborne to send burgesses'. It interpreted the 1556 charter as evidence that the town had 'grown into a better estate'; but insisted that it was not until 'a few years past, searching among the records of the Tower' that it was realized that these privileges included parliamentary representation.[13] This unlikely story was accepted by the House, as one historian has remarked, with 'remarkably little discussion'; the only recorded objection came from Sir Humphrey May, chancellor of the duchy of Lancaster.[14] The acceptance of this petition, and another submitted at the same time for the re-enfranchisement of Pontefract, Yorkshire, constituted a significant precedent for the expansion of the Commons' membership by reviving the obsolescent franchises of medieval boroughs.[15] The nature of the renewed franchise was not recorded, but in 1688 it was described by the king's electoral agents as 'popular'.[16] This may have suited Phelips personally, since he seems to have been at odds with the ruling oligarchy: by the end of the decade he was 'championing' the cause of the 'inferior burgesses', in direct confrontation with some of Ilchester's leading businessmen.[17]

Although Ilchester's corporation may have wished to challenge Phelips's electoral influence, there is no evidence that they did so – the early years of Ilchester's representation are a chronicle of Phelips's electoral patronage. The choice of candidates in 1621 was relatively small, as most of those who wanted seats had already found them at the general election. Sir Richard Wynn, a Welsh courtier who had suffered a humiliating defeat in the Caernarvonshire election, had already been disappointed in his approach to Sir Thomas Wentworth*, for a seat at Pontefract. He may have been more fortunate at Ilchester because of a recommendation from Nathaniel Tomkins, Phelips's Court correspondent, who was, like Wynn, a member of Prince Charles's Household. The other Member, Arthur Jarvis, was an Exchequer official who had information about the activities of Henry Spiller*, clerk of recusancy fines, who some in Phelips's circle hoped to investigate during the session.[18] Following its enfranchisement, Ilchester was mentioned once more in debate in 1621: when the bill for the paving of Colchester was debated on 5 May, it was cited as an example of a town which had previously benefited by

such a measure; yet this seems to have been a garbled reference to another town.[19]

As part of the preparations for the 1624 Parliament, Prince Charles and the duke of Buckingham sought the support of Phelips, among others, in pursuing an anti-Spanish foreign policy. It was thus particularly appropriate that Wynn, a committed hispanophobe, should have been returned for Ilchester once again. Phelips offered the other seat to Tomkins, but when the latter opted to sit for Christchurch, Dorset, the place went to Tomkin's brother-in-law Edmund Waller.

Wynn had hopes of securing a seat in Wales in 1625, but in the event he was returned for Ilchester once more. While attending the Oxford sitting he shared a house with Tomkins. Phelips bestowed the other seat upon his brother-in-law Sir Robert Gorges of Redlynch, Somerset. During the brief session Phelips obstructed Buckingham's efforts to secure a large grant of supply to fund war with Spain, and in November 1625 he was pricked as sheriff of Somerset in order to prevent him from sitting in the next Parliament. On this occasion, the return of Edward Kirton of Castle Cary, Somerset, and the prominent lawyer John Selden, both of whom went on to play a significant part in Buckingham's impeachment, looks very much like a gesture of defiance – though in the event, both men opted to sit for constituencies controlled by their chief patron, William Seymour*, 2nd earl of Hertford.[20] Phelips's endorsement of two known troublemakers for the Ilchester seats may have earned him a rebuke from the favourite, as Kirton was replaced by the Privy Council clerk William Beecher, one of Buckingham's few defenders during the session. Selden's replacement, however, was the Chancery clerk Robert Caesar, who had been employed by the Commons in 1625 to check the enrolments of the oaths of the treasurers of the 1624 subsidies, with a view to establishing whether funds had been misused.[21]

1628 saw the election of two of Phelips's closest local allies. The first was Sir Henry Berkeley of Yarlington, Somerset, an 'old friend and most constant supporter',[22] who had replaced Phelips as knight of the shire in 1626, and with whom Phelips had initially hoped to pair for the county seats. The second seat went to Sir Robert Gorges, who had been returned for Taunton in 1626, who seems to have shared Phelips's political sympathies: both men had been expelled from the Somerset commission of the peace in the government purge following the dissolution of the 1626 Parliament.[23]

[1] *VCH Som.* iii. 185. [2] Ibid. 185-7; J. Leland, *Itinerary* ed. L. Toulmin-Smith, i. 156. [3] *VCH Som.* iii. 192. [4] T. Barnes, *Somerset 1625-40*, p. 9. [5] *VCH Som.* iii. 185. [6] Ibid. 189. [7] Barnes, 69. [8] J. Stevens Cox, *Ilchester Monographs*, 92. [9] *VCH Som.* iii. 188, 194. [10] Merewether and Stephens, *Hist. Boroughs*, iii. 1591. [11] E. de Villiers, 'Parlty. Boroughs Restored by the House of Commons', *EHR*, lxvii. 188. [12] *CJ*, i. 572b. [13] Nicholas *Procs. 1621*, i. 221. [14] Villiers, 177; *CJ*, i. 572b, 576a. [15] Villiers, 176. [16] G. Duckett, *Penal Laws*, ii. 230. [17] *VCH Som.* iii. 192-3; Barnes, 216. [18] *Strafforde Letters* (1739) ed. W. Knowler, i. 14; CAERNARVONSHIRE; ARTHUR JARVIS. [19] Nicholas, *Procs. 1621*, ii. 25. Such Acts had previously been passed to benefit Ipswich (13 Eliz. I, c. 24) and Chichester (18 Eliz. I, c. 19). [20] *CJ*, i. 821b; J.K. Gruenfelder, *Influence in Early Stuart Elections*, 181 n. 75. [21] R. Cust, *Forced Loan*, 192-3; W. Prest, *Rise of the Barristers*, 239. [22] Barnes, 217. [23] *CJ*, i. 891a.

G.Y.

MILBORNE PORT

Right of election: ?in the inhabitants paying scot and lot

Number of voters: at least 20 in 1628

26 May 1628	PHILIP DIGBY
	SIR NATHANIEL NAPPER

Situated in south-eastern Somerset, Milborne Port was recorded as a substantial borough in the Domesday book, and returned Members to the Commons five times under Edward I. It declined thereafter as nearby Sherborne, Dorset, grew. By the time Leland visited Milborne in the 1530s, its market was defunct, although it 'retaineth privileges of a franchised borough'. A century later a local man observed that 'there remains nothing but a straggling town', the population of which was probably around 400-500 in the seventeenth century.[1] Milborne was governed by a corporation of two stewards and seven assistants, which had evolved from the medieval merchant guild.[2] By 1702 the parliamentary franchise was vested in the town's ratepayers, but in 1628 the return was signed by only 20 men, among whom were the deputy bailiffs and the town's constables.[3]

Milborne probably owed its enfranchisement in 1628 to its neighbour, the 1st earl of Bristol (Sir John Digby*), who was anxious to secure the passage of legislation to confirm his grant of the manor of Sherborne under letters patent of 1616. This bill was necessary because Carew Ralegh*, whose brother Sir Walter†, had forfeited the estate for his part in the Main Plot of 1603, had a tenuous legal claim to the property. In 1621 Ralegh's draft restitution bill had included a proviso safeguarding Bristol's title, but similar legislation in 1624 and 1626 had attempted to exploit the earl's fall from favour by omitting this guarantee.[4] Ralegh reintroduced his restitution bill in the Lords on 1 May 1628, but Bristol managed to replace it with a draft which preserved his own interests on 5 May. Furthermore, on 20 May, the earl tabled another bill confirming his letters patent, which was swiftly passed and sent to the Commons two days later.[5]

Bristol, who himself attended the Lords to promote his bill,[6] already had a substantial party of supporters in the Commons, including his stepson Sir Lewis Dyve, Sir John Strangways (Dyve's father-in-law), Sir Robert Phelips, who had served with him during the time he was ambassador in Madrid, and Edward Kirton, who had helped to defend him against the attacks of the duke of Buckingham in 1624 and 1626. However, Bristol was keen to increase his following to secure the passage of his private legislation, and therefore must have prompted one of his allies, all four of whom were members of the committee for privileges, to propose the re-enfranchisement of Milborne Port. The borough's case, which strongly resembled that of Ilchester (enfranchised at Phelips's behest in 1621), was upheld in committee on 29 Apr., and confirmed by the Commons on 1 May.[7] The fact that Bristol did not present the Sherborne bill to the Lords for two weeks after his draft of the Ralegh restitution bill was committed on 5 May suggests that he initially intended to wait until the Members for Milborne had taken their seats before sending both bills to the Commons.

On 26 May the borough returned Bristol's brother Philip Digby, together with a local man, Sir Nathaniel Napper, who owned property in the town.[8] However, the return arrived too late to allow Digby to take part in the passage of the Sherborne bill, which received two readings in the Commons on 23 May and was assigned to a committee which included Phelips, Dyve and Kirton. The bill was reported by Hakewill on 31 May, who informed the House that three unnamed knights, 'Members of this House' (conceivably Phelips, Dyve and Strangways) had signified that the bishop of Salisbury, who had exchanged Sherborne with the Crown in 1592, approved of the measure. Ralegh's restitution and the Sherborne bill. Both received the Royal Assent at the end of the session without any known intervention on the part of the Milborne MPs.[9]

[1] S.G. McKay, *Milborne Port in Som.* 1-6, 31-2, 113-14; J. Leland, *Itinerary* ed. L.T. Smith, v. 109-10; T. Gerard, *Particular Description of Som.* ed. E.H. Bates (Som. Rec. Soc. xv), 153 [2] J. Collinson, *Hist. and Antiqs. of co. Som.* (1791), ii. 352-5; McKay, 22-5. [3] McKay, 117-18; C219/41A/68. [4] For the complex provenance of Sherborne, see Kyle thesis, 442-8. [5] *Lords Procs. 1628*, v. 367-8, 376, 473-4. [6] C66/2093/2; 66/2115/2; *Procs. 1628*, vi. 210. [7] *CD 1628*, ii. 28-9; iii. 154, 185; *Procs. 1628*, vi. 107-9. [8] C219/41A/68; E179/172/403. [9] *CD 1628*, iv. 36, 503-5; *Lords Procs. 1628*, v. 706.

S.H.

MINEHEAD

Right of election: in the inhabitant householders

Number of voters: at least 19 in 1628

10 Mar. 1604	SIR AMBROSE TURVILE
	SIR MAURICE BERKELEY
1614	No returns made
c.Dec. 1620	(SIR) ROBERT LLOYD
	FRANCIS PEIRCE
	Lloyd expelled 21 Mar. 1621
	but not replaced
16 Jan. 1624	SIR ARTHUR LAKE
	ARTHUR DUCK
c.May 1625	THOMAS LUTTRELL
	EDMUND WYNDHAM
30 Jan. 1626	SIR JOHN GILL
	THOMAS HORNER
1 Mar. 1628[1]	THOMAS HORNER
	EDMUND WYNDHAM

Minehead probably derived its name either from a Celtic phrase meaning 'the haven under the hill' or from the Anglo-Saxon for 'main head', which alluded to its location on one of Somerset's most prominent coastal headlands. Following the Norman Conquest, the settlement enjoyed manorial status, and became part of the honour of Dunster. Although well placed for trade with Wales and Ireland, Minehead played only a limited role as an outport.[2] Its principal exports were beans and cloth, especially the local cottons manufactured in Dunster, though the total volume of this trade was very small.[3] In the early seventeenth century, fishing formed a major element in the town's economy, and accordingly its overseas trade centred on importing salt from the Bay of Biscay. Following a slump during the Elizabethan war with Spain, trade picked up in the early Jacobean period, only to decline again from the mid-1610s. A subsequent recovery in the early 1620s was associated with an increase in Irish wool imports, whereupon the town became a centre for the distribution of wool. This in turn encouraged local cloth manufacture, which led to 'Minehead dozens' being regularly exported to the Bay of Biscay for the first time.[4]

Before the mid-sixteenth century Minehead's trading position was never substantial enough for the town to establish itself as an independent political unit, and it therefore remained in the shadow of the Luttrell family, who had been lords of the manor of Minehead since the end of the fourteenth century. Based at Dunster Castle, three miles south of the town, the Luttrells were the dominant landowners in north-west Somerset. However, the town resented their domination, and in 1559 its inhabitants obtained a charter of incorporation, which created a new municipal government comprising a portreeve, 12 principal burgesses and a steward.[5] This charter was granted on the condition that the new town government kept its harbour in good repair. The Luttrells were displeased at this blatant assertion of municipal independence and in 1601, probably at the instigation of George Luttrell, a royal commission was established to inquire into the maintenance of the harbour, which was by now decayed.[6] Although Minehead asserted that its recent trade slump had greatly reduced the funds available for essential repairs, Luttrell successfully argued that as the corporation lacked other sources of income with which to offset this loss of mercantile revenues, it was incapable of carrying out its duties, and that the charter was therefore void. The inquiry upheld Luttrell's claims, and in the summer of 1604 the charter was revoked and the town council dissolved.[7]

George Luttrell now embarked on the building of a new harbour at his own cost.[8] However, he soon found the work to be prohibitively expensive, and in October 1609 he invited 40 of his neighbours to dinner with the aim of asking for financial contributions. Not surprisingly, only five of the invited guests promised to attend, and as a result little money was raised.[9] In the following year Luttrell turned to Parliament for a solution. At his instigation, a bill 'for repairing and maintaining the harbour at Minehead' was introduced into the Commons and given a first reading on 21 February.[10] This explained that a new harbour was needed as the old one had become 'choked up with gravel and stones', and that to meet the expense statutory authority was required to lay a series of duties on shipping.[11] Although the bill encountered opposition from some Welsh Members (presumably because of the duties intended to be levied on commodities from Wales),[12] it passed through its final stages in the Commons on 28 Mar. and received a first reading in the Lords on 2 April.[13] However, thereafter no more was heard of the measure. Nothing daunted, Luttrell subsequently established the new quayside duties by other means. By 1622 he was asserting a right to levy them by virtue of his ownership of the land on which the new harbour was being built. Anyone who refused to pay was to be dealt with 'by way of distress as damage feasant for the passing upon my soil there'. The new harbour evidently proved highly successful, as it was at about this time that Minehead's trade revived.[14]

Although not explicitly enfranchised by the charter of 1559, Minehead first sent Members to Parliament at the next available opportunity, in 1563. The revocation of the charter in the summer of 1604 occurred too late to effect the election held that same year, and therefore two Members were returned in the manner which had become usual since 1563, that is to say in the name of 'the portreeve and burgesses with the consent of the commons'.[15] In 1614 the town ostensibly made no returns, which suggested that the borough believed that the franchise had been forfeited along with the charter. However, the townspeople thought otherwise and later claimed that an election did take place in 1614, but that Luttrell had prevented the return by intercepting the indentures. As Parliament had been dissolved soon thereafter, the town had not had time to seek redress.[16]

In December 1620 Minehead again elected two Members, somehow outmanoeuvring Luttrell, who promptly tried to get the return declared void. On 20 Feb. 1621 he presented a petition to the Commons arguing that the election should be quashed as the franchise had depended on the charter, which was now forfeit.[17] When the matter was debated again the following day, Minehead's representatives riposted that Luttrell's argument was flawed as the charter did not mention the franchise.[18] They were probably encouraged by the opinion of Sir Edward Coke that a franchise need not depend on a charter or patent but might be based on prescriptive right or custom.[19] However, the Commons stated that it would only be satisfied that such a right existed if it could be demonstrated that the town had enjoyed the franchise before 1563. The town was therefore given time to search the records.[20] It was subsequently discovered that the Commons had queried Minehead's return in 1563, when the town had been listed among several boroughs which had 'not lately returned in Chancery'. The searcher who made this finding noted, however, that satisfaction must have been given, as the town's burgesses continued to sit and were not questioned in the succeeding assembly.[21] This was scarcely a convincing argument, and when Sir George More reported the case from the privileges committee on 3 Mar. he gave a stern warning that unless the town could produce concrete precedents the election of its Members would be declared void. Furthermore, he noted that though the town had requested more time to continue its search, the committee doubted whether there was any point in this.[22] The situation was saved by Sir Robert Lloyd, one of the town's Members and its leading spokesman in the matter, who appealed to the House for 'liberty till Tuesday next, and then to be heard by his counsel'. The House agreed to this postponement, but stressed that this would be the last chance for Minehead to prove its case.[23]

The town was never able to find evidence that it had returned Members to Parliament before 1563. However, it was determined not to give up the fight without a struggle, and it therefore fell back on the argument that the records of parliamentary returns were simply not adequate to determine the issue either way. Lloyd pointed out that 'from Ed. IV till 33 Henry VIII no records of this kept; and from 33 Henry VIII ill kept'. He concluded that it was only in 1563 itself that the keeping of records became reliable.[24] This did not seem to add up to a very powerful case, but when Sir George More came to make his final report on 16 Mar. he found in favour of the town. Three things seem to have swayed him and the rest of the committee in reaching their conclusion. First, they acknowledged that Minehead's franchise did not rest upon the charter, which had been merely concerned to erect a municipal government 'for the maintenance of the harbour only'. Secondly, they accepted the argument that poor record keeping could indeed make it impossible to demonstrate that Minehead had enjoyed a prescriptive right to the franchise before 1563. Thirdly, and perhaps most importantly, they had come to realize that if the Members for Minehead were unseated so too would the representatives of 30 other ancient boroughs then sitting in the House, as there were no records extant to prove that these boroughs had anciently sent burgesses to Parliament either.[25] However, the committee's recommendation was not quite the end of the matter. On 7 May, after Lloyd had been expelled as a monopolist and a motion had been made to send out a writ for a by-election,[26] Luttrell renewed his petition against the franchise. This provoked a response from some of the most influential figures in the House, such as John Glanville, who reiterated the reasons which had earlier led the Commons to find in favour of the town. Sir George More, too, spoke of the town having been hampered in the presentation of its case because 'their records have been embezzled'. Four days later, William Noye and Sir Edwin Sandys persuaded the House not to hear Luttrell's counsel.[27] Luttrell's sole achievement may have been to delay proceedings to such an extent that the intended by-election was never held.

Nothing more was heard of the franchise dispute thereafter. From 1624 the town's parliamentary indentures assumed a settled form which differed in some respects from those which had been used before 1604. They were now made out between the sheriff of Somerset on the one hand and the constables, burgesses and inhabitants of Minehead on the other. Each indenture was witnessed by at least ten 'burgesses and inhabitants', and the election was said to have been carried out in 'public and open assembly in the presence of divers others the burgesses and inhabitants of the said borough with a free and voluntary consent'.[28]

In view of the long-running dispute between George Luttrell and the town over the charter, it is not surprising that Luttrell apparently exercised no influence in the borough's parliamentary election of 1604. Sir Ambrose Turvile, who took the senior seat, was a Buckinghamshire gentleman who undoubtedly owed his election not to Luttrell but to the prominent Somerset lawyer Sir Edward Phelips, whose marriage into another Buckinghamshire family meant that he was a close neighbour and friend of Turvile's mother. Sir Maurice Berkeley, who obtained the junior seat, was a prominent parliamentarian who had recently been one of Somerset's knights of the shire and was probably elected for Minehead at his own request. Appointed to the committee for the Minehead harbour bill, he played no active part in managing it so far as is known. There is no clue as to the identity of the men whom the town claimed it had elected in 1614, but both they and the Members chosen in 1620 would obviously have been chosen without Luttrell's approval. Of the latter, Francis Peirce was a prominent Minehead resident who had advanced money to help the town a few years earlier. He was the only townsman to be elected in this period. His presence at Westminster was undoubtedly necessitated by the need to defend the franchise against Luttrell. Peirce's fellow Member, Sir Robert Lloyd, is not known to have had a personal connection with the town. His election should perhaps be seen as part of a bargain, whereby he agreed to help defend the franchise in return for an opportunity to defend a cause of his own in Parliament. This other cause involved a patent for the sole engrossing of wills, which he enjoyed. In this personal battle he proved unsuccessful, and on 21 Mar. 1621 he was expelled as a monopolist.

The election of 1624 appears to have been held without a confrontation between Luttrell and the town, but even so the candidates returned seem not have owed their seats to the squire of Dunster Castle. It is true that Arthur Duck was loosely connected with Luttrell, as his father-in-law was tenant of a manor held by Luttrell, but Duck's electoral patron was undoubtedly his employer, the bishop of Bath and Wells. Duck was chancellor of the diocese, and was entrusted with guiding through the Commons the bill to confirm the foundation of Wadham College, Oxford, in which the bishop had an interest as the college's ecclesiastical visitor. The bishop's influence in this election is underlined by the identity of Duck's fellow Member, the bishop's nephew and namesake, Sir Arthur Lake.

It was only from 1625 that Luttrell's influence can be clearly perceived as the determining force in Minehead elections. The completion of the new harbour not only gave Luttrell control of the town's major trading facility, but also enabled the trade expansion of the 1620s. Many of Luttrell's former enemies among Minehead's citizens may have been grateful to him for their new-found prosperity, but even if they were not they could now scarcely afford to ignore his views. The 1625 election saw the return of Thomas Luttrell, the heir to Dunster and the first member of the family to sit in the Commons since 1589. He was accompanied by Edmund Wyndham, who also sat in 1628. A relative and neighbouring landowner, Wyndham was a close associate of the Luttrells. Wyndham's father was overseer to Thomas Luttrell's marriage settlement in 1621, and Luttrell's father performed the same service for Wyndham in 1623.[29] John Gill, a royal equerry who sat in 1626, was another distant kinsman of the Luttrells, as well as being a Somerset magistrate based a few miles from Minehead. The precise identity of his fellow Member, Thomas Horner, who also sat in 1628, is uncertain, but he belonged to another prominent Somerset family, and most likely also relied for his returns on his cousins, the Luttrells.[30]

[1] OR. [2] F. Hancock, *Hist. Minehead*, 138-41, 230, 232-4. [3] E190/1081/1; 190/1082/5; 190/1083/1, 24; 190/1084/7, 17, 23; 190/1085/5. [4] E190/1084/7, 17, 23; 190/1085/5, 7, 13; 190/1086/8, 15, 19; 190/1087/1, 14, 16; Som. RO, DD/L 1/55/1. [5] Hancock, 242-5; Som. RO, DD/L/P 29/34. [6] E178/1994; H.C. Maxwell-Lyte, *Hist. Dunster*, 174. [7] Som. RO, DD/L/P 30/50; L/P 55/1; E159/425, Trinity term, 1 Jac. I, memo. 25; Hancock, 254. [8] Som. RO, DD/L 1/55/1, letter from John Luttrell, n.d. but c.1604. [9] Ibid. letter of 9 Oct. 1609. [10] *CJ*, i. 398a. [11] Som. RO, DD/L 1/55/1, 'Draft Act for Minehead Quay'; *CJ*, i. 398a-b, 416a. [12] *CJ*, i. 398b, 403a. [13] *CJ*, i. 416a; *Procs. 1610*, pp. 63, 207. [14] Som. RO, DD/L 1/55/1, docket of quay duties, 1622. [15] Som. RO, DD/L 1/59/1. [16] *CD 1621*, ii. 87; v. 481. [17] Ibid. ii. 82; Nicholas, *Procs. 1621*, i. 68. [18] *CD 1621*, ii. 87. [19] Ibid. i. 73. [20] Ibid. v. 481. [21] SP12/77/44. [22] *CJ*, i. 536b. [23] Ibid. 537b. [24] Ibid. 556b. [25] Nicholas, i. 175. [26] *CJ*, i. 612a. [27] *CD 1621*, iii. 190-1, 372; *CJ*, i. 617a. [28] C219/41A/65; Som. RO, DD/L 1/59/1: 16 Jan. 1624, 31 Jan. 1626. [29] Som. RO, DD/L/P 3/4; C142/568/120. [30] *Vis. Som.* (Harl. Soc. xi), 103, 125; Collinson, *Som.* ii. 12; *Misc. Gen. et Her.* n.s. iv. 162.

G.Y.

TAUNTON

Right of election: in the inhabitants not receiving charity

Number of voters: at least 21 in 1626

c. Feb. 1604[1]	EDWARD HEXT
	JOHN BOND
c. Mar. 1614	JOHN DONNE
	JAMES CLARKE I
c. Jan. 1621	THOMAS BRERETON
	LEWIS POPE
c. Jan. 1624	THOMAS BRERETON
	ROGER PROWSE
c. Apr. 1625	SIR HUGH PORTMAN, bt.
	THOMAS BRERETON
20 Jan. 1626	SIR ROBERT GORGES
	GEORGE BROWNE
19 Feb. 1628[2]	SIR HUGH PORTMAN, bt.
	GEORGE BROWNE

Originally an Anglo-Saxon foundation, Taunton was dominated throughout the Middle Ages by the bishops of Winchester, who owned the principal manor of Taunton Dean.[3] Accordingly, at the start of the seventeenth century, the town's considerable economic prosperity and regional importance contrasted sharply with its primitive municipal government. On the one hand, it was now both a major market town, and a thriving centre of the cloth trade, specializing in 'Taunton cottons', as well as the home of Somerset's autumn assizes and midsummer quarter sessions.[4] On the other hand, the town was still only a borough by prescription, presided over by the bishops' bailiffs, with the assistance of two constables elected annually at the manorial court leet.[5] Despite this anomaly, Taunton's leading residents were more than capable of asserting their own self-interest. In 1615 the town was rebuked by the Privy Council after many of its wealthiest inhabitants refused to contribute to the Benevolence. Unbowed by the government's displeasure, the local merchants threatened in 1620 to withdraw their trade from Lyme Regis, Dorset, if they were compelled to help with that port's contribution towards the forthcoming Mediterranean naval expedition.[6]

Taunton was badly affected by the slump in the cloth trade in the early 1620s. This crisis was cited in 1622 as an excuse for the town's predictably small contribution towards the Palatine Benevolence. Two years later, economic hardship prompted the borough to apply for a charter of incorporation.[7] Such a grant would inevitably reduce the bishops' influence, and Lancelot Andrewes presumably used his influence at Court to block it. Not until March 1627, six months after Andrewes' death, was a new charter issued, which established a corporation consisting of a mayor, recorder, 14 capital burgesses, and ten inferior burgesses.[8]

Taunton first returned Members to Parliament in 1295. The franchise was broad, embracing all adult male residents who were not receiving charitable support, but the parliamentary borough covered only part of the town, the parish of St. Mary Magdalen. At the start of the seventeenth century the two constables acted as returning officers, but under the 1627 charter, this role passed to the mayor.[9] Only the indentures for the 1626 and 1628 elections survive from this period. Both were written in Latin. The pre-charter return was made in the name of the constables, bailiffs and burgesses, with 21 individuals listed altogether. The later indenture was returned by the mayor, and on this occasion was signed by at least 17 voters. It is not known whether the signatories in 1628 were specifically members of the new corporation.[10]

There is no clear evidence that the bishops of Winchester influenced the choice of Members during this period. Ordinarily, the two burgess-ships were taken by local residents or the Somerset gentry. In the former category was John Bond, a former Taunton schoolmaster, who had represented the borough in 1601, and retained his seat in the first Jacobean Parliament. His son-in-law Roger Prowse was returned in 1624, while Lewis Pope, a Taunton merchant, sat in 1621. George Browne, the junior Member in 1626 and 1628, was clerk of Taunton castle, and became the borough's recorder under the 1627 charter.[11] Of the gentry, James Clarke (1614) lived just outside the town, as did Sir Hugh Portman (1625 and 1628), who was also Browne's cousin. Edward Hext, the senior Member in 1604, hailed from 12 miles away, but as an active local magistrate he was presumably well known in the borough, and indeed had already represented Taunton in 1597. The remaining Members were all nominated by one of Somerset's most important gentry families, the Phelipses of Montacute. Sir Robert Gorges, who sat in 1626, was Sir Robert Phelips'* brother-in-law, while Thomas Brereton (1621-5) was one of his principal allies in county politics.[12] The only complete outsider was John Donne in 1614, who benefited from the patronage of Sir Edward Phelips*, although the latter also initially considered handing the seat to Sir Edwin Sandys*.[13]

Taunton rarely featured in the Commons' records. Indeed, in March 1624, when Brereton was requested by one of the town's merchants to seek parliamentary action over the threat posed to West Country trade by French privateering, he instead passed the letter to Sir Robert Phelips, who secured government intervention without taking the matter before the House.[14] However, the borough did briefly come under the Commons' scrutiny in the 1628 session. During the previous winter, 100 soldiers from Sir Richard Grenville's* regiment had been billeted in the town. Shortly before the shire election, (Sir) John Stawell* canvassed for votes in Taunton, but failed to attract much support, and was subsequently outpolled by Sir Robert Phelips. In revenge, he used his powers as a Somerset deputy lieutenant to reorganize the billeting in Taunton, allocating soldiers to the houses of leading residents, including the mayor and the recorder, George Browne. The latter raised this abuse in the House on 2 Apr., and the matter was referred to a committee. The initial report by Sir Walter Earle on 19 Apr. suggested that the disruption to Browne's household might constitute a breach of his parliamentary privilege, and Stawell was accordingly summoned to Westminster to explain himself. On closer inspection, though, the committee concluded that the privilege complaint could not be proved, and despite further evidence that Stawell had abused his position as a deputy lieutenant, he was discharged again on 15 May.[15]

[1] SP14/7/82.II. [2] OR. [3] J. Toulmin, *Hist. Taunton* ed. J. Savage, 18, 47. [4] T.G. Barnes, *Som. 1625-40*, pp. 8-9; *CSP Dom.* 1611-18, p. 206; *HMC Cowper*, i. 171. [5] Toulmin, 310-11. [6] *APC*, 1615-16, pp. 49-50; *CSP Dom.* 1619-23, p. 156. [7] *CSP Dom.* 1619-23, p. 389; *HMC Cowper*, i. 171; [8] *HMC Cowper*, i. 466-7; *CSP Dom.* 1627-8, p. 101; M. Weinbaum, *British Bor. Chs. 1307-1660*, p. 104. [9] T.H.B. Oldfield, *Hist. Bors. of Gt. Britain*, ii. 447-8, 455-6; Toulmin, 310-11. [10] C219/40/133; 219/41A/64. [11] *Som. Par. Reg.* ix. 19. [12] *Vis. Dorset Addenda* ed. F.T. Colby and J.P. Rylands, 8; *Vis. Som.* (Harl. Soc. xi), 42; Barnes, 287. [13] R.C. Bald, *John Donne*, 285; E. Farnham, 'Som. Election of 1614', *EHR*, xlvi. 581. [14] *CSP Dom.* 1623-5, p. 173; T. Cogswell, *Blessed Revolution*, 160-1. [15] *CD 1628*, ii. 254-5, 264-5, 564, 573; iii. 419-20.

J.P.F.

WELLS

Right of election: in the burgesses

Number of voters: 75 in 1626

25 Feb. 1604	JAMES KIRTON II, recorder	
	SIR ROBERT STAPLETON	
13 Nov. 1606[1]	EDWARD FORSETT *vice*	
	Stapleton, deceased	

8 Mar. 1614	THOMAS SOUTHWORTH, recorder	
	SIDNEY MONTAGU	
21 Dec. 1620[2]	THOMAS SOUTHWORTH, recorder	
	SIR EDWARD RODNEY	
24 Jan. 1624[3]	THOMAS SOUTHWORTH, recorder	
	SIR EDWARD RODNEY	
26 Apr. 1625[4]	SIR THOMAS LAKE II	
	SIR EDWARD RODNEY	
	?John Paulett	
	Henry Southworth	
13 Jan. 1626[5]	SIR THOMAS LAKE II	62
	SIR EDWARD RODNEY	44
	John Baber*, recorder	39
	Hugh Mead	3
	Virtue Hunt, mayor	3
	Bartholomew Cox	2
	Henry Baron	1
25 Feb. 1628[6]	RALPH HOPTON	
	JOHN BABER, recorder	

Wells had long been dominated by the bishops of Bath and Wells, lords of the manor, liberty and hundred. In 1201 a royal charter vested municipal authority in an annually elected master (or steward) and a council of Twenty-Four. Successive bishops aimed to erode this independent jurisdiction, forcing the cancellation of the town's first two charters of incorporation (1341 and 1574). Nevertheless, the burgesses re-confirmed their privileges in 1577 and secured a fresh charter in 1589, which established a corporation composed of a mayor, seven 'masters', and 16 capital burgesses, assisted by a recorder (often one of the 'masters') and a town clerk. The parliamentary franchise was initially restricted to the corporation, but freemen were later given the vote.[7]

Payment of the 40s. entry fine for freemen was occasionally commuted or remitted altogether, as with Sir Edward Rodney* whose father, Sir John*, had been 'a great friend of the city'.[8] Such fines, and market tolls, were the borough's principal source of income. Salaries were restricted to the mayor and recorder (40s. each); the 12d. per day formerly paid as parliamentary wages had been discontinued by the 1520s. The first mention in the Act Books of such a payment thereafter was in August 1607, when James Kirton, having served in Parliament 'to his great charge', was reimbursed £5.[9]

Wells had first sent representatives to Parliament in 1295. By the sixteenth century the seats were usually shared between borough officials, episcopal nominees and the local gentry. The extent of the diocesan interest depended upon the interests of the individual bishop: no such nominations seem to have been made between 1593 and 1604, but in 1614 the borough returned Sidney Montagu, brother of Bishop Montagu, while in 1625 Bishop Lake secured the election of his nephew Sir Thomas Lake II. Other outsiders included Sir Robert Stapleton, from whose estate at Lacock Abbey, Wiltshire, the corporation drew a small income; he was perhaps recommended by Sir John Thynne*, who had solicited his support for the Wiltshire county election.[10] The corporation preferred such men to have some local connection. In 1628 the non-resident Ralph Hopton* obtained a seat because his father was a freeman,[11] and following Stapleton's death in October 1606 the corporation accepted Edward Forsett on condition that he was sworn a freeman beforehand. Forsett, a client of secretary of state Robert Cecil[†], 1st earl of Salisbury, was nominated for the place by his patron and by lord chancellor Ellesmere (Thomas Egerton[†]). The swearing-in ceremony was performed in London before Ellesmere and several existing freemen.[12]

From 1601 the senior seat at Wells was reserved for the town's recorders, the lawyers James Kirton II and Thomas Southworth. At the 1625 election, however, Southworth chose not to stand, probably because of ill health – he died only four months later. In the absence of suitable alternatives, two councillors were nominated, one of whom, Southworth's frail elder brother, Henry, was to die within the month.[13] Under these unusual circumstances, the corporation invited Bishop Lake to 'commend some discreet and sufficient worthy burgess', and duly returned his nephew, together with the local magistrate Sir Edward Rodney.[14] In 1626 Southworth's successor as recorder, John Baber, was one of five councillors to contest the election, among them the mayor and town clerk. Sir Thomas Lake comfortably topped the poll, with Rodney, who received the votes of 36 of Lake's supporters, coming second, which enabled him to beat Baber by the narrow margin of five votes.[15]

At the 1628 general election, neither Lake nor Rodney stood again, which allowed Baber to be returned along with another local man, Ralph Hopton. Baber's success was somewhat marred by complaints made in the Commons in April 1628 about his role in the billeting of troops upon the town a few months earlier. When it emerged that he had advised the corporation to 'yield to necessity rather than law' in admitting the troops without proper warrant or means of payment, there were loud calls for his expulsion from the House.

This did not happen, but Baber was suspended for two months, while his constituents took advantage of the ruling to evict the soldiers from their houses.[16]

[1] *Wells Convocation Acts Bks. 1589-1629* ed. A. Nott and J. Hasler (Som. Rec. Soc. xc), 194. [2] Ibid. 333-4. [3] Ibid. 378. [4] Ibid. 407. [5] Ibid. 429. [6] Ibid. 469. [7] Ibid. 1-5. [8] Ibid. 333. [9] Ibid. 200. [10] Ibid. 22-3 Longleat, Thynne Pprs. (IHR microfilm), viii. f. 310. [11] *Wells Convocation Act Bks. 1589-1629*, p. 469. [12] Ibid. 193-4. [13] J. Collinson, *Hist. Som.* i. 219; *Vis. Som.* (Harl. Soc. xi), 102. [14] *Wells Convocation Act Bks. 1589-1629*, p. 407. [15] Ibid. 427-9. [16] *CD 1628*, ii. 370-1, 374-5; iv. 124-19, 345; T.G. Barnes, *Som. 1625-40*, pp. 256-8.

H.J.L.

STAFFORDSHIRE

?15 Mar. 1604	SIR ROBERT STANFORD SIR EDWARD LITTLETON I
27 *Aug. 1607*	SIR JOHN EGERTON *vice* Stanford, deceased
15 Nov. 1610	FRANCIS TRENTHAM *vice* Littleton, incapacitated
1614	(SIR) WALTER CHETWYND THOMAS CROMPTON
30 Nov. 1620	SIR WILLIAM BOWYER II THOMAS CROMPTON
22 Jan. 1624	SIR WILLIAM BOWYER II SIR EDWARD LITTLETON II
?5 May 1625[1]	SIR SIMON WESTON RICHARD ERDESWICKE
19 Jan. 1626	SIR SIMON WESTON SIR WILLIAM BOWYER II
14 Feb. 1628	SIR HERVEY BAGOT, bt. THOMAS CROMPTON

Described by Camden as 'in form of a lozenge, broader in the midst and growing narrow at the ends', Staffordshire 'for the most part consisteth of barren land' and 'doth ... abound with poor people', or so said the county's magistrates on attempting to obtain a reduction in the county's Ship Money quota in 1637. While the northern part of the county was certainly hilly, 'and so less fruitful', the central region was, according to Camden, 'more plentiful, clad with woods and embroidered gallantly with corn fields and meadows', being 'watered with the river Trent'. Moreover, in the south coal and iron was mined.[2] The settlement pattern reflected the varying geography, with compact villages in the central arable region and small hamlets and isolated farms in the largely pastoral north and south. The years between 1610 and 1630 were periods of frequent dearth and widespread social dislocation in the county, with destitute travellers frequently appearing in the better-kept parish registers.[3]

As in the late Elizabethan period, elections were almost certainly held at the shire hall in Stafford.[4] In 1610 the corporation of Stafford purchased 'a pottle of sack' for the sheriff's refreshment at the election of Trentham.[5] The precise date of the 1604 election is a matter for conjecture, as the indenture does not survive. The Staffordshire gentry were well aware that elections were meant to be held on the next county day after the sheriff received the writ, for in 1604 Sir Robert Stanford argued that if the sheriff received the writ on a county day he was obliged to proceed to an election then and there.[6] On 5 Feb. the sheriff, Walter Bagot[†], was informed that the next county court would be held on 16 Feb.,[7] but he did not receive the writ until about the 24th. As county days were held every 28 days, this suggests that the election took place on 15 March.[8] That date is certainly compatible with an undated letter from one of the candidates in which it is stated that the election was held on a Thursday.[9] However, the requirement to hold elections at the next county day was not always observed in practice. On 14 Apr. 1625, at the county day in Stafford 'when the knights of Parliament should have been elected', Ralph Sneyd delivered to the sheriff a new commission of the peace,[10] as a result of which the election seems to have been delayed by three weeks.

In contrast to the 1590s, the electoral politics of early seventeenth-century Staffordshire appear to have been marked by peace and, outwardly at least, consensus. The execution in 1601 of Robert Devereux, 2nd earl of Essex, the dominant magnate in late Elizabethan Staffordshire, had removed the prime cause of conflict, as Essex had attempted to nominate both knights of the shire in the teeth of gentry opposition. However, political conflict was contained rather than eliminated.

At the beginning of this period the county was deeply divided by religion. Under Elizabeth Staffordshire had been notorious for its recusants, and Catholics remained a powerful force under James. In the aftermath of the 1604 election, Sir Edward Littleton I* remarked that 'the common speech is that the assembly at Stafford on Thursday was rather to choose a pope then a knight for the Parliament because they were all of that tribe'. Before 1601, Protestant interests in the county coalesced around Essex. Indeed, the

Protestant credentials of the earl's supporters gave his faction a coherence which undoubtedly contributed to its continuance as a political force after Essex's execution.[11] Among the most notable members of this group was Sir Thomas Gerard I[†], who had been one of Essex's nominees in 1593. Gerard stayed loyal to the queen during Essex's rising and had consequently been rewarded with the position of *custos rotulorum*. He also sat for Staffordshire in 1601.

During the Jacobean period the Devereux faction regained their leader. Essex's son was restored to his father's lands and titles in 1604, was appointed lord lieutenant in 1612 and succeeded Gerrard as *custos* in 1617.[12] As lord lieutenant, Essex frequently appointed deputies from families that had been associated with his father. His earliest deputies were Sir Walter Aston, Walter Bagot, Sir Simon Weston* and Thomas, 4th Lord Cromwell. Aston and Bagot were both sons of men to whom the 2nd earl had written in 1593 to promote his parliamentary nominations, and Cromwell's father and Weston had been knighted by the 2nd earl in Dublin. Cromwell's father and Littleton had been fined for their parts in Essex's rising, in which Weston was also accused of having played a part.[13]

In the 1604 election conflict was avoided, mainly because the Devereux faction proved willing to accommodate the local Catholic community. The sheriff Walter Bagot, was one of their number, whose partisanship initially caused alarm among other sections of the Staffordshire gentry. On 20 Jan. the recusant Philip Draycourt urged Bagot to 'work it mildly and not with too great forwardness'.[14] Bagot's own legal advisor, William Browne, reinforced this advice on 5 Feb. when he suggested that 'if Sir Edward Littleton and Sir Robert Stanford carry off the election [it] will be well enough liked of and is least trouble'.[15] By this Browne meant that such a result would see both sides of the religious divide represented, as the Protestant Littleton had been the unsuccessful Essex candidate of 1597, while Stanford, who came from a largely recusant family, would be acceptable to Catholic sympathizers. Bagot accordingly contacted Stanford, who had agreed to stand after being urged to do so by William Paget, son of Thomas, Lord Paget, the major patron of Staffordshire Catholics until his attainder in 1587.[16]

The pairing of Littleton and Stanford was clearly ideal, but Bagot's plans were almost wrecked by Sir Walter Harcourt[†], who had upset the applecart in 1593, when he had forced one of the 2nd Earl of Essex's candidates to withdraw.[17] Despite claiming that his name had been put forward by his friends without his knowledge, Harcourt was heavily indebted and needed the protection conferred by parliamentary privilege. Writing to Bagot on 17 Feb. he protested that, on trying to pull out, rumours had been spread that he was withdrawing to avoid certain defeat, and consequently he was forced to stand to avoid disgrace. However, his constant letters to Bagot inquiring whether the sheriff had received the election writ, and an attempt to have Sir Edward I outlawed, suggest that his purported reluctance to stand was insincere. Bagot subsequently arranged a meeting to reconcile Littleton and Harcourt, who evidently regarded Bagot as his friend, but, as it turned out, Bagot kept Littleton informed of Harcourt's actions.[18] Moreover, Bagot, who knew that he was heavily indebted, seems to have exerted pressure on Harcourt to stand aside. He may have reminded him that in January a Proclamation had been issued forbidding the election of bankrupts to Parliament.[19] This would explain why, on 11 Feb., Harcourt assured Bagot that he was in the process of settling all his debts, and why he repeatedly argued that the Proclamation did not have the force of law. However, as executions for debt against him accumulated in Bagot's hands, Harcourt was ultimately forced to withdraw.[20]

There is no evidence that the county came this close to a contest again during this period. Indeed, the indentures for 1620, 1624, 1626 and 1628 suggest that a consensus was reached. Three men – (Sir) Walter Chetwynd, Matthew Cradock* and Ralph Sneyd – were parties to all four indentures, and several others, among them Thomas Crompton, appear more than once. The indentures for the 1607 and 1610 by-elections were signed by minor figures. Of the eight men named in the 1607 indenture, for example, five were yeomen, of whom two were illiterate.[21] The fact that such minor individuals were permitted to sign suggests that turnout was low, and that these by-elections were uncontroversial.

After 1604, consensus was established through preliminary meetings of the magistrates, who selected the candidates. The 1620-1 accounts of the corporation of Stafford include payments for wine for the justices of the peace when the county Members were chosen as well as for burnt sack for Chetwynd, the deputy custos rotolorum, and the sheriff, who all apparently met together in the 'office' about the election.[22] In 1628 the magistrates ordered the high constables 'to bring in the freeholders to the county town, and to entreat them to attend and give their voices for such gentlemen as shall be agreed upon by the more part of the magistrates'.[23] These meetings provided a mechanism to enable factions among the Staffordshire gentry to avoid contests by parcelling out the two county seats among themselves.

Until 1628 one seat always went to the Devereux faction. After Littleton became incapacitated by illness in 1610 he was replaced by Francis Trentham, whose father had been a trustee for Littleton's father-in-law, Sir William Devereux.[24] In 1614 and 1621 the Essex candidate was Thomas Crompton, one of Essex's deputy lieutenants in the early 1620s and 1630s, whose mother was an Aston. In 1624 the Essex candidate was the son of Sir Edward Littleton I. Each of these men held the junior seat, and it is possible that Crompton's success in twice becoming the Devereux candidate was due to the reluctance of higher status members of the faction, such as Sir Walter Aston, to accept the less prestigious position. However, in 1625 the Essex candidate, Sir Simon Weston, one of the trustees appointed by Essex to manage his estates when he was abroad in the early 1620s, took the senior place, which he retained in 1626.

The non-Essex element in Staffordshire politics seems to have been a rather diverse force. Stanford's election in 1604 suggests that the Pagets were still significant, and Sir Walter Chetwynd, elected in 1614, was the son of a close ally of Thomas, Lord Paget.[25] Lord chancellor Ellesmere may also have played an important part in the early Jacobean period, as Sir John Egerton of Wrinehill, Stanford's replacement in 1607, was his kinsman. Ellesmere was also responsible for Chetwynd's appointment as deputy custos rotulorum of Staffordshire.[26] In 1621, 1624 and 1626 the non-Essex seat went to Sir William Bowyer, who lived close to the border with Cheshire and does not seem to have been attached to any particular faction in Staffordshire during the 1620s, perhaps making him an acceptable compromise candidate.

The election of Richard Erdeswicke in 1625 suggests that for a short period the duke of Buckingham became a force in Staffordshire politics. The death of Ellesmere in 1617 left Chetwynd temporarily without a patron at Court to counter Essex's influence. However, in 1623, at Buckingham's instigation, Chetwynd married his daughter to Erdeswicke's half-brother, George Digby, a client of the duke's.[27] In 1624 Chetwynd helped ensure the election of Buckingham's client, Charles Glemham, at Newcastle-under-Lyme, and in 1625 he probably provided the main support for Erdeswicke. However, Erdeswicke's rapid slide into insolvency meant that Buckingham's excursion into Staffordshire politics was brief.

In 1628 Essex achieved the goal that had eluded his father, succeeding in filling both the Staffordshire places with his nominees. Walter Bagot's son, Sir Hervey, took the first seat while Thomas Crompton took the second. Essex's success was undoubtedly due mainly to the fact that he had refused to pay the Forced Loan, for which offence he was removed from the Staffordshire lieutenancy and commission of the peace.[28] However, he may also have benefited from showing more tact than his father. In the elections for the Long Parliament, Essex let it be known that he was leaving the selection of the Staffordshire knights of the shire to the county's free choice, whereupon one prominent Staffordshire gentleman inquired of one of the deputy lieutenants which individuals Essex wanted to see elected.[29]

[1] J.C. Wedgwood, 'Parl. Hist. of Staffs. 1603-1780', *Staffs. Hist. Colls.* (Wm. Salt Arch. Soc. 1920 and 1922), 44. However Wedgwood gives no source for this date and the indenture does not survive. [2] W. Camden, *Britannia* (1610), p. 581; SP16/345/76. [3] D. Palliser, 'Dearth and disease in Staffs.' *Rural Change and Urban Growth* ed. C.W. Chalkin and M.A. Havinden, 55, 64. [4] STAC 5/L11/24. [5] Staffs. RO, D1323/E/1, f. 58. [6] FSL, L.a.296, 527, 886. [7] FSL, L.a. 296. [8] FSL, L.a. 528; J.J. Alexander, 'Dates of county court days' *BIHR*, iii. 89. [9] *Staffs. Hist. Colls.* ed. A.G. Petti (Wm. Salt Arch. Soc. ser. 4. ix), 77; FSL, L.a.528. [10] Staffs. RO, Q/SO/2, f. 44. [11] *Staffs. Hist. Colls.* (Wm. Salt Arch. Soc. ser. 4. ix), x, 43, 77; *Letter-Books of Sir Amias Poulet* ed. J. Morris, 98, 103, 251, 269, 275. [12] *Staffs. Hist. Colls.* ed. J.C. Wedgwood (Wm. Salt Arch. Soc. 1912), pp. 326, 327; Sainty, *Lords Lieutenants*, 32. [13] FSL, L.a. 469-70; 751; Longleat, Devereux Pprs. (IHR microfilm), Box. vii. no. 106; *CP*, iii. 558. [14] FSL, L.a.429; *Recusant Roll, 1592-3* ed. M.M.C. Calthrop, (Cath. Rec. Soc. xviii), 303. [15] FSL, L.a.296. [16] FSL, L.a.886. [17] FSL, L.a.81. [18] FSL, L.a.525-8, 623-4. [19] *Stuart Royal Procs.* ed. J.F. Larkin and P.L. Hughes, i. 68. [20] FSL, L.a. 525, 527-9. [21] C219/35/2/42, 50; 219/37/227; 219/38/213; 219/40/109; 219/41A/19. [22] Staffs. RO, D1323/E/1, f. 112. [23] Wedgwood, 54. Unfortunately Wedgwood does not give a source. [24] C142/191/119. [25] FSL, L.a. 886; C. Harrison, 'Fire on the Chase', *Staffs. Hist. Colls.* ed. P. Morgan and A.D.M. Phillips (Wm. Salt Arch. Soc. ser. 4. xix), 114; J. Sutton, 'Loyalty and a "Good Conscience"', Ibid. 131. [26] FSL, L.a. 382. [27] *Staffs. Hist. Colls.* ed. S.A.H. Burne (Wm. Salt Arch. Soc. 1941), 91-3. [28] Sainty, 32; *Cal. of Docquets of Ld. Kpr. Coventry, 1625-40* ed. J. Broadway, R. Cust and S.K. Roberts (L. and I. Soc. spec. ser. xxxiv-vii), 61. [29] *HMC 2nd Rep.* 47.

B.C.

LICHFIELD

Right of election: in the corporation

Number of voters: 29 in 1624

1604	ANTHONY DYOTT, ?steward
	THOMAS CREWE
1614	SIR JOHN EGERTON
	WILLIAM WINGFIELD
May 1614	ANTHONY DYOTT, ?steward, *vice* Egerton, died 27 Apr.
Dec. 1620	WILLIAM WINGFIELD
	RICHARD WESTON

22 Jan. 1624	(SIR) JOHN SUCKLING
	WILLIAM WINGFIELD
15 Apr. 1624	SIR SIMON WESTON, recorder, *vice* Suckling, chose to sit for Middlesex
1625	RICHARD DYOTT, steward
	WILLIAM WINGFIELD
1626	RICHARD DYOTT, steward
	WILLIAM WINGFIELD
14 Feb. 1628	SIR WILLIAM WALTER
	RICHARD DYOTT, steward

Lichfield lies in south-east Staffordshire, between the high ground of Cannock Chase to the west and the Tame valley to the east. The origins of its name are obscure. Once thought to signify 'a field of corpses', after the massacre of early Christians by the Romans, a more likely meaning is 'a common pasture in (or beside) a grey wood'.[1] In the mid-seventh century the king of Northumberland, having conquered the Mercians, established a bishopric at Lichfield, and at the end of the eighth century the bishop briefly enjoyed metropolitan authority. Under Saxon rule Lichfield was little more than a village, but in the midtwelfth century a town was laid out on a ladder plan by the bishop, who became lord of the manor.[2] This enlarged settlement was granted a guild to govern its affairs by Richard II in 1387, when he visited Lichfield to attend the enthronement of a new bishop.[3] By 1563 there were around 400 households living there,[4] whose economic fortunes depended upon agriculture, sheep-farming, leatherworking, textile production, metalworking and the bishop's Consistory Court, which provided employment and attracted litigants and witnesses in large numbers.[5] In April 1612 the Anabaptist Edward Wightman of Burton-on-Trent was burnt in the market square after being tried in the Consistory Court as a heretic. His execution, carried out on the orders of the king, was the last recorded instance of burning at the stake in England.[6] During the later sixteenth and early seventeenth centuries several new trade companies sprang up, but even so, in 1582 Bishop Overton claimed that Lichfield 'is not the city that it hath been'. One reason for the decline was the nationwide collapse in demand for cloth caps. In 1575 the city's cappers had brought their plight to the attention of the queen,[7] and in 1604 they probably played a part in the unsuccessful agitation to revive legislation requiring the wearing of caps which had been repealed in 1597.[8]

The balance of power at Lichfield shifted in 1548, when the town guild was abolished and the bishop was compelled to grant his lordship of the town to a new corporation, consisting of two bailiffs and 24 burgesses, established by Edward VI. One bailiff had seniority to the other, and both were elected annually. In October 1553 the corporation established an additional 24-strong common council to assist it. Two months later, as a reward for supporting Mary against the duke of Northumberland, the city was made a county borough and allowed to elect its own sheriff and recorder.[9] The bishop initially resented his loss of authority, but in 1598 he surrendered his rights to the queen, who later that year leased the lordship of the manor to the corporation.[10] In return, the corporation agreed to present him each year with at least two names from which he would nominate the senior bailiff.[11] However, tension remained over the administrative status of the 16-acre cathedral close within the heart of the city. In 1441 the Close had been granted extensive powers of self-government, which had remained unaffected by the charters of 1548 and 1553. Sometime before 1622 the corporation insisted that the Close lay within its jurisdiction. Bishop Thomas Morton naturally disagreed, and in May 1623 the corporation disclaimed all privileges within the Close.[12] By way of compensation, perhaps, James granted Lichfield a fresh charter four months later whereby its 24 burgesses were replaced with 21 brethren.[13]

The corporation's chief legal adviser was not its recorder but its steward, who was mentioned in the charter of 1553. This had not always been the case, for in 1583 the recorder was Thomas Egerton I[†], solicitor-general and later lord chancellor. However, during the early seventeenth century the recorder performed the functions of high steward. By 1606 Egerton had been succeeded by his son (Sir) John Egerton[†], who held office until 1622 and was created Earl of Bridgwater in 1617. Unlike his father, Bridgwater was no lawyer; nor was his successor, the exceptionally wealthy Sir Simon Weston. The corporation seems never to have considered conferring the recordership on successive earls of Essex. Robert Devereux, 2nd Earl of Essex, was Staffordshire's most prominent peer, whose seat at Drayton Basset lay about six miles east of Lichfield. Essex enjoyed the right to walk with the town bailiffs at an annual fair,[14] and it was through his influence that in 1598 the bishop surrendered his manorial rights to the Crown. In return the corporation promised to grant Essex the fee farm of the manor, but it never did so, and in July 1604 it was sharply rebuked by the Privy Council for its negligence. Soon thereafter the

corporation bestowed the fee farm upon Essex's son, the 3rd Earl, who paid £40 annually to the corporation for the privilege.[15] The latter stayed in Lichfield in November 1614 when, as lord lieutenant, he held musters for Staffordshire.[16]

In 1547 Lichfield recovered a long forgotten right to return Members to Parliament. The precise nature of the franchise is uncertain, and parliamentary indentures are unhelpful: those of 1614, 1625 and 1626 are no longer extant, while the returns for 1604, 1620 and January 1624 are so damaged as to be illegible.[17] However, indentures for April 1624 and February 1628 do survive, and these omit any mention of the borough's ordinary freemen. It seems likely that the franchise resided exclusively in the corporation, which seems to have included municipal officers like the town clerk, Michael Noble[†], whose name appears on the 1628 indenture.[18] The real question is whether the assistants to the corporation appointed in 1553 were also entitled to vote. The return for April 1624 suggests that they were as, apart from the Steward, Richard Dyott, 28 individuals signed the indenture with the sheriff, of whom only 23 at the most can have been bailiffs or brethren.[19] The indentures for April 1624 and February 1628 differ slightly in layout. In the former, all individuals named as parties to the return signed their names, but in the latter more than 18 signatures appear although only 12 men were named in the text.[20] This variation may suggest that in 1628 a conscious effort was made to distinguish between different sorts of voters, but it is more likely that it simply reflects differences in the physical form of the returns. In 1624 the indenture took the form of an L-shaped piece of parchment, which afforded plenty of space for signatures, whereas the rectangular design adopted in 1628 restricted the available space for signing.[21]

None of the elections during this period are known to have been contested, although controversy evidently surrounded Anthony Dyott's return at a by-election in May 1614, as the House ordered that his election should stand.[22] Towards the end of Elizabeth's reign a habit of returning the borough steward appears to have developed. Richard Broughton, who was certainly steward in 1583, was returned in 1586, 1588 and 1593, and in 1601 and 1604 the lawyer Anthony Dyott occupied the senior seat. There is no evidence that Dyott was Broughton's successor as steward, except that he was the lawyer who advised the corporation when it attempted to gain control of the cathedral close. Dyott was passed over for a seat at the general elections of 1614 and 1621, although he was returned at a by-election in May 1614. Dyott died in 1622 whereupon the stewardship passed to his son, Richard. The latter did not come in for Lichfield until 1625, however, because he preferred to be returned for Stafford, where he was recorder. Thereafter Dyott continued to represent Lichfield, although in 1628 he had to settle for the junior place. Both Dyotts were resident in Lichfield, as was Sir Simon Weston, the recorder, who came in at a second 1624 election. The only Parliament in which no resident represented Lichfield was that of 1621, although the junior member, Richard Weston, lived about six miles to the north-west at Rugeley.

At the beginning of Elizabeth's reign the bishop had exercised limited electoral influence at Lichfield, but this was replaced by the 2nd earl of Essex. Following Essex's execution in 1601 the Devereux interest temporarily disappeared, leaving a vacuum that was filled by lord chancellor Ellesmere, the former recorder, whose son now held the recordership. In 1604 the junior seat was occupied by Thomas Crewe, the brother of Ellesmere's client Ranulphe Crewe, and at the general election in 1614 the senior seat was conferred on Sir John Egerton, Ellesmere's distant cousin, whose extensive estates straddled the Staffordshire/Cheshire border. Egerton influence over Lichfield's parliamentary elections seems to have ended on Ellesmere's death in 1617, by which time Essex's son had attained his majority. The revival of the Devereux interest was signalled by the return of the earl's estate steward, William Wingfield, who was awarded the senior seat in 1621. Wingfield also sat in the next three successive parliaments, though he was relegated to the junior position, and in 1628 he was replaced by his friend Sir William Walter, who may have had a kinsman on the corporation. Another Lichfield Member connected with Essex was the recorder, Sir Simon Weston, a trustee of the earl's estates in 1620-1. It is unclear how the comptroller of the Household, Sir John Suckling, came to be elected for Lichfield in 1624, as he had no known links with Staffordshire, but an Essex connection cannot be ruled out.

Lichfield is not known to have preferred any legislation during this period, although the cappers' bill of 1604 may have been supported by many of the town's tradesmen. In 1621 and 1626 the bishop introduced unsuccessful bills to annex the prebend of Freeford, which lay a few miles south-east of the city, to the vicarage of St. Mary's, Lichfield, with a view to better provision for the vicar.[23]

[1] T. Harwood, *Hist. and Antiqs. of Lichfield*, 2; *VCH Staffs.* xiv. 37-8. [2] *VCH Staffs.* xiv. 5-6, 9, 67. [3] N. Saul, *Richard II*, 171; Harwood, 311. [4] *VCH Staffs.* xiv. 39. [5] *CSP Dom.* 1635, pp. 454-5. [6] Harwood, 304-5; *CSP Dom.* 1611-18, p. 123; Bodl. Ashmole 1521. [7] *VCH Staffs.* xiv. 16, 121. [8] NLS, Adv. MS 34.2.15, f. 71, petition addressed to Sir Edward Hoby, Member for Rochester. For the bill, see *CJ*, i. 161b, 189a. [9] Harwood, 311, 335, 337, 342. [10] Harwood, 336, 338. [11] Lichfield RO, D77/10/1. [12] Lichfield RO, D30/8/2, 5; *VCH Staffs.* xiv. 84. [13] Harwood, 344. [14] P.E.J. Hammer, *Polarisation of Elizabethan Pols.* 271 n. 6. [15] Harwood, 340-1, 384. [16] *CSP Dom.* 1611-18, p. 259; Harwood, 341. [17] For the 1604, 1620 and Jan. 1624 indentures, see C219/35/2/52; 219/37/321; 219/38/219. [18] C219/41A/117. On Noble, see *VCH Staffs.* xiv, 78; C2/Chas.I/L25/2. [19] C219/38/221. [20] It is impossible to be more specific about the number signing as part of the return is torn away. [21] The L-shape format is rare, but was adopted by Lichfield in Jan. 1624 and by Warwickshire in 1621 and Callington in 1628. For the latter, see C219/37/266; 219/41B/142. [22] *CJ*, i. 502b. [23] Lichfield RO, D30/5/30; *CJ*, i. 505b, 631a; *Procs. 1626*, ii. 32, 70, 151, 214, 217.

A.D.T.

NEWCASTLE-UNDER-LYME

Right of election: in the corporation to 1624; thereafter in the freemen

Number of voters: 27 to 1624; 155 on 28 Apr. 1624[1]

28 Feb. 1604	WALTER CHETWYND	
	JOHN BOWYER	
c.Oct. 1605	ROWLAND COTTON *vice* Bowyer, deceased	
19 Mar. 1614[2]	EDWARD WYMARKE	
	ROBERT NEEDHAM	
19 Dec. 1620[3]	SIR JOHN DAVIES	
	EDWARD KIRTON	
19 Jan. 1624	SIR EDWARD VERE	16
	RICHARD LEVESON	26
	John Keeling	9[4]
28 Apr. 1624[5]	CHARLES GLEMHAM *vice* Vere, disabled	
	John Keeling	
11 May 1625[6]	EDWARD MAINWARING	
	JOHN KEELING	
23 Jan. 1626	SIR JOHN SKEFFINGTON	
	JOHN KEELING	
23 Feb. 1628	SIR GEORGE GRESLEY, bt.	
	(SIR) ROWLAND COTTON	

Situated in north-west Staffordshire, close to the borders with Cheshire and Shropshire, Newcastle-under-Lyme grew up around a castle built in the 1140s in a lake fed by Lyme Brook, a tributary of the Trent. The town, which lay on the main road from London to the north-west, hosted a weekly market, three annual fairs, and perhaps also a separate corn market.[7] In the seventeenth century the dominant industry was the making of felt hats, but iron-working and tanning were also important.[8] The town's population was probably growing rapidly. In the early Elizabethan period it had an estimated 390 or so inhabitants, a figure which rose to about 870 by the eve of the Civil War.[9]

Newcastle-under-Lyme was represented in Parliament from 1354.[10] A new charter was granted in 1590 through the intercession of Robert Devereux, 2nd earl of Essex. Political authority was vested in a common council of 27, consisting of the mayor, two bailiffs and 24 capital burgesses. The mayor and bailiffs held office for a year, while the capital burgesses served for life. Former mayors were styled aldermen, but enjoyed no specific powers. New capital burgesses were co-opted by the council, which was empowered to regulate the election of officers. In 1599 the council agreed that eight freemen, to be chosen by the council itself, should join the capital burgesses to elect officers. However, in 1620 this limited element of popular participation was abolished. Before 1590 the franchise at parliamentary elections lay with the freemen, but thereafter the corporation, believing that its exclusive right under the new charter to elect borough officers also extended to the election of Members of Parliament, confined the franchise to itself. If the vote was tied, the mayor was entitled to cast a second vote.[11] The oligarchy was not universally respected, as is shown by a steady stream of offenders who were fined for showing contempt towards the town's officers. There was also probably considerable factionalism on the council, and in the 1590s regulations were made to ensure secrecy of its proceedings and to prevent the bribing of electors and canvassing of votes.[12] Despite his role in procuring the 1590 charter, Essex appears to have nominated only one of the borough's Elizabethan MPs.[13]

More influential in the Elizabethan elections were the local gentry. Newcastle was, in theory, an urban oligarchy, but in practice it could not afford to ignore the local gentry, from among whom the mayor was frequently chosen. Gentry mayors were so common that, in 1596, the borough ordered that 'if any foreigner dwelling without the town be chosen mayor or burgess of the Parliament for the town, by means whereof he is burgess for his life … his children … shall not have any freedom within us in respect of their father's burgess-ship'. The inclusion of Members of Parliament in

this ordinance indicates that it was common for the borough to choose members of the gentry as its parliamentary representatives, and indeed, probably for this reason, there is no evidence that any of the borough's Members was ever paid. It also suggests that those chosen from among the gentry were routinely created freemen on election. However, this is certainly known to have happened only to Sir George Gresley during this period; Richard Leveson was not made free until he was re-elected in 1640.[14]

Another significant factor in the borough's electoral politics in the sixteenth century was the duchy of Lancaster,[15] whose influence over the borough derived from Henry III's grant of the manor of Newcastle-under-Lyme to Edmund, 1st earl of Lancaster in 1267. Technically the borough was distinct from the manor, but the townsmen were obliged to grind their corn at the castle mills and many townsmen and local gentlemen were copyholders in the manor. For instance, John Brett, three times mayor, had 41 acres of copyhold.[16] Up until 1624 the duchy continued to play a part in the borough's electoral politics, but no letters of nomination from the chancellor of the duchy have survived, and it is not always clear through whom the duchy operated.

The Sneyd family, local landowners who lived at Keele, three miles from Newcastle, may have played an important role as power brokers between the duchy and the borough. When the 1st earl of Salisbury (Robert Cecil[†]), a former chancellor, tried to influence the 1605 by-election, he contacted the then head of the family, Ralph Sneyd the elder.[17] Ralph had been mayor in 1574, as had his brother George in 1592 and his eldest son William in 1599. The Sneyds held an important stake in the manor of Newcastle, as they were connected with the castle mills from 1537, and were lessees of the castle and farmers of the manorial court from 1609. Walter Chetwynd, who secured the prime seat in 1604, was closely connected with the Sneyds. His aunt had married Ralph Sneyd the elder, and he made Ralph Sneyd the younger the overseer of his will. It is possible that Ralph Sneyd the elder utilized the duchy's influence on Chetwynd's behalf. However, Chetwynd also had other family connections with the borough, which he had represented in the 1580s.[18]

Following the earl of Essex's disastrous rising in 1601 the Devereux interest, such as it was, was entirely in abeyance. Consequently, in 1604 the second seat went to a prominent local figure, John Bowyer, who lived seven miles away and worked closely with the corporation. Following Bowyer's death in 1605,

Salisbury tried to nominate the replacement, but the corporation had already promised the place to Rowland Cotton. Cotton's family owned considerable property in the borough, where his uncle endowed a school. The corporation seems also to have rebuffed lord treasurer Dorset (Thomas Sackville†). The borough's determination to keep control of the junior seat adds weight to the supposition that Chetwynd was regarded as the duchy's nominee.[19]

In 1614 Chetwynd, then mayor, secured for himself a county seat, leaving the borough to find a suitable replacement. There can be little doubt that the chancellor of the duchy of Lancaster, Sir Thomas Parry*, was responsible for nominating Edward Wymarke in his stead, since Wymarke was one of Parry's clients and had no known connection with the borough.[20] The second seat was bestowed on Cotton's erstwhile brother-in-law, Robert Needham.

Sir John Davies, a prominent lawyer originally from Wiltshire, took the first seat in 1621, and was probably also a duchy of Lancaster nominee. However, he may have owed his return to William Herbert, 3rd earl of Pembroke rather than to the chancellor of the duchy. Pembroke had been appointed steward of the manor of Newcastle in 1616 as successor to his father-in-law, the 7th earl of Shrewsbury (Gilberty Talbot†), and is known to have been electorally active in other constituencies where he had inherited influence from Shrewsbury. Moreover, Davies and his family had long-standing connections with the Herberts.[21] On the other hand Davies was also connected with the Sneyds through his wife's family. The 1621 election saw the first example of Devereux influence in this period, as Edward Kirton, who took the remaining seat, was the servant of William Seymour, Lord Beauchamp*, brother-in-law of Robert Devereux, 3rd earl of Essex.

Like Davies, Sir Edward Vere, a professional soldier who may have been in the Netherlands at the time of the 1624 elections, had connections with both Pembroke and the Sneyds. In addition, he may have had been known to Essex, who also served in the Netherlands in the early 1620s. However, his election in 1624 proved highly controversial, and the resulting dispute overthrew the restricted franchise and the influence of the duchy.

The election took place in the upper room of the guildhall, and involved no contest in respect of the second seat, which went to Richard Leveson, a prominent local landowner. However, the first seat was contested by Vere and John Keeling, a London lawyer and the son of a member of the Newcastle corporation. On losing the poll of the capital burgesses Keeling

called out of the window to the assembled inhabitants, 30 or 40 of whom then entered the guildhall to protest at the result. Unmoved by this tactic, the corporation returned Vere and Leveson. However, the privileges' committee later ruled that, despite the 1590 charter, the corporation had no right to monopolize the franchise, which was restored to the freemen. The election of Vere was therefore quashed.[22]

In the subsequent election 155 men participated, including 27 non-resident freemen. However, many of the electors were freemen of very recent standing: in 1623-4 21 sons of existing freemen and seven non-residents were made burgesses. This was many more than was usual, for the previous year only one new freeman had been admitted. As all the newly created foreign freemen and all but three of the freemen's sons participated in the election, this looks suspiciously like an attempt to pack the vote. Prominent among the foreign freemen attending the election were Ralph Sneyd the younger and Walter Chetwynd, who may have influenced the outcome in favour of Charles Glemham, a Buckingham client who had decided to stand. Glemham probably enjoyed the support of the duchy, as Pembroke was in an uneasy alliance with Buckingham in 1624. It is striking that Chetwynd's daughter had recently married George Digby at Buckingham's instigation. Perhaps Chetwynd and Sneyd used their influence to bring in new freemen in order to prop up the duchy's influence. If so, they enjoyed only short-term success. It is almost certain that Keeling again contested the election for, on 25 May, he again petitioned the privileges committee. However, there was not sufficient time to hear his case, despite the fact that the House acknowledged that his grounds of complaint were 'very considerable'.[23]

Keeling's candidacy may have been part of a campaign to allow more popular participation in the government of Newcastle, although Keeling himself clearly had the support of elements within the ruling oligarchy, of which his family were a part. In the first election in 1624 he received support from nine of the capital burgesses. Discontent about the running of the corporation from around this time is be found in a council order suspending the payment of the £4 p.a. gratuity previously given to their minister Nicholas Richardson until 'he clear himself of certain wrongs and abuses, which he hath attempted against Mr. Mayor and the rest of the town, concerning the government of this corporation'. However, in all respects other than the election of Members of Parliament the powers of the capital burgesses remained intact until 1834.[24]

After 1624 there is no evidence of duchy influence. Keeling's complaint against Glemham's election may have led to a reluctance to use what remaining power the duchy still had. Certainly, by the late 1620s most of the non-resident freemen seem to have ceased participating in elections. In 1625 and 1626 the local gentry took control of the senior seat, while Keeling held the junior. Edward Mainwaring, elected in 1625, was a student at the inns of court, but his father lived close to the borough, which he had himself served, both in Parliament and as mayor. It is perhaps significant, too, that Mainwaring's father had not participated in the second 1624 election. In 1626 the first seat went to Sir John Skeffington, brother-in-law of Sir William Bowyer*, the son of the 1604 Member. In 1628 the pattern of influence changed again, as a client of the earl of Essex, Sir George Gresley, took the first seat, while the second went to Rowland Cotton, who was presumably the choice of the borough. The numbers participating in elections fell to 116 in 1626 and 92 in 1628.[25]

[1] T. Pape, *Newcastle-Under-Lyme*, 259, 265-6. [2] Ibid. 252. [3] Pape, 259. The indenture is dated 6 January. *OR*. [4] *CJ*, i. 759a. [5] Pape, 265-6. [6] Ibid. 269. [7] *VCH Staffs*. viii. 2, 45, 47; Pape, 1. [8] *VCH Staffs*. viii. 51-2. [9] P. Clark and J. Hosking, *Population Estimates of English Small Towns* (Cent. for Urban Hist. Working Pprs. v), 133. [10] *VCH Staffs*. viii. 42. [11] Pape, 53-61, 66-7, 217-18, 228, 252, 257. [12] Ibid. 215, 217-8, 258, 259, 261. [13] *HP Commons, 1558-1603*, i. 242-3. [14] Pape, 219, 276, 304. [15] *HP Commons, 1558-1603*, i. 243. [16] *VCH Staffs*. viii. 15; DL43/8/34, f. 2; C142/289/97; Pape, 2, 78. [17] *HMC Hatfield*, xvii. 358. [18] *Staffs. Hist. Colls*. ed. H.S. Grazebrook (Wm. Salt Arch. Soc. v. pt. 2), p. 274; PROB 11/181, ff. 31v-2; Pape, 201, 213, 229, 256; *VCH Staffs*. viii. 14, 48, 184-5. [19] *HMC Hatfield*, xvii. 358. [20] R.C.L. Sgroi, 'Electoral Patronage of the Duchy of Lancaster', *PH*, xxvi. 316. [21] *Duchy of Lancaster Office-Holders* ed. R. Somerville, 161. See EAST RETFORD; NOTTINGHAM; DERBY. [22] Pape, 265; *CJ*, i. 714b-15a, 759a, 798a; 'Pym 1624', i, f. 55; DL43/8/34, f. 1. [23] Pape, 264-6; *CJ*, i. 714b-15a, 798a; T. Cogswell, *Blessed Revolution*, 156. [24] Pape, 71, 267, 270. [25] Ibid. 270-1, 275-6.

B.C.

STAFFORD

Right of election: in the freemen

Number of voters: 80 in 1614; 120 in 1624

15 Mar. 1604	HUGH BEESTON GEORGE CRADOCK
1 Nov. 1609	ARTHUR INGRAM *vice* Beeston, deceased
1614	SIR WALTER DEVEREUX THOMAS GIBBS John Cooper
30 Nov. 1620	MATTHEW CRADOCK, recorder RICHARD DYOTT
21 Jan. 1624	MATTHEW CRADOCK, alderman RICHARD DYOTT, recorder Sir William Walter* Election declared void, 22 Mar. 1624
1 Apr. 1624	MATTHEW CRADOCK, alderman RICHARD DYOTT, recorder
1625	MATTHEW CRADOCK, alderman (SIR) ROBERT HATTON
4 July 1625	SIR JOHN OFFLEY *vice* Hatton, chose to sit for Sandwich
23 Jan. 1626	SIR JOHN OFFLEY BULSTRODE WHITELOCKE
21 Feb. 1628[1]	MATTHEW CRADOCK, alderman WILLIAM WINGFIELD

For an English county town, Stafford in the early seventeenth century was surprisingly small. In 1622 its entire population was just 1,550, having increased perhaps by as little as 50 per cent over the previous 250 years,[2] whereas that of contemporary Worcester was four times greater, while Exeter in 1638 boasted more than 10,000 souls. Moreover, Stafford was quite eclipsed by the cathedral city of Lichfield, which lay 15 miles distant. Whereas Lichfield was rated at £250 for Ship Money in 1635, Stafford, which enjoyed an annual income of less than £100, was assessed at just £50.[3]

During the early seventeenth century Stafford's inhabitants were mainly 'men of trade or mechanics, as maltsters, innkeepers, vintners, butchers, tailors, clothworkers, glaziers, plumbers, tanners, mercers, shoemakers, glovers, and the like'.[4] The predominant industry was evidently the cloth trade, but the town did not prosper, as its cloth was inferior in both quality and quantity to Worcester's and it had not yet recovered from the collapse in the capping industry that occurred sometime before 1570. By 1575 the town was so decayed that, despite being conveniently located in the centre of the shire, it temporarily ceased to host the assizes.[5] The circuit judges were subsequently lured back by the erection of a new shire hall, and hence in 1606 the town witnessed the trial and execution of two of the Gunpowder plotters.[6] However, despite the town's restoration as the county's administrative centre, it continued to experience severe economic hardship, occasioned by the slump in the cloth trade following the failure of the Cockayne Project. In 1621 rising unemployment led the municipal authorities to acquire the former county gaol as a house of correction. By the following year no less than a quarter of the town's inhabitants were eligible for poor relief.[7] It is scarcely surprising that, under such conditions, the borough seems never to have paid parliamentary wages during this period. Nevertheless, attempts were made to conceal the town's underlying poverty when James I visited Stafford in August 1617 on his return from Scotland. The borough council resolved to give James the 'most royalst' [sic] reception it could, and accordingly it instructed the citizens to paint their houses, repair their roofs and sand the streets. It also had the windows of the town hall glazed and emblazoned with the royal arms, comfortable chairs and stools were purchased for the king and his entourage, and a specially made triangular scaffold was erected in the market-place,

> whereupon was placed in the fore part a table covered with a carpet of broad green cloth, hanging down to the ground and fringed with Naples silk, and in the middle of the same the arms of all the kingdoms richly embroidered, and of either side the king's arms were the arms of the town, richly embroidered.

On entering the market square, James acknowledged the efforts made to beautify the town by announcing loudly 'that he was come into Little London'.[8]

Incorporated in 1206, Stafford was, by 1476, governed by two bailiffs and 25 capital burgesses. The bailiffs, elected each October by all the freemen, were chosen from among the capital burgesses. In 1604, for reasons which are unclear, the borough resolved that the number of capital burgesses should be reduced to 21. A fresh charter, costing more than £100, a sum greater than the corporation's entire annual income, was accordingly obtained in March 1605.[9] However,

it soon became apparent to those who were dismayed that the multitude of voters 'never made election of the worthiest sort',[10] that a much more radical overhaul of municipal government was needed. The trouble evidently began in 1599, when a lowly shoemaker inflicted a humiliating defeat on Hugh Beeston, a gentleman originally from Cheshire who had settled in Stafford after marrying into the wealthy Dorington family.[11] Matters took a turn for the worse in 1604, when bailiff John Towers, a man described by the town's coroner, Thomas Worswick, as irreligious and 'a common adulterer', caused the town acute embarrassment by being arrested by the county sheriff 'with the white staff in his hand'. By about 1610, Stafford's reputation for electing alehousekeepers as its bailiffs was widely lampooned by travelling players throughout the shire. The straw which broke the camel's back, however, was the announcement by Towers in 1612 that he would seek re-election, alongside Nicholas Seckerson *alias* Woodhouse, the keeper of an unruly alehouse. In vain a horrified group of Stafford's leading dignitaries, among them the Clement's Inn lawyer Richard Drakeford, tried to persuade Towers to withdraw as they were concerned that, having recently been outlawed, he would heap further disgrace on the town. It was not long before Towers and Seckerson, both of whom were elected, revealed themselves to be as incompetent and irresolute as Drakeford and his allies had feared. They countermanded each other's orders, failed to bind over one man who reviled them to their face, released a suspected horse thief and neglected to keep proper records.[12] This was all too much to bear, and in April 1613 the rest of the corporation resolved to petition the king for a new charter that would establish a better form of town government. In place of the single body of capital burgesses it was proposed to erect a corporation consisting of 11 aldermen and ten chief burgesses, and to replace the office of bailiff with that of mayor, whose holder would be elected annually from the ranks of the aldermen. All corporation members would be entitled to vote in mayoral elections, but the rest of the borough's freemen would be disfranchised. The recorder and six members of the corporation, including Drakeford, described by one of his colleagues as 'the primo motor of all this business',[13] were assigned to pursue the matter.

Over the next 12 months Drakeford and his allies aroused widespread hostility. The ordinary freemen naturally objected to the plan to disfranchise them, while those on the corporation who realized that they would not be appointed aldermen (and thus mayor) were equally vociferous, fearing perhaps, as Worswick alleged, that 'such men will be governors as will punish their disorders and idleness, suppress the multitude of alehouses and draw them and their children to spin and card'.[14] In July 1613 no less than 60 of the borough's 80 freemen petitioned the king to be allowed to retain their old charter.[15] At around the same time the widow of Sir Thomas Crompton[†], who nursed a personal grudge against one of the charter's key supporters, Matthew Cradock, notified the bishop of Coventry and Lichfield, Richard Neile, that a clause in the charter would, in effect, turn the parish of St. Mary, Stafford, into an ecclesiastical peculiar. Neile was furious and threatened to use his influence with the king to stop the charter dead in its tracks.[16] However, Drakeford and his friends had their own allies at Court, in particular the lord privy seal, the earl of Northampton, 'who above any others' they desired to be their high steward.[17] By cultivating Northampton and inserting a proviso to protect Neile's interests,[18] they smoothed the charter's passage. Meanwhile, back in Stafford, they suborned one of their principal opponents by adding his name to the list of prospective aldermen.[19] Consequently, in April 1614, despite a last-ditch opposition mounted by some of its former supporters in the wake of that year's parliamentary election (see below), the charter was finally enrolled. However, the difficulties associated with its passage had caused costs to spiral out of control, so that the final bill exceeded £300.[20] This sum lay quite beyond the town's own meagre resources, and were it not for the fact that Cradock, Worswick and (to a lesser extent) Drakeford pledged their own credit the charter would have proved unaffordable.[21]

Stafford had enjoyed the right to parliamentary representation from at least 1295. During the sixteenth century elections were dominated by two local noble families, the Staffords of Stafford Castle and the Devereux of Chartley. Consequently, no townsmen represented the borough in Parliament apart from the wool merchant Matthew Cradock the elder in 1554, and his son Francis, who served on four consecutive occasions between 1584 and 1593. This pattern of representation changed dramatically in 1604 as a result of the execution of the 2nd earl of Essex in 1601 and the death in October 1603 of the 3rd Lord Stafford (Edward Stafford I[†]). The 3rd earl of Essex was a minor, while the 4th Lord Stafford, who inherited a much diminished estate, proved unable or unwilling to exert the electoral influence formerly enjoyed by his father, leaving his kinsman Sir Edward Stafford, who had represented the borough in 1597 and 1601, to find a seat elsewhere. The borough's choice instead fell on the former bailiffs Hugh Beeston and George Cradock.

Following the death of Beeston in May 1608, the borough was again obliged to surrender one of its seats to an outsider. Elected in November 1609, Arthur Ingram had no known connection with Stafford and was almost certainly nominated by Robert Cecil[†], 1st earl of Salisbury, whose advocacy of the Great Contract led him to use his influence to return as many of his friends and supporters to the Commons as possible. At the next general election, in 1614, the borough again hoped to return Members without outside interference. It was widely expected that Matthew Cradock would sit, for having succeeded his father George in 1611 he was almost certainly the wealthiest man in the borough. The remaining place was set aside for John Cooper who, though neither a freeman nor a resident, was nephew to two of Stafford's leading corporation members, the grocer Richard Dorington and the stapler Thomas Cradock. Shortly before the election, however, the borough received letters of nomination from the earl of Northampton and the 3rd earl of Essex, who had now reached his majority, in favour of two strangers, Thomas Gibbs and Sir Walter Devereux. These letters have not survived, but it seems likely that Northampton nominated Gibbs and that Essex supported his Warwickshire kinsman, Devereux. Thomas Cradock responded by urging his fellow voters to disregard the earls' requests, 'saying it was ordinary to deny noblemen's letters'. However, Matthew Cradock announced that, in view of the earls' nominations, he would not be standing. He clearly understood that it would be dangerous and ungrateful to rebuff Northampton, whose support in the continuing charter negotiations remained crucial, and that it would also be unwise to upset their near neighbour Essex, who was, after all, only reasserting his family's traditional right of nomination. Thomas Cradock and Richard Dorington nevertheless refused to withdraw their backing from Cooper. In the ensuing contest the earls' candidates were elected, whereupon Cooper's sponsors threatened to prevent the passage of the new charter, despite having previously been among its keenest advocates.[22] However, by the time Dorington and Cooper reached London the charter had passed the great seal.[23]

Before the intervention of Northampton and Essex wrecked their carefully laid plans, Stafford's leaders had intended that the election result should reflect the balance of power between Matthew Cradock and Richard Dorington, the two most substantial men in the borough. In the event this balance was not achieved until the next parliamentary election, which was held in November 1620. Cradock, now recorder, was elected to the senior seat while the junior place was conferred on Dorington's son-in-law, the Lichfield lawyer Richard Dyott, who had settled in Stafford after his marriage in 1615. Essex, who had replaced Northampton as the borough's high steward on the latter's death in June 1614, evidently failed to send the borough a letter of nomination, probably because he was then serving in the Palatinate. This result was repeated at the general election of January 1624, although Cradock had by then lost the recordership to Dyott after falling out with his corporation colleagues over the use of his malt mill. However, the outcome was questioned by an unsuccessful challenger for the second seat, Sir William Walter, a Surrey resident but a friend of the earl of Essex's steward, William Wingfield*.[24] Walter claimed to have received more voices than Dyott, whom he accused of securing his return 'upon promise of saving the mayor harmless'. His complaint was duly investigated by the privileges committee, which said nothing about the distribution of votes but found that the election had indeed been flawed, 'for the warning was given but at seven or eight of the clock in the morning, and within an hour or two they went to election, and of about 120 burgesses in the whole there were 24 absent'. The man responsible for this irregularity appears to have been none other than Richard Dorington, who had unexpectedly produced the precept from the sheriff during a meeting of the town council. In view of these findings, the Commons had little choice but to invalidate the entire election, thereby depriving Cradock as well as Dyott of his seat, although there was no suggestion that he had acted improperly.[25] However, a fresh election held at the beginning of April merely confirmed the earlier result.

In 1625 Matthew Cradock retained the senior borough seat. Richard Dorington, on the other hand, briefly lost control of the junior place as Richard Dyott, though still recorder, preferred to represent Lichfield, where he had lived since the death of his father in 1622. The vacancy was filled, not by another of Dorington's relatives, but by the archbishop of Canterbury's steward, (Sir) Robert Hatton, who lived in Kent. It is not clear by what route Hatton secured election, but it may be significant that the bishop of Coventry and Lichfield, Thomas Morton, had once been a house guest of his late brother, Sir Christopher Hatton*.[26] Another possibility is that Hatton was nominated by the earl of Essex, a former comrade in arms of the 18th earl of Oxford, with whom the Hattons were closely connected. In the event, Hatton decided to represent Sandwich, where he had also been elected, enabling Dorington to reassert his interest. Hatton's replacement was Sir John Offley of Madeley, in north-west Staffordshire, whose ancestors had

originated in Stafford. Although the borough continued to benefit from a couple of charitable bequests left by members of his family in the sixteenth century, Offley was loosely connected to Dorington through Richard Dyott, having in 1619 presented Dyott's younger brother Robert to the Staffordshire rectory of Darlaston. In 1640 Dyott would, in turn, be a party to the contract drawn up on the marriage of Offley's eldest daughter, Elizabeth.[27]

Offley was not only re-elected in January 1626 but advanced to the senior seat. His progression was made possible because Matthew Cradock, who also served as clerk of the assize for the Oxfordshire circuit, decided not to stand, but to assign his interest to the young Bulstrode Whitelocke, the son of his colleague, the assize judge (Sir) James Whitelocke*. Cradock resumed his tenure of the senior seat in 1628, though by this time had settled ten miles away, at Caverswall Castle. Cradock's junior partner that year was William Wingfield, Essex's steward, who undoubtedly owed his return to his employer. Essex had failed to exert any influence over the previous two elections, probably because he was abroad when these were held. The return of Wingfield may have disappointed Sir Edward Littleton II, who had represented the county in 1624, as he may have approached Stafford for a seat. Certainly the borough's accounts record that a letter was sent to him 'concerning the choice of a burgess for the Parliament'.[28]

[1] OR. [2] VCH Staffs. vi. 186; HP Commons 1386-1422, i. 610. [3] K.R. Adey, 'Seventeenth-Cent. Stafford', Midland Hist. ii. 152-4, 166. Annual income based on accounts for 1612, as this is one of the few years for which both bailiffs' and chamberlains' accounts survive: Staffs. RO, D1323/E1, ff. 62r-4v, 70v-1v. [4] VCH Staffs. vi. 215. [5] E. Kerridge, Textile Manufactures in Early Modern Eng. 21; VCH Staffs. vi. 186, 216. [6] VCH Staffs. vi. 201; 'Expenses of Judges of Assize' ed. W.D. Cooper, Cam. Misc. IV (Cam. Soc. o.s. lxxiii), 53-7; J.S. Cockburn, Hist. of English Assizes, 35; M. Nicholls, Investigating Gunpowder Plot, 73. [7] VCH Staffs. vi. 215; Staffs. RO, D1323/E/1, f. 111. [8] J. Nichols, Progs. of Jas. I, iii. 414, 416; Staffs. RO, D1323/E/1, f. 89. [9] VCH Staffs. vi. 222-3; T.J. Davies, 'Ancient Stafford', Birmingham Arch. Soc. Trans. xlv. 147; Charters of Stafford ed. J.W. Bradley, 108-32. Bradley mis-dates the charter to 1606. [10] Staffs. RO, D(W)1721/1/4, f. 27v (2nd numbering). [11] Ibid. f. 40. [12] Ibid. ff. 12-13v, 134. Shortly after they left office they were amerced for their offences. [13] Ibid. ff. 14r-v, 16. [14] Ibid. ff. 22v, 24r-v. [15] Ibid. f. 23r-v. [16] Ibid. ff. 18r-v, 23, 38. [17] Ibid. f. 18v. [18] Ibid. f. 27. [19] Ibid. ff. 29r-v, 30v. [20] Ibid. ff. 11v, 29r-v. [21] Ibid. ff. 20v-1, 112-13. [22] Ibid. f. 37r-v. [23] Ibid. f. 43. [24] PROB 11/164, f. 137. [25] J. Glanville, Reps. of Certain Cases (1775), 25-7; 'Earle 1624', ff. 47, 91; CJ, i. 745b. [26] DNB sub Morton. [27] PRO, Institution Bks. ser. A, iv. 15; C2/Chas.I/O11/40. [28] Staffs. RO, D1323/E/1, f. 162. We are grateful to Matthew Blake for this ref.

A.D.T.

TAMWORTH

Right of election: in the corporation

Number of voters: 24

1 Mar. 1604	SIR PERCIVAL WILLOUGHBY SIR JOHN FERRERS
27 Mar. 1604	SIR THOMAS BEAUMONT II *vice* Willoughby, chose to sit for Nottinghamshire
1614	SIR THOMAS ROE SIR PERCIVAL WILLOUGHBY
28 Dec. 1620	SIR THOMAS PUCKERING, bt. JOHN FERRAR
22 Jan. 1624	JOHN WOODFORD JOHN WIGHTWICK
13 May 1625	SIR THOMAS PUCKERING, bt. SIR RICHARD SKEFFINGTON
20 Jan. 1626	SIR THOMAS PUCKERING, bt. (SIR) WALTER DEVEREUX
16 Feb. 1628	SIR THOMAS PUCKERING, bt. (SIR) WALTER DEVEREUX

Situated at the confluence of the rivers Tame and Anker, Tamworth was a Saxon foundation once favoured as a residence by the monarchs of Mercia. It was fairly small, even by early modern standards: by 1640 around 300 households clustered around its privately owned castle.[1] Little is known of its economy, but by 1589 several inhabitants had erected corn mills to compete with those already there belonging to the queen.[2] During the early seventeenth century Tamworth was considered a centre for recusancy. Its most prominent recusant was Humphrey Comberford, of the Moat House, in Lichfield Street. In 1606 Comberford's property was searched after it was rumoured that seminary priests had resorted to his house. This led to the apprehension of three strangers, and to the discovery of a surplice, vestments and several popish books, all hidden under a bed.[3] In 1626 Tamworth experienced a severe outbreak of plague, but neighbouring areas proved reluctant to contribute towards emergency poor relief.[4] The borough received royal visits in 1619, 1621 and 1624, but details of these are scanty.[5]

Tamworth straddled the Staffordshire and Warwickshire border. Until 1560 both parts of the town enjoyed their own self-government, but in that year they were brought under one jurisdiction by a charter of incorporation, which created a governing body of 26 capital burgesses, of whom two were to be elected annually as bailiffs.[6] Despite its incorporation, the borough continued to enjoy a curiously schizophrenic existence. Each bailiff was chosen from different sides of the town and at parliamentary elections the borough made two returns. Under Elizabeth one Member served for the Warwickshire side of the town, while the other represented the Staffordshire side.[7] By 1604 the notion that each Member represented a different part of the town had broken down. Nevertheless the sheriffs of both Warwickshire and Staffordshire continued to receive separate writs and to make separate returns, even in the case of the second March 1604 election, which concerned only one of the borough's two seats.[8]

Before its incorporation, Tamworth lacked parliamentary representation. The charter itself did not change this situation, but perhaps emboldened by its new-found status, in 1563 two Members were dispatched to Westminster; thereafter the borough enjoyed the franchise by prescription. Voting was restricted to members of the corporation. In 1640 Tamworth's householders complained that they too 'ought to have their voices in the election of the burgesses', but significantly they did not claim that they had ever actually exercised this right. When, in 1669, it was suggested that the commonalty was entitled to vote, the committee for privileges ruled that the franchise lay exclusively in the corporation.[9]

Under Elizabeth, control of Tamworth's parliamentary seats lay largely in the hands of the owner of nearby Drayton Bassett manor. Before 1588 this interest was exercised by Robert Dudley, earl of Leicester; thereafter it passed to his step-son Robert Devereux, 2nd earl of Essex. In 1586 Sir Humphrey Ferrers of Tamworth Castle, the borough's hereditary high steward, exploited Leicester's absence in the Netherlands by obtaining the junior seat for his son John. Mindful of this intrusion, Leicester's successor, Essex, had himself named high steward of Tamworth by the queen in 1588. At the same time, he obtained both parliamentary seats for his nominees. Essex was subsequently forced to share control of the constituency with Ferrers, however, following the marriage of John Ferrers to a daughter of the lord keeper (John Puckering[†]). On the earl's execution in February 1601, the Drayton Bassett interest temporarily fell into abeyance.

In 1604 Sir John Ferrers took the junior seat. The senior burgess-ship was conferred on Sir Percival Willoughby, whose property at Middleton lay five miles from Tamworth in Warwickshire. Willoughby subsequently plumped for Nottinghamshire, but nominated in his stead Sir Thomas Beaumont II, the cousin of his colliery manager. At the following general election Willoughby again came in for Tamworth, having given way at Nottinghamshire to Sir Gervase Clifton. His fellow Member was Sir Thomas Roe, whose patrimony lay in Gloucestershire. Roe is not known to have been connected to either Ferrers or the young 3rd earl of Essex, who was by now active as a parliamentary patron. By the time of the elections to the third Jacobean Parliament, Willoughby was so impoverished that he probably could not afford to stand again. He might otherwise have stood a good chance of securing a seat, as Essex was then serving as a volunteer in the Palatinate. Essex's absence, and Willoughby's financial difficulties, meant that Ferrers can have encountered little difficulty in obtaining the senior seat for his brother-in-law, Sir Thomas Puckering. The junior seat was bestowed on an outsider, John Ferrar, deputy governor of the Virginia Company. Ferrar may have been nominated by his fellow Virginia Company member William, 5th Lord Paget, whose seat at Beaudesert lay four miles north-west of Lichfield. In 1624 the electoral situation echoed that of 1593 and 1597, when the Devereux and Ferrers' interests had shared the nominations. Essex put in John Woodford, secretary to his cousin by marriage, the earl of Carlisle, while Ferrers, unable to select Puckering, who was serving as sheriff of Warwickshire, nominated his lawyer, John Wightwick.

Essex was again abroad at the general election of 1625. This may have left the way clear for Ferrers to fill both seats. Puckering took the senior place, and the junior burgess-ship was bestowed upon Sir Richard Skeffington, who may have been connected to Ferrers through his fellow Coventry resident, John Wightwick. Essex returned to England in the summer of 1625 and resumed his role as a parliamentary patron. In both 1626 and 1628 he returned his half-brother (Sir) Walter Devereux, who was no longer able to find a place at Pembroke Boroughs. Ferrers, meanwhile, continued to oblige Puckering with the senior seat.

[1] C.F. Palmer, *Hist. Tamworth*, app. p. xxvii. [2] H. Wood, *Tamworth Bor. Recs.* 11. [3] M.B. Rowlands, 'Catholics in 1676', in *English Catholics of Par. and Town 1558-1778* ed. M.B. Rowlands (Cath. Rec. Soc. monograph ser. v), 105; *HMC Hatfield*, xviii. 172-3. [4] Palmer, 121; *Warwick County Recs. I: Q.S. Order Bk. 1625-37* ed. S.C. Ratcliffe and H.C. Johnson, 43. [5] J. Nicholas, *Progs. of Jas. I*, iii. 561; iv. 713, 995. [6] *CPR*, 1560-3, pp. 7-8. [7] *HP Commons 1558-1603*, i. 245. [8] C219/35/2/47-8, 59, 92-3. [9] D.G. Stuart, 'Parliamentary Hist. of Tamworth, 1661-1837', (Univ. of London M.A. thesis, 1958), p. 40.

A.D.T.

SUFFOLK

27 Feb. 1604	SIR JOHN HEIGHAM
	SIR ROBERT DRURY[1]
c. Mar. 1614	SIR THOMAS JERMYN
	SIR ROBERT GARDENER
11 Dec. 1620	SIR ROBERT CRANE
	THOMAS CLENCH
	Sir Lionel Tollemache, bt.
2 Feb. 1624	SIR WILLIAM SPRING
	SIR ROGER NORTH
25 Apr. 1625	SIR EDMUND BACON, bt.
	THOMAS CORNWALLIS I
30 Jan. 1626	(SIR) ROBERT NAUNTON
	SIR ROBERT CRANE
25 Feb. 1628[2]	SIR EDWARD COKE
	SIR NATHANIEL BARNARDISTON
Apr. 1628	SIR WILLIAM SPRING *vice* Coke, chose to sit for Buckinghamshire

The divided administrative geography of Suffolk reflected the privileges enjoyed in medieval times by two great monastic foundations. The eight-and-a-half hundreds of West Suffolk formed the franchise of Bury St. Edmunds, while the eastern half of the county was divided between the liberty of St. Audry, or St. Etheldred, and the 'geldable'. Stowmarket was the most centrally situated town in Suffolk, and it was here that the county's deputy lieutenants usually met; but, lying off the main roads, it failed to develop facilities for large gatherings.[3] The quarter sessions were divided between four towns – Bury St. Edmunds, Beccles, Woodbridge, and Ipswich – and it was at the latter, in the south-east of the county, that shire elections were always held, giving a disproportionate weight to the puritan townsmen under the influence of such notable preachers as Samuel Ward.[4] In 1624 the corporation employed 14 labourers to clear snow from a hill in preparation for the county election. The following year, although the election was held in the spring, it was moved indoors, probably to the Ipswich town hall.[5]

In addition to its administrative divisions, Suffolk was divided economically between the long-enclosed agriculture of the east and the open champaign country of the franchise. Moreover, Ipswich and Aldeburgh were important ports: in 1621 Thomas Clench, the only knight of the shire from a coastal parish in the early Stuart Parliaments, told the Commons that 'above 3,000 men upon the coast of Suffolk' earned their livelihood from fishing.[6] Furthermore, the Stour valley, in the south of the county, was a major centre for the production of new draperies. Sir Robert Crane, who lived in that part of the county, may have owed his electoral success, in part, to his advocacy of the interests of the clothing interests in the Commons.[7]

The eastern half of the county was almost certainly the wealthiest part of Suffolk. The geldable division was traditionally assessed to pay half of county rates, the franchise of Bury St. Edmunds a third and the liberty of St Audrey's a sixth.[8] Nevertheless, of the 13 Members elected in the period only four were resident in east Suffolk. The imbalance may partly be attributed to the greater number of borough seats available for the gentry of the geldable, but was probably mostly due to the greater cohesion among the west Suffolk gentry. Drawing up his will in 1614, Sir Robert Jermyn[†] of Rushbrooke wrote of his neighbours, Sir Nicholas Bacon[†] of Culford, Sir Robert Gardener of Elmswell and Sir John Heigham of Barrow: 'we have lived together in sweet and Christian society, and by our unity have much furthered the peace and profit of our country in the administration of justice and other public duties'.[9] In 1620 this unity was reflected in a pre-election meeting of the western gentry held at Bury St. Edmunds. One reason for this cohesiveness was doubtless that Jermyn and his friends were all generally puritan, a fact which may have won them the support of the Ipswich townsmen.[10]

In 1604 Jermyn's friend Heigham was returned with Sir Robert Drury who, aside from being a soldier, courtier and aspiring diplomat, was also Sir Nicholas Bacon's son-in-law. Ill health caused Heigham to be absent from the Commons for much of 1610 and, although he survived until 1626, he does not seem to have sought re-election. Drury, on the other hand, proved happy to serve again. In February 1614 he wrote to Sir Robert Cotton* that he would willingly sit for a borough and leave the county seat to 'some younger spirit which may be ambitious of it' in the forthcoming Parliament, but as the outcome of an approach to Thetford had proved unproductive Cotton was asked to approach Henry Howard, earl of Northampton, on his behalf so that, if 'forced to seek a knightship of the shire', Northampton 'will do me the favour to let his tenants know his favour to me'. However, to avoid appearing too solicitous, Drury hastened to add that the voters should be left to 'their own disposition, as in the general I think it honest and honourable for every man to proceed no otherwise'.[11]

In the event, Drury found a place at Eye, leaving the shire seats to Jermyn's son, Sir Thomas, and another of Sir Robert Jermyn's friends, Sir Robert Gardener.

Gardener and Drury died before the next election, in 1620, by which time Bacon and Heigham were both in their eighties. By 14 Nov. Sir Robert Crane, who had been brought up in the Jermyn household, had been adopted at a meeting of the gentry of the franchise at Bury. Crane subsequently sent a circular to the freeholders of west Suffolk to inform them of his (almost certainly feigned) reluctant acceptance of the nomination and to give his assurance that he would 'omit no opportunity wherein I may show a requital' were he to be elected.[12]

On 23 Nov. Crane's father-in-law, Sir Henry Hobart, informed Crane that he had asked Sir Henry North[†], the outgoing sheriff of Suffolk, to keep the writ in his hands, presumably to give Crane time to canvass the county, only to find that the writ had already been sent to North's successor, Sir William Spring. North, who had died three days previously had, however, apparently told Hobart that the next county court was not due for more than a fortnight, giving Crane 'leisure to make your means'.[13] Six days later Samuel Ward, the Ipswich preacher, notified Crane 'of the good affection and inclination of town and country' towards the latter's nomination. Ward added that 'it is here generally wished you incline your mind and voices of such as you bring with you to the election of a sufficient and suitable colleague', perhaps as a warning to Crane not to ally himself with anyone who would alienate his godly supporters.[14] Joseph Mead subsequently reported that Ward had preached that 'a religious care was to be taken in such elections, and heed to be taken of such as were of suspected affection to our religion'.[15]

Crane's supporters included Sir Robert Hitcham, a prominent east Suffolk lawyer. On 10 Dec. Hitcham wrote to Crane informing him that, having written letters on his behalf to Ipswich (where he lived) and the surrounding villages, he had been 'certainly informed the first voice will be yielded to you [Crane] without competition'. Now his thoughts were turning to the question of Crane's colleague, not least because he had been 'earnestly entreated by one of especial rank' to win support for 'Sir L.', probably the county's vice-admiral Sir Lionel Tollemache, for the second place. The 'person of especial rank' may have been Tollemache's superior, the marquess of Buckingham, who was lord admiral. In fact, Tollemache had already, at his own suggestion, paired with Crane, to whom he wrote on 6 Dec. stating that the sheriff had decided to hold the election the following Monday. 'I hear not of any that will stand against us', he declared, before offering to provide a supper at Ipswich the night before the election for the sheriff and Crane, presumably to arrange the following day's events.[16] However, late in the day a new candidate emerged. Thomas Clench, an east Suffolk lawyer with strong links to Ipswich, was connected to the puritan sheriff, Spring, his eldest son having married the niece of Spring's former step-father, Sir Robert Gardener. Despite the belated nature of his candidacy, Clench went on to secure the second seat alongside Crane. Among the parties to the indenture were Clench's son-in-law, Sir Roger North; John Clench (either a son or brother); Sir Henry Glemham*; Brampton Gurdon*; and Robert Snelling, the last having just secured his re-election for Ipswich.[17] A doubtless disappointed Tollemache was subsequently returned for Orford and Sir Thomas Jermyn for the newly enfranchised Bury St. Edmunds.

As the first untitled knight of the shire in this period, as well as the first easterner, Clench, who was not a young man, probably entertained no further political ambitions. He may have proposed Sir Roger North as his successor for the county in 1624, but he died before the year was out. Crane was returned for the borough of Sudbury in 1624 and North was returned by another zealous puritan sheriff, Sir Nathaniel Barnardiston, with Spring as his senior partner.

In 1625 North and Spring sat for Eye and Bury St. Edmunds respectively, while Crane and Jermyn were re-elected for Sudbury and Bury St. Edmunds. The senior knight of the shire in the first Parliament of the new reign was Sir Nicholas Bacon's son, Sir Edmund, while the occupant of the junior seat was Thomas Cornwallis I of Earl Soham. Cornwallis had been added to the county bench less than a year before, but his role as executor of the estate of Sir Michael Stanhope, a prominent Suffolk courtier, seems to have propelled him into the front rank of county society. Cornwallis may also have benefited from the fact that he lived at Ipswich; certainly the strong Calvinist piety evident from his will must have won him the support of the town's puritans.[18] The return of Bacon and Cornwallis meant that, for once, the franchise of the Liberty of Bury St. Edmunds could claim neither Member as a resident, Bacon having left Culford to a younger brother and established himself at Redgrave in east Suffolk.

In the second Caroline Parliament Suffolk was the only county to be represented by a privy councillor. Sir Robert Naunton, the master of the Court of Wards, had inherited and enlarged a modest estate in east Suffolk, but since boyhood he had only occasionally resided there, and he had never held county office. His candidacy was first proposed by Brampton Gurdon, a west Suffolk puritan, who quickly won the support of his neighbour, John Winthrop, later governor of Massachusetts. In a letter to Sir Robert Crane, Winthrop argued that Naunton was eminently suitable for election, having 'suffered for the commonwealth', a reference to Naunton's disgrace in 1621 for proposing a French alternative to the Spanish Match. Winthrop also pointed out 'the favour and help' that 'such an honourable person may be in the causes of our country, especially for our clothiers', and asked Crane to propound Naunton's candidacy 'to the other gentlemen at sessions'. This was a reference to the quarter sessions, which were presumably then being held at Bury St. Edmunds, where Winthrop's letter to Crane was directed.[19]

Naunton's nomination met with a cool reception from the corporation of Bury St. Edmunds, who objected that Sir Robert 'was tied in so particular an obligation to His Majesty as if there were occasion to speak for the country he would be silent, and in general they would give no voice to any courtiers especially at this time of all others'. For this reason Crane, in his reply to Winthrop, recommended that Naunton should not 'proceed ... any further lest he should suffer in it'. However, he assured Winthrop that he was 'ready to afford him what success lieth in my power'. Despite these doubts, Naunton was returned on 30 Jan. alongside Crane himself. Winthrop and Gurdon were both parties to the indenture and the former was subsequently appointed one of the attorneys in the Court of Wards.[20]

In December 1626 Naunton was one of the privy councillors sent to execute the Forced Loan in Suffolk, where resistance was led by Sir Nathaniel Barnardiston and two sons of Sir Edward Coke*, who had acquired an estate in the north-east of the county.[21] Following the 1628 election, which he attended, Winthrop wrote to his eldest son that 'what our success was you may know by my letter to either of your uncles', but quite what this means is unclear, as neither of the letters referred to have survived.[22] According to John Wilson, a puritan lecturer at Sudbury, 'the country' wanted to elect Sir William Spring and Sir Nathaniel Barnardiston, but Spring seems to have refused to stand, and the county, 'not without a kind of unwillingness, gave way to the other, whom yet they thought it would be a heinous thing to refuse'.[23]

The 'other' was the renowned jurist and parliamentarian Sir Edward Coke, who had long owned property in the county. Sir Martin Stuteville, a Suffolk knight who had been a party to the 1624 indenture, complained that Coke's election 'is against the express words of the statute which said the electors and elected must be residing in the same shire at the time of the date of the writ', and as a consequence refused to have anything to do with it.[24] A correspondent of Edward Nicholas*, clerk of the Privy Council, wrote that 'there was not ten gentleman at this election ..., neither was there the tenth man [present] which formerly there had been', and it was thought that had more of the Suffolk gentry turned up Coke and Barnardiston would not have been elected, 'for neither the town of Ipswich had any great affection to either of them nor yet most of the country'.[25]

Coke had also been returned for Buckinghamshire, and therefore on 28 Mar. he waived his Suffolk seat: a writ for a fresh election was issued on 2 April.[26] This time Spring was persuaded to stand, but Sir John Rous I*, a member of the east Suffolk gentry, was also proposed by William Cage*, Member for Ipswich. Rous, Spring thought, was sure to be able to 'sway that town' [Ipswich], whose inhabitants were likely to be 'the strongest if not sole actors in it'. Spring suggested an approach to Samuel Ward 'or some of that town' to find a compromise candidate. However, Spring's concerns were misplaced. When Sir Francis Barrington, the senior Essex knight of the shire, proposed an unnamed candidate to John Wilson, the Sudbury lecturer, the latter replied that 'the eyes of the country for ought I can learn are bent on Sir William Spring' and that the 'justices and gentlemen all have pitched upon this said knight (so much as lieth in them)'. Whether Ward intervened or not, it is likely that, faced with this formidable opposition, Rous was persuaded not to stand. The date of the election is unknown, but Spring had taken his seat in the Commons by 5 May.[27]

[1] *Life and Letters of John Winthrop* ed. R.C. Winthrop, i. 419. [2] Ibid. 249-50. [3] *HMC 13th Rep. IV*, 438. [4] *CSP Dom.* 1628-9, p. 478; C219/37/233; 219/38/223; 219/40/176; C. Thompson, 'New Light on the Suff. Elections to the Parl. of 1628', *Suff. Review*, n.s. x. 22. [5] Suffolk RO (Ipswich), C/3/2/1/2, ff. 317v, 323v. [6] *CJ*, i. 588b. [7] *HMC 13th Rep. IV*, 439-40; Nicholas, *Procs. 1621*, ii. 255. [8] *HMC 13th Rep. IV*, 433. [9] *Rushbrook Par. Regs.* ed. S.H.A. Hervey, 153. [10] W.S. Appleton, *Mems. of Cranes of Chilton*, 69. [11] A.R. Campling, *Hist. of Fam. of Drury*, 62. [12] Bodl., Tanner 69, f. 151; Appleton, 69. [13] Bodl., Tanner 290, f. 54. [14] Ibid. f. 37. [15] T. Birch, *Ct. and Times of Jas. I*, ii. 232. [16] Bodl., Tanner 69, f. 150. [17] C219/37/233; *Frag. Gen.* xii. 126. [18] PROB 11/151, f. 465. [19] Appleton, 75-6. [20] *Winthrop Pprs.* i. 326; C219/40/176; Oxford *DNB* sub Winthrop, John. [21] *APC*, 1626, pp. 426-7. [22] *Life and Letters of John Winthrop*, i. 249. [23] Thompson, 19, 21-2, 24. [24] *Procs. 1628*, vi. 167; C219/38/223. [25] *Procs. 1628*, vi. 148. [26] Ibid. ii. 169; C231/4, f. 243. [27] Thompson, 21-4; Harl. 378, f. 29v.

J.P.F./B.C.

ALDEBURGH

Right of election: ?in the inhabitants

Number of voters: 11 in 1610[1]

4 Mar. 1604	SIR WILLIAM WOODHOUSE
	THOMAS RIVETT
	ALEXANDER BENCE (elected on a separate indenture with Rivett but evidently not retured)[2]
24 Apr. 1610	SIR JOHN GREY vice Rivett, deceased
21 Mar. 1614[3]	SIR WILLIAM WOODHOUSE
	SIR HENRY GLEMHAM
20 Dec. 1620	SIR HENRY GLEMHAM
	CHARLES GLEMHAM
22 Jan. 1624	NICHOLAS RIVETT
	JOHN BENCE
15 Apr. 1625	SIR THOMAS GLEMHAM
	CHARLES GLEMHAM
19 Jan. 1626	SIR THOMAS GLEMHAM
	WILLIAM MASON
c. Mar. 1628[4]	SIR SIMEON STEWARD
	MARMADUKE RAWDON

Of the three coastal boroughs of Suffolk, only Aldeburgh retained any economic significance in the seventeenth century. Coastal erosion, which had swept away the greater part of Dunwich and blocked access to Orford, left it open to the sea with deep water at hand. Ships of 200 tons and upwards were built, a fishing fleet of 50 or 60 sail was dispatched every year to Icelandic waters and the Westmann Isles, and the port claimed a share in the Newcastle coal trade.[5]

Aldeburgh was contained within one parish, which, according to the corporation, had 'above 1,000 communicants' in the early 1640s.[6] There were no municipal institutions in the Middle Ages and consequently the town was still under manorial government at the start of the sixteenth century. At the Dissolution of the Monasteries Thomas Howard, 3rd duke of Norfolk, acquired the manor of Aldeburgh, which was forfeited to the Crown on his attainder in 1546. The following year a charter was issued conferring borough status on the town and establishing a corporation consisting of two annually elected bailiffs and an unspecified number of burgesses.[7] Norfolk was restored in 1553, and it was probably his son, the 4th duke, who secured the borough's enfranchisement in 1571. However, Howard influence in the borough was curtailed by the duke's execution for treason the following year. Subsequently members of the prominent local merchant families, such as the Bences and the Johnsons, provided representatives for the borough in Elizabethan Parliaments along with the local gentry.[8] Shortly after the accession of James I the manor was granted to the fourth duke's younger sons, Thomas, 1st earl of Suffolk and Lord William Howard, who subsequently made it over to their nephew, Thomas, earl of Arundel.[9]

In 1606 a new charter created a more sophisticated urban structure. Ten capital burgesses were named, including three Bences and one Johnson, who, together with the bailiffs, formed the common council. The capital burgesses served for life and were recruited from a body of 24 inferior burgesses. The charter also provided for a recorder, and Robert Barker*, the son of a Suffolk clothier, was named as the first incumbent.[10]

Returns were usually made in the name of the bailiffs and burgesses, although that of 1625 also included the commonalty. The latter document also states that the election took place at the town hall, by which was presumably meant the early sixteenth-century 'Moot Hall'. Generally only the bailiffs were specifically named, although in the return for the 1610 by-election nine other names were included, these being of those ostensibly described as 'burgesses': all but one had been appointed either bailiff or capital burgess in the 1606 charter. The identity of these signatories suggests that in practice the common council controlled elections.[11]

In 1604 two election indentures were drawn up and survive among the borough archives, both dated 4 March. In one the successful candidates are given as Thomas Rivett, a west Suffolk squire, and Alexander Bence, whose brother William had represented the borough in the Elizabethan period. In the other those chosen are named as Sir William Woodhouse, a courtier connected with the Howards, and Rivett.[12] Duplicates of neither survive among the Chancery returns, but it was clearly Woodhouse and Rivett who took their seats in the Commons.[13] It is possible that both indentures were submitted to Chancery, but there is no record of a ruling by the Commons on the election and, in the aftermath of the Buckinghamshire election dispute, it is unlikely that Chancery suppressed the Rivett/Bence return on its own initiative. It is more probable that only the Woodhouse/Rivett indenture was returned.

The most likely scenario is that Rivett and Bence were the original choices, their indenture being signed by the sheriff, but that subsequently the borough received a nomination in favour of Woodhouse, probably from the new lord of the manor, the earl of Suffolk. The corporation persuaded Bence to stand aside, whereupon they quietly suppressed the first election and drew up a new, backdated return.[14]

On Rivett's death in 1610 Sir John Grey, his kinsman as well as a courtier and friend of Woodhouse's, filled the vacancy. Alexander Bence, who had been listed first among the capital burgesses in the 1606 charter, was a party to the return.[15] Woodhouse was re-elected in 1614, but by this date Grey had died. Instead the borough returned Sir Henry Glemham, an important local member of the Suffolk gentry and one of the earl of Suffolk's deputy lieutenants.

The earl of Arundel was almost certainly in possession of the manor by 1620, when he nominated both Glemham and the latter's courtier kinsman Charles Glemham. Charles Glemham was doubtless the son of Edward Glemham, who had been employed by the earl's father to manage his Suffolk estates. After the 1621 Parliament Sir Henry seems to have shown no inclination to serve again, and at the next election Arundel nominated Charles Glemham and a certain 'R.G.', probably another member of the Glemham family, as 'men worthy of your choice, who shall willingly serve you at their own charge'.[16] However, Aldeburgh preferred to return Rivett's cousin Nicholas, who by this date had succeeded Barker as recorder, and Bence's son John. The latter was a prominent member of the corporation and was the only Aldeburgh Member known to have been paid in this period, receiving £18 14s. 8d. for 'his charges when he was burgess at the Parliament' in June 1625.[17]

Arundel seems to have been more successful in 1625 when Sir Henry's son, Sir Thomas, took the senior seat with Charles Glemham (who died soon after the dissolution) as his colleague. Sir Thomas Glemham was re-elected in 1626, this time alongside William Mason, an official of the King's Bench and friend of the attorney-general, (Sir) Robert Heath*. Mason had settled in Suffolk, but had no discernable interest in Aldeburgh of his own. It is possible that he owed his election to Arundel as in the same year the earl nominated another friend of Heath's, Nicholas Jordan, at Arundel.[18]

Aldeburgh suffered heavy losses in the wars of the late 1620s. The corporation submitted a list of 13 vessels wrecked (two of them in the king's service) or taken by the Dunkirkers between 1625 and 1627, with a loss of 200 men and £6,800. They were granted a convoy for their fishing fleet for the 1627 season and ten pieces of ordnance for the defence of the town.[19]

There is no evidence that Sir Thomas Glemham sought re-election in 1628, by which date Mason was dead. Arundel may have nominated Sir Simeon Steward, the brother-in-law of Sir Thomas Monson*, the disgraced former client of the earl of Suffolk, while the junior seat was taken by an enterprising London merchant, Marmaduke Rawdon, who had connections among the Aldeburgh sea captains.[20] Both Steward and Rawdon came to Aldeburgh at about the time of the election, possibly to be made free. On 12 June the corporation celebrated the king's acceptance of the Petition of Right by paying 5s. 'for ringing for joy for good news from the Parliament'.[21]

[1] C219/35/2/55. [2] HMC Var. iv. 304. [3] Ibid. [4] 'Aldeburgh. Extracts from chamberlain's acct. bk.' ed. A.T. Winn N and Q (ser. 12), viii. 387. [5] CSP Dom. 1625-6, pp. 530, 532; APC, 1627, p. 2; HMC Var. iv. 290. [6] HMC Var. iv. 307 [7] CPR, 1548-9, p. 106. [8] W.A. Copinger, Manors of Suff. v. 95-6; HMC Var. iv. 279, 281; HP Commons, 1558-1603, i. 246-7. [9] Add. 19100, f. 91v; Copinger, 96. [10] C66/1708, mm. 23-8. [11] C219/35/2/56; 219/37/239; 219/39/192; R. Tittler, Architecture and Power, 34; C66/1708, m. 24. [12] HMC Var. iv. 304; C78/363/5. [13] H. Hulme, 'Corrections and additions to the Official 'Return' of Members of Parliament, 1603/4', BIHR, v. 103; CJ, i. 154b. [14] Copinger, v. 96. [15] C219/35/2/55; C66/1708, m. 24. [16] SP14/135/42; APC, 1587-8, p. 161. [17] 'Aldeburgh. Extracts from chamberlain's acct. bk.', 225 [18] Arundel, autograph letters 1617-32, Peers to Spiller, 16 Jan. 1626. [19] HMC Var. iv. 290-4; APC, 1627, pp. 2-3; 1627-8, p. 183; CSP Dom. 1625-6, p. 226. [20] CSP Dom. 1628-9, p. 197. [21] Suff. RO (Ipswich), EE1/I2/2, f. 50; 'Aldeburgh. Extracts from chamberlain's acct. bk.', 387-8.

J.P.F./B.C.

BURY ST. EDMUNDS

Right of election: in the corporation

Number of voters: 37

2 Jan. 1621	SIR THOMAS JERMYN	
	JOHN WOODFORD	
2 Feb. 1624	SIR THOMAS JERMYN	
	ANTHONY CROFTS	
25 Apr. 1625	SIR THOMAS JERMYN	
	SIR WILLIAM SPRING	
11 Jan. 1626	SIR THOMAS JERMYN	
	EMMANUEL GIFFARD	
c. Feb. 1628	SIR THOMAS JERMYN	
	SIR WILLIAM HERVEY II	

The town of Bury St. Edmunds, having grown up around a Benedictine abbey founded before the Conquest, not only survived but flourished after the Dissolution of the Monasteries, retaining its position as the venue of assizes and quarter sessions and the capital of West Suffolk.[1] Though distant from any navigable waterways, Bury boasted a thriving market, and was known as 'a great malting place', where beer was brewed far above strength 'to the extraordinary waste of malt and wheat', and 300 alehouses found willing customers at 8d. a gallon (four times the statutory price).[2] The town, noted by Bishop Bancroft for its firm alliance between 'magistracy and ministry', leaned towards puritan nonconformity; it was in a sermon preached there in 1599 that the term 'Sabbatarian' was coined.[3] The strong religious views of many leading inhabitants fostered a spirit of independence, as Sir Robert Jermyn[†] wrote to Sir Robert Cecil[†] in 1601, 'the townsmen of Bury, being mechanical and tradesmen, thirst for a corporation, not only to draw unto themselves their popular government ... but also to exempt themselves from the common charges of the country, which now, being rich and able, they are subject to'.[4] Their efforts are recorded in a memoranda book kept by one Thomas Bright, who held meetings at his house and raised subscriptions totalling £68 to cover the costs of lobbying for a charter. However, Jermyn, an influential puritan magistrate and landowner whose estate at Rushbrooke was less than four miles distant, staunchly opposed Bury's bids for incorporation.[5] Thomas Howard, 1st earl of Suffolk was granted the stewardship of the borough soon after the accession of James I, and may have helped the townsmen finally to obtain a charter in 1606. Two years later, after an outbreak of fire that destroyed many buildings, James granted the appropriation of tithes to the corporation.[6] Regular royal visits to neighbouring Newmarket encouraged the growth of amenities which attracted both courtiers and local gentry to take up residence in Bury, though not to universal satisfaction, for it was claimed that prices rose in consequence. A Venetian physician set up practice in the town, a tennis court was licensed, and the enterprising corporation established a volunteer corps on the lines of the artillery company in London.[7]

Several of Bury's demands, for example for a coroner, and its own court of quarter sessions, had not been met by the first charter; the corporation, headed by Bright, therefore continued to lobby for further privileges, petitioning King James, lord chancellor Ellesmere (Thomas Egerton[†]) and lord treasurer Dorset (Thomas Sackville[†]), and sending delegations to attend the king at London and Royston.[8] These efforts led to factional divisions between those for and against a new charter, since some argued that the first had been 'obtained by only a few persons against the will of the majority, and is made only a means for extorting money'.[9] It was not until after Jermyn's death in April 1614 that a second charter fulfilling the townsmen's requests was finally granted. Dated September 1614, this enfranchised the borough, allowing the head alderman, 12 'capital burgesses' and 24 common councilmen to elect two Members to the next Parliament.[10] Jermyn's successor, Sir Thomas Jermyn, apparently did not share his father's disapproval of the charter, or was perhaps mollified by the offer of nominations in future elections. He took the senior seat at Bury in the first seven Parliaments after enfranchisement; at the 1621 general election he also bestowed the other seat on John Woodford, a diplomat and secretary to Lord Hay, Viscount Doncaster. Jermyn had accompanied Hay's embassy to Paris in 1616, and undoubtedly became acquainted with Woodford during the visit. They were 'freely and indifferently elected' according to the indenture exchanged with the sheriff, which was signed by the head alderman, the coroner, eight 'capital burgesses' and 15 others.[11]

Ahead of the next general election, on 7 Jan. 1624, Prince Charles's Council wrote to the corporation, nominating Sir Francis Cottington* for a seat at Bury, on the grounds that a small amount of property and some rent-charges in the borough were parcel of the duchy of Cornwall. The town clerk, John Mallowes, replied on behalf of the corporation that while they would be willing to elect Cottington on condition he take the freeman's oath, they had already promised the first seat to Jermyn. The prince's Council wrote again on 14 Jan. to accept these terms, but took the precaution of also nominating Cottington at three other boroughs.[12] In the event Cottington was returned for Camelford on 30 Jan., and three days later, before the prince's Council could substitute another candidate at Bury, Anthony Crofts, a younger son of a local gentry family, was elected as Jermyn's colleague.

The duchy of Cornwall interest vanished with the accession of Charles I, and at the general election in 1625 Jermyn was joined by the puritan Sir William Spring, of Pakenham, five miles east of the town. The elections in the following year took place in two stages, with Jermyn's re-election confirmed on 6 Jan. 1626, followed by the return of Emmanuel Giffard, a minor courtier presumably nominated by Jermyn, five days later.[13] In an attempt to conceal this 'straggling election' Mallowes dated the return 30 Jan., the day on which the county court was to meet. On 23 Jan., however, Giffard was taken in execution by a creditor,

and he was in detention when Parliament met. Privilege was claimed for him, but could not be granted until the sheriff and town clerk had altered the date on the indentures to 11 January.[14] In 1628 Jermyn was able to secure the second seat for his brother-in-law, Sir William Hervey II of Ickworth. A bill was introduced in 1629 for paving the streets of the town and connecting it with the Great Ouse by a navigable canal, but never advanced beyond its first reading.[15]

[1] R.S. Gottfried, *Bury St. Edmunds and the Urban Crisis*, 5, 8. [2] *HMC 14th Rep. VIII*, 142, 143; *CSP Dom.* 1619-23, p. 484; *APC*, 1615-16, p. 623. [3] P. Collinson, *Eliz. Puritan Movement*, 188, 338, 436. [4] *HMC Hatfield*, xi. 351, 396. [5] M. Statham, *Book of Bury St. Edmunds*, 57-60. [6] R. Yates, *St. Edmunds Bury*, 243; app. 7, 14, 38. [7] Add. 39245, f. 21; *Life and Letters of Sir Henry Wotton* ed. L. Pearsall Smith, ii. 467-8; *Bury Wills* ed. S. Tymms (Cam. Soc. xlix), 200; *CSP Dom.* 1611-18, p. 230; *APC*, 1615-16, pp. 101-2; 1621-3, p. 344. [8] J. Craig, *Ref., Pols. and Polemics: the Growth of Protestantism in E. Anglian Market Towns, 1500-1610*, pp. 127-32. [9] *HMC 14th Rep VIII*, pp. 140-1. [10] Yates, 80; C66/2031. [11] Suff. RO (Bury St. Edmunds), D13/1; *Accts. of Feoffees of the Town Lands of Bury St. Edmunds* ed. M. Statham (Suff. Rec. Soc. xlvi), 282. [12] DCO, Prince Chas. in Spain, ff. 35v-6; P.M. Hunneyball, 'Prince Charles's Council as Electoral Agent 1620-4', *PH*, xxiii. 317-18, 327, 329, 332, 335. [13] Suff. RO (Bury St. Edmunds), D13/3. [14] *Procs. 1626*, ii. 44-5, 55, 64. [15] *CJ*, i. 931b.

J.P.F./R.C.L.S.

DUNWICH

Right of election: in the freemen

12 Feb. 1604	SIR VALENTINE KNIGHTLEY PHILIP GAWDY[1]
31 Mar. 1604	SIR THOMAS SMYTHE I *vice* Knightley, chose to sit for Northants.[2]
21 Mar. 1614[3]	PHILIP GAWDY HENRY DADE
18 Dec. 1620	CLEMENT COKE THOMAS BEDINGFIELD
24 Jan. 1624	SIR JOHN ROUS I SIR ROBERT BROOKE
20 Apr. 1625	SIR JOHN ROUS I SIR ROBERT BROOKE
18 Jan. 1626[4]	SIR JOHN ROUS I THOMAS BEDINGFIELD
?24 Feb. 1628[5]	SIR ROBERT BROOKE FRANCIS WINTERTON Sir John Rous I[6]

Dunwich had been one of the most important Saxon ports in East Anglia and the seat of a bishopric, but coastal erosion and the silting of the harbour had reduced it to a shadow of its former self by the early seventeenth century.[7] In 1628 the corporation stated that their entire town had been 'swallowed up by the sea, save one parish whose inhabitants are grown so poor that they live only by fishing upon the sea coast in small boats'.[8]

Incorporated as a royal borough by King John, Dunwich claimed in 1628 to be 'one of the ancientest corporations of this kingdom'. In the medieval period a mayor governed the town, but by the sixteenth century the corporation consisted of 12 capital burgesses, called the portmen, from whom two bailiffs were annually elected, and a subordinate body known as the Twenty-Four.[9] It had sent two Members to Parliament since 1298. The indentures, or at least those which have survived, were signed by the two bailiffs on behalf of the 'burgesses' and the 'proved' or 'honest' men – presumably the freemen – of the borough.[10]

Canvassing for the first Stuart election began within a month of the death of Elizabeth. (Sir) Robert Brooke, a newcomer to the neighbourhood, applied for a seat on his own behalf, but on 19 Apr. 1603 the corporation resolved in favour of (Sir) Valentine Knightley, a Northamptonshire knight proposed by Sir Edward Coke*, the attorney-general, who owned property nearby and had controlled the nomination of a seat at Dunwich since 1597. The deputy vice-admiral of Suffolk, John Talbot, whom the corporation had recently decided to reward for his friendship to the town, put forward for the remaining seat one of the Stanhopes, almost certainly the vice-admiral, (Sir) Michael*. The corporation agreed to this request, but only if Stanhope would undertake to 'serve and supply the place in his own person, and by no other by his appointment'. However, 'if he should refuse to serve as before' they would elect Brooke. Presumably a seat had been offered to Stanhope previously and he had nominated a third party, whom the borough had felt obliged to return.[11]

In the event the first Jacobean Parliament was not summoned until 1604. There is no evidence that either Stanhope or Brooke tried to renew their candidacies, and on 12 Feb. the borough elected Knightley together with Philip Gawdy, a Norfolk courtier whose brother was a friend of Coke's. Gawdy was presumably referring to himself when he wrote to his elder brother, Sir Bassingborne* eight days later that 'I know a poor younger brother that had a free election for a place without the opposition of any one body'.[12] Knightley was also returned for Northamptonshire and

consequently waived the lower status borough seat. Ironically, in view of the borough's previous insistence on Stanhope not nominating a third person, it was presumably Knightley who persuaded the borough to return Sir Thomas Smythe I at the ensuing election on 31 March. Smythe had been a close friend of Knightley's brother, Edward, whose son Richard*, Knightley's heir, was in his care.[13]

On 6 Feb. the borough had received a proposal from the bailiffs of the neighbouring town of Southwold and the inhabitants of Walberswick for a joint petition to Parliament to allow them to appeal for funds to every parish in England to pay for the repair of the harbour. The borough seems to have been mostly concerned with protecting its privileges, which formed the first two of the 'special points' they outlined for a proposed meeting between the three towns. Nevertheless, on 31 Mar. they agreed to a combined suit, on condition that it was made in the name of the 'port of Dunwich', and their neighbours shared the costs. On 18 Apr. the borough sent a representative to London with instructions to consult Smythe and Gawdy and to lobby for the harbour repairs. He was also to seek a renewal of the town's charter. In the event only the latter was forthcoming. Indeed there is no evidence that the repair of the harbour was ever broached in the first Jacobean Parliament. In 1609 the cliffs crumbled to the south of the town, and the main highway disappeared beneath the sea.[14]

In 1614 Smythe was returned for Sandwich on the nomination of Henry Howard, earl of Northampton. Gawdy was re-elected with the support of Coke, by now chief justice of King's Bench and a privy councillor, alongside Henry Dade, who had replaced Talbot as deputy vice-admiral. Dade was nominated by the lord chamberlain, Thomas Howard, 1st earl of Suffolk and 'others', who probably included Stanhope. Six days after the election, the borough agreed to levy a rate of £10 towards the cost of sending another representative to London to lobby for the repair of the harbour. On 24 May they resolved to write to one of their former bailiffs, John Harper, who may have been the representative sent two months earlier, to petition the king and Parliament for assistance in improving the harbour, and it was agreed that 'for the better furthering thereof we perceive some gratuity is to be bestowed'. However, the Addled Parliament was dissolved a fortnight later, and there were no recorded proceedings on this matter in the Commons.[15]

On 23 Feb. 1619 the Privy Council initiated a national collection to raise money for the repairs, and in the following year it was ordered that the receipts should be deposited in Fishmongers' Hall in London. The result was disappointing. An undated note in the corporation records that whereas £6,000 was needed only £33 3s. 6d. was received, of which £17 3s. 6d. was incurred in expenses.[16]

Sir Edward Coke was dismissed from office in 1616, but he was partially rehabilitated the following year. The Dunwich corporation continued to believe he was worth cultivating, and in 1618 they expended 30s. 2d. on wine and sugar for his sons and their friends.[17] Consequently, when Parliament was summoned again in 1620 the borough elected Sir Edward son Clement, possibly one of the 1618 visitors, along with Thomas Bedingfield, a young lawyer whose father and namesake was an influential member of the local gentry. Bedingfield was described as 'junior' in the return to distinguish him from his parent. Once again the borough Members made no documented efforts to aid their constituency, but the bill for repair of the haven received a first reading on 11 May 1621, possibly thanks to Speaker Richardson, the town's recorder. It was supported by William Denny, a Norwich lawyer who was later himself recorder of Dunwich, but made no further progress before the summer recess. During the second reading debate on 3 Dec. Sir Thomas Riddell, the Member for Newcastle-upon-Tyne, objected to the proposed Imposition on coal, corn and other produce intended to finance the project. The bill was rejected, although only after the question was put three times 'because the voices [where] doubtful'.[18]

Sir Edward Coke seems to have lost his electoral interest at Dunwich after the 1621 Parliament, possibly because he was again removed from the Privy Council and suffered a period of imprisonment. In 1624 the borough elected two local knights, Sir John Rous and Sir Robert Brooke. There was no attempt to revive the bill for repairing the haven in the remaining parliaments of this period. Rous and Brooke were re-elected in 1625, but Bedingfield, who by 1627 was the borough's recorder, replaced Brooke in 1626.[19]

Brooke was re-elected in 1628, but by that date the town had lost a significant proportion of its maritime population as a result of the wars with France and Spain. Consequently, the corporation, fearing that the local economy would be ruined if more of their fishermen were pressed into service, was anxious to please the lord admiral, the duke of Buckingham. They therefore rejected Sir John Rous, who complained bitterly on 3 Mar. 'how vilely they have used me', and elected instead Francis Winterton, a servant of Buckingham's sister, the countess of Denbigh. A damaged entry in

the corporation minute book records the admission of Winterton to the freedom on 24 Feb., and also refers to his election, which presumably took place on that day. On 4 Apr. 1628 the corporation drew up a petition to Buckingham asking for their seamen to be exempted from royal service, but the upshot is not known.[20]

[1] HMC Var. vii. 89. [2] C219/35/2/71. Omitted from OR. [3] HMC Var. vii. 93. [4] Suff. RO (Ipswich), HD1538/208/6. [5] Suff. RO (Ipswich), EE6:1144/11, f. 7. [6] Procs. 1628, vi. 145. [7] J.A. Steers, 'Suff. Shore', Procs. Suff. Inst. Arch. xix. 9-11; T. Gardner, Historical Acct. of Dunwich, 43. [8] Suckling, Suff. ii. 251-6; SP16/100/38. [9] A. Ballard, Brit. Bor. Chs. p. cxl; Suckling, 251; T.H.B. Oldfield, Rep. Hist. of Gt. Brit. and Ireland, iv. 561; HMC Var. vii. 86. [10] OR; C219/37/234; 219/38/337; Suff. RO (Ipswich), HD1538/208/6. [11] HMC Var. vii. 86, 88; HP Commons, 1558-1603, i. 247. [12] Letters of Philip Gawdy ed. I.H. Jeayes, 142. [13] PROB 11/92, f. 317v [14] HMC Var. vii. 89-91. [15] Ibid. 93. [16] HMC Var. vii. 93, 95; APC, 1618-19, p. 378; 1619-21, p. 245; CSP Dom. 1619-23, p. 17. [17] HMC Var. vii. 95. [18] C181/3, f. 9; CJ, i. 616b, 655a. [19] C181/3, f. 236. [20] CSP Dom. 1627-8, p. 584; Procs. 1628, vi. 145; SP16/100/38.

J.P.F.

EYE

Right of election: in the freemen

1604	EDWARD HONING
	SIR HENRY BOKENHAM[1]
7 Feb. 1610	SIR JOHN KAY vice
	Honing, deceased
1614	SIR ROBERT DRURY
	HUNTINGTON COLBY
21 Dec. 1620	SIR ROGER NORTH
	SIR JOHN CROMPTON
5 Feb. 1624	SIR HENRY CROFTS
	FRANCIS FINCH
28 Apr. 1625	SIR ROGER NORTH
	FRANCIS FINCH
26 Jan. 1626	SIR ROGER NORTH
	FRANCIS FINCH
1628	SIR ROGER NORTH
	FRANCIS FINCH

Eye is situated in 'High Suffolk', the predominantly pastoral region to the north of the county, which takes its name from the honour of 'Heya' or Eye, a Crown possession from the mid-sixteenth century. It allegedly first received privileges as early as the reign of King John, but was not incorporated until 1575, under the name of 'Heya alias Eye', a formula still sometimes used in the election indentures of the early seventeenth century. The charter of that year confirmed the borough's enfranchisement, which had actually taken place four years earlier, and established a town government consisting of two bailiffs, ten other 'principal burgesses' and 24 common councillors. The election indentures were generally made in the name of the bailiffs, burgesses and commonalty, although only the bailiffs were personally named.[2]

Elizabethan elections were dominated by the Bacon family, whose influence in the latter part of the reign was wielded by Sir Nicholas Bacon[†] of Redgrave.[3] Consequently, at James's accession in March 1603, Philip Gawdy* asked his brother Sir Bassingbourne* to 'make sure with Sir Nicholas Bacon that I may be burgess of Eye' in the imminently expected first Jacobean Parliament.[4] In the event, however, Parliament was not summoned until 1604, whereupon Eye elected not Gawdy, who was returned for Dunwich, but Edward Honing and Sir Henry Bokenham. Honing and Bokenham were both local men and closely connected, as Honing's mother and Bokenham's mother-in-law were the coheirs of Nicholas Cutler[†], one of Eye's original Members, while Bokenham was described as the 'especial friend and near kinsman' of Honing's father. Moreover, both men were in a position to deploy the Crown's interest in the borough: Honing leased the manor of Eye from the king and was the Exchequer's receiver-general for Suffolk, while Bokenham was a gentleman pensioner and presumably had good connections at Court.[5]

Honing was buried on 7 May 1609, leaving his eldest son under-age. The writ for the by-election was issued the following September, and shortly thereafter lord treasurer Salisbury (Robert Cecil[†]) sent a letter of nomination to the corporation, probably in favour of Sir John Kay, a courtier and Ordnance official. On 16 Oct. the corporation replied that, at the 'motion' of their 'near worthy neighbour', Sir William Cornwallis[†] of Brome Hall, they had intended to elect one Mr. Kempe. The latter was probably Robert Kempe of Gissing, a lawyer closely connected to Sir Nicholas Bacon's half brother, Sir Francis*, and related to Bartholomew Kempe, who had represented the borough in 1586. However, having gained Cornwallis' acquiescence, they agreed to accept Salisbury's nominee. They stipulated that he should come to Eye to be made free 'as in the like have always been accustomed' and that he would serve without payment. These conditions were presumably acceptable as Kay was elected the following February.[6]

There is no evidence that either Bokenham or Kay sought re-election in 1614, and indeed by then Bokenham had fled abroad to escape his father's creditors. Instead, Sir William Cornwallis' brother Sir Charles* applied for a seat, although probably not on the family interest as Sir Charles was then involved in litigation with Sir William's widow. It seems more likely that Sir Charles hoped that his patron, the lord privy seal, Henry Howard, earl of Northampton, would intervene on his behalf, but stopping at Ipswich on his way from London to the borough, he learned that the election had already taken place. The successful candidates were Sir Robert Drury, who had married the daughter of Sir Nicholas Bacon, and Huntington Colby, who had been appointed muster master of Suffolk by Northampton's nephew, the lord chamberlain, Thomas Howard, 1st earl of Suffolk.[7]

Both Drury and Colby were dead by 1620. Neither of their replacements had any obvious connections with the borough. Sir Roger North owned extensive estates in Suffolk, but they were located in the west of the county and around Stowmarket, about ten miles south of Eye. His colleague, Sir John Crompton, was from even further afield; his estates were in Yorkshire. Possibly Crompton owed his election to Prince Charles, who had been granted the honour and manor of Eye in 1617, as Crompton had been reappointed joint steward of the manor of Beverley by the prince in 1618. However, except at Chester, there is no evidence that the Prince's Council made nominations outside the West Country in 1620.[8]

Crompton had died by 1624, while Sir Roger North was returned for the more prestigious county seat. On this occasion the Prince's Council did make a nomination, in favour of Francis Finch, the brother of Charles's serjeant-at-law, Heneage Finch*. Sir Henry Crofts, whose sister was the widow of Sir John Crompton, was returned for the other seat. Crofts came from a Suffolk family, but he lived near Bury St. Edmunds, and consequently was not local to the borough.[9] During the Parliament the Commons' recusancy committee investigated the activities of Simon Dormer, a popish schoolmaster in Eye. 'It was not much denied by him that he did pervert boys, his scholars, from the Protestant religion', and he was declared unfit to continue in his place. More seriously, it was complained that Bishop Harsnett, the diocesan, had done nothing. The complaints were transmitted to Archbishop Abbot, and Dormer was removed before the end of the year. Neither of the borough Members took any known part in this business.[10]

After the accession of Charles, the honour of Eye became part of Henrietta Maria's jointure, but this seems to have had no impact on electoral patronage in the borough, which re-elected North and Finch without known opposition to the remaining Parliaments of this period. There is no evidence that Crofts sought re-election for the borough, although he was returned for Derby in 1626.[11]

[1] H. Hulme, 'Corrections and Additions to the Official 'Return' of Members of Parl., 1603/4', *BIHR*, v. 104. [2] *HMC 10th Rep. IV*, 513-14, 521; W.A. Copinger, *Manors of Suff*. iii. 259; *HP Commons, 1558-1603*, i. 248; *OR*; C219/37/236; 219/39/191. [3] *HP Commons, 1558-1603*, i. 248, [4] *Letters of Philip Gawdy* ed. I.H. Jeayes, 142. [5] 'Description of a picture of the fam. of Honing' *Coll. Top. et Gen.* vii. 399; C2/Jas.I/B34/22. [6] C219/35/2/70; SP14/48/109; *Vis. Norf.* (Harl. Soc. xxxii), 176; *Works of Francis Bacon* ed. J. Spedding, iii. 74; iv. 40. [7] *Collectanea Curiosa* ed. J. Gutch (1781), i. 161; P.B. Whitt, 'New Light on Sir William Cornwallis the Essayist' *Rev. Eng. Studies*, viii. 156; A.R. Campling, *Hist. of Fam. of Drury*, 62; Add. 39245, f. 8v. [8] E371/724/126, m. 61; DCO, EP1, ff. 171-2, 178v-81; P.M. Hunneyball, 'Prince Charles's Council as Electoral Agent, 1620-24', *PH*, xxiii. 318, 327, 334-5. [9] DCO, 'Prince Charles in Spain', f. 35. [10] *CJ*, i. 707b; 'Nicholas 1624', ff. 213-14; *VCH Suff.* ii. 338. [11] Copinger, iii. 259.

J.P.F.

IPSWICH

Right of election: in the freemen

Number of voters: 126 in 1628[1]

3 Mar. 1604	SIR HENRY GLEMHAM SIR FRANCIS BACON ?Edward Grimston
17 Mar. 1614	SIR FRANCIS BACON ROBERT SNELLING, alderman[2]
27 Apr. 1614	WILLIAM CAGE, alderman *vice* Bacon, chose to sit for Cambridge University[3]
6 Dec. 1620[4]	ROBERT SNELLING, alderman WILLIAM CAGE, alderman
29 Jan. 1624[5]	ROBERT SNELLING, alderman WILLIAM CAGE, alderman
20 Apr. 1625[6]	ROBERT SNELLING, alderman WILLIAM CAGE, alderman
12 Jan. 1626[7]	ROBERT SNELLING, alderman WILLIAM CAGE, alderman
3 Mar. 1628[8]	WILLIAM CAGE, alderman EDMUND DAY

Situated at the head of the Orwell estuary in east Suffolk, with a population estimated at about 4,300 in 1603, Ipswich was the most important shipbuilding centre in the country after London. It was estimated in 1625 that there had been an annual average of 12 launchings for the past 30 years. A head port with resident customs and Admiralty officials, Ipswich played an important part in the Newcastle coal trade, with 50 colliers of between 200 and 300 tons burthen plying regularly between Tyne and Thames around six times a year.[9] In 1621 the Ipswich Member Robert Snelling promoted a navigation bill to compel merchants to use English shipping, and in that same year Snelling's colleague, William Cage, presented the Shipwright Company's patent as a grievance. However, a report that the ship owners of Ipswich had promoted a bill to dissolve the latter Company seems to have been unfounded.[10]

Although not itself a major centre for textile production (apart from sailcloth), about one-sixth of the Eastland Company's exports of Suffolk broadcloth were shipped from Ipswich to the Baltic and Scandinavia. However, in the early seventeenth century this trade was in long-term decline, so that the corporation was obliged to explore alternative forms of commerce. In 1605 it applied to the lord treasurer for permission to establish a staple for the re-export of grain from the Baltic. Eleven years later it sponsored a project to establish a sugar refinery, and in the early 1620s the permission of the royal favourite, the marquess of Buckingham, was sought to establish a staple, this time of 'of all manner of East [i.e. Baltic] commodities'.[11] Neither these proposals, nor the 1621 navigation bill, which included a provision to allow merchants to re-export grain, came to anything.[12]

Ipswich's corporation resented interference from the county magistrates, despite the fact that the borough did not enjoy separate county status, and in 1615 it protested that the town lay outside the jurisdiction of the Suffolk deputy lieutenants.[13] Nevertheless, the borough was a significant social and administrative centre, since it was one of the four sessions towns in Suffolk and the usual site for county elections. In addition the registrar and the commissary of the archdeaconry of Suffolk were based in Ipswich.[14] The presence of these ecclesiastical officials did not prevent the borough from becoming a major centre for puritanism: there appears to have been a separatist congregation in the early part of the period, and in one parish in 1615 the churchwardens had to be ordered to make provision for communion to be received kneeling. The late

Elizabethan town preacher, John Burges, was a notorious nonconformist. In 1605 the corporation appointed Samuel Ward, at a salary of £73 6s. 8d., subsequently increased to £100. Ward was imprisoned in the early 1620s for designing an anti-Spanish engraving, but he was probably more moderate than Burges, as charges of nonconformity were smoothed over by lord keeper Williams in 1622, and the Court of High Commission did not condemn him until the changed circumstances of the 1630s. The leaders of the corporation almost certainly shared Ward's hispanophobia, expending 24lb of gunpowder in firing the town's guns to celebrate the return of the still unwed Prince Charles from Spain in 1623. The grammar school had received a royal charter in 1566, and Ipswich was one of the first English towns to establish a public library, open to all the freemen. The corporation made efficient, if conventional, provision for the poor in Christ's Hospital and elsewhere, and instituted a water supply for household purposes in 1614.[15]

The town's first charter dates from 1200, although the borough was not incorporated until 1446. Municipal government was headed by two annually elected bailiffs, who were usually chosen from among the 12 'portmen' or aldermen. The bailiffs and four other senior portmen served as the borough's magistrates and deputy lieutenants. The portmen, together with 24 common councilmen, formed the 'Assembly'. Before the Civil War control was exercised by a closely linked oligarchy, 'generally recommended for the orderly government of that town', as a report of a committee of the Privy Council stated in 1620. Opposition to the oligarchy found expression in an attempt by the small tradesmen and artisans to organize themselves into a Clothworkers and Tailors' Company. They obtained a charter in 1606, but King's Bench did not approve their restrictions on entry into the trade and the Company was dissolved by order of the assize justices in 1620. The borough was represented in Parliament from at least 1298. Elections took place at the 'General Court', consisting of all the freemen of the borough, although the Assembly, which in this period dominated the General Court, nominated the candidates. The bailiffs made the return, which was usually dated a few days after the election. In 1626, however, eight days elapsed between the election and the dating of the indenture.[16]

During the Elizabethan period the borough had striven to maintain its electoral independence, but with mixed results, and by the 1590s one seat had fallen under the control of the high steward, who, by 1601, was lord treasurer Buckhurst (Thomas Sackville†). In

that year Buckhurst nominated (Sir) Francis Bacon, while the other seat went to (Sir) Michael Stanhope, a Suffolk courtier closely connected to the Cecils.[17]

In 1604 Buckhurst, shortly to become 1st earl of Dorset, nominated both his son-in-law Sir Henry Glemham, a Suffolk knight, and Bacon. The corporation responded by agreeing to accept Glemham, so long as he took the freedom, but complained that it had already been approached by Stanhope for a seat. Buckhurst was therefore asked to mediate between Stanhope and Bacon. The corporation presumably also hoped that Buckhurst would come to an agreement with Stanhope's patron, Lord Cecil (Robert Cecil†). In the event Stanhope was returned for Orford, but there may still have been opposition to Bacon, as on 24 Feb. Edward Grimston, whose father had represented the borough under Elizabeth, was made free with Glemham. Nevertheless, Glemham and Bacon were elected on 3 March.[18]

On 6 Feb. a proposed bill to regulate the taking of lodgers, probably intended to assist the corporation's attempts to restrict the numbers of poor migrants, was read at the Assembly. The measure was referred to the borough's law officers for redrafting, in addition it was agreed to raise £100 to cover the costs of promoting it in the forthcoming Parliament. The bill clearly had considerable support among the rulers of Ipswich as on 9 Mar. various members of the Assembly offered to lend money to cover costs until the £100 was raised. However, on 4 Apr. the town clerk, who had been sent to Westminster to lobby for the measure, and had presumably consulted sympathetic members, reported that it was not thought suitable to proceed with and the bill was abandoned before it had even received a first reading.[19]

Dorset died in 1608 and his successor as high steward, Thomas Howard, 1st earl of Suffolk, played no known part in Ipswich elections.[20] In 1614 Glemham was returned for Aldeburgh. The Assembly seems to have hoped to return two of their number, but they received a letter from Bacon, by now attorney-general, who requested re-election. The Assembly agreed on 22 Feb. to nominate Bacon to the General Court, along with a townsman, and on 17 Mar. Bacon was duly returned with Robert Snelling, an Eastland merchant and portman, by a court consisting of 89 freemen. Bacon, however, had also been returned for Cambridge University, and was willing to waive his Ipswich seat, thereby enabling the borough to elect another portman, the attorney William Cage. Snelling was serving as bailiff when he was returned, and consequently was not eligible to sit. In theory there was no difference between his case and that of the bailiff of Ludlow, Robert Berry, who was ejected from the House on 14 Apr. for contravening the rule against mayors and bailiffs returning themselves. However, although the House was aware that Berry was by no means alone in his offence, there were no further expulsions. Thereafter Snelling and Cage were re-elected to every subsequent Parliament until they died.[21]

In the Parliaments of the 1620s Snelling and Cage worked closely together to advance the economic interests of their constituency. In 1621, for instance, they combined to attack the lighthouse patentees.[22] That same year, and again in 1624, Snelling attacked patents restricting the coal trade, a theme Cage took up in 1628.[23] Moreover, Snelling attacked the Muscovy Company's monopoly of the whale fisheries in 1624, the subject of Cage's attacks in 1628.[24]

By late 1625 the Ipswich shipping industry was being adversely affected by war, particularly the depredations of the Spanish privateers operating from Dunkirk.[25] Edmund Day, the borough's senior Member in the third Caroline Parliament, may have had an interest in an Ipswich privateer, the *Heart's Desire*, which was commanded by his son in 1628, but in general the port's participation in English privateering was intermittent and small scale, and consequently of limited benefit to the local economy.[26] In the 1626 Parliament Cage complained that 'there is no fleet at sea to defend the coasts'.[27] In the aftermath of the Parliament it was reported that Ipswich's preacher, Samuel Ward, had attacked Buckingham, the lord admiral, by saying that 'the breaking of the Parliament was done by a great person', whom God would cut off in his time. Ward naturally hastened to deny having uttered these words.[28] In the same year the corporation gave a gift of wine to Buckingham's opponent, Archbishop Abbot.[29] Nevertheless, in early 1628 the 2nd earl of Suffolk (Theophilus Howard, Lord Howard de Walden*), described the borough as 'conformable and ready to do His Majesty service on all occasions'.[30]

After five successive parliaments, the partnership of Snelling and Cage was broken by the death of the former in 1627, leaving Cage the dominant political force in Ipswich. Bells were rung in the town on the summoning of Parliament in 1628, and at the ensuing election, attended by 126 freemen, the vacant seat was taken by Edmund Day, the senior member of the town's common council and in all likelihood a Forced Loan refuser.[31] Cage and Snelling were paid wages by the corporation for their parliamentary services. Both

men received £50 for the 1621 Parliament and £30 for the 1624 Parliament, although Snelling's widow was still receiving money for her late husband's services in 1632.[32]

[1] Suff. RO (Ipswich), C/2/2/2/1, f. 218. [2] N. Bacon, *Annalls of Ipswche* ed. W.H. Richardson, 454. [3] Ibid. 455. [4] Ibid. 475. The return is dated 11 Dec.: *OR*. [5] Bacon, 482. The return is dated 31 Jan.: *OR*. [6] Bacon, 484. The return is dated 21 Apr.: *OR*. [7] Suff. RO (Ipswich), C/2/2/3/2, f. 209, misdated to 11 Jan. in Bacon, 486. The return is dated 20 Jan.: *OR*. [8] Suff. RO (Ipswich), C/2/2/3/2, f. 218, misdated to 1 Feb. in Bacon, 490. [9] M. Reed, 'Economic Structure and Change in Seventeenth-Century Ipswich', *Country Towns in Pre-Industrial England* ed. P. Clark, 92, 97, 104-5; *CSP Dom.* 1625-6, p. 415. [10] *CD 1621*, vii. 267-9; *HMC Cowper*, i. 111; *CJ*, i. 563b. [11] Reed, 104, 107, 125. [12] *CD 1621*, vii. 267-9. [13] Add. 39245, f. 27. [14] Reed, 92, 96-7. [15] Reed, 92, 96, 124; *CSP Dom.* 1611-18, p. 314; Bacon, 424; *Oxford DNB sub* Burges, John; Ward, Samuel; Suff. RO (Ipswich), C/3/2/1/2, f. 317v. [16] *Ipswich Bor. Archives*, pp. xvii, xxvii; Reed, 89-1, 122; Add. 39245, f. 10v; *APC*, 1619-21, pp. 122, 147-8, 208; Coke, *11th Rep.* 53; C219/40/179. [17] *HP Commons, 1558-1603*, i. 248-9. [18] *HMC 9th Rep.* pt. 1, p. 253; Bacon, 417. [19] Suff. RO (Ipswich), C/4/3/1/3, ff. 165, 168-9; Bacon, 418; Reed, 121. [20] Bacon, 436. [21] Suff. RO (Ipswich), C/4/3/1/4, f. 123v; C/2/2/3/2, f. 77. [22] *CJ*, i. 573b, 611a. [23] Ibid. 609a; 794b; *CD 1628*, iii. 453. [24] 'Spring 1624', p. 40; *CD 1628*, iv. 474. [25] *CSP Dom.* 1625-6, p. 415; *APC*, 1626, pp. 140-1. [26] J.C. Appleby, 'Eng. Privateering during the Spanish and French Wars, 1625-30' (Hull Univ. Ph.D. thesis, 1983), 211. [27] *Procs. 1626*, ii. 204. [28] *CSP Dom.* 1625-6, pp. 399, 458. [29] Suff. RO (Ipswich), C/3/2/1/2, f. 329v. [30] *APC*, 1627-8, p. 295. [31] Harl. 378, f. 29v; D. Hirst, *Representative of the People?*, 49; Suff. RO (Ipswich), C/2/2/3/2, f. 218; *APC*, 1627, p. 48; 'Extracts from the Churchwardens' Bks. of St. Clement Ipswich', *East Anglian*, n.s. iii. 356. [32] Suff. RO (Ipswich), C/4/3/1/5, ff. 30, 64-v; Bacon, 501.

J.P.F.

ORFORD

Right of election: in the freemen

by 11 Mar. 1604	SIR MICHAEL STANHOPE SIR WILLIAM CORNWALLIS[1]
1614	SIR WILLIAM CORNWALLIS SIR FRANCIS BAILDON
23 Dec. 1620	SIR LIONEL TOLLEMACHE, bt. SIR ROGER TOWNSHEND, bt.
28 Jan. 1624	SIR ROBERT HITCHAM WILLIAM GLOVER
9 May 1625	SIR ROBERT HITCHAM SIR WILLIAM WITHYPOLL
28 Jan. 1626	SIR ROBERT HITCHAM SIR CHARLES LE GROS
1628	SIR CHARLES LE GROS SIR LIONEL TOLLEMACHE, bt.

Orford was an important East Anglian port in the early Middle Ages and had received its first its charter in 1256.[2] It was represented in the reign of Edward I, but subsequently ceased to return Members until the early sixteenth century.[3] Incorporated in 1579, with a mayor, recorder, town clerk, eight portmen and 12 'capital burgesses', it enjoyed the privilege of a weekly market, but was no longer of economic significance, being described as 'now lying in the greatest ruin and decay.[4] The returns were made in the name of the mayor and commonality.[5]

By the accession of James I the dominant interest in the borough belonged to Sir Michael Stanhope, who owned the manor and castle of Orford and lived two miles away at Sudbourne.[6] Stanhope presumably had little difficulty in securing his return in 1604, when he may also have been responsible for the election of Sir William Cornwallis. The latter had no obvious connection with the borough, but was, like Stanhope, a gentleman of the privy chamber. Moreover, the two men may have been distantly related, for in his will Stanhope described Cornwallis' second cousin, Thomas Cornwallis I*, whom he appointed one of his executors, as his friend and kinsman.[7] Neither Member seems to have attended the election, for they were afterwards sworn in as freemen by the recorder of the borough, Sir Edward Coke*, in the Middle Temple on 11 March.[8]

The charter was confirmed in 1605, and in the following year Thomas Shaw, Stanhope's steward, was elected town clerk.[9] Shaw was unable to prevent disputes arising between his master and the corporation,[10] which may explain why Stanhope was not re-elected in 1614. In addition to Cornwallis, who was chosen again, the borough elected Stanhope's friend Sir Francis Baildon, a Yorkshireman who had married a Suffolk heiress. Cornwallis, who had moved up to the senior seat, died soon after the dissolution, and Baildon was outlawed for debt in 1617.[11]

Whatever loss of influence Stanhope had suffered seems to have proved purely temporary, as he agreed to endow six almshouses and pay compensation to the corporation for demolishing without permission St. Leonard's Hospital. Consequently, he was almost certainly responsible for nominating both Members elected in 1620.[12] The senior place on the return was taken by his niece's husband, Sir Lionel Tollemache, bt., Stanhope's colleague as joint vice-admiral of Suffolk, who was subsequently appointed one of the executors of his will.[13] Stanhope's great-nephew and trustee Sir Roger Townshend was returned for the second seat.[14]

On 3 Dec. 1621 Sir Robert Hitcham, who was closely connected with Stanhope's son-in-law, Sir William Withypoll, replaced Coke as recorder of Orford. It seems likely that Withypoll, a partisan of Coke's estranged wife, Lady Hatton, engineered Coke's removal.[15] Withypoll inherited Stanhope's Suffolk estates on the latter's death 17 days later. However, by the terms of the latter's will, the executors, Thomas Cornwallis and Tollemache, were given considerable control over the estate for three years following Stanhope's decease. This may explain how William Glover, a local man who had appointed Cornwallis trustee of his son's marriage settlement, came to be returned in 1624 alongside Hitcham.[16]

Presumably on Hitcham's advice, the corporation instituted a Chancery suit against Withypoll on 10 May 1624; this seems to have been a collusive action, designed to confirm the diversion of a highway through 'Chapman's tenement' (renamed Sudbourne Park by Stanhope). They alleged that the new half-mile detour was 'scarce passable in summer-time ... for carts with any reasonable lading', and that the effect on their market in winter would be so disastrous to the economy of the borough that they could not wait for 'the ordinary remedy which the course of the common laws of this realm doth afford'. Withypoll replied by citing letters patent of 4 Aug. 1597, under which he had acted, and assured the court that the sandy subsoil of the new road would be good for all seasons.[17]

Withypoll had presumably secured control over his wife's inheritance by 1625, when he was returned to the first Caroline Parliament with Hitcham. He was not re-elected the following year, but was probably responsible for the return of his friend Sir Charles Le Gros. Le Gros's Suffolk connections were slight, but he was re-elected at every subsequent election until his death. Hitcham was returned again in 1626, but not in 1628, when Le Gros secured the first seat despite the higher rank of his colleague, Tollemache.[18]

[1] Suff. RO (Ipswich), EE5/2/2, f. 70. [2] R.A. Roberts, 'Bor. Business of a Suff. Town', TRHS (ser. 4), xiv. 95; HMC Var. iv. 256. [3] OR; HP Commons, 1509-58, i. 192. [4] Roberts, 97-102. [5] C219/37/238; 219/38/229; 219/39/193. [6] W.A. Copinger, Manors of Suff. v. 150. [7] PROB 11/139, f. 77. [8] Suff. RO (Ipswich), EE5/2/2, f. 70. [9] HMC Var. iv. 257, 267; PROB 11/139, f. 76v. [10] Roberts, 113-14. [11] Bodl. Tanner 283, f. 83v; W.P. Baildon, Baildon and the Baildons, iii. 31. [12] HMC Var. iv. 277. [13] Vice-Admirals of the Coast comp. J.C. Sainty and A.D. Thrush (L. and I. Soc. cccxxi), 44; PROB 11/139, f. 77. [14] WARD 7/68/178. [15] HMC Var. iv. 268; CSP Dom. 1628-9, p. 151. [16] PROB 11/139, f. 77; Suff. RO (Ipswich), IC/AA1/65/102. [17] C2/Jas.I/03/67. [18] Knyvett Letters ed. B. Schofield (Norf. Rec. Soc. xx), 75.

J.P.F.

SUDBURY

Right of election: in the corporation

Number of voters: 31

22 Feb. 1604	SIR THOMAS BECKINGHAM
	THOMAS EDEN I[1]
1614	SIR ROBERT CRANE
	HENRY BYNG
29 Nov. 1620[2]	EDWARD OSBORNE
	BRAMPTON GURDON
	?Philip Bell
26 Jan. 1624	SIR ROBERT CRANE
	SIR WILLIAM POLEY
6 May 1625	SIR ROBERT CRANE
	SIR NATHANIEL BARNARDISTON
30 Jan. 1626	SIR NATHANIEL BARNARDISTON
	THOMAS SMITH, alderman
	?John Winthrop
1628	SIR ROBERT CRANE, (bt.)
	SIR WILLIAM POLEY

Sudbury is situated in the extreme south of Suffolk on the left bank of the River Stour, which forms the border with Essex. In this period the Stour valley was a major cloth-producing region, which brought considerable wealth to the town. Sudbury was an ancient borough, which first received a charter in the mid-thirteenth century, but despite having a mayor by 1331 it was not incorporated until 1554, when the town was rewarded for its support of Queen Mary at her accession.[3] The 1554 charter seems to have done little more than to confirm the existing borough constitution. In addition to a mayor, the corporation consisted of a self-selecting oligarchy of six aldermen and 24 capital burgesses, plus a steward who presided over the borough court.[4]

The lordship of the borough was annexed to the duchy of Lancaster in 1558, and it was probably thanks to the chancellor of the duchy, Sir Ambrose Cave[†], that the town was enfranchised the following year. Not surprisingly, therefore, the duchy was an important electoral patron in the Elizabethan period, as was the Waldegrave family, since it had been the local landowner Sir Edward Waldegrave, a member of Mary's Household, whose leadership of the town's inhabitants had secured the 1554 charter. The borough remembered its debt to Sir Edward as late as the 1590s, despite his Catholicism, while Sir

William Waldegrave[†], the head of the Protestant branch of the family, had a significant electoral interest in the borough.[5] The mayor, aldermen and capital burgesses exercised the franchise and the indentures were generally made in their name.[6]

In 1604 Thomas Eden I of Ballingdon, a suburb of Sudbury on the Essex side of the Stour, was elected together with Sir William Waldegrave's son-in-law, Sir Thomas Beckingham. In 1610 the duchy property at Sudbury was sold to Sir Robert Crane, who lived at Chilton, one-and-a-half miles from the borough. However, Sudbury remained under the lordship of the duchy, to which it continued to pay a fee farm.[7] Three years later both Sir William Waldegrave and his son died within barely more than three months of each other, leaving a ten-year-old as heir to the estate and effectively extinguishing the Waldegrave interest in this period.[8]

Crane presumably had little difficulty securing his election for the borough in 1614 alongside Henry Byng, a Cambridgeshire lawyer who had recently been appointed steward of the borough, possibly thanks to the patronage of Suffolk's lord lieutenant, Thomas Howard, 1st earl of Suffolk. If so Suffolk may also have nominated Byng for Parliament. The borough accounts record payment for the accommodation of a servant of the chancellor of the duchy, Sir Thomas Parry, at around this time, but it is not known whether his presence had any connection with the election.[9]

There is no evidence that Byng sought re-election and, in 1620, Crane decided to run for a county seat.[10] Consequently the latter's father-in-law, Sir Henry Hobart*, receiver for the duchy in Suffolk, hoped to procure the return of his wife's nephew, Philip Bell, for Sudbury. It is striking that Hobart approached the chancellor of the duchy, by now Sir Humphrey May*, rather than Crane, for a letter of nomination; he informed his son-in-law of his actions on 23 November. This indicates that the duchy was still seen as the 'natural' patron of the borough despite the loss of its landed interest, although matters are confused by the fact that May had married the granddaughter of Sir Robert Jermyn[†], Crane's guardian. Hobart assured Crane that, if needed, the seat at Sudbury would be available to him, which may suggest that Crane had actually been a duchy nominee in 1614.[11]

The election is recorded in the borough records as having taken place on 3 Jan. 1621, although the return was backdated to 29 November. The corporation elected Brampton Gurdon, a prominent member of the local gentry whose father had represented the borough half a century before.[12] His colleague was almost certainly Edward Osborne of the Inner Temple, although the return records his address as Sudbury. Osborne presumably owed his election to Gurdon, with whom he may already have been connected by marriage. It is possible the return was backdated to make it appear that the election had taken place before the borough received May's nomination of Bell. Alternatively, the election may have been delayed to ensure that Crane had a place in the Commons if he failed to secure a county seat. Once assured of success, Crane may then have persuaded Hobart and May to put the seat at Gurdon's disposal in reward for the latter's support at county level.

Neither Gurdon nor Osborne seems to have sought re-election. In 1624 Sudbury again returned Crane, who had given the borough a messuage in Friar Street as a workhouse, alongside May's brother-in-law Sir William Poley, whose election was presumably assisted by his residence eight miles from the borough.[13] At the next election Crane was elected for a third time, along with the leading puritan Sir Nathaniel Barnardiston, who lived at Kedington, 11 miles from the borough. The following year Crane was again chosen to sit for the county. In his stead he seems to have hoped to secure a seat at Sudbury for John Winthrop of Groton in Suffolk, who subsequently became governor of Massachusetts. In a letter probably dating from February 1626, Brampton Gurdon told Winthrop that the mayor complained Crane had 'never made his mind so known to him', and that consequently the corporation had been unaware of his preference for Winthrop.[14] Instead of Winthrop the borough re-elected Barnardiston, together with one of its aldermen, Thomas Smith. The borough accounts record payments for a copy of a petition presented by the freemen concerning the election and a counter-petition from the corporation, indicating that there was a franchise dispute. Regrettably, copies of neither document have survived and there were no recorded proceedings about the dispute in the 1626 Parliament. In 1628 it was Barnardiston who was elected for the county, while Crane and Poley were returned for Sudbury, without any recorded controversy.[15]

[1] E. Stokes and L. Redstone, 'Cal. of the Muns. of the Bor. of Sudbury', *Suff. Arch. Inst. Procs.* xiii. 287. [2] Date of return, which was probably backdated. [3] W.W. Hodson, *Short Hist. of Bor. of Sudbury* comp. C.F.D. Sperling, 9, 23, 33, 35; *HP Commons, 1509-58*, iii. 534-5. [4] Stokes and Redstone, 264-5. [5] Hodson, 45; *HP Commons, 1558-1603*, i. 250; Stokes and Redstone, 285. [6] Suff. RO (Bury St. Edmunds), EE501/2/3, p. 195; EE501/2/5, p. 103; C219/37/235; 219/40/178. [7] W.A. Copinger, *Manors of Suff.* i. 234-5; Hodson, 46. [8] *HP Commons, 1558-1603*, iii. 564; *Chamberlain Letters* ed. N.E. McClure, i. 491. [9] Suff. RO (Bury St. Edmunds), EE501/2/3, pp. 418,

430. [10] Bodl. Tanner 72, f. 69. [11] Bodl. Tanner 290, f. 54; *Vis. Norf.* (Harl. Soc. xxxii), 34. [12] Suff. RO (Bury St. Edmunds), EE501/2/5, p. 103. [13] Stokes and Redstone, 272. [14] *Winthrop Pprs.* i. 317. This letter is dated only 19 Feb., but the year can be established from Gurdon's report that he had heard two days previously that Sir John Deane, who died on 17 Feb. 1626, was not expected to live 'one hour'. [15] Stokes and Redstone, 290.

J.P.F.

SURREY

Number of voters: unknown

Feb. 1604	SIR ROBERT MORE
	SIR EDMUND BOWYER
c. Mar. 1614	SIR GEORGE MORE
	SIR EDMUND BOWYER
6 Dec. 1620	SIR GEORGE MORE
	SIR NICHOLAS CAREW
c. Jan. 1624	SIR ROBERT MORE
	SIR THOMAS CRYMES
20 Apr. 1625	SIR GEORGE MORE
	SIR FRANCIS LEIGH II
25 Jan. 1626	SIR GEORGE MORE
	SIR FRANCIS VINCENT, bt.
c. Feb. 1628	SIR AMBROSE BROWNE, bt.
	SIR RICHARD ONSLOW

Writing in 1627 the deputy lieutenants of Surrey complained of the 'smallness and poverty of this county'. An Elizabethan petition from some of Surrey's inhabitants also described the county as 'one of the least shires' and 'one of the barrenest'.[1] However, both of these complaints were made in order to reduce financial burdens on the county. Camden, by contrast, stated that Surrey was 'wealthy enough', especially around the Thames valley and towards the border with Sussex, although he admitted that the centre of the county was infertile.[2] Speed, too, described Surrey as 'better stored with game than with grain' and also praised the 'sweet and delectable' air, which he thought explained why the county contained so many royal palaces and parks, including Nonsuch, Oatlands and Richmond.[3]

Surrey's attractiveness to the English monarchy had disadvantages for the local inhabitants, particularly as it was heavily burdened with purveyance. As a consequence the county was one of the first to compound with the Household in the Elizabethan period, though this arrangement only mitigated that burden. Counties close to London had to pay a higher price for their agreements than those more distant, and they did not cover all forms of purveyance. In particular Surrey suffered from a high demand for carts, excluded from the county agreements, not only for moving the royal Household between various palaces but also for transporting goods to government departments, including timber and iron from the Weald to the Ordnance Office in the Tower. In addition, during the Elizabethan period the inhabitants complained of being heavily burdened by the subsidy. This they attributed to their proximity to the centre of authority, which made 'both gentlemen's living and others ... very well known' to the officials of the Exchequer.[4]

Surrey contained the London suburb of Southwark and was consequently affected by the rapid growth of the metropolis. Several Surrey Members in this period, including Sir Edmund Bowyer and Sir Thomas Crymes, who both lived close to Southwark, had important connections with the City of London. The growth of Southwark presumably explains why the Surrey Members were appointed to consider a bill to regulate new building and lodgers on 27 Apr. 1604, and another concerning lodgers on 16 May 1610. Surrey's position on the doorstep of London may also explain why its Members were included in the committee to consider the bill concerning retailing brokers 11 days later.[5]

The surviving indentures indicate that county elections were held at Guildford.[6] Until the end of this period the senior seat was monopolized by the More family from neighbouring Loseley. Between 1597 and 1626 Sir George More, the head of the family, generally took the senior place on the return. However, every third Parliament his eldest son Sir Robert replaced him, and he sat for Guildford instead. Consequently, in 1604 it was Sir Robert More who was elected for the senior seat, Sir George having been returned for the two last Elizabethan parliaments. Sir Robert's partner on this occasion was Sir Edmund Bowyer of Camberwell, who probably owed his place to Surrey's lord lieutenant, lord admiral Nottingham (Charles Howard[†]). Though not then knight of the shire, it was Sir George More who nevertheless spoke up during the first Jacobean Parliament for the Surrey clothiers on 27 Mar. 1604,[7] and who took a lively interest in the issue of purveyance.[8] On this latter subject he was aided by Bowyer, who was one of the Members named on 7 May to 'make more pregnant proof' of the articles drafted by the Commons against the abuses of the purveyors.[9]

As well as its demands for composition money and carts, the Crown seems to have contributed to the deterioration in the county's roads. In the 1605-6 session a bill was introduced for the repair of part of the highway between Nonsuch and Kingston-upon-Thames, which was said to be virtually impassable. According to the preamble to the Act, the road was the main thoroughfare for supplying the royal palaces in the county and for bringing timber and other provisions to the Tower. On 2 Apr. 1606 the Surrey Members were appointed to the committee to consider the bill, which was subsequently enacted.[10]

In 1614 Sir George More was re-elected for the county and his son sat for Guildford. Bowyer was also returned again, but on 20 Apr. More had to ask leave of the House for him to go to Bath 'for prevention of the palsy'.[11] He recovered sufficiently to be elected for Gatton in 1624, but there is no evidence that he ever sought re-election for the county, possibly due to the declining status of his patron, Nottingham, who relinquished the Admiralty to the marquess of Buckingham in 1619.

The last two Jacobean elections were dominated by the Mores. In 1620 Sir George More was re-elected along with his former son-in-law, Sir Nicholas Carew, who had inherited extensive Surrey estates. Sir Robert More was the first of the 20 or so freeholders to sign the 1620 indenture.[12] Carew seems to have been absent from the election as More wrote to him informing him of the outcome six days later.[13] In 1624 Sir Robert More was re-elected with his brother-in-law Sir Thomas Crymes.

In the following three elections a new interest emerged centred on the Browne family of Betchworth castle near Dorking. In 1625 Sir George More's colleague was Sir Francis Leigh II, the grandson of (Sir) Thomas Browne[†] who came from an old but undistinguished Surrey family. In 1626 More was elected for the last time with Sir Francis Vincent, the first Surrey baronet whose sister had married Sir Thomas's son Sir Matthew[†].

Surrey was the second county, after Middlesex, in which the Forced Loan was implemented in late 1626.[14] On 24 Nov. the first receipts from the Loan were paid into the Exchequer, and over the following 12 months nearly £3,000 was received from the county.[15] Sir George More, Sir Francis Carew and Sir Francis Vincent served as collectors, and Sir Thomas Crymes was an active commissioner.[16] There is no sign of a purge of Loan refusers on the county magistracy. Nevertheless, the response of the deputy lieutenants in December 1627 to orders from the Council for billeting soldiers sent from the West Country shows that the 'great sums lately disbursed for the Loan', coming on top of military charges and the existing burden of purveyance, had increased tensions within the county. The deputy lieutenants stated that the inhabitants of the county complained of 'want of monies' and also referred to the 'great difficulty to raise money for necessary and ordinary services'.[17] The complaints proved unavailing, and in the 1628 Parliament Edward Bysshe, sitting for Bletchingley, protested at the disorder of the soldiers billeted in the county.[18]

There is no sign that either the Forced Loan or billeting were significant issues at the 1628 Surrey election, which was distinguished by the fact that, for the first time since 1588, no member of the More family secured a county seat. Sir Robert More was now dead, and his father Sir George, being in his mid-70s and in poor health, did not seek re-election. Instead, he appears to have tried to secure the return of his friend Sir Richard Onslow, a wealthy deputy lieutenant. Sir Ambrose Browne, the son of Sir Matthew, also sought election and some kind of meeting, presumably of the Surrey gentry, seems to have been convened at Dorking, near Browne's residence. Browne agreed to stand with Onslow, fully expecting More's support, but on 16 Feb. Browne wrote to the latter accusing him of endeavouring 'by all means possible to oppose me'. Browne stated that he had acted 'fairly and respectfully' at the 'election' at Dorking, although it had been 'in my power to have done otherwise', by which he was presumably referring to his acquiescence to Onslow's candidacy. Although Browne said he could not 'certainly know' on whose behalf More was opposing his candidacy, he may have suspected either that More had changed his mind about standing himself or that he wanted a seat for his grandson Poynings More*. However, Browne secured the senior seat anyway, leaving Onslow to take the junior place. Poynings More had to settle for Guildford.[19]

[1] Manning and Bray, *Surr*. iii. 669-70. [2] W. Camden, *Britain* trans. P. Holland (1610), p. 294. [3] J. Speed, *Theatre of the Empire of Great Britaine* (1611), p. 11. [4] *VCH Surr*. i. 367-8, 398; Manning and Bray, iii. 669-70; E.N. Lindquist, 'King, the People and the House of Commons: the Problems of early Jacobean Purveyance', *HJ*, xxxi. 551, 554, 555; A. Woodworth, 'Purveyance for the Royal Household in the Reign of Queen Elizabeth', *Trans. Am. Phil. Soc.* n.s. xxxv. 39, 41, 52, 71-2. [5] *CJ*, i. 188a, 429a, 444a. [6] C219/37/242. [7] *CJ*, i. 154a-155b. [8] P. Croft, 'Parl., Purveyance and the City of London 1589-1608', *PH*, iv. 18. [9] *CJ*, i. 202a. [10] Ibid. i. 288a, 292a; *SR*, iv. 1094-5. [11] *Procs. 1614 (Commons)*, 109. [12] C219/37/242. [13] Berks. RO, D/ELL/C1/111. [14] *Historical Collections* ed. J. Rushworth, i. 455. [15] E407/1386, m. 32; SP16/84/89. [16] *CSP Dom*. 1627-8, p. 31; SP16/67/4. [17] Manning and Bray, iii. 669-70. [18] *CD 1628*, ii. 127-8. [19] *HMC 7th Rep* 676; Surr. Hist. Cent. LM/6729/1/23.

A.D./B.C.

BLETCHINGLEY

Right of election: in the burgage-holders

Number of voters: 24 in 1624[1]

9 Mar. 1604	SIR JOHN TREVOR I
	RICHARD BELLINGHAM I
16 July 1610	CHARLES HOWARD *vice*
	Bellingham, deceased
c. Mar. 1614	SIR JOHN TREVOR I
	(SIR) CHARLES HOWARD
17 Dec. 1620	JOHN HAWARDE
	HENRY LOVELL
22 Jan. 1624	SIR MILES FLEETWOOD
	JOHN HAWARDE
	Henry Lovell
c. Mar. 1624	EDWARD BYSSHE *vice* Fleetwood,
	chose to sit for Launceston
19 Apr. 1625	SIR THOMAS GRESHAM
	EDWARD BYSSHE
18 Jan. 1626	EDWARD BYSSHE
	HENRY LOVELL
21 Feb. 1628	EDWARD BYSSHE
	JOHN EVELYN

Although a flourishing market town which returned Members from 1295, Bletchingley was never incorporated and had no governing body other than the manorial court. There was a bailiff but he was not a public officer, being described in 1624 as 'only a rent-gatherer' for the lord of the manor. The returning officer was the sheriff, who exchanged indentures with the burgage-holders – the resident owners of property by burgage tenure – who held the franchise. The manor of Bletchingley was purchased by William Howard, 1st Lord Howard of Effingham, in 1560. It was inherited in 1573 by Charles Howard[†], subsequently lord admiral and 1st earl of Nottingham who, by 1602, had settled it on his eldest son, Sir William Howard[†].[2]

Sir William Howard was ineligible to stand in 1604 as he was summoned to the Upper House in his father's barony as Lord Howard of Effingham; nevertheless he was undoubtedly responsible for the return of the two clients of Nottingham's in that year, Sir John Trevor I and Richard Bellingham I.[3] Trevor, who had sat for the borough in 1597, was a naval official and Bellingham was Nottingham's secretary, a position that Trevor had previously held. Neither man had any other connection with the borough. Bellingham died in July 1610 and in the consequent by-election was replaced by Nottingham's nephew (Sir) Charles Howard, a youth of 19 or 20. Nineteen burgage-holders are named in the indenture as electors, including one who voted in the right of his wife.[4]

Trevor and Howard were re-elected in 1614. Lord Howard died on 28 Nov. 1615 without male heirs, having in the previous August settled Bletchingley on his wife Anne.[5] By 1616 Lady Howard had quarrelled with her husband's family over property at Bletchingley, which she claimed as part of her jointure.[6] This may have made her reluctant to support Trevor and Howard in 1620. Consequently they had to find other seats; the former stood at Bodmin and the latter at New Windsor. Lady Howard secured the junior seat for her trustee Henry Lovell, who lived in Bletchingley and was about to become involved in a protracted lawsuit in the Court of Wards; she seems to have been obliged to forego the other seat, which went to John Hawarde, a local lawyer whose father had purchased the nearby manor of Garston in 1577. Only 12 burgage-holders signed the indenture.[7]

In 1624 Lady Howard seems to have tried to control both seats, nominating Lovell and Sir Miles Fleetwood, the receiver-general of the Court of Wards, whose wife was Lady Howard's cousin.[8] The burgage-holders were willing to elect Fleetwood, who may also have had the support of Edward Bysshe, a prosperous local lawyer and a fellow official of the Court of Wards, but they rejected Lovell in favour of Hawarde. This may have been because Lovell was suspected of having Catholic sympathies, although this had not prevented his election in 1620; alternatively it is possible that the electors were unwilling to let Lady Howard monopolize both seats. In the ensuing dispute two separate election meetings were held and appeals were made to the committee for privileges, which read petitions from both sides on 2 March.[9]

The privileges committee found that on 17 Jan. 1624 the sheriff had delivered his precept for the election to one of the burgage-holders. It also learned that although there had been no formal summons of an election meeting, news had quickly spread to other the burgage-holders, who had agreed to hold the election five days later. Seventeen burgage-holders participated at the meeting, allegedly held at an inn, which elected Fleetwood and Hawarde.[10] Lovell had been dissatisfied with the result, but he failed to persuade the sheriff to issue a new precept. Lady Howard evidently also shared his disappointment, and

on 8 Feb., a Sunday, her bailiff had announced in the parish church that a second election meeting would be held the following day which would be open to the inhabitants of the borough generally, not just the burgage-holders. Lovell was supported by the rector of Bletchingley, Dr. Nathaniel Harris, who may have been one of his wife's kinsmen and had taken offence after Hawarde had told him that his curate was not eligible to vote in the election. Harris had responded by saying that if the 'clergy and temporalty made not one body, he would never come into the pulpit'. On the day of the new meeting, Harris read from the pulpit a letter from Lady Howard commending Lovell and Fleetwood, and reminded the congregation that she might withdraw her annual benevolence to the poor of the parish.[11] The next day, at a meeting attended by 30 inhabitants of the borough, Fleetwood and Lovell were elected. It was subsequently alleged that Lovell had used bribery, although Glanville thought the sums involved were 'very little'. Indeed, the *Journal* states that Lovell gave voters only 6d. for beer. However, he apparently also threatened some of the inhabitants with actions for breach of promise if he was not elected and repeated Harris' warning that Lady Howard would withdraw her charity.[12]

Lovell's next problem was to secure the acceptance of the return, to which there was no counterpart. The under-sheriff very properly refused to be a party to his proceedings; but, with what seems like singular ingenuity, he agreed to meet Lovell in the clerk of the Crown's office, and was thus present, albeit 'at the farthest end of that office', at the delivery of the false indenture.[13]

When Parliament assembled, Fleetwood chose to sit for Launceston, having also been returned for that borough, thereby necessitating a fresh election at Bletchingley. After the petitions on behalf of Lovell and his opponents had been read by the privileges committee, its chairman, John Glanville, made a preliminary report to the Commons on 3 Mar. in which he successfully moved that the writ for a new election should be delayed until after the election dispute had been resolved.[14]

Before the privileges committee Lovell argued that the first election had been invalid because no summons had been issued by the bailiff or any other public officer. Moreover, he argued that the wording of previous indentures, which sometimes referred to 'others' in addition to the burgage-holders, implied a wider franchise. However, Lovell and his supporters were unable to find any evidence that a wider franchise had ever actually been used in earlier elections; indeed all the witnesses before the privileges committee seem to have confirmed that the franchise had been exercised by the burgage-holders at all elections 'holden within the memory of man now living'. The committee ruled that the 'others' referred to in the indentures were those burgage-holders who failed to subscribe their names either because they were absent or because they had voted for unsuccessful candidates. It was also ruled that the bailiff was not an appropriate person to organize elections because he was the servant of the lord of the manor who 'hath nothing to do in the matter'. The original election meeting was deemed valid because all the burgage-holders had been given notice, albeit informally.[15]

The hearing before the privileges committee revealed significant questions about Lovell's religious allegiances. It was demonstrated that he had not received Anglican communion in over a year, and it was alleged that his mother was a recusant, his brother a priest and his daughter a nun. The printed edition of Glanville's reports, not published until the eighteenth century, states that 'no hold was taken in point of judgment' concerning his 'ill affection in religion', but the accusations feature prominently in contemporary accounts of Glanville's final report to the Commons from the privileges committee on 22 Mar. and the consequent hostility to Lovell may help to explain why the Commons agreed to uphold a restricted franchise at Bletchingley.[16] Following Glanville's report on 22 Mar. the Commons agreed that the franchise lay only with the burgage-holders. The original election of Fleetwood and Hawarde was upheld and Lovell was declared ineligible for election to the present Parliament, ostensibly for electoral malpractice but perhaps in reality because of his religion, clearing the way for the election to replace Fleetwood. Lovell appeared at the bar of the Commons on 3 Apr. and was sent to the Tower.[17]

After Glanville had made his report, Thomas Fanshawe I drew his colleagues' attention to a 'very invective sermon' preached by Dr. Harris on 21 Mar. against the proceedings of the privileges committee. Fanshawe read notes of the sermon in the House and the paper was referred to the privileges committee. Fanshawe, who had no known connection with Surrey, may have been a friend of Hawarde, as both men were members of the Inner Temple. In addition to clashing with Hawarde over the participation of the clergy in the election, Harris had been heard to say that Hawarde's testimony before the privileges committee 'was nothing but lies'. It seems likely that Hawarde passed his notes of Harris' sermon, taken by himself or one of his supporters, to Fanshawe in order to exact revenge. The sermon preached by Harris was against 'false witnesses and false judges', and when Harris was

examined before the privileges committee it was ruled to have been directed not just against those who had testified in the case but against the committee itself. On 30 Apr. Harris was brought before the Commons and ordered to confess his sins, both concerning the election and sermon, before his parishioners from the pulpit the following Sunday.[18]

No accusations were levelled against Lady Howard over the 1624 election dispute. Indeed, Lovell was accused of having 'abused' her name in suggesting that she would withdraw her charity from the borough. However, there is no evidence that she was unhappy with Lovell's tactics and Lovell appears to have remained in her employment until the 1630s.[19]

Edward Bysshe was returned at the election to choose Fleetwood's replacement. Bysshe lived at Burstow, just south of Bletchingley, and his wife's family were prominent in the borough, which his father-in-law, John Turner†, had represented in 1601. Whether this local influence was sufficient to secure his return is unclear. An alternative possibility is that he was recommended to Lady Howard by Fleetwood, for as feodary of Surrey he was the local representative of the Court of Wards. Having had their independence vindicated by the Commons, it is just possible that the burgage-holders were willing to let Lady Howard nominate for the other seat.

Bysshe was re-elected in 1625 with Sir Thomas Gresham, a local landowner who had previously sat for Gatton and who may have owed his election to the influence of his friend Hawarde.[20] The electors, some 15 of whom were named, described themselves as 'of the commonalty of the borough', and claimed to have made their choice 'for and in the name of themselves and the rest of the borough'.[21]

In 1626 Lady Howard may have succeeded in nominating both Members, as Bysshe was re-elected with Lovell. Bysshe was again re-elected in 1628, this time with John Evelyn, the gunpowder monopolist, who lived two miles away at Godstone. It is possible that the election occasioned another dispute, as one diary records that on 8 May the privileges committee 'debated the cause of Bletchingley', but no details are known.[22]

[1] 'Earle 1624', f. 91v. [2] VCH Surr. iv. 253, 257; 'Earle 1624', f. 91v. [3] CP, v. 10. [4] C219/35/2/61. [5] C142/352/122. [6] APC, 1615-16, pp. 659-60. [7] C219/37/246. [8] CJ, i. 695b. [9] 'Earle 1624', f. 47. [10] J. Glanville, Reps. of Certain Cases Determined and Adjudged by the Commons in Parliament (1775), 32; 'Earle 1624', f. 91. [11] Glanville, 33, CJ, i. 695b; 'Nicholas 1624', f. 187. [12] Glanville, 33, 39-40; CJ, i. 745b. [13] Glanville, 49; 'Earle 1624', ff. 91v-2; 'Nicholas 1624', f. 106. [14] CJ, i. 716a, 726a; Glanville, 30-1. [15] Glanville, 34-9. [16] Ibid. 39; CJ, i. 745b; 'Nicholas 1624', ff. 105v-6; 'Spring 1624', p. 170; Holles 1624, p. 60; D. Hirst, Representative of the People?, 72-3. [17] CJ, i. 745b, 754a. [18] Ibid.

695b, 745b; 'Pym 1624', i. f. 37v; Glanville, 43-6; 'Hawarde 1624', p. 224. [19] 'Nicholas 1624', f. 106. [20] Berks. RO, D/ELL/C1/112. [21] C219/39/199. [22] CD 1628, iii. 329.

A.D./B.C.

GATTON

Right of election: in the inhabitants

Number of voters: 8 in 1624; 12 in 1628

?29 Feb. 1604	SIR THOMAS GRESHAM	
	SIR NICHOLAS SAUNDERS	
c. Mar. 1614	SIR THOMAS GRESHAM	
	SIR JOHN BROOKE	
12 Dec. 1620	JOHN HOLLES[1]	7[2]
	(SIR) HENRY BRITTON[3]	7[4]
	Sir Thomas Gresham	10[5]
	Sir Thomas Bludder	10[6]
	GRESHAM and BLUDDER vice Holles and Britton, seated on petition, 7 Feb. 1621[7]	
16 Jan. 1624	SIR EDMUND BOWYER	
	SAMUEL OWFIELD	
16 May 1625	(SIR) CHARLES HOWARD	
	(SIR) THOMAS CREWE	
23 Jan. 1626	(SIR) CHARLES HOWARD	
	SAMUEL OWFIELD	
11 Mar. 1628	SAMUEL OWFIELD	
	(SIR) CHARLES HOWARD	
	SIR THOMAS LAKE II	
	JEROME WESTON	

Double return. OWFIELD and HOWARD seated, 26 Mar. 1628

Situated two miles from Reigate in east Surrey, Gatton was described by William Camden in the late sixteenth century as 'scarce a small village'. Camden also stated that Gatton had previously been 'a famous town', but there is no evidence that the village was considered a borough until it started to return Members to the Commons in 1450. Never incorporated, it had no borough officials and consequently the returning officer was the high constable of Reigate hundred.[8]

The manor of Gatton was in the possession of the Copley family by the early sixteenth century. In 1547 the Members were elected by Sir Roger Copley as 'burgess and sole inhabitant of the borough'.[9]

However Sir Roger's son Thomas[†], his widow, and his son William, were Catholics, and spent much of the reign of Elizabeth in exile. In their absence, parliamentary patronage was exercised by Lord Burghley (Sir William Cecil[†]) and Lord Howard of Effingham (Charles Howard[†]), subsequently 1st earl of Nottingham, the latter being lord lieutenant of Surrey and part owner of Reigate manor.[10]

William Copley returned from exile and took possession of his lands shortly after the accession of James I, but his prospects of exerting electoral influence were compromised by his continued recusancy.[11] Both the Members elected in 1604, Sir Thomas Gresham and Sir Nicholas Saunders, were Surrey gentlemen. Saunders may have had the support of Nottingham, with whom he had served on the Cadiz expedition of 1596. He may also have enjoyed the backing of Copley, for although he conformed to the Church of England he had strong Catholic connections.

Gresham was re-elected in 1614, along with Sir John Brooke, who was connected to Nottingham by marriage.[12] Brooke was returned for Oxford at the next election, but may have recommended to Nottingham John Holles, the son of his friend the Nottinghamshire peer Lord Houghton (Sir John Holles*), in his stead.[13] At the request of the high constable the rector of Gatton announced from the pulpit that the election would be held on 13 December. But on the previous day Copley called to his house six of his tenants, 'inhabitants and no freeholders', where they elected Holles along with (Sir) Henry Britton. The latter was a Surrey recusant who was involved in a number of patents and was presumably Copley's candidate. Copley may have hoped to get Nottingham's support by securing the election of Holles. The indenture was sealed at Reigate, an irregularity made much of in the resulting dispute, and was returned by the sheriff. Meanwhile, at the meeting held on 13 Dec. 'one or two inhabitants [of the borough] and divers other possessors of freehold land ... but not inhabitant' re-elected Sir Thomas Gresham, along with Sir Thomas Bludder, another local gentleman. An indenture was drawn up, which named about ten parties, but was rejected by the sheriff.[14]

On the first day of business, 5 Feb. 1621, Sir George More, who had been returned for Surrey, preferred a petition against the return of Holles and Britton and moved for a committee for privileges.[15] The case was heard at the committee the following day, and on the 7th More reported back to the Commons, recommending that the election be overturned. Britton was allowed to attend both the committee and the House while the case was under discussion, and defended his patron very ably. He maintained that all but one of the freeholders 'dwelt out of the town', and were therefore, from a dozen indentures dating back to the reign of Henry VIII, disqualified. However, he failed to convince the House, presumably because of suspicions about his religion. Sir Edward Montagu moved for a fresh election but was opposed by Sir Henry Poole 'in respect of the danger from Copley', and consequently the Commons agreed to seat Gresham and Bludder.[16] On 23 Feb. More reported that the privileges committee had received a petition 'against the burgess of Gatton', but this was rejected.[17] None of the four candidates ever sat for Gatton again. Gresham and Bludder withdrew to Bletchingley and Reigate respectively, and Holles to East Retford, Nottinghamshire, while Britton disappeared into obscurity.

At the election of 1624 a new interest made its appearance, that of Samuel Owfield who had purchased the manor of Upper Gatton.[18] He was elected with Sir Edmund Bowyer, who was connected to both the earl of Nottingham and William Copley. Copley himself and the rector signed the indenture with six others of the 'burgesses and commonalty'.[19]

Nottingham died in December 1624 and was succeeded by his son, Sir Charles Howard*.[20] The following year the latter's cousin (Sir) Charles Howard took the senior seat together with the Speaker-designate (Sir) Thomas Crewe, with the consent of Owfield, who signed the indenture together with Copley and the rector.[21] In 1626 'the commonalty of the borough', seven men headed by Copley and the rector, returned Howard and Owfield.[22] The following August Howard, a Surrey deputy lieutenant, clashed with Owfield over musters for the county militia, but the two interests continued to co-operate in the borough, and they were re-elected in 1628, though in reverse order. Twelve 'inhabitants' of the borough signed the return,[23] although they did not include Copley, who made a last effort to regain control by sending up a separate return. His candidates were Sir Thomas Lake II*, the son of the former secretary of state Sir Thomas Lake I*, and Jerome Weston*, the son of the chancellor of the Exchequer Sir Richard Weston*, both of whom were probably crypto-Catholics. William Hakewill reported from the privileges committee on 26 Mar. that Copley, citing the 1547 return as a precedent, claimed to be able to elect the borough's Members as 'sole inhabitant', despite having conceded the right of his tenants to participate in elections in 1621. He also reported that Copley claimed that the borough was limited to the area 'within the castle and a certain precinct'. The House,

however, took the borough to be coterminous with the parish of Gatton, which included Upper Gatton, and found that previous returns had been made in the name of the inhabitants. Copley argued that these returns were irrelevant, as they had been made when he was living in exile, but this claim was presumably only true of the Elizabethan elections. Following Hakewill's report the return of Lake and Weston was declared invalid and was ordered to be taken off the file.[24]

[1] Nicholas, *Procs. 1621*, i. 20. [2] *CJ*, i. 511b. [3] Nicholas, i. 20. [4] *CJ*, i. 511b. [5] C219/37/249. [6] C219/37/249. [7] *CJ*, i. 512b. [8] *VCH Surr.* iii. 196-7; W. Camden, *Britain*, trans. P. Holland (1610), p. 29; Nicholas, i. 20. [9] *VCH Surr.* iii. 197-8. [10] *Letters of Sir Thomas Copley* ed. R.C. Christie (Roxburghe Club 1897), xli-xliii; *HP Commons, 1558-1603*, i. 252. [11] *Letters of Sir Thomas Copley*, xliii. [12] *CP*, iii. 349. [13] G. Holles, *Mems. of Holles Fam.* ed. A.C Wood (Cam. Soc. ser. 3. lv), 111-12. [14] *CJ*, i. 511b; *CD 1621*, iv. 24-5; vi. 356-60; C219/37/249. [15] *CJ*, i. 507b. [16] *CD 1621*, ii. 34-5; iv. 24-5; vi. 359-60, 443-4; *CJ*, i. 512a-b; D. Hirst, *Representative of the People?*, 73-74. [17] *CD 1621*, vi. 4. [18] *VCH Surr.* iii. 199. [19] C219/38/236. [20] *CP*, ix. 786. [21] C219/39/203. [22] C219/40/223. [23] C219/41A/17. [24] *CD 1628*, ii. 112, 119-20, 136.

A.D.

GUILDFORD

Number of voters: c.30 in 1624; 17 in 1625[1]

5 Mar. 1604	SIR GEORGE MORE
	GEORGE AUSTEN
c.Mar. 1614	SIR ROBERT MORE
	GEORGE STOUGHTON
6 Dec. 1620	SIR ROBERT MORE
	JOHN MURRAY
26 Jan. 1624	SIR GEORGE MORE
	NICHOLAS STOUGHTON
25 Apr. 1625	SIR ROBERT MORE
	ROBERT PARKHURST
	Nicholas Stoughton
3 Feb. 1626	SIR RICHARD SHILTON
	ROBERT PARKHURST
c.Feb. 1626	SIR WILLIAM MORLEY *vice* Shilton, chose to sit for Bridgnorth
25 Feb. 1628	POYNINGS MORE
	ROBERT PARKHURST
	(SIR) FRANCIS CAREW II
	Double return of PARKHURST and CAREW

Guildford, the county town of Surrey, is situated on the river Wey 30 miles south of London. It received its first recorded charter in 1257, and was incorporated in 1488. The corporation consisted of the 'approved men' who annually elected the mayor from among their number. A self-selecting oligarchy controlled entry to the ranks of the 'approved men', who usually numbered around 25, by insisting on previous service as a bailiff, an office chosen by the 'approved men'. In 1603 the borough was granted a separate commission of the peace, consisting of the current and previous mayors, two of the 'approved men', annually elected by the others, and one other person, also elected by the 'approved men' and 'learned in the law'. The latter also fulfilled the functions of a recorder. In 1627 the borough secured, at a cost of £75 15s., a further charter extending its jurisdiction to the suburbs, although apparently without effect.[2] The 1st earl of Nottingham (Charles Howard†) was high steward of the borough until his death in 1624 but does not seem to have influenced the elections in this period, and was not replaced until the 1660s.[3]

A bill to make the Wey navigable between Guildford and the Thames, promoted by the corporation in 1621, described the town as one that 'hath been and yet is very populous, and the inhabitants thereof in former times have lived in good plenty by the trade of clothing'. However, this staple industry was now in decline.[4] Indeed, Archbishop Abbot, who was born in the town, wrote in December 1614 that the borough no longer had 'that flourishing estate for trade and traffic which I have known it sometime to have'. He recommended a change from kerseys to broadcloth, and the growing of hemp and flax. He donated £100 in 1614, founded Trinity Hospital in 1622, and purchased land worth £100 *per annum* for the setting up of 'some manufacture' in 1628.[5]

The town of Guildford was regularly represented in Parliament from 1295. However, it was not until 1689, following a dispute, that the Commons ruled the franchise lay with the freemen and freeholders paying scot and lot.[6] The necessary qualification for voting previous to that date is uncertain. The indentures were always made in the name of the mayor, who acted as returning officer, and the 'approved men'. In addition they frequently, although not invariably, also referred to the burgesses and commonality, suggesting that townsmen outside the corporation participated in elections. This is apparently confirmed by the 1624 indenture, which was signed by about 30 townsmen, although the following year only 17 subscribed.[7]

In the Elizabethan period the most important electoral influences in the borough were two neighbouring gentry families, the Mores of Loseley and the Stoughtons of Stoughton. These families continued to dominate the borough's elections in the Jacobean period, although the Stoughtons do not seem to have had much influence in 1604.[8] On this occasion Sir George More, who had previously been returned four times for the borough, took the first place. His junior colleague, George Austen, the only townsman elected in the period, was a former mayor but, perhaps more importantly, also a former servant of the Mores and still closely connected with the family.

In 1614 More was returned for the county and there is no evidence that Austen sought re-election. Instead More's eldest son Sir Robert secured the senior seat. The junior place went to George Stoughton, heir to (Sir) Lawrence Stoughton† who had represented the borough four times under Elizabeth, and nephew of Adrian Stoughton*, the justice 'learned in the law'.[9] Sir Robert More was re-elected in 1620, but George Stoughton appears not to have been interested in standing again. His younger brother Nicholas, then studying at the Inner Temple, therefore sought his support for the seat, but by then George had already promised his backing to John Murray, a naturalized Scottish courtier who had recently purchased Guildford Park from the Crown. Murray was also on good terms with the Mores and was consequently able to secure the junior seat.[10]

The Wey navigation bill was introduced in the Commons on 22 Feb. 1621 and committed on 6 March. However, on the latter occasion Edward Alford, who owned property close to the Wey, protested that he was unconvinced that the bill would benefit those parts of the county up river from Guildford compelled to contribute towards the improvements. In addition a petition to Parliament against the bill was organized. In reply, the supporters of the bill produced their own petition, signed by Sir George and Sir Robert More and George Stoughton. Sir George More, who had been re-elected for Surrey, reported the bill on 17 Mar., when it was ordered to be engrossed, but there were no further proceedings.[11]

Sir Robert More was re-elected for Surrey in 1624. Consequently, it was Sir George who sat for Guildford in the last Jacobean Parliament. Murray received a Scottish peerage in 1622 and subsequently showed no further interest in pursuing an English parliamentary career, enabling Nicholas Stoughton to secure the junior seat. There were no recorded moves to reintroduce the Wey navigation bill.

In 1625 it was Sir Robert More who was elected for Guildford and Sir George for the county. Nicholas Stoughton sought re-election for Guildford's junior seat and, according to his nephew who wrote a history of the family, 'the town' promised to oblige him. However, Robert Parkhurst, a London alderman of Guildford origin, wanted the seat for his son, and wrote to the corporation 'promising them what great matters he would do for the town if they choose his son, and threatening what prejudice he could do against them if they did not'. The indenture electing More and Parkhurst was signed by Parkhurst's uncle Thomas, who had served four terms as mayor. The drop in the number of signatories suggests that Stoughton and his supporters refused to accept defeat gracefully. Indeed, Stoughton's nephew wrote that Stoughton 'intended to have troubled them [the borough] for it, and made them ashamed of it; but that Parliament was quickly dissolved, and so his prosecution fell to the ground'.[12]

Parkhurst was re-elected in 1626, but for the first time since 1571 no member of the More family represented the borough. Sir Robert More died shortly before the election, Sir George More was returned for Surrey and Sir Robert's son Poynings* obtained a seat at Haslemere. Uncertain who to choose, the borough, perhaps at the prompting of the attorney-general (Sir) Robert Heath*, a former justice of the peace 'learned in the law' and still closely connected with Guildford, decided to leave the name of the senior Member blank in the original indenture. The name that was eventually inserted was that of Heath's colleague Sir Richard Shilton, the solicitor general. However, after Shilton chose to sit for Bridgnorth in Shropshire, where he had also been returned, Heath's son-in-law Sir William Morley filled the vacancy. The date of the election is unknown but it was presumably shortly after the issuing of the writ on 11 February.[13]

Poynings More was elected in 1628, apparently without opposition, but the junior seat seems to have been contested by Parkhurst and More's cousin (Sir) Francis Carew II. Two indentures were returned, both naming More first and now largely illegible. The one for More and Parkhurst was signed by at least two future mayors and carries the borough seal, suggesting that this combination had the support of the corporation. Indeed the Crown Office list gives Parkhurst's name rather than Carew's. However, there is no evidence that the dispute was resolved, or indeed discussed, by the Commons and neither Carew nor Parkhurst left any trace on the parliamentary records.[14]

1625-6, p. 474; Surr. Hist. Cent. BR/OC/1/2, f. 103v. [3] Manning and Bray, Surr. i. 41. [4] CD 1621, vii. 40. [5] Hist. Guildford (1801), pp. 11-20, 203; Surr. Hist. Cent. BR/OC/1/2, ff. 84, 101v; VCH Surr. iii. 548. [6] CJ, x. 100. [7] C219/37/243; 219/38/236; 219/39/197. [8] HP Commons, 1558-1603, i. 253. [9] Surr. Hist. Cent. BR/OC/1/2, f. 66v. [10] Add. 6174, f. 138v. [11] CD 1621, ii. 117; vii. 40-6; CJ, i. 539b, 561a; Surr. Hist. Cent. LM/1331/32. [12] Add. 6174, f. 144v; C219/39/197. [13] C219/40/219; Surr. Hist. Cent. BR/OC/1/2, f. 103v; C231/4, f. 195v. [14] C219/41A/13, 20; Manning and Bray, i. 39.

A.D./B.C.

HASLEMERE

Right of election: in the inhabitant freeholders

7 Mar. 1604	EDWARD FRAUNCEYS
	WILLIAM JACKSON
c. Mar. 1614	SIR THOMAS CRYMES
	SIR WILLIAM BROWNE
6 Dec. 1620	SIR THOMAS CRYMES
	SIR WILLIAM BROWNE
29 Jan. 1624	FRANCIS CAREW II
	POYNINGS MORE
20 Apr. 1625	FRANCIS CAREW II
	POYNINGS MORE
24 Jan. 1626	FRANCIS CAREW II
	POYNINGS MORE
c. Feb. 1628	GEORGE CRYMES
	SIR THOMAS CANON

Haslemere was a small market town which owed some of its modest prosperity to the iron and woollen industry in its neighbourhood. It was enfranchised in 1584, and a charter of 1596 confirmed its market and fairs. In 1601 Sir George More* purchased the lordship of the manor from the Crown, together with the hundred and manor of Godalming, of which Haslemere had originally been a tithing. More's bailiff, who seems to have been the only officer of the borough, acted as returning officer and consequently More dominated the electoral patronage of the borough in this period. The franchise was vested in the freeholders of the borough who, since they held their land by burgage tenure, are described in the indentures as burgesses. The number of parties varied from at least a dozen in 1624 to over 20 in 1626.[1]

In 1604 More put his influence in the borough at the disposal of two aristocratic friends, Henry 9th earl of Northumberland and the lord admiral, the 1st

[1] C219/38/236; 219/39/197. [2] VCH Surr. iii. 547, 560; Guildford Bor. Recs. ed. E.M. Dance (Surr. Rec. Soc. xxiv), p. xxiiii; CSP Dom.

earl of Nottingham (Charles Howard[†]). The senior Member for Haslemere in the first Jacobean Parliament, Edward Fraunceys, was Northumberland's steward at Petworth, the earl's house eight miles from Haselmere. His junior colleague, William Jackson, was either receiver-general or secretary to Nottingham, a long-standing friend and associate of More.[2]

More seems to have responsible for all the Members subsequently elected for this borough until 1628. By 1614 William Jackson had left Nottingham's employment and Edward Fraunceys had acquired property near the Sussex borough of Steyning, where he was elected to the Addled Parliament. Consequently More nominated his son-in-law Sir Thomas Crymes and also Sir William Browne, a trustee of More's lands since 1609. In 1620 More received a request from another son-in-law, Sir Nicholas Carew*, on behalf of his cousin Sir Nicholas Saunders*. More replied on 12 Dec. that 'many days before' he had received Carew's letter he had nominated Crymes and Browne and that they had already been returned.[3] This was despite the fact that Browne had moved to Warwickshire three years earlier.

By the time of the last Jacobean Parliament both seats at Haslemere were going begging as Browne no longer took any interest in Surrey electoral affairs and Crymes was returned for the county. Carew again wrote to More, on 23 Dec. 1623, but this time on behalf of his son Francis, More's grandson, who had recently come of age. Carew wrote that a seat in the Commons for Francis 'would do him good and get him some experience', but if More thought him unsuitable then he begged to have the place himself, 'for I would very fain have him or myself in the next Parliament'. More evidently did consider the young man suitable, however, and consequently Francis was elected as senior partner to another of More's grandsons, Poynings More, aged just 18.[4]

Francis Carew and Poynings More were re-elected in both 1625 and 1626, but in 1628 they were returned at Guildford, where the More interest was also strong. The Haslemere representatives in 1628 were another of Sir George More's grandsons, Sir Thomas Crymes' son George, who had just turned 23, and a Welshman, Sir Thomas Canon. The latter was presumably nominated by More at the request of the earl of Northumberland, with whom Canon had longstanding links.

[1] *VCH Surr.* iii. 45-47; C219/37/248; 219/38/234; 219/40/221. [2] *Loseley MSS* ed. A.J. Kempe, 372, 496-7. [3] Berks. RO, D/ELL/CI/111. [4] Add. 29599, f. 20.

A.D.

REIGATE

Right of election: in the freeholders

c. Mar. 1604	SIR EDWARD HOWARD I
	HERBERT PELHAM
c. Mar. 1614	SIR EDWARD HOWARD I
	JOHN SUCKLING
12 Dec. 1620	SIR THOMAS GLEMHAM
	ROBERT LEWIS
16 Jan. 1624	SIR THOMAS BLUDDER
	ROBERT LEWIS
13 Apr. 1625	SIR THOMAS BLUDDER
	SIR ROGER JAMES
20 Jan. 1626	SIR THOMAS BLUDDER
	SIR WILLIAM MONSON
11 Feb. 1628	SIR THOMAS BLUDDER
	CHARLES COCKAYNE

Reigate first returned Members to the Model Parliament of 1295,[1] but received no charter until 1863. Consequently it remained under the jurisdiction of the lord of the manor and all public officers were chosen by the court leet, including the bailiff, who acted as returning officer. It was nonetheless a reasonably prosperous market town, particularly noted for the manufacture of oatmeal. The franchise was vested in the freeholders, returns usually being made in the name of the 'burgesses', although in 1620 the term 'inhabitants' of the borough was used. Between a dozen and 25 freeholders were normally parties to the indentures.[2]

In the late Elizabethan period Charles Howard[†], 2nd Baron Howard of Effingham and, from 1597, 1st earl of Nottingham, owned half the manor of Reigate, plus the former Augustinian priory, which had been converted into a more desirable residence than the decaying castle. Up until 1600, when it was sold to Thomas Sackville[†], 1st Lord Buckhurst, created 1st earl of Dorset in 1604, the other part of the manor was owned by the earls of Derby.[3]

In the first three elections of this period the seats were divided between the Howard and Sackville interests. In 1604 Sir Edward Howard, a nephew of Nottingham's was returned for the senior seat, while the junior place was taken by Herbert Pelham, a Sussex kinsman of the Sackvilles. Howard was re-elected to the Addled Parliament, his partner being John Suckling, a rising official who had begun his career as secretary to the 1st earl of Dorset. Although the latter was by now dead, Suckling probably owed his seat to the influence of Dorset's grandson, Richard, 3rd earl of Dorset.

Sir Edward Howard's death in 1620 resulted in the senior seat going to the Sackville candidate, Sir Thomas Glemham, another grandson of the 1st earl of Dorset and a close associate of the 3rd earl. The junior seat went to Robert Lewis, a Welsh lawyer who acted as steward of the manor and may have been the Howard candidate. Glemham was the last Sackville nominee at Reigate, probably due to the 3rd earl of Dorset's financial problems. The earl died in March 1624, his share of the manor and was sold four years later to help clear his debts.[4]

In 1624 Robert Lewis was re-elected, this time with Sir Thomas Bludder. The latter lived at Flanchford, a sub-manor of Reigate purchased by his father in 1601. However, it is not clear whether this gave him sufficient influence in the borough to secure his election on his own interest and consequently he may have owed his return to Nottingham. Bludder's father had been victualler of the Navy when Nottingham had been lord admiral, and had served on the earl's embassy to Spain in 1605.[5]

Nottingham died in December 1624 having settled his share in Reigate manor on his second wife Margaret, daughter of James Stewart, earl of Moray, as part of her jointure. It was therefore presumably the countess of Nottingham who nominated Bludder for re-election in April 1625, together with Sir Roger James, her tenant at Reigate Castle.[6] Bludder was again chosen in 1626, when his partner was the countess' new husband and former page, Sir William Monson. Bludder seems to have been on good terms with the countess and Monson; his widowed sister-in-law subsequently alleged that in the late 1620s he had persuaded the couple to allow him to enter property at Flanchford that rightfully belonged to her.[7] Bludder was elected for a fourth time in 1628, when he was paired with Charles Cockayne, whose sister had married the countess' stepson, the 2nd earl of Nottingham (Sir Charles Howard*).[8]

[1]OR.[2]VCHSurr.iii.229,233;C219/37/245;219/39/186;219/41A/15. [3]W. Hooper, *Reigate*, 29-30, 46, 71, 131; *VCH Surr.* iii. 236 [4]*CP*, iv. 422-4; *VCH Surr.* iii. 236; Hooper, 30; Manning and Bray, *Surr.* i. 280. [5]*VCH Surr.* iii. 237. [6]*CP*, ix. 786; Hooper, 29; *VCH Surr.* 232. [7]C78/435/3. [8]*CP*, ix. 789.

A.D./B.C.

SOUTHWARK

Right of election: ?in the ratepayers

c. Mar. 1604	GEORGE RIVERS WILLIAM COWNDEN
7 *Feb. 1610*	WILLIAM MAYHEW *vice* Cownden, deceased ?John Marshall
c. Mar. 1614	EDWARD COXE RICHARD YEARWOOD
4 Dec. 1620	RICHARD YEARWOOD ROBERT BROMFIELD
22 Jan. 1624	RICHARD YEARWOOD FRANCIS MYNGAYE ROBERT BROMFIELD
	Double return of MYNGAYE and BROMFIELD, whose election was declared void, 2 Mar. 1624
c. Mar. 1624	ROBERT BROMFIELD
11 Apr. 1625	RICHARD YEARWOOD WILLIAM COXE
23 Jan. 1626	RICHARD YEARWOOD WILLIAM COXE
15 Feb. 1628	RICHARD YEARWOOD WILLIAM COXE

Southwark owed its existence to its situation at the southern end of London Bridge. Its major highways linked the metropolis to Kent and Surrey, and made Southwark a prime location for shops and taverns. Indeed, writing in the late Elizabethan period, John Stow wrote of its 'many fair inns'.[1] The borough was also a convenient location for industries officially discouraged within the City of London itself, such as leather-dressing, tanning and the theatre. It also housed many breweries, soaphouses and dyehouses.[2]

Of the four Southwark parishes, the most southerly and least urbanised was St. George's, which contained the prisons of the courts of King's Bench and Marshalsea and the Surrey county gaol called the White Lyon. The smallest and wealthiest parish was St. Thomas', which centred round the hospital of the same name. Along the river to the east of the bridge was St. Olave's, which, as Stow remarked, contained many foreigners and poor inhabitants. Textiles, especially felt-making, played an important part in the parish's economy as did shipbuilding and seafaring. To the west of the bridge was the parish of St. Saviour's, created in 1540 by Act of Parliament from two former parishes. Only one part of the parish, the eastern district of Borough-side, was officially within the borough, but this area, which included the market, was the second wealthiest part of Southwark and its inhabitants dominated local office-holding in the borough as a whole. The local economy was dominated by the production and retailing of food and drink. The western part of the parish, consisting of the Paris Garden and Clink liberties, contained numerous bear gardens and theatres, and there were many watermen among the inhabitants. The population of Southwark, including the liberties outside the borough proper, grew from about 19,000 in 1603 to over 25,000 in 1631.[3]

Southwark enjoyed borough status from at least the twelfth century and returned Members to Parliament from 1295,[4] but its proximity to the City of London stunted the development of urban self-government. From 1326 London's corporation began to acquire jurisdiction over its southern neighbour, a process consolidated and confirmed by the charter of 1550. Shortly thereafter Southwark became the twenty-sixth ward of the City, called Bridge Without, and was given its own alderman. However, the residents received no representation on the court of common council, and from 1557 the corporation appointed the alderman who, though active in the borough's government, was not a Southwark resident and seems never to have played any part in its parliamentary elections. The alderman, who for part of this period was Sir Maurice Abbot*, was assisted by three deputies, all of whom were evidently local inhabitants, but the London corporation clearly felt the need of a resident justice and, in 1606, the Court of Aldermen agreed to exercise their long standing, but previously unused, right to nominate a Surrey justice. To ensure that the justice would reside in the borough and remain under corporation control he was given free accommodation in the Bridgehouse and an annual salary of £20.[5]

Those borough institutions as Southwark did possess, such as the borough court, were firmly under the control of the corporation, which appointed the steward, who presided over the borough court's proceedings, and the bailiff. Corporation control was widely resented; John Donne* remarked on the residents' 'scorn' of the lord mayor's authority, though this was far from complete, as Southwark remained under the jurisdiction of Surrey's lord lieutenant, sheriff, and justice of the peace. Moreover, while many London livery companies had the right to search in the

borough they could not prevent non-freemen trading and working there. Both the Surrey and London justices held sessions in the borough, using the former parish church of St. Margaret's at Hill.[6]

The evidence for the impact of the unpopularity of corporation control on elections is ambiguous. It may have contributed to the opposition to Francis Myngaye, the justice resident in the Bridgehouse in 1624, but George Rivers, steward of the borough court, was elected in 1604 despite being a corporation appointee. Moreover, Edward Coxe was returned in 1614 even though he was one of the alderman's deputies, and both he and at least two other Members, his son William Coxe and Richard Yearwood, were freemen of the City. In addition, Robert Bromfield, elected in 1624, was the son a deputy alderman and brother of the future lord mayor.

In the absence of independent borough institutions the Southwark parish vestries, particularly those of St. Saviour's and St. Olave's, played an important role in the government of the borough. In the late Elizabethan period both parishes employed salaried officials to search for lodgers who might prove a burden on the poor rates if allowed to settle, and the vestries supported the Crown's efforts to restrict new building and sub-division of properties.[7] In St. Saviour's the vestry was a tightly knit self-selecting oligarchy of 30 wealthy parishioners, mostly from Boroughside, who, according to their critics, spent large sums feasting together and granted each other valuable leases of parish property at low rates; as a consequence it became known as the 'sharing house'.[8] They constituted the dominant electoral influence in Southwark. Four Members in this period, William Cownden, William Mayhew, Richard Yearwood and Robert Bromfield, were St. Saviour's vestrymen resident in Boroughside. Only Rivers and the Coxes were from outside this circle, the latter being members of the equally oligarchical St. Olave's select vestry.

It is likely that elections were held at the former parish church of St. Margaret's at Hill, although this location is specified only in the indenture for the 1610 by-election.[9] It was probably the bailiff who supervised the elections, just as he had in the Elizabethan period, as the 1625 indenture specifically states that the election took place by virtue of a warrant to the bailiff. However, the bailiff was a party to only one of the surviving indentures, that of 1628.[10] Elections were made by a show of hands, a procedure described as being of 'ancient usage' in 1624, and generally between 15 and 20 electors were named in the returns.[11] The extent of the franchise is uncertain.

The indentures were usually made in the name of the burgesses, but that for 1625 was drawn up in the name of the burgesses and inhabitants. By the late-seventeenth century the vote lay with all the inhabitant householders, but before the Civil War it may have been restricted to ratepayers, at least in theory. In 1624, however, it was alleged that 'divers watermen and others' who had not been eligible to vote had been present at the election, and the privileges committee ruled that a formal poll should have been held to identify those who legitimately had the franchise.[12]

In 1604 the borough elected George Rivers and William Cownden. Both men were inhabitants of Boroughside, and the latter was a member of the St. Saviour's vestry. The former may have secured his election despite his employment by the corporation because he was a client of the 1st earl of Dorset (Thomas Sackville†), the lord treasurer. The St. Saviour's vestry probably wanted Dorset's favour as they then rented the rectory of their parish from the Crown and their lease was shortly due for renewal.[13] During the 1604 session the borough members were appointed *en bloc* to consider bills for the true making of hats and felts (31 Mar.), alehouses, inns and taverns (23 May) and the leather industry (28 June), all measures with important implications for the local economy. In addition they were instructed to consider the bill concerning new building, lodgers and subdivided tenements on 27 Apr. and another measure concerning lodgers on 2 July, measures which presumably had the support of the vestries of St. Saviour's and St. Olave's.[14]

Far from being renewed, the lease of the St. Saviour's rectory was bestowed in May 1605 on a Scotsman, and the vestry did not regain control until 1611, when it purchased the fee-farm for £800.[15] In the 1605-6 session the Southwark Members were appointed to consider a bill 'to reform Multitudes of unnecessary and inconvenient Buildings in or near the City of London, and to avoid the numbers of dangerous Inmates and Lodgers within the same' (24 Jan. 1606). They were also appointed to consider measures concerning watermen (28 Jan. 1606), while the brewers of the borough were presumably interested in measures to prevent the haunting of alehouses (11 Feb.), to stop brewers from selling beer to unlicensed alehouse keepers (3 Apr.), and to naturalize a brewer resident in the Middlesex suburbs of London (17 April).[16]

During the session opposition to the St. Saviour's vestry came to a head. This seems to have originated in a dispute about pews in the church but widened into an attack on the structure of the parish government,

and on 2 Apr. 1606 the vestry decided to seek counsel over its right to elect the churchwardens. According to the vestry itself these critics were no more than 'some ten or twelve' malcontents who thought that they themselves should have been chosen vestrymen. The dispute resulted in a Chancery case in which the vestry was accused of misappropriating parish funds and the following October the court ordered Rivers and Sir Edmund Bowyer*, who lived near Southwark and sat for Surrey, to audit the parish accounts. However, the critics of the vestry clearly thought this unsatisfactory as they prepared a bill for the third session of the first Jacobean Parliament.[17]

The bill, ostensibly 'for the strengthening, explanation, and enlarging' of the 1540 Act which had created the parish, was intended to enlarge the vestry to 40 members, who would be elected by the wealthier subsidymen, and open the churchwardens' accounts to public scrutiny. The vestry naturally denied the charge of misappropriation, and defended its 'sociable meetings' as 'more profitable to the encouraging and drawing men together about the parish business than chargeable to the parish'. It justified its oligarchic constitution on the ground that election would lead to disorder and, since 'every one will covet to name and elect his friend', the choice of men unworthy of office. As for the opening of the accounts, this would lead to 'a dissembled poverty in the idler sort of people'. The proponents of the bill countered that throughout the realm civic officers were chosen 'by the inhabitants and commonalty', unless otherwise ordered by charter, and Members of Parliament 'by the freeholders, which in most places consist of greater multitudes'. The bill received its first reading on 21 Feb. 1607 and four days later was referred to a committee whose members included Rivers. Reported on 12 May, the Commons completed its passage in the Commons four days later but failed to progress in the Lords.[18] During the third session the Southwark Members were appointed to consider another bill concerning building in and around London, and also measures concerning the Court of Marshalsea and the curriers of London's suburbs.[19]

Cownden died shortly before the opening of the fourth session in 1610, and was replaced by his friend and fellow-vestryman William Mayhew, a brewer. It is possible that there was a contest as, three weeks after Cownden's death, Mayhew and John Marshall both appear to have been anxious to win vestry support as each offered to build galleries in the transepts of St. Saviour's parish church to increase the seating. These offers were accepted and the galleries built, but there is no evidence of a poll. Edward Coxe* was the first named of the 15 'burgesses' on the indenture.[20]

In 1614 Rivers was elected for East Grinstead and Coxe, who was a member of the London Cloth-workers' Company, secured the senior seat. Mayhew having died in 1612, Coxe was accompanied in the Addled Parliament by Richard Yearwood, a Grocer and a member of the St. Saviour's vestry. Coxe died in 1618, and Yearwood moved up to the senior place in 1620. His fellow Member in the third Jacobean Parliament, Robert Bromfield, was also a vestryman of St. Saviour's and seems to have had interest in the timber trade. By 1624 he held a position in Star Chamber. A further bill to regulate building around London, which specifically included Southwark, was prepared by the corporation of London and received a first reading on 12 May 1621, but progressed no further.[21] In the following November Yearwood, who had an interest in the drinks trade, spoke forcefully in favour of a petition of the London Brewers' Company against a composition for purveyance which its members were forced to pay.

Yearwood and Bromfield stood again in 1624, but faced a challenge from Francis Myngaye, a nephew to Sir Edward Coke*. According to John Glanville's subsequent report from the committee for privileges, Yearwood was re-elected unanimously, leaving Bromfield to face Myngaye alone. Myngaye subsequently produced two witnesses who stated that he received a majority of the votes cast, but a third witness declared that Myngaye only won the initial show of hands. He added that when Myngaye got on a table to make a speech of thanks the assembled voters cried 'for what?' and then 'No Myngaye! no Myngaye! a Bromfield! a Bromfield!' The witness further stated that Bromfield was judged to have had the most support after a second show of hands. However, an indenture was subsequently drawn up in which Myngaye was returned first with Yearwood taking the second place. A rival indenture was also drawn up which named Yearwood first and Bromfield second. Both documents were dated 22 Jan., but that for Bromfield was apparently drafted after the election. Accusations of malpractice soon flew back and forth between the two sides. It was alleged that Myngaye had obtained possession of the key to the building in which the election was held and prevented voters from gaining access, while his side claimed many of those present had not been eligible to vote and that a demand for a formal poll had been denied. Myngaye was also accused of having altered one or other indenture. Neither accusation against Myngaye was ever proven, whereas the committee for

privileges agreed that the failure to hold a poll made the eligibility of the voters impossible to judge.[22]

Following the election Bromfield agreed to relinquish his claims to Myngaye who, perhaps believing that the settling of his election in his favour was now only a formality, raised the matter at the privileges committee on 26 February.[23] However, to his undoubted dismay, the committee ruled that it was not possible for Bromfield to waive his election. After confirming Yearwood's return, the committee divided equally between seating Bromfield on the one hand and declaring his election void on the other. This was reported by Glanville on 2 Mar. to the Commons, which agreed to seat Yearwood. Moreover, on Coke's motion, a writ for a fresh election to fill the other place was issued the following day. Bromfield was subsequently returned, but whether Myngaye opposed him is unknown.[24]

Neither Bromfield nor Myngaye are known to have subsequently sought re-election. In the Caroline parliaments Yearwood's colleague was Edward Coxe's son William. Like his father, Coxe was a vestryman of St. Olave's, but he had connections with St. Saviour's as he was soon to be related to Yearwood by marriage, and would remember one of the ministers of St. Saviour's in his will. In 1625 Coxe moved to have Southwark included in the bill against petty larceny.[25] The following year the borough was again included in another unsuccessful bill to regulate building, first read on 24 February. The Southwark burgesses were also appointed to consider a bill concerning the London Apothecaries' Company (4 Mar.) and to help draft a measure to prevent the spread of the plague (29 April).[26]

[1] J. Boulton, *Neighbourhood and Soc.* 62-4, 69; J. Stow, *Survey of London* (1598), p. 238. [2] Boulton, 62, 78-9; *CD 1621*, vii. 154; L.A. Clarkson, 'Organization of the English Leather Industry in the Late Sixteenth and Seventeenth Centuries', *EcHR*, n.s. xiii. 256. [3] Boulton, 19, 62-5, 69-71, 265, 267; Stow, 340. [4] *VCH Surr.* iv. 139. [5] Ibid. iv. 136-8; D.J. Johnson, *Southwark and the City*, 147-51, 229-30. [6] *VCH Surr.* iv. 138-9; Johnson 317; *CD 1621*, vii. 155. [7] I. Archer, *Pursuit of Stability*, 184-5. [8] Boulton, 142-3, 265, 267; J. Stow, *Survey of London* ed. J. Strype, ii. bk. 4, pp. 9-10; LMA, P92/SAV/787-98. [9] C219/35/2/73. The 1624 election was said to have taken place at 'usual place for such purposes': J. Glanville, *Reps. of Certain Cases* (1775), p. 7. [10] C219/39/201; 219/41A/16; *HP Commons, 1558-1603*, i. 254. [11] Glanville, 8; C219/35/2/73; 219/39/201. [12] *CJ*, x. 119; Glanville, 8. [13] *VCH Surr.* 153-4. [14] *CJ*, i. 160b, 188a, 222b, 247b, 251a. [15] *CSP Dom.* 1603-10, p. 218; *VCH Surr.* iv. 154; LMA, P92/SAV/450, p. 436. [16] *CJ*, i. 259b, 260b, 266b, 292b, 299b. [17] Archer, 73; LMA, P92/SAV/450, pp. 398, 400; C33/112, f. 21. [18] *CJ*, i. 339a, 340b, 372b, 374b; LMA, P92/SAV/787-98; Johnson, 229-30, 320-1. [19] *CJ*, i. 328b, 329a, 365a. [20] LMA, P92/SAV/450, p. 425; C219/35/2/73. [21] *CJ*, i. 619a; *CD 1621*, vii. 272. [22] 'Earle 1624', f. 31r-v; *CJ*, i. 724b; 'Holland 1624', i. f. 18. [23] 'Earle 1624', f. 31r-v. [24] *CJ*, i. 724b; C219/38/231. [25] *Procs. 1625*, p. 411. [26] *Procs. 1626*, ii. 113, 194; iii. 97.

A.D./B.C.

SUSSEX

Number of voters: unknown

1 Mar. 1604	ROBERT SACKVILLE
	SIR CHARLES HOWARD
2 Nov. 1609	HENRY CAREY *vice* Sackville,
	called to the Upper House
c. Mar. 1614	SIR WALTER COVERT
	SAMPSON LENNARD
14 Dec. 1620	SIR EDWARD SACKVILLE
	CHRISTOPHER NEVILLE
5 Feb. 1624	ALGERNON PERCY, Lord Percy
	THOMAS PELHAM
28 Apr. 1625	(SIR) THOMAS PELHAM, (bt.)
	SIR JOHN SHURLEY
2 Feb. 1626	SIR WALTER COVERT
	SIR ALEXANDER TEMPLE
28 Feb. 1628	RICHARD LEWKNOR
	SIR WILLIAM GORING, bt.

The notoriously bad Wealden roads meant that Sussex was more isolated from London than its geographical proximity would suggest and ensured that the assizes were usually held at East Grinstead, near the Surrey border. For most administrative purposes the county was divided between its eastern and western parts. In accordance with an early sixteenth-century statute, the county court met alternately at Chichester, in the west, and Lewes, in the east, and although in theory there was a single commission of the peace the county bench only met at midsummer; at Epiphany, Easter and Michaelmas separate sessions were held for the western and eastern divisions.[1]

Of the surviving indentures, those that are legible suggest that the elections were usually held at Lewes. Perhaps as a consequence, the eastern division, which was both more populous and more puritan, provided ten of the 13 knights of the shire returned in this period. A 1603 petition from the Sussex gentry against the enforcement of ceremonies and calling for a further reformation attracted widespread support in east Sussex, the subscribers including Sir Walter Covert and Sir John Shurley. In addition, at least half of them had interests in the Wealden iron industry, then at its apogee.[2]

In the Elizabethan period the county possessed an abundance of peers, 'more', according to Richard Curteys, bishop of Chichester, 'than one shire can well bear'.[3] The Jacobean Members included three heirs to peerages, three younger sons, and one (Sampson Lennard) married to a peeress in her own right. The pattern changed in the next reign, but less dramatically than might at first appear, since there had been much intermarriage between gentry and peerage families. Despite the profusion of powerful families there were no known contests in the period. Friendship and intermarriage, which crossed religious barriers to an unusual degree, may have kept families from fighting over the county representation. In particular the Sackvilles and the Howards, the two most powerful noble families, were closely related following the 1580 marriage of Robert Sackville to Margaret Howard. Moreover, those disappointed of a county seat could fall back on no less than 18 borough and six Cinque Port seats.

For most of this period Sussex had three lords lieutenant. In 1604 these were lord treasurer Buckhurst (Thomas Sackville[†]), soon to become 1st earl of Dorset and the major magnate in the east of the county; Henry Percy, 9th earl of Northumberland, who lived at Petworth in west Sussex; and Charles Howard[†], 1st earl of Nottingham, whose estates lay chiefly in Surrey. Nottingham had probably been appointed as a proxy for the senior branch of the Howard family, important west Sussex landowners, whose interests were in abeyance after the attainder of Philip Howard, earl of Arundel in 1589. Nevertheless, he remained in office until his death in 1624. Northumberland was omitted from the commission in 1608, having been imprisoned following his kinsman, Sir Thomas Percy's, involvement in the Gunpowder Plot. His replacement was Philip Howard's son, Thomas, who had been restored in blood and to his father's titles in 1604. The same commission also added Robert Sackville, who had recently succeeded his father as 2nd earl of Dorset. However, Robert died the following year, and as his son, Richard, was still a minor the latter was not appointed to the lieutenancy until 1612. Richard himself died in 1624 and was promptly succeeded as both earl and lord lieutenant by his brother, Sir Edward Sackville.[4]

In 1604 the county's representation was monopolized by the sons of the lord lieutenants, just as it had been in the last Elizabethan Parliament, although their places on the return were reversed, possibly as the result of an agreement reached in 1601. Consequently, Robert Sackville took the senior seat, while Sir Charles Howard, Nottingham's younger son, took the second. The latter had acquired a modest stake in the county by marrying an ironmaster's widow and, like his colleague, lived in the eastern part of the county.

Sackville succeeded as 2nd earl of Dorset in April 1608, but a writ to replace him was not issued till 13 Sept. 1609, by which time he had been dead six months.[5] The replacement, Henry Carey, the son of a Hertfordshire peer, was probably recommended by Nottingham, whose first wife had been Carey's great-aunt. Despite being an outsider, Carey was probably generally acceptable in Sussex, as his father-in-law, Sir Thomas Pelham[†], was an important east Sussex land-owner who had sat for the county in 1586. Sackville's son, Richard, 3rd earl of Dorset, was still under-age at the time of the election, which presumably limited the influence of the Sackville interest. Nevertheless it is notable that Pelham's mother had been a Sackville.[6]

Carey was returned for Hertfordshire in 1614 while Howard sat for New Shoreham. Instead the county returned two septuagenarian brothers-in-law, Sir Walter Covert and Sampson Lennard, both of whom lived in the eastern part of the county. Covert had already sat twice for the county, and over 30 years had established himself as the most effective of the deputy lieutenants and an energetic county administrator. Lennard, on the other hand, was a newcomer who had acquired Hurstmonceaux, through his wife, Baroness Dacre of the South, and had only just been appointed to the Sussex bench.

The poor response of the county to the Benevolence, initiated following the failure of the Addled Parliament to vote supply, brought a stinging rebuke in July 1615 from the Privy Council. It informed the bench that 'the backwardness of yourselves and the rest of the inhabitants by your example will be interpreted as a measure of your affections' to James, and that only three people had 'expressed their love and duty' in a 'reasonable proportion'. In total only about £875 was raised, significantly less than the nearly £1,400 which a single subsidy yielded in the mid-1620s.[7]

Lennard died in 1615, and as Covert showed no interest in seeking re-election, this left both seats in the third Jacobean Parliament to a younger genera-tion. Robert Sackville's second son, Sir Edward was returned alongside Christopher Neville, Lennard's nephew and the younger son of Lord Bergavenny (Edward Neville[†]). Neville maintained a house in Lewes, but lived mostly in London. Sackville and Neville were connected by marriage, the latter's elder brother, Sir Henry Neville II*, having wed the former's aunt. Sir Thomas Bishopp* headed the list of electors named in the indenture, who included two later representatives of the county, Pelham's son

Thomas and Richard Lewknor, and at least five other Members, among them the earl of Northumberland's former steward (Sir) Edward Fraunceys.[8]

The 1622 Benevolence initially faced consider-able resistance in Sussex. Twenty-three members of the county gentry, mostly from the eastern part, were ordered before the Privy Council for failing to subscribe, including Sir Walter Covert, Sir John Shurley and Sir Alexander Temple. Nevertheless, about £1,300 was eventually raised.[9]

Sackville was overseas at the time of the 1624 elec-tion, and shortly afterwards succeeded his brother as 4th earl of Dorset, while Neville was returned for Lewes. This meant that both seats were available. The senior place went to the 22-year old Lord Percy, heir to the earl of Northumberland, and the first Member to be returned from the west of the county since 1593. His colleague was the eldest son of Sir Thomas Pelham[†], who came of an old Sussex family, with extensive iron interests and strong Protestant connec-tions. Having succeeded to his father's estates and baronetcy in late 1624, Pelham took the senior place in the return in 1625. His colleague was Sir John Shurley, his cousin and fellow-puritan, was also the father of Covert's second wife.

The following year two nominees were agreed at a general assembly of the county gentry at the Epiph-any sessions held at Lewes on 17 January. This was the only occasion on which a pre-election meeting is known to have taken place during this period. The day before John Peers, Arundel's steward, wrote that Covert, now in his eighties, was seeking re-election, apparently without opposition. He was unsure who would get the other seat but thought that, if Pelham and Shurley did not want to stand again, Sir Alexander Temple would be nominated. Temple, a younger son in the Buckinghamshire family, had acquired property in east Sussex and a connection with the Sackvilles through his recent third marriage. On the 18th Covert wrote to Arundel and Dorset announcing his nomina-tion and tactfully asking for their approbation. Pelham and Shurley having presumably declined re-election, Covert was subsequently returned with Temple.[10]

The Crown's attempt to raise a fresh Benevolence in August 1626 aroused widespread hostility in Sussex, the deputy lieutenants recording that 'the whole county ... did crave a Parliament by general consent'.[11] In a letter subscribed by Covert, Pelham, Shurley and Temple among others, the bench informed the Council that the inhabitants had answered that 'they are not willing to give as is required' because of 'their wants and poverty occasioned by the late great expenses in many public charges', although they were willing to 'strain themselves beyond their abilities' in 'a parliamentary course'. Only £120 had been raised, which they thought was 'not worthy the presenting'.[12] Nevertheless the Forced Loan, initiated towards the end of 1626, proved relatively successful in Sussex, yielding the equivalent of at least three subsidies. This was largely due to Dorset, who obtained permission for the county to pay the cost of billeting soldiers out of the receipts. Nevertheless the Loan exacerbated political tensions in the county, and the concession on billeting was initially greeted with widespread scepticism, causing Dorset to write to the commissioners indignantly denying that he had been 'made the instrument of deception', and to say that he was 'sorry that any of the country should apprehend His Majesty's would by me have promised the thing which he had not first fully resolved to perform'. He also announced that he had instruction to billet soldiers on refusers, which no doubt hastened compliance.[13]

Neither Covert nor Temple sought re-election in 1628 when, for the only time in the period, both Members came from West Sussex. Richard Lewknor, a country gentleman, had sat in the four previous Parliaments for Midhurst. Though untitled he took precedence over the less experienced Sir William Goring, bt., a second cousin of the courtier Sir George Goring*, who had married the daughter of (Sir) Edward Fraunceys*, the steward of his neighbour the earl of Northumberland.

---

[1] A. Fletcher, *County Community in Peace and War*, 3, 5, 134-6; *SR*, ii. 665. [2] C219/35/2/74, 91; 219/39/205; Fletcher, 3, 17, 61; T.W.W. Smart, 'Extracts from the Mss of Samuel Jeake', *Suss. Arch. Colls.* ix. 45-7. [3] R.B. Manning, *Religion and Soc. in Eliz. Suss.* 222. [4] Sainty, *Lords Lieutenants*, 34-5. [5] C219/35/2/75. [6] *CP*, ix. 786; *HP Commons, 1558-1603*, iii. 194. [7] Harl. 703, f. 115v; E351/1950; Fletcher, 196. [8] C219/37/256. [9] Fletcher, 213; SP14/127/81; 14/135/62. [10] Arundel, Autograph Letters 1617-32, Peers to Spiller, 16 Jan. 1626, Covert to Arundel and Dorset, 18 Jan. 1626. [11] E.S. Cunliffe, '"Booke Concerning the Deputy Leiuetennantshipp"', *Suss. Arch. Colls.* xl. 20. [12] SP16/33/109. [13] Fletcher, 195-6; E. Suss. RO, LCD/EW1, f. 40v.

A.D./B.C.

ARUNDEL

Right of election: in the inhabitants[1]

Number of voters: ?more than 76 in 1624[2]

6 Mar. 1604	THOMAS PRESTON		
	JOHN TEY		
13 May 1610	SIR JOHN DANVERS *vice*		
	Preston, deceased		
c. Mar. 1614	HENRY SPILLER		
	EDWARD MORLEY		
8 Jan. 1621	SIR LIONEL CRANFIELD		
	(SIR) HENRY SPILLER		
22 Nov. 1621	SIR RICHARD WESTON *vice*		
	Cranfield, called to the		
	Upper House		
23 Jan. 1624	(SIR) HENRY SPILLER		
	SIR GEORGE CHAWORTH	37	
	William Mill	29	
	MILL *vice*		
	Chaworth, on petition,		
	24 Mar. 1624		
27 Apr. 1625	(SIR) HENRY SPILLER		
	WILLIAM MILL		
31 Jan. 1626	NICHOLAS JORDAN		
	WILLIAM MILL		
29 Feb. 1628	HENRY FREDERICK HOWARD,		
	Lord Maltravers		
	JOHN ALFORD		

The market town of Arundel, in west Sussex, grew up at the lowest point that the river Arun could be bridged. According to a visitor in the 1630s it was 'relieved with a convenient pretty haven, and graced with an ancient, strong and stately castle'.[3] Despite a lack of social amenities, relatively good communications made it the regular venue for the West Sussex epiphany sessions.[4] The town enjoyed borough status by 1086, but it did not break free from manorial control completely until the nineteenth century. Nevertheless, by the end of the thirteenth century it had a borough court and a mayor. In the mid-sixteenth century Arundel was governed by a self-perpetuating oligarchy consisting of no more than 12 burgesses. The mayor continued to be officially elected by the annual court leet, although in practice the burgesses controlled the choice.[5] The castle, manor and borough formed part of the honour of Arundel, which was inherited, together with the earldom of Arundel, by Philip Howard on the death of his maternal grandfather in 1580. He converted to Catholicism in 1584 and, after his capture trying to flee abroad the following year, was attainted. He died in the Tower in 1595.[6] The town governors took advantage of the earl's fall to procure a judgment on a writ of *quo warranto* in 1587, which, although ostensibly only confirming the borough's existing rights, in fact substantially enhanced them.[7]

Arundel had returned Members to the Parliament since at least 1295. The right of election lay in all the inhabitants, and the indentures were exchanged between the sheriff of Sussex and the mayor, burgesses and commonalty, who were generally said to have made election 'of their common consent and assent'. Usually the mayor was the only voter named in the return. An exception was the 1624 election when, probably because there was a contest, about 20 names were listed. These probably represented fewer than half the number of actual voters.[8]

In the late Elizabethan period the borough fell under the influence of Lord Buckhurst, joint lord lieutenant of Sussex. In 1604 he nominated his servant John Tey, deputy alnager of London, promising that Tey would serve without wages.[9] The election of Thomas Preston for the senior seat marked the revival of the Howard interest. Although Philip's son Thomas was not yet officially restored to his father's estates or titles, the family had regained favour on the accession of James I and there was consequently a widespread assumption that Thomas, who was then still only in his teens, would be rehabilitated.[10] This belief proved correct, for in 1604 a bill was passed restoring Thomas Howard to the earldom of Arundel, while in July the king granted the new earl the manor of Arundel.[11] In Arundel and elsewhere, Thomas' interest seems to have been wielded by his uncle, Lord William Howard, with whom Preston was closely connected.[12]

Preston died sometime before 27 Apr. 1610, upon which date a writ for a by-election was moved by Sir Robert Harley*. The vacancy was filled in May by Sir John Danvers, the stepfather of Harley's friend Sir Edward Herbert*. Danvers may have been recommended to Arundel by his father-in-law, the 7th earl of Shrewsbury (Gilbert Talbot†), with whom he had been connected. Interestingly, his name was inserted in the return in an ink different from that in which the rest of the document was written.[13] The following month a petition from the town of Arundel, complaining that Tey was suing them for wages he had promised not to accept, was referred to the privileges committee, but no further proceedings in the matter are recorded.[14]

Tey was probably dead by the time the next Parliament was summoned in 1614, when Danvers was returned for Montgomery Boroughs. Both the new Members for the Addled Parliament were returned on the Howard interest. Henry Spiller, an Exchequer official, was the brother of the dowager countess of Arundel's steward. The latter kept the earl's courts in Sussex, and is known to have acted as a Howard agent in later elections.[15] The junior Member, Edward Morley, was the stepson of one of Arundel's trustees.[16]

Spiller was re-elected for the next three parliaments. Morley died in 1620, and in the third Jacobean Parliament Arundel nominated his friend and creditor Sir Lionel Cranfield, who had entered government service as a protégé of his great uncle, Henry Howard, earl of Northampton. Cranfield was created a baron in July 1621 and made lord treasurer in September, and as such presumably had a hand in the choice of the newly appointed chancellor of the Exchequer, Sir Richard Weston, as his replacement. On the other hand, Weston was a friend of Arundel's and was also known to Spiller.[17]

In 1624 Weston was returned for Bossiney, meaning that he was no longer available at Arundel, where Spiller was 'elected in the first place ... without contradiction'.[18] Sir George Chaworth, took the second place on the return, subsequently writing that 'Arundel who would have me be at his dispose caused me to be chosen in his own town Arundel (as he called it)'. Like the earl, he was an opponent of war with Spain and was the countess' kinsman by marriage. However, the choice of Chaworth was not universally popular, for he was opposed by William Mill, a member of the local gentry.[19]

A petition from Mill's supporters, objecting to Chaworth's return, was read at the privileges committee on 2 Mar., and on 24 Mar. the chairman, John Glanville, reported the case to the Commons. Glanville stated that an initial 'private enumeration' of the voters had shown that Chaworth had 37 voters to Mill's 35, but subsequently four more Mill supporters had arrived and consequently, when the formal poll was held at midday, the latter had a lead of two votes. The mayor not only refused to accept the result, but according to one account 'sent into the town and fields and called in the inhabitants from their work', even though Mill's supporters had by now dispersed. By five or six in the evening Chaworth had the advantage, whereupon the mayor closed the poll and made out the return. Glanville argued that the mayor's behaviour was wholly improper. Chaworth had clearly lost the formal poll at midday, and the mayor could not be allowed to 'continue the election at his pleasure; and ...

gain his own purpose by wearying out the electors with attendance'. The mayor, moreover, had put the town to a good deal of expense, sending a legal representative to the committee hearing, and therefore Glanville moved for a committee to assess the costs.[20]

Following Glanville's report Chaworth rose to defend his return, stating that he was 'so confident of the justice of the House, that upon this cause, he shall not go out'. He protested that the meeting of the privileges committee had been held at 'a late and unseasonable hour', that he had not had a proper hearing, and that the mayor's counsel 'spake against him'. He demanded that his own counsel be heard, but the House was unimpressed, Edward Alford declaring that 'nothing [had been] said, but said before'. The following day Sir Francis Nethersole* wrote that by his defence Chaworth had got 'nothing but red cheeks'. Chaworth's outspoken opposition to the war with Spain had done nothing to help his cause, for as Nethersole remarked, he had thereby 'lost the goodwill' of the House. Had he been less forthright he might have been afforded the opportunity of fighting a new election. Instead, the Commons ordered the mayor to return Mill.[21]

Spiller and Mill were also elected to the first Caroline Parliament, but another contest threatened in 1626 when Arundel tried to find a seat for Nicholas Jordan, a Chichester lawyer and friend of the attorney-general Robert Heath*. At the Epiphany sessions Jordan had disclaimed any interest in standing. However, he reconsidered his decision after receiving a letter from Heath and applied to John Peers, the earl's steward, to secure his return at Arundel, believing that Mill, being in poor health and having recently lost his wife, would not stand again. Peers, however, found Mill 'resolved to serve if he be chosen'. Consequently Mill and Jordan were returned together, while Spiller was elected at Midhurst, where Weston was influential. The suggestion of Alford, then serving as sheriff, that the earl nominate (Sir) Francis Crane*, Arundel's unsuccessful candidate at New Shoreham, was apparently not taken up.[22]

It seems likely that neither Jordan nor Mill were in sufficiently good health to stand in 1628, while Arundel nominated Spiller at another family borough, Thetford, in order to give his heir, Lord Maltravers, a seat in the Commons. Maltravers, a member of the committee for the bill successfully promoted by his father to entail the manor of Arundel and other properties on the earldom of Arundel,[23] was joined in the Commons by Alford's son John, subsequently Mill's trustee and executor.

[1] CJ, i. 748b. [2] Ibid. 748a. [3] VCH Suss. v. pt. 1, p. 10; 'Relation of a Short Survey of the Western Counties' ed. L.G. Wickham Legg Cam. Misc. XVI (Cam. Soc. ser. 3. lii) pt. 3, p. 30. [4] A. Fletcher, County Community in Peace and War, 135, 220. [5] VCH Suss. v. pt. 1, pp. 73-5, 77; G.W. Eustace, Arundel, 217. [6] M.A. Tierney, Hist. and Antiqs. of Castle and Town of Arundel, 19-20; Oxford DNB sub Howard, Philip, earl of Arundel. [7] VCH Suss. v. pt. 1, p. 74; Eustace, 122, 127; Tierney, 697-8. [8] VCH Suss. v. pt. 1, p. 83; C219/35/2/88; 219/38/244. [9] Procs. 1610 ed. E.R. Foster, ii. 373. [10] HMC Hatfield, xv. 283. [11] HLRO, HL/PO/PB/1/1603/1J1n38; CSP Dom. 1603-10, p. 129. [12] CJ, i. 973a. [13] Ibid. i. 422a; C219/35/2/77. [14] Procs. 1610, ii. 373; CJ, i. 427b. [15] Lives of Philip Howard, Earl of Arundel, and of Anne Dacres, his Wife ed. Henry Granville, 14th duke of Norfolk, 240-1; Cal. N. Wales Letters. ed. B.E. Howells (Univ. Wales, Bd. of Celtic Studies, Hist. and Law Ser. xxiii), 218. [16] Tierney, 20n. [17] M. Prestwich, Cranfield, 421n, 521, 524. [18] Glanville, 72. [19] Add. 72368, f. 11. [20] CJ, i. 748a; Harl. 159, f. 98v; Glanville, 74-5. According to the edn. of Glanville's reports printed in the 1770s, the votes in the initial poll were 25 for Mill and 27 for Chaworth. This edition also states that four more Mill supporters had arrived by midday and that a further ten Chaworth supporters were subsequently found. However, both the Journal and Pym's diary agree that the midday poll result was 39 votes for Mill and 37 for Chaworth, although Pym does not give the total for the initial poll and neither state the final result. CJ, i. 748a; Glanville, 72-3; 'Pym 1624', i. f. 39v. [21] CJ, i. 748a-b; 'Spring 1624', p. 158; 'Pym 1624', i. f. 40v; SP14/161/36. [22] Arundel, Autograph Letters 1617-32, Peers to Spiller, 16 Jan. 1626. [23] CD 1628, iv. 236; Tierney, 132-5.

A.D./B.C.

BRAMBER

Right of election: ?in the inhabitants

14 Feb. 1604	SIR JOHN SHURLEY
	HENRY SHELLEY I
c.Mar. 1614	SIR JOHN LEEDES
	HENRY SHELLEY II
16 Dec. 1620	THOMAS BOWYER
	ROBERT MORLEY
23 Jan. 1624	THOMAS BOWYER
	ROBERT MORLEY
c.Apr. 1625	THOMAS BOWYER
	WALTER BARTTELOT
16 Jan. 1626	WALTER BARTTELOT
	THOMAS BOWYER
23 Feb. 1628	(SIR) THOMAS BOWYER, (bt.)
	(SIR) SACKVILLE CROWE, (bt.)

Situated four miles from the sea on the west bank of the River Adur, Bramber gave its name to one of the six rapes of Sussex, at a time when it was presumably the principal settlement in the Adur valley. Its prosperity was not of long duration as a port, New

Shoreham, situated at the mouth of the river, replaced it and by 1595 it had ceased even to be a market town. Unincorporated, it came under the lordship of the barony of Bramber, and the administration of the borough was in the hands of a constable, chosen annually by the steward at the manorial court leet from two candidates put forward by the borough jury and the retiring constable.[1]

In the early Elizabethan period the barony belonged to the 4th earl of Norfolk, but was confiscated by the Crown on his downfall in 1572. The duke's grandson, Thomas Howard, was restored to the lesser title of earl of Arundel in 1604 but had difficulty recovering the family estates. In 1608 the barony was granted to the 1st earl of Suffolk and Lord William Howard of Naworth, younger sons of the last duke, who in turn sold it to Arundel in 1619.[2]

Bramber returned Members to Parliament in 1295, but subsequently enjoyed only intermittent representation, sometimes in conjunction with the adjoining borough of Steyning, and was only consistently represented from 1453.[3] Indentures were exchanged between the sheriff of Sussex and up to 18 named 'burgesses' headed by the constable, who were described in the returns for 1604 and 1628 as acting with others. In an election dispute in 1640 the Commons ruled that the franchise lay with all the inhabitants, including lodgers, and this may have been the practice earlier.[4]

In the later Elizabethan period, in the absence of the Howard interest, the 1st Lord Buckhurst (Thomas Sackville†), one of the lord lieutenants of Sussex, emerged as a significant electoral patron in Bramber.[5] He may have been responsible for the election of his kinsman, Henry Shelley I, in 1604, but Shelley owned significant property in adjoining parishes and may not have needed outside support. Shelley's partner was Sir John Shurley, who, though he lived in east Sussex, was also the son-in-law of Sir Thomas Shirley I*, another important local landowner.

Neither Shelley nor Shurley seem to have sought re-election in 1614. The senior place in the Addled Parliament went to Sir John Leedes, who owned property in Bramber and was the son-in-law of the Howard client, Sir Thomas Monson*. The junior place was bestowed upon Shelley's second son and namesake, as Shelley himself was then sick. The sale of lands to meet Thomas Shelley's debts had destroyed the Shelley interest by 1620, when Leedes was returned for New Shoreham. Thomas Bowyer, who took the senior seat, lived over 20 miles to the west and had no obvious connection with Bramber, but he was nonetheless re-elected to the next six parliaments. In 1620 and 1624 Robert Morley, a member of the east Sussex gentry, who may have owed his return to his neighbour Sir John Shurley, took the junior seat. Meanwhile John Middleton* had taken control of the Shelley property and in the next two elections it was presumably he who was responsible for nominating his son-in-law Walter Barttelot, first as junior Member in 1625 and then as senior Member in 1626. Barttelot may also have had the support of Arundel, who almost certainly employed his brother. In 1628 Middleton apparently transferred his interest to (Sir) Sackville Crowe (bt.), who was one of his trustees.[6]

[1] VCH Suss. vi. pt. 1, pp. 206, 210; Add. 28252, f. 110. [2] Ibid. 5; M.A. Tierney, *Hist. and Antiqs. of Castle and Town of Arundel*, 416-17; Arundel, Suss. deeds, D2838, info. from Mrs. Sara Rodger. [3] VCH Suss. vi. pt. 1, 211. [4] C219/35/2/86; 219/41B/85; D. Hirst, *Representative of the People?*, 99. [5] *HP Commons, 1558-1603*, i. 257. [6] C.F. Trower, 'Findon', *Suss. Arch. Colls.* xxvii. 17.

A.D.

CHICHESTER

Right of election: in the inhabitant ratepayers

Feb. 1604	ADRIAN STOUGHTON, recorder GEORGE BLINCOWE
5 Apr. 1610	SIR JOHN MORLEY *vice* Blincowe, deceased
c. Mar. 1614	SIR JOHN MORLEY ADRIAN STOUGHTON, recorder
14 Dec. 1620	SIR EDWARD CECIL THOMAS WHATMAN, recorder
Feb. 1624	SIR THOMAS EDMONDES THOMAS WHATMAN, recorder
28 Apr. 1625	ALGERNON PERCY, Lord Percy HUMPHREY HAGGETT
13 Jan. 1626	ALGERNON PERCY, Lord Percy HUMPHREY HAGGETT
c. Apr. 1626	EDWARD DOWSE *vice* Percy, called to the Upper House
29 Feb. 1628	WILLIAM CAWLEY HENRY BELLINGHAM

Described in 1635 as a 'pleasant and sweet little city ... in a pleasant, fertile level and not far from the main sea', Chichester, situated in the extreme west of Sussex, had a population of about 2,500.[1] Despite being the seat of a bishopric, poor communications with the east of the county meant that it was obliged by statute to share the county court alternately with Lewes in the east, 'the same shire being 70 miles in length'.[2] The coast was five miles away, but the town was said to possess 'the best haven between Portsmouth and the Thames', and enjoyed an increasingly flourishing trade in corn with Ireland and the Low Countries.[3] There were resident gentry and 'goodly seats of lords, knights and gentlemen ... not far off', notably those of the Howards at Arundel and the Percys at Petworth. Thomas Howard, restored to the earldom of Arundel in 1604, was the city's *custos rotulorum* by 1612. In 1618 he procured for the corporation a new charter, in which he was named high steward. His friend Henry Percy, 9th earl of Northumberland, was imprisoned in the Tower for alleged complicity in the Gunpowder Plot between 1605 and 1621, but retained control of his lands.[4]

A mayor and two bailiffs had governed Chichester since the early thirteenth century. In addition there was a council of 'free citizens enfranchised', of uncertain number, which had evolved out the medieval merchants' guild. By the early part of this period the corporation had acquired a recorder, although his office, like that of alderman, bestowed on former mayors, was not sanctioned by charter. Sessions of the peace for the city were held under commissions issued periodically by the Crown. However, as the bishop complained in 1617, these allowed outsiders 'hateful to the whole incorporation' to involve themselves in the city's affairs. The new charter issued the following year formalized many of the existing arrangements, and made the recorder, the mayor and four aldermen justices of the peace for the city. It also created a common council, consisting of former civic officeholders, who elected the mayor; again this probably merely confirmed existing practice, with the common council taking the place of the 'free citizens enfranchised'.[5]

Chichester had been represented in Parliament since 1295. During a disputed Elizabethan election it had been admitted that the franchise lay in those inhabitants who paid scot and lot, but only one of the surviving indentures (1620) for this period mentions the participation of 'the commonalty'. Indentures were normally exchanged between the sheriff of Sussex and the mayor, aldermen and citizens who, in 1604, were said to 'have assembled themselves together in their council house and guildhall'.[6] In the early Elizabethan period Henry Fitzalan, earl of Arundel had been a major electoral force in the city. After his death in 1580 his interest in Chichester passed to his son-in-law, John, 1st Lord Lumley, who had inherited Arundel's house at Stanstead, seven miles from the city.[7]

In 1604 the indentures record the election 'with one consent and assent' of two freemen, Adrian Stoughton, the recorder, and George Blincowe, described as resident, who had probably lived in the city since his brother had been appointed chancellor of the diocese in 1590.[8] It is likely that Blincowe was a Lumley nominee, as it was almost certainly he who had recommended William Ashby[†] to Lumley in 1593, when Ashby had been returned for Chichester at the latter's nomination.[9] The death of Blincowe was certified to the Commons by the city on 2 Apr. 1610, when the writ for his replacement was issued; the by-election was held three days later. Lumley having died the previous year without surviving children, it is likely that Blincowe's successor, Sir John Morley, was nominated by Thomas Howard, earl of Arundel, the great-grandson of Henry, earl of Arundel. Morley lived near Chichester, but perhaps more significant was the fact that his father-in-law, Sir Edward Caryll, had been closely connected with the Howards.[10]

Both Stoughton and Morley were re-elected in 1614. Stoughton died later that year, and was replaced as recorder by Morley's brother, Edward*, but the latter had been sacked by the corporation for absenteeism by the time the 1618 charter was granted. Presumably as a result of his brother's disgrace, Morley decided not to seek re-election in 1620. He was returned instead for New Shoreham, probably at Arundel's nomination, early in the New Year.[11] The city elected Edward Morley's replacement, Thomas Whatman, alongside the soldier Sir Edward Cecil, a first cousin of Northumberland. Whatman was re-elected to the last Jacobean Parliament, together with the treasurer of the Household, Sir Thomas Edmondes, who was presumably the nominee of Arundel, a privy councillor.

Whatman was not returned again in 1625, an early sign, perhaps, of declining relations between him and the corporation. In his absence the city's elections came completely, albeit temporarily, under the control of its aristocratic neighbours. In 1625 Northumberland's eldest son, Lord Percy was elected with Arundel's secretary, Humphrey Haggett. They were again elected in 1626, but Percy was called up to the Lords in his father's barony on 28 Mar., and a week later the Commons ordered the writ for the by-election.[12] The return has not survived, but Bishop William Laud's annotations on a contemporary printed list of Members of Parliament indicate that Percy's replacement was the latter's former tutor Edward Dowse.[13]

In August 1626 Whatman complained to the Privy Council that he had been sacked by Chichester's corporation and procured an order for his reinstatement. In the ensuing war of words Whatman alleged 'some indirect carriage and fraudulent speeches used at the last election of a burgess for Parliament'. However there is no evidence that this accusation was pursued and it may have been intended merely to discredit his opponents. On 12 Sept. the Council ordered the corporation to restore Whatman, who was instructed to behave respectfully to the mayor and aldermen.[14]

By the end of 1627 billeted soldiers were proving a major burden on Chichester, and were blamed for an outbreak of the plague.[15] Thoroughly disgruntled, Chichester unanimously returned two residents to the third Caroline Parliament. William Cawley, the son of a wealthy brewer who had served three terms as mayor, had just founded an almshouse for impoverished tradesmen. He was accorded the senior seat, although his colleague Henry Bellingham was an older man from a recognized county family. During the first session complaint was made to the Commons against the mayor for his acceptance of billeting, possibly by one of the justices who had been intruded onto the city bench in 1617 and who may have had a grudge against the corporation.[16]

In the following October Bellingham and Cawley were summoned before the Privy Council for having encouraged the inhabitants 'to shut the gates of the city' against soldiers, and for saying that 'by law there could be no more billeting of soldiers'. They also stood accused of having warned the city's authorities 'to take heed what you did, for that the Parliament would call you to account for it'. The Privy Council found such behaviour, 'strange and unheard of from persons living under a civil government', but the day after Bellingham and Cawley made their appearance on 14 Oct. they were discharged, the Council having perhaps belatedly realized that they were Parliament men.[17]

[1] 'Relation of a Short Survey of the Western Counties' ed. L.G. Wickham Legg *Cam. Misc.* xvi. (Cam. Soc. ser. 3. lii), pt. 3, pp. 33, 35; A. Fletcher, *County Community in Peace and War*, 8. [2] *SR*, ii. 665. [3] J. Dallaway, *Hist. of Western Div. of Co. of Suss.* i. pt. 1, p. 1; *SR*, iv. 729; Fletcher, 20; *VCH Suss.* iii. 102. [4] Fletcher, 8-9; 'Relation of a Short Survey', 35; C181/1, f. 169v; Dallaway, i. pt. 1, p. 153. [5] *VCH*, iii. 90-6; Dallaway, i. pt. 1, pp. 153-4; C181/1, f. 47v; 181/3, ff. 169v, 294v; M.A. Tierney, *Hist. and Antiqs. of Castle and Town of Arundel*, 433; F.W. Steer, *Chichester City Chs.* (Chichester Pprs. iii), 18-20. [6] *VCH Suss.* iii. 98; J.E. Neale, *Eliz. House of Commons*, 267; C219/35/2/87; 219/37/259. [7] *HP Commons, 1558-1603*, i. 258. [8] C219/35/2/87. [9] *HP Commons, 1558-1603*, i. 353. [10] *CJ*, i. 417b; C219/35/2/78-9; *Oxford DNB sub* Lumley, John, first Bar. Lumley; H. Ellis, 'Certificate concerning Justices of the Peace in 1587', *Suss. Arch. Colls.* ii. 60; M.A. Tierney, *Hist. and Antiqs. of Castle and Town of Arundel*, 20n. [11] SP16/35/74-5. [12] *Procs. 1626*, ii. 427. [13] SP16/20/36. [14] *CSP Dom.* 1625-6, p. 414; *APC*, 1626, pp. 223, 256, 264; SP16/35/74-6. [15] *APC*, 1627-8, pp. 173, 180. [16] *CD 1628*, iii. 185, 511. [17] *APC*, 1628-9, pp. 187-8, 197.

A.D./B.C.

EAST GRINSTEAD

Right of election: in the inhabitant burgage-holders

Number of voters: 15 in 1621

8 Feb. 1604	SIR HENRY COMPTON
	SIR JOHN SWINARTON
c. Mar. 1614	SIR HENRY COMPTON
	(SIR) GEORGE RIVERS
1 Jan. 1621	SIR HENRY COMPTON
	THOMAS PELHAM
	?Robert Goodwin
7 Feb. 1624	(SIR) ROBERT HEATH
	MATTHIAS CALDICOTT
c. Apr. 1625	SIR HENRY COMPTON
	(SIR) ROBERT HEATH
c. Jan. 1626	SIR HENRY COMPTON
	(SIR) ROBERT HEATH
c. Mar. 1626	ROBERT GOODWIN, gent. *vice* Heath, ineligible to sit
18 Feb. 1628	SIR HENRY COMPTON
	ROBERT GOODWIN

East Grinstead, situated close to the Surrey border, was only 30 miles from London. Thanks to the notoriously impassable Sussex roads it accordingly shared the assizes with Horsham (and occasionally, in dry summers, with Lewes). In addition the town lay on the edge of Ashdown forest, a centre of the Wealden iron industry.[1] An unincorporated borough, East Grinstead had returned Members since 1301, the right of election being in the inhabitant burgage-holders. The chief officer was the bailiff, who was annually elected at the court leet. He probably drew up the returns, in which his name generally headed the list of electors, who usually numbered no more than 15.[2]

At the beginning of this period the borough was part of the duchy of Lancaster, as was Ashdown Forest. However, the Duchy's property in Sussex was administered by the head of the Sackville family as steward of the honour of Eagle. The Sackvilles also owned the advowson of the parish church and considerable property in and around the borough. In the sixteenth century they lived at nearby Buckhurst, from where Thomas Sackville† took the title of his barony when he was raised to the peerage in 1567. Consequently, during the Elizabethan period it was the Sackvilles rather than the chancellors of the Duchy who were the dominant electoral patrons in the borough. At the beginning of the seventeenth century the Sackvilles moved to Knole in Kent, but they continued to use Withyham church, some six miles from the borough, as their mausoleum, and in 1606 Buckhurst, by now lord treasurer and 1st earl of Dorset, purchased the lordship of the borough.[3]

Sir Henry Compton, who had sat for the borough in the last Elizabethan Parliament, was the stepson and son-in-law of the lord treasurer's heir, Robert Sackville*. He was accompanied to the first Jacobean Parliament by Sir John Swinarton, a London alderman whose farm of the French and Rhenish wines brought him into frequent contact with the lord treasurer. Compton subsequently took up residence at Brambletye, just outside the town, and was re-elected throughout the period, except in 1624. However, Swinarton, who had no connection with the Sackvilles after the death of lord treasurer Dorset in 1608, was not returned again.

Robert Sackville, 2nd earl of Dorset, died less than a year after his father. In his will he instructed his executors to build a 'college or hospital' for the poor in East Grinstead, which he endowed with a rent charge of £330 a year. One of the executors was (Sir) George Rivers, who had already sat for the borough in the last two Elizabethan parliaments and was re-elected in 1614 with Compton.[4] The 3rd earl of Dorset promoted a bill, which was introduced in the Commons, to confirm the establishment of the hospital. It received a second reading on 16 May and was ordered to be engrossed eight days later, but there were no further proceedings.[5]

There is no evidence that Rivers sought re-election in 1621, by which time he may have been in poor health. Instead, Compton's partner was Thomas Pelham, heir to a major east Sussex estate. It seems likely that Pelham was the nominee of the 3rd earl of Dorset, to whom he was related. It also seems possible that Dorset endorsed his candidacy in return for the support of Pelham's father for the earl's steward, Richard Amherst*, at Lewes. There is no contemporary evidence that either Compton or Pelham were forced to contest their seats. There is a slim possibility that Robert Goodwin, who was to be returned in 1626

and was the son of an important local gentleman, may have stood against them, as 60 years later he recalled that he had been elected for East Grinstead in 1621, but it seems much more likely that, with the passage of time, he had become confused about the date of his successful election.[6] During the course of the 1621 Parliament Dorset again sought statutory confirmation of Sackville College. A bill to that effect was introduced in the Commons, where it was committed on 4 May, but not reported.[7]

Neither Compton nor Pelham were re-elected for East Grinstead in 1624. The latter was returned for the county, but the reason for Compton's decision not to stand again is unknown, although it may have been connected with the death of his wife that same year. The junior seat went to Matthias Caldicott, a favourite servant of Dorset's, while the senior seat was bestowed upon the solicitor general (Sir) Robert Heath. Heath had family connections with the East Grinstead area and had purchased property in the borough from Caldicott, but he almost certainly owed his election to Dorset, whom he attended on his deathbed on 28 Mar. and whose will he witnessed. As in 1614 and 1621, Dorset proved eager to secure statutory recognition of Sackville College, and early in the Parliament a bill to that effect was laid before the Lords.[8] However, by the time the bill was given a second reading Dorset had died and the measure was quietly forgotten. There were no further attempts to secure statutory confirmation of the hospital, which was instead incorporated by letters patent in 1631.[9]

There is no evidence that Caldicott sought re-election after the death of his employer. By the time of the elections for the 1625 Parliament the 4th earl of Dorset (Sir Edward Sackville*) was a rising figure at Court and was presumably happy to nominate Heath again at East Grinstead. On this occasion Heath took the second place, leaving the senior position free for Sir Henry Compton, who was closely associated with the fourth earl. Compton and Heath were re-elected the following year, but the latter had been promoted to attorney-general in the intervening period, and on 10 Feb. 1626 the Commons declared his election void in accordance with the resolution of 1614. The ensuing election saw the first crack in the Sackville's domination of East Grinstead's electoral patronage with the election of Robert Goodwin, whose father owned four burgages in the borough but had no known connection with Dorset. Goodwin succeeded to his father's estate the following year and was re-elected with Compton in 1628.[10]

[1] A. Fletcher, *County Community in Peace and War*, 136; E. Straker, *Wealden Iron*, 238-41. [2] W.H. Hills, *Hist. East Grinstead*, 22, 60-1; C219/37/260; 219/38/240. The bailiff certainly drew up the returns in the 1640s, see *CJ*, iv. 432a. [3] Hills, 10, 75; *Duchy of Lancaster Office-Holders* ed. R. Somerville, 216-17; *HP Commons, 1558-1603*, i. 259; *CSP Dom.* 1603-10, p. 338; 1611-18, p. 5. [4] PROB 11/113, f. 182-v [5] *Procs. 1614 (Commons)*, 81, 258, 331; PROB 11/143, f. 210. [6] *CJ*, ix. 587b. [7] *CJ*, i. 607a. [8] PROB 11/143, ff. 210-11; Kyle thesis, 382-3; *LJ*, iii. 269, 284. [9] C66/2571/17. [10] *Procs. 1626*, ii. 14.

A.D./B.C.

HORSHAM

Right of election: in the burgage-holders

Number of voters: 27 in 1628[1]

12 Mar. 1604	JOHN DODDRIDGE
	MICHAEL HICKS
c. Mar. 1614	SIR THOMAS VAVASOUR
	JOHN MIDDLETON
c. Jan. 1621	THOMAS CORNWALLIS II
	JOHN MIDDLETON
22 Jan. 1624	JOHN BOROUGH
	JOHN MIDDLETON
19 Apr. 1625	(SIR) JOHN BOROUGH
	JOHN MIDDLETON
24 Jan. 1626	(SIR) JOHN BOROUGH
	JOHN MIDDLETON
29 Feb. 1628	SIR DUDLEY NORTH
	JOHN MIDDLETON

Situated on the River Arun and the edge of St. Leonard's forest in the west Sussex rape of Bramber, Horsham prospered in Elizabethan times as a centre of the Wealden iron industry. It was also the seat of the county gaol and sometimes hosted the summer assizes and quarter sessions.[2] The manor and borough of Horsham descended with the barony of Bramber in the Howard family until it passed to the Crown on the attainder of the 4th duke of Norfolk in 1572. The duke's grandson, Thomas Howard, earl of Arundel, was restored in blood in 1604, but had difficulty regaining the family estates. In 1608 a moiety of the barony of Bramber and the attached properties formed part of a grant of former Howard lands to Arundel's uncles, the 1st earl of Suffolk and Lord William Howard. Three years later a survey of Horsham, conducted by Arundel's steward, declared that Arundel was the 'lord paramount' of the borough. However, it was not until 1619 that the earl bought out Suffolk and Lord William Howard's claim to the borough.[3]

Horsham enjoyed borough status by 1235, but was never incorporated. Nevertheless it developed relatively sophisticated institutions of self-government, headed by two bailiffs chosen annually in the manorial court leet by the lord's steward, who was selected from four candidates presented by the burgesses. Horsham faced *quo warranto* proceedings in 1614, but its claim to be a borough by prescription was acknowledged by the Crown three years later.[4]

The borough was represented in Parliament from 1295. The franchise lay with the burgesses, who owned the burgage plots held directly from the lord of the manor. Although there were originally 52 plots, sub-division accounts for the fact that 54 owners are recorded in the 1611 survey. The indentures were made in the name of the two bailiffs, who presumably supervised elections, and up to 25 named burgesses.[5]

In 1604 the borough was still under Crown control, and lord treasurer Buckhurst (Thomas Sackville[†]), joint lord lieutenant of the county, probably nominated both Members on the recommendation of Sir Robert Cecil[†]. Consequently Cecil's friend Michael Hicks was re-elected, together with the rising Crown lawyer John Doddridge. By 1614 Hicks had died and Doddridge was a judge. The earl of Arundel was in Italy and, whatever his claims to the lordship of Horsham may have been, he was in no position to exercise electoral patronage in the borough. The earl of Suffolk was consequently able to secure the return of his wife's cousin, Sir Thomas Vavasour, the knight marshal, to the Addled Parliament. The junior Member, John Middleton, was a local ironmaster, and was the first resident known to have been returned for the borough since 1529. He went on to be re-elected to every Parliament in this period.[6]

Vavasour died in 1620, and it is likely that Arundel, by now returned to England and confirmed in the lordship of the borough, nominated Thomas Cornwallis II to the third Jacobean Parliament. Cornwallis probably owed this nomination to his kinswoman Lady Katherine Cornwallis, a Surrey neighbour of Arundel's mother.[7] There is no evidence that Cornwallis sought re-election in 1624, when (Sir) John Borough, a client of Arundel's, was returned. Borough was re-elected in 1625 and 1626, but in 1628 was replaced by Sir Dudley North, the young heir of a Cambridgeshire peer. He had spent the previous three years soldiering in the Netherlands, and his only apparent link with Arundel was through his uncle, Capt. Roger North, who had mounted an expedition to Guiana in 1619 with the earl's backing.[8]

[1] C219/41B/81. [2] *VCH Suss.* vi. pt. 2, pp. 129-35, 178. [3] Ibid. vi. pt. 2, pp. 156; M.F.S. Hervey, *Thomas Howard, Earl of Arundel*, 21-24, 40, 464; M.A. Tierney, *Hist. and Antiqs. of Castle and Town of Arundel*, 416; W. Albery, *Millennium of Facts in Hist. of Horsham and Suss.* 50, 53; Arundel, Suss. deeds, D2838, info. from Mrs. Sara Rodger. [4] *VCH Suss.* vi. pt. 2, p. 180; Albery, 63-71. [5] *VCH Suss.* vi. pt. 2, 180, 189; Albery, 44; W. Albery *Parlty. Hist. of Ancient Bor. of Horsham*, 18; C219/41B/81. [6] *Oxford DNB sub* Howard, Thomas, 14th earl of Arundel; *VCH Suss.* vi. pt. 2, p. 163. [7] Manning and Bray, *Surr.* iii. 34; Hervey, 248. [8] J.A. Williamson, *English Colonies in Guiana and on the Amazon*, 83.

A.D.

LEWES

Right of election: in the inhabitants[1]

Number of voters: 147-50 in 1628[2]

21 Feb. 1604	JOHN SHURLEY
	SIR HENRY NEVILLE II
c. Mar. 1614	CHRISTOPHER NEVILLE
	RICHARD AMHERST
21 Dec. 1620	SIR GEORGE GORING
	RICHARD AMHERST
20 Jan. 1624	CHRISTOPHER NEVILLE
	SIR GEORGE GORING
20 Apr. 1625	SIR GEORGE GORING
	(SIR) GEORGE RIVERS
18 Jan. 1626	SIR GEORGE GORING
	(SIR) GEORGE RIVERS
26 Feb. 1628	SIR GEORGE GORING
	GEORGE RIVERS 61
	ANTHONY STAPLEY 69[3]

Double return of Rivers and Stapley. STAPLEY declared elected, 3 Apr. 1628

c. *July 1628*	JEROME WESTON *vice* Goring,
	Goring, called to the
	Upper House

Camden described Lewes as 'for largeness and populousness one of the chief towns' of Sussex, and it has been estimated that its population at this period may have substantially exceeded 2,000. This considerable figure was due less to commerce than to its functions as a sessions' town and as the social centre for the three rapes of East Sussex: the appalling local roads almost required even minor gentry families to maintain houses in Lewes for winter use. Thomas Twyne,

the distinguished physician and astrologer, settled in the town under the patronage of lord treasurer Dorset (Thomas Sackville[†]) and played a prominent role in the town's government.[4]

An unincorporated borough which had been represented in Parliament since 1295, Lewes and the lordship of which it formed a part lay within the honour or barony of the same name. In this period half the barony was held by the Nevilles of Birling in Kent, while the other half was divided between the senior branch of the Howard family and the Sackvilles. The Howards played no discernable role in the borough's politics in this period, but the Sackvilles were more influential. Earls of Dorset from 1604, they were the dominant aristocratic family of East Sussex and used the town as an administrative centre for their estates, being for most of the period in the charge of Richard Amherst. Although without a charter, the townsmen enjoyed a degree of self-government under the Twelve, described by John Rowe, the Neville's steward, as 'a society of the wealthier and discreeter sort of townsmen'. Despite the name, Rowe states that the membership of the Twelve generally exceeded a dozen, although they were never more than 24. The Twelve were a self-selecting oligarchy that controlled local taxation and issued the borough's bye-laws. The chief officers of the borough were the two annually elected constables, the most senior of whom was selected on the basis of length of service from among the Twelve; the senior constable then chose his junior partner.[5] According to an account of proceedings at the privileges committee in 1628 'the constable', probably meaning the senior of the two, 'was to make the return'.[6] Indentures were exchanged between the sheriff and the constables and about a dozen named 'burgesses and inhabitants', probably members of the Twelve, acting 'by the consent of the greatest part of all the burgesses and inhabitants'.[7]

John Shurley, who took the senior seat in the first Jacobean Parliament, was a younger son of a family seated at Isfield, five miles from Lewes, and the only Member in the period who did not obviously belong by blood, marriage, or service to the seigneurial family circle. A recently created serjeant-at-law, he had sat for the borough in three Elizabethan parliaments and resided there when the exigencies of his profession allowed. Sir Henry Neville united the two family interests as heir to the Birling estate and the 1st earl of Dorset's (Thomas Sackville[†]) son-in-law, but took the junior seat.

Dorset died in 1608 and bequeathed £1,000 to Lewes to build a granary for the poor and a further £2,000 to stock it with wheat, which must have strengthened the Sackville interest in the borough.[8] The date of the 1614 election is unknown as the indenture is missing, but the sheriff's precept, dated 17 Mar., survives and the election presumably took place shortly thereafter.[9] There is no indication that Shurley or Sir Henry Neville sought re-election. Advancing age may have deterred the former, as he was now probably in his late 60s, while Neville had been removed from the county bench, presumably because of suspicions of Catholicism. The Neville interest was instead transferred to Sir Henry's younger, more Protestant, brother, Christopher, who took the first place in the return. His partner was the Sackville's steward, Amherst.

In 1620 Christopher Neville was returned for Sussex, and it is likely that his family's influence at Lewes went to his brother-in-law, Sir George Goring. The latter, a rising courtier and a client of the favourite the marquess of Buckingham, had his own interest in the borough as owner of a large town house and other property in Lewes, 11 miles from his principal estate at Hurstpierpoint. Both his father and grandfather had sat for the borough in Elizabethan parliaments. Amherst was re-elected for the junior seat.

By 1624 the Sackville interest seems to have fallen into abeyance in Lewes, possibly due to the increasing indebtedness of Richard, 3rd earl of Dorset. Christopher Neville was re-elected for the senior seat with Goring taking the junior. The third earl died in April of that year and the Sackville interest revived under his successor, Sir Edward Sackville*, who like Goring, was an adherent of Buckingham's. Consequently, in 1625 Sir George Rivers*, who had long been connected with the Sackville family and was one of the 3rd earl's executors, was elected for the second seat, while Goring was re-elected for the first.

Goring and Rivers were chosen again in 1626, but in 1628 there was a contest for the second seat between Rivers and Anthony Stapley. The latter was Goring's brother-in-law, although Goring did not support him in the Commons. Stapley may have had the support of Sir Thomas Pelham*, the head of an important local family, with whom he founded a puritan lectureship in Lewes at around this time. The sheriff sealed and returned two indentures, one naming Goring and Rivers and the other Goring and Stapley, but only the second gave the names of the constables and the participating inhabitants.[10] The case was raised in the committee for privileges on 20 Mar. and debated seven days later. According to the evidence presented to the committee 'an equality being in the number of voices' a poll was called. The constable counted 69

voters for Stapley and 61 for Rivers, but in addition a further 20 Rivers supporters were polled by a local minister, who 'came hither to see the election' and had been appointed by some of Rivers' faction. A further 17 or 20 Rivers supporters 'would not go out as the rest did, but said they would number themselves'. An offer by the constable to poll the additional Rivers supporters formally was apparently refused. It seems to have been agreed that in total between 78 and 81 voters supported Rivers, giving him a majority of the electors, but there was considerable doubt as to the validity of the votes not counted by the constable.

In addition, Stapley's supporters alleged that various acts of skulduggery had been committed on Rivers' behalf; 'one Shepley' apparently said that Stapley did not want to be elected 'by which he drew some away', while another Rivers supporter threatened that soldiers would be billeted on the town, presumably by the 4th earl of Dorset, one of the lord lieutenants of Sussex, in revenge for rejecting his candidate. It was further claimed that 'when those that stood for Stapley were altogether fast, that they could not stir, one goes about the town proclaiming if any would give their voices for Rivers that they should come in'. Nevertheless, the case rested on the legality of the additional Rivers voters. The committee divided 27 to 22 between those who supported Stapley's return and those who wanted the election declared void, and on 29 Mar. William Hakewill reported to the Commons in favour of seating Stapley. Further debate was deferred, but when Goring moved for a new writ on 3 Apr. the Commons resolved that Stapley had been duly elected.[11]

Goring was created a peer on 14 Apr. 1628 and on 1 May the House ordered a warrant for a by-election, but the writ was not issued by Chancery until 13 June. The return has not survived, but it is likely that it was Jerome Weston, the son of the chancellor of the Exchequer, Sir Richard Weston*, who was elected. Weston was certainly a Member of the Commons by March 1629. It is possible that the impecunious courtier Goring nominated Weston as a favour to the latter's father, or he may have been nominated by the earl of Dorset, who was on good terms with his father in the 1630s.[12]

[1] CD 1628, ii. 188. [2] Ibid. 163. [3] Ibid. (Counting only those voters polled by the constable.) [4] Camden, Britannia (1695), p. 173; A. Fletcher, County Community in Peace and War, 9, 134-5; C.E. Brent, 'Urban Employment and Population in Suss. between 1550 and 1660', Suss. Arch. Colls. cxiii. 36, 47-50. [5] J. Goring, 'Fellowship of the Twelve in Elizabethan Lewes', Suss. Arch. Colls. cxix. 157-72; VCH Suss. vii. 4-7, 19-31, 48; Bk. of John Rowe ed. W.H. Godfrey (Suss. Rec. Soc. xxxiv), 120. [6] CD 1628, ii. 163.

[7] C219/35/2/85; 219/38/243. [8] PROB 11/113, f. 19v. [9] E. Suss. RO, LEW/C5/1/2. [10] C219/41B/84,86. [11] CD 1628, ii. 37, 163, 188, 275, 282. [12] Ibid. iii. 190; C231/4, f. 247; CD 1629, p. 262; D.L. Smith, 'Fourth Earl of Dorset and the Personal Rule of Charles I', JBS, xxx. 278-9.

A.D./B.C.

MIDHURST

Right of election: in the burgage-holders

c. Feb. 1604	WILLIAM TWYNEHO FRANCIS NEVILLE I
29 Mar. 1604	SIR RICHARD WESTON *vice* Twyneho, chose to sit for Bishop's Castle
c. Mar. 1614	THOMAS BOWYER WILLIAM COURTMAN
2 Jan. 1621	RICHARD LEWKNOR JOHN SMITH
31 Jan. 1624	SIR ANTHONY MAYNEY RICHARD LEWKNOR
23 Apr. 1625	SIR WALTER TICHBORNE RICHARD LEWKNOR
c. June 1625	SAMUEL OWFIELD *vice* Tichborne, chose to sit for Wootton Bassett
23 Jan. 1626	(SIR) HENRY SPILLER RICHARD LEWKNOR
29 Feb. 1628	CHRISTOPHER LEWKNOR EDWARD SAVAGE II

The West Sussex market town of Midhurst, situated 11 miles north of Chichester, was an ancient but unincorporated borough, ownership of which was attached to the adjacent manor of Cowdray. It was governed by a bailiff, who was elected by the burgage-holders, seven of whom also enjoyed the right to collect the market tolls and appoint the steward of the borough's manorial court. The borough first returned Members of Parliament in 1301, but was only consistently represented from 1382. The franchise was held by the burgage-holders, and about a dozen of them, headed by the bailiff, exchanged indentures with the sheriff of Sussex.[1]

In 1542 the manor of Cowdray was inherited by Sir Anthony Browne[†], from whom it passed to his son and namesake, created 1st Viscount Montagu in 1554. Montagu, who died in 1592, and his grandson and heir, the 2nd viscount, were both staunch Catholics. Under their protection the borough constituted by far the strongest Catholic community in Sussex, able to patronize its own recusant schoolmasters, physicians and midwives.[2] The viscounts' faith made it difficult for them to play an active role in public affairs and consequently the Cowdray interest was generally exercised through or by others, principally the family of the 1st viscount's legal advisor, Sir Richard Lewknor[†] of West Dean but also Sir Richard Weston[*], who was related to the 2nd viscount via the latter's mother. The 2nd viscount's unwillingness to intervene directly was no doubt enhanced by his experience in the first Jacobean Parliament, when he was twice imprisoned, first for a defiantly Catholic speech in the Lords in 1604 and then for alleged complicity in the Gunpowder Plot.[3]

In the initial election to the first Jacobean Parliament the senior seat was taken by Francis Neville, who had married Sir Richard Lewknor's cousin and was himself described as cousin by Lewknor in the latter's will.[4] The other seat was taken by William Twyneho, a friend of Montagu's brother-in-law, Robert Sackville[*].[5] Twyneho, however, chose to sit for Bishop's Castle, where he had also been returned, and at the ensuing election on 29 Mar. he was replaced by Weston.

By the time of the next election, in 1614, Neville was in poor health. Weston was returned for his native county of Essex, but was undoubtedly responsible for nominating William Courtman, who had witnessed his father's will.[6] Thomas Bowyer, who filled the other seat, perhaps owed his election to his first wife's great-uncle, Sir Richard Lewknor. Alternatively he may have been recommended by Viscount Montagu's Sackville kinsmen, as he had shared chambers at the Middle Temple with his cousin Robert Bowyer[*], who had been closely connected to Robert Sackville.[7]

Courtman died in 1615, and Bowyer was returned to the third Jacobean Parliament for Bramber. As Weston was then abroad on diplomatic business, the Lewknors seem to have been able to secure both seats. The first was taken by Richard Lewknor, the eldest son of Sir Richard, who had died in 1616. The second place was filled by John Smith, the renowned steward and biographer of the Berkeleys. It seems likely that Sir Richard Lewknor had known Smith, as both men had worked for the 9th earl of Northumberland and belonged to the Middle Temple, where Richard Lewknor had studied.[8] It may also be relevant that Smith supervised a west Sussex property held in jointure by the widow of Sir Thomas Berkeley[*]. She was a London neighbour of Richard Lewknor's kinsman, Sir Lewis Lewknor*, who had himself represented Midhurst in 1597.

Smith showed no sign of seeking re-election in 1624, when Sir Anthony Mayney, a Kentish knight, took the first place on the return. He was a close friend of Weston, and acted with him as trustee for Montagu's daughter Mary on her marriage to William Paulet, Lord St. John, the eldest son of the 4th marquess of Winchester. Lewknor moved down to the junior seat, for which he was re-elected for the next two Parliaments.[9]

Sir Walter Tichborne, elected to the first Caroline Parliament with Lewknor, was Weston's first cousin and a Catholic. He chose to sit for Wootton Bassett, where he had also been elected, and under a writ issued on 24 June 1625 was replaced by Samuel Owfield, a Surrey gentleman whose connection with Midhurst is unknown. The latter was returned for Gatton in 1626, and consequently Midhurst elected (Sir) Henry Spiller, an Exchequer official who had previously sat for Arundel at the nomination of Thomas Howard, earl of Arundel. In 1626 Arundel wanted to secure the election of Nicholas Jordan and probably asked his friend Weston, who was chancellor of the Exchequer, to find a seat for Spiller. In 1628 both Spiller and Lewknor were returned as knights of the shire, the former for Middlesex and the latter for Sussex. Richard Lewknor secured the return of his younger brother Christopher, a lawyer. The other Member was Edward Savage, whose cousin, Sir Thomas Savage, had been a friend of Sir Anthony Mayney and, through him, was probably acquainted with Weston.[10]

---

[1] *VCH Suss.* iv. 75-7; *Cowdray Archives* ed. A.A. Dibben, i. pp. xviii-xxvi; C219/35/2/81; 219/38/247; 218/39/212; 219/40/102; 219/41B/82. [2] T.J. McCann, 'Midhurst Catholics and the Protestation Returns of 1642', *Recusant Hist.* xvi. 320. [3] *LJ*, ii. 328-9; *CP*, ix. 100. [4] PROB 11/127, f. 491v. [5] PROB 11/113, f. 183 [6] PROB 11/104, f. 281v. [7] *MTR*, 461; PROB 11/113, f. 182. [8] J. Smyth, *Berkeley MSS* ed. J. Maclean, ii. 426, 432-4; *Household Pprs. of Henry Percy, Ninth Earl of Northumberland* ed. G.R. Batho (Cam. Soc. ser. 3. xciii), 34. [9] T. Birch, *Ct. and Times of Jas. I*, ii. 306; PROB 11/124, f. 360. [10] C231/4, f. 189v; A.F. Upton, *Sir Arthur Ingram*, 69; PROB 11/151, f. 131v.

A.D.

NEW SHOREHAM

Right of election: in the inhabitants

23 Feb. 1604	SIR BARNARD WHETSTONE SIR HUGH BEESTON
c. Mar. 1614	SIR CHARLES HOWARD THOMAS SHELLEY
4 Jan. 1621	SIR JOHN MORLEY SIR JOHN LEEDES
16 Feb. 1621	INIGO JONES *vice* Leedes, expelled the House
21 Jan. 1624	ANTHONY STAPLEY WILLIAM MARLOTT
2 May 1625	ANTHONY STAPLEY WILLIAM MARLOTT
13 Jan. 1626	JOHN ALFORD WILLIAM MARLOTT
5 Mar. 1628	ROBERT MORLEY WILLIAM MARLOTT

Founded at the mouth of the River Adur in the eleventh century, New Shoreham soon became one of the most important of the Channel ports, though it suffered a severe decline in the fourteenth century. In the late sixteenth century Camden reported that 'the greatest part' of it was 'ruined and under water, and the commodiousness of its port ... wholly taken away', and one of its own Jacobean Members called it 'a town as poor and poorer than any in the realm'. It was nonetheless then entering upon a new period of prosperity. Engaged primarily in the coastal trade, it was also the chief centre in Sussex for shipbuilding.[1]

New Shoreham had the status of a borough by 1235 and, although not incorporated, evolved sophisticated structures of urban self-government, almost all of which fell into abeyance in the late Middle Ages. By the seventeenth century there was little to distinguish it from an ordinary manor. The principal public officer was the constable elected annually by the manorial court leet, while the borough court dealt only with tenurial business. The borough was represented in Parliament from 1295. Indentures were exchanged between the sheriff of Sussex on the one hand and up to 35 named townsmen (sometimes including the shipbuilder Robert Tranckmore) 'and other burgesses' on the other.[2]

The manor or borough formed part of the barony of Bramber, and as such had been forfeited by Thomas

Howard, 4th duke of Norfolk on his attainder in 1572. In the late Elizabethan period the lord admiral, the 2nd Lord Howard of Effingham (Charles Howard[†]), head of a junior branch of the Howard family based in Surrey, served as lord lieutenant of Sussex and seems to have exercised at least some of his family's traditional electoral influence, especially in New Shoreham which, as a port, was presumably particularly susceptible to Admiralty influence.[3] Norfolk's grandson, Thomas, earl of Arundel, was restored in blood in 1604, but he had some difficulty in obtaining possession of all of his family's lands. In 1608 Arundel's uncles, the 1st earl of Suffolk and Lord William Howard of Naworth were granted various parts of the estates, including the barony of Bramber, and he did not buy them out until 1619.[4]

The two Members returned in 1604 probably owed their election to Lord Howard, by now 1st earl of Nottingham. Sir Barnard Whetstone, from Essex, was the stepfather of Nottingham's secretary, Richard Bellingham I[*]. He also leased the manor of Hangleton, four miles from the borough, and was a member of the county bench. His colleague, Sir Hugh Beeston, was a client of Sir Robert Cecil[†], Nottingham's principal ally at Court, and was the son of a man knighted by Nottingham during the Armada campaign. His election may have represented a favour done by Nottingham for Cecil.[5]

There is no evidence that Beeston and Whetstone initially sought re-election in 1614, although the former was returned at Liverpool. Instead, the Howard interest went to Nottingham's second son, Sir Charles Howard. His colleague was Thomas Shelley, the eldest son of Henry Shelley I[*], who owned property in the nearby parish of Findon. By 1621 Howard was the heir to the Nottingham earldom and showed no apparent interest in sitting in the Commons again, while Shelley had been outlawed for debt. It is possible that the earl of Arundel, now back in England, nominated Sir John Morley, who had previously sat for the borough in 1601, because Morley's father-in-law and stepfather, Sir Edward Caryll, had been steward to Arundel's father. Moreover Morley's younger brother Edward[*] was closely connected with the earl, having sat for the borough of Arundel on the earl's nomination in 1614. The second seat went to Sir John Leedes, a courtier and local landowner. Interestingly, Edward Morley was one of Leedes' trustees.[6] The principal signatory to the indenture was the vicar of New Shoreham, William Greenhill.[7]

Leedes was expelled from the House on 10 Feb. for taking his seat unsworn, and was replaced by the great architect Inigo Jones, who was presumably nominated by his patron Arundel. Jones's name is more faded than the main text of the indenture and it is probably in a different hand, suggesting that it was a later insertion. Greenhill again led the electors.[8] Morley died before the next election, and Jones does not seem to have sought re-election.

There is no evidence that Arundel tried to influence the election for the 1624 Parliament, when the puritan Anthony Stapley, who lived about nine miles from the borough, took the senior seat. His junior colleague was William Marlott, a New Shoreham merchant. If Marlott was already serving as deputy vice-admiral of Sussex to Sir Charles Howard, by now 2nd earl of Nottingham, it raises the possibility of a revival of the Nottingham interest.

In 1625 Arundel apparently nominated Evan Edwards[*], secretary to Arundel's fellow joint lord lieutenant of Sussex, the 4th earl of Dorset (Sir Edward Sackville[*]), but the borough re-elected Stapley and Marlott.[9] The following year Arundel tried again, this time nominating (Sir) Francis Crane, who had recently participated in the negotiations for the marriage of the earl's heir, Henry Frederick Howard[*], Lord Maltravers. The earl sought the support of Edward Alford[*], who was sheriff of Sussex and lived near New Shoreham. However, Alford claimed he had already recommended his son John to the borough and that he did not know of the earl's nomination of Crane until it was too late. There is no evidence that Stapley sought re-election and John Alford was elected with Marlott.[10]

In the late 1620s the maritime economy of Sussex was being adversely affected by the war. In July 1626 'the inhabitants and fishermen' of Shoreham called for better protection to be provided against the ravages of the Dunkirkers. In August 1628 Edward Alford wrote to the lord lieutenants complaining that French warships had taken a vessel in Shoreham haven and had anchored off the port all night. The war probably helped to raise the local prominence of Marlott, as deputy vice-admiral, as he was re-elected in 1628. John Alford, however, was returned for Arundel. Marlott's partner this time was Robert Morley, who lived at Glynde in east Sussex. Unrelated to the 1621 Member, Morley was instead a kinsman of the Alfords and Stapley.[11]

[1] VCH Suss. vi. pt. 1, pp. 138, 157-9, 162, 165; W. Camden, Britannia (1695), p. 173; Bowyer Diary, 92; C.E. Brent, 'Urban employment and population in Suss. between 1550 and 1660' Suss. Arch. Colls. cxiii. 44; H. Cheal, Story of Shoreham, 32, 149. [2] VCH Suss. vi. pt. 1, pp. 164-5, 167; C219/35/2/90; 219/39/207. In February 1628

Tranckmore was contracted to build the *Tenth Lion's Whelp* for the Navy: Cheal, 149. ³ *VCH Suss*. vi. pt. 1, p. 149; R. W. Kenny, 'Parlty. Influence of Charles Howard, Earl of Nottingham', *JMH*, xxxix. 220-1, 224. Howard had inherited the manor of Eastbrook, two miles east of Shoreham, but sold it in 1595. W. Bray, *Collections Relating to Henry Smith* (1800), pp. 85-7. ⁴ M.A. Tierney, *Hist. and Antiqs. of Castle and Town of Arundel*, 416-17; M.F.S. Hervey, *Thomas Howard, Earl of Arundel*, 21-23, 40, 464: Arundel, Suss. deeds, D2838, info. from Mrs. Sara Rodger. ⁵ G.K. Gruenfelder, *Influence in Early Stuart Eng*. 40. ⁶ H. Ellis, 'Certificate concerning Justices of the Peace in 1587', *Suss. Arch. Colls*. ii. 60; *Suss. Manors and Advowsons* ed. H.W. Dunkin (Suss. Rec. Soc. xx), 463. ⁷ C219/37/258. ⁸ C219/37/254. ⁹ *Cal. N. Wales Letters* ed. B.E. Howells (Univ. Wales, Bd. of Celtic Studies, Hist. and Law ser. xxiii), 218. ¹⁰ Arundel, Autograph Letters 1617-32, Peers to Spiller, 16 Jan. 1626. ¹¹ *CSP Dom*. 1625-6, p. 390; 1628-9, p. 250; A. Fletcher, *County Community in Peace and War*, 189.

A.D./B.C.

STEYNING

Right of election: in the inhabitants

Number of voters: 36 in 1624[1]

17 Feb. 1604	SIR THOMAS SHIRLEY I
	SIR THOMAS BISHOPP
c. Mar. 1614	SIR THOMAS SHIRLEY II
	(SIR) EDWARD FRAUNCEYS
22 Dec. 1620	SIR THOMAS SHIRLEY II
	(SIR) EDWARD FRAUNCEYS
	Philip Mainwaring*
	William Gardiner
23 Jan. 1624	(SIR) EDWARD FRAUNCEYS
	SIR THOMAS FARNEFOLD
	Philip Mainwaring
	William Gardiner
	Sir Edward Greville*
30 Apr. 1625	(SIR) EDWARD FRAUNCEYS
	SIR THOMAS FARNEFOLD
Jan. 1626	(SIR) EDWARD FRAUNCEYS
	SIR EDWARD BISHOPP
	Sir Thomas Farnefold
	Sir John Leedes*
25 Feb. 1628	SIR THOMAS FARNEFOLD
	EDWARD ALFORD

Situated close to the River Adur on the boundary between the downland and wealden regions of Sussex, Steyning remained an important market town in this period, with a significant tanning and leather industry. However, as a port it, like Bramber, had long been eclipsed by New Shoreham, situated at the mouth of the river. The population grew from about 300 in 1565 to roughly 1,000 by the early 1640s.[2] The borough was unincorporated, and therefore administration was in the hands of a constable, elected annually at the manorial view of frankpledge. However, the extent of the manor was ambiguous. The original manor of Steyning had been divided in the mid-fifteenth century, one part consisting of the borough and the other becoming the manor of Charlton. The boundary between the two manors was unclear which meant that the owners of Charlton had a significant interest in the borough. Before the Dissolution the borough manor belonged to Syon Abbey and was granted by Elizabeth to Thomas Howard, 4th duke of Norfolk in 1562, but forfeited on his attainder after the Ridolfi Plot a decade later. In the absence of the Howard interest Sir Thomas Shirley I, whose seat at Wiston was situated two miles away, became an important electoral force in the borough during the Elizabethan period, which was no doubt consolidated by his acquisition of Charlton and the advowson of the parish church in 1593.[3]

Steyning was frequently represented in Parliament in the fourteenth century, but always in conjunction with the nearby borough of Bramber. Their joint representation was discontinued in 1399 and Steyning did not return Members separately until 1453.[4] In this period indentures were exchanged between the sheriff of Sussex and up to 36 named burgesses, headed by the constable; these were described as acting with others, on at least one occasion (1628) with 'other the inhabitants within the borough'.[5]

In 1604 Sir Thomas Shirley I was re-elected for the borough, despite having since been forced to surrender all his local property to the Crown in part settlement of his debts. His colleague was his wife's friend Sir Thomas Bishopp of Parham, who had previously represented the borough in 1586. Bishopp was closely connected with Lord Buckhurst (Thomas Sackville†) who, as lord treasurer and lord lieutenant of Sussex, may have had influence in the borough, which was still in the possession of the Crown. Shirley, who was in favour with King James I, was restored to Wiston during the Parliament, albeit as a Crown tenant. He died in 1612, and was replaced in the Addled Parliament by his eldest son, Sir Thomas II. Bishopp, an important figure in county administration, seems to have been content not to sit again, and so the junior seat went to (Sir) Edward Fraunceys, estate steward to Henry Percy, 9th earl of Northumberland at Petworth, 12 miles from Steyning. He had sat in previous parliaments on his master's interest, but it is by no means certain that he owed his election in 1614 to Northumberland, who was imprisoned in the Tower. Indeed, Fraunceys was active on his own account in the Sussex land-market, and acquired property near Steyning. In 1618 he also became trustee for Sir John Leedes* and took up residence at Leedes' home at Wappingthorne, in the parish of Steyning. In 1619 Thomas Howard, earl of Arundel, the grandson of the duke of Norfolk, acquired possession of the borough of Steyning, and at the parliamentary elections the following year he nominated the courtier Philip Mainwaring* and William Gardiner. However, the borough re-elected Shirley and Fraunceys.[6]

Shirley sold up in 1622, and when a fresh Parliament was summoned two years later Arundel attempted to take advantage of the lapse in the Wiston interest. On 9 Jan. 1624 he wrote to the constable and inhabitants of the borough, affecting to believe that their previous refusal 'rather proceeded out of ignorance than neglect towards me'. After acknowledging that 'every borough should elect members of their own body' to Parliament, he claimed that depopulation and impoverishment had led many to accept 'able men' nominated 'by their chief lords', such as his ancestors. He therefore recommended his two former nominees, Mainwaring and Gardiner, both of whom, he declared, would serve without wages. He ended by stating that, while 'I neither may nor will press you further ... I desire and expect that you give me speedy notice what resolution you take in this behalf'.[7] Arundel was not the only peer who sought the right of nomination, however, as the earl of Middlesex (Sir Lionel Cranfield*), who had purchased the Wiston estate, nominated Sir Edward Greville*, an elderly Warwickshire gentleman who had been a business associate of the Shirleys.[8] The borough rejected both approaches, though, and re-elected Fraunceys together with Sir Thomas Farnefold, who lived just outside Steyning and owned property in the borough.

Farnefold and Fraunceys were re-elected in 1625. The following year Middlesex made a further attempt to secure the nomination of one Member. He wrote to his Sussex steward, Richard Gravett, to that purpose, but the latter had been entrusted with letters of nomination from Arundel on behalf of Nicholas Jordan* and 'one Mr. Garrett', possibly George Garrard*. Gravett replied to Middlesex in early January that he had tried to promote Arundel's nominees by 'underhand' means, but with so little success that he was planning to return the latter's letters. The borough, he stated, was 'resolved to make choice' of Sir Thomas Bishopp's son Sir Edward, and 'young Alford', almost certainly John Alford*, the son of the sheriff Edward* and son-in-law of Sir Thomas. He also reported that Fraunceys was 'desperately sick' and that Farnefold, who was in dispute with Sir Thomas Bishopp, would be 'denied for himself'.[9] In the event John Alford was returned for New Shoreham on 13 January. The date of the Steyning election is unknown, but it must have been on or shortly before 16 Jan., when the earl of Arundel's steward, writing from Arundel, reported that he had 'heard this day' that Sir Edward Bishopp had been elected with Fraunceys and that Farnefold had been 'cashiered'. According to the same account, Fraunceys had tried to secure a seat for Sir John Leedes, 'but the townsmen rejected him because he had been put out of the House'.

Fraunceys did not survive the Parliament and was buried at St. Margaret's, Westminster on 23 May, but the Parliament was then nearing its end and no writ was issued for a by-election. In October 1627 Bishopp killed Sir Thomas Shirley II's son, Henry, for which he was found guilty of manslaughter. Not surprisingly he was not re-elected in 1628. He presumably supported the candidacy of Edward Alford, who had previously sat for Colchester but was now unsure whether he would be re-elected, but as Alford lived only five miles from the borough he probably did not require Bishopp's support. With the eclipse of the Bishopp interest Farnefold was re-elected for the senior seat.[10]

[1]C219/38/241. [2]VCH Suss. vi. pt. 1, pp. 220-1, 234; J. Pennington and J. Sleight, 'Steyning Town and its Trades 1559-1787', Suss. Arch. Colls. cxxx. 164-5, 173. [3]VCH Suss. vi. pt. 1, pp. 226-7, 237, 241. [4]Ibid. vi. pt. 1, 240. [5]C219/41B/79. [6]Arundel, Suss. deeds, D2838, info. from Mrs Sara Rodger; H.A. Merewether and A.J. Stephens, Hist. of Boroughs and Municipal Corporations of UK (1835), iii. 1513-14. [7]Merewether and Stephens, iii. 1513-14. [8]R.E. Ruigh, Parl. in 1624, p. 331n. [9]Procs. 1626, iv. 253. [10]Arundel, Autograph Letters 1617-32, Peers to Spiller, 16 Jan. 1626.

A.D.

WARWICKSHIRE

Number of voters: maximum 3,511 in Dec. 1640

1604	SIR EDWARD GREVILLE SIR RICHARD VERNEY
1614	SIR THOMAS LUCY SIR RICHARD VERNEY
25 Dec. 1620	SIR FULKE GREVILLE SIR THOMAS LUCY
26 Nov. 1621	SIR FRANCIS LEIGH I vice Greville, called to the Upper House
1624	SIR THOMAS LUCY SIR CLEMENT THROCKMORTON
1625	SIR THOMAS LUCY SIR CLEMENT THROCKMORTON
16 Jan. 1626	SIR THOMAS LUCY SIR CLEMENT THROCKMORTON
1628	SIR THOMAS LUCY SIR THOMAS LEIGH, bt.

Early seventeenth-century Warwickshire was a divided community, geographically and socially. The southern third of the county, with its 'fertile fields of corn and verdant pastures', was notable for its settled communities and traditional manorial structures. To the north, however, lay a heavily wooded region, Shakespeare's Forest of Arden, where a more mobile population combined agricultural pursuits with industrial enterprise, particularly around the north-eastern coalfields and the thriving iron-works of Birmingham. The only other economically important town, the cloth-producing centre of Coventry, was a liberty within Warwickshire, and stood proudly aloof from county life despite its declining prosperity.[1] The bulk of the wealthiest gentry resided in the south, and took little interest in Arden's burgeoning industry. Conversely the few prominent gentlemen who lived in the north rarely participated in public affairs outside their own districts, such as the assizes at Warwick, or indeed the county's parliamentary elections. Not surprisingly, the knights of the shire were almost invariably drawn from the leading southern families, such as the Grevilles, Verneys and Lucys, dominant landowners with long pedigrees who typically also engaged actively in local or even national government.[2]

Election to the county seats was primarily a reflection of personal status, and Warwickshire's knights only rarely voiced the concerns of their constituents in the Commons. On 2 May 1610 Sir Edward Greville successfully moved to have the county exempted from a bill about the burning of moorland, and it was presumably either Sir Thomas Lucy or Sir Thomas Leigh who certified on 24 Apr. 1628 that Warwickshire had no recusant office-holders. Lucy may also have been the anonymous speaker who offered evidence on 14 May 1621 on the local impact of Sir Robert Mansell's* glass patent.[3] There is no evidence that either Lucy or Sir Fulke Greville were involved in the short-lived 1621 bill to improve the lot of ironworkers in the Birmingham region, while it was an Oxford Member, Thomas Wentworth, who on 19 June 1607 requested financial help to restore a ruined Warwickshire church. When, on 23 June 1625, Sir Clement Throckmorton condemned 'the infinite confluence of priests and Jesuits into this kingdom', he was voicing his personal convictions, although his views would have struck a chord with Warwickshire's voters, as the danger posed by Catholics had been brought home forcibly in 1605, when the county witnessed an abortive rising in the aftermath of the Gunpowder Plot.[4]

As the county lacked a resident peer with sufficient local influence to dictate the course of shire elections, the selection process rested with the gentry. There is no firm evidence that there were contests between 1604 and 1628, though it is possible to detect some tensions and rivalries. In 1601 the sheriff had attempted to manipulate the election in a bid to block the fifth consecutive return of (Sir) Fulke Greville, reflecting local resentment at his monopoly of one seat. On that occasion the government intervened on behalf of Greville, but his fall from favour after Elizabeth's death removed any hope of a sixth victory.[5] Instead, the choice in 1604 fell on two other well-established local figures, Sir Edward Greville and Sir Richard Verney, both of whom had represented Warwickshire before. The fact that both were close relatives of Sir Fulke was probably coincidental. Verney sat again in 1614, when Sir Edward's rapidly deteriorating finances presumably ruled him out. His place was taken by Sir Thomas Lucy, a generous and godly magistrate whose immense local popularity enabled him to win six consecutive elections, thus outdoing Sir Fulke Greville. The latter in fact staged a comeback in 1620, doubtless boosted by his position as chancellor of the Exchequer, though his elevation to the Lords in the following summer necessitated a by-election. A poor turnout favoured Sir Francis Leigh I, who, by rallying his neighbours in east Warwickshire, became the only resident outside the county's southern zone to serve as a knight during this period.[6] From 1624 to 1626 Lucy was partnered by another puritan squire, Sir Clement Throckmorton, but in 1628 the junior seat was claimed instead by Sir Thomas Leigh, a cousin of the 1621 Member. On this occasion the sheriff, Sir Robert Fisher, delayed making his return. No explanation was offered when this negligence was reported in the Commons on 20 March, and there are no contemporary reports of a contest, but the fact that Fisher was Throckmorton's brother-in-law may be significant. If Sir Clement stood again that year, his failure to secure a seat might be explained by his support for the Forced Loan, which was unpopular in Warwickshire. By contrast, both Lucy and Leigh had distanced themselves from the Loan's collection.[7]

[1] W. Camden, *Britannia* (1772), i. 446, 450, 452; A. Hughes, *Pols. Soc. and Civil War in Warws.* 4-5, 8, 10, 12, 16. [2] Hughes, 5, 9, 52, 55, 59, 91; *Vis. Warws.* (Harl. Soc. xii), 25, 29, 288; C142/293/75; 142/300/172; WARD 7/86/148; PROB 11/154, ff. 285-9. [3] *CJ*, i. 423b; *SR*, v. 1172; *CD 1621*, iii. 257; *CD 1628*, iii. 64; Hughes, 91. [4] *Procs. 1625*, p. 231; *CSP Dom.* 1603-10, p. 242; *CD 1621*, ii. 206; vii. 141-3; *CJ*, i. 385b. [5] Hughes, 21-4, 26; *APC*, 1601-4, pp. 247-8; J.E. Neale, *Eliz. House of Commons*, 52-3. [6] C219/37/266; Hughes, 32, 45, 59, 71, 91 n. 140; Verney sat for Warws. in 1589, Greville in 1593. [7] *Vis. Warws.* 217; *Vis. Warws.* (Harl. Soc. lxii), 10-11; C193/12/2, ff. 60v-1; SP16/50/54; Hughes, 59, 95-7.

P.M.H.

COVENTRY

Right of election: in the freemen

Number of voters: c.600 in 1628

20 Feb. 1604	HENRY BRERES, alderman	
	JOHN ROGERSON, dep. alderman	
5 Mar. 1610	SIR JOHN HARINGTON *vice*	
	Rogerson, vacated his seat	
c. Mar. 1614	SIR ROBERT COKE	
	SAMPSON HOPKINS	
5 Dec. 1620	SAMPSON HOPKINS, alderman	
	HENRY SEWALL, alderman	
27 Jan. 1624	SIR EDWARD COKE, recorder	
	HENRY HARWELL, dep. alderman	
1625	SIR EDWARD COKE, recorder	
	HENRY HARWELL, dep. alderman[1]	
1626	HENRY HARWELL, alderman	
	ISAAC WALDEN, dep. alderman	

by 1 Mar. 1628[2]	RICHARD GREENE	367
	WILLIAM PUREFOY	
	ISAAC WALDEN, alderman	29
	THOMAS POTTER, dep. alderman	

Double return. GREENE and PUREFOY declared elected, 9 Apr. 1628

A town existed at Coventry by the mid-eleventh century, when it belonged to the famous Godiva. Made rich by the cloth trade, in 1377 it was England's third biggest provincial centre, with perhaps 9,000 inhabitants. Growth continued into the fifteenth century, and in 1451 it was granted the status of both city and county. Around this time, however, the market for the local broadcloth contracted, and despite the development of alternative manufactures such as caps and blue thread economic decline set in. In the severe depression of the 1520s, the population shrank to about 6,000. Recovery was slow, as there were only 6,502 inhabitants in 1586, and a major outbreak of plague in 1604 claimed 494 lives. However, in 1611 the number of communicants in the city was estimated at 6-7,000.[3] One factor behind this increase was apparently an influx of radical Protestants, who were attracted by the plethora of sermons in the city's churches, and the corporation's enforcement of religious observance. In 1605, for example, the court leet banned the playing of football in the street on Sundays. Four years later, it observed that although 'by order from Mr. Mayor and his brethren, the constables and churchwardens … have taken pains in procuring and compelling the poorer sort of people to come to their parish church on the sabbath days', nevertheless 'many of them do lie in bed, and others do use to resort unto divers villages and alehouses near adjoining, there to spend the sabbath very profanely in tippling and drinking'. A fine of 12d. was introduced for this offence.[4]

The economy of early seventeenth-century Coventry remained largely stagnant. In 1609 the corporation refused to raise the local subsidy assessments, complaining to the Privy Council of 'the general and great decay of our city … since the beginning of Her late Majesty's reign, by reason that such as formerly used to traffic at Coventry now turn all or the most part of their dealings to London'. Although in 1615 a shortage of fullers obliged the court leet to relax restrictions on strangers, there was a general drive to protect the local workforce from external competition. In 1598 and 1602 the sale of cloth anywhere but in the appropriate cloth halls was banned so as to restrict openings for country traders, while in 1610 the aldermen were ordered to report any strangers taking up residence in the city.[5] However, these measures did nothing to prevent increasingly cut-throat rivalries between Coventry's trading companies within Coventry. In 1607 the Drapers surreptitiously obtained a new charter giving them a monopoly over the sale of all woollen cloth. This underhand move was designed to prevent the Mercers from participating in the lucrative market in new draperies, which had been developing in the city since around 1570. After a three-year battle, the Mercers managed to overturn the charter, but in the process found themselves accused of poaching business from the local hosiers.[6] Defeated on this front, the Drapers went in search of new markets, and in 1608 obtained a 'toleration' from the Privy Council that allowed them to produce 1,000 cloths a year specifically for export. This grant had been intended by the government to benefit Coventry's cloth producers in general, but the Drapers conspired to suppress this fact until 1622, instead managing the toleration solely in their own interests.[7]

At the start of the seventeenth century Coventry was governed by a tripartite structure of Great (or Mayor's) Council, common council and court leet. By far the most important component was the great council, which consisted of the mayor, all ten aldermen and approximately ten other leading citizens. Although the election of civic officers and the enactment of by-laws remained the preserve of the *ad hoc* jury assembled for the bi-annual court leets, it was the great council which made policy, and indeed made up the bulk of the jury. The common council still held a key to the chest containing the city's seal, but between 1605 and 1614 a series of court leet rulings effectively reduced it to a rubber-stamping body. In June 1623, apparently as a token protest, the common council walked out of a meeting with the great council where the seal was to be used, and deliberately left their key behind.[8]

The 1451 city charter remained in force until 1621, even though the framework of local government had changed markedly in the interim. An attempt to obtain a new city charter in 1611-12 was abandoned, probably because of spiralling costs.[9] However, in November 1620 the great and common councils resolved to try again, and their efforts were rewarded in the following July. The 1621 charter confirmed the existing arrangements, but also designated the mayor, recorder and aldermen as magistrates within the county of Coventry, and established two new fairs.[10]

The city jealously guarded its privileges and independence. In April 1623 the great council had little choice but to comply when the king and two Warwickshire-based privy councillors, Lord Brooke (Sir Fulke Greville*) and Sir Edward Conway I*, requested the post of Steward for John Verney. However, all efforts to persuade Coventry to increase the scale of its contributions towards the militia and similar levies in Warwickshire were vigorously resisted, except in 1625 when the impressment quota was exceeded in order to rid the city of some 'loose and unthrifty persons'.[11] Between 1619 and 1622 the corporation held out against demands from Prince Charles's Council for a rent-charge, which it believed was not justified in law.[12] The city was equally reluctant to compromise over religion. When James I demanded an end to the local puritan practice of standing or sitting to receive communion in 1611, some of the more obdurate offenders responded that their behaviour was condoned by learned divines, and that the sheer number of communicants rendered kneeling impractical. Although the king got his way, he was still smarting over this affront when he visited Coventry six years later, and in 1621 he insisted on proof that his wishes were still being enforced before he agreed to grant the new charter.[13] In general, the great council successfully maintained a common front against rival jurisdictions of all kinds, but it was also occasionally riven by bitter internal discord. In one extreme case which erupted in 1617, a dispute between Sampson Hopkins* and Matthew Collins led to the latter's expulsion from the Council for three years, during which time he sued the corporation for alleged misappropriation of charitable funds.[14]

Given Coventry's assertiveness, it is surprising that the city did not engage more fully with Parliament. In 1610 a bill to restrict the conditions under which chapmen and pedlars could sell cloth was introduced in the Commons, but it was rejected at its first reading on 24 February. While this measure reflected the interests of trading companies such as the Drapers, who wished to drive the chapmen out of business, the corporation probably donated £40 towards its costs. In the following May, the great council again set aside £40 to promote a bill 'for the better relief of cities and corporations', but nothing at all seems to have come of this. Possibly it was the lack of return on these investments which discouraged the Council from further efforts of this kind. In 1621, for reasons that are unclear, Coventry provided a certificate on the rising price of glass, which was produced in the Commons during a debate on 14 May about Sir Robert Mansell's* glass-making patent.[15]

Until 1628 the great council maintained an iron grip on the selection of Coventry's MPs. The normal practice was apparently for the mayor and some of his colleagues to nominate candidates in the guildhall, where the Council met. The names were then submitted to the assembled freemen, roughly one-tenth of the population, for ratification. In the unlikely event of a poll, votes were gathered in the nearby churches of St. Michael and Holy Trinity. The indenture recording the 1610 by-election was signed by the two sheriffs, but those for 1604 and 1620 were sealed instead. In the latter year the sheriffs also returned the election writ, annotated with the result.[16] Wages were normally paid to Members chosen from within the city, but not to gentlemen such as Sir Robert Coke. The level of payment varied considerably. In 1604, 1605-6 and 1626 both Members received 5s. a day. However, Sampson Hopkins was paid at a daily rate of only 4s. in 1614 and 5s. 6d. in 1621, while Henry Sewall claimed 6s. 8d. a day during the first phase of the 1621 Parliament. Relative experience and seniority within the corporation may have been deciding factors, but Sewall in 1621 was almost certainly paid more because he was simultaneously conducting negotiations in London about the new charter.[17]

In each Parliament between 1604 and 1626, at least one of Coventry's representatives belonged to the great council. Henry Breres in 1604 and Henry Sewall in 1621 both enjoyed the prestige of being its senior member, while John Rogerson (1604), Hopkins, Henry Harwell (1624-6) and Isaac Walden (1626-8) all achieved at least the rank of deputy alderman. However, seats were also distributed to other important officers or associates of the city. Sir Edward Coke secured a place for his son, Sir Robert, upon becoming recorder in 1614, and was himself elected in 1624 and 1625, although on the latter occasion he plumped for Norfolk instead, creating a vacancy that was apparently left unfilled. Similarly, when Rogerson became too infirm in 1610 to attend the Commons, the city replaced him with Sir John Harington, son of the then recorder.[18] The great council did not welcome approaches from complete outsiders. In 1624 Sir Thomas Edmondes* was nominated for a seat by the Prince's Council, but although the corporation made Edmondes a freeman to render him eligible for election, this was merely an act of diplomacy, and his candidacy went no further. The privy councillor Sir John Suckling* was similarly fobbed off in 1625 when he applied 'divers times' to fill the vacancy left by Sir Edward Coke, despite securing letters of commendation from the bishop of Lichfield and Coventry's lord lieutenant, the earl of Northampton.[19]

In 1628 the great council's control was finally broken. On election day, the mayor's nomination of two of its members, Isaac Walden and Thomas Potter, met with a challenge from two rival candidates, Richard Greene and William Purefoy, the former a gentleman living at Wyken in the county of Coventry, the latter a Warwickshire squire based around eight miles away at Caldecote. As neither of these outsiders was a resident or freeman of the city of Coventry, they were not strictly eligible to stand. However, notwithstanding subsequent claims that Walden and Potter easily secured majority support inside the guildhall, the mayor was twice forced to concede a full poll, and amid chaotic scenes Greene and Purefoy emerged as convincing winners. The details of Purefoy's victory have not survived, but Green overwhelmed Walden by 367 votes to 29. One of the city's sheriffs, Richard Knipe, refused to accept these results because neither man was resident, and therefore returned Walden and Potter as properly elected. The other sheriff, Godfrey Legge, had no such qualms, and made out a rival indenture for Greene and Purefoy. The dispute was then passed to Parliament for a final decision.[20]

Several explanations have been proposed for these tumultuous events. The letter-writer Joseph Mead attributed the outcome to the political fall-out from the previous year's Forced Loan. Writing on 1 Mar. 1628 to Sir Martin Stuteville, he observed: 'at Coventry they have … admitted two gentleman recusants [ie. Loan refusers] in the county to be of their corporation [ie. freemen], that they might choose them and pass by, against their custom, all their own [citizens], as being not that way qualified'.[21] This statement was inaccurate, insofar as Greene and Purefoy were never made freemen of Coventry, but Purefoy was indeed a Loan refuser, who had appeared before the Privy Council in February 1627. This doubtless raised his local profile, and may therefore have contributed to his election victory. However, there is no evidence that Greene refused to lend, although as late as January 1627 neither he nor Godfrey Legge had yet contributed. By comparison, Richard Knipe paid up promptly, along with most members of the great council. This is suggestive of the future electoral divisions, but it should be noted that another of the late payers was Isaac Walden. Thus the Forced Loan may have had some impact on the 1628 election, but it is unlikely that it was a decisive factor.[22]

Another possibility is that the election dispute was a product of long-standing resentment among Coventry's poorer residents against the corporation, and in particular the way in which the Great

Council managed the city's common lands. Certainly this issue was a source of local friction. One consequence of the neutering of the common council was a steady increase in the Great Council's control over the issuing of leases. This encouraged fears that the ordinary residents would lose their grazing rights, and the late 1620s saw rioting against enclosures erected on the commons.[23] Even so, it is clear from accounts of the 1628 elections that they were not a straightforward battle between the local oligarchy and the wider population. During the polls, sheriff Legge and at least one member of the Great Council, the former MP Henry Harwell, rallied support for Greene and Purefoy, and presumably they and their allies also orchestrated the initial opposition to the nominations of Walden and Potter. Clearly there was a split within the corporation itself, and it is this which holds the key to the election dispute.[24]

It is important to understand precisely what Walden and Potter represented to the average Coventry voter in 1628. In addition to serving on the Great Council, they were also leading figures within their companies, the Drapers and the Dyers respectively. As such they were prime movers in a trade dispute which polarised opinion within the city in the latter part of the decade. Walden was closely involved with the implementation of the 1608 toleration for local cloth manufacture, and at least until 1622 seems to have kept possession of the grant himself. The government's intention had clearly been to boost local employment by permitting surplus production for export, but the Drapers had utilised this concession primarily to boost their own profits. Walden in particular was an active partner in a consortium which brought in unfinished cloth from other areas such as Gloucestershire, so that it could be finished and sold on as Coventry cloth, ostensibly within the terms of the toleration. This operation resulted in heavy financial losses and unemployment among the city's weavers and clothiers, and when it finally emerged in 1622 that the toleration had been granted, somewhat imprecisely, to Coventry's 'clothiers', as opposed to the Drapers' Company, the Weavers appealed to the Privy Council for redress.[25] A compromise agreement was reached later that year to give the Weavers a greater share of the market, but the Drapers failed to honour it, and in 1626 the government was once again drawn into the quarrel. A fresh commission of inquiry was launched, and both sides in the dispute set about trying to influence its outcome. Here, Walden and the Drapers possessed a significant advantage, as they enjoyed a controlling majority on the Great Council. In June 1627 the corporation wrote to the Privy Council, backing the Drapers' arguments,

and forwarding supportive petitions from two allied companies, the Clothworkers and Dyers. It subsequently emerged that this initiative was the work of the Drapers on the Great Council, abetted by the then mayor, Walden's brother, and that their colleagues had not been informed about the letter.[26] Nevertheless, the Privy Council was taken in by this stratagem, and its final decision in November was relatively favourable to the Drapers. It was subsequently alleged that the Drapers had offered secret concessions to the Weavers which they then failed to honour. Whether or not this was correct, within months it was clear that the new settlement was not being implemented, and that no redress would be forthcoming from the Great Council. Consequently, the nomination of Walden and Potter as parliamentary candidates by the new mayor, Richard Clark, another leading figure in the Gloucestershire cloth consortium, amounted to an act of provocation against Coventry's long-suffering weavers and clothiers.[27] The tensions generated by this dispute within the Great Council explain why Henry Harwell broke ranks. Quite apart from the fact that he was overlooked as an MP, despite having served in the three previous Parliaments, as a Mercer he had been a key figure in his Company's battle against the Drapers in 1607-10, and was therefore highly unlikely to sympathize with Walden's faction. Similarly, the frustration felt by those who had repeatedly lost out in the cloth dispute accounts for the scale of the vote against Walden, who was regarded by the weavers and clothiers as being principally responsible for their misery.[28]

The election dispute caused considerable consternation in the Commons. Discussed by the committee for privileges on 20 Mar., the case was presented to the House on the following day, and the dilemma at its core was immediately apparent. Greene and Purefoy had a clear popular mandate, but if the statutes governing elections were applied strictly neither man was eligible to sit, since they were not resident freemen of Coventry. This was by no means the first time that this issue had been debated, and consequently Richard Taylor was able to cite the 1621 Leicestershire dispute to support his argument that the residence requirement was merely a guideline. Even Sir Richard Shelton, the solicitor-general, gave his backing to the majority verdict. However, Henry Sherfield warned that if the Commons upheld the election of Greene and Purefoy an important precedent would be set, and he successfully moved for the debate to be adjourned until the House was fuller.[29] On 24 Mar. a petition arrived from supporters of Walden and Potter, alleging electoral malpractice, and the case was promptly referred back to the privileges committee, where it was considered on 8 April. The next day the committee's verdict was reported in the House, and this time Sir Edward Coke, Coventry's recorder, gave his backing to the popular vote, pointing out that he himself had served for Liskeard without being a resident freeman, and asserting that such qualifications were not obligatory if the corporation concerned chose to dispense with them. The House was not minded to argue with Coke, and Greene and Purefoy were therefore confirmed as Members. As Sherfield had predicted, a precedent was set, and the centuries-old requirement for the election of resident freemen, long obsolete in practice, was finally and formally abandoned.[30]

[1] *Names of Knights, Citizens, Burgesses and Barons of House of Commons, 1625* (London, 1625), unpag. *OR* incorrectly states that Harwell replaced Coke in a by-election. [2] Harl. 390, f. 356v. [3] *VCH Warws.* viii. 256, 263; A. Dyer, *Decline and Growth in English Towns, 1400-1640*, pp. 28-9; B. Poole, *Coventry: its history and antiquities*, 401; Add. 11364, f. 13v; Coventry Archives, BA/H/Q/A79/97. [4] Coventry Archives, BA/H/C/17/1, ff. 173v, 181v-2v, 259v; BA/H/Q/A79/97; BA/E/F/37/2, pp. 35, 49. [5] *HMC Hatfield*, xxi. 42; Coventry Archives, BA/E/F/37/2, pp. 20, 28, 77; BA/H/C/17/1, f. 177v. [6] E. Kerridge, *Textile Manufactures in Early Modern England*, 34-5; C66/1750; 66/1846/8; *HMC Hatfield*, xix. 435, 438-9; Coventry Archives, PA/15/1, ff. 481-2v. [7] SP14/40/25; Coventry Archives, PA/100/12/23. [8] *VCH Warws.* viii. 263-5; Coventry Archives, BA/H/C/Q/1, ff. 143v, 149, 194r-v, 264; BA/E/F/37/2, pp. 23-4, 37-8, 51, 74-6. [9] Coventry Archives, BA/H/C/17/1, ff. 186v, 188v; BA/H/Q/A79/105-6. [10] Ibid. BA/H/C/17/1, ff. 236, 244; A.A. Dibben, *Coventry City Charters*, 31-2. [11] Coventry Archives, BA/H/C/17/1, f. 259; BA/H/Q/A79/126, 141a-b; *APC*, 1601-4, pp. 191-2; Add. 11364, f. 15v. [12] Coventry Archives, BA/H/Q/A79/128; BA/G/A/34/36; Bodl. ms Eng. misc. b.27, ff. 151-2; C2/Jas.I/W8/35. [13] Coventry Archives, BA/H/Q/A79/35, 97; *CSP Dom.* 1611-18, p. 424; Bodl. ms Eng. misc. b.27, ff. 149-50v. [14] Coventry Archives, BA/H/C/17/1, ff. 220v, 221v-2v, 223v, 228, 234v; C2/Jas.I/C12/35. [15] Salop RO, 1831/14; Coventry Archives, BA/H/C/20/2, p. 97; BA/H/C/17/1, f. 176; *CJ*, i. 399a; *CD 1621*, iii. 257; *Nicholas 1621*, ii. 71. [16] Hants RO, 44M69/L39/35; C219/35/2/95, 97; 219/37/270-1. [17] Coventry Archives, BA/H/C/20/2, pp. 82, 114, 181, 186, 191, 239, 244; BA/H/Q/A79/92b-c. [18] Ibid. BA/H/C/17/1, ff. 175v, 201v-2; *CJ*, i. 396b, 404a. [19] Coventry Archives, BA/H/C/17/1, ff. 268, 276v. [20] Hants RO, 44M69/L39/35; *CD 1628*, ii. 376. [21] Harl. 390, f. 356v. [22] *APC*, 1627, p. 52; Coventry Archives, BA/H/M/17/1; BA/H/M/24/1-2. [23] D. Hirst, *Representative of the People?*, 51-2; Coventry Archives, BA/E/F/37/2, pp. 51, 92, 127; Add. 11364, f. 15v. [24] Hants RO, 44M69/L39/35. [25] SP14/40/25; C2/Chas.I/W39/53; Coventry Archives, PA/100/12/2, 7, 14. [26] Coventry Archives, PA/100/12/3, 12, 15, 18, 26; *APC*, 1626, p. 383; 1627, p. 297; SP16/66/3. [27] *APC*, 1627-8, pp. 152-3; Coventry Archives, PA/100/12/23, 29, 35; SP16/105/102. [28] Coventry Archives, PA/15/1, f. 482v; PA/100/12/18, 31. [29] *CD 1628*, ii. 37, 44-5, 49-50. [30] Ibid. ii. 78, 91, 368, 374-6, 390.

P.M.H.

WARWICK

Right of election: in the bailiff and burgesses

Number of voters: 24 in 1620

8 Mar. 1604	JOHN TOWNSEND
	WILLIAM SPICER
c. Mar. 1614	GREVILLE VERNEY
	JOHN TOWNSEND
26 Dec. 1620[1]	(SIR) GREVILLE VERNEY
	JOHN COKE
23 Jan. 1624	SIR EDWARD CONWAY II
	FRANCIS LUCY
10 May 1625	SIR FRANCIS LEIGH, bt.
	FRANCIS LUCY
1626	SIR FRANCIS LEIGH, bt.
	FRANCIS LUCY
1628	SIR THOMAS PUCKERING, bt.
	ROBERT GREVILLE
3 Apr. 1628	FRANCIS LUCY *vice* Puckering, chose to sit for Tamworth Both elections declared void, 31 May 1628
30 Jan. 1629	ANTHONY STOUGHTON
	FRANCIS LUCY

Warwick's strategic location on a 'rocky ascent' above the Avon made it an important military and administrative centre from Saxon times. As the county town of seventeenth-century Warwickshire, it played host to the quarter sessions and assizes, and housed the local militia's magazine. However, although it possessed a thriving market in local agricultural produce, it lagged behind both Coventry and Birmingham in terms of commercial and industrial development. The growing population stood at around 3,000 in 1600, but poverty levels were relatively high.[2] Social tensions were exacerbated by the oligarchical character of Warwick's corporation. Under the terms of its 1554 charter, executive power was vested in the bailiff and 12 principal burgesses, the common council. The wider population was allowed little say in the borough's affairs beyond the choice of bailiff. Assistant burgesses were initially recruited purely at the common council's discretion, and their numbers were intermittently reduced when they proved too unmanageable. A revised charter in 1613 finally guaranteed a role for the assistants, but allowed for only a dozen rather than the more usual 24. This routine stifling of dissent within the corporation simply encouraged other forms of popular protest, including occasional riots and, in 1615, the erection of a mock 'court' which summoned the principal burgesses to account for their abuses of power.[3] At the same time, the common council's chronic financial weakness left it vulnerable to the attentions of the local gentry, who might themselves stir up trouble in the town if the corporation resisted their demands. After Sir Thomas Leigh of Stoneleigh failed in his bid to become recorder in 1610, he encouraged complaints of financial malpractice, then persuaded his kinsman, lord chancellor Ellesmere (Thomas Egerton[†]) to order an inquiry into the allegations. As a result, in 1615 the corporation was ordered to increase its provision for the poor, and to allow the sheriff of Warwickshire to inspect its annual accounts.[4]

Warwick's parliamentary history stretched back to 1275. The 1554 charter awarded the franchise to the bailiff and burgesses, which was at first interpreted to mean the common Council alone, although in 1573 the corporation conceded this privilege to the 12 assistant burgesses. Elections became another focus for popular dissent, and in 1586 the commonalty put forward their own candidate, the puritan Job Throckmorton. The corporation, unable to ignore this development, eventually agreed to endorse him themselves rather than acknowledge the precedent for a broader franchise. In the early seventeenth century, elections were held in the Court House at the shire hall. Once the bailiff, principal and assistant burgesses had voted, the whole corporation formally consented to the outcome, and the borough's common seal was applied to the election indenture. In 1620 the indenture was drawn up on the day after the vote.[5]

For the last two Elizabethan parliaments the corporation returned two of its senior members, John Townsend and William Spicer, and it did so again in 1604. A few months later, however, Warwick Castle was granted to Sir Fulke Greville*, who became recorder in 1610 and acquired significant amounts of property in the town. Although Townsend again secured a burgess-ship in 1614, that marked the last gasp of corporation independence during this period.[6] Greville commanded at least one seat in every election from then until 1628. His nephew, Greville Verney, was returned both in 1614 and 1620. In the latter year, the second place went to John Coke, Greville's former secretary. Two more distant kinsmen, Sir Edward Conway II in 1624 and Sir Francis Leigh in 1625-6, were followed in 1628 by Sir Fulke's cousin

and heir, Robert Greville. However, from 1624 the corporation also accepted nominations from another leading Warwickshire figure, Sir Thomas Lucy* of Charlecote, whose brother Francis represented the borough continuously from 1624 to 1626. The Lucy interest was so strong that Sir Fulke felt unable to request the second seat for Sir Edward Conway in 1626.[7] Given this apparent stranglehold, Prince Charles's Council failed to obtain a place in 1624 for Sir Francis Cottington.[8] Several local gentlemen proved equally unsuccessful during this decade when they appealed to the commonalty. This tactic was first attempted in 1620 by Sir Bartholomew Hales of Snitterfield, one of the town's j.p.s, and Sir Clement Throckmorton*, son of the 1586 Member. When the common council produced their charter as proof of the narrow franchise, Hales and Throckmorton withdrew.[9] A more determined candidate emerged in 1625. Sir Thomas Puckering, who lived at the Priory, just outside the town, had fallen out with the corporation in the previous year over tithe payments, though it is debatable whether he stood for election out of a desire to cause trouble, or because, as a firm puritan, he genuinely favoured a broader franchise. Although the corporation's records are ambiguous, he probably sought a seat at Warwick in both 1625 and 1626. As his overtures were rejected, he sat for Tamworth on each occasion. On 21 June 1625 he tendered a petition from the borough of Warwick, which was referred to the committee for privileges, but no more was heard of it.[10] Puckering presumably also presented a second petition about Warwick on 9 Feb. 1626. This time the privileges committee pursued the matter of the franchise, summoning witnesses from both sides, but the final verdict, which allegedly favoured the corporation, was never reported to the House.[11] In 1628 the corporation tired of this harassment, and actually returned Puckering, but he promptly opted for Tamworth again and resumed the struggle. This time, even though the privileges committee acknowledged the common council's customary monopoly over voting, the verdict went in favour of the wider franchise. The elections of both Greville and Puckering's replacement, Francis Lucy, were declared void on 31 May. However, no writ for a fresh election was issued until the following January, by which time Greville's succession as 2nd Lord Brooke had rendered him ineligible. This allowed Lucy to resume his seat, the other burgess-ship going to Puckering's friend Anthony Stoughton.[12]

[1] Black Bk. of Warwick ed. T. Kemp, 411. [2] W. Dugdale, Antiqs. of Warws. (1730), i. 372; VCH Warws. viii. 418; A. Hughes, Pols.

Soc. and Civil War in Warws. 9, 17; *APC*, 1626, p. 77; P. Clark and P. Slack, *Eng. Towns in Transition*, 83, 121. [3] *CPR*, 1554-5, pp. 18-20; C66/2141/17; *Black Bk. of Warwick*, 56-7, 60-1, 104-6, 360; *VCH Warws.* viii. 493; D. Hirst, *Representative of the People?*, 210-11. [4] Clark and Slack, 130; *VCH Warws.* viii. 495-6. [5] *CPR*, 1554-5, p.21; *Black Bk. of Warwick*, 106, 409-11; *HP Commons, 1558-1603*, iii. 492; *VCH Warws.* viii. 478. [6] *HP Commons, 1558-1603*, i. 264; *CSP Dom.* 1603-10, p. 128; 1611-18, p. 444; *VCH Warws.* viii. 493. [7] *Vis. Warws.* (Harl. Soc. xii), 25, 29; *Vis. Warws.* (Harl. Soc. lxii), 9, 93; *HMC Cowper*, i. 26; PROB 11/154, ff. 286-90; *Procs. 1625*, p. 703; *CSP Dom. Addenda* 1625-49, p. 94 [8] DCO, 'Prince Charles in Spain', f. 34v. [9] *Vis. Warws.* (Harl. Soc. xii), 207, 210; *Black Bk. of Warwick*, 409-10. [10] W. Cooper, *Hist. Lillington*, 19; PROB 11/175, f. 295; Hughes, 92 n. 143; *Procs. 1625*, pp. 206, 703. [11] *Procs. 1625*, p. 703; *Procs. 1626*, ii. 7, 16, 105-6, 281, 300; iii. 190, 377. [12] *CD 1628*, ii. 169; iv. 37-8, 46; *Procs. 1628*, vi. 169-70; C231/4, f. 263.

H.J.L./P.M.H.

WESTMORLAND

Number of voters: unknown

1 Mar. 1604	SIR THOMAS STRICKLAND SIR RICHARD MUSGRAVE
c. Mar. 1614	HENRY CLIFFORD, Lord Clifford SIR THOMAS WHARTON
11 Jan. 1621	HENRY CLIFFORD, Lord Clifford SIR THOMAS WHARTON
5 Feb. 1624	JOHN LOWTHER I ROBERT STRICKLAND
28 Apr. 1625	JOHN LOWTHER I SIR HENRY BELLINGHAM, bt.
2 Feb. 1626	JOHN LOWTHER I SIR HENRY BELLINGHAM, bt.
28 Feb. 1628	(SIR) JOHN LOWTHER I JOHN LOWTHER II

Westmorland had long been free from Scottish incursions before the Union of the Crowns in 1603, by which time 'the old breed of northern magnates who saw their tenants as armed retainers rather than mere entries on a rent roll' was practically extinct.[1] Nevertheless, the early Stuart period was dominated by wrangling over tenant-right, the custom of rendering an uneconomic rent in consideration of the obligation to serve on the now non-existent border. Landlords regarded the change of circumstances as an opportunity to overthrow all customary tenures and increase entry fines, although this met with considerable resistance from their tenants.[2] Traditionally Westmorland, a 'little mountainous county', was divided into two

parts; the barony of Appleby in the north, dominated by the Clifford earls of Cumberland who also held the hereditary shrievalty of Westmorland; and the barony of Kendal in the south, comprised mainly of Crown estates.[3] Elections were held at Appleby and seats were shared out between a handful of local gentry families; the Cliffords remained the main patron of elections, but in four out of seven Parliaments one Member was selected from each side of the county. There were no electoral contests in this period, and it is notable that the same Members tended to be re-elected to consecutive Parliaments, perhaps reflecting the 'relative poverty of the border areas and the proportionately smaller number of noteworthy families' who were willing to bear the expense of parliamentary service.[4]

In 1604 Sir Thomas Strickland of Sizergh, three miles south of Kendal, who had served in Elizabeth's last Parliament, was returned as the senior knight of the shire, with Sir Richard Musgrave of Hartley, on the north Yorkshire border, as his colleague. At the next general election in 1614 the 4th earl of Cumberland (Francis Clifford*), as sheriff, returned his own son, Henry, Lord Clifford, and nephew Sir Thomas Wharton, in first and second places respectively. Both were from the northern half of the shire. Wharton and his father had recently won a significant victory in a Chancery case concerning agreements with 279 tenants on six manors that set a precedent against tenant-right.[5] Customary tenures were further shaken up by two events that occurred in 1616. First, the heirs of the countess dowager of Cumberland, who died in that year, discovered to their dismay that lands worth £3,000 a year would yield little more than a tenth of that sum unless the terms of tenant-right were altered, which would require an Act of Parliament. Clifford not surprisingly announced his intention to proceed with a bill, although there is no evidence that he ever did so.[6] Secondly, the Crown lands in the barony of Kendal were granted to Prince Charles upon his creation as Prince of Wales. The prince's newly appointed steward, John Lowther I, immediately applied himself to the overthrow of tenant-right both in the barony and on his own newly purchased manor of Crosby Ravensworth.[7] In 1618 the lord chancellor Sir Francis Bacon* issued a decree requiring the prince's tenants to pay £2,700 for confirmation of their right of inheritance. There followed on 28 July 1620 a Proclamation abolishing tenant-right as incompatible with the Union of the Crowns, which provoked organized protests across the region.[8]

The next election took place against a backdrop of insurrection over tenures, led by Crown tenants in the barony of Kendal. A Remonstrance was drawn up by the vicar of Kirkby Stephen and read in Staveley chapel on 2 Jan. 1621 to a gathering described by the landlords as a 'riotous assembly'.[9] Nine days later Clifford and Wharton were re-elected. Two tenants' bills were tabled in the Commons, one concerning the prince's Kendal estates (26 Feb. 1621), and another 'for enabling and confirmation of certain lands and tenements within the county of Westmorland to be customary lands and tenements of inheritance, according to the purport of decrees heretofore made within the space of two years last past in the High Court of Chancery, or within seven years hereafter' (27 February).[10] Clifford and Wharton were both appointed on 10 Mar. 1621 to consider the first of these bills, which was steered through committee by the prince's solicitor, (Sir) Thomas Trevor*, and sent to the Lords on 26 May. It passed, but failed to be enacted at the abrupt end of the Parliament.[11] The second bill was an attempt by the tenants of various private landlords in the county, including the Bellinghams of Over Levens, to protect themselves against high entry fines and rack-renting. However, the bill was not only rejected on second reading because of objections raised against its 'future authority', but the landlords also later sued the tenants responsible in Star Chamber.[12] Clifford refused to stand again, and so Westmorland was represented in the last Jacobean Parliament by Lowther, a substantial landowner in northern Westmorland, together with Strickland's son Robert.[13]

In 1625 and 1626 Lowther was re-elected, along with Sir Henry Bellingham, whose estates lay to the south of Kendal; the latter took the opportunity while in London to appear as a plaintiff in the Star Chamber tenant-right case. The tenants, who had engaged Sir Heneage Finch* as legal counsel, finally emerged triumphant from prolonged litigation with a ruling confirming their inheritance of their estates; the Bellinghams and other landlords were ordered to set agreed rates of fines.[14]

Perhaps because of the tradition of border service, there seems to have been no serious opposition either to the Forced Loan or to the pressing and billeting of soldiers in Westmorland.[15] At the general election in 1628 both Members came from the north of the shire. Lowther was elected for the fourth time in succession, together with his son John, though the latter was then in London pursuing his legal studies.[16] The choice of Lowther and his son was a unique honour for the family.

[1] A.R. Appleby, 'Agrarian Capitalism or Seigneurial Reaction?', *AHR*, lxxx. 586-7. [2] M. Campbell, *Eng. Yeoman*, 148-50; J. Scott, 'The Kendal Tenant Right Dispute, 1619-26', in *Trans. Cumb. and Westmld. Antiq. and Arch. Soc.* n.s. xcviii. 169-82. [3] *CSP Dom.* 1627-8, p. 198. [4] R.E. Ruigh, *Parl. of 1624*, p. 106. [5] C78/505/10. [6] *Lowther Fam. Estate Bks.* ed. C.B. Phillips (Surtees Soc. cxci), 224-5. [7] Ibid., 226. [8] *Stuart Royal Procs.* ed. Hughes and Larkin, i. 488-90; Campbell, 150-2; J. Nicholson and R. Burn, *Westmld. and Cumb.* i. 51-5. [9] STAC 8/34/4; S.J. Watts, 'Tenant Right in Early Seventeenth-Cent. Northumb.', *NH*, vi. 74-7. [10] *CJ*, i. 526b, 529a. [11] Ibid. 548b; *CD 1621*, iv. 142, 379; vii. 65-70, 75-77; Watts, 75-6. [12] *CSP Dom.* 1619-23, p. 216; 1623-5, p. 107. [13] *Strafforde Letters* (1739) ed. W. Knowler, i. 19. [14] STAC 8/34/4; Nicholson and Burn, i. 56-9; Scott, 174-80. [15] *CSP Dom.* 1627-8, pp. 48, 198, 312. [16] *Lowther Fam. Estate Bks.* 27.

J.P.F./R.C.L.S.

APPLEBY

Right of election: in the freemen

Number of voters: c.85 in 1614[1]

1 Mar. 1604	SIR JOHN MORICE
	SIR WILLIAM BOWYER I
c.Mar. 1614	SIR GEORGE SAVILE
	SIR HENRY WOTTON
11 Jan. 1621	(SIR) ARTHUR INGRAM
	THOMAS HUGHES
5 Feb. 1624	(SIR) ARTHUR INGRAM
	THOMAS HUGHES
28 Apr. 1625	SIR JOHN HOTHAM, bt.
	THOMAS HUGHES
2 Feb. 1626	SIR WILLIAM SLINGSBY
	WILLIAM ASHTON I
28 Feb. 1628	RICHARD LOWTHER
	WILLIAM ASHTON I

Situated in the north of Westmorland, Appleby received its first royal charter in the late twelfth century, and sent two Members to the Model Parliament.[2] Geographically and politically dominated by its castle, one of the many homes of the Clifford earls of Cumberland and hereditary sheriffs of Westmorland, the town had, by the early Stuart period, been outstripped by Kendal, both as an economic and administrative centre.[3] Municipal government lay in the hands of a mayor, eight aldermen, and a common council of 16. Surviving returns from this period were made by the mayor in the name of the freemen, a list of whom, probably drawn up for the election to the Addled Parliament, contains about 85 names.[4] The borough was so poor that it could not afford to cover its Members' travelling expenses to distant Westminster, let alone parliamentary wages, although it did manage to find the money to have its charters confirmed in 1607.[5] None of the ten Members returned in this period resided in the town, or even in the county. Five were Yorkshiremen, while the rest came from as far south as Essex, Buckinghamshire, Bedfordshire, Middlesex, and Kent.

The two Members returned in 1604 were presumably nominated by the 3rd earl of Cumberland; although, as hereditary sheriff of Westmorland, the earl was also the returning officer, this does not appear to have prevented him from exercising patronage in the election. Sir John Morice, who was re-elected, was a kinsman of the countess, while Sir William Bowyer I, an Exchequer official, was probably recommended to Cumberland by Sir Robert Cecil[†]. Cumberland died in 1605 and was succeeded by his brother, Francis Clifford*. In 1614 neither he, nor the dowager countess, who had recently made an unpopular attempt to obstruct the holding of the assizes in the castle, appear to have put forward candidates.[6] Instead, both Members were probably nominated by the dowager countess' nephew, Henry, Lord Clifford*. The first, Sir George Savile, was the brother-in-law of Clifford's friend and schoolfellow, Sir Thomas Wentworth*, while the second place went to Sir Henry Wotton, Clifford's friend and former travel companion.

Before the next general election Wentworth had 'an absolute promise of my Lord Clifford' to reserve one seat for him at Appleby, which, were he to be re-elected for Yorkshire, he would transfer to Christopher Wandesford*.[7] In the event Wentworth did retain the county seat, while Wandesford was also successful at Aldborough, Yorkshire, leaving the senior seat at Appleby available for (Sir) Arthur Ingram, who handled Clifford's business at Court and in the city.[8] The junior seat went to Clifford's maternal uncle, Thomas Hughes. The same pair were re-elected in 1624. However, Ingram was also returned at Old Sarum and York, opting to serve for the latter. A fresh election was ordered at Old Sarum, but surprisingly there is no evidence of formal steps to fill the Appleby vacancy. Nevertheless the Crown Office list, the official record of returns, was temporarily amended to indicate that the Appleby Member was in fact Ingram's eldest son and namesake. Ingram himself was presumably behind this unsuccessful subterfuge, for in October 1624, when a second session was expected, he explored the possibility of securing a writ for a new election at Appleby, with a view to returning Sir Arthur junior. Again, nothing came of this, so Hughes alone sat for the borough during this Parliament.[9]

In the first election of Charles I's reign, Wentworth persuaded Clifford to nominate Sir John Hotham, who chose to sit for Beverley; yet, again no new writ was issued to find a replacement. In 1626 the first seat went to Sir William Slingsby, the brother of one of Wentworth's trustiest adherents, and in second place Lady Clifford proposed William Ashton, who had acted as surety in her 'necessities'. Hughes was re-elected in 1628, still as junior Member. For the senior seat, Richard Lowther, the cousin of local magnate Sir John Lowther I*, was presumably nominated by Clifford.[10]

[1] Cumb. RO (Kendal), WSMB/A/2/1. [2] M. Weinbaum, *Brit. Bor. Charters*, 118; M.W. Holdgate, *Hist. Appleby*, 22-3, 26. [3] *Trans. Cumb. and Westmld. Antiq. and Arch. Soc.* xi. 282-3. [4] Cumb. RO (Kendal), WSMB/A/2/1. [5] Cumb. RO (Kendal), WSMB/A/2/2. [6] *CSP Dom.* 1603-10, pp. 408, 435. [7] *Strafforde Letters* (1739) ed. W. Knowler, i. 9. [8] A.F. Upton, *Sir Arthur Ingram*, 154. [9] *CJ*, i. 617b; SP14/159/54; C193/32/14, f. 10; *Wentworth Pprs.* ed. J.P. Cooper (Cam. Soc. ser. 4. xii), 213. Sir Arthur Ingram jun. is misidentified as the Appleby Member in R.E. Ruigh, *Parl. of 1624*, pp. 56, 413. [10] *Wentworth Pprs.* 288.

J.P.F./R.C.L.S.

WILTSHIRE

Number of voters: unknown

13 Mar. 1604	SIR FRANCIS POPHAM
	SIR JOHN THYNNE
22 Oct. 1605	(SIR) THOMAS THYNNE *vice*
	Sir John Thynne, deceased
11 Feb. 1606	SIR WALTER VAUGHAN *vice* Thynne,
	disqualified as he was already
	a Member
c.Mar. 1614	SIR THOMAS HOWARD
	SIR HENRY POOLE
29 Dec. 1620	SIR EDWARD BAYNTUN
	SIR FRANCIS SEYMOUR
20 Jan. 1624	EDWARD HUNGERFORD
	SIR JOHN ST. JOHN, bt.
10 May 1625	SIR FRANCIS SEYMOUR
	(SIR) HENRY LEY
17 Jan. 1626	WALTER LONG II
	SIR HENRY POOLE
11 Mar. 1628	SIR FRANCIS SEYMOUR
	SIR WILLIAM BUTTON, bt.

Wiltshire can be divided into two main regions: the chalk downlands of the Marlborough Downs and Salisbury Plain, dominated by sheep-corn husbandry; and the cheese district of the northern and western parts of the county. There was also a separate 'butter' region in the south-west, and two royal forests, Savernake in the north, and Clarendon in the south-east. Wiltshire was a major centre for cloth manufacture, concentrated in the west of the county and along the Wyley, Avon and Nadder valleys in the south.[1]

By 1604 Wiltshire contained 16 parliamentary boroughs, more than any other shire except Cornwall. The larger boroughs sometimes returned inhabitants, but most were amenable to the influence of neighbouring gentry such as the Thynnes of Longleat, Hungerfords of Corsham, Bayntuns of Bromham, and Pophams of Littlecote. This tended to reduce the pressure on the county seats, where election contests were usually avoided before the Civil War. The fact that no candidate was returned at two consecutive elections during the period suggests there may have been an informal agreement to rotate the shire seats among the leading families. The county court was held at Wilton, the ancient shire town in the south of the county, yet it is worth noting that 10 of the 13 men returned as knights of the shire in this period came from families based in the north of the county.[2]

As might be expected, resident peers enjoyed considerable influence over the shire seats: in 1604 Sir Robert Stapleton* advised one of the candidates that whatever he was promised by the freeholders, they would 'observe the dispositions of my very good lords, the earls of Hertford and Pembroke' before making their decision.[3] As Stapleton claimed, the shire's chief aristocratic patrons were William Herbert, 3rd earl of Pembroke, based at Wilton, and Edward Seymour, 1st earl of Hertford, and his grandson William Seymour*, the 2nd earl, whose seat at Great Bedwyn lay in the north of the county. The only newcomer who had a significant impact on the shire elections was Thomas Howard, 1st earl of Suffolk, whose marriage to Catherine Knyvett had brought him large estates in the county. His patronage was chiefly restricted to the boroughs of Malmesbury and Cricklade, but in 1614 he secured a county seat for one of his younger sons, Thomas Howard*, later 1st earl of Berkshire.

Under Elizabeth the Herberts had dominated Wiltshire politics, but the balance of local power shifted when Hertford succeeded the 2nd earl of Pembroke as lord lieutenant in 1601. Sir John Thynne, the wealthiest commoner in Wiltshire, had a good claim to Hertford's patronage, as the latter's grandfather,

Lord Protector Somerset, had set the Thynnes on the path to prosperity. However, in 1601 his quest for a county seat was undermined by Hertford's nomination of two other candidates, while in 1604, when Thynne sought to pair with Sir Edmund Ludlow*, the senior seat went to Sir Francis Popham, son of chief justice Sir John Popham[†]. The main Popham estates lay in neighbouring Somerset; but as Sir Francis was a Wiltshire deputy lieutenant he was quite possibly endorsed by Hertford. Thynne took the junior county seat, but Ludlow had to content himself with a seat at Hindon, in partnership with Thynne's son Thomas. The Hindon return was dated to the day before the shire election, which probably allowed Ludlow to withdraw from the county contest without losing face.[4] Thynne died in November 1604, and at the ensuing by-election held in October 1605 his son Thomas was returned in his stead. This result was overturned by the Commons on 9 Nov., on the grounds that Thynne was already sitting for Hindon and could not, therefore, be returned for the county.[5] A fresh election held on 11 Feb. 1606 saw the return of Sir Walter Vaughan, who was presumably a Pembroke nominee, as his great-uncle Charles Vaughan[†] had served the Herberts in the previous reign.

In 1614 the senior county seat went to Sir Thomas Howard, whose family were then at the height of their influence at Court; one of his kinswomen had also recently become Sir Thomas Thynne's second wife. Howard was paired with a local landowner, Sir Henry Poole. Suffolk's fall in 1618 precluded Howard's re-election, but a similar combination of gentry and aristocratic influences occurred in 1621, when Sir Henry Bayntun was returned along with Hertford's younger grandson Sir Francis Seymour – whose elder brother William Seymour*, Lord Beauchamp, had stood unsuccessfully for a county seat in Somerset. At the next election in 1624, the county seats were shared by two half-brothers, Sir Edward Hungerford and Sir John St. John. The latter's sister was married to Sir Edward Villiers*, half-brother to the royal favourite, the duke of Buckingham, whose stock was then riding high as leader of the anti-Spanish 'patriot' cause, a consideration which may have assisted their election.

The 1625 election saw the return of Sir Francis Seymour once again, paired with Henry Ley, son of the lord treasurer, Lord Ley (Sir James Ley*). Seymour apparently dissuaded (Sir) Thomas Thynne from standing by claiming that his elder brother, now 2nd earl of Hertford, and the earl of Montgomery (Sir Philip Herbert*) 'would give their assents for none but myself'.[6] Seymour's efforts in wrecking royal attempts to secure a large grant of supply during the parliamentary session persuaded the king to prick him as sheriff of Wiltshire in November 1625, thus ensuring that he could not stand for Parliament in the election which followed shortly thereafter. He approached Sir Thomas Wentworth* for a nomination in a northern constituency, in order to evade the prospect of having to return himself, but nothing came of this scheme, and rumours that he had been returned for Wiltshire proved equally unfounded.[7] In his stead was returned Walter Long II, a landowner of rather lesser standing than was normal for a shire knight, who was also in financial difficulties. His cause was doubtless promoted by his stepfather Henry Sherfield*, recorder of Salisbury, and seems to have been supported by the earl of Pembroke, who found Long's brother-in-law, Sir John Evelyn, a seat at Wilton at this election. Long repaid his patron by vigorously promoting the earl's anti-Buckingham agenda in the Commons. The junior knight on this occasion was Sir Henry Poole, who consistently doubted the wisdom of attempting the duke's impeachment.

In 1628 Long was sheriff, while Poole, who had served as a Forced Loan commissioner in Wiltshire and Oxfordshire, seems to have decided not to stand for election at a time when the Loan was a divisive political issue.[8] This allowed Seymour to resume the senior county seat, paired on this occasion with Sir William Button, 1st bt., whose family had long been tenants of the Herberts.

[1] D. Underdown, *Revel, Riot and Rebellion*, 73-105; G.D. Ramsay, *Wilts. Woollen Industry*, 1-30, 122-38. [2] *VCH Wilts.* iii. 111-13, 117, 123-4. [3] Longleat, Thynne pprs. (IHR microfilm), vii. f. 310. [4] Ibid. vii. ff. 212, 310. [5] C142/290/110; *CJ*, i. 257a. [6] Longleat, Thynne pprs. (IHR microfilm), viii. ff. 121-3. [7] *List of Sheriffs* comp. A. Hughes (PRO, L. and I. ix), 154; *Strafforde Letters* (1739) ed. W. Knowler, i. 29-31. [8] *List of Sheriffs*, 154; C193/12/2, f. 20.

H.J.L./S.H.

CALNE

Right of election: in the burgesses

Number of voters: 17 in 1621

5 Mar. 1604	WILLIAM SWADDON JOHN NOYES
13 Jan. 1606[1]	SIR EDMUND CAREY *vice* Swaddon, vacated his seat
c. Mar. 1614	SIR EDMUND CAREY RICHARD LOWE

23 Dec. 1620	JOHN DUCKETT JOHN PYM
29 Jan. 1624	SIR EDWARD HOWARD II JOHN DUCKETT
6 May 1625	SIR EDWARD HOWARD II GEORGE LOWE
25 Jan. 1626	SIR JOHN EYRE GEORGE LOWE
13 Mar. 1628	(SIR) JOHN MAYNARD GEORGE LOWE

Situated on the main road from London to Bristol, Calne was already a significant settlement by the late Anglo-Saxon period, and formed part of the Crown's ancient demesne. However, from the tenth century the original manor was divided into two, with one portion passing into ecclesiastical hands. The borough of Calne straddled the boundary between these smaller manors, and this dual patronage perhaps hindered its municipal development. Although its residents enjoyed the basic privileges associated with the royal demesne, Calne remained merely a borough by prescription until it was finally incorporated in 1685.[2] Early seventeenth-century records occasionally mention the renewal of the borough's charter, but in practice this meant little more than the confirmation of its limited existing rights. Administrative autonomy was almost entirely lacking. Calne's two constables were elected each year at the local hundred court, while new burgesses had to be sworn in at the manorial court of Ogbourne St. George, over 14 miles away. From at least the mid-sixteenth century the borough's principal officers were the two stewards of the town's merchant guild, who were also appointed annually, and managed the borough's property and finances.[3] Calne possessed a weekly market and a yearly fair, but its economy in the early Stuart period revolved around cloth production. Ordinarily this guaranteed the town's prosperity, but the district was badly hit by the trading slump of the early 1620s.[4]

Calne's parliamentary record dated from 1295, though the borough was not regularly represented in the Commons until the late 1300s. The franchise was vested in the burgesses, who seem not to have numbered more than 20 at any time during the seventeenth century.[5] Elections were held at the borough's guildhall, or church house, as the 1606 indenture confirms. All seven returns surviving from this period once bore the borough seal, but only those of 1604 and 1606 were signed. The guild stewards are normally described as being the borough's returning officers, but during the early Stuart period most of the indentures were made out in the name of the constables and burgesses. The stewards headed the list of voters only in 1624, though they did also sign the 1606 return.[6]

In 1604 Calne elected two residents of the borough, William Swaddon and John Noyes, both of whom were clothiers and former guild stewards. When Swaddon stood down through ill health two years later, he was replaced by Sir Edmund Carey, a minor courtier living some six miles away at Dauntsey.[7] Thereafter, a regular pattern emerged, with one seat in each election going to a complete outsider, while the other was controlled by the owners of Calne's two manors. John Duckett, who held the former royal manor, sat in 1621 and 1624. Richard Lowe, lessee of the second, or prebendal manor, had already represented the borough in 1597 and 1601, and secured re-election in 1614. He died ten years later, but his brother George then revived the family's interest, sitting in each Parliament from 1625 to 1628.[8] The patronage of the remaining seats was much less predictable. Sir Edmund Carey was again elected in 1614, but is not known to have sought a Commons' place after that. In 1624 and 1625 the borough accepted Sir Edward Howard, whose father, the 1st earl of Suffolk, was a major landowner in north Wiltshire. Sir John Eyre and Sir John Maynard, who sat in 1626 and 1628 respectively, were both related to the Bayntuns, one of the most important gentry families in the Calne area.[9] John Pym, the junior Member in 1621, was a Somerset gentleman, whose role as receiver-general of Crown lands in Wiltshire gave him jurisdiction over Bowood Park, just outside the borough. Whether this was sufficient to secure him his seat, or whether he also enjoyed the backing of a local patron, remains uncertain.[10] Of all these Members, only Noyes is known to have pursued his constituents' interests in the Commons, gathering the details of legislation that might affect them. Noyes is also the only one of the ten who definitely received parliamentary wages. Given that his expenses of £19 in 1607 accounted for nearly half of the borough's annual budget, it is perhaps understandable that Calne normally accepted external nominees who were unlikely to expect payment.[11]

---

[1] Election held on 13 Jan. 1606, but return made on 14 Jan.: C219/35/2/107. [2] VCH Wilts. xvii. 32, 64; Guild Stewards' Bk. of Bor. of Calne ed. A.W. Mabbs (Wilts. Arch. and Nat. Hist. Soc. recs. branch, vii), p. x; Wilts. Bor. Recs. ed. M.G. Rathbone (Wilts. Arch. and Nat. Hist. Soc. recs. branch, v), 1. [3] Guild Stewards' Bk. pp. xii-xvi, 39, 47; Wilts. Bor. Recs. 1-2. [4] VCH Wilts. xvii. 83-4; CSP Dom. 1619-23, p. 149. [5] OR; Guild Stewards' Bk. p. xv. [6] C219/35/2/107,121;219/37/301;219/38/303;219/39/225;219/40/91;

219/41B/68; Guild Stewards' Bk. pp. xiv-xv. [7] PROB 11/109, f. 245v; Wilts. N and Q, iv. 368-9, 421-2; CJ, i. 257a. [8] VCH Wilts. xvii. 100-1; HP Commons, 1558-1603, i. 269; Vis. Wilts. (Harl. Soc. cv-cvi), 120-1. [9] King's Coll. Lib., Camb., KCAR/1/2/16, vol. iv, no. 59; Wilts. N and Q, viii. 446-50; Vis. Wilts. 60; Vis. Essex (Harl. Soc. xiv), 595. [10] J.E. Jackson, 'Calne', Wilts. Arch. Mag. xxiv. 188. [11] HMC Var. iii. 263-4; Guild Stewards' Bk. 39.

H.J.L./P.M.H.

CHIPPENHAM

Right of election: in the burgesses

Number of voters: 46 in 1624

c. Mar. 1604	JOHN HUNGERFORD	
	JOHN ROBERTS	
	Edward Wymarke*	
16 Mar. 1614[1]	SIR ROGER OWEN	
	THOMAS CULPEPER	
15 Apr. 1614[2]	SIR WILLIAM MAYNARD, (bt.) vice Owen, chose to sit for Shropshire	
11 Dec. 1620	EDWARD HUNGERFORD	
	JOHN BAILIFFE	
23 Jan. 1624	JOHN MAYNARD (not returned)	13
	SIR FRANCIS POPHAM	39
	JOHN PYM	7
	CHARLES MAYNARD returned vice Maynard. John Maynard seated, 12 Mar. 1624	
	Double return of Popham and Pym.	
	POPHAM seated, 9 Apr. 1624	
c. May 1625	JOHN MAYNARD	
	SIR FRANCIS POPHAM	
13 Jan. 1626	SIR EDWARD BAYNTUN	
	SIR FRANCIS POPHAM	
7 Mar. 1628	SIR FRANCIS POPHAM	
	SIR JOHN EYRE	

Located on the River Avon, close to the royal forest of Pewsham, the settlement of Chippenham dates from at least the ninth century, and was the scene of a famous peace treaty between the Saxons and Danes in 879. In the early Stuart period the town was noted for its corn market, though its prosperity depended primarily on the manufacture of broadcloth. There were at least 94 households in 1604, and Chippenham was substantial enough to host quarter sessions in its town hall.[3] A corporation, consisting of a bailiff and 12 capital burgesses, was created in 1554, at which time the Crown also granted the town more than 200 acres, the revenues from which were intended to be used for maintaining a bridge over the Avon and to help fund the costs of sending Members to Parliament. The town lands were a frequent source of controversy, and in 1574 certain corporation members were sued in Chancery for misappropriating the revenues. More seriously, in the early years of James's reign the grant itself was called into question by the Crown, which claimed that over a quarter of this property was assart land within Pewsham forest and therefore liable to rent. In 1607 the borough was obliged to compound and obtain a fresh charter which resolved this issue.[4]

Chippenham first returned Members to the Commons in 1295. Under the Marian charter the franchise was vested in the corporation, but prior to this the freemen in general had enjoyed the vote. Consequently, at several Elizabethan elections the ordinary freemen asserted their right to this privilege, but without success.[5] The matter was not forgotten, however, for when, at the start of James's reign, a fresh dispute arose over the corporation's management of the town lands, the freemen took the opportunity to claim in Chancery that by long tradition they both elected and funded the borough's Members. Certainly, when wages were required during the first Jacobean Parliament, every householder was rated in order to raise this money, though it is unclear whether this was the usual practice. The question of the franchise was only incidental to the Chancery suit, but significantly, in February 1604, the court upheld the freemen's complaints. This issue must therefore have been at the forefront of residents' minds when a parliamentary election was held just weeks later.[6]

Over the previous decade the borough's dominant patron had been Sir Anthony Mildmay of Apethorpe, Northamptonshire, who had acquired by marriage a half-share in the lordship of Chippenham, and who received £4 a year from the profits of the town's market.[7] When the 1604 election was called, Mildmay nominated Edward Wymarke, who had represented the borough in the previous two Parliaments. However, in the aftermath of the Chancery ruling the corporation evidently felt that it had to consult the freemen, and consequently when the election was held 'most of the inhabitants were called and assembled in the lower hall to signify their allowance and approbation of the choice and election'. At this meeting Wymarke was rejected 'because the freemen would not admit of him'. Instead, one of the

townsmen, John Roberts, was chosen, 'being proposed by the generality'.[8] In a further blow to Mildmay, the senior seat was awarded to John Hungerford, a Wiltshire gentleman living some five miles away at Bremhill. He may have been returned on the strength of his own local standing, but he probably received backing from his kinsman, Sir Edward Hungerford[†], who not only owned Sheldon manor in Chippenham, but had also recently purchased a seat at Corsham, just three miles away. Roberts received parliamentary wages of 2s. a day, but Hungerford doubtless covered his own expenses.[9]

Undeterred, Mildmay took steps to reassert his authority over the borough, in 1608 collecting his market rents in person. In 1614 he again demanded one seat, and at the request of his son-in-law, Sir Francis Fane*, nominated Thomas Culpeper. However, he faced competition from three other directions. Sir Edward Hungerford was now dead, and his heir, Edward Hungerford*, was still a minor. The family's interest was therefore exercised by Sir Edward's widow, who had since become countess of Rutland. She recommended one 'Mr. Letet', who has not been identified. Henry Bailiffe [Bayly][†], who had just inherited the seat of Monkton on the edge of the town, also put himself forward. Finally, another outsider, Sir Roger Owen, was proposed by his Wiltshire kinsman, Sir Henry Bayntun* of Bromham, a former Chippenham Member who had recently acquired the nearby manor of Rowden.[10] On 20 Feb. the countess withdrew her initial request, having heard that Letet would be supplied with a seat elsewhere by the 2nd earl of Salisbury (William Cecil*), and instead nominated her own brother, Humphrey Tufton[†]. At this juncture the corporation apparently resolved to accept Bailiffe and Tufton, and accordingly it wrote to Mildmay explaining that it would be unable to oblige him. By return of post they received a clear statement of Sir Anthony's displeasure, and Fane also pitched in by letter to pile pressure on the borough. Meanwhile, Bailiffe proved to be no match for the much wealthier Bayntun. On 16 Mar. the borough finally settled on Owen and Culpeper. The freemen again requested to participate in the election, but there was clearly too much at stake for the corporation to risk another upset, and the narrow franchise was restored.[11] The emergence of the Bayntun interest was confirmed a month later, when Owen opted to sit for Shropshire, and he was replaced at Chippenham by Sir William Maynard, whose sister had just married Sir Henry's son, Sir Edward*.[12]

By December 1620, when the next election was held, both Mildmay and Sir Henry Bayntun had died, leaving the way clear for their rivals. Consequently, the senior seat was taken by Edward Hungerford, who was now of age, while the junior place went to John Bailiffe, Henry's younger brother.[13] However, the picture in 1624 was different again. Hungerford sat as a Wiltshire shire knight, and seems not to have nominated anyone at Chippenham. Instead, the Bayntun interest revived, in the shape of Maynard's brother John. The borough was also approached by John Pym, the local Crown receiver, who probably hoped to exploit the Exchequer's interest in Pewsham forest. Another outsider to express interest in a seat was Sir Francis Popham, a gentleman resident at Littlecote, on the opposite side of Wiltshire. Popham was later a major benefactor of Chippenham, but his connection with the borough at this time has not been established.[14] On 21 Jan. 12 members of the corporation assembled at the town hall. Some of the ordinary freemen also turned up, but without attempting to participate in proceedings. The corporation agreed unanimously to elect Maynard as the senior Member, but there was a tie between Pym and Popham for the remaining seat. Accordingly, a further gathering was held two days later, at which, with the entire corporation present, Pym won the contest by a margin of one vote. A body of freemen had again gathered in the lower hall, and the bailiff, who favoured Popham, now invited them to state their own preference, ignoring any questions about the legality of this move. When Sir Francis received the entire popular vote, the bailiff made out an indenture returning Maynard and Popham, endorsed with the names of the six dissenting capital burgesses and those of 33 freemen. However, Pym's seven supporters refused to accept defeat, and returned Maynard and Pym as the choice of the majority of the corporation.[15]

To complicate matters further, Maynard had learnt that he was also being nominated by Prince Charles's Council for a seat at St. Albans, Hertfordshire, and decided that he had no use for the seat at Chippenham. Accordingly, his brother William, now Lord Maynard, contacted Sir Edward Bayntun, their brother-in-law, who arranged for John's name to be erased from both indentures and replaced with that of another sibling, Charles Maynard. No attempt was made to hold a fresh election before the rival returns were dispatched to London. Unfortunately for John Maynard, the Prince's Council heard that he had been elected at Chippenham and promptly withdrew its own nomination of him, thus leaving him without a seat at all.[16]

When the Parliament assembled Sir Robert Phelips moved for Popham to be admitted. Pym, who had also

been returned for Tavistock but had not yet formally opted for either borough, objected, at which point the matter was referred to the committee for privileges. On 2 Mar. Bayntun, himself a Member, unfolded to the committee the delicate problem of his brother-in-law's fraudulent return, whereupon it was agreed both that John Maynard must be reinstated and that the facts of the case should be firmly suppressed to avoid scandal.[17] A week later the committee addressed the equally tricky question of the double return of Pym and Popham, hearing counsel for both sides on the history of the borough's franchise. On 10 Mar. Pym finally chose to sit for Tavistock, seemingly leaving the field clear for Popham. The next day the committee decided that the broad franchise was legitimate, though this was deemed not to affect Maynard's return. However, Sir Francis then failed to prove that the freemen had participated in the election on 23 Jan., rather than merely voiced their preference afterwards. As this cast doubt on his victory, the committee cautiously decided to recommend a by-election for the second seat.[18] On 12 Mar. the Commons, falsely informed by the committee for privileges that Charles Maynard had been returned purely by accident, agreed that John Maynard should be recognized as the rightful Member. Three days later, the House also decided that the bailiff must amend the relevant indenture. However, no verdict was reached concerning Popham, who was left in limbo for another three weeks. On 1 Apr. the committee for privileges finally concluded that he should be allowed to sit without the formality of a fresh election, an opinion that was endorsed on 9 Apr. by the Commons, which also ruled that in future the borough's elections should be conducted under a broad franchise.[19]

Popham, having evidently established a popular base at Chippenham, retained his seat at the next three elections. John Maynard sat again in 1625, and Sir Edward Bayntun himself represented the borough in the following year. In 1628 the second place went to Sir John Eyre, another Wiltshire gentleman, whose mother was a Bayntun. Elections were clearly viewed within the borough primarily as an opportunity to gratify its assorted patrons, and at no stage during this period did any of Chippenham's Members demonstrably seek to advance the town's interests in Parliament.[20]

[1] Wilts. RO, G19/1/30/257. [2] Ibid. G19/1/30/262. [3] J.J. Daniell, Hist. Chippenham, 4, 20, 29, 66-7, 69, 90-1; Recs. of Chippenham Bor. ed. F.H. Goldney, 191. [4] Recs. of Chippenham Bor. 266, 269-71, 284, 286, 288; Daniell, 61. [5] Daniell, 67; J. Glanville, Reps. of Certain Cases Determined and Adjudged by the Commons in Parl. (1775), pp. 49-50. [6] Recs. of Chippenham Bor. 30, 191, 272-83. [7] HP Commons,

1558-1603, i. 270; *Recs. of Chippenham Bor.* 189, 292, 323-4, 339; *CP*, xii. pt. 2, p. 567. [8] *Recs. of Chippenham Bor.* 328; 'Earle 1624', ff. 109v-10. [9] *Vis. Wilts.* (Harl. Soc. cv-cvi), 91, 94; *Recs. of Chippenham Bor.* pp. xii, 2, 195. [10] *Recs. of Chippenham Bor.* pp. xviii, 197; *Vis. Wilts.* 13-14, 91; Daniel, 52; PROB 11/82, f. 228; Wilts. RO, G19/1/30/252-3; 473/87, 90. [11] Wilts. RO, G19/1/30/253-5, 258, 260; 'Earle 1624', f. 110. [12] C142/366/189. [13] *Vis. Essex* (Harl. Soc. xiii), 251; *Recs. of Chippenham Bor.* 44; *Vis. Wilts.* 13-14, 91-3. [14] *Vis. Essex* (Harl. Soc. xiv), 679; *Recs. of Chippenham Bor.* 18, 58; Daniell, 143. [15] Glanville, 51-3. Glanville incorrectly states the number of freemen as being 32; cf. Wilts. RO, G19/1/30/264. [16] DCO, 'Prince Charles in Spain', f. 37; C219/38/306; 'Hawarde 1624', p. 169. [17] *CJ*, i. 717b; 'Hawarde 1624', p. 169. [18] 'Earle 1624', ff. 64-5; *CJ*, i. 681b; 'Hawarde 1624', p. 191. [19] *CJ*, i. 684b, 686a-b, 759a; 'Earle 1624', ff. 109v-110. [20] *Vis. Wilts.* 60.

H.J.L./P.M.H.

CRICKLADE

Right of election: in the burgage-holders

3 Mar. 1604	SIR JOHN HUNGERFORD
	SIR HENRY POOLE
c. Mar. 1614	SIR THOMAS MONSON
	SIR JOHN EYRE[1]
26 Dec. 1620	SIR THOMAS HOWARD
	SIR CAREW REYNELL
24 Jan. 1624	SIR WILLIAM HOWARD
	SIR NEVILLE POOLE
3 May 1625	SIR WILLIAM HOWARD
	EDWARD DOWSE
18 Jan. 1626	SIR WILLIAM HOWARD
	SIR ROBERT HYDE
4 Mar. 1628	(SIR) EDWARD HUNGERFORD
	ROBERT JENNER

Situated in north Wiltshire, near the border with Gloucestershire, and lying strategically on both the Thames and Ermine Street – the principal road connecting Gloucester and Cirencester with Winchester – Cricklade was originally developed as a Saxon royal borough. It received its first charter in the twelfth century and was represented in Parliament from 1275. However, it was never incorporated and it continued to be governed by the annual manorial court leet.[2] The election indentures were made in the name of the bailiff, burgesses and freeholders of the borough and were signed by the former, who presumably supervised the election. The burgesses and freeholders held the burgage plots in the borough, the former as tenants, the latter as owners. The bailiff was appointed by the

lord of the manor, who thereby exercised considerable control over parliamentary elections.[3]

Cricklade belonged to the Crown in the Elizabethan period, when successive Lords Chandos, who controlled the borough elections, exercised the stewardship of the manor.[4] However, on the death of William, 4th Lord Chandos, in November 1602, Elizabeth appointed as steward Thomas Howard, Lord Howard de Walden, subsequently 1st earl of Suffolk, who had acquired a substantial property in north Wiltshire by his marriage to the daughter of (Sir) Henry Knyvet[†].[5] James I, in 1611, sold the borough to two Londoners, who in turn sold it seven years later to Edmund Maskelyne, a Wiltshire barrister who owned it at his death in 1630.[6] Nevertheless, Suffolk clearly remained the dominant electoral patron until he died in 1626. When, in January of that year, his countess stated that her sons were 'all sure of places in the west country which never have denied my lord', she was presumably principally referring to Cricklade, which had consistently elected her sons since 1620.[7]

In 1604 the Members chosen were both prominent local men: Sir John Hungerford, who lived at Down Ampney in Gloucestershire, three miles away, and Sir Henry Poole, who lived at Kemble in north Wiltshire. It is possible that Suffolk, who had been steward of the borough for less than two years, was uncertain of the extent of his patronage and agreed to let the two important local men have a free run. Thereafter Hungerford showed no sign of seeking re-election, while in 1614 Poole was returned for the county alongside Sir Thomas Howard. It is possible that Poole came to some form of accommodation with Suffolk, whereby the latter agreed to support the former's son Sir Neville at Malmesbury in return for control over both seats at Cricklade. Sir Thomas Monson, who took the first place in the return, was a Lincolnshire courtier described in a Chancery suit as someone Suffolk 'might command and had power over'.[8] His colleague, Sir John Eyre, was a Wiltshire man, but probably also owed his election to Suffolk, whose henchmen had aided Eyre in the attempted murder of Sir Edward Herbert* in 1610.[9]

Monson's political career was brought to an end by his alleged involvement in the murder of Sir Thomas Overbury, for which he was arrested in 1615, while Eyre was, by 1620, ambassador to the Ottoman Empire. In their room Suffolk nominated his son Sir Thomas Howard and Sir Carew Reynell, who had owed his election at Wallingford in 1614 to the earl's son in law William, Lord Knollys (William Knollys[†]). Reynell had married into the Hungerford family and may consequently have had Sir John's support.

Sir Thomas Howard was raised to the peerage in 1622, and was consequently ineligible to sit in the Commons again, while Reynell may have been in poor health at the time of the 1624 election, as he made his will on 12 Jan. and died in the following September.[10] Instead, Suffolk nominated another of his sons, Sir William, who was returned with Sir Neville Poole, the son of Sir Henry. Sir William was re-elected in 1625 and 1626. His colleague in 1625 was Edward Dowse, the former tutor of Algernon, Lord Percy* and a member of the household of Percy's father, Henry, 9th earl of Northumberland.[11] It is possible that Dowse was recommended to Suffolk by Northumberland's cousin, Sir Edward Cecil*, whose niece had married Sir Thomas Howard. In 1626 the second place was filled by Sir Robert Hyde, a Berkshire gentleman and ranger of the nearby forest of Braydon, where Suffolk was keeper and Sir Thomas Howard, by now earl of Berkshire, was lieutenant.[12]

Suffolk died during the 1626 Parliament and with him the Howard influence at Cricklade ended. In 1628 the borough returned (Sir) Edward Hungerford, who owned property in the borough and was the nephew of Sir John Hungerford, and Robert Jenner, a wealthy London Goldsmith who had purchased property nearby, including the manor of Widhill, situated just outside the borough.[13]

[1] *Procs. 1614 (Commons)*, 464. [2] T.R. Thomson, 'Early Hist. and Topography', *Materials for a Hist. of Cricklade*, ed. T.R. Thomson, 63-80; T.R. Thomson, 'Manors', *Materials for a Hist. of Cricklade* ed. T.R. Thomson, 46; W.B. Crouch, 'Parlty. Hist.', in *Materials for a Hist. of Cricklade* ed. T.R. Thomson, 127. [3] C219/37/297; 219/39/227; Thomson, 'Early Hist. and Topography', 79; *HP Commons, 1508-58*, i. 220. [4] *HP Commons, 1558-1603*, i. 270-1. [5] *CP*, iii. 127; E315/309, f. 149. [6] C66/1870/3; Thomson, 'Manors', 45; 'Cricklade manor' (unpublished *VCH Wilts.* draft); *Wilts. IPMs* ed. G.S. and A.E. Fry (Brit. Rec. Soc. xxiii), 112. [7] C66/1870/3; Thomson, 'Manors', 45; King's Coll. Lib., Camb., ms KCAR/1/2/16, vol. iv. no. 59. [8] C78/363/5. [9] *Life of Edward, 1st Lord Herbert of Cherbury* ed. J.M. Shuttleworth, 61-5. [10] PROB. 11/144, f. 202. [11] *Corresp. of John Cosin* ed. G. Ornsby, (Surtees Soc. lii), 73. [12] E315/310, f. 56; SO3/7, unfol., Apr. 1621. [13] *CP*, xii. pt. 1, p. 465; Thompson, 'Manors', 55.

H.J.L./B.C.

DEVIZES

Right of election: in the burgesses

Number of voters: c.80-100

5 Mar. 1604	SIR HENRY BAYNTUN ROBERT DREWE
8 Mar. 1614[1]	SIR EDWARD BAYNTUN WILLIAM KENT
29 Dec. 1620	(SIR) HENRY LEY JOHN KENT
23 Jan. 1624	SIR EDWARD BAYNTUN JOHN KENT
9 May 1625	SIR EDWARD BAYNTUN ROBERT DREWE
7 Jan. 1626[2]	(SIR) HENRY LEY JOHN DREWE
17 Mar. 1626	ROBERT LONG *vice* Ley, called to the Upper House
7 Mar. 1628	ROBERT LONG THOMAS KENT

Situated on a rocky outcrop in the centre of Wiltshire, Devizes was described by Thomas Fuller in the mid-seventeenth century as 'the best and biggest town for trading' in the county next to Salisbury.[3] The town was celebrated for its twice-weekly markets, at which corn, wool, yarn, fish, butter and cheese were sold,[4] but its principal industry, since at least the late thirteenth century, was the manufacture of textiles. An important source of white broadcloths under the Tudors, it responded to the trade depression of the 1620s by turning to the manufacture of serge and felt, though in the short term many of its spinners and weavers were forced to rely on handouts from the corporation to subsist.[5] The town was also an important judicial centre. Quarter sessions had been held there since 1383, and until about 1631 the town held the only bridewell in Wiltshire.[6]

First styled a borough by charter in 1141, Devizes enjoyed the parliamentary franchise intermittently from 1295 and almost without a break from 1459.[7] By the late fourteenth century a distinct form of government had emerged, consisting of a mayor and three grades of burgess – the common councillors (who were generally former mayors), the Twelve, or capital burgesses, and the inferior burgesses. The size of each tier was inconsistent: in 1584 there were 12 councillors,

13 capital and 35 inferior burgesses, whereas in 1630 there were 21, 30 and 42 respectively.[8] Parliamentary elections were held in the guildhall.[9] The mayor and around half a dozen of the burgesses were party to the indentures (in Latin), as was the sheriff of Wiltshire, who acted as returning officer. Outsiders chosen to represent the borough were sworn in as members of the corporation on the day of their election.[10]

Before 1606 the corporation enjoyed only a modest annual income of less than £100, most of which derived from rents.[11] However, for reasons that remain unclear, its receipts increased sharply thereafter, rising to £190 in 1608 and increasing to £481 two years later before settling down to an average £200 p.a. This sudden prosperity encouraged the corporation to design a new seal and purchase other emblems of municipal identity, including richly decorated copies of its charter and constitutions.[12] It also enabled it to clear its debts, increase the salary of its principal officials,[13] and embark upon ambitious building projects. A new Market House, for instance, became the meeting place for the quarter sessions, which had previously met in the ruins of the town's castle.[14] Municipal election dinners, too, became more elaborate and expensive, increasing from £3 6d. in 1604 to £5 1s. 6d. in 1613.[15]

Devizes' new-found prosperity did not go unnoticed. In 1613 James I paid the first of three visits to the town, on which occasion the fees payable to the officers of the royal Household alone cost more than £20.[16] The following year the borough was one of just three Wiltshire towns to which the Crown appealed for a benevolence following the failure of the Addled Parliament, and in 1622 the town contributed £21 towards the recovery of the Palatinate.[17] A threat to the borough's continued prosperity emerged in 1609, when the Exchequer official (Sir) Edward Wardour* obtained from the Crown a lease in reversion of the profits to the borough's markets for 40 years. Although this grant would not fall in for another 18 years, the corporation was so alarmed that by the end of 1610 it had bought out Wardour's reversion for £300.[18] It may have been to prevent the Crown from making any further grants of this nature that in July 1624 the corporation obtained from the king a charter granting it the fee-farm of the profits arising from its courts, fairs and markets in return for an annual rent of £5. In theory the new charter cost just £120, but the true amount, taking into account the fees payable to various royal officials, was actually around £400.[19] Though the corporation was wealthy, this sum was more than it could easily afford, and consequently

it had to offer longer leases to its tenants to raise the money.[20]

During this period the corporation generally returned one prominent townsman and one member of the local gentry to Parliament. In 1604 the corporation initially tried to keep both seats for its own members, just as it had in 1597, for on 25 Feb. it originally agreed to return both Robert Drewe and John Kent.[21] However, a member of the local gentry, Sir Henry Bayntun, chose this moment to reassert his family's interest, which had been in abeyance since 1593, and Kent was forced to step aside. In 1614, most unusually, two outsiders were returned. However, the man chosen for the junior seat, William Kent, who helped manage the estates of William Herbert, 3rd earl of Pembroke, may have been regarded as an honorary townsman, as it seems likely that he was a kinsman of the town clerk, John Kent, and possibly also an associate of another key corporation member, Robert Drewe.

Members of the Kent and the Drewe families supplied all of the townsmen-MPs during this period. John Kent, who sat in 1597, 1621 and 1624 (and was almost elected in 1604), had trained as an attorney and often carried out legal work for the town. He held several key offices in the borough, most notably that of town clerk, which he held from 1592 until his death. His son and heir Thomas, chosen mayor in 1626, was elected in 1628. Like John Kent, Robert Drewe also enjoyed a legal training, and though never called to the bar he occupied chambers in the Middle Temple. He represented the borough in 1597-8, 1601 and 1604-10, and may have gone on to do so again in 1625. However, there is a strong possibility that the Member on this occasion was actually Drewe's third son, also named Robert, who had just turned 21 and was then studying at the Middle Temple. Certainly the elder Robert Drewe's second son, John, did a stint as the borough Member in 1626.

The senior seat was habitually reserved for prominent local landowners, the most conspicuous of whom were the Bayntuns, whose seat at Bromham lay four miles from Devizes. The family had long enjoyed ties with Devizes, an ancestor, Sir Edward Bayntun[†], having been steward of the castle in the 1520s. In 1604, when he caused the corporation to abandon its original plan of returning John Kent, Sir Henry Bayntun seems to have been particularly keen to secure election, having been overlooked by the borough before the previous two parliaments. Following the Parliament he retained close links with the town, and in his will he left the corporation £30 as a stock to support several apprentices.[22] At the following election Bayntun waived his interest in favour of his eldest son, Sir Edward Bayntun, who was technically under-age. Sir Edward, who entered into his inheritance in 1616, lent money to the corporation on at least one occasion, and even though he chose to sit for the county in 1621 the corporation offered him a bottle of 'Muscadyn' wine.[23]

The temporary removal from the scene of Sir Edward Bayntun in December 1620 allowed (Sir) Henry Ley to establish an interest at Devizes. Although Ley had no property in the town, his father, Sir James Ley*, was a major Wiltshire landowner, whose seats at Westbury and Heywood lay about ten miles distant. It had been to Sir James that the borough had turned for legal advice in 1609 after Edward Wardour had secured a reversion to the lease of the profits arising from the town's courts, markets and fairs.[24] Bayntun reasserted his interest in 1624 and 1625, but in 1626 he transferred to Chippenham, thereby freeing up the senior seat again for Ley. The latter was called to the Upper House on 2 Mar. 1626, and at the ensuing by-election the corporation chose instead Ley's brother-in-law, Robert Long, who, then training to be a barrister, was secretary to Ley's father, by now lord treasurer Marlborough.[25] Long was re-elected in 1628, as Bayntun evidently showed no interest in returning to Parliament that year.

Given the local economic and administrative importance of Devizes it is surprising that there were no parliamentary matters of direct concern to the town in this period. However, John Kent and both Bayntuns were named to committees concerned with the sale of gentlemen's estates in the area.[26] Payments were occasionally made by the borough to its Members. Following the 1621 assembly John Kent received £19 in expenses, while in 1624 he and Sir Edward Bayntun shared £28 between them.[27] In 1628-9 Thomas Kent, who made no recorded impact on the Parliament in which he sat, was paid a total of £15.[28]

¹ Wilts. RO, G20/1/16, f. 272. ² Wilts. RO, G20/1/17, f. 39v. ³ VCH Wilts. x. 225; T. Fuller, Worthies of Eng. ed. J. Freeman, 609-10. ⁴ VCH Wilts. x. 264; E. Bradby, Bk. of Devizes, 51; Wilts. Arch. Mag. i. 180. ⁵ E. Kerridge, Textile Manufacturers in Early Modern Eng. 15, 115, 156; Wilts. Arch. Mag. i. 180; Wilts. RO, G20/1/17, f. 48. ⁶ VCH Wilts. x. 251. ⁷ Ibid. 238, 268; Bradby, 41. ⁸ Wilts. RO, G20/1/16, f. 69; G20/1/17, f. 72v. ⁹C219/39/235.¹⁰Wilts.RO,G20/1/16,ff.272,275,324v.¹¹Ibid.ff.185v, 190, 198, 201, 206, 266, 218, 224v. ¹² Ibid. ff. 237, 211-12v; G20/6/1. ¹³Wilts. RO, G20/1/16, ff. 263,274v. ¹⁴VCH Wilts. x. 245; Bradby, 59. ¹⁵ Wilts. RO, G20/1/16, ff. 206v, 270. ¹⁶ B.H. Cunnington, Some Annals of Bor. of Devizes, i. pt. 2, p. 49. ¹⁷E351/1950; SP14/156/14. ¹⁸ Cunnington, i. pt. 2, pp. 45-6; ii. 142. ¹⁹ Ibid. i. pt. 2, pp. 64-5, 76-7; Add. 15663, ff. 188-94; VCH Wilts. x. 270-1. ²⁰ Wilts. RO, G20/1/17, f. 31. ²¹ Wilts. RO, G20/1/16, f. 203. ²² Ibid. f. 293v.

²³ Ibid. ff. 18v, 323. ²⁴Cunnington, i. pt. 2, p. 45. ²⁵ Ibid. G20/1/17, f. 40. ²⁶ CJ, i. 281b, 291b, 438b, 688b. ²⁷ Wilts. RO, G20/1/17, ff. 4, 11v, 29. ²⁸ Ibid. ff. 60, 69v.

H.J.L./A.D.T.

DOWNTON

Right of election: in the burgage-holders

Number of voters: 24 in 1620

27 Feb. 1604	SIR CAREW RALEGH
	WILLIAM STOCKMAN
c. Mar. 1614	GILBERT RALEGH
	JOHN RYVES
28 Dec. 1620	SIR CAREW RALEGH
	SIR THOMAS HINTON
19 Jan. 1624	SIR WILLIAM DODINGTON II
	SIR CLIPPESBY CREWE
3 Jan. 1625	EDWARD HERBERT vice
	Dodington, deceased
19 Apr. 1625	SIR CLIPPESBY CREWE
	EDWARD HERBERT
16 Jan. 1626	HERBERT DODINGTON
	EDWARD HERBERT
16 Feb. 1626	WILLIAM TRUMBULL vice
	Dodington, chose to sit for
	Lymington
11 Mar. 1628	SIR BENJAMIN RUDYARD
	EDWARD HERBERT

Located on the banks of the Avon in Wiltshire's south-east corner, Downton was owned from Saxon times by the bishops of Winchester, who founded a settlement there in the early 1200s. With few medieval privileges, the town developed slowly. At the start of the seventeenth century, Downton was still only a borough by prescription, presided over by an alderman, a tithingman and a constable. Its market and fairs had apparently fallen into abeyance, and the local economy was almost entirely agricultural, with little discernible industry apart from the small-scale manufacture of leather goods.[1]

Downton first returned Members to Parliament in 1275, but the borough was regularly represented in the Commons only from 1442. The franchise was vested in the burgage-holders. Their actual number in the early Stuart period is unclear, but 24 voters were listed on the 1620 election return.[2] By long-established custom, the returning officer was the bishop's local bailiff. This office was held by the owners of the minor local manor of Barford, who at this juncture were the Stockman family. Nevertheless, there is no evidence that the bishops made nominations at Downton in the opening decades of the seventeenth century, the borough's most important patron instead being the 3rd earl of Pembroke, the lessee of Downton manor.[3]

Surprisingly, the earl's influence was not greatly felt in the first three Jacobean elections. On each occasion, the senior seat was taken by a member of the Ralegh family, who owned the local rectory and a significant quantity of property within the borough.[4] In 1604 the junior place went to William Stockman, owner of Barford manor, whose father had been a servant to the 2nd earl of Pembroke.[5] Ten years later Stockman was replaced by John Ryves, a lawyer with a Dorset gentry background, who may have been resident in the borough. In 1620 the second seat was taken by another outsider, Sir Thomas Hinton, whose seat lay in north-east Wiltshire. His connection with Downton has not been established, but he was presumably a Pembroke nominee.[6]

In 1624 the borough's senior Member was Sir William Dodington II, whose father was a major landowner at Breamore, three miles away across the Hampshire border. However, the second seat was awarded to Sir Clippesby Crewe, almost certainly the choice of Pembroke, who is known to have placed him at Callington, Cornwall in 1626.[7] When Dodington died between the prorogation and dissolution of the 1624 Parliament, he was replaced by the earl's kinsman, Edward Herbert, who, because the Parliament never reconvened, did not actually take his seat on this occasion. However, Herbert continued to represent the borough for the remainder of the period. Crewe sat again in 1625. In the following year the senior place was briefly taken by Dodington's brother, Herbert, but after he opted to sit for Lymington, Hampshire, the vacancy was filled by William Trumbull, another outsider who was probably nominated by Pembroke. Edward Herbert's colleague in 1628 was Sir Benjamin Rudyard, one of the earl's most prominent clients.[8]

[1] R.C. Hoare, *Hist. Modern Wilts.* iii. 'Downton', 13-14, 19; *VCH Wilts.* xi. 41-4. [2] *VCH Wilts.* xi. 45; C219/37/292. [3] Hoare, iii. 'Downton', 38-9; *VCH Wilts.* 28-9, 45. [4] Hoare, iii. 'Downton', 36-7. [5] *CSP Dom.* 1598-1601, p. 218; Harl. 7186, f. 27v. [6] *Vis. Dorset* (Harl. Soc. xx), 80-1; E115/193/11. [7] *Cardiff Recs.* ed. J.H. Matthews, iii. 512; SP16/523/77. [8] V.A. Rowe, 'Influence of the Earls of Pembroke on Parlty. Elections', *EHR*, l. 242-4, 251.

H.J.L.

GREAT BEDWYN

Right of election: in the freemen

Number of voters: c.12

9 Mar. 1604	SIR JOHN RODNEY ANTHONY HUNGERFORD
c.Mar. 1614	ROBERT HYDE GILES MOMPESSON
22 Dec. 1620	SIR FRANCIS POPHAM (SIR) GILES MOMPESSON
8 Mar. 1621	THOMAS CAREY *vice* Mompesson, expelled the House
26 Jan. 1624	HUGH CROMPTON WILLIAM CHOLMLEY
24 Apr. 1625	SIR JOHN BROOKE WILLIAM CHOLMLEY
1 Feb. 1626	MAURICE BERKELEY JOHN SELDEN
7 Mar. 1628	EDWARD KIRTON SIR JOHN TREVOR II

Situated in north-east Wiltshire, Great Bedwyn at the time of the Domesday survey was a thriving community with its own mint. However, the local economy, based on the wool and clothing industries, went into severe decline in the Middle Ages.[1] Despite being incorporated by charter in 1468, the borough dwindled into insignificance, and was described as 'a poor thing to sight' by John Leland in the early sixteenth century. The town was governed by a single bailiff, who enjoyed the powers of a magistrate, but no other municipal officers or institutions were mentioned when the charter, which is not extant, was confirmed in 1673.[2] Members were returned to Parliament intermittently from 1295. In the Elizabethan and early Stuart period the borough was owned by Edward Seymour, 1st earl of Hertford, whose seat at Wolf Hall lay nearby. Hertford often nominated both Members, although the Hungerford family of Stock manor, less than a mile north of the town, had laid claim to the senior seat in 1593, 1597 and 1601.[3] Election indentures were signed by up to 12 inhabitant 'burgesses'.[4] There is no evidence that Great Bedwyn contributed towards the expenses of any of its Members during this period.

In 1604 Hertford nominated his cousin's husband, Sir John Rodney, with the intention of furthering a private bill 'for the quiet establishing and settling of the lands and possessions late of Sir George Rodney, deceased', in which both parties had an interest. Anthony Hungerford, who had served as the borough's senior Member in Elizabeth's last two parliaments, took the second seat. Rodney's bill received its first reading on 23 Apr. 1604; and two days later another private measure to confirm Hertford's possession of Bedwyn was also reported and passed.[5] At the next general election Robert Hyde, whose father, father-in-law and brother had successively served as Hertford's auditors, was returned in first place. Giles Mompesson, the husband of Hungerford's stepdaughter, took the junior seat.

Another leading member of the local gentry, Sir Francis Popham, was returned as the senior Member in December 1620; his Wiltshire home at Littlecote was only four miles from Bedwyn, and as Hertford's long-serving deputy in the lieutenancy and militia he presumably had the latter's support. Mompesson was re-elected, but as a notorious monopolist he was expelled early in the session, when the Commons launched an attack on grievous patents and corruption. By this time Hertford, aged around 83, was on his deathbed; probably his grandson and successor William Seymour, Lord Beauchamp* was responsible for nominating the courtier Thomas Carey, who had no local connections, to replace Mompesson at a by-election on 8 March.

In 1624, at the next general election, Seymour, now 2nd earl of Hertford, returned of two of his associates to James's last Parliament; by this time Hungerford had left Stock to take up residence on his Oxfordshire estates. Hugh Crompton, who filled the first seat, was formerly a gentleman usher to Arbella Stuart, Hertford's first wife, and had remained in his service since her death in 1615. In second place was William Cholmley, brother-in-law and close associate of John Pym*, the Exchequer's receiver-general for Wiltshire. In the 1625 Parliament the courtier Sir John Brooke, a court acquaintance of both the 1st and 2nd earls of Hertford, was elected in first place, while Cholmley sat again in second. Hungerford's relation, (Sir) Maurice Berkeley took the first seat in 1626, together with John Selden, a lawyer presumably chosen by Hertford for political reasons. The connection between the two remains obscure; Hertford perhaps wished to ensure Selden, a known critic of the duke of Buckingham, a seat in the Lower House in anticipation of, and to encourage, Buckingham's impeachment. In 1628 Hertford nominated Edward Kirton, his servant, as the senior Member, and was probably also responsible

for the election in second place of Sir John Trevor II, a courtier.

[1] *VCH Wilts.* xvi. 11. [2] C66/3140/15; *VCH Wilts.* xvi. 11, 42. [3] *VCH Wilts.* xvi. 43-4. [4] C219/37/279, 302. [5] *CJ*, i. 181b-182a, 182b, 184a.

H.J.L./R.C.L.S.

HEYTESBURY

Right of election: in the freemen

Number of voters: 12 in 1620[1]

8 Mar. 1604	SIR WILLIAM EYRE WALTER GAWEN
c. Mar. 1614	HENRY LUDLOW II WALTER GAWEN
28 Dec. 1620	(SIR) THOMAS THYNNE (SIR) HENRY LUDLOW II
20 Jan. 1624	(SIR) THOMAS THYNNE (SIR) HENRY LUDLOW II
7 May 1625	(SIR) CHARLES BERKELEY EDWARD BISSE
20 Jan. 1626	(SIR) CHARLES BERKELEY WILLIAM BLAKE
4 Mar. 1628	(SIR) CHARLES BERKELEY WILLIAM ROLFE

A small town in south-west Wiltshire lying on the principal road between Warminster and Salisbury, Heytesbury was, like many settlements in the region, dependent upon the cloth trade. As part of the royal forest of Selwood, there was also some trade in timber. At its heyday in the late Middle Ages the town had a market, and two annual fairs.[2] Enfranchised as a proprietary borough in 1449, it had never been incorporated.[3] The franchise rested in the freemen, up to a dozen of whom usually signed election indentures. Elections were held at the *Angel* inn, a local landmark that dated back to the early fifteenth century.[4] Throughout the early Stuart period the electorate deferred entirely to gentry patrons. The manor was owned by Thomas Hawker, but since at least the 1570s elections had been dominated by the Thynne family based at nearby Longleat.[5]

In 1604 the first seat went to Sir William Eyre, a kinsman of Sir John Thynne*, while the second

Member was Walter Gawen of Imber, whose estate lay less than five miles north of the borough. At the next general election the Thynnes were again responsible for the choice of at least one, and probably both Members, returning their close neighbour Henry Ludlow II, together with Gawen. Ludlow, who was knighted sometime before the next general election, was returned to the Parliaments of 1621 and 1624 but pushed into second place, while Sir John Thynne's successor, Sir Thomas, took the first seat for himself on both occasions.

Although Hawker sold Heytesbury manor to William Blake in 1624 as part of a marriage settlement involving one of his daughters and Blake's son, the 1625 election saw the first assertion of electoral patronage by the Hawker family.[6] The second seat went to another of Hawker's sons-in-law, Edward Bisse. In first place Thynne nominated Charles Berkeley, a Somerset landowner based at Bruton, 17 miles south of the borough. Berkeley, who later became a Selwood forest official, was re-elected to the next two Parliaments. In 1626 Blake himself took the second seat, which in 1628 went to his nephew, William Rolfe, to whom he had by this time sold the manor.[7]

[1] C219/37/304. [2] E.D. Ginever, *Ancient Wilts. Village of Heytesbury*, 23-5; *Wilts. Arch. Mag.* xxiii. 283. [3] R.C. Hoare, *Hist. Wilts.* 'Heytesbury Hundred', 122; *VCH Wilts.* v. 114. [4] Ginever, 25. [5] *VCH Wilts.* v. 121-3. [6] C78/489/20. [7] C2/Chas.I/B77/56.

H.J.L.

HINDON

Right of election: in the burgage-holders

Number of voters: 10-30

12 Mar. 1604	SIR EDMUND LUDLOW THOMAS THYNNE
by 3 Apr. 1614[1]	SIR EDMUND LUDLOW SIR EDWIN SANDYS
aft. 9 Apr. 1614	HENRY MERVYN *vice* Sandys, chose to sit for Rochester
22 Dec. 1620	SIR JOHN DAVIES JOHN ANKETILL SIR EDMUND LUDLOW
	Double return of Anketill and Ludlow. Ludlow's election declared void 18 Apr. 1621
30 May 1621	(SIR) HENRY MERVYN *vice* Davies, chose to sit for Newcastle-under-Lyme
16 Jan. 1624	LAWRENCE HYDE II MATTHEW DAVIES
25 Apr. 1625	(SIR) THOMAS THYNNE THOMAS LAMBERT
13 Jan. 1626	(SIR) THOMAS THYNNE THOMAS LAMBERT
3 Mar. 1628	(SIR) THOMAS THYNNE LAWRENCE HYDE II

Still little more than a village in the seventeenth century, Hindon, which had regularly sent Members to Parliament from 1448, was an early thirteenth-century settlement planned by the bishop of Winchester and built on his manor of East Knoyle. Although close to the market towns of Wilton and Warminster, it boasted a market place and hosted a Michaelmas fair. By the mid-1630s its principal trades were weaving and the manufacture of gunpowder. The bishop's bailiff headed the town's administration, and acted as returning officer at parliamentary elections. As at Downton, another Wiltshire borough controlled by the see of Winchester, the right to participate in borough administration probably depended upon the ownership of plots of land in free burgage tenure. Certainly it was this form of ownership which provided the basis of the franchise.[2] Returns were signed by each of the participating burgesses, whose numbers tended to vary. Ten appended their names in 1604 while 30 did so in 1624. However, the illiteracy rate among the burgesses was high: in 1625, 11 of the 28 participating burgesses were obliged to make their mark rather than sign, while in 1626 only 12 or 13 could do so out of 22 or 23. Not surprisingly, it was felt necessary for three or four individuals to attest the validity of the returns, which they did by placing their signatures on the back of the indenture.[3]

Before 1584 the bishop controlled both parliamentary seats, but thereafter episcopal authority waned. Archbishop Whitgift assumed the bishop's right of nomination to one seat, but at the price, it would seem, of allowing the other place to fall under the control of the local gentry. This arrangement persisted until the end of Elizabeth's reign, and would doubtless have continued under James had Whitgift not died less than two weeks before Hindon held its election to the first Jacobean Parliament. The inability or unwillingness of the then bishop of Winchester, Thomas Bilson, to fill the void created by Whitgift's death on 29 Feb. 1604, meant that both seats were now targeted by members of the local gentry.

Chief among the local landowners was Sir James Mervyn[†] [Marvyn], whose seat at Fonthill Gifford lay a few miles north of the borough. In 1597 Mervyn had secured his own return for Hindon, and in 1601 and 1604 he used his influence for the benefit of Thomas Thynne, his granddaughter's husband and heir to the Longleat estate. The senior place in 1604 was bestowed upon Sir Edmund Ludlow, whose seat lay at Hill Deverill, six miles north-west of Hindon. Ludlow, a familiar figure about Hindon no doubt, may have possessed sufficient interest to procure the seat unaided, but in all likelihood he replied upon the Thynnes, as earlier in the month Thomas' father, Sir John Thynne, had unsuccessfully tried to drum up support for Ludlow, who had cherished ambitions of serving as a knight of the shire for Wiltshire.[4]

Following the death of Sir James Mervyn in 1611, ownership of Fonthill Gifford passed to George Tuchet, 11th Lord Audley, the brother of Thomas Thynne's wife Maria Tuchet. Despite Maria's death that same year, Thynne, now knighted, retained a residual interest at Hindon. In 1614 Thynne chose not to exercise this interest in his own behalf, possibly because he was then busily preparing for the christening of his son by second wife.[5] Instead he apparently threw his support behind Ludlow, who was accordingly re-elected. Ludlow's partner was Sir Edwin Sandys of Northbourne, Kent, a leading Member of the first Jacobean Parliament who was finding it difficult to obtain a seat nearer to home. How Sandys came by the Hindon seat is unclear, but it may be significant that the Wiltshire magnate, the 3rd earl of Pembroke, was then an ally of Sandys's patron, the earl of Somerset. Whatever the truth may have been, Sandys ultimately chose not to serve for Hindon, for soon after he was elected he learned that he had been returned for Rochester, which borough he preferred to represent.[6] At the ensuing election Sandys was replaced by Lord Audley's son-in-law, Henry Mervyn.

Audley was elevated to the Irish peerage in 1617 as earl of Castlehaven. Later that same year he died, whereupon his titles and estates passed to his son, Sir Mervyn Audley *alias* Tuchet*. At the parliamentary election of 1620, the new earl of Castlehaven had the burgesses of Hindon return his brother-in-law Sir John Davies and his page John Anketill. Sir Thomas Thynne, who seems not to have enjoyed the same

favour with Castlehaven that he had with Castlehaven's father, found a seat at Heytesbury instead, but Sir Edmund Ludlow, who had previously relied on Thynne to procure him a place, was left high and dry. On the morning of the election, an angry Ludlow, though now 80 years old, gathered together some 'out-dwellers' and various other individuals and, 'in a chamber', got them to sign a separate indenture naming himself.[7]

Shortly after the Commons assembled, Anketill, who had never served in Parliament before, attempted to take his seat, whereupon he was ordered to forbear the House until the matter of his election was resolved.[8] No such prohibition was directed at Ludlow, an experienced Member who knew the rules, or at Davies, who preferred to serve for another borough for which he had also been elected. During the course of the ensuing investigation it became apparent that Hindon had, most unusually, sent in no less than three returns. The first, signed by 23 burgesses, named Sir John Davies alone, and appears to have been produced as the result of an administrative error, the sheriff having mistakenly directed his precept to the burgesses rather than to the bailiff. The second return was drawn up after the sheriff, alerted to his earlier mistake, sent his precept to the bailiff. In this fresh document the same burgesses who had signed the earlier indenture now returned both Davies and Anketill. The final return was, of course, the one drafted by Ludlow and 17 of his supporters.[9]

On 27 Mar. the three candidates were instructed to attend the committee for privileges 'or else the House will proceed to take some final course in it.'[10] Three weeks later, on 18 Apr., the chairman of the committee, Sir George More declared that none of the three had attended its proceedings. Nevertheless, it was clear that Ludlow's election 'could not be good', as his supporters included 'some freeholders that were not dwellers in the town', as well as women and boys, 'who ought not to deal in the election of burgesses'. Consequently, the House ordered that Anketill be seated and that a writ for a fresh election be moved to replace Davies, who had plumped for Newcastle-under-Lyme.[11]

The House's ruling cemented Castlehaven's control over Hindon. At the subsequent election held in May, the earl's brother-in-law Sir Henry Mervyn took the seat, apparently without a contest. Mervyn's influence over Castlehaven may help to explain the election in 1624 and 1628 of the Salisbury lawyer Lawrence Hyde II, whose seat at Woodford lay ten miles west of Hindon. At any rate, Hyde can be linked to a bill that was laid before the Commons in 1624 by Mervyn's maternal kinsman, Sir John Ryves.[12] Hyde's partner in 1624 was another lawyer, Matthew Davies, whose parents lived a few miles south-east of Hindon at Chicksgrove and whose uncle was the borough's former Member Sir John Davies. Sir Thomas Thynne resumed his representation of Hindon in 1625, 1626 and 1628, presumably with the blessing of Castlehaven, whose kinsman by marriage, Thomas Lambert, took the junior seat in the first two Caroline Parliaments. Lambert lived at Boyton, a village situated a few miles north of Hindon. Sir Edmund Ludlow, whose attempt to gain a seat for a third successive occasion had back-fired so badly, never sat again, and died in November 1624.

[1] *Procs. 1614 (Commons)*, 458; Staffs. RO, D593/S/4/60/12. [2] *VCH Wilts.* v. 112; *VCH Wilts.* xi. 98, 100-1; *Wilts. Arch. Mag.* xxxvi. 51-2; M. Beresford, *New Towns of Middle Ages*, 505. [3] C219/39/232; 219/40/94. The 1626 indenture is badly faded on the right hand side. [4] Longleat, Thynne Pprs. vii. f. 310. [5] Longleat, Thynne Pprs. viii. ff. 110, 111v. [6] Staffs. RO, D593/S/4/60/12; *Procs. 1614 (Commons)*, 37. [7] Nicholas, *Procs. 1621*, i. 268. [8] *CJ*, i. 516b. [9] Nicholas, i. 268; *CJ*, i. 580a. [10] *CJ*, i. 576b; *CD 1621*, ii. 270. [11] C219/37/289; *CJ*, i. 576a, 580a. [12] *CJ*, i. 772a.

A.D.T.

LUDGERSHALL

Right of election: in the burgesses until 1624; in the burgesses and freeholders thereafter

Number of voters: c.12 until 1624; 32 in 1626

12 Mar. 1604	JAMES KIRTON I	
	HENRY LUDLOW I	
c.Mar. 1614	JAMES KIRTON I	
	CHARLES DANVERS	
14 Dec. 1620	ALEXANDER CHOCKE II	
	WILLIAM SOTWELL	
19 Jan. 1624	EDWARD KIRTON	
	WILLIAM SOTWELL	
16 Apr. 1625	SIR ROBERT PYE	
	SIR THOMAS HINTON	
26 Jan. 1626	SIR WILLIAM WALTER	
	ROBERT MASON II	15
	SIR THOMAS JAY	14

Double return of Mason and Jay. Election declared void, 10 Mar. 1626

18 Mar. 1626	SIR THOMAS HINTON	16
21 Mar. 1626	SIR THOMAS JAY	16

Double return of Hinton and Jay. Unresolved at dissolution

3 Mar. 1628	JOHN SELDEN
	SIR THOMAS JAY

Ludgershall lies on the principal road between Marlborough, Salisbury and Winchester. The Normans had constructed a castle on its northern edge by 1103, which later became a garrisoned provincial treasury. A planned town was laid out on a grid pattern focused upon a central market square, though economic growth was restricted by the larger markets at nearby Marlborough and Salisbury.[1]

Urban government at Ludgershall was rudimentary: the inhabitants occasionally claimed to possess a charter, but the town was run by a bailiff (originally the castle bailiff), assisted by a manorial court.[2] Despite this, the borough first returned Members to Parliament in 1295, and was represented continuously from 1421.[3] The franchise was exercised by around a dozen 'freeholders and burgesses'. No returning officer was mentioned, but the task was presumably performed by the bailiff. The format of the indentures changed from 1625, being attested by 20 to 30 signatories variously described as the 'constable, burgesses and free-holders' or 'burgesses, freeholders and inhabitants'.[4] This wider franchise was confirmed in 1699, when freeholders and inhabitants with inherited leasehold property were granted voting rights.[5]

No townsman had represented the borough since 1558, when Robert Brydges, the lord of the manor, returned himself. In 1593 the manor passed to Sir George Browne, a relative of the Brydges family by marriage. As a recusant, he had little electoral influence even before two-thirds of his property was seized in 1610, but despite this setback he can probably be credited with the 1614 return of Charles Danvers, who managed his cousins' Wiltshire estates.[6] Browne may also have had a hand in the 1620 election of Danvers's cousin Alexander Chocke II. The other influence in the borough during this period was Edward Seymour, 1st earl of Hertford, whose Wiltshire seat at Great Bedwyn lay eight miles to the north. Hertford had recommended his steward James Kirton I to the borough in 1601, and the latter's continuing service with the earl explains his re-election in 1604 and 1614.[7]

Most of the borough's remaining Members owed their seats their own local standing. Henry Ludlow's family had represented Ludgershall in several

Parliaments, most recently in 1597, when his father Edmund was also returned, while two ancestors of William Sotwell, from the nearby village of Chute, had represented the borough in the Middle Ages.[8] Sir Thomas Jay and Sir Thomas Hinton were local gentlemen whose estates lay within a few miles of the borough, while Hinton had already sat for a Wiltshire constituency. Only two Members, Sir Robert Pye and Sir William Walter, had no connection with the borough or county. At the 1625 election, Pye's name was entered on a blank return endorsed by tenants of William (Seymour*), 2nd earl of Hertford, who presumably nominated Pye at the behest of George Villiers, duke of Buckingham.[9] Walter's election was based upon his friendship with Pye, whom he succeeded in 1626.

There was only one contested election at Ludgershall during this period. On 10 Mar. 1626 the Commons accepted Walter for one seat, but voided the rival returns of Jay and Robert Mason II for the second seat, on the grounds that the voting intentions of a single burgess could not be determined, leaving the result tied. Mason, not to be confused with his namesake who sat for Christchurch in this Parliament, was Buckingham's secretary, and his candidacy was evidently an attempt to exploit the borough's earlier willingness to accommodate Buckingham's nominees. However, Mason dropped out before the election was re-run, leaving Jay to face a fresh contest against Hinton. It is not known whether Hinton stood at the general election, but the dispute afforded him time to launch his own challenge. Both candidates were returned on separate indentures, Hinton's dated 18 Mar. and Jay's dated three days later. No obvious pattern can be discerned from the rival groups of electors, for of the 32 signatures at least ten of Jay's supporters had signed Hinton's indenture in 1625, while five of Hinton's men came out for Jay in 1628. The committee for privileges failed to determine the outcome of this election before the dissolution in June.[10] Although the circumstances of this contest are uncertain, the experience apparently dissuaded Hinton from standing against Jay at the next election.

[1] VCH Wilts. xv. 119, 121, 124. [2] Ibid. 129. [3] Wilts. Arch. Mag. xxxiv. 151-6. [4] C219/39/231; C219/40/56-7; C219/41B/61. [5] T. Carew, Rights of Elections, 354-6. [6] C2/Chas.I/B126/60; Burke Dorm. and Extinct Baronetcies, 88-9; Burke, Peerage, Baronetage and Knightage (1916 edn.), 2132. [7] HMC Bath, iv. 202, 207, 213. [8] Vis. Wilts. (Harl. Soc. cv-cvi), 185; Wilts. Arch. Mag. xxxiv. 151-6. [9] C219/39/231. [10] Ibid.; C219/40/56-7; Procs. 1626, ii. 246, 248; CJ, i. 834a; Carew, 354.

H.J.L.

MALMESBURY

Right of election: in the burgesses

Number of voters: 8 in 1604[1]

1 Mar. 1604	SIR ROGER DALLISON SIR THOMAS DALLISON
1614	SIR ROGER DALLISON SIR NEVILLE POOLE
16 Dec. 1620	SIR HENRY POOLE SIR EDWARD WARDOUR
12 Feb. 1624[2]	SIR EDWARD WARDOUR SIR THOMAS HATTON ?Sir Edward Cecil*
10 May 1625	SIR EDWARD WARDOUR SIR THOMAS HATTON ?Sir Henry Moody, bt.
27 Jan. 1626	SIR HENRY MOODY, bt. (SIR) WILLIAM CROFT
7 Mar. 1628	(SIR) WILLIAM CROFT SIR HENRY MOODY

The ancient market town of Malmesbury, sited on a defensive position on the upper reaches of the Avon, grew up in the shelter both of its castle and a Benedictine abbey founded in the mid-seventh century. The development of the town's clothing industry, which processed wool produced in north Wiltshire and south Gloucestershire, was facilitated by its good trade links, for the main road between Bristol and Oxford ran through Malmesbury, while other routes linked it to nearby Chippenham and Tetbury. A mint was established in the tenth century, suggesting the town's early economic and strategic importance, and a market was licensed in the western suburb of Westport in 1252.[3]

Malmesbury was held in fee farm by a guild merchant from at least the early thirteenth century, originally from the abbey and subsequently, after the Reformation, from the Crown. The guild evolved into the Malmesbury corporation, which received a confirmatory charter in 1381. By the sixteenth century a body of 13 burgesses, headed by an alderman and two stewards, governed the town. Below the burgesses the corporation consisted of three further groups: the Twenty-Four, the landholders and the commoners. In the early seventeenth century a proposal by the burgesses to enclose 100 acres of the town lands led to conflict with the other three groups. The quarrel was settled by a general agreement in 1609, but three years later an attempt was made to establish a rival governing body consisting of 12 overseers selected from all the members of the corporation. This failed, although subsequently the number of stewards increased to four – one to represent each of the four groups, namely the burgesses, the Twenty-Four, the landholders and the commoners.[4]

From 1616 the burgesses met every June in St. John's hospital, purchased by the corporation in 1580, to elect the alderman and admit commoners.[5] The corporation's meagre income was principally derived from rents and entry fines from its own members. The gradual decline in this income during this period, from £23 in 1600 to just 3s. in 1629, was reflected in the low payments made by the corporation to its officials – 10s. to the alderman who also acted as treasurer, and 6s. to a steward. Although a collection of £20 was made in 1618 towards the school and almshouse, ten years later payments to the schoolmaster were replaced by providing him with an allotment for his maintenance. There is no indication that the corporation paid a fee to its representatives in Parliament.[6] The borough had been represented in Parliament since 1275. The indentures were made in the name of the alderman and burgesses but were usually only signed by the former. However, the indenture for 1604 bears eight signatures, all of which were presumably made by burgesses.[7]

The parliamentary elections of Elizabethan Malmesbury were dominated by Sir Henry Knyvet[†] until his death in 1598. Knyvet owned the site of the old abbey and a good deal of the former monastery's property in the town and the surrounding area, including the manor of Charlton situated two-and-a-quarter miles from the borough. Knyvet's daughter and heir, Catherine, married Thomas Howard, a younger son of the 4th duke of Norfolk, who was created Lord Howard in 1597 and earl of Suffolk in 1603; Howard seems to have nominated both Members in 1601. In 1614 Suffolk transferred his Wiltshire estate to his second son, Sir Thomas Howard*, but he apparently continued to exercise the parliamentary patronage that it conferred until his death in 1626.[8]

Suffolk was almost certainly responsible for the nomination in 1604 of Sir Roger Dallison, an Ordnance Office official from Lincolnshire and a Howard client. Sir Roger presumably also persuaded Suffolk to recommend his cousin, Sir Thomas Dallison who, like Sir Roger, had no known connections with Wiltshire. Sir Roger was re-elected in 1614, but by then Sir Thomas had suffered a major crisis in his

finances that had led to a period of imprisonment in Lincoln gaol, and consequently was in no position to seek re-election. Instead, Sir Roger had as his colleague Sir Neville Poole, the son of Sir Henry Poole, a major north Wiltshire landowner based at Kemble near the border with Gloucestershire. It is not known whether Suffolk consented to Poole's candidacy. On the face of it, this seems unlikely, as Poole had previously feuded with Sir Henry Knyvet. However, in 1604 Poole had been returned for Cricklade, where Suffolk was also influential, and in 1614 he had been returned for Wiltshire alongside Suffolk's son, Sir Thomas Howard. Possibly Suffolk had decided to come to an accommodation with a potentially powerful local rival rather than risk a conflict.

Sir Henry Poole himself was returned for Malmesbury in 1620 along with Sir Edward Wardour. The latter was an important Exchequer official who would have worked with Suffolk when the earl was lord treasurer between 1614 and 1618. In addition Wardour had a lease on the profits of Malmesbury's markets and fairs as well as a number of copyhold tenements in the town.[9] Wardour was re-elected in 1624, when Sir Thomas Hatton, a courtier with no known local connections, took the other seat. Hatton presumably owed his election to Suffolk, whose son Sir Thomas had married the niece of Lady Hatton, the estranged wife of Sir Edward Coke* and widow of Hatton's kinsman Sir William Hatton[†]. A petition from one Thomas Baskerville and 'divers others' inhabitants of Malmesbury was presented to the privileges committee complaining that the indenture had been tampered with and that Sir Edward Cecil* had originally been elected along with Wardour. A day was appointed for a hearing, but the committee's chairman John Glanville, reported to the Commons on 4 May that despite being summoned the complainants 'came not to prosecute'. The Commons consequently resolved that Hatton's election should stand. The failure of Baskerville and his allies to press their case makes it difficult to establish what was going on. It is unlikely that there had been contest between Cecil and Hatton, as the former was Lady Hatton's brother and had already been returned for Dover on 20 January. It seems much more likely that Cecil had been Suffolk's original nominee but that, on hearing of Cecil's election elsewhere, the earl had decided to replace him with Hatton. News of his change of mind must have reached the borough only after the indenture had been drawn up, creating confusion in the minds of Baskerville and his adherents, who presumably failed to attend the privileges committee under pressure from Suffolk.[10]

Wardour and Hatton were re-elected in 1625, when the alderman present was Thomas Waite, one of those who had been accused of tampering with the indenture the year before. On this occasion there is no evidence that the return was altered, but in the Crown Office list Hatton's name was substituted for Sir Henry Moody's, which was deleted. There is no evidence that anyone complained about the election and the alteration may have been intended to correct a clerical error.[11]

Moody was returned in 1626, probably on the strength of his local standing: his family had been tenants of Malmesbury abbey from the end of the fifteenth century, having acquired many of its estates at the Dissolution. Wardour may have decided not to stand again because of deteriorating relations between him and the town, which culminated in a Chancery suit in 1628. Instead, the other seat went to Sir William Croft, a courtier from Herefordshire who was probably nominated by Suffolk. Croft's father, Sir Herbert*, had been a client of the earl's son-in-law, Robert Carr, earl of Somerset. As Suffolk died during the 1626 Parliament it was presumably Sir Thomas Howard, by now earl of Berkshire, who nominated Croft in 1628. Croft's partner was once again Sir Henry Moody, although on this occasion both men are shown in reversed positions on the return.[12]

[1] C219/35/2/110. [2] C219/38/290A. [3] VCH Wilts. xiv. 127-32. [4] Ibid. 149-50; J.M. Moffatt, Hist. of Town of Malmesbury, 123. [5] VCH Wilts. xiv. 151. [6] Malmesbury corp. bk. ff. 21, 58, 65, 65, 69, 80. [7] VCH Wilts. xiv. 154-5; C219/35/2/118; 219/40/88. [8] HP Commons, 1558-1603, i. 275; CP, xii. pt. 1, 462-6; King's Coll. Lib., Camb., ms KCAR/1/2/16, vol. iv. no. 59. [9] C2/Chas.I/W37/43; 2/Chas.I/W18/8. [10] J.K. Gruenfelder, Influence in Early Stuart Elections, 139; J. Glanville, Reports of Some Cases, (1775), pp. 115-16; CJ, i. 783a. The 1624 indenture is now no more than a fragment. C219/38/290A. [11] C219/39/236; Glanville, 115; OR. [12] C2/Chas.I/W37/43; 2/Chas.I/W18/8; CP, xii. pt. 1, p. 465.

H.J.L./B.C.

MARLBOROUGH

Right of election: in the freemen

Number of voters: c.50-70

2 Mar. 1604	RICHARD DIGGES, recorder LAWRENCE HYDE I
c.Mar. 1614	RICHARD DIGGES, recorder SIR FRANCIS POPHAM
22 Dec. 1620	RICHARD DIGGES, recorder WILLIAM SEYMOUR, Lord Beauchamp
14 Feb. 1621	SIR WALTER DEVEREUX vice Seymour, called to the Upper House
22 Jan. 1624	RICHARD DIGGES, recorder SIR FRANCIS SEYMOUR
11 May 1625	RICHARD DIGGES, recorder EDWARD KIRTON
1 Feb. 1626[1]	RICHARD DIGGES, recorder EDWARD KIRTON
10 Mar. 1628	RICHARD DIGGES, recorder SIR FRANCIS SEYMOUR
c.20 Mar. 1628[2]	HENRY PERCY vice Seymour, chose to sit for Wilts.

Marlborough was founded by the Saxons on the site of a Roman fortified settlement. Situated on the River Kennet, the town was an axis for communications between London and Bristol, and from the southern ports via Winchester and Salisbury to Gloucester. Its favourable location enabled the town to develop into one of the principal trading centres in the area, while its strategic importance was recognized in the eleventh century with the construction of a castle, which was also used as a provincial mint and treasury.[3] In King John's charter of 1204 the town was granted an eight-day annual fair, a Wednesday and Saturday market, and exemption from certain tolls modelled upon similar privileges enjoyed by the burgesses of Winchester. The main local industries were the manufacture of pins, lace, clay, leather, gloves, cloth and pipes.[4]

Marlborough was first styled a borough in 1086. The town's earliest administrators, the constables of the castle, were gradually superseded by the members of an influential merchant guild, principally comprised of fullers and weavers, established in 1163. A town steward was first mentioned in 1280 and a mayor in 1312. To these offices were later added two bailiffs, two chamberlains to manage the corporation's finances, a coroner, and two serjeants-of-the-mace. Finally, a town clerk, or recorder, was instituted in 1579 to handle the town's legal affairs. In 1514 the merchant guild, which had enjoyed an ill-defined and limited authority, was replaced by a two-tiered governing body of around 16-20 common councillors.[5] An annually elected mayor also served as escheator, coroner, and clerk of the market. There was a discernible decline in the number of freemen in the early Stuart period, from about 80 in the late sixteenth century to 75 in 1614, 59 in 1623, 52 in 1636 and 32 by the 1700s.[6]

The corporation's income – derived from entry fines, tolls, pasturage on neighbouring downland, rent from numerous houses and inns, and charges made for grazing stock on Portfield, an 80-acre tract of common land – amounted to £96 in 1572, but had declined to £88 by 1604. This was partly due to lax management of the corporation's properties, for in that year it was noted that £34 was yet due from tenants listed in old rent rolls who 'have not paid ... of late years and part of them are thought to be lost'.[7] In the beginning of James's reign the corporation made greater efforts to exploit its resources, and by 1628 the income of the borough had reached £294; however, expenditure increased commensurately, and the surplus in any year was rarely more than £6.[8] Much was spent on an ambitious building programme, including a new town hall in 1612.[9] An almshouse and grammar school, founded in 1550 in the former buildings of the hospital of St. John, were also maintained out of municipal coffers.[10] Miscellaneous gifts, usually of money, wine and sugar, were made to neighbouring gentry such as Sir John St. John*, Sir Gilbert Prynne and Sir Francis Seymour, as also to Sir Francis Bacon*, presumably to gain his favour towards the town's bid for a new charter in 1609, on which it expended £22. In 1611 wine was bestowed upon Sir John Bennet*, then a master in Chancery, perhaps for similar considerations, and three years later the corporation gave £32 towards the feudal aid for Princess Elizabeth's wedding.[11] The lords of the manor, the earls of Hertford (Edward Seymour and his grandson William, Lord Beauchamp*), also benefited from regular gifts. The corporation's relations with the first earl were cordial, but after the latter's death the second earl resisted the townsmen's attempts to confirm various rights. In October 1625 it was finally agreed that the Seymours owned all streets and wastes in the town, could claim the profits from fairs, and could nominate one of the two bailiffs. In turn, the corporation confirmed its right to a court leet, its control over the twice-weekly and other markets, and its rent of the Portfield.[12]

Marlborough had been represented in Parliament since Edward I's reign. The franchise rested in the freemen, although by the early seventeenth century the Seymours' influence was sufficient to guarantee the return of at least one nominee in every election. In each Parliament of this period the corporation's choice was Richard Digges, Marlborough's recorder since 1597. His chambers at Lincoln's Inn meant that he was well placed to carry out various legal duties for the town, including the renewal of the charter, but his activity in the House never directly concerned the borough.[13] The separation of the Seymours' parliamentary patronage from that of the corporation is indicated by the fact that the latter's payments for parliamentary wages and expenses were made to Digges alone: he received 23s. in 1604, followed by regular payments of 16s. in 1607, 1609 and 1610, and 6s. to cover expenses in 1614.[14] By 1621 it was formally established that he should receive 40s. as parliamentary wages, together with incidental expenses. The Members recommended by the Seymours presumably served free of charge.

The 1st earl of Hertford's nominee in 1604 was his auditor Lawrence Hyde I; in 1614 it was his neighbour Sir Francis Popham, who had accompanied him on an embassy to Brussels in 1605.[15] Hertford's grandson and heir, William Seymour, Lord Beauchamp, was returned to the third Jacobean Parliament, but was called to the Upper House before the Commons assembled, and subsequently succeeded as 2nd earl in April 1621.[16] As a replacement he nominated Sir Walter Devereux, a kinsman of his brother-in-law Robert Devereux, 3rd earl of Essex. In 1624 the junior seat went to Hertford's younger brother, Sir Francis Seymour. Edward Kirton, nephew of James Kirton I*, a long-standing servant of the Seymour family, took the second seat both in 1625 and 1626. Seymour was Hertford's initial choice again in 1628, but after he decided to serve as a knight of the shire another of Essex's kinsmen, Henry Percy, was returned in his stead.

[1] Wilts. RO, G22/1/20, f. 102. [2] Wilts. RO, G22/1/20, f. 118; *Procs. 1628*, vi. 123. [3] A. Stedman, *Marlborough and the Upper Kennet Country*, 25, 39, 41; *VCH Wilts.* xii. 199, 201. [4] Stedman, 93-4, 96; Wilts. RO, G22/1/20, f. 1. [5] Stedman, 123; Wilts. RO, G22/1/20, ff. 12, 57, 61, 120. [6] *VCH Wilts.* xii. 212; Wilts. RO, G22/1/39. [7] Wilts. RO, G22/1/228; *VCH Wilts.* xii. 207. [8] Wilts. RO, G22/1/39, no. 53; G22/1/205/2, ff. 26, 66v, 69; G22/1/228. [9] Ibid. G22/1/39, no. 54. [10] *HMC 4th Rep.* 351; *VCH Wilts.* xii. 216; Wilts. RO, G22/1/205/2, ff. 40v, 54v, 55v. [11] Wilts. RO, G22/1/205/2, ff. 43v, 45v, 46v, 48, 50v, 59v, 66v; E351/1950. [12] Wilts. RO, G22/1/268. [13] Ibid. G22/1/205/2, ff. 43v, 58, 59v. [14] Ibid. ff. 36v, 40v, 45; *Marlborough Mun. Recs.; Chamberlains' Accts.* ed. B.H. Cunnington, 9-11. [15] *HMC Bath*, iv. 200; NLW, Carreglwyd I/643. [16] *CP*, ix. 733-4.

H.J.L.

OLD SARUM

Right of election: in the burgage-holders

Number of voters: 11 in 1626

13 Mar. 1604	WILLIAM RAVENSCROFT EDWARD LEECH
9 Mar. 1614[1]	WILLIAM RAVENSCROFT WILLIAM PRICE
23 Dec. 1620	GEORGE MYNNE THOMAS BRETT
22 Jan. 1624[2]	(SIR) ARTHUR INGRAM MICHAEL OLDISWORTH
12 Mar. 1624[3]	SIR ROBERT COTTON, (bt.) *vice* Ingram, chose to sit for York
23 Apr. 1625	MICHAEL OLDISWORTH SIR JOHN STRADLING, bt.
18 Jan. 1626	SIR BENJAMIN RUDYARD MICHAEL OLDISWORTH
12 Mar. 1628	MICHAEL OLDISWORTH CHRISTOPHER KEIGHLEY

Old Sarum was an ancient hill-fort known to the Romans as Sorbiodunum. A military refuge for the residents of nearby Wilton during Saxon times, a mint was established there by the late tenth century. After the Conquest a royal castle was constructed, to which William I famously summoned all the landowners of England to swear fealty to him in 1086. A cathedral was built inside the walls following the creation of the diocese of Sarum in 1075, and this in turn encouraged the development of a town. A market existed by 1130, and Henry I granted a charter around the same time. However, decline set in after Bishop Poore moved his episcopal seat to Salisbury in 1220, and although a new charter was secured in 1229, the town never recovered from this setback. The municipal offices of mayor and bailiff were recorded as late as the 1420s, but by now the castle was crumbling into ruins, and within decades the whole site was deserted. By the early seventeenth century, nothing remained within the old ramparts except a rabbit warren.[4]

Old Sarum first returned Members to Parliament in 1295, finally achieving regular representation in the early fifteenth century, not long before the town itself ceased to exist. In the absence of actual inhabitants, the franchise descended to the owners of the final vestiges of settlement, a handful of burgage tenements in the vicinity of the old castle. With no borough officers, the sheriff was obliged to deal directly with one or more of these burgesses. The format of the returns varied from one election to the next during this period, the majority being in English but with Latin employed in 1620 and 1626. The indentures normally referred simply to 'the burgesses' of Old Sarum, but the phrasing 'burgesses and electors of the burgesses' was adopted in 1604, while in 1625 the form used was 'freeholders and burgesses'. The usual practice was apparently for all the participating voters to sign the indentures, and in the later 1620s their names were also listed as part of the text. With fewer than a dozen electors, and no meaningful community for the two Members to represent, the borough had already achieved notoriety by this period, and in 1624 James I refused to contemplate the creation of new constituencies in county Durham unless Old Sarum was disenfranchised and its seats reallocated elsewhere.[5]

Since the mid-sixteenth century the dominant electoral patrons of Old Sarum had been the powerful Herbert earls of Pembroke, who not only lived just three miles away at Wilton House, but also leased the manor of Milford, directly adjacent to the borough.[6] This pattern was maintained in 1604, when the 3rd earl successfully nominated his servant Edward Leech, and William Ravenscroft, a Chancery official probably recommended to Pembroke by lord chancellor Ellesmere (Sir Thomas Egerton[†]).[7] In 1614, however, Pembroke's monopoly was challenged by the 2nd earl of Salisbury (William Cecil, Viscount Cranborne*), who now owned the freehold of Old Sarum castle and borough. On 17 Feb. Pembroke wrote to the burgesses as usual, nominating Ravenscroft again, but pairing him this time with William Price, one of his Welsh land agents. Meanwhile, one of the burgesses, Henry Sherfield*, an up-and-coming lawyer, had contacted Salisbury's receiver-general, Thomas Brett*, offering to make at least one seat available to the earl. Brett conveyed this message to Salisbury, who promptly recommended him to the borough. On this occasion Pembroke maintained his hold over the borough, which duly returned Ravenscroft and Price. Nevertheless, Salisbury had now been alerted to a possible interest at Old Sarum, and moved to consolidate his position. Sherfield, who was clearly willing to act as his local agent, was made sub-tenant of the castle site in May 1614, and steward of the earl's Wiltshire lands three years later.[8]

In November 1620, with fresh elections imminent, Brett again successfully approached Salisbury for a nomination. However, Pembroke was no more willing than before to accommodate a rival patron, and when Salisbury requested Sherfield to mobilize support for him, the lawyer initially declined, hinting that Pembroke had threatened him. Undeterred, Salisbury sought legal advice, establishing to his own satisfaction that the right of election at Old Sarum actually belonged to him personally, rather than to the burgesses. He evidently communicated this opinion to Pembroke, who replied on 10 Dec. in outraged tones:

> I cannot conceive how you can claim any right ... The dwellers of that borough have ever since my memory showed their respect to my father and myself in choosing those ... whom we have recommended unto them. Neither do I understand why your lordship's having the castle, or rather the stones, should make it a matter of right. If out of their respect to you they will choose whom you have recommended, I shall not take it unkindly; and if they will continue their former respect to me, in doing as they have done these threescore years, I know not why I may not receive it without wrong to you.

Salisbury responded by forcing the issue. A week later he wrote again to Sherfield, instructing him to inform the other burgesses that while, as owner of Old Sarum, he was legally entitled to determine the election by himself, he was prepared to allow the customary forms to continue, providing that both of his nominees were accepted. This message had the desired effect, and the voters returned Brett and George Mynne, clerk of the hanaper, whose brother-in-law, (Sir) George Calvert*, may have introduced him to Salisbury.[9]

Far from settling the issue, this outcome merely spurred Pembroke to reassert his customary influence. In real terms his local strength far outweighed Salisbury's alleged rights at Old Sarum. Sherfield clearly recognized this, and when the next Parliament was summoned he invited Pembroke to make one nomination, the earl's choice falling on his secretary, Michael Oldisworth.[10] Salisbury perhaps suspected Sherfield of double-dealing, for he made a direct approach to another of the prominent Old Sarum burgesses, Thomas Hooper, reminding him that the borough had returned both of his nominees at the previous election, and seeking his assistance in achieving the same success this time.[11] However, this intervention came too late. On 14 Jan. 1624 the under-sheriff, John Puxton*, requested Sherfield 'to send down the indentures for the burgesses for Old Sarum'; by now, Pembroke had formally nominated Oldisworth, and Puxton merely wished to know who Salisbury would be recommending for the remaining vacancy. When the election was held eight days later, the second seat went to a long-standing Cecil client, Sir Arthur Ingram, and after he opted to sit for York he was replaced by Sir Robert Cotton, presumably also on Salisbury's nomination.[12]

Relations between Sherfield and Salisbury were now deteriorating, and in late 1624 the earl dismissed Sherfield's brother, who had been working as his deputy-steward in Wiltshire.[13] Not surprisingly, when the next parliamentary elections were called, Salisbury found Sherfield even less co-operative than before, and on 12 Apr. 1625 he berated him for his disloyalty:

> I cannot but remember that I have more than once heard you say that you had so settled your lands within the borough of Old Sarum that you had half the voices (at least) at your own command ... so that none ... without your consent is likely to have either of those places. But now I perceive by your letter that you make it doubtful (in regard of some other voices) that if you should insist upon both for me, you may be in danger to lose both, and to incur the displeasure of some great ones, who have sent unto you about them.[14]

Now convinced that Sherfield could not be trusted, Salisbury again approached Hooper. However, the latter merely confirmed that, while he could offer the earl two votes, his own and one other, 'all the rest ... are wholly at Mr. Sherfield's command, who hath ... of late made choice of whomsoever it pleased him'. Hooper optimistically predicted that Salisbury's nominees were bound to be accepted, but in the event the voters handed both seats to Pembroke clients, Oldisworth and Sir John Stradling.[15]

Salisbury and Sherfield effectively parted company following this débâcle, but the latter remained sub-tenant of Old Sarum, the role that allowed him to act as arbiter in elections. As Hooper explained in January 1626 to Salisbury's receiver-general, Christopher Keighley*, Sherfield had exploited his power to make new freeholders within the borough, thereby multiplying the number of voters under his control. As things now stood, four of the burgesses were Pembroke's officers, while Salisbury might be able to call on Hooper, his brother, and another of the earl's tenants, a Mr. Servington. However, the remaining four burgess-ships belonged to Sherfield's relatives, which meant that he held the balance of power. As Hooper observed, even if Salisbury solicited Sherfield's support, 'it had been all in vain, as ... it was in the last election'. He therefore recommended that the earl negotiate directly with Pembroke, as the only practical means of securing a seat.[16] This clearly did not happen at the 1626 election, when Pembroke successfully nominated both Oldisworth and another of his principal clients, Sir Benjamin Rudyard. However, the rival patrons apparently reached an accommodation in 1628. Pembroke as usual secured the first seat for Oldisworth, but the second went to Keighley, although this was not quite what Salisbury had intended. The decision to elect the earl's receiver was taken locally, and Keighley wrote in some agitation to Hooper that he would have preferred not to be awarded this place, 'in regard my lord had appointed it for another'. Precisely why the voters used their own initiative in this way has not been established.[17]

[1] Hants RO, 44M69/L4/3. [2] Ibid. 44M69/G2/48. [3] Harl. 354, f. 86v. [4] R.C. Hoare, *Hist. Modern Wilts.* iv. (Salisbury), 1, 3; *VCH Wilts.* vi. 52-3, 58-60, 62-3; *Anglo-Saxon Chronicle* ed. D. Whitelock, 162; Hants RO, 44M69/L4/9. [5] *OR*; *VCH Wilts.* vi. 66; Hants RO, 44M69/L4/4; C219/35/2/126; 219/37/288; 219/39/226; 219/40/95; 219/41B/65; *HMC Hatfield*, xxiv. 263-4; *CSP Dom.* 1623-5, p. 266. [6] *HP Commons, 1509-58*, i. 229; 1558-1603, i. 276. [7] C66/1691, m. 9; T.D. Hardy, *Chancery Officials*, 127; L. Dwnn, *Vis. Wales* ed. S.R. Meyrick, ii. 315-16. [8] *VCH Wilts.* vi. 65; Hants RO, 44M69/L2/1; L4/1-2, 9; *Glam. Co. Hist.* ed. G. Williams, v. 165, 173; L. Stone, *Fam. and Fortune*, 130; *HMC Hatfield*, xxii. 135. [9] *HMC Hatfield*, xxii. 102, 135-6; xxiv. 262; Hants RO, 44M69/L4/5; 44M69/L33/22; *CSP Dom.* 1623-5, p. 87. [10] Arundel, Autograph Letters 1617-32, no. 261; *CSP Dom.* 1623-5, p. 233. [11] *HMC Hatfield*, xxiv. 262 (undated letter misassigned to Jan. 1626). [12] Hants RO, 44M69/L37/26; L. Stone, 'Electoral Influence of 2nd Earl of Salisbury', *EHR*, lxxi. 396. [13] *HMC Hatfield*, xxii. 20. [14] Hants RO, 44M69/L4/7 (a draft of this letter is calendared in *HMC Hatfield*, xxiv. 262, but misdated to c. Jan. 1626, and with incorrect authorship). [15] *HMC Hatfield*, xxiv. 261; V.A. Rowe, 'Influence of the Earls of Pembroke on Parl. Elections', *EHR*, l. 243; L. Bowen, *Politics of the Principality*, 15. [16] *HMC Hatfield*, xxiv. 263-4; Stone, 'Electoral Influence', 398-9. [17] J.K. Gruenfelder, *Influence in Early Stuart Elections*, 128; *HMC Hatfield*, xxii. 229.

H.J.L./P.M.H.

SALISBURY

Right of election: in the aldermen

Number of voters: 24

7 Mar. 1604	GILES TOOKER, alderman
	RICHARD GODFREY I, alderman
c. Mar. 1614	GILES TOOKER, recorder
	ROGER GAUNTLETT, alderman
15 Dec. 1620	ROGER GAUNTLETT, alderman
	LAWRENCE HORNE, alderman
16 Jan. 1624	ROGER GAUNTLETT, alderman
	HENRY SHERFIELD, recorder
	?Thomas Hancock, alderman
25 Apr. 1625	HENRY SHERFIELD, recorder
	WALTER LONG II
16 Jan. 1626	HENRY SHERFIELD, recorder
	JOHN PUXTON, alderman
	?Sir John Evelyn*

7 Mar. 1628	HENRY SHERFIELD, recorder
	BARTHOLOMEW TOOKIE, alderman
	(Sir) Thomas Morgan*

Salisbury was founded in the tenth century by the bishops of Old Sarum on water meadows by the river Avon, but it was only fully developed in the 1220s, when Bishop Poore began construction of a new cathedral. Immediately to the north of this site, burgages were laid out in a series of rectangular blocks, later called chequers.[1] Salisbury boomed during the Middle Ages, but its principal industry, the manufacture of broadcloths derived from the flocks of sheep which grazed on the surrounding downs, suffered considerably during the early seventeenth century. Economic depression was compounded by war in the 1620s, which affected exports to the German states and the Low Countries. Salisbury was not wholly reliant upon the cloth trade, however, for its craftsmen also made bonelace, cutlery and leather goods, while the city's situation on the main route between Bristol and Southampton sustained a significant service industry. It also enjoyed an administrative role, being the south Wiltshire centre for the assizes and quarter sessions.[2]

In 1225 the bishop of Salisbury granted the townsmen a charter which established their property rights and his claims to taxes and tolls. These rights were confirmed by a royal charter two years later, which additionally freed the citizens from certain tolls.[3] By 1249 the town had a mayor, two coroners and two bailiffs (whose main responsibility was to collect the bishop's rents), while four aldermen were charged with oversight of the town's four wards. However, these officials remained subordinate to the bishop's bailiff, whose control of their functions and powers inhibited the development of a more settled system of government: municipal elections did not occur until 1417, while the subordinate body of assistants, from which all lesser officials were appointed, only emerged later in the century.[4] From 1411 a city clerk was appointed to give legal advice, but retained lawyers generally handled work of this nature until Sir John Penruddock[†] was appointed fee'd counsel in 1587.[5]

From its inception, the corporation was intermittently at loggerheads with the bishop about its respective rights and responsibilities.[6] Towards the end of the sixteenth century the corporation secured allies by appointing a series of Elizabethan privy councillors – Sir Francis Walsingham[†], Sir Christopher Hatton I[†], Sir Thomas Heneage[†] and Sir John Puckering[†] – to the newly created post of chief steward.[7] At the same time, the city lobbied for a charter of incorporation, which would compel the bishop to relinquish his interest in the city in return for compensation, secure county status for the municipality, and formalize the guild structure of the numerous trades.[8] In 1591 the queen agreed to this proposal in principle, and two years later a writ of *quo warranto* challenged the bishop's franchise. Yet while aldermen were frequently dispatched to London to further these negotiations, it was not until 1612 that a fresh charter was granted.[9] This established a mayor and two tiers of corporate government: the aldermen, called the Twenty-Four; and the assistants, or the Forty-Eight. Other officials included a recorder, bailiff and two chamberlains, while the mayor, recorder and six aldermen served as municipal justices. Episcopal authority, once unassailable, was now restricted to the cathedral close, although the mayor still took his oath before the bishop's bailiff.[10] However, it soon became apparent that the council created by the 1612 charter was unwieldy, for in 1624 it was proposed that the corporation's numbers be halved. In the event it was not until 1675 that any reduction was achieved. Meanwhile, the 1630 charter freed the mayor from being 'tied to any kind of tradesmen or artificer', and altered the date of municipal elections to November.[11]

The city's revenues, from tenements, market stalls and dues from the racecourse, paid for its mayor and recorder, while other officers were remunerated according to their services.[12] In 1615 the corporation raised contributions towards the building of a new assize court and council house, while efforts were also made to build an infirmary, establish a public brewhouse, relocate the free school, and improve the workhouse. Other signs of civic pride included the wearing of formal gowns at meetings, the commissioning of a portrait of recorder Giles Tooker holding the 1612 charter, and a 1623 order that the mace be enlarged 'and made greater than that of Marlborough or the Devizes.'[13]

All but one of the Members returned during this period were residents, the exception being Walter Long II. All the townsmen made significant contributions to municipal affairs: Giles Tooker, the city's first recorder, lobbied tirelessly to secure the 1612 charter, making him a natural choice in the parliaments of 1604 and 1614.[14] Godfrey, Gauntlett, Horne, Puxton and Tookie were city merchants and aldermen, while Gauntlett and Tookie had also been instrumental in negotiating the charter.[15] Sherfield, appointed recorder a few weeks before his election, was also a natural choice as MP, and on 23 Jan. 1624, soon after he had accepted his nomination, he was thanked 'for your kind offers and friendly advice ... hoping you will continue your good endeavours to effect such matters as shall be conceived to be good for our city.'[16]

Corporation membership was restricted to resident freemen; an order of 1592 disenfranchised any councillor absent from the city for more than a year.[17] The parliamentary franchise lay with the Twenty-Four, who were supposed to return two suitable freemen. Despite the formality of this procedure, perhaps intended to forestall contested elections, there may have been as many as three contests during this period.[18] The background to the first of these, in 1624, lay in the establishment the previous year of a public brewhouse which aimed to raise funds for poor relief. The scheme was supported by the majority of the puritan-minded council, including Henry Sherfield, Bartholomew Tookie and Roger Gauntlett, but generated significant opposition from the city's brewers, one of whom, a future mayor, procured a writ of *quo warranto* against the corporation. Nine days before the 1624 election, Thomas Hancock, another brewer and member of the Twenty-Four, wrote to Sherfield at Lincoln's Inn, informing him of his impending election, and offering 'to join with you I am very willing, if so be that I am chosen, which I think will be if you desire it by letter to Mr. Mayor'. It is uncertain whether Hancock withdrew or was defeated in a contest, but in this instance the corporation, perhaps affronted by Hancock's soliciting on his own behalf (he was subsequently voted off the municipal bench), elected Gauntlett, who had been returned in 1621.[19]

The brewhouse was one of two factors to cause the corporation concern at the 1626 election. Despite the requirement that freemen should be resident, outsiders had been sworn as freemen on the day of their election. However, after Walter Long II, assisted by his father-in-law Henry Sherfield, had benefited from this process in 1625, the council determined that 'none [shall] be hereafter chosen to serve as citizens of this city for any Parliament but such is [sic] at the time of the election shall be free citizens and of the common council of this city and then residing there'. This order was soon put to the test, for in 1626 the attorney-general, (Sir) Robert Heath*, asked the council to return Sir John Evelyn*, while another, unnamed, candidate was put forward by the city's chief steward, William Herbert, 3rd earl of Pembroke. The council rejected both Heath's and Pembroke's nominees, arguing that because it desired to have the brewhouse confirmed by Act of Parliament, 'as well as of other provisions of great importance to our city, which it were impossible to accomplish by strangers', it was necessary to send 'two of our own company to this Parliament'.[20] This brewhouse bill, initially referred to as a bill for the relief of the poor, was introduced on 11 Mar. 1626 by Sherfield, who kept notes of its numerous provisions and how it was to differ from the Elizabethan poor laws. Sherfield also headed the committee appointed on 2 May following, but the bill went no further thereafter.[21]

In 1628 Pembroke nominated his steward Sir Thomas Morgan. He was seconded by Sherfield and the mayor, who proposed that Morgan be made a freeman to permit him to represent the city, despite the 1625 forbidding such manoeuvres. However, Alderman Thomas Squibb wrote to Sherfield on 5 Feb. reiterating that 'it is requisite by the words of our charter … that Sir Thomas Morgan should be an inhabitant before we elect him. We would willingly preserve our privileges and yet give our most noble and honourable friend all the content and satisfaction that his lordship [Pembroke] shall require of us. There are some opponents, yet not many'. However, these opponents held sway, rejecting Morgan in favour of one of their own, Alderman Bartholomew Tookie.[22]

Members were reimbursed *pro rata* for their travel and expenses while in London, but such retrospective payments were often delayed and incomplete: Giles Tooker's expenses during the 1597 Parliament were only repaid to him in 1608; in the same year Richard Godfrey accepted £15 'notwithstanding by His Majesty's writ there is due to him £42 6s. for his expenses for 535 days' (although the Parliament in which he served had only been in session for 344 days), while Gauntlett and Horne waited five years to be paid for their parliamentary expenses.[23]

[1] *VCH Wilts.* vi. 94-5. [2] Ibid. 124-7. [3] T. Carew, *Hist. Acct. of Rights of Elections*, 111. [4] Wilts. RO, G23/1/1, f. 62; *VCH Wilts.* vi. 96. [5] Wilts. RO, G23/1/3, ff. 99, 167. [6] Wilts. RO, G23/1/222PC. [7] Wilts. RO, G23/1/226; R.C. Hoare, *Hist. Wilts.* 'Salisbury', 296. [8] Wilts. RO, G23/1/3, f. 174; G23/1/223/15, 38, 42. [9] Wilts. RO, G23/1/223/31; G23/1/3, ff. 122v, 125, 127, 214v. [10] Wilts. RO, G23/1/223/10, 20. [11] Hants RO, 44M69/L37/25; *VCH Wilts.* vi. 105. [12] Wilts. RO, G23/150/36; G23/1/3, ff. 223, 235, 322. [13] Ibid. G23/1/3, ff. 219v, 243, 292, 294, 301v. [14] Wilts. RO, G23/1/9, f. 7. [15] Wilts. RO, G23/1/3, f. 208. [16] Hants RO, 44M69/L37/21. [17] Wilts. RO, G23/1/3, f. 197v; Hoare, 365. [18] Hants RO, 44M69/L37/27. [19] Hants. RO, 44M69/L37/21; *Crisis and Order in English Towns 1500-1700* ed. P. Clark and P. Slack, 186-8. [20] Hants RO, 44M69/L37/40. [21] *Procs. 1626*, ii. 238, 255, 288; iii. 120; iv. 118-26. [22] Wilts. RO, G23/1/3, f. 355; Hants RO, 44M69/L37/37-8, 40. [23] Wilts. RO, G23/1/3, ff. 200v, 330.

H.J.L.

WESTBURY

Right of election: in the 'mayor and burgesses'

Number of voters: unknown

Mar. 1604	SIR JAMES LEY MATTHEW LEY
17 Oct. 1605	ALEXANDER CHOCKE I *vice* Ley, appointed to office
18 Sept. 1609	SIR JAMES LEY *vice* Chocke, deceased
c. Mar. 1614	HENRY LEY MATTHEW LEY
2 Jan. 1621	SIR JAMES LEY SIR MILES FLEETWOOD
1 Mar. 1621	WALTER LONG I *vice* Ley, called to the Upper House as a legal assistant
3 Feb. 1624	(SIR) HENRY LEY SIR HENRY MILDMAY
6 May 1625	WALTER LONG I GIFFORD LONG
6 Jan. 1626	THOMAS HOPTON WALTER LONG I
4 Mar. 1628	MAXIMILIAN PETTY CHARLES THYNNE

Westbury was a small market town in the centre of Wiltshire's clothing area. The borough, apparently restricted to the precinct in which the ancient burgage tenements lay, was never chartered, but a municipal structure had evolved by the reign of Elizabeth, which included a mayor and a town seal. Enfranchised from 1448, the parliamentary indentures for the early Stuart period were signed by the 'mayor and burgesses' and authenticated with the town seal; the 1625 indenture was additionally witnessed by 'Edward Greenhill, Thomas Style, John Greenhill and others'. At its dissolution in 1835 the corporation consisted of a mayor, recorder, and 13 capital burgesses, but it is impossible to say how far this structure had developed two centuries earlier.[1]

The most influential local landowner at Westbury was Sir James Ley, whose father had acquired the nearby manor of Teffont Evias. From 1599 Ley began to purchase property in Westbury, which ultimately gave him a preponderant interest in the parliamentary elections there.[2] During the early Stuart period four of the borough's MPs were his relatives: his brother Matthew, son Henry, brother-in-law Maximilian Petty, and son-in-law Walter Long I. Sir Miles Fleetwood, returned in 1621, was professionally connected with Ley, being receiver-general of the Court of Wards, of which Ley was then attorney.

Though their election presumably needed Ley's approbation, other Members had independent influence as local landowners. The family of Alexander Chocke I, who was returned at Westbury after Ley was appointed chief justice of Ireland, had long owned property in the area.[3] On the day after his election, Chocke was invested with the manor of Westbury St. Maur.[4] Gifford Long, whose maternal grandfather and great-uncle had represented the borough in the previous reign, inherited property in Westbury, of which at least one manor – Westbury Stourton – was sold to Ley;[5] and Thomas Hopton's brothers had recently acquired an interest in Westbury rectory.[6] Charles Thynne is the only Member who had no known connection with Ley or the borough. He probably relied for his seat upon his half-brother (Sir) Thomas Thynne*, whose estate at nearby Longleat presumably gave him some influence with Ley.

[1] *VCH Wilts.* viii. 186; C219/39/230. [2] *VCH Wilts.* viii. 149-51, 155, 157-8, 161-2. [3] *CJ*, i. 323b; *Bowyer Diary*, 188. [4] *VCH Wilts.* viii. 150; C142/211/186; R.C. Hoare, *Hist. Wilts.* 'Westbury Hundred', 39. [5] *VCH Wilts.* viii. 150. [6] C3/358/7.

H.J.L.

WILTON

Right of election: in the freemen

Number of voters: 28 in 1628

13 Mar. 1604	SIR THOMAS EDMONDES
	HUGH SANFORD
2 June 1607	THOMAS MORGAN *vice*
	Sanford, deceased
c. Mar. 1614	SIR ROBERT SIDNEY
	THOMAS MORGAN
16 Dec. 1620	SIR THOMAS TRACY
	THOMAS MORGAN
8 Nov. 1621	SIR HENRY NEVILLE III *vice*
	Tracy, deceased
26 Jan. 1624	PERCY HERBERT
	(SIR) THOMAS MORGAN
18 Apr. 1625[1]	SIR WILLIAM HERBERT
	(SIR) THOMAS MORGAN
c. June 1625	SIR WILLIAM HARINGTON *vice*
	Herbert, chose to sit for
	Montgomeryshire
17 Jan. 1626[2]	SIR JOHN EVELYN
	(SIR) THOMAS MORGAN
5 Mar. 1628	SIR WILLIAM HERBERT
	(SIR) THOMAS MORGAN
2 Apr. 1628[3]	JOHN POLEY *vice* Herbert,
	chose to sit for Montgomeryshire

Wilton was the seat of the Wessex kings until the ninth century, and thereafter the administrative centre of Wiltshire, although the rise of nearby Salisbury restricted its economic growth.[4] Originally a borough by prescription, the town was governed by a merchant guild until 1350, when a charter appointed a mayor, recorder, town clerk, five aldermen, three capital burgesses, 11 common councilmen and other minor officials.[5] Wilton first returned MPs to Parliament in 1275. The freemen held the franchise, while the mayor acted as returning officer.[6] In 1544 the borough was acquired by the Herbert earls of Pembroke, who made it their main country seat and thereafter controlled the electoral patronage.

All the early Stuart Members owed their places to William Herbert, 3rd earl of Pembroke or his clients. Sir Robert Sidney was Pembroke's brother-in-law, while Sir William Herbert was his cousin. Percy Herbert was the latter's son, and Sir William Harington was the brother-in-law of Sir Richard Moryson*, a distant relation of Pembroke's. Thomas Morgan had been the family steward since at least 1596. Hugh Sanford, formerly William's tutor, served the earl as secretary and helped to negotiate his 1604 marriage to a daughter of the 7th earl of Shrewsbury (Gilbert Talbot†), as did Sir Thomas Edmondes. Sir Thomas Tracy was a client of Pembroke's brother Philip Herbert*, later earl of Montgomery, and joined the East India Company on Pembroke's recommendation. Montgomery may also have been responsible for recommending Sir Henry Neville III, as he later appointed him to the privy chamber. (Sir) Humphrey May*, a longstanding Pembroke associate, was probably behind the election of his brother-in-law John Poley. No specific connection with Pembroke can be established in respect of Sir John Evelyn, but as a Wiltshireman Evelyn was doubtless known to the earl, who nominated him after he failed to secure a place at nearby Salisbury.[7]

[1] Wilts. RO, G25/1/21, f. 337. [2] Ibid. f. 341. [3] Ibid. f. 347. [4] R.C. Hoare, *Hist. Wilts.* 'Branch and Dole', 55, 117. [5] *VCH Wilts.* vi. 1, 9; Hoare, 131. [6] Hoare, 'Branch and Dole', 55. [7] M.F. Keeler, *Long Parl.* 169.

H.J.L.

WOOTTON BASSETT

Right of election: ?in the corporation

Number of voters: ?15

10 Mar. 1604	HENRY MARTYN
	ALEXANDER TUTT
c. Mar. 1614	SIR WILLIAM WILLOUGHBY
	EDWARD HUNGERFORD
18 Dec. 1620	RICHARD HARRISON
	JOHN WRENHAM
22 Jan. 1624	SIR ROLAND EGERTON, bt.
	JOHN BANKES
5 May 1625	SIR ROBERT HYDE
	SIR WALTER TICHBORNE
c. Jan. 1626	SIR JOHN FRANKLIN
	SIR THOMAS LAKE I
10 Mar. 1628	SIR JOHN FRANKLIN
	ANTHONY ROUS

Although little more than an agricultural village lying in the northern 'cheese' district of Wiltshire, Wootton Bassett returned Members to the Commons from 1446, at which time it was held by the dukes of York. In 1631 the residents produced a copy of an alleged charter of 1561 which vested authority in a mayor, two aldermen and 12 capital burgesses. The original grant has not been found, but the format of the early Stuart indentures – which were sealed with the borough seal and describe the electorate as the 'mayor and burgesses' – suggests that the franchise then lay with the corporation, however dubious its legal status.[1]

From 1555 Wootton Bassett manor was held by the Catholic Englefield family, whose head, Sir Francis[†], a Marian courtier, opted for exile on the Continent

under Elizabeth, and was attainted in 1585. The estate was swiftly re-granted to his nephew, also Sir Francis Englefield, who ran into serious financial problems in James's reign; the only early Stuart MP who seems to have been connected with his interests was John Wrenham, who made several interventions on his behalf in the 1621 Parliament.[2]

With the decline of the Englefield patronage, the borough accepted a number of strangers with no known connection to the area.[3] These included Sir John Franklin and Sir Thomas Lake I, both seated in Middlesex; Sir Roland Egerton of Northamptonshire; Sir William Willoughby from Buckinghamshire; and the Dorset lawyer John Bankes. Indeed, the only early Stuart Member with local connections was Henry Martyn, who held three manors on the outskirts of nearby Swindon.[4] Four Members are known or are suspected to have owed their election to the influence of others: Edward Seymour, 1st earl of Hertford, advanced his agent Alexander Tutt in 1604; Sir Robert Hyde's position as steward of Crown lands in neighbouring Chippenham doubtless assisted his return;[5] and the family of the young Edward Hungerford held extensive property in north Wiltshire. Finally, the return of Anthony Rous, joint clerk of the Pipe with Henry Croke*, was probably engineered by Croke to help resist an attack on their office launched in Parliament by Edmund Sawyer*.[6]

In only one instance are Members known to have served the borough's interests. In March 1621 Richard Harrison and John Wrenham responded to a petition signed by the mayor and freeholders against the enclosure by Sir Francis Englefield of Vasterne Great Park, which restricted access to common pasture.[7]

[1] *VCH Wilts.* ix. 191, 198-9; C219/35/2/125; 219/37/300. [2] *VCH Wilts.* ix. 191; JOHN WRENHAM. [3] Wilts. RO, 212A/27/12/1; *Diaries of the Eng. Coll. Douai* ed. T.E. Knox, 299; J.A. Williams, *Cath. Recusancy in Wilts. 1660-1791*, p. 14; *Recs. of Eng. Province of Soc. of Jesus* ed. H. Foley, iv. 334, n. 3. [4] *Wilts. IPMs* ed. G.S. and A.E. Fry (Brit. Rec. Soc. xxiii), 395; DL4/57/63. [5] *CSP Dom.* 1625-6, pp. 154, 552. [6] *CD 1628*, iii. 298. [7] HLRO, main pprs. 22 Feb. 1621; *CJ*, i. 554a; *Top. and Gen.* iii. 22-5.

H.J.L.

WORCESTERSHIRE

Number of voters: unknown

29 Feb. 1604	SIR HENRY BROMLEY
	SIR WILLIAM LIGON
	Sir Edmund Harewell
1 Nov. 1609	SIR SAMUEL SANDYS *vice*
	Ligon, deceased
c. Mar. 1614	SIR THOMAS BROMLEY
	SIR SAMUEL SANDYS
13 Dec. 1620	SIR THOMAS LITTLETON
	SIR SAMUEL SANDYS
c. Jan. 1624	SIR WALTER DEVEREUX, (bt.)
	SIR THOMAS LITTLETON
27 Apr. 1625	SIR THOMAS LITTLETON
	WILLIAM RUSSELL
1 Feb. 1626	SIR THOMAS LITTLETON
	SIR JOHN ROUS II
27 Feb. 1628	THOMAS COVENTRY
	SIR THOMAS BROMLEY

Worcestershire lies on the border between the highland and lowland zones of England. One of the wealthiest and most densely populated counties in seventeenth-century England, it was predominantly pastoral, though the south-east was mainly arable.[1] A substantial cloth industry, mostly concentrated in Worcester, produced high quality broadcloths, in addition from 1600 Kidderminster started manufacturing quantities of linsey-woolsey stuffs.[2] Worcestershire's most important rural industry, iron-working, was based in the north-east of the county, where coal and iron ore was mined.[3]

The most consistent factor in elections was the influence of the Littleton-Bromley connection. A member of one or other family was returned in every election in this period, usually for the senior seat. The Littletons owned a substantial estate based around Frankley. Indeed, their freeholders numbered 192 in 1602, giving them a sizeable block of voters.[4] John Lyttleton[†] married Meriel Bromley, the sister of Sir Henry Bromley, but was attainted for his part in the Essex rising. The estate was returned to his widow in 1603, and the following year she mobilized her tenants in support of her brother and Sir William Ligon. It seems likely that she also supported Sir Henry Bromley's son, Sir Thomas, in 1614. By 1620 her own son,

Sir Thomas Littleton, had come of age, allowing him to be returned that same year and in the following three elections. In 1628 it is likely that Sir Thomas Littleton stood down in favour of his cousin Sir Thomas Bromley.

Aristocratic and Court influence on the politics of the county was rare and seldom had the power to disrupt the established patterns of Worcestershire politics. In 1604 the only resident peer was Henry, 5th Lord Windsor, who lived at Hewell in the north-east of the county. A Catholic, he supported Sir Edmund Harewell at the 1604 election.[5] In the 1590s the 2nd earl of Essex had a significant following in Worcestershire, but two of his leading supporters, Sir Henry Bromley and John Lyttleton, probably relied primarily on their local standing to secure their election. Essex's son, the 3rd earl, was a minor at the start of this period, and did not play an active part in electoral politics until 1614. Even then he seems to have on concentrated on Staffordshire, as the only county election in Worcestershire in which his family's influence is apparent is that of 1624, which saw the return of his cousin, Sir Walter Devereux. The extent to which Devereux relied directly upon Essex for support is unclear, but it seems likely that other factors were more important, as he had purchased an estate at Leigh and was connected with the Littletons. The only other peer in Worcestershire was lord keeper Sir Thomas Coventry*, who was not ennobled until April 1628. Coventry emerged as a significant electoral patron in the county's boroughs, but he had no discernable influence on county elections until 1628, when he secured the return of his son.

The elections of 1624 and 1628 were the only occasions on which neither a Bromley nor a Littleton was returned for the first seat. In their place gentlemen from the south of the county were chosen. This was highly unusual, as Worcestershire's southern gentry were generally forced to settle for the junior seat, and sometimes, as in 1614 and 1620, both places were taken by northerners. However, those chosen for the senior seat in 1624 and 1628 – Devereux and Thomas Coventry respectively – were hardly typical of south Worcestershire's gentry.

The importance of regional divisions ought not to be overstated. It seems likely that Sir Samuel Sandys, who sat three times for the county, was popular because he helped lead the campaign against the Council in the Marches rather than because he was a northerner. Moreover, by the late Elizabethan period, religion was the dominant factor: Catholicism in particular played an important role in the electoral politics of Elizabethan Worcestershire. In 1596 the bishop of Worcester complained to Sir Robert Cecil[†] of the number of recusants in his diocese, and that many were 'not only of good wealth but of great alliance'.[6] His proposal to establish a commission to combat recusancy was implemented two years later, and included Bromley, Ligon and Sandys among its members.[7] Catholic fear of increasing persecution, reflected in the correspondence of Humphrey Pakington, the recusant head of the junior branch of one of Worcestershire's most prominent county families, may have led local Catholics to seek an increased role in parliamentary elections, despite the obstacles in their way.[8] To sit in the Commons Members had to take the Oath of Supremacy, but this does not seem to have deterred Ralph Sheldon, elected in 1563, John Talbot, returned in 1572, and John Lyttleton, elected in 1584, 1586 and 1597, all of whom were notorious for their Catholic sympathies. In 1597 both seats were taken by Catholics, reflecting the fact that the sheriff, Edmund Harewell, was himself a leading member of the Catholic faction.[9] Harewell's friends included the Catholic antiquary Thomas Habington, who later hinted that Harewell converted to Rome on his deathbed.[10] In 1601 the Privy Council was so worried by Catholic electoral influence in Worcestershire that it wrote to Ralph Sheldon and John Talbot warning them not to oppose the election of the strongly Protestant Sir Thomas Leighton.[11]

Soon after James's accession the Catholic faction decided to promote candidates sympathetic to their cause in the forthcoming Worcestershire election.[12] They therefore chose Edmund Harewell, now a knight of the Bath, and John Talbot. Harewell, who came from a well-established county family and was a prominent member of the bench, may have sought election in order to avoid his creditors, as serious financial problems eventually forced him to sell his estate. Talbot did not require a seat so urgently, and soon developed qualms about taking the Oath of Supremacy.[13] His decision not to stand made it necessary to find a suitable replacement, but this proved difficult. At first Worcestershire's Catholics seem to have considered as an alternative his cousin, Sharington Talbot[†], but their preferred candidate was Sir John Pakington,[14] who had attracted Queen Elizabeth's favour and was the *custos rotulorum*.[15] Though not Catholic himself, Pakington seems to have been considered a sympathizer for some while, for in 1592 while under arrest for refusing to conform, John Talbot asked to be committed to his custody.[16] However, despite supporting Harewell, Pakington refused to stand. Talbot and his allies nevertheless remained hopeful that he would still be elected.[17]

Campaigning in Worcestershire began during the summer of 1603. Soon after Christmas Day as many as 200 members of the Catholic faction, erroneously believing that the sheriff of Worcestershire, Sir Thomas Russell[†], had received the writ, assembled at Worcester.[18] The bishop of Worcester, Gervase Babington, was so alarmed by this development that he turned to Sir William Ligon, who had represented the county in 1589. Although married to Harewell's sister, Ligon was 'known to be one that professed and favoured the established religion'.[19] Ligon agreed to stand again, and was initially paired with Sir William Walsh[†], another firm Protestant, who had been arrested in 1593 for supporting the puritan Peter Wentworth's[†] attempt to raise the issue of the succession in Parliament. However, shortly before the election, Walsh was persuaded to withdraw in favour of Sir Henry Bromley who, apart from owing an extensive estate with land in both Worcestershire and Shropshire, had recently been appointed as a gentleman of the privy chamber. According to John Talbot, Walsh realized that his supporters were too few and that it was necessary to strengthen the Protestant faction 'by one that was of greatest power and authority in Court'. Bromley's greater standing also meant that, if necessary, he was better able to intimidate the sheriff. John Talbot later alleged that Sheriff Russell, who subsequently converted to Catholicism, was over-awed by Bromley, but this is difficult to believe, for as late as November 1605 Russell was described as one of the most loyal Protestants on the bench. His undoubted support for Bromley and Ligon in 1604 must therefore have arisen from religious conviction.[20]

About five days before the election, which was held on 29 Feb., Ralph Sheldon sent Francis More, Ligon's brother-in-law, to persuade Ligon not to stand, 'assuring him ... that he was like receive a disgrace (if he stood out to the election) for want of voices'. This prompted Ligon to estimate the extent of his support. Aided by another of his brothers-in-law, Robert Walwyn, he drew up lists of his supporters and opponents on the county bench. He assured himself that his supporters were 'of great kindred, alliance and men of great command in the county', including the bishop, the dean and chapter and the sheriff, whereas his opponents were mostly concentrated in Halfshire Hundred, in the north-east of the county, which, with the neighbouring Dodingtree Hundred, comprised only about a third of Worcestershire. Moreover, even in Halfshire, Meriel Lyttleton, the widow of John Lyttleton, 'a gentlewoman of great estate of living ... had promised her tenants and friends voices to Sir William Ligon'.[21] However, Ligon and Walwyn underestimated Harewell's support in other parts of the county. Those overlooked included Henry Russell in the south-west and Thomas Habington in central Worcestershire, both of whom mobilized their tenants and servants in support of Harewell, who lived in the south. Harewell seems to have had little support in the hundreds of Blackenhurst and Doddingtree, in the south-east and north-west, where Ligon and Bromley were strong.[22]

There was extensive canvassing in the run-up to the election, much of it underhand. In the summer of 1603 Stephen and Humphrey Littleton tried to mobilize the tenants of their late brother John Lyttleton for the Catholic faction while Meriel was away in London, telling them that they had the support of Mrs. Lyttleton, even though she was Protestant. However, when Meriel returned she instructed her tenants to vote for Bromley and Ligon. Having recently negotiated the return of her late husband's estate, which had been forfeit owing to the latter's part in the Essex rising, she was undoubtedly hoping that the forthcoming Parliament would restore her children in blood, an objective which might not be realized if she were seen to support the Catholic faction.[23]

Ligon employed his servant William Addis to canvass in Powick, a manor owned by his stepmother, Margaret, Lady Ligon, who also happened to be John Talbot's aunt. Addis initially targeted the freeholders, but was not overly scrupulous: one week before the election, finding a freeholder away, he recruited his son instead.[24] On the day before the election Addis, together with his son and servants, went round the households in Powick indiscriminately urging copyholders, craftsmen and labourers to come to Worcester to support Ligon.[25] When Richard Man, a tailor, replied 'that he was no freeholder nor copyholder but a poor man and therefore he needed not to come',[26] Addis promised to pay the expenses of those who turned out and to compensate them for the loss of a day's work. He does not seem to have made good this promise, although he did provide food and drink in Worcester.[27]

Some of those recruited by Addis left for Worcester the evening before the poll. The sheriff appointed Sir Henry Bromley's brother, Edward, to guard Castle Green, where the election was to be held, and, to exclude Harewell supporters, he was instructed to let in only those who could supply a password.[28] Many of Bromley and Ligon's supporters spent the night on the Green, warmed by fires provided by Addis.[29] In the morning they were joined by larger crowds. Those who came from Powick were woken before dawn by

Addis and his servants, and in Pershore, near Harewell's residence at Besford, orders were given for the bells to be rung at three in the morning to summon the inhabitants to vote for Harewell.[30] As the numbers began to swell, the sheriff's organization began to break down. An oversight had left several of Bromley and Ligon's supporters unaware of the password. They were therefore not allowed through the gate and instead had to find a way into the Green over a broken pale. This route also enabled Harewell's supporters to enter, and more gained access to the Green by taking boats across the Severn. Harewell himself and a body of his supporters got in through a gap in the hedge. The resulting disorder was considerable, as the supporters of the rival candidates clashed and several people were injured.[31] During these tumultuous proceedings Sheriff Russell, accompanied by Edward, 11th Lord Zouche, president of the Council in the Marches, declared that Bromley and Ligon had the most voices. When Harewell requested a poll he was refused.[32]

In the aftermath of the election Talbot, who had been forced to watch the proceedings from a neighbouring hill, tried to recruit support to appeal against the result: he wrote to his kinsman, the 7th earl of Shrewsbury (Gilbert Talbot†), with an account of the election,[33] and contacted Sir Arnold Ligon, the husband of Margaret, Lady Ligon. Sir Arnold is not known to have participated in the election on either side, but he objected to the participation of non-freeholders and had his own reasons for disliking Addis, who had supported one of his tenants against him in a suit in the Council of the Marches.[34] In January 1605 Sir Arnold preferred a bill against Addis in Star Chamber, which included the charge of recruiting non-freeholders to vote in the election.[35] No attempt was made to bring the matter to the attention of the House of Commons.

The 1604 election saw the end of Catholicism as a powerful electoral force in Worcestershire. The discovery of the Gunpowder Plot the following year discredited their cause, especially as the plotters included Stephen Littleton, a leading member of the Catholic faction in 1603-4, and Robert Winter, a Harewell supporter and Talbot's son-in-law. Moreover, Thomas Habington was attainted for sheltering Garnet and others, including Talbot, came under suspicion.[36] By the time of the next election, in 1609, the dominant theme in Worcestershire politics was the jurisdiction of the Council in the Marches. This issue had initially erupted as a clash between the Council and King's Bench, but in December 1605

Lord Zouche complained to Robert Cecil, now 1st earl of Salisbury, about a petition from 'four gentleman protectors of the four shires of Gloucester, Hereford, Worcester and Salop' against the Council. The leaders of the campaign against the Council's jurisdiction in Worcestershire were Sir John Pakington and Sir Samuel Sandys, who had been on opposing sides in the 1604 election.[37] In January 1608, Ralph, 3rd Lord Eure, Zouche's successor as president of the Council in the Marches, complained to Salisbury that Sir William Ligon was the only Worcestershire deputy lieutenant willing to visit him.[38]

Ligon died later that year and, on 13 Nov. 1609, Eure wrote to Salisbury stating that 'the better sort of gentlemen' of Worcestershire 'repine and complain of' the election of Sandys, who had been returned for the county at the resulting by-election. According to Eure, the election writ had been sent to the under-sheriff, who did not declare its existence until the next county court, which was attended by only a few coroners, one magistrate (William Ingram) and between 40 and 50 suitors, most of whom were not freeholders. When one of the coroners protested that the election was illegal because the writ had not been published he failed to receive any support and therefore withdrew his objection.[39] Eure's account of the election, in which the only candidate nominated was Sandys, is corroborated by the return. Of the 19 parties mentioned, only William Ingram was a justice of the peace and five are described as yeomen.[40]

In 1614 Sandys was re-elected alongside Sir Thomas Bromley, the son of Sir Henry,[41] and in 1620 with Sir Thomas Littleton, the son of Meriel Littleton. In 1620 the Council in the Marches prohibited the carrying of weapons at the election, although there is no evidence of any controversy, and at least nine magistrates were parties to the indenture.[42] In 1624 Sir Thomas Littleton was elected with Sir Walter Devereux, the cousin of the 3rd earl of Essex, again without a contest.[43] Littleton was returned for a third time in 1625, this time alongside William Russell, the son of the man who had served as sheriff in 1604, and a year later he was elected again, together with Sir John Rous, a respected and wealthy gentleman from the south-east of the county. There is no evidence of controversy until the re-election of Sir Thomas Bromley in 1628. On 20 Mar. the privileges committee was informed that Bromley was 'unrightfully chosen', probably because he had been outlawed for bankruptcy.[44] There is no evidence that the election of Thomas Coventry, the son of the lord keeper and heir to a significant estate in south Worcestershire, was controversial.

[1] R.H. Silcock, 'County Govt. in Worcs.' (London Univ. Ph.D. thesis, 1974), pp. 11-13, 20. [2] A.D. Dyer, *City of Worcester in Sixteenth-Cent.* 93, 117; E. Kerridge, *Textile Manufactures in Early Modern Eng.* 87. [3] *VCH Worcs.* ii. 264, 267, 271-2. [4] J.M.J. Tonks, 'Lyttletons of Frankley and their estates 1530-1640', (Oxford Univ. B.Litt. thesis, 1978), p. 139. [5] STAC 8/201/17, ff. 18v, 19. This document is double foliated; refs. are to the stamped numbering on the verso, which is the more consistent of the two. [6] *HMC Hatfield*, vi. 265-6. [7] C66/1478, mm. 8-11. [8] Worcs. RO, 705:24/BA81/576/6, 12. [9] *List of Sheriffs* comp. A. Hughes (PRO, L. and I. ix), 158. The 1597 MPs were John Lyttleton, who was dead by 1604, and Edmund Colles, who supported Harewell in 1604, STAC 8/201/17, f. 19. [10] Shaw, *Knights of Eng.* i. 155; *VCH Worcs.* iv. 21, 73, 140; *Survey of Worcs. by Thomas Habington* ed. J. Amphlett (Worcs. Hist. Soc. 1893-9), i. 49; ii. 28-9; STAC 8/201/17, ff. 17, 19v. [11] *APC*, 1601-4, p. 251. [12] STAC 8/201/17, f. 18v. [13] Ibid. f. 16. [14] Ibid. ff. 16, 17, 18v; T. Nash, *Colls. for Hist. Worcs.* i. p. xxviii. [15] E.A.B. Barnard, 'Pakingtons of Westwood', *Trans. Worcs. Arch. Soc.* n.s. xiii. 36; Add. 38139, ff. 163-4. [16] *HMC Hatfield*, xiii. 472. [17] Nash, i. p. xxviii; STAC 8/201/17, f. 19. [18] STAC 8/201/17, ff. 16, 17v, 18v. This is almost certainly the incident referred to in Worcs. RO, 705:24/BA81/576/3. [19] STAC 8/201/17, ff. 17v, 18v. [20] Nash, i. p. xxviii; STAC 8/201/17, f. 18; SP14/216/131; *CJ*, i. 706. [21] STAC 8/201/17, f. 19; *Worcs. Vis.* (Harl. Soc. xxvii), 91. [22] STAC 8/201/17, ff. 16, 17, 17v, 18v, 19. [23] Ibid. ff. 16v, 17v, 18. Meriel appears to have declared her opposition to Harewell before her brother entered the lists. [24] Ibid. f. 10v. [25] Ibid. f. 9. [26] Ibid. f. 10. [27] Ibid. ff. 9, 9v, 10, 11. [28] Ibid. f. 10. [29] Ibid. f. 9v. [30] Ibid. ff. 7v, 10, 17. [31] Ibid. ff. 7v, 8, 8v. [32] Nash, i. p. xxviii. [33] Ibid. [34] *HMC Var.* ii. 319. [35] STAC 8/201/17, f. 23. [36] Ibid. f. 16; *CSP Dom.* 1603-10, pp. 242, 243, 253, 267. [37] P. Williams, 'Attack on the Council in the Marches', *Trans. Hon. Soc. Cymmrodorion* 1961, pp. 2-3; *HMC Hatfield*, xvii. 552; Silcock, 216-20. [38] Cott. Vitellius C.I, f. 206v. [39] SP14/49/26. [40] C219/35/2/138. [41] Gruenfelder's statement that Sandys' canvassing in 1614 aroused opposition in Worcestershire is based on a misreading of an undated letter by (Sir) William Russell* concerning William Sandys† of Fladbury. The letter concerned must relate to one of the 1640 elections. J.K. Gruenfelder, *Influence in Early Stuart Elections*, 16; Worcs. RO, BA81 705:24/647(3). [42] *HMC Rye and Hereford*, 260; C219/37/311; C66/2234. [43] Hirst erroneously states that there was a contest in 1624. D. Hirst, *Representative of the People?*, 222. See M.A. Kishlansky, *Parlty. Selection*, 76. [44] *CD 1628*, ii. 37.

B.C.

BEWDLEY

Right of election: in the freemen[1]

?1605	?RICHARD YOUNG
c.Mar. 1614	JAMES BUTTON
19 Feb. 1620	SIR THOMAS EDMONDES
c.Jan. 1624	RALPH CLARE
6 May 1625	RALPH CLARE
22 Jan. 1626	RALPH CLARE
5 Mar. 1628	(SIR) RALPH CLARE

Bewdley is situated where the River Severn meets the Forest of Wyre as it enters north-western Worcestershire. 'Not anciently famous', as a contemporary remarked, the town owed its rise to prominence to the construction of the bridge over the Severn in the mid-fifteenth century. The bridge wardens, who were responsible for the upkeep of bridge, managed the finances of the borough.[2] The manor of Bewdley became Crown land in 1461, and in 1472 Edward IV granted the borough its first charter. The manor house, called Tickenhall, was enlarged by Henry VII for Prince Arthur, and subsequently became the principal summer residence of the Council in the Marches.[3]

Bewdley was enfranchised by charter in September 1605.[4] The new charter was primarily justified on account of the cost of maintaining the bridge, and placed the government of the town in the hands of a bailiff, elected annually by the common burgesses, and 12 capital burgesses who served for life, vacancies being filled by co-option. The bailiff, his predecessor, and the recorder were *ex officio* justices. Sir Francis Eure* and Sir James Whitelocke* are mentioned as chief recorders of the town in 1615 and 1621 respectively.[5] In October 1619 it was agreed that 25 'of the most substantial and discreet burgesses' be added to the dozen capital burgesses, and that they should 'have their voices in election of officers and in the orders to be made'. Officially known as the Common Council, the lesser burgesses were more usually called the 'Twenty Five'.[6] Unusually the 1605 charter only granted Bewdley a single Member, who was to be elected by the burgesses. The surviving indentures were made out in the name of the bailiff and burgesses, but in fact name only the bailiff.[7] In 1677 Edmund Waller* recalled that John Selden* 'grumbled' at Bewdley's enfranchisement.[8] Perhaps Selden feared that the Crown's influence over the borough would inevitably be considerable.

It is not known when the first writ was issued for an election at Bewdley. The appointment on 31 Mar. 1604 of the burgess of Bewdley to a committee for the bill for the true making of hats must surely be an error, for though the town was a major centre for the manufacture of caps, the appointment predates the borough's enfranchisement by 18 months.[9] A writ was probably issued at about the same time as the charter, as the bridge wardens' accounts record that in 1606 a payment of £5 was 'laid out to Mr. Young for his being a burgess in the Parliament House'.[10] There are numerous references to 'Mr. Yong' in the Journal, some of which probably refer to John Young, the Member for Rye. However the Mr. Yong who defended the Council in the Marches and its lord president (10 Mar. 1606) is more likely to have been the Member for Bewdley. Indeed, he was probably Richard Young*, a client of Lord Zouche, the president of the Council of Wales at the time of Bewdley's enfranchisement.

In 1624 the Lord President of the Council in the Marches nominated Ralph Clare at the prompting of the Prince's Council. Clare was a gentleman of the Prince's Privy Chamber and the keeper of Tickenhall House.[1f] The influence of the Prince's Council over the borough was derived from the fact that the manor of Bewdley had been transferred to Prince Charles in 1617, and it is likely that that his council also nominated Sir Thomas Edmondes, treasurer of the Household in 1620.[12] In 1614 the manor was still under the control of the Exchequer, and consequently it is possible that Button owed his election to his brother Sir William Button, a client of the lord chamberlain and treasury commissioner, Thomas Howard, 1st Earl of Suffolk.[13]

Clare remained a member of the Privy Chamber after Charles's accession, and therefore it is likely that he was elected in 1625 and 1626 with royal support. However Clare lived locally and had been granted the lease of Bewdley manor in 1623. Consequently, he was re-elected in 1628, even though he had been suspended from his position in the Privy Chamber two years earlier.

---

[1] T. Nash, *Colls. for Hist. Worcs.* ii. 293. [2] *Survey of Worcs. by Thomas Habington* ed. J. Amphlett (Worcs. Hist. Soc. 1893-5), i. 530-2; P. Styles, 'Corporation of Bewdley under the later Stuarts', in P. Styles, *Studies in Seventeenth-Cent. Midlands Hist.* 45; Worcs. RO, Bewdley Bridge and Chapel Wardens Accts., BA8681/236(i). [3] H.M. Colvin, *History of the King's Works*, iv. 279-82; *VCH Worcs.* iv. 301, 303, 309. [4] C661676/10; a translation is printed in Nash, ii. 285-94. [5] Soc. Antiq., Prattinton Coll., Top. IV(i) (Bewdley), p. 347. [6] Soc. Antiq., Prattinton Coll., Top. IV(iiB) (Bewdley), pp. 98-108. [7] C219/37/316; 219/39/243 [8] A. Grey, *Debates of House of Commons*, iv. 300. [9] *CJ*, i. 160b; *VCH Worcs.* iv. 305. [10] Worcs. BA8681/236(i), p. 317. The forename 'John' is deleted. [11] DCO, 'Prince Charles in Spain', f. 35. [12] *VCH Worcs.* iv. 309. [13] *Chamberlain Letters* ed. N.E. McClure, i. 358.

G.R./B.C.

DROITWICH

Right of election: in the freemen[1]

Number of voters: c.100[2]

14 Mar. 1604	GEORGE WYLDE I
	JOHN BRACE
c. Mar. 1614	EDWIN SANDYS
	RALPH CLARE
11 Dec. 1620	SIR THOMAS COVENTRY
	JOHN WYLDE
17 Feb. 1621	RALPH CLARE *vice*
	Coventry, declared ineligible
c. Jan. 1624	WALTER BLOUNT
	JOHN WYLDE
2 May 1625	JOHN WYLDE, recorder
	THOMAS COVENTRY
24 Jan. 1626	THOMAS COVENTRY
	JOHN WYLDE, recorder
28 Feb. 1628	JOHN WYLDE, recorder
	GEORGE WYLDE II

Droitwich, six miles north-east of Worcester, had a population of about 760 in the 1560s, rising to over 1,000 a century later.[3] It had been famous since Anglo-Saxon times for the production of salt, a trade which continued to dominate the town in the early seventeenth century, although only one brine-pit at Upwich and two in Netherwich remained in operation.[4] Town government and the salt industry were closely interconnected, as the corporation organized the trade. Shares were measured in the numbers of 'phats', or bullaries, of brine that an owner received yearly from the borough's officials, which were inherited like freehold land and could be bought and sold. The borough's freedom was generally acquired through the inheritance of bullaries, although the eldest son of a freeman was entitled to the freedom on reaching the age of 21, whether or not he had inherited. Moreover, freemen by inheritance could make their siblings and children burgesses by granting them a quarter of a bullary, and women who possessed the right to the freedom could confer the franchise on their husbands. Purchasers of bullaries could only become free with the unanimous consent of the corporation.[5]

A charter of 1554 revived the borough's representation in Parliament, which had lapsed in the fourteenth century. The franchise was placed in the hands of the freemen, who also elected two bailiffs annually. Together, the bailiffs and freemen ran the borough, although by the early seventeenth century an informal oligarchy had emerged, as the bailiffs tended to be drawn from a small clique of between six and eight freemen. A further charter granted in November 1624 gave the borough its own magistrates, and also appointed a recorder.[6] Participation at elections may have been limited. Although there were about 100 freemen in the early seventeenth century, only 28, including the two bailiffs, were parties to the 1620 return, and by 1628 the number had fallen to 16.[7]

During the sixteenth and seventeenth centuries a number of Worcestershire gentry and noble families acquired the freedom and became influential in borough affairs,[8] among them Sir John Pakington, 1st bt.*, who was party to the February 1621 indenture.[9] Gentry influence explains the outcome of a number of elections in this period. The Brace and Sandys families lived nearby and were influential in the borough, while Sir Thomas Coventry, who resided at Croome d'Abitot, in the south of the county, purchased several bullaries and was made a freeman. The Commons unseated Coventry on 8 Feb. 1621 after he had been appointed attorney-general, but he secured the election of his eldest son in 1625 and 1626.[10] Ralph Clare may have owed his election to his mother's family, the Sheldons, who owned bullaries in Droitwich. The most influential family at Droitwich were the Wyldes, whose members combined the town's freedom with legal eminence in London. They represented the borough in every Parliament except 1614, and in 1624 both John Wylde and his brother-in-law, Walter Blount, were returned. The Wyldes took both seats in 1628, when John was elected with his brother George, who had participated in the 1620 election.[11] The 1628 election was the only occasion when there is evidence of controversy, as 'an unfit letter' was brought to the attention of the Commons by one of the Wylde brothers on 4 April. The issue was apparently unresolved, and Wylde renewed his complaint on 28 Jan. 1629.[12]

[1] *CPR*, 1553-4, p. 404; T. Nash, *Collections for Hist. of Worcs.* i. 314. [2] Worcs. RO, BA1006/32b/452, is a late 16th or early 17th cent. list of c.100 freemen liable for the fee-farm and other taxes. [3] P. Clark and J. Hosking, *Population Estimates of English Small Towns* (Cent. for Urban Hist. Working Ppr. v), 165 [4] Nash, i. 298. [5] F.W. Large, 'Economic and Social Change in North Worcs.' (Univ. Oxf. D.Phil thesis, 1980), pp. 191-6. [6] *CPR*, 1553-4, pp. 402-4; Nash, i. 308-16; Large, 190, 197-8. [7] C219/37/315; C219/41B/30. [8] Large, 190, 196. [9] C219/37/306. [10] Large, 190, 201. [11] C219/37/315. [12] *CD 1628*, ii. 296; *CJ*, i. 923b.

G.R./B.C.

EVESHAM

Right of election: in the freemen[1]

Number of voters: 18 in 1605[2]

15 Mar. 1604	SIR THOMAS BIGG SIR PHILIP KIGHLEY ?Sir Francis Egioke[3]
31 Oct. 1605	ROBERT BOWYER *vice* Kighley, deceased
26 Feb. 1610	EDWARD SALTER *vice* Bowyer, appointed clerk of the Parliaments
1614	THOMAS BIGG ANTHONY LANGSTON
15 Dec. 1620	(SIR) THOMAS BIGG, (bt.) ANTHONY LANGSTON
5 July 1621[4]	SIR EDWARD CONWAY I *vice* Bigg, deceased
4 Feb. 1624	SIR EDWARD CONWAY I RICHARD CRESHELD, recorder
27 Apr. 1625	RICHARD CRESHELD, recorder ANTHONY LANGSTON
17 Jan. 1626[5]	SIR JOHN HARE ANTHONY LANGSTON
27 Feb. 1628	SIR ROBERT HARLEY RICHARD CRESHELD, recorder

Lying 15 miles south-east of Worcester, close to the borders with Gloucestershire and Warwickshire, Evesham grew up around Evesham Abbey. Though it sent representatives to Parliament in 1295 and 1337, it did not do so subsequently.[6] Lewis Bayly, the vicar of All Saints, Evesham, since 1600, was appointed chaplain to Henry, prince of Wales soon after James's accession,[7] so enabling the town to acquire its first royal charter, issued on 2 Mar. 1604. This restored the borough's parliamentary representation, vesting the franchise in the freemen, whose number is unknown, but the 1604 election took place under the unincorporated town government, since the new officers of the corporation had not yet been sworn. The parties to the indenture were the two bailiffs, who were confirmed in their offices in the charter, and 10 other inhabitants –presumably prominent freemen of the old municipality – of whom six were appointed aldermen in the new incorporation and one was made a capital burgess.[8]

The senior seat was bestowed on Sir Thomas Bigg, a prominent local landowner, while the second place went to Sir Philip Kighley, who had assisted Bayly in procuring the charter. However, according to Bayly, Sir Francis Egioke, 'affecting to be the other burgess', thereupon had Kighley indicted for riot. This suggests that there may have been a contest for the junior seat. Egioke was the brother of Kighley's deceased first wife, his trustee and a colleague in the Exchequer, and probably expected Kighley to support his candidacy. His anger suggests that Kighley supported Bigg, who was also connected to Kighley.[9]

The new charter was rapidly found to be inadequate and a second was issued in April 1605. In the new charter the town's government was vested in a common council of 21, consisting of seven aldermen, 12 capital burgesses, a recorder and a chamberlain, of whom one was to be mayor. The charter also appointed as high steward Sir Thomas Chaloner*, a Buckinghamshire man who, though he had no previous connection with Evesham, was governor to Prince Henry, so strengthening the connection between the prince's Household and the borough.[10]

In the same month as the new charter was issued Kighley died, thereby necessitating the holding of a by-election. Although the franchise continued to lie with all the freemen, the subsequent return states merely that Kighley's successor, Robert Bowyer, was elected by the mayor, aldermen and capital burgesses. Furthermore, all except one of the signatories to the return had been named to the common council in the 1605 charter. Bowyer seems to have been the nominee of Chaloner,[11] and when he was forced to relinquish his seat following his appointment as clerk of the Parliaments it was presumably Chaloner's influence which accounts for the election of Edward Salter, another member of the prince's Household, in 1610. On this occasion only members of the common council were parties to the indenture.[12]

By 1614 Prince Henry was dead; the borough returned two local men, Thomas Bigg and Anthony Langston, both of whom were re-elected in 1620. It was by now clear that the corporation had effectively taken control of the borough's parliamentary elections, for although the return reiterated the passage in the charter vesting the franchise in the burgesses and claimed that the election took place at a meeting of the mayor, aldermen and burgesses at the town hall, only members of the corporation were signatories to the return and the election was recorded in the minutes of the common council.[13] After Bigg died in June 1621 he was replaced by Sir Edward Conway

I, a rising soldier-diplomat from Ragley across the Warwickshire border. The election was held at a meeting of the common council in July, but Conway could not be formally returned until after the writ for Bigg's replacement was issued in November. Only eight parties were named in the return, the mayor, two aldermen and five capital burgesses, although 16 had been present at the July meeting.[14] Conway had been connected with Prince Henry and may have been elected through the influence of Bayly, who had been high steward since 1615.[15]

In February 1624 the corporation re-elected Conway and, for the first time, the recorder, Richard Cresheld, was also returned. From 1624 the returns do not name the parties and use the formula mayor, aldermen and burgesses in describing the election.[16] Conway became the borough's high steward in March 1625, at which time he was also raised to the peerage.[17] Unable by virtue of his ennoblement to stand for re-election the following month, Conway was replaced as senior Member by Cresheld, who was joined by Langston.

Although two local men were returned in 1625, this did not establish a pattern for the future. In 1626 a Norfolk gentleman, Sir John Hare, took the senior seat. Hare was the son-in-law of Sir Thomas Coventry*, the lord keeper, and though Coventry did not yet own property near the town, he was an important south Worcestershire landowner who had, in 1622, supported various members of the corporation against Cresheld when the latter stood for election as recorder.[18] Conway regained control of Evesham in 1628, when the corporation elected his nominee, Sir Robert Harley. At first the corporation wanted to re-elect Cresheld and Langston, but the elderly Langston was reluctant to serve again. The corporation's next choice was a Mr. Savage, but the latter's heavily pregnant wife opposed his election and Conway's agent was confident he could get the support of Cresheld and Langston for Harley.[19]

The Evesham Members may have been paid before 1620, when Langston and Bigg agreed to relinquish their salaries.[20] There is no evidence that the corporation promoted legislation in Parliament.

[1] G. May, *Descriptive Hist. of Town of Evesham*, 472. [2] Ibid. 280; C219/37/308 [3] E178/3832. [4] *Evesham Bor. Recs. of Seventeenth Cent.* ed. S.K. Roberts (Worcs. Hist. Soc. n.s. xiv), 23. The return is dated 8 November. OR. [5] *Evesham Bor. Recs.* 27. The return is dated 1 February. OR. [6] *VCH Worcs.* ii. 371-7. [7] O.G. Knapp 'Evesham Parsons', *N and Q Concerning Evesham and Four Shires* ed. E.A.B. Barnard, ii. 79; T. Birch, *Life of Henry Prince of Wales*, 455. [8] E178/3832; C2/Jas.I/A6/3; May, 279, 451-2. [9] E178/3832. [10] R. Strong, *Henry, Prince of Wales and England's Lost Renaissance*, 31.

[11] May, 280, 457, 472, 462; C219/35/2/136. [12] C219/35/2/134. [13] C219/37/317; *Evesham Bor. Recs.* xv, 22. [14] *Evesham Bor. Recs.* 23; C219/37/308. [15] Harl. 7002, f. 69. [16] C219/38/261; C219/39/245; C219/40/80; C219/41B/28. [17] *Evesham Bor. Recs.* 25. [18] *VCH Worcs.* ii. 413; SP14/134/74. [19] *Procs. 1628*, vi. 149; *CSP Dom.* 1627-8, pp. 562, 583. [20] *Evesham Bor. Recs.* 22.

B.C.

WORCESTER

Right of election: in the freemen

Number of voters: several hundred

2 Mar. 1604[1]	JOHN COUCHER
	CHRISTOPHER DIGHTON
10 Jan. 1605[2]	ROLAND BERKELEY (BARTLETT) *vice* Dighton, deceased
Mar. 1614[3]	THOMAS CHETTLE
	JOHN COUCHER
15 Dec. 1620	JOHN COUCHER
	ROBERT BERKELEY (BARTLETT), recorder
3 Feb. 1624	ROBERT BERKELEY (BARTLETT), recorder
	JOHN COUCHER, alderman
26 Apr. 1625	SIR WALTER DEVEREUX, bt.
	SIR HENRY SPELMAN
10 Jan. 1626[4]	JOHN SPELMAN
20 Jan. 1626[5]	JOHN HASELOCK
26 Feb. 1628[6]	JOHN COUCHER, alderman
	JOHN HASELOCK, alderman

An inland port, Worcester benefited from trade along the Severn between Shrewsbury and Bristol, and also acted as an *entrepot* for the pastoral Marcher counties and the arable west Midlands. It was also a centre of the cloth industry, producing high quality broadcloth, mostly for export, and as a cathedral city and county capital it was a significant administrative centre. Between the 1560s and 1640s the population rose from around 4,000 to about 8,000. In 1590 the clothiers, fullers and weavers were incorporated into a new united company, which played an important role in Worcester politics; four of the city's MPs were prominent members.[7]

At the beginning of the seventeenth century Worcester was governed in accordance with a charter it had been granted in 1555. At the centre of the corporation was the common council, usually called the chamber or convocation, consisting of a senior and junior branch, known as the Twenty-Four and Forty-Eight respectively. Vacancies were filled by co-option. Each year the chamber elected two bailiffs and two aldermen from the Twenty-Four who, together with the recorder, comprised the city bench. In addition two chamberlains, administered the corporation's finances.[8]

From the 1590s the corporation began lobbying for a new charter to extend its powers.[9] On 2 Mar. 1604 the chamber established a committee, including its newly elected Members, Christopher Dighton and John Coucher, to discuss 'the defects and imperfections in the charter of this city and to consider reducing this corporation to a mayoralty and certain number of aldermen and for enlarging the liberties'. Three weeks later the chamber agreed to lobby the king to make the city a county borough, and referred the matter to Roland Berkeley, who had been appointed to the earlier committee.[10] However the bishop of Worcester, fearing that the enlarged corporation would encroach on his powers, successfully opposed the city.[11] A new charter was eventually procured in 1616, but as it merely established a court of record and gave the justices the right of gaol delivery it made little difference to the government of the city. Consequently in January 1621 a new committee was established to campaign for an extension of their liberties.[12] This proved successful, for on 2 Oct. 1621 a new charter was issued which elevated the city to county status. Moreover a mayor replaced the bailiffs and the number of aldermen increased to six.[13]

The 1555 charter placed the franchise in the hands of the chamber, whose minutes record every election except that of 1624.[14] However under Elizabeth, in accordance with pre-charter practice, an assembly of freemen was called at the Guildhall to endorse the chamber's decision.[15] It is likely that elections continued to be conducted in this way during this period. This may explain why the 1605 and 1628 indentures bear dates later than the elections themselves. Both candidates were normally elected on the same day, but in 1626 Spelman and Haselock were chosen at two different meetings of the chamber, ten days apart. Before the 1621 charter, returns were made in the name of the bailiffs, aldermen, chamberlains and citizens of Worcester, although only the six officeholders were personally named.[16] Although the 1621 charter did not mention parliamentary elections, subsequent indentures took a different form. In 1625 14 people were named 'with many other persons'. Those named

included the mayor, three aldermen, six members of the Twenty-Four and at least two of the Forty-Eight, but one of the remaining parties, the city's attorney in the Common Pleas, was not a member of the chamber.[17] In 1628 24 parties are named, including the mayor, two aldermen, four members of the Twenty-Four and at least seven from the Forty-Eight. The others, including the sword-bearer, do not seem to have been members of the chamber. The post 1621 indentures perhaps made explicit the existing practice, namely that a wider group of citizens participated in elections, if only to rubber stamp the chamber's decision.[18]

In the Jacobean period Worcester retained the electoral independence that had been established in the late sixteenth century.[19] All its Members belonged to the corporation and were clothiers, except the recorder, Robert Berkeley, who owned property locally. The election of Berkeley in 1620 and 1624 established a precedent that the recorder had a right to a seat, and consequently the city temporarily lost its independence after the attorney-general Sir Thomas Coventry* was appointed recorder in 1624. Although Coventry was not eligible for election to the Commons, he clearly considered that he now exercised rights of patronage. In 1625 the city returned Sir Henry Spelman, a friend of Coventry's son-in-law, Sir John Hare*.[20] The following year Spelman's son John was elected at Coventry's request.[21] Coventry's influence may have created something of a backlash, for in 1625 the city returned Sir Walter Devereux, who had served for the country the previous year, suggesting that the chamber was seeking allies among the county gentry to counter-balance its recorder. A further factor which may have influenced the 1625 and 1626 elections was a dispute between the corporation and the foundation of the 'Six Masters', the governors of the free school and almshouses. The masters, who included the former Members John Coucher and Thomas Chettle, were appointed by the corporation, but in 1624 the chamber procured a commission of charitable uses to investigate the administration of certain bequests by the masters. The commission, whose members had been nominated by the chamber and included Sir Walter Devereux, concluded that the bequests should be administered directly by the corporation. The 'Six Masters' appealed, but in November 1626 the lord keeper, by this date Sir Thomas Coventry, ruled in favour of the chamber. This dispute may explain why Coucher was not elected in 1625 and 1626. On the latter occasion John Haselock, who had acted on behalf of the chamber in the dispute, was chosen instead.[22] There is no evidence that Coventry made a nomination in 1628, and the election of Haselock and Coucher together may have been a conscious attempt to mend the rift between the chamber and the six masters.

The corporation took an active interest in parliamentary proceedings, writing to Coucher in 1628 to thank him for keeping them up to date with his parliamentary activities as well as informing him of the disorders of locally billeted soldiers.[23] There is no evidence that the chamber sponsored any legislation, but in 1621 Coucher and Berkeley worked together to amend the bill for free trade in wool in the interests of Worcester's clothiers.[24] In 1606 Worcester weavers promoted a bill to confirm an order made by the justices of the assizes. This was intended to enforce provisions in a Henrician statute which fixed the rents of those working in the cloth industry in Worcester.[25] However rather than going through the city's Members the bill was introduced in the Lords on 19 February. It is possible that Coucher and Berkeley, who owned property in Worcester, did not support the bill. The Lords did not like it either and drew up another in its place, which would have empowered the lord chancellor to appoint a commission to fix the rents. This bill received its first reading on 13 May but proceeded no further.[26]

Members were paid at the rate of 2s. 6d. a day, and, as was usual in cases of Worcester's municipal expenditure, the costs were divided equally between the members of the chamber and the commoners of the city, on whom a fifteenth was levied.[27]

[1] Chamber Order Bk. of Worcester ed. S. Bond (Worcs. Hist. Soc. n.s. viii), 82. [2] 31 Dec. 1604 in bor. mins. Ibid. 87. [3] Ibid. 125. [4] Ibid. 202. [5] Ibid. 203. [6] 18 Feb. in bor. mins. Ibid. 222. [7] A.D. Dyer, City of Worcester in Sixteenth Cent. 26-7, 58-62, 93, 115. [8] CPR, 1554-5, pp. 81-6; Chamber Order Bk. of Worcester, 26. [9] Chamber Order Bk. of Worcester, 5. [10] Ibid. 83. [11] Ibid. 6-7. [12] Ibid. 8-9, 168. [13] V. Green, Hist. and Antiqs. of City and Suburbs of Worcester, ii. pp. lxxxi-xcvi; Chamber Order Bk. of Worcester, 12. [14] Chamber Order Bk. of Worcester, 82, 87, 125, 167, 196, 202, 222. [15] Dyer, 215-16; HP Commons 1558-1603, i. 279-80. [16] C219/35/2/132; C219/37/321. [17] C219/39/214; Chamber Order Bk. of Worcester, 54-67, 192-3. [18] C219/41B/32; Chamber Order Bk. of Worcester, 219, 54-67. [19] Dyer, 214. [20] Norf. RO, Hare 5633. [21] Chamber Order Bk. of Worcester, 202. In the bor. mins. 'Henry' is deleted and 'John' interlined. [22] Ibid. 41-2, 189, 190, 215-18; Dyer, 168-9. [23] CD 1628, ii. 402. [24] CJ, i. 552b (13 Mar.), 627b (26 May). [25] HMC Hatfield, xix. 487-8; J.S. Cockburn, History of English Assizes, 268; SR, iii. 459-60. [26] LJ, ii. 377, 392, 423, 431. [27] Chamber Order Bk. of Worcester, 49.

G.R./B.C.

YORKSHIRE

Number of voters: almost 7,000 in 1597

12 Mar. 1604[1]	FRANCIS CLIFFORD
	SIR JOHN SAVILE
7 Apr. 1606	SIR RICHARD GARGRAVE vice
	Clifford, called to the
	Upper House
28 Mar. 1614[2]	SIR JOHN SAVILE
	SIR THOMAS WENTWORTH
	Sir John Mallory*
25 Dec. 1620	(SIR) GEORGE CALVERT
	SIR THOMAS WENTWORTH, (bt.)
	Sir John Savile
	Sir Thomas Savile
19 Jan. 1624	SIR JOHN SAVILE
	SIR THOMAS SAVILE
9 May 1625[3]	SIR THOMAS WENTWORTH, (bt.)
	SIR THOMAS FAIRFAX I
	Sir John Savile
	?Sir Thomas Savile
1 Aug. 1625	SIR THOMAS WENTWORTH, (bt.)
	SIR THOMAS FAIRFAX I re-elected
	after being unseated on petition
	Sir John Savile
	?Sir Thomas Savile
16 Jan. 1626[4]	SIR JOHN SAVILE
	SIR WILLIAM CONSTABLE, bt.
	?Sir Francis Wortley*
by 12 Mar. 1628[5]	SIR THOMAS WENTWORTH, (bt.)
	HENRY BELASYSE
	Sir John Savile
	?Sir Thomas Savile
9 Feb. 1629	SIR HENRY SAVILE, (bt.) vice
	Wentworth, called to the
	Upper House
	?Sir Francis Wortley

The largest county in England, Yorkshire is a region of enormous topographical variety.[6] The early Stuart economy reflected this diversity, with the lowlands dominated by arable farming, the Wolds and the Ryedale given over to large-scale sheepwalks, and the dales in the Moors and northern Pennines used for cattle grazing.[7] The Aire and Calder valleys contained one of the country's fastest-growing cloth industries, while Richmond and Doncaster specialized in hand-knitted stockings,[8] and Sheffield in cutlery; meanwhile, coal and lead mining proliferated along the eastern fringes of the Pennines, and alum shale deposits were exploited on the Cleveland coast.[9] Yorkshire was fully integrated into both the national and international economy. York's access to the sea via the River Ouse made it a regional distribution centre,[10] while the West Riding clothing industry acquired its wool from across the north and north Midlands. Yorkshire cattle were sold in London, and their hides were returned north for tanning.[11] Cloth and lead were shipped to the Baltic and the Low Countries through Hull, and lead, grain and cutlery to London. In return came whale oil from the Arctic, grain, timber and iron from the Baltic, wine, salt and oil from France and Spain, finished goods from Amsterdam and London and coal and salt from Tyneside and Scotland.[12]

Administratively, Yorkshire was dominated by the lord president of the Council in the North, the county's *ex officio* lord lieutenant, who was assisted by a law court staffed by four judges, and a professional secretariat.[13] At a lower level, the county was divided into a multitude of overlapping jurisdictions: each of the three Ridings had a separate bench of justices, as did York, Hull and the three ecclesiastical liberties of Ripon, Cawood and Beverley. The ancient feudal lordships still retained some significance; most belonged to the Crown, except for the honour of Skipton, held by the Clifford family, and that of Holderness, held by the Constables of Burton Constable.[14] Geography shaped the administrative contours of the shire: the North Riding was customarily divided into three parts covering the Pennines, the Vale of York and the Moors, while in the West Riding each of the dales was run by a different group of gentry. Despite this fragmentation, York remained the focal point of county society, both because of its economic significance, and also because it was the seat of a multiplicity of administrative and judicial bodies: the Council in the North, ecclesiastical courts for the diocese and archdiocese of York, an Admiralty Court, the assizes and (usually) the county gaol.[15]

The shock waves of the Reformation reverberated longer in Yorkshire than in most counties. Except at Hull and Beverley, Protestantism struck few deep roots before the Northern Rising of 1569, but by the end of the century the corporations of Doncaster, Halifax, Leeds, and York had acquired godly reputations, although many rural areas still lacked access to a preaching ministry.[16] Recusancy and occasional conformity remained a serious problem at the end of Elizabeth's reign,[17] notwithstanding the efforts of a small but energetic group including (Sir) John Ferne*, Sir Thomas Hoby* and John Thornborough, dean of York, who harried the political unreliable during the 1590s.[18] There were fewer problems with Protestant nonconformity, partly because of official connivance. Archbishop Neile's rigorous enforcement of conformity drove Sir William Constable*, Sir Matthew Boynton* and Sir Richard Saltonstall into exile in the 1630s, but long before this there was plenty of evidence of both puritanism and outright heterodoxy: Dr. John Favour ran a clerical exercise at Halifax; Hoby and (somewhat later) Boynton provided patronage for ejected ministers; Sir John Savile's chaplain, James Nutter, twice fell foul of the authorities, while one of his parishoners, James Nayler, went on to become a leading Quaker in the 1650s; and there were separatist conventicles in Craven and Cleveland.[19]

I. Yorkshire's Electoral Geography

Despite its size, Yorkshire returned only two knights of the shire before 1820. However, aspiring MPs could look to the county's 11 borough constituencies (12 from 1621), as well as to East Retford, in Nottinghamshire, Clitheroe in Lancashire and Appleby in Westmorland. Perhaps for this reason there was only one known contest for the shire under Elizabeth, in 1597. However, this situation changed abruptly following the accession of James I. One reason for this was electoral geography: the southern part of the West Riding, where many of the wealthiest gentry lived, had no parliamentary boroughs until the enfranchisement of Pontefract in 1621, and the majority of candidates for the shire seats came from this area throughout the early modern period.[20] Hence it was no accident that rivalry among the West Riding elites played a major part in the eight contested elections between 1597 and 1629. Another factor in the growth of electoral controversy was the personality of the lord president, who was generally reluctant to allow factional disputes to boil over at election time, for the sake of public order as much as for political reasons. Vice-president Sir Thomas Gargrave[†] and lord president Huntingdon had kept a tight rein on the county elections for much of Elizabeth's reign, but thereafter electoral disputes occurred in 1597, in 1614 and repeatedly throughout the 1620s, during the incumbency of the often ineffectual Lord Scrope.[21] A third factor prompting some to contest elections was the prestige which the knighthood of the shire conferred, particularly upon rising families or newcomers to the shire. Sir Thomas Hoby was an ambitious newcomer looking to prove himself in 1597; Wentworth aspired to favour at Court in return for securing the election of secretary of state

(Sir) George Calvert* in 1620; Henry Belasyse's transfer from Thirsk in 1626 to the county in 1628 reflected his father's recent elevation to the peerage; while Sir Henry Savile* may have felt that his defeat of Wentworth's candidate in 1629 repaid the latter for his failure to help him find him a borough seat in December 1620.[22]

As no individual wielded a preponderant influence in any one of Yorkshire's three Ridings, let alone throughout the shire, candidates for the county seat were obliged to construct a coalition from among their relatives, friends and neighbours, a complex task even in the absence of a contest. The individual best placed to do this was the lord president, who was accustomed to playing local factions off against each other. Lord Sheffield went to considerable lengths to arrange an uncontested election in 1604, and Scrope made an abortive attempt to impose his own candidates when an election was called in November 1620.[23] Several extended family networks could combine their forces to produce an impressive turnout at the hustings. These included the Cliffords, Wentworths and Saviles of Thornhill, whose West Riding tenants formed the core of Sir Thomas Wentworth's support throughout the 1620s; the Constables of Burton Constable and Fairfaxes of Gilling, who held over 60,000 acres in the East and North Ridings; and the Belasyses, Cholmleys and Fairfaxes of Denton, whose estates were less extensive than those of the other two affinities, but lay (for the most part) much closer to York. Aspiring candidates could also seek the support of the shire's many noble landowners. Lords Sheffield and Scrope had private estates in Cleveland and the Wensleydale respectively, while lords Darcy and Eure held lands in the Vales of York and Pickering. There were also three absentee magnates with substantial Yorkshire estates: the earls of Rutland, with estates at Helmsley; Gilbert Talbot[†], 7th earl of Shrewsbury and (after his death in 1616) his sons-in-law the earls of Arundel and Pembroke, who held the manor of Sheffield; and (at least in theory) the disgraced 9th earl of Northumberland, who owned a dozen manors in the North and East Ridings.[24]

The only key electoral player in Yorkshire who was unable to rely upon an extended family network, aristocratic or official support was Sir John Savile, whose estate of 5,000 acres in the Leeds area was unremarkable by Yorkshire standards. His influence was grounded upon his tenure as steward of the duchy of Lancaster honour of Wakefield, which he took over from his father-in-law, Sir Edward Carey[†], in 1588. This jurisdiction covered much of the hinterland of Halifax and Huddersfield, two of the most rapidly expanding cloth manufacturing districts in the West Riding, where Savile earned substantial goodwill by enfranchising large numbers of copyhold tenants at nominal rents. He reinforced the loyalty of this quasi-feudal following by maintaining cordial relations with the influential puritan clergy of the area, and by his vigorous advocacy of the clothiers' economic interests at Court, in the law courts and in Parliament.[25] Substantial as his personal following was, it is worth noting that Savile's most notable electoral successes, in 1597 and 1614, were achieved with the assistance of the earl of Shrewsbury and influential gentry allies; Wentworth's skill in co-opting the gentry vote during the 1620s caused Savile immense problems which he never entirely solved.

II. Electoral History to 1614

Savile's early interests and much of his landed inheritance lay in Lincolnshire, where he served as sheriff in 1590-1. Later in the decade, however, he built up his influence in Yorkshire, and in 1597 he picked a fight with Sir John Stanhope I* and Sir Thomas Hoby over the county seats, almost certainly at the behest of Stanhope's enemy, the 7th earl of Shrewsbury. Stanhope was backed by Archbishop Hutton (acting head of the Council in the North), Lords Cumberland, Darcy and Scrope, 86 gentry and an estimated 3,000 freeholders. However, Savile, whose supporters were dismissed as 'a few gentlemen and a great multitude of clothiers, woolmen and other freeholders of the West Riding', carried the day with the assistance of Shrewsbury's tenants and four of the county's greatest gentry: Sir William Fairfax[†] of Gilling (with whom he paired on the morning of the election), Sir Richard Mauleverer, William Wentworth and Richard Gargrave*. This upset provoked a flurry of anguished protests, both from the supporters of the defeated parties and from the leading dignitaries of the Council in the North, who had been prepared to abandon Hoby and concede the junior seat to Savile, but pronounced themselves 'much grieved that Sir John Savile should think to prefer himself and others in this way, and still more that he should express publicly against Sir John Stanhope, born in this country, *custos rotulorum* of the North Riding and a large landowner, that he is uncapable to election'.[26] Savile's efforts availed him little at the time: Fairfax died a week into the session, and Savile later recalled that he was 'taken at the bar, coming into the House [of Commons], and was brought to the [Privy] Council Chamber and therein committed' to the Fleet prison for three weeks.[27] However, his achievement in defeating candidates backed by both the Council in the North and the overwhelming majority of the gentry overshadowed the shire's electoral politics for the next 30 years.

The 1601 election seems to have passed without incident, with lord president Burghley (Thomas Cecil[†]) securing the apparently uncontested return of his vice-president, Sir Thomas Fairfax I*, and Sir Edward Stanhope[†]; the election indenture was a roll-call of those who had supported the Stanhope-Hoby ticket four years earlier.[28] When the writs for James's first Parliament were sent out in February 1604, Lord Sheffield, who had succeeded to the presidency only seven months previously, looked to achieve a compromise with a circular letter recommending two candidates he described as 'persons against whom no exceptions can be made': the former Stanhope supporter Francis Clifford, heir to the earldom of Cumberland, and Sir John Savile. Furthermore, Sheffield avoided controversy by offering no suggestions as to which man should be given precedence. To the palpable relief of all, this question was resolved on the eve of the election, when Savile informed the Council that

> he then was well contented that in the indentures Mr. Clifford should be first set down, and himself for the second, howsoever the freeholders should be affected towards him. … And upon the election, he being carried upon the freeholders' shoulders, cried himself, "a Clifford", and with that cry went to Mr. Clifford's company, and so went they to the [York Castle] hall to have the indentures for that election sealed, still crying, "a Savile, a Savile".[29]

Clifford's seat fell vacant when he succeeded his brother as 4th earl of Cumberland in October 1605. It was nearly six months before a by-election was held, a delay which, intentionally or otherwise, ensured the eligibility of the man returned, Sir Richard Gargrave, who only completed his term of office as sheriff in February 1606. The list of attestors on the indenture suggests that ill-feeling generated by the 1597 election had finally subsided: Gargrave had supported Savile on the former occasion, but in 1606 the sheriff was Archbishop Hutton's son Sir Timothy, and the return was witnessed by the erstwhile Stanhope supporters Sir Henry Jenkins*, Sir Conyers Darcy and Christopher Constable as well as Savile adherents such as Sir John Jackson[†], Sir Thomas Bland and John Mauleverer.[30]

By 1614 Gargrave's profligacy had obliged him to alienate many of his estates, and he was no longer a plausible candidate for the knighthood of the shire.[31] Sir George Savile[†], then sheriff, was probably the moving force behind the nomination of his great-

nephew Sir Thomas Wentworth, the 21-year-old heir to the Wentworth Woodhouse estate, whose candidacy was apparently endorsed by Sir John Savile, who proposed to stand again. However, at the county court Wentworth was challenged by a man almost 40 years his senior, Sir John Mallory* of Studley Royal, a member of the Council in the North, whose father had represented the shire in 1584. Mallory naturally commanded the support of his immediate neighbours such as William Aldeburghe*, the mayor of Ripon and the crypto-Catholic Thomas Tankard, but he also won over the Fairfaxes of Denton, their cousins the Belasyses of Coxwold, and even Christopher Wandesford*, the only occasion on which the latter is known to have opposed his future patron. Furthermore, presumably with the backing of his brother-in-law Ralph, 3rd Baron Eure[†], Mallory managed to assemble an impressive coalition of East Riding families including Sir William Constable, 1st bt.*, the recusant Sir Henry Constable, John Hotham* and John Legard*. The election was clearly a tumultuous affair, with the sheriff drowning out Mallory's supporters 'by sounding of trumpets and other practices' to ensure the return of his candidates. At the start of the parliamentary session Mallory submitted a petition 'about the election of the knights of the shire'. This was 'respited till Sir John Savile's coming up' and nothing further was heard of the complaint during the session.[32]

III. The Election of December 1620

By the time the writs for the next Parliament were sent out in November 1620, the political landscape of Yorkshire had undergone considerable changes. Savile had been ordered to resign as *custos rotulorum* of the West Riding in December 1615, following a Star Chamber case in which one of his neighbours accused him of abusing his powers as a justice.[33] He was replaced by Wentworth, who had just succeeded his father and was apparently intended to have been a temporary substitute. To Savile's undoubted dismay, Wentworth was confirmed in office when he declined to resign the position two years later.[34] The presidency of the Council in the North also changed hands in January 1619, when Sheffield, an associate of the 3rd earl of Southampton and a supporter of a Protestant foreign policy, was removed at the behest of the Spanish ambassador, Gondomar. His replacement, Lord Scrope, was well known for his Catholic sympathies, which recommended him to the advocates of a Spanish Match at Court, but hardly suited the ethos of an institution which had consistently championed the fight against recusancy since the Northern Rising.[35]

These local upheavals explain why Scrope felt able to ignore Savile's inherent claim to one of the Yorkshire seats in November 1620. He recommended a pairing between his vice-president, Sir Thomas Fairfax II*, and Secretary of State Sir George Calvert, one of the keenest proponents of the Spanish Match, who had recently purchased a small estate at Kiplin in the North Riding but had virtually no personal influence within the shire. While Savile did not declare formally his candidacy for some weeks, he signalled his intentions by announcing 'that he will be at York the day of the election', and it quickly became apparent that Fairfax, son of Savile's partner in 1597, was reluctant to pick a fight with such a redoutable adversary. At this point Wentworth, who was keen to boost his standing at Court, and could hardly afford to have Savile questioning his conduct as *custos* in Parliament, clamoured to be allowed to take up the challenge. The issue was swiftly resolved when Wentworth sent Sir Peter Middleton to Fairfax, who willingly resigned his interest in the county election in favour of a seat at Hedon, a borough dominated by his brother-in-law, Sir Henry Constable, Viscount Dunbar.[36]

Wentworth's first move was to secure control of the election writ, which was brought down from London by his cousin George Radcliffe*. Unhappily, the only county court day before the Parliament was due to convene fell upon 25 Dec., and despite consulting the judges over the possibility of an adjournment, Wentworth was obliged to ask his supporters to 'eat a Christmas pie with me' at York. Although his pairing with Calvert was a naked bid for preferment at Court, custom required him to present himself as a disinterested patriot:

> In truth, I do not desire it [a seat] out of any ambition, but rather to satisfy some of my best friends and such as have most power over me. Yet if the country make choice of me, surely I will zealously perform the best service for them that my means or understanding shall enable me unto.

Wentworth gave the lie to this false modesty by his willingness to use Calvert's influence to further his cause. He pressed his partner to secure a Privy Council letter (along the lines of the one used at Middlesex in 1614) advising Savile to stand aside, and warned Scrope that 'if this old veteran [Savile] should carry it against Mr. Secretary (without whom neither will I be [elected]) it were some touch to our own estimations above'. Sir Henry Belasyse (1st bt.)[†] was informed that 'in my next letters I will ... let Mr. Secretary know your good respect and kindness towards him' (an undertaking Wentworth apparently failed to keep),

while the York alderman (Sir) Robert Askwith* was promised an introduction to Calvert when he came up to London.[37]

Wentworth's campaign followed the conventional tactic of seeking the maximum turnout among the tenantry of the shire's greatest landowners. He confidently relied on his friend Christopher Wandesford to mobilize the Swaledale, and on Lord Darcy and Sir Richard Cholmley to do likewise in the Vale of York and Whitby Strand, but in other areas of the North and East Ridings, where his personal influence was slight, he was obliged to appeal to more distant acquaintances. Bishop Neile of Durham provided him with a letter of recommendation which was presumably aimed at episcopal tenants in Allertonshire and Howdenshire. Scrope's secretary, George Wetherid*, was urged to ensure the support of his master's tenants in the Wensleydale and those of the earl of Rutland at Helmsley, and asked to procure a letter from Scrope to Sir Thomas Fairfax II and Sir Henry Constable, 'that they will labour their friends and further our elections' in the Vale of York and Holderness. Sir Henry Belasyse mobilized the Vale of Pickering, while Sir Matthew Boynton was flattered into acting on Wentworth's behalf in the Flamborough area by the latter's reference to a fictitious 'ancient and near acquaintance' of their two families.[38]

However much Wentworth canvassed for voices in the North and East Ridings, the precedent of 1597 suggested that Savile might still carry the day if he managed turn out the West Riding clothiers in sufficient numbers. Consequently it was this area which became the main battleground between the two men. Wentworth promised Calvert 'a thousand voices of my own besides my friends', and began by securing the support of his immediate neighbours at the southern end of the West Riding in Strafforth, Osgoodcross and Staincross wapentakes. He also took considerable pains to mobilize the Hallamshire tenants of the earls of Pembroke and Arundel, and the freeholders of the honour of Pontefract, where Pembroke had succeeded Shrewsbury as steward in 1619. Further north, Wentworth could count upon the Clifford interest in Craven, while in Claro wapentake and Knaresborough liberty he used Sir Henry Slingsby* to further his cause; in Skyrack wapentake he looked to Sir Thomas Fairfax I, Sir Henry Savile and (Sir) Arthur Ingram*. Even in the heart of the clothing district, Wentworth took the fight to his opponent with the aid of Samuel Casson, deputy steward of the manor of Leeds Kirkgate, and two local landowners, Sir Richard Beaumont* and Sir John Ramsden*.[39]

Savile's campaign is more difficult to reconstruct, as almost none of his correspondence survives. He kept his opponents guessing about his intentions for several weeks, and when he finally declared himself, it was upon the unlikely pretext that he 'had received three hundred letters in two days from gentlemen of worth to move him to stand for one at the election'. In fact, it is very difficult to identify more than a handful of gentry who supported him: he was almost certainly backed by William Mallory*, and probably by Sir Thomas Bamburgh, Sir Robert Monson*, Sir John Jackson and Richard Darley*, whose names headed his return in 1624. However, his key supporters, who signed the petition against the election of Wentworth and Calvert which was submitted to the committee for privileges in February 1621, were almost exclusively West Riding clothiers, leavened by only a few clothier-gentry such as John Kaye and Gregory Armytage.[40] Thus it is not surprising that early in the campaign Sir Henry Savile, one of Wentworth's staunchest supporters, believed that 'when he [Savile] shall well understand his friends' and neighbours' engagements he will think it more wisdom and safety for his reputation to go to his grave with that honour the country hath already cast upon him than to hazard the loss of all at a farewell'.[41] Savile confounded such expectations by staking his chances almost exclusively upon a direct appeal to the freeholders, which he disseminated through his friends among the clothiers, and clerics such as Dr. John Favour, vicar of Halifax. He made great play of the fact that Calvert was not resident within the shire, and thus technically disqualified under a statute of 1413, and may also have insinuated that the ruling of 1614 excluding the attorney-general from the Commons extended to other government officials. Moreover, having been detained at the end of the Addled Parliament, he was able to present himself to the freeholders as 'their martyr, having suffered for them, the patron of the clothiers, of all others the fittest to be relied upon'.[42]

Wentworth treated his adversary's efforts with the utmost seriousness. Following Savile's attacks on Calvert for his pro-Spanish sympathies, and for the slightness of his connections with the county, Wentworth circulated a detailed refutation of these charges among the high constables of the West Riding. Never one to shrink from a confrontation, Wentworth also visited Halifax in a fruitless attempt to win over Daniel Foxcroft, one of Savile's key supporters.[43] Two weeks before the election, when it seemed that Savile would only contest the senior seat, Wentworth planned to face his adversary in a poll, but then to reverse the order of precedence and have Calvert's name entered first on the indenture.[44] Wentworth also sought to ensure the maximum turnout among his own supporters, requesting the high constables to ask the parish constables to draw up lists of freeholders who intended to vote for him, on the disingenuous grounds that 'we may keep the note as a testimony of their good affections and know whom we are beholden unto'; it would also have allowed him to identify those who had betrayed him at a poll.[45] Finally, Wentworth mustered his supporters at Tadcaster on the eve of the election and led them into York in a body to impress waverers, while he warned Sir Richard Beaumont, who planned to spend the night in York, to ensure that 'there be no working underhand with your freeholders'.[46]

Election day was, inevitably, a confused and controversial affair. As in 1597, Savile appears to have surprised his opponents by making a last-minute pairing with his son, Sir Thomas*, which rendered Wentworth's plans to secure an unopposed election for Calvert worthless.[47] The election seems to have been decided by the sheriff's decision to shut the gates of York Castle before all of Savile's supporters had entered: if testimony from both sides is to be believed, only a few hundred Savile supporters were present in the castle yard, while over a thousand more clamoured for admission outside the gates.[48] The Saviles subsequently raised a petition against the election, which was signed by 362 freeholders and claimed the support of 'many hundreds more', while Wentworth's allies spread a countervailing rumour 'that the said complaints hath rather proceeded from some particular differences of some private persons than for any general grievance'.[49]

The committee for privileges heard evidence about the election on 6 and 8 Feb. 1621. Both Calvert and Wentworth had powerful friends on the committee, and only Mallory, who still resented Wentworth's defeat of his father in 1614, advocated overturning the result.[50] The House took a more serious view of the charge of labouring for voices, which turned on the semantic issue of whether Wentworth had instructed the high constables either to 'entreat and request' or to 'will and require' the freeholders to give their voices for Calvert and Wentworth. A canny political operator such as Wentworth was never likely to have left such a hostage to fortune in writing, and two of the constables, George Shilleto* and Walter Stanhope, produced copies of the offending letter which exonerated Wentworth.[51] It eventually emerged that two other constables had exceeded their remit by sending out warrants to their petty constables in the usual form to 'will and require' the freeholders to attend and give their voices for Wentworth. After a heated debate, 'the voice and dislike of each party crying down and hindering the speech of those that were of another opinion', it was these constables who became scapegoats for the whole affair, being required to make a public submission both before the Commons and also at the next West Riding quarter sessions.[52]

IV. Elections of 1624-6

Wentworth appeared to be on the verge of a break-through at Court in July 1622, when he was mentioned as a contender for the comptrollership of the House-hold, but over the next two years he lost his wife, his health and his putative career to repeated outbreaks of tertian fever. Still recuperating when the next Parliament was summoned, in January 1624, he contented himself with a seat at Pontefract. This left the Saviles with a clear run at the shire seats, although Wentworth recorded a brief alarm on the eve of the election, 'upon a sudden noise in the country of an intention in some to have elected persons suspected in religion, which to us all would have been full of danger and scandal'. On the eve of a Parliament which was intended to over-turn the Spanish Match and lead the country into the confessional conflict then raging on the Continent, even Wentworth claimed to be prepared to turn out on behalf of his old adversary, whose 'soundness in religion' he freely acknowledged. The identity of the potential challengers is not known; it is possible that Scrope attempted to promote Sir Thomas Fairfax II and Sir Thomas Belasyse*, both of whom had Catho-lic wives, as official candidates.[53] The crisis blew over as quickly as it had arisen, and the most notable feature of the county court was the conspicuous absence of the greater gentry, who followed Wentworth's example in staying at home: of the 30 men who attested Went-worth's return in 1620 only one, Sir Peter Middleton, also signed the Saviles' in 1624.[54]

The death of King James in March 1625 was quickly followed by writs for a fresh Parliament. Savile, who had undoubtedly enhanced his local reputation by his opposition to war with Spain in the 1624 session, was the obvious candidate for the shire, leaving Wentworth pondering 'how to set my cards upon this new shuffle of the pack'. Having arranged to discuss tactics with Wandesford and Sir Francis Trappes at the militia musters for Claro wapentake on 12 Apr., Wentworth changed his mind and took horse for London, where he assessed the altered balance of power at Court. Before leaving he instructed Trappes, Sir Peter Middleton and Sir John Jackson* to canvass privately for him as senior knight among their friends, and 'not to engage themselves anywhere else till they hear

further'. However, he kept his options open, asking the mayor of Pontefract for one of the borough's seats in case he failed to be returned for the shire.[55]

With Wentworth's intentions still unclear, two other contenders, Sir Thomas Fairfax I and William Mallory, joined forces to challenge the Saviles. The source of Fairfax's opposition to Savile, a leading opponent of war in the 1624 session, is easily surmised. Fairfax was one of the few Yorkshire gentry who was unequivocally in favour of a continental war, having volunteered to help defend the Palatinate in 1620, while in 1624 he had petitioned James to raise an army to assist in the defence of the Low Countries. Mallory's motivation is more difficult to compre-hend: a supporter, like Savile, of the anti-war stance in the 1624 session, he may have felt that Savile was too willing to abandon his principles in pursuit of favour at Court. Savile directed his main effort against Mallory, using his chaplain, James Nutter, to savage his rival's reputation by circulating 'scandalous and seditious letters' accusing Mallory of Catholic sympa-thies. Fairfax was confident that his partner would 'most substantially acquit himself of the guilt, for he doth daily make good testimony of his sincerity', but the smear was effective because it was founded upon the truth: Mallory's mother had recently been indicted for recusancy by the York High Commission, one of his brothers was a Catholic exile, and he was first cousin to William, 4th Baron Eure[†], a recusant convict, half of whose fines he had been granted in 1619.[56] As Fairfax justifiably complained to Scrope, 'they [the Saviles] will no doubt accumulate such a multitude of people in those well disposed towns of trades as they will be powerful. Neither can the falsehood of the suggestions [against Mallory] appear, for at the day of elections shouts, not reasons, must be heard'.[57]

Meanwhile Wentworth, having resolved to stand against Savile during his sojourn in London, returned to Yorkshire at the end of April to find that he was facing not one but two pairs of rivals. He also had to respond to Savile's mischievous allegation that the findings of the recent inquisition *post mortem* into the lands of Sir George Savile had lost him control of the Thornhill estate, which he held as guardian to his underage nephews, George and William Savile[†]. These problems aside, he now concentrated on the further reaches of the county. Having been endorsed by Lord Henry Clifford*, he wrote to the latter's steward at Skipton, and asked George Boteler* to go to Londesborough to solicit the support of Clif-ford's father, the 4th earl of Cumberland. Boteler and Sir John Hotham were then delegated to canvass the

East Riding and Henry Stapleton the Ainsty, while the steward of the 9th earl of Northumberland was approached for the voices of the Percy tenants in the North and East Ridings. Despite his exertions, Wentworth's candidacy was undoubtedly hampered by lack of preparation, and by his status as a single candidate facing two rival pairs. He was saved by Mallory's decision to accept the offer of a burgess-ship from his neighbours at Ripon on 3 May. Three days later Mallory asked Sir Francis Trappes to ensure that 'Sir Thomas Fairfax may be joined to some worthy gentleman, which I leave to be considered of amongst friends'. As Trappes was Wentworth's uncle, the identity of Fairfax's new partner was a foregone conclusion.[58]

Even with this new infusion of strength, Wentworth could hardly have been assured of victory at the county court without the connivance of the sheriff, Sir Richard Cholmley. The latter acceded to a request for a poll from the Savile supporter Sir Christopher Hildyard*, but had only tallied 35 voices when he learned that the gate of the castle yard had been broken open 'and many freeholders gone out upon Sir John Savile's persuasions that the taking of the poll would last many days'. Cholmley abandoned the poll and declared Wentworth and Fairfax elected, both of whom, he subsequently claimed, had 'double the number of freeholders' mustered by the Saviles. The dispute was further complicated by controversies over whether (as in 1620) some of Savile's supporters had been shut out of the castle yard, and whether the poll had been demanded before eleven o'clock, as the statute required.[59]

Wentworth and his allies tacitly conceded the weakness of their cause by doing everything in their power to delay judgment when the issue came before the Commons. On 21 June, the first day of business in the new session, Mallory and Wentworth responded to Sir Edward Giles's submission of a petition on Savile's behalf by moving 'to adjourn till Michaelmas, in respect of the plague', while Sir Robert Phelips and Wandesford suggested 'an adjournment to another place'. The House shrugged off what one diarist called an 'untimely motion', and Savile's petition was expedited by the committee for privileges. Sir George More's report on 4 July accepted Wentworth's claim that the blame for any misconduct at the election lay entirely with Sheriff Cholmley, but the latter sought to delay the proceedings by asking for permission to summon witnesses. The committee refused this request by 17 votes to 25, but the question was reopened on the floor of the House by Sir

Edward Coke and a northern chorus: Wentworth, Hoby, Wandesford and John Lowther I. Eventually, at Coke's suggestion, a compromise was agreed whereby Wentworth, Fairfax and Cholmley were to set down their version of events; if Savile verified their claims the case was to proceed to judgment, otherwise witnesses were to be called. Savile wrong-footed his rivals by accepting their account without demur on the following day, which, as (Sir) John Eliot* later recalled, 'although desired, was no satisfaction unto Wentworth, who came unwillingly so near the determination of the question'. Clearly flustered, Wentworth renewed his call for counsel and witnesses, but the House disapproved of such a transparently self-serving motion, rejecting it by 133 votes to 94 and ordering a warrant for a new election.[60]

Wentworth's first instinct was to play for time by asking lord keeper Williams to delay the issue of the election writ. The failure of this gambit left him with the gargantuan task of mobilizing his supporters in Yorkshire in little over two weeks, a prospect which was not assisted by Fairfax's apparent apathy: having written to his partner on 16 July, Wentworth had heard nothing in return nine days later. As hitherto, Wentworth looked to the earls of Cumberland, Arundel and Pembroke for support in Craven and Hallamshire, while he secured Viscount Dunbar's backing by means of a letter from Williams. He encountered some trouble from his neighbour Sir Francis Wortley*, who canvassed for him but refused to back Fairfax, but his chief concern was the fear that Savile would sow confusion among his supporters by laying the blame for the overturning of the earlier election at his door. In his letter to Fairfax on 16 July, he proposed to counter this accusation at two levels: to the gentry he offered the consideration that 'the whole kingdom looks not only whether Sir John [Savile] be able to carry it against you and me, but indeed against all the gentlemen too besides'; while lower down the social scale, he advocated that

> The other freeholders should, by some fit instruments, be let to understand that they have reason to stand to the first election, by reason we were put forth by a faction for serving them honestly and boldly; the little cause they have to choose Sir John, that did so apparently wrong them by bringing in apprentices and such as had not voice, much to their danger and prejudice, and that since hath been the author of putting the country to this second trouble.

At a practical level, Wentworth arranged to provide two hogsheads of wine and 10 of beer at York Castle 'for the freeholders, who will be forced to stay long, to refresh themselves with this hot season'. This precaution proved to be wise, as Cholmley was obliged to hold a 'tedious and troublesome polling' before declaring Wentworth and Fairfax returned.[61]

Wentworth's efforts earned him just four days service in the Commons before the Parliament was dissolved. During that time he managed to damage his standing at Court by refusing to add to the existing grant of two subsidies, a stance which proved sufficient to have him pricked as sheriff in November.[62] This excluded him from the Parliament summoned to meet in the following February, but in the event it allowed him to play a pivotal role in the county election of January 1626. Despite misgivings, he was unable to resist the opportunity to make trouble for his old adversary when Wandesford proposed to mount a challenge to the Saviles in conjunction with Fairfax's son-in-law Sir William Constable:

> I [Wentworth] ... find in my judgment Sir John Savile stronger than formerly, for besides his own number ... it will be impossible to draw so great a part from him out of this country, nay I fear not possible to keep them at home .... Yet I confess I wish old [Savile of] Howley were put to it, so it were not at your cost.

Having himself been approached about the county election by his neighbour Sir Francis Wortley, who had come to blows with Sir Thomas Savile a few days after the 1625 election, Wentworth advised Wandesford to content himself with a borough seat at Richmond, allowing Wortley to join Constable in opposition to the Saviles,

> for I foresaw if he [Wortley] gained it, Savile were lost forever, and if he failed, the other got no conquest much to brag of; besides, being his countryman, these parts would be more easily drawn with him than with a stranger, and consequently more weaken the old fox in his earth than any other I can think of.

Wentworth's assessment of Savile's growing strength in the West Riding was borne out only a few weeks later, when Sir Henry Savile, who had enthusiastically supported Wentworth in 1620, declared for Sir John Savile, on the grounds that the latter's patronage had done a great deal for Leeds. Wentworth ironically observed that 'the supremacy of Agbrigg and Morley[63] will scorn to have any partners in an election of knights for the shire', and offered his erstwhile supporter the glib assurance that 'you frame imagination of an opposition, whereof there is little ground'. The duplicity of this statement must have been obvious to Sir Henry, but Wentworth's conciliatory tone was probably intended to suggest that he was not entirely

committed to the Constable-Wortley ticket, and left room for a deal to avoid a repetition of the events of the previous year, in which the sheriff's intervention had robbed the Saviles of victory. The issue was ultimately resolved 'at the very hour of the election', when Sir Thomas Savile found himself 'surprised with a sudden sickness which enforced me to keep to my chamber and to resign my interest in that business to another'. This well-timed indisposition allowed Sir John Savile to ensure his own election by conceding the junior seat to his rival, Constable, an arrangement that left only Wortley without a seat.[64]

V. The Forced Loan and the Elections of 1628-9

In the 18 months which elapsed before the next election, local and national politics intermeshed to an unprecedented degree as Wentworth, Savile and their respective allies vied with each other for the confidence of the Court while striving to retain that of their countrymen. Savile secured a two-thirds' reduction in the Privy Seal loans charged upon Yorkshire in April 1626, but lost face when criticisms of the Commons' attacks on Buckingham, which he had made in a letter to the West Riding clothiers, came to light in the following month.[65] After the Parliament was dissolved on 15 June, Savile was named to the Privy Council, and at the summer assizes he displaced his rival as *custos* of the West Riding. Moreover, at his behest, Sir William Alford* succeeded Sir William Constable as *custos* in the East and Sir David Foulis replaced Sir Thomas Hoby in the North.[66] Savile helped alleviate the Crown's financial problems by inaugurating a scheme to allow recusants to compound for their fines, while his implementation of the Forced Loan in 1626-7 pushed Constable, Sir John Hotham and (rather more reluctantly) Wentworth into defiance, arrest and, ultimately, internal exile.[67] Meanwhile, the Belasyses and Fairfaxes of Denton, who might also have refused the Loan, were brought to acquiescence with timely offers of peerages, while Viscount Dunbar was offered the leading role in East Riding politics which he had hitherto been denied because of his Catholicism.

At a time when Savile had, to all intents, succeeded Scrope in charge of the north of England, those who refused to co-operate with him could only pin their hopes upon a fresh Parliament, a prospect which came closer after the failure of the expedition to the Île de Ré in the autumn of 1627. In November Wandesford discussed the issue with Mallory, who insisted that Wentworth was the only man to challenge Savile, and suggested a pairing with Henry Belasyse, heir to the recently ennobled Lord Fauconberg (Sir Thomas Belasyse). As Mallory saw it, the only problem with this arrangement was the possibility that Belasyse, as a peer's son, might demand the senior seat. Wandesford hastened to set his mind at rest with the assurance that Wentworth 'never expected that but when it was your [Wentworth's] right; in this case it was not, unless Mr. Belasyse were pleased to resign it. And so the dialogue [with Mallory] concluded with a mutual promise to send to one another upon the first notice of a summons'. Hopes for a Parliament grew after the release of the Loan refusers on 2 Jan. 1628. Wandesford worried about the electoral consequences of 'the universal dependence Sir John Savile hath from the Catholics' following the success of the recusant composition policy, but Wentworth probably faced a greater challenge from those Wandesford characterized as 'poor and low spirits that devote themselves to a servile adoration of any temporary greatness': beneficiaries of Savile's regime such as Dunbar, Hildyard, Alford and Foulis, whose tenants would augment Savile's clothier vote. Another danger was the possibility that the Fairfaxes of Denton and the Belasyses, having acquired their peerages upon Savile's recommendation, might abandon Wentworth, leaving him only Constable or Sir Arthur Ingram as possible partners, but any such fears were quickly laid to rest when Sir Ferdinando Fairfax* offered a partnership between Wentworth and Belasyse. Wandesford leapt at the chance, advising Wentworth 'you must join with a man gracious with the papists, which only Henry is'.[68]

The 1628 election was possibly the most close-run of the entire decade. The sheriff, Sir Thomas Fairfax II, brother-in-law of Viscount Dunbar, might have been expected to be a Savile partisan, but he resented the fact that the junior (Denton) branch of the family had acquired a peerage while he had not. Moreover, the Commons' investigation of Cholmley's conduct in 1625 undoubtedly obliged him to behave more responsibly than Savile might have wished. A poll was held, probably at Savile's request, but some of the freeholders, when tendered the oath, refused to declare their names. According to the report from the committee for privileges, the contest was so tight that 'Sir Thomas Wentworth had the major number at the poll, but the major number of them who put down their names in writing were for Sir John Savile'. Under the circumstances, Savile must have been astonished when Fairfax declared Wentworth and Belasyse elected, a decision which was ratified by the Commons on 17 April.[69]

Wentworth's performance in the 1628 session, which was critical of the government but notably more responsible than that of many of his colleagues,

earned him a peerage, a seat on the Privy Council and (in December) the presidency of the Council in the North. According to Wandesford, news of Wentworth's preferment was poorly received in the Yorkshire, 'the common opinion passing you now under Sir John Savile's character, and that there is a Thomas as well as a John for the king'. Such discontent counted for little in the long term, as Wentworth quickly set about removing Savile's men from office and installing his own, but before he could begin this task, he had to organize the by-election brought about by his own elevation to the Lords. By the time he arrived in York to take up the presidency at the end of December, Sir Henry Savile had already declared his intention to stand. Although a Savile supporter in 1626 and 1628, Sir Henry had remained on good terms with Wentworth, congratulating him on his victory on the latter occasion, and insouciantly observing that if both Sir John and Sir Thomas Savile were to be rejected by the freeholders (as they ultimately were), 'in good faith our case will be lamentable'.[70]

Savile approached the 1629 by-election in the same light-hearted vein, sending Wentworth a long and rather disingenuous account of his motives for seeking election, which included

> hope of better and more free times, a desire to see my honourable friends in the south ... a desire to keep this honour deposited for this time in that name which hath often enjoyed it, until your lordship's nephew and my young cousin Sir Willam [Savile] be more capable thereof ... an ambition to serve my country with a good heart, which must serve to supply all other defects in a man not qualified for such an assembly.

Wentworth made it clear that he intended to promote an official candidate, apparently his neighbour Sir Francis Wortley, whose dignity he had undoubtedly offended by dropping him so suddenly at the 1626 election, and Sir Henry Savile gave every impression of having yielded gracefully:

> though it were but for your little neighbour (who of himself is able to do so little) yet ... I could never be drawn to oppose any design of your lordship's when you were in our rank ... much less may I be seen to oppose a known design of your lordship's, and that the first after the entry to your government.

However, three weeks later, Savile returned to the fray, allegedly at the behest of the Leeds clothiers, rescinding his earlier withdrawal on the grounds that Wentworth was supporting Wortley only 'as a private friend, but not as a lord president'. Although Wortley could presumably count on the sympathy of the sheriff,

Wentworth's ally Sir Matthew Boynton, his personal interest was (as Wentworth had himself observed in 1626) relatively slight, and at the county court some of Wentworth's friends apparently deserted him: Trappes and Sir Peter Middleton both signed Savile's return. Sir Henry vehemently denied that the Saviles of Howley had had anything to do with his decision to stand: 'upon my salvation I have nothing to do with them or they with me in this affair. They neither send me a voice, nor did I beg any of them; it may be true that many of my neighbours and wellwillers are of the old bands of reiters'. The first part of this statement is unverifiable, but the second was undoubtedly true: among those who signed Savile's election indenture, the majority were either gentry who had signed the Saviles' return in 1624, or clothiers such as John Kaye, Gregory Armytage and John Harrison, who had backed the petition against Wentworth's election in 1621.[71]

VI. Local Issues in Parliament

With Savile basing much of his electoral appeal upon his reputation as 'the patron of the clothiers, of all others the fittest to be relied upon', neither Wentworth nor any other potential challenger for local pre-eminence could afford to neglect the freeholders' interests. Thus there was a consensus about the significance of Parliament as a forum for the airing and resolution of local grievances: in a speech at Rotherham in April 1621 Wentworth assured the subsidymen who were footing the bill for the Commons' speedy grant of two subsidies for defence of the Palatinate that 'we have not been idle in performance of our duties towards our great mother, the commonwealth'; while on the last day of the 1624 session, in a debate sparked by the king's criticism of the Commons for its relentless attacks on monopoly patents, Savile insisted 'that none can judge of a grievance to the kingdom as this House, which is composed of all the kingdom'.[72] Rhetorical flourishes aside, in a county as large, prosperous and diverse as Yorkshire it was inevitable that much parliamentary business, particularly over issues relating to administrative and economic affairs, would be either sponsored by or relevant to local interests.

The most straightforward issues promoted in Parliament by Yorkshire Members were bills to resolve local problems. In 1610 Savile secured statutory confirmation of copyholds held of the honour of Wakefield (agreed under a duchy of Lancaster initiative in 1607-8), while in 1624 he tabled the bill to allow the Hallamshire cutlers to form a trade gild independent of the Sheffield manorial court. The Saviles, Hoby and Wandesford were all named to the committee for the bill to confirm copyholds on the duchy of Cornwall manor of Goathland (15 Mar. 1624), but, unlike several other items of legislation then before the House, the bill did not have the personal backing of Prince Charles and was never reported. In the following year Sir Thomas Fairfax I received a petition from freeholders who objected to being fined for nonattendance at the county assizes due to sickness or old age, and he was presumably sponsor of a bill to this remedy this problem, which received a first reading on 25 June; his subsequent unseating meant that the measure progressed no further.[73]

The clothing interest was, after agriculture, Yorkshire's largest employer, and was a perennial concern for the county's MPs. Crises occurred regularly within the industry, as its supply and manufacturing processes were vulnerable to interruption by war, disease, the vagaries of the trading cycle, government interference and changes in fashion and technology, any combination of which could have a significant impact on the local economy. Thus in both May 1614 and February 1626 Savile warned of the consequences of slumps in the cloth trade, advising the House on the latter occasion that there were '30,000 men within ten miles of his house who, if they have not relief shortly, will take it where they can get it'.[74] Furtherance of the cloth trade was an issue over which many interests could co-operate, as is demonstrated by the 1606 bill to confirm a 20 per cent discount on the customs for northern cloths. Savile drew attention to 'an abuse in the custom of cloths' on 11 Feb., and a bill to rectify the situation was tabled two days later. Reported by the York MP Christopher Brooke on 5 Mar., it was smothered in the Lords despite the best efforts of Anthony Cole* of Hull, but the discount was later confirmed by means of a petition to the earl of Salisbury (Robert Cecil†).[75]

In 1614, Members were almost unanimous in their condemnation of the New Merchant Adventurers, who had been granted a monopoly of cloth exports on the understanding that they would develop the dyeing industry and discontinue shipments of white cloth. Trade halved within months, to the despair of many Members, including Savile, who protested that poorer clothiers were being driven to bankruptcy.[76] The new Company ignored these criticisms, but its failure to improve the balance of trade led to the revocation of its patent in 1617, when the old Merchant Adventurers were allowed to buy back their former rights. The substitution of one monopoly for another was not universally welcomed, and the Adventurers were criticized in the Commons in 1621 for imposing charges upon exports to recoup the cost of their new patent. Their detractors included William Mallory, an inveterate opponent of all monopolies, and alderman John Lister* of Hull, who was not a Merchant Adventurer and resented the obligation to pay their charges; the government, however, was grateful for the Company's financial support, and Wentworth, following Calvert's lead, sought to defuse the situation. The Merchant Adventurers came under attack again in 1624, this time for their monopoly of the export of coloured cloths, when Savile, who numbered many Adventurers among his closest supporters, came to the Company's defence, warning that 'if we labour too much to prune this Company we may destroy them, and so bring a great mischief to the kingdom'. During May 1624 he twice extolled the benefits the Company had brought to the cloth trade, blaming declining exports on increases in wool prices and customs dues, and the growth of a rival industry in Silesia.[77] Controversy over the cloth trade subsided during the war years of the later 1620s, but in 1629 the Leeds clothiers, who had been the driving force behind Sir Henry Savile's return at the Yorkshire by-election, gathered a petition against the town corporation's attempts to force them into a trade guild. The sudden dissolution meant that Savile was unable to bring this to the Commons' attention, but Wandesford later submitted it to the Privy Council.[78]

The clothing debates of the early 1620s highlight the way in which economic interests engendered as much controversy as co-operation in the Commons. The middle years of James's reign saw a similar upheaval in the wool trade, with the Merchants of the Staple and a consortium of patentees led by Viscount Fentoun fighting for control.[79] Both groups came under attack in the Commons in 1621, when the Staplers' patent was condemned, Fentoun's was censured, and the pretermitted custom on cloth was heavily criticized. Wentworth and Calvert moved to safeguard Halifax's exemption from regulation, secured by statute in 1555, but were opposed by Sir Thomas Belasyse, a North Riding woolgrower, and Mallory, who (in pursuance of his feud with Wentworth), unreasonably asked 'that a knight of the shire would not move for a particular place for exemption'. To Wentworth's undoubted satisfaction, the House resolved to throw the domestic wool trade open to all, but brought in a bill to ban exports, at the third reading of which Northumbrian MPs pressed for exemption for Berwick wool on the grounds of its extreme coarseness. With an eye to his constituents' interests, Wentworth, among others, insisted that Berwick wool should not be exported, as its quality had improved, 'and [it] is now bought by Yorkshire clothiers'.[80]

If the knights of the shire often served the interests of the West Riding clothiers in debates on wool and cloth, their attitude to the grain trade was dominated by a more obviously self-interested determination to secure the highest possible price for their crops. The only MPs who did not welcome the 1621 bill to ban grain imports were Brooke and Lister, who protested that Polish rye was the only commodity which York and Hull merchants could trade for northern cloth in the Baltic. Wandesford, by contrast, argued that a ban on grain shipments would encourage the Eastland merchants to look for new imports. The bill was lost at the dissolution, which was just as well, as the glut of 1621 turned to shortage by 1624, when restrictions on the export of grain was debated as part of the statutes' continuance bill. Savile advocated maintenance of a good price, 'that the farmer and husbandman be encouraged, for then the poor will not want', whereas Hoby approached the problem from the opposite direction, urging that the poorest should be relieved by lowering the price of pease and beans, from which the cheapest bread was made.[81]

The improvement of river navigation was an issue which had a potentially enormous impact upon the economies of both York and the West Riding clothing district, but the projected costs and the reluctance of either area to see its rivals prosper created a good deal of tension in the Commons. There were no recorded objections to the proviso for the River Ouse which Robert Askwith appended to the weirs bill on 23 June 1604, but the draft was not reported before the prorogation. From about 1614 the York corporation promoted a much more radical scheme to cut a new 25-mile channel across the East Riding, which gave rise to a navigation bill in 1621. This was opposed by Wentworth, who refused to pay for the scheme through a county-wide rate, although it was agreed that funds might be raised by means of a duty upon goods shipped upriver. In 1626 the York corporation hoped to reintroduce the bill, now shorn of its contentious county rate, but their intentions came to nothing, probably because enthusiasm for local legislation dwindled as the session came to be dominated by the duke of Buckingham's impeachment.[82] Meanwhile, Savile promoted a rival measure to canalize the rivers Aire and Calder. Although plans were laid in 1624 and 1625, no legislation reached the Commons until 1626, when a bill was rejected at the second reading 'after long debate'. The proposal avoided a county levy, laying most of the charge for the work on an imposition on trade, but faced objections from the York corporation, which feared the project would be 'a great impoverishment to this ancient city'. Shortly before the 1628 session the Saviles discussed the prospects for fresh legislation, but with both father and son defeated in their attempts to secure election, none was introduced.[83]

Yorkshire MPs welcomed attacks on patents and patentees as warmly as any, particularly in the case of the locally unpopular Sir Stephen Procter, who was called before the House as much because of his long-standing feud with his neighbour Sir John Mallory as for his patent as collector of recusancy fines. The case of Sir John Bennett*, who had made many friends in Yorkshire during his years as diocesan chancellor, was somewhat different: charged with bribery as judge of the Prerogative Court of Canterbury in 1621, it was more in sorrow than in anger that Mallory and Sir John Gibson* called for his expulsion from the House.[84] The fact that Bennett's misdemeanours had been visited upon litigants in Canterbury archdiocese only may help to explain why his crimes aroused relatively little anger among northern MPs. The same could not be said of John Lepton, whose monopoly of drafting lawsuits submitted to the Council in the North had significantly raised the price of litigation at York. Wentworth, Hoby and Lister attacked Lepton at the committee of grievances on 7 May 1621, although (Sir) Talbot Bowes* later tried to secure him a more sympathetic hearing at the bar of the House. This patent was subsequently revived for the benefit of Sir Thomas Monson*, and it is hardly surprising that Wentworth and Wandesford were tellers in the vote which censured it afresh in 1628.[85]

The key role of the Council in the North meant that its affairs loomed large in the priorities of the county's MPs. Unlike the residents of the Marcher shires, northerners were not concerned to free themselves from the Council's jurisdiction, but on 18 May 1614 Savile moved to include its court within the remit of a bill to restrict the use of writs of *supersedeas* by Westminster courts, a proviso which would have substantially reduced the volume of litigation referred to York from local courts. He was opposed by Sir Richard Williamson*, one of the York justices, who, as Christopher Brooke observed, almost undoubtedly spoke 'intending his private [interest]'. The same arguments were deployed when a similar bill was tabled in 1624: Wentworth and Sir Thomas Savile both revived the proviso for York, which was opposed on this occasion by Sir Christopher Hildyard, a Council member.[86]

While Yorkshiremen largely accepted the Council's authority, the Commons was used as a platform for a series of increasingly outspoken attacks on lord president Scrope during the 1620s, all but one of which were promoted by Savile and Wentworth, who both aspired to discredit Scrope and secure the presidency for themselves. The sole exception was a petition of June 1621, in which a dissatisfied litigant charged Scrope with corruption: the accusation was discounted by Mallory, Wentworth, Ingram and Hoby, who suggested that Scrope's accuser be kept in custody lest the accusation prove frivolous.[87] Three years later the Commons received a petition of complaint about the support given to Catholics by Scrope, Rutland and Dunbar. It was said that 'the men most violent against these lords are Wentworth, Hoby, Savile and Wandesford', a claim supported by the fact that it was Sir Thomas Savile who named Scrope to the recusant officeholders' petition. Although an embarrassment to Scrope, the political impact of these accusations was muted by the Lords' contention that the charges were based upon hearsay, and a week before the end of the session it was agreed that the petition should be presented to the king privately by Prince Charles. Any chance that it might be heeded were presumably dashed by Buckingham, whose wife was niece to Scrope's wife.[88]

With Wentworth and Savile at each others' throats during the 1625 session neither had time to attack Scrope, but the latter's fate became an issue during the next election, when Wentworth worried that unless Sir William Constable stood, 'a great part of the East Riding will voice with Savile in opposition of the president, whom they persuade themselves he [Savile] would question in Parliament'. As he was by this stage angling for Buckingham's favour, Savile can have had little intention of acting upon this threat, and he is unlikely to have been 'the knight of Yorkshire' who cited Scrope among the county's recusant officials at the end of February 1626; the troublemaker must therefore have been Constable. Meanwhile, a separate petition, which revived the charges levelled at Scrope in 1624, and claimed that recusant convictions in the north had more than doubled since Scrope took office, was forwarded to the king on 11 March, but this elicited no response.[89] Hoby subsequently used the charges against Scrope, Dunbar and Rutland to illustrate the allegation that the duke of Buckingham had systematically promoted recusants to positions of authority. Eliot gleefully reported this to the House on 24 Mar., but the accusation was strenuously opposed by a number of the duke's clients. It was at this point that Savile, who had held aloof from the debate about Scrope, intervened to defend the duke, blaming any increase in recusancy on the inadequacies of the clergy in the North and East Ridings and belittling the lord president, who was, he claimed, 'not so great a man as to carry a faction in Yorkshire'. The duke took the hint, and while Scrope remained in office and secured an earldom after the dissolution of the Parliament, Savile assumed executive power in the north.[90]

Having been excluded from influence for 18 months, Wentworth and his associates inevitably regarded the 1628 Parliament as a golden opportunity to settle scores with Scrope, Savile and Dunbar. On the second day of business, Hoby called for an inquiry into the increase in the numbers of recusants, while Mallory observed that the relevant statistics could be collated from the papers of Savile's composition committee. Despite the efforts of the lord president's secretary, James Howell*, Scrope, Rutland and Dunbar were once again included on the list of recusant officeholders, while on 24 May John Pym* and Hoby secured an investigation of Savile's composition committee. Finally, on 6 June, as the Commons anxiously awaited the king's second answer to the Petition of Right, Hoby, Hotham and Wentworth attacked the activities of the recusancy commission, which Wentworth portrayed as an attempt 'to pervert the law, and will amount to a toleration'. Although Wentworth's performance in the Commons earned him favour at Court and a viscountcy in July 1628, it did nothing to dislodge Scrope from office, and it was only after Buckingham's assassination that Wentworth finally secured the presidency, which he offered to buy for £20,000.[91]

VII. Yorkshire and War in the 1620s

The knights of Yorkshire were broadly similar to other MPs in terms of their willingness to defend and promote a range of interests in Parliament, and while the rivalry between Savile and Wentworth may have given a competitive edge to their advocacy, it would be wrong to assume that either was solely motivated by a cynical desire to manipulate local opinion for their own benefit. The issues which best illustrate the complex interplay of principle and self-interest upon the actions of the shire knights are the interrelated questions of the nation's involvement in and financing of the continental wars of the 1620s. Although most MPs regarded the spectre of Habsburg hegemony as a serious threat to national security, there were profound disagreements over strategy between those unwilling to condone anything more than a defensive war, others who cast covetous glances towards the wealth of Spain and the Indies, and the small number who were prepared to face the burden of raising or subsidising an army to intervene in Germany and the Low Countries.

One of the few Yorkshiremen who welcomed the prospect of intervention in the war in Germany was Sir Thomas Fairfax I, who briefly served in the Low Countries among the English volunteers organized to defend the Palatinate in 1620, and was subsequently the author of a petition urging King James to hire Count Mansfeld's services to assist the beleaguered Protestant forces on the Continent. Hence it is no surprise that his only recorded speech in the 1625 Parliament supported a grant of two subsidies rather than the single subsidy facetiously proposed by Sir Francis Seymour. This offer, although hardly enough to fund a major campaign, was at least a gesture of support to assist the preparations for what would clearly be a lengthy commitment, and it was generally assumed that a fresh grant would be offered at another session in the spring.[92] John Lister and George Shilleto both spoke approvingly of a 'blue water' strategy involving an attack on Spanish possessions in the Caribbean,[93] but once the question of cost was raised most Yorkshiremen were reluctant to commit themselves to anything more expensive than a defensive policy. This attitude may have arisen in part from a natural parsimoniousness, but also owed something to a realistic calculation of local interests: as Lister and others persistently reminded the House during the later 1620s, war with Spain left the Yorkshire coast and the region's main trading routes to London, the Low Countries and the Baltic dangerously vulnerable to attacks by privateers based at Dunkirk.[94]

The provision of supply to bring the kingdom to readiness for war began auspiciously enough on 15 Feb. 1621, when a swift consensus emerged for a grant of two subsidies, although Christopher Brooke and John Carvile grounded their assent upon the expectation that the House would be allowed to attack monopolists in return. This was duly permitted, and Wentworth used the Commons' proceedings against patentees as the centrepiece of the speech he made to the Rotherham subsidymen at Easter 1621, claiming that the impeachment of (Sir) Giles Mompesson* was 'of more safety to the Commonwealth in the example than 6 of the best laws that have been made in 6 of the last parliaments', and a more than adequate justification for an early vote of supply.[95] While Wentworth was prepared to bankroll James's diplomatic initiatives, he was probably one of the few pro-Spanish Members of the House, and during the autumn sitting both his personal inclinations and his concern for the Commonwealth led him to argue that domestic issues should be given priority over foreign policy. On 26 Nov., during a debate on the king's demands for a fresh grant of subsidy for relief of the Palatinate, he urged that the question be thrust aside, 'and tomorrow patiently to fit ourselves for the end of a session, and not to lose the fruits of a Parliament'. The motion would have put legislation before supply, exactly the opposite of what the government wished, a stance which cut across Wentworth's energetic attempts to curry favour at Court over the preceding year. He reiterated this point in a speech drafted about two weeks later, in which he sought to persuade the House to abandon the cessation of business which ultimately wrecked the session.[96]

Wentworth maintained a lower profile in 1624 than he had in previous parliaments. This stance was partly forced upon him by ill-health, but probably also owed something to political calculation, as the lot of representing the county's views on war thereby fell to Savile. In a session in which the war party was led by Prince Charles, Buckingham, and the Privy Council, assisted (or at least not hindered) by many of those who had spoken in favour of domestic priorities in 1621, opposition was a daunting prospect, but Savile rose to the occasion.[97] On 5 Mar., during a debate about the 3rd earl of Southampton's motion to offer the king open-ended assistance if the abandonment of the Spanish Match should result in war, he echoed Edward Alford's criticism of the undertaking, observing that 'it was a great engagement, and that having once passed it, it was not in our power to revoke it nor moderate it', as the king would be left to judge the scale of the funds he required. While Savile gave general assurances of support and spoke of the need to prepare for a defensive war, the effect of his speech was entirely obstructive of official efforts. He was presently supported by Wandesford, who argued that the House should ignore Southampton's motion and wait until the end of the session to vote a specific grant of subsidies, and Mallory, who overplayed his hand by moving that Sir Edwin Sandys, who had raised the motion, be expelled from the House.[98]

Savile launched his most powerful attack on the 'patriot' coalition during the supply debate of 19-20 March. Initially primed by a series of official and semi-official speakers, the House was thrown into confusion by a brief interjection from Savile, who demanded 'first to know what we shall do in this business; 2. what the charge of it will come to; 3. to consider how to levy it'. Pym, himself a hawk, wryly summarized the effect of this speech:

he [Savile] was seconded by Mr. Alford, Sir Arthur Ingram, Mr. Mallory and others, among which there were no doubt those who wished this order for the better perfecting and establishing of our counsels, and perchance there wanted not [those] who in this variety affected delay or an opportunity of crossing that in some privative or subordinate question which they would not oppose in the main.

Thanks to a timely intervention from Sir Edward Coke the proposal for supply was eventually restored to the agenda, but Savile continued to play for time, first by deferring the debate until the next morning, and then by proposing to appropriate the three subsidies agreed upon to 'Holland, Ireland, the ports and the Navy', an essentially defensive strategy. It was objections such as these which provided the impetus for the relatively unusual stipulation that the disbursement of the funds raised should be supervised by a six-man committee nominated by the Commons.[99]

James's equivocations over the breach with Spain made many MPs understandably reluctant to offer liberal supply for a war which would, at best, have been pursued half-heartedly. If this had been the chief fear of those who opposed a war in 1624, their attitudes should have been transformed at the accession of King Charles, who undertook preparations for an attack on Spain and summoned a fresh Parliament to provide funds for the war effort. In fact, the vigorous approach Charles demonstrated towards a war with Spain had very little impact upon the attitudes of Yorkshire Members. Sir Thomas Hoby spent most of the 1625 session venting his outrage at the relaxation of the recusancy laws consequent upon the king's marriage to Henrietta Maria, while the efforts of Mallory and Wandesford to secure an immediate adjournment to delay consideration of Savile's petition about the Yorkshire election were hardly supportive of royal policy. In the supply debate of 30 June Wentworth agreed to the emerging consensus for two subsidies, but ominously insisted that these be given 'only as a testimony of the duty of the subject towards His Majesty', not as an indication of any long-term obligation to support a war.[100] Distracted for the next month by the need to secure his own re-election, Wentworth, arriving late at the Oxford sitting, was asked by the chancellor of the Exchequer, Sir Richard Weston*, to be more accommodating in his attitude to the Crown's needs. Although he agreed to serve Buckingham 'in the quality of an honest man and a gentleman', Wentworth could hardly afford to be seen as neglectful of his constituents' interests in the immediate aftermath of a hard-fought by-election, and in the key debate of 10 Aug., as in the autumn of 1621, he called for a pardon and 'some good bills' to be given precedence over any increase in supply. In what was clearly an attempt to square his views with his undertaking to Weston, he added the rider that 'when it shall please His Majesty to call us together again, be it within a day [after the prorogation], and to propound supply, we shall entertain it with all cheerfulness'. However, his stance was clearly regarded as a betrayal at Court, and resulted in his exclusion from the next Parliament.[101]

During the 1626 Parliament Savile gradually moved into Buckingham's orbit, a development which encouraged him to modify his earlier opposition to the war. However, this did not oblige him to demonstrate a slavish devotion to every aspect of government policy, and his desire to lighten the financial burdens heaped upon his constituents remained undimmed. On 24 Feb. he demanded to know whether there were 'any enclosures' of policy which were not to be debated, a motion which harked back to the confusion sown by the roundabout means the 'patriots' had used to advocate war in 1624. More constructively, he went on to urge 'that the Privy Council may lead the way', a motion which resulted in chancellor Weston being ordered to present a projected budget of the Crown's expenses to the House. While this was being prepared, the Commons considered ways in which to increase royal revenues. Voicing the grievances of his neighbours, Savile spoke of the burdens laid upon poorer taxpayers: 'the £5 man in subsidy who is the farmer and copyholder ... is the third or fourth part of England; he languishes and [is] ready to give up the last gasp, and by raising of the [land]lords' fines worse'. He estimated the annual cost of the subsidy to the Danish army at £600,000, and demanded to know 'are we able to bear this? If the king of Denmark withdraw [from Germany], what estate will the Low Countries be [in]?'. The alarmist tone of this speech was unhelpful to the government, and Secretary of State (Sir) John Coke was obliged to reassure the House that the Danish subsidies were 'not so great as Sir H. [sic J.] Savile [thinks]'. However, Savile seems to have been aiming to support the commitment to Denmark, and advocating nothing more controversial than the shifting of the fiscal burdens of war away from subsidy by exploring other revenue-raising schemes. He may have gone some way towards redeeming his reputation in official circles two days later, when he was one of the few Members who spoke in favour of an early grant of supply.[102]

Savile's constructive criticism of official policy allowed him to retain credibility in a House which was overwhelmingly hostile to Buckingham's conduct of both the war with Spain and the rapidly deteriorating diplomatic relations with France. He was less guarded in a letter he sent to his associates at Leeds on 27 Feb.,

in which he advised that his efforts to raise the clothiers' grievances in Parliament had been ignored by Members 'so resolutely bent and with such eagerness in pursuit of a great man as rather than they will fail or surcease they are resolved to hazard the whole estate of the Commonwealth'. This letter was widely circulated in the West Riding over the following weeks, during which time Savile stood out in the Commons as one of the few independent Members who counselled moderation as the duke's opponents began to gather charges against him. He dismissed Buckingham's arrest of the *St. Peter* of Le Havre as 'an error, but no grief', made light of the alleged misuse of Crown revenues, and insisted that the duke was doing his best to protect English shipping. His attitude to supply also became more accommodating. He welcomed Secretary Coke's war budget of 23 Mar., and was probably the unidentified Yorkshire MP who was prepared to endorse a grant of three subsidies and three fifteenths in return for a reduction in the Privy Seal loan of £10,000 then being collected within the county, a *quid pro quo* he duly obtained from the Privy Council a few days later. However, his support for the government reached its limits on 26 Apr., when he flatly refused to add to the existing grant of supply and recommended other methods of raising revenue which did not fall so heavily upon the poorer subsidymen, such as composition for wardship and a Poll Tax on the gentry. He also moved that all those rated at above £4 in the subsidy books should pay half the total at the first subsidy, offering £15 as his own share. On 3 May he moved that 'the king should know the state of his subjects and that he should not presume of more from them than can be paid', advice he was presumably also offering the government in private. On the following day he was one of those appointed to draft a petition imploring the king to allow the House to discuss revenue reform.[103]

Savile's drive for fiscal efficiency survived the dissolution of the 1626 Parliament: within weeks he had been appointed to the Privy Council commission for revenue reform, whereupon he recommended schemes to compound for fines for both recusancy and feudal tenures.[104] However, his willingness to impose a Forced Loan worth five subsidies upon his countrymen sat rather uneasily with his objection to any increase in a grant of three subsidies only months before, and must have made some contribution to his defeat at the 1628 election. By contrast, Wentworth's refusal of the Loan and subsequent imprisonment burnished his local reputation, while his disinclination to speak out publicly against the legality of the levy earned him the respect of the Privy Council.[105]

Wentworth's reputation as one of the more moderate Loan refusers put him in an ideal position to assist in the negotiations whereby Parliament traded the Petition of Right for five subsidies in 1628. This did not mean that he was prepared to compromise the principles for which he had so recently suffered, and he was resolutely set against an early grant in the supply debate of 2 Apr., insisting that 'I cannot forget that duty I owe to my country, and unless we be secured against our liberties we cannot give'. However, once the king signified his willingness to exchange a confirmation of the liberties of the subject for cash two days later, he hastened to secure a vote of supply, helping to talk the House around to a grant of five subsidies rather than the four originally mooted. In a letter to Sir Edward Stanhope on 6 Apr. he spoke of his hopes for 'a very happy Parliament', but made it clear that this presupposed a satisfactory resolution of the constitutional crisis: 'the grand committee hath voted for five subsidies, but [these] are not as yet to be reported to the House, nor will not I think, at least by my consent, till we be in something a better readiness for the security of the subjects in those fundamental liberties'.[106] It was quickly resolved (with Wentworth's support) that all five subsidies should be paid within a single year, but House held Charles to his bargain: the bill did not receive its first reading until 12 May, and the committee stage was dragged out until 10 June, after the Commons had received the king's second answer to the Petition of Right.

With the exception of Sir Thomas Hoby, Yorkshire's MPs were generally less vociferous in 1629 than in previous sessions. As Wentworth and Savile had both 'turned courtier', each had an obvious interest in restraining their allies in the Commons. Eschewing his former reputation as a firebrand, Wandesford made valiant attempts to moderate proceedings against the customs farmers on 19 Feb., and to defend Wentworth's new patron, lord treasurer Weston, on 2 March. As for the knights of the shire, Sir Henry Savile, who cannot have sat for more than two weeks between his election and the dissolution, had little impact upon the House, while Henry Belasyse, still only 24 years old, is not recorded to have spoken until the final day. On this occasion, fired with youthful ardour by Sir John Eliot's dramatic declaration against Tunnage and Poundage, he moved 'that the Speaker, if he would not put it to the question, should come out of the chair and the House should choose another'.[107]

and Lincs.; W. Edwards and F.M. Trotter, *British Regional Geology: Pennines and Adjacent Areas.* [7] *Agrarian Hist. Eng. and Wales* ed. J. Thirsk, v. pt. 1, 59-86. [8] H. Heaton, *Yorks. Woollen and Worsted Industries*; W.B. Crump and G. Ghorbal, *Hist. Huddersfield Woollen Industry*; R.T. Fieldhouse and B. Jennings, *Hist. Richmond and Swaledale*, 158-62, 169-60, 177-82; STAC 8/230/20, f. 2. [9] D. Hey, *Fiery Blades of Hallamshire*; A. Raistrick and B. Jennings, *Hist. of Lead Mining in Pennines*; J.U. Nef, *Rise of British Coal Industry*, i. 57-64; Borthwick, Reg. Test. 23, f. 787v; Fieldhouse and Jennings, 160-1; R.B. Turton, *Alum Farm*. [10] B.F. Duckham, *Yorks. Ouse*, 13-42; D. Palliser, 'York under the Tudors: the trading life of the northern capital', in *Perspectives in Eng. Urban Hist.* ed. A. Everitt, 39-59; D. Palliser, *Tudor York*, 179-200; *VCH Yorks. (E. Riding)*, vi. 80-1, 105-6. [11] P.J. Bowden, *Wool Trade in Tudor and Stuart Eng.* 68-71, 87n.1; D. Hey, *Yorks. from AD1000*, p. 137. [12] KINGSTON-UPON-HULL. [13] R. Reid, *Council in the North*, 243-371. [14] R.B. Smith, *Land and Pols. in the Eng. of Henry VIII*, 50-61; map at rear of Reid; B. Dobson, 'Crown, Charter and City, 1396-1461', *Gov. of Medieval York* ed. S. Rees Jones (Borthwick Studies in Hist. iii), 34-55; *Hull Charters* trans. J.R. Boyle, 34-45. [15] Palliser, 3-4; Reid, 344. Sir Richard Gargrave kept the county gaol at Wakefield in 1604-6: LPL, ms 708, f. 93; ms 709, f. 61. [16] A.G. Dickens, *Lollards and Protestants in the Diocese of York*; C. Cross, *Puritan Earl*, 247-69; P. Lake, 'Matthew Hutton – Puritan Bishop?', *Hist.* lxiv. 182-204; Palliser, 226-259; C. Cross, *Urban Magistrates and Ministers* (Borthwick Ppr. lxvii); *Reformation in Eng. Towns* ed. P. Collinson and J. Craig; P. Marshall, *Face of the Pastoral Ministry in the E. Riding* (Borthwick Ppr. lxxxviii). [17] See primarily the works of J.H. Aveling: *Northern Catholics*; *Catholic Recusancy of W. Riding*; *Post-Reformation Catholicism in E. Yorks.*; *Catholic Recusancy in City of York*. [18] M. Questier, 'Practical Anti-Papistry during the reign of Elizabeth I', *JBS*, xxxvi. 371-96; SIR RICHARD CHOLMLEY; SIR HENRY CONSTABLE. [19] R.A. Marchant, *Puritans and Church Courts in the Dioc. of York*, 15-43; D. Como, *Blown by the Spirit*, 266-324; SIR MATTHEW BOYNTON, 1st Bt.; SIR WILLIAM CONSTABLE, 1st Bt.; SIR THOMAS POSTHUMOUS HOBY. [20] Map in *HP Commons, 1558-1603*. [21] Particularly in 1597: *HMC Hatfield*, vii. 412-13. [22] SIR THOMAS POSTHUMOUS HOBY; *Strafforde Letters*, i. 8; HENRY BELASYSE; J.J. Cartwright, *Chapters in Yorks. Hist.* 203-4; *Wentworth Pprs.* ed. J.P. Cooper (Cam. Soc. ser. 4. xii), 144-6. [23] *Wentworth Pprs.* 47-8; *Strafforde Letters*, i. 10. [24] *Wentworth Pprs.* 143-5; *Fairfax Corresp.* ed. G.W. Johnson, i. 7-8; C142/185/40; 142/310/79. Northumberland's estates had changed little since the 15th century, for which see A.J. Pollard, *North-East Eng. during Wars of the Roses*, 96. [25] C142/476/141; R. Somerville, *Hist. Duchy Lancaster*, 523; Crump and Ghorbal, 31 – 50; B. Jennings, *Pennine Valley*, 41-57; STAC 5/S10/16; 5/S32/1; 5/S33/11; 5/S43/14; 5/S71/32; 5/S73/23; 5/S79/9; 5/S81/31; 5/S83/9; 5/W14/31; 5/W32/21; 5/W40/3; 5/W47/7; 5/W49/14; 5/W69/24; 5/W70/14; 5/W71/12. [26] *HMC Hatfield*, vii. 412-17; *Wentworth Pprs.* 37, 39; M. Kishlansky, *Parl. Selection*, 49-55. [27] *HMC Hatfield*, vii. 426-7, 436-7; *Procs. 1626*, iii. 244; *APC*, 1597-8, pp. 46, 114. [28] *HMC Hatfield*, vii. 413-16; C219/34/116. [29] *Wentworth Pprs.* 47-8; LPL, ms 708, f. 131. [30] *List of Sheriffs* comp. A. Hughes (PRO, L. and I. ix), 163; C219/35/2/145. Darcy, Constable and Mauleverer were close relatives of men who had participated in the 1597 election. [31] SIR RICHARD GARGRAVE. [32] W. Yorks. AS (Bradford), 32D86/38/2, f. 14; *CJ*, i. 457b; *Procs. 1614 (Commons)*, 471. [33] The case was presumably STAC 8/225/12. [34] *Strafforde Letters*, i. 2-4; *Wentworth Pprs.* 84-6, 100-1, 105; C231/4, f. 13; *Fortescue Pprs.* ed. S.R. Gardiner (Cam. Soc. n.s. i), 23-8; R. Cust, 'Wentworth's "change of sides" in the 1620s', in *Pol. World of Thomas Wentworth* ed. J.F. Merritt, 66-7. [35] Reid, 387-8; S.L. Adams, 'The Protestant Cause ... 1585-1630' (Oxf. Univ. D.Phil. thesis, 1973), pp. 433-7. [36] *Strafforde Letters*, i. 10; N. Yorks. RO, ZBL1, 1/1/1-2, 9-10. [37] *Strafforde Letters*, i. 8-9; *Wentworth Pprs.* 144. [38] *Wentworth Pprs.* 143-4; *Strafforde Letters*, i. 8-9; Surr. Hist. Cent. LM1331/25. [39] *Strafforde Letters*, i. 11-13; *Wentworth Pprs.* 144-5; *Beaumont Pprs.* ed. W.D. Macray

[1] LPL, ms 708, f. 131. [2] W. Yorks. AS (Bradford), 32D86/38/2, f. 14. [3] Ibid. f. 19. [4] *HMC Hodgkin*, 43. [5] *Strafforde Letters* (1739) ed. W. Knowler, i. 44. [6] V. Wilson, *British Regional Geology: E. Yorks.*

(Roxburghe Club cxiii), 43-4; *Duchy of Lancaster Office-Holders* ed. R. Somerville, 149; *Manor and Bor. of Leeds* ed. J.W. Kirby (Thoresby Soc. lvii), 248. [40] *Strafforde Letters*, i. 13; C219/38/269; Surr. Hist. Cent. LM1331/26; Crump and Ghorbal, 43-7. For Mallory, see below. [41] *Beaumont Pprs*. 43-4. [42] *Strafforde Letters*, i. 11; *SR*, ii. 170; *Procs. 1614 (Commons)*, 52-8; *APC*, 1613-14, p. 457; *HMC Portland*, ix. 138; R. Cust, 'Pols. and the Electorate in the 1620s', in *Conflict in Early Stuart Eng.* ed. R. Cust and A. Hughes, 144-6. [43] W. Yorks. AS (Bradford), Sp St 11/5/3/1; Surr. Hist. Cent. LM Corresp., 14 Dec. 1620. [44] *Strafforde Letters*, i. 11. [45] Ibid., 13; *CD 1621*, iv. 48-9; Surr. Hist. Cent. LM1331/25. [46] *Wentworth Pprs*. 145. [47] Sir Thomas Savile's candidacy may be deduced from his role in the subsequent complaints to the committee of privileges: *CD 1621*, ii. 45, 260; iv. 187; Nicholas, *Procs. 1621*, i. 38-9, 61; *CJ*, i. 571b. [48] Surr. Hist. Cent. LM1331/25; Nicholas, i. 175; *CD 1621*, iv. 23; vi. 69. [49] Surr. Hist. Cent. LM1331/26. [50] *CJ*, i. 556-7. [51] *CD 1621*, iv. 48-9; Surr. Hist. Cent. LM1331/25. Stanhope's copy of the letter is in W. Yorks. AS (Bradford), Sp St 11/5/3/1. [52] *CD 1621*, iv. 161; *CJ*, i. 571b. [53] *Chamberlain Letters* ed. N.E. McClure, ii. 446; *Wentworth Pprs*. 202-3; SIR THOMAS BELASYSE, 2nd bt.; SIR THOMAS FAIRFAX II. Visct. Dunbar would also have been eligible, but unlikely to stand, as he was a Catholic. [54] C219/37/321; 219/38/269. [55] *Wentworth Pprs*. 229-31; *Strafforde Letters*, i. 25-6. [56] Borthwick, HCAB 16, ff. 322-3; WILLIAM MALLORY; C66/2209/4. [57] Bodl. Fairfax 34, f. 71, repr. in *Fairfax Corresp*. i. 6-7. [58] *Radcliffe Corresp*. ed. T.D. Whitaker, 176-7; Add. 25463, f. 72; *Strafforde Letters*, i. 27; *Wentworth Pprs*. 231-2; Bodl. Fairfax 34, f. 47. [59] *Procs. 1625*, pp. 295-7, 300. [60] Ibid. 206-7, 209, 211, 213, 296-7, 314-15, 513-15. Savile's petition is in W.Yorks. AS (Bradford) 32D86/38/2, f. 19. [61] *Fairfax Corresp*. i. 7-10; H. Cholmley, *Mems*. (1787), pp. 23-4. [62] *List of Sheriffs*, 163. [63] The two wapentakes which comprised the heart of the clothing district, in which Howley lay. [64] *Strafforde Letters*, i. 32-3; *Wentworth Pprs*. 246; *HMC Hodgkin*, 43, 285-8. [65] *APC*, 1625-6, pp. 169-70, 421-2, 424; *Wentworth Pprs*. 249-50; *Procs. 1626*, ii. 301, 303-4, 306-8, 392-401; iv. 289; *Fairfax Corresp*. i. 30-1. [66] *APC*, 1626, p. 100; Som. RO, DD/PH 219/66; *Wentworth Pprs*. 255-6; *Strafforde Letters*, i. 36; C231/4, f. 209v. [67] SP16/60/51-2; *APC*, 1627, pp. 382, 418; 1627-8, pp. 17, 75, 217; *Fairfax Corresp*. i. 59-61; *Wentworth Pprs*. 256-62; *Strafforde Letters*, i. 36-9; R. Cust, *Forced Loan*, 221-3, 227. [68] *Wentworth Pprs*. 278, 283, 287; *APC*, 1627-8, p. 217; Cust, *Forced Loan*, 72-90. [69] *CD 1628*, ii. 507-8, 510-11, 517. [70] SIR THOMAS WENTWORTH,; *Wentworth Pprs*. 301; SCL, Strafford Pprs. 12/50; *Strafforde Letters*, i. 44. [71] *Strafforde Letters*, i. 48-9; *Wentworth Pprs*. 312-14; C219/41A/106. [72] *Wentworth Pprs*. 153; 'Nicholas 1624', f. 245v. [73] *CJ*, i. 403a, 686a, 750a; HLRO, O.A. 7 Jas. I, c.25; main pprs. (suppl.) 13 Mar. 1624; R.W. Hoyle, 'Vain Projects: the Crown and its Copyholders in the reign of Jas. I', *Eng. Rural Soc.* ed. J. Chartres and D. Hey, 86-7; Hey, *Hallamshire*, 54-7; C.R. Kyle, 'Prince Charles in Parl.', *HJ*, xli. 614-19; Bodl. Fairfax 34, f. 25; *Procs. 1625*, p. 245. [74] *Procs. 1614 (Commons)*, 299-300, 304, 306; *Procs. 1626*, ii. 137. [75] *CJ*, i. 267, 269b, 277b; *LJ*, ii. 394a; *HMC Hatfield*, xxiii. 220-1; xxiv. 52; Hull RO, L.159-60; SP14/111/69. [76] A. Friis, *Alderman Cockayne's Project*; *Procs. 1614 (Commons)*, 299-300, 304, 306. [77] *CJ*, i. 620b, 698-9; *CD 1621*, ii. 363; 'Holland 1624', ii. f. 79; 'Nicholas 1624', ff. 192v, 206; 'Pym 1624', f. 36. [78] *Wentworth Pprs*. 311-12; *Seventeenth Cent. Ec. Docs.* ed. J. Thirsk and J.P. Cooper, 223-4; SP16/139/57. [79] *Stuart Royal Procs*. i. 344-5; Bowden, 164-74. [80] *SR*, iv. 288; *CJ*, i. 520-1, 624-5, 653; *CD 1621*, ii. 381, 478-9; v. 456-8; Nicholas, ii. 255-6. [81] *CJ*, i. 544-5; *CD 1621*, iii. 281; 'Nicholas 1624', ff. 136-7, 141-2. [82] *CJ*, i. 245, 605b; Duckham, 43-8; York City Archives, House Bk. 34, ff. 218, 220-2v, 291; House Bk. 35, ff. 6, 9. [83] York City Archives, House Bk. 34, f. 291; House Bk. 35, f. 6; *Procs. 1626*, ii. 288, 266, 269; W. Yorks. AS (Bradford), 32D86/19, ff. 89-90. [84] C.C.G. Tite, *Impeachment and Parl. Judicature*, 64-72, 133-6; *CJ*, i. 583b; *CD 1621*, v. 339-40. [85] Reid, 383-5, 390-2; *CD 1621*, iii. 194, 244; *CJ*, i. 620a; *CD 1628*, iii. 345; iv. 22-3, 28-33. [86] *Procs. 1614 (Commons)*, 281, 284, 290-1; 'Spring 1624', p. 157; *CJ*, i. 747b. [87] *CD 1621*, iii. 387; *CJ*, i. 635a.

Nicholas, ii. 149-50. [88] Bodl. Eng. Misc. c.855, ff. 131-2; *HMC Hodgkin*, 42; *CJ*, i. 708, 776a; 'Holland 1624', ii. f. 52; 'Nicholas 1624', ff. 214v-15; *LJ*, iii. 394-5. [89] *Strafforde Letters*, i. 32; *Procs. 1626*, ii. 102, 138, 179, 264-7. [90] *Procs. 1626*, ii. 334-5, 357-9, 362-3; Reid, 398. [91] *CD 1628*, ii. 48; iii. 63, 595, 599; iv. 143-4, 151, 156-7, 162-3, 166-7, 169, 324; J. Howell, *Epistolae Ho-Elianae* (1727) 5 Aug. 1629 [sic June 1628]; C. Russell, *PEP*, 380-2; *Wentworth Pprs*. 309. [92] *Strafforde Letters*, ii. 288; Add. 28326; Bodl. Fairfax 34, f. 7; *Procs. 1625*, pp. 274-6; Russell, *PEP*, 225. [93] *CJ*, i. 648a, *CD 1621*, ii. 455 (named as 'Mr. Solicitor': identified as Shilleto from *CD 1621*, v. 217); Hull Trinity House, ATH/47/1, letter of 14 Mar. 1625/6. [94] *Procs. 1625*, pp. 458, 468 (Lister); *Procs. 1626*, ii. 56 (Wandesford), 323 (Lister); *CD 1628*, iii. 308, 310 (Hoyle, Lister). [95] *CD 1621*, ii. 86-7; Nicholas, i. 48-9; *Wentworth Pprs*. 155. [96] *CD 1621*, iii. 457-8; *Wentworth Pprs*. 165-8; C. Russell, 'Wentworth and Anti – Spanish Sentiment, 1621-4', in *Wentworth*, 53-6; Cust, 'Wentworth's "change of sides"', in *Wentworth*, 69-70. [97] *Wentworth Pprs*. 205; Russell, *PEP*, 145-53, 168-71; T. Cogswell, *Blessed Revolution*, 145-65. [98] *Ferrar 1624*, p. 61; *Rich 1624*, p. 24; 'Lowther 1624', f. 24; Russell, *PEP*, 179-82; Cogswell, *Blessed*, 184-6. [99] 'Jervoise 1624', f. 72; 'Pym 1624', f. 32v; *CJ*, i. 743b; 'Spring 1624', pp. 148-9; Cogswell, *Blessed*, 203-15. [100] Russell, *PEP*, 204-13; T. Cogswell, 'Phaeton's Chariot', in *Wentworth*, 24-46; *Procs. 1625*, pp. 207, 209-11, 213, 231, 246, 249, 276, 278-9. [101] *Strafforde Letters*, i. 34-5; *Procs. 1625*. p. 423; *Wentworth Pprs*. 236-9; Russell, *PEP*, 257-9; Cust, 'Wentworth's "change of sides"', in *Wentworth*, 72-4; S.P. Salt, 'Wentworth and the Parl. Representation of Yorks.', *NH*, xvi. 154-5. [102] *Procs. 1626*, ii. 116, 122, 126, 129-30, 137. [103] Ibid. 298-9, 352, 361, 381; iii. 74, 76-8, 147, 156, 303; *APC*, 1625-6, pp. 421-2. [104] *APC*, 1626, p. 51; *HMC Cowper*, i. 273; Univ. London, Goldsmiths' ms 195/1, ff. 2v-4. [105] Cust, 'Wentworth's "change of sides"', in *Wentworth*, 74-6; *Wentworth Pprs*. 260-1. [106] *CD 1628*, ii. 250, 300-2, 307-8, 318-19; *Wentworth Pprs*. 290. [107] *CD 1629*, pp. 85, 156, 172, 222, 255, 266.

S.H.

ALDBOROUGH

Right of election: in the burgage-holders

Number of voters: 9

9 Mar. 1604	SIR HENRY SAVILE
	SIR EDMUND SHEFFIELD
c.Mar. 1614	SIR HENRY SAVILE, (bt.)
	GEORGE WETHERID
15 Dec. 1620	CHRISTOPHER WANDESFORD
	JOHN CARVILE
	Sir Henry Savile, (bt.)
15 Jan. 1624	CHRISTOPHER WANDESFORD
	JOHN CARVILE
	William Peaseley
19 Apr. 1625	RICHARD ALDBURGHE
	JOHN CARVILE
15 Jan. 1626	RICHARD ALDBURGHE
	JOHN CARVILE
12 Feb. 1628	HENRY DARLEY
	ROBERT STAPLETON
	?Richard Aldburghe

Aldborough enjoyed its heyday as the residence of Queen Cartimandua of the Brigantes, and then as a Roman town, but declined after the main bridge over the river Ure was re-sited a mile upstream, at Boroughbridge, in the twelfth century. A duchy of Lancaster borough, it was enfranchised in 1558, but with an electorate comprising a mere nine burgage-holders, several of whom could not sign their names on the election indentures, it was hardly a constituency to be proud of; Sir Henry Savile, the only magistrate who represented the borough during the early Stuart period, was outraged at his rejection in December 1620.[1]

By the second half of Elizabeth's reign, the most significant electoral force at Aldborough was the Council in the North. A local family, the Aldburghes of Ellenthorpe Hall, who held three of the electoral burgages, also wielded influence, while the duchy of Lancaster retained some modest interest: in 1601 Richard Theakston of nearby Masham was returned at the behest of Sir John Fortescue I*, chancellor of the Duchy.[2] The 1604 general election saw the return of Sir Edmund Sheffield, a kinsman of the lord president of the north, and Sir Henry Savile, heir to the Exchequer baron Sir John Savile†. Savile's father was dead by the time of the 1614 election, but by then

Savile had married the step-daughter of Sir Julius Caesar*, chancellor of the Exchequer, whose interest may have helped to secure his return. On this occasion he was paired with lord president Sheffield's secretary, George Wetherid*.

When the next Parliament was called in November 1620, Savile initially looked to his ally Sir Thomas Wentworth* for a seat, but when the latter advised 'it were not amiss if you tried your ancient power with them of Aldborough', he applied to William Aldburghe of Ellenthorpe. To his annoyance, 'Aldburghe played the knave with me': after Wetherid found a vacancy at nearby Boroughbridge, Aldborough returned two other Wentworth associates, Christopher Wandesford and John Carvile. Savile sought revenge by promoting a petition to have Aldborough disenfranchised in favour of a more populous borough – his suggestion was Wakefield, which lay close to his own estates, but Wandesford threatened to 'spend mountains' to avoid such an eventuality, and Wentworth eventually resolved the situation by leaving Aldborough alone, and securing the enfranchisement of Pontefract, which he was better placed to control.[3]

Wandesford and Carvile were re-elected at Aldborough in 1624, seeing off a rival nomination from Prince Charles, whose duchy of Cornwall had inherited the duchy of Lancaster estates in Yorkshire in 1617; the prince's nominee was William Peaseley, a servant of Secretary of State (Sir) George Calvert*.[4] In 1625, Aldburghe put forward his grandson Richard, only 18 years of age, which forced Wandesford to find another seat, at Richmond. Curiously, the return was signed by 11 men, including the manorial bailiff and an intruder 'who lived in part of one of the old burgage houses'. Richard Aldburghe and Carvile were re-elected in 1626, but in 1628, following William Aldburghe's death, neither Carvile nor Richard Aldburghe was returned; the latter may have been a candidate, but Carvile, who had serious debt problems, is unlikely to have stood. On this occasion the senior seat was taken by Henry Darley, who, having been rejected three times at Scarborough, may have been recommended at Aldborough by Sir William Sheffield*, son of the 1604 MP; while the junior seat went to Robert Stapleton, whose uncle Brian Stapleton† had recently bought the neighbouring manor of Myton-on-Swale, and was engaged in litigation with the Aldburghes.[5]

[1] T. Lawson-Tancred, *Recs. Yorks. Manor*, 10; J.W. Walker, 'Recs. relating to a Seventeenth Century Parlty. Election', *Yorks. Arch. Jnl.* xxxiv. 24-30; J.J. Cartwright, *Chapters in Yorks. Hist.* 199; A.D.K. Hawkyard, 'Enfranchisement of Constituencies, 1509-58', *PH*, x. 18. [2] Walker, 30-1. [3] *Strafforde Letters* (1739) ed. W. Knowler, i. 8;

Beaumont Pprs. ed. W.D. Macray (Roxburghe club cxiii), 43-4; A.J. Fletcher, 'Sir Thomas Wentworth and the Restoration of Pontefract', NH, vi. 89-91. [4] DCO, Prince Charles in Spain, f. 34; R.E. Ruigh, Parl. of 1624, p. 62. [5] Wentworth Pprs. ed. J.P. Cooper (Cam. Soc. ser. 4. xii), 230; T. Lawson-Tancred, 'Ellenthorpe and the Brooke Fam.' Yorks. Arch. Jnl. xxxiv. 74; xlix. 106, 108.

J.P.F./S.H.

BEVERLEY

Right of election: in the corporation

Number of voters: 26

8 Mar. 1604	ALLAN PERCY
	WILLIAM GEE, recorder
c. Mar. 1614	WILLIAM TOWSE
	EDMUND SCOTT
29 Dec. 1620	SIR CHRISTOPHER HILDYARD
	EDMUND SCOTT
	Sir John Hobart II*
15 Jan. 1624	SIR HENRY VANE
	EDMUND SCOTT
	Sir William Alford
	?Sir John Hotham, bt.
3 Mar. 1624	SIR HENRY CAREY II vice
	Vane, chose to sit for Carlisle
26 Apr. 1625	SIR JOHN HOTHAM, bt.
	SIR WILLIAM ALFORD
23 Jan. 1626	SIR JOHN HOTHAM, bt.
	SIR WILLIAM ALFORD
19 Feb. 1628	SIR JOHN HOTHAM, bt.
	SIR WILLIAM ALFORD

Site of the shrine of St. John of Beverley, a former archbishop of York, Beverley had been a national centre of pilgrimage before the Reformation, and remained the chief market for wool and agricultural produce in the East Riding thereafter, while its Cross Fair attracted merchants from London and across the north of England. Its population, estimated at about 5,000 in 1600, still almost equalled that of Hull.[1] Beverley returned MPs during the reign of Edward I, but its representation lapsed after 1328. Elizabeth granted the manor to her favourite Robert Dudley[†], who secured the town's re-enfranchisement in 1563, a privilege which was confirmed by the borough's charter of incorporation in 1573. This charter assigned the franchise to the mayor, governors (equivalent to aldermen) and burgesses. The latter were customarily defined as the 13 'select burgesses', who came to assume the functions of common councillors.[2]

Unlike York and Hull, Beverley rarely returned townsmen to Parliament. The corporation regularly sent representatives to York and London on legal business, and would have been able to afford parliamentary expenses, but its interests rarely clashed with those of its neighbours, and the domination of the corporation by local gentry meant that it was disinclined to promote trade interests. The only measure which could have vexed the Beverlonians was a proposal from the York corporation in the early 1620s to secure a statute barring Londoners from the fairs at Beverley and Howden. However, the York MPs warned that 'there is no way by Parliament to take away the liberty of any subject from going and merchandising where he list', and the plan was dropped.[3] In the absence of a corporation interest, several other parties claimed an electoral influence at Beverley. The Ellerkers and Alfords were returned at times when the heads of their respective families were members of the corporation. The 9th earl of Northumberland had a local base at Leckington, three miles north of the town, and his steward, Edward Fraunceys*, was returned in 1597 and 1601. The steward of the manor, (Sir) Thomas Crompton[†], who collected lucrative tolls (valued at £274 p.a. in 1628) was returned in 1597. Finally, Sir John Stanhope*, farmer of former church lands within the town, had his servant Ralph Ewens[†] elected in 1601.[4]

In 1604 Northumberland, then riding high in the king's favour, had his younger brother Allan Percy returned at Beverley. With Ewens ineligible following his appointment as under-clerk of the Parliaments, the corporation chose William Gee, who had several claims on their allegiance: the town's recorder since 1597, he rented property near the Minster, and was brother-in-law to Sir Thomas Crompton. Both Members were dead by 1614, as was the Percy interest following the family's involvement in the Gunpowder Plot, while Gee's son, born in 1604, was far too young to stand. Edmund Scott, returned at the next three elections, cannot be identified: no-one of this name has been connected with the corporation or any known electoral patrons; but as he was returned during Sir John Crompton's* tenure as manorial steward, he was presumably nominated by the latter. William Towse, a lawyer from Essex, had two possible patrons with local links: Crompton, a fellow Inner Templar, and Sir Lancelot Alford[†], whose second cousin Edward Alford* (himself returned Beverley in 1593) subsequently served with Towse as MP for Colchester.[5]

The manor of Beverley had passed to the duchy of Cornwall by the general election of December 1620, when Sir Henry Hobart* apparently used his position as a member of Prince Charles's Council to nominate his son Sir John Hobart II*. The corporation signified 'our common desire to satisfy so great and noble a friend', but disingenuously claimed that it could not make a firm offer of a seat until the writ arrived. It also warned 'that [because] the election consists in the voices and votes of many, we dare not assure your lordship of more than what rests in our own particular power'. Disappointed at Beverley, Hobart was eventually returned at a by-election for Cambridge in March 1621. The candidate for whom the corporation saved a seat was Sir Christopher Hildyard, who owned the manor of Routh, four miles east of Beverley, and had served as a magistrate for the town's liberty since 1604.[6]

In 1624 Hildyard was returned at Hedon, leaving the senior seat at Beverley open to fresh contenders. One of these was Hildyard's neighbour Sir William Alford of Meaux Abbey, while another was Sir John Hotham. The latter presumably hoped for a nomination from Sir William Constable*, briefly tipped to succeed Crompton as steward of Beverley in December 1623.[7] However, the corporation favoured the duchy of Cornwall, returning first Sir Henry Vane and then, after he elected to serve for Carlisle, Sir Henry Carey II. This sudden tractability was due to the duchy's victory in *quo warranto* proceedings brought against the corporation in Easter 1623. The town thereby lost possession of assets including the market tolls, which the corporation agreed to lease back for £40 p.a. in February 1625.[8]

The conclusion of the *quo warranto* dispute freed the corporation from any electoral obligation to the duchy council at the general election of April 1625, while the new manorial steward, Sir Robert Yaxley*, was also unable to exercise any patronage, having been shipwrecked on Anglesey while *en route* to Ireland. Lord President Scrope, who wrote to Scarborough on Alford's behalf at this election, may have sent a similar nomination to Beverley, and while Alford and Hotham had recently snubbed one of the town's governors for abusing his position as a subsidy assessor, the pair were apparently returned unopposed for the remainder of the decade. Alford's electoral influence was eventually to be undermined by the duchy's lease of Beverley manor to the Warton family in January 1628.[9]

[1] *VCH Yorks. (E. Riding)*, vi. 2-10, 34-5, 39-42, 80-83, 105-6; Hull RO, WT1. [2] *VCH Yorks. (E. Riding)*, vi. 19-22, 63-5, 73-6; *CPR*, 1572-5, pp. 120-1. [3] Yorks. ERRO, BC/II/6/43-55; D.

Lambourn, *Reformation in English Towns* ed. P. Collinson and D. Craig, 63-78; York City Archives, House Bk. 34, ff. 217v-18, 291v. [4] Yorks. ERRO, DDBC 19/19. [5] Yorks. ERRO, BC/II/5/1, ff. 7v, 9; BC/II/6/45-52; Clay, *Dugdale's Vis. Yorks.* iii. 22; C142/332/165; J.G. Alford, *Alford Fam. Notes*, 10, 16, 24. [6] Yorks. ERRO, BC/II/6/51, 'common expenses'; BC/II/7/4/1, f. 17, mistakenly dated to 1604 (when Hobart was 10 years old) in *VCH Yorks. (E. Riding)*, vi. 91-2; C181/1, f. 94. [7] Yorks. ERRO, DDCC/144/1, Dunbar to John Kirton; HUL, DDHA/18/12. [8] DCO, 'Prince Charles in Spain', ff. 34, 39v; Yorks. ERRO, DDBC 2/17, 19/18; BC/II/7/4/1, f. 36; E401/2445, unfol. (3 Dec. 1628). [9] *CSP Dom.* 1625-6, p. 41; PROB 11/155, f. 13; *Scarborough Recs. 1600-40* ed. M.Y. Ashcroft (N. Yorks. Co. RO xlvii), 142; SP14/170/42; Yorks. ERRO, DDBC 19/19.

S.H.

BOROUGHBRIDGE

Right of election: in the burgage-holders

Number of voters: 64

25 Feb. 1604	JOHN FERNE
	SIR HENRY JENKINS
14 Dec. 1609	SIR THOMAS VAVASOUR *vice*
	Ferne, deceased
	?Sir Ferdinando Fairfax
c. Mar. 1614	SIR FERDINANDO FAIRFAX
	GEORGE MARSHALL
18 Dec. 1620	SIR FERDINANDO FAIRFAX
	GEORGE WETHERID
16 Jan. 1624	SIR FERDINANDO FAIRFAX
	PHILIP MAINWARING
	?Sir Edmund Verney*
19 Apr. 1625	SIR FERDINANDO FAIRFAX
	PHILIP MAINWARING
16 Jan. 1626	SIR FERDINANDO FAIRFAX
	PHILIP MAINWARING
	Bulstrode Whitelocke*
26 Feb. 1628	SIR FERDINANDO FAIRFAX
	FRANCIS NEVILLE II

Established in the eleventh century when the bridge at Aldborough was re-sited upstream, Boroughbridge returned two Members to Parliament in 1300, and was re-enfranchised in 1553. The town was part of the duchy of Lancaster honour of Knaresborough, which was granted to Anne of Denmark and later Prince Charles, though the government interest was usually exercised by the Council in the North.[1] The dominant local family, the Tankards, were Catholics who were implicated in the 1569 rebellion, but in 1598 Thomas Tankard, the new head of the family, conformed to escape recusancy fines. He filled one of the parliamentary seats with a succession of his relatives, while from 1614 the other was monopolized by Sir Ferdinando Fairfax, whose main estates lay some miles to the south. As the only gentry family among the electorate, the Tankards took precedence in the seven surviving indentures, in which almost half of the 20 voters could sign or at least initial their names, suggesting a better educated electorate than at Aldborough.[2]

In 1604 the borough returned John Ferne, deputy secretary to the Council in the North, and Sir Henry Jenkins, whose wife was a Tankard. Following Ferne's death, a by-election was ordered on 8 Sept. 1609. Lord Treasurer Salisbury (Robert Cecil[†]) nominated the knight marshal, Sir Thomas Vavasour, who was a Yorkshireman by birth. Although Salisbury was rebuffed elsewhere, Tankard and four other electors acceded to his request in extraordinarily obsequious terms:

> thinking ourselves more than twice happy to be moved by your favourable letters for the grant of a burgess-ship, the refusal whereof (even in our simplest judgments) were worse to us than death itself: since the never dying fame of your renowned virtues do of right claim in us no denial. And since we know your godly care of the commonwealth both in public and private to be so singular as the world doth justly admire your prudence and wisdom in the uniform settling of the same, the consideration of which your worthiness hath won us (most unworthy your love) to grant you your request, which otherwise (but that it was your honour's pleasure) you might have commanded.

Vavasour was returned 'of our free and general consent', but his name was entered over an erasure. Ferne, the original nominee, had been backed by the Council in the North, and thus lord president Sheffield may have nominated a replacement before hearing of Salisbury's request; if so, the candidate was presumably his new son-in-law, Sir Ferdinando Fairfax. The misunderstanding clearly created some confusion, as the indenture had not reached Chancery by the eve of the next session.[3]

In 1614 Vavasour found a seat at Horsham, Sussex, on the earl of Arundel's interest. He was replaced at Boroughbridge by the Yorkshire-born equerry George Marshall, whose wife's Catholic sympathies may have recommended him to Tankard; the other Member was Sir Ferdinando Fairfax. By the time of the next election in December 1620 Fairfax's wife was dead and Sheffield out of office, but Sir Ferdinando

retained his seat for the rest of the decade, accompanied in 1621 by George Wetherid, lord president Scrope's secretary. Tankard's interest was not eliminated, however, as his wife's nephew Philip Mainwaring, a royal cupbearer and another Arundel client, was returned in 1624, despite a challenge from Sir Edmund Verney*, nominee of the duchy of Cornwall, which had acquired the honour of Knaresborough in 1619. Fairfax and Mainwaring were returned to the next two parliaments, though in 1626 Bulstrode Whitelocke* was nominated by his father's friend, (Sir) Humphrey May*, chancellor of the duchy of Lancaster. Whitelocke later insisted he had been returned, a plausible claim, as there were only 11 signatures on the surviving return for Fairfax and Mainwaring. A petition came before the committee for privileges, but was never reported. Mainwaring may have felt his tenure threatened, particularly after the death of his cousin Tankard in 1627, as he transferred to Derby at the next election. His seat at Boroughbridge was taken by Francis Neville II, brother-in-law of Tankard's heir.[4]

[1] Sir T. Lawson-Tancred, *Recs. Yorks. Manor* 3-14, 141, 174-5; A.D.K. Hawkyard, 'Enfranchisement of constituencies, 1508-1558', *PH*, x. 14-19. [2] *Misc.* (Cath. Rec. Soc. liii), 97, 346-7, 377-8; E368/493, recorda rot.185; C142/600/124. [3] SP14/49/10; Surrey Hist. Cent. LM 1331/15. [4] J.P. Earwaker, *East Cheshire*, ii. 566; DCO, Prince Charles in Spain, f. 34; *Whitelocke Diary* ed. R. Spalding, 53; *Procs. 1626*, ii. 55.

S.H.

HEDON-IN-HOLDERNESS

Right of election: ?in the corporation

Number of voters: 13 or 14

5 Mar. 1604	SIR HENRY CONSTABLE SIR CHRISTOPHER HILDYARD
by 3 Mar. 1610	SIR JOHN DIGBY vice Constable, deceased Election of Digby declared void, 26 Mar. 1610[1]
7 Apr. 1610	SIR JOHN DIGBY vice Digby, return rejected by the House
c. Mar. 1614	WILLIAM SHEFFIELD CLEMENT COKE
c. Dec. 1620	SIR THOMAS FAIRFAX II SIR MATTHEW BOYNTON, 1st bt.
18 Jan. 1624	SIR CHRISTOPHER HILDYARD SIR THOMAS FAIRFAX II
28 Apr. 1625	SIR CHRISTOPHER HILDYARD SIR THOMAS FAIRFAX II
16 Jan. 1626	SIR THOMAS FAIRFAX II SIR CHRISTOPHER HILDYARD
3 Mar. 1628	SIR CHRISTOPHER HILDYARD THOMAS ALURED

Hedon was founded in the twelfth century on a haven two miles from the Humber, as a convenient point for the export of produce from Holderness. The town boasted an imposing chapel known as the 'King of Holderness', but in 1540 Leland noted 'the haven is very sorely decayed', and by the 1620s the town's modest remaining trade was being unloaded a mile downstream at Paull. With a population of only 400 by the 1670s, the town lacked any significant manufacturing base: a handful of merchants dealt in corn, cloth and coal, and a leather industry developed during the seventeenth century.[2]

The town possessed a well-developed corporate structure: the charter of 1348 specified a mayor, two bailiffs, a coroner and 'other fit officers', which included a recorder and ten aldermen by 1603.[3] Like many Yorkshire boroughs, Hedon had returned Members to Parliament in 1295. However, it was not properly enfranchised until 1547, when the right to return Members was almost certainly obtained at the behest of Sir Michael Stanhope[†], groom of the stool to Edward VI, who had been granted chantry property in the vicinity of the town. After his execution in 1552, Stanhope's lands and electoral interest were transferred to the Constable family, who owned vast estates in Holderness. Their influence explains why, as the mayor stated in 1609, Hedon's MPs 'have always been gentlemen of the best sort and esteem in the country about us'.[4]

In the absence of electoral contests the franchise was ill-defined: the 1604 and 1610 indentures, which cite the 'community of the burgesses' as the electorate, bear no signatures, and are validated only by the town seal; while those from 1624 were signed by corporation members alone. Although after the Restoration the franchise was exercised by the burgesses, during the early Stuart period it was probably restricted to the corporation. Members are unlikely to have received wages or expenses: in 1609, the corporation asked that the nominee for the forthcoming by-election should be 'such a one as shall in every respect defray his own charges and in no ways be burdensome unto us'.[5] The surviving returns for the period are in Latin, perhaps an indication of the corporation's self-esteem, and all include a clause giving their MPs powers to assent to all that was done in their name in the Commons, a standard phrase elsewhere, but rarely found in Yorkshire indentures.

Sir Henry Constable's return for Hedon in 1604 was a sign of political rehabilitation: although a conformist in religion, he had been removed from local office and missed the last three Elizabethan parliaments after his wife and brother, both obdurate Catholics, had been arrested for their involvement with priests connected to the exiled 5th earl of Westmorland. The earl's affinity was regarded with particular suspicion during the 1590s because of their support for a Stuart succession, a threat which James could obviously indulge in a way that his predecessor could not. The junior Member in 1604 was Sir Christopher Hildyard, a local landowner representing the borough for the fifth time. He had recently inherited a substantial Holderness estate from his uncle, also Sir Christopher Hildyard[†], whose wife had been Constable's aunt.[6]

Constable died in December 1607, but no by-election was moved until November 1609, shortly before the Parliament reassembled, when Lord Treasurer Salisbury (Robert Cecil[†]), wrote to the mayor asking for the right of nomination. The corporation, 'thinking ourselves greatly blessed of God and highly graced by your honour in having a patron so worthy who hath such a special care of us and our poor corporation', volunteered to send a blank indenture, 'although we had partly promised it before to another'. This may refer to Constable's son, also Sir Henry, a crypto-Catholic who had recently conformed to avoid recusancy fines on his estates, although Sheffield might have preferred the return of Constable's brother-in-law Sir Thomas Fairfax II, one of the vice-presidents of the Council in the North.[7] For some reason the by-election had not been held by the time Parliament reassembled in February 1610. Salisbury, clearly impatient, sent another letter to the mayor via (Sir) William Gee*, secretary of the Council in the North, at the end of the month. On 3 Mar. the corporation insisted that they had already sent their return up to Hildyard (who was presumably then at Westminster) 'which assuredly will be speedily returned to your honour when it shall come to his hands'. This indenture, which returned Sir John Digby, a courtier who was clearly Salisbury's nominee, reached the Commons on 26 Mar., but was rejected upon a motion from Sir George More*, the chairman of the committee for privileges. The reason for this decision went unrecorded, but the committee may have objected to the use of a blank indenture. A new writ was dispatched, and Digby was eventually returned on 7 Apr., by which time the corporation had clearly been informed of Salisbury's choice, as Digby's name was entered on the indenture at the time of the election.[8]

None of the obvious candidates was returned at Hedon in 1614. Constable may already have reverted to Rome; he had certainly done so by 1626, when the Commons complained that his conviction for recusancy was being delayed by removal of the prosecution into King's Bench. He compensated for his removal from political life by purchasing the Scottish title of Viscount Dunbar in 1620. Digby lost his patron when Salisbury died in 1612, but he was in any case unavailable as a candidate in 1614 as he had become resident ambassador in Spain.[9] Hildyard's absence is curious, as this was the only Parliament of his adult life in which he did not sit. Neither of the Members returned in 1614 had any traceable links with the Constable interest. William Sheffield was distantly related to the lord president; his great-aunt, Magdalen Frodsham, had served Sheffield's mother; and in 1615 he married the widow of one of Lord Sheffield's sons. The other Member, Clement Coke, was one of the sons of lord chief justice Sir Edward Coke*, whose legal advice had saved Constable's estates from wardship. Coke, however, opted to sit for Clitheroe, where he had also been elected, on 14 May; no by-election is known to have taken place at Hedon before the dissolution on 7 June.[10]

The matrix of Yorkshire politics was changed in January 1619, when Constable's second cousin Emanuel, 10th Lord Scrope replaced Sheffield as lord president. At the general election of December 1620 Scrope volunteered Fairfax as a partner for Secretary of State (Sir) George Calvert*. Fairfax, reluctant to contest the county seats against Sir John Savile*, resigned his interest to Sir Thomas Wentworth* and saved his pride by obtaining a seat at Hedon.[11] Hildyard, who was returned at Beverley, may have been moved at short notice to accommodate Fairfax. The junior Member for Hedon, Sir Matthew Boynton, was probably sponsored by Henry Alured of Sculcoates, who was married to Boynton's first cousin. Although Boynton and Alured were both Puritans, and thus unlikely allies of the Constable family, Alured was Dunbar's third cousin and owned a farm on the outskirts of Hedon.[12]

Boynton, having inherited his estates in 1617, probably only sought election in 1620 to enhance his local status; having achieved his aim, he is not known to have stood again until 1645. Hildyard was thus able to return to Hedon from 1624.[13] Fairfax, who was returned as Hildyard's partner until 1626, was prevented from standing in 1628 by his appointment as sheriff of Yorkshire. Henry Alured probably intervened to secure the election of his brother Thomas in 1628, although the latter may also have received official support from (Sir) John Coke* and Lord Brooke (Sir Fulke Greville*), a relative of Dunbar's who had sat for Hedon himself in 1584.[14]

[1] CJ, i. 414b. [2] VCH Yorks. (E. Riding), v. 168-77. [3] Ibid. 178-9; G.R. Park, Hist. Hedon, 25-33. [4] A.D.K. Hawkyard 'Enfranchisement of Constituencies, 1504-58', PH, x. 20; VCH Yorks. (E. Riding), v. 174; SP14/49/25. [5] C219/35/2/146, 155; 219/38/275; 219/39/212; 219/40/125; 219/41B/36; SP14/49/25. [6] Vis. Yorks. ed. J. Foster, 51, 57-8. [7] C142/310/79; CSP Dom. 1603-10, p. 438; HMC Var. ii. 111. [8] SP14/53/2-3; CJ, i. 414b; C219/35/2/46-7. [9] DCO, 'Parl. Procs. Chas. I, 1625-6', unfol.; Handlist of Brit. Diplomatic Representatives comp. G.M. Bell, 258. [10] Coke, 8th Rep. Sir Henry Constable's case; CJ, i. 485b. [11] R. Reid, Council in the North, 488; Clay, Dugdale's Vis. Yorks. iii. 304-6; Strafforde Letters (1739) ed. W. Knowler, i. 10. [12] Vis. Yorks. ed. J. Foster, 57-8, 120-1, 144; C142/452/42; VCH Yorks. (E. Riding), v. 188, 192. [13] C142/367/59; DCO, Prince Charles in Spain, f. 34. [14] List of Sheriffs comp. A. Hughes (PRO, L. and I. ix), 163; THOMAS ALURED.

S.H.

KINGSTON-UPON-HULL[1]

Right of election: in the freemen

Number of voters: c.750-1000[2]

11 Mar. 1604	JOHN EDMONDES ANTHONY COLE, alderman Robert Tailler, alderman John Lister[†], alderman
9 Mar. 1607	JOSEPH FIELD vice Cole, deceased [Robert] Tailler, alderman Sir Edward Michelborne[†]
c.Mar. 1614	SIR JOHN BOURCHIER RICHARD BURGIS, alderman
25 Dec. 1621	JOHN LISTER, alderman MAURICE ABBOT
19 Jan. 1624	(SIR) JOHN SUCKLING MAURICE ABBOT
15 Mar. 1624	JOHN LISTER, alderman vice Suckling, chose to sit for Middlesex Sir William Constable, bt.* Emmanuel Giffard*
9 May 1625	JOHN LISTER, alderman (SIR) MAURICE ABBOT
16 Jan. 1626	JOHN LISTER, alderman (SIR) MAURICE ABBOT
13 Mar. 1626	LANCELOT ROPER, alderman vice Abbot, chose to sit for London
10 Mar. 1628[3]	JOHN LISTER, alderman JAMES WATKINSON, alderman Lancelot Roper, alderman Joshua Hall, alderman

Chartered by the Crown as Kingston-upon-Hull in 1299, the borough regularly returned MPs thereafter. A charter of incorporation in 1440 conferred jurisdiction independent of the East Riding.[4] Its economy originally depended almost entirely upon the loading of Yorkshire wool onto seagoing ships, and it probably bore the brunt of the fifteenth-century decline in the wool trade. To bolster its position, the borough ordered that no alien could buy or sell except through a Hull burgess. This prohibition on 'foreign bought and sold' goods was extended to all non-freemen (except at markets and fairs) by letters patent in 1532,

encouraging a revival of trade which made Hull one of the busiest ports on the east coast by 1603.[5]

Early Stuart Hull had one of the highest export trades of any outport, shipping upwards of 40,000 northern cloths and 2,000 fothers of lead to the Baltic, the Low Countries and France each year. The town also maintained a vigorous coastal trade, particularly with London for manufactures and Tyneside for coal.[6] Much of the profit accrued to outsiders, particularly York merchants, who had an uneasy relationship with their neighbours. Hull's 1598 charter exempted York men from the obligation to land their goods at Hull, but tensions remained over enforcement of the 'bought and sold' rule, and York's reluctance to share the burden of fitting out ships for service against the Armada.[7] Other rivals included the West Riding clothiers, 'which have got their freedoms [to trade at Hull] by the Merchant Adventurers ... [and] have great advantage of the merchants of this town in buying of their cloth and their easy charge withal'; London merchants, who were criticized for monopolizing Yorkshire's fairs in defiance of government orders;[8] aristocratic mineowners such as William Cavendish[†], 1st earl of Devonshire, who ignored an order of 1587 that all lead was to be landed and weighed at Hull;[9] and Scottish and Dutch merchants. The Hull Trinity House regularly fined local merchants for using foreign shipping, and in 1621 the corporation asked the Privy Council to order foreign merchants and mariners to repatriate their profits in the form of English goods rather than coin.[10]

Hull's complaints were reciprocated by its rivals, who attacked its privileges in the law courts and Parliament, and lobbied the Council in the North and the Privy Council. Such threats were countered by an influential network of supporters. From 1584 the town selected a privy councillor as its high steward, and in 1596 it chose Sir Robert Cecil[†], who was distantly related to two aldermen. In 1594 Peter Proby[†] was appointed solicitor for the town's business at Court: he rendered invaluable service during the charter renewal of 1608-11, and was succeeded by (Sir) William Beecher*, clerk to the Privy Council, in 1629. However, most lobbying was done by the aldermen, who were regularly sent to York and London both in and out of parliamentary sessions.[11] Despite considerable effort, Hull's MPs largely failed to obtain parliamentary redress for their grievances, even though they sometimes worked with their counterparts from York and Newcastle: during a debate of 8 Mar. 1621 on a measure to prohibit the import of corn, John Lister protested 'that this bill may do much hurt, because much cloth transported into the east countries, whence the only return rye'. This point was picked up by Sir Thomas Riddell of Newcastle, and amplified by Christopher Brooke on behalf of his York constituents.[12]

Under its 1598 charter, Hull was run by a corporation comprising a mayor and 12 aldermen, assisted by a sheriff and two chamberlains. There was no common council, although prominent burgesses were occasionally asked to endorse important decisions, especially those involving expensive lawsuits. During the early Stuart period the recordership was held successively by two local lawyers, William Gee* and William Dalton, both of whom were sons of Hull aldermen. Almost two-thirds of the 58 aldermen who served between 1585 and 1645 were merchants, some of whom probably earned their living from retailing or property rental; the remainder included a handful of drapers and mariners.[13] MPs were usually elected in the manner prescribed for municipal officials by letters patent of 1443, that is to say the corporation nominated two candidates for each vacancy, from which the burgesses chose one. Thus the freemen exercised a real (albeit restricted) choice at elections, except when a nomination was offered to one of the town's political patrons. In 1604 lord president Sheffield secured a seat for his secretary, John Edmondes, while ten years later he nominated Sir John Bourchier, his associate in the Cleveland alum business.[14] In 1620 the town's high steward, Archbishop Abbot, proposed his brother, the London merchant Maurice Abbot, promising he would 'give help to any business which may belong unto your town'. As a Levant and East India merchant, Abbot, who represented the borough in three parliaments, had little to offer the corporation, although his speech of 21 Apr. 1621 about Dutch interlopers in the Eastland trade certainly echoed local opinion. However, the corporation clearly judged that the archbishop's support on the Privy Council justified their choice. In 1626 Abbot also stood for one of the London seats, whereupon the corporation resolved that if he waived his election at Hull, 'there shall be one other burgess of the town ... elected ... and not any dwelling out of the town for any respect whatsoever. This resolution seems to have discouraged further outside nominations, and he was replaced by alderman Lancelot Roper. At the 1628 election the corporation reverted to its customary selection of four aldermen as candidates: Lister was once again returned, but on this occasion Roper was replaced by James Watkinson.[15]

Although for much of the period the town disregarded the legal requirement that Members should be resident in the constituencies for which they served, it paid lip-service to the requirement that all borough Members should be freemen: John Edmondes was admitted two weeks before his election; and after (Sir) John Suckling was returned in 1624, the corporation arranged to swear him in at Westminster, and undertook 'that Mr. Sheriff should be kept harmless' for returning a stranger.[16] Parliamentary expenses are only recorded for 1626, but the corporation probably offered payment to all of its aldermen Members; certainly each year in which Parliament sat, 'knights' silver' of 47s. 4d. was levied on the country districts within the corporation's jurisdiction. While York's Members were regularly sent to Westminster with formal written instructions, Hull's are only known to have received them in 1628 and 1629. However, between 1621 and 1626 John Lister went to Westminster armed with numerous documents, from which the corporation's priorities may be judged. Hull expected regular reports from its lobbyists and MPs. As early as 1587 alderman Edward Wakefield† noted his activities in the margin of the instructions he took to London, while ten years later Leonard Willan† and Anthony Cole* informed the mayor of their efforts to lobby for the preservation of the salt monopoly which the town had recently purchased from (Sir) Thomas Wilkes†.[17] The corporation also expected news of political developments: in the aftermath of the Gunpowder Plot, Cole promised to send a copy of 'the articles (some 22) that are agreed upon to frame two bills against the traitorous recusants', and he asked that the town preacher be told of 'divers good bills put in to try against swearing, against drunkenness and against profaning the Sabbath, for a learned ministry and against good men deprived'. Lister delighted in reporting the arrest of the projector (Sir) Giles Mompesson* in 1621, hoping that 'more of that kind will follow'; he subsequently recounted proceedings against Sir John Bennet* and lord chancellor St. Alban (Sir Francis Bacon*). He also sent news of foreign affairs, obtained through contacts at the Custom House and the Exchange, and of economic developments, which were of considerable importance to the Hull merchants, especially during the grain shortage of 1623, when he forwarded details of the latest London prices for Dutch and Polish rye.[18]

At the 1604 general election the corporation presumably supported Lord Sheffield's nominee John Edmondes, but intended the other seat for a townsman. Recorder William Gee*, who had represented the town in 1589, may have had designs upon this place, as three days before the election he sent the corporation the deeds of the almshouse his father had recently bequeathed to the town. In the event this approach proved unnecessary, however, as he was returned for Beverley on the same day, but it may help to explain why his cousin alderman Anthony Cole, who had recently been out of favour with the corporation, subsequently defeated John Lister[†] at the hustings. During the 1604 session Cole was named to the committee for the bill restricting the processing of spices to London garblers (30 May 1604), but there is no evidence that he attempted to win exemption for Hull's spice imports from the Low Countries.[19]

In 1606 the survival of two of his letters to the corporation demonstrate that Cole undertook several projects in the Commons. The most important of these was a bill to allow the merchants of York, Newcastle and Hull the discount on the customs duty on cloth which had been granted to all northern merchants in 1592, but which the customs farmers now refused to accept. The burgesses for the northern towns presumably drafted the bill, which was reported on 5 Mar. by the York Member Christopher Brooke.[20] Five days later, Cole informed the Hull corporation that the measure

> hath been twice read, committed and now engrossed, and if time will serve I do mean to call tomorrow [for it] to be put to the question [for the third reading] ... I do hear the clothiers have made a petition which we mean to show to the Parliament House.[21]

The bill was one of several dispatched to the Lords on 13 March. Cole later sent a list of the Lords' committee to Hull, assuring the mayor that 'as yet we can do no more if our lives did [re]lly of [sic] it'. Although not a cloth merchant himself, Cole may have attended the committee, as Lord Treasurer Dorset (Thomas Sackville[†]) was instructed to invite 'such merchants or others as his lordship shall think meet to be heard concerning this bill'. Objections from the customers or other ports probably overwhelmed the bill, which was never reported, but undaunted the northern corporations sent a joint petition to Cecil, now 1st earl of Salisbury, who had the former discount restored.[22] At the same time as he was pursuing this measure, Cole proposed another bill to reform the drainage around Hull and avoid pollution of the town's drinking water, an issue which had provoked an Exchequer suit with a neighbouring landowner in 1599. Cole assured the corporation that Sir Francis Barrington*, owner of the Darringham spring from which the town drew its main water supply, supported the bill, and promised that the cost would 'not come to £40', but there is no evidence that his suggestion was accepted.[23] Cole also reported the controversial vote of 18 Mar. 1606 which

granted the king three subsidies and six fifteenths. Anticipating displeasure at the size of the grant, he recalled the magnitude of the king's debts and a royal undertaking that the first subsidy was to be used to repay the Privy Seal loans of 1604-6. He suspected that 'there are divers will make suit to have assistance or taxes abated, as York and other places, [though] they will not tell me of it', and looked for a share of the £36,000 rebates provided for 'impoverished towns' in the preamble to the bill.[24]

Cole died in January 1607, and was replaced at a by-election on 9 March. Salisbury recommended Sir Edward Michelborne[†] for the vacancy, but sheriff Richard Burgis put forward the names of two aldermen, Joseph Field and Robert Tailler instead. Burgis eventually agreed to include Michelborne in the poll, and the corporation tried to dissuade the freemen from choosing Field who, they claimed, 'was altogether unwilling to take it upon him'. However, the towns freemen would not hear of Michelborne and chose Field regardless. This, at any rate, was the version of events related to Salisbury by the corporation, whose members may secretly have welcomed Michelborne's rejection; they certainly felt no animosity towards Burgis, who was elected alderman four months later.[25] This unwillingness to oblige Salisbury was probably caused by the latter's failure to secure compensation for the loss of four Hull whaling ships which had been seized in Norwegian waters by the king of Denmark in 1599. Diplomatic efforts on the whalers' behalf had failed to secure restitution, but the 120 mariners involved, who reckoned their losses at £7,000, were eventually compensated with a £3,000 Star Chamber fine due from Sir Robert Stapleton*. When this fine was waived they were left without any relief, a grievance the corporation highlighted by sending Salisbury a fresh petition with their letter bearing news of Michelborne's defeat.[26]

Having apparently protested at his election that parliamentary service would interfere with 'his own private affairs in trade of merchandise', Field left no trace on the records of the sessions in which he sat, and was replaced by Burgis in 1614. However, during his sojourn at Westminster, Field was 'employed about the confirmation of the charters and liberties', negotiations for which were begun by Peter Proby and John Lister in 1608-9. The corporation lobbied on a lavish scale, spending £500 'about their charter and charges at the Parliament'. Field was probably responsible for obtaining the confirmation of the 'Hull bought and sold' privilege and the charter of the Hull Merchants' Company which were granted by letters patent on

21 June 1610. He also helped to secure the town charter of March 1611, delivering Salisbury a timely gift of lead three weeks before it passed the Great Seal.[27] The new charter settled several disputes unlikely to have been resolved by Parliament. Most significantly, it confirmed that Derbyshire lead passing down the Humber was required to pay duty at the Hull woolhouse whether it was landed there or not. It also gave the town a permanent grant of the right to collect dues on wool, leather, tin and lead. Though normally leased by the town, when the customer of Hull had secured a grant of these tolls in 1607, the corporation, fearing that they would threaten their other tolls, had been obliged to buy him out. Finally, the charter gave the corporation the right to choose the town's schoolmaster and lecturer, and granted a fee-farm of the shipyards to the north of the walls known as the Trippett.[28]

While the new charter solved many of Hull's municipal problems, another dispute was brewing over whaling rights. Undaunted by the Danes, Hull ships continued to fish off Norway, and in 1611 a consortium of Hull and York merchants (including Richard Burgis) sent an expedition to 'Greenland' (Spitzbergen), which rescued the crew of a Muscovy Company whaler. The rivals returned to the islands in 1612, and in the following year nearly 30 ships from London, Hull, France, Spain and the Low Countries competed for the catch.[29] While there was little the Muscovy Company could do about well-armed foreign fleets, they managed to secure the exclusion of English interlopers in their charter of 1613. This was contested by the Hull Trinity House, which petitioned London at the end of the year, while two Hull ships were defiantly sent to Spitzbergen in the following summer. The whalers' grievances were raised in the Commons in 1614, probably by Burgis or one of the York Members, and the Muscovy Company charter was on the Commons' agenda by the end of May, but consideration was delayed by the political dispute over Bishop Neile; the 'Hull and Muscovy' question was to have been raised on the day of the dissolution.[30]

Hull's trade was disrupted by two separate disputes over staple rights between 1614 and 1619. The first was the closure of the Eastland Company's staple at Elbing in the summer of 1614 which, when combined with a Polish embargo on the city's trade in 1616, forced English merchants to seek new markets. Most switched their business to Danzig or Riga, but others, such as Field, shifted their trade to Amsterdam.[31] The other dispute, concerning the supersession of the Merchant Adventurers' cloth monopoly by alderman

Cockayne's company in 1614, initially had little effect on the Hull merchants, many of whom had been systematically bypassing the staple at Middelburg by shipping cargoes to Amsterdam in vessels falsely registered for San Lucar or Lisbon. However, the reinstatement of the Merchant Adventurers had a significant impact at Hull, as from January 1618 Company members were permitted to ship goods to non-staple ports for a nominal fee. Hull Merchant Adventurers were thus allowed to trade legitimately with Amsterdam for the first time, and in January 1619 they secured a Privy Council order forbidding interlopers from shipping any cloth or lead to the Low Countries. Those affected by this embargo included John Lister (son of the earlier alderman), then mayor and the town's biggest lead merchant, who complained to the Council in June, claiming that members of the Hull Merchants' Company were entitled to trade lead freely under their 1577 charter. After hearing testimony from Lister and Field (governor of the Hull Merchant Adventurers), the Council reopened the lead trade to all Hull merchants in December 1619.[32]

Lister's championship of the Hull merchants' cause recommended him as the ideal replacement for the recently deceased Richard Burgis at the parliamentary election of December 1620. Lister was Hull's keenest advocate at Westminster: in 1625 he promised the corporation that, although 'never so weary of London in all my life, yet my conscience and affection to my country will not give [me] leave to come away till I see things brought to some perfection'. Resolving to stay for debates on the Tunnage and Poundage bill, he criticized MPs who had fled the plague: 'if all men do as some do, what might become of these things if none but the courtiers were remaining?'.[33] Almost all of Lister's lobbying activity can be linked to local interests. Many of the grievances he raised related to mercantile affairs, such as excessive customs fees, a bill to redress which was laid before the Commons in 1624. Lister attended the bill's committee, presumably to complain about the Hull custom house, a grievance York's MPs had been instructed to raise. The issue was subsequently investigated by the Privy Council, which issued a new table of fees at the end of the year after discussion with Hull and York.[34] Lister also lobbied for the Hull Trinity House while at Westminster. He was feasted by the brethren before his departure in 1621, and was doubtless the anonymous Member who called for 'consideration of the privileges of Kingston-upon-Hull' on 27 Feb. 1621, at the second reading of the bill to assign fees for maintenance of the lighthouse at Winterton Ness, Norfolk to the Deptford Trinity House. The Hull brethren were probably concerned about a project to erect a similar lighthouse on Spurn Point at the mouth of the Humber, which they had rejected in 1618. In 1626 the brethren briefed him to secure alterations to their charter, whereupon he advised them that a confirmation would cost only £20, whereas a new charter with additional privileges would cost £70.[35]

Lister naturally participated in the Commons' attack on the Merchant Adventurers in 1621: on 13 Mar., when deputy governor William Towerson* defended the Company's imposition of a lead duty to help recoup the £60,000 paid to secure its 1617 charter, Lister insisted, 'that the said eight pence on a fother of lead is not paid by consent; or if it be, it is a compulsory consent, and by such as are not of the said company of merchants'. Two months later, Lister (probably unjustly) blamed the Adventurers for a brief slump in Hull's cloth trade, claiming 'that 40,000 kersies heretofore transported [from Hull] and now there is but few'.[36] While criticism of the pretermitted custom imposed on cloth exports in 1619 was muted in the Commons in 1621, the duty was seen as a particular grievance by the northern merchants because of its impact upon the thin profit margins on their cheap cloths. The Hull, York and Newcastle corporations jointly petitioned for exemption in 1619, and lord treasurer Mandeville (Sir Henry Montagu*) authorized a 40 per cent discount for northern cloths in May 1621. The Hull corporation clearly aimed for a complete exemption in its submission to the Privy Council on the decay of trade in October 1621, but it correctly assumed that 'more will be expected for the decay of His Majesty's customs'.[37] At Christmas 1622 Hull's discount was halved by lord treasurer Middlesex (Sir Lionel Cranfield*), but despite an offer of help from Middlesex's associate (Sir) Arthur Ingram*, other rivalries between York and Hull forestalled any agreement between the northern towns over a petition. The duty was investigated by the Commons in 1624, when Lister moved 'to proceed to judgment of the pretermitted custom' (3 May), securing its inclusion among the trade grievances to be presented to the king. Another petition submitted by the northern towns at the end of the year secured the restoration of the 40 per cent discount, and the repayment of the surplus duties collected in 1623-4.[38]

Although Hull's dispute with the Muscovy Company was raised in Parliament in 1621, most of the important decisions on this issue were made by the Privy Council. In 1617, when two Hull mariners were summoned before the Council upon charges of interloping, the corporation claimed 'that the Hollanders

and other nations do freely fish the whale there ... which liberty His Majesty's subjects here [at Hull] hope they might exercise as well as strangers'. The Council proved immune to this argument, but accepted Hull's claim to the fishing around Trinity Island (Jan Meyen Land), allegedly discovered by a Hull mariner in 1611. The town's whalers thereafter confined themselves to this area, although Lister unsuccessfully attempted to overthrow their rivals' monopoly with a motion to add the Spitzbergen whaling grounds to the bill for free fishing in 1621.[39] The Hull whalers announced their intention to return to Spitzbergen in the spring of 1623, when alderman Ralph Freeman of London, farmer of the Muscovy Company's rights, convinced the Privy Council to revoke the Hull monopoly of the fishing around Trinity Island. Abbot brokered a temporary deal allowing four northern whalers access to Spitzbergen and a monopoly of train oil sales in the north; Freeman's consortium also promised 'that upon our fair carriage this year, we [the Hull whalers] shall find their favours hereafter'.[40]

As the Hull whalers reached an accommodation with their London rivals, the town suffered a serious reversal at the hands of the York merchants. Relations had soured in 1619, when the York Merchant Adventurers attempted to withhold payment for lead tolls at Hull. Another attack was clearly expected in 1621, when Lister was sent to Westminster with documentation which would have allowed him to defend the town's rights. Having raised the matter with the York MP (Sir) Robert Askwith*, Lister recommended that James Watkinson*, weighmaster of Hull, negotiate with a group of York merchants. A compromise proved elusive, but when Lister received a draft of 'a bill intended for lead' which was presumably meant to confirm Hull's rights, he advised the mayor that 'there is little to do us good in parliamentary courses'. Consequently, the issue was only settled after arbitration by Sir Arthur Ingram in the autumn of 1623.[41] The dispute over trading privileges was rekindled at Hull in July 1622, when 'certain corn sold by the merchants of York unto country chapmen' was seized for breach of the 'foreign bought and sold' rule. Alderman Joshua Hall was sent to London to defend Hull against the resulting lawsuit, but, having consulted precedents, Francis Thorpe[†] and William Noye* advised him to seek arbitration by the Privy Council. Proby, then lord mayor of London, agreed, warning Hall 'not to trust too much of the lawyers, lest they opened gaps that could not be shut', while Archbishop Abbot promised his support.[42] The York men arranged the Privy Council hearing for the same day on which Hull's whaling case was considered, and their counsel's arguments prevailed: attorney-general Coventry* claimed that Hull's privilege 'rather deserved p[rohibition] than relief'; while Heneage Finch*, recorder of London, 'justified against us the usage of London in the matter of corn'. Lister optimistically ventured that the order granting York merchants free trade in grain at Hull 'is rather a restraint than an enlargement to what they have formerly used', but was relieved to have avoided Coventry's threat of a *quo warranto*, as patchy evidence of the enforcement of the 'bought and sold' claim made it difficult to prove at law. The York corporation wrongly assumed their rivals would attempt to confirm their privilege by statute in 1624, and advised their Members to defend the city's rights against any such bill.[43]

Hull's defeat in the dispute with York probably cost Lister his seat at the 1624 general election. His replacement, the comptroller of the Household, Sir John Suckling, was selected for 'divers considerations', foremost among which was the need to acquire new allies at Court. The junior seat was bestowed upon Archbishop Abbot's brother, even though no nomination had been received at the time of the election. Suckling, however, opted to sit for Middlesex, and 'refused to write his letters for any other to have that place'. Instead, perhaps with Lister in mind, he merely suggested that the town replace him with an inhabitant. He was later persuaded to back lord admiral Buckingham's nominee, Emmanuel Giffard, while letters were also received from Ingram and Middlesex on behalf of Sir William Constable*. However, as Ingram and Cranfield had previously supported the York merchants, their candidate received short shrift from the corporation. As was probably always the intention, the corporation therefore turned to Lister once more, using Suckling's first letter to justify its decision.[44]

By the time Lister arrived at Westminster at the end of March 1624, the Commons had already moved the king to break off negotiations for a Spanish Match. Lister had supported the Palatine cause in 1621, when he had lamented that 'I can write no good news from Bohemia, both Morosia [Moravia] and Silesia ... being revolted [from the Elector Palatine] to the Emperor', and sent the corporation a digest of official speeches which revealed the failure of diplomatic attempts to settle 'the bleeding business [of the] Palatinate'.[45] However, several Hull ships had since been seized by the Dunkirkers, and Lister's earlier inclination to belligerence was quickly tempered by concern for the safety of the town and its trade. Learning of the breach with Spain in 1624, the corporation sent Lister documents relating to the town's fortifications, probably

with the intention that he should procure a licence to replace ordnance removed during Elizabeth's wars.[46] In August 1625, with hostilities against Spain imminent, Lister interrupted a debate on the release of a Sallee pirate detained in the Channel to remind the House that 'the northern coasts [are] as much infested by the Dunkirkers', and to ask for a committee to consider the safety of all ports.[47] As England went to war with Spain, relations with France also deteriorated. In December 1625 the French seized the *Gift of God* of Hull in retaliation for Buckingham's detention of the *St. Peter* of Le Havre. Lister, one of those whose goods had been seized by the French, joined in a petition to the Privy Council, and when the issue of the *St. Peter* was raised in the Commons in February 1626, he moved 'that those poor [French] merchants may be relieved, and that our merchants' goods may not be sold'.[48]

The outbreak of war with Spain in the autumn of 1625 allowed the Dunkirkers to prey on English shipping, which reduced Hull's trade by a third. Thus while Lister commended plans for a privateering company to wage war against Spain in the West Indies in March 1626, security remained uppermost in his mind. He informed the Hull Trinity House that the question of trade protection 'hath been moved in Parliament, and divers of the lords of the Council have been acquainted with the Dunkirkers their spoils on our coasts, but as yet nothing is done either for the restraining of them, or securing our commerce'. He voiced his frustration in the Commons three days later, moving 'that a natural and genuine cause of the stopping of trade [is] the want of wafters and convoy for merchants' ships', and asking for consideration of the safety of the ports.[49] His pleas were quickly heeded: a convoy to London was arranged during the winter of 1625-6, and in March a warrant was issued for the arming of 22 Hull ships. The town's MPs presumably raised the issue with the Privy Council on 7 Apr. 1626, when three armed colliers were ordered to escort Hull's Baltic cloth fleet to the Sound; convoys were later arranged to the Texel, and in the following year Sir John Savile* organized a squadron to protect the Yorkshire coast. However, Lister continued his 'pitiful complaints' in 1628, warning that 'we that have given laws to others are now kept in by two paltry towns [Dunkirk and Ostend]; merchants dare not set forth. We must never hope to be a brave nation again without speedy reformation'.[50]

Hull's dependence on naval protection during the war years denied the corporation the luxury of dissent from the Crown's demands. The town lodged and transported 2,000 recruits to the Low Countries in 1625, but apparently balked at the £6,000 worth of Privy Seal loans demanded from the county at the same time: its MPs joined a deputation which successfully lobbied the Privy Council for a 60 per cent reduction in April 1626. These reduced Privy Seals were promptly collected by Lister, who delivered 90 per cent of the town's quota of just over £200 to the Exchequer on 16 August. The levy was eventually replaced by the Forced Loan, which Hull collected with a minimal number of defaulters and only one refuser, who was certified to the Privy Council.[51] In 1626 the town was ordered to find two ships for the Navy. The corporation protested its inability, blaming both the towns of the West Riding and the Yorkshire coast for refusing to contribute, and also the reluctance of townsmen to bear charges beyond the Forced Loan and improvements to the town's defences.[52] However, where prospects of repayment existed, the corporation was prepared to exert itself: in 1627 £2,200 was raised to ship 2,500 reinforcements to Germany, including loans of £300 from the Forced Loan collectors and £200 from the Trinity House. When town officials encountered 'long stay and much suit' in recovering their outlay from the Exchequer, Sir John Savile* offered his assistance, but then promptly borrowed £200 of the sum repaid for his own uses.[53]

During the 1628 parliamentary session, Lister brokered a fresh settlement of the long-running whaling dispute. The 1623 agreement over quotas and markets had broken down by 1626, when the Hull and London whalers attacked each other. The Council, mindful that northern merchants were 'almost wholly barred from foreign trade elsewhere', permitted them to send 600 tons of shipping to the Arctic in 1627, but the Hull whalers provocatively sent out one ship more than their quota allowed.[54] The dispute was raised in the Commons in 1628, when Lister's nomination to the committee for the free fishing bill (17 Apr.) suggests that he hoped to revive his 1621 plan to abrogate the Muscovy Company charter by statute. This clearly failed, as the issue was referred to the committee for grievances, where alderman Freeman eventually agreed to allow fishing rights to 500 tons of Hull shipping for the coming season. The committee's report criticized the Muscovy Company for its claims 'to restrain all men from fishing without their licence, and to imprison men without their conviction', and Lister underlined the reasonableness of his constituents' claims by reminding the House that 'it is not intended that the Muscovy Company should be excluded, but it is desired that the Hull men and others may have liberty as well as they'. The House

condemned the Muscovy Company patent as a grievance, and a committee was charged to draw up a petition calling for its revocation (25 June), though this was dashed by the prorogation, which took place the next day.[55]

While the whalers had cause to celebrate, Hull's MPs failed to implement any of the written instructions they received from the corporation in 1628 and 1629. They were ordered to arrange for the shipment of guns for the town defences, which had been authorized by the Privy Council in 1627, or if these were not available, to buy others. However, it was not until the summer of 1629, when Lister recruited the support of Sir William Beecher, the town's new solicitor, that a licence was granted for the purchase of 12 sakers for the castle and blockhouses.[56] Watkinson was charged with the recovery of the £100 which Savile still owed the corporation, but this sum was not recovered from Savile's estate until 1633. Lister even failed to deliver Archbishop Abbot's fee as high steward, which the latter refused 'in respect (as he said) he could do the town no pleasure'. His one positive achievement was the release of the crew of the *Gift of God*, who were presumably the Hull mariners exchanged for French prisoners in the summer of 1628.[57]

While Lister was added to the committee investigating the seizure of the goods of the merchant John Rolle* on 3 Feb. 1629, he played no recorded part in the furore stirred up over the issue by (Sir) John Eliot*. It is possible that Edmond Cooper of Hull, summoned before the Privy Council on 10 Apr.,[58] had joined the customs strike inspired by Eliot's propositions of 2 Mar., but the most important issue for most of the townsmen until the end of the war continued to be the disruption of trade: with many mariners out of work, the corporation permitted unofficial alehouses (often run by mariners' wives) to buy licences because of 'the interruption of the trade at sea by the Dunkirkers and otherwise'.[59]

[1] This article has been written with assistance from Prof. Donald Woodward, Geoffrey Oxley and Sarah McCrow. [2] Hull RO, Freemen's Reg. 1442-1645 shows 20-30 men taking up the freedom each year. [3] Hull RO, Bench Bk. 5, f. 91. [4] D. Hey, *Yorks. from AD 1000*, pp. 48-9; E. Gillett and K.A. MacMahon, *Hist. Hull*, 1-6, 24-5, 85-6; *VCH Yorks. (E. Riding)*, i. 13-21, 39-40; *Charters of Hull* trans. J.R. Boyle, 1-5, 35-6, 54-6. [5] *Medieval Hull* ed. R. Horrox (Yorks. Arch. Soc. rec. ser. cxli), 12, 16-17; R. Davies, *Trade and Shipping of Hull, 1500-1700* (E. Yorks. Local Hist. Ser. xvii), 4-7; *VCH Yorks. (E. Riding)*, 77-82, 99-101; J.K. Fedorowicz, *England's Baltic Trade*, 156-7; *Charters of Hull*, 64-5. [6] Hey, 151-2; Davies, 22, 24; W.B. Stephens, 'Cloth exports of provincial ports, 1600-40', *EcHR* (ser. 2), xxii. 244-7; A. Raistrick and B. Jennings, *Hist. of Lead Mining in the Pennines*, 55-65; D.M. Palliser, *Tudor York*, 189-90. [7] Davies, 28-9; Hull RO, Bench Bk. 4, ff. 263, 297-8, 300v, 318, 331v; Palliser, 272-3, 282; *APC*, 1588, p. 282; *York Civic Recs.* ed. A. Raine (Yorks.

Arch. Soc. rec. ser. cxix), 162-3; *Charters of Hull*, 128-30. [8]Hull RO, Bench Bk. 5, f.47r-v; Hull RO, WT1; *APC*, 1591-2, p. 531. [9]D. Kiernan, *Derbys. Lead Ind.* (Derbys. Rec. Soc xiv), 227-30; Hull RO, Bench Bk. 4, ff. 249v-50, 370. [10]*Order Bk. of Trin. House* ed. F.W. Brooks (Yorks. Arch. Soc. rec. ser. cv); *Trin. House of Deptford Trans.* ed. G.G. Harris (London Rec. Soc. xix), 44-5; Hull RO, Bench Bk. 5, f. 45v. [11]Hull RO, Bench Bk. 4, ff. 234, 258v, 265v, 288, 300, 321, 359, 370, 375-6v; Bench Bk. 5, ff. 1, 10, 32v, 95v, 98, 154-5; *HMC Hatfield*, xx. 148, 252. [12]*CJ*, i. 544b-5a. [13]*Charters of Hull*, 106-13; Hull RO, Bench Bk. 4, ff. 293, 343, 360v, 371-2. The aldermen comprised: merchants 38; mariners 7; drapers 5, others 3; unknown 5. [14]*Charters of Hull*, 52; Hull RO, Bench Bk. 4, f. 357v; R.B. Turton, *Alum Farm*, 70-4. [15]Hull RO, Bench Bk. 5, ff. 45v-6v, 70v, 91; Hull RO, L.166; *CD 1621*, iii. 47-9; iv. 229. [16]Hull RO, Bench Bk. 5, ff. 41, 60v, 72v; BRF/2/470, 472, 474-5, 477, 482, 485, 487, 488; Freemens' Reg. 1396-1645, f. 139. [17]Hull RO, Bench Bk. 4, ff. 264v-5, 269v, 272v, 274; Bench Bk. 5, ff.41, 61, 67, 70v; Hull RO, L.128, M.89; E. Hughes, *Studies in Admin. and Finance*, 45-56. [18]Hull RO, L.159, 169-71, 180, 200. [19]Hull RO, Bench Bk. 4, ff. 315, 340v, 343, 357r-v; PROB 11/101, f. 281; *CJ*, i. 228b, *SR*, iv. 1036-7. [20]*LJ*, ii. 394a; L.H. Zins, *Eng. and the Baltic in the Elizabethan Era*, 180-1; Stephens, 237, 244-6; *HMC Hatfield*, xxiii. 220-1; xxiv. 52; *CJ*, i. 277b. [21]Hull RO, L.159. The petition was perhaps Hatfield House, Petition 2048. [22]*CJ*, i. 283b; Hull RO, L.160; *LJ*, ii. 396b; Hatfield House, Petition 2070. [23]Hull RO, Bench Bk. 4, ff. 292-3, 323v, 338v; E134/40 Eliz/Hil.12; Hull RO, L.159. [24]*CJ*, i. 286; E401/2584-5; Hull RO, L.160; *SR*, iv. 1109. [25]Yorks. ERRO, PE158/1, p. 402; *HMC Hatfield*, xix. 65; Hull RO, Bench Bk. 4, ff. 370, 375. [26]SP12/271/68; SP75/3, f. 154; *45th DKR*, 54-5; H.E. Chetwynd-Stapylton, *Stapletons of Yorks.* 225; *HMC Hatfield*, xvii. 195; xix. 66; xx. 312. [27]Hatfield House, ms 115, f. 137; *HMC Hatfield*, xx. 80; Hull RO, Bench Bk. 5, ff. 1, 7; *Charters of Hull*, 131-2; SP14/61/109. [28]*Charters of Hull*, 134-9, 145-9; Hull RO, Bench Bk. 4, ff. 371v-2; Gillett and MacMahon, 151. [29]Hull Trinity House, Accts. 3, ff. 39v, 40v, 72, 100, 107-8v, 119; E190/312/6-7, 190/313/5; S. Purchas, *Purchas his Pilgrims* (1906 edn.), xiv. 37-9, 44-5, 57; *Early Dutch and Eng. Voyages to Spitsbergen* ed. W.M. Conway (Hakluyt Soc. ser. 2. xi), 3-8; *CSP Ven.* 1613-15, p. 61. [30]*CD 1628*, iii. 122, n. 1; Hull Trinity House, Accts. 3, f. 144r-v; E190/313/8; *CJ*, i. 494b, 502a; *Procs. 1614 (Commons)*, 339-88, 444-5. [31]Fedorowicz, 145-50, 155-6. [32]A. Friis, *Alderman Cokayne's Project*, 121-7; E190/312/6, 7; 190/313/5, 8; *APC*, 1618-19, pp. 351-2, 482-3; 1619-21, pp. 90-1; *Charters of Hull*, 91-6; Lansd. 162, ff. 1-3. [33]Yorks. ERRO, PE185/1, unfol. (17 Apr. 1620); *Procs. 1625*, pp. 717-8. [34]C.R. Kyle, 'Attendance Lists', *PPE 1604-48* ed. Kyle, 217-19; E190/315/3; York City Archives, House Bk. 34, f. 292; *APC*, 1623-5, pp. 354, 368-9, 371. [35]Hull Trinity House, Accts. 3, ff. 248, 346, ATH/47/1, letter of 17 Mar. 1626; *CJ*, i. 529b; *CD 1621*, vii. 6-17; *Charters of Hull*, 57-8; *Trinity House Trans.* 33-6. [36]Nicholas, *Procs. 1621*, i. 152-3; *CD 1621*, ii. 365; iv. 339; vi. 60; Stephens, 237, 247; *CJ*, i. 620b improbably ascribes the cloth statistics to King's Lynn. [37]C. Russell, *PEP*, 60; SP14/111/69; *APC*, 1623-5, pp. 382-3; Hull RO, Bench Bk. 5, ff. 45-8; L.176. [38]*APC*, 1623-5, pp. 377-8, 382-3; Hull RO, L.190-1, 200; *CJ*, i. 782a; E190/316/1. [39]J.D. Benson, *Co-operation to Competition*, 128-33; *CSP Ven.* 1613-15, p. 146; 1617-19, pp. 296-7, 331; *APC*, 1616-17, pp. 329-30, 344; 1618-19, pp. 2, 45-6; SP14/94/71; *Early Voyages to Spitsbergen*, 83; E190/314/14, ff. 4, 17; *CD 1621*, ii. 386; *CJ*, i. 626a. [40]Hull RO, L.200; L.173 [dated 9 May 1623]; *APC*, 1621-3, pp. 459, 488-9. For the whalers, see E190/315/3, ff. 18v-19v; Hull Trinity House, Accts. 3, f. 293. [41]Hull RO, Bench Bk. 5, ff. 34v, 41, 59v; L.169, L.170, L.200, 202A; York City Archives, House Bk. 34, f. 270. [42]Hull RO, Bench Bk. 5, f. 51v, L.189-91; York City Archives, House Bk. 34, f. 266; *APC*, 1621-3, pp. 405-6; *CSP Dom.* 1619-23, p. 505. [43]Hull RO, L.190-1, L.197, L.200; York City Archives, House Bk. 34, ff. 266, 291. [44]Hull RO, L.203-4; Hull RO, Bench Bk. 5, ff. 60v-1. [45]Hull RO, L.168, L.178; Russell, 124-6, 171-90. [46]*CSP Dom.* 1623-5, pp. 265, 500; *APC*, 1623-5, pp. 238-9; Hull RO, Bench Bk. 5, f. 61. [47]*Procs. 1625*, pp. 458, 460, 468.

[48]SP16/42/136; *Procs. 1626*, ii. 95. [49]*CSP Dom.* 1625-6, pp. 135, 140; Hull Trinity House. Accts. 3, ff. 333-47, ATH/47/1, letter of 17 Mar. 1626; Stephens, 247; *Procs. 1626*, ii. 323. [50]Hull Trinity House, Accts. 3, f. 346r-v, ATH/47/1, letter of 17 Mar. 1626; SP16/16/30; *APC*, 1625-6, pp. 421-2, 462; 1627, pp. 312-13, 365; *CSP Dom.* 1625-6, p. 306, 402, 420; *CD 1628*, iii. 308, 310. [51]*APC*, 1625-6, pp. 58-74; 1626, pp. 421-2, 424, 426; *CSP Dom.* 1625-6, pp. 23-46; E401/1913, unfol. (16 Aug. 1626); Hull RO, Bench Bk. 5, ff. 78-80v. [52]SP16/55/9; *APC*, 1626, pp. 48, 108, 146-8, 243-5, 253. [53]*APC*, 1626-7, pp. 101, 104-5, 312-3; 1627, pp. 125, 155-6, 159-61; Hull RO, Bench Bk. 5, ff. 80v, 89v; *CSP Dom.* 1627-8, pp. 133, 156. [54]*CD 1628*, iii. 343; *CSP Dom.* 1625-6, p. 475; 1627-8, pp. 10, 40, 190; *APC*, 1626, pp. 367-8, 395, 406, 436; 1627, pp. 13-14, 273-4. [55]*CJ*, i. 884b, 919a; *CD 1628*, iv. 59, 474. [56]Hull RO, Bench Bk. 5, ff. 70v, 91v, 109v; M.150; *APC*, 1627, p. 137. [57]Hull RO, Bench Bk. 5, ff. 89, 94, 139v, 142, 143, 150v, 154v, 162; *CSP Dom.* 1628-9, pp. 39, 47, 110, 213. [58]*CJ*, i. 926a; *APC*, 1628-9, pp. 381-2, 394. [59]Stephens, 244, 247; Hull RO, Bench Bk. 5, f. 106v.

S.H.

KNARESBOROUGH

Right of election: in the burgage-holders

Number of voters: 59 (reduced to 46) in 1628

5 Mar. 1604	SIR HENRY SLINGSBY	
	SIR WILLIAM SLINGSBY	
?21 Mar. 1614[1]	SIR HENRY SLINGSBY	
	WILLIAM BEECHER	
	?[Walter] Bethell	
27 Dec. 1620	SIR HENRY SLINGSBY	
	RICHARD HUTTON	
20 Jan. 1624	SIR HENRY SLINGSBY	
	RICHARD HUTTON	
	Sir Arthur Mainwaring*	
23 Apr. 1625	RICHARD HUTTON	
	HENRY SLINGSBY	
20 Jan. 1626	(SIR) RICHARD HUTTON	
	HENRY BENSON	
	?Henry Slingsby	
3 Mar. 1628	(SIR) RICHARD HUTTON	
	HENRY BENSON	31
	Henry Slingsby	28[2]

The thriving market town of Knaresborough was subject to the manorial government of the duchy of Lancaster's honour of Knaresborough, which covered one-third of Claro wapentake. There was 'great resort to it in summer time by reason of the wells' at nearby Harrogate, discovered by the Slingsby family in about 1570. It was, however, a source of limited profit to the Crown: the duchy surveyors acknowledged the wealth of the copyholders of Knaresborough forest in 1608, but noted that 'they … stand upon it that their fines are certain' – they were fixed by decree in 1562 – which meant that there was little hope of increasing the honour's rental income of around £200 p.a.[3] Knaresborough may have returned Members to the Commons once in 1300, but its permanent enfranchisement in 1553 almost certainly came about because of its role as a duchy administrative centre. A survey of 1611 identified 88 burgage tenements, but owners of multiple burgages were only allowed one vote at the hustings. Indentures for the early Stuart period were signed by between 15 and 40 individuals. The only poll held during this period, in 1628, saw 59 burgesses claim the vote, 13 of whom were disallowed.[4]

At the turn of the century the dominant interest in the borough was held by Sir Henry Slingsby of Scriven, the leading local landowner and also a holder of multiple offices within the honour. These included the post of borough bailiff, although the election indentures of 1601 and 1604, in which he returned both himself and his brother Sir William, failed to mention this.[5] His influence was challenged on the latter occasion, though, as in October 1603 lord president Sheffield approached him for a nomination at the forthcoming election. Slingsby's reply, a seamless blend of fact and fiction, claimed that some tenants had pledged their voices to George Clifford, 3rd earl of Cumberland, steward of the honour, who, he said, had 'never heretofore, nor now to my knowledge required it of us'. As for the other seat, he awaited the customary nomination of Sir John Fortescue*, chancellor of the duchy, while an accompanying letter from some of the burgesses made it clear that this candidate would be Slingsby himself; Sheffield does not appear to have pressed his case.[6]

Slingsby strengthened his hold over the township with the purchase of £2,000 worth of lands from Sir Francis Trappes in 1606, but in 1609 Fortescue's successor as duchy chancellor, Sir Thomas Parry*, suspended Slingsby from the office of receiver of the honour, apparently on charges of embezzlement. In July 1611 the duchy interest was transferred to the appanage of Prince Henry, to whom Slingsby quickly applied for reappointment; he seems to have been reinstated to at least some of his offices, albeit conditionally, during good behaviour.[7] The Prince's Council also included Slingsby on a commission of August 1611 to survey the honour, which commission established that the best opportunity for profit lay in the enclosure and sale of the manorial wastes to the tenants. In 1612, 40-year leases of 15,000 acres of common pasture were assigned to agents for the tenants at 12d. per acre, but

this speculative venture quickly collapsed.[8] The honour reverted to the Crown on Henry's death in November 1612, but the prince's surveyor, Richard Connock*, continued work, and in May 1613 he calculated that the enclosure of 21,000 acres of commons would produce fee-farm rents of almost £750 p.a., plus entry fines of £10,000 and timber sales worth £1,500. The problem with the duchy's proposal was that the compliance of the majority of the tenants – gentry, smallholders and cottagers – had to be secured before it could be implemented, but with each of these conflicting interests attempting to maximize their share of the spoils, it was almost impossible to obtain agreement.[9]

Surveyors began dividing the commons in the autumn of 1613, and thus the general election held the following March came at a particularly sensitive time for the burgesses of Knaresborough. Slingsby, heavily involved in promoting the enclosure plan, assured both the tenants and the Crown that he was furthering their interests, but he also attempted to gain the best share of the commons for himself in his capacities as freeholder, copyholder and local official. Meanwhile, only weeks before the election, he learned that the duchy of Lancaster had begun a fresh investigation into his financial irregularities, while chancellor Parry, lord president Sheffield and Lord Henry Clifford* all made inquiries about parliamentary nominations. Slingsby's letter of 9 Mar. to two borough officials confronted the enclosure issue directly:

> I understand that it is conceived in the country that matter of enclosure of wastes and enfranchising of copyholders will amongst other things be handled at this Parliament, and I think it is not unknown to my neighbours … that I do very much affect the enclosing of commons as a matter beneficial to the commonwealth …

Cottagers enfranchised by the enclosures, he insisted, should not expect exemption from jury service, and he gave fair warning 'that if I be chosen my voice must go according to my heart and conscience, and that if they do not like of this opinion of mine I will be well pleased they choose another'. This missive was read to the burgesses on the eve of the election, and while Slingsby was returned, it seems likely that he faced a challenge at the hustings. His partner was the diplomat William Beecher, who had been Clifford's tutor in Paris several years earlier, and who may also have been backed by Parry. However, a 'Mr. Bethell' who was present at the election – perhaps Walter Bethell, sometime deputy surveyor of woods for the Duchy's northern estates – may also have been a candidate.[10]

Under a new enclosure commission of August 1615, the poorer tenants of the honour were to be shown particular consideration; 150 tenants eventually agreed to compound for over 5,000 acres of commons. However, in May 1616 the Privy Council instructed the commissioners to review these agreements, and the entire project appears to have failed by the time the honour was assigned to Prince Charles in the following year.[11] The local man whose standing improved most during these troubled times seems to have been the lawyer Serjeant Richard Hutton, a justice of Common Pleas from 1617, who had clashed with Slingsby over grist rights at the local mills; the burgesses returned his son Sir Richard Hutton to Parliament throughout the 1620s. Slingsby was his partner in 1620, and the pair were re-elected in 1624, seeing off a challenge from Prince Charles's servant Sir Arthur Mainwaring*, while in the following year Slingsby passed his seat to his heir, Henry Slingsby.[12]

The Slingsby interest was finally overthrown in 1626 by a townsman named Henry Benson, whose father owned 16 burgages within the town and had donated a house and garden for the use of the new grammar school in 1616. Benson may have been related to Robert Benson, a servant of Sir John Savile*. If so it would explain his willingness to challenge Slingsby, whose father was a supporter of Savile's arch-rival, Sir Thomas Wentworth*. Although no contest is known to have occurred in 1626, it seems unlikely that the Slingsbys failed to defend their interest; and the inclusion of at least four women as attestors to Benson's return suggests that the result may have been close.[13] The 1628 election certainly went to a poll. Slingsby initially mustered almost as many voices as his opponent, but was comfortably defeated after a number of his supporters, including eight widows and a clergyman, were excluded by the bailiff; he does not seem to have appealed to the Commons against this decision.[14]

[1] Date inferred from York. Arch. Soc. DD56/B2/1 [Henry Thompson to Sir Henry Slingsby, 5 May 1614]. [2] 15 votes allowed. [3] Hist. Harrogate and Knaresborough ed. B. Jennings, 125-30, 165-70; Slingsby Diary ed. D. Parsons, 330; SP14/37/107. [4] A.D.K. Hawkyard, 'Enfranchisement of Constituencies, 1504-58', PH, x. 14, 19; York Arch. Soc. DD56/A2/1; W.A. Atkinson, 'Parlty. Election in Knaresborough in 1628', Yorks. Arch. Jnl. xxxiv. 213-17. [5] York Arch. Soc. D56/A2/1; C219/34/109; 219/35/2/160. [6] York Arch. Soc. DD56/M2/21. [7] York Arch. Soc. DD56/C2; DD56/A5/1-2. [8] York Arch Soc. DD56/A2/1; E317/Yorks./32, ff. 22-3. [9] LR2/194, ff. 34-6, 159; York. Arch. Soc. DD56/A5/2; J. Thirsk, 'The Crown as Projector on its own Estates' in Estates of the Eng. Crown, 1558-1640 ed. R.W. Hoyle, 364-6. [10] York Arch. Soc. DD56/A5/2; DD56/B2/1; Duchy of Lancaster Officeholders ed. R. Somerville, 80; WILLIAM BEECHER. [11] Thirsk, 365-6; APC, 1615-16, pp. 532-5. [12] Slingsby Diary, 23; DCO, 'Prince Charles in Spain', f. 34. [13] Atkinson, 213-17; C219/40/116. [14] C219/41B/37.

K.E.B./S.H.

PONTEFRACT

Right of election: in the inhabitant householders

Number of voters: at least 60 in 1624

14 Apr. 1621	(Sir) Edwin Sandys	
	George Shilleto	
	(Sir) Henry Rich*	
	?Sir Henry Savile*	
20 Jan. 1624	Sir Thomas Wentworth, (bt.)	
	Sir Henry Holcroft	
11 Mar. 1624	Sir John Jackson	c. 40
	Sir Richard Beaumont	c. 20
	Robert Mynne	
	Double return vice Holcroft, chose to sit for Stockbridge. Jackson seated, 1 Apr. 1624. Election declared void, 28 May 1624	
17 June 1624	Sir John Jackson Following rejection of previous return	
c. May 1625	Sir John Jackson	
	Sir Richard Beaumont	
25 Jan. 1626	Sir John Jackson	
	Sir Francis Foljambe, bt.	
5 Mar. 1628	Sir John Jackson	
	Sir John Ramsden	

Under the Tudors much of the Yorkshire woollen industry migrated to the Pennines, a source of abundant water power. Pontefract – frequently pronounced Pomfret – lay just outside the principal industrial area, 'in a very pleasant place that bringeth forth liquorice and skirrets [parsnips] in great plenty'. It contained 'fair buildings, and hath to show a stately castle as a man shall see, situated upon a rock no less goodly to the eye than safe for the defence'. The honour of Pontefract, consisting of 18 manors reaching to the Lancashire border, was a fiefdom of the duchy of Lancaster. The borough had been chartered as early as 1194, and in 1484 it was incorporated under a mayor and 12 other comburgesses. Its parliamentary record, however, was miniscule, consisting only of three Parliaments in the reign of Edward I.[1]

James I visited Pontefract Castle on his journey south in 1603, and assigned the honour to Anne of Denmark's jointure estate. In 1607 a new charter provided for the use of a secret ballot at municipal elections, and confirmed all liberties and privileges enjoyed by the corporation at any time, irrespective of discontinuance, forfeiture, or misuse. After Anne's death in 1619, the castle and honour were assigned to Prince Charles, while William Herbert, 3rd earl of Pembroke was appointed constable, steward, and master forester. Pontefract was an important battleground in the hard-fought Yorkshire election of December 1620. There, with Pembroke's backing, Sir Thomas Wentworth, (2nd bt.), enjoyed the assistance of the honour's steward learned, Christopher Banester, and the receiver-general, George Shilleto.[2] The latter had ambitions to secure the enfranchisement of Pontefract, for which there was a strong case: the southern half of the West Riding was probably the fastest-growing industrial area in the country, but entirely lacked parliamentary representation. Doncaster, on the Great North Road, had sought enfranchisement in 1593 and 1597 by offering blank indentures to leading courtiers, and more formally in 1614 via a new charter, but neither scheme had succeeded.[3]

Shilleto's unaided efforts were unlikely to persuade the Commons to agree to an enfranchisement – a procedural innovation in 1621 – and it was only when he attracted Wentworth's support that the plan came to fruition. As part of his quest for the knighthood of the shire in December 1620, Wentworth had promised borough seats to more supporters than he could provide for. One of the unlucky candidates was Sir Henry Savile*, who lost out at Aldborough to Wentworth's closest associate, Christopher Wandesford*. Seeking revenge against the voters who had 'played the knave with me', Savile circulated a petition calling for the disfranchisement of the tiny village and the transfer of its seats to Wakefield. Wentworth would have been doubly alarmed by this proposal, first because Wandesford threatened to 'spend mountains' to avert the loss of his seat, and secondly because this plan would have delivered patronage into the hands of his arch-rival Sir John Savile*, whose son Sir Thomas* was steward of the honour of Wakefield.[4] Wentworth initially suggested Doncaster as a neutral alternative, but the experience of defending his own return before the privileges committee may have convinced him that the entire project was unfeasible. At the same time he had a chance to consult Shilleto, who, as high constable of Agbrigg wapentake, had attended the privileges' committee as one of his witnesses (13 February). Wentworth's return was confirmed on 23 Mar., and only three days later Sir Edwin Sandys* – brother-in-law of Shilleto's wife – moved for the restoration of Pontefract's medieval franchise, on the grounds that the 1607 charter revived all privileges, however long they had lain dormant, a feat one historian has termed

'a dazzling and rhetorical display of inaccurate antiquarianism'. On 27 Mar. Sir George More reported that the privileges' committee had endorsed this claim, and a writ was ordered for an election.[5]

No sooner had the decision for enfranchisement been made than Wentworth was approached for a seat by the courtier (Sir) Richard Wynn*, defeated after a bruising campaign in Caernarvonshire.

> I told him [Wynn] that the town had already chosen two, and that if they would be persuaded to alter their choice I assured myself they would give me the nomination of one; but therein lies the difficulty, for I fear the town will unwillingly disappoint those they have formerly elected, having put themselves to charge and trouble in effecting the business.

The two men selected by the townsmen were almost certainly Shilleto and Sandys's nephew and namesake, (Sir) Edwin Sandys, who were returned on 14 Apr., by which time Wynn had sensibly transferred his ambitions to Ilchester, Somerset, the other borough 'restored' in this Parliament. However, the return was almost certainly contested, as the duchy of Cornwall, upon learning of the enfranchisement, resolved to nominate two more courtiers, (Sir) Henry Rich* and Sir Francis Blundell*, 1st bt. The duchy council made their intentions known to Sir Henry Savile, who presumably advised them of his own aspirations for a seat, as Blundell's name was struck out in the final draft of the letter; but if Rich and Savile stood, they were clearly defeated. In the absence of any specific franchise, Shilleto and Sandys were elected by the mayor, aldermen and burgesses on an indenture bearing 20 signatures.[6]

Sandys died in 1623, while Shilleto did not stand again. At the 1624 election the senior seat was taken by Wentworth, then recovering from a protracted illness, who had resolved not to contest the county seats with Sir John Savile. Though presumably supported by Shilleto and Banester, he admitted that there was 'labour made against me' – perhaps by Sir Henry Savile, although the latter is not known to have stood. Wentworth told Sir Richard Beaumont*, 'I should have been glad of such a partner at Pontefract as yourself', but the second seat went to the duchy nominee, Sir Henry Holcroft, who quickly opted to sit for another borough, prompting a fresh election.[7] On this occasion the duchy nominated Robert Mynne, brother-in-law of Wentworth's ally Secretary of State (Sir) George Calvert*. Mynne stood little chance, as Wentworth had clearly decided to throw his interest behind Beaumont, but the latter was in turn challenged by Sir John Jackson. At the election on 11 Mar., Jackson seemed likely to carry the day: the mayor, William Oates, declared for him, and barred the doors, thus denying entry to Beaumont's supporters. A return was signed and authenticated with the borough seal, but at this point Beaumont insisted upon a poll. When it became clear that his supporters were outnumbered by around two to one, he interrupted the proceedings, and had his supporters, led by Alderman William Tatam, draft a second indenture. Sheriff Sir Henry Jenkins* wisely avoided any accusation of partisanship by forwarding both returns to Westminster.[8]

Once this dispute reached the Commons, the rival candidates looked to bigger figures to support their cause. With Beaumont backed by Wentworth, Jackson naturally turned to Savile, who delivered a petition on his behalf on 22 Mar., and called 'to know the resolution of the House'. Wentworth promptly claimed that Jackson had been returned 'by a popish faction in the town, and by the unlawful practice of temporary burgesses', and moved that both returns be suspended pending investigation. With the clerk of the Crown apparently unable to offer any definitive ruling in this case, the question was referred to the privileges' committee.[9] Over the Easter recess, Wentworth procured a petition from Beaumont's supporters which catalogued the mayor's malpractices, but the committee's report, on 1 Apr., was sympathetic towards Jackson, on the grounds that he had been returned by the 'mayor, aldermen and burgesses' to whom the writ had been directed, whereas Beaumont's indenture contained a number of technical flaws. Sir Edward Coke moved to have the petition from Beaumont's supporters heard in committee that afternoon, but William Mallory – no friend to Wentworth – successfully insisted that it should take its turn behind the many other election disputes then under consideration, with Jackson allowed to take his seat in the mean time.[10] John Glanville eventually reported the committee's decision on 28 May, the penultimate day of the session. Over the franchise dispute, the committee ruled that in the absence of 'constant and certain custom ... all the inhabitants, householders, and residents within the borough ought to have voice in the election', a decision which was adopted as a definitive precedent. However, because of the interruption of the poll the election itself was declared void. A third election was accordingly held on 17 June, at which Mayor Oates, four aldermen and about 35 burgesses returned Jackson; Tatam and Beaumont's other supporters were conspicuous by their absence. Despite all this effort, Jackson never got to take his seat, as King James's death dissolved the Parliament before it was reconvened.[11]

There is no evidence that Beaumont stood against Jackson at the election of June 1624, while Jackson's use of Savile during the 1624 dispute was more a convenience than a declaration of partisanship. In April 1625 Jackson volunteered to assist Wentworth against Savile in any contest for the county seats, an offer which was gratefully accepted. Wentworth informed Jackson of his intention to guard against a possible defeat at Savile's hands by keeping a seat for himself at Pontefract, and informed the mayor that 'I do exceeding much desire Sir John Jackson may be my partner in that service; and in case I should serve in the other place that you would then join Sir Richard Beaumont with Sir John Jackson, ... so that all breaches may be made up'. Wentworth's victory in the county election allowed Jackson and Beaumont to be returned, but the latter, apparently resentful at incurring an obligation to Jackson, ungratefully informed Wentworth that 'I do not intend to serve in that rank; I am much beholden to them [of Pontefract] for the matter, but not for the manner'. He advised Wentworth to procure a new writ, and suggested Sir Henry Savile or Shilleto as his replacements. As there was no formal procedure for resignation, it is doubtful this would have been allowed, and in any case, Wentworth's troubles over the county election left him with no time to argue Beaumont's case.[12]

In 1626 Wentworth was barred from election by his appointment as sheriff; he therefore nominated Sir Francis Foljambe, 1st bt., a neighbour of his in Hallamshire, to serve with Jackson. On 22 May Foljambe showed the Commons a copy of a letter in which Savile attacked the House for wasting its time in pursuing Buckingham rather than attending to the needs of the cloth trade. Savile was one of the few Members willing to defend the duke during his impeachment, and this letter undercut his credibility. He emerged as a Buckingham partisan after the dissolution, and one of the offices with which he was rewarded was the stewardship of the honour of Pontefract, which offered the possibility of influence at subsequent parliamentary elections.[13] Jackson was certainly aware of this prospect at the 1628 election, and when Wentworth suggested the re-election of the previous Members, he advised him

> I had a long conflict with myself before I could resolve to stand; yet not so much out of fear of the grandees' opposition as in favour of my own purse, which ... required some more ease than the ordinary expenses attending parliamentary service will afford me. For my joining with Sir Francis Foljambe, I protest I desire his company in that service, and will endeavour it; yet not in so public a

manner as you seem to wish, as conceiving it would prove extremely prejudicial to both, and cause the adverse party to stand closer upon their guards.

Wentworth took the hint, and replaced Foljambe with Sir John Ramsden, who lived only four miles from the borough. During the autumn, the two Members visited their constituency, ostensibly 'to know what service the townsmen would command them', but actually to infuriate Savile, recently ennobled as Baron Savile of Pontefract, by hunting the hares that his office as gamekeeper required him to preserve.[14]

[1] H. Heaton, *Yorks. Woollen and Worsted Industries*, 21, 49; W. Camden, *Britannia* (1610), i. 695; SP14/37/107; *Vis. Yorks.* ed. J. Foster, 311. [2] G. Fox, *Pontefract*, 33, 35-36, 39, 162; *Strafforde Letters* (1739) ed. W. Knowler, i. 11; *Duchy of Lancaster Office-Holders* ed. R. Somerville, 149. [3] *HMC Hatfield*, vii. 442; *Doncaster Bor. Courtier* ed. A. Brent, 211. [4] A. Fletcher, 'Sir Thomas Wentworth and the Restoration of Pontefract as a Parl. Bor.', *NH*, vi. 89-93; *Strafforde Letters*, i. 8-9; *Beaumont Pprs.* ed. W.D. Macray (Roxburghe club, cxiii), 43-4; *Duchy of Lancaster Office-Holders*, 152. [5] *CD 1621*, ii. 263, 270; iv. 49, 192, 201; *CJ*, i. 572b, 576a; Surr. Hist. Cent. LM1331/29; Nicholas, *Procs. 1621*, i. 230; Fletcher, 92-6. [6] DCO, Letters and Warrants, 1620-1, f. 98; *Strafforde Letters*, i. 14; C219/37/319. [7] *Strafforde Letters*, i. 19; *Wentworth Pprs.* ed. J.P. Cooper (Cam. Soc. ser. 5. xii), 202-3; DCO, Prince Charles in Spain, f. 34. [8] DCO, 'Prince Charles in Spain', f. 39; C219/38/280-1; *CJ*, i. 751a. [9] 'Pym 1624', f. 37; *CJ*, i. 745a; 'Earle 1624', f. 102. [10] *CJ*, i. 751a; 'Pym 1624', f. 44; 'Earle 1624', ff. 107v-8; *Holles 1624*, p. 54; J. Glanville, *Reports of Certain Cases* (1775), pp. 134-9. [11] *CJ*, i. 714b; 'Earle 1624', f. 196v; 'Hawarde 1624', p. 302; Glanville, 140-3; C219/38/282. [12] *Strafforde Letters*, i. 25-7; SIR THOMAS WENTWORTH. [13] *Procs. 1626*, iii. 301-8, 392-401; C. Russell, *PEP*, 320-1; DCO, Letters and Warrants 1626-32, f. 74. [14] *Strafforde Letters*, i. 34; *Star Chamber Cases* ed. S.R. Gardiner (Cam. Soc. n.s. xxxix), 147.

K.E.B./S.H.

RICHMOND

Right of election: ?in the corporation

Number of voters: 13

5 Mar. 1604	TALBOT BOWES	
	RICHARD PERCIVAL	
c. Mar. 1614	TALBOT BOWES	
	SIR RICHARD WILLIAMSON	
3 Jan. 1621	(SIR) TALBOT BOWES	
	WILLIAM BOWES	
	Christopher Pepper	
	Sir Henry Savile, (bt.)*	
26 Jan. 1624	CHRISTOPHER PEPPER	
	JOHN WANDESFORD	
27 Apr. 1625	(SIR) TALBOT BOWES	
	CHRISTOPHER WANDESFORD	

15 Jan. 1626	CHRISTOPHER WANDESFORD	
	MATTHEW HUTTON	
11 Mar. 1628	(SIR) TALBOT BOWES	
	JAMES HOWELL	
	Christopher Wandesford	
	Matthew Hutton	

Situated on a strategic promontory where the River Swale emerges from the Pennines, Richmond was founded in 1071 as the administrative centre of the vast honour of Richmond. The town became the focal point for the distribution of corn from the Vale of York to the Dales, and for the collection of Pennine wool for export through Newcastle, Hartlepool and Hull. The town's population reached 1,600 in 1563, but was thereafter affected by repeated plague epidemics, the worst of which, in 1597-8, carried off at least 1,050 victims.[1] The mainstays of Richmond's economy were the cloth and leather industries. From the fifteenth century, locally knitted caps and stockings were fulled and dyed within the town, which came to be dominated by a clique of wealthy hosiers who controlled the supply of wool to the knitters and disposed of the finished product. The development of this industry was disrupted by the 1552 Act limiting the buying and selling of wool, which rendered the hosiers' role as middlemen illegal. However, the town was granted an exemption in 1585, and by the end of the century it was producing an estimated 200,000 pairs of stockings a year.[2] The leather industry was based upon the growing number of dairy cattle being grazed in Swaledale. The town held major cattle fairs fortnightly between Palm Sunday and Christmas, and a significant proportion of the burgesses were butchers and tanners.[3]

Richmond's medieval charters specifically exempted the borough from the obligation of sending burgesses to Parliament, a right upheld when the town received writs of summons in 1294 and 1328. The potential benefits of representation had become far more obvious by 1536, when the duke of Norfolk was instructed to promise the Yorkshire Pilgrims of Grace that Richmond and six other boroughs in the north were to be enfranchised.[4] However, no action was taken until January 1577, when the borough's new charter granted parliamentary representation: the vote was given to 'the burgesses', which was later held to include all ratepayers, although the surviving returns for the early Stuart period cite the corporation alone, an alderman (mayor) and 12 head burgesses, as the electorate.[5] None of the sparse borough records suggest that the hosiers who dominated the corporation were interested in securing their own return to Parliament, perhaps because the town could not afford to pay wages. Furthermore, there is little to suggest that the corporation had a parliamentary agenda during the period, despite James Howell's undertaking of 1628 to promote 'anything that may concern the welfare of your town and the precincts thereof'. Outside the Commons, however, (Sir) Talbot Bowes, the borough's senior MP, may have helped to promote a petition to Bishop Neile of Durham against an expansion of the rival cattle markets at nearby Darlington in 1621.[6]

This lack of local candidates left Richmond open to the influence of the Council in the North and the local gentry. Talbot Bowes, senior Member in the first Stuart Parliament, had been returned for the borough in 1593 on the interest of his uncle Robert Bowes[†] of Aske, a mile to the north of the town. By 1604, Bowes had acquired his own interest, both as a resident and as one of the town's head burgesses.[7] The other local man with parliamentary experience was the town's recorder, Sir Cuthbert Pepper[†], surveyor of the Wards, whose estate at Long Cowton lay seven miles to the east of the town. Either Pepper or his cousin and deputy as recorder, Christopher Pepper, a lawyer who lived just outside the borough, could have claimed the junior seat for themselves, but they deployed their interest on behalf of Richard Perceval, the secretary who handled wardship business for the master of the Wards, Lord [formerly Sir Robert] Cecil[†].[8] By 1614, Bowes had left Richmond for his family's main seat at Streatlam Castle in county Durham, but he remained a member of the corporation, and was duly returned to the Addled Parliament. Perceval's interest expired with the deaths of Sir Cuthbert Pepper in 1608, and of his own master in 1612; Christopher Pepper may have expected the offer of a seat, but the corporation chose Sir Richard Williamson, one of the justices at York, who was probably nominated by Sir Thomas Lascelles, another of the town's head burgesses, who was also a member of the Council in the North.[9]

While Sir Talbot Bowes was once again assured of the senior seat at the election of January 1621, the other was coveted by an outsider, Sir Henry Savile*, who correctly surmised that his 'ancient power' would not suffice to secure his re-election at Aldborough. Savile's ally Sir Thomas Wentworth* procured a letter of recommendation for Richmond from Secretary of State Sir George Calvert*, his partner for the county election, who had recently purchased a small estate at Kiplin, seven miles south-east of the borough.[10] A further nomination, perhaps for Savile, was received from lord president Scrope, whose official influence was reinforced by the proximity of his

Wensleydale estates and his tenure as steward of the honour of Richmond.[11] The corporation was encouraged to decline these recommendations 'in respect of some clause in the late proclamation'. This probably referred to the stipulation that voters should 'make choice of them that best understand the state of their countries, cities or boroughs', which could hardly be true of Savile, whose estates lay near Wakefield. Undaunted by this rejection, Savile used the judge Sir Richard Hutton to secure the support of Christopher Pepper, who hoped 'that considering the several answers to the forenamed honourable persons [Calvert and Scrope] I myself should have had the offer [of a seat] before any foreigner', and promised, if elected, to yield his place to Savile. As he could not be present at the election, Pepper asked for a postponement until the following morning. However, on returning to the borough, he discovered that the choice had already taken place, and that the second seat had been given to William Bowes on the advice of Sir Thomas Wharton*, a newcomer to the area who had recently purchased the manor of Aske from Bowes's father. Pepper was certain that it was Wharton who had encouraged opposition to Savile, whose return on Wentworth's interest would have represented a victory for the Cliffords, the Whartons' chief political rivals in Westmorland.[12]

Pepper finally managed to secure a seat in 1624, shortly after Wharton's death, replacing Sir Talbot Bowes, who had been chosen as alderman (mayor) two weeks previously, and was thus barred from returning himself as an MP. William Bowes, whose father had died in 1623, does not appear to have stood again, and was replaced by John Wandesford, Sir Talbot Bowes's great-nephew.[13] Neither of these Members appears to have stood in 1625, when Sir Talbot regained the senior seat. The other went to Christopher Wandesford, John's brother, who had been obliged to relinquish the seat at Aldborough which he had taken from Savile in 1621.

While Wandesford was returned again in the following year, Bowes, beset by financial problems, used his interest on behalf of his nephew, Matthew Hutton, as part of an agreement for the settlement of Bowes's debts: Sir Talbot and his brother Thomas were to pass Barforth manor to Hutton, who was to pay off debts, and return the remainder of the purchase price of £2,340 to his uncles.[14] A deed of sale was drawn up in January 1626, but its implementation was delayed until the following May, to allow Hutton sufficient time to secure a private Act of Parliament adding Barforth to his entail in place of his wife's jointure estate, which was to be sold to raise the cash to pay Bowes's creditors.[15] Hutton duly signed an indenture for the purchase of Barforth on 31 May, the day before his estate bill completed its second reading, but the bill's passage was wrecked by the dissolution on 15 June.[16] One of Bowes's most persistent creditors quickly foreclosed on his loan, and, after the failure of a last-minute attempt at arbitration by lord justice Hutton, Thomas Bowes was arrested at Richmond in September. He spent the next 15 months languishing in York Castle, to the increasing agitation of his brother, who, fearing a similar fate, pleaded for Hutton to complete his purchase of Barforth.[17]

By the time a new Parliament was summoned in January 1628, it was clear that Sir Talbot would seek to resume his seat at Richmond, to secure temporary protection from his creditors. Wandesford, seeing his chances at Richmond evaporating, appealed to Sir Thomas Wentworth to approach friends for a seat in the West Country, while Hutton asked his father, a member of the Richmond corporation, to canvass for himself and particularly for Wandesford, as, in the latter's absence, he saw no chance of obtaining the passage of his estate bill.[18] However, their hopes of securing the second seat were wrecked by lord president Scrope, who pressured the corporation into choosing his secretary, James Howell. The latter's presence in the House was required to prevent a revival of the 1626 recusant officeholders' petition, which had condemned his master's Catholic sympathies.[19]

[1] R.T. Fieldhouse and B. Jennings, *Hist. Richmond and Swaledale*, 11-33, 102-7. [2] Ibid. 158-62, 169-70, 177-82, partly citing SP12/252/18; E134/2 Chas.I/Michs. 38; *SR*, iv. 141-2. [3] Fieldhouse and Jennings, 184-6; N. Yorks. RO, DC/RMB/II/1/1, unfol. petitions of 1620-1. [4] Fieldhouse and Jennings, 410; A.D.K. Hawkyard, 'Enfranchisement of constituencies, 1504-58', *PH*, x. 13-14. [5] *CPR*, 1575-8, pp. 294-6; Fieldhouse and Jennings, 411. [6] J. Howell, *Epistolae Ho-Elianae*, letter of 24 Mar. 1627[/8]; N. Yorks. RO, DC/RMB/II/1/1, unfol., petitions of 1620-21. [7] Durham RO, D/St/D8/1/62; N. Yorks. RO, DC/RMB/V/1/95-121. [8] N. Yorks. RO, DC/RMB/II/1/1, unfol. (13 Jan. 1604); C142/160/51; 142/310/64; A.G.R. Smith, 'Secretariat of the Cecils' *EHR*, lxxxiii. 482, 493, 498. [9] C142/310/64; R. Reid, *King's Council in the North*, 496-7. [10] *Strafforde Letters* (1739) ed. W. Knowler, i. 8; *VCH Yorks. (N. Riding)*, i. 307. [11] SO3/4, unfol. Oct. 1609; *Procs. 1626*, ii. 264-5. J.K. Gruenfelder, 'Electoral patronage of Sir Thomas Wentworth' *JMH*, xlix. 570 assumes that Scrope backed Savile. [12] *Stuart Royal Procs.* ed. J.F. Larkin and P.L. Hughes, i. 494; Harl. 7000, f. 41, repr. in J.J. Cartwright, *Chapters in Yorks. Hist.* 203-4. [13] C219/38/274; *Dur. Vis. Peds.* ed. J. Foster, 38-9; DURH 3/189/110. [14] C2/Chas.I/W16/20. [15] For the bill, see N. Yorks. RO, MIC 1286/8521-4, 8640. A breviate may be found in Harl. 6847, ff. 66v-67. [16] N. Yorks. RO, MIC 1513/1710; *Procs. 1626*, iii. 341-2. [17] C2/Chas.I/B82/8; 2/Chas.I/S96/8; *Hutton Corresp.* ed. J. Raine (Surtees Soc. xvii), 312-16. [18] *Wentworth Pprs.* ed. J.P. Cooper (Cam. Soc. ser. 4. xii), 278-9; *Hutton Corresp.* 316-17. [19] *Procs. 1626*, ii. 264-7.

S.H.

RIPON

Right of election: in the burgage-holders

Number of voters: over 100[1]

c. Feb. 1604	SIR JOHN BENNET SIR JOHN MALLORY
c. Mar. 1614	SIR THOMAS POSTHUMOUS HOBY WILLIAM MALLORY
c. Dec. 1620	SIR THOMAS POSTHUMOUS HOBY WILLIAM MALLORY
20 Jan. 1624	SIR THOMAS POSTHUMOUS HOBY WILLIAM MALLORY
3 May 1625	SIR THOMAS POSTHUMOUS HOBY WILLIAM MALLORY
c. Jan. 1626	SIR THOMAS POSTHUMOUS HOBY THOMAS BEST
1 Mar. 1628	SIR THOMAS POSTHUMOUS HOBY WILLIAM MALLORY

An ecclesiastical peculiar founded by St. Wilfrid in the seventh century, Ripon returned MPs to three Parliaments under Edward I. The Crown offered representation to Ripon and five other northern boroughs in negotiations with the Pilgrims of Grace in 1536, but Ripon was only re-enfranchised in 1553, by which time the Minster estates had passed to the duchy of Lancaster; control of the liberty returned to the archbishop of York in 1556. Borough government, under a prescriptive charter only codified in 1598, was consigned to a wakeman [mayor] and around 30 aldermen. The franchise was technically vested in the burgage-holders, who numbered well over 100. There were no contested elections during the early Stuart period, and surviving election returns were signed by up to three dozen corporation members and burgesses.[2]

Under Elizabeth, electoral influence at Ripon was managed by the archbishops of York: the diocesan chancellor (Sir) John Bennet was returned in 1597; the 7th earl of Shrewsbury applied to Archbishop Piers on behalf of one of his wife's relatives in 1593; while in 1597 and 1601 Sir Robert Cecil[†] obtained a seat for the diplomat (Sir) Christopher Parkins*. Other intermediaries within the diocesan administration also obtained seats: in 1588 Sir William Mallory[†], steward of the liberty, nominated his wife's relative Peter Yorke; chancellor Bennet obtained a seat for his brother in 1593; and dean Thornborough of York secured the election of one of his relatives in 1601.[3] In 1604 chancellor Bennet, defeated in a contest at York, found a seat at Ripon, while the second place went to Sir John Mallory, who had succeeded to his father's estates at nearby Studley Royal a year earlier. The wakeman subsequently accompanied the two men to London in search of a charter of incorporation, which passed the great seal on 24 June, at a cost of £64: this may explain why on 18 May Mallory moved the Commons for legislation to confirm all letters patent granted since the start of the reign. The resulting bill was reported by Sir Thomas Hoby on 11 June, but set aside at the Speaker's request 'upon some special exception', while a similar bill, initiated in the Lords on 21 June, failed for lack of time. The new charter replaced the old governing body with a mayor (still habitually called the wakeman), 12 aldermen and 24 assistants, but made no mention of parliamentary representation or the franchise. The balance of power changed little, as the corporation felt obliged to ask Archbishop Matthew for permission to hold the borough court granted by the new charter.[4]

By the 1614 general election Bennet had moved to London. In his stead the archbishop nominated his friend Sir Thomas Hoby, who came from the other end of the shire but had recently lost his interest at Scarborough. Sir John Mallory, in the midst of an unsuccessful bid for a knighthood of the shire, secured the return of his son William at Ripon. Hoby was appointed steward of Ripon in 1617, and along with William Mallory he was returned at the next three elections. In 1621 the two men combined to attack Sir John Townshend*, whose concealed lands patent had been used to question the title of Ripon's hospital lands: Mallory drew attention to the town's plight on 23 Mar., while on 24 Apr. Hoby secured a first reading for a bill to confirm the exemption of hospital lands from seizure under the 1547 Chantries' Act. This measure was dropped after the king revoked Townshend's patent by proclamation on 10 July.[5]

There may have been some dissension at Ripon during the general election of 1625, as the corporation sent two letters to Archbishop Matthew, although the indenture recorded the 'unanimous assent' of the electors to the return of Hoby and Mallory. At the next election Mallory, perhaps unwilling to get involved in attacks on the duke of Buckingham, resigned his interest at Ripon to his brother-in-law, Thomas Best of Middleton Quernhow, although he resumed the junior seat with no apparent difficulty in 1628.[6]

[1] *Yorks. Arch. Jnl.* xxxii. 78-80; *Hist. of Ripon* (1801), p. 45; C219/41B/34. [2] A.D.K. Hawkyard, 'Enfranchisement of Constituencies', *PH*, x. 13-17, 25; Borthwick, Rev. RGA 1628; *Ripon* (1839), p. 42; *Yorks. Arch. Jnl.* xxxii. 82; N. Yorks. RO, DC/RIC,

Ripon Town Bk, 1598; C219/39/95. [3] LPL, ms 3200, f. 158; *HMC Hatfield*, vii. 404; ix. 409, 442. [4] *CJ*, i. 237a, 974; *LJ*, ii. 325b; N. Yorks. RO, DC/RIC/1/1/2, ff. 4, 20. [5] YORKSHIRE; N. Yorks. RO, DC/RIC/1/1/2, f. 78; Nicholas, *Procs. 1621*, i. 218-19; *CD1621*, v. 346; vi. 83; *CJ*, i. 588a; SIR JOHN TOWNSHEND; *Stuart Royal Procs.* ed. J.F. Larkin and P.L. Hughes, i. 514-15. [6] N. Yorks. RO, DC/RIC/1/1/2, f. 219; C219/39/95.

S.H.

SCARBOROUGH[1]

Right of election: ?in the corporation

Number of voters: 44

6 Mar. 1604	FRANCIS EURE
	SIR THOMAS POSTHUMOUS HOBY
	?Matthew Dodsworth
	?Nominee of Lord Sheffield
c.28 Mar. 1614[2]	EDWARD SMYTHE
	WILLIAM CONYERS
	John Suckling*
1 Jan. 1621	SIR RICHARD CHOLMLEY
	WILLIAM CONYERS
20 Jan. 1624	HUGH CHOLMLEY
	WILLIAM CONYERS
	John Legard
	Richard Osbaldeston
c.30 Apr. 1625	JOHN LEGARD
	?HUGH CHOLMLEY
	?Sir William Alford*
	Sir Edward Coke*
	?William Conyers
	Sir Guildford Slingsby
	William Thompson
	Nominee of Lord Sheffield
2 May 1625	HUGH CHOLMLEY
	WILLIAM THOMPSON *vice*
	Legard, refused to serve
	Henry Darley*
	Sir Edward Waterhouse
25 Jan. 1626	HUGH CHOLMLEY
	STEPHEN HUTCHINSON
	Sir John Brooke*
	William Cholmley*
	Henry Darley*
	William Turner
26 Feb. 1628	SIR WILLIAM CONSTABLE, bt.
	JOHN HARRISON
	Thomas Alured*
	Henry Darley*

The largest port on Yorkshire's North Sea coast, numbering about 450 households, Scarborough was governed by two bailiffs, two coroners (by convention, the retiring bailiffs), four chamberlains and 36 common councillors.[3] The corporation was dominated by merchants and shopkeepers, the most prominent of which, the Thompson family, provided one of the bailiffs at least 18 times between 1603-40; only two non-residents held municipal office during this period.[4] Under the Tudors Scarborough steadily declined relative to Hull, and by 1603 its mercantile fleet comprised only 30 small vessels shipping Tyneside coal and Yorkshire cloth to the Low Countries and returning fish, grain, wine, spices and dyestuffs. Shipping dues and profits of a train oil patent helped to maintain the harbour.[5] The town also had a thriving market, briefly threatened at the end of Elizabeth's reign when the Gates family established a rival at nearby Seamer, a move which cost them their electoral influence at Scarborough. Sir Richard Cholmley and John Legard courted similar unpopularity in 1625-6 when they aimed to close the market to prevent the spread of the plague.[6]

The town returned MPs from 1295, although the parliamentary franchise, governed by custom rather than charter, was ill-defined: surviving indentures cite 'the bailiffs, burgesses and commons' as the electorate, and the bailiffs claimed that 'the commonalty had a great sway' in the 1625 election; but this may have signified the common council rather than the freemen. In 1614 MPs were returned by 'the whole house', suggesting a corporation vote, and the council minute book, begun in 1622, records elections as regular meetings. Letters of nomination and support for candidates were apparently read out on election morning, but as with many corporations the issue was often decided earlier: in 1604, Sir Thomas Hoby was told the result of the election six days before the date of the return.[7] The surviving indentures, all in Latin, follow the form of that of 1614, 'sealed with the town's seal, Mr. bailiffs', Mr. coroners' [and two common councillors'] hands and seals, though all counterfeited except Mr. bailiff Thompson's'. The corporation worried about this minor deceit, and about their election of two outsiders 'in which choice although we have directly gone against the statute'. When non-residents were elected in 1601, 1614 and 1624, the corporation had them sworn as freemen before they took their seats. In 1604 Hoby assured the bailiffs 'that in choosing me, I will be your warrant that therein you shall not offend either law or proclamation; for that by law I am eligible, being both a freeholder and a free burgess of the town'.[8]

The Scarborough corporation often required their MPs to promote a corporate agenda: Hugh Cholmley expected to receive instructions in 1624 and 1626, and during the latter year Stephen Hutchinson lobbied for protection against Dunkirk privateers. In 1621 Sir Richard Cholmley consulted the bailiffs over his plans to seek legislation for the repair of Whitby pier, a project they strongly opposed: five years later Hugh Cholmley warned 'that obligation which is first and chiefly to your town must not tie me from doing any public and good service to other parts of my country'. The corporation did not pay parliamentary wages: aspiring candidates often volunteered to serve without charge, or, in the case of the wily Sir Edward Coke*, 'at as little charge to the town as any that shall be joined with me'.[9]

Parliamentary lobbying at Scarborough began promptly in 1603, in a letter from Sir Thomas Hoby informing the corporation of Queen Elizabeth's death. When the summons was delayed due to the plague, Hoby renewed his suit to the new bailiffs, and a similar request followed from Ralph, 3rd Lord Eure†, who recommended his brother Francis. In August 1603 the corporation offered first refusal to their high steward, lord admiral Nottingham (Charles Howard†), who ordered

> that you pleasure my Lord Eure with one [seat] and that you appoint my officer, your recorder Mr. Dodsworth [vice-admiralty judge for Yorkshire] to be the other, the rather because I have appointed him to attend some services concerning His Majesty in Michaelmas term.

Hoby, having presumably learnt of this threat to his candidacy, entertained the vicar of Scarborough and other townsmen in the succeeding months, and, writing to the corporation eight days before the election, he dismissed rival nominations by Nottingham and Lord President Sheffield, promising

> I will take upon me to satisfy my lord admiral, who will not, I know prefer any that are named in his honour's letters before me, in respect that his honour and mine only brother married two sisters. And for my lord president, as soon as I did hear that his lordship had written, I did ... signify unto his honour that I stood for a place in Scarborough ... so as I hope you shall hear no more from his lordship.

Hoby was duly returned, and feasted by the corporation before his departure for London.[10]

Despite serving as senior bailiff of Scarborough in 1610-11, Hoby found a parliamentary seat at Ripon in 1614. With Lord Eure having moved to Shropshire as president of the Council in the Marches, the rivalry of the previous decade evaporated. Lord President Sheffield renewed his suit for a nomination, 'the like courtesy having been often afforded to my predecessors', promising the nominee, his lawyer Edward Smyth, would be 'to your liking, serviceable for his country, and careful upon all occasions for the good of your corporation'.[11] At the same time, two Scarborough merchants, sent to lobby the Privy Council for funds to repair the town's damaged pier, turned for assistance to Tristram Conyers, a Court of Wards' official and brother to a corporation member. Conyers, having sought a nomination at Scarborough upon rumours of a Parliament in 1612, now renewed his request, promising that his nephew William Conyers, newly called to the bar, would serve without charge.[12] Shortly before the election, a third nomination arrived from Sir Henry Griffiths of Burton Agnes, recommending John Suckling* as 'very sufficient ... to supply that place if you have not already disposed thereof to some other'. This lukewarm recommendation failed, but Tristram Conyers showed gratitude for his nephew's return with a loan of £50, which enabled the townsmen to secure a levy on east coast shipping for the repair of Scarborough's pier.[13]

At the beginning of 1620 the corporation sought a confirmation of their charter 'upon occasion of being questioned for their [market] tolls' by the patentee Sir John Townshend*. Their draft aimed to recover privileges lost when the town's Yorkist charter of incorporation was quashed in 1485: the corporation was to be restricted to a mayor (William Thompson being named as the first), 12 aldermen, and 12 capital burgesses; the town was to acquire head port status separate from Hull; and the pier levy of 1614 was to be confirmed. The most important reason for the proposed confirmation was apparently the clause granting the town its own Admiralty jurisdiction: lord admiral Nottingham apparently delegated Admiralty rights, but lord admiral Buckingham offered no similar agreement following his appointment in 1619. The draft charter passed the signet and privy seal in February 1620, but was then halted on the instructions of Thomas Aylesbury, Buckingham's Admiralty secretary.[14] Although no longer Lord President, Sheffield, still vice-admiral of Yorkshire, was prevailed upon to intercede with Buckingham, who refused to allow the charter to pass, but offered the corporation a grant of Admiralty rights for the duration of his tenure of office similar to that allowed by Nottingham. The town's negotiators explained that 'there will be nothing but the charge and renewing [under] every lord admiral, and we shall hold the same thing'. However, William Conyers, asked for his opinion, warned against conceding the

principle of the town's claim: 'if you should now give way to so great a loss, I know you will never hereafter have means to regain it'. This advice was vindicated in March 1621 when Sir Henry Marten*, judge of the Admiralty Court, advised Aylesbury that the town's claim was indeed valid, though 'an inconvenience fit to be reformed'. However, the corporation failed to press its advantage, possibly because of lack of funds.[15]

Conyers's assistance over the charter guaranteed him a parliamentary seat at Scarborough in 1621, but the other was open to newcomers. No letters of nomination survive, but among likely patrons, the 4th Lord Eure was a recusant, and Sheffield's influence had diminished following his dismissal as Lord President. The return of Sir Richard Cholmley of Whitby, whose family had long been in disgrace for their Catholic sympathies and their feud with Sir Thomas Hoby, was presumably arranged by his cousin lord president Scrope.[16] In November 1623 the corporation enlisted Conyers in a fresh suit against Sir John Townshend*, despite his advice that any action was likely to prove pointless, as Townshend was living in sanctuary near the inns of court. Conyers also noted the likelihood of a Parliament, 'for that the Spanish business doth not go forward as the king and state expected', and asked for a seat. Sir George Ellis and Sir Thomas Tildesley, justices of the Council in the North, subsequently recommended Richard Osbaldeston, a York lawyer who 'by reason of his practice at London may have opportunity to do you service ... and that without any charge unto you', while Sir Richard Cholmley nominated his son Hugh, then living with his wife's family in London; he probably also supported the candidacy of his cousin, John Legard of Ganton. At the election in January 1624 the corporation rejected Osbaldeston, but attempted to please the remaining candidates by returning Cholmley and Conyers, and promising Legard a seat at the next election. This obliged Sir Richard Cholmley and Conyers to compete for the continuation of the corporation's affections: Cholmley sent a fulsome letter of thanks for his son's return, and Conyers promised the bailiffs 'a buck for you out of Pickering or Danby forest'.[17]

In the summer of 1624 the corporation clashed with Lord Sheffield over their claim to an autonomous Admiralty jurisdiction. First, the bailiffs and the town's mariners were ordered to attend a muster at the Vice-Admiralty Court at Bridlington: the bailiffs refused to appear, and were fined £10 by the court. A few days later, two Dutchmen were arrested and fined for buying fish in the town by Luke Fox, the Admiralty marshal for Yorkshire, who contemptuously announced that 'he cared not for the bailiffs nor never a man in the town'. The bailiffs seized Fox's warrant and complained to Sheffield's deputy, Sir Francis Gargrave, about the affront to the town's liberties. The latter was unrepentant: 'the admiral hath a jurisdiction to preserve, no less than your liberties are to be continued ... if anything hereupon have fallen out otherwise than you expected, I am confident the fault will appear to be in yourselves'. The corporation finally capitulated in November, asking Buckingham 'to be pleased to receive our corporation into protection as formerly the lords admiral of this kingdom have done', and offering him the nomination of a burgess at the next election.[18]

Unfortunately for the corporation, the 1625 election was the most hotly contested of the period. Some of the aspiring candidates were easily discounted. Sir Edward Coke, who had not had any contact with the town since 1615, based his appeal upon his acquaintance with members of the Privy Council. Sir Guildford Slingsby, suspended as navy comptroller since 1618, was recommended by his brother-in-law Edward Cayley of Brompton; heavily indebted, he probably sought membership of the Commons for protection from his creditors.[19] The serious contenders for the senior seat were Sir William Alford*, nominated by lord president Scrope as 'one who is known to you all to be religious, discreet and fit for the place', and the unspecified candidate of vice-admiral Sheffield, who was probably claiming the seat offered to Buckingham the previous autumn. Writing on Sheffield's behalf, Gargrave emphasized that his choice would be 'both powerful by himself and friends to do you kind respect and favours as any other'. Sir Richard Cholmley, then sheriff, wrote from York to recommend his son's re-election, but the bailiffs disobligingly complained of his unhelpfulness as sheriff, and advised that 'they would put it as far as they could, but the commonalty had a great sway in it'. As for the second seat, promised to Legard the previous year, Cholmley's messenger confessed that he had not dared remind the bailiffs of their undertaking while a cousin of his rival William Conyers was also present. Conyers was annoyed at complications in the establishment of charitable bequests made to the corporation by his uncle, and there is no evidence that he sought re-election in 1625, although in the following year he recalled that 'I should have been ready to have done you service this Parliament if you had thought so well of me'. A candidate with much stronger claims appeared in 1625 in the person of corporation member William Thompson, who was supported by the earl of Holderness, governor of Scarborough Castle.[20]

Hearing of his son's likely rejection on 25 Apr., an irate sheriff Cholmley rebutted the bailiffs' accusations of unhelpfulness, reminding them of a previous letter to Lord Scrope

wherein they did intimate that they had chosen Sir Richard's son, though he was not named, and so his lordship and Sir Richard did both conceive of it, in which letter there was some distaste taken by my lord president for making my Lord Sheffield his competitor.

Cholmley ended with the ominous warning that if his son were rejected, 'instead of a worthy friend they will find a shrewd adversary'. The bailiffs, apparently unmoved by this threat, advised Alford of their 'friendly intentions', but he declined the seat following his return for Beverley on 26 April. The election, held before the end of April, apparently saw the return of Legard and Hugh Cholmley, but Legard, when informed, 'upon some present occasions of his own ... did utterly refuse the same', probably having heard how close he had come to rejection.[21] The corporation then decided to hold a fresh election: news of the unexpected vacancy encouraged Richard Darley of Buttercrambe to nominate his son Henry* on 1 May 'if you be not formerly engaged to others'. On the same day Gargrave, aghast to discover that Sheffield's expected nomination had failed to arrive, explained that the latter's candidate was his neighbour Sir Edward Waterhouse of Lythe, 'one that both in Court and country is able to do his friend a courtesy'. However, the corporation resolved 'never to choose any afterwards without their handwriting for the same', which presumably disqualified Waterhouse, and on 2 May Cholmley and Thompson were returned on the existing indenture by an alteration of the date and names.[22]

The looming war with Spain arrived on Scarborough's doorstep on 26 Oct. 1625, when rival Dutch and Dunkirker squadrons clashed off the coast.[23] Following this incident, the town sent Luke Fox to ask Buckingham for protection in return for a nomination at the next election; he recommended Sir John Brooke* and William Turner, promising

if you shall on this my request and first trial of your affections in this kind give a good success to their desires and mine, it shall oblige me henceforth upon all occasions to requite your loss, and further anything that may tend to the advancement of your corporation.

Both men had been investors in the Yorkshire alum industry, were doubtless known to Sheffield, from whose lands most of the alum shale was extracted.[24] Richard Darley also renewed his son's candidacy, improbably recalling 'much willingness and good respect from the town' in the previous year, while Henry Darley himself wrote promising to serve at his own charge. He secured further recommendations from Sir William Sheffield*, and from William Thompson's nephew, who nominated Darley for 'the second voice, for I suppose my uncle Thompson will stand again and well deserves the prime voice'.[25] Thompson in fact yielded his interest to Stephen Hutchinson, a relative by marriage, who also promised to serve without charge, and to further 'any occasions you have for the common gain of the town'.[26] Sir Richard Cholmley recommended his 'kinsman' William Cholmley, an Exchequer official, though 'if his being a stranger to your town should oppose his election' he asked for his son to be considered instead.[27] Despite careful lobbying, the election of Henry Darley, a grandson of Edward Gates†, was unlikely to be sanctioned by a corporation whose senior members could still recall the Seamer market dispute. The return of William Cholmley at Thirsk on 17 Jan. reduced the field to a contest between local and Admiralty interests. Buckingham's nomination of two candidates where only a single seat had been offered may have offended the corporation, which proposed to send Hutchinson to London with an extensive agenda of town business. His candidates were thus rejected in favour of Hutchinson and Hugh Cholmley, who needed parliamentary immunity from his creditors, and may have enlisted the aid of Lord Scrope, or lobbied the corporation in person.[28]

Cholmley, who offended the corporation with his plans to petition Parliament for the repair of Whitby pier, does not appear to have been asked to undertake any business for Scarborough. Hutchinson, however, wrote to the corporation to warn of reprisals taken by the French for the seizure of the *St. Peter* of Le Havre, and to explain his plans for lobbying for defence of the Yorkshire coast. He was supported in his endeavours by Sir Thomas Hoby, who complained of 'the want of ships to keep the Narrow Seas'.[29] In May 1626 a fresh attempt was made to secure the passage of the charter denied the town in 1620, which was presumably supervised by Hutchinson, named as the town's first mayor in the draft charter. Once again, the draft passed the signet and privy seal only to be refused the great seal, presumably on renewed objections from the Admiralty.[30]

Though suffering from the dual affliction of plague and privateers, the corporation complied with the Forced Loan in 1626-7.[31] The town's need for naval defence may have been one of the factors behind the eventual success of the Admiralty interest at the general election of 1628, when neither of the previous Members appear to have stood for re-election. Cholmley, having forced his creditors to a settlement, no longer needed a parliamentary seat, while Thompson's son Francis, customs collector at Scarborough, apparently secured his family's influence for John Harrison, a London customs official, who claimed the backing of 'some friends amongst you'; Harrison also had connections with Buckingham's circle.[32] Darley stood again, together with his uncle Thomas Alured*, but as both were related to the Gates family they were unlikely to be returned.[33] Rather surprisingly, Sheffield, now earl of Mulgrave, nominated Sir William Constable, one of the county's most prominent Loan refusers. In a letter probably intended to strike a note of humility, Constable acknowledged

> I can neither press such a request further than you shall well like of, nor hold it to stand with the liberty of your choice to be importuned in it, but I shall acknowledge your kind respect in particular to me ... for your town or any person whose kind respect I find in this.

Mulgrave supported Constable with a letter which unashamedly flattered the bailiffs for 'your respects towards me both while I had that place of government in your country [the presidency] and at all times since'.[34] This cautious approach, together with a lack of suitable alternative candidates, secured the return of Constable together with John Harrison.

[1] M.Y. Ashcroft, archivist of N. Yorks. RO, assisted with the dating of election corresp. and provided a list of corp. members. [2] *Scarborough Recs.* ed. M.Y. Ashcroft (N. Yorks. RO, xlvii), 57. [3] *VCH N. Riding*, ii. 551; J.B. Baker, *Hist. Scarbrough*, 28, 45, 195. [4] From corp. list. [5] E190; *Scarborough Recs.* 1, 11, 23, 36, 210, 214; *VCH N. Riding*, ii. 553. [6] *CSP Dom.* 1580-1625, p. 343; *HMC Hatfield*, ix. 388; *APC*, 1600-1, pp. 5-6; *Scarborough Recs.* 13, 134, 143-4, 169. [7] *Scarborough Recs.* 57, 116, 143, 146, 160, 188; Baker, 195; *Scarborough Recs. 1641-60* ed. M.Y. Ashcroft (N. Yorks. RO, xlix), 49-50; *Diary of Lady Margaret Hoby* ed. D.M. Meads, 210. [8] *Scarborough Recs.* 4, 32, 57-8, 116-17, 121. [9] Ibid. 80, 118, 143, 160-2. [10] *Scarborough Recs.* 32; *Diary of Lady Hoby*, 207, 210-11. [11] *Scarborough Recs.* 56. Sheffield also requested a seat in the Parl. rumoured to be imminent in Nov. 1615: ibid. 62. [12] *Scarborough Recs.* 52-57; *Vis. Essex* (Harl. Soc. xiv), 649; C66/1393; E215/587; C. Roberts, *Schemes and Undertakings*, 11-14. [13] *Scarborough Recs.* 57-8; *APC*, 1613-14, pp. 417-18. [14] Baker, 41-42; SO3/7, PSO2/42 and PSO5/4 (all Feb. 1620); *Scarborough Recs.* 69-71, 73, 141; R. Lockyer, *Buckingham*, 275. For Nottingham's agreement with Hull, see Bodl. North. a.1, f. 79. [15] R. Reid, *Council in the North*, 488; *Scarborough Recs.* 72-3, 75. [16] C66/2209/4; Reid, 386-8, 488; H. Cholmley, *Mems.* (1787), p. 22. [17] *Scarborough Recs.* 70, 73, 80, 14, 116, 118, 121, 146; Reid, 497-8; Cholmley, 24, 39-40. [18] *Scarborough Recs.* 69, 127-31, 141. [19] Ibid. 61-2, 142-3; Clay, *Dugdale's Vis. Yorks.* ii. 67; iii. 297; Add. 64882, f. 31. Slingsby's poor rate assessment for St. Martin-in-the-Fields par. fell from 26s. in 1613-14 to 4s. in 1624-5: WCA F340, F351. [20] *Scarborough Recs.* 93, 114, 142-4, 162; Baker, 224-5. Holderness's letter is now lost. [21] *Scarborough Recs.* 143-6. The date on the indenture was altered after the second election, see C219/39/286. [22] *Scarborough Recs.* 145-6; N. Yorks. Co. RO, MIC 1320/459-61; *Vis.*

Yorks. ed. Foster, 353; C219/39/286. [23] *CSP Dom.* 1625-6, pp. 135, 140; *Scarborough Recs.* 151-3, 155-7. [24] *Scarborough Recs.* 141, 186 (dated to 1625/6); R.B. Turton, *Alum Farm*, 72-74, 86-87, 94, 120. [25] *Scarborough Recs.* 159, 198 (redated to 17 Jan. 1625/6); N. Yorks. RO, MIC 1320/500-6. [26] N. Yorks. RO, MIC 1320/502, cal. in *Scarborough Recs.* 159. [27] *Scarborough Recs.* 197 (redated to 12 Jan. 1625/6). [28] *Vis. Yorks.* ed. Foster, 60, 87; C219/40, f. 118; *Scarborough Recs.* 161; Cholmley, 42, 44-46. [29] *Scarborough Recs.* 160-2; *Procs. 1626*, ii. 203. [30] SO3/8; PSO2/65 and PSO 5/5 (all May 1626). [31] *CSP Dom.* 1625-6, p. 275; *Scarborough Recs.* 171-2, 174, 177-9. [32] Cholmley, 45; *APC*, 1627, p. 229; *Scarborough Recs.* 187; *Fanshawe Mems.* ed. T. Fanshawe, 18; *CSP Dom.* 1625-6, p. 573. [33] *Scarborough Recs.* 188; *Vis. Yorks.* ed. Foster, 60, 87, 144. [34] N. Yorks. RO, MIC 1320/582, cal. in *Scarborough Recs.* 187.

S.H.

THIRSK

Right of election: in the burgage-holders

Number of voters: 52

c. Feb. 1604	SIR EDWARD SWIFT
	TIMOTHY WHITTINGHAM
c. Mar. 1614	SIR THOMAS BELASYSE
	SIR ROBERT YAXLEY
12 Dec. 1620	SIR THOMAS BELASYSE
	SIR JOHN GIBSON
22 Jan. 1624	WILLIAM SHEFFIELD
	SIR THOMAS BELASYSE
19 Apr. 1625	HENRY BELASYSE
	HENRY STANLEY
17 Jan. 1626	HENRY BELASYSE
	WILLIAM CHOLMLEY
12 Mar. 1628	CHRISTOPHER WANDESFORD
	WILLIAM FRANKLAND

Thirsk had returned Members to the Parliament of 1295, but was not permanently enfranchised until the reign of Edward VI, shortly after the Crown acquired former monastic property within the town. The town was unincorporated, but earls of Derby, lords of the manor, had little influence on borough politics during the early Stuart period because of a dispute between the 6th earl and his sister-in-law, the dowager countess, over the manorial stewardship: in 1609 there was violence when the countess's choice as steward, Sir John Mallory*, attempted to overthrow the earl's nominee, his 'mortal enemy' Sir Stephen Procter. This dispute was eventually resolved, as by 1627 the manor was settled on James (Stanley*) Lord

Strange, the heir to the earldom. Electoral influence was divided between the Council in the North and a group of local gentry, by far the most significant of which was the Belasyse family, resident at Newborough Priory since its dissolution. Returns were made by the bailiff, elected annually by a variable number of free burgesses at the manorial court.[1]

In 1604 Sir Henry Belasyse (Bellasis[†]) was serving as sheriff, while his heir Sir Thomas was under suspicion for his clandestine marriage to a Catholic daughter of Henry Cholmley[†]. In this year the borough returned Sir Edward Swift, a son-in-law of Lord President Sheffield, and Procter's friend Timothy Whittingham, who owned a small Yorkshire estate and controlled the rectory of Thirsk as guardian of his wife's nephew William Askwith. By the time of the 1614 election Swift had quarrelled with his father and gone into hiding, while Whittingham had moved to his new estate in county Durham. Sir Thomas Belasyse was returned on the family interest, while Sir Robert Carey* probably secured the Council in the North's backing for Sir Robert Yaxley, a soldier from the Low Countries garrisons. Belasyse was elected again in 1621, the bailiff and 18 others signing his return, while the other MP, for whom no indenture survives, was Sir John Gibson, who lived near Malton, 20 miles from Thirsk; a member of the Council in the North, he was presumably its nominee.[2]

In 1624 Belasyse was re-elected, but Gibson, probably suffering from ill-health, was replaced by a near neighbour, Sir William Sheffield, a relative of Belasyse's uncle Sir Thomas Fairfax II*. Belasyse, who inherited the family estates later in the year, probably considered the representation of such a minor borough beneath his newly enhanced dignity, and at the 1625 election he procured the return of his eldest son in his stead. The other Member on this occasion, Henry Stanley, was auditor of the Mint and a distant relative of the earl of Derby. His return was signed by two men who may have been the earl's manorial steward and his deputy, but his patron is likely to have been Henry Belasyse, who had recently married his niece. Belasyse was re-elected in 1626, his partner on this occasion being the Exchequer official William Cholmley, who was father-in-law to William Askwith, lay rector of Thirsk.[3] At the next election in 1628, Sir Thomas Belasyse, newly created Lord Fauconberg, secured his son's return as knight of the shire in partnership with Sir Thomas Wentworth* on the understanding that Wentworth's ally Christopher Wandesford, whose electoral interest at Richmond was in doubt, should fill the vacancy at Thirsk. On this occasion the second seat went to William Frankland, a recent arrival in the area whose descendants came to dominate the borough's representation. The return was the only one from the period to name both Members on a single indenture.[4]

[1] *VCH Yorks (N. Riding)*, ii. 19, 61, 64; A.D.K. Hawkyard 'Enfranchisement of Constituencies, 1504-58', *PH*, x. 20; W. Grainge, *Vale of Mowbray*, 62-3, 91, 93, 109; SP14/47/104. [2] H. Aveling, *Northern Catholics*, 183; *HMC Hatfield*, xi. 379; xvii. 45; Grainge, 100, 136-7; *Chamberlain Letters* ed. N.E. McClure, i. 547; Surtees, *Co. Pal. Dur.* ii. 326; C219/37/229. [3] C219/39/290; *APC*, 1623-5, p. 223; *Vis. Essex* (Harl. Soc. xiv), 602-3; E. Baines, *County Palatine of Lancs.* iii. 157; *Mdx. Peds.* (Harl. Soc. lxv), 140. [4] C219/41B/40; *Wentworth Pprs.* ed. J.P. Cooper (Cam. Soc. ser. 4. xii), 278-9, 287.

S.H.

YORK

Right of election: in the freemen

Number of voters: 111 in 1604; over 300 in 1628

		1st seat	2nd seat
5 Mar. 1604	ROBERT ASKWITH, alderman	61	
	CHRISTOPHER BROOKE		60
	Sir John Bennet*	14	29
	Thomas Moseley†, alderman	13	12
	Sir Robert Watter, alderman	8	8
	William Robinson†, alderman	3	1
	Robert Paycock, alderman	1	1
21 Mar. 1614	ROBERT ASKWITH, alderman		
	CHRISTOPHER BROOKE		
18 Dec. 1620	(SIR) ROBERT ASKWITH, alderman		
	CHRISTOPHER BROOKE		
6 Feb. 1624	(SIR) ARTHUR INGRAM		
	CHRISTOPHER BROOKE		
7 May 1625	(SIR) ARTHUR INGRAM		
	CHRISTOPHER BROOKE		
c. Jan. 1626	(SIR) ARTHUR INGRAM		
	CHRISTOPHER BROOKE		
3 Mar. 1628	(SIR) ARTHUR INGRAM		
	SIR THOMAS SAVILE		
	Thomas Hoyle, alderman		
	William Robinson		

HOYLE *vice* Savile, seated
on petition 23 Apr. 1628

Early Stuart York, still reckoned the second city of England, had a population of around 10,000. Its archbishop, styled 'primate of England', supervised four northern dioceses, while the Council in the North, a small but permanent bureaucracy based at the King's Manor, managed civil affairs north of the Trent. The city, chartered under Henry II, sent two citizens to the Model Parliament of 1295, who by custom sat next to the privy councillors and London citizens in the Commons. Incorporated as a county borough in 1396, York thereby gained jurisdiction over its immediate hinterland, the Ainsty. It was the only provincial city to be governed by a lord mayor, who was assisted by 12 aldermen, the 'Twenty-Four' comprising all those who had served as sheriff (generally less than 24 in number) and a common council of 41 men drawn from the city's guilds.[1] The medieval city had been an occasional venue for parliaments, particularly during campaigns against the Scots, and in April 1607 the Venetian ambassador reported that James, disgusted at the Commons' obstruction of the Union, intended to 'dissolve Parliament and summon another in York, which, being incommodious, will make the Houses dispatch their business the quicker'.[2]

Although 40 miles inland, York was accessible to small seagoing ships and barges via the River Ouse (at least at high tide) and was classified as a 'member' of Hull by the customs service. Formerly a major centre of cloth manufacture, by 1600 the city had become more dependent on service industries, and while no longer as prosperous as it had been in the fifteenth century, it still catered to a hinterland comprising much of the north of England. Above its artisan base stood a mercantile elite who controlled a significant proportion of the West Riding cloth industry, and also held a stake in the northern lead trade. Much of this output was shipped through Hull, a situation which led to conflicts of interest, although both communities united to prevent the encroachment of Londoners.[3]

From 1581 the parliamentary franchise at York was restricted to a group of 40-50 freemen, who nominated four *lites*, from whom the corporation chose two MPs; this system was discontinued in 1597, when the freemen regained the vote, giving their voices in advance of the corporation members, the better to avoid partiality. The change was not necessarily significant, as the lord mayor was allowed a view of those assembled before they were admitted to the election in the Guildhall, and it was only at the contest of 1628 that the generality of the freemen exercised their franchise. Members customarily received generous expenses of 6s. 8d. a day while at Westminster, far more than the statutory allowance of 2s. *per diem*. They were, however, expected to work hard for their constituents: the corporation drafted an agenda of business to be handled both in and out of Parliament; and expected to be kept abreast of developments in a regular correspondence. Not surprisingly, almost all of the city's Elizabethan MPs were aldermen who were thoroughly familiar with the city's business, the only exception being (Sir) John Bennet, the archdiocesan chancellor, who was returned in 1601 after failing to secure a seat at the archiepiscopal liberty of Ripon.[4]

At the 1604 general election five aldermen (two with previous parliamentary experience) stood for election alongside Bennet (backed by a letter from Archbishop Hutton) and Christopher Brooke, a York-born lawyer well known in London literary circles. By a comfortable margin, the senior seat went to Robert Askwith, a recent arrival on the aldermanic bench who had been one of the candidates for lord mayor a few weeks earlier. Bennet garnered only 14 voices, but though he went on to pick up 29 for the second seat, he lost the contest to Brooke. However, the most important part of the electoral process was the preparation of detailed instructions which followed the hustings. In 1604 the city's Members were urged to consult with Yorkshire's other MPs to establish a Common Law court north of the Trent, presumably to supersede the judicial functions of the Council in the North, which operated as a prerogative court. Secondly, Yorkshire's contributions under the Dover Harbour Act of 1581 were to be diverted to one of the corporation's pet projects, the improvement of the Ouse navigation. Thirdly, the city was to secure its customary discount of £50 from each of the fifteenths then being collected, and more aldermen were to be added to the subsidy commission. The city's butchers, pewterers, cordwainers and tanners added their own requests, and the tapestry-makers asked for the repeal of a Henrician statute which gave the weavers a monopoly of coverlet manufacture. Ten days after the election, the corporation dispatched additional instructions requiring its Members to seek modifications to the city charter.[5] In the event, however, little of this ambitious agenda was realized. The tax rebate was secured, but the project for a Common Law court sank without trace and Askwith advised against a new charter on grounds of cost. Moreover, while Brooke moved to repeal the Dover Harbour Act on 5 June, the Act was eventually confirmed by a fresh statute. Later that month Askwith, doubtless in an attempt to promote the Ouse navigation, added a proviso for York and the Ainsty to the bill to remove weirs on navigable rivers, and he may also have hoped to obtain some local benefits as a member of the committee for the tanners' bill (28 Apr.), although the resulting statute contained no proviso for York.[6]

Elected lord mayor in January 1606, Askwith missed the next parliamentary session, although he retained his seat, despite the recent prohibition on mayors serving in the Commons. It was therefore left to Brooke to assist in a collaborative bid to recover for the merchants of York, Newcastle and Hull a 20 per cent discount on the customs duties on cloth. This reduction had been granted to the northern towns by the Crown in 1592, but was disallowed by the London consortium which had recently taken over the Great Farm. Brooke chaired the committee, reporting the bill on 5 Mar. 1606. Lord Treasurer Dorset (Thomas Sackville[†]) ensured that the bill fell asleep in the Lords, but after the prorogation a petition to Robert (Cecil[†]), 1st earl of Salisbury, secured the restoration of the former discount.[7]

Askwith returned to Westminster at Easter 1607, bearing detailed instructions for a renewal of the city's charter, which was secured at a cost of £120. Having undertaken a survey of the Ouse during his mayoralty, he may have been particularly interested in the clause granting Admiralty rights over the Humber and its Yorkshire tributaries to the lord mayor. However, this privilege was already held by the mayor of Hull, and the claim was dropped before the charter reached the seals. York's corporation is not known to have issued any instructions to its MPs in 1610, although it was presumably Askwith who procured a renewal of the city's commission for surveying the Ouse in June. In October he was asked to renew the lease of part of the city's commons during the autumn session, when he and Brooke also compounded for a parcel of concealed lands on the corporation's behalf.[8]

While they had achieved little in 1610, Askwith and Brooke received parliamentary wages, and both men continued to be elected to Parliament until their deaths, a notable break with precedent. In 1614 their instructions covered the Ouse navigation, the control of vintners, and legislation to restrain Londoners from selling goods in fairs anywhere north of the Trent. They were also told to co-operate with other Yorkshire Members in restricting lord president Sheffield's control over town militias. However, the swift dissolution meant that nothing was achieved, and they do not appear to have received any expenses.[9]

Further attempts to improve the Ouse were mooted in 1616, which may have included an ambitious plan to divert the course of the river altogether. When the king visited the city on his way to Scotland in the following year, Askwith, again serving as lord mayor, saluted him with an ode on the need to improve the Ouse navigation, a view he believed James had endorsed. Askwith and Brooke tabled a bill for this purpose in 1621, but, to their frustration, it received only a single reading before Easter. They blamed this on

the slow proceedings of private things ... in regard so many public grievances and [an]noyances of the commonwealth are on foot, and that those whom we mean to use for moving the king to be a burgess for us, as he pleased to say he would have been so employed, that it was not possible for them to act our desires.

The bill received a second reading on 3 May, but Sir Thomas Wentworth* and other landowners objected to the proposal to fund the project through a charge upon the whole county, and it never emerged from committee. The other issue which Askwith and Brooke pursued during the 1621 session was the procurement of relief from the economic downturn which had badly affected the north. They welcomed the Commons' decision to investigate the problem, which they ascribed to 'the pretermitted customs, the impositions upon cloth, the wars in Germany, and the more frequent making of cloth beyond the seas', but they confessed that 'in this we have found a deep ocean of matter not to be waded through in a whole Parliament'. At a practical level, they hoped to have London merchants barred from the fairs at Beverley and Howden, a measure they found other northern MPs were willing to support. Advised that 'there is no way by Parliament to take away the liberty of any subject from going and merchandizing where he list', they approached a master of Requests to secure a Proclamation, but they were disappointed, and their plans to make a personal appeal to the king came to nothing.[10]

During the 1621 session, rivalry between York and Hull simmered just beneath the surface. Relations had soured in 1619, when the York merchants had attempted to withhold payment for lead tolls at Hull, and a confrontation was anticipated in 1621. Askwith and the Hull MP John Lister arranged negotiations, but after these collapsed, the Hull corporation drafted a bill to uphold their rights. This was dropped on Lister's advice that 'there is little to do us good in parliamentary courses', and the dispute was eventually settled through the mediation of Sir Arthur Ingram in the autumn of 1623.[11] Another dispute broke out in July 1622, when several York merchants had their goods seized at Hull for selling to 'country chapmen' in breach of the 'foreign bought and sold' rule, which specified that a Hull burgess had to be party to every sale which took place in the town. The York men brought their case for restitution in Common Pleas, but the dispute was referred to the Privy Council for arbitration. Both sides marshalled an impressive array

of legal advisers, but the York men apparently won the day with the support of Lord Treasurer Middlesex (Sir Lionel Cranfield*), who had been briefed by Ingram, his former business partner.[12]

Having rendered himself useful to the York corporation, Ingram, a financier who had built himself a palatial residence in the city, aspired to a parliamentary seat at the 1624 election, supporting Brooke as his partner and undertaking 'to show my willingness in all things that may concern the good of the city'. Brooke's own letter of nomination waived any sums due for his service in the previous Parliament, beyond the £20 he had been obliged to contribute to the Palatine Benevolence raised after the dissolution, and expressed the hope that 'by serving as well and faithfully as I can, I might haply save the city a great deal of charge, which (if the Parliament continue long, as it is like to do) must needs be spent'. Although Ingram had insured himself against disappointment by securing nominations at two other boroughs, he was in fact returned for the senior seat. The instructions issued by the city to its Members concentrated on economic issues: the Ouse navigation was to be pursued, and a rival project for the River Aire was to be stopped; bills were to be promoted to prevent Londoners attending northern fairs, to enclose the city's commons and to establish a court of orphans like that at London; Hull was to be prevented from enforcing its 'foreign bought and sold' claims; an abatement of the pretermitted custom on cloth was to be sought; free trade was to be promoted; and complaint was to be made about customs fees. When Parliament assembled, Ingram and Brooke certainly kept the corporation informed about the debates on free trade and the attack on the pretermitted custom, but otherwise they achieved nothing: Ingram, a former customs farmer himself, was unlikely to exert himself over the pretermitted custom, and both men were distracted by Middlesex's impeachment.[13]

Ingram and Brooke were re-elected in 1625 'by general and free consent', but no instructions are known to have been drafted by the city, either because of the failures of the previous session, or because the king made it clear that the Parliament was being called for supply, with a legislative session to follow in the autumn. Brooke wrote to the corporation in July, but only to recommend a York lawyer as assistant to the city's ailing recorder.[14] The 1626 election was not recorded in the corporation minutes, but the instructions issued to both Members were carefully noted. The Ouse navigation scheme was to be revived, but the contentious county-wide rate was dropped; the rival navigation project for the Aire and Calder, sponsored by Sir John Savile*, was to be opposed as 'a great impoverishment to this city'; any attempt by the Hull corporation to confirm their 'foreign bought and sold' rights was to be opposed; an abatement in the pretermitted custom on northern kerseys was to be sought; the Hull whalers were to be supported in their efforts to break the Londoners' monopoly of the trade; and shipping was to be protected against the depredations of the Dunkirk privateers. Significantly, the corporation also decided not to rely solely on the efforts of its MPs, neither of whom was a corporation member: on 6 Mar. Brooke was asked 'whether he think fit to send up a solicitor this Parliament time'; and two weeks later Robert Belt and Robert Hemsworth were dispatched to Westminster.[15]

Writing to the corporation on 15 Apr., Belt and Hemsworth asked for instructions about the Ouse navigation scheme, and warned that Savile had tabled his bill for the Aire navigation; they were clearly unaware that it had been rejected at its second reading on 25 March. Much as they may have disliked Savile's navigation project, the citizens of York had cause to thank him for securing another of their desires, a reduction in the city's Privy Seal loan quota. York's quota had initially been set at £1,800, equivalent to ten parliamentary subsidies, but during the subsidy debate of 27 Mar., an anonymous Yorkshireman (probably Savile) had called for a discount to encourage prompt payment. During the Easter recess Savile led a delegation, including the York MPs, to lobby the Privy Council, which granted a two-thirds reduction for the whole shire. Belt and Hemsworth commended this deal to the corporation, and also undertook to advance £400 from the county's Privy Seal money to Sir William Russell*, the Navy treasurer, who promised to dispatch three ships to Hull as convoy escorts in return.[16] Under these circumstances, it is not surprising that the corporation quickly raised £350 of the city's reduced Privy Seal quota of £400, which was paid into the Exchequer on 4 July; ratepayers were also asked for £90 to defray the costs of lobbying. While the corporation subsequently dragged its feet over demands that the Yorkshire raise three ships for service with the Navy, they demonstrated a co-operative attitude to the Forced Loan: Hemsworth delivered 82 per cent of his quota of £877 to the Exchequer, a figure comfortably above the national average of 72 per cent.[17]

At the 1628 election Savile, who by then dominated Yorkshire politics as both a privy councillor and vice-president of the Council in the North, looked to York to return his son, Sir Thomas*. At first it seemed as though the latter had no rivals, for although Ingram had a secure claim on the senior seat, the junior seat was going begging, its previous occupant, Brooke, having died four weeks before the election. William Robinson, son of a recently deceased alderman, acquired his freedom shortly before the election with a view to standing, but he had little support. Meanwhile, two aldermen, Hemsworth and William Cowper, canvassed for Savile among the city's guilds and the merchant adventurers, insisting that anyone who voted for Savile would be 'saved harmless' if they voted for a stranger (Savile only became a freeman on the day of his election). They also claimed that it would be wise to support Savile as 'the Parliament would not hold', which would leave Savile's father with an unquestioned sway over the north of England.[18] With a hard fought contest in prospect, Lord Mayor Belt (a Savile supporter) apparently decided to waive all the restrictions on the electorate, and over 300 freemen turned up to the hustings. The names of Sir Thomas Savile, Ingram and Robinson were initially put to the question, and while Robinson demanded a poll, 'three or four shouts' established that his supporters were outnumbered by those of his rivals. Following a modest altercation, Savile yielded the senior seat to Ingram, the result was proclaimed by sheriff Henry Thompson, and the return sealed. At this point, however, another alderman informed Thompson that as it was not yet eleven o'clock the hustings were not yet legally closed. Robinson, meanwhile, resigned his interest to Thomas Hoyle, his father's successor as alderman. As more freemen arrived at the hustings, Hoyle's supporters came to outnumber Savile's (they claimed) by two to one. Thompson, however, declined to alter his initial decision, and returned Ingram and Savile.[19]

At Westminster, the Commons' committee for privileges had only just been named (20 Mar.) when an allegation was received that 'Sir Thomas Savile … kept the townsmen from coming in at a right door, and brought those that chose him through a wall purposely broken down, to keep out others and let in whom he pleased'. Savile's supporters secured 150 signatures to a rival petition endorsing his return, including those of Belt, Cowper and Hemsworth, and even Hoyle's old master, Alderman Matthew Topham. It is therefore hardly surprising that the 'long and tedious business' occupied the committee for at least three afternoons. The antipathy many MPs felt towards the duke of Buckingham and his clients doubtless influenced the eventual decision to unseat Savile and declare Hoyle elected in his stead (23 April). Thompson and Hemsworth were subsequently required to make a formal submission to the Commons, and to pay Hoyle £20 towards the cost of his witnesses.[20]

Under the tumultuous circumstances of the election, the York corporation had, understandably, neglected to draft any instructions for its MPs. Nevertheless, on 7 May 1628 Hoyle informed the House that ten ships had lately been captured off the Yorkshire coast by Dunkirkers, news which provoked 'pitiful complaints by the aldermen of London, Mr. Lister and others'. Ingram subsequently joined in the attack on Sir Thomas Monson's* patent for the drafting of bills before the Council in the North, but as this patent affected his income as secretary to the Council, his protest was clearly lodged more for the benefit of himself than his constituents. In October the corporation belatedly considered 'what might be fitting to be done for the good of this city in this Parliament', but laid the matter aside until the next session, when the early dissolution rendered their efforts unnecessary. Hoyle's inaction on the corporation's behalf presumably explains why he subsequently had difficulty in securing payment of his parliamentary wages.[21]

[1] R. Reid, *King's Council in the North*; R.A. Marchant, *Church Under the Law*; *York Civic Recs. IX* ed. D. Sutton (Yorks. Arch. Soc. rec. ser. cxxxviii), 1-7. [2] *CSP Ven.* 1603-7, p. 488. [3] B.F. Duckham, *Yorks. Ouse*, 13-42; D.M. Palliser, *Tudor York, passim.* [4] York City Archives, House Bk. 31, ff. 297v-8; House Bk. 32, f. 313v; House Bk. 34, ff. 32, 208v; SIR JOHN BENNET. [5] York City Archives, House Bk. 32, ff. 313v-14v, 318-19; *SR*, iv. 1062. [6] *CJ*, i. 189a, 242a, 986a, 997a; York City Archives, House Bk. 32, f. 331v. [7] *LJ*, ii. 394a, 396b; *HMC Hatfield*, xxiii. 220-1; xxiv. 52-3; *CJ*, i. 277b, 283b; Hull RO, L.159-60; Hatfield House, Petition 2070. [8] York City Archives, House Bk. 33, ff. 27v, 62, 203v, 221, 229v-30; C181/2, f. 127v. [9] York City Archives, House Bk. 34, ff. 34-5. [10] Ibid. ff. 217v-23; *Recs. Early Eng. Drama, York* ed. A.F. Johnston and M. Rogerson, i. 549-56; Duckham, 44-7; *CJ*, i. 605b. [11] Hull RO, Bench Bk. 5, ff. 34v, 41, 59v; Hull RO, L.169-70, 200, 202A; York City Archives, House Bk. 34, f. 270. [12] Hull RO, Bench Bk. 5, f. 51v; Hull RO, L.189-91, 197, 200; York City Archives, House Bk. 34, f. 266; Hull RO, L.190-1; *APC*, 1621-3, pp. 405-6; *CSP Dom.* 1619-23, p. 505. [13] York City Archives, House Bk. 34, ff. 282v-3, 290-2. [14] Ibid. 34, ff. 314, 317. [15] Ibid. 35, ff. 5v-6. [16] Ibid. ff. 8v-10; *APC*, 1625-6, pp. 421-4; *Procs. 1626*, ii. 366, 381. [17] York City Archives, House Bk. 35, ff. 13, 16-20, 33v, 37v; E401/2586, pp. 283-6; E401/1913-14, 401/2443-5. [18] York City Archives, House Bk, 35, ff. 24v, 56v; *CD 1628*, iii. 146-9. [19] *CD 1628*, iii. 42, 45-6, 49-50, 53, 55. [20] Ibid. ii. 37, 296; iii. 28, 42, 64, 146-9, 171, 178, 208, 224; W. Yorks. AS (Leeds), GA/B10. [21] *CD 1628*, iii. 308-11; iv. 24, 29; York City Archives, House Bk. 35, ff. 63-4; *VCH York*, 196.

J.P.F./S.H.

THE CINQUE PORTS[1]

LORD WARDENS

1 Jan. 1604	Lord Henry Howard (subsequently 1st earl of Northampton)
20 July 1615	Edward Zouche, 11th Lord Zouche
Nov. 1624	George Villiers, 1st duke of Buckingham
22 July 1628	Theophilus Howard*, 2nd earl of Suffolk

LIEUTENANTS OF DOVER CASTLE

1588	(Sir) Thomas Fane[†]
1603	Sir Thomas Waller* (jt.)
1606	Sir Thomas Waller (sole)
1613	Sir Robert Brett*
1615	Sir John Brooke*
1615	Sir Thomas Hammon*
1620	Sir Henry Mainwaring*
1624	Sir John Hippisley*
1629	Sir Edward Dering*

The Cinque Ports of Kent and Sussex, to which were early added the two 'ancient towns' of Rye and Winchelsea, controlled the shortest sea routes to the Continent, and during the medieval period their responsibilities for defence and the provision of shipping was recognized by the grant of exceptional privileges. They were exempt from subsidies, for instance, and provided representatives who helped carry the canopy at the Coronation. Moreover, the county authorities had no power over them.[1] Instead, the Crown was represented by a lord warden, invariably in this period a great nobleman, who had at his disposal a whole range of special law courts situated at Dover. Following the death of the earl of Northampton in June 1614, the wardenship was left vacant for 13 months, during which time the duties of the office were performed by the king's favourite, Robert Carr, earl of Somerset.[2]

By the late sixteenth century it was hard to see why the Ports should continue to be exempt from taxation, as by then most of them had shrunk to mere fishing harbours. Besides, at a time of declining subsidy yields the Ports' status as a tax haven had obvious drawbacks for the Crown. In 1593 Sir Thomas Cecil*, eldest son of lord treasurer Burghley (William Cecil†) advised the Commons to end the Ports' exemption because 'it hath been the use of men having any lands in the Cinque Ports to take sanctuary there' whenever subsidies were levied.[3] The Ports themselves were keen to retain their tax exemption and, *inter alia*, pleaded poverty and the fact that they were required to provide fish for the royal Household as grounds for its continuance. However, their representatives frequently harmed their own cause by supporting grants of subsidy to which they and their constituents would not be required to contribute. During the supply debate of 1610, some Members were so infuriated by the Ports' representatives that they proposed that their purses 'should walk as well as their voices'.[4] Not surprisingly, repeated attempts were made in this period to end the Ports' exemption. Though never successful, these challenges often aroused considerable alarm. In May 1614 the Ports drew up a series of points to be used by their representatives to counter the arguments of their opponents, while in March 1624 the corporation of Dover sent its Member, Edward Nicholas, detailed instructions on what to say should the Ports' privilege be challenged.[5]

The Ports possessed their own representative institutions, the Guestling and the Brotherhood (Brodhull), which met annually at New Romney. Although regularly summoned to elect Members of Parliament from 1322,[6] they contrived to evade this burdensome duty until 1366. To the considerable annoyance of the Upper House, they insisted that their representatives should be styled not 'burgesses' but 'barons'. In March 1607 the peers were afforded an opportunity to express their irritations after Sir Edward Hoby*, in the course of conveying a message to the Lords, carelessly referred to the Members sitting for the Cinque Ports as 'the barons of the Commons House of Parliament'. Quite correctly, the Lords observed that no Member of the Lower House sat 'as a baron of Parliament', but they conceded that there were some who 'may be termed barons of the Cinque Ports'.[7]

Hastings, Hythe, and New Romney were incorporated under Elizabeth; but in all the Ports the municipal organization took a similar form, with a council consisting of mayor, 'jurats' or aldermen, and commoners. In Dover, Hythe and Sandwich this body had, by the beginning of the early seventeenth century, succeeded in usurping the parliamentary franchise from the freemen. However, beginning at Dover in 1621, the freemen took back control of the franchise in all three cases during the 1620s.

One of the most unusual features of the Cinque Ports was that the lord warden distributed the writs and returned a consolidated list of Members to Chancery. This enabled him to nominate one Member in each port, and usually to leave the other to the electorate. Normal procedure seems to have been for the lord warden, who was invariably an absentee, to send his letters of nomination to the clerk of Dover Castle. The clerk then had the messenger for the Ports – known as the boder – distribute these documents, along with the writ and the lord warden's precept. However, in December 1620 the clerk of Dover Castle, Richard Marsh, went down with these documents to the town of Dover in person, for which courtesy he was given 2s. by the corporation, before riding over to Hythe (having an errand there), where he delivered the writ and the lord warden's letters.[8] Once each borough had held its election, it made its return to the clerk, who sent it up to the lord warden once all the others were in. This procedure was longstanding, but at New Romney at least it was not well understood, for in January 1621 the town clerk claimed that his town normally had one of its Members make its return to Chancery. An astonished Richard Marsh told him to re-read the writ more carefully, 'for', as he informed the lord warden's secretary, 'they have no return of writs to Westminster from their town'.[9] However, one week later Marsh had still not received the borough's return, 'so as for want of it and Dover's I cannot now send all away as I projected'.[10]

The lord warden was represented locally by a deputy, the lieutenant of Dover Castle, who was frequently able to 'come in upon my own strength'.[11] The two most compliant constituencies were Dover and Rye. Dover was not only directly under the lieutenant's eye, but also dependant on recurrent legislation for the maintenance of its harbour; whereas the Rye electorate may have been unnerved by their sudden descent from Elizabethan prosperity to impoverishment and depopulation. Sandwich, with its 'schismatical sectaries', and Hythe, with an abundance of neighbouring gentry, were the most difficult constituencies for the lord warden to control.

Following the accession of James I in March 1603 a Parliament was widely believed to be imminent. In May the lord warden, Henry Brooke†, 11th Lord Cobham, dispatched a note to the borough of Rye announcing that he expected it to yield him the nomination of one of its Members at the next election.[12] In fact, however, a Parliament was not summoned for another ten months. During the interim Cobham fell from office after his participation in the Main Plot was discovered. By the time that writs of election were issued in January 1604 a new lord warden, Lord Henry Howard, had been installed.

As was his right, Howard proceeded to nominate candidates to one seat in at least six of the seven Ports under his control. At Dover his choice lit upon Sir Thomas Waller, a kinsman of the lieutenant of Dover Castle who had been acting as his deputy, while at Sandwich he selected Sir George Fane, the nephew of the lieutenant, Sir Thomas Fane. For Hastings he chose the queen's vice chamberlain, Sir George Carew, while at New Romney he offered a place to Sir Robert Remington, a Hampshire gentleman closely associated with the Irish peer Lord Clanricarde. At Winchelsea he nominated his own servant Thomas Unton, while at Rye he chose the town's absentee joint water-bailiff John Young, who seems to have regarded Howard as his patron. Only at Hythe is there no direct evidence of a Howard nomination. The Members chosen were Sir John Smythe I, who lived at nearby Westenhanger and Christopher Toldervey, a former servant of Smythe's father. Both men had twice previously represented the town.

Howard might have encountered little difficulty in placing his nominees were it not for the fact that in July 1603, in the aftermath of the Main Plot, the brodhull had declared that 'no baron shall be chosen for the Parliament out of the Five Ports and two ancient towns' except 'such persons as are freemen resident and inhabiting the said ports and ancient towns' or were 'of counsel with the Ports'.[13] A further, if related, problem was the king's Proclamation of 11 Jan. 1604, which required enfranchised boroughs to 'make open and free election according to the law'.[14] At Hastings and New Romney at least, this Proclamation was interpreted to mean that outsiders nominated by the lord warden were barred from standing because of the fifteenth-century laws prohibiting non-residents from serving in Parliament. Howard was horrified, but with the help of Sir Thomas Fane and his nephew Sir George Fane, both boroughs were browbeaten into submission. It was a different story at Winchelsea, though, where townsmen were elected for both seats. A furious lord warden entered the name of his candidate on the list returned to Chancery regardless. Adam White, the townsman elected by the borough, was consequently forced to resign, but only after the Parliament had begun and only after he had gone to the expense of sending his personal effects by boat to Westminster.

Despite these difficulties, Howard, created earl of Northampton six days before the Parliament commenced, had secured at least six of the 14 available seats. He subsequently took advantage of a couple of by-elections to improve his position. At Rye in 1607 he secured the election of the London lawyer Heneage Finch in place of the townsman Thomas Hamon, who had died, while at Sandwich the following year he snapped up the seat previously held by Edward Peake, who had also expired, for his secretary, John Griffith. Elsewhere, Northampton ensured that he retained his interest, securing the return for Hastings of the wealthy north Kent gentleman Sir Edward Hales after Carew was elevated to the peerage, and the election of his servant William Byng at New Romney after Remington died. However, Hythe as yet seems to have remained beyond his grasp: at the election held in October 1609 to replace Smythe, who had died the previous year, it was a member of the local gentry, Sir Norton Knatchbull, who was returned.

At the general election of 1614, Northampton greatly improved upon his performance ten years earlier. Dover permitted him to nominate both Members after Sandwich made difficulties about accepting Sir George Fane, while at least five of the other Ports, including Hythe, all accepted candidates put up by the lord warden. As in 1604 they were a varied group. Dover returned both the lieutenant of Dover Castle, Sir Thomas Brett, and also Fane; Hythe agreed to take the London merchant and financier Sir Lionel Cranfield; while New Romney accepted the nomination of the London businessman Sir Arthur Ingram. At Sandwich, where the electors would have preferred to have been offered John Griffith rather than Sir George Fane, who was widely disliked, Northampton inserted his 'dear friend' Sir Thomas Smythe, a London merchant with property in the town but resident on the other side of Kent. Northampton's servant William Byng, who had represented New Romney in 1610, now came in for Winchelsea, while Sir Edward Hales was returned a second time for Hastings. Only at Rye is there no clear evidence of nomination by Northampton. Both seats were certainly bestowed on outsiders: Thomas Watson was an Exchequer teller from north Kent, and Edward Henden was a Gray's Inn barrister so unfamiliar to Rye's corporation that it referred to him as 'Edmund' Henden in its minutes. It is not impossible that both men owed their seats to Northampton, but Watson at least is likely to have been nominated in the first instance by secretary of state Sir Thomas Lake I, his fellow contractor in the sale of Crown rectories.

Only two of the 14 Members returned in 1614 were townsmen: James Lasher I, who sat for Hastings, and Robert Wilcocks, who came in for New Romney. Thomas Godfrey, who took one of the seats at Winchelsea, had previously been a jurat of

Winchelsea, and had even risen to the rank of deputy mayor, but by the time of the election he was living in London with his brother. His election may have been particularly acceptable to Northampton, as he was one of the earl's former servants. At Sandwich the second seat was bestowed not on a townsman but on Sir Samuel Peyton, a member of the local gentry.

In the aftermath of the Addled Parliament, the success of the lord warden in obtaining additional places for his nominees, and the incursion of the local gentry into seats traditionally reserved for townsmen, gave rise to concern within the Ports. On 25 July 1615, five days after the patent appointing Lord Zouche as lord warden was enrolled, the Brotherhood increased the penalty for the election of outsiders from £20 to £50.[15] Despite this edict, Zouche became the most effective electoral manager of the period, perhaps because he held no other major office and was able to reside for considerable periods at Dover Castle. Before the next election he drew up a schedule of the candidates he wished to place:[16]

The names of such as I have promised to offer to the towns for burgess-ships this Parliament.

Dover — Mr. Neville, son to the Lord Abergavenny

Hythe — Sir Guy Palmes

Sandwich — Sir Robert Hatton

Rye — Mr. Emmanuel Giffard, His Majesty's sworn servant

Romney — Mr. Francis Fetherston[haugh], one of His Majesty's pensioners

Sir Edward Zouche

Winchelsea Edward Nicholas

Hastings Samuel More

these two latter being my servants.

The names of such as I promised to place if any of them failed by choice elsewhere.

Sir Richard Young

Richard Zouche, doctor of law

Sir William Monyns

Sir Samuel Peyton

Sir Roger Nevinson

Zouche's plans were ambitious, and, despite an attempted intervention by the king, who hoped to use the lord warden's electoral patronage himself,[17] generally successful. Of his first choices, Christopher Neville and Sir Guy Palmes were elected knights of the shire for Sussex and Rutland, making way for two of his second-stringers at Dover and Hythe respectively, while Nicholas, Gifford, Featherstonhaugh and More were all placed without difficulty. Only Sir Robert Hatton ran into trouble, for although

returned with the aid of a sympathetic mayor he was unseated on petition. Sir Edward Zouche, the knight marshal, appears to have made no use of his cousin's offer.

Zouche also managed to secure both seats at Rye, for as well as nominating Gifford there he also sent a letter in favour of John Angell, the son of the king's fishmonger. He assured the borough that it was not his intention to deprive it of the right to nominate its second Member, but having been entreated by the young man's father he had not known how to refuse. Zouche achieved further electoral success by endorsing the candidacy of two members of the local gentry, Sir Thomas Finch at Winchelsea and Sir Peter Heyman at Hythe. One individual whom Zouche conspicuously failed to support, however, was the lieutenant of Dover Castle, Sir Henry Mainwaring. The lieutenant had customarily been the recipient of a nomination from the lord warden – Sir Thomas Fane appears to have been acting voluntarily when he surrendered his interest in 1604 to his nephew – but Mainwaring was a former pirate, and may have aroused Zouche's dislike. Despite being passed over, Mainwaring persuaded the corporation of Dover to grant him their senior seat.

Largely as a result of Zouche's success, but also because of the increasing poverty of most of the Ports, not a single townsman secured a seat in 1621. It is true that James Thurbarne[†], counsel to the Cinque Ports and a resident of New Romney, was initially adopted as a candidate by his home town, but he subsequently stood down in favour of Sir Peter Manwood, a Kentish gentleman ruined by his hospitality. It was also the case that at Hastings James Lasher II, the son of the jurat who had represented the borough twice previously, was selected. However, Lasher was hardly a resident, having lived in London since the mid-1590s. Attempts by leading inhabitants of a couple of the 'limbs' of the Cinque Ports to fill the void created by the absence of townsmen candidates failed: Samuel Short of Tenterden and James Berry of Lydd were defeated at Rye and Winchelsea respectively. Seven candidates contested Sandwich, but only one of them – John Jacob – was a townsman. Though popular with his fellow residents, Jacob was ultimately squeezed out by the lord warden's candidate (Hatton) and a member of the local gentry, Sir Edwin Sandys of Northbourne. Although Hatton was subsequently unseated on petition, his replacement, John Borough, was also an outsider, despite having been born at Sandwich.

At the general election of 1624 most of Zouche's

previously successful candidates were re-elected, with the exception of the Catholic Giffard, who was obliged to give way to a son of Secretary Conway at Rye. In addition, the lord warden also secured both seats at Dover, one of which was bitterly contested by Sir Henry Mainwaring, whom Zouche had dismissed from the lieutenancy the previous year. Although Mainwaring persuaded the Commons to overturn the Dover return, he failed to obtain a seat at the ensuing election, which was won by the two previously successful candidates. It is unclear to whom the Surrey gentleman and Household official Francis Drake owed his seat at Sandwich, but if Zouche was responsible then both Members were placed by the lord warden.

Members of the local gentry also continued to make inroads on the Ports in 1624. At Hastings Nicholas Eversfield, who lived two-and-a-half miles away at Hollington, was returned out of gratitude for his help in raising money for the repair of the town's pier, while at Winchelsea Sir Thomas Finch assigned his interest to his younger brother John, the deputy recorder of London. However, at Rye neither Sir William Twysden, from West Kent, nor Richard Tufton, whose family's ancestral seat lay at nearby Northiam, proved successful. As in 1621, there were no genuine townsmen Members, and Samuel Short failed for a second time to get elected at Rye. On the other hand, at New Romney the freemen returned Richard Godfrey II, the son of a jurat of Lydd, who agreed to serve without wages.

Well before the next general election Zouche sold the lord wardenship to the duke of Buckingham. The latter is usually considered to have been a poor electoral patron, but in 1625 at least he fared rather better in the Cinque Ports than Northampton had done in 1604. Of the 12 men nominated by him for seats, no less than eight were successful. However, in only one of the Ports – Dover – did Buckingham secure both places for his candidates; at Hythe, Rye, Sandwich and New Romney, his efforts to gain complete control were rebuffed. Of the eight successful candidates, three were close dependants of the duke: Thomas Fotherley, who came in for Rye, and Sackville Crowe, who was elected at Hastings, were both members of Buckingham's household, while Edward Clarke, returned for Hythe, was one of the duke's intimate servants. As in 1624, outsiders rather than townsmen took all those seats not controlled by the lord warden. The sole exception, perhaps, was at New Romney, where the junior seat once again went to Richard Godfrey II.

Buckingham proved unable to repeat the success of his first general election in 1626. This must have been partly due to his growing unpopularity, but matters were not helped by the fact that many of his letters of nomination failed to arrive before the Ports conducted their elections. The reason for this has never been satisfactorily established, but it may be significant that in early December 1625 his secretary for the Cinque Ports, Edward Nicholas, lay ill at his parents' house in Wiltshire.[18] Whatever caused the delay, only three of Buckingham's eight nominees were accepted, these being Sir John Suckling at Sandwich; Sir Nicholas Saunders at Winchelsea; and Sir Dudley Carleton at Hastings. In addition, the lieutenant of Dover Castle, Sir John Hippisley, scraped in at Dover. Those who relied upon Buckingham for a seat, only to be disappointed, were Sir William Beecher (at Dover); Sir Richard Weston (at Hythe); Walter Montagu (at New Romney) and Thomas Fotherley and Thomas Alured (both at Rye).

The outcome of the 1626 general election was nothing less than a disaster for Buckingham in the Cinque Ports, but worse was soon to follow. Shortly after the Parliament opened Suckling opted to sit for Norwich, for which borough he had also been returned. When Buckingham nominated as Suckling's replacement the master of the Jewel House, Sir Henry Mildmay, the freemen chose to bestow the seat instead on a member of the local gentry, Sir Edward Boys. Matters got worse in May, when Sir Dudley Carleton was elevated to the peerage. Buckingham selected as Carleton's replacement Walter Montagu, whom he had originally earmarked for a seat at New Romney. By now, however, impeachment proceedings against the duke were underway and Nicholas Eversfield persuaded the freemen of Hastings to return Sir Thomas Parker instead. By the time the Parliament was dissolved, only one of the Cinque Ports' representatives, aside from the lieutenant of Dover Castle, owed his seat to the duke.

Buckingham's failure to ensure that his letters of nominations were dispatched promptly ahead of the 1626 general election allowed the Ports to recover some of the ground they had lost since the end of Elizabeth's reign. For the first time since 1614 a couple of townsmen were returned: Dover elected John Pringle, a jurat and master of the town's fellowship of lodemanage, while Sandwich chose its former town clerk, Peter Peake. At New Romney, where Richard Godfrey II was returned for a third time in a row, the Thurbarne family appear to have used their influence to ensure the election of their kinsman by marriage of the Tenterden-born Thomas Brett.

From so low a point, Buckingham's performance at the next election could only improve. Even so, the outcome of the 1628 general election must have been deeply disappointing to the duke. Seats were regained at Dover and Hastings, but perhaps only four of the Cinque Ports' Members were the duke's nominees: Edward Nicholas (Dover), John Ashburnham (Hastings), Thomas Fotherley (Rye) and Sir Ralph Freeman (Winchelsea). In addition Sir John Hippisley again came in for Dover, while John Philipot, a supporter of Buckingham's, got himself elected at Sandwich. However, two of the duke's nominees suffered defeats: Sir Edwin Sandys saw his distinguished parliamentary career brought to an ignominious end at Sandwich, while Sir Edward Dering was thwarted at New Romney by Thomas Godfrey. It apparently became known during the first session of Parliament that Buckingham had been sufficiently moved by criticism of his secular pluralism to resign the wardenship. 'I know not who is lord warden', declared Coke in the debate of 11 June on the Remonstrance.[19] However, it was not until after the prorogation that the earl of Suffolk was appointed, presumably as a reward for declaring that John Selden*, the principal legal expert among those opposed to the duke, deserved hanging.[20]

[1] K.M.E. Murray, *Cinque Ports*, 6. [2] *HMC Downshire*, iv. 452. [3] *Procs. in Parls. of Eliz. I* ed. T.E. Hartley, iii. 110. [4] T. Birch, *Ct. and Times of Jas. I*, i. 130. [5] *Cal. White and Black Bks. of Cinque Ports* ed F. Hull (Kent Recs. Soc. xix), 405, 407; *CSP Dom.* 1623-5, p. 182. [6] Murray, 30. [7] *Bowyer Diary*, 212-13; *HMC Hatfield*, xviii. 456. [8] SP14/119/3. For Hythe's payment to Marsh, see E. Kent Archives Cent. H1209, f. 140v. [9] SP14/119/3. [10] *CD 1621*, vii. 569. [11] *Procs. 1628*, vi. 143. [12] *HP Commons 1558-1603*, i. 305. [13] *Cal. White and Black Bks. of Cinque Ports*, 375. [14] *Stuart Royal Procs.* ed. Larkin and Hughes, 69. [15] C66/2075/2; *Cal. White and Black Bks. of Cinque Ports*, 409. [16] SP14/118/26. [17] SP14/118/27. [18] *CSP Dom. Addenda 1625-49*, p. 73. [19] *CD 1628*, iv. 258. [20] *CSP Dom.* 1628-9, p. 224.

P.J.L./J.P.F./A.D.T.

DOVER

Right of election: in the corporation to 1621; in the freemen from 1624

Number of voters: 48 in 1621; 252 in 1624[1]

10 Mar. 1604[2]	SIR THOMAS WALLER
	GEORGE BYNG
14 Mar. 1614[3]	SIR GEORGE FANE
	SIR ROBERT BRETT
20 Dec. 1620[4]	SIR HENRY MAINWARING
	(SIR) RICHARD YOUNG
20 Jan. 1624[5]	SIR EDWARD CECIL
	(SIR) RICHARD YOUNG
	Sir Henry Mainwaring
	Election declared void,
	24 Mar. 1624
31 Mar. 1624[6]	SIR EDWARD CECIL
	(SIR) RICHARD YOUNG
	Sir Jasper Fowler
	Sir Henry Mainwaring
	Sir Thomas Wilsford*
19 Apr. 1625[7]	SIR JOHN HIPPISLEY
	(SIR) WILLIAM BEECHER
Jan. 1626	SIR JOHN HIPPISLEY
	JOHN PRINGLE
	(Sir) William Beecher
	Stephen Monins
25 Feb. 1628[8]	SIR JOHN HIPPISLEY
	EDWARD NICHOLAS

Commanding the shortest sea passage to France, Dover, described by one observer in 1635 as a 'long town ... indifferently well built', was the only Cinque Port to retain much economic importance, boasting as it did a substantial fleet of trading vessels.[9] Its prosperity, however, was achieved only at the price of constant maintenance work on pier and harbour. Under the Dover Harbour Act of 1581, periodically renewed, the cost was met by a general levy on English-owned shipping of 3d. a ton. The work was regarded as of national interest, and the necessary legislation was included among the public Acts.[10] The strategic importance of the castle required a garrison under the command of a resident lieutenant, who acted throughout the Cinque Ports as the lord warden's deputy. Unlike the funding for the pier and harbour, the cost of maintaining Dover Castle was not provided for by Act of Parliament. The Crown spokesman who told the House of

Commons in 1614 that the castle was so decayed that it was 'like to fall down' was ignored, and the king was subsequently obliged to foot the repair bill himself.[11]

There had been 'burgesses' and a guildhall in Dover before the Norman Conquest, and a charter was granted by Henry II.[12] At a general assembly of the freemen, or 'hornblowing', in 1561, the franchise, both municipal and parliamentary, was conceded exclusively to the corporation, consisting of the mayor, ten jurats, and a self-perpetuating oligarchy of 37 commoners, and since 1581 the elections had been held in the principal parish church.[13] The requirement that Members should take out their freedom was strictly enforced, though the £5 fee was invariably returned to them in consideration of past or future services to the town.[14] From 1584 it had become customary for the senior seat to be conferred upon the lieutenant of Dover Castle, although in 1601 the lieutenant was too ill to serve and the place was bestowed upon his nephew instead.

When the 11th Lord Cobham (Henry Brooke *alias* Cobham†) was dismissed in the early months of the new reign, the lord warden's duties were performed by his deputy (Sir) Thomas Fane† of Burston, who brought in his cousin Sir Thomas Waller to assist him as lieutenant of the castle.[15] The new lord warden, Lord Henry Howard, subsequently earl of Northampton, recommended Waller to the corporation for election to the first Stuart Parliament. Waller's colleague, chosen by the corporation, was George Byng, a brewer and jurat with extensive experience of the Brotherhood and Guestling, who was to be paid 6s. a day. The corporation's first concern, after the Parliament assembled, was for the renewal of the Harbour Act, which in recent years had encountered opposition in the Commons from spokesmen for the northern and western ports. One month into the Parliament the corporation gave Byng *carte blanche* 'to invite certain of the burgesses of the Parliament he shall think meet to a dinner or supper' to garner support.[16] A proviso concerning Dover harbour to the statutes renewal bill was 'much disputed' in June by Waller and others, but it was 'disliked' and referred back to committee. A separate bill to extend the levy for seven years 'and no longer' was subsequently introduced and became law at the end of the session.[17] Byng duly reported to the corporation in July, presenting his bill 'for extraordinary expenses', while Waller, who had refused all remuneration, was voted half a tun of wine for his efforts.[18] Two years later, the establishment of the Dover Harbour Board, under the *ex officio* chairmanship of the lord warden, removed the issue from the parliamentary arena.[19]

By the time of the next election, in 1614, Sir Robert Brett was lieutenant of the castle. A Somerset man by birth, he had married the sister of Sir George Fane, who had succeeded his uncle, the late lieutenant, to the Burston estate and leased a house in the town.[20] When Fane was rejected at Sandwich, Northampton was 'upon the grounds of an extraordinary occasion' compelled to 'entreat' Dover for both seats.[21] The corporation made no difficulty, and apparently returned Fane as the senior Member,[22] the only election in the period in which the lieutenant gave precedence to his colleague.

Northampton's successor as lord warden was Edward, 11th Lord Zouche. Unlike previous lord warden's, Zouche refrained from nominating the lieutenant of Dover Castle for one of the borough seats. On the contrary, shortly before the next general election, in December 1620, he listed Christopher Neville*, the eldest son of Lord Bergavenny, as his preferred nominee, with his own former secretary (Sir) Richard Young as his second string.[23] Consequently, when Neville was returned as knight of the shire for Sussex, Zouche transferred his choice to Young, to whom the Dover corporation had presented a silver cup in 1616,[24] rather than to the newly appointed lieutenant, Sir Henry Mainwaring. The corporation, however, concluded that the lieutenant should be one of the borough's representatives, especially after a leading townsman, William Leonard†, declined to put himself forward. As a result Mainwaring was asked to stand by the mayor.[25] Mainwaring proved only too willing to fill the vacancy, but took care to notify Zouche of his plans in advance.[26] On the day of the election Young, unlike Mainwaring, failed to attend the hustings, but instead presented his £5 fee for the freedom of the borough (which was returned to him) through another man. The corporation was clearly piqued at this behaviour, but rather than risk offending Zouche, Young was allowed to swear the oath of a freeman in London, a courtesy never extended to any of the port's former representatives.[27]

Dover sent its Members to the 1621 Parliament against a backdrop of trade depression. In 1618 the corporation had complained that it was indebted and that trade was 'very much decreased'. At the same time it sought exemption from the charges for the lighthouses at Winterton and Dungeness, and also access to the cloth markets of Germany and Flanders, an objective they had found 'so strongly opposed by the Merchant Adventurers … and their great friends as there is little hope'.[28] Young, a complete landlubber, was out of his element, and wrote to the corporation on 29 Mar. 1621 to send up 'some knowledgeable person' to represent the Cinque Ports before the free trade committee.[29] As a reformed pirate, Mainwaring was better equipped: he spoke during the debate on the lighthouse monopoly,[30] and in 1622 the corporation presented him with a hogshead of wine 'towards his charges, he requiring no allowance'.[31] The corporation was also anxious to obtain a bill redrawing parish boundaries in the town, which was given a second reading on 18 April. However, the speakers in the debate, particularly Sir George Newman†, who had represented Dover in the last Elizabethan Parliament, were mostly hostile, and the bill never emerged from committee.[32]

Mainwaring was dismissed from the lieutenancy in 1623, ostensibly for scandalous absence from his post and 'women's matters', but almost certainly for 'too much affecting Buckingham's desires'.[33] Zouche kept the post in his own hand, and for the last Jacobean Parliament nominated Young for re-election, together with Sir Edward Cecil, a professional soldier high in favour with Buckingham. Mainwaring, anxious to have his revenge on Zouche, wrote to the corporation on his own behalf, but when the election was held on 20 Jan. 1624 he received no votes, but rather a polite reply, 'acknowledging his former kindness and pains taken at the last Parliament', and asking him 'not to take it unkindly that he was not elected'.[34] His lack of support on the corporation probably came as no great surprise to Mainwaring, for a few days before the election one of the jurats, Stephen Monins, along with Sir Jasper Fowler, a local customs officer with a house in the town, had unsuccessfully pressed the mayor to allow the ordinary freemen the vote.[35] Mainwaring, it seems, was convinced that though Zouche disapproved of him, 'the inhabitants there do all love him'.[36]

Although Mainwaring had now been rejected, he had, by questioning the narrow franchise, found the perfect way to challenge the election result. Shortly after the Parliament assembled a petition signed by Fowler, the vicar of St. James, and 19 freemen, was presented to the Commons complaining that only the councilmen had received warning of the election and that others who attended had been denied the vote. At Young's suggestion, the corporation hastily drafted a counter-petition defending the borough's accustomed electoral practice, which was sent up to London with the 1604 Member George Byng and two other leading townsmen.[37] However, the committee for privileges ruled on 23 Mar. that 60 years' usage could not validate the surrender of the inalienable right of the commonalty. It also decided that the mayor should

not be punished, since he had followed precedent and acted in good faith. The following day the Commons accepted the committee's recommendations and declared the election void, though it found the sitting Members 'altogether innocent of any practice'.[38]

Cecil was bitter at being so unceremoniously turfed out of the House, telling Zouche that if the law requiring the commonalty to participate in elections 'were so generally followed as it hath been against us … there would be but few sit in Parliament'. He initially intended to resume his military command in the Low Countries, having recently been recalled by Prince Maurice, but on reflection he resolved to delay his departure, announcing that 'if there be any means for us to recover the honour' the lord warden should consider it.[39] Young, too, was determined to stand again, if only because he was anxious to ensure that the monopolies bill did not adversely effect an office he held in Chancery. The day after the election was quashed he informed Zouche that one of the jurats named Garrett 'can do much with the seamen that are freemen'. He subsequently sent the lord warden a copy of the Commons' order suppressing the earlier election, 'by which your lordship may see that there is no exception taken, but rather an implicit approbation of our persons, with some tacit intimation unto the freemen to choose us again'. This ruling, he advised, ought to be read aloud at the forthcoming election so as to dispel any suggestion that he and Cecil had been unseated because they were disliked.[40]

Young affected outrage on learning that Mainwaring also intended to stand, believing that the former lieutenant aimed at reinstatement by demonstrating his popularity in the port. Never, he told Zouche, had he suspected that Mainwaring would be 'so mad as to stand for himself' given 'your lordship's disaffection to him'.[41] However, Mainwaring not only put himself forward for the senior seat, but enlisted the help of Sir Thomas Wilsford*, who stood for the junior place. There was 'earnest labouring' for them both by Monins and Sir Edwin Sandys*, Wilsford's father-in-law.[42] Thanks to Young, who pointed out that neither Mainwaring nor Wilsford were capable of election because they were not freemen, their campaign foundered at the end of March. The subservient mayor refused first to admit them to the freedom, and then denied them the poll, as unqualified to represent the port. Fowler also 'stood to be one',[43] but customs officials were seldom popular in a seafaring community, and his efforts on behalf of the commonalty went for nothing. It was perhaps only natural that in the aftermath of the election Wilsford should have called the mayor 'an arrant knave, rogue, cuckold, wittol, and many other uncivil words', but the occasion was ill-chosen, and he had to apologize.[44] Zouche, meanwhile, was so incensed at Mainwaring's behaviour that on the transfer of the lord wardenship to Buckingham a few months later it was explicitly provided that his former lieutenant should hold no office in the Cinque Ports.[45]

After these excitements the 1625 election passed off peacefully. Wilsford found a seat at Canterbury, while Cecil, Mainwaring and Young all pursued careers under Buckingham's patronage, without further experience in the Commons. Sir John Hippisley, the new lieutenant of Dover Castle, took the senior seat in the first Caroline Parliament, and obtained from Buckingham a letter for the election of Sir William Beecher, his father-in-law's first cousin and a clerk of the Privy Council. The corporation admitted him to the freedom, but pointed out that with the wider franchise it was not possible to guarantee his election.[46] However, the corporation's fears proved groundless, as both nominees were duly returned. It was a different story when they stood for re-election in the following year. Dover's shipping had suffered heavy losses, and the Dunkirkers were so active in the Channel that the town's fortifications had to be strengthened.[47] Hippisley complained of the tardiness of the lord warden's nominations, but admitted that he himself, trusting in the efficacy of the mayor's good offices, 'had no man busy' canvassing the freemen, and that 'a faction was made upon a sudden to put us out'. This time Monins, the only Member of the corporation to be styled 'esquire', offered himself as a candidate, and it may have been in the hope of dividing his supporters that John Pringle, another jurat and Hippisley's colleague in the Dover prize commission, was persuaded to stand. If so, the stratagem failed; Beecher finished at the foot of the poll, and it was only by three votes that Hippisley avoided a similar failure.[48] Pringle, a baker by trade, may have owed his success to the fact that he was then serving as master of Dover's fellowship of lodemanage, the organization which provided pilots for the Channel crossing. As such he was well placed to speak for Dover's maritime community, and once in the Commons he lost no opportunity in doing so.

For the general election of 1628 the lord warden's interest was better organized. Beecher withdrew to Windsor, Berkshire, and was replaced by Edward Nicholas, Buckingham's Admiralty secretary and former secretary to lord warden Zouche. Although not a freeman, he had been invited as long ago as 1620 to stand for the port.[49] The remaining seat was bestowed upon Hippisley, who was re-elected 'on my own

strength'. After the election, which was 'most free and general', the corporation nominated commissioners to swear in Nicholas as a freeman, and expressed their sense of 'many engagements to yourself for sundry favours, and great hope of your best endeavours for the good and benefit of this township and the Ports in general'.[50] On 4 June it was reported to the House that 19 Dover ships of 100 tons and upwards had been taken by the enemy or cast away since the last Parliament.[51] After Buckingham's assassination, the corporation seem to have given up hope of any effective help from the town's Members. Its petition against the water-bailiff was rejected by the Privy Council, and shortly before the second session Pringle was chosen 'to be a solicitor to Parliament' in the case. The results of his lobbying do not appear.[52]

[1] Add. 29625, ff. 36-60. [2] Add. 29623, f. 5. [3] Add. 28036, f. 115v. [4] Add. 29623, f. 51. [5] Ibid. f. 63v. [6] Eg. 2120, f. 2. [7] Ibid. [8] Add. 29763, f. 79. [9] 'A Relation of a Short Survey of the Western Counties' ed. G. Wickham Legg, in *Cam. Miscellany XVI* (Cam. Soc. ser. 3. lii), 26. For the size of Dover's fleet, see SP14/140/68; Eg. 2584, ff. 375-80v. [10] *Hist. King's Works* ed. H.M. Colvin, iv. 756; *SR*, iv. 811, 854-6, 918, 973-4. [11] *Procs. 1614 (Commons)*, 62; E351/3590. [12] S.P.H. Statham, *Dover Charters*, xv; A. Ballard, *British Bor. Charters 1042-1216*, p. 114. [13] J. Glanville, *Reps.* 64-5; E. Hasted, *Kent*, ix. 512-13. [14] Add. 29623, ff. 5, 82. [15] *CSP Dom.* 1603-10, p. 25; *HMC Hatfield*, xv. 279. [16] Add. 29623, f. 4. [17] *CJ*, i. 241b, 986a, 994a-b; *SR*, iv. 1062. [18] Add. 29623, f. 5. [19] J.B. Jones, *Annals of Dover*, 99-100. [20] Add. 29623, f. 12. [21] Add. 28036, f. 115v. [22] The return does not survive, but Fane's name appears before Brett's in two contemporary lists: *OR*; *Procs. 1614 (Commons)*, 464. [23] SP14/118/26. [24] Add. 29623, f. 35; SP14/119/2. [25] SP14/118/20; *CSP Dom.* 1619-23, p. 192. [26] SP14/118/20. [27] Add. 29623, f. 52; SP14/119/2. [28] Add. 29623, ff. 44-5, 49. [29] *HMC 13th Rep. IV*, 159. [30] *CJ*, i. 529b; *CD 1621*, ii. 284. [31] Add. 29623, f. 58. [32] *CD 1621*, ii. 202, 298; SP14/120/123. [33] SP14/139/121; 14/154/23. [34] Add. 29623, f. 64. [35] SP14/161/32. On Fowler, see E351/619-24; Add. 29625, f. 53v; PROB 11/154, f. 127. [36] SP14/161/38. [37] Add. 29623, ff. 64-5; SP16/160/94. [38] Glanville, 66-70; *CJ*, i. 748a. [39] *Life and Times of Sir Henry Mainwaring Vol. I* ed. G.E. Manwaring (Navy Recs. Soc. liv), 127; SP14/161/32. [40] SP14/161/38, 51. [41] SP14/161/38. [42] SP14/161/51. [43] Eg. 2120, f. 2. [44] Add. 29623, ff. 65-6; *CSP Dom.* 1623-5, p. 245. [45] SP14/170/16. [46] Add. 29623, f. 67. [47] *CJ*, i. 845a, 871b. [48] *Procs. 1626*, iv. 234-5; SP16/19/33. [49] *CSP Dom.* 1619-23, p. 192. [50] *Procs. 1628*, vi. 145. [51] *CD 1628*, iv. 93. [52] Add. 29623, ff. 79-80.

P.J.L./A.D.T.

HASTINGS

Right of election: in the freemen

Number of voters: c.40

1 Mar. 1604[1]	RICHARD LYFFE SIR GEORGE CAREW I
20 Oct. 1605	SIR EDWARD HALES *vice* Carew, called to the Upper House JAMES LASHER I *vice* Lyffe, deceased
7 Mar. 1614	SIR EDWARD HALES, (bt.) JAMES LASHER I
25 Dec. 1620	SAMUEL MORE JAMES LASHER II
24 Jan. 1624	NICHOLAS EVERSFIELD SAMUEL MORE
c. 1 May 1625[2]	NICHOLAS EVERSFIELD SACKVILLE CROWE
21 Jan. 1626[3]	(SIR) DUDLEY CARLETON NICHOLAS EVERSFIELD
31 May 1626	SIR THOMAS PARKER *vice* Carleton, called to the Upper House Walter Montagu
29 Feb. 1628	JOHN ASHBURNHAM NICHOLAS EVERSFIELD

One of the original five members of the Cinque Ports, the ancient coastal town of Hastings can trace its history back to the early tenth century. By the early modern period the town consisted of two parallel streets that met at the upper end. A stream, known as the Bourne, divided the two roads, which were connected by several small lanes.[4] During the early medieval period Hastings enjoyed great prosperity owing to its natural harbour, and from 1369 it claimed to be chief among the Cinque Ports.[5] However, subsequent coastal erosion reduced the town to little more than a fishing port. The local fishing industry nevertheless prospered, despite competition from French trawlers and the danger of piracy. In 1587 the town could muster 106 mariners and 15 vessels of between 20 and 50 tons.[6] In 1621 the lord warden of the Cinque Ports, Lord Zouche, threatened to withdraw the town's special privileges after he discovered that its fishermen were illicitly exporting its best fish to France and slighting the authority of the king's purveyor.[7]

Hastings first received a charter in about 1155, and in 1589 it was incorporated.[8] From 1603 elections took place in the Ancient Court House, beside the Bourne stream,[9] and were conducted by the mayor, who replaced the bailiff under the Elizabethan charter. The franchise was held by the borough's 12 jurats and all the freemen, of whom there were about 30 at any one time, but attendance at the hustings naturally varied. Perhaps not surprisingly, the by-elections of 1605 and 1626 were relatively poorly attended, by 26 and 24 voters respectively. The best attended elections of the period appear to have been those of January 1626 and February 1628, when 38 and 37 voters respectively turned out. However, it is not known how many of the electors voted in 1604. Townsmen occupied one seat until 1621, and except at the by-election of 1626, the lord warden's nomination was accepted for the other.

Outsiders chosen to sit were normally expected to take the oath of a freeman. In so doing, they promised to bear 'faith and truth ... to the mayor, jurats and commonalty of the town and port of Hastings' and to uphold 'the charters, liberties and franchises and customs and usages' of the Cinque Ports, and 'specially of the said town of Hastings'. However, as strangers chosen by the borough were rarely willing to travel to Hastings take their oath, it was not unusual for the corporation to make arrangements for them to do so in London. In 1625 the mayor travelled to London for the express purpose of administering the oath to Sackville Crowe, while in 1620 authority to tender the oath to Samuel More was granted to More's fellow Member, the London resident James Lasher II, and to the lieutenant of Dover Castle, Sir Henry Mainwaring*. In addition to taking the oath of a freeman, all Members chosen by the borough were issued with a commission under the common seal of the town whereby they were assigned 'full power and authority ... to do and consent unto such things and matters as at the said Parliament (by God's permission) shall happen to be ordained'. However, the granting of such a commission was made conditional on the taking of the oath of a freeman.[10]

For the first election of the period the newly appointed lord warden, Lord Henry Howard, soon to be created earl of Northampton, recommended the queen's vice-chamberlain, Sir George Carew. However, at a meeting of the corporation on 14 Feb. some of those present, mindful of the recent Proclamation for the election of residents (and also of a similar decree issued by the Brotherhood of the Cinque Ports), and resentful of Howard's minatory tone, jibbed at the nomination. 'We paused to proceed to any such election', the corporation's minute book records, 'till we might understand how other places of the Ports resolve to do'. Faced with this threat to the lord warden's patronage, the lieutenant of Dover Castle, Sir Thomas Fane[†], wrote to the corporation at the end of February. After insisting that there was no need to heed either the Proclamation or the decree of the Brotherhood, Fane warned of the inconveniences that might follow unless the borough complied with Howard's request. An identical letter addressed to the corporation of New Romney, which like Hastings had also threatened to break ranks, succeeded in its objective on 29 Feb., and the following day Hastings, too, yielded, 'being in some sort persuaded that his lordship rather requested than challenged de jure'. Four days later Northampton sent a letter of thanks.[11]

Carew's colleague was the septuagenarian townsman Richard Lyffe, who had a long record of municipal and parliamentary service. At the time of the 1604 election he was serving as mayor for the second time. After the first session he asked to be paid parliamentary wages, which he had received in 1597 and 1601. Affronted by this request, the corporation declared that Lyffe 'ought not to have challenged any fee or wages … but to have served gratis'. However, in return for agreeing to waive his rights, Lyffe was allowed £5 as a present, of which sum 20s. was to be levied on nearby Pevensey and 10s. on neighbouring Seaford (both towns being 'members' of Hastings).[12]

Shortly before the next session a double by-election was caused by the elevation of Carew to the Lords (May 1605) and the death of Lyffe (August 1605). The lord warden recommended Sir Edward Hales, a Kent gentleman, who was chosen 'sed non jure', while Lyffe was replaced by James Lasher, a prominent jurat. Hales and Lasher were re-elected in 1614, and the corporation ordered that Lasher was to be paid both wages (at 7s. 6d. per day) and riding expenses (at 5s. per day).[13]

At the next general election the corporation broke with tradition by failing to return a townsman. Instead, its choice for the second seat settled upon Lasher's eldest son. An amateur soldier with a stake in the Sussex iron industry, the younger James Lasher had retained his links with Hastings despite living in London, and consequently was now captain of the town's militia. The first seat was bestowed upon Samuel More, the servant and kinsman of the new lord warden, Lord Zouche. In his letter of nomination to the borough, Zouche praised More's 'honesty and soundness in religion'.[14]

It is not clear why Hastings failed to return a townsman to the 1621 Parliament, but the answer almost certainly lies in the state of the borough's finances. From at least 1611 the corporation had been trying to repair the town's pier, upon which the continued prosperity of the port depended but which periodically suffered destruction by the sea.[15] In 1619 matters had become so desperate that it was decided to petition the king, and to approach the new lord warden, Lord Zouche, for support.[16] Faced with the prospect of a large bill for the repairs, it seems likely that the borough decided that it could no longer afford to pay parliamentary wages. Under these circumstances, it is hardly surprising that the borough opted to return the younger James Lasher, whose residence in the capital meant that he might serve without cost. However, Lasher may have subsequently blotted his copybook, for once in the Commons he proposed that a bill to prevent trawling be committed. Although the fishermen of Rye and Hythe were opposed to the use of trawl nets, those of Hastings were most emphatically not.[17]

Shortly before the 1621 Parliament opened, the corporation succeeded in obtaining letters patent from the king authorizing it to raise money for the pier by means of a collection. These evidently proved so successful that repairs began later that year, and though the corporation was forced to petition the Privy Council in February 1622 after the collectors held back half the money raised, work continued into the summer of 1622.[18] One of those who helped the borough obtain the letters patent was Nicholas Eversfield, whose seat at Hollington lay two-and-half miles from the town. The borough was evidently grateful for his assistance, as at the next general election in 1624 it chose him rather than the younger Lasher, whose father was now dead, to serve in Parliament. It also re-elected the lord warden's nominee, Samuel More. The corporation, fearing that the 1621 bill against trawl fishing would be reintroduced to the Commons, ordered that all its manuscript books concerning its right to fish with trawl nets were to be delivered to Eversfield.[19]

Eversfield was re-elected to all the remaining parliaments of this period, but More lost his interest on Zouche's resignation as lord warden in the autumn of 1624. Shortly before death of the king, an irritated corporation learned 'by common report, not by writ or other ordinary course anciently used', that the duke of Buckingham had succeeded as lord warden. Nevertheless, at the next election, which was held at the end of April or beginning of May 1625, it accepted without demur Buckingham's nomination of Sackville Crowe, a member of his household of Sussex origin. It also returned Buckingham's choice in 1626, this being the vice-chamberlain of the king's Household, (Sir) Dudley Carleton. However, during the course of the Parliament Carleton was raised to the Upper House to avert the wrath of the Commons. On 22 May, the day before a new writ was issued, Buckingham thereupon wrote to the corporation, nominating Walter Montagu, who had been unsuccessful at New Romney, and may have relied on the local influence of John Ashburnham.[20] Although the mayor and the three jurats who were present seem to have been willing to accept Montagu – the corporation's minute book, which they controlled, describes the duke's letter to them as 'very kind' – the freemen were not. On the contrary, 'by means made to some of them by Mr. Eversfield' they chose instead a Sussex gentleman from an ancient family, Sir Thomas Parker, although Parker himself had never requested the seat.[21] At the next election Ashburnham stood himself, though the estate that had been in the family since at least 1166 had been sold in 1611, and he relied principally on his kinsman and master, Buckingham.[22] He replaced Parker, and established an interest in the port that only negligence could undermine.

[1] Dates of election, 1604-24, taken from E. Suss. RO, HAS/DH/B98/1, ff. 89v, 107v, 174, 221; HAS/DH/B98/2, f. 15. [2] The date given in the corporation minute book, 19 Jan., is clearly a clerical error. The borough dated its return 1 May: E. Suss. RO, HAS/DH/B98/2, ff. 19v, 20v. [3] Dates of election, 1626-8, taken from ibid. f. 24v, 31, 38v. [4] VCH Suss. ix. 5, 8. [5] K.M.E. Murray, Constitutional Hist. of Cinque Ports, 18. [6] W.D. Cooper and T. Ross, 'Notices of Hastings', Suss. Arch. Colls. xiv. 86-7. [7] Add. 37818, f. 59. [8] CPR, 1587-8 ed. S.R.R. Neal (L. and I. Soc. ccc), 8. [9] VCH Suss. ix. 5. [10] E. Suss. RO, HAS/DH/B98/1, f. 221; HAS/DH/B98/2, ff. 20v, 38v. [11] E. Suss. RO, HA/DH/B98/1, ff. 88v-90. For Fane's letter, see Murray, 98-9. [12] E. Suss. RO, HAS/DH/B98/1, f. 94; J.M. Baines, Historic Hastings, 41. [13] E. Suss. RO, HAS/DH/B98/1, ff. 107v, 174. [14] SP14/118/50. [15] HMC 13th Rep. IV, 360; E. Suss. RO, HAS/DH/B98/1, ff. 151, 197v; A. Fletcher, A County Community in Peace and War: Suss. 1600-60, p. 20; VCH Suss. ix. 10. [16] Baines, 203. [17] CJ, i. 558b; CSP Dom. 1611-18, p. 457. [18] E. Suss. RO, HAS/DH/B98/1, f. 211v; Cooper and Ross, 90; APC, 1619-21, p. 346; 1621-3, p. 136. [19] CSP Dom. 1623-5, p. 208. [20] Procs. 1626, iii. 312; iv. 237. [21] E. Suss. RO, HAS/DH/B98/2, f. 31. [22] VCH Suss. ix. 127.

P.J.L./A.D.T.

HYTHE

Right of election: in the corporation to 1624; in the freemen from 1625

Number of voters: 35 in 1640[1]

16 Mar. 1604	SIR JOHN SMYTHE I
	CHRISTOPHER TOLDERVEY
4 Oct. 1609[2]	SIR NORTON KNATCHBULL vice
	Smythe, deceased
9 Mar. 1614	SIR RICHARD SMYTHE
	SIR LIONEL CRANFIELD
29 Dec. 1620	SIR PETER HEYMAN
	RICHARD ZOUCHE
17 Jan. 1624	SIR PETER HEYMAN
	RICHARD ZOUCHE
18 Apr. 1625	SIR EDWARD DERING
	EDWARD CLARKE
	Sir Allen Apsley
8 Jan. 1626	SIR PETER HEYMAN
	BASIL DIXWELL
	Sir Richard Weston*
25 Feb. 1628	SIR PETER HEYMAN
	(SIR) EDWARD SCOTT
	?Basil Dixwell

Hythe received its first charter in 1156, and in 1575 became the first Cinque Port to be formally incorporated, under a mayor, nine jurats, and an undefined common council in whom the franchise was vested. By the early seventeenth century the obstruction of the haven by shingle had reduced the town, described in 1613 by the mayor and jurats as 'much decayed', to a mere fishing port.[3] Its difficulties were compounded during the mid-Jacobean period by competition from French trawlermen.[4] The absence of a secure economic foundation not surprisingly left the borough vulnerable to the local gentry. Indeed, no townsman was elected in this period. After 1614 the dominant gentry interest passed from the Smythes of nearby Westenhanger to the borough's near neighbour Sir Peter Heyman of Sellinge. Sir Norton Knatchbull of Mersham Hatch could probably always have commanded a seat, but he preferred to exercise his interest behind the scenes. Successive lord wardens were able to exercise their power of nomination only intermittently. Elections were held in the town's common hall.[5]

In 1604 Sir John Smythe I, the eldest son of 'Customer Smythe', was elected, together with his father's old servant and friend Christopher Toldervey. When Smythe died in 1608, he was replaced by Knatchbull, who declined the honour of re-election in 1614, by which time Toldervey was also dead. The corporation accepted lord warden Northampton's nomination of Sir Lionel Cranfield, surveyor-general of the customs, 'whose quality both for worth and sufficiency I know to be void of all exception'. As Smythe's heir was still under age, his brother Sir

Richard was elected to the remaining seat, fortified with the recommendation of Sir John Scott*.[6]

After 1614 the Westenhanger interest was in eclipse, owing to the incapacity of Sir John Smythe's son Thomas, and Sir Richard's disdain for politics.[7] On 28 Nov. 1620 lord warden Zouche wrote to the corporation at the request of Sir Peter Heyman, who desired a seat. Zouche was willing that Heyman should supply one of the seats, but as he had already promised his support for another he asked the borough to bestow upon him the place reserved 'for the burgess of whom yourselves have the sole nomination'. This arrangement, he promised, would 'be no prejudice to your privilege in future times'. It was not until 18 Dec., however, that Zouche was in a position to announce his official candidate. His choice fell upon his kinsman Dr. Richard Zouche, a civil lawyer, 'whom I will boldly commend unto you for a very sufficient, religious, worthy gentleman'.[8] Although entirely unacquainted with Dr. Zouche, the borough elected him the following day without demur. Heyman too was chosen, having brought the lord warden's letter of nomination to the town in person.[9]

On 17 Apr. 1621 the corporation wrote to Lord Zouche asking that the Dungeness lighthouse, 'being called in question in Parliament', might be committed to the custody of the Cinque Ports. It may have been in response to this letter that the lord warden's cousin rose to his feet in the debate on sea-marks of 7 May.[10] Although no speech was ever delivered, the corporation was well enough satisfied with both its Members to re-elect them in 1624. In April the corporation asked for a subsidy for the repair of the haven, whereupon Lord Zouche recommended that it petition Parliament. However, although two men were appointed to solicit the business, no such petition had been submitted by the time Parliament adjourned the following month.[11] Heyman had been vocal in defence of the tax exemption enjoyed by the Cinque Ports. In May the corporation sent him a dozen fish, and in June it resolved to let him have 'a billet in the town for the freeing of his goods and chattels'.[12]

By the time of the 1625 election Heyman was overseas, probably in Ireland. On 3 Apr., the day after the writs of summons were issued, Knatchbull approached the corporation and asked that Sir Edward Dering, a gentleman 'without exception, religious, learned [and] stout', be elected. He added that it was 'without question' that the new lord warden, the duke of Buckingham, would approve of this choice, as Dering had 'lately matched in his family'. Eight days later Buckingham nominated the courtier Edward Clarke. On 14 Apr. the corporation approved both candidates, but the following day, to general consternation, it received a further letter of nomination from the duke. In addition to Clarke, Buckingham desired the town to bestow a seat on Sir Allen Apsley, the lieutenant of the Tower and victualler of the Navy. 'If you shall now thus doubly gratify me at my entrance in my office', he declared', it would 'be no prejudice to your privilege and freedom of this kind for the future'. It was in these circumstances that the corporation decided to strengthen its position by widening the franchise. An assembly was held in the town hall late in the evening of Easter Monday, to which the freemen were summoned, and 'the said mayor, jurats, commons, and freemen, being all particularly called by their names, did freely elect, choose, and confirm the said Sir Edward Dering and Edward Clarke, esq. their burgesses to the said next Parliament'. They then wrote to Apsley to assure him that his candidature had been properly presented to the electorate, but that at this second meeting they had 'elected, or at the least confirmed, the said persons before mentioned for their burgesses to the next Parliament'.[13] A separate letter of explanation was also sent to Buckingham.[14] Three days after the election Dering came down to Hythe and demonstrated his gratitude by spending £3 6s. on white wine and sugar 'upon the mayor and jurats and freemen'.[15]

Although the corporation had refused to allow Buckingham both seats in 1625, it had at least accorded him the right to nominate one of the candidates. In 1626, however, the borough failed to wait for Buckingham's letter of nomination before proceeding to an election. On 7 Jan. the writ reached the town, and the following day it was resolved to return Heyman, who had now returned from overseas, along with a newcomer to the neighbourhood, Basil Dixwell of Folkestone. Buckingham's nomination of Sir Richard Weston*, the chancellor of the Exchequer, arrived four days later. At a second meeting the corporation resolved to adhere to its original choice, whereupon the grateful Dixwell 'gave liberty to all the inhabitants of this town at all times hereafter to carry and recarry, go and return over his land called the Slip at the east end of the town ... without paying anything for the same'. A letter of apology, explaining the circumstances, was sent to Buckingham, and another was dispatched to the lieutenant of Dover Castle, Sir John Hippisley*, one of the duke's closest allies.[16] Following the dissolution, Heyman sent the borough some rabbits and venison.[17]

Buckingham may not have been overly displeased at the borough's refusal to elect Weston, as Dixwell, apart from being a friend of Hippisley's, was also the godson of his kinsman by marriage, Basil Feild-ing. However, he had now twice failed at Hythe, and therefore not surprisingly he seems not to have both-ered to nominate anyone at all there in 1628. Heyman, however, was unaware that his seat was safe, for on 26 Jan. he wrote to Buckingham's Admiralty secretary, Edward Nicholas*, complaining that 'my lord the duke takes something ill at my hand (which I am not able to guess at)'.[18] The borough turned for the other seat to (Sir) Edward Scott, who had twice stood for the county. On 25 Feb. they notified him of his election in a letter in which he was praised for his 'worthiness and integrity both to God and the country' and for having shown his 'special love to us'.[19] Five weeks after the election six companies of Irish soldiers were billeted upon Hythe. Heyman's tacit support in Parliament for billeting may have redounded to the advantage of his constituents, for not long after he addressed the Commons on the matter the Privy Council ordered the number of troops stationed at Hythe to be reduced by more than half.[20] His constituents were evidently kept closely informed of events in Parliament, for on learn-ing of the passage of the Petition of Right the town fired off its guns in celebration.[21]

Although no wages were paid to its Members during this period, the borough was unable to avoid incurring some expenditure in relation to Parliament. In 1620/1 4s. was paid to the messenger who brought down the writ of summons and two proclamations, and who carried the return to Dover Castle. A further 2s. was also bestowed upon the clerk of Dover Castle, Richard Marsh. In November 1620 the corporation bought Heyman dinner after he produced the lord warden's letter of nomination in person, and in 1626 both Heyman and Dixwell were dined at the corporation's expense after it was decided to disregard Bucking-ham's nomination of Weston.[22] However, such social events were rare, as those chosen were often unwill-ing to journey to Hythe to be sworn in as freemen. In 1614 the corporation delayed making its return in the hope of forcing its newly elected Members to come down to be sworn, but it was ignored and had to beat a retreat. In December 1620 lord warden Zouche bluntly informed the borough that he thought it 'need-less' for his kinsman Dr. Zouche to journey all the way from London, and demanded that a commission be issued allowing the latter to take the oath of a freeman in the capital 'as other towns that will have it so do'.[23] Reluctantly the corporation agreed to this request, and following both the 1625 and 1628 elections it issued similar commissions regarding Edward Clarke and Sir Edward Scott respectively.[24]

[1] G. Wilks, *Barons of Cinque Ports and Parlty. Rep. of Hythe*, 80. [2] Dates of elections 1609-28 taken from E. Kent Archives Cent. 1209, ff. 3v, 45v, 129v, 181; 1210, ff. 19v, 22, 61. [3] E. Hasted, *Kent*, viii. 236-7; HCA 30/4, unnumb. item, 19 Apr. 1613, mayor and jurats to Northampton. [4] *CSP Dom.* 1611-18, pp. 349, 365, 433; 1619-23, p. 345. [5] Wilks, 69. [6] Ibid. 66-8. [7] *Chamberlain Letters* ed. N.E. McClure, ii. 228. [8] Wilks, 69-71. [9] E. Kent Archives Cent. H1209, f. 140v. [10] *CSP Dom.* 1619-23, p. 247; *CJ*, i. 610a. [11] E. Kent Archives Cent. 1209, f. 191v. [12] 'Nicholas 1624', f. 100v; E. Kent Archives Cent. 1209, f. 192; 1210, f. 5. [13] Wilks, 75-9. [14] E. Kent Archives Cent. H/01/01. [15] Cent. Kent. Stud. U350, E4, f. 51. [16] Wilks, 72-3; *Procs. 1626*, iv. 240-1. [17] E. Kent Archives Cent. H1210, f. 56. [18] SP16/91/63. [19] *Procs. 1628*, vi. 151. [20] *APC*, 1627-8, pp. 370, 383-4, 389. [21] E. Kent Archives Cent. H1210, f. 81. [22] E. Kent Archives Cent. H1209, f. 140v; 1210, f. 33. [23] Wilks, 67-70. [24] E. Kent Archives Cent. H1210, f. 73r-v.

P.J.L./A.D.T.

NEW ROMNEY

Right of election: in the freemen

Number of voters: 18 in 1628[1]

29 Feb. 1604[2]	SIR ROBERT REMINGTON JOHN PLOMER
17 Sept. 1610	WILLIAM BYNG *vice* Remington, deceased
9 Mar. 1614	(SIR) ARTHUR INGRAM
14 Mar. 1614	ROBERT WILCOCKS
5 Nov. 1620	JAMES THURBARNE
9 Jan. 1621	SIR PETER MANWOOD *vice* Thurbarne, refused to serve
12 Jan. 1621	FRANCIS FETHERSTONHAUGH
23 Jan. 1624	FRANCIS FETHERSTONHAUGH RICHARD GODFREY II
18 Apr. 1625	RICHARD GODFREY II SIR EDMUND VERNEY Sir William Twysden, (bt.)*
11 Jan. 1626	RICHARD GODFREY II THOMAS BRETT Walter Montagu
16 Feb. 1628	THOMAS GODFREY THOMAS BRETT Sir Edward Dering, (bt.)*

New Romney lost its access to the sea after the violent storm of 1286, and dwindled into a mere market town, often at odds with its 'limb' of Lydd. It nevertheless served as the meeting place of the Cinque Ports' two representative assemblies, the Brotherhood and the Guestling, received a charter in 1352, and in 1563 was incorporated under a governing body consisting of a mayor and a maximum of 12 jurats.[3] In this period no more than half this number can be traced at any one time, and most of those recorded as participating in parliamentary elections were mere freemen. This small electorate clung with much determination to its right to return at least one townsman, whom, before the 1620s, it somehow found the means to pay despite the diminished economic status of the town. Only in 1621 and 1628 were both seats conferred on outsiders, and in each case the place normally reserved for a townsman went to men closely associated with the town and its immediate neighbourhood rather than on strangers.

Outsiders were required to take the oath of a freeman each time they were returned. Before the 1620s they were expected to journey to the town for this purpose, but in 1621 Francis Featherstonhaugh was sworn at London by his colleague Sir Peter Manwood, and by the borough's standing counsel, James Thurbarne. A similar commission was issued in 1625 to swear in Sir Edward Verney. In 1628 Thomas Brett, who had taken the trouble to journey to New Romney two years earlier after his first election by the borough, also took his oath in the capital.[4]

At the 1604 general election the corporation initially rejected as non-resident the candidate nominated by the newly appointed lord warden of the Cinque Ports, Lord Henry Howard. This was Sir Robert Remington, a Yorkshire-born administrator with a wife in Hampshire and interests chiefly in Ireland. On 13 Feb. the corporation explained that the Brotherhood of the Cinque Ports had resolved only seven months earlier to impose a fine of £20 on any of its members who failed to elect a resident freeman as one of its parliamentary representatives. It also drew attention to the king's recent Proclamation, which required enfranchised boroughs to observe electoral law, which forbade the return of non-residents.[5] Sir Thomas Fane[†], lieutenant of Dover Castle and thus deputy to Howard, was shocked at the 'unkindness' shown by the corporation to his superior. Other boroughs in Kent, he remarked on 28 Feb., had disregarded the ancient law on non-residence. Moreover, so far as the 1603 instruction was concerned, the borough was at liberty to dispense with any order that it had helped to make. Unless Remington was returned, New Romney would suffer many 'inconveniences', as Fane's nephew, Sir George Fane*, would explain

verbally.[6] The corporation was so intimidated by these threats that it immediately capitulated, returning Remington along with one of their own number, John Plomer.[7] It also fired off an apologetic letter to the lord warden. It had not known how other boroughs had responded to the royal Proclamation, it explained, and had only declined the lord warden's request out of fear of punishment. Far from entertaining hostile intentions towards Howard, it had delayed its election until it had received a response to its letter of 13 February. These explanations proved so satisfactory that on 4 Mar. the lord warden promised the corporation that 'hereafter' he would show 'care for your good'.[8]

Plomer's wages, originally fixed at 2s. a day like those granted to his immediate predecessors, were doubled for the third and fourth sessions.[9] The cost of these payments averaged over six per cent of the borough's total income between 1604 and 1610.[10] On Remington's death during the last recess of this Parliament the freemen accepted without demur one of Northampton's servants, William Byng, who was at least Kentish-born.[11]

Plomer and another jurat, Robert Wilcocks, were delegated in 1612 to protest to Northampton against the new charter sought by Lydd because 'it may be prejudicial to this corporation'.[12] They were apparently successful, as no objection was raised to Northampton's nomination of the parvenu London businessman and concessionaire, Sir Arthur Ingram, to replace Byng, who transferred to Winchelsea, Sussex, in 1614. Since Plomer was in poor health, the remaining seat was conferred on Wilcocks, who received payment at the reduced rate of 3s. a day.[13]

Plomer and Wilcocks were dead before the next general election, leaving the way clear for the borough's standing counsel, James Thurbarne, to regain the seat he had occupied in 1597. As a partner of (Sir) Giles Mompesson* in the unpopular alehouse patent, Thurbarne might have had good reason to seek election to the third Jacobean Parliament. He offered his services to the corporation on 5 Nov. 1620, and declared his willingness to accept 'what wages they think fit'. He was duly adopted 'with one consent', and it was agreed to allow him a salary of 4s. a day

> because he is a very able and sufficient man to do the Ports goods service at the said Parliament and also this town in particular if there shall be occasion to employ him, and because his charges for himself and his man lying there and attending at the Parliament will be more than former burgesses have been.[14]

However, on 4 Jan. 1621, having perhaps been advised that it would go better with him in Parliament if he kept his head down, Thurbarne was discharged at his own request 'because of special occasions'. His withdrawal paved the way for the Kent squire Sir Peter Manwood, who had previously owned property in Romney Marsh and now needed protection from his creditors. On 9 Jan. he was elected at his 'earnest request'. The remaining seat, which lay in the gift of Northampton's successor Lord Zouche, was bestowed three days later upon a courtier, Francis Fetherstonhaugh, whose chief interest in Parliament was the enfranchisement of County Durham.[15]

Fetherstonhaugh was nominated for re-election by Zouche in 1624, and shortly after being returned he wrote to the corporation promising 'his care in performing that service'.[16] The second place was taken by Richard Godfrey, the younger son of a jurat of Lydd, as by this time Manwood had fled overseas. Godfrey was quickly sworn in as freeman and jurat and agreed to serve without wages, to the delight and astonishment of the corporation.[17] Not surprisingly, Godfrey was returned to the next two Parliaments. In 1625 the new lord warden, the duke of Buckingham, attempted to take both seats, nominating the courtiers Sir Edmund Verney and Sir William Twysden*. The corporation rejected the Kentish magnate Twysden in favour of the more distant Verney, who could not threaten to establish a personal interest in the borough.[18] They also showed their appreciation of Godfrey's parliamentary services (which remained free but minimal, so far as official records show) by promoting him from 'gent.' to 'esquire' on the next return, and later by a gift of plate.[19] In 1626 the corporation returned Godfrey for a third time, and celebrated the event at a cost of 12s. 10d.[20] Godfrey was paired with Thomas Brett, a former soldier and Kentish-born kinsman of Thurbarne, much to the surprise of Buckingham, whose nomination of the aspiring diplomat Walter Montagu (son of Sir Henry Montagu*) came fractionally too late. The corporation explained that it had thought that the duke had decided not to make a nomination, but on its own admission it had waited only three days after it had received formal notification that there was to be a Parliament before proceeding to election.[21] Not surprisingly, therefore, this excuse was not accepted, and the town was punished by the billeting of soldiers.[22] During the course of the Parliament the corporation sent letters to Godfrey, but their contents are unknown.[23]

In 1628 Buckingham nominated Sir Edward Dering*, who had already been rejected by the county.

Godfrey stood down, to be replaced by his older half-brother Thomas, but Brett, who had sent the corporation a buck following the dissolution of the 1626 assembly,[24] held his ground, and Dering was rejected on the poll. This time the corporation aggravated its offence by returning no answer to the lord warden's letter;[25] and Buckingham aggravated its punishment by billeting Irish soldiers previously destined for Hythe on the town.[26] The corporation responded by petitioning the Commons, but the troops were not finally removed until the end of July.[27] At least one New Romney man was among those who toasted Buckingham's assassin a few months later.[28]

[1] E. Kent Archives Cent., NR/AC/2, p. 84. [2] Dates of election from New Romney assembly bks.: E. Kent Archives Cent., NR/AC/1, ff. 135v, 191v, 209, 267; NR/AC/2, pp. 27, 41, 51, 84. [3] E. Hasted, *Kent*, viii. 447; W. Holloway, *Romney Marsh*, 81; *CPR*, 1560-3, p. 499; M. Teichman Derville, *Annals of New Romney*, 5, 10; K.M.E. Murray, *Constitutional. Hist. of Cinque Ports*, 56. [4] SP14/119/19; *Procs. 1628*, vi. 156; *Top. and Gen.* ii. 461. [5] E. Kent Archives Cent., NR/AC/1, ff. 134v-5; *Cal. of the White and Black Bks. of Cinque Ports* ed. F. Hull (Kent Recs. xix), 375; *Stuart Royal Procs.* ed. J.F. Larkin and P.L. Hughes, i. 69. [6] Murray, 98-9. See also E. Kent Archives Cent., NR/AEp/41. [7] E. Kent Archives Cent., NR/AC/1, f. 135v. [8] E. Kent Archives Cent., NR/AEp/42-3. [9] E. Kent Archives Cent., NR/AC/1, ff. 138v, 152v, 161. [10] V.J. Hodges, 'The Electoral Influence of the Aristocracy 1604-41' (Columbia Univ. Ph.D. thesis, 1977), p. 143. [11] E. Kent Archives Cent., NR/AC/1, f. 191v; NR/AZ32/9. [12] E. Kent Archives Cent., NR/ACo/1, f. 28v. See also NR/FA/c8, f. 152. [13] E. Kent Archives Cent., NR/AC/1, ff. 209-10v. [14] Ibid. f. 265r-v. [15] Ibid. ff. 266v-7v; NR/AEp/44; SP14/118/26; 14/119/19. [16] E. Kent Archives Cent. NR/AC/2, pp. 27, 30. [17] Ibid. 47. [18] Ibid. 41. [19] Cent. Kent. Stud., PRC 16/240, f. 362. [20] E. Kent Archives Cent. NR/FA/c8, f. 236. [21] *Procs. 1626*, iv. 246. [22] Add. 37819, f. 17v; E. Kent Archives Cent., NR/CP/c110. [23] E. Kent Archives Cent., NR/FA/c8, f. 240. [24] Ibid. f. 242. [25] *Procs. 1628*, vi. 156. [26] *APC*, 1627-8, pp. 370, 389. [27] E. Kent Archives Cent., NR/AC/2, f. 45; *APC*, 1628-9, pp. 29, 57. [28] *CSP Dom.* 1628-9, p. 325.

P.J.L./A.D.T.

RYE

Right of election: in the freemen

Number of voters: 50 in 1604; 29 or 30 bet. 1621 and 1628

12 Mar. 1604[1]	THOMAS HAMON
	JOHN YOUNG
17 Oct. 1607	HENEAGE FINCH *vice*
	Hamon, deceased
7 Mar. 1614	EDWARD HENDEN
	THOMAS WATSON
23 Dec. 1620	EMMANUEL GIFFARD
	JOHN ANGELL
	Samuel Short
25 Jan. 1624	SIR EDWARD CONWAY II
	JOHN ANGELL
	Sir William Twysden, (bt.)*
	Samuel Short
	Richard Tufton
28 Feb. 1624	THOMAS CONWAY *vice*
	Conway, chose to sit for Warwick
21 Apr. 1625	THOMAS FOTHERLEY
	JOHN SACKVILLE
	Sir John Franklin*
	John Angell
	Emmanuel Giffard
16 Feb. 1626	THOMAS FOTHERLEY
	JOHN SACKVILLE
	Thomas Alured*
27 Feb. 1628	RICHARD TUFTON
	THOMAS FOTHERLEY
	John Sackville

Rye had obtained charters from its overlords, the Norman abbots of Fécamp, in the twelfth century, and by the reign of Henry III it had been added to the original Cinque Ports.[2] The only major natural harbour between Portsmouth and the Thames, it reached the zenith of its commercial prosperity in the mid-sixteenth century, when it emerged as 'the most important urban economy in eastern Sussex'.[3] London's cloth merchants took advantage of the short sea crossing to northern France and the Netherlands to export their goods from Rye, which also boasted one of the largest fishing fleets in southern England.[4] However, in the last decade of Elizabeth's reign the town experienced total and irretrievable economic collapse. The draining of marshland by commercial farmers in the nearby Rother levels caused the haven to silt up, and forced London's merchants to export their cloth directly to France instead. As the haven declined so too did the fishing fleet, which by 1629 had been reduced to nine small barks.[5] The inability of Rye's corporation to prevent the plundering of the town's fishing grounds by those who used the illegal trawl net, such as the French, merely hastened the process.[6] In the late 1590s a desperate corporation spent over £1,400 on a scheme to deepen the channel, but the project failed and between 1600 and 1602 the town was forced to sell most of its properties to pay off its loans.[7] As Rye's economy spiralled downwards, so too its population shrank, from more than 3,500 in the early 1570s to fewer than 1,300 by 1600. Among those who fled were most of the enterprising Protestant refugees who had previously flooded into the town to escape persecution.[8] By 1624 more than a hundred houses were uninhabited.[9] A reduced population meant that the corporation's total receipts, which had regularly exceeded £300 in the 1580s, fell by more than a third by 1600.[10]

Protestants formed a majority in Rye long before the Elizabethan settlement, under which it became a stronghold of puritanism, though a traditionalist faction survived at least until the middle of the reign.[11] The governing body consisted of the mayor and up to 12 jurats, but all the freemen were part of the assembly and were entitled to vote at parliamentary elections. An attempt to limit the franchise to the magistrates and the short-lived common council in 1580 had ended in failure.[12] The number of voters at parliamentary elections tended to fluctuate. In 1604 there were 50, whereas in 1614 there were only 26. However, in the 1620s the figure settled at around 30.[13] From 1571 the lord warden of the Cinque Ports enjoyed the right to nominate one of the borough's two Members. What was left of the Crown revenues – the petty customs and the rents of assize – was collected by the water-bailiff, while the customer of Chichester, who was responsible for all the Sussex ports, maintained an office on the quayside with a resident searcher.[14]

Following the accession of James I it was widely expected that a Parliament would be called immediately. In May 1603 the lord warden, Henry Brooke, 11th Lord Cobham, dispatched a note to Rye in which he curtly demanded 'the nomination of one of your burgesses for the next Parliament'. In the event, however, no Parliament was summoned until 31 Jan. 1604, by which time Cobham had been replaced by Henry Howard, earl of Northampton. On 20 Feb. the corporation, having learned of the impending Parliament, sent two of its jurats to wait on Northampton, presumably to know the name of his nominee, but also to request his aid in the 'repair of our decayed haven',[15] as the town was now incapable of paying for any further repairs itself. At the ensuing election, held on 12 Mar. and attended by the mayor, three jurats and 25 members of the commonalty, the borough elected as its senior Member its former mayor, Thomas Hamon, who had been one of the two jurats sent to consult Northampton in the previous month. The junior seat was bestowed on the former customer of Chichester, John Young, who had once lived in Rye and was now its water-bailiff. It seems likely that Young was Northampton's nominee, as he subsequently regarded Northampton as his patron. Despite the town's poverty, the assembly agreed to pay Hamon parliamentary wages.[16]

Soon after Parliament assembled Hamon and Young sent the corporation a letter, which was read out at a meeting of the assembly on 2 April. Its contents are unknown, but it seems likely that the two Members proposed that the town should lobby vigorously for the repair of its harbour. On 21 Apr. the land chamberlain paid out 5s. to one Robert Burdet for engrossing 'certain letters ... sent to the nobility about our harbour'. The following day, at a meeting of the corporation, a petition addressed to the king and drafted by Hamon and Young was read out and approved, as were several other letters 'sent by our lord warden and our burgesses to the Parliament ... which letters do concern our harbour, for the amendment thereof'. On 23 Apr. the land chamberlain reimbursed one William Harvey the £6 which he had 'laid out at London to Mr. Hamon by the appointment of Mr. Mayor'.[17] This lobbying campaign seems to have borne fruit, for on 27 June, shortly before Parliament was prorogued, the king appointed a special sewer commission to which both Hamon and Young were named. Procured at the cost of the corporation, it was granted for the sole purpose of preserving Rye's haven.[18] Several of the local landowners complained about this development, however, and in November Hamon was sent back to London armed with 'all necessary decrees and ordinances' in order to rebut their objections.[19]

Hamon returned home early from the third session of Parliament, and died soon after submitting a request for the payment of his outstanding parliamentary wages. Shortly after learning of Hamon's death, a local landowner, Sir William Twysden* (bt.), desired the mayor and his brethren to defer the subsequent by-election until he had consulted the lord warden. These consultations produced a letter from Northampton recommending Twysden's brother-in-law Heneage Finch, who as a barrister of the Inner Temple would 'ease you of that daily and large allowance which was before allotted to his predecessor'. Twysden himself pointed out that Finch would be 'very willing and able to advise, as well as aid and plead for you, if need shall be'.[20] The assembly yielded to these arguments, and in October 1607 elected Finch, who took his seat when Parliament finally reassembled in 1610. By that time it had become clear that the 1604 sewer commission had failed to halt the decline of the harbour.[21] On the contrary, recent storms had brought in more silt than ever, the town's jetties and quays were on the verge of collapse and the roadway leading to Rye had been almost completely washed away, threatening 'the utter ruin and decay of this whole town'.[22] Unable to pay for repairs itself, the mayor and jurats resolved to lay a bill before Parliament. A previous attempt in 1601 to secure legislation had failed,[23] but the Rye corporation was encouraged by the fact that the Dover authorities had succeeded in renewing their harbour preservation Act of 1581, which gave them the right to levy a duty from passing ships to pay for repairs. Consequently, on 29 Mar. 1610 the mayor and jurats asked Northampton to further a bill in Parliament. However, both Houses were then preoccupied with the Great Contract and it was therefore not until November that lobbying began in earnest. The mayor and jurats wrote to Northampton's secretary, John Griffith II*, James Thurbarne* (counsel to the Cinque Ports), Serjeant John Shurley (counsel for Rye and one of the Members for Lewes) and Twysden, as well as to Finch and Young, for assistance. They also dispatched four of their number to London to confer 'with such gents as have taken upon them to be our solicitors to follow our suit by bill into the Parliament House'. Yet despite these efforts the bill was not granted even a first reading by the Commons.[24]

Following this failure Rye evidently tried to work with the marsh-drainers rather than against them. In October 1613 the local sewer commissioners declared that the salt marshes near Rye harbour might be drained without prejudice to the haven, while in November Rye's mayor entered into an agreement with one of the drainers to recover 27 acres of marshland near the town.[25] This change of tactics may explain why Rye failed to reintroduce its harbour bill when Parliament met again in 1614. By that time Young had evidently emigrated while Finch did not put himself forward for election. As the borough was unable any longer to pay parliamentary wages, its choice of representatives necessarily fell on two outsiders, Thomas Watson, an Exchequer official who had purchased a small estate in Kent, and Edward Henden, a barrister of local origin, both of whom were instructed to 'bear their own charges'.[26] It has been suggested that both men were the nominees of the lord warden,[27] but Watson at least may have had access to other sources of patronage, as he was a friend of Sir Francis Fane*, who had headed the 1604 sewer commission, and a former business associate of the privy councillor Sir Thomas Lake I*. Henden was clearly a stranger to Rye before he was elected, as his first name was initially recorded in the corporation minutes as 'Edmund'. Following the election, Watson and Henden were ordered to visit Rye before Parliament commenced to be sworn as freemen, but it seems that only Henden actually did so.[28] Both men were subsequently named to the committee for the cancellation of the fish-packing monopoly, but neither is known to have performed any direct service for their constituents.

By the time of the next general election neither Watson nor Henden seem to have been interested in serving again. Shortly after writs were dispatched the borough was contacted by the yeoman purveyor of fish for the royal Household, William Angell, who had been trading with the town in an official capacity since at least 1594.[29] Moreover, in 1606-7 he had paid part of Thomas Hamon's parliamentary wages out of his own pocket, for which he had been subsequently reimbursed.[30] On 22 Nov. 1620 he asked the borough to bestow one of its seats on his 30-year old son John, a gentleman pensioner who had 'spent his time to good purpose both in the university and inns of court, as he will be ready to give demonstration thereof'. In order to improve John's chances, Angell went to see the lord warden, Lord Zouche, whom he asked for a letter of nomination. He also remonstrated with Zouche on behalf of the borough about various French fishermen whose use of the trawl net was ruining the fishing grounds off Rye. Zouche, however, had already promised his support to 'his ancient acquaintance', Emanuel Gifford, a crypto-Catholic courtier, and was initially reluctant to yield to Angell's request. Nevertheless, 'considering how worthy the son is and how well his father has deserved of you', he asked the borough to elect John Angell, promising that this request for the second seat would not become a precedent.[31] William Angell, however, was clearly dissatisfied with this arrangement, for if Rye refused to allow Zouche the right to nominate two candidates his son might be left empty-handed. Consequently he also obtained letters of nomination from his departmental superiors, the treasurer of the Household, Sir Thomas Edmondes*

and the lord steward, the duke of Lennox.[32] Angell may have had good grounds for concern, for on 4 Dec. Samuel Short, a local lawyer from Tenterden, offered 'to do your town and the rest of the Ports some service for the maintenance of your liberties, which are daily attempted to be infringed'.[33] Short's interest in standing may have stemmed from the insistence of the Privy Council that the Cinque Ports should contribute to the cost of the attack on the Algerian corsairs, a levy that would include Tenterden, which, through its links with Rye, was considered a member of the Cinque Ports. However, his candidature was unsuccessful, as Gifford and John Angell were elected in their absence.

By the time the 1621 Parliament met, Rye was once again desperately concerned at the state of its harbour. The earlier improvement in relations with the local marsh drainers had not halted the decline, and consequently, as Parliament was assembling, the mayor and jurats sent letters to the lord warden, to its newly elected Members and to William Angell asking them 'to move for us the tonnage which was formerly granted unto Dover'.[34] They also instructed their parliamentary representatives to seek some remedy for 'the injurious and disorderly fishing of the French trawlers'.[35] In response John Angell declared his willingness to cooperate, but on 9 Feb. suggested that the town 'send someone up to London ... that Mr. Giffard and myself may be strengthened with some good reasons in behalf of that cause'.[36] Neither Member was well acquainted with the borough, and in 1610, when the town had last sought legislation, it had sent up several 'solicitors' to assist its parliamentary representatives. However, this sensible request caused unexpected difficulties. On 26 Feb. the Rye assembly chose Richard Gilberidge to travel to London with instructions for Giffard and John Angell.[37] The mayor and jurats were appalled, as a few days earlier they had learned that Gilberidge had been selling licences to French fishermen giving them permission to fish with whatever nets they chose.[38] Declaring that they had little confidence in Gilberidge's willingness to help the town seek parliamentary redress against the trawl fishermen, they appealed to Lord Zouche.[39] However, it was not until mid-April that the lord warden intervened to bring about the replacement of Gilberidge by the town's mayor, John Palmer, by which time the Parliament was well advanced. Although Palmer was subsequently paid expenses by the borough, he soon found that he needed more help, and at the end of April two assistants were dispatched to London to consult with him and the town's Members.[40] By the time that Parliament rose for the summer, neither Palmer nor Rye's Members had succeeded in laying a bill to preserve its haven before the Commons, though other towns, such as Colchester, had managed to do so. A bill to preserve sea fry by restraining unlawful fishing with trawls was certainly read on 19 Mar., but it was the work of a group of London Fishmongers rather than Rye's Members, neither of whom spoke in the ensuing debates. Committed some five weeks later, it was never reported, possibly because it smacked too much of the restrictions on trade that were so unpopular in this Parliament.[41]

By the time that a new Parliament met, in 1624, Rye's authorities had evidently decided to leave the parliamentary campaign against trawl fishing to others and to concentrate instead on a bill to pay for the repair of the harbour. Rather than seek the right to lay a charge on shipping, as it had done in the past, however, Rye now sought to gain control of the duties paid by shipowners to Dungeness lighthouse, which was situated at the mouth of the harbour. This lighthouse had allegedly been the brainchild of one of Rye's own freemen, but the right to erect it had been granted to the courtier Sir Edward Howard I*, who had subsequently sold his interest to another. A bill to transfer ownership of the lighthouse to the town would enable its authorities to pay for the repair of the harbour and restore the borough to its former prosperity.[42] This idea was by no means far-fetched, as in 1621 there had been many in the Commons who had regarded private owners of lighthouses as greedy monopolists, and who might be willing to look with approval on a scheme to convert the revenues of Dungeness lighthouse to the public good.

Rye's sudden interest in Dungeness lighthouse probably explains why Richard Tufton, the younger brother of Sir Nicholas Tufton*, owner of the land on which the lighthouse stood, applied to the borough for one of its parliamentary seats. Tufton urged the mayor 'to signify unto the jurats of Rye how much I desire to do them service, and to give them assurance that I shall do my best endeavour to advance the good of the town',[43] but his protestations of goodwill are unlikely to have been believed, as it must have been obvious that Tufton's main concern was to protect the rents paid by the lighthouse patentees to his brother. Another local applicant for a seat was Sir William Twysden, who had not sat in Parliament since 1614 and who reminded the borough that it was he who had recommended that his brother-in-law Heneage Finch, serve as their MP in 1607.[44] The lawyer Samuel Short of Tenterden also cast his hat into the ring, this time with the support of the Tenterden corporation, which commended him 'both for the care he hath to religion and his love to the commonwealth'.[45] However, both Twysden and Short lacked the sort of poweful connections that would help the borough gain control of the revenues paid to Dungeness lighthouse. The same was not true of John Angell, though, whose father William, now serjeant of the acatry, renewed his former approach for his son. William was at first anxious that the borough would not consider his request as John had failed to obtain legislation in 1621, and consequently pointed out that the 1621 Parliament had failed to pass any bills apart from the Subsidy Act, 'so as no man's service appeared what it was or would have been unto the place he were burgess of'. He promised that if Rye re-elected his son, he and his friends would rally to the borough's assistance, 'because your town hath of all others most need of help'. He further pledged that if Rye sent up a solicitor to assist its Members, as it had done in the past, he would 'entertain him in my own house at bed and board' and that every evening, when they were altogether, they would 'confer and consider the best way to do you service'.[46] This was clearly music to the ears of Rye's voters, and not surprisingly the borough once again bestowed its second seat upon John Angell. The senior place was, as always, conferred upon the lord warden's nominee. This time the Zouche's favour was bestowed not on Emmanuel Giffard, who asked William Angell to intervene with Zouche on his behalf, but on Sir Edward Conway II, the eldest son of Secretary Conway, whose patron was the royal favourite, the duke of Buckingham. If anything, Conway's connections must have made him seem even more useful to Rye than John Angell. The day after the election the Rye corporation wrote to the successful candidates, neither of whom had been present on the hustings, to ask them to come down to take the oath of a freeman and to 'receive such information from us as [to] what is to be moved in Parliament for the good and benefit of our town'.[47]

Following the opening of the Parliament, however, Conway elected to serve for Warwick, for which borough he had also been returned. On 24 Feb. Conway's father sent an apology to Rye's corporation, and explained that he had not intended that they should return his eldest son at all, but his youngest son Thomas. As a fresh election would now be held, he asked the town to elect Thomas instead. As an incentive for it to do so, he added that he had persuaded Buckingham to join him in speaking with the king on their behalf, 'so that I doubt not but that you will have a good end of it to your liking'.[48] This was exactly what the corporation must have wanted to hear, and four days later, after receiving confirmation from Lord Zouche that he was happy with the new arrangement,

Thomas Conway was elected and sworn as a freeman.[49] Shortly thereafter the mayor, Mark Thomas, who had served as one of the town's 'solicitors' in Parliament in 1610, instructed a local lawyer named Robert Foster to prepare a bill concerning Dungeness lighthouse.[50] Foster, who had evidently drafted legislation before, provided two copies and advised the mayor to 'make the Speaker as much yours as you can'.[51]

On 8 Mar. 1624 the town assembly resolved to send the bill to its Members for 'the advice of their expert and skilful friends, who are well acquainted with the former method of bills of this nature'.[52] Two days later the assembly also wrote to Lord Zouche requesting his support for the bill, which was carried up to London by the mayor, at a cost of 4s. 3d.[53] The timing of the submission of the bill was left to the discretion of the borough's parliamentary representatives, but by 20 May, following a reminder sent to him two weeks earlier, John Angell confessed that nothing had been done. He apologized for the sickness that had lately made him 'an ill Member of the House, and a bad servant to you', but added that as Parliament was engrossed with 'matters of so great importance and high a nature ... these ordinary businesses are put off from time to time and infinitely delayed'. There was no need to worry, however, as the Dungeness patent was still before the committee and, until the House had resolved either to condemn or modify it, a bill would be premature. Besides, he observed, 'I make no question that this Parliament will be of so long continuance that we shall find leisureable time to effect our desires for you'. This was a disastrous miscalculation, however, for not merely had the Commons already announced that it would not receive any more bills that session 'without order of the House', but just nine days after this letter was written the Parliament was prorogued, never to meet again.[54]

The failure to secure a hearing for the lighthouse bill in 1624 marked not only the end of Rye's legislative ambitions during this period, but also of John Angell's parliamentary career. Following the summons of a fresh Parliament in 1625, Angell was deserted by his father, who was clearly bitterly disappointed with his son. Angell himself admitted that his earlier performance had proved disappointing, but in a letter to the corporation applying for re-election he protested that 'I did you as faithful and effectual a service as those times would give me leave'. His request was supported by his cousin and neighbour, John Halsey, who had recently donated premises to Rye for use as a house of correction and who claimed that Angell would prove to be much more useful in Parliament 'than any man that

has had no experience in that high court'.[55] However, the failure to promote the Dungeness lighthouse bill had severely tarnished the reputation of both Angell and Thomas Conway, who did not seek re-election, having resumed his military career abroad.

The field was now wide open for other candidates, among them Emanuel Gifford, who now obtained a letter of recommendation from the lord treasurer, Sir James Ley*. In his letter to the corporation, Ley stated that Gifford should only be provided for after the new lord warden, the duke of Buckingham, had been satisfied. Buckingham characteristically sought to expand the lord warden's interest by nominating two candidates, his steward Thomas Fotherley and Sir John Franklin*, 'a deserving friend' from Willesden, Middlesex. However, the duke's admiralty secretary Edward Nicholas* made it clear that Fotherley, who was also brother-in-law of the lieutenant of Dover Castle, Sir John Hippisley*, was to be preferred, as 'in very great esteem with his grace, beyond most of his grace's servants'. Rye's assembly, which had only granted Buckingham's predecessor the privilege of naming the candidates to both seats in 1620 as a favour, was naturally reluctant to surrender its rights over the junior seat. Besides, the 4th earl of Dorset (Sir Edward Sackville*), the patron of Rye's church, had also applied for a seat on behalf of his cousin, John Sackville, an officer in the Dutch army like Thomas Conway. Some of the townsmen were evidently sceptical that Sackville would prove any more active on their behalf than Conway had been, for it was the middle of the campaigning season and there was every likelihood that he would soon rejoin his unit in the Low Countries.[56] However, Rye urgently needed Dorset's co-operation as their vicar, Bryan Twyne, a non-resident, was seeking a new curate.[57] Consequently, at the election, which was held on 21 Apr., the borough returned not only Fotherley but also Sackville, who attended the proceedings and was sworn in as a freeman.[58] Shortly after the Parliament began, on 22 June, Sackville wrote to the mayor and jurats from Dorset House to let them know that he had been in touch with Twyne, and to assure them that no clergyman contrary to their good liking would be sent to serve the cure. He also stated that, 'according to your order', he had sworn in Fotherley as a freeman. Patience was needed in respect of a curate, however, as the town was still unfitted of an able and sufficient minister to conduct the national day of fasting and prayer ordered on the Dutch model for 20 July.[59] Nevertheless Sackville was re-elected in 1626, when Buckingham again sent in two nominations. The assembly naturally preferred Fotherley who, through Hippisley, had great influence in the local Cinque Ports' administration, to the lord keeper's secretary Thomas Alured*, who was put forward merely in fulfilment of a promise by Buckingham's client, (Sir) John Coke*.[60]

The outbreak of war with France found Rye virtually defenceless against the old enemy. Consequently, in March 1627 the corporation applied to Buckingham through Sackville for ordnance and (less successfully) for the return of the town gunner from London.[61] Sackville continued to remain eager to demonstrate his willingness to serve the town, for in January 1628, 'by his pains and importuning his noble friends', he evidently obtained for the corporation a royal licence to collect money in southern England for the repair of their harbour, a courtesy which the earl of Dorset described as being 'not ordinary in these times'. However Dorset's account of his cousin's services proved of no avail at the election of 1628.[62] The freemen, it seems, were more concerned to conciliate Sir Nicholas Tufton as ground landlord of the Dungeness lighthouse. He reminded them that he had a claim for damages caused by their harbour works, and that he and his ancestors had spent money on the maintenance of the London road through his property, on which their sole remaining economic activity depended. He also sent the borough £30 to spend on further improvements and instructed his clerk of the ironworks to deliver as much cinder as he could spare.[63] Consequently, when Tufton's brother Richard again offered himself for election, he pushed Fotherley, still the lord warden's nominee, into second place, and Sackville was left out in the cold. Following the election, the mayor and the land chamberlain journeyed to London to administer the freeman's oath to both burgesses, although Fotherley had been sworn in three years earlier.[64]

[1] Dates of elections from E. Suss. RO, RYE 1/7, f. 507v; 1/8, f. 68; 1/9, f. 423v; 1/10, f. 209; 1/11, ff. 15, 22, 67, 100v, 196v. [2] L.A. Vidler, *New Hist. of Rye*, 4, 6; *VCH Suss*. ix. 50. [3] S. Hipkin, 'Closing Ranks', *Urban Hist*. xxii. 321; S. Hipkin, 'The Impact of Marshland Drainage on Rye Harbour, 1550-1650', *Romney Marsh: the Debatable Ground* ed. J. Eddison, 138. [4] S. Hipkin, 'Buying Time: Fiscal Policy at Rye, 1600-40', *Suss. Arch. Colls*. cxxxiii. 242-3. [5] *HMC 13th Rep. IV*, 192. [6] Ibid. 137, 139, 143; *CSP Dom*. 1611-18, p. 354; 1623-5, p. 228; SP14/127/45; *APC*, 1627-8, p. 341. [7] Hipkin, 'Buying Time', 246; G. Mayhew, *Tudor Rye*, 268. [8] Mayhew, 81, 83, 89. [9] *HMC 13th Rep. IV*, 167. [10] Hipkin, 'Closing Ranks', 321; Hipkin, 'Buying Time', 421. [11] Mayhew, 61, 79, 134. [12] Hipkin, 'Closing Ranks', 325-6. [13] For the 1604 figure, see Hipkin, 'Closing Ranks', 334; for the others, see endnote 1. [14] Mayhew, 103. [15] E. Suss. RO, RYE 61/12, f. 19v; RYE 1/7, f. 506v. [16] E. Suss. RO, RYE 1/7, ff. 507v-8. [17] Ibid. ff. 506v, 508v, 509v; RYE 61/12, f. 21. [18] *Recs. Rye Corporation* ed. R.F. Dell, 89-90; *HMC 13th Rep. IV*, 131. [19] E. Suss. RO, RYE 1/7, f. 535. [20] E. Suss. RO, RYE 47/71/2; *HMC 13th Rep. IV*, 134-5. [21] Hipkin, 'Marshland Drainage', 139-40. [22] *HMC 13th Rep. IV*, 144; *Recs. Rye Corporation*, 95. [23] Hipkin, 'Closing Ranks', 332.

[24] *HMC 13th Rep. IV*, 144, 146; E. Suss. RO, RYE 1/8, ff. 250, 264v; RYE 61/16, f. 8. [25] *CSP Dom*. 1611-18, p.201; *Recs. Rye Corporation*, 134. [26] E. Suss. RO, RYE 1/9, ff. 423v-4. [27] Hipkin, 'Closing Ranks', 333. [28] E. Suss. RO, RYE 1/9, ff. 431-2. [29] E. Suss. RO, RYE 47/59/10. [30] E. Suss. RO, RYE 61/13, ff. 73, 76v. [31] E. Suss. RO, RYE 47/96/1-3. [32] E. Suss. RO, RYE 47/96/4, 5. [33] E. Suss. RO, RYE 47/96/6. [34] E. Suss. RO, RYE 1/10, f. 211. [35] SP14/119/85. [36] E. Suss. RO, RYE 47/96/10. [37] E. Suss. RO, RYE 1/10, f. 217v. [38] *CSP Dom*. 1619-23, p. 228. [39] SP14/119/110. [40] E. Suss. RO, RYE 47/98/11; 1/11, f. 22. [41] *CJ*, i. 562a, 588b; GL, ms 5570/2, pp. 405, 408; *CD 1621*, iii. 64, n. 2). It has been suggested that Rye was probably behind bills to prevent unlawful fishing in 1606 or 1610, but there is no evidence for this: J.K. Gruenfelder, 'Rye and the Parl. of 1621', *Suss. Arch. Soc*. cvii. 27-8. [42] SP14/160/60; SP16/89/26 (the latter is a set of miscalendared notes on this matter). [43] E. Suss. RO, RYE 47/99. Tufton's letter is undated, but it describes Mark Thomas as mayor and states that the writs had only just been issued, indicating that it was written in late Dec. 1623 or early January 1624. We are grateful to Christopher Whittick for drawing this dating evidence to our attention. [44] *HMC 13th Rep. IV*, 162. [45] E. Suss. RO, RYE 47/98/6. [46] E. Suss. RO, RYE 47/98/7. [47] SP14/158/50. [48] E. Suss. RO, RYE 47/98/16. [49] E. Suss. RO, RYE 47/98/11; 1/11, f. 22. [50] E. Suff. RO, RYE 61/30, f. 13. [51] *HMC 13th Rep. IV*, 166. [52] E. Suss. RO, RYE 1/11, f. 22v. [53] SP14/160/60; E. Suss. RO, RYE 61/30, f. 13v. [54] *HMC 13th Rep. IV*, 171; *CJ*, i. 702b. [55] *Procs. 1625*, pp. 697-9; *HMC 13th Rep. IV*, 172. [56] *Procs. 1628*, vi. 161. [57] *Procs. 1625*, pp. 696-8; *Suss. Arch. Colls*. xiii. 274. [58] E. Suss. RO, RYE 1/11, f. 67. [59] *HMC 13th Rep. IV*, 174. [60] *Procs. 1626*, iv. 249; *HMC Cowper*, i. 240; E. Suss. RO, RYE 1/11, f. 100v. [61] *HMC 13th Rep. IV*, 181; *CSP Dom*. 1627-8, pp. 112, 220. [62] *Procs. 1628*, vi. 160-1; *Recs. Rye Corporation*, 95. [63] E. Suss. RO, RYE 47/109/31. [64] E. Suss. RO, RYE 1/11, f. 197v; RYE 61/34, f. 13.

P.J.L./A.D.T.

SANDWICH

Right of election: in the common council 1603-20; in the freemen from 1621

Number of voters: 37 in 1620; c.250 in 1640[1]

2 Mar. 1604[2]	SIR GEORGE FANE
	EDWARD PEAKE
11 Jan. 1608	JOHN GRIFFITH II *vice*
	Peake, deceased
	William Wood
18 Mar. 1614	SIR THOMAS SMYTHE
	SIR SAMUEL PEYTON, bt.
29 Dec. 1620	SIR EDWIN SANDYS
	(SIR) ROBERT HATTON 18
	John Jacob
	John Borough
	Francis Drake
	Sir Peter Manwood*
	Sir Samuel Peyton, bt.
	Sir Thomas Smythe
12 Apr. 1621	JOHN BOROUGH *vice*
	Hatton, election declared void
27 Jan. 1624	(SIR) ROBERT HATTON
	FRANCIS DRAKE
5 May 1625	SIR HENRY WOTTON
	(SIR) ROBERT HATTON
	Henry Sandys*
27 Jan. 1626	(SIR) JOHN SUCKLING
	PETER PEAKE
21 Feb. 1626	SIR EDWARD BOYS *vice*
	Suckling, chose to sit for Norwich
	Sir Henry Mildmay*
29 Feb. 1628	JOHN PHILIPOT
	PETER PEAKE
	Sir Edwin Sandys

Sandwich was a chartered borough before Domesday. The easternmost of the Cinque Ports, its limbs included Deal, Fordwich, Ramsgate and even Brightlingsea in Essex. Its harbour decayed in Tudor times because of the growth of a sandbank across the entrance, preventing the entry of all but the smallest ships.[3] During the early seventeenth century the borough frequently lobbied for a new haven to be built, but the estimated cost – more than £50,000 – was prohibitive.[4] Despite its decline, Sandwich remained, with Dover and Rye, Sussex, one of the three authorized passenger ports for the short sea crossing to

the Continent.[5] From 1561 religious refugees from the Continent began to arrive in large numbers. Welcomed by the government as 'men of knowledge in sundry handicrafts', they were allowed their own church, which attracted Englishmen who found the Elizabethan settlement insufficiently radical, including separatists living in the United Provinces.[6] The Hispanophile Sir William Monson† declared 'their religion truly Hollandish' and complained that 'the country thereabouts swarms as much with sects as Amsterdam'. In May 1605 the people of Sandwich allegedly cursed Monson for intervening with his naval warship to prevent a Dutch squadron from seizing the departing Spanish ambassador.[7] Crown dues were collected by a bailiff, whose office was sufficiently profitable to generate considerable competition. Owing to the disorder of the commonalty at municipal elections, the lord warden and Privy Council ordered in 1603 that the franchise be confined to the governing body, which was reduced to a mayor, 12 jurats and a self-renewing common council of 24 rather than the 48 which had been established in the mid-1590s.[8] These changes had a marked effect on the parliamentary representation of the port, which throughout the Elizabethan period had never accepted a stranger. Between 1604 and 1629 only Edward Peake and his son Peter could be classed as residents; the lord warden (who began to demand the right at the end of the Elizabethan period) was usually able to nominate to the senior seat, while the other fell into the hands of the East Kent magnates (including the archbishop of Canterbury).

Elections were held at the 'Court Hall', to which voters were summoned by 'the sound of the Common Horn'.[9] Although the borough's limbs were excluded from the franchise, they were evidently expected to contribute financially, for in 1622 Brightlingsea paid £3 'for charge of Parliament wages for the last session of Parliament'.[10] Often the borough swore in their parliamentary representatives as freemen on the hustings, but in 1626 the absentee Sir John Suckling's oath 'was respited until another time'. Those elected seem also to have been required to swear an additional oath, whether or not they were freemen. In February 1626, for instance, Sir Edward Boys took 'the oath of an advocate of this town', and 'also the oath of a baron to the Parliament'.[11]

At the 1604 general election the earl of Northampton was still new to his office as lord warden, and so it was left to his lieutenant, Thomas Fane†, to nominate his own nephew and heir Sir George for the senior seat. The remaining place was bestowed upon the jurat Edward Peake, who was returned 'according to the ancient custom of pricking' to his eighth successive parliament and granted wages of 4*s.* a day.[12] On Peake's death in 1607 one of his colleagues on the town council, William Wood, aspired to succeed him, but at the by-election in January 1608 he was rejected in favour of Northampton's secretary, John Griffith II. Northampton thanked the electorate for choosing his dependant 'before one of your own', as he was not entitled to fill the second seat, and promised that it should not constitute a precedent.[13] Such harmonious relations could scarcely endure, and by 1609 Northampton's staff were complaining of lack of co-operation from the municipal authorities.[14] When Fane was nominated by the lord warden for re-election in 1614, Northampton was told that 'we know he is so disliked of the most part of our assembly as that upon nomination he was no way pleasing to them', and was asked to substitute Griffith, 'who is well-affected and beloved among us'. Perhaps the councillors were unaware that Griffth had already been returned for Portsmouth, but Northampton was visibly annoyed. He nominated instead his 'dear friend' Sir Thomas Smythe, a leading figure in most of the great London trading companies and a younger brother of the Westenhanger family, who owned property in the town but lived on the other side of the county, at Sutton-at-Hone, near Gravesend. The second seat was conferred on Sir Samuel Peyton, bt., of Knowlton, a much closer neighbour, who also seems to have owned property in Sandwich.[15]

By the 1620 general election Northampton was dead and Smythe's brother, Sir Richard*, was engaged in a boundary dispute with the corporation. This quarrel may have suggested to Smythe's principal business rival, Sir Edwin Sandys, the idea of supplanting Smythe at Sandwich. Sandys had been living at nearby Northbourne since 1602, and in 1608 had offered to cut a new channel for the haven.[16] Well-informed about Sandwich's problems, he seems to have hoped to carry both seats at the next election as his late wife's brother, Sir Roger Nevinson of nearby Eastry, obtained a recommendation for the senior seat from the crypto-Catholic Lord Wotton to Northampton's successor, Lord Zouche. However, Zouche preferred to nominate the archbishop's steward, (Sir) Robert Hatton, and placed Nevinson on his reserve list of candidates for seats in the Cinque Ports, along with the former Sandwich Member, Sir Samuel Peyton.[17] Nothing more was heard of Nevinson. For the remaining seat the first choice of the corporation seems to have fallen on one of their own number, John Jacob, 'a man generally there beloved'.[18]

As the second seat was now apparently unavailable, it became clear that Sandys and Hatton would have

to fight over the senior burgess-ship. In the run-up to the election, however, Sandys was in London, engaged upon Virginia Company business. He did not write to Sandwich for the place, and even affected an air of casual indifference, saying that 'he could have been for a town in Yorkshire'. However, he sent down Thomas Gookyn of Ripple Court, Kent, a man 'very conversant in Sandwich and a great talker' who 'laboured all his acquaintance for Sir Edwin, even jurats as well as others'. Through Gookyn, Sandys resorted to the populist arguments that had enabled him to win control of the Virginia Company from Smythe. He announced that he held Sandwich in great affection, and was saddened that the townsmen had 'lost some of their liberties', which, he assured them, 'would be recovered again'. So far as a new haven was concerned, he said 'there was hope some good might be done for them by their good friends'. He also announced through Gookyn his opposition to the East India Company, which he described as 'a pernicious matter to them and the whole kingdom'.[19] Support for Sandys was also canvassed by Thomas Brewer, a wealthy Kent Brownist, who until recently had lived at Leiden and who was exploring with Sandys the possibility of settling members of the Leiden congregation in Virginia.[20] Without Brewer, Sandys's credentials as a radical Protestant would have been unconvincing. Instead it was reported that Sandys stood 'in the good liking of the rabble ... of schismatical sectaries with whom that town aboundeth'.[21]

Sandys's electioneering greatly alarmed the mayor, who wanted the senior seat to go to the lord warden's candidate as custom required. Consequently, on the day of the election he altered the procedure, directing the voters 'to choose one burgess first and not both together'. In this way he hoped that 'my lord would be respected for Sir Robert to have the first place, or if not, yet that Jacob should have carried the place from Sir Edwin'. His decision was challenged by the previous mayor, Peake's eldest son, who also objected that the word 'commonalty' had been omitted from the writ. These complaints were ignored by the mayor, who nominated Hatton, Sandys and Jacob for the first seat, but his plan backfired, as Sandys triumphed easily.

The mayor then turned his attention to the junior seat and announced that Jacob could not resubmit his name. Jacob himself 'utterly disclaimed to stand again', whereupon 'some of the company would no further proceed'. Hatton, however, was again proposed in his absence, although he too had been defeated for the first seat. Also nominated were Smythe, Peyton (who may by now have been seriously ill),[22] Sir Peter Manwood* (who had represented the borough in the last four

Elizabethan Parliaments), Francis Drake and John Borough. Drake had no known local connection, but may have been backed by the town lecturer, Thomas Marston, 'a precise preacher' who 'gaddeth up and down' and 'cannot abide a bishop'. Marston's influence probably weakened support for Hatton, the archbishop of Canterbury's household steward, but perhaps his most serious challenger was John Borough, secretary to the lord chancellor (Francis Bacon*), as he had been born in the town, the son of a Dutch immigrant. The mayor, unable to prevent the commonalty from participating in the election for the senior seat, now made one last effort on behalf of the lord warden's candidate by insisting, in accordance with the Privy Council's ruling of 1603, that only corporation members could vote. In the ensuing tumult 18 electors gave their votes for Hatton, six chose other candidates and seven abstained. Those excluded from voting were furious: 'Some raved of breach of liberties, others plainly told the mayor they would make a certificate to the Parliament against him, and that he should, or deserved to be, fined at £100'.[23]

These were not idle threats. On 3 Feb. 1621 the town clerk, Edward Kelk, wrote to Lord Zouche that a petition to the Commons (which he incorrectly described as a bill) had been set on foot by Borough's supporters 'to disannul our late choice of burgesses, which was done (as they say) both against our charters and the law, because they were not admitted to have any voice in the election'. Kelk had assisted the mayor at the election, and had been abused after the election for the second seat, being told by one member of the commonalty that 'he deserved to have his ears nailed' for 'breaking their liberties'. Kelk was unrepentant, and sent Zouche a copy of the 1603 Council order, along with a judicial decision reported by Sir Edward Coke* approving the restriction of the franchise in corporations 'for avoiding of popular disorder and confusion'.[24] However, the petitioners were not alone in wanting to quash the return. Sir Edwin Sandys, having belatedly concluded that his Virginia Company business precluded him from serving in the Commons, disingenuously announced on 7 Feb. that he had been chosen without his knowledge or consent, and claimed that his election was invalid as he had refused to be sworn a freeman.[25] However, the House was unwilling to lose one of its most important Members. On 22 Mar. Sir George More, reporting from the committee for privileges and returns, upheld the petitioners' claim to a wider franchise but dismissed Sandys's objections. The freemen had assented to Sandys's election, he stated, and would have chosen Borough had they not been denied further participation, but he recommended that the second election should be declared void rather than reversed. The

House accepted these findings, and thereby widened the franchise, although Sir Dudley Digges argued that no new writ should be issued until Borough had been cleared of the charge of corruption brought against him as one of Bacon's secretaries.[26] It is not known whether Hatton, Peyton or Drake stood in the ensuing election, when Borough was returned 'by most voices by the pricking of the mayor, jurats, and commonalty'.[27]

Shortly after this election Sandwich joined the parliamentary clamour for free trade. On 23 Apr. the corporation ordered that a petition concerning restrictions on buying and selling cloth in Blackwell Hall and the prisage of wine should be followed in Parliament by its author, Arthur Rucke, a former mayor of the borough, assisted by Mr. Raworth of Dover. One week later Sandwich proposed that the Cinque Ports should apply to Parliament for statutory confirmation of their privileges, and use the services of Rucke and Raworth, 'who are already both there employed about some affairs'. Most of the Ports agreed to help, and on 16 May Sir Edwin Sandys preferred one petition from the Cinque Ports in general complaining, *inter alia*, that the Merchant Adventurers excluded them from Blackwell Hall, and another from the mayor and jurats of Sandwich.[28] Sandys also spoke for his constituents during the subsidy debate on 12 Mar., when he argued for the continuation of the Cinque Ports' traditional exemption because of their decayed condition. Sandwich in particular was unable to afford to contribute, he said, as many of the Dutch settler families there, 'such as did set the poor a work', had quit the town because of its unwholesome air.[29]

By the time of the 1624 general election, when Sandwich was in the midst of a smallpox epidemic,[30] the number of candidates requiring seats in the borough had lessened. Peyton was now dead and Smythe was living in retirement, while Sandys moved up to represent the county, and Borough transferred to Horsham, Sussex, having found a new patron, the earl of Arundel. Relations between Sandwich and the lord warden were now strained, as they had quarrelled over the choice of a town clerk on Kelk's death. In June 1623 Zouche's recommendation of one of the turbulent Verrall family was rejected by 19 votes to eight in favour of Peake's youngest son, Peter, although the corporation subsequently tried to heal the breach by sending Zouche a present.[31] On 23 Jan. 1624 the corporation noted that they had received a letter from Zouche 'touching the choosing of a burgess'. Its members seem to have been dissatisfied with its contents, however, as Peter Peake was chosen, rather tactlessly, to 'confer with him about the matter'. Four days later the borough chose 'by the major part of the voices' Robert Hatton (presumably Zouche's nominee) for the senior seat and Drake as his colleague 'by pricking'. So transient was the effect of the earlier Commons resolution that they were returned in the name of the mayor, jurats, and common council only.[32]

At the first general election held after Buckingham became lord warden, the duke sought to capture both seats at Sandwich through the interest of his hench-man Sandys, who stood for the county. On 8 Apr. 1625 he wrote to the corporation that he had been

> entreated by Sir Edwin Sandys to desire you to elect his son a burgess to this Parliament to serve in the second place for the town (reserving still to me, as you have done to my predecessors, the nomination of the first). I have not been forward to yield to his request in regard you might [fear] that I purpose by this to gain too much ground on your liberty and freedom. ... But being credibly informed how hopeful and likely his son is to merit your respect, and considering how well his father hath deserved of you, and his good neighbourhood and readiness at all times to further the good of your town, I thought I could do no less than desire you to add to the consideration of these reasons ... the esteem I hold of them both.

His esteem was now shared by very few in Kent; Sandys was defeated in the county election, and the candidature of his son, who was still under age, so cautiously propounded, was hardly likely to be taken seriously in Sandwich, even though the way had been partially cleared by Drake's decision to trans-fer to the newly enfranchised borough of Amersham, Buckinghamshire. Buckingham's motive was to exclude Hatton, as servant of his enemy Archbishop Abbot, and consequently he nominated Lord Wotton's Protestant half-brother, Sir Henry, for the senior seat. However, with the franchise reverting to the commonalty he could not prevent them from electing Hatton for the other.[33]

By the next election Wotton had determined to take orders and it was rumoured, probably falsely, that Hatton would stand for the county. Buckingham nominated (Sir) John Suckling, the comptroller of the Household, who was elected 'with great applause', and Peter Peake, who had resigned the town clerkship, was chosen for the second place. When Suckling opted for Norwich, Norfolk, the duke complimented Sand-wich for 'the better measure of respect' shown to him 'than from most of the Cinque Ports', and nominated Sir Henry Mildmay*, master of the Jewel House, instead. However, Mildmay was rejected in favour of Sir Edward Boys the younger, who lived nearby and owned property in the borough.[34] Consequently, in the second Caroline Parliament Sandwich was for the only time in this period represented by two local men.

The 1628 election occurred against a backdrop of renewed tension between the corporation and commo-nalty. Although the commonalty had by now been restored to the franchise in both municipal and parlia-mentary elections, the corporation refused to allow them a say when the living of St. Peter's, which was in their gift, fell vacant in November 1627. Secretary Conway and the dean of Rochester pressed them to appoint the former chaplain of Sir Henry Mervyn*, who was acceptable to the commonalty, but the corpo-ration installed Thomas Warren, 'a most seditious man' who had given much trouble as town preacher at Rye.[35] At the general election in February 1628, the commonalty, which may also have been incensed at the billeting of Irish troops in the town,[36] exacted its revenge. Buckingham, who was closely associated with the billeting of troops, nominated for the senior seat Sir Edwin Sandys, no longer widely popular, who wrote from London on his own behalf. 'We spared no pains', the mayor and jurats replied, 'to incite so many as we could to join with us therein; but the generality of voices amongst the commons bred such a distraction that we could have no power over them'.[37] Instead, Peake was re-elected, with a new colleague, John Philipot, the Herald, whose father had been mayor of Folkestone. His 'particular interest' in the borough, however, arose from his place as bailiff for the Crown, which he had held since 1623, and he promised to serve 'at my own charge, and so save the town's exhibition'.[38]

[1] W. Boys, *Sandwich*, 702; *CD 1621*, vii. 568; M.F. Keeler, *Long Parl.* 77. [2] Dates of elections from Boys, 410-11. [3] Boys, 684. [4] E. Kent Archives Cent. Sa/AC7, f. 49v; SP16/154/31. [5] *CSP Dom.* 1603-10, p. 473. [6] Boys, 740; D. Gardiner, *Historic Haven*, 174, 183; *APC*, 1613-14, pp. 304, 614; Add. 33512, ff. 18-19. [7] *Naval Tracts of Sir William Monson III* ed. M. Oppenheim (Navy Recs. Soc. xliii), 29-31. [8] *CJ*, i. 568b; Boys, 702. [9] E. Kent Archives Cent. Sa/AC6, f. 329; Sa/AC7, f. 85v. [10] E. Kent Archives Cent. Sa/AC7, f. 96. [11] Ibid. ff. 127v, 132A. [12] E. Kent Archives Cent. Sa/AC6, f. 329. [13] Ibid. ff. 370, 373. [14] SP14/57/31. [15] E. Kent Archives Cent. Sa/AC7, ff. 31v-2. [16] Boys, 703. [17] SP14/117/72; 14/118/26. [18] *CD 1621*, vii. 568. [19] Ibid. 567, 569. On Gookyn's identity, see *Vis. Kent* (Harl. Soc. xlii), 48. [20] P. Clark, *Eng. Prov. Soc.* 327, 332; Nicholas, *Procs. 1621*, ii. app. [21] *CD 1621*, vii. 567. [22] WARD 7/68/8. [23] *CD 1621*, vii. 568-9. For Marston's appointment as town lecturer, see E. Kent Archives Cent. Sa/AC7, f. 66r-v. [24] *CD 1621*, vii. 568, 571-2. [25] *CJ*, i. 513a; *CD 1621*, iv. 26. [26] *CD 1621*, iv. 181; *CJ*, i. 568b. [27] E. Kent Archives Cent. Sa/AC7, f. 87. [28] Ibid. f. 88r-v; *CJ*, i. 620a-b; *CD 1621*, iv. 337-8; vii. 593-6, 598-9. [29] *CJ*, i. 550b; *CD 1621*, iv. 146. [30] *CSP Dom.* 1623-5, p. 146. [31] Gardiner, 157-8; E. Kent Archives Cent. Sa/AC7, f. 107; SP14/146/46; 14/153/100. [32] E. Kent Archives Cent. Sa/AC7, f. 115. [33] Add. 37819, f. 11v; E. Kent AO, Sa/AC7, f. 125v. [34] E. Kent Archives Cent. Sa/AC7, ff. 127v, 132A; SP16/19/17; Add. 37819, f. 19v. [35] *CSP Dom.* 1627-8, pp. 433, 436; E. Kent Archives Cent. Sa/AC7, ff. 150, 156v; SP14/91/22, 27. [36] *APC*, 1627-8, p. 384; *Procs. 1628*, vi. 114; *CD 1628*, iv. 164. [37] *Procs. 1628*, vi. 162-3. [38] Ibid. 162; E. Kent Archives Cent. Sa/AC7, f. 154.

P.J.L./A.D.T.

WINCHELSEA

Right of election: in the inhabitant freemen

Number of voters: 19 in 1624[1]

20 Feb. 1604[2]	THOMAS EGLESTON (not returned)	
	ADAM WHITE	
12 Apr. 1604	THOMAS UNTON *vice*	
	Egleston, resigned	
8 Mar. 1614	WILLIAM BYNG	
19 Mar. 1614	THOMAS GODFREY	
5 Jan. 1621	SIR THOMAS FINCH, bt.	
	EDWARD NICHOLAS	
	?John Berry	
23 Jan. 1624	EDWARD NICHOLAS	
	JOHN FINCH I	8
	Sir Alexander Temple*	8
	Election of Finch declared void, 18 Mar. 1624	
25 Mar. 1624	JOHN FINCH I	11
	Sir Alexander Temple	7
26 Apr. 1625	SIR RALPH FREEMAN	
	SIR ROGER TWYSDEN	
16 Jan. 1626	SIR NICHOLAS SAUNDERS	
	SIR ROGER TWYSDEN	
25 Feb. 1628	SIR WILLIAM TWYSDEN, (bt.)	
	SIR RALPH FREEMAN	
c. *Jan. 1629*	THOMAS HENEAGE *vice*	
	Twysden, deceased	

Old Winchelsea, one of the ancient towns added to the original Cinque Ports, was destroyed by the sea in the thirteenth century and rebuilt on a nearby hill. Although the new town enjoyed a brief period of prosperity based on the wine trade, it fell into decay in the fifteenth century as its haven gradually silted up. By the middle of Elizabeth's reign there were reportedly not 'above sixty households standing, and those, for the most part, poorly peopled'.[3] This sorry state of affairs continued under James: in 1621 Sir Dudley Digges* remarked that Winchelsea presented 'a lamentable spectacle', with 'scarce any sign or memory of its haven'. As there were so few inhabitants the town struggled to find the requisite number of 12 jurats to manage its affairs. By 1621 there were only four, a number so insufficient that, as the 11th Lord Zouche

observed, were the town to send the correct number to the Brotherhood of the Cinque Ports it would be left entirely without magistrates.[4]

The franchise was vested in the freemen, and parliamentary elections were held in the Court Hall.[5] Normally both candidates were chosen on the same day, but in 1614 there was an unexplained interval of 11 days between the election of both candidates. Outsiders chosen to serve in Parliament were expected to swear the oath of a freeman following their election. As such men rarely attended the hustings in person, it sometimes proved necessary to issue a commission under the town's common seal that allowed them to be sworn in as freemen in London. In 1625 and 1628 commissions were granted to townsmen, but in 1621 the task of swearing in Edward Nicholas was entrusted to Nicholas' parliamentary colleague John Finch, and to Sir Henry Mainwaring, the newly elected Member for Dover. Outsiders who were returned more than once were expected to take the oath of a freeman following each election.[6]

By tradition each of the Cinque Ports conferred one seat on the nominee of the lord warden, while the other remained at the disposal of the town. For the first election of the period, in February 1604, the new lord warden, Henry Howard, earl of Northampton, nominated his servant Thomas Unton. However, perhaps as a result of the king's recent Proclamation requiring the return of residents only, Winchelsea's voters decided to choose both Members themselves. Northampton was furious, and when he came to compile his return for all the Cinque Ports on 16 Mar. he entered Unton's name in place of the townsman Thomas Egleston. By the time the borough discovered what had happened, Parliament had already begun. Rather than 'increase his lordship's indignation' by appealing to the committee for privileges and returns, the corporation decided, at a town meeting held on 12 Apr., to accept Egleston's offer to step down in favour of Unton, and to reimburse Egleston the money he had spent in sending his clothes to London by boat. The remaining Member, Adam White, was unaffected by these decisions, and in 1607 was voted wages of 4s. a day. However, in June 1608, White having by then received £30, it was decided to cap the amount payable to White, who was to have only £20 more 'during the whole Parliament unless that this corporation shall voluntarily give him any more, and that without any motion of Mr. White or any other by his procurement'.[7] This order effectively marked the end of parliamentary wages in Winchelsea.

The 1604 election saw the townsmen of Winchelsea act in unison, but by early 1607 they were riven with factional strife. There were complaints that there were not enough freemen and jurats, and that the same three individuals monopolized the mayoralty. In March 1607 the Privy Council ordered the town to appoint eight new freemen in order to increase the pool of men available to serve as jurats and mayor,[8] but despite conciliar intervention the faction-fighting continued. It was soon apparent that the good offices of the lord warden would be needed, and consequently efforts were made by the town to improve its relations with Northampton. In April 1607 the corporation offered the next reversion to the town clerkship to William Byng, one of the earl's servants. When Byng declined the place due to his necessary attendance on his master, the corporation permitted him to nominate another man instead. In September 1607 the corporation also bestowed 'a silver cup of 20 nobles' on Northampton's client Unton, ostensibly in recognition of his service for the town in Parliament.[9] These attempts to mollify Northampton evidently paid dividends, for in May 1609 the earl issued instructions for the election of the mayor on a strict rotational basis. These orders, which were immediately adopted, were reiterated in April 1610, and a few months later the corporation appointed Unton its standing counsel.[10]

Mindful perhaps of the debt it now owed to Northampton, and also of the angry reaction it had provoked in 1604, the corporation made no qualms about electing the earl's nominee, William Byng, at the 1614 general election. For the remaining seat it chose one of the earl's former servants, Thomas Godfrey, a former resident of Winchelsea who had recently served as the town's deputy mayor and had helped liaise with Northampton during the dispute over the election of the town's mayor. Both Members undertook to serve 'gratis and without wages of Parliament'.[11]

In the short term, the settlement reached in 1609 helped to dampen down the internal conflicts in Winchelsea, but by the time of the next general election these quarrels had reignited. In June 1620 Robert Butler, mayor at the time of the dispute over the mayoral elections, complained to Northampton's successor as lord warden, Lord Zouche, that he had been disfranchised because he was non-resident. Butler was now lieutenant of nearby Camber Castle, and by ancient custom any freeman who removed himself from the town or its liberties for more than a year and a day was required to lose his franchise.[12] At around the same time the borough was embroiled in a fresh dispute over the election of jurats. Following mediation by the lieutenant of Dover Castle, Sir Henry Mainwaring, and the Brotherhood of the Cinque Ports, a settlement to these problems was reached in July, but only at the cost of stripping two of the men involved of their position as jurats.[13] By the time that a fresh parliamentary election was ordered in November 1620 it was clear that much ill feeling remained, and that it would no longer be possible to return a townsman.

On 6 Dec. an alarmed mayor, John Collins, informed Lord Zouche that three of the chief townsmen, 'contrary to all due proceedings, have hunted for, wrought and gotten the voices, or the promise of the voices, of most part of the freemen' for 'one Mr. Anscombe, a lawyer ... a man that as I have understood never sought for it, one who is altogether unacquainted with the customs and liberties of the Ports, and one who by reason of a caution in His Majesty's Proclamation your lordship by reason of his profession only may perhaps think not fit to be chosen'.[14] The lawyer referred to by Collins was almost certainly Thomas Aynscombe, who lived either at Buxted, near Uckfield, or Mayfield, both of which lay in Sussex. A bencher of the Inner Temple, Aynscombe, the brother-in-law of Nicholas Eversfield*, was not unknown to Winchelsea, having served as counsel for the borough in 1617.[15] Rather than allow the seat that was traditionally reserved for a townsman to be taken by Aynscombe, Collins preferred that it should be bestowed upon one or other of 'two gentlemen of worth and credit, well-willers unto the said town'. The first of these 'well-willers' was Sir Thomas Finch, bt., whose father had represented the borough in Parliament in 1601. Finch had recently become head of his family, but since his mother continued to live on the family's main property at Eastwell, in Kent, he was obliged to dwell near Winchelsea, on the manor of Icklesham, of which he was the lord. The second man favoured by Collins was John Berry, captain of the foot company in Lydd, Kent, and cousin of the former Winchelsea jurat Thomas Godfrey.[16] Collins appealed to Zouche to decide which of the three candidates the borough should select, as this would 'free the town of a great deal of perplexity'. The following day the field may have unexpectedly narrowed, as Thomas Aynscombe of Mayfield died.[17] Unaware of this development, though, Zouche replied:

I affect Captain Berry well for his own particular and the acquaintance I have with him. I know not Mr. Aynscombe, but have heard him much commended for a discreet gentleman. Though the king admonished that you elect no wrangling lawyer, yet he forbade not such as are modest and discreet. For Sir Thomas Finch he is a gentleman of worth and quality, and one who dwelling near you may do you good hereafter.

If he had been asked for a recommendation before other candidates were in the field, he went on, he would have nominated Finch. As it was, he added diplomatically, he left the town to a free election.[18]

Zouche's support for Finch evidently proved decisive, although as Finch attended the hustings in person on the day of the election it may be that the threat posed by Berry remained right up until the last moment.[19] Finch's colleague was Edward Nicholas, whom the lord warden nominated for the remaining place. Nicholas was secretary to Zouche, and as such was obliged to draft a letter of modest self-commendation for the lord warden's signature himself. In this Zouche declared that 'though perhaps he is not well known to you all', Nicholas was nevertheless 'acquainted with the business and occasions of the Ports' and was both 'honest and trusty'. Like their predecessors, both Members agreed to forego parliamentary wages.[20]

Following the 1621 parliamentary election, the truce brokered by Mainwaring and the Brotherhood in July 1620 quickly broke down. In May 1621 fresh arguments broke out over the suitability to serve as jurats of Robert Butler and Giles Waters, who like Butler formed part of the garrison of Camber Castle.[21] Matters came to a head in April 1623, when John Collins and nine of his fellow townsmen refused to elect Waters as mayor, thereby disregarding the 1609 settlement, which provided for the annual election of the mayor on a strict rotational basis. Collins claimed that such drastic action was justified because Waters had recently been declared bankrupt. While this was certainly true, Lord Zouche was incensed, and in August Collins, who had been re-elected mayor by his supporters, was stripped of office, disfranchised and imprisoned in Dover Castle, along with two of his chief accomplices. Waters, meanwhile, was sequestered as a jurat until such times as he demonstrated that he was fit to hold office. Instead, the lord warden placed the mayoralty in the hands of the former incumbent, Paul Wymond.[22]

It was against the backdrop of these turbulent events that the king summoned a fresh Parliament. Once again, the townsmen of Winchelsea, while happy to accept the lord warden's nominee, Edward Nicholas, for one seat, were divided over which man to choose for the other. One group within the town, led by the mayor, was willing that the Finch family should be allowed to provide the successful candidate, as it had in 1621. Since Sir Thomas Finch was no longer willing to stand, his younger brother John, deputy recorder of London, put his hat into the ring. Another group

of townsmen, however, wished to elect Sir Alexander Temple, who had acquired an east Sussex estate by marriage and whose younger brother, Peter, had served as captain of Camber Castle between 1610 and 1618.[23] It seems likely that at least some of Temple's supporters may have been drawn from among those townsmen who were closely connected with Camber Castle.

From evidence later submitted to the committee for privileges, it seems clear that both before and during the election held on 23 Jan. 1624 the mayor, Paul Wymond, employed underhand means to thwart Temple. First, he delayed calling a town meeting until seven o'clock the previous evening. Then he announced, disingenuously, that the purpose of the forthcoming meeting was to consider the business of the town in general rather than to hold a parliamentary election. When these tactics failed to prevent Temple's supporters from turning out, Wymond refused to read out the election writ until two of the jurats present, the brothers Jonathan and Daniel Tilden, withdrew, as they had not been summoned to the meeting. Wymond claimed that, by virtue of a town edict issued in November 1609, the Tildens were not entitled to participate in the election, having been non-resident for the past three months, and declared that they had only come to the meeting to raise a tumult. However, the Tildens were reluctant to depart, and spent the next hour remonstrating with the mayor, supported by another of the jurats, an innkeeper named Richard Martin. After denouncing Temple as a man 'of suspected religion, and allied to an arch-papist, the earl of Clanricarde', Wymond threatened Martin, telling him that he should 'look better to his small pots, which had loose bottoms'. Unable to make any headway, the Tildens were eventually forced to leave, but not before they had publicly declared their support for Temple. Their departure left the two sides evenly matched: the mayor and seven of the freemen supported Finch, while four jurats and four freemen gave their voices for Temple. However, rather than announce that a stalemate had been reached, Wymond declared Finch elected, on the grounds that, being mayor, he was entitled to a casting vote.[24] Wymond's fellow jurats were incensed, and consequently it was not until 27 Jan. – four days after the election – that the return was drawn up. Even then it was not sealed until the next day.[25]

Following the election, Temple and the jurats sent separate letters of protest to Lord Zouche. The lord warden was initially horrified at the information contained within these reports, particularly as he had recently worked so hard to restore peace and good government in Winchelsea, and one week after the election he warned Wymond that he would be punished by the Commons 'if the present House refuse or dislike your election'. However, by early February he had concluded that Wymond was not as culpable as he had been led to believe, and therefore advised Temple to drop his complaint, as Parliament would have 'many more weighty businesses to consider'. He also tried to persuade Nicholas Eversfield, who had supported the candidacy of Thomas Aynscombe in 1621 and had also protested at the mayor's behaviour, to use his influence with Temple to ensure that the matter went no further.[26]

Temple refused to heed Lord Zouche's advice, however, and on 2 Mar. he petitioned the Commons' elections committee.[27] The following day, after a preliminary hearing in committee, the House summoned the mayor as a delinquent.[28] A full hearing took place on 16 Mar., as a result of which the committee recommended that, for several reasons, the election of Finch should be declared void. First, it was observed that the town's by-law of November 1609 was 'utterly void', for no private ordinance was capable of restraining 'the manner, or right, of election of barons or burgesses to the Parliament'. Secondly, it was noted that, quite apart from the illegality of the 1609 bye-law, the grounds for barring the Tildens from voting were insufficient, for although neither the Tildens nor their families lived within the borough they still owned houses there. Besides, if three months' absence was to be cited as a qualification for voting, what was to prevent a town from passing by-laws that barred a man from voting if he was absent for a month or less? The committee further condemned the election on the grounds that the mayor had given insufficient warning of the election, had concealed the true purpose of the town meeting, and had falsely claimed the right to a casting vote. Finally, the committee observed that in 'seeking to draw the said Sir Alexander into scandal touching his religion, without cause', Wymond had committed 'an offence against the liberties and privileges of the Commons in Parliament'. The House agreed with these damning conclusions, and consequently Wymond was committed to prison for two days and ordered to acknowledge his fault publicly, both at the bar of the House and at the forthcoming election.[29]

Wymond returned to Winchelsea within a week, and held a second election on 25 Mar, which was attended both by Temple and by two of Finch's brothers, Sir Thomas Finch and Francis Finch. This time the Tildens were permitted to cast their votes, but at least one elector evidently abandoned Temple, who was now only able to muster nine votes in total rather than the ten he might have expected to receive. As a result, support for John Finch increased to 11. However, some time during the course of the proceedings, six of the freemen who had been disfranchised in 1623 burst into the hall and declared their support for Temple. They claimed that they were entitled to vote on the grounds that Paul Wymond, who had disfranchised them, had no right to the mayoralty as he had never been elected to office but had been installed by the lord warden. None of the freemen or jurats present were willing to accept this argument, however, but rather than allow the proceedings to descend into chaos it was decided that a letter should be directed to the lord warden asking whether the votes of the six disfranchised men should be allowed.[30] Naturally Zouche proved unwilling to endorse their claims, as it had been on his instruction that they had lost the franchise in the first place, and as a result Temple once again petitioned the Commons' elections committee. However, on 11 May the committee swept aside his complaint on the grounds that it was sufficient that Wymond was *de facto* mayor, and that the six disfranchised men had not claimed the right to vote in the previous contest. The House agreed with this conclusion, and on 28 May, the day before the Parliament ended, it declared Finch's election good.[31]

Following these tumultuous events, the divisions within Winchelsea seem largely to have subsided. Nevertheless, as late as February 1629 Giles Waters, by then mayor, complained that aspersions were being cast on his probity behind his back by some of his fellow townsmen.[32] By the time of the 1625 election the duke of Buckingham had replaced Lord Zouche as lord warden. Buckingham nominated his kinsman by marriage, Sir Ralph Freeman, a master of Requests from Surrey, for one seat, while the Finch interest, which now seems to have been firmly established, went to the Kentish gentleman Sir Roger Twysden, who was re-elected in 1626. The lord warden's choice in 1626 fell on Sir Nicholas Saunders of Ewell, in Surrey.[33] Saunders seems to have needed parliamentary privilege to stave off his creditors, and may have been recommended to Buckingham by his neighbour Freeman. The latter regained the Winchelsea seat in 1628, but Twysden was replaced by his father Sir William, an opponent of the Forced Loan. Neither writ nor indenture survives for the by-election caused by Sir William Twysden's death on 8 Jan. 1629, nor is there any record of the election in the corporation's minute book, which is blank for the period between mid-August 1628 and September 1630. However, by 12 Feb. 1629 Twysden's kinsman Thomas Heneage, whose sister-in-law was the widow of Thomas Egleston, had taken a seat in the Commons, presumably for this constituency.[34]

[1] 'Earle 1624', f. 46v. [2] Dates of elections from E. Suss. RO, WIN 55, ff. 82, 84, 190r-v, 234, 279, 283v-4, 298, 307; 58, f. 2. [3] W.D. Cooper, *Winchelsea*, 107; *VCH Suss.* ix. 67, 69-70. [4] E. Suss. RO, WIN 55, f. 274; Add. 37818, f. 63v. [5] J. Glanville, *Reps.* (1775), pp. 13-15. [6] E. Suss. RO, WIN 55, ff. 235, 280, 298; 58, f. 2. [7] E. Suss. RO, WIN 55, ff. 82, 84, 110v, 120; *OR*. [8] Add. 11402, f. 125. [9] E. Suss. RO, WIN 55, ff. 117, 124, 143. [10] Ibid. ff. 151, 162, 164v; *Top. and Gen.* ii. 452. [11] E. Suss. RO, WIN 55, f. 190r-v. [12] Ibid. ff. 208v, 232v; Add. 37818, f. 42; Add. 5705, f. 91. [13] E. Suss. RO, WIN 55, ff. 231, 233, 241r-v. [14] SP14/118/9. [15] *CITR*, 88; *I. Temple Admiss.* 122; E. Suss. RO, WIN 55, f. 214; STAC 8/195/28, f. 10. [16] *Top. and Gen.* ii. 459. [17] *Suss. Inquisitions* (Suss. Rec. Soc. xiv), 12. The will of Thomas Aynscombe of Mayfield contains nothing that would lead to the conclusion that he was a lawyer: PROB 11/137, ff. 286v-9. [18] Add. 37818, f. 51r-v. [19] E. Suss. RO, WIN 55, f. 234. [20] Add. 37818, f. 52v. [21] Ibid. ff. 63v, 64v-5; *CSP Dom.* 1619-23, pp. 255, 258. [22] *CSP Dom.* 1619-23, p. 351; E. Suss. RO, WIN 55, ff. 267-8, 273; Add. 37818, ff. 129v-30. It may be significant that hostility between Collins and Waters predated Waters' bankruptcy. In Jan. 1621 Collins killed Waters' dog, and then had him arrested for publicly subjecting him to 'unadvised speeches': *CSP Dom.* 1619-23, p. 218; Add. 37818, f. 54. [23] *CSP Dom.* 1603-10, p. 579; 1611-18, p. 554. [24] Glanville, 15-17; 'Earle 1624', ff. 46v-7, 88r-v; Bodl. Tanner 392, f. 21. [25] E. Suss. RO, WIN 55, ff. 279v, 280. [26] Add. 37818, ff. 145v-6, 147v-8. [27] 'Earle 1624', ff. 46v-7. [28] Bodl. Tanner 392, f. 21. [29] Glanville, 17-24; 'Earle 1624', ff. 90v-1. [30] E. Suss. RO, WIN 55, ff. 283v-4. [31] 'Earle 1624', ff. 179v, 196v. [32] E. Suss. RO, WIN 58, f. 1v. [33] *Procs. 1625*, p. 704; *Procs. 1626*, iv. 254-5. [34] *CJ*, i. 714b; *Vis. Bucks.* (Harl. Soc. lviii), 132.

P.J.L./A.D.T.

WALES

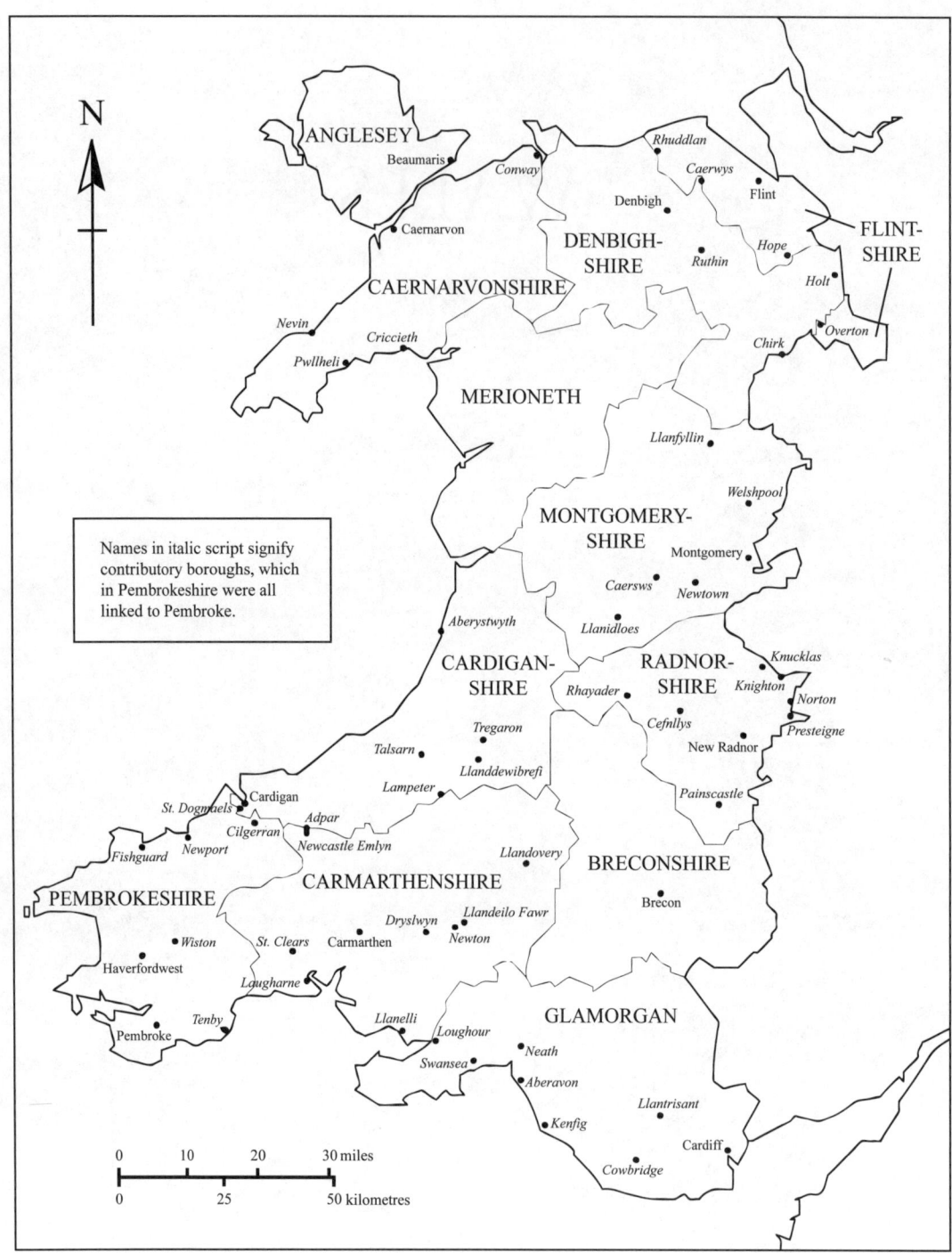

N

ANGLESEY

Beaumaris

Conway

Rhuddlan

Caerwys

Flint

Denbigh

FLINT-
SHIRE

DENBIGH-
SHIRE

Ruthin

Hope

Caernarvon

CAERNARVONSHIRE

Holt

Chirk

Overton

Nevin

Criccieth

Pwllheli

MERIONETH

Llanfyllin

Welshpool

MONTGOMERY-
SHIRE

Montgomery

Names in italic script signify
contributory boroughs, which
in Pembrokeshire were all
linked to Pembroke.

Caersws

Newtown

Aberystwyth

Llanidloes

CARDIGAN-
SHIRE

RADNOR-
SHIRE

Knucklas

Rhayader

Knighton

Norton

Tregaron

Cefnllys

Presteigne

Talsarn

Llanddewibrefi

New Radnor

Lampeter

Painscastle

St. Dogmaels

Cardigan

Adpar

Cilgerran

Newcastle Emlyn

Llandovery

BRECONSHIRE

Fishguard

Newport

CARMARTHENSHIRE

Brecon

PEMBROKESHIRE

Wiston

St. Clears

Carmarthen

Dryslwyn

Llandeilo Fawr

Newton

Haverfordwest

Laugharne

Llanelli

Loughour

GLAMORGAN

Tenby

Swansea

Neath

Pembroke

Aberavon

Llantrisant

Kenfig

Cardiff

Cowbridge

0   10   20   30 miles

0   25   50 kilometres

4. The Welsh constituencies

ANGLESEY

Number of voters: several hundred

23 Feb. 1604	SIR RICHARD BULKELEY
c. Mar. 1614	SIR RICHARD BULKELEY
4 Jan. 1621	RICHARD WILLIAMS
29 Jan. 1624	JOHN MOSTYN
21 Apr. 1625	SIR SACKVILLE TREVOR
c.23 Feb. 1626	RICHARD BULKELEY
21 Feb. 1628	RICHARD BULKELEY

A low-lying, though comparatively sparsely populated island off the north coast of Wales, Anglesey was
commended by the Beaumaris-born merchant Lewes
Roberts as 'having plenty of all food and other provision necessary to preserve the life of man, out of which
is yearly sent 3,000 head of cattle to supply the wants of
other countries adjoining, together with a good quantity of corn, butter, cheese'.[1] From the government's
viewpoint, the island's strategic significance considerably outweighed its economic importance: it had
been the base for Edward I's conquest of Gwynedd,[2]
and in 1625 the bishop of Bangor suspected that plans
for an invasion from Ireland were being abetted by
the local Catholics. These fears were taken seriously
by the Privy Council, which exempted the island
from contributing to the levies for the Irish army, and
arranged for the trained bands of north Wales to be
mustered there in the event of an invasion scare.[3]

The parliamentary representation of the island's
county and borough seats was dominated by the Bulkeley family of Baron Hill from the time of the 1543 Act
of Union. Sir Richard Bulkeley, an Elizabethan courtier
and the greatest landowner on the island, obtained the
return of relatives and friends at every election from
1584. It is just possible that Richard Williams, the only
Member returned under the early Stuarts who lacked a
London address, was paid expenses by his constituents,
which would explain why his successor, John Mostyn,
was urged to attend the next assize following his return
to 'give the gentlemen of that country thanks ... and
remit the mise'.[4] The islanders did not initiate any legislation during the period, but on 7 May 1604 Sir Richard
Bulkeley was among those named to give evidence
regarding local abuses of purveyance, and in 1606 he
was probably the sponsor of a proviso which exempted
Anglesey from a bill which would have entailed the
destruction of most of the county's watermills.[5]

In 1604 Bulkeley sought election for the first time
since 1563, probably in order to demonstrate his
loyalty to the new monarch. He was re-elected in 1614,
and although nearly 80 years old he was presumably
intending to stand again in 1621. However, he was
taken seriously ill a few days before the election, and
a substitute was hastily provided in the person of
Richard Williams, a minor landowner married to one
of his nieces.[6] After Bulkeley's death on 28 June 1621,
three factions among his descendants began fighting
for their share of the spoils, and in 1622 the family's
Anglesey estates were sequestrated by order of the
Court of Wards until a permanent settlement could be
arranged.[7] Bulkeley's grandson and designated heir,
another Richard Bulkeley, then well under age, did
not stand for election during the inheritance dispute,
although he re-established the family's hold on the
county seat in 1626, when only 19 years old.[8]

With the Bulkeley interest temporarily in abeyance,
other contenders quickly emerged in 1624: Rowland
Whyte of Friars apparently began canvassing by New
Year's Day, and Sir Sackville Trevor was also said to
be considering his chances.[9] Arrangements proceeded
at a leisurely pace, probably because the islanders had
become accustomed to seeking a lead from Baron Hill.
Thus John Mostyn, who had been denied a seat in

Flintshire by the gentry's early agreement on candidates for both shire and borough seats, was able to begin canvassing for the Anglesey seat before a local candidate had been agreed upon. Sir Roger Mostyn*, resolving to 'rest wholly upon my cousin Richard Bulkeley's power' wrote to Baron Hill on his son's behalf, though he emphasized that 'if it may not be had without any contesting with any country gentleman, I hold it not worth the having'. While this recommendation was at best lukewarm, the bearer of this letter, Sir Roger's brother-in-law Owen Wynn, had grandiose plans to 'carry the day wholly in North Wales'. Wynn, as one of the administrators of Bulkeley's sequestrated estates,[10] encountered no problems in securing the latter's support for Mostyn, and it was Bulkeley who suggested canvassing the gentry at the funeral of David Owen Theodor of Penmynydd.[11] Though those canvassed expressed concern, 'lest Sir Sackville Trevor being now above forth should move for it, who dwelling in the country, and one of them, must be preferred before a stranger', Wynn secured the support of the previous Member, Richard Williams. He also recruited Bulkeley's uncle Sir Thomas Holland†, who advised that Wynn's brother-in-law Sir John Bodvel could campaign at the Epiphany sessions, and that a letter of nomination from Sir James Whitelocke*, chief justice of the Chester circuit and father-in-law of Mostyn's elder brother, 'would strike it dead'. Meanwhile, Robert Whyte, archdeacon of Anglesey, also present at the funeral, detected the groundswell of support for Mostyn, and persuaded his brother to step down.[12]

Though Mostyn was almost certainly returned for Anglesey unopposed, his local standing was diminished by his father's refusal to let him attend the summer assizes at Beaumaris to thank the gentry for his election and waive any claim to parliamentary wages, on the dubious grounds 'that they chose him when they had none other to supply the place'.[13] Intending to seek re-election in 1625, Mostyn secured the backing of his patron Lord Keeper Williams, who wrote letters of recommendation to some of the gentry. Among his erstwhile opponents, Rowland Whyte, although 'somewhat offended ... that Jack Mostyn should gain the knightship of the Parliament from him', did not put his name forward, but Sir Sackville Trevor was 'resolved to stand for it against all men', and quickly secured the written support of the local justices.[14] While Trevor had learned from his previous mistakes, Mostyn's campaign undoubtedly suffered from the absence of Owen Wynn, who was in London on legal business. In Wynn's stead, Sir Roger Mostyn, realizing that his son's only chance lay in weaning a faction among the gentry from their

undertaking to Trevor, made an ill-advised attempt to lobby the bishop of Bangor, who, being married to Trevor's step-daughter, did his best to persuade the Mostyns that they stood no chance of victory.[15] It is unlikely that Mostyn allowed his son to stand in the face of almost certain defeat.

[1] L. Roberts, *The Merchants Mappe of Commerce* (1638/9), pp. 219-20; *Welsh Port Books, 1550-1603* (Cymmrodorion Soc. rec. ser. xii), pp. xix-xxxviii; *Agrarian. Hist. Eng. and Wales* ed. H.P.R. Finberg, iv. 129-30. [2] R.R. Davies, *Age of Conquest*, 334, 351-2. [3] SP16/11/37; *APC*, 1580-1, pp. 140, 364; 1595-6, p. 449; 1597-8, p. 223; 1626, pp. 89, 100. [4] NLW, 9059E/1242. [5] *CJ*, i. 202a; *SR*, iv. 1126. [6] STAC 8/76/3, ff. 4, 5; J.E. Griffith *Peds. Anglesey and Caern. Fams.* 114. [7] NLW, 9058E/1050. [8] NLW, Carreglwyd III/10. [9] NLW, 9059E/1172; 9060E/1276. [10] NLW, 9058E/1050; 9059E/1172 (should be dated 2 Jan. 1623/4), 1186. [11] Owen's distant kinship with the royal Tudor line gave him a social significance which outweighed his economic standing. We owe this point to Prof. Antony Carr. [12] NLW, 9059E/1172; 9060E/1276. [13] NLW, 9059E/1242; 9060E/1276. [14] *Procs. 1625*, p. 684; NLW, 9059E/1198; 9060E/1324. [15] NLW, 9060E/1294, 1324, 1335; *DWB* (Lewis Bayly).

S.H.

BEAUMARIS

Right of election: in the corporation

Number of voters: 24

23 Feb. 1604	WILLIAM JONES I, recorder
c. Mar. 1614	WILLIAM JONES I, recorder
c. Jan. 1621	SAMPSON EURE
c. Jan. 1624	CHARLES JONES
21 Apr. 1625	CHARLES JONES, recorder
23 Feb. 1626	CHARLES JONES, recorder
21 Feb. 1628	CHARLES JONES, recorder

Sited at the eastern end of the Menai straits, Beaumaris was the last of the Welsh fortresses to be founded by Edward I. Sacked and then captured by Owen Glyndŵr in 1403-5, it was quickly repaired. By the sixteenth century the borough, which commanded 'a fair, safe, and capacious haven and road', had become the main port on the north coast of Wales, trading with Lancashire for grain, general merchandise from Chester and salt and wine from France, Ireland and Scotland.[1] The borough's government evolved rapidly after the Union of 1536-43: a hall book was probably commenced around 1550,[2] and a recorder and town clerk were appointed under Elizabeth.[3]

Beaumaris was not enfranchised in 1536, as Newborough had been designated the county town under Henry VII. This arrangement was overturned by an Act of 1549, which awarded Beaumaris parliamentary representation, though Newborough remained a contributory borough.[4] In 1562, following a promise to maintain the town walls and sea defences at their own charge, the townsmen secured a charter appointing a mayor and two bailiffs, to be elected annually by the incumbents and the 21 chief burgesses. It also confirmed that the borough was 'to have a burgess in Parliament, elected by the bailiffs and chief burgesses'. Subsequent indentures suggest that this franchise was taken to include the mayor, but it excluded Newborough, making Beaumaris the only corporation franchise in Wales.[5] There is no explicit evidence that the borough's MPs lobbied on behalf of its interests under the early Stuarts, although Owen Wynn, broker for the Gwydir electoral interest, made inquiries about the town charter in 1622.[6]

Throughout the later Elizabethan and Jacobean periods, the borough was dominated by the local magnate, Sir Richard Bulkeley*, who was both constable of the castle and the owner of extensive property within the town. Several of his relatives were chief burgesses, and, perhaps most significantly, he leased over one-third of the town lands.[7] He wielded his electoral influence on behalf of his brother, Thomas†, but after the latter's death in 1593 the seat was held by his lawyer, William Jones of Castellmarch, Caernarvonshire. Jones's father may have been town clerk from 1585, and Jones had probably succeeded Thomas Bulkeley as recorder by the time of his election in 1597, though the indenture merely cited him as 'learned in law'.[8] On his return for Caernarvonshire in 1601, Jones was replaced by another Caernarvonshire squire, Sir William Maurice*, but the pair swapped seats in 1604, when the Beaumaris return referred to Jones as 'burgess and recorder'.[9]

Jones sat for Beaumaris again in 1614, but declined to seek re-election in the autumn of 1620. On this occasion Sir Richard Wynn* offered him first refusal of the Caernarvonshire seat; Jones declined, and initially agreed to support to Wynn as knight for Caernarvonshire, but changed his mind when he learned that his first wife's nephew, John Griffith III*, was a rival contender.[10] Jones may have intended to keep Beaumaris free for Griffith in case he was defeated at the Caernarvonshire election, but Griffith's resounding victory allowed the Beaumaris seat to go to an outsider, Sampson Eure. The latter's father was chief justice of the Anglesey circuit, and his stepmother, Maurice's granddaughter, had been Griffith's most

energetic lobbyist. In 1624, with both Maurice and Sir Francis Eure* dead, Jones replaced Eure's son with his own, who, as recorder, continued to represent the borough until his death in 1640.[11]

[1] I. Soulsby, *Towns of Medieval Wales*, 78-80; E.A. Lewis, *Medieval Bors. Snowdonia*, 204, 206; L. Roberts, *The Merchants Mappe of Commerce* (1638/9), pp. 219-20; *Welsh Port Books, 1550-1603* (Cymmrodorion Soc. rec. ser. xii), pp. xix-xxxviii. [2] Fragments of which survive in UCNW, Bangor 478D; NLW, 1546E/iii; NLW, 9081D. [3] UCNW, Bangor 478B, ff. 36v, 43; NLW, 9081D, pp. 122-3. [4] A.D.K. Hawkyard, 'Enfranchisement of Constituencies', *PH*, x. 9-10. [5] *CSP Dom.*, 1547-80, pp. 194-5; *CPR*, 1560-63, pp. 346-50; Hawkyard, 9-10. [6] NLW, 9058E/1050. [7] *CPR*, 1560-3, pp. 130, 347; *CSP Dom.* 1611-18, p. 443; UCNW, Baron Hill 4694; NLW, 9081D, pp. 137-46. [8] UCNW, Baron Hill 28; UCNW, Bangor 478B, f. 43; C219/33/253. [9] NLW, Brogyntyn 468; C219/35/2/182. [10] NLW, 9057E/916; Brogyntyn 399. [11] CAERNARVONSHIRE; NLW, 9081D, pp. 122-3.

S.H.

BRECONSHIRE

Number of voters: unknown

7 Mar. 1604	SIR ROBERT KNOLLYS I
c. Mar. 1614	SIR CHARLES VAUGHAN
20 Dec. 1620	SIR HENRY WILLIAMS
30 Dec. 1623	SIR HENRY WILLIAMS
2 Apr. 1625	SIR CHARLES VAUGHAN
11 Jan. 1626	JOHN PRISE
5 Mar. 1628	HENRY WILLIAMS

Breconshire was one of the counties created by the Henrician Acts of Union, centred on the old lordship of Brecon, which had escheated to the Crown following the attainder of the 3rd duke of Buckingham (1523). The county was dominated by the upland ranges of the Brecon Beacons and the Black Mountains, one seventeenth-century author observing that the 'high hills' were 'so thick together ... in a manner of high bulwarks and compact joints of this county' that it was a 'fit place of refuge for the Britons'.[1] This geography meant that the farming of cattle and sheep dominated, although there was scope for producing corn and grain in the fertile river valleys and in the more forgiving topography towards the border with England on the county's eastern fringe. Such an economic profile did not produce a crop of wealthy gentlemen, and so early Stuart Breconshire was stocked with only a small number of gentry families of the first rank. Parliamentary elections for the county were held at Brecon Castle.

In electoral terms the interest of the Vaughans of Porthaml had been decisive during the Elizabethan era, and their large family estates meant that they continued to hold sway under James I. This was evidenced in the 1604 return of Sir Robert Knollys I, who had married the Porthaml heiress. Knollys' poor financial situation may have dissuaded him from sitting again, however, for in 1614 his son-in-law, Sir Charles Vaughan, who lived in Wiltshire, replaced him. After Knollys' death in 1619, the seat passed to the new powerhouse of Breconshire politics, Sir Henry Williams of Gwernyfed, whose family had previously sat for the borough seat. Williams' father, Sir David†, was a lawyer who spent most of his time in London or Berkshire, but Sir Henry resided within the shire, serving as chairman of the county bench and as a member of the Council in the Marches. He took the county seat in 1621 and 1624 with support from a broad spectrum of gentry allies, including the Gameses of Aberbrân, Newton and Buckland, the Walbeoffs of Llanhamlach, and the Aubreys of Abercynrig.[2] Probably through contacts forged by his father, he was also on good terms with another leading figure in Breconshire politics, (Sir) Walter Pye I* of the Mynde, Herefordshire, who became chief justice of the Breconshire circuit in 1617.

There seems not to have been a particularly vibrant parliamentary political culture amongst the Breconshire gentry, for in 1625 the county's electors were happy to return the absentee Sir Charles Vaughan once more, while in 1626 they chose the inexperienced John Prise of The Priory. The latter, a scion of one of the shire's most respected political families, was not an active representative, and perhaps owed his return to his father's contacts with Sir Henry Williams, or possibly to a family connection with Sir Walter Pye I, whose father-in-law was Prise's grandfather. It is likely that Vaughan, too, was chosen at the behest of, or at least with the blessing of, Sir Henry Williams, who endorsed his election indenture and who, for reasons that are unknown, seems never to have stood for re-election after sitting in 1624. Sir Henry's son and heir took the county place in 1628, aided by his father, who was then serving as sheriff. An impressive array of the county's leading gentlemen were contracting parties at his election, among them the 1626 Member, John Prise.[3]

There were few issues on which the county MPs were active in Parliament. An exception, however, was the question of purveyance. This was a comparatively novel levy in Wales, having only been introduced in the later years of Elizabeth's reign. Although the burden of composition was comparatively light, being set at only £30 for each county, the fact that the charge covered stirks (young bullocks or heifers) and 'fat cattle', seems to have caused disquiet.[4] In 1604 Sir Robert Knollys I was one of the Welsh Members who petitioned Parliament 'in the name of the commons of those parts', that the charge was a grievance.[5] He was also among those named to a committee in May 1604 to give evidence 'either by experience in their own particular, or by testimony of their country neighbours' of the impact of purveyance in their localities.[6]

[1] Harl. 7017, f. 244. [2] C219/37/336; C219/38/312. [3] C219/41B/5. [4] NLW, 14699B; Add 10609, f. 117; L. Bowen, *Pols. of the Principality*, 52-6. [5] Add. 5847, ff. 163v-4. [6] *CJ*, i. 202b.

L.B.

BRECON BOROUGHS

Right of election: in the freemen

4 Mar. 1604	Sir Henry Williams
c. Mar. 1614	Sir John Crompton
18 Dec. 1620	Walter Pye I
14 Jan. 1624	(Sir) Walter Pye I
4 May 1625	(Sir) Walter Pye I
12 Jan. 1626	(Sir) Walter Pye I
aft. 11 Feb. 1626[1]	Sir Humphrey Lynde *vice* (Sir) Walter Pye I, chose to sit for Herefordshire
18 Feb. 1628	Walter Pye I
31 Mar. 1628	Walter Pye II *vice* (Sir) Walter Pye I, chose to sit for Herefordshire

The county town, Brecon was a fairly prosperous market town located in the centre of post-union Breconshire at the confluence of the Honddu and the Usk. Its liberties ran in a rough ellipse outside the walled town some three miles in length and one mile in width, but they also comprehended the detached ward of Llywel, some 11 miles to the east. In the early seventeenth century Brecon's population numbered around 2,000, making it one of the largest of early modern Wales's small urban centres.[2] It held three markets a week, including a cattle market every Friday, and hosted three fairs per year.[3] The preponderant trades of the town, which supported six guilds, were the production of leather goods, textiles and cloth.[4] Brecon was also the administrative centre of south-east Wales. Forming the hub of the judicial circuit which encompassed Glamorgan and Radnorshire, it housed the Chancery and Exchequer of these three counties as decreed by the Acts of Union. The town's governing structure was established by a charter of 1556, which provided for a bailiff and two aldermen to be elected annually from among 15 capital burgesses, who constituted the town's common council.[5]

Unlike most other Welsh boroughs, Brecon was evidently able to elect its Member without reference to any of its 'contributory boroughs'. Returns were made by the bailiff in the presence of the aldermen, and a small number of burgesses – probably the capital burgesses – also witnessed returns. The loss of its records makes it difficult to be sure, but Brecon seems not to have enjoyed an energetic or autonomous political life. The Member in the first Jacobean Parliament, Sir Henry Williams, was son of the borough's recorder, Sir David, who had represented the town in 1601. Thereafter, outsiders were chosen. Sir John Crompton was son of the 1593 Member for New Radnor, and his connection with the lingering remnants of an Essex interest in mid-Wales (which would have included the New Radnor Member in the Addled Parliament, Rowland Meyrick) probably accounts for his return in 1614.

During the 1620s the chief justice of the Brecon circuit, Walter Pye I*, became the key figure in Brecon's parliamentary politics. In choosing Pye or his associates the borough probably wished to keep on the right side of a powerful local figure, but it also thereby obtained a powerful advocate at the centre, as Pye was a client of lord chancellor St. Alban (Sir Francis Bacon*) and the duke of Buckingham. Another consideration may have been the fact that Pye seems to have established good contacts with the leading gentry figure in Breconshire, Sir Henry Williams of Gwernyfed, who had represented the borough in 1604. At any rate, an important marriage was contracted between the two families in 1631. Pye himself was elected for all the Parliaments of the 1620s, but does not appear to have lobbied on behalf of his constituents. Indeed, his eye was on the greater prize of a county seat in his native Hereford-shire, and when he succeeded in obtaining this, both in 1626 and 1628, he chose it over Brecon.[6] In his stead came his eldest son (in 1628) and Sir Humphrey Lynde (in 1626). Lynde was a scholar and theologian, whose interests lay in Surrey and Middlesex, but he also had contacts with officials in the Court of Wards, where Pye was attorney. In 1623 Lynde dedicated a volume to Pye, whom he described as 'my much honoured friend'.[7]

[1] CJ, i. 818a. [2] N.M. Powell, Urban Hist. xxxii. 50. [3] Hugh Thomas' Essay Towards the Hist. of Brec. 1698 ed. J. Jones-Davies, 23. [4] W.S.K. Thomas, Brecon, 1066-1660, pp. 63-4, 115. [5] CPR, 1555-7, pp. 76-81. [6] Add. 70001, ff. 195-6; Add. 70108, no. 39(i). [7] Sir Humphrey Lynde, The Book of Bertram the Priest (1623), sig. A2.

L.B.

CAERNARVONSHIRE

Number of voters: c.1,100 in 1620.[1]

14 Mar. 1604	SIR WILLIAM MAURICE
c. Mar. 1614	RICHARD WYNN
27 Dec. 1620	JOHN GRIFFITH III
	Griffith Jones
21 Jan. 1624	THOMAS GLYNNE
11 May 1625	THOMAS GLYNNE
	(Sir) Peter Mutton*
18 Jan. 1626	JOHN GRIFFITH III
c. Feb. 1628	JOHN GRIFFITH III

Caernarvonshire is divided into three by the massif of Mount Snowdon: to the east, the Creuddyn peninsula and the Conway valley; Arfon and Arllechwedd Isaf along the Menai Strait to the north; and Eifionydd and the Llŷn peninsula to the south and west. During the early modern period the shire's economy was of the conventional upland type, mixing subsistence crops of rye and barley with the commercial farming of livestock, a combination which left the freeholders' ability to meet tax demands heavily dependent upon the state of the cattle trade. Industrial activity was modest: Caernarvon had a small cloth industry, and there were a number of millstone, slate, coal and lead mines on the slopes of Snowdon.[2]

The politics of early Tudor Caernarvonshire were dominated by the Griffiths of Penrhyn, but their subsequent decline allowed Elizabeth's favourite, Robert Dudley[†], earl of Leicester, to intervene in local affairs, polarizing the county over his vigorous pursuit of concealed tenures within the Forest of Snowdon.[3] After his death in 1588 control of the shire devolved upon the two greatest local landowners, Sir John Wynn[†] of Gwydir and Sir William Maurice. In a county divided by geography, faction and religion, it is surprising that parliamentary elections in Elizabethan Caernarvonshire were largely uncontested, as similar circumstances produced bruising clashes in Denbighshire and Montgomeryshire. The fact that Leicester was an absentee may have helped to defuse the situation, although the underlying tensions probably explain why Wynn, one of the earl's most active local allies, did not stand after 1586, and his younger brother Ellis Wynn[†] failed in his ambition to secure the knighthood of the shire at the end of Elizabeth's reign.[4]

At the general election of 1604 Sir William Maurice, who had sat for Beaumaris in 1601, changed places with the lawyer William Jones I*, knight for Caernarvonshire in Elizabeth's last Parliament. This was probably an amicable arrangement, as Maurice had headed the list of attestors to Jones's return in 1601, and the sheriff who supervised his own return three years later was Jones's brother-in-law, John Griffith the elder of Cefnamwlch. Maurice probably faced a challenge from Gwydir at some stage of the proceedings in 1604: the Wynns were conspicuously absent from the election return, which was signed almost exclusively by men from the western end of the shire, while Sir John Wynn had spoken of nominating his brother when a Parliament was first mooted in June 1603. However, the disgruntled tone of a letter written by Ellis Wynn shortly before the county day suggests that his brother had failed to stand by his earlier undertakings, from which it may be inferred that the family ultimately shied away from a contest.[5]

It is unlikely that Maurice contemplated standing for the shire at the next general election in 1614: he was by then over 70 years old, and the king's cherished project for a full Union with Scotland, to which he, almost alone among MPs, had given his wholehearted support, had long since been laid aside. As soon as the summons was announced, Wynn (whose heir was then in France) nominated his second son Richard, a courtier in the household of lord chamberlain Suffolk. Confident of the backing of his own tenants in the Conway valley, Wynn appealed to at least three key figures at the western end of the shire, John Griffith of Cefnamwlch, Henry Bodvel of Maes y Castell and John Jones of Castellmarch, who assured him of their support on the (well-founded) understanding that William Jones was prepared to settle for the burgessship at Beaumaris. The only other candidate who may have put himself forward was Sir William Glynne[†] of Glynllivon, who was later said to have withdrawn upon receiving Wynn's promise to support either him or his heir at the next election.[6]

Any joy Wynn may have felt at this electoral success turned to ashes six months later with the news of the sudden death of his heir in Italy, while his local prestige suffered a mortifying blow in November 1615, when he was fined 1,000 marks by the Council in the Marches for attempting to intimidate the Crown tenants of

the manor of Llysvaen, Caernarvonshire.[7] Wynn had no intention of paying the fine without appeal, but in the meantime his servants were arrested, his lands seized, and the justices of the Council in the Marches called for his removal from local office. Forced to flee to London to avoid arrest, he procured the remission of all but £200, at the price of a public submission at Ludlow in March 1616.[8] The memory of this humiliation presumably explains why Wynn welcomed an opportunity to restore his local standing when a fresh general election was called in November 1620.

Much as Sir John Wynn may have been inclined to pick a fight over the county seat, the initiative for the 1620 contest came from London, where his son (Sir) Richard had decided to stand by 3 Nov., the day on which the Privy Council ordered the writs sent out. Sir Richard probably hoped his early declaration of intent would discourage any rival candidates, to which end he offered first refusal of the seat to (Sir) William Jones; the latter, being on the verge of appointment as a justice of Common Pleas, declined, and, as courtesy demanded, offered Wynn 'his goodwill and assent'. There was also a remote possibility that the aged Sir William Maurice might choose to 'run a-madding again', in which case Wynn proposed to yield precedence and content himself with the borough seat. Having carefully guarded against a confrontation with the two most senior figures in county society, Wynn was taken aback by a challenge from a completely different quarter when John Griffith III, a Lincoln's Inn lawyer and son of the 1604 sheriff, declared himself.[9]

Griffith's entry into the fray threw Wynn's calculations into disarray: he correctly surmised that any promises made by Jones and Maurice should now be discounted, while Griffith could look for further support from his father-in-law, Sir Richard Trevor[†], who had recently purchased a large slice of the Penrhyn estate. In all the excitement, Wynn, having earlier lobbied Sir Lionel Cranfield* to get his brother-in-law Sir John Bodvel excused from the shrievalty, now forgot to countermand the request, thus losing the chance to secure himself a favourable returning officer at the election. Griffith's supporters regarded the new sheriff, Robert Owen of Ystumcegid, as their man, but the Wynns seem to have neutralized his influence by delaying the dispatch of the writ appointing him sheriff until after the election, which was thus presided over by the previous year's incumbent, Robert Wynn of Glascoed. Wynn's uncle Sir William Thomas doubted whether either man would be willing to serve the Wynns' cause, advising that 'the best kindness we are to expect of them is but indifferency'.[10]

Griffith, also working from London, lobbied just as hard as his rival, approaching Sir William Maurice with particular care:

> You know best the experience that is obtained by being of a Parliament, and that every true lover of his country should endeavour to do service there; in that desire I now am bold to entreat your voice for me to be knight of the shire, whereby you shall make me beholding to you, and I shall rejoice in a better thought of myself by your election of me.

This overture failed, as Wynn had already secured Maurice's support, but Griffith responded by pressing Maurice 'to grant me your favour in leaving your friends to their liberty … if without injury to yourself it may be so', an appeal which was quickly reinforced by another from Maurice's favourite granddaughter, wife of the assize judge Sir Francis Eure*, who urged him to 'labour and endeavour for other voices in his behalf as you would do for me, if I were a man and fit for the place'. To Wynn's annoyance, Griffith also managed to secure control of the writ for the election, despite promises to the contrary from lord chancellor St. Alban (Sir Francis Bacon*). Finally, Griffith's opponents accused him of employing nefarious means to achieve his ends, including the interception of Wynn's correspondence and the use of the lawyer Simon Parry as a spy within the Gwydir camp.[11]

The efforts of the two contenders in London were more than matched by those of their supporters in Wales. Sir John Wynn quickly dispatched his younger son Owen, his servant Edward Lloyd and his cousin William Wynne of Melai, Denbighshire, to canvass the freeholders of the Conway valley, the Creuddyn peninsula, Llysvaen and the lowlands along the Menai Strait as far as Caernarvon, where they were assisted by Sir William Thomas.[12] The latter's calculations, based upon these efforts, provide some of the most detailed psephological data of any early Stuart election:

CAERNARVONSHIRE CANVASSING RETURNS, 1620[13]

Commotes	Freeholders	Projected Wynn support
Conway, Creuddyn and Arllechwedd Isaf	300	All but 'scattered voices' (assuming Bulkeley support)
Arllechwedd Uchaf	40	All but 'scattered voices'
Is Gwyrfai, Bangor and Caernarvon	140	All but 'scattered voices'
Uwch Gwyrfai	120+	Half
Eifionydd	70+	Three-quarters
Llŷn peninsula	350-400	About 50

On these projections, the Wynns looked as though they might carry the day by a comfortable majority of up to 200 votes, but, like any modern pollster, Thomas warned of a substantial margin of error, particularly as Wynn's adversaries had engaged a Caernarvon scrivener to draft leases enfranchising additional freeholders to swell their numbers at the county day, a tactic that was promptly emulated by Sir John Wynn among his Gwydir tenants. Thomas's prediction for Eifionydd suggests that he believed Sir William Maurice's tenants would vote for Wynn, an assumption Griffith's supporters were ultimately to undermine.

Allegiances in the remainder of the shire varied according to the cross-currents of local politics. Lewis Bayly, bishop of Bangor, having commenced his episcopate by picking a fight with Sir John Wynn, thereafter sparred more regularly with his dean, Edmund Griffith of Cefnamwlch. Some weeks before the election Bayly surprised even Owen Wynn with the vehemence of a post-sermon oration in which he exhorted his Bangor congregation 'to pass their voices for my brother'. Bayly's neighbour, William Williams of Vaynol, who had recently clashed with the bishop over his wife's Catholic sympathies, declared for Griffith, although neither he nor his wife (Sir John Wynn's aunt by her previous marriage) were prepared to pressure their tenants on behalf of either side.[14] The Wynns looked for additional support among Merioneth gentry families who had estates in Caernarvonshire, such as the Vaughans of Corsygedol and Robert Lloyd† of Rhiwgoch, but there were fears that Sir Richard Bulkeley's* promises to Wynn on behalf of his tenants in the Conway valley might not hold good, probably because of the ill usage they had hitherto received at Sir John Wynn's hands. At the western end of the shire, Sir John Bodvel lobbied on behalf of his brother-in-law, Sir Richard Wynn, apparently making headway with Arthur Williams of Meilionydd, who had recently been feuding with his Cefnamwlch neighbours.[15]

After a whirlwind campaign lasting three weeks, the freeholders converged upon Caernarvon for the county court at the end of November. Sir William Thomas leased the Shire Hall on behalf of Wynn's supporters, stocking it with beer, food and bedding, while it seems that both sides independently sought to encourage a good turnout among their own tenants by arranging a muster of the county militia at Caernarvon on the same day. This provoked a shrill protest from Thomas Glynne: 'the election of the knight of the shire should proceed from the free will of the freeholders according to the statute and by His Majesty's

Proclamation ... and not from the threats of these musters'. Sir William Thomas unsuccessfully urged an ailing Sir John Wynn to make a personal appearance at the hustings, promising him that 'your countenance will carry the matter clear away by dashing and daunting the adverse part'. However, if the election looked doubtful, Thomas planned to object to both candidates on the grounds that they were not resident within the shire, and to impose a third man at the last moment, a ploy he assured Wynn 'will grieve and gall them more than the losing of it by competition with you'. In the event the election was postponed, presumably because the writ had not arrived, although Griffith's supporters, doubting the prospect of a clear-cut victory without the benefit of their newly minted freeholders, may simply have advised the sheriff not to publish the writ.[16]

Surprisingly, it was the Wynns who experienced a loss of nerve in the aftermath of this abortive contest, perhaps because they had come to believe their own predictions of an easy victory. Sir William Thomas admittedly remained confident: he assured Sir John Wynn that 'I will not spare for any pains or labour in the defence of your credit', even though the next county day would fall during the Christmas holidays, and he advised Wynn to canvass his followers once again. Owen Wynn, by contrast, urged his father to reconsider, reminding him of 'the trouble and charge you will put your friends unto in such a time as everyone would willingly take his rest', and hinting that some of the Gwydir faction were inclined to put him forward as a candidate in place of his brother. Meanwhile, Sir John wrote an angry letter to his son William Wynn* in London, castigating Sir Richard Wynn's failure to mobilize official support from the Council in the Marches and the Prince's Council. By the middle of December the strain had broken Sir John's health, and Owen Wynn returned to Gwydir to care for his father, advising Thomas that 'my case now admits no gadding abroad about an imaginary cause'. Morale at Gwydir improved a little with the arrival of letters from Sir Richard Wynn and the family's close ally John Williams, dean of Westminster, and on 19 Dec. Sir John Wynn sent to Sir William Maurice, urging him to maintain his support 'to the end'. Meanwhile, Owen Wynn sought to improve the family's chances by passing a bribe to the sheriff's wife. However, by this stage Wynn was looking to salvage some shreds of his reputation rather than to score an outright victory, and legal advice he received at the time suggest that his options included ruling both candidates unfit through non-residence, or, at worst, standing aside in a last-minute show of generosity to Griffith.[17]

The Llŷn men, scenting victory, pressed home their advantage, warning Sir William Thomas and Sir John Bodvel that they would face charges in Star Chamber for attempting to impose militia rates upon Griffith's supporters, and threatening to proceed against Bishop Bayly in Parliament and to terminate his lease of a farm held from the Cochwillan estate as a punishment for pressuring his tenants to support Wynn. Bayly also received a letter of admonition from Lord President Northampton, warning him that the lord chancellor had received a complaint about his activities, and urging him to ensure that the election was not marred by violence. With increasingly contradictory signals emerging from Gwydir, support for the Wynns faded even among their closest allies: Sir John was particularly shocked to be deserted by his son-in-law Sir Roger Mostyn*, who may have agreed to back Griffith as the price for the Trevors' endorsement of his own uncontested election for Flintshire.[18]

At the county court, which took place on 27 Dec., John Griffith III was returned on an indenture which was, as might be expected, dominated by Llŷn families: Griffith's father, his uncle Dean Edmund Griffith of Bangor, Henry Bodvel of Maes y Castell, Griffith Jones of Castellmarch, the Madryns and Bodurdas; further east, he was also supported by the Glynnes of Glynllivon and Nanlley, and Thomas Williams, heir to the Vaynol estate. On the morning of the election the Gwydir camp, faced with this huge array, was thrown into a panic. Assuming Sir Richard Wynn's cause to be lost, Bishop Bayly suggested that Sir John Wynn stand instead, at which Sir John Bodvel objected that a rebuff for the head of the family would be even more humiliating than the defeat of the heir. His solution was to propose Owen Wynn as their candidate, but at this Sir William Thomas demurred, 'saying he would not adventure his credit upon any younger brother'. He moved instead to revive Sir John Wynn's long-forgotten promise of 1614 in favour of Thomas Glynne of Glynllivon, who, as a declared supporter of Griffith's, might be used to divide the opposing vote. Owen Wynn endorsed the principle behind this plan, but persuaded his colleagues to adopt another Cefnamwlch partisan, Griffith Jones of Castellmarch, on the grounds that the latter's father-in-law, William Griffith† of Caernarvon, was backing the Gwydir interest, and his father, Sir William Jones, had initially pledged his support to Sir John Wynn if the latter chose to stand in person. The logic of this tortuous argument clearly eluded the freeholders, and the Wynns' failure to petition the Commons about the election suggests that Griffith won by an overwhelming margin.[19]

The ignominious collapse of the Gwydir interest provoked angry recriminations among the Wynns: taunts about Sir Richard's non-residence struck a particularly raw nerve in Sir John, who had always regretted his son's decision to neglect his Welsh patrimony in favour of an English wife and a Court career. The latter, reduced to the shrill assertion that 'I ... cannot find the least cause ... wherein I have been faulty', found a more level-headed advocate in Dean Williams:

> The opposition grew not here at London ... but it began at home in the country, against the greatness not of your son, but of yourself and your house. This I know very well as having taken no small pains in reconciling your son and Mr. Griffith betimes, which I had soon effected but that I found (by a little disputation) that the root of the opposition lay hid in Wales, and the gentleman was only set up as an active instrument to advance the designs of closer opposites.

Some historians have suggested that the roots of this electoral clash may be found in a conflict between the modernizing social and religious values of Gwydir and the conservatism of the Llŷn gentry. This interpretation gives too much weight to the Wynns' extensive correspondence, which tends to present the family as the focus of a public-spirited struggle against obscurantist forces, a view founded upon the paranoia which increasingly coloured Sir John Wynn's outlook in the last decade of his life as ill-health and old age confined him to Gwydir. As Williams suggested, the key issue was the conflict between Wynn and the gentry from the western end of the shire, who resented taking orders from a man who was both impossibly high-handed and virtually a stranger in their part of the world. This tension was exacerbated as Wynn's poor health led him to sustain his authority through a clique of close relatives, such as Thomas, Bodvel and Owen Wynn, who wielded only a fraction of his social and political authority. Under Elizabeth, the grievances of the Llŷn men would have coalesced around the Bodvel family, but with the heir to the estate married to one of Wynn's daughters, the Griffiths seized the chance to carve out a leading role for themselves in county society.[20]

Neither side was disposed to bury the hatchet in the months following their electoral clash. For some time, supporters of Griffith, whom Sir John Wynn ironically dubbed 'the lord of Llŷn', held weekly victory rallies at Pwllheli, largely to annoy Sir John Bodvel. Meanwhile, Owen Wynn, in London to explore potential avenues for revenge, discovered that he could not bring a credible lawsuit against the Llŷn men, even for acceptance of the bribe he had himself given to the sheriff's wife, as there was no proof it had been received, and anyway, it had evidently failed to procure a victory for the Wynns.[21] Moreover, a plainly vexatious charge would encourage the Wynns' adversaries to raise the issue in Parliament, where Griffith was already boasting to Sir Roger Mostyn that he would file a complaint against Bodvel and Thomas for abusing their powers as deputy lieutenants. Shortly thereafter, in June 1621, the Wynns had an unexpected stroke of luck when Dean Williams of Westminster became lord keeper. Williams immediately took Sir John Wynn's son William and grandson John Mostyn* into his service, and the family had high hopes that 'by degrees we shall be sufficiently revenged of our adversaries', a portent of which was the swift removal of three of their adversaries from the subsidy commission. However, hopes for a purge of the Llŷn faction from the commission of the peace came to nothing, as did efforts to secure the attorneyship of North Wales for Ellis Lloyd* in place of Owen Griffith of Cefnamwlch, while it took nine months of lobbying merely to get Owen Wynn added to the county bench. Williams was too canny a politician to serve as a mere catspaw for Gwydir's ambitions, and, well aware of the way in which his predecessor had met his downfall, he warned his servants that 'he will have no favourites as the Lord St. Albans had'. Both sides talked endlessly about litigation, and after many months of preparation the Wynns sponsored a Star Chamber bill against the Llŷn faction; to deprive Griffith of the opportunity to claim immunity, the suit was only entered on file four days before the Parliament was dissolved in February 1622.[22]

Williams's reluctance to take sides in the endless quarrels of his native shire eventually served to take some of the heat out of the disputes. Griffith procured a referral of his lawsuits with the Wynns to the Council in the Marches, where he hoped for a favourable hearing, but his adversaries responded with an injunction from Williams revoking the most important charges, relating to the sealing of the Caernarvonshire election indenture, back to Chancery; the case was eventually brought to a composition by Sir Peter Mutton and Edward Littleton II*, the assize judges for North Wales, in the autumn of 1623. In November 1622, anticipating another general election, the Wynns had Sir John Bodvel pricked as sheriff, while Owen Wynn spent much of the following year trying to forge himself a marriage alliance, first with Williams's sister and then with the lord keeper's niece. Meanwhile, John Griffith stirred up trouble between Griffith Jones and Owen Wynn, culminating in a public quarrel at the Beaumaris assizes. He also aimed to build up an interest in the Caernarvon Boroughs seat by procuring a grant of the constableship of Caernarvon Castle, a deputation of which had hitherto been held by Sir William Thomas.[23]

When a fresh Parliament was finally summoned at Christmas 1623, the Caernarvonshire factions were more evenly balanced than they had been in the aftermath of the previous election, although the memory of that humiliation encouraged the Wynns to focus their efforts on Merioneth, Anglesey and Caernarvon Boroughs. However, Owen Wynn and Sir William Thomas, upon learning that the Griffiths backed the return of Thomas Williams of Vaynol, developed an opportunistic plan to divide their enemies by securing a rival nomination from Sir James Whitelocke*, chief justice of Chester, on behalf of his son-in-law Sir Thomas Mostyn. Wynn had no particular brief for his Mostyn relatives, who had abandoned the Gwydir cause at the 1620 election, but the scheme promised to sow dissension in the ranks of the family's adversaries at little cost. In the event, Whitelocke misguidedly resolved to back Mostyn for the Flintshire seat against the express wishes of the latter's own father, while an even more improbable attempt to promote the candidacy of one of the Wynns' obscurer neighbours, Hugh Hughes of Cefn Garlleg, came to nothing. In a final twist to the proceedings, on the morning of the election Thomas Williams resigned his interest in favour of Thomas Glynne of Glynllivon. Once again, the indenture was dominated by the gentry of Llŷn and Uwch Gwyrfai, although they were joined by Sir William Thomas, who was present in the hope that a last-minute rival might enter the fray.[24]

The Wynns received two unwelcome scares during the 1624 Parliament, one over the investigation of their patron lord keeper Williams for judicial malpractice, and the other when Sir Eubule Thelwall* persuaded a majority of Welsh MPs to sign a petition against a lease of the Welsh greenwax fines to Sir Richard Wynn, thus delaying a grant on which the family had already expended 18 months of effort and £150.[25] The lord keeper's survival apparently disheartened John Griffith, who was reported to be on the verge of giving up his career ambitions at the end of the year, but the king's death in March 1625 threw everything back into the melting pot, not least because it held out the prospect of fresh parliamentary elections. Williams, who hoped to organize the return of sympathetic candidates across North Wales, intended to leave Merioneth and Caernarvonshire to the Wynns. Sir John initially approached Sir William Thomas for the Caernarvonshire seat, but Thomas, mindful of the Wynns' previous electoral humiliations, declined the offer,

protesting that 'I am not yet ready for the Parliament, and therefore whomsoever you shall nominate, I am for him'.[26] Wynn's choice next lighted upon Sir Peter Mutton, the chief justice of North Wales, an outsider whose estates lay in Flintshire. He announced his intention to stand on a visit to Sir John Wynn, 'thinking that if I opposed it not, no other would do', a stance which naturally delighted his host. It was presumably Wynn who suggested that Mutton write to Sir William Thomas for support, as well as Thomas Williams and Thomas Glynne, the two candidates at the previous election. However, Wynn somehow neglected to advise his guest to approach the Llŷn gentry, an omission which verged on electoral suicide and suggests that his protestations of support for Mutton's cause were less than sincere. Shortly thereafter, when Mutton learned of Glynne's intention to contest the seat 'might and main', he recalled that at the 1624 session his rival had assured him 'that if any of my friends had desired the place for me he would have yielded with many protestations of his love and respect unto me'. This disingenuous misinterpretation of what had clearly been only a casual pleasantry as a firm promise cannot have assisted his cause. Wynn acknowledged 'I would not willingly that Thomas Glynne should carry the place', but he showed no real inclination to exert himself on Mutton's behalf, and seems to have lost patience with his inept ally when it emerged that the latter's failure to muster at least a token presence at the county court on 13 Apr. would have cost him the election if the writ had arrived in time. At the actual election four weeks later, Glynne 'came with all the forces of Llŷn, Eifionydd and Uwch Gwyrfai' to trounce an opponent who may already have given up the fight. Sir William Thomas, who attended the hustings, probably reflected Wynn's views in observing with studied indifference that Glynne 'laboured as if it had been to obtain a great prize'.[27]

By the time of the next election, in January 1626, changes at Whitehall had profoundly altered the political balance in Caernarvonshire. Lord Keeper Williams had been sacked and had retired to his episcopal palace at Buckden, Huntingdonshire, while Sir William Jones, although still in office, was reported to have fallen foul of the all-powerful favourite, the duke of Buckingham. The Wynns had no hope of mounting a credible challenge to the Llŷn faction, and Mutton showed no sign of wishing to repeat the electoral annihilation of the previous year. However, Glynne was replaced by John Griffith, in an arrangement which was clearly consensual, as he endorsed the latter's return, which comprised, as usual, a roll call of the leading families from the western end of the shire.[28]

Griffith's quest for preferment continued unabated, as was made evident by his obsequious defence of Buckingham in a session largely devoted to the preparation of the duke's impeachment charges. From a local viewpoint, the session was more remarkable for the vigorous attack on Bishop Bayly led by Sir Eubule Thelwall, who accused his diocesan of offences ranging from the appointment of non-Welsh speaking clergy to fornication with his maidservants. Bayly may well have regretted the fact that, for the first time in over a decade, his Wynn allies were not represented in the Commons, and while the charges made against him were never pressed to a hearing, they were taken sufficiently seriously in official circles that he was still answering enquiries about his alleged shortcomings four years later.[29]

The Caernarvonshire gentry dragged their feet over the payment of Privy Seal loans to the total of £540 which were levied during the 1626 Parliament, the more so because the government was then laying plans to assess the four subsidies of 1606 and 1610 which had never been collected within the principality. Griffith used his influence to exempt his father, Glynne and Sir Thomas Williams from the loans, while Sir William Jones simply refused to pay those demanded from his family; Sir John Wynn was perhaps in the most fortunate position, in that the collector, Sir William Thomas, omitted to pressure him for payment. None of this augured well for the collection of the Forced Loan in 1627, but with Griffith by then firmly rooted in Buckingham's service, Sir John Wynn dead, and Sir William Jones, as a judge, expected to set an example of prompt payment, would-be refusers lacked a figurehead, and the issue did not become as divisive as it would have only a few years earlier. Griffith's dependence upon the favourite had no perceptible effect on his electoral prospects, as he was returned for the shire once again in 1628.[30]

[1] NLW, 9057E/921. [2] *Agrarian Hist. Eng. and Wales* ed. J. Thirsk, v. pt. 1, pp. 396-7; A.H. Dodd, *Hist. Caern.* 34-5; J. Gwynfor Jones, *Law, Order and Govt. in Caern.* 14-15, 24-9; NLW, 9056E/889, 9057E/922, 964, 466E/905; J. Gwynfor Jones, *Wynn Fam. of Gwydir*, 65-8. [3] P. Williams, *Council in the Marches*, 237-9; Gwynfor Jones, *Wynns*, 214-17. [4] J.E. Neale, *Elizabethan House of Commons*, 93-121; Gwynfor Jones, *Wynns*, 217; NLW, 9052E/195, 197. [5] C219/34/91; 219/35/2/191; J.E. Griffith, *Peds. Anglesey and Caern. Fams.* 191; NLW, 9052E/250, 271. [6] NLW, 466E/644-5, 940; 9055E/650. [7] Llysvaen was detached from the rest of the shire on the coast of Denb., near Abergele. [8] NLW, 9055E/672, 749, 758; NLW, Wynnstay 106/88; *CSP Dom.* 1611-18, p. 336; Gwynfor Jones, *Wynns*, 89-90. [9] NLW, 9057E/915, 916; *Stuart Royal Procs.* ed. J.F. Larkin and P.L. Hughes, i. 493-5. [10] C2/Jas.I/T9/55; NLW, 9057E/916, 921, 923; NLW, Brogyntyn 399; *List of Sheriffs* comp. A. Hughes (PRO, L. and I. ix), 248; C219/37/339. [11] NLW, Brogyntyn 398-400, 402; NLW, 9057E/923, 926, 933, 466E/1000.

[12] NLW, 9057E/918; Griffith, 281, 376. [13] Derived from NLW, 9057E/921. [14] A.H. Dodd, 'Bp. Bayly', *Trans. Caern. Hist. Soc.* xxviii. 23-4; NLW, 9057E/918; Griffith, 190, 281. [15] NLW, 9057E/921, 925, 932; 466E/1000; A.D. Carr, 'Gloddaith and the Mostyns', *Trans. Caern. Hist. Soc.* xli. 48; Gwynfor Jones, *Wynns*, 88; STAC 8/31/3; Griffith, 171, 380. [16] NLW, 9057E/921, 933, 940; NLW, Brogyntyn 401. [17] NLW, 9057E/924-8, 930-3, 948. [18] NLW, 9057E/925, 932, 934. [19] C219/37/339; NLW, 9057E/940; 466E/1000. [20] NLW, 9057E/926, 933, 937; 466E/940, 1000; A.H. Dodd, 'Wales's Parliamentary Apprenticeship', *Trans Cymmrodorion Soc.* (1942), p. 42; Dodd, *Caern.* 70-1. [21] NLW, 9057E/944, 948. [22] NLW, 9057E/966, 968, 971, 975, 979, 988, 994; 9058E/1002-3, 1008, 1011, 1020; 466E/1024; C66/2245; STAC 8/31/3; *JPs in Wales and Monm.* ed. Phillips, 26. [23] NLW, 9058E/1025, 1028, 1038, 1043, 1046, 1050, 1062, 1065, 1067, 1082, 1096, 1115; 9059E/1169; Griffith, 186, 194, 281. [24] NLW, 9059E/1172 (which should be dated 2 Jan. 1624), 1189; Griffith, 77; C219/38/324. [25] NLW, 9058E/1062, 1070; 9059E/1198, 1206, 1218; 466E/1235; 9060E/1276. [26] NLW, 9060E/1311. [27] *Procs. 1625*, pp. 674-8; C219/39/275. [28] NLW, 9061E/1389; C219/40/13. [29] JOHN GRIFFITH III; *Procs. 1626*, ii. 28; iii. 3, 5, 11; UCNW, Baron Hill 3230; NLW, 9061E/1411; *CSP Dom.* 1629-31, p. 231. [30] NLW, 9061E/1412, 1422; E401/2586, p. 337; E179/224/598; E401/1386, m. 7; *CSP Dom.* 1627-8, p. 224.

S.H.

CAERNARVON BOROUGHS

Right of election: in the burgesses of Caernarvon, Conway, Criccieth, Nevin and Pwllheli

Number of voters: over 100 in 1584

14 Mar. 1604	JOHN GRIFFITH I
15 Nov. 1609	CLEMENT EDMONDES *vice* Griffith, deceased
c. Mar. 1614	NICHOLAS GRIFFITH
30 Dec. 1620	NICHOLAS GRIFFITH
21 Jan. 1624	(SIR) PETER MUTTON
29 Apr. 1625	EDWARD LITTLETON II
c. July 1625	ROBERT JONES *vice* Littleton, chose to sit for Leominster
18 Jan. 1626	EDWARD LITTLETON II
6 Mar. 1626	ROBERT JONES *vice* Littleton, chose to sit for Leominster
c. Feb. 1628	EDWARD LITTLETON II

Probably founded by the Normans in about 1090, *Caer yn Arfon* [the fort in Arfon *cantref*] quickly reverted to Welsh control until its capture by Edward

I, whose heir, the first Plantagenet prince of Wales, was born there in 1284. In the same year the Statute of Rhuddlan established the new town as the administrative centre of the principality of North Wales; hence Sir John Wynn's[†] description of the inhabitants as 'the lawyers of Caernarvon'. Afer a slow start, the town grew under the Tudors, having a population of perhaps 1,000 in 1600. Caernarvon was dominated by its castle, the constable of the latter being *ex officio* mayor of the former, while the burgesses annually elected two bailiffs from among their own number to run their internal affairs. Under Elizabeth the constabulary became a sinecure held by absentees, although several deputy constables wielded sufficient local influence to earn a seat in Parliament during the period.[1]

By the terms of the Henrician Act of Union, the franchise in each Welsh borough constituency was shared between all the chartered boroughs within the county. In the case of Caernarvonshire this included Conway and Criccieth, both fortress towns founded by Edward I, and the Welsh fishing ports of Nevin and Pwllheli, chartered by the Black Prince in 1355. Nevin and Criccieth faded into insignificance after the Glyndŵr revolt, but Conway, Pwllheli and (particularly) Caernarvon enjoyed modest economic success, importing grain and cattle from Ireland and salt from Lancashire. The only significant town excluded from the franchise was Bangor, which was never chartered by its episcopal lords.[2]

Whatever the legal definition of the franchise, surviving election indentures from the first half of the seventeenth century demonstrate a notable lack of consistency about voting rights: those for 1604, 1609, 1625 and 1626 were made in the name of the burgesses of Caernarvon alone; that for 1597 cited electors from Caernarvon, Pwllheli and Criccieth; and although the indenture of December 1620 described the electorate as 'the burgesses here [Caernarvon] and ... the burgesses of the said towns and liberties of Conway, Pwllheli, Nevin and Criccieth', it returned Nicholas Griffith as 'burgess for our said borough of Caernarvon' and received no further endorsement apart from the Caernarvon borough seal. The indenture of December 1640 was punctiliously attested by no less than 55 burgesses, including the bailiffs of all five boroughs, but this hotly contested election spawned an inquiry which only served to highlight the lack of any settled electoral custom.[3] Two of the witnesses to the Commons' investigation of 1640 noted that the contributory boroughs levied a charge for parliamentary expenses, and recalled that Clement Edmondes had accordingly received £30 in 1610. This was an unusual gesture to make towards a Member who was a stranger to the shire, and Edmondes may have been expected to return all or part of this sum to his constituents. In notifying him of his election in 1624, Sir Peter Mutton was advised by the Caernarvon corporation to 'take out a writ for the levy of the fee due for serving that place, though you mean not to take any thereof to yourself, and to bestow it towards the repair of our ruinous quay'.[4]

Under Elizabeth, the Caernarvon borough seat was dominated by the Griffith family of Plas Mawr, Caernarvon, a junior branch of the once powerful Griffiths of Penrhyn. John Griffith I, the head of the Caernarvon family, was elected in 1604. He apparently absented himself from the 1605-6 session and was dead by 15 Nov. 1609, when Clement Edmondes, recently appointed one of the clerks of the Privy Council, was returned at a by-election. Edmondes was almost certainly nominated by Lord Treasurer Salisbury (Sir Robert Cecil[†]), who was at the time attempting to build support for the Great Contract by securing the election of courtiers and government officials to every available seat. Salisbury usually canvassed borough corporations on his own initiative, but in this case he may also have approached Sir John Harington[†], constable of Caernarvon castle, who had virtually retired from public life, for support. If he did so, Harington missed the point, as the reply he wrote to the lord treasurer on the day of the by-election merely offered to surrender the constabulary in exchange for some other form of remuneration.[5] Electoral patronage at Caernarvon reverted to local hands in 1614 with the return of Nicholas Griffith, a younger son of the 1604 Member. Griffith's eldest brother William, who had served as knight of the shire in 1597, would have been a more obvious candidate, but he may have felt the borough seat to be beneath his dignity.

When another Parliament was summoned in November 1620, (Sir) Richard Wynn* considered seeking a seat at Caernarvon in the unlikely event that Sir William Maurice* should chose to stand for knight of the shire. Wynn soon diverted his energies into an unsuccessful contest for the shire seat with John Griffith III* of Llŷn, allowing Nicholas Griffith to be returned once again for the borough.[6] Unfortunately for the latter, one of the long-term consequences of the county election dispute of 1620 was that it engendered a lasting breach between the Wynns of Gwydir and the Llŷn faction, which quickly spilled over into municipal politics. In September 1622 John Griffith III was appointed constable of Caernarvon Castle, partly to enable him to strip the fortress of building materials, but also with one eye on the patronage the town's mayoralty might afford him as returning officer at parliamentary elections. At the corporation elections of the following month, Griffith, supported by the sheriff, Thomas Glynne*, clashed with the incumbent mayor, the Wynns' cousin and close ally Sir William Thomas of Coed Helen, who reluctantly relinquished his office, but spent the next year supporting the Wynns' fruitless efforts to quash the borough's charter by means of a *quo warranto*.[7]

Control of the Caernarvon corporation remained unresolved at the time of the parliamentary election of January 1624, when William Wynn* approached Sir William Thomas and William Griffith to secure the return of himself or his brother Owen. Griffith waived any claims his brother Nicholas might have to re-election, and Owen Wynn prepared to canvass at Conway, while strengthening his family's standing at Caernarvon by offering charity to the prisoners in the castle gaol. Surprisingly, there is no evidence that the Llŷn faction promoted a rival candidate, perhaps because their energies were concentrated on securing the county seat. However, the Wynns' plans were dashed by the emergence of another contender in the form of Sir Peter Mutton, chief justice of North Wales and brother-in-law to the Wynns' patron, lord keeper Williams, a connection which explains his unopposed return.[8]

At the next election in April 1625, Mutton and his fellow judge, Edward Littleton II, aspired to make a clean sweep of both the county and the borough seats. Mutton made an early approach to Sir John Wynn, who endorsed this plan largely in the hope that it would break the Llŷn men's grip upon the county seat, presumably being unaware of the plans his son William had already set in motion to secure the borough seat. Upon learning of a potential rival for the borough seat, Littleton wrote to Sir William Thomas 'to know the truth in these particulars', although, being confident of his return for Leominster, he was able to assure his supporter that 'if the electors find one more worthy, or that they more affect than myself (as they may easily do), their refusal shall not break myself'. Thomas relayed this letter to Sir John Wynn with the observation that, if crossed in this matter, the judges could punish the boroughs by choosing to remove the assizes from Caernarvon and Conway. He also warned that, in the event of a contest with the Wynn interest, Littleton was capable of raising 'a great faction in Pwllheli, Nevin and Criccieth', largely due to the influence of his father-in-law, Justice (Sir) William Jones I*. The result of Thomas's appeal was never in doubt: three days later Wynn wrote to assure Littleton that his son William had abandoned his candidacy.[9]

Littleton's return for Leominster enabled him to resign the Caernarvon burgess-ship at the start of the 1625 session, whereupon he was replaced by his brother-in-law Robert Jones. A similar arrangement was reached in 1626, but in 1628 Littleton plumped for the Caernarvon seat, enabling Sir Thomas Littleton, 1st bt. to take his place at Leominster.[10]

[1] K. Williams-Jones, 'Caernarvon', *Bors. Medieval Wales* ed. R.A. Griffiths, 73-100; I. Soulsby, *Towns of Medieval Wales*, 88-91; J. Wynn, *Hist. Gwydir Fam.* ed. J. Gwynfor Jones, 49; L. Owen, 'Population of Wales', *Trans. Cymmrodorion Soc.* (1959), p.109; M. Gray, 'Castles and Patronage in 16th Century Wales', *WHR*, xv. 491-2. [2] *SR*, iii. 568, 935-6; Soulsby, 76-8, 110-15, 117-19, 192-4, 221-2; *Cal. Clenennau Letters* ed. T. Jones Pierce, 54, 133; E.A. Lewis, *Welsh Port Bks. 1550-1603*; E190/1330/12, 16, 190/1331/9, 190/1332/2. [3] A.H. Dodd, *Hist. Caern.* 70-4; NLW, 9062E/1677; C219/33/284, 219/34/92, 219/37/340, 219/43/3/182; *D'Ewes* ed. W. Notestein, 455-6, 475-6. [4] *D'Ewes* ed. Notestein, 456; Flints. RO, D/GW 2128. [5] NLW, Clennenau 213; *CSP Dom.* 1603-10, pp. 535, 560. [6] NLW, 9057E/916. [7] NLW, 9058E/1033-4, 1037, 1041, 1043, 1068, 1112; J.E. Griffith, *Peds. Anglesey and Caern. Fams.* 125, 202, 280-1; *Trans. Caern. Hist. Soc.* xlviii. 11-13. [8] NLW, 9059E/1172 (should be dated 2 Jan. 1624), 1176, 1189; Flint. RO, D/GW 2128. [9] *Procs. 1625*, pp. 672-3, 684, 686; Griffith, 191; NLW, 9060E/1329. [10] *Procs. 1625*, p. 205; *Procs. 1626*, ii. 60; *CD 1628*, ii. 144.

S.H.

CARDIGANSHIRE

c. Mar. 1604	JOHN LEWIS
c. Mar. 1614	SIR RICHARD PRICE
3 Jan. 1621	SIR RICHARD PRICE
28 Jan. 1624	JAMES LEWIS
20 Apr. 1625	JAMES LEWIS
c. Jan. 1626	JAMES LEWIS
20 Feb. 1628	JAMES LEWIS

Cardiganshire, a 'proto-county' under royal control from the 1240s, was given formal status by the Statute of Rhuddlan in 1284.[1] Its boundaries largely followed the native territory of Ceredigion, but it was somewhat enlarged by the Henrician Acts of Union. Most commentators concurred that it was sparsely populated and difficult to farm: with forbidding uplands in the north and east and open pasture to the south and west, the local economy was dominated by cattle farming. It had significant mineral and metallurgical reserves, however, and Richard Gough believed that the county's wealth 'lies in its mines and scarce shows itself above ground'.[2]

This sparse economy did not support a prosperous gentry class. Parliamentary representation under the early Stuarts, as in the Elizabethan era, was dominated by the Prices of Gogerddan, and families connected to them by marriage and kinship.[3] The leading county magnate was Sir Richard Price, deputy lieutenant, *custos rotulorum* and county representative in four Elizabethan Parliaments. Barred from standing in 1604 as the serving sheriff, he returned his son-in-law, John Lewis of Abernantbychan. The normal pattern of representation was resumed in 1614 and 1621, when Price was elected. After Price's death in 1623, the Gogerddan estate went to his grandson (Sir) Richard Price[†], then under-age. In this situation there were few candidates outside the Price-Lewis axis who could step into the breach. As a result, in 1624 and for the remainder of the decade the county seat went to another of Price's grandsons, James Lewis. It is unclear why the latter's father, John Lewis, did not sit again.[4]

Cardiganshire's Members had little known concern with advancing local business in Parliament, but it is likely that there was an interest in the 1621 initiative to prevent the importation of Irish cattle, which was seen as damaging to the local economy.[5]

[1] J.G. Edwards, 'The Early Hist. of the Cos. of Carm. and Card', *EHR*, xxxi. 90-8. [2] R. Gough, *Addits. to Camden's Brittania* (1789), 526. [3] W.O. Williams, *Ceredigion*, vi. 142. [4] C219/38/316. [5] L. Bowen, *Pols. of the Principality*, 68-9.

L.B.

CARDIGAN BOROUGHS

Right of election: in the freemen of Cardigan, Aberystwyth, Tregaron, Talsarn, Lampeter, Trerhedyn (Adpar) and Llanddewibrefi

c. Mar. 1604	WILLIAM BRADSHAW, alderman
	RICHARD DELABERE
	Double return. Bradshaw seated, 13 Apr. 1604
c. Mar. 1614	ROBERT WOLVERSTON
23 Dec. 1620	WALTER OVERBURY
26 Jan. 1624	ROWLAND PUGH
2 May 1625	ROWLAND PUGH
c. Jan. 1626	WALTER OVERBURY
18 Feb. 1628	JOHN VAUGHAN

Cardigan was founded as a Norman military centre, occupying a strategic position on the banks of the Teifi where the river flows into the Irish Sea. In the 1240s and 1250s, following a turbulent period when the borough became a battleground between Welsh and English interests, it acquired a wall and an impressive castle. In 1279 Edward I made Cardigan the political and administrative capital of Ceredigion, and gave it a charter of incorporation in 1284 modelled on that of Carmarthen.[1] Thereafter, until 1527, the borough received several charters of confirmation. Municipal government was vested in the hands of a mayor and two bailiffs, who were chosen from a common council of burgesses.[2]

Cardigan did not flourish in the later medieval period, however, as Aberystwyth increasingly usurped its trading and administrative functions. Although the Acts of Union had constituted Cardigan the county town, a private act of 1553 allowed for the county court to be shared in rotation with Aberystwyth.[3] This complicating factor at elections was compounded by the fact that, as in many of the Welsh borough constituencies, a number of small contributory boroughs could claim an interest.[4] All of these towns, including Cardigan itself, were small and many were decaying, allowing neighbouring gentry a considerable influence over a fragile corporate system.[5] In 1547 both Cardigan and Aberystwyth had tried to return their own candidates without reference to any other contributory boroughs.[6] Difficulties surfaced again in 1601, when there was a double return. At Aberystwyth one 'Dr. Awbrey' was elected, apparently at the instigation of a partial sheriff, whose voters acted independently of the other boroughs. This prompted Cardigan to elect Richard Delabere* without any warrant from the sheriff.[7]

This rivalry between the two principal boroughs, coupled with the behaviour of another partisan sheriff, was at the heart of fresh confusion in 1604, when the two rival boroughs returned Members for the single constituency. The sheriff, the county's leading magnate and regular shire Member, Sir Richard Price of Gogerddan, issued his precept to the mayor of Cardigan, Richard Mortimer, a man supposedly 'devoted' to Price.[8] The town elected one of their aldermen, William Bradshaw, whose residence at St. Dogmaels, Pembrokeshire, just across the Teifi from Cardigan, allowed him scope for influence in the borough's affairs. However, as later reported in the Commons, Price, 'minding to make choice of a friend of his', then held a second election at Aberystwyth using electors 'unduly procured' by him, as a result of which Richard Delabere, attorney-general of south-west Wales and Cardigan's choice in 1601, was awarded the seat. The Commons debated both returns on 13 Apr. 1604, and decided to admit Bradshaw and order Price's arrest for partiality.[9] What happened to Price after he was thus censured, or what he said in his own defence, is unknown.

Aside from being determined to elect a 'friend', Price, in holding a rival election at Aberystwyth, may have been trying to extend his influence over the disparate constituency. Aberystwyth, where he held at least 35 acres, was close to his home of Gogerddan, and much more amenable to his influence than Cardigan which lay at the opposite end of the shire.[10] A Star Chamber case of 1599 seems to support this hypothesis, as Price was then accused of using his local influence to remove the apparatus of county administration from Cardigan to Llanbadarn Fawr, a small settlement in the precincts of Aberystwyth, by building a new shire hall and transferring the county armoury.[11]

Whatever Price's motives may have been, Bradshaw's election apparently left a legacy of ill-feeling: in 1607 he brought an Exchequer suit against the shire town and contributory boroughs, including Aberystwyth, claiming that his 'fees and wages' as Member were being withheld. Cardigan was said to owe him £14; Aberystwyth, £10; Tregaron, £3; Lampeter: £3 10s.; Talsarn, 30s.; and Trerhedyn, 20s.[12] It is possible that Price, sore at having been thwarted in 1604, was behind this stratagem. Bradshaw's bill was frustrated, as the boroughs successfully claimed that the matter was determinable at Common Law rather than in a court of equity.[13] Bradshaw naturally appealed against this verdict, and the case was still being heard as late as 1611. Interestingly, counsel for the contributory boroughs was one 'Mr. Delabere', undoubtedly Richard Delabere, the defeated candidate in 1604.[14] The case was eventually adjourned, and it seems unlikely Bradshaw was ever paid.

Perhaps because of the problems encountered in 1604, the contributory boroughs were explicitly invited to participate in later elections. At the election of December 1620 the mayor of Cardigan claimed that he had 'sent sufficient notice to all boroughs within the said county to be at Cardigan'.[15] The 1625 return states that 'open notice and public proclamation' had been given in respect of the forthcoming election 'upon a market day', while the indenture for the 1628 election mentions 'all others claiming voice and interest therein'.[16] It is difficult to know, however, how many burgesses from the contributory boroughs actually met at the county court in Cardigan or Aberystwyth to give their voices. The contracting parties for the most part were Cardigan burgesses, and it would seem that few, if any, burgesses from the smaller boroughs exercised their right to vote; certainly none indicated that they were such on the election indentures.

Despite this preponderance of Cardigan electors in the 1620s, the constituency chose Members who reflected the political interests of the greater gentry rather than local townsmen. Richard Delabere, the Price candidate in 1604, certainly fitted this profile. The 1614 Member, Robert Wolverston, was a minor courtier, while Walter Overbury, elected in 1621 and 1626, probably obtained his seat through his father, (Sir) Nicholas*, chief justice of south Wales and, like Sir Richard Price, a member of the Council in the Marches. Rowland Pugh of Montgomeryshire, who sat in 1624 and 1625, was a landed gentleman who enjoyed good relations with the heirs to the Gogerddan mantle, the Lewises of Abernantbychan. His return on a blank indenture in 1625 strengthens the argument that elections were orchestrated by a gentry oligarchy rather than by the boroughs themselves. John Vaughan of Trawsgoed, who obtained the place in 1628, possessed the advantages of a local landed estate and a family which was on good terms with the Abernantbychan interest. There is no evidence that any of the Members pursued local business within Parliament.

[1] R.A. Griffiths, 'The Making of Medieval Cardigan', *Ceredigion*, xi. 97-124. [2] S.R. Meyrick, *Hist. and Antiqs. of Co. of Cardigan*, 162-7. [3] HLRO, O.A. 1 Mary St 2, c.23; L. Bowen, 'Wales at Westminster ... 1542-1601', *PH*, xxii. 111-12. [4] P.S. Edwards, 'The Parlty. Representation of the Welsh Bors. in the mid-Sixteenth Cent.', *Bull. Bd. Celtic Studs*. xxvii. 428-9. [5] N.M. Powell, 'Do Numbers Count?', *Urban Hist*. xxxii. 50. [6] P.S. Edwards, 'The Mysterious Parlty. Election at Cardigan Bors. in 1547', *WHR*, viii. 172-87. [7] *Procs. in Parls. of Eliz. I* ed. T.E. Hartley, iii. 323. [8] STAC 5/L2/10. [9] *CJ*, i. 170a-b. [10] E112/145/42. [11] STAC 5/L2/10; 5/L9/26. [12] E112/151/29. [13] The mayor of Cardigan claimed that his town had levied the money, and it was the out-boroughs which were in default. [13] E124/5, f. 45. [14] E124/13, f. 8. [15] C219/37/346. [16] C219/39/274; C219/41B/9.

L.B.

CARMARTHENSHIRE

Number of voters: over 160 in 1545.[1]

15 Mar. 1604	SIR ROBERT MANSELL
c. Mar. 1614	SIR ROBERT MANSELL
28 Dec. 1620	SIR JOHN VAUGHAN
22 Jan. 1624	RICHARD VAUGHAN I
12 May 1625	RICHARD VAUGHAN I
19 Jan. 1626	RICHARD VAUGHAN I
14 Feb. 1628	RICHARD VAUGHAN I

Carmarthenshire antedated the Statute of Rhuddlan (1284) and historically was the area subject to the control of the royal castle at Carmarthen. The union legislation of 1536 added seven outlying lordships to the existing county, but omitted districts immediately west of the town of Carmarthen, which were annexed to Pembrokeshire. This anomalous situation was addressed by statute in 1543, when Llanstephan, Ystlwyf and Laugharne were amalgamated as the new Carmarthenshire hundred of Derllys.[2] The county thus became the largest of the Welsh shires, covering a diverse natural environment from the lowland plain of the Towy to the upland pastures of the north and east. Butter, cheese and cloth-making were mainstays of the local economy,[3] but contemporary commentators also noted the county's 'fruitful' soils: even in the upland margins, rye, oats and wheat were cultivated, supporting one of the largest populations of any Welsh shire.[4] A net exporter of grain, Carmarthenshire, even in the famine years of 1629-31, produced a surplus which was used to alleviate shortfalls in Ireland and the West Country.[5] In addition, the south-east of the county, especially the area around Llanelli, had easily accessible coal deposits which had been worked for many decades.[6]

The site of the Carmarthenshire election was not specified by the statute of enfranchisement, but hustings were held at Carmarthen regularly in the sixteenth century, and the elections of 1624, 1625 and 1626 took place at the town's guildhall.[7] In 1621, however, the election was held in the town of Llandeilofawr, in the north-west of the county, while in 1628 it took place at Pontargothi, four miles east of Carmarthen.[8] There does not appear to have been any political motive behind this perambulation, which was also a feature of elections in later years, but the 1628

site was equidistant from Carmarthen and Golden Grove and so may have been conveniently located for the Vaughan family to select one of their number.[9]

In the Elizabethan period the Jones family of Abermarlais had dominated the county's parliamentary representation, but the death of Sir Thomas Jones† in 1604 ended their influence. After a brief interlude their place was taken by the Vaughans of Golden Grove. The *paterfamilias*, Sir John, had won the county seat in 1601, but did not seek the place in the next two elections, perhaps because he desired to maintain a low profile after being implicated in the Essex revolt. This allowed the shire to accommodate the naval official Sir Robert Mansell in 1604 and 1614, a Glamorganshire native who only acquired an estate at Laugharne in south-western Carmarthenshire in 1615.[10] Mansell had influential kinsmen within the county including his brother-in-law, Sir Walter Rice* of Newton, who endorsed the 1604 election indenture, and he was presumably on good terms with Rice's nephew, Sir John Vaughan.[11]

Mansell subsequently transferred his electoral interests to Glamorgan, and following his departure, the Vaughans of Golden Grove dominated Carmarthenshire's representation for the remainder of the period. Sir John Vaughan was returned in 1621 with the support of his brothers Henry Vaughan of Derwydd – who was returned for the borough seat – and Walter Vaughan of Llanelli. The endorsement of Sir Henry Jones, head of the Abermarlais clan, testifies to the wide support he enjoyed among the leading gentry of Carmarthenshire.[12] Vaughan's elevation to an Irish peerage in July 1621 raised questions about his eligibility to sit in the Commons, a controversy which may explain why he did not sit again. His heir, Richard, served as knight of the shire in the remaining parliaments of the 1620s.

---

[1] In 1545, the elected Member possessed a majority of 80. [2] *Carm. County Hist.* ed. J.E. Lloyd, i. 12-13, 207, 264; R.A. Griffiths, *Principality of Wales in Later Middle Ages*, i. 6-7, 14-17; *SR*, iii. 936. [3] H.A. Lloyd, *The Gentry of S.W. Wales, 1540-1640*, pp. 71-2; R.I. Jack, 'Cloth Manufacture in the Medieval Lordship of Kidwelly', *Carm. Antiquary*, xix. 9-15. [4] *Carm.* ii. 276, 290, 313-15; *Progs. of 1st Duke of Beaufort Through Wales* ed. T. Dinley, 172; *Agrarian Hist. Eng. and Wales* ed. J. Thirsk, iv. 121, 143. [5] *Carm.* ii. 282; *APC*, 1629, pp. 410-11; 1630-1, pp. 126-7; SP16/175/119. [6] M.V. Symons, *Coal Mining in Llanelli Area*, i. 26-35. [7] C219/38/314v; 219/39/269; 219/40/10. [8] C219/37/342; 219/41B/12. [9] *HP Commons, 1660-90*, i. 510 [10] S. Thomas, 'Descent of the Lordships of Laugharne and Eglwyscummin', *Carm. Antiquary*, vi. 41-3. [11] C219/35/2/188. [12] C219/37/342.

L.B./S.H.

CARMARTHEN BOROUGHS

Right of election: in the freemen of Carmarthen, Laugharne, Llandovery, St. Clears, Llandeilo Fawr, Llanelli, Newcastle Emlyn, Newton and Dryslwyn (to 1604); freemen of Carmarthen (aft. 1604)

Number of voters: at least 128 in 1659[1]

5 Mar. 1604	SIR WALTER RICE
c. Mar. 1614[2]	WILLIAM THOMAS, recorder
8 Jan. 1621	HENRY VAUGHAN
2 Feb. 1624	HENRY VAUGHAN
24 Apr. 1625	HENRY VAUGHAN
12 May 1625	SIR FRANCIS ANNESLEY Double return
30 Jan. 1626	HENRY VAUGHAN
25 Feb. 1628	HENRY VAUGHAN

Carmarthen was founded by the Romans and reoccupied by the Normans, who built a castle to secure their dominion over the Welsh. The borough served as the administrative centre of the principality of South Wales down to the Stuart period.[3] The town enjoyed good trading links, both by land and via the navigable River Tywi (Towy): it was the staple port for Welsh wool from 1353, and in return for the wool and cloth shipped to Bristol and the Continent, French wine was imported.[4] In the reign of James I the Tywi was described as 'sore pestered with sands and shelfs,' but as neighbouring ports such as Laugharne and Kidwelly were experiencing similar difficulties, Carmarthen's economy suffered little dislocation.[5] Carmarthen's trading links made it the largest town in Wales, with a population in the early seventeenth century in excess of 2,000; in 1602 the antiquary, George Owen, described the borough as 'fair and good in estate.'[6]

The borough of Carmarthen received its first royal charter in the mid-thirteenth century, which confirmed existing customs.[7] The early Stuart town was governed under a charter of 1546, which incorporated a mayor and 20 burgesses, who elected a mayor and two bailiffs annually, and appointed a recorder, town clerk and sword-bearer. The rights of the town's other resident burgesses provoked 'popular strife and controversies' under Elizabeth and James.[8] The 1546 charter recognized Carmarthen's status in South Wales and was adopted as a model by other

towns such as Cardigan.[9] Under the Henrician Acts of Union, Carmarthen became the site for the county's Great Sessions courts.[10] As the county town it was also enfranchised, together with representatives from eight other 'ancient boroughs' who attended elections at Carmarthen's guildhall. By 1604 all of these contributory boroughs were in decline.[11] The largest, Kidwelly, suffered from the silting up of the Gwendraeth: in 1615 its inhabitants lamented that 'there is neither shipping nor trade to maintain the town', and over 140 burgages lay deserted.[12] The borough paid nearly £80 for a new charter in 1619, but continued to be overshadowed by Carmarthen.[13]

The contributory boroughs seem to have played little part in parliamentary elections, even though the indentures for 1589 and 1604 listed their names. Ostensibly made out in the name of the burgesses of 'all the boroughs of the county', the 1604 indenture was actually signed only by the local magnate Sir John Vaughan*, and by the mayor and bailiffs of Carmarthen.[14] The Member returned, Sir Walter Rice, had represented the borough in 1601 and headed a once-mighty family which had been weakened by a series of attainders under the Tudors. His election was doubtless assisted by the fact that the mayor of Carmarthen was his nephew.

The electoral politics of Carmarthen were fundamentally changed by the grant of a new borough charter on 14 June 1604. Obtained with Vaughan's assistance, this conferred county status on the borough, and created two sheriffs in place of the bailiffs.[15] From this point onwards, it would seem that Carmarthen enjoyed the same position as the other Welsh county borough – Haverfordwest – in returning Members without any reference to the contributory boroughs, in effect disenfranchising them through a royal grant. The endorsement of the writ of summons for the 1621 election does refer to the other boroughs of the county, but this was probably only because the confused election of 1614 brought the matter into question; the returns of 1625 and 1626 omit any such reference.[16] Carmarthen's control of parliamentary elections is confirmed by a comparison of those endorsing the election returns in the 1620s with the town's 1625 subsidy roll: most witnesses can be identified as borough residents, with a high proportion of aldermen in evidence.[17] The political significance of this administrative change was, however, modest: leading gentry families, particularly the Vaughans, had considerable influence in the contributory boroughs, but continued to control nominations at Carmarthen after 1604. The corporation's primary motive may simply have been to raise the borough's prestige.

The new charter apparently contributed to the confusion in 1614, when William Thomas, the town's recorder, was elected. On 12 Apr. the Cardiff Member Mathew Davys complained that Carmarthenshire's sheriff, Rees Williams of Edwinsford, had failed to forward Thomas's return on the grounds that the new charter removed Carmarthen from the jurisdiction of the surrounding county, which thus no longer contained a 'shire town' from which a burgess could be elected as required by law.[18] It is possible that sheriff Williams aimed to frustrate Thomas's election, but Davys seems to have intended to rectify the procedural anomaly without casting blame. The problem was circumvented at the next election, when an endorsement on the writ of summons scrupulously identified the borough as being 'called the shire town of the county of Carmarthen.'[19]

Throughout the 1620s, the town returned Henry Vaughan of Derwydd, head of a cadet branch of the Vaughans of Golden Grove. Vaughan was a member of the common council and served as mayor in 1623-4, which should, perhaps, have disabled him from election. However, no investigation appears to have been undertaken, either because the Commons was unaware of his status or because the town's sheriffs had acted as returning officers since 1614.[20] There was only one electoral contest in this period: on 24 Apr. 1625 Henry Vaughan was returned for the third time in succession, while on 12 May a separate indenture was made out in favour of Sir Francis Annesley, principal secretary in Ireland. It is difficult to uncover the circumstances behind this double return. On the face of it the electors appear to have been divided, as Vaughan was returned, as was customary, by the borough's sheriffs, whereas Annesley was returned by the mayor. However, Henry Vaughan actually endorsed Annesley's indenture.[21] This second return was presumably arranged by Annesley's father-in-law, John Philipps of Picton Castle, Pembrokeshire, who endorsed the return even though he was not a resident burgess and never signed any other indentures for Carmarthen. This device placed the onus of resolving the matter upon Parliament: upon receipt of Annesley's indenture, Vaughan's name was crossed off the Crown Office list, but the case remained undecided at the dissolution.[22]

[1] *CJ*, vii. 617a, 620b. [2] C219/330/31. [3] R.A. Griffiths, 'Carmarthen', in *Medieval Bor. Wales* ed. R.A. Griffiths, 132-52. [4] Ibid. 152-3; *Welsh Port Bks.* ed. E.A. Lewis (Cymmrodorion Rec. Ser. xii), pp. xix-xx. [5] T.H. Lewis, 'Carm. Under the Tudors', *W. Wales Hist. Recs.* viii. 5; DL44/983; NLW, Duchy of Cornw. CS3. [6] G. Williams,

'Carm. and the Reformation', in *Carm. Studies* ed. T. Barnes and N. Yates, 137. [7] Griffiths, 131; Hatfield House, (BL, microfilm 485) ms 93/88. [8] *Letters and Pprs. Hen. VIII*, xxi. pt. 1, p.484; STAC 5/P33/19; 5/P25/4; 5/P52/37; STAC 8/20/14; *Carmarthen Bk. of Ordinances* ed. J. Davies, 8, 30-1, 47-8. [9] NLW, Noyadd Trefawr 1663. [10] STAC 9/2/5, f. 2v; NLW, Derwydd 251. [11] *Hist. Carm.* ed. J.E. Lloyd, ii. 8-16; *HP Commons 1558-1603*, i. 313. [12] DL44/983, f. 10v; *Survey Duchy of Lancaster Lordships* ed. W. Rees (Univ. Wales, Bd. of Celtic Studs., Hist. and Law ser. xii), 178. [13] NLW, 12367E, p. 224; D.D. Jones, *Hist. Kidwelly*, 131-56. [14] C219/35/189. [15] C66/1645/17. [16] C219/37/343v; 219/39/267, 270; 219/40/9. [17] E179/220/120; C219/39/267; 219/40/9; 219/41B/11. [18] *Procs. 1614 (Commons)*, 59. [19] C219/37/343v. The phrase was also included in Annesley's 1625 return: 219/39/270. [20] Carm. RO, Mus. 155, ff. 38, 43, 58; Mus. 611; E179/220/120. [21] C219/39/270. [22] C193/32/16, f. 13v.

L.B./S.H.

DENBIGHSHIRE

Number of voters: unknown

c.14 Mar. 1604	PETER MUTTON
c. Mar. 1614	SIMON THELWALL
	Henry Salusbury
27 Dec. 1620	SIR JOHN TREVOR II
21 Jan. 1624	SIR EUBULE THELWALL
	?Sir John Trevor II
11 May 1625	SIR THOMAS MYDDELTON II
	Sir Eubule Thelwall
18 Jan. 1626	SIR EUBULE THELWALL
13 Feb. 1628	SIR EUBULE THELWALL

Denbighshire was created by the 1536 Act of Union, which amalgamated those of the Marcher lordships of North Wales that had not already been assigned to existing shires. However, the lordship of Mold and the parishes of Hawarden and St. Asaph were surrendered to Flintshire only five years later.[1] Administrative fiat thus joined a number of disparate regions: the uplands of Rhos and Rhufoniog in the west; the vale of Clwyd in the north-west; mountainous Yale in the centre and Chirkland in the south; and the lowlands of Bromfield in the east. All except the last were upland areas with livestock-based economies: sheep provided wool for the Welsh cloth marketed at Oswestry, and cattle were sold at fairs at Denbigh, Ruthin, Wrexham and Holt to provide leather for Chester and meat for London and the south-east of England. The division of the county by a central range of mountains had a significant impact on local society: quarter sessions, assizes and parliamentary elections were held alternately on either side of the county at Denbigh and Wrexham, and political differences sometimes reflected the geographical split.

Since the conquest of 1282, the lordships of Denbighshire had been held by the Crown and absentee magnates. Under Elizabeth the most influential of these was Robert Dudley[†], earl of Leicester, whose vigorous assertion of his feudal rights in the lordships of Denbigh and Chirk created trouble for his local allies, the Salusburys of Lleweni, and frustrated their attempt to secure the return of William Almer[†] as knight of the shire in 1588. A decade of tension followed, which came to a head at the general election of October 1601, when the rival factions backed Sir John Salusbury[†] and Sir Richard Trevor[†], a client of lord treasurer Buckhurst (Thomas Sackville[†]), for the county seat. Mutual insults degenerated into swordplay in Wrexham churchyard, and the sheriff, fearing a riot, abandoned the county court; Salusbury was eventually returned at an election held just before the end of the Parliament.[2] The protagonists of 1601 apparently fought shy of a fresh contest at the general election of 1604, which saw the return of Peter Mutton of Lleweni, a rising Flintshire lawyer who had inherited a 1,600-acre Denbighshire estate from an uncle in 1601. This was not a particularly large holding by local standards, and he clearly owed his seat to the support of his neighbours, the Salusburys.[3]

By the 1614 election many of the key players of 1601 were dead, including Sir John Salusbury, Edward Thelwall of Plas y Ward, Sir John Lloyd[†] of Bodidris and Capt. John Salesbury of Bachymbyd. The heirs of the first two men, Harry Salusbury and Simon Thelwall, contested the shire seat, probably more for reasons of social rivalry than political preferment. The Thelwalls had supported Sir John Salusbury in 1601, and factional alignments within the county underwent some adjustment in the changed circumstances of 1614: Sir Richard Trevor now backed his old rival's son, whereas his son-in-law Evan Lloyd of Bodidris, whose father had been one of Sir John Salusbury's opponents, backed Thelwall, his second cousin. William Salesbury* of Bachymbyd and Sir John Wynn[†] of Gwydir, Caernarvonshire probably promised their voices to Thelwall, a close relative, which left only the Myddeltons of Chirk Castle uncommitted. Andrew Brereton, steward of the Chirk estate, who was related to the Salusburys, assured Sir Thomas Myddelton II* that 'if it come to election there will be hard tongueing, but it is thought Mr. Salusbury will carry it away'. In the event, Thelwall was returned, which suggests that the Myddeltons either supported him or remained aloof from the contest.[4]

Sir Richard Trevor may have backed Salusbury in 1614 on the understanding that the favour would be reciprocated at the next election. His was undoubtedly the decisive influence in the return of his nephew Sir John Trevor II in December 1620, as the latter's main estates lay in Flintshire and Surrey. The election was apparently uncontested, and there was clearly no challenge from Thelwall, whose name headed the list of signatures on the indenture.[5] Trevor may have hoped for re-election three years later, but if so, he was to be disappointed; he ultimately secured a seat at the Flintshire by-election of December 1624. The knighthood of Denbighshire went to Sir Eubule Thelwall, a master in Chancery, who required a seat to defend recent increases in Chancery fees, for which offence he had been attacked by the Commons in 1621. He may have requested a letter of nomination from his departmental chief, lord keeper Williams, an active parliamentary patron in North Wales, but his election clearly owed most to the efforts of his immediate relatives: the return was signed by three of his brothers, a nephew and his more distant cousin Simon Thelwall of Plas y Ward.[6]

The summons of a fresh Parliament in 1625 brought forth an unprecedented number of candidates. Doubtless anticipating that Thelwall would stand again, Sir Thomas Myddelton II appealed to Gwydir for support on 6 Apr., only to find that Wynn had already promised his interest to Sir Thomas Wynne of Melai, then serving as a soldier in the Low Countries. Sir John Wynn excused himself to Myddelton with the explanation that he had undertaken to support his 'cousin' of Melai in the aftermath of the 1624 election, 'else I can assure you there is not anyone within the county of Denbigh that I would more freely and willingly bestow the same [upon] than on yourself'. A week later, Sir Roger Mostyn* approached Wynn (his father-in-law) with a proposal from Williams to nominate (Sir) Peter Mutton for the Denbighshire seat, but the latter, who was presumably aware that he would face at least three challengers, preferred to try his chances against the Cefnamwlch interest in Caernarvonshire.[7]

All three candidates canvassed the freeholders vigorously, but, as one of Myddelton's supporters observed, the impact of their efforts was impossible to predict, as 'many of the freeholders will stay at home for fear of displeasing any man which makes of our part'. Faced with this prospect, Myddelton sent his neighbour Robert Wynn of Maes Mochnant (Sir John Wynn's younger brother) to Melai at the end of April to seek the support of the Wynnes against Thelwall. Sir Thomas Wynne's nephew John revealed that he had already been approached by Sir Eubule's nephew John Thelwall of Plas Einion with a request 'to slacken in the business', and made a tentative offer of support for Myddelton if the latter would allow Sir Thomas Wynne to come in for his borough seat at Weymouth and Melcombe Regis. The deal was quickly agreed, and it was apparently also arranged that the freeholders of Melai and Gwydir would still be encouraged to turn out for Wynne rather than Myddelton, so as to maximise the numbers present on the day of the election. Robert Wynn confidently believed that 'the Thelwalls when all comes to all will not stand for the election', and claimed that Simon Thelwall had already abandoned all hope of victory and left for London. Myddelton's plan worked perfectly: on the day of the election, Sir Eubule found himself hopelessly outnumbered, and conceded the election without a fight after Myddelton promised to recommend him for the Weymouth seat, which was no longer reserved for Sir Thomas Wynne, who had been killed in action on 2/12 May.[8]

Myddelton proved unable to honour his promise to Thelwall, as a local man, Giles Greene, was returned at Weymouth, but this failure may have persuaded him to allow Sir Eubule Thelwall a clear run in Denbighshire at the general elections of 1626 and 1628. The indenture for 1626, which was signed by William Salesbury of Bachymbyd, Simon and Edward Thelwall of Plas y Ward, John Thelwall of Bathafarn Park, John Lloyd of Bodidris and Richard Thelwall of Llanbedr, points to the continuity of at least one of the county's electoral factions throughout the period.[9]

[1] SR, iii. 568, 849; G. Williams, Recovery, Reorientation and Reformation: Wales c.1415-1642, pp. 268-9. [2] Cal. Salusbury Corresp. ed. W.J. Smith (Bd. of Celtic Studs., Univ. Wales Hist. and Law ser. xiv), 7-9; A.H. Dodd, 'N. Wales in the Essex Revolt of 1601', EHR, lix. 348-70; APC, 1601-4, pp. 342-3, 379; STAC 5/T15/33. [3] C142/592/81. [4] NLW, Chirk F.10751; J.E. Griffith, Peds. Anglesey and Caerns. Fams. 7, 59, 222, 274, 280-2; Glynde Place Archives ed. R.F. Dell (Trevor fam. ped.). [5] C219/37/348. [6] C219/38/319; Griffith, 274, 369; SIR EUBULE THELWALL. [7] Procs. 1625, pp. 682, 684; Griffith, 376. [8] NLW, Chirk F.12837; NLW Jnl. x. 37; NLW, 9060E/1340; Wentworth Pprs. ed. J.P. Cooper (Cam. Soc. ser. 4. xii), 235. [9] C219/40/1/17.

S.H.

DENBIGH BOROUGHS

Right of election: in the burgesses of Denbigh, Ruthin, Holt and Chirk

Number of voters: 13-17 or more

c.14 Mar. 1604	HUGH MYDDELTON, recorder of Ruthin
c.Mar. 1614	HUGH MYDDELTON
27 Dec. 1620	HUGH MYDDELTON, recorder of Denbigh
21 Jan. 1624	(SIR) HUGH MYDDELTON, bt., recorder
c.11 May 1625	(SIR) HUGH MYDDELTON, bt., recorder
c.18 Jan. 1626	(SIR) HUGH MYDDELTON, bt., recorder
13 Feb. 1628	(SIR) HUGH MYDDELTON, bt., recorder

The four contributory towns of the Denbigh Boroughs seat were all founded in the aftermath of the conquest of 1282 and prospered to varying degrees as centres of clothmaking and tanning. The boroughs gradually declined under the Tudors with the movement of the cloth industry into the countryside and the shift of the staple for Welsh cloth to Oswestry. By James's accession Chirk and Holt had shrunk to insignificance; Denbigh and Ruthin retained small leather and cloth finishing industries, but were eclipsed by the unchartered town of Wrexham, which by the 1620s contained almost as many subsidymen as the four contributory boroughs combined.[1]

Under the 1536 Act of Union, all four of the ancient boroughs of Denbighshire were understood to contribute to both the election and the expenses of the single Member returned to Parliament. In practice, the elections, which alternated between Denbigh and Wrexham, seem to have been dominated by the Denbigh corporation. The surviving returns for 1620, 1624 and 1628 describe the attestors as 'burgesses of the borough called the shire town', and of the 28 individuals named in these indentures, 16 can be identified from subsidy rolls as residents of Denbigh, one was from the neighbouring parish of Henllan, and the others remain unidentified.[2] Until 1588 the lordships of Denbigh and Chirk were held by Robert Dudley†, earl of Leicester, but thereafter electoral patronage reverted to local interests. The last two Elizabethan parliaments saw the election of the recorder of Denbigh, John Panton*, a London lawyer and servant of lord keeper Sir Thomas Egerton†. He only represented the borough in a notional sense in 1601, as he was returned a mere three days before the end of the parliamentary session, the original election having been abandoned following a brawl between rival candidates for the knighthood of the shire.[3]

The uproar in 1601 may have encouraged Panton to seek a seat elsewhere in 1604. His place was taken by another Londoner with local connections, Hugh Myddelton, whose brother Charles was governor of Denbigh castle. Myddelton was appointed to the Denbigh corporation under the 1597 charter and secured the recordership of Ruthin in February 1604, a post he may have obtained with the specific intention of enhancing his prospects, as he swiftly relinquished it to (Sir) Eubule Thelwall* after the election. His regular promotion of the interests of the Denbigh corporation apparently secured him the borough's recordership after Panton's death, and he was returned for the parliamentary seat at every subsequent election until his own death in 1631.[4]

[1] I. Soulsby, *Towns of Medieval Wales*, 121-3, 144-7, 232-4, 269-71; D.H. Owen, 'Denbigh' and R.I. Jack, 'Ruthin', *Bors. Medieval Wales* ed. A. Griffiths, 165-88, 245-62; T.C. Mendenhall, *Shrewsbury Drapers and Welsh Wool Trade*, 1-14; E179/220/193-5, 198; 179/221/202-3. [2] *SR*, iii. 568, 935-6; C219/37/349; 219/38/320; 219/41B/17; E179/220/193-5, 198; 179/221/202-3. [3] STAC 5/T15/33. [4] J. Williams, *Recs. Denbigh Lordship*, 76, 128; E315/310, ff. 22, 24; HUGH MYDDELTON.

S.H.

FLINTSHIRE

Number of voters: unknown

27 Feb. 1604	ROGER PULESTON
c. Mar. 1614	ROBERT RAVENSCROFT
c.11 Dec. 1620	SIR ROGER MOSTYN
2 Feb. 1624	SIR JOHN HANMER, bt. ?Sir Thomas Mostyn
6 Dec. 1624	SIR JOHN TREVOR II *vice* Hanmer, deceased
28 Apr. 1625	SIR JOHN TREVOR II
1 Feb. 1626[1]	JOHN SALUSBURY Sir Thomas Hanmer†, bt.
c.25 Feb. 1628	ROBERT JONES

Founded in 1284 and enlarged in 1541, Flintshire returned a knight of the shire and a burgess to Parliament from 1542.[2] Although one of the smallest counties in Wales, it was among the least mountainous, and its population, perhaps 20,000 in 1600, was larger than that of Merioneth, Anglesey or Radnor.[3] While the shire was predominantly agricultural, coal, mined in the north of the county, was sold both locally and shipped to Ireland via Chester: Sir Roger Mostyn* valued his mines at £700 a year in 1620.[4]

In the last two Elizabethan parliaments Flintshire was represented by William Ravenscroft*, an Exchequer official whose family had considerable local influence: his eldest brother was *custos rotulorum*, and one of his aunts had been the first wife of lord keeper Sir Thomas Egerton†, whose main estates lay just across the Dee in Cheshire and Shropshire. It was doubtless at Egerton's behest that Ravenscroft was accommodated at Old Sarum in 1604 and 1614, and it is likely that the return of Ravenscroft's second cousin Roger Puleston for Flintshire in 1604, and his nephew Robert Ravenscroft in 1614, owed something to Egerton's influence.[5] Egerton died in 1617, and while his son, John Egerton†, earl of Bridgewater, helped to secure the Flintshire boroughs seat for William Ravenscroft at the general election of December 1620, he does not appear to have claimed any interest in the county seat. This therefore went to Sir Roger Mostyn, the greatest landowner in the north of the shire, who had been active in county politics for 20 years, although he only became head of his family in 1618.[6]

Never truly happy when away from north Wales, Mostyn probably only sought the knighthood of the shire to maintain his family's prestige. In early December 1623, when the next Parliament was first mooted, his eldest son Sir Thomas, then in London, was encouraged to stand for the county seat by his father-in-law (Sir) James Whitelocke* and his uncle (Sir) Richard Wynn*. However, by Christmas, when his relatives' letters of recommendation reached Flintshire, the gentry had already decided to return Sir John Hanmer. If Sir Roger Mostyn had wished, he might have been able to persuade Hanmer to stand aside, but he was determined that his eldest son should not be seduced by the delights of the capital, proclaiming 'had I been a free man to dispose of the place at my pleasure, I would have been well advised before I would have conferred the same upon my son Thomas'. The election indenture eschewed the usual reference to the 'unanimous assent and consent' of the freeholders, ascribing Hanmer's return to '*maior[em] partem totius com.*' [the greater part of the whole county], which suggests that there was a contest. However, with Mostyn bereft of any local support, Hanmer presumably carried the day with ease.[7]

Hanmer died on the penultimate day of the 1624 session. The subsequent by-election was held on 6 Dec., in anticipation of a fresh session scheduled for the New Year. It was presumably uncontested, as Sir Thomas Mostyn headed the list of those who returned Sir John Trevor II, a cousin of Hanmer's widow. In 1621 Trevor had sat for Denbighshire, where his family's main estates lay, but he was acceptable to the freeholders of Flintshire, as his father held property at Plas Têg in the south of the county.[8] King James's death dissolved the Parliament before Trevor was able to take his seat, but he was the obvious candidate at the general election called within days of Charles's accession. However, he was challenged by Sir Thomas Mostyn, who wrote to his relative Robert Davies of Gwysaney as soon as news of the election reached north Wales, asking for support for the Flintshire seat 'if you have not passed your word to another'. Mostyn presumably canvassed others, but he stood no chance of success unless Trevor released his former supporters from their obligations. Furthermore, as in the previous year, Mostyn's father was reluctant to support his cause, observing that 'to make a show to seek it [the seat] and fail were a greater disgrace than the benefit thereof would be to him that had it'. Unlike the return for the 1624 general election, that for 1625 provides no evidence of a contest, and it is likely that Sir Thomas Mostyn withdrew before the day of the election.[9]

Little is known about the background to the next election of 30 Jan. 1626, which was decided by a poll of the voters, who consisted of the supporters of John Salusbury of Bachegraig, head of the Flintshire branch of a powerful Denbighshire family, on the one side and the supporters of Sir Thomas Hanmer†, 2nd Bt., the 13-year old heir to the 1624 Member, on the other. Although the eventual contenders differed from those of 1625, the factional interests at work were largely unaltered. Hanmer was probably a last minute substitute for Sir John Trevor, who had presumably declared his intention to stand again when the Parliament was first summoned. However, whereas Trevor had easily rebuffed the earlier half-hearted challenge from the Mostyns, he now faced Salusbury, a much sterner prospect as an opponent. This was both because of lingering rivalry between the two families – arising from the Denbighshire election of 1601 – and also because Salusbury, unlike Mostyn, could call upon wider support. The Salusbury family's main estates lay in Denbighshire, but their ally Sir Peter Mutton* was a substantial Flintshire landowner, and Salusbury presumably also obtained the voices of his wife's family, the Ravenscrofts. Moreover, he would probably not have put himself forward without some indication of support from his immediate neighbours in the north of the shire, although the most important of these, the Mostyns, ultimately seem to have deserted him. While Trevor's position was not as strong as it had been in 1625, it was hardly desperate, as he could call upon the support of his Hanmer relatives, including the tenants of John Hanmer, bishop of St. Asaph, and he must have hoped to garner voices from the other major families in the south of the county. However, he was open to the criticism that his main interests lay outside the shire, an accusation which could not be brought against Hanmer, the eventual candidate. Furthermore, if Trevor's prospects looked doubtful, the last-minute substitution of a callow youth, too young to be a credible candidate for the shire seat, saved him from the personal disgrace of a defeat at Salusbury's hands.[10]

The election was clearly a disorderly affair. In what was possibly a reference to the Denbighshire election of 1601, Salusbury's supporters were alleged to have said 'that their master would have it by the sword if he could not otherwise have it'. Moreover, the sheriff, Thomas Evans, was reported to have excluded many freeholders (presumably Hanmer supporters) and boasted 'that how many soever here, yet is the election in my power. I may choose whom I will'. Despite Evans's partiality, the contest went to a poll, following which Salusbury was returned on 1 February.

Sir Roger Mostyn was soon reported to be considering a protest, and Hanmer's supporters ultimately complained to the committee for privileges. On 5 May 1626 William Coryton* reported the petition, and the House summoned Evans to explain his conduct, but his testimony seems not to have been heard before the dissolution on 15 June.[11]

In the absence of an election indenture the Robert Jones who was returned in 1628 cannot be conclusively identified. It is possible that he was the local landowner who held just under 400 acres in the vicinity of Halkin, but as this man was rated at a mere 30s. in lands in the 1626 subsidy,[12] it is much more likely that he was the younger son of the Caernarvonshire landowner (Sir) William Jones I*, a justice of king's bench. Justice Jones's son had been returned for Caernarvon Boroughs at by-elections in 1625 and 1626, and on this occasion Sir William Jones presumably asked his fellow judge Sir James Whitelocke to use his connections with the Mostyns in order to arrange a seat for his son in Flintshire. This was a notable break with tradition, as the shire had returned local men since its enfranchisement, but the scars of recent controversies presumably made the gentry more willing to sink their differences by returning an outsider, apparently without a contest.

[1] P. Roberts, Y Cwtta Cyfarwydd ed. D.R. Thomas, 111. [2] R.R. Davies, The Age of Conquest: Wales 1063-1415, pp. 364-5; SR, iii. 849. [3] L.E. Owen, 'Population of Wales', Trans. Hon. Soc. Cymmrodorion (1959), pp. 99-113. [4] J.U. Nef, Rise of the British Coal Industry, i. 55-6, app. D; UCNW, Mostyn 5486. [5] L. Dwnn, Vis. Wales ed. S.R. Meyrick, ii. 310, 315-16; JPs in Wales and Monm. ed. Phillips, 99. [6] NLW, Gwysaney transcript; C142/368/117; SIR ROGER MOSTYN. [7] NLW, 9059E/1172, 1177, 1185-7; C219/38/326. [8] E. Suss. RO, GLY/554, Richard Prythergh to Sir John Trevor II; C219/38/290. [9] Procs. 1625, p. 684; JRL, Ry. Ch. 1200. [10] STAC 5/T15/33; NLW, 9061E/1359. [11] Roberts, 111; C142/447/45; Procs. 1626, iii. 167, 171, 175. [12] Flints. RO, D/LE/780; NLW, Bettisfield 904.

S.H.

FLINT BOROUGHS

Right of election: in the burgesses of Flint, Rhuddlan, Hope, Caerwys and Overton.

Number of voters: ?10-20

27 Feb. 1604	ROGER BRERETON
c.Mar. 1614	JOHN EYTON
11 Dec. 1620	WILLIAM RAVENSCROFT
2 Feb. 1624	WILLIAM RAVENSCROFT
c.28 Apr. 1625	WILLIAM RAVENSCROFT
c.30 Jan. 1626	WILLIAM RAVENSCROFT
26 Feb. 1628	WILLIAM RAVENSCROFT
1 Dec. 1628	PETER WYNNE vice Ravenscroft, deceased ?a Ravenscroft candidate

The 1536 Act of Union enfranchised the shire town of each Welsh county except Merioneth; in the case of Flintshire, representation was extended to include four other boroughs, only one of which, Rhuddlan, was of any consequence.[1] The extent to which the 'contributory boroughs' were involved in the electoral process is an open question, as surviving election returns are inconsistent in their description of the electors: that of 1604 described those named as burgesses of 'the town called the shire town'; while that of 1624 mentioned four gentlemen, none of whom lived in Flint, 'and many other burgesses of the towns of the aforementioned county', some 14 of whom signed the return.[2] Those who attested the returns may have owned or leased property in the contributory boroughs, but in practice, patronage was dominated by local landowners, and the franchise was not so carefully defined as in some other Welsh borough constituencies.

Flint boroughs was habitually represented by minor figures among the county gentry, although outsiders may have exercised some influence. These included the Stanley family, whose extensive Flintshire estates included the two contributory boroughs of Hope and Overton, and lord chancellor Ellesmere (Sir Thomas Egerton†), whose chief estates lay in the adjacent counties of Cheshire and Shropshire, and whose first wife had been a member of the Ravenscroft family of Bretton; it was under his patronage that the Ravenscrofts were first appointed to the office of custos rotulorum in Flintshire, which they held from 1596 until the Civil War.

Ellesmere's third wife had a local interest of her own in the form of an extensive jointure estate from her first husband, Ferdinando Stanley, 5th earl of Derby.[3]

Unusually, the 1604 MP, Roger Brereton, came from a Denbighshire family, albeit one which owned 150 acres in a detached part of Flintshire in the parish of Marchwiel, near Wrexham.[4] Brereton lived at Halghton in Maelor Saesneg (the eastern portion of Flintshire), and Hinton, just over the Shropshire border, where he leased lands from Ellesmere, who may conceivably have backed his candidacy.[5] In 1614 the seat went to John Eyton, who had just succeeded to a small estate in the parish of Mold and was related by marriage to Brereton and Roger Puleston, the 1604 shire knight.[6]

Brereton and Puleston were both dead by the time of the next election in December 1620, which saw the return of William Ravenscroft, clerk of the Petty Bag, who had spent many years in Ellesmere's service; he was also closely involved with Ellesmere's son John [Egerton†], 1st earl of Bridgewater, who wrote him a letter of recommendation when the Parliament was first called in November 1620.[7] However, the key factor behind Ravenscroft's return at five successive general elections was almost certainly his family: Bridgewater addressed his nomination letter to Ravenscroft's eldest brother Thomas, his cousin George Hope and his brother-in-law Robert Davies, and it was probably read to the voters on the day of the election by the MP's nephew Robert Ravenscroft*, who signed the surviving returns of 1620, 1624 and 1628.[8]

William Ravenscroft died in October 1628. The subsequent by-election saw the return of Peter Wynne, the owner of a small amount of property in Mold and a neighbour of John Eyton, one of the signatories of the election indenture. Wynne had recently been appointed steward of the contributory borough of Caerwys, but his chief patron was undoubtedly James Stanley, Lord Strange*, heir to the earldom of Derby, whom he served as an estate steward.[9] This intrusion probably upset the Ravenscrofts, who may have fielded a rival candidate: the family, most unusually, were not listed among the electors on the return. They were probably also responsible for the protest 'that the writ was unduly executed' which reached the committee for privileges at the start of the 1629 session. William Hakewill* reported the case on 9 Feb., but this dealt only with a separate allegation that the clerks in the Crown Office had issued the writ for the by-election without a written warrant from the lord keeper. As a result of the early dissolution, the charge of electoral malpractice was never aired on the floor of the House.[10]

[1] *SR*, iii. 568, 935-6. [2] C219/35/2/44; 219/38/147. [3] CHES 3/84/2; L. Dwnn, *Vis. Wales* ed. S.R. Meyrick, ii. 315-16; *JPs in Wales and Monm.* ed. Phillips, 99-111. [4] C142/282/47. [5] STAC 5/B39/27; STAC 8/61/62; E179/221/223; 179/264/42. [6] Dwnn, ii. 310, 320, 353. [7] Lansd. 163, f. 278; HEHL, EL6470, 6701; PROB 11/154, f. 269; NLW, Gwysaney typescript. [8] C219/37/356; 219/38/147; 219/41B/19. [9] C219/41B/124; C66/2440/17; C2/Chas.I/S89/20; 2/Chas.I/W43/69. [10] *CJ*, i. 917b; *CD 1629*, p. 181.

S.H.

GLAMORGAN

Number of voters: over 700 in 1634[1]

5 Mar. 1604	SIR PHILIP HERBERT
aft. *4 May 1605*	SIR THOMAS MANSELL *vice* Herbert, called to the Upper House
c. Mar. 1614	SIR THOMAS MANSELL
16 Jan. 1621	WILLIAM PRICE
9 Feb. 1624	SIR ROBERT MANSELL
2 May 1625	SIR ROBERT MANSELL
6 Feb. 1626	SIR JOHN STRADLING, bt.
c. Feb. 1628	SIR ROBERT MANSELL

The medieval lordship of Glamorgan was formed after the Norman invasion of the Welsh kingdom of Morgannwg in the last years of the eleventh century. The lordship extended from the River Rhymni in the east to the upper reaches of the Tawe in the west, and was bounded to the north and south by the lordship of Brecon and the Bristol Channel respectively.[2] The Union legislation of the mid-sixteenth century enlarged the lordship to form the new county of Glamorgan by uniting it with the western lordships of Gower and Kilvey. This western territory had a greater affinity with the area which became Carmarthenshire, but was amalgamated with Glamorgan as a concession to Henry Somerset, 2nd earl of Worcester, who held Gower but also administered Glamorgan for the Crown.[3] There remained a fundamental division after the union, however, which was reflected in the organization of the county bench into Western and Eastern justices.[4]

The new county was also disparate in its physical geography, something which affected the patterns of Normanisation, language, settlement and agriculture.

The essential division was between the uplands or *blaenau* of the north and the smaller area of *bro* or Vale lowlands in the southern coastal plain, although a zone of transition or border Vale cut east-west through the county.[5] The uplands were given over to the grazing of cattle, which John Speed described as 'the best means unto wealth which this shire doth afford', and also sheep, though oats and other grains were also grown as well, especially in the *blaenau's* southern reaches. In the Vale area the cultivation of corn and other crops was much more prevalent, leading one local squire to describe it as 'the garden of Wales', although this region also relied heavily on dairy cattle.[6] The sheep of the northern pastures provided wool for the clothiers of the west of England, but also supported an indigenous cloth-making industry. The dairy herds of the Vale, meanwhile, produced great quantities of butter and cheese, which supplied the large market of Bristol and other towns in western England.[7] The county also possessed rich deposits of coal, which had been mined since the medieval period. The most accessible outcrops were in the south west of the county near Neath, Swansea and Llansamlet, exports of which dominated trade from the Glamorgan's western ports. The production of iron in some of the eastern valleys was stimulated by an influx of Sussex ironmasters in the sixteenth century. The county's produce was traded to Bristol, Somerset and Devon, while France provided the major overseas destination for butter and coal.[8]

On the death of the 2nd earl of Worcester in 1549, many of his offices and much of his influence in Glamorgan passed to William Herbert[†], later 1st earl of Pembroke. Herbert was rewarded for his role in suppressing the western rebellion of 1549 with enormous grants of land, which left him as lord of most of Glamorgan; his family consequently became one of the most powerful political influences in the shire down to the Civil Wars, despite their residence at Wilton, in Wiltshire. Herbert influence did not go unchallenged, however, and the sixteenth century saw a good deal of feuding between various gentry groups in the shire, although this had largely dissipated by Elizabeth's death.[9] The election of Sir Philip Herbert, brother of William, 3rd earl of Pembroke, as knight of the shire in 1604 demonstrates the continuing potency of the family's electoral influence. The return, which was witnessed by representatives of most of the county's leading families, marked the end of the conflicts of previous decades.[10]

After the king ennobled Herbert as earl of Montgomery in May 1605, Sir Thomas Mansell of Margam, sheriff the previous year, and head of the most powerful gentry interest in Glamorgan, was returned at the ensuing by-election; he also took the county seat again in 1614. Mansell was related through his mother to the earls of Worcester, and served as their steward in the lordship of Gower, but there is no evidence to suggest that his return demonstrates electoral rivalry between Worcester and Pembroke.

Mansell's advancing age probably dissuaded him from seeking re-election in 1621, at which time his brother, Sir Robert[*], was absent leading an expedition against Algerian pirates. This left the county seat open for William Price of Britton Ferry. Price enjoyed the support not only of Sir Thomas Mansell, whose son and stepson witnessed his return, but also the representatives of the county's most prominent families.[11] He may also have been backed by Pembroke: he had previously been elected at Old Sarum through the earl's influence, and had served as Member for Cardiff, where Pembroke had a dominant interest, in the three subsequent parliaments.

Having returned from the Mediterranean, Sir Robert Mansell secured election for Glamorgan in 1624, and again in 1625 and 1628. On each occasion his elder brother, Sir Thomas, lent his support, as did his nephews Arthur and Sir Lewis Mansell.[12] Most of the other leading families also witnessed Sir Robert's returns, but from the look of the documents the 1624 and 1628 indentures were prepared beforehand. Mansell's name appears to have been included when the text was drawn up, and spaces were left for the names of the contracting parties to be inserted.[13] Rarely present in his native shire, Mansell is unlikely to have attended the hustings in person, so the prepared nature of the indentures suggests that agreements were reached prior to the election.

How far Mansell owed his return for Glamorgan to Pembroke's influence is uncertain, but Herbert supporters such as William Price of Britton Ferry and William Herbert[*] of Grey Friars were certainly signatories to all three returns. Moreover, in 1626 Pembroke provided Mansell with a seat at Lostwithiel, having recruited him to assist to assist in the parliamentary attacks on the duke of Buckingham.[14] In Mansell's absence that same year, the Glamorgan seat was taken by Sir John Stradling of St. Donat's, a Pembroke client who had previously sat for Old Sarum and had dedicated a tract to the earl in 1625.[15]

Glamorgan's elections were consistently held at Bridgend, a location probably chosen for its centrality, allowing ease of access for the gentry from both the east and west of the shire. Although there were more than 700 freeholders in the early seventeenth century, it is not known how many attended the hustings at any given election. Generally the parties contracting with the sheriff were comprehended under the heading 'all other free tenants of the shire', but the signatories were limited usually to between 10 and 20 representatives of the county's major families.

Glamorgan business was brought occasionally before Parliament during this period. During the debates over the subsidy bill in 1606, one unnamed Member, probably Sir Thomas Mansell, put the case for delaying the collection in Glamorgan on account of the concurrent levying of mises which were due after James's accession.[16] Flooding in South Wales in 1607 caused widespread devastation along the Glamorgan coast, and Sir Thomas Mansell, along with his brother Sir Robert (who then sat for Carmarthenshire), were nominated to a committee to consider the best course for repair and the relief of those affected (3 Mar. 1607).[17] In the 1621 Parliament, debate over the export of Welsh butter, one of Glamorgan's principal commodities, also exercised William Price. He urged that the provisions of the bill for the free export of butter should apply to Welsh ports (26 Mar.), and it was later noted that he had 'earnestly protested' against the patent limiting export of Welsh butter.[18] The issue of Glamorgan trade also brought a contribution from Sir John Stradling in 1626, when he described how the county had been 'ransacked by pirates', costing it between £2,000 and £3,000 in lost revenue (16 February).[19] As well as drawing attention to his constituency's plight, Stradling's speech provided support to his patron, Pembroke, in the latter's attempt to impeach Buckingham, who, as lord admiral, was charged with guarding the coasts.

---

[1] *Names of all the Freeholders within Glam. in 1634* ed. H.H. Knight. [2] *Glam. Co. Hist.* ed. T.B. Pugh, iii. 1-11. [3] Ibid. 571. [4] SP16/31/44; P. Jenkins, *Hist. Modern Wales*, 6. [5] *Glam. Co. Hist.* ed. G. Williams, iv. 2-3; R. Meyrick, *Morganiae Archaiographia* ed. B.Ll. James (S. Wales Rec. Soc. i.), 125. [6] *Glam.* iv. 2-9; D.J. Davies, *Economic Hist. of S. Wales*, 57. [7] *Glam.* iv. 25, 46-8, 65; M.I. Williams, 'A Further Contribution to the Commercial Hist. of Glam.', *NLW Jnl.* xi. 334-9; E178/3445, 4143. [8] *Glam.* iv. 48-55; *Welsh Port Bks. 1550-1603* ed. E.A. Lewis (Cymmrodorion Rec. Ser. xii.), 1-48; *Port Bks. for Cardiff and its Members, 1606-10* ed. W. Rees (S. Wales and Mon. Rec. Soc. iii.), 71-2; C.D.J. Trott, 'Coalmining in the Bor. of Neath in the 17th and early 18th centuries', *Morgannwg*, xiii. 48-53; W. Glam. AS, D/D RE 1/236-7. [9] *Glam.* iv. 175-91. [10] C219/35/2/194. [11] C219/37/351. [12] C219/38/328; 219/39/261; 219/41/13; NLW, Mansel-Franklen 75 (3), pt.1a. [13] C219/38/328; 219/41/13. [14] SP16/523/77. [15] NLW, 5666C. [16] *CJ*, i. 300b. [17] Ibid. 346a; *God's Warning to His People of Eng.* (1607). [18] *CJ*, i. 575b; *CD 1621*, ii. 389, iii. 305; Cent. Kent. Stud. U269/1/OE126. [19] *Procs. 1626*, ii. 56-7. See also SP16/18/5.

L.B.

CARDIFF BOROUGHS

Right of election: in the burgesses of Cardiff, Swansea, Cowbridge, Kenfig, Neath, Loughour, Llantrisant and Aberavon.

Number of voters: at least 322 in 1604.[1]

5 Mar. 1604	MATTHEW DAVYS
c. Mar. 1614	MATTHEW DAVYS
15 Jan. 1621	WILLIAM HERBERT I
9 Feb. 1624	WILLIAM PRICE
2 May 1625	WILLIAM PRICE
c. Feb. 1626	WILLIAM PRICE
c. Feb. 1628	LEWIS MORGAN

Situated in south-eastern Glamorganshire, near the mouth of the River Taff, Cardiff flourished during the medieval period as the commercial centre of the lordship of Glamorgan,[2] but was sacked during Glyndŵr rebellion and had not recovered its prosperity by the sixteenth century.[3] Nevertheless, with a population of around 1,300 it remained an important administrative and commercial centre, described as 'very well compacted, beautified with many fair houses and large streets'.[4] Under Henry IV Cardiff became the head port for most of South Wales, shipping produce such as butter, livestock and coal from the surrounding countryside.[5]

From 1340 Cardiff was governed by the constable of the castle, the *ex officio* mayor, who chose two portreeves (later bailiffs) annually from among the burgesses. This municipal government was augmented by a council of 12 aldermen in 1421,[6] and in 1608 William Herbert, 3rd earl of Pembroke, procured a fresh charter which appointed a common council of 12 capital burgesses and a steward as legal adviser. In addition, the corporation was granted a large measure of autonomy from the county administration.[7] The borough nevertheless remained closely tied to its manorial lords. Under the early Stuarts these were, respectively, Mary, dowager countess of Pembroke, and after her death in 1621, her son, William, the 3rd earl,[8] whose nominees, the constables, chose the bailiffs and approved elections to the aldermanic bench.[9]

The Union legislation of 1536-42 constituted Cardiff as the shire town of Glamorgan and gave it the right to return a burgess to Parliament, in association with seven 'ancient boroughs', which were required to contribute to the payment of the Member's wages. Unlike many other Welsh borough constituencies, which saw the link between payment and contributory voting wane as the sixteenth century progressed, Cardiff kept up the practice of demanding these contributory payments. The deputy sheriff of Glamorgan certainly approached Swansea for proportional payments for the expenses of the Members elected in 1586 and 1593.[10] Moreover, all but one of the boroughs voted in the election of 1604, as did at least two in 1621 (Cowbridge and Llantrisant) and 1624 (Neath and Aberavon), and one in 1626 (Neath).[11] This is known from lists of voters attached to the indentures, where those named can often be identified as residents of the respective boroughs from other sources.[12] The full involvement of the out-boroughs was evidently the norm rather than the exception in this period; some of the surviving 1604 voting lists also acknowledged the out-boroughs as being 'contributory to the pay' of parliamentary wages.[13]

All of the elections for which indentures survive in this period took place at Bridgend, which was not a contributory town. This arrangement may have served to discourage partisan activity at the time of the election, but Bridgend, being more centrally located, was also better situated for electors from the county's western boroughs (Loughor, Swansea, Neath and Aberavon) than Cardiff. Despite the active role played by the contributory boroughs, the single most powerful electoral influence in the constituency during the early Stuart period was the 3rd earl of Pembroke, manorial lord of Cardiff and of five of the seven contributory boroughs: Aberavon, Cowbridge, Kenfig, Llantrisant and Neath.[14] The earls of Worcester held the remaining boroughs of Swansea and Loughor, but there is no evidence that they claimed any electoral influence, or attempted to cross the Herbert interest: the 1604 voting lists actually show a greater number of Swansea burgesses endorsing the Member than those of Cardiff itself.[15]

The Member in 1604 and 1614 was a London attorney, Matthew Davys, a native of the county who had family in the Swansea area. He also maintained close contacts with the county gentry over matters such as the 1604 Privy Seal loan and the 1614 Benevolence. Moreover, it was probably the fact that he was counsel for Pembroke's kinsmen, the Herberts of Cogan Pill, Glamorgan, that allowed him to gain the borough seat. He defended the interests of his constituents in debates over the bill for the repair of Minehead

harbour (23 Feb. and 1 and 28 Mar. 1610), but there is little evidence that he prosecuted any business in the House which was concerned solely with Cardiff's interests.

Another Herbert kinsman, William Herbert of Grey Friars, took the seat in 1621, probably in the hope that he could defend his family's role in the patent for the exportation of Welsh butter. A letter to his cousin of Cogan Pill reveals the operation of Pembroke influence within the constituency: he recounted how the dowager countess of Pembroke had written to 'her bailiff [sic] and townsmen of Cardiff that they should make choice of me for their burgess the next Parliament'.[16] However, other interests in the shire opposed the Welsh butter patent, including William Price of Britton Ferry, who transferred from the county seat to Cardiff Boroughs in 1624.[17] Price managed the Pembroke estate of Caergurwen in west Glamorgan, while his return at Old Sarum in 1614 further demonstrates his reliance on the earl's electoral patronage.[18] Price's death in 1627 left a vacancy for the borough place at the 1628 election, which was filled by Lewis Morgan, the heir of Pembroke's steward, Sir Thomas Morgan*.

[1]C219/35/2/195-201. [2]D.G. Walker, 'Cardiff', in *Bors. of Medieval Wales* ed. R.A. Griffiths, 125-6. [3]W. Rees, *Cardiff*, 1-15; I. Soulsby, *Towns of Medieval Wales*, 98. [4]R. Merrick, *Morganiae Archaiographia* ed. B.L. James (S. Wales Rec. Soc. i.), 87. [5]M.E. Thomas, 'Glam. 1540-1640: Aspects of Social and Economic Hist.' (Univ. of Wales M.A. thesis, 1973), pp. 239-71; *Port Bks. for Cardiff and its Members 1606-10* ed. W. Rees (S. Wales and Mon. Rec. Soc. iii.), 70-1. [6]Rees, 54-7. [7]Ibid. 63-4; *Cardiff Recs.* ed. J.H. Matthews, i. 61-72. [8]STAC 8/183/35-6; *HMC Hatfield*, xii. 279, 576-7. [9]STAC 8/183/35, f. 6; STAC 5/L8/3, f. 1; 5/M27/40; Merrick, 88-9; R. Lewis, *A Breviat of Glam. 1596-1600* ed. W. Rees (S. Wales and Mon. Rec. Soc. iii.), 99. [10]W. Glam. AS, B/S Corp. J1, pp. 27, 29, 45. [11]C219/35/2/195-201; 219/37/353-4; 219/38/329-30; 219/30/263. Another indenture for 1624 survives, but is illegible: 219/38/331. [12]E.g. comparisons of the Cowbridge voters of 1604 with the bailiff's accts. for 1600 and 1609, the Llantrisant voters of 1621 with a survey of 1631, as well as subsidy lists of 1604 and 1628 for all boroughs: NLW, Bute M9/28-9, M21/15; E179/221/274; 179/221/286. [13]C219/35/2/198, 201 (?Neath, Loughor). [14]*Breviat of Glam.* 96; *HP Commons, 1558-1603*, i. 318-19. [15]C219/35/2/195, 200. [16]NLW, Bute L3/84. [17]Cent. Kent. Stud. U269/1/OE126. [18]L. Stone, 'Electoral Influence of the 2nd Earl of Salisbury,' *EHR*, lxxi. 395.

L.B./S.H.

MERIONETH

Number of voters: over 600 in 1597[1]

6 Mar. 1604	SIR EDWARD HERBERT
c. Mar. 1614	ELLIS LLOYD
19 Dec. 1620	WILLIAM SALESBURY
10 Feb. 1624	HENRY WYNN
c. May 1625	HENRY WYNN ?Edward Vaughan
7 Feb. 1626	EDWARD VAUGHAN Henry Wynn
c. Feb. 1628	RICHARD VAUGHAN II

Early modern Merioneth was the poorest and most isolated shire in Wales, a fact which induced the architects of the 1536 Act of Union to deny the county a borough seat in Parliament. Its population of about 19,500 was smaller than any except Anglesey and Radnor, and the assessment quotas imposed upon the county after 1640 were lower than elsewhere. This was unsurprising in a shire which consisted almost entirely of mountain and summer pasture, punctuated only by the narrow valleys of the Dyfi, Dysynni and Mawddach in the west, and the area around Lake Tegid and the upper Dee in the north-east. Urban settlement was minimal, with Dolgellau, the only town of note, numbering no more than 150 households, while the other medieval boroughs, Bala and Harlech, had dwindled to negligible proportions: in 1610 John Speed depicted the latter as a few dozen cottages sheltering in the lee of the castle.[2]

Although poor by comparison with the arable regions of lowland England, Merioneth sustained a successful upland economy based upon stock-rearing and clothing. Each summer several thousand cattle were fattened for sale at the autumn fairs along the Dee valley and the Vale of Clwyd, from whence they supplied the leather industry at Chester and the meat markets in the south-east of England.[3] The other staple of the local economy was coarse wool, used to make cheap cloth. The vitality of this industry may be gauged by the large number of fulling mills operated within the county, and the vigorous resistance the clothiers mounted against any signs of interference with their market at Oswestry.[4]

For half a century after the Union of 1536 Merioneth was dominated by Dr. Ellis Price[†] and his brother,

who controlled parliamentary representation in conjunction with the Owens of Dolgellau. However, Dr. Price's role as agent for the earl of Leicester's rights in the Forest of Snowdon, which covered much of the north of the county, made him unpopular, and in 1586 there was delight when Robert Lloyd broke Price's hold on the shire seat:[5]

Aethost gwr a thyst geirwir
Er serch yn Farchog o'r sir ...
Tra enwog lew trwy naw gwlad
Tynnaist y beilchion tanad

You went as a man of conviction and duty to become a knight of the shire. ... Most famous leader throughout nine countries [commotes of Merioneth?], you overcame the proud upstarts [i.e. the Prices].[6]

Despite this setback, Cadwalader Price[†] and John Lewis Owen[†] used their powers as deputy lieutenants to keep much of the shire in awe for the next decade, and attempted to win the county seat back at the general election of 1597. A chorus of protest finally secured their removal from office in the following year, and they were kept occupied in Star Chamber until their deaths early in the next reign.[7]

The neutralization of the Price-Owen faction left a political vacuum in Merioneth at the end of Elizabeth's reign. This could have been filled by Sir William Maurice*, but he preferred to sit for his native Caernarvonshire, and during the early Stuart period electoral patronage devolved upon four leading county families: the Salesburys of Rûg, Lloyds of Rhiwgoch, Nanneys of Nannau and Vaughans of Cors-y-Gedol. At least until 1604 the primary interest this group had in parliamentary elections was the exclusion of the Price faction, and even thereafter they were little concerned to use Parliament to further their particular interests. Most of the local men returned for the shire were elected when still in their twenties, while the heads of the Nanney and Vaughan family did not sit at all, preferring to put their heirs forward for election in 1593 and 1628. This low level of interest in the parliamentary politics meant that the gentry were occasionally willing to return outsiders, including the London merchant (Sir) Thomas Myddelton I* in 1597, and the Montgomeryshire landowner Sir Edward Herbert in 1604. Herbert required a seat after voluntarily yielding the representation of his own shire to his relative Sir William Herbert of Powis, and while his lands lay along the Montgomery-Shropshire border at some distance from Merioneth, this may have worked to his advantage, as it meant that he was unlikely to become a permanent fixture on the local political scene. This proved to be the case: at the next general election in

1614 Herbert was preparing for service in the English army in the Low Countries, and was replaced by Ellis Lloyd, heir to the Rhiwgoch estate.[8]

Lloyd stood aside voluntarily in December 1620, when he, his father and his cousins the Vaughans of Cors-y-Gedol all attested the return of William Salesbury of Rûg. Aged 40, Salesbury was by far the most active of Merioneth's MPs in the Commons during this period, which makes it rather surprising that he was replaced as knight of the shire in 1624 by Henry Wynn of Gwydir, a newcomer to the shire who was 20 years his junior. Wynn had married the heiress of Rhiwgoch in 1620, at which time he had also been granted immediate possession of part of his own father's 8,000 acre estate in the Trawsfynydd area. His return also reflected the burgeoning ambitions of the Wynn family, who attempted to influence the choice in four counties during this election. However, in a shire where the gentry liked to establish a consensus well before the county day, the crucial factor may well have been the speed and determination with which (Sir) Richard Wynn* promoted his brother's candidacy: he warned his father of the imminence of the election some days before the official Proclamation was issued, hoping that he would gain 'much advantage in the knowledge', and he later worked to secure the support of both the sheriff and Sir William Herbert, whose Montgomeryshire estates extended across the Dyfi valley into Merioneth. The election is unlikely to have been contested, as the heads of the Lloyd, Vaughan and Nanney families all endorsed the return, and Salesbury was the only notable figure whose name was absent from the indenture.[9]

Wynn was re-elected in 1625, but circumstantial evidence suggests that his victory was achieved only with difficulty. Sir John Wynn[†] canvassed Salesbury as soon as news of King James's death reached North Wales, but the latter's reply of 4 Apr. contrived to be simultaneously reassuring yet evasive: he claimed that after the 1624 election he had promised to endorse whoever Hugh Nanney and William Vaughan should nominate at the next election, 'those two houses having never been contrary in voices, and I had their voices formerly for myself'. Both men were related to Wynn's wife, and duly offered their support some ten days later, but the fact that the issue was resolved in such a roundabout way suggests that the local gentry were not entirely happy about the growing influence of Gwydir within their shire. There was almost certainly some kind of contest at the county court, and although it was clearly resolved in Wynn's favour by the sheriff (his wife's grandfather Robert Lloyd) he spent the

opening weeks of the session fearing that his return would be challenged.[10] Once Wynn judged the danger of an electoral petition had passed, he sued out a writ for payment of his expenses from the 1624 session. While such claims were rare in England, they were not unknown in Wales – Griffith Nanney had received £16 for his service in the 1593 session – but Wynn anticipated that 'the gentlemen of the country perhaps would take exceptions at it', and had delayed serving the writ to avoid any unnecessary complications if a by-election were called.[11]

Wynn's calculations were thrown out by the king's decision to dissolve the Parliament and call fresh elections only six months later, leaving him to face an electorate undoubtedly annoyed by his duplicity. The news of 'great bustling in Merionethshire' reached Wynn's brother Owen in London, and the fall of the family's patron, lord keeper Williams, in November 1625, cannot have helped his already slender prospects. Wynn retained the support of his Rhiwgoch relatives, but the indenture returning his rival, Edward Vaughan of Llwydiarth, Montgomeryshire, was signed by virtually every other gentleman of note within the shire: William Vaughan of Cors-y-Gedol (as sheriff), William Salesbury, Hugh Nanney, John Price of Rhiwlas, John Lloyd of Rhiwaedog, John Vaughan of Caergai, Piers Meyrick of Ucheldre and over a dozen others. The Llwydiarth estate in Merioneth – about 1,000 acres – was relatively modest, and Vaughan was presumably nominated by his brother-in-law, William Salesbury; indeed, he may have been Wynn's adversary in 1625, which would explain why Salesbury tried to avoid committing himself to Wynn's cause on that occasion.[12] Any hopes for a revival of the Gwydir electoral interest at the next election died with Sir John Wynn[†] on 1 Mar. 1627, and in the following year Richard Vaughan II, son of the 1626 sheriff, was probably returned unopposed.

Merioneth's MPs had little known interest in furthering local issues in Parliament, which was hardly surprising in view of their youth and inexperience. The only exception to this rule was Salesbury: on 19 Apr. 1621 he recommended that the provisions of a bill for the annual drafting of lists of freeholders liable for jury service should be extended to cover Wales; while he also opposed the customary exemptions from the subsidy bill, which probably reflected local dissatisfaction that Wales had not been excused payment during collection of the mise for Prince Charles.[13] In 1624 Henry Wynn failed to sign a petition against the proposed farm of Welsh greenwax fines which was circulated among the principality's

MPs at Westminster by Sir Eubule Thelwall*, an evasion which was hardly surprising, as the beneficiary of the farm was to have been his brother, Sir Richard.[14]

The sole item of legislation mooted for the benefit of the shire during the early Stuart period was a bill for the improvement of Harlech, part of a wider plan to revive the town's economic fortunes. Significantly, the man chosen to further this project was not the county's own MP, Sir Edward Herbert, but the Caernarvonshire MP Sir William Maurice, who lived at Clenennau, Caernarvonshire, only seven miles from Harlech. On the eve of the 1604 session the town's leading burgesses asked Maurice to obtain a confirmation of their charter, with a view to changing the date of one of their cattle fairs, fixing the assizes and quarter sessions at the town, and securing the grant of a parliamentary seat in line with the other Welsh shires. Under the circumstances a bill was hardly appropriate, but towards the end of the session the burgesses wrote again, offering Maurice £100 to secure an Act for the assizes, quarter sessions and parliamentary seat. By this stage the townsmen had recruited the support of the local gentry, as Griffith Vaughan of Cors-y-Gedol and Robert Lloyd of Rhiwgoch each undertook to pay £10 of this sum. With only a month of the session remaining, there was no time to lay a bill before the Commons, and the scheme was allowed to lapse.[15]

What was clearly regarded as the most important part of the Harlech project was revived in another form in March 1609, when lord president [Ralph] Eure†, newly appointed constable of Harlech Castle, was petitioned separately by the burgesses and a group of JPs to procure an order for the assizes and quarter sessions to be kept at Harlech rather than the 'very filthy dirty town' of Bala. The cause of this sudden flurry of activity seems to have been the promotion of a rival scheme by the sheriff, John Price of Rhiwlas, to make Dolgellau the assize town. Having assured Eure that that their proposal would relieve him of much of the cost of maintaining the castle, the magistrates undertook to build new lodgings for themselves, while the burgesses offered Eure £50. Eure quickly forwarded these petitions to master of requests Sir Daniel Dunne*, but in case this proved insufficient, Maurice also engaged Sir Patrick Murray, a gentleman of the Privy Chamber, to further the cause, and in June 1609 the town's petition was granted under a Signet letter. The long-term effectiveness of this granted came to less than the protagonists might have hoped, as by the 1620s the assizes were being held at Dolgellau.[16]

[1] STAC 5/L45/6, f. 1 states that the loser mustered 300 voters. [2] L. Owen, 'Population of Wales', *Trans. Hon. Soc. Cymmrodorion* (1959), 111, 113; I. Soulsby, *Towns of Medieval Wales*, 74-6, 131-3, 138-9. [3] C2/Chas.I/W36/65; *Cal. Wynn Pprs.* no. 1610. [4] T.C. Mendenhall, *Shrewsbury Drapers and Welsh Wool Trade*, esp. 193-5; SP14/121/58, 131/21, 22.I. [5] H.G. Owen, 'Fam. Pols. in Eliz. Merion.', *Bull. Bd. Celtic Studies*, xviii. 185-9; J. Gwynfor Jones, *Concepts of Order and Gentility in Wales, 1540-1640*, pp. 178-9. [6] Translation by Dr. Margaret Escott. [7] *APC*, 1597-8, pp. 551-2; STAC 5/L45/36; STAC 8/225/15. [8] C142/247/84; *Life of Edward, First Lord Herbert of Cherbury* ed. J.M. Shuttleworth, 39, 68. [9] C219/37/35; 219/38/292; NLW, 9059E/1177, 1190; Denb. RO, DD/WY/6555; C142/562/82. [10] *Procs. 1625*, pp. 692-3; Griffith, 180, 200, 279; NLW, 9060E/156; *Sheriffs of Merion.* in *Arch. Camb.* o.s. ii. 130. [11] NLW, 9060E/1356; STAC 5/W28/2. [12] *Procs. 1626*, iv. 322; C219/40/19; C142/380/136. [13] *CJ*, i. 544a, 551a, 582a; *CD 1621*, iii. 19. For lists of jurors, see also *Clenennau Letters and Pprs.* ed. T. Jones Pierce, 60, 70. [14] NLW, 9059E/1217, 1228. [15] *Cal. Clenennau Pprs.* 61-2; *Arch. Camb.* o.s. i. 254-5. [16] *Cal. Clenennau Pprs.* 73, 132, 138; *Arch. Camb.* o.s. i. 255-8; SP14/43/58, 14/44/30; *CSP Dom.* 1603-10, p. 495; SO3/4, unfol. (June 1609); G.D. Owen, *Wales in the Reign of Jas. I*, 54-8; Exeter Coll. Oxf. ms 168.

S.H.

MONTGOMERYSHIRE

Number of voters: between 1,600 and 2,100 in 1588.[1]

c. Mar. 1604	SIR WILLIAM HERBERT
c. Mar. 1614	SIR WILLIAM HERBERT
9 Dec. 1620	SIR WILLIAM HERBERT
31 Jan. 1624	SIR WILLIAM HERBERT
21 May 1625	SIR WILLIAM HERBERT ?Edward Vaughan*
28 Jan. 1626	SIR WILLIAM HERBERT
?3 Mar. 1628	SIR WILLIAM HERBERT ?Edward Vaughan

Montgomeryshire was created by amalgamation of the Marcher lordships of Powis, Montgomery, Ceri and Cedewain under the 1536 Act of Union. One of the wealthier shires of early modern Wales, it encompassed not only the mountainous pastures of Powis, but also the fertile upper reaches of the Severn valley. The county's economy was typical of much of upland Wales, being dominated by the fattening of livestock for the markets of south-eastern England, and the manufacture of coarse cloth, which was sold to the Shrewsbury Drapers at the nearby staple town of Oswestry, Shropshire.[2]

From about 1550 Edward Herbert† of Montgomery, a distant relative of the earls of Pembroke whose immediate forbears had amassed a local estate of over 20,000 acres, dominated Montgomeryshire politics. The family's local influence was reinforced during the 1580s, when their kinsman Sir Edward Herbert† purchased the castle and lordship of Powis, comprising 150,000 acres of upland pasture and the boroughs of Welshpool and Llanfyllin. This led to conflict with the greatest of the native families, the Vaughans of Llywidiarth, whose 100,000 acre estate lay in the same area, provoking a hard-fought county election contest in 1588 and a struggle for control of Llanfyllin in 1602.[3]

The local balance of power within the Herbert family changed in 1604, when Sir Edward Herbert* of Montgomery resigned his claim to the county seat in favour of Sir William Herbert of Powis Castle. Sir Edward subsequently made a career as a courtier and diplomat, while Sir William remained at home and served as knight of the shire throughout the early Stuart period. Lesser gentry families, such as the Pughs of Mathafarn, the Prices of Newtown and the Lloyds of Berthllwyd, were happy to sign the election returns, although the Vaughans of Llwydiarth were conspicuous by their absence. Sir Robert Vaughan, who might have mounted a serious challenge to the Herbert interest in the early 1620s, was neutralized by a marriage with one of Sir William Herbert's daughters. The bad blood between the two families resurfaced after Sir Robert's death in July 1624, with a dispute over the legitimacy of the latter's posthumous son. It seems likely that Sir Robert's brother Edward Vaughan, the rival claimant to the Llywidiarth estate, mounted an electoral challenge to the Herberts in 1625, when Sir William played safe by securing a seat at Wilton, Wiltshire from his cousin the 3rd earl of Pembroke. This precaution turned out to be unnecessary, as Montgomeryshire's electors returned Herbert anyway, obliging Vaughan to look for a seat in neighbouring Merioneth. As Herbert took the same precaution three years later, it seems likely that Vaughan challenged him again for the county seat at the 1628 election, but with equal lack of success.[4]

Issues relating to Montgomeryshire were rarely raised in the Commons. Herbert endorsed the 1621 bill to ban imports of Irish cattle on the grounds that this would benefit Welsh graziers, and his nomination to the committee for the bill to allow free trade in Welsh cloth (2 Mar. 1621) permitted him to support the attacks on the Shrewsbury Drapers' monopoly of the Oswestry staple, although it was the local clothiers themselves who lobbied hardest over this issue.[5] From 1624 Sir William Herbert was obliged to name himself as a recusant officeholder within the shire because of the Catholicism of his wife, a daughter of

the 8th earl of Northumberland. Not surprisingly, in 1626 Edward Vaughan maliciously attempted to make trouble for his enemy with a motion to overturn the House's decision to remove Herbert from the resulting petition to the king.[6]

[1] J.E. Neale, *Eliz. House of Commons*, 102-3. [2] *Agrarian Hist. Eng. and Wales* ed. J. Thirsk, iv. 133, 470-2; T.C. Mendenhall, *Shrewsbury Drapers and the Welsh Wool Trade*, 26-47. [3] C142/242/107; 142/247/84; 142/380/136; Neale, 93-104; *Montgoms. Collections*, lxxxv. 28-9. Herbert ped. at back of *Herbert Corresp.* ed. W.J. Smith (Univ. Wales, Bd. of Celtic Studs. (Hist. and Law ser. xxi). [4] *Life of Lord Herbert of Cherbury* ed. J.M. Shuttleworth, 39; EDWARD VAUGHAN. [5] *CJ*, i. 534b, 615b; Mendenhall, 181, 183. [6] *Procs. 1626*, iii. 146, iv. 215.

S.H.

MONTGOMERY BOROUGHS

Right of election: in the burgesses of Montgomery, Caersws, Llanfyllin, Llanidloes, Newtown and Welshpool.

Number of voters: 30-40

c. Mar. 1604	EDWARD WHITTINGHAM
c. Mar. 1614	SIR JOHN DANVERS
19 Dec. 1620	EDWARD HERBERT
c. Feb. 1624	GEORGE HERBERT
7 May 1625	GEORGE HERBERT
26 Jan. 1626	SIR HENRY HERBERT
3 Mar. 1628	RICHARD LLOYD

According to the terms of the 1536 Act of Union, every Welsh county (except Merioneth) was to have an MP returned by the burgesses of all the shire's chartered boroughs. This enfranchised six towns in the east of Montgomeryshire, along the upper reaches of the Severn valley. Two of these, Llanfyllin and Welshpool, were prosperous market towns with substantial populations of 1,000 each. Montgomery and Llanidloes, each a little over 500 strong, retained a formal corporate structure and were wealthy enough to secure confirmations of their borough charters at the beginning of Elizabeth's reign, but Newtown and Caersws dwindled into insignificance. Machynlleth, the sole town in the west of the shire, had important cloth and cattle markets but no charter, and its manorial government was extinguished by *quo warranto* during the 1630s.[1]

Notwithstanding the legal formula, during the early Stuart period the franchise was apparently confined to the burgesses of Montgomery. As late as 1601, borough and shire elections were held together, alternating between Montgomery and Machynlleth, but by the 1620s the borough elections became fixed at the shire town. At the same time the wording of the returns, which under Elizabeth had generally located the franchise among 'all the burgesses of the county', was altered to redefine the electorate as 'the burgesses of Montgomery'. This distinction was only reversed when three of the other boroughs fought to reassert their voting rights in 1679. The narrowing of the franchise undoubtedly took place with the encouragement of the Herbert family, who dominated the county's parliamentary representation in the century between the Union and the Civil War: the last thing they would have wanted to see was an influx of voters from Llanfyllin, where their enemies the Vaughans of Llywidiarth had influence, or Newtown, residence of the Price family, who had challenged their authority at the county election of 1588.[2]

Under Elizabeth the county's electoral patronage had been dominated by the Herberts of Montgomery, but from 1604 the knighthood of the shire became the exclusive preserve of their kinsman Sir William Herbert of Powis Castle. The Montgomery Herberts' ownership of 16 burgages in the town of Montgomery gave them an enduring interest in the latter seat, and the return of lesser figures in the four elections between 1593 and 1604 almost certainly owed more to a shortage of adult male Herberts rather than any decline in the family's electoral influence. Edward Whittingham, the Member returned in 1604, was a minor gentleman resident at Court Culmore, a mile to the west of Montgomery, and a member of the town corporation, but his claim upon the seat was doubtless assisted by the fact that he was a servant of Sir Edward Herbert* of Montgomery.[3]

Although Whittingham continued to play an active part in the borough's affairs until the 1630s, he is not known to have sought election to Parliament again. The next five parliaments saw the return of four close relatives of Sir Edward Herbert: Sir John Danvers (1614) was Herbert's stepfather; Edward Herbert (1621) his cousin; while George and Sir Henry Herbert (1624-6) were his youngest brothers.[4] The supply of family candidates dried up once again in 1628, with Danvers and Edward Herbert being provided for elsewhere, George Herbert ineligible since his ordination, and Sir Henry Herbert presumably disinclined to stand following his marriage to a Worcestershire heiress. This left room for a local candidate, Richard Lloyd of Marrington, a small town situated two miles east of Montgomery in Shropshire. Lloyd was a distant cousin of the Herbert family by marriage, and his father, Priamus Lloyd, was one of the witnesses to his return.[5]

[1] SR, iii. 568, 935-6; I. Soulsby, Towns of Medieval Wales, 93-4, 167-8, 170-2, 180-1, 185-7, 209-11, 265-8; Montgoms. Colls. xxiii. 192-4; lxxviii. 100; lxxix. 11-16; Agrarian Hist. Eng. and Wales ed. J. Thirsk, iv. 535. [2] J.E. Neale, Eliz. House of Commons, 93-104. [3] C142/247/84; PROB 11/90, f. 195; C3/297/34. [4] See ped. at end of Herbert Corresp. ed. W.J. Smith (Univ. Wales Bd. of Celtic Studs., Hist. and Law ser. xxi). [5] RICHARD LLOYD; C219/41B/21.

S.H.

PEMBROKESHIRE

Number of voters: at least 400

c. Mar. 1604	ALBAN STEPNETH
c. Mar. 1614	JOHN WOGAN
12 Dec. 1620	JOHN WOGAN
3 Feb. 1624	SIR JAMES PERROT / John Wogan
26 Apr. 1625	JOHN WOGAN / Sir James Perrot
c. Jan. 1626	JOHN WOGAN
26 Feb. 1628	JOHN WOGAN

Pembrokeshire was among the smallest of the Welsh counties, having been reduced in size by statute in 1543. In 1626 its magistrates claimed, with only slight exaggeration, that it was nowhere more than 18 miles wide.[1] However, the county's smallness was not always appreciated. One of its chief inhabitants, George Owen, lord of Cemais, complained that the mapmaker Christopher Saxton, in devoting as much space in his 1575 book of maps to Pembrokeshire as to Cardiganshire, Carmarthenshire, Breconshire and Radnorshire combined, had misled the Crown as to the county's true size and caused Pembrokeshire to be overburdened with taxes.[2] Owen was on safer ground when he observed that Pembrokeshire was a poor county, all of whose boroughs, apart from Haverfordwest, were in economic decline. That said, the shire was hardly devoid of significant economic activity. 'Corn', meaning oats, wheat, barley, peas, beans and rye, was one of its main commodities, and was grown not only for local consumption but also for export to Ireland, France and Spain.[3] The cornfields around Milford Haven were so fertile that in 1595 the county's magistrates feared that these alone would suffice to feed an invading Spanish army.[4] Pembrokeshire's farmers also earned a good living from the woollen industry. By the end of Elizabeth's reign the shire abounded in sheep, the keeping of which, according to Owen, 'yieldeth great profit with little charge'. Bristol and several other English ports along the Severn depended heavily for their prosperity on wool grown in southern Pembrokeshire.[5]

Pembrokeshire society was sharply divided between Welsh speakers, who lived mainly in the north, and English speakers, who were chiefly located in the south and west. Despite the passage of five centuries, the members of both nations barely intermingled, 'differing in manner, diet, buildings and tilling of the land'. Where intercourse between the two did occur the language barrier created an insuperable obstacle, as was apparent whenever juries formed from both English and Welsh speakers were empanelled. Sprinkled among the English speakers were large numbers of Irish-born inhabitants, many of whom were refugees from the Elizabethan war in Ireland.[6] In 1592 a government surveyor reported that all the residents of the western coastal parish of Nolton were Irish-born 'except two or three'.[7] Dearth in Ireland in the later 1620s created a fresh influx of refugees from across the Irish Sea, who were smuggled in at night on small boats, to the despair of Pembrokeshire's magistrates.[8]

At the beginning of the seventeenth century Owen remarked that there were 'scarce 400 freeholders' capable of jury service.[9] His observation provides a clue as to the size of the county's electorate, but whether attendance at the hustings ever approached this figure is impossible to say, since the surviving election indentures almost certainly do not contain the signatures of all those who voted. Elections were normally held at Haverfordwest rather than the shire town, Pembroke, which was decayed. The customary venue appears to have been the castle (1601, 1625), but in 1620 the election took place at the Guildhall. In 1624 voting occurred just outside Haverfordwest at Prendergast, the seat of the then sheriff, Sir John Stepneth, while in 1628 the sheriff made his return from Llawhaden, a minor borough seven miles east of Haverfordwest.[10]

The pattern of electoral politics in Pembrokeshire under the early Stuarts is clear. Towards the end of Elizabeth's reign the leaders of the Perrot and Essex factions in Pembrokeshire were removed from the scene, thereby allowing John Philipps of Picton Castle, whose uncle William Philipps had represented the shire in 1559 and 1572, to occupy the county seat in 1601. In 1604 the Philipps interest again prevailed with the return of Alban Stepneth, the squire of Prendergast and the cousin by marriage of John Philipps. In 1614, however, the Philipps family lost control of the county seat to their arch-enemies, the Wogans of Wiston. Whether this happened without a contest is unknown, for although Stepneth was now dead John Philipps was capable of standing and might have expected to enjoy the assistance of the sheriff, Stepneth's son John.

John Wogan secured the knighthood of the shire again in 1620, but his hold on the county seat was temporarily broken in 1624, when he was defeated by Sir James Perrot of Haroldston, whose late father, Sir John Perrot, had once counted the Wogans among his allies. Sir James had represented Haverfordwest in four of the five previous parliaments, but in 1624 he was incapable of standing for re-election there because he held office as the borough's mayor. Details of the contest between Perrot and Wogan are wanting, but as the election was held at Prendergast rather than Haverfordwest it seems likely that the sheriff, Sir John Stepneth, colluded with Perrot to defeat Wogan, who subsequently complained to the committee for privileges. On the other hand, the report made to the Commons by the committee on 28 May indicates that it was Wogan rather than Perrot who was suspected of certain 'misdemeanours'. In the event, the question of which candidate had abused the electoral process proved irrelevant to the committee, which decided to uphold the election on the grounds that Wogan's petition had been submitted after the deadline for receiving such complaints had passed.[11]

Wogan ruthlessly exacted his revenge at the 1625 election, which was well-attended by members of his immediate family. A defeated Perrot subsequently complained that he was the victim of a concerted campaign involving serious electoral malpractice. A rumour of his death had been spread before the election, and many of his followers had been threatened with impressment; several others had been beaten or prevented from reaching the hustings. Those who attended had allegedly found themselves 'interrupted and refused'. However, Perrot failed to persuade the Commons to eject Wogan. He omitted to lay before the privileges committee the evidence needed to substantiate his claims, and although he told the House on 7 July that he had 'very sufficient' witnesses to corroborate his story, he admitted that it would take some time to produce them. In desperation, he argued that Wogan's election should immediately be declared void, as the authority of the sheriff who had overseen the election had been ended by the death of James I. This was a specious argument, because immediately after James's death a Proclamation had been issued confirming all officeholders in their posts. Nevertheless, it caused momentary disquiet as Members realized that their own elections were invalid if Perrot was correct. The Commons refused to make a hasty ruling, however, and referred the matter back to the privileges' committee.[12] By the time the Parliament was dissolved the issue had still not been settled.

Defeat at the hands of Wogan in 1625 left Perrot without a parliamentary seat for the first time since 1601. It was clearly not an experience that he wished to repeat, and therefore he left the knighthood of the shire to Wogan in both 1626 and 1628, when he concentrated instead on winning the seat at Haverfordwest. It is not known whether the decision of the sheriff, Charles Bowen, to hold the 1628 county election at Llawhaden rather than Haverfordwest was intended to help or hinder Wogan.

[1] SP16/33/57. [2] G. Owen, *Description of Penbrokshire* ed. H. Owen (Cymmrodorion Rec. Ser. i.), i. 2-4. [3] Ibid. 55-6; *Agrarian Hist. of Eng. and Wales* ed. J. Thirsk, iv. 135-6. [4] *Arch. Camb.* (ser. 3), viii. 15. [5] Owen, 56-7; B.E. Howells, 'Pemb. Farming c.1580-1620', *NLW Jnl.* ix. 241-2; *Merchants and Merchandise in Seventeenth-Cent. Bristol* ed. P. McGrath (Bristol Rec. Soc. xix), 142. [6] Owen, 39-40. [7] LR2/260, f. 67. [8] *CSP Dom.* 1628-9, pp. 258, 358, 519, 573; *APC*, 1629-30, pp. 389-90. [9] G. Owen, *Taylor's Cussion* ed. E.M. Pritchard, ii. f. 50v. [10] C219/35/2/188; 219/37/67; 219/38/337; 219/39/265; 219/41B/23. The returns for 1604 and 1614 are wanting; that for 1626 is illegible. [11] *CJ*, i. 714b, 798a. [12] *Procs. 1625*, pp. 335-6, 340-1.

A.D.T.

HAVERFORDWEST

Right of election: in the freemen

Number of voters: 94 in 1571 (of whom 12 were allegedly ineligible)[1]

6 Mar. 1604	SIR JAMES PERROT, ?alderman
1614	SIR JAMES PERROT, alderman
19 Dec. 1620	SIR JAMES PERROT, alderman
10 Feb. 1624	LEWIS POWELL Sir Thomas Canon, alderman
1625	SIR THOMAS CANON, alderman
31 Jan. 1626	SIR THOMAS CANON, alderman Sir James Perrot, alderman
1628	SIR JAMES PERROT, alderman

Situated near the centre of Pembrokeshire, at the head of the Cleddau estuary and with roadways emanating from it in every direction, Haverfordwest was easily the most prosperous and populous town in the county. Its thriving Saturday market was reputed to be the best in all Wales for fish, and the town carried on a flourishing coastal trade with several English ports along the Severn, chief among which was Bristol, whose clothiers relied heavily on woollen shipments from the Milford Haven area. In addition, skins, sack and salt were exported to Ireland in return for coal and corn, while wines and salt were imported from France.[2] No long term economic damage appears to have been caused by neglect of the town's quay, which for 30 years prior to 1615 was in such a ruinous condition 'that no barque could ride safe there'.[3] Haverfordwest's prosperity helps to explain why the borough continued to pay parliamentary wages until at least 1606,[4] and contrasts with the declining fortunes of neighbouring Pembroke, which was economically decayed and heavily depopulated. By the early sixteenth century Haverfordwest had effectively displaced Pembroke as the county's administrative centre, although formally at least Pembroke remained the shire town.[5]

Unique among Welsh boroughs, Haverfordwest enjoyed the distinction of being a separate county. This privilege was obtained at its incorporation in 1479, and was confirmed by the 1543 Act of Union, which also awarded the borough the franchise. By the terms of the 1479 charter, borough administration was placed in the hands of a common council comprising

24 burgesses, which each year elected from its own ranks a mayor and a sheriff. In 1610, after several years of lobbying and at a cost of more than £83, the town was granted a new charter whereby, *inter alia*, the borough's ordinary burgesses were accorded a say in which council members should occupy these two key offices.[6] The ordinary burgesses already participated in the town's parliamentary elections, which were presided over by the borough's sheriff and held at the guildhall.

During the first three Jacobean parliaments, and in 1597 too, Haverfordwest was represented by Sir James Perrot, whose father had sat for the borough in 1589. As the squire of nearby Haroldston, Perrot was one of only two members of the local gentry living outside the borough who were entitled to become a freeman. His godly enthusiasm was undoubtedly attractive to many of the borough's residents who, during the 1620s were willing to employ the puritan Stephen Goffe as their lecturer.[7] By 1605 at the latest Perrot was a member of the town council. He was not re-elected for the borough in 1624 but chose instead to sit for the county. Apart from the greater prestige attached to the county seat, Perrot presumably decided not to stand at Haverfordwest because, being then mayor he was the borough's returning officer. His departure from the scene created an opening for the fiercely litigious crypto-Catholic Sir Thomas Canon, who lived in the borough and had served as its mayor on four occasions. However, Canon was defeated by Lewis Powell, who in the previous Parliament had represented Pembroke Boroughs. An outsider, Powell lived on the southern shore of Milford Haven, some distance from Haverfordwest, and presumably owed his election to someone powerful inside the borough. That someone was almost certainly Sir James Perrot. Both men hated Canon – in 1622 the latter had prosecuted Powell in Chancery – and they probably knew each other well, having both been educated at Jesus College, Oxford and the Middle Temple (though not at the same time). Moreover, Powell's father had once leased property at a preferential rate from Perrot's father. Whatever the truth behind Powell's election, Canon complained to the Commons that he had been cheated of victory. The committee for privileges carried out an investigation, but on finding that it could not proceed to judgment without first establishing the validity of a legal instrument produced by Canon it appointed two senior members of the Pembrokeshire gentry to examine the matter. Before their report could be submitted, however, the Parliament was adjourned, never to reconvene.[8]

Canon's failure did not discourage him from standing in 1625, and this time he took the seat, apparently unopposed: Perrot had stood once more for the knighthood of the shire, only to be beaten by John Wogan of Wiston, while Powell had reverted to his former constituency of Pembroke Boroughs. In the following year, however, Canon was again confronted with opposition, this time from Perrot, whose earlier defeat at the hands of Wogan, who had decided to stand again for the shire, undoubtedly persuaded him that he stood a better chance of achieving victory at Haverfordwest than he did at the county election. However, Canon was determined that Perrot should not prevail, and in mid-January Perrot reported his rival for having secretly obtained possession of the election writ, and for concealing it from the sheriff 'at the late county day'.[9] Despite these protests, it was Canon's name and not Perrot's that was entered on the borough's election return. Perrot subsequently travelled to London with the aim of overturning the result,[10] but he failed and was forced to find another seat. It is not known whether Haverfordwest witnessed a further contest between Canon and Perrot in 1628, when Perrot recovered the seat and Canon was elected for Haslemere.

[1] STAC 8/S79/34, ff. 12, 14. [2] *Cal. of Recs. of Bor. of Haverfordwest, 1539-1660* ed. B.G. Charles (Univ. of Wales, Bd. of Celtic Studies, Hist. and Law Ser. xxiv), 2, 9; *Merchants and Merchandise in Seventeenth-Cent. Bristol* ed. P. McGrath (Bristol Rec. Soc. xix), 140-3. [3] *Pemb. Life: 1572-1843* ed. B.E. and K.A. Howells (Pemb. Rec. Soc. Ser. i.), 11-12. [4] B.G. Charles, 'Haverfordwest Accts. 1563-1620, *NLW Jnl.* ix. 170. [5] PEMBROKE BOROUGHS. See also G. Owen, *The Taylor's Cussion* ed. C.M. Prichard, pt. 2, f. 48. [6] *Recs. of Haverfordwest*, 2-3; Charles, 'Haverfordwest Accts.' 172. Charles puts the cost at £40, but the items of expenditure listed appear to give the higher figure. [7] J. Phillips, *Hist. Pemb.* 481. [8] J. Glanville, *Reps. of Certain Cases* (London, 1775), pp. 112-14; 'Earle 1624', f. 196. [9] SP16/18/63. [10] *CSP Ire.* 1625-32, p. 91.

A.D.T.

PEMBROKE BOROUGHS

Right of election: in the freemen of Pembroke, Tenby, Wiston, Newport, Fishguard, Cilgerran and St. Dogmaels

Number of voters: c.230

c. Mar. 1604	RICHARD CUNY
c. Mar. 1614	WALTER DEVEREUX
28 Dec. 1620	LEWIS POWELL
	Henry Wogan
2 Feb. 1624	(SIR) WALTER DEVEREUX
May 1625	LEWIS POWELL
c. Jan. 1626	HUGH OWEN
25 Feb. 1628	HUGH OWEN

By the beginning of the seventeenth century Pembrokeshire's boroughs were, with the exception of prosperous Haverfordwest, in an advanced state of economic decay. Pembroke was in places 'very ruinous' and severely depopulated, John Speed recording in 1611 that it had 'more houses without inhabitants than I saw in any one city'. Though nominally the shire town, it had long since been eclipsed by Haverfordwest as the county's administrative centre. Pembroke's near neighbour Tenby, on the south coast, helped to distribute wine throughout west Wales, but it too was in decline by 1586, despite having been incorporated five years earlier, and was badly affected by the trade depression of the early 1620s. Newport, to the north, had ceased to hold a weekly market by the end of the sixteenth century, a disappearance which the lord of the manor supposed to be 'the chiefest cause of the decay of that town'. Nearby Cilgerran retained its market, but was also decayed, as was Wiston which, situated in the centre of the county, nevertheless continued to host one of the shire's two great annual livestock fairs.[1]

The 1536 Act of Union enfranchised all but one of the county towns of Wales, granting to each the right to return a single Member to Parliament. The responsibility for meeting the cost of parliamentary wages, however, was not exclusively fixed on the newly enfranchised county towns, but was extended to the other ancient boroughs within the affected shires. Throughout Wales this statutory provision was interpreted to mean that these 'contributory boroughs' were entitled to vote in parliamentary elections for the borough Member. In Pembrokeshire the contributory boroughs excluded Haverfordwest, which in 1543 was granted county status and the right to choose its own representative at Westminster, but until February 1621, when the committee for privileges ruled on the matter, it remained unclear which of the remaining towns were to be regarded as contributory boroughs. The committee's decision was that the list should include Tenby, Wiston, Newport, Fishguard, Cilgerran and St. Dogmaels. However, the surviving election indentures suggest that in the early seventeenth century only Wiston and Tenby – being geographically closest to Pembroke – ever exercised voting rights.[2]

During the first Jacobean Parliament, Pembroke Boroughs was represented at Westminster by Richard Cuny, who twice obtained formal leave of absence and seems rarely to have attended the House. Settled at St. Florence, a few miles west of Tenby, Cuny was a former servant of Robert Devereux, 2nd earl of Essex (d.1601), whose ownership of Lamphey manor, near Pembroke, in the late Elizabethan period had given him electoral influence over the constituency. Cuny undoubtedly owed his election to the mayor of Pembroke, Nicholas Adams[†]. Like Cuny, Adams had been a member of the Devereux faction, and by 1609 at the latest the two men were brothers-in-law. When, in 1620, Cuny was himself appointed mayor of Pembroke, he chose Adams to be his deputy. Cuny was succeeded in 1614 as Member for Pembroke Boroughs by Walter Devereux, the younger brother of the 3rd earl of Essex and squire of Lamphey. Aged about 23, Devereux was old enough to exert his family's influence over the seat on his own.

Devereux did not seek re-election in December 1620, when he probably served alongside Essex in the Palatinate. His absence left the way open for an alternative candidate. Richard Cuny was out of the reckoning, for being then mayor of Pembroke he was barred from standing. The former mayor, Lewis Powell, on the other hand, was a different proposition. In the run-up to the election, Powell, whose seat at Greenhill lay a few miles west of the town, received vigorous support from both Cuny and Nicholas Adams, both of whom were his brothers-in-law. However, a challenger to Powell emerged in the form of Henry Wogan of Wiston, whose elder brother John had served as knight of the shire in the previous Parliament. On learning that Wogan intended to stand, an alarmed Cuny declared that he 'would admit no election unless Mr. Lewis Powell should be named'. He is also said to have 'threatened the burgesses of the town of Pembroke that they were forsworn if they did not give their voices as he did, alleging the charter of the town for warrant thereof'. However, several burgesses refused to be intimidated. Their defiance prompted Nicholas Adams to summon before him the recalcitrant burgesses, whom he urged 'with divers menaces and railings to give their voices as the mayor did'. If they refused to do so, he added, 'they should be disgraded of their burgess-ships'.

These tactics may have overawed the electors of Pembroke, but the latter numbered at most around 70 individuals, whereas the contributory boroughs were reckoned to be capable of fielding around 160 voters between them. It seems unlikely that Cuny wielded much influence outside Pembroke, even over Tenby, where he was nominally deputy constable of the local castle, as his position there had effectively been usurped by another man.[3] Certainly, neither he nor Adams was capable of influencing the Wogan stronghold of Wiston. Nevertheless, Cuny attempted to intimidate the outboroughs by nominating Powell in the formal notification of the impending election that he sent to each of them. This clumsy tactic probably did more harm than good, and by the time the election came round a desperate Cuny refused to allow the electors from the contributory boroughs to cast their votes.[4] His decision was upheld by the sheriff, Alban Philipps, whose return bears only the names of Pembroke's electors.[5] This highly partisan behaviour by the sheriff was undoubtedly motivated by personal considerations, as the Philipps family of Picton Castle had long been enemies of the Wogans of Wiston. Moreover, Alban Philipps' brother, (Sir) John Philipps†, bt.,[6] had particular reason to detest the Wogans, as in 1616 they had engineered his removal from the captaincy of the local company of the trained band, an insult which he deeply resented and which eventually caused him to complain in Star Chamber.[7]

The manner in which the election was managed by Cuny and Philipps inevitably provoked howls of protest from the outboroughs, which claimed that Wogan would have won had their votes been admitted. Their evidence was compelling. On 27 Feb. 1621 the committee for privileges dismissed Pembroke's claim that the outboroughs were not entitled to participate in parliamentary elections for the borough seat, and condemned the outrageous behaviour of Cuny and Adams.[8] However, these findings were not reported to the House until 18 May, when the committee also recommended that Powell's election be quashed. Judgment was further delayed after Sir Samuel Sandys, who observed that there was no evidence that

Powell himself had behaved improperly, persuaded the House to grant Powell and Cuny a hearing. Ignoring the advice of Sandys's brother Sir Edwin, who pointed out that Powell had already told the committee all it needed to know, the Commons decided to allow Powell three weeks in which to answer as he had been permitted leave to return to Pembrokeshire four days earlier.[9] This delay proved fatal: before the three weeks had elapsed, Parliament was adjourned, and by the time it had reconvened in November the question of Powell's election had been quietly forgotten.

In 1624 Lewis Powell was obliged to look to Haverfordwest for a parliamentary seat rather than Pembroke Boroughs, where Sir Walter Devereux, no longer squire of Lamphey, made himself available for re-election. The damaged condition of the 1624 election indenture[10] makes it impossible to establish whether the voters of Pembroke's outboroughs were restored to their electoral rights. In 1625 the electorate's choice fell once more on Lewis Powell, as Devereux was again absent, this time serving alongside his brother in the Netherlands. Although Powell presumably enjoyed the backing of Cuny, who was in his third term as mayor of Pembroke, his election was a surprising result. No less than 27 of the 44 freemen who voted were from Wiston, of whom three were Wogans.[11]

Neither Powell nor Devereux was returned again. Instead, Pembroke Boroughs was represented in 1626 and 1628 by the young Hugh Owen. As squire of Orielton, a manor situated two miles south-west of Pembroke, and as lessee of Pembroke's former priory lands at Monkton, Owen was well placed to dominate the shire town, whose freemen formed the majority of the voters in 1628 at least.[12] In 1626 he may have encountered opposition from Devereux, who certainly required a seat, as he was returned for Tamworth on his grandmother's interest. However, in 1628 Devereux may have allowed Owen a free hand at Pembroke, as he was elected at Tamworth nine days before the voters of Pembroke Boroughs went to the hustings.

[1] *Pemb. County Hist. III: Early Modern Pemb. 1536-1815* ed. B. Howells (Pemb. Rec. Soc.), 18-20, 27-8; G. Owen, *Description of Penbrokshire* ed. H. Owen (Cymmrodorion Rec. Ser. i. pt. 3), p. 359; B.E. Howells, 'Pemb. Farming c.1580-1625', *NLW Jnl.* ix. 242; G. Dyfnallt Owen, *Wales in Reign of Jas. I*, 132; B.G. Charles, 'Recs. of Bor. of Newport', *NLW Jnl.* vii. 136; Anon. *An Acct. of Tenby*, 40-4; J. Phillips, *Hist. Cilgerran*, 46. [2] C219/39/264; 219/41B/24. The indentures for 1604 and 1614 are missing. The compilers of *OR* mistook the 1604 return relating to Poole, Dorset for that of Pembroke Boroughs. [3] *Exch. Procs. concerning Wales in Tempore Jas. I* comp. T.I. Jeffrey Jones (Univ. of Wales, Bd. of Celtic Studs., Hist. and Law ser. xv), 308. [4] Som. RO, DD/PH 216/6, f. 11. [5] C219/37/363. [6] L. Dwnn, *Vis. Wales* ed. S.R. Meyrick, i. 115. [7] *HP Commons* 1558-1603, iii. 217; STAC 8/239/20. [8] Som. RO,

DD/PH 216/6, ff. 11-12. ⁹ CJ, i. 621a, 624a, 624b; Nicholas, *Procs.*
1621, ii. 89-90; *CD 1621*, iii. 285-6. ¹⁰ C219/38/336. ¹¹ C219/39/264.
¹² C219/41B/24. The 1626 indenture is illegible.

A.D.T.

RADNORSHIRE

Number of voters: c.1,000 in 1621.[1]

c. Mar. 1604	JAMES PRICE I
c. Mar. 1614	JAMES PRICE I
12 Dec. 1620	JAMES PRICE I
	William Vaughan
c. Jan. 1624	JAMES PRICE II
26 Apr. 1625[2]	JAMES PRICE II
c. Jan. 1626	JAMES PRICE II
26 Feb. 1628	RICHARD JONES

Radnorshire was created from an agglomeration of several marcher lordships by the Act of Union of 1536. As practically all of these territories had been held by the monarch, the Crown enjoyed an enduring presence in the post-Union shire, but there is no evidence that this landholding was ever translated into electoral influence. Under the second union statute of 1543 the venue of the county court was meant to alternate between Presteigne and New Radnor. However, most of the early Stuart election returns are damaged or lost, making it impossible to assess whether this practice was observed at times of election. In 1620, however, it was claimed in a Star Chamber suit that it had not been.

Radnorshire was a small county, dominated by large tracts of upland, interspersed with steep river valleys; its towns and villages congregated on the shire's eastern fringes. Pastoral farming, often on unenclosed commons, dominated the local economy, with the trade in cattle and wool being of central importance. The county had few gentry, and those who were resident were proverbially poor, as described in one mid-seventeenth-century rhyme:

> Radnorshire, poor Radnorshire
> Never a park and never a deer,
> Never a squire of five hundred a year.[3]

Partly because of this lack of social competition, two families, the Prices of Mynachdy and the Lewises of Harpton Court, dominated the shire's parliamentary representation throughout the Elizabethan period. However, their influence faced challenges from the Vaughan family of Clyro Court, followers of the earls of Essex. Nonetheless, James Price I of Mynachdy managed to orchestrate a remarkable period of parliamentary ascendancy from 1593 through a network of dependent families and kinsmen whose members pulled most of the administrative strings in the county. These families included the Prices of Pilleth, the Joneses of Trewern, the Bradshaws of Presteigne and the Phillipses of Llanddewi. Price's ascendancy was undermined by financial troubles, reportedly caused by his own extravagance. The Vaughans, meanwhile, expanded their influence within the county elite, which led Roger Vaughan[†] to challenge to Price at the 1597 election – in his Star Chamber lawsuit following the election, Vaughan made considerable play of the fact that his income equalled that of any magistrate in the county.[4] George Owen's 1602 list of Radnorshire landholders placed the Vaughans above the Prices, and it was only a matter of time before Mynachdy faced another challenge.[5]

The next contest, in 1620, took place between Price and William Vaughan, grandson of the 1597 contender.[6] A member of the Llowes branch of his family, Vaughan took over the family interests in Radnorshire after the head of the Clyro branch married an English heiress.[7] His bid failed, but the Star Chamber bill he filed against Price reveals many details of the contest. Vaughan claimed that Price had entered into an 'unlawful plot, practice and combination' with the sheriff, Thomas Rea, and the under-sheriff (and Price's brother-in-law), Richard Phillips of Llanddewi, to make a fraudulent return. The bill describes conventional 'sheriff's tricks', including concealment of the writ until the last possible moment, and delaying the election. Price and his associates were also alleged to have offered threats and bribes, and to have bestowed bogus freeholds upon his supporters, whose ranks had been further swelled by clergymen who 'unlawfully exhorted and persuaded their ... parishioners' to vote for Price. Finally, the bill paints an interesting portrait of Radnorshire's electoral topography: Price's main support came from Radnor hundred, site of the election venue at Presteigne, whereas Vaughan's backers came from Painscastle hundred – the area in which the Clyro and Llowes estate lay. On election day Price was allegedly elected by around 40 freeholders; Vaughan claimed that 800 had given a 'great shout' for him, only to be ignored by the sheriff. The return was witnessed by a Price clique numbering 11 electors, including James Price II* and Richard Jones*.[8]

Vaughan's appeal to Star Chamber during a parliamentary session was decidedly irregular, as the Commons had claimed to be the sole arbiter in cases of disputed elections since 1604. On 18 May 1621 his bill was brought to the Commons' attention, whereupon the Member for Haverfordwest, Sir James Perrot, described Vaughan's bill as 'a wrong to our privileges ... [and] a wrong to this House'. Vaughan was summoned to answer for his contempt, but nothing further was heard of the matter.[9]

It has been claimed that the Price family's monopoly of county representation continued down to the Long Parliament.[10] This is strictly correct, but overlooks the fact that it was a different branch of the family, the Prices of Pilleth, who took over the county seat in 1624. James Price II was a kinsman of the Mynachdy family, but his mother Catherine was daughter of Roger Vaughan, the man who had challenged the Prices in 1572 and 1597.[11] William Vaughan's ambitions seem to have been fulfilled by his appointment as *custos rotulorum* of Radnorshire in 1622, while the debt problems of James Price I led to his removal from the county bench shortly thereafter.[12] The thesis that the respective factions became reconciled is strengthened by the fact that Hugh Lloyd of Caerfagu, a Vaughan supporter in 1621, witnessed the county election indentures for 1624 and 1625 alongside Price stalwarts such as Richard Phillips.[13] James Price II may have derived further strength from his position as a deputy steward to the 3rd earl of Pembroke in several Radnorshire lordships, but there is insufficient evidence to be certain of the extent to which he operated as a client of the earl in or out of Parliament.[14] The Member elected in 1628, Richard Jones of Trewern, was the brother-in-law of James Price II and an executor of the will of his brother, Charles Price*.[15]

Radnorshire pursued no legislative programme in the early Stuart era, but several representatives of the county and borough seats appear to have been involved in discussions about the Welsh wool trade, a key component of the local economy.

[1] STAC 8/288/9. [2] C219/39/280. The day date is now illegible and has been taken from *OR*. [3] R.A. Suggett, *Houses and Hist. in March of Wales*, 3-10; *Cal. Reg. Council in the Marches, 1569-91* ed. R. Flenley (Cymmrodorion Rec. Ser. viii.), 105-7. [4] STAC 5/V7/39. [5] G. Owen, *Description of Penbrokeshire* ed. H. Owen (Cymmrodorion Rec. Ser. i.), ii. 336-7. [6] G.T. Clark, *Limbus Patrum Morganiae et Glamorganiae*, 238; L. Dwnn, *Vis. Wales* ed. S.R. Meyrick, i. 255, 258. [7] *Exch. Procs. in Temp. Jas. I* ed. T.I. Jones (Bd. Celtic Studs. Hist. and Law ser. xv), 326. [8] STAC 8/288/9; C219/37/368. [9] *CD 1621*, ii. 380; iii. 285-6; v. 172-3; *CJ*, i. 624b; Nicholas, *Procs. 1621*, ii. 90. [10] J.K. Gruenfelder, 'Radnorshire's Parlty. Elections, 1604-40', *Trans. Rad. Soc.* lxvii. 25-31. [11] J. Williams, *Hist. Rad.* 313. [12] *JPs in Wales and Monm.* ed. Phillips, 328. [13] C219/30/2/280; 219/38/339. Hugh Lloyd was no friend of the Prices, and was highly critical of Charles Price* of Pilleth's conduct in raising composition monies for the grant of the lordship of Maelienydd in 1633: *HMC Var.* viii. 34-5. [14] E112/278/3. [15] PROB 11/196, f. 375v.

L.B.

NEW RADNOR BOROUGHS

Right of election: in the freemen of New Radnor, Cefnllys, Knighton, Knucklas (Cnwclas), Rhayader, ?Presteigne, ?Painscastle and ?Norton

c. Mar. 1604	SIR ROBERT HARLEY
c. Mar. 1614	ROWLAND MEYRICK
28 Dec. 1620[1]	CHARLES PRICE
3 Feb. 1624[2]	CHARLES PRICE
26 Apr. 1625[3]	CHARLES PRICE
c. Jan. 1626	CHARLES PRICE
c. Feb. 1628	CHARLES PRICE

The English plantation borough of New Radnor had taken over the mantle of its declining neighbour, Old Radnor, in the thirteenth century. It suffered badly during the Glyndŵr rebellion, and did not receive a full charter until 1562, when the townsmen apparently joined with the Anglesey borough of Beaumaris to lobby for incorporation. The charter provided for a council of 25 capital burgesses, from which a bailiff and two aldermen were selected annually. The borough's jurisdiction included the neighbouring parishes of Old and New Radnor and Llanfihangel Nant Melan, along with parts of Cascob and Llandegley, an area which encompassed about a fifth of the shire. New Radnor was not a flourishing settlement, however: the charter referred to its dwindling market, and the situation does not appear to have improved subsequently.[4] This was partly because of the prosperity of nearby Presteigne, the population of which, at around 600, was over twice that of New Radnor.[5] Camden noted that Prestigne had 'now grown to be so great a market town and fair withal that at this day it dammereth and dimmeth the light of Radnor', while a petition from 1641 noted that the quarter sessions rarely met at New Radnor, having presumably been drawn to its thriving neighbour.[6] An Exchequer deposition of 1622 claimed that the corporation of New Radnor was 'dissolved' or 'suspended' around 1618, which suggests serious disruption within the borough's elite, although the complete loss of corporation records makes this impossible to ascertain.[7]

Under the terms of the Henrician union legislation, a substantial number of out-boroughs were allowed to participate in parliamentary elections. The indentures testify that 'all bailiffs of all boroughs and shire towns ... which be contributory to the payment of the burgess' wages' were summoned to vote at election times, but the surviving returns are in such a poor condition that it is difficult to ascertain whether this was for form's sake only. The 1620 and 1625 elections suggest that the electors were drawn from New Radnor and its vicinity. The contracting parties on these occasions included John Bull of Old Radnor; Thomas Howell of New Radnor; William Knill of Womaston, Evenjobb, a hamlet located between New Radnor and Presteigne and within the capacious boundaries of the corporation; and Richard Jones* and his son and namesake who, residing in Llanfihangel Nant Melan, were also within the territorial ambit of the borough liberties, as were Hugh Lewis of Harpton Court and his son Charles.[8] However, the presence of Hugh Lewis, who lived at Dolley (Discoed) in the parish of Presteigne in 1620, and James Duppa of Whitney, Herefordshire, who held land in Painscastle in 1625, suggests that some participation by the contributory boroughs may have occurred.[9] The role of these outboroughs was hotly contested in elections later in the seventeenth century, but even then their number and rights were confused and disputed.[10] From the fragmentary evidence of the Jacobean and Caroline elections, it seems that that for the most part it was the burgesses of Radnor who attended, with the bailiff acting as the returning officer.

The 1604 Member, Sir Robert Harley, resided just across the English border at Brampton Bryan, around 13 miles from New Radnor. His influence certainly extended into Radnorshire: he served as sheriff in 1606-7; and was later described as 'a man largely estated' in the county,[11] while his father leased the manor of Gladestry, a mere four miles south of New Radnor, after the attainder of (Sir) Gelly Meyrick† in 1601. Harley was perhaps more closely associated with Prestigne than with Radnor itself, however, buying the rectory in 1619 in order to convey it to the Puritan feoffees of impropriations, and assisting the town during a severe outbreak of the plague in 1636-7.[12] He also appears as a witness in a land transaction involving the Bradshaw family of Presteigne, associates and kinsmen of the powerful Price dynasty of Mynachdy, who held the county seat in 1604.[13]

Robert Devereux, 2nd earl of Essex, had cultivated a considerable following in Radnorshire. His steward, Sir Gelly Meyrick, had obtained the Gladestry estate after marrying into the powerful Lewis family, and while his estates were still under attainder in 1604, his son and heir, Rowland Meyrick, obtained restitution by a private Act in 1606. The latter probably mobilised

the considerable remnant of Essex's local affinity (the earl had been constable of Radnor castle) to secure his return for the borough in 1614.[14]

The borough Member throughout the 1620s was Charles Price of Pilleth, brother of the knight of the shire between 1624 and 1626. The family's influence over the shire seat, principally by the parent branch at Mynachdy, reached back into the Elizabethan period, but after the collapse of James Price I's political and financial power in the latter part of James's reign, the Pilleth family emerged as the dominant force in Radnorshire politics. Charles Price was a military man involved with the war effort of the 1620s, and was probably returned *in absentia* on several occasions. The surviving indentures for 1624 and 1625 indicate that local figures associated with the Mynachdy supremacy, including Charles Price's brother-in-law, Richard Jones* of Trewern, were important in securing his return.[15] It may also be significant that Price acted as deputy steward for the 3rd earl of Pembroke in the lordship of Maelienydd throughout the 1620s.[16] The constableship of Radnor Castle, and influence over several of the contributory boroughs which lay within the lordship, came with the stewardship, so Price probably enjoyed some control over the admission of burgesses. The relationship between Price and Pembroke should not be overstated, however, for Price emerged as a vocal Buckingham supporter and showed few signs of any close attachment to Pembroke's circle in the later 1620s.

None of New Radnor's representatives pressed local legislative business in the House, although Charles Price did concern himself with measures relating to the Welsh wool trade, important for the market centres of the county. Additionally, Rowland Meyrick's restitution bill of 1606 seems to have been supported by a circle of old Essex associates, but neither the borough nor the shire Member appear to have been involved.

[1] C219/37/369. [2] C219/38/340. [3] C219/39/281; Add. 70109, no. 59. [4] SP12/21/2; *CPR*, 1560-3, pp. 343-6; STAC 5/D11/3; I. Soulsby, *Towns of Medieval Wales*, 206-8. [5] N. Powell, *Urban Hist.* xxxii. 50, 52. [6] W. Camden, *Britannia* (1610), p. 623; Add. 70003, f. 136. [7] E178/5136. [8] L. Dwnn, *Vis. Wales* ed. S.R. Meyrick, i. 262, 264-5; NLW, James Coleman Deeds, D.D. 952-3. [9] PROB 11/98, f. 19v. [10] *CJ*, x. 87b-88a, 469a; Harl. 6846, ff. 294-7; *HP Commons 1660-90*, i. 521-2; *HP Commons 1690-1715*, ii. 820-2. [11] Add. 70003, f. 132v. [12] Brampton Bryan, ms 8/34/1; Add. 70002, ff. 122-4, 127, 135. [13] NLW, James Coleman Deeds, D.D. 954. [14] M. Gray, 'Castles and patronage in sixteenth century Wales', *WHR*, xv. 489-93. [15] C219/30/340; Add. 70109, no. 59. [16] K. Parker, *Hist. Presteigne*, 65.

L.B.